Allen's Dictionary of
English Phrases

Allen's Dictionary of
English Phrases

Robert Allen

PENGUIN BOOKS

PENGUIN BOOKS

Published by the Penguin Group
Penguin Books Ltd, 80 Strand, London WC2R 0RL, England
Penguin Group (USA) Inc., 375 Hudson Street, New York, New York 10014, USA
Penguin Group (Canada), 90 Eglinton Avenue East, Suite 700, Toronto, Ontario,
Canada M4P 2Y3 (a division of Pearson Penguin Canada Inc.)
Penguin Ireland, 25 St Stephen's Green, Dublin 2, Ireland
(a division of Penguin Books Ltd)
Penguin Group (Australia), 250 Camberwell Road, Camberwell,
Victoria 3124, Australia (a division of Pearson Australia Group Pty Ltd)
Penguin Books India Pvt Ltd, 11 Community Centre,
Panchsheel Park, New Delhi – 110 017, India
Penguin Group (NZ), cnr Airborne and Rosedale Roads, Albany,
Auckland 1310, New Zealand (a division of Pearson New Zealand Ltd)
Penguin Books (South Africa) (Pty) Ltd, 24 Sturdee Avenue,
Rosebank, Johannesburg 2196, South Africa

Penguin Books Ltd, Registered Offices: 80 Strand, London WC2R 0RL, England

www.penguin.com

First published 2006
1

The author and publishers would like to thank Anne Seaton
for her contribution to the research work for this project.

Quotations from the *Oxford English Dictionary* are reproduced
by kind permission of Oxford University Press.

The moral right of the author has been asserted

Typeset in England by Data Standards Ltd
Printed in England by Clays Ltd, St Ives plc

ISBN-13: 978-0-141-00672-7
ISBN-10: 0-141-00672-2

Publishing Director: Nigel Wilcockson
Commissioning Editor: Georgina Laycock
Editorial Managers: Ellie Smith, Sophie Lazar
Copy-editor: Rosalind Fergusson
Editorial Assistant: Emma Brown
Proofreaders: Sophia Kingshill, Deirdre Clark
Design: Richard Marston
Production: Kristen Harrison
Cover: Jim Stoddart

For Alison

Contents

Preface

This book is intended to fill a major gap in the record of the English language. It offers, for the first time on this scale, a scholarly and systematic treatment of thousands of idiomatic phrases that play a crucial role in modern spoken and written English, and seeks to provide a comprehensive picture of their use and history. If words are the building blocks of language, then phrases are the walls and windows, providing a shape and structure and allowing the daylight of metaphor and imagery into the darkened rooms of everyday language.

The treatment of phrases in the major historical dictionaries is far less rigorous than the coverage of individual words; many are given with a sketchy or incomplete record or are merged into the ordinary senses of words, and some are not included at all. There are many books of idioms, clichés, and catchphrases, all invariably entertaining but falling well short of a complete narrative and making little attempt to go beyond conventional anecdote to trace the history and usage of phrases in systematic ways, which is a key feature of this book. Nor, generally, do they provide evidence in the form of quotations in support of their history and development, except opportunistically and spasmodically. There have been more scholarly books, such as the *Oxford Dictionary of English Proverbs* (third edition, 1970), which lists proverbial language in a broader sense than is generally understood by the term *proverb* and gives copious citations but virtually no editorial comment. Then, most famously of all, there is *Brewer's Dictionary of Phrase and Fable* (originally by Ebenezer Cobham Brewer, first published in 1870 and in many editions since) but despite its great appeal this is more about 'fable' than 'phrase', makes only occasional attempts to explain the evolution and history of phrases, and rarely dates them. In this book, I have attempted to supply as full a record as possible at all levels: historical, philological, and anecdotal.

Compiling this book has taken several years and involved considerable amounts of original investigation. Assembling the list of phrases to be treated was the simplest part of the task, as such lists exist in other places and can easily be collated and then edited into a coherent form. More important, as with all historical lexicography, is the reading of primary sources (chiefly fiction, drama, and poetry, but also biography and other works of non-fiction) to establish what really exists in the language and at what dates. This evidence of actual usage is the life-blood of any treatment of the language. Many phrases can be traced back to older forms of English, even to Anglo-Saxon, and some (such as *busy as a bee* and *be at one's wits' end*) are found in Chaucer and other writers of the period after the Norman Conquest known as Middle English. References to

Shakespeare in this book run into several hundred, as do those to the Authorized Version of the Bible (1611). The rise of the novel in the late 18th and 19th centuries provided a vehicle for the rapid spread of very many phrases that are now fully absorbed into everyday English. Notable among these are the set similes such as *good as gold*, which occurs frequently in the writing of Dickens, Wilkie Collins, Charlotte Yonge, and others. The prolific use of idioms by Dickens (*take one's secret to the grave, like grim death, lose one's grip, eat one's hat, take it into one's head*) was perhaps less of a surprise than the rich yield from Jane Austen (*throw cold water on, be dying to, dog tired, done for, with one's eyes open, act the fool*) and, at an earlier date still, from Henry Fielding (*kick one's heels, draw in one's horns, a fine kettle of fish, a likely story, leave somebody in the lurch*).

During the compiling of this book, I made some interesting discoveries. Most of these concerned the origins of phrases, which (as with words of obscure origin such as *OK* and *posh*) were quite evidently devised long after the event and have been repeated in print with a persistence that is in inverse proportion to their likelihood. They were usually disproved by investigation or at least weakened by a lack of historical evidence: that the *brass monkeys* invoked in cold weather related to the storage of cannon balls on ships (which shrank and became dislodged in cold weather), that the *cats and dogs* of heavy rain were a corruption of a phrase in ancient Greek (*kata doxan* meaning 'contrary to belief'), or that *setting the Thames on fire* had something to do with a tool called a *temse* (which overheated with excessive use). In many cases, such as the last, these stories were invented in the face of straightforward explanations that made perfect sense in themselves (and historical evidence for *setting the Thames on fire* establishes an explicit link with the river at an early stage of its use). In the case of the brass monkeys, an early use of the phrase by Herman Melville in 1847 ('hot enough to melt the nose off a brass monkey') clearly involves a meaning directly opposite to the usual one and seriously undermines the traditional theory about its origin. As far as I am aware, this evidence has not been adduced before.

Many phrases are a great deal older then one might expect, and others again are much more recent. Those for which I was expecting to find earlier evidence than in fact emerged include *Achilles' heel* (19th cent.), *as honest as the day is long* (20th cent.), *a knight in shining armour* (20th cent.), and *the luck of the draw* (20th cent.). There were also some surprises in the opposite direction: *chop and change* has a modern ring but goes back to Tyndale's translation of the New Testament in the early 16th century; *cool as a cucumber* is found in early 17th century drama; *like mad* occurs in its modern sense as early as the work of Aphra Behn later in the same century; and *son of a bitch*, for all its modern American resonance, is the way Lord Byron refers to Robert Southey in a letter written in 1818. A most interesting byway of my investigation into usage of the late 16th century was the setting of Shakespeare in the context of his time. Some phrases closely associated with him or regarded as his inventions are also found in the work of his contemporaries and in some cases precede his use; a notable example is *nip in the bud*, which we owe to John Fletcher and Thomas Dekker and not to Shakespeare (who uses it in the form *blasted in the bud*). Other phrases (such as *cock-and-bull story* and *the straight/strait and narrow*) emerge gradually from the mists of usage.

I was also struck by the abundance of recent coinages, of phrases with a modern resonance that form a linguistic commentary on our own times: *smoking gun, be economical with the truth, her indoors, be unfit to run a whelk stall, joined-up government, ladies who lunch, a level playing field, get a life, over the limit, the bottom line, get the message, mission creep, the full monty, name and shame, pass one's sell-by date.*

In the Introduction I have explained the principles that underlie the choice of material included. Despite these attempts to establish boundaries to keep the book within manageable proportions, the reader will find a fair number of entries that defy the selection principles as I have outlined them. I have usually included them because I could not resist it. Serendipity and personal idiosyncrasy help to make a book like this – and language in general – a lot more interesting and a lot more fun.

I should like to thank all those who helped me to write this book, and to improve earlier versions of the text: in particular Anne Seaton, who contributed hugely to the task of establishing chronology and tracking down early uses of phrases, and Rosalind Fergusson, who copy-edited the book and brought greater order to a mass of detailed information. Any remaining inconsistencies or errors are entirely my fault. I am also very grateful for the support and encouragement of the publishers, especially Nigel Wilcockson and Sophie Lazar. Everyone involved in the project became aware of how much the book represents work in progress and can never be the last word. I am sure there are readers who will have suggestions and improvements to offer, and these – especially when backed up by evidence – will always be welcome. Please write to the publisher at the address on the title verso.

Robert Allen
Edinburgh 2006

Introduction

The terms 'phrase' and 'idiom' (*an idiom*, as a unit of language, as distinct from *idiom*, the natural way of using language) reinforce each other, and I have no wish to argue a distinction between the two. For our purposes a *phrase* is a group of words, and an *idiom* is a group of words that occur regularly together, forming what linguists call a fixed (or semi-fixed) expression, such as *round the bend* and *pass the buck*. Another characteristic of the phrases explained here – in addition to their constant occurrence in the same form or in similar forms – is that they have a special meaning that is not (in varying degrees) deducible from the words from which they are formed.

Phrases may also contain a verb and form a complete idea, such as *mind one's own business, sit on one's hands*, and *talk through one's hat*. Some indeed cannot be captured as dictionary headings at all but have to be expressed as a statement, for example *the ball is in so-and-so's court* and *the jury is still out on such-and-such*. Many of the phrases dealt with here, however, are prepositional, i.e. they consist of a preposition followed by a noun, as in *over the moon* and *under the weather*. (These can also be expressed with a preceding verb such as *be* or *become* or *seem*.) A more difficult type to distinguish as an idiom is the compound noun or noun phrase: in general I have included these when they are phrasal in the sense of strongly implying a state or action, i.e. are dynamic in terms of meaning and structure (and usually constitute a total metaphor, as with *a red herring, a rule of thumb*, and *the bee's knees*), and not when they are relatively static and usually comparatively transparent in meaning or based on the figurative meaning of a single word (as with *war baby* and *pearls of wisdom*).

Most of the idioms we are concerned with here are productive, that is to say they can be fitted into sentences and altered as necessary in functional ways to suit the context in which they are being used, just as individual words can. For example, you can say *I told him to mind his own business, Why don't you mind your own business, I was just minding my own business*, and so on, which are all forms of the basic phrase *mind one's own business*. The least productive (and in many ways least interesting) phrases are those that allow little or no variation, notably catchphrases (such as *flavour of the month*), on which more is said below. Other phrases that appear to be fixed in form are subject to variation: for example we can say *a piece of the action, a slice of the action*, or *a share of the action*. (These word-based variants are noted in the entry headings.) The phrase based on a *ball rolling* can be launched with any of the verbs *get, set*, or *start*, as well as (with a shift in meaning) *keep*. Even freer variation is possible when the image suggests it. The typical form of the phrase *the jury is still out on such-and-*

such, meaning that it is still under consideration, might be modified in the form *the jury remains out on such-and-such* or even *the jury has ordered sandwiches on such-and-such*. Phrases are based on imagination, and are subject to extensive free realization. The modern phrase *a sandwich short of a picnic*, for example, meaning 'stupid or crazy', has been modified in all sorts of ways (beyond what can be listed in the entry) both within and outside its original image domain: *two sandwiches short of a picnic, two slices short of a toast rack, a few pickles short of a jar, one card short of a full deck, one side short of a pentagon*, and (with a nod to the surreal) *one tree short of a hammock*. We also see a mock adaptation of register (level of formality) in mutations such as *extract one's digit* (from *pull one's finger out*) and *extract the michael* (from *take the mickey*), and irony influences forms such as *as clear as mud*.

A recurring feature of the phrases included here is, as we have seen, that their meanings cannot be explained in terms of their constituent words. This aspect is not, however, an absolute: some phrases are more understandable than others, and what we are dealing with here is a spectrum of transparency. At one end of the spectrum are phrases that are totally opaque – that is to say, an individual who did not know them would have no idea of what they meant by analysing their content and in many cases might be struck by their literal absurdity: *bite the bullet, bury the hatchet, give somebody the cold shoulder, off the cuff, go Dutch, no hard feelings, sit on the fence, pull one's finger out, fly off the handle, lead somebody up the garden path*, and *lose one's head*. A fair number of idiomatic phrases are based on words or meanings that are no longer (or, less usually, have never been) used outside the phrase: familiar examples are *run amok, kith and kin, at somebody's beck and call, hale and hearty, betwixt and between, bide one's time, bear the brunt of, lie doggo, in fine fettle*.

Other phrases are 'semi-transparent', which is to say that a speaker of English might be able to work out from the image presented by the phrase what it is meant to signify. Examples of this type are *see the colour of somebody's money, call it a day, be all ears, end in tears, have eyes in the back of one's head, fair and square, take to one's feet, make somebody's flesh creep, be as good as one's word, move the goalposts, with all guns blazing*, and *throw in the towel*. The transparency of some of these phrases depends on knowledge about the real world: anyone who knows how a football game is played might be able to work out what *move the goalposts* means, and a corresponding situation arises with *throw in the towel*, which is an image from boxing. But a sporting ignoramus would remain baffled. Contrast these with *bite the bullet* and *fly off the handle*, from the 'opaque' group, where no amount of special knowledge will lead to an explanation. Indeed, special knowledge might lead one astray in the matter of 'losing one's head', which is the traditional fate of traitors in a very literal sense. Some phrases are now better known for their generalized meanings than for their technical origins, for example *in the offing*, one of many idioms to do with the sea (the *offing* is the part of the horizon in which ships are visible and therefore shortly to put into harbour). I was struck during the writing of this book by the large number of phrases that have nautical origins: as well as those already mentioned there are *give somebody a wide berth, broad in the beam, go by the board, push the boat out, cut and run*, and many others.

Another important group consists of allusive phrases, i.e. phrases that allude (whether knowingly or not on the part of the user) to an identifiable first use or coinage, often in translations of the Bible or in the works of Shakespeare. Examples of these are *kill the fatted calf* (from the Bible), *it is all Greek to me* (from Shakespeare's *Julius Caesar*), *in one fell swoop* (from Shakespeare's *Macbeth*), and *an albatross round one's neck* (from *The Rime of the Ancient Mariner* by Coleridge). Some phrases become altered to suit the pragmatics of language (and there is nothing wrong with this despite the protestations of language purists): a classic example is *every dog has its day* (Hamlet's words to Laertes in Shakespeare's play are 'Let Hercules himself do what he may, | The cat will mew, and dog will have his day'). A common occurrence with these types is the long interval between the locus classicus and the first allusive uses. Many phrases based on Shakespeare, for example, first appear as late as the 19th century, some three hundred years after his works became known. This is true of *be cruel to be kind* and *this mortal coil* (both from *Hamlet*), *one's pound of flesh* (from *The Merchant of Venice*), and *one's salad days* (from *Antony and Cleopatra*). Readers will understand that the dates normally given in these cases are of the allusive uses, and only exceptionally of the original use (for example, in cases where this does not differ markedly in form or sense from the later uses).

Some other special kinds of phrase are worth mentioning as they form an important part of the picture. These include set similes (e.g. *as drunk as a lord, as merry as a grig*, etc) and proverbs (phrases that give advice or state a general truth, e.g. *if you can't beat them, join them* and *the end justifies the means*). The principle I have followed in including proverbs has been to concentrate on those that have given rise to truncated allusive free forms, often with the free form itself as the heading (as with *be an early bird*, which alludes to the proverb *the early bird gets the worm*, and *count one's chickens*, which originates in the admonition *don't count your chickens until they are hatched*). Thirdly there are catchphrases, fairly rigid phrases that allude to well-known historical events and to areas of public life such as literature, entertainment, sport, and politics: examples include *cut the Gordian knot* (associated with Alexander the Great), *like Caesar's wife* (Pompeia), *meet one's Waterloo* (the fate of Napoleon), and in more recent times *flavour of the month* (derived from American marketing of ice cream in the 1940s), *be economical with the truth* (a euphemism for lying, redolent of the Thatcher years in Britain), and *don't ask, don't tell* (denoting tolerance in moral behaviour, from the end of the 20th century).

The phrases mentioned so far are predominantly based on metaphor, drawing on images from the real world. Others, which for our purposes belong to a different class of phrase, are more abstract, not drawing at all on physical images but using basic function words in special ways, often in ways that do not conform to the normal patterns of English (for example, *stay put*). Within this class are many transparent formulae of the type *by all means, I'm sorry to say, more or less,* etc, which are idiomatic and fit the criteria of fixedness but have no special significance in terms of meaning and are not based on metaphor or any distinct imagery. These more abstract idioms are of interest to learners of English and form an important part of the dictionaries written for them, but fall outside our present scope, whereas (for example) *by and large* is included because of its origin and the fact that it is grammatically anomalous (what linguists call 'ill-formed'); and *hale and hearty,* which we noted above, is also included because the word *hale* is, in current use, restricted to this phrase. The emphasis here is on metaphor and anecdote, as well as special behaviour within the phrase. I have also been sparing with so-called phrasal verbs (verbs consisting of a base verb and an adverb), except where these form part of a more extended phrase (so *turn over* is not included but *turn over a new leaf* is), or show some other special feature of interest.

The citations from literature are an important part of the treatment. They are meant to support the conclusions reached and to show the historical development of each phrase, and draw on sources ranging in date from Middle English (the English in use after the Norman Conquest of the 11th century) to the present. Throughout, the emphasis is on early rather than current usage, and to give this more substance I have exercised some freedom regarding the form a phrase takes in a particular quotation, which will not always be identical to that given in the heading. Normally I have tried to illustrate phrases with citations from the literature of the century in which the phrase first occurs in a form now recognizable. Where I have been unable to trace material of my own, I have (with permission) used quotations given in the *Oxford English Dictionary* or other published sources. Other material has been drawn from language databases, including the *British National Corpus* (a collection of about 100 million words of printed and spoken British English of many kinds made by a number of academic institutions) and the Chadwyck Healey database *Literature Online*. A small amount of material has been sent in by contributors, to whom I am most grateful.

The most important and familiar authors, such as Chaucer, Shakespeare, Scott, Dickens, and Hardy, are cited by surname alone; others are given with first names or initials to enable identification. Chaucer, who lived from *c*1343 to 1400, is cited without specific dates from the Riverside edition (Oxford, 1988), and Shakespeare from the Oxford text edited by Wells and Taylor (second edition, 2005). References to the Bible are to the Authorized Version of 1611 unless another edition (such as the New English Bible) is specified. Older English spellings have been modernized when necessary to aid comprehension or avoid confusion, and glosses in square brackets have been added to quotations to explain words that will not be familiar to most readers. In 17th and 18th century printing, common nouns were often given initial capital letters; these have been modified in places to conform with modern practice.

It might be helpful to add a few words on some of the less well-known early sources that are cited throughout the book. In particular, English versions of the Bible formed a key medium for the early development of phrase and idiom. In the 14th century, the

Bible was translated into English by John Wyclif (c1330–84), although how much of the work was done by Wyclif himself is disputed. Two centuries later, William Tyndale (c1495–1536), who communicated with Thomas More and Martin Luther, produced a translation of the New Testament in Cologne in 1525, and his contemporary Miles Coverdale (1488–1568), a Lutheran priest who had studied at Cambridge, translated the Bible in Antwerp, using German and Latin versions and drawing on the work of Tyndale. Early non-biblical sources cited frequently include the works of John Lydgate (c1370–1449), a monk from Suffolk who visited Paris, spent most of his life in the monastery at Bury, and wrote poetry in the style of Chaucer. His *Troy Book*, published c1420, was a translation of a 13th-century Sicilian writer of romances named Guido delle Colonne (who was also an important source for English writers on the theme of Troilus and Cressida). The *Cursor Mundi* is a poem from the North of England dating from about 1300 based on earlier works written in Latin and dealing with the seven ages of mankind's spiritual course from the Creation to the Last Judgement. The Middle English poem *Piers Plowman*, a work attributed to William Langland (about whom very little is known), is an allegorical series of dream visions narrated by 'Will', which describe the progress of the ploughman Piers to serenity and salvation. It was written down in the second half of the 14th century.

Some phrases are recorded for the first time in numerous collections of phrases and proverbs dating from the 16th century onwards. The most important of these are shown below. Readers should be aware that the distinction between *phrase* and *proverb* was not always as rigorous as it is today. Most collections understood the term *proverb* in much broader terms, and consequently included a wider range of expressions that we would describe as idiomatic rather than proverbial. Some collections, such as Hazlitt's and Apperson's, included the term 'proverbial phrases' in their titles. This broadened concept extends to the third edition (1970) of the *Oxford Dictionary of English Proverbs* (a revision by F P Wilson of a work compiled in 1935 by William George Smith), which admitted items that are not by any stretch of the imagination proverbs in the way now understood: *by a long chalk*, *to chop logic*, and many set similes such as *flat as a pancake* and *merry as a grig*.

Some important collections of phrases and proverbs

R Taverner, *Proverbs or adagies with newe addicions gathered out of the Chiliades of Erasmus*, 1539

John Heywood, *Dialogue conteinyng the nomber in effect of all the prouerbes in the englishe tongue*, 1546

George Herbert, *Outlandish Proverbs*, 1640

John Ray, *Collection of English Proverbs*, 1670

W Carew Hazlitt, *English Proverbs and Proverbial Phrases*, 1869

James Main Dixon, *Dictionary of Idiomatic English Phrases*, 1891

G L Apperson, *English Proverbs and Proverbial Phrases*, 1929

W G Smith, *The Oxford Dictionary of English Proverbs*, 1935

M P Tilley, *Dictionary of the Proverbs in England in the Sixteenth and Seventeenth Centuries*, 1950

B J Whiting, *Early American Proverbs and Proverbial Phrases*, 1977

J Speake, *The Oxford Dictionary of Proverbs*, 2003

Abbreviations used

cent.	century
NAmer	North American
NZ	New Zealand
OED	*Oxford English Dictionary*
transl	translating, translation

Layout of entries

Phrases by their nature defy a rational ordering, and no arrangement has been found that satisfies everybody. In this book, they are grouped for convenience under keywords. The keyword chosen is normally the most significant word in the phrase, where such a word can be identified; otherwise, the first significant word that is a stable feature of the phrase. Accordingly, **in the act** and **put on an act** are given at ACT, but **act one's age** and **act the fool** are given at AGE and FOOL respectively, and **read the riot act** is given at RIOT. Normal dictionary practice is adopted for homographs, such as LAST as an adjective (meaning 'final') and as a noun (meaning 'a shoemaker's tool'), but keywords are not normally divided by wordclass (part of speech): for example, BACK is a single keyword combining its uses as noun, adjective, adverb, and verb.

Variants and alternative words are shown by means of parentheses and slashes, so that (for example) **put on / give oneself airs (and graces)** embodies the forms *put on airs, put on airs and graces, give oneself airs,* and *give oneself airs and graces.* Set similes are normally entered at the first word, so that **(as) bold as brass** is given at BOLD. But **(as) merry/lively as a grig** will be found at GRIG because neither *merry* nor *lively* is a stable element in the phrase.

Cross-references are given at the ends of entries to direct readers who look in the wrong place: for example, anyone looking for **rain cats and dogs** at the entry for RAIN will be redirected to the entry for CAT. In these references, the target keyword is given in small capitals, either embedded in the phrase when the form is the same or given separately when it is not:

See also ... rain cats and dogs *at* CAT; rain on somebody's PARADE.

Phrases are dated according to the century for which the earliest datable evidence has been found, e.g. *17th cent.* Phrases first recorded in the 20th century are allocated, when the evidence permits, to early (1900–30), mid (1931–1970), or late (1971–2000) parts of the century. The explanations are followed in many cases by examples of use arranged historically. The date of each citation is given after the title of the work cited. In the case of works published before about 1800 these dates are not always so well established, and in these cases I have tried to find a consensus. The dates given for Shakespeare's plays follow the ones given in *The New Penguin Encyclopedia* (2003 edition).

A

The first letter of the alphabet, used to denote a starting point or the highest level in a system of grades.

A1

first-class, excellent. First used in Lloyd's Register of Shipping to indicate ships in the best condition. *A* classifies the hull of the ship and *1* classifies its stores. *19th cent.*

> Dickens *Pickwick Papers* 1837
> *'I s'pose the other gen'l'men as sleeps here, are gen'l'men.' 'Nothing but it,' said Mr. Roker. 'One of 'em takes his twelve pints of ale a-day, and never leaves off smoking, even at his meals.' 'He must be a first-rater,' said Sam. 'A 1,' replied Mr. Roker.*

from A to B

from one place to another, representing a whole journey from the starting-point (A) to the destination (B). Occasionally used figuratively about lengthy tasks and ventures that are compared to journeys. *18th cent.*

> T Mathias *The Pursuits of Literature* 1798
> *Be regular: from A to B proceed; I hate your zig-zag verse, and wanton heed.*

from A to Z

from beginning to end; in every detail; over the whole range. The phrase has often been used in the titles of books that deal with the essentials of a subject, e.g. *Wines and Liqueurs from A to Z*, but this use is now dated. *19th cent.*

> Jane Austen *Persuasion* 1818
> *This very awkward history of Mr. Elliot, was still, after an interval of several years, felt with anger by Elizabeth, who had liked the man for himself, and still more for being her father's heir, and whose strong family pride could see only in him, a proper match for Sir Walter Elliot's eldest daughter. There*

was not a baronet from A to Z, whom her feelings could have so willingly acknowledged as an equal.

aback

be taken aback

to surprise or disconcert somebody. *Aback* is an Old English word meaning 'backward', 'to the rear', and survives in modern English only in this phrase: earlier phrases, such as *hold aback* and *stand aback*, which correspond to the modern forms *hold back* (= restrain oneself) and *stand back* (= remain aloof or uninvolved), have fallen out of use. *Take aback* originated as a nautical term (18th cent.) used to describe a ship that is prevented from moving forward by a headwind pressing the sails against the mast. *19th cent.*

> Charlotte Brontë *Shirley* 1849
> *Mr. Helstone, thus addressed, wheeled about in his chair, and looked over his spectacles at his niece: he was taken aback. Her father and mother! What had put it into her head to mention her father and mother, of whom he had never, during the twelve years she had lived with him, spoken to her?*

ABC

(as) easy/simple as ABC

very easy or straightforward. The use of *ABC* to mean the alphabet as a whole dates from Middle English, and expressions such as *know one's ABC* and *learn one's ABC* are found from an early date. *As easy as ABC* occurs as the title of a book by Kipling (1912). *Early 20th cent.*

abdabs

give somebody the (screaming) abdabs

informal to make somebody feel extremely agitated or irritated: *abdabs* (or *habdabs*) is a fanciful word of elusive origin, or more likely of no origin at all, being plain invention. *Late 20th cent.*

about

know what one is about

informal to be well aware of what one is doing or what is happening and its implications.

that's about it

an expression of relief or satisfaction at the conclusion of a task or discussion. The notion is that everything has been done or considered, although there is often the implication that more might have been done, given the opportunity. *Late 20th cent.*

Michael Frayn *Sweet Dreams* 1976
One is who one is. That's about it, I suppose.

above

be/get above oneself

to be or become conceited and arrogant. This is possibly an extension of the notion of marrying or forming friendships 'above oneself', i.e. at a higher social level than one's own, which occurs often in romantic literature. There is also the idea of rising above oneself in excelling one's own normal level of achievement. Finally there is the meaning 'out of control from high spirits', which is used of horses as well as people. All these meanings probably influenced each other and affected the main meaning we are concerned with here. *19th cent.*

J H Ingraham *The Gipsy of the Highlands* 1843
Paul's intimacy with Duncan Powell, had early initiated him into the first steps of dissipation; and, by bringing him into the social circle of young men, whom his humble condition would prevent him from afterwards associating with, inspired him with ideas above himself and his circumstances, which would prevent him from engaging, with proper feelings, in the pursuit for which his mother designed him.

Kipling *From Sea to Sea* 1900
I have seen more decent men above or below themselves with drink, than I care to think about.

not be above (doing) something

to be quite prepared to do something unworthy or disreputable.

See also above BOARD.

Abraham

in Abraham's bosom

in heaven, or in a state of eternal happiness. Used with allusion to Luke 16:22 'And it came to pass, that the beggar died, and was carried by the angels into Abraham's bosom.' The reference is to the Old Testament father of the Hebrews, and ancestor of the three great religions that profess one God (Judaism, Christianity, and Islam). In

the Genesis account he was born in the Sumerian town of Ur (of the Chaldees) in Mesopotamia (modern Iraq), and moved with his family to the city of Mari on the Euphrates and then on to the promised land of Canaan. *18th cent.*

Thomas Holcroft *The Adventures of Hugh Trevor* 1794
You may guzzle wine here, but you shall want a drop of water to cool your tongue hereafter! You may guttle, while righteous Lazarus is lying at your gate. But wait a little! He shall soon lie in Abraham's bosom, while you shall roast on the devil's great gridiron, and be seasoned just to his tooth!

absence

absence makes the heart grow fonder

(proverb) one becomes nostalgically fond of a person or place after a period of separation. The sentiment can be found as early as the 1st cent. BC in a poem by the Roman poet Propertius (*Elegies* II.xxxiii): *semper in absentes felicior aestus amantes* ('Passion is always stronger in absent lovers'). In English the phrase appears as a line in a mid 19th cent. song 'The Isle of Beauty' by T Haynes Bayly (1797–1839). The emotional effects of absence feature in much earlier writing, e.g. a 16th cent. source offers the assurance that 'Absence works wonders' and, more specifically, the diplomat and poet Sir Henry Wotton wrote in 1589 that 'nothing was able to add more to [affection] than absence'. But contrary notions are also found: 'three things there be that hinder love, that's absence, fear, and shame' (W Averell, *Charles and Julia*, 1581); and there is an implicit contradiction in *out of sight, out of mind* (see SIGHT). In the current form the phrase dates from the 19th cent.

absence of mind

an inability to concentrate or remember everyday things. *18th cent.*

Smollett *The Adventures of Ferdinand Count Fathom* 1753
He was blind to the objects that surrounded him; he scarce ever felt the importunities of nature; and had not they been reinforced by the pressing entreaties of his attendant, he would have proceeded without refreshment or repose. In this absence of mind did he traverse a great part of Germany, in his way to the Austrian Netherlands, and arrived at the fortress of

Luxemburg, where he was obliged to tarry a whole day on account of an accident which had happened to his chaise.

absolutely

absolutely fabulous

excellent, first-class: representing an upper-class utterance, often used ironically. The phrase was given prominence as the title of a television sit-com broadcast from 1992 and featuring a pair of women friends who behave outrageously, one an ostentatiously neurotic and socially aspiring PR agent, the other a hard-drinking chain-smoking mutton-dressed-as-lamb type. Some recent uses of the phrase allude to this association. *Absolutely* has several strands of meaning, of which the one relevant here ('completely, perfectly') is 16th cent. (occurring in Shakespeare), and it occurs with *fabulous* in their separate meanings without the connotations of the present usage. *Late 20th cent.*

Ann Pilling *Henry's Leg* 1987
She thought his attic bedroom was absolutely fabulous.

abyss

look/stare into the abyss

to be faced with catastrophe: *abyss* (from Greek *abussos* (*a* = without) meaning 'bottomless') dates from Middle English in the sense 'bowels of the earth, primal chaos' and then 'a bottomless chasm or gulf'. Figurative uses date from the 17th cent.; in the Brontë passage below the use seems to be in a positive sense. *19th cent.*

Charlotte Brontë *Jane Eyre* 1847
I thought Miss Ingram happy, because one day she might look into the abyss at her leisure, explore its secrets and analyse their nature.

Michael Dobbs *Wall Games* 1990
The fruits of success were well known to him; he needed to remind himself of the cost of getting it wrong, to take a long, deliberate look into the abyss before deciding whether to jump.

acceptable

See the acceptable FACE.

accident

accidents will happen (in the best regulated families)

(proverb) one cannot always prevent things from going wrong. Use of *accident* in the sense 'an unfortunate occurrence or misfortune', which is now dominant, emerges in the 17th cent. The phrase dates from the 18th cent. and the full form occurs in 19th cent. literature. It was a favourite expression of Charles Dickens, who used it in varying forms in *Pickwick Papers* (1837), *Dombey and Son* (1848), and *David Copperfield* (1850: see below).

Richard Graves *The Spiritual Quixote* 1773
'A whole heap of soot has fallen down into the fish-kettle, and entirely spoiled the carps. I very providentially caught up the loin of veal upon the spit; or else that would have been covered with dust and ashes.' 'Well, well,' (says Mr. Slicer) 'accidents will happen; it is well it is no worse; we must dine without the carp, then.'

Dickens *David Copperfield* 1850
'Copperfield,' said Mr Micawber, 'accidents will occur in the best-regulated families; and in families not regulated by ... the influence of Woman, in the lofty character of Wife, they must be expected with confidence, and must be borne with philosophy.'

an accident waiting to happen

informal a situation that was bound to lead to disaster or misfortune, especially because of negligence or neglect. The phrase is constantly used with hindsight by those who are wise after the event (*see* WISE). It was much heard in the 1980s after a succession of disasters that were attributed to negligence or incompetence, including the capsizing of the Zeebrugge ferry, a fire at Kings Cross underground station in London, and crowd deaths at Hillsborough football stadium. *Mid 20th cent.*

The Times 1988
The crash that began on Wall Street on October 19 is traceable to two simple and related causes. It was not, as Mr Alan Greenspan, chairman of the Federal Reserve Board, suggested, 'an accident waiting to happen'; primarily it was caused by the determination of Americans to consume more than they produce.

a chapter of accidents

a series of unfortunate events or mishaps: from an earlier (18th cent.) phrase *the chapter of accidents* meaning 'the unpredictable way events unfold'. It is the heading of a chapter in Sir Walter Scott's *Waverley* (1814), and of a section of Thomas Hughes' *Tom Brown's Schooldays* (1857). *19th cent.*

R L Stevenson *New Arabian Nights* 1882
He was reckoning without that chapter of accidents that was to make this night memorable above all others in his career.

more by accident than design

by chance rather than deliberately: also in variant forms. The two words occur together in contrastive form from the 18th cent.

Henry Fielding *The Life and Death of Jonathan Wild* 1743
I rejected them often with the utmost Indignation, till at last, casting my eye, rather by accident than design, on a diamond necklace, a thought, like lightning, shot through my mind, and, in an instant, I remembered, that this was the very necklace you had sold the cursed Count, the cause of all our misfortunes.

accidentally

See accidentally on PURPOSE.

according

See according to COCKER; according to HOYLE; according to one's lights *at* LIGHT[2].

account

The noun is particularly prolific in the generation of idioms, the notion being of a person's 'account' representing their standing in relation to another individual or to society as a whole. Some phrases are derived from another branch of meaning, 'a statement or narrative of a thing or an event': *by all accounts* belongs here, whereas *give a good account of oneself* overlaps in meaning.

by all accounts

as a general consensus; in the opinion of most people. *18th cent.*

Smollett *The Adventures of Peregrine Pickle* 1751
It is now high time for you to contract that unbounded spirit of gallantry, which you have indulged so long, into a sincere attachment for the fair Emilia, who, by all accounts, deserves the whole of your attention and regard.

give a good account of oneself

to be successful, to do well. To *give a good account of* something occurs from the 17th cent. in the meaning 'to do well by' or 'to be successful by', and the reflexive use is a development of this sense. *18th cent.*

Fanny Burney *Cecilia* 1782
He assured her he doubted not giving her shortly a good account of himself, and that living in the country was a resource of desperation which need not be anticipated.

on no account / not on any account

not in any circumstances. *18th cent.*

Fanny Burney *Cecilia* 1782
The physician declined giving any positive opinion, but, having written a prescription, only repeated the injunction of the surgeon, that she should be kept extremely quiet, and on no account be suffered to talk.

settle/square accounts with somebody

to have one's revenge on somebody. Derived from the more concrete meaning 'to pay a debt owed to somebody'. *18th cent.*

John Cleland *Memoirs of a Woman of Pleasure* 1748
After dinner, which we eat a-bed in a most voluptuous disorder, Charles got up, and taking a passionate leave of me for a few hours, he went to town, where concerting matters with a young sharp lawyer, they went together to my late venerable mistress's, from whence I had but the day before made my elopement, and with whom he was determin'd to settle accounts in a manner that should cut off all after-reckonings from that quarter.

take account of something / take something into account

to consider something as a factor when making a decision. *16th cent.*

Brian Melbancke *Philotimus* 1583
Philotimus began to recounte Archaretos his letters, & to take account of his passed life, howe he should deserve his passing goodwill.

there is no accounting for taste(s)

(proverb) people's tastes and preferences differ. Usually said with reference to an individual's strange or unusual liking or appetite. It is a version of the Latin tag *de gustibus non est disputandum* 'there is no disputing about tastes', which is found in English literary contexts from the 16th cent. The phrase is susceptible to variation and extended uses. *18th cent.*

Ann Radcliffe *The Mysteries of Udolpho* 1794
I have often thought the people he disapproved were much more agreeable than those he admired; – but there is no accounting for tastes. He was always so much influenced by people's countenances.

Barbara Whitehead *Sweet Death Come Softly* 1993
There was no accounting for the strange behaviour of females.

turn something to good account

to derive an advantage or profit from something. From the general meaning 'profit or advantage', as in St Paul's Epistle to the Philippians 4:17 'I desire fruit that may abound to your account.' *17th cent.*

Head & Kirkman *The English Rogue Described* 1668
I was entrusted with 100l. worth of commodities, with which I set up another trade in the country: this turned to good account: for I seldom ventured on any thing, but it was effectual and to purpose.

---

ace

Ace originally denoted the one on a dice, and was later extended to refer to a playing card which has the numerical value of 'one' but often ranks highest of all. This ambiguous status of the ace in cards has led to two strands of idiom, its low nominal value giving rise to phrases associated with misfortune or bad luck (it occurs in this sense in Chaucer), and its high value being reflected in more recent idioms as the dominant underlying meaning. The latter is reflected also in the 20th cent. meaning 'something outstandingly good', which is also found in quasi-adjectival use (*it's ace*). An ace is also (19th cent.) an unbeatable serve in tennis, and was used in the First World War as a term for a crack airman.

an ace up one's sleeve / in the hole

an effective argument or advantage held in reserve. The variant *ace in the hole* is chiefly North American; it was the title of a 1940 Cole Porter song and of a 1951 film about a man trapped in a cave, his rescue unscrupulously delayed by a journalist who wanted to keep the story going and claim a scoop. Both versions of the phrase allude to card playing: in the first version to a cardsharp keeping a card literally up his sleeve, and in the second to stud poker, in which a card is kept face down until after the betting is completed, and then turned over in the hope of its being an ace. The phrase is alluded to in the title of a novel by Annie Proulx, *That Old Ace in the Hole* (2002). *Early 20th cent.*

M Ondaatje *In the Skin of a Lion* 1987
There was always, he thought, this pleasure ahead of him, an ace of joy up his sleeve so he could say you can do anything to me, take everything away, put me in prison.

have/hold all the aces

to have all the advantages. *Late 20th cent.*

The Times 1985
Bairn, runner-up to Shaweed in the 2,000 Guineas and the fluent winner of the St James's Palace Stakes at Ascot, went smoothly into the lead a quarter of a mile out but it was immediately obvious that Starkey was holding all the aces in the shape of Rousillon's superior speed.

play one's ace (card)

to use a decisive argument or stratagem. This uses the same image as *an ace up one's sleeve* above. *Late 20th cent.*

Guardian 1985
Hopes in the White House that Mr Reagan's illness would encourage the Congress to pass the budget this week out of sympathy for his plight appear to have been dashed, though there were hints yesterday that the President may still play his ace card – a presidential phone call.

within an ace of something

on the point of something, very close to something. *18th cent.*

Thomas Brown *Amusements Serious and Comical* 1700
Their rashness makes me tremble, when I see brute heavy beasts hurry through so many streets, and run upon slippery uneven stones, where the least false step brings them within an ace of death.

Achilles

Achilles' heel / Achilles heel

a single vulnerable spot or weakness. The allusion is to the story of the Greek hero Achilles, who was dipped into the River Styx by his mother Thetis to render him invulnerable. But the water did not cover the heel by which she held him, and it was in this spot that he was fatally wounded by an arrow fired by the Trojan Paris. Early figurative uses of the phrase (which is surprisingly recent) referred to Ireland in relation to Britain (Coleridge) and divorce in relation to marriage (G B Shaw). It was deplored by George Orwell in 1946 as a 'lump of verbal refuse': see the ACID test. The *Achilles' tendon*, which connects the heel and calf, carries the same allusion. *19th cent.*

Anna Cora Ritchie Armand 1855
Ah! you touch us nearly when you talk of her! Our love for the 'illusive sex' – for such we deem them – is our Achilles' heel – our vulnerable point!

acid

Francis Bacon, in his natural history miscellany *Sylva Sylvarum* (1627), described sorrel as 'a cold and acid herb', an adjectival use of *acid* that predates the noun. The chemical meaning is first recorded in Phillips' *Dictionary* of 1696 but it does not appear in a real context until the early 18th cent. The 1960s slang use relating to the drug LSD underlies some modern uses.

acid house

extremely loud repetitive music produced originally by sampling existing songs and featuring strong complex percussion patterns; such music is played at gatherings often associated with the activities of drug-pushers. *House* is derived from *Warehouse*, the name of a Chicago nightclub where this kind of music was played; and *acid* here may be taken from *Acid Trax*, the name of a rock record produced in Chicago, rather than being directly associated with the drugs term. *Late 20th cent.*

acid rain

rain containing high levels of acid, especially sulphur and nitrogen compounds and other pollutants released by industrial fossil fuels into the atmosphere. There is a stray use of this term in

the 19th cent., but it came into real prominence in the 1970s, when concern for the environment and awareness of the dangers to it intensified. *19th cent.*

the acid test

a conclusive or searching test. The meaning is developed from the slightly older physical sense of a test for gold using nitric acid, to which gold reacts. Fowler in *Modern English Usage* (1926) listed the expression among his 'popularized technicalities' and identified it as 'the term of this sort most in vogue at the time of writing'. Some twenty years later, George Orwell in his uncompromising article *Politics and the English Language* (first published in the periodical *Horizon* in 1946 and reprinted in several collections of his essays) included it among the 'verbal refuse' – along with *Achilles' heel, hotbed, melting pot*, and other phrases – that should be consigned 'to the dustbin where it belongs'. *Early 20th cent.*

Woodrow Wilson in The Times 1918
The treatment accorded Russia by her sister nations in the months to come will be the acid test of their good will.

come the (old) acid

informal to be offensive or unpleasant; literally, to speak in an 'acid' manner: originally forces' slang. *Early 20th cent.*

H Hodge Cab, Sir? 1939
Any attempt to 'come the acid', so far from frightening the cabman, will probably result in the cabman's giving him a little fatherly advice.

put the acid on somebody

Australian, informal to apply pressure on somebody for a favour. The connection, if any, with *acid test* is uncertain. *Early 20th cent.*

acquaintance

make the acquaintance (of somebody)

to come to know somebody (replacing *take acquaintance with*, which referred to knowledge of people and things). *18th cent.*

Fanny Burney Camilla 1796
She then spoke of the ball, public breakfast, and raffle; chatting both upon persons and things with an easy gaiety, and sprightly negligence, extremely amusing to Camilla, and which soon, in despight of the unwillingness with which she had entered her

house, brought back her original propensity to make the acquaintance, and left no regret for what Lionel had done.

scrape (an) acquaintance with somebody
to become acquainted with somebody with difficulty or by making great efforts. *17th cent.*

John Dunton *A Voyage Round the World* 1691
Ben't earth and heaven enough, that thou must go | To view the kingdoms of the world below; | Both of thy pockets and thy self take care, | For sholes of booksellers will scrape acquaintance there.

See also be on nodding terms / have a nodding acquaintance with somebody *at* NOD.

acre

God's acre
a churchyard: the phrase is a translation of German *Gottesacker*, 'God's field' in which the bodies of the dead are regarded as being 'sown' (as in 1 Corinthians 15:36). This corresponds to the earliest meaning of *acre* in English, 'tilled field', although it seems not to have meant 'cemetery' specifically until the 19th cent.

Hardy *A Pair of Blue Eyes* 1873
There was no wall, the division between God's Acre and Lord Luxellian's being marked only by a few square stones.

across

See across the BOARD.

act

The dominant meaning is 'something done, a deed'. The meaning 'division of a theatrical performance' (16th cent.) gave rise to the sense 'each of a series of short pieces in a programme of entertainment' which is the basis of some of the phrases below. The verb is 17th cent.

an act of God
a sudden event brought about by natural forces that only God is supposedly able to control, especially a catastrophe such as a flood or earthquake. *17th cent.*

John Reynolds *The Triumphs of Gods Revenge* 1635
Her guilty thoughts and conscience (like so many blood-hounds) still pursuing her, she seeing this unlookt for disaster and death of her Bernardo to be

an act of God, and a blow from heaven, which infallibly predicted both her danger and death.

C Allmand *The Hundred Years War* 1991
A factor which could be regarded as an act of God now intervened.

be/get in on the act
to become involved in an enterprise, especially to gain an advantage. *Mid 20th cent.*

Mario Puzo *The Godfather* 1969
The author … came west on Johnny's invitation, to talk it over without agents or studios getting into the act.

clean up one's act
to stop behaving badly or irresponsibly and start to act in a more acceptable or proper way. *Late 20th cent.*

Daily Mirror 1992
A judge ordered him to clean up his act by watching Gary Lineker videos.

do a disappearing/vanishing act
to leave a place suddenly without leaving information about one's whereabouts: usually in the context of dishonest or underhand activities. A metaphor from conjuring. *Early 20th cent.*

Rachel Elliot *Lover's Charade* 1992
Well, tonight she'd do something about it, she pledged silently. Tonight she wouldn't give him the chance to do his disappearing act.

get one's act together
to organize oneself to undertake or achieve something. *Late 20th cent.*

Today 1992
When is the United Nations going to get its act together in Bosnia?

a hard act to follow
an achievement that sets a high standard for the future. The phrase is based on a theatrical metaphor alluding to the difficulty faced by an entertainer coming on stage immediately after a popular or successful act. *Late 20th cent.*

Accountancy 1993
Sir John Harvey-Jones, who led ICI to its first billion-pound profit in 1984, was always going to be a hard act to follow.

in the act
in the process of doing something, especially something wrong or illicit. In early use the mean-

ing was often sexual: e.g. in Shakespeare's *The Merchant of Venice* (1598) I.iii.82 'And when the work of generation was | Between these woolly breeders [i.e. sheep] in the act, | The skilful shepherd peeled me certain wands.' This sense survives in modern informal use. *16th cent.*

put on an act
to make an elaborate show or pretence. *Mid 20th cent.*

> Monica Dickens *Happy Prisoner* 1946
> *This girl's not naturally like that. She's putting on an act.*

See also act one's AGE; act the GOAT; a CLASS act; play/act the FOOL; read the RIOT act.

action

actions speak louder than words
(proverb) it's what people do that matters, not what they say they will do. *17th cent.*

> Hannah Foster *The Coquette* 1797
> *I go on finely with my amour. I have every encouragement that I could wish. Indeed my fair one does not verbally declare in my favor; but then, according to the vulgar proverb, that actions speak louder than words, I have no reason to complain.*

action stations
a state of readiness: originally (in singular and plural) the positions taken by a military force preparing for military action. *Early 20th cent.*

> Michael Munn *Hollywood Rogues* 1991
> *Bogie was very cool and returning insults with a smile while Mayo was rising in anger and waiters were circling warily around taking up action stations.*

a piece/share/slice of the action
involvement in an interesting activity. *Mid 20th cent.*

> Michael Dibdin *Dirty Tricks* 1991
> *Nation shall speak peace unto nation, and I shall grab a piece of the action.*

where the action is
informal where the most interesting or important activities are going on. *Mid 20th cent.*

> New Statesman 1992
> *An officer at Scotland Yard's Obscene Publications Squad tells me there isn't much interest in magazines these days: videos are where the action is.*

actress

as the actress said to the bishop
used to suggest a sexual innuendo or ambiguity in an innocent remark. The phrase also appears in the reverse form *as the bishop said to the actress*, without any apparent difference of nuance. *Mid 20th cent.*

> Kingsley Amis *Lucky Jim* 1954
> *If you don't know what to do I can't show you, as the actress said to the bishop.*

> Esquire 1992
> *Size, as the actress said to the Bishop, is part of the problem.*

actual

your actual
informal used to indicate something that is genuine or typical: first used in the radio comedy programme *Round the Horne* in the 1960s. *Mid 20th cent.*

> Fiona Cooper *I Believe in Angels* 1993
> *'Is this a drop of your actual feminine intuition?' he asked, pretending to chew gum.*

Adam

The name of the first man in Genesis 2–3, it is probably derived from the Hebrew word *adama* meaning earth, reflecting the divine creation of humans by forming them from the earth and then breathing life into them (see Genesis 2:7). In Hebrew, *Adam* is a generic name for 'man' (see Genesis 5:2), which is reflected in the phrases.

Adam's ale
water, man's first drink. Also called *Adam's wine*. *17th cent.*

> Prynne *Sovereign Power of Parliament* 1643
> *They have been shut up in prisons and dungeons ... allowed only a poor pittance of Adams Ale, and scarce a penny bread a day to support their lives.*

Adam's apple
the projection of the thyroid cartilage in front of the neck, more prominent in men and traditionally associated with part of the forbidden fruit that is said to have stuck in Adam's throat (*see* FORBIDDEN fruit). The name was earlier given to varieties of lime and orange, and in the current

meaning was first recorded by Dr Johnson (1755), although *Adam's morsel* is recorded earlier (16th cent.) in the same meaning. *18th cent.*

not know somebody from Adam
to have no knowledge of somebody, or be unable to recognize them. *18th cent.*

> **Mrs Gaskell** *Wives and Daughters* 1866
> *And there's Osborne, who takes after his mother, who couldn't tell her great-grandfather from Adam, bless her; and Osborne has a girl's delicate face, and a slight make, and hands and feet as small as a lady's.*

the old Adam
the obstinately bad side of human nature, in Christian theology represented by the first Adam whereas Christ was the second Adam and redeemer (Romans 6:6 'Knowing this, that our old man is crucified with him [Christ]'). In the first scene of Shakespeare's *Henry V* (1599), which is a conversation about the King between the Archbishop of Canterbury and the Bishop of Ely, Canterbury declares (I.i.28–30) that 'at that very moment [i.e. his father's death] | Consideration like an angel came | And whipped th'offending Adam out of him'. *19th cent.*

> **Walter Besant** *Dorothy Forster* 1884
> *Yet I confess to you, Miss Dorothy, that there have been moments, before Mr. Forster came of age, when I have had a vehement yearning upon me to put on, as I may say, the old Adam. That temptation has now disappeared.*

add
See add FUEL to the fire; add INSULT to injury.

adder
See (as) DEAF as an adder.

admirable

the admirable Crichton
a person of great abilities or excellence. The original of the name was James Crichton, a 16th cent. Scottish nobleman noted for his scholarship and physical prowess, called 'the admirable Crichton' by Sir Thomas Urquhart in *The Jewel* (1652). It is also the title of a novel by Harrison Ainsworth (1827) and of a play (1902) by J M Barrie about a butler named Crichton who assumes responsibility when the household is shipwrecked (filmed in the UK in 1918 and 1957). *19th cent.*

> **Trollope** *The Prime Minister* 1876
> *'I rather fancy I picked up more Greek and Latin at Bohn than I should have got here, had I stuck to nothing else.' 'I dare say; – I dare say. You may be an Admirable Crichton for what I know.'*

ado

without further/more ado
without any delay or pause for consideration. *Ado*, which is a northern dialect form of *to do*, dates from Middle English in the sense 'business' or 'fuss' (and in the Authorized Version of the Bible (1611), e.g. at Mark 5:39 'Why make ye this ado and weep?'). It occurs from the 16th cent. in now obsolete uses such as *much ado* and *little ado*, and survives in modern English only in the present phrase, which is also found in Middle English literature.

> **Richard Mulcaster** *The Elementarie* 1582
> *And yet all this great confusion is easilie to be certained, without anie more ado.*

> **Rider Haggard** *King Solomon's Mines* 1885
> *Without further ado Gagool plunged into the passage, which was wide enough to admit of two walking abreast.*

adrift

cast/cut/turn somebody adrift
to desert or abandon somebody: the image is of a boat drifting helplessly out to sea. *19th cent.*

> **Julian Barnes** *Flaubert's Parrot* 1985
> *He had a passion for the dreamy knight cast adrift in a vulgar, materialist society.*

advantage

have the advantage of/over somebody
to be aware of something about another person that can be used to embarrass or compromise them. *17th cent.*

> **Sheridan** *The Rivals* 1775
> *Really, Sir, You have the advantage of me. I don't remember ever to have had the honour. – My name is Saunderson, at your service.*

take advantage of somebody/something

to benefit from an advantage or opportunity: often in unfavourable senses, to exploit somebody's goodwill or good nature. *Middle English* (in Gower)

> Shakespeare *The Merry Wives of Windsor* III.iii.102 (1597)
>
> *Your husband's coming hither, woman, with all the officers in Windsor, to search for a gentleman that he says is here now in the house, by your consent, to take ill advantage of his absence.*

adversity

adversity makes strange bedfellows

(proverb) in times of difficulty people support each other who would not normally be associates. *17th cent.*

> Shakespeare *The Tempest* II.ii.37 (1613)
>
> *Misery acquaints a man with strange bedfellows.*

> Trollope *Phineas Redux* 1874
>
> *They say that 'misfortune makes men acquainted with strange bedfellows.' The old hereditary Whig Cabinet ministers must, no doubt, by this time have learned to feel themselves at home with strange neighbours at their elbows.*

advocate

See play devil's advocate *at* DEVIL.

aegis

under the aegis of somebody

with the support or protection of a person, organization, etc: the *aigis* (in Latin *aegis*) was an attribute of Zeus and Athena that took various forms, principally a shield covered with a goatskin. In later representations it had a fringe of snakes and a Gorgon's head, making it more effective in protecting friends and frightening off enemies. *19th cent.*

> William Barry *The New Antigone* 1887
>
> *I tell you, then, that if Mrs. Malcolm has thrown herself under the ægis of the revolution, I may hunt out where she is, but to bring her back I cannot give a pledge. Is it understood?*

affluent

the affluent society

coined by the American economist J K Galbraith (b 1908), as the title of a book (1958): based on the (18th cent.) meaning of *affluent* that is now the most current, 'abounding in wealth', itself a figurative development of the meaning 'flowing copiously', which dates from Middle English. Galbraith's theme was the imbalance between 'private affluence and public squalor' in modern societies. The phrase has been subject to irreverent variation, notably as *the effluent society* in a poem of 1964 called 'Never So Good' by Stan Gooch. *Mid 20th cent.*

> G Pearson *Hooligan* 1983
>
> *What is altogether remarkable is the way in which these rough working-class youths who donned Ted suits in the 1950s, and slicked back their hair in a greasy imitation of Elvis Presley, could be mistaken for the children of the 'affluent society'.*

afraid

See afraid of one's own SHADOW.

after

after all

1 used to introduce a contrary point or argument. *17th cent.*

> Locke *An Essay Concerning Human Understanding* 1690
>
> *A man may find an infinite number of propositions, reasonings, and conclusions, in books of metaphysics … and, after all, know as little of God, spirits, or bodies as he did before he set out.*

> R H Dana *Two Years Before the Mast* 1840
>
> *To work hard, die hard, and go to hell after all, would be hard indeed!*

2 used to reinforce a point in the sense 'may I remind you'. *17th cent.*

> Dryden *All for Love* 1678
>
> *For, after all, though the one were a woman and the other a queen, they were both women.*

> Michael Falk *Part of the Furniture* 1991
>
> *Life did, after all, have to go on.*

after you

a formula used when yielding precedence: in early use in an extended form *after you is manners*. *17th cent.*

Richard Brome *The Queen and Concubine* a1652
[Andrea] *After you is manners.* [Curate] *Now, by mine intellect, discreetly spoken.*

James Fenimore Cooper *The Pioneers* 1823
The veteran landlord was requested to … taste the liquor he presented, by the invitation of 'after you is manners'.

Dickens *Great Expectations* 1861
At last we came to the door of a room, and she said, 'Go in.' I answered, more in shyness than politeness, 'After you, miss.'

be after somebody or something

to be in determined pursuit of a person or thing. *19th cent.*

R L Stevenson *Treasure Island* 1883
Now, if I can't get away nohow, and they tip me the black spot, mind you, it's my old sea-chest they're after; you get on a horse – you can, can't you? Well, then, you get on a horse, and go to – well, yes, I will! – to that eternal Doctor.

Frederick Thomas *Howard Pinckney* 1840
'No, he suspects nothing; he's disguised as a farmer.' 'Disguised as a farmer – here, and suspects nothing.' 'He's after me, then – and only me.' 'Do your own revenge then, Jack.'

be after doing something

1 *Anglo-Irish* to have just done something. The phrase is derived from a construction in Irish Gaelic, in which the preposition *ar* (= after) is used with the verb *be* and a verbal noun to express the perfect tense; in its Anglicized form *he's after dying* means 'he's died'. *19th cent.*

J M Synge *Shadow of Glen* 1904
He's after dying on me, God forgive him.

Conan Doyle *The Valley of Fear* 1915
I'm a Freeman myself. I'm after telling your father about it.

James Joyce *Ulysses* 1922
Sure, I'm after seeing him not five minutes ago.
2 (with a meaning effectively opposite to the first) to be bent on doing something; influenced by *be after somebody or something*. *Early 20th cent.*

J B Cooper *Coo-oo-ee* 1916
'Gorrah!' exclaimed Mrs O'Callaghan. 'Is he after making me drunk?'

Celia Brayfield *The Prince* 1990
I suppose you're after picking your girlfriend some strawberries now?

Aga

Aga saga

a popular novel about middle-class village people, typically those who live in the shire counties and own an Aga stove (a heavy-duty stove, the name of which is derived from that of the original manufacturers, [Svenska] A[ktienbola-get] G[as]a[ckumulator] = Swedish Gas Accumulator Company). The feeling evoked by the phrase is one of bourgeois nostalgia, and the novels of Joanna Trollope, Jilly Cooper, and other writers of popular fiction that are largely preoccupied with the tribulations of domestic affairs, are often cited in this context. The coinage of the phrase *Aga saga* has been claimed by the writer and newspaper columnist Terence Blacker, but the phrase occurred coincidentally in a totally different context referring to the racing activities of the Aga Khan – and his long-running dispute with the Jockey Club – in newspaper stories from 1992. *Late 20th cent.*

Evening Standard 1993
Jilly Cooper is a thumping success. Her sexy romps shift off shelves like billyo. As a Cotswold-based scribbler, she gave kind advice to a great admirer from that part of the country, Joanna Trollope, who composed what Graham Lord in the Telegraph calls 'Aga sagas' about village life.

against

See be/run UP against something.

age

act/be one's age

to behave or think in a mature way. Often as a generalized imperative or to reinforce an assertion made to correct somebody. The phrase also occurs in humorous extensions such as *act your age, not your shoe size* (i.e. between 4 and 12 in the system in use in Britain). *Early 20th cent.*

Nevil Shute *No Highway* 1948
Do you think the Inspection would have let this aircraft fly if there was any danger of that sort of thing? Be your age.

age before beauty
young people should give precedence to their elders. Usually as a humorous or casual remark when holding a door open for somebody (not necessarily older) or yielding the right of way. The phrase pays a compliment to the person giving precedence. The corollary sometimes found is *the dog follows its master*, and an anecdote attributes to the American writer and wit Dorothy Parker the retort 'pearls before swine', although this is thought to be apocryphal. Eric Partridge (*A Dictionary of Catch Phrases*, 1977), defined the phrase in a way that is not now familiar ('a girl's mock courtesy addressed to an old – or, at best, an elderly – man') and regarded it as 'rarely heard' after 1960; the second edition, edited by Paul Beale (1985) correctly notes that it is still very much in use. *19th cent.*

Charles Hale Hoyt *A Midnight Bell* 1889
Why, age before beauty – no, no, I mean beauty before age!

age of consent
the age at which a person may legally agree to marriage or to sexual intercourse. *19th cent.*

age of discretion
the age at which a person is legally regarded as being responsible for their own actions, usually 14. *18th cent.*

Henry Fielding *The History of Tom Jones* 1749
My Sister, tho' many years younger than me, is at least old enough to be at the age of discretion.

age of reason
in Christianity, the age at which a child is held to be capable of distinguishing right from wrong. *17th cent.*

John Reynolds *The Flower of Fidelitie* 1650
The physnomie of his face, as true almanacks of future qualities, did perfectly prognosticate that his princely self would at the age of reason undoubtedly merit to be triumphantly crowned with the superlative laurel garlands of Olympian dignified fame.

the awkward age
a person's adolescence, when no longer a child but not yet an adult: also commonly in the form *at*

an awkward age = during adolescence (with the implication of suffering emotional problems). *The Awkward Age* is the title of a novel by Henry James (1899) about an adolescent young woman. *19th cent.*

Mrs Gaskell *Wives and Daughters* 1866
'How old is Miss Gibson?' 'Seventeen. It's a very awkward age for a motherless girl.'

Iain Banks *The Crow Road* 1993
'Why do you think he doesn't want to talk with us?' Prentice's thin face looked genuinely puzzled ... 'I think,' Rory said, 'it's called being at an awkward age.'

come of age
to reach the legal status of an adult (also in early use in the form *come to age*). Also in extended uses of countries and organizations that become fully established or recognized. *18th cent.*

Defoe *Roxana* 1724
I assur'd him, I had made my will, and that I had left it 5000l. and the interest of it till he shou'd come of age.

L S Dorman et al *Leonard Cohen* 1990
In the century which Canadians believed belonged to them, poetry had come of age.

feel/look one's age
(as a resigned or despairing admission, or in the negative as a compliment) to feel or look as old as one actually is. *19th cent.*

Louise Chandler Moulton *Juno Clifford* 1856
The boy of almost sixteen, who answered the summons, was quite a different looking person. He was well, though not richly dressed, handsome, and manly – looking his age, with an honest yet fearless expression of countenance.

See also a GOLDEN age; UNDER age.

agenda

a hidden agenda
concealed motives or intentions. *Agenda* (plural of *agendum*) is found alongside *agends* (plural of the disused form *agend*) from the 18th cent. In its collective countable meaning, often treated as a singular, it is early 20th cent. *Late 20th cent.*

Guardian 1984
For women ministers, the first hurdle is to get a parish. A minister is 'called' to a church by the congregation, who form a vacancy committee to

interview applicants and invite selected candidates to preach as guests. The greatest difficulty for a woman minister is to get herself selected by a committee which normally has a preponderance of men. 'Quite often there is a hidden agenda, and the ideal is a married man, 35-plus with two children.'

agony

agony aunt
a newspaper or magazine columnist, traditionally a woman, who advises readers on personal problems. See also *agony column*. *19th cent.*

Alice T Ellis *Unexplained Laughter* 1985
Dear agony aunt, said Lydia in her head, I have a person staying with me whose presence disinclines me from food.

agony column
a column written by an agony aunt in a newspaper or magazine. The agony column of a newspaper originally advertised details of missing friends and relatives and therefore involved more genuine *agony* than in the modern trivialized use. *19th cent.*

Conan Doyle *The Sign of Four* 1890
I tossed the paper down upon the table, but at that moment my eye caught an advertisement in the agony column.

pile on the agony
to make a bad situation much worse. *Mid 20th cent.*

Guardian 1984
The Minister for the Arts ... has delayed the issuing of an export licence to give a British public collection a chance to match the valuation – £436,800. He has already embargoed the export of 12 drawings valued at about £13 million, from the Duke's collection. The latest embargo piles on the agony for the British Museum and other bodies anxious to keep the drawings in this country.

prolong the agony
to make an unpleasant situation or experience last longer than is necessary. *Mid 20th cent.*

The Times 1985
Mr Gow ... could not support the Government's change of policy on Northern Ireland. That change, including the involvement of the foreign power in a consultative role in the administration of the

province, 'will prolong and not diminish the agony of Ulster', Mr Gow said.

agree
See agree to DIFFER.

agreement
See a gentleman's agreement *at* GENTLEMAN.

ahead
See ahead of the GAME; streets ahead *at* STREET.

aid

aid and abet
to help and encourage somebody to do something wrong or ill-advised. *Abet* is now used only in this phrase: it is cognate with *bait* and *bite* and is derived from an Old French word meaning 'to urge on hounds' in hunting. *18th cent.*

Frances Sheridan *Memoirs of Miss Sidney Bidulph* 1761
Mr. Faulkland and I correspond, and I know how all matters stand. You are not made acquainted, perhaps, that I was aiding and abetting to a certain scheme.

Stephanie Howard *Miracles Can Happen* 1992
Was she actually planning to aid and abet him in this unexpected, meaningless sexual dalliance?

what's all this in aid of?
British, informal what is the purpose of this idea, activity, etc? The phrase in aid of (= supporting) dates from the 18th cent., and the present phrase is recorded from the mid 20th cent.

Michael Innes *Old Hall, New Hall* 1956
He couldn't quite make out what Olivia's questions and speculations were in aid of.

air

in / up in the air
(said of ideas) hypothetical or speculative; (said of issues) still under discussion, unresolved. *In the air* also has the meaning 'in people's minds, under general consideration'. *19th cent.*

F W Farrar *The Life and Work of St Paul* 1879
The appreciation of Shakspere and the dramatic art perceptible in both these great writers was, as the

phrase is, in the air, – in the air, i.e., breathed by those who stood on the height of European culture.

Joan Beech One WAAF's War 1989
There was a general feeling of change in the air.

into / out of thin air

(with reference to sudden appearance or disappearance) completely; as though by magic; without any trace at all. *17th cent.*

Shakespeare The Tempest IV.i.150 (1613)
These our actors | As I foretold you, were all spirits, and | Are melted into air, into thin air.

National Trust Magazine 1991
We needed a washing line to dry some tea towels and within minutes one had been created almost out of thin air.

on/off the air

being (or not being) broadcast on radio or television. *Early 20th cent.*

New Musical Express 1992
The BBC almost took Pinky & Perky off the air on Election Day for fear of its 'political content' (i.e. the two jolly piglet puppets get into Downing St) but changed their minds.

put on / give oneself airs (and graces)

to act in a superior or pretentious way. In early use the phrase had the more neutral meaning of taking on an assumed, and not necessarily superior, manner. *18th cent.*

William Oldisworth Volpone, Or the Fox 1715
The wolves, for sure they hate and fly, | You know the cause as well as I. | If they'd succeeded, as they thought, | Then you and I had come to nought, | So we have reason to look shy, | And put on airs, when they are by.

Thackeray The Adventures of Philip 1862
I know what sort of company I prefer myself: but that is not the point. What I would hint is, that we possibly give ourselves patronizing airs before small people, as folks higher placed than ourselves give themselves airs before us.

take the air

dated to go out of doors, to walk in the open air. *16th cent.*

tread/walk on air

to be conspicuously elated or jubilant. *18th cent.*

Jane Austen Northanger Abbey 1818
If Wednesday should ever come! … It came – it was fine – and Catherine trod on air.

See also build castles in the air *at* CASTLE; CLEAR the air; HOT air.

---

aisle

have people rolling in the aisles

informal to cause great laughter or mirth: with reference to the aisles or passageways of a theatre or cinema, the notion being of the audience falling into these areas in their state of helplessness. *Mid 20th cent.*

P G Wodehouse Quick Service 1940
I made the speech of a lifetime. I had them tearing up the seats and rolling in the aisles.

knock them in the aisles

to make an overwhelming impression on people. The image is of an entertainer having a powerful effect on an audience in a theatre. *20th cent.*

walk / lead somebody up the aisle

to be married in a church. It is sometimes pointed out that the idiom is incorrect, since the bride walks up the nave of the church and not any of the aisles (which are at the sides of the building); but idiom is frequently based on such misapprehensions. There are many fanciful and romantic variants of the phrase: *see also* get / lead somebody to the ALTAR. *19th cent.*

Kate Wiggin The Old Peabody Pew a1923
If I had courage enough to wait for you all this time I've got courage enough to walk up the aisle with you, and marry you besides.

Fiona Cooper I Believe in Angels 1993
She dreamed of floating up the aisle in frothy white, to stand beside a dark-suited figure.

---

aitch

drop one's aitches

to fail to pronounce an aspirated h at the beginning of a word. *Aitch* as a name for the letter H is 19th cent. An earlier form *ache*, with play on the more familiar word of that spelling, dates from about 1600. *19th cent.*

G B Shaw Man and Superman 1903
This man takes more trouble to drop his aitches than ever his father did to pick them up.

Aladdin

an Aladdin's cave
a collection of priceless or valuable things, especially one encountered by chance or after a search: from the name of a hero of the stories in the *Arabian Nights*, used allusively from the early 19th cent.

> Lydia Child *A Romance of the Republic* 1867
> *High above our heads were great rocks of sapphire, deepening to lapis-lazuli at the base, with here and there a streak of malachite. 'It seems like Aladdin's Cave,' remarked Flora.*

> John Braine *Room at the Top* 1957
> *I was taking Susan not as Susan, but as a Grade A lovely, as the daughter of a factory-owner, as the means of obtaining the key to the Aladdin's cave of my ambitions.*

an Aladdin's lamp
a means of getting anything one wants, with allusion to the story of the genie of the lamp invoked by Aladdin in the *Arabian Nights*. *19th cent.*

> Byron *Don Juan* 1823
> *Yes! ready money is Aladdin's lamp.*

alarm

Originally (in Middle English) a call to arms (from Italian *all' arme!*). The spelling *alarum* represents an earlier pronunciation with the rolling sound of the *r* fully articulated.

alarm bells sound / start to ring
there are clear warnings of trouble or danger. The phrase has been used in various forms. *Late 20th cent.*

> *Guardian* 1984
> *Dr David Owen ... said the dispute showed how difficult it was to reduce the monopoly power of public sector unions. The outcome was still uncertain but once the National Coal Board started to back off, the alarm bells sounded for those who had watched successive governments retreat under pressure from industrial action.*

alar(u)ms and excursions
wild confusion or fighting: originally used as a stage instruction in Shakespearean drama, especially in the battle scenes (e.g. in *Richard III*, 1593) and usually in the form 'Alarum. Excursions'. An *alarm* is a call to arms (see introduction above), and an *excursion* is the ensuing attack on the enemy. *16th cent.*

albatross

an albatross round one's neck
a source of encumbrance or guilt. An albatross was supposed to bring good luck at sea. In Coleridge's narrative poem *The Rime of the Ancient Mariner* (1798), the mariner shoots an albatross whose earlier appearance had freed the ship from being trapped by ice. The shooting brings a curse on the ship and its crew, and the dead albatross is hung round his neck as a punishment: 'Instead of the cross, the albatross | About my neck was hung'. One by one the crew members die, leaving the mariner alone (and eventually freed of the albatross and the curse) to sail the world telling his tale. Allusive uses date from the early 20th cent.

> Ogden Nash in *McCall's* 1955
> *For when you're cross, Amanda, I feel an albatross | Around my neck.*

alight
See SET the world alight.

alive

alive and kicking
alive and flourishing. *19th cent.*

> James Fenimore Cooper *Ned Myers* 1843
> *The next day a doctor's boat came alongside, and we were ordered to show ourselves, and flourish our limbs, in order to make it evident we were alive and kicking.*

alive and well
flourishing, often despite contrary rumours or suspicions. Originally used in answer to casual queries about a person one has lost touch with, the phrase surely received a powerful boost from Sir Arthur Conan Doyle, who prefaced his final set of detective stories (*His Last Bow*, 1917) with the assurance 'the friends of Mr Sherlock Holmes will be glad to learn that he is still alive and well', despite having been killed off – to all appearances – in an earlier adventure. The phrase was extended to figurative contexts of ideas and institutions, and since the mid 20th cent. has often

had an extension introduced by 'and' (typically *and living in such-and-such a place*). The use in the *New Statesman* (see below) was in response to a cover for *Time Magazine* published in 1966 with the heading 'Is God Dead?' Other replies included 'God is not dead – but alive and well and working on a less ambitious project.' A similar anecdotal extension to the phrase appeared in the title of a revue *Jacques Brel is Alive and Well and Living in Paris*, which opened at the Village Gate in New York in 1968, with songs by the eponymous Belgian singer and songwriter, who died ten years later – in Paris, as it happens. *18th cent.*

Jane Barker *Exilius* 1719
The poor girl was wet, fatigu'd, and faint, otherwise alive and well; for the young monster had found her when she first fell into the water.

New Statesman 1966
Much of today's wittiest and most significant writing can be found scrawled on walls ... How would the Englishman react to 'God is alive and living in Argentina', or 'God is Dead: Nietzsche', countered by 'Nietzsche is dead: God'?

all

all along
during the whole course of a period or activity: originally with neutral meaning, later in the context of a contrary suggestion or expectation. *17th cent.*

Addison in the *Spectator* 1712
It was certainly a very bold thought in our author, to ascribe the first use of artillery to the rebel angels. But as such a pernicious invention may be well supposed to have proceeded from such authors, so it entered very properly into the thoughts of that being, who is all along described as aspiring to the majesty of his maker.

all along the line
at every point, continuously: originally with reference to a line of battle. *19th cent.*

Macaulay *History of England* 1855
All along the line ... there was long a disputed territory.

all and sundry
people or things of every kind. The phrase appears earlier in other forms: *all and some* is the oldest and occurs in Chaucer (*The Knight's Tale* 2187: 'And in this wise thise lordes, alle and some, | Been on the Sonday to the citee come'). *19th cent.*

Scott *Old Mortality* 1816
The Duke pronounced sentence of death upon him ... and adjudged him to be carried from the bar to the common place of execution, and there hanged by the neck; his head and hands to be stricken off after death, and disposed of according to the pleasure of the Council, and all and sundry his moveable goods and gear escheat [= forfeit] and inbrought to his Majesty's use.

all comers
everybody who is present or chooses to be present, especially as a competitor or rival. *16th cent.*

Henry Roberts *Honours Conquest* 1598
The princesse humbly thanking them for their loue and fauor, calling Alynda vnto her, commanded her to go to the Emperor, and to craue at his hands, to trie against all comers, his strength.

all ears
attentive to anything that might be said or suggested. *19th cent.*

Robert Montgomery Bird *The Hawks of Hawk Hollow* 1835
Come, begin; I am all ears – that is, metaphorically speaking; though a viler metaphor, to come from men of rational imagination, could not have been invented.

all eyes
the watchful attendance or observation of everybody present. *17th cent.*

Shakespeare *The Tempest* iv.i.59 (1613)
[Prospero] Now come, my Ariel! ... Appear, and pertly. (To Ferdinand and Miranda) No tongue, all eyes! Be silent.

all in
worn out from work or effort, exhausted. *Early 20th cent.*

A D McFaul *Ike Glidden* 1903
The horse was holding steady up to his clip, but it could be easily seen that he was 'all in'.

all of
used ironically of amounts that are surprisingly or significantly small. *19th cent.*

Mark Twain *Life on the Mississippi* 1883
It must have been all of fifteen minutes ... of dull, homesick silence.

all's well that ends well

(proverb) a situation is well if the circumstances end satisfactorily, even if all has not been well along the way. *Middle English*

> Shakespeare *All's Well That Ends Well* IV.iv.35 (1603)
> *All's well that ends well. Still the fine's* [= end is] *the crown.*

all things come to those that wait

(proverb) patience is rewarded. The sentiment dates in English from the 16th cent., although the present form of the phrase does not appear until the 19th cent.

> Longfellow *Tales of a Wayside Inn* 1863
> *Monna Giovanna, his beloved bride,* | *Never so beautiful, so kind, so fair,* | *Enthroned once more in the old rustic chair,* | *High-perched upon the back of which there stood* | *The image of a falcon carved in wood,* | *And underneath the inscription, with a date,* | *'All things come round to him who will but wait.'*

— and all

in addition, as well. *Late 20th cent.*

> Alice Grey *Hearts in Hiding* 1993
> *She asked me if I'd hold the baby while she went, as it might be cumbersome taking the bag and all.*

for all —

despite, notwithstanding: used as a preposition and conjunction. Common in the expressions *for all one cares* and *for all one knows. Middle English*

> Tyndale *Bible* Acts 16:39 1525
> *They have beaten us openly… for all that we are Romans.*

> Fay Weldon *Darcy's Utopia* 1991
> *'My brother,' said Nerina, 'can go to Saudi Arabia for all I care.'*

give somebody the all-clear

to tell somebody that a danger or difficulty has passed, or to give them authorization to proceed. To *get the all-clear* is to receive this information or authorization. The phrase alludes to the wartime signal that sounded when an air raid was over. *20th cent.*

> Financial Times 1982
> *How soon aerial advertising will get the all-clear is anyone's guess. All the Department of Trade will say is 'shortly, depending on ministers' minds'.*

See also all BEHIND, like a cow's tail; all girls together *at* GIRL; all hands *at* HAND; all MOUTH and (no) trousers; (all) of a SUDDEN; all of a TISWAS; all over bar the shouting *at* SHOUT; all over the MAP; all over the PLACE; all over the SHOP; all over the SHOW; all the RAGE; all SET; all-singing all-dancing *at* SING; all systems go *at* SYSTEM; all very WELL; all the WORLD and his wife; and all that JAZZ; be all fingers and (all) thumbs *at* FINGER; be all GO; be all ONE; be all OVER somebody; be all THERE; be all things to all men *at* THING; for all one is WORTH; it's all UP with —; my EYE/all my eye and Betty Martin; on all fours (with something) *at* FOUR; ONCE (and) for all.

---

alley

a blind alley

a choice or course of action that leads nowhere, i.e. is fruitless or unsuccessful: from its physical meaning, a road closed at one end, a cul-de-sac. Also (with hyphen) used descriptively before a noun. In its literal meaning the term dates from the 16th cent., and the figurative meaning dates from the early 20th cent.

> George Orwell *The Road to Wigan Pier* 1937
> *The youth who leaves school at fourteen and gets a blind-alley job is out of work at twenty, probably for life; but for two pounds ten on the hire-purchase system he can buy himself a suit which, for a little while and at a little distance, looks as though it had been tailored at Savile Row.*

up somebody's alley

suited to somebody: *cf* (right) up somebody's STREET. *Mid 20th cent.*

> W H Auden *New Year Letter* 1941
> *All vague idealistic art* | *That coddles the uneasy heart,* | *Is up his alley.*

---

allowance

make allowance(s) for somebody or something

to take special circumstances into consideration when dealing with somebody or something: based on the (17th cent.) meaning of *allowance* 'taking circumstances into account'. *19th cent.*

> Trollope *The Way We Live Now* 1875
> *As long as his father would make fair allowance for his own peccadilloes, – he also would make allowances for his father's roughness.*

alpha

alpha and omega

the beginning and the end. The phrase combines the names of the first and last letters of the Greek alphabet, and occurs in Wyclif's and Tyndale's translations of the Bible to denote eternity (Revelations 1:8 'I am alpha and omega, the beginning and the end, saith the Lord God'). *Middle English*

also

an also-ran

a person or thing that is uncompetitive or unsuccessful: originally with reference to a horse that fails to finish among the first three in a race. *19th cent.*

> Denman Thompson *Our New Minister* 1903
> [Strong] *You have an odd way of expressing yourself.* [Skeezicks] *Can't scratch it! I was brought up in that way. In New York you've got to be up to date, an' talk in ragtime, or they class you with the also-rans. So long!*

altar

get / lead somebody to the altar

to get married, especially in a determined or calculating way. There are many variants of the phrase, and figurative uses referring to other forms of alliance: *see also* walk / lead somebody up the AISLE. *19th cent.*

> Jane Austen *Pride and Prejudice* 1813
> *'I am not now to learn,' replied Mr. Collins, with a formal wave of the hand, 'that it is usual with young ladies to reject the addresses of the man whom they secretly mean to accept, when he first applies for their favour; and that sometimes the refusal is repeated a second or even a third time. I am therefore by no means discouraged by what you have just said, and shall hope to lead you to the altar ere long.'*

> Andrew Morton *Diana: Her True Story* 1993
> *As the hysterical media juggernaut pushed Charles and Diana along to the altar, she had to try and come to terms with her own feelings and thoughts about the Prince of Wales.*

sacrifice happiness/feelings, etc on the altar of love/desire, etc

to allow an intense or obsessive love or passion to destroy one's happiness or well-being. *18th cent.*

> M G Lewis *The Monk* 1796
> *As yet, my heart is free; I shall separate from you with regret, but not with despair. Stay here, and a few weeks will sacrifice my happiness on the altar of your charms; you are but too interesting, too amiable!*

altogether

the altogether

a state of nakedness: usually *in the altogether*. The noun is first recorded in the 17th cent. in the meaning 'a whole, a whole collection of something'; the current use is 19th cent.

> George Du Maurier *Trilby* 1894
> *It soon seemed as natural to sit for people as to run errands for them, or wash and mend their clothes ... I have sat for the 'altogether' to several other people ... and for the head and hands to lots of people.*

> Robin Smith *The Encyclopaedia of Sexual Trivia* 1990
> *Accommodating mainly mothers and children, the village had a warden and first-aid post and included tuition in basic skills like cooking (with special emphasis on careful use of the frying pan) 'in the altogether'.*

always

See always verify your references *at* REFERENCE.

American

the American dream

the ideals of democracy and equality of opportunity for everybody, seen as representing American social values and aspirations. It was coined by J T Adams in *The Epic of America* (1931), who wrote 'If the American dream is to come true and to abide with us, it will, at bottom, depend on the people themselves'; but it was surely Ernest Hemingway's use in 1937 that gave rise to the popular usage of the term, as well as its later use as the title of a play by Edward Albee (1961) and, in the form *An American Dream*, of a novel by Norman Mailer (1965). *Mid 20th cent.*

> Ernest Hemingway *To Have and Have Not* 1937
> *The Colt or Smith and Wesson ... so well designed to end the American dream when it becomes a nightmare.*

amiss

take something amiss

to take offence at something: originally, to mis-understand in more neutral senses. The phrase occurs in Middle English (Wyclif), but uses date predominantly from the 16th cent.

Edward Howard *The Man of Newmarket* 1678
[Bowser] *I have enough of this sort of Game, I thank you.* [Swiftspur] *Let me perswade thee; I know there are some here may take it amiss.*

— would not come/go amiss

it might be advisable or beneficial to do the thing specified. The phrase is derived from a physical meaning that describes a blow or aim finding its target. *18th cent.*

Addison in the *Spectator* 1712
Since none of the Criticks have considered Virgil's Fable, with relation to this History of Æneas, it may not, perhaps, be amiss to examine it in this Light, so far as regards my present Purpose.

amok

run amok

to create violent havoc, to behave uncontrollably. The phrase is used both figuratively and in phys-ical meanings close to the original meaning. *Amok* is derived via Portuguese from a Malay word *amoq* meaning 'a frenzied attack' and is also applied to the person carrying out such an attack; it sometimes appears in the more phonetic form *amuck*. It is normally used only in the phrase, but there are occasional uses outside it (as in the 1993 example below). *17th cent.*

Andrew Marvell *The Rehearsal Transpros'd* 1672
He would take it ill if we should not value him as an enemy of mankind: and like a raging Indian (for in Europe it was never before practised) he runs a mucke (as they cal it there) stabbing every man he meets, till himself be knockt on the head.

Albyn Leah Hall *Deliria* 1993
Her body's intact but her mind's amok, though if you're askin' me, I'd say that was nothin' new.

analysis

in the final analysis

when everything has been considered or evalu-ated: used to state a general conclusion (often a platitude or cliché) about a complex situation: *cf* when all is said and done *at* SAY. *19th cent.*

G H Lewes *The Principles of Success in Literature* 1891
Thus liberty, equality, humanity (the three-fold form of this century's mission) are not, so to speak, 'doctrinal points' in the formalised religion of the epoch; but inasmuch as they express (in the final analysis) the object and faith of the crusade in which all Europe is now sensibly or insensibly engaged, and as they have to complete a great social end, so may they be considered as eminently religious.

Vladimir Nabokov *The Gift* 1963
'And what's her nose like?' asked Alexandra Yakovlevna. 'You know, to tell you the truth I didn't look at it very carefully and in the final analysis all girls aspire to be beauties. Let's not be catty.'

ancient

the Ancient of Days

a biblical name for God (Daniel 7:9), occurring also in Robert Grant's hymn 'O worship the King' (1833): 'Our Shield and Defender, the Ancient of Days, | Pavilioned in splendour, and girded with praise.' *16th cent.*

be ancient history

to belong to the past, to be no longer relevant or important. The meaning evolved during the 19th cent. from political references to more trivial everyday uses.

William Morris *News From Nowhere* 1891
All this seemed very interesting to me, and I should like to have made the old man talk more. But Dick got rather restive under so much ancient history: besides, I suspect he wanted to keep me as fresh as he could for his great-grandfather.

See also (as) old/ancient as the hills *at* HILL.

and

See and HOW!; and that's OFFICIAL.

angel

Figurative and allusive uses are recorded from the 16th cent. (and Romeo addresses Juliet as a 'bright angel' in Shakespeare's *Romeo and Juliet* (1596) II.i.68).

the angel in the house

a devoted wife and mother: after the title of a collection of poems in praise of married love by Coventry Patmore (published from 1854 to 1863). *19th cent.*

Louisa M Alcott *Work: A Story of Experience* 1873
I didn't find out why I liked my friend so well till I lost her. I had just begun to feel that you were very dear, – for after the birthday you were like an angel in the house, Christie, – when you changed all at once, and I thought you suspected me, and didn't like it.

Michael Dibdin *Dirty Tricks* 1991
It's a bit late to be coming on like the Angel in the House now.

enough to make the angels weep

very distressing or embarrassing. The locus classicus is Isabella's speech in Shakespeare's *Measure for Measure* (1605) II.ii.126: 'But man, proud man, | Dressed in a little brief authority, | Most ignorant of what he's most assured, | His glassy essence, like an angry ape | Plays such fantastic tricks before high heaven | As makes the angels weep.' *17th cent.*

John Philip Kemble *Alexander the Great* 1796
'Twas but a dream; and yet I saw and heard | My royal parents, who, while pious care | Sat on their faded cheeks, pronounc'd with tears, | Tears such as angels weep, this hour my last.

Mary Wollstonecraft *Mary* 1788
Shade of my loved Ann! dost thou ever visit thy poor Mary? Refined spirit, thou wouldst weep, could angels weep, to see her struggling with passions she cannot subdue; and feelings which corrode her small portion of comfort!

Dickens *Oliver Twist* 1838
Although within such walls enough fantastic tricks are daily played to make the angels weep hot tears of blood, they are closed to the public, save through the medium of the daily press.

(fools rush in) where angels fear to tread

(proverb) being precipitate or impulsive is no substitute for prudent consideration: also in many variant forms. The phrase is taken from Pope's *Essay on Criticism* (1711): 'Nay, fly to altars; there they'll talk you dead; | For fools rush in where angels fear to tread. | Distrustful sense with modest caution speaks.' *Where Angels Fear to Tread* is the title of E M Forster's first novel (1905), which has as its theme the tragic consequences of impulsive romance. *18th cent.*

Edmund Burke *Reflections on the Revolution in France* 1790
What ought to be the heads, the hearts, the dispositions that are qualified or that dare … at one heat to strike out a totally new constitution for a great kingdom…? But – 'fools rush in where angels fear to tread'.

Hardy *The Woodlanders* 1887
He felt shy of entering Grace's presence as her reconstituted lover – which was how her father's manner would be sure to present him – before definite information as to her future state was forthcoming: it seemed too nearly like the act of those who rush in where angels fear to tread.

James Joyce *Ulysses* 1922
Later on, at a propitious opportunity he purposed (Bloom did), without anyway prying into his private affairs on the fools step in where angels principle advising him to sever his connection with a certain budding practitioner.

on the side of the angels

supporting what is right: originally used by Benjamin Disraeli in a speech in 1864 defending the spiritual nature of human origins against Darwin's theories published in *The Origin of Species* (1859): 'Is man an ape or an angel? Now I am on the side of the angels.' *19th cent.*

Ann Wroe *Lives, Lies and the Iran-Contra Affair* 1991
Somebody ought to stand up and acknowledge what we have done because we are on the side of the angels.

---

angry

an angry young man

a young man who scornfully rejects conventional social values, with reference to the title of a work by the Irish writer Leslie Paul (1951). The term *Angry Young Men* was used to refer to a group of British writers and playwrights in the 1950s, especially in connection with John Osborne's play *Look Back in Anger* (published in 1957). *Mid 20th cent.*

Hot Press 1991
Long past his angry young man stage, Dave Couse has embraced the era of the paranoid, terrified, unsure, disgruntled, disillusioned slightly older man.

(as) angry as a wasp

extremely angry: based on the proverbial aggressiveness of wasps. *16th cent.*

Annie

up in Annie's room

informal used in answer to an enquiry about a person's whereabouts, either because the speaker doesn't know or because they are unwilling to say. The phrase dates from forces' slang in the First World War, when it was most likely used about soldiers who were missing or had been killed. The choice of Annie is unexplained, and was probably just a random use of a common enough name in the sense of 'any woman'. Later the phrase was extended with the addition ... *and behind the clock*, which suggests an altogether more furtive association. *Early 20th cent.*

another

See in another PLACE.

answer

the answer to a maiden's prayer

an eligible bachelor. Although the phrase in this specific form is fairly recent, the notion of women needing help by means of a *maiden's prayer* appears in literature from the 19th cent. *Mid 20th cent.*

> J Fleming *Maiden's Prayer* 1957
> You're the answer to a maiden's prayer, dear heart. No need for you to do a stroke of work, you can marry money and live the life of a gentleman.

know all the answers

to be well-informed or experienced: usually (with unfavourable overtones) to be glibly clever or precocious. *Mid 20th cent.*

> Angus Wilson *Anglo-Saxon Attitudes* 1956
> She'd been a glamour girl, but she knew all the answers.

See also the answer's a LEMON.

ant

have ants in one's pants

informal to be impatient or restless. *Mid 20th cent.*

ante

raise/up the ante

chiefly NAmer to increase what is at stake or intensify what is at issue: originally with reference to the stake placed in a game of poker. *19th cent.*

> Melville D Landon *Eli Perkins* 1875
> The Rev. Winfield Scott, a devilish good old minister from Denver, was takin' a quiet game of poker with another passenger at the time. He had just got four queens and was raisin' the ante to fifteen dollars when one of the robbers pointed his pistol at him.

any

See any PORT in a storm.

anybody

See anybody's/anyone's GUESS.

anything

anything goes

anything can be done or is acceptable; there are no rules or restrictions. The currency of the phrase was enhanced by its use as the title of a musical and song title by Cole Porter (1934). *Everything goes* is a common variant still sometimes found. *19th cent.*

> George Meredith *The Egoist* 1879
> 'Patrick will be sure to aspirate the initial letter of Hibernia.' 'That is clever criticism, upon my word, Miss Middleton! So he would. And there we have two letters dropped. But he'd do it in a groan, so that it wouldn't count for more than a ghost a one; and everything goes on the stage, since it's only the laugh we want on the brink of the action.'

if anything can go wrong, it will

a proverb underlining the perverseness of life, known as *Murphy's law* (*see* MURPHY) or *Sod's law* (*see* SOD).

See also (do) anything for a quiet LIFE.

apart

See be poles apart *at* POLE; come/fall apart at the seams *at* SEAM.

ape

go ape
informal, originally NAmer to go crazy; to be crazily keen on something; to go wildly wrong; to malfunction. The phrase may have been influenced by early 20th cent. stories and films about human dealings with wild animals, notably the film *King Kong* (1933) about a giant ape. *Mid 20th cent.*

lead apes in hell
to suffer the traditional fate of unmarried women when they die. Shakespeare uses the expression on two noteworthy occasions. In *The Taming of the Shrew* (1592), Katherine protests that her father is favouring her sister's marriage before her own (II.i.32): 'She is your treasure, she must have a husband. I I must dance barefoot on her wedding day, I And for your love to her lead apes in hell.' And in *Much Ado About Nothing* (1598), Beatrice, dismissing the possibility of marriage, declares (I.iii.36) 'I will even take sixpence in earnest of the bearherd and lead his apes into hell.' A bearherd was a keeper of tame bears, and the reference here suggests that bears and perhaps other animals were also involved in the notion. *16th cent.*

Alexander Oldys *The Female Gallant* 1692
You shall either marry me, or dye of the Pip, and so lead apes in Hell.

apology

an apology for —
a pitiful specimen of, or inadequate substitute for, something. *18th cent.*

James Fenimore Cooper *The Last of the Mohicans* 1826
Leaning with one elbow on the blanket that concealed an apology for a saddle.

Henry James *The Ambassadors* 1903
Do you consider her even an apology for a decent woman?

with apologies to —
used to name an author or source that has been adapted or parodied in quotation: a specific application of a general use. *Late 20th cent.*

Jack Caplan *Memories of the Gorbals* 1991
With apologies to Winston Churchill I venture to mis-quote: 'Never has so much rubbish been written by a few, against so many.'

appeal

appeal from Philip drunk to Philip sober
to appeal to somebody in authority to reconsider an unfavourable decision. The phrase is based on an anecdote concerning King Philip II of Macedon (4th cent. BC, father of Alexander the Great): a poor woman appealed to the king for justice but was refused, whereupon she exclaimed 'I appeal.' 'To whom do you appeal?' asked the astonished king, to which the woman replied 'from Philip drunk to Philip sober'. The story is recorded among the historical anecdotes collected in the 1st cent. AD by Valerius Maximus (VI.2.1: *Provocarem ad Philippum, inquit, sed sobrium* 'She would appeal to Philip, she said, but to Philip sober'). *19th cent.*

Mrs Gaskell *Wives and Daughters* 1866
Mr. Preston turned to Roger, as if appealing from Philip drunk to Philip sober, and spoke in a tone of cool explanation, which, though not insolent in words, was excessively irritating in manner.

appeal to Caesar
to appeal to the highest authority. The phrase refers to the action of St Paul in invoking his right as a Roman citizen to appeal to the Emperor against the outcome of his trial before M Porcius Festus in Caesarea, known from Acts 25:11–12 'I [Paul] appeal unto Caesar. Then Festus, when he had conferred with the council, answered, Hast thou appealed unto Caesar? unto Caesar shalt thou go.' *19th cent.*

Edward Eggleston *The End of the World* 1872
But so long as it's nobody but Goshorn, I'm goin' to stay and litigate the question till the Millerite millennium comes. I appeal to Cæsar or somebody else.

appearance

appearances are deceptive
(proverb) circumstances are not always what they appear to be. The form *appearances are deceiving* is also used, especially in North America. The proverb is entered in collections of the 17th cent.

and 18th cent., but does not appear in literature before the 19th cent.

Mrs Humphry Ward *Robert Elsmere* 1888
'The men of action are to be found with us.' 'It hardly looks just now as if the upper class was to go on enjoying a monopoly of them,' he said, smiling. 'Then appearances are deceptive. The populace supplies mass and weight – nothing else.'

keep up appearances
to maintain an outward show of normality or respectability. The phrase appears earliest in the form *save appearances*. The related phrase *for the sake of appearances* dates from the same time and was common in the 19th cent. *18th cent.*

Richardson *Pamela* 1741
The poor Gentleman has been oddly affected at our coming; tho' the good Breeding of the Lady has made her just keep up Appearances.

Angela Carter *The Magic Toyshop* 1967
She put plastic holly in the windows, to keep up appearances.

put in an appearance
to appear at a place in person, usually briefly and for form's sake. *19th cent.*

Conan Doyle *Resident Patient* 1893
Our visitors arrived at the appointed time, but it was quarter to four before my friend put in an appearance.

to/by all appearances
as it seems to be; apparently. The form *to all appearance* is recorded earlier. *17th cent.*

Anon *The London Jilt* 1683
They came upon me like devils, and seem'd as if they would have torn me in pieces; and according to all appearances I should have been swing'd of, if in that extream necessity I had not invented a piece of cunning.

---

apple

Apple appears from Middle English in similes and proverbial expressions (e.g. *as sure as God made little apples*). It has various symbolic attributes: dissension in the story of Eris (*apple of discord*), a thing of great value (*the apple of one's eye*), temptation in the biblical story of the creation, and homeliness in the American fondness for apple pie.

an apple a day keeps the doctor away
(proverb) an exhortation to eat a healthy diet. Also used in shortened and allusive forms. Recorded as a Pembrokeshire proverb in *Notes & Queries* (February 1866, p.153): 'Eat an apple on going to bed. And you'll keep the doctor from earning his bread.' *19th cent.*

apple of discord
something bitterly contended over: from the story that Eris, goddess of strife, threw a golden apple inscribed 'for the fairest' amongst the Greek gods, whereupon it was claimed by three goddesses, Hera, Athene, and Aphrodite. *17th cent.*

Samuel Holland *Don Zara del Fogo* 1656
The British bards (forsooth) were also ingaged in quarrel for superiority; and who think you, threw the apple of discord amongst them, but Ben Johnson, who had openly vaunted himself the first and best of English Poets.

Charlotte Brontë *Jane Eyre* 1847
The very name of love is an apple of discord between us – if the reality were required, what should we do?

the apple of one's eye
a precious or highly cherished person or thing. In English from the time of King Alfred, the *apple of the eye* was a name for the pupil, and served as a powerful image of a cherished thing or (more usually) person. Shakespeare in *A Midsummer Night's Dream* (1595) makes Oberon squeeze magic juice into the eye of the lover Demetrius with the incantation (III.ii.104) 'Flower of this purple dye, | Hit with Cupid's archery, | Sink in apple of his eye'. The pupil was mistakenly thought to be a solid ball, a notion which gave rise to the current meaning. The locus classicus in this sense is the biblical use in Proverbs 7:2: 'Keep my commandments, and live; and my law as the apple of thine eye', and Deuteronomy 32:10, where God is said to have protected Jacob and 'kept him as the apple of his eye'. *16th cent.*

Willa Cather *O Pioneers!* 1913
Marie was his youngest child, by a second wife, and was the apple of his eye.

apple-pie bed
a bed made with the sheets folded back halfway down as a practical joke, preventing the occupant's legs from being properly stretched out. The origin is as obscure as it is for *apple-pie*

order (see the following phrase), and we cannot even be sure that there is any historical connection between the two phrases. *Apple-pie* could be a corruption of the French phrase *cap-à-pie* meaning 'from head to foot', which fits the context of the English phrase in a vague way, though hardly with any close relevance to what is going on in an apple-pie bed. Elaborate explanations of this kind are always suspicious in their neatness; a more likely origin, feeble though it may seem, is the shallow form of an apple-pie, resembling the shortness of the bed, in the minds of early users of the phrase. *18th cent.*

apple-pie order
perfect order or organization. It is tempting to align this phrase with the orderliness of American mothers baking their apple pies (see elsewhere in this entry), but the phrase is found earliest in British and not American English. The earliest evidence is from the journals of a seaman named Thomas Pasley, in an entry for 1780 where he wrote that the sailors were 'clean and in apple-pie order on Sundays'. This is followed by a letter of Sir Walter Scott quoted in the memoirs of Scott by John Lockhart published in 1839, which contains the description 'the children's garden is in apple-pie order'. An alternative suggestion, that apple-pie is a corruption of *cap-à-pie* meaning 'from head to foot' (see the previous phrase), is too neat to be believable (and in this regard much too reminiscent of the suggestions made for *raining cats and dogs*), and is undermined by the absence of any early evidence for a form *cap-à-pie order* (or any intermediate forms), which we would surely expect if this were the true origin. *18th cent.*

James Kenney *Sweethearts and Wives* 1823
You gave me the key, you know, sir, and I have been setting them all to rights. When you go, you'll find everything in apple-pie order.

Jeffrey Archer *As the Crow Flies* 1991
Becky turned out to be as good as her word, keeping the accounts in what she described as 'apple-pie order'.

(as) American as apple pie
Apple pie is used in various phrases as a stock symbol of American motherhood and traditional family life. *Mid 20th cent.*

Joseph Heller *Catch-22* 1961
The hot dog, the Brooklyn Dodgers. Mom's apple pie. That's what everyone's fighting for.

she's apples
informal, chiefly Australian and NZ everything is fine, all is well: from rhyming slang *apples and rice* or *apples and spice* for 'nice'. *Mid 20th cent.*

J Binning *Target Area* 1943
If everything is running smoothly 'she's apples'.

upset the apple cart
to ruin a carefully laid scheme, or undermine the status quo where there are interests in maintaining it. *18th cent.*

Thomas Fessenden *Political Squib* 1806
Simon Spunkey, Esq. showeth, that the prayer of a certain 'Memorial', from Matthew Lyon, stating his pre-eminent qualifications for a seat in our national legislature, is just and reasonable. – Talketh big words to congress, and threateneth to overturn their apple-cart, and set his foot in it!

See also a ROTTEN apple.

approval

on approval
(said of goods) sent to a customer for inspection without an obligation to buy. *19th cent.*

seal/stamp of approval
an authoritative statement that something is satisfactory or acceptable: from the practice of putting an official seal or stamp on a document to authenticate it. *Early 20th cent.*

Charles Klein *The Third Degree* 1909
I refuse to be engulfed in this wave of hysterical sympathy with criminals. I will not be stamped with the same hall-mark as the man who takes the life of his fellow being – though that man is my son. I will not set the seal of approval on crime – by defending it.

April

April fool
a trick played on All Fools' Day (1 April), or a person tricked in this way. The link between trickery and this date is first found in the 1690s, although this kind of exploitation of the gullible is seen earlier, for example in Thomas Dekker's *Seven Deadlie Sinnes of London* (1602),

which describes the actual pinning of a hoax note on the back of an unsuspecting passer-by: 'The booke-seller ever after when you passe by, pinnes on your backes the badge of fooles to make you be laught to scorne, or of sillie Carpers to make you be pittied.' *17th cent.*

> **Congreve** *The Old Batchelour* 1693
> *What, has he been here? That's one of Love's April-fools, is always upon some errand that's to no purpose, ever embarking on adventures, yet never comes to harbour.*

> **New Scientist** 1991
> *Commiserations to all readers who were taken in by our April fool.*

apron

tied to somebody's apron strings
unable to break free from the protection or domination of a woman, especially one's mother or wife, or from any over-protective person or dominant influence. The compound *apron strings* dates from the 16th cent., with early connotations of legal or emotional ties. A man had *apron-string tenure* or *apron-string hold* on property if he held it through his wife, or for her lifetime only. *17th cent.*

> **Thomas Tomkis** *Lingua* 1607
> *In the Court your gentlewomen hang me at their apron strings, and that makes them answer so readily.*

> **Dickens** *The Chimes* 1844
> *If I was a fine, young, strapping chap like you, I should be ashamed of being milksop enough to pin myself to a woman's apron-strings!*

area

See GREY area; no-go area *at* NO.

argue

argue the toss
informal to dispute a clear-cut decision: from the tossing of a coin to decide a matter according to the side facing up when the coin lands. The phrase is recorded first as military and naval slang. *Early 20th cent.*

ark

out of the ark
primitive, out of date, old-fashioned: with reference to the Jewish Ark of the Covenant and the vessel built by Noah in the biblical story (Genesis 6–9) of the Flood. *Late 20th cent.*

arm

an arm and a leg
a very high or exorbitant price. The phrase usually occurs in the form *cost an arm and a leg*, meaning 'to be exorbitantly expensive'. Another variant, *give an arm and a leg (for something)*, merges this phrase with *give one's right arm for* — (see below). *Mid 20th cent.*

> **Billie Holiday** *Lady Sings the Blues* 1956
> *Finally she found someone who sold her some stuff for an arm and a leg.*

at arm's length
at a distance, so as to be inaccessible or less of a threat: from the notion of holding something unpleasant or dangerous away from oneself with the arm outstretched. The phrase is found earlier in the form *at arm's end. 16th cent.*

> **Sir Philip Sidney** *The Countesse of Pembrokes Arcadia* a1586
> *Such a one as can keep him at arms end, need never wish for a better companion.*

> **Charles Lamb** *Essays of Elia* 1823
> *No person ... can, with any prospect of veracity, conduct a correspondence at such an arm's length.*

> **D H Lawrence** *Sons and Lovers* 1913
> *It tortured her, and so she tortured him. For a month at a time she kept him at arm's length.*

chance one's arm
to do something adventurous or risky. The phrase is entered in slang dictionaries (including Barrère and Leland's *Dictionary of Slang, Jargon and Cant* of 1889) from the end of the 19th cent.

give one's right arm for —
to want something very badly, especially something unattainable, and be willing to make a great sacrifice for it. The earliest use is in *Sharpe's London Journal* of 1849: 'He felt as if he could gladly give his right arm to be cut off if it would make him, at once, old enough to go and earn money instead of Lizzy.' The phrase

also makes an appearance in a play by W S Gilbert (*Dan'l Druce*, 1876): 'Thou'rt comely, lass, and mebbe, ere long, some smart young lad will whip thee from my arms, and carry thee away to t'other side o' the sunrise. There's mor'n one within a mile o' this who'd give his right arm to do it now.' *19th cent.*

the long arm (of the law)

the far-reaching and inescapable power of the police or other authorities to administer justice. The phrase dates in its present form from the middle of the 19th cent., but the image is somewhat older. Scott, for example, wrote in *Rob Roy* in 1817: 'The arm of the law was also gradually abridging the numbers of those whom I endeavoured to serve, and the hearts of the survivors became gradually more contracted towards all whom they conceived to be concerned with the existing government.' The phrase was picked up by Dickens, who seems to have been fond of it. In *Pickwick Papers* in 1837, we find: 'These are two cut-throats from London, who have come down here to destroy his Majesty's population: thinking that at this distance from the capital, the arm of the law is weak and paralysed.' The phrase also occurs in the slightly different form *the strong arm of the law*, and Dickens combined both forms in *The Old Curiosity Shop*, published four years after *Pickwick* (see below). Also used figuratively and extended to other contexts. *19th cent.*

Dickens *The Old Curiosity Shop* 1841
The gamblers, Isaac List and Jowl, with their trusty confederate Mr. James Groves of unimpeachable memory, pursued their course with varying success, until the failure of a spirited enterprise in the way of their profession, dispersed them in different directions, and caused their career to receive a sudden check from the long and strong arm of the law.

Emily Pfeiffer *The Wynnes of Wynhavod* 1882
Poor soul, she does not know | The long arm of the Law has hold of him!

Saki *Reginald in Russia* 1910
The long arm, or perhaps one might better say the long purse, of diplomacy at last effected the release of the prisoners.

Aldous Huxley *Letters* 1963
Talk about the long arm of coincidence! The mail which brought your note ... brought ... at the same time a letter from Betty Wendel.

put the arm on somebody

informal, originally NAmer to coerce somebody to do something: originally in a physical sense, to restrain or apprehend somebody with force. *Early 20th cent.*

one's right arm

1 one's most loyal or devoted friend or supporter. *17th cent.*

Southey transl *El Cid* 1637
Now the Cid ... made ready to go to the Cortes and with him went Alvar Fanez Minaya, who he called his right arm.

2 one's physical strength or stamina. *19th cent.*

Byron *Don Juan* 1824
Cervantes smiled Spain's chivalry away; a single laugh demolished the right arm of his own country; seldom since that day has Spain had heroes.

G B Shaw *Caesar and Cleopatra* 1901
Lend me your sword and your right arm for this campaign.

throw up one's arms

to express horror, outrage, or despair: from the physical reflex often arising in reaction to sudden fear or alarm. *20th cent.*

twist somebody's arm

to coerce somebody: often used with ironic humour in contexts where persuasion is hardly needed, e.g. in accepting an offer of a drink. *Mid 20th cent.*

with open arms

with warmth or enthusiasm: originally in the physical sense of an embrace. *17th cent.*

Dryden transl Plutarch's *Dion* c1690
But Speusippus and the rest of his friends assisted and encouraged him, bidding him deliver Sicily, which with lift-up hands implored his help, and with open arms was ready to receive him.

Mary Davys *The Lady's Tale* 1725
I have a Request to make to you both; which is, to let me wait upon you to see my poor Mother, who will, I am sure, receive us all with open arms.

Dickens *David Copperfield* 1850
I ... was received by her, and Mr Dick, and dear old Peggotty ... with open arms.

See also a BABE in arms.

armchair

an armchair critic/historian/philosopher
somebody who takes a theoretical or academic interest in a subject without becoming involved in its practical aspects or applications. The idea underlying the phrase appears in other forms in the 19th cent. For example, in George Eliot's *Middlemarch* (1872) the author remarks that 'a great historian ... glories in his copious remarks and digressions ... where he seems to bring his armchair to the proscenium and chat with us in all the lusty ease of his fine English'. In the British general election of 1886, according to *The Times Register of Events*, the radical leader Joseph Chamberlain (1836–1914) rounded on his opponents as 'armchair politicians'.

> **C Day Lewis transl Virgil's Aeneid 1952**
> *We don't want big talk from an armchair critic.*

armed

armed at all points
fully armed; ready for the affray. *Middle English* (in Lydgate)

> **Shakespeare Hamlet I.ii.200 (1601)**
> *A figure like your father, | Armed at all points exactly, cap-à-pie, | Appears before them, and with solemn march | Goes slow and stately by them.*

> **Henry James The Portrait of a Lady 1881**
> *Familiarity had modified in some degree her first impression of Madame Merle, but it had not essentially altered it ... That personage was armed at all points; it was a pleasure to see a character so completely equipped for the social battle.*

armed to the teeth
fully armed. Why the teeth? Either because the teeth are themselves weapons or, more likely, because pirates and brigands used to be shown in illustrations holding knives and daggers in their teeth, leaving their hands free for other work. *19th cent.*

> **Wilkie Collins The Moonstone 1868**
> *In the wild regions of Kattiawar (and how wild they are you will understand, when I tell you that even the husbandmen plough the land armed to the teeth), the population is fanatically devoted to the old Hindoo religion.*

> **Kenneth Grahame The Wind in the Willows 1903**
> *One dark night ... a band of weasels, armed to the teeth, crept silently up to the front entrance.*

> **Mark Twain Speeches 1906**
> *Let us abolish policemen who carry clubs and revolvers, and put in a squad of poets armed to the teeth with poems on Spring and Love.*

arms

a call to arms
a summons to action in support of a cause, originally to take up weapons (*to be called to arms*) in defence of one's home or country. In Fletcher and Shakespeare's *The Two Noble Kinsmen* (a1616), Palamon says of Theseus' friend Pirithous (II.ii.252–4) 'He shall see Thebes again, and call to arms | The bold young men that, when he bids 'em charge, | Fall on like fire.' *17th cent.*

> **William Hawkins The Siege of Aleppo 1758**
> *For thou shalt sally forth before yon Sun | Has dipp'd his Beams in Ocean – rouse their Souls | To Christian Fortitude; remember them, | Life, Liberty, Religion, call to Arms.*

> **Andrew Walker Enemy Territory 1988**
> *We need to recapture the vision of the primitive church, for if only we could drag ourselves away from our television sets and unhook our headphones from our portable stereos we would hear the clear call to arms.*

up in arms
armed and mustered ready for the fight. Also in figurative uses: prepared to resist opposition or challenge disagreement. *16th cent.*

> **Shakespeare 2 Henry VI IV.i.100 (1591)**
> *The commons here in Kent are up in arms.*

> **Dryden All for Love 1678**
> *Oh, thou has fired me; my soul's up in arms, and mans each part about me.*

> **Henry Fielding The History of Tom Jones 1749**
> *Allworthy was of a cooler disposition than the good woman, whose spirits were up in arms in the cause of her friend.*

army

Figurative meanings, with reference to large bodies of people supporting a cause or organized for a special purpose, date from the 16th cent.

the forgotten army
a group of people who, unnoticed or unpaid, do the actual work for which others take the credit. *20th cent.*

the tartan army
supporters of Scotland abroad, especially at international football matches. *Late 20th cent.*

> The Times 1986
> *Roxburgh has seized a golden opportunity for experiment. Luxembourg are perhaps the weakest of all the countries in the European championship. Scotland's disappointed tartan army has had enough of the old guard.*

> Stuart Cosgrove Hampden Babylon 1991
> *As the tartan army drowned its sorrows in the bars of Soho, Frank preferred a candlelit dinner.*

you and whose army?
informal used to question somebody's ability to carry out a threat or challenge unaided. *Late 20th cent.*

> Susan Gates The Lock 1990
> *Gazzer had been afraid that she would say something like: 'Well, you needn't have bothered!' or 'You and whose army!'*

See also Dad's Army at DAD.

around

have been around
1 to have been in existence. *Early 20th cent.*

> She 1989
> *As W Somerset Maugham once pointed out, short stories have been around for a long time.*

2 to have had a wide experience of life. *Early 20th cent.*

> Celia Brayfield The Prince 1990
> *Look, kid, I've been around, I know what happens with kids like you.*

arrow

a straight arrow
a square-dealing, transparently honest person. *Mid 20th cent.*

> Mike Ripley Angel Hunt 1991
> *There was absolutely no reason why I shouldn't be straight arrow and honest with them.*

arse

go/fall arse over tit/tip
to fall over in a spectacular way, especially head over heels: also in figurative meanings. *Early 20th cent.*

> M Gist Life at the Tip 1993
> *Unluckily, neither the inspector nor myself spotted the stray soap and after slipping arse over tit he put his head through the water tank.*

not know one's arse from one's elbow
to be a complete innocent or ignoramus. *Mid 20th cent.*

> Nevil Shute Pastoral 1944
> *I wish I'd had a crowd like that for my first crew. We none of us knew arse from elbow when they pushed me off.*

See also ASS²; LICK somebody's boots/arse.

art

Concrete senses to do with the application of skill, most notably to the creation of visual images and designs, date from the 17th cent.

art concealing art
skill and ingenuity that is most effective when it is not obvious or applied ostentatiously: also as a proverb *art consists in concealing art*, from a Latin maxim *ars est celare artem*. *16th cent.*

be art and part of something
to be actively involved in something. The phrase originated as a Scottish legal term referring to participation in an act: to be *art* was to be involved in planning it and to be *part* was to participate in carrying it out. *Middle English*

> Henry Brooke The Fool of Quality 1766
> *He had neither art nor part in this frightful discomfiture.*

> R L Stevenson New Arabian Nights 1882
> *Madame Berthelini … was art and part with him in these undignified labours.*

have/get something down to a fine art
to perfect a means of doing something effectively and with economy of effort. *19th cent.*

> Robert Williams Buchanan Poetical Works 1878
> *How busily the peddling knave | Searches about for souls to save; | Yet Conscience, to a fine art turn'd, | Loses the wisdom fools have learn'd.*

state of the art
the latest stage of development in something, especially if incorporating the most recent technology: commonly used (with hyphens) as a modifier before another noun. *Early 20th cent.*

article

an article of faith
a firm or strong belief: originally in matters of religion, later in extended uses. Based on the use of *article* denoting sections of a prayer or creed (notably the *Apostles' Creed*) and to the provisions of legal statutes. *16th cent.*

> **Arthur Golding transl Philippe De Mornay's** *Trueness of the Christian Religion* 1587
> *The thing which had aforetimes bene disputable among the Heathen, is now admitted as an article of faith.*

> **Samuel Butler** *The Way of All Flesh* 1903
> *Of course he read Mr. Darwin's books as fast as they came out and adopted evolution as an article of faith.*

> **National Trust Magazine** 1991
> *Small is beautiful is almost an article of faith in Britain.*

the genuine article
an authentic or dependable thing or person. *19th cent.*

> **Joseph Neal** *Charcoal Sketches* 1838
> *There are, it is true, many delightful versifiers at the present moment, but we fear that though they display partial evidences of inspiration upon paper, the scintillations are deceptive. Their conduct seldom exhibits sufficient proof that they are touched with the celestial fire, to justify the public in regarding them as the genuine article.*

ascendant

in the ascendant
having increasing power or influence: the original meaning was 'supreme, dominant' (i.e. denoting a state achieved rather than a process leading to it), with reference to the astrological meaning of a planet reaching its zenith. The *OED* has a stray quotation from the 17th cent., but usage is predominantly from the 19th cent. on.

> **Hardy** *Far from the Madding Crowd* 1874
> *There are occasions when girls like Bathsheba will put up with a great deal of unconventional behaviour. When they want to be praised, which is often; when they want to be mastered, which is sometimes … Just now the first feeling was in the ascendant with Bathsheba, with a dash of the second.*

ash

Allusive and figurative uses referring to ruins and destruction date from the 16th cent.

rise/emerge (like a phoenix) from the ashes
to reappear or be renewed after destruction: from the myth of the phoenix rising reborn and rejuvenated from the ashes of its own funeral pyre. The phrase also appears in forms referring directly to the phoenix. *16th cent.*

> **Shakespeare** *1 Henry VI* iv.vii.93 (1590)
> *[Charles] Go, take their bodies hence. [Lucy] I'll bear them hence, but from their ashes shall be reared | A phœnix that shall make all France afeard.*

> **Milton** *Paradise Lost* iii.334 (1667)
> *Mean while the world shall burn, and from her ashes spring | New Heav'n and Earth, wherein the just shall dwell.*

turn to (dust and) ashes (in one's mouth)
to turn into something worthless, especially a cause of great disappointment after high expectations. The phrase alludes to biblical uses of dust and ashes as a symbol of something that has been reduced to nothing (e.g. Job 30:19 'He hath cast me into the mire, and I am become like dust and ashes') and to the legend of the Dead Sea Fruit, or apple of Sodom, which according to the Jewish historian Josephus (1st cent. AD) had an attractive appearance but dissolved into smoke and ashes when put in the mouth. *19th cent.*

> **William Hickling Prescott** *The History of the Conquest of Mexico* 1843
> *Unhappily, they were fast falling under the dominion of the warlike Aztecs. And that people repaid the benefits received from their more polished neighbours by imparting to them their own ferocious superstition, which, falling like a mildew on the land, would soon have blighted its rich blossoms of promise, and turned even its fruits to dust and ashes.*

Herman Melville *Typee* 1846
Had the apples of Sodom turned to ashes in my mouth, I could not have felt a more startling revulsion.

See also rake over the ashes *at* RAKE[1].

---

ask

ask me another
informal used when unable to answer a question. The phrase has been given added currency as the title of television quiz shows. *Early 20th cent.*

Arnold Bennett *Clayhanger* 1910
'Why's he wearing his best clothes?' Clara demanded ... 'Ask me another!' said Edwin.

ask no questions (and you'll hear / be told no lies)
(proverb) it is better to remain silent than to risk hearing something unwelcome or unreliable. *18th cent.*

Oliver Goldsmith *She Stoops to Conquer* 1773
Ask me no questions and I'll tell you no fibs.

Ann Radcliffe *The Romance of the Forest* 1791
The moment they were alone, Madame seized the opportunity of entreating her husband to explain the scene she had witnessed. 'Ask me no questions,' said La Motte sternly, 'for I will answer none.'

Dickens *Great Expectations* 1861
'Drat that boy ... What a questioner he is. Ask no questions and you'll be told no lies.' It was not very polite to herself, I thought, to imply that I should be told lies by her, even if I did ask questions.

ask a silly question (and you get a silly answer)
used on getting a useless or unhelpful answer to a question. The phrase can be traced back to Middle English (in Caxton) in forms close to this, with earlier occurrences of the notion expressed differently.

be asking for trouble
to be risky or dangerous, or (said of a person) to act in such a way, usually unintentionally: also informally *be asking for it*. Cf be looking for trouble *at* LOOK. *Early 20th cent.*

H V Esmond *Eliza Comes to Stay* 1913
It may be all very well for a man to marry a woman who loves him – but for a man to marry a woman who doesn't love him just because he's ass enough to love her seems to me to be asking for trouble.

Conan Doyle *The Valley of Fear* 1915
You've been asking for it this many a day, Ted Baldwin – now you've got it!

don't ask, don't tell
a catchphrase denoting a policy of tolerance towards practices carried on in private that might be disapproved of if made public. The phrase was originally used in US military contexts with reference to homosexual members of the services, who are allowed to continue to serve as long as they are not open about their sexual orientation. Similar versions of the phrase occur in freer guises in other contexts of tacit withholding of information. *Late 20th cent.*

The Times 1993
Congress appears to be rallying around the more likely outcome, proposed by Senator Sam Nunn, chairman of the Senate armed services committee, a continuation of the present "don't ask, don't tell" policy under which gays can enter the military but face a ban if they publicly admit their homosexuality.

don't ask me
I've no idea, I cannot say: used when unable or unwilling to explain or comment on a point. *19th cent.*

Dickens *The Haunted Man* 1847
'My little woman, what has put you out?' 'I'm sure I don't know ... Don't ask me. Who said I was put out at all? I never did.'

for the asking
on demand, without any difficulty. *19th cent.*

Wilkie Collins *The Woman in White* 1860
Go, if you like – there are plenty of housekeepers as good as you, to be had for the asking.

I ask you!
informal an exclamation of surprise or disapproval: typically used to accompany a statement that the speaker questions or rejects. *19th cent.*

Conan Doyle *The Beryl Coronet* 1892
I ask you now, is such a theory tenable?

Julian Barnes *A History of the World in 10½ Chapters* 1990
I ask you, forty of us slogging into the Jungle all because we bought his line about needing to work

our way into the reality of a couple of deeply dead Jesuit priests.

if you ask me

used to introduce a suggestion or a piece of advice, or as a tag phrase following this. *19th cent.*

James Joyce *A Portrait of the Artist as a Young Man* 1916

'That is the language of the Holy Ghost.' 'And very bad language if you ask me,' said Mr Dedalus coolly.

See also ask no ODDS; cry/ask for the MOON.

askance

look askance at somebody/something

to regard somebody or something with disfavour or disapproval: from the physical meaning of *askance* 'oblique, askew'. *16th cent.*

Shakespeare *The Taming of the Shrew* II.i.242 (1592)
Thou canst not frown. Thou canst not look askance, | *Nor bite the lip, as angry wenches will.*

asleep

asleep at the switch/wheel

neglecting one's responsibilities: the switch (chiefly North American) is the lever that changes a set of railway points, and the wheel is the steering wheel of a motor vehicle. *19th cent.*

Shipp & Dunbar *In Dahomey* 1902
I've got a contract with a medicine shark, in all cases of sea sickness, we split the purse fifty-fifty. If anybody pegs out on the trip, I've got an undertaker waitin' at the wharf that gives me 35 percent of the net. Am I asleep at the switch, ask me?

aspersion

cast aspersions

to make disparaging remarks, especially by innuendo rather than direct accusation: recorded earlier in the form *lay aspersions*. An *aspersion* (from *asperse* meaning 'to sprinkle') was originally a sprinkling of water, especially in ritual contexts. In Roman Catholic ritual, the *asperges* are the sprinkling of holy water. *16th cent.*

Henry Fielding *The History of Tom Jones* 1749
I defy all the world to cast a just aspersion on my character: nay, the most scandalous tongues have never dared censure my reputation.

ass¹

make an ass of somebody

to make somebody appear foolish or stupid: from Shakespeare's use in *A Midsummer Night's Dream* (1595) III.i.112, where the speaker, Bottom, has been temporarily transformed into a figure with an ass's head: 'I see their knavery: this is to make an ass of me; to fright me, if they could.' The name for the beast of burden is from Old English. It has been a symbol of awkwardness, stupidity, and stubbornness in many languages since ancient times. *16th cent.*

Robert Howard *The Committee* 1665
O, are you at your ifs again; d'you think they | *Shall make a fool of me, though they make an ass of you.*

ass²

This spelling is a primarily American form of *arse*, and all the phrases originating in North America therefore tend to be spelt in this way. These are mostly to do with control of and aggression towards people. In some phrases *ass* stands for one's person, as in the phrases beginning *get your ass … See also* ARSE.

break/bust/kick/whip (some/somebody's) ass

informal to beat or bully somebody. *Mid 20th cent.*

John Steinbeck *The Grapes of Wrath* 1939
With that kind of a son-of-a-bitch, if I was God I'd kick their ass right outa heaven.

bust (one's) ass

informal to do one's utmost to achieve something difficult or challenging. *Late 20th cent.*

Guitarist 1992
He knew that we were all willing to bust ass on this record and so he really drove us hard.

chew somebody's ass

informal to scold or reprimand somebody: also used in more literal senses. *Mid 20th cent.*

Muriel Gray *The First Fifty* 1991
The perfect weather for camping – a still, warm night with a gigantic pastel-coloured moon reflecting dreamily in a glassy loch – is coincidentally the perfect night for the midges to chew your ass off.

drag/haul/tear (somebody's) ass
informal to move or deal with somebody quickly or promptly. *Late 20th cent.*

> Alastair MacNeill *Time of the Assassins* 1992
> *It won't be the first time I've had to come to your rescue and haul your ass out of trouble.*

get your ass here/home, etc
informal (usually as an imperative) to come or go promptly or obediently, to hurry in a specified direction: there are many variants. *Ass* here is used as equivalent to 'oneself'. *Mid 20th cent.*

> Toronto Star 1975
> *I protested at being told to 'get your ass home'.*

> Ben Elton *Stark* 1992
> *'Yeah, I got the message to get my ass over here, on the car phone,' Aristos said pointlessly.*

not give a rat's ass
informal not to care about something. *20th cent.*

put/have somebody's ass in a sling
NAmer, informal to cause somebody trouble. *Mid 20th cent.*

work one's ass off
informal to work very hard: also with other verbs and in more literal senses, and with the spelling *arse*. *Mid 20th cent.*

> T Bell *There Comes Times* 1946
> *Here's a smart apple like you working your ass off for a lousy forty bucks a week.*

See also be a PAIN in the neck/arse/ass; it's no SKIN off my ass; KISS ass; a PIECE of ass.

asset

asset stripping
the practice of selling off a company's assets to raise capital, disregarding the likely need for them in the future: also used figuratively and as *asset-strip* (verb). The form of the noun was originally *assets*, treated at first as a singular but later as a collective plural, giving rise to the singular form *asset*; this form has predominated since the 20th cent. in compounds such as *asset card* and *asset stripping*. The meaning 'an advantage or resource' is 17th cent. *Late 20th cent.*

astray
See lead somebody astray *at* LEAD[1].

at

at it
informal busy doing something, especially working or fighting. *17th cent.*

> Shakespeare *Troilus and Cressida* v.iii.98 (1602)
> *They are at it, hark. Proud Diomed, believe, | I come to lose my arm or win my sleeve.*

where it's at
informal a fashionable scene of activity. *Early 20th cent.*

> Esquire 1992
> *Pretty much what happened was that I'd been waiting all this time to be successful, to achieve whatever I was going to achieve, now I had and I was sitting in this flippin' hotel thinking: This is not where it's at.*

atmosphere
See a feeling/atmosphere, etc that one could CUT with a knife.

attendance
See DANCE attendance on somebody.

attitude
See STRIKE an attitude.

augur

augur well/ill
to engender good (or bad) expectations for an outcome: originally with a person as subject, later with a situation. The verb is 17th cent. and is derived from the noun meaning 'soothsayer, diviner', from the name of the Roman official who took omens from the flight of birds and other signs (*see also* AUSPICES). First-person uses occur in the 18th cent., with the corresponding meaning 'I divine good (or bad) consequences'. *18th cent.*

> Richard Cumberland *The Box-Lobby Challenge* 1794
> *I have not seen him, but from his friend's report I augur well of his qualifications.*

> Edgar Rice Burroughs *The Beasts of Tarzan* 1914
> *What had brought the beast to him? The fact that he had come augured well for what he might accomplish.*

auld

for auld lang syne

for old times' sake (literally 'for old long since'): used by Robert Burns as the title of a song. *Auld* is a Scottish and northern English form of *old*. *17th cent.*

> Byron *Don Juan* 1824
> *Floating past me seems my childhood in this childishness of mine: I care not – 'tis a glimpse of 'Auld Lang Syne'.*

auspices

under the auspices of somebody

with the protection or support of somebody: an *auspice* was originally an observation of birds as omens in ancient Rome (Latin *auspicium*; a seer was *auspex*). In the 17th cent. the term developed (in singular and plural forms) the more generalized meaning 'token or indication of a good outcome' and hence the concrete meaning 'favour, protection' which underlies the phrase. *18th cent.*

> Jane Austen *Emma* 1816
> *The idea of her being indebted to Mrs. Elton for what was called an introduction – of her going into public under the auspices of a friend of Mrs. Elton's – probably some vulgar, dashing widow … The dignity of Miss Woodhouse, of Hartfield, was sunk indeed!*

authority

on good authority

from a reliable source of information. *18th cent.*

> Mary Wollstonecraft *A Vindication of the Rights of Woman* 1792
> *The very confessions which mere children were obliged to make, and the questions asked by the holy men, I assert these facts on good authority, were sufficient to impress a sexual character.*

avail

to no/little avail

having no or little effect or benefit. The noun is derived from the verb (as in *to avail oneself*); both are related to a noun *vail* meaning 'advantage, profit', which is also the primary meaning of *avail*

as a noun. Earlier idioms are *of avail* and *without avail*. *18th cent.*

> Harriet Beecher Stowe *Uncle Tom's Cabin* 1852
> *Miss Ophelia had several times tried to awaken her maternal fears about Eva; but to no avail.*

awakening

a rude awakening

a sudden arousal from self-delusion or complacency. *19th cent.*

> Kate Chopin *The Maid of Saint Philippe* 1889
> *The Spaniards may any day they choose give a rude awakening to those stolid beings who are living on in a half-slumber of content.*

away

away with —

an instruction to be rid of something: an elliptical use with a verb such as *be* or *get* understood. The first recorded use is in Tyndale's translation of Matthew 27:23 'Away with him, away with him, crucify him.' *16th cent.*

> Dickens *Our Mutual Friend* 1865
> *If I indicated such a programme to any worthy and intelligent tradesman of your town – nay, I will here be personal, and say Our town – what would he reply? He would reply, 'Away with it!' That's what he would reply, gentlemen.*

get away with you

an expression of doubt or scepticism about what somebody has said. An extension of *get away*, and originally an instruction to leave: earlier in the form *go away with you*. *19th cent.*

> D H Lawrence *Sons and Lovers* 1913
> *Then Paul was cross with her for not answering with more dignity. 'You go away with you!' she exclaimed.*

See also FAR *and away; get away with* MURDER; HAVE *it away;* HAVE *it away/off;* OUT *and away.*

awkward

Meanings to do with clumsiness and lack of dexterity date from the 16th cent.

the awkward squad

people who are difficult to deal with or unwilling to acquiesce in a situation. The term was applied originally to military recruits who had not yet been trained, and it was attributed in this meaning to the Scottish poet Robert Burns, whose dying words in 1796 are said to have included the appeal: 'John, don't let the awkward squad fire over me' (probably referring to his fear of a metaphorical gun salute from the literary establishment after his death). In extended use the phrase dates mainly from 19th cent.

Byron Don Juan 1824

It is an actual fact, that he, commander in chief, in proper person deign'd to drill the awkward squad.

Dickens Our Mutual Friend 1865

A considerable capital of knee and elbow and wrist and ankle, had Sloppy, and he didn't know how to dispose of it to the best advantage, but was always investing it in wrong securities, and so getting himself into embarrassed circumstances. Full-Private Number One in the Awkward Squad of the rank and file of life, was Sloppy, and yet had his glimmering notions of standing true to the Colours.

See also the awkward AGE.

aye

the ayes have it

there is a majority in favour of a proposal. *Aye* is a 16th cent. dialect and northern word for 'yes', in general use only as a term in voting. *Cf* the noes have it *at* NO (recorded earlier). *19th cent.*

Dickens Our Mutual Friend 1865

'My dear Mrs. Veneering, do let us resolve ourselves into a Committee of the whole House on the subject.' Mrs. Veneering, always charmed by this rattling sylph, cries, 'Oh yes! Do let us resolve ourselves into a Committee of the whole House! So delicious!' Veneering says, 'As many as are of that opinion, say Aye, – contrary, No – the Ayes have it.'

axe

Idioms based on the physical meaning date from the Middle English, but figurative uses of the word itself, in the sense 'a reduction or cutting back (especially of expenditure)' are modern.

have an axe to grind

to have private (and usually suspect) motives or intentions in doing something. The phrase has a different meaning in a story related by the American statesman Benjamin Franklin (1706–90). George Orwell in 1946 condemned the phrase (listed in the form *no axe to grind*) as a 'dying metaphor' in his essay *Politics and the English Language* (*see* the ACID test). *19th cent.*

John William De Forest Honest John Vane 1875

She perceived that her husband was right in affirming that everybody in Washington 'had an axe to grind'; the natural result being, that gentlemen would not spend their time in paying court to ladies whose male relatives had no favors to confer.

B

plan B

an alternative plan or strategy. The identification of a series of plans by letters of the alphabet dates from the 19th cent., and idiomatic uses of *plan B* in the generalized sense of any alternative plan occur from the mid 20th cent.

> **The Times 1987**
> *We knew it was important to get to half-time with a clean sheet. Our thoughts were to keep it tight and build our way into the game but the penalty wrecked all that. After that we had to switch to plan B.*

> **Climber and Hill Walker 1991**
> *So on the basis of a mis-spelt name and a single hazy photo, we rang our travel agent to book our flight to La Paz and put Plan B into action.*

See also from A to B *at* A.

---

babe

Figurative meanings referring to inexperience and innocence date from the 16th cent.

a babe in arms

a baby that is too young to crawl or walk and has to be carried. *19th cent.*

> **Nathaniel Hawthorne The Scarlet Letter 1850**
> *Pearl, too, was there; first as the babe in arms, and afterwards as the little girl, small companion of her mother, holding a forefinger with her whole grasp, and tripping along at the rate of three or four footsteps to one of Hester's.*

babes in the wood

young or inexperienced people in a challenging situation. The phrase alludes to an old ballad, *The Children in the Wood*, in which two children are abandoned in a wood by a wicked uncle who wants to rob them of their inheritance. *Babes in the Wood* is also the title of a pantomime. The phrase

is occasionally used in the singular, as in the 1993 example below. *18th cent.*

> **Herman Melville Typee 1846**
> *I could not avoid comparing our situation with that of the interesting babes in the wood. Poor little sufferers! – no wonder their constitutions broke down under the hardships to which they were exposed.*

> **Paula Marshall An American Princess 1993**
> *She's a regular babe in the wood in the East End, however knowledgeable she might be in her own world – wherever that is.*

---

baby

baby bunting

a term of endearment for a young child or baby, familiar from the nursery rhyme that begins *Bye, baby bunting, Daddy's gone a hunting*. It first appears in collections of rhymes from the 18th cent. The word *bunting* may be simply alliterative, or may be related to a Scottish word *buntin* meaning 'plump and stout'. It is recorded in the *OED* as a term of affectionate address with a single 17th-cent. quotation from Sir William D'Avenant's comic drama *The Wits*. *18th cent.*

be somebody's baby

to be a particular person's idea or creation and be closely associated with them. *Late 20th cent.*

> **M Kilby Man at the Sharp End 1991**
> *'But the Business Plan is his baby, Randy.'*

carry / hold / be left holding the baby

to have to bear an unwelcome responsibility: with reference to a parent's responsibility for a child. The phrase is sometimes used with simultaneous figurative and literal reference. *Early 20th cent.*

> **Daily Express 1927**
> *Disclaiming responsibility for all the financial misfortunes of the country, he found himself confronted by Mr. Jack Jones, who told him that he was 'carrying the baby' anyhow.*

throw/empty the baby out with the bath-water

to reject or discard something useful or valuable along with things no longer wanted or desirable. The phrase was often used by G B Shaw and his circle, and was originally a proverb, *don't throw the baby out with the bath water*. In this form it was derived from a German maxim (*nicht das Kind mit dem Bad ausschütten*) that was known to Thomas Carlyle; he translated it in a work on the abolition of slavery in 1853 as 'you must empty out the bathing-tub, but not the baby along with it'. *19th cent.*

G B Shaw *Getting Married* (Preface) 1908
We shall in a very literal sense empty the baby out with the bath by abolishing an institution which needs nothing more than a little ... rationalizing to make it ... useful.

Alasdair Heron *A Century of Protestant Theology* 1993
In the process everything distinctively Christian was eliminated: the baby was thrown out with the bath water.

See also WET the baby's head.

---

back

at/to the back of one's mind
vaguely but persistently occupying part of one's mind. Early uses are in the form *at the back of one's head*. *19th cent.*

Joseph Conrad *Lord Jim* 1900
I suppose there had been at the back of my head some hope yet.

Somerset Maugham *Of Human Bondage* 1915
Constantly now at the back of his mind was the thought of doing away with himself, but he used all the strength he had not to dwell on it.

a back number
an out-of-date idea or thing, or somebody who is no longer useful or needed: originally an issue of a magazine or journal earlier than the current one. *19th cent.*

Henry James *The American* 1877
[Claire] *I was only seventeen. But let that horrible time alone!* [Newman] *I speak of it only to remind you that it's a reason the more for your having a better time now. The joys we've missed in youth are like back numbers and lost umbrellas; we mustn't spend the rest of life wondering where they are!*

Frank Dumont *A Girl of the Century* 1904
Don't get off your base! Get in the push, you know – be a blood, not a back number – don't be a jay all your life.

James Joyce *Ulysses* 1922
You once nobble that, congregation, and a buck joy ride to heaven becomes a back number.

Rose Macaulay *Told by an Idiot* 1923
Bicycle bolts are a back number, and that's a fact.

the back of beyond
a remote or inaccessible place. *19th cent.*

Scott *The Antiquities of Scotland* 1816
You ... whirled them to the back of beyont to look at the auld Roman camp.

back the wrong horse
to make a wrong choice, especially by supporting an unsuccessful candidate: originally with reference to betting. *Early 20th cent.*

behind somebody's back
without somebody knowing or seeing, or in their absence: often in the phrase *go behind somebody's back*. The earliest use in this meaning is from Malory's *Le Morte d'Arthur* (c1485): 'To say of me wrong or shame behind my back.' *15th cent.*

Shakespeare *Romeo and Juliet* IV.i.28 (1596)
[Juliet to Paris] *If I do so* [admit that I love you], *it will be of more price | Being spoke behind your back than to your face.*

be on / get off somebody's back
to be on somebody's back is to be constantly harassing or nagging them, and to get off somebody's back is to leave them alone (the negative form typically being in the form of an angry interjection from the victim). The phrase has many variations. *19th cent.*

George Eliot *Silas Marner* 1861
I may as well tell the Squire everything myself – I should get you off my back, if I got nothing else.

Joseph Heller *Catch-22* 1961
Stop picking on me, will you? Get off my back, will you?

break the back of somebody/something
1 to crush somebody with a heavy burden or responsibility. *17th cent.*

Shakespeare *Henry VIII* I.i.84 (1613)
O, many have broke their backs with laying manors on 'em | For this great journey.

2 to get the most difficult part of a task done: there are connotations of sense 1 in some uses (e.g. the 1989 example below). *19th cent.*

Virginia Woolf *The Voyage Out* 1915
'What Hewet fails to understand,' he remarked, 'is that we must break the back of the ascent before midday.'

Guardian 1989
The Colombo government believes it has broken the back of the rebellion in the south.

by/through the back door

by an indirect or devious route or method: from the notion of gaining surreptitious access to a building. The phrase is common with reference to political measures introduced in a disguised manner. *Backdoor* (usually one word) is used as a modifier with the same meaning, as in the example from 1992 below. *19th cent.*

Edgar Allan Poe *Criticism* 1831
He either jumps at once into the middle of his subject, or breaks in at a back door, or sidles up to it with the gait of a crab.

Today 1992
Treasury chiefs refused yesterday to rule out the backdoor tax rise.

get/put somebody's back up

to irritate or offend somebody: with reference to a cat's arching its back when angered or threatened. *19th cent.*

James Kirke Paulding *Madmen All* 1847
Now I should calcerlate that Bill would naterally get his back up at that.

Somerset Maugham *Of Human Bondage* 1915
'You are a fool to put her back up,' said Dunsford.

know something like the back of one's hand

to know something well or in great detail. *Mid 20th cent.*

Michael Clynes *The White Rose Murder* 1992
Our guide was a dour-faced taciturn little man who had as much chatter and wit as a dumb-struck oaf, though he knew the bridle paths and trackways of Leicestershire like the back of his hand.

on one's back

recovering from injury or illness: also in figurative meanings. Earlier uses include *lay somebody on their back*, meaning 'to leave them prostrate'. *19th cent.*

R H Dana *Two Years Before the Mast* 1840
He confessed the whole matter; acknowledged that he was on his back.

put one's back into something

to devote oneself energetically to a task: originally in physical senses. *19th cent.*

Rider Haggard *King Solomon's Mines* 1885
'Now, Curtis,' he said, 'tackle on, and put your back into it; you are as strong as two.'

see the back of somebody/something

to be rid of somebody or something unwanted. *19th cent.*

Mrs Humphry Ward *Robert Elsmere* 1888
Edward Meyrick would come whirling in and out of the hamlet once a day. Robert was seldom sorry to see the back of him.

turn one's back on somebody/something

to forsake or abandon somebody or something: *turn one's back* occurs earlier. *17th cent.*

Shakespeare *King Lear* I.i.174 (1606)
[Lear to Kent, banishing him] *Five days we do allot thee for provision | To shield thee from disasters of the world, | And on the sixth to turn thy hated back | Upon our kingdom.*

Louisa M Alcott *Little Women* 1868
If Amy had been here, she'd have turned her back on him forever, because, sad to relate, he had a great appetite, and shovelled in his dinner in a manner which would have horrified 'her ladyship'.

when / as soon as somebody's back is turned

(seizing the moment) when somebody is not watching or listening. *18th cent.*

Richardson *The History of Sir Charles Grandison* 1753
The Italian surgeons and Mr. Lowther happily agree in all their measures: They applaud him when his back is turned; and he speaks well of them in their absence. This mutual return of good offices, which they hear of, unites them.

Joseph Conrad *Lord Jim* 1900
They said 'Confounded fool!' as soon as his back was turned.

with one's back to / (up) against the wall

in a desperate situation, under a great threat: from the notion of fighting off attackers with a wall at one's back cutting off further retreat. There is a historically isolated 16th cent. use given in the *OED*, but the developed figurative usage is found mainly in 19th cent. literature. A memorable use of the phrase occurs during the First World War, in the order issued to the troops on 12 April 1914 by Earl Haig, commander-in-chief on the Western Front: 'Every position must be held to the last man: there must be no retirement. With our backs to the wall, and believing in the justice of our cause, each one of us must fight on to the end.'

> **R L Stevenson** *Kidnapped* 1886
> *'But, for all that,' says he, 'I can be sorry to see another man with his back to the wall.'*

See also back on one's FEET; back to basics *at* BASIC; back to the DRAWING board; be back to SQUARE one; get/go back to NATURE; GET one's own back; make a ROD for one's own back; MIND your backs; not in my back YARD; on the back BURNER.

backbone

put backbone into somebody
to increase somebody's stamina the hard way. *Backbone* is a common image for strength of character. *19th cent.*

> **Joseph Conrad** *Lord Jim* 1900
> *I managed to put some backbone into them that time, and no mistake.*

back-handed

See a back-handed/left-handed COMPLIMENT.

backroom

The physical meaning 'a room at the back of a building' dates from the 16th cent. In recent usage it has come to be associated with clandestine research or other secret activity.

the backroom boys / boys in the backroom
people engaged in research, especially of a secret nature. *The boys in the back rooms* was used in a speech by Lord Beaverbrook, Minister of Aircraft Production, in 1941, reported in *The Listener* for 24 March of that year: 'Now who is responsible for this work of development on which so much depends? To whom must the praise be given? To the boys in the back rooms. They do not sit in the limelight. But they are the men who do the work.' Beaverbrook is said to have been a devotee of the 1939 film *Destry Rides Again*, which memorably included Marlene Dietrich's rendition of the song 'See what the boys in the backroom will have'. *Mid 20th cent.*

> **J R L Anderson** *Death in the City* 1980
> *I think you'd better be a financial adviser – one of the bank's backroom boys.*

a backroom deal
a clandestine or secret deal or agreement. *Late 20th cent.*

> **The Times** 1985
> *Mr Bush, while welcoming Israel's release of more Shia Muslim prisoners yesterday denied once more that there had been any backroom deal over the release of the TWA hostages.*

back seat

a back-seat driver
a person sitting at the back of a vehicle who pesters the driver with unwanted advice on driving: also in extended uses of unwanted advice in other contexts. *Early 20th cent.*

> **P G Wodehouse** *Very Good, Jeeves!* 1930
> *Quite suddenly and unexpectedly, no one more surprised than myself, the car let out a faint gurgle like a sick moose and stopped in its tracks … The back-seat drivers gave tongue. 'What's the matter? What has happened?' I explained. 'I'm not stopping. It's the car.'*

> **S Morgan et al** *Childcare: Concerns and Conflicts* 1989
> *No amount of back-seat driving will persuade new parents to change their basic way of running their family.*

take a back seat
to assume a minor or subordinate role: originally with reference to the seats in a vehicle. *19th cent.*

> **John William De Forest** *Honest John Vane* 1875
> *To try to carry Jim Bummer would break down the organization. Jim must take a back seat, at least until this noise about him blows over, and give some fresh man a chance.*

> **James Joyce** *A Portrait of the Artist as a Young Man* 1916
> *Draw it mild now, Dedalus. I think it's time for you to take a back seat.*

backward(s)

backward in coming forward
reluctant to draw attention to oneself, shy: now usually in negative contexts. *19th cent.*

> **Alonzo Delano** *A Live Woman in the Mines* 1857
> *Come down, gentlemen. Fortune to the brave – don't be backward in coming forward – down – down – all down?*

Trollope *Orley Farm* 1862
I must say you're rather backward in coming forward.

bend/fall/lean over backwards
to make every effort to be helpful, or to be fair or impartial and avoid bias. *Early 20th cent.*

R G Bayly *Patrol* 1989
It was a classic illustration of how our laws often seem to lean over backwards to protect the law-breakers.

know something/somebody backwards
to know something or somebody very well. *Early 20th cent.*

Martin Amis *Time's Arrow* 1991
We made our own way there (somehow Tod knows this town backwards), and we didn't stay long, thank God.

bacon

A Middle English word that rapidly acquired associations from its denoting the principal meat of rural England.

bring home the bacon
to return home with a prize, to be successful in an undertaking: possibly with reference to former pig-catching competitions at fairs. Also, more generally: to earn an income, to be the bread-winner. *Early 20th cent.*

Conan Doyle *His Last Bow* 1917
'You can give me the glad hand to-night, mister,' he cried. 'I'm bringing home the bacon at last … It's the real goods, and you can lay to that.'

save one's/somebody's bacon
to escape harm or injury. The origin of the expression is obscure: Brewer referred to the need to protect bacon stored for the winter from being plundered by stray dogs, but it is just as likely that bacon refers to a person's own flesh, i.e. to the human body (compare other phrases no longer current, which support this: to sell one's bacon, to baste somebody's bacon = to beat them). *17th cent.*

T Ireland *Momus Elenticus* 1654
Some fellowes there were … To save their bacon penn'd many a smooth song.

Edward Ward *Hudibras Redivivus* 1705
And they write Truth to save their Bacon; | The wiser Sort would still deceive 'em, | And none but Blockheads, sure, believe 'em.

bad

a bad quarter of an hour
a brief but very unpleasant experience: translating the French phrase *mauvais quart d'heure* (also used in English contexts). *19th cent.*

Trollope *The Way We Live Now* 1875
He was prepared himself to bear all mere ignominy with a tranquil mind, – to disregard any shouts of reprobation which might be uttered, and to console himself when the bad quarter of an hour should come with the remembrance that he had garnered up a store sufficient for future wants and placed it beyond the reach of his enemies.

Frances Hodgson Burnett *A Little Princess* 1905
She returned home and, going to her sitting room, sent at once for Miss Amelia … and it must be admitted that poor Miss Amelia passed through more than one bad quarter of an hour.

have a bad hair day
informal, originally NAmer to have a day when everything seems to go badly, beginning with not being able to get one's hair into shape. The phrase is much associated with the 1990s, with Hillary Clinton, and with Buffy the Vampire Slayer: in the 1992 film, Buffy, played by Kristy Swanson, delivers the line 'I'm fine, but you're obviously having a bad hair day'. *Late 20th cent.*

Guardian 1993
She [Hillary Clinton] *stopped saying 'two-fer-one' and 'vote for him, you get me' – but still, one bad hair day was following the next. Soon she started making jokes about it with her campaign staff. 'How 'bout it?' she'd say. 'Another bad hair day?'*

in bad
in bad odour; out of favour. *Mid 20th cent.*

Kingsley Amis *Lucky Jim* 1954
This ought to put me nicely in bad with the Neddies.

in a bad way
in an unfortunate state, especially from illness or injury, or from mental anxiety or depression. *18th cent.*

Fanny Burney *Cecilia* 1782
We must get rid of his fever, and then if his cold remains, with any cough, he may make a little excursion to Bristol ... I don't send him to Bristol because he is in a bad way, but merely because I mean to put him in a good one.

take the bad with the good
to accept misfortune and disadvantage along with good fortune. The use of *bad* as a quasi-noun dates from the 16th cent.: Shakespeare in *The Two Gentlemen of Verona* (1593) has Proteus declare (II.vi.13) 'And he wants wit that wants resolvèd will | To learn his wit t'exchange the bad for better.'

See also bad BLOOD; a bad EGG; badly OFF; a bad PATCH; a bad WORKMAN blames his tools; be good/bad NEWS; come to a bad END; have got it bad/badly *at* GET; in somebody's bad/good books *at* BOOK; turn up like a bad PENNY.

---

bag

bag and baggage
with all one's belongings. It is originally a military term for the personal belongings carried in soldiers' bags plus the regiment's movable equipment; to march out with bag and baggage was to retreat without loss of this equipment. Also in figurative use in the sense 'entirely, wholesale'. *16th cent.*

Shakespeare *As You Like It* III.ii.158 (1599)
Come, shepherd, let us make an honourable retreat; though not with bag and baggage, yet with scrip and scrippage [= a shepherd's satchel and its contents: the coinage is a fanciful variation].

Dickens *Hard Times* 1854
Whether she would instantly depart, bag and baggage ... or would positively refuse to budge from the premises ... Mr Bounderby could not at all foresee.

Elizabeth Bailey *Hidden Flame* 1993
It was one thing to ask for a reference, quite another to throw herself, bag and baggage, on the lady's mercy!

bag lady
originally NAmer a homeless woman who carries all her possessions with her in bags. *Late 20th cent.*

S R Curtin *Nobody Ever Died of Old Age* 1972
Letty the Bag Lady ... would pack all her valuables in two large shopping bags and carry them with her.

a bag of bones
a thin and scrawny person or animal. *19th cent.*

Dickens *Bleak House* 1853
I didn't say much to you, commander, then, for I was took by surprise, that a person so strong and healthy and bold as you was, should stop to speak to such a limping bag of bones as I was.

Samuel Butler *The Way of All Flesh* 1903
At thirteen or fourteen he was a mere bag of bones, with upper arms about as thick as the wrists of other boys of his age.

a bag / the whole bag of tricks
everything, or (figuratively) every expedient: possibly with reference to the fable of the Fox and the Cat, or to the traditional conjuror's bag. *19th cent.*

Edward Dyson *Rhymes from the Mines* 1898
Round the spurs very daintily crawling, | With one team pulling out in a row, | And another lot heavenward hauling, | Lest the whole bag-of-tricks should go sprawling | Into regions unheard of below.

Kipling *Kim* 1901
This is fine ... You have ... swiped the whole bag of tricks – locks, stocks, and barrels.

H R F Keating *Writing Crime Fiction* 1986
The puzzle of how a murder could have been committed in what John Dickson Carr used to call a 'hermetically sealed chamber' is perhaps the most intriguing one in the detection writer's whole bag of tricks.

bags I
a formula used by children to claim something: from the verb *bag* in its meaning 'to take hold of, to steal'. *19th cent.*

Kipling *Stalky & Co* 1899
There's a Monte Cristo in that lower shelf. I saw it. Bags I, next time we go to Aves!

in the bag
achieved, accomplished: originally with reference to a bag of game killed in a shoot. In earlier use it means 'in reserve, available if needed' (see the 1872 example below). *19th cent.*

George Eliot *Middlemarch* 1872
Mr. Farebrother's prophecy of a fourth candidate 'in the bag' had not yet been fulfilled.

P G Wodehouse *Hot Water* 1932
We're sitting pretty. The thing's in the bag.

See also a bag of nerves *at* NERVE; let the CAT out of the bag.

---

bait

rise to the bait

to react to a challenge or provocation in the way intended: with reference to fish rising in the water to take the bait at the end of a line. *Cf* get/take a RISE out of somebody. *19th cent.*

> Disraeli *Coningsby* 1844
> *As the prey rose to the bait, Lord Monmouth resolved they should be gorged. His banquets were doubled; a ball was announced; a public day fixed; not only the county but the principal inhabitants of the neighbouring borough were encouraged to attend.*

---

baker

See a baker's DOZEN.

---

balance

balance of mind

due proportion in one's mental or emotional make-up; sanity. *18th cent.*

> Pope *An Essay on Man* 1734
> *Love, hope, and joy, fair pleasure's smiling train, | Hate, fear, and grief, the family of pain, | These mixt with art, and to due bounds confin'd, | Make and maintain the balance of the mind.*

> Henry Adams *The Education of Henry Adams* 1907
> *His duties and cares absorbed him and affected his balance of mind.*

the balance of power

a state of equal power between nations, such that none is in a position to threaten another. The phrase, which appeared originally in the form *balance of (power in) Europe*, is used in other political and social contexts (e.g. of the representation of parties in a legislative assembly, and of equality of the sexes) and also occurs in variations such as *the balance of terror*. *17th cent.*

> Robert Wood *The Ruins of Palmyra* 1753
> *Odenathus, a Palmyrene, ... made so proper a use of this situation ... as to get the balance of power into his hands.*

> Abraham Lincoln *First Inaugural Address* 1861
> *Resolved, That the maintenance inviolate of the rights of the States, and especially the right of each State to order and control its own domestic institutions according to its own judgment exclusively, is essential to that balance of power on which the perfection and endurance of our political fabric depend.*

> Virginia Woolf *The Voyage Out* 1915
> *To hear him engaged with her husband in argument about finance and the balance of power, gave her an odd sense of stability.*

lose one's balance

to fall or stumble. *19th cent.*

> Scott *A Legend of Montrose* 1819
> *An arrow whistled from the bow of one of the Children of the Mist, and transfixed him with so fatal a wound, that, without a single effort to save himself, he lost his balance, and fell headlong from the cliff on which he stood, into the darkness below.*

on balance

all things considered. In early use the phrase has the form *upon a balance*, which is an elliptical use of the fuller form *upon the balance of* [matters to be considered]. *19th cent.*

> Ainsworth's Magazine 1843
> *Upon the 'balance', as the betting men say, women are quite as mercenary as men.*

redress the balance

to restore an equilibrium; to compensate for one extreme by introducing an opposite one. The phrase seems to have been first used by the British Tory statesman George Canning in 1826, in a speech on the affairs of Portugal (see below). *19th cent.*

> Robert Montgomery *The Runaways* 1828
> *What was that to the arrogance of Mr Canning's unfounded boast; – 'I called a new world into existence, to redress the balance of the old.'*

strike a balance

to achieve a middle course or compromise: from the notion of reconciling a set of accounts. *17th cent.*

> Wilkins *New World* 1638
> *Those rewards and punishments by which ... the balance of good and evil in this life is to be struck.*

Thomas Holcroft *Anna St Ives* 1792
Whether this be the motion of my superb and
zealous sister, or of the arrogant peer, is more than I
can divine. But I shall know some day, and shall
then perhaps strike a balance.

weigh something in the balance

to assess carefully the factors affecting a situation, as though weighing them to determine
the most persuasive or powerful. The earliest
use is in the biblical account of the dream of
Belshazzar (6th cent. BC King of Babylon) as
interpreted by Daniel (5:27, in the Authorized
Version of 1611): 'Thou art weighed in the balances, and art found wanting.' The phrase draws
on the common image of a pair of balances as a
symbol of justice. *17th cent.*

Head & Kirkman *The English Rogue Described* 1674
For his own part he had been, and was again
searched, but none found about him, and he in all
respects pleaded innocency: This, though considered
and weighed in the balance of justice, he could not
think that the countrey-man had it, and therefore to
commit him would be injustice.

Harriet Beecher Stowe *Uncle Tom's Cabin* 1852
Those temptations to hardheartedness which always
overcome frail human nature when the prospect of
sudden and rapid gain is weighed in the balance,
with no heavier counterpoise than the interests of
the helpless and unprotected.

See also HANG *in the balance; tip the scales/bal-
ance at* TIP[1].

bald

(as) bald as a coot

completely bald. The bald coot or baldicoot
(*Fulica atra*) has a white patch on its forehead.
The English word *bald* may be cognate with Germanic words to do with 'shining' or 'having
white patches', although an alternative etymology based on its early form *balled* associates it
with the word *ball* in the sense of 'rounded like a
ball'. *Bald as a coot* goes back to Middle English,
and occurs in John Lydgate's *Troy Book* of c1420.

Robert Burton *The Anatomy of Melancholy* 1621
I have an old grim sire to my husband, as bald as a
cout.

Lewis Carroll *Sylvie and Bruno* 1889
'The old gentleman was as bald as a coot.' 'How bald
would that be?' ... 'As bald as bald,' was the
bewildering reply.

Virginia Woolf *The Voyage Out* 1915
Can't you imagine him – bald as a coot with a pair of
sponge-bag trousers, a little spotted tie, and a cor-
poration?

go (it) bald-headed

originally NAmer to act recklessly: from the
notion of casting one's hat (or wig) aside in a
rush of impetuosity. *19th cent.*

---

ball[1] (spherical object)

Applications connected with games and play are
among the earliest meanings recorded. The
notion of a ball as representing an opportunity
or responsibility is recorded in phrases from the
16th cent. onwards.

a ball and chain

a severe hindrance: from the heavy ball attached
by a chain to the leg of a convict to prevent
escape. *19th cent.*

Melvyn Bragg *Rich* 1989
His childhood, far from seeming a ball and chain in
this airy court of privilege, glowed into a magic
kingdom.

the ball is in —'s court

it is a particular person's turn to act or respond: a
metaphor from tennis. *Mid 20th cent.*

A Newman *Three into Two* 1967
No doubt she would play safe and ... the ball would
be back in his court.

a ball of fire

a lively or enthusiastic person: often used in
negative contexts. *Mid 20th cent.*

Nancy Mitford *Don't Tell Alfred* 1960
Yes, I know her. Not a ball of fire, is she?

be on the ball

to be alert and attentive. *Late 20th cent.*

Simon Romain *How to Live Safely in a Dangerous*
World 1989
Soldiers are also very much on the ball when it
comes to 'night vision'.

get/start/set/keep the ball rolling

to initiate or maintain progress in an activity.
Early 20th cent.

James Joyce *A Portrait of the Artist as a Young Man* 1916

Everyone of us could do something. One fellow had a good voice, another fellow was a good actor, another could sing a good comic song ... another could tell a good story and so on. We kept the ball rolling anyhow and enjoyed ourselves.

grab/have somebody by the balls

to have somebody at one's mercy, or put them in an extremely awkward predicament. *Early 20th cent.*

have the ball at one's feet

to be presented with a good opportunity: the image is from football or other ball games. *16th cent.*

Trollope *Phineas Finn* 1869

I know no one so young who has got the ball at his feet so well. I call it nothing to have the ball at your feet if you are born with it there. It is so easy to be a lord if your father is one before you.

keep one's eye on / take one's eye off the ball

to concentrate (or lose concentration) on the matter in hand. *Early 20th cent.*

make a balls of something

to bungle or make a mess of something. The phrase makes a surprisingly early appearance in slang glossaries from the end of the 19th cent., notably in Barrère and Leland's *Dictionary of Slang, Jargon and Cant* of 1889. *Balls* here are the testicles, on which the slang meaning 'nonsense' or 'mess' is based. *19th cent.*

a new / different / whole new ball game

a completely different experience or situation. *Ball game* as a generic term for any game or sport played with a ball appeared in American use in the mid 19th cent., and was eventually applied specifically to football and baseball. *Late 20th cent.*

The Times 1988

To a Tory member who seemed stand-offish to the Russians, Mr Skinner said: 'Doesn't 'e realise it's a different ballgame between the Prime Minister and Gorby? She meets 'im at Brize Norton all the time and goes gallivantin' with 'im down the streets of Moscow.'

play ball

to be supportive or cooperative: from the mutual cooperation of a team playing a ball game. *Early 20th cent.*

Today 1992

Charlie Chaplin was without doubt a major figure during Hollywood's inception, a star who stoutly refused to play ball with Senator Joe McCarthy's communist witch-hunt in the dark days of the Fifties.

run with the ball

to take advantage of an opportunity: a metaphor from American football (or in Britain, rugby). *Mid 20th cent.*

J Didion *Run River* 1963

He had asked her to call him 'Buzz' ... and had announced that although she was no Jinx Falkenburg she had a lot of class and for his money ($75 a week) the ball was hers to run with ... Although Lily never learned exactly where the ball had been dropped, Martha had worked only one full week and three days of last week.

the way the ball bounces

informal, chiefly NAmer how things are or how they turn out. To *see which way the ball bounces* is to wait on events. *See also* the way the COOKIE crumbles. *Mid 20th cent.*

G Mandel *Flee Angry Strangers* 1952

Women can kick that habit easier than men; that's the way the ball bounces.

Guardian 1991

Similar difficulties will be faced by the architectural press which at the moment appears to be suspending judgment, otherwise known as sitting on the fence while waiting to see which way the ball bounces.

---

ball² (formal dance)

have a ball

informal, originally NAmer slang to have an enjoyable or exciting time. *Mid 20th cent.*

Michael Frayn *Sweet Dreams* 1976

We're really going to have a ball together on this one.

ballistic

go ballistic
informal to lose one's temper: a metaphor from military language. *Late 20th cent.*

> Daily Telegraph 1992
> *Just as he will not tolerate questions about his private life, so he will also go ballistic if bureaucrats attempt to meddle in his creative decisions.*

balloon

when the balloon goes up
informal when the action or trouble begins: probably from the practice of releasing a balloon or balloons to open an outdoor event. *Early 20th cent.*

> P G Wodehouse Hot Water 1932
> *This was the moment when he must put his fortune to the test, to win or lose it all. Now or never must the balloon go up.*

> Sebastian Faulks Birdsong 1993
> *The day the balloon goes up I'm aiming to have dinner off the regimental silver in Bapaume.*

See also go down like a lead balloon at LEAD².

ballpark

a ballpark figure
an approximate figure or estimate. From the original North American meaning 'a baseball stadium', *ballpark* developed its figurative meaning to do with broad estimation or approximation in the 1960s, in early use denoting the intended landing area of a spacecraft returning to earth. Similarly, *in the right/wrong ballpark* indicates how accurate (or inaccurate) an estimate or judgement is. *Late 20th cent.*

> Independent 1989
> *The proposed buildings sale value is estimated at £120m. A spokeswoman for Hammerson said: 'If we are not allowed to use the whole basement area for plant, a ball park figure lost to the group would be anything up to £20 to £25m immediately in the event of us wanting to sell the building.'*

> Oxford Economic Papers 1993
> *We exclude from the analysis those five observations where the output decision was quite clearly in the wrong ballpark.*

bamboo

the bamboo curtain
a perceived barrier to political and economic contact between China and the non-Communist countries of the West in the 1950s. Based on IRON curtain. *Mid 20th cent.*

banana

banana republic
a derogatory name for a small tropical country, especially one in Central or South America, that is economically dependent on its export of fruit: often used allusively to refer to weak or corrupt political and social conditions of the kind associated with such countries. *Mid 20th cent.*

> Daily Telegraph 1992
> *The audacity of criminals faced with ineffective and ill-equipped police forces, not just in their East European homelands, is turning crime levels in Germany into 'banana republic' proportions.*

go bananas
informal to become angry or excited. *Mid 20th cent.*

> Michael Aspel In Good Company 1989
> *She went bananas when I said I was going to leave nursing.*

slip/tread on a banana skin
to make an obvious and embarrassing mistake. *Mid 20th cent.*

> Kenneth O Morgan The People's Peace 1990
> *The Thatcherite band-wagon rolled on relentlessly, though with crises, errors, and 'banana skins' aplenty littering the route.*

top banana
informal the most senior or most important person in an organization. The term originated in North American theatrical slang, where it referred to the chief act in a burlesque entertainment. *Mid 20th cent.*

band

when the band begins to play
when things get difficult or serious. *19th cent.*

> Kipling Barrack-room Ballads 1890
> *It's 'Thank you, Mister Atkins', when the band begins to play.*

bandwagon

jump/climb on the bandwagon

to join in a fashionable or popular activity for one's own advantage. In the US in the 19th cent. a band wagon was a wagon large enough to carry the members of a band. *19th cent.*

Theodore Roosevelt *Letter* 1899

When I once became sure of one majority they tumbled over each other to get aboard the band wagon.

Esquire 1992

I would have expected Esquire to be a little more imaginative than to jump on the anti-Essex bandwagon and to realize that you don't have to be brainless to live in Braintree.

bane

the bane of one's life

one's greatest source of trouble or difficulty: often used in trivialized contexts. *Bane* is Old English in its original meaning 'killer or murderer'. The meaning reflected in the phrase, 'a cause of ruin or trouble', dates from the 16th cent.

Gabriel Harvey *Foure Letters* 1592

He that like a Lacedemonian, or Romane, accounteth Infamy worse then death, would be loath to emproue his courage, or to employ his patience, in digestinge the pestilent bane of his life.

Jack London *White Fang* 1906

But the bane of his life was Lip-lip. Larger, older, and stronger, Lip-lip had selected White Fang for his special object of persecution.

Rachel Elliot *Lover's Charade* 1992

It's always been the bane of my life that you can eat your way through a tuckshop without gaining a pound while I only have to look at a picture of a cream cake to make the scales groan.

bang

bang goes —

used to express distress at a suddenly lost opportunity or hope. The phrase is derived from literal uses to do with the shock caused by collisions and explosions. *19th cent.*

Harriet Beecher Stowe *The Mayflower* 1843

Tired and drowsy, you are just sinking into a doze, when bang! goes the boat against the sides of a lock, ropes scrape, men run and shout.

William James *Letter* 1886

The moment I get interested in anything, bang goes my sleep.

Christopher Morley *Parnassus on Wheels* 1917

I was frightened to death that he'd take me right on the nail and bang would go my three years' savings for a Ford.

get a bang out of something

informal to derive pleasure or excitement from an experience. *Mid 20th cent.*

J D Salinger *Catcher in the Rye* 1951

I hate the movies like poison, but I get a bang imitating them.

New Musical Express 1992

'Boom, Boom,' says the boogieman, as he coolly shoots his lady down, rams her into his car, steers off to his house, gets a bang out of watching her walking the floor, and then settles down for a bit of baby talk.

not with a bang but a whimper

used with allusion to T S Eliot's line (*Hollow Men*, 1925): 'This is the way the world ends | Not with a bang but a whimper.' *Mid 20th cent.*

New Statesman 1992

It seemed fitting for Thatcherism to end, not with a bang, but with the protracted whimper of a 'hung' parliament.

with a bang

with eclat or conspicuous success: with reference to the report made by a gun or bomb. *19th cent.*

Wilkie Collins *The Moonstone* 1868

Everything the Miss Ablewhites said began with a large O; everything they did was done with a bang.

See also bang one's head against a BRICK wall; bang heads together *at* HEAD; bring somebody / come back (down) to EARTH (with a bang).

bank

be crying/laughing all the way to the bank

informal to enjoy success or reward while mocking (by 'crying') or ignoring (by 'laughing') disapproval of criticism of the activities that have earned it: also used with variation of the verb.

The phrase is especially associated with the popular pianist and entertainer Liberace (1919–87), who was noted for his glamour and flamboyance and was much derided by his critics for vulgarity and lack of talent. His reply, as he noted in his autobiography (1973), was 'When the reviews are bad I tell my staff that they can join me as I cry all the way to the bank'. A similar remark was attributed to him in an article in the American national weekly *Collier's* in 1954. *Late 20th cent.*

Richard Dawkins *The Selfish Gene* 1989
The law courts at least preserve the decencies of debate. As well they might, since 'My learned friend and I' are cooperating very nicely all the way to the bank.

Punch 1992
I don't know if they're laughing all the way to the bank, but they can certainly afford to get there in a cab.

break the bank
to cost more than one can afford. The phrase was originally used in the meaning 'to become bankrupt' (i.e. to break one's own bank); later usage refers to winning more in gambling than the bank can pay, and the phrase is now common in informal use in negative contexts. There is a stray quotation from the early 17th cent. in the *OED* in the original sense 'to become bankrupt', but evidence in the current meaning is mainly from the 18th cent.

Thackeray *The Newcomes* 1854
So they travelled by the accustomed route to the prettiest town of all places where Pleasure has set up her tents; and … where young prodigals break the bank sometimes, and carry plunder out of a place which Hercules himself could scarcely compel.

Penelope Fitzgerald *Offshore* 1988
'We can go round by Arthur's in Covent Garden and get a sandwich, if you want,' he said, 'that won't break the bank.'

banner

join/follow the banner
to join or follow a particular cause: from the historical meaning of a standard under which an army marches to war. *16th cent.*

W K Marriott transl Machiavelli's *The Prince* 1517
It is seen also that she [Italy] is ready and willing to follow a banner if only someone will raise it.

under the banner of something
as a representative of something; under the auspices of or serving the interests of a person or organization. *19th cent.*

Charlotte Brontë *Jane Eyre* 1847
God … is the All-perfect. It seems strange to me that all round me do not burn to enlist under the same banner – to join in the same enterprise.

F Mort *Dangerous Sexualities* 1987
Under the banner of health education, the Ministry's aim was for the creation of an enlightened public opinion.

banns

forbid the banns
to make an objection to a proposed marriage. *19th cent.*

Hardy *Tess of the D'Urbervilles* 1891
But to know that things were in train was an immense relief to Tess notwithstanding, who had well nigh feared that somebody would stand up and forbid the banns on the ground of her history.

J M Barrie *Peter Pan* 1904
Wendy was married in white with a pink sash. It is strange to think that Peter did not alight in the church and forbid the banns.

baptism

a baptism of fire
a harsh or unpleasant first experience of a new situation or undertaking: originally applied to a soldier's first experience of battle (translating French *baptême de feu*). Earlier meanings relate to the Holy Spirit in Christian teaching (see Matthew 3:11 'I [John the Baptist] indeed baptize you with water unto repentance: but he that cometh after me is mightier than I … he shall baptize you with the Holy Ghost, and with fire.'). *19th cent.*

George Eliot *Adam Bede* 1859
It seemed to him as if he had always before thought it a light thing that men should suffer; as if all that he had himself endured, and called sorrow before, was only a moment's stroke that had never left a bruise. Doubtless a great anguish may do the work of years,

and we may come out from that baptism of fire with a soul full of new awe and new pity.

D H Lawrence *Sons and Lovers* 1913
She saw what he was seeking – a sort of baptism of fire in passion, it seemed to her.

---

bar

bar none

with no exceptions. This use of the verb *bar* (= prevent) as a preposition dates from the 18th cent. It is used in racing to specify the number of runners that have special odds apart from the rest of the field (*bar one, bar two,* etc). Its main modern use, apart from in the phrase *bar none*, is in the participial form *barring* (= except for). *19th cent.*

Augustin Daly *Love in Harness* 1886
Am I, or am I not, the kindest, gentlest, quietest, best fellow in the world – bar none.

New Musical Express 1992
Rosie Perez is the sexiest actress in the world bar none.

behind bars

in prison. *19th cent.*

Thackeray *The Virginians* 1858
Poor as he was, he always found means to love and help his needy little sister, and a more prodigal, kindly, amiable rogue never probably grinned behind bars.

Liza Goodman *Gemini Girl* 1992
If I don't go along with Roman I could well land in gaol, and I wouldn't be any good to anyone behind bars, would I?

---

bare

the bare bones

the essentials of a situation, description, etc, without any details or elaboration. The image is of a carcass being stripped to its skeleton. *19th cent.*

William Gilmore Simms *Helen Halsey* 1845
I found him always thus capricious; – at one moment gloomy, even to ferocity, and sometimes touched with a sort of religious fanaticism that would have done honor to the ruggedest bare-bones of the Long Parliament.

See also bare one's SOUL.

barefaced

a barefaced lie

a shameless or impudent lie or piece of deceit. *Barefaced* originally meant 'having no beard' or 'with the face uncovered'; it occurs in this sense in Shakespeare's *A Midsummer Night's Dream* (1595) I.ii.90 '[Quince to Bottom] Some of your French crowns have no hair at all, and then you will play bare faced', and in *Hamlet* (1601) IV.v.164, where Ophelia sings in her mad scene 'They bore him barefaced on the bier'. From this it was a short step to the meaning 'undisguised' or 'blatant' in unfavourable contexts such as effrontery, villainy, and tyranny. Addison wrote in the *Spectator* in 1712 that 'hypocrisy is not so pernicious as bare-faced irreligion', and in *Things As They Are* (*The Adventures of Caleb Williams*, 1794) by William Godwin (the husband of Mary Wollstonecraft and father of Mary Shelley), one character accuses another (the tyrannical squire Tyrrel, who has sent his own niece to an early grave) with the words 'They will laugh at so barefaced a cheat. The meanest beggar will spurn and spit at you'. Dickens in *Oliver Twist* (1838) makes Mr Bumble castigate Oliver as 'of all the artful and designing orphans that ever I see … one of the most bare-facedest'. *Barefaced lie* first appears in North American usage in the mid 19th cent., but *bare-faced liar* is found a little earlier (see below). In North America, variant forms *baldfaced lie* and (later) *boldfaced lie* came into use in the mid 20th cent., but these forms have not gained a foothold in British English. *19th cent.*

John Neal *Errata, Or the Works of Will. Adams* 1823
I found no drunkards; no scoundrels – (scoundrels, I mean, that have been convicted in a court of justice) – no downright, bare faced liars, nor thieves, among them.

Charles White *The Mischievous Nigger* 1874
You lying vagabond, do you mean to tell me such a bare-faced lie. Where's the chicken?

---

bargain

into the bargain

in addition; furthermore. The notion is of an additional item being introduced into an existing arrangement or 'bargain'. Lord Clarendon's *History of the Rebellion* (17th cent.) includes the statement that 'He paid much too dear for his wife's fortune, by taking her person into the bargain'. The phrase in its generalized sense dates from the 19th cent.

See also drive a HARD bargain.

bargepole

not touch something with a bargepole
to refuse to have anything to do with something. A bargepole is a long pole used for moving or directing a barge and pushing obstacles out of the way. Early uses have the form *with the end of a bargepole*. *19th cent.*

> Lady Monkswell *Diary* 1893
> *It will be a long while before any political party touches Home Rule again with the end of a barge pole.*

bark

—'s bark is worse than their bite
somebody is less fierce or aggressive than they seem to be. The contrast between *bark* and *bite* appears earlier, notably in a proverb of French origin, *a barking dog never bites*. *19th cent.*

> Scott *The Black Dwarf* 1816
> *'Hout, mother,' said Hobbie, 'Elshie's no that bad a chield; he's a grewsome spectacle for a crooked disciple, to be sure, and a rough talker, but his bark is waur than his bite.'*

be barking up the wrong tree
to be following an erroneous line of thought or course of action; to seek the wrong objective. The image is associated with raccoon hunting, which is conducted in the dark. Dogs are trained to mark the tree in which there is a raccoon, but they can choose the wrong tree in the dark. *19th cent.*

> James Hall *Legends of the West* 1832
> *I must say, when I hear you talk of spirits and such like, that I am sorry to find you are still barking up the wrong tree.*

See also bark at/against the MOON.

barn

See round Robin Hood's barn *at* ROBIN.

barrel

a barrel of fun/laughs
a person or thing that is a source of great amusement or enjoyment: *see also* BUNDLE. *Early 20th cent.*

> She 1989
> *When all things are said and done, life – as any self-respecting Capricorn will readily admit – is not exactly a barrel of laughs at the moment.*

get/have somebody over a barrel
to find or put somebody in an impossibly weak position in dealings, negotiations, etc: the origin is thought to lie in the practice of putting a person rescued from drowning over a barrel to clear the lungs. *Mid 20th cent.*

> Raymond Chandler *The Big Sleep* 1939
> *We keep a file on unidentified bullets nowadays. Some day you might use that gun again. Then you'd be over a barrel.*

> Mike Ripley *Angel Touch* 1991
> *I always like doing business with a man who knows he's over a barrel.*

scrape (the bottom of) the barrel
to have to use the last and least adequate of one's resources: in early uses also in the form *scrape the bucket*. *Mid 20th cent.*

> New Statesman 1992
> *Also, below the surface among the grass-roots leadership, it was usually plain to see that the party was scraping the barrel for competent politicians.*

with both barrels
with great force or feeling: a metaphor from shooting with a double-barrelled rifle. *20th cent.*

base

The meaning involved in all these phrases is the one in American baseball, 'a station at each of the four corners of the inner part of the field, to which the batter must run in turn in order to score a run'.

get to/past first base
to accomplish the first part of an objective. *Mid 20th cent.*

> F Scott Fitzgerald *Letter* 1938
> *I made some bad mistakes in choosing my own curriculum on silly careless premises … I thought*

I'd read Italian to read Dante and didn't get to first base. I should have known from my wretched French that I had no gift for languages.

off (one's) base
in error, wildly mistaken. *19th cent.*

touch base
to make brief contact with one's people or customary surroundings after an absence, especially to remind them of one's existence or to get further information. *Mid 20th cent.*

---

basic

back to basics
a call to return to decent and honest values, especially as a political slogan. The phrase is recorded from the 1970s, originally in American use; in Britain it is now invariably associated with its ill-fated adoption by the Conservative Prime Minister John Major in a speech to the Party conference in 1993, when he declared: 'It is time to get back to basics: to self-discipline and respect for the law, to consideration for others, to accepting responsibility for yourself and your family, and not shuffling it off on the state.' Although the emphasis in the speech was on personal responsibility rather than moral behaviour, it was widely taken up by the mass media in the second sense, especially when members of the Conservative Party itself were shown to be falling short in this regard. *Late 20th cent.*

> **Guardian 1984**
> *Mr Murray thinks that if the unions are forced back on the defensive they must protect their members as best they can. 'And if that means becoming more interested in their occupational problems, so be it. We have got to get back to basics and there is nothing wrong with that. In spite of being excluded from government, we must not spend the time burying our heads in the sand.'*

---

basket

a basket case
informal a person or organization that is incapable of functioning: from an earlier meaning 'a soldier who has lost all four limbs'. The earliest uses are North American, in the context of military hospitals, and also referring to mentally ill patients. The explanation of the term in this meaning may

be that these patients were given basket weaving to occupy their time, and in the sense of physical disability that injured patients, because they had no limbs, had to be transported in baskets. *Early 20th cent.*

> **Esquire 1993**
> *I asked Stephen – one of the two hapless fathers and himself reduced to a mulberry-eyed basket case – if he still had enough marbles to drive me to the station at Orvieto.*

See also put all one's eggs in one basket *at* EGG.

---

bat[1] (implement for hitting)

off one's own bat
British on one's own initiative, unprompted. The origin of the phrase is neatly encapsulated in the colourful citation in extended metaphor from Trollope below, and is an association from the game of cricket, referring to a positive score a batsman makes by hitting the ball with his bat, as distinct from runs earned from byes and other extras. Literal uses occur in the 18th cent. *19th cent.*

> **Trollope The Duke's Children 1880**
> *But in this political mill of ours in England, a man cannot always find the way open to do things. It does not often happen that an English statesman can go in and make a great score off his own bat. But not the less is he bound to play the game and to go to the wicket when he finds that his time has come.*

> **Nigel Williams The Wimbledon Poisoner 1990**
> *Donald would issue a death certificate for any cause you suggested to him; this case, Henry felt, might be so staggeringly self-explanatory as to allow him to come to a diagnosis off his own bat.*

(right) off the bat
NAmer without delay, immediately: from the hitting of the ball in baseball. *19th cent.*

---

bat[2] (animal)

have bats in the/one's belfry
to be crazy or possessed: also in the shortened form *to be bats*. The image is of bats flying about in a frenzy when disturbed in an enclosed space. The American writer Ambrose Bierce (1842–1914) mentioned the phrase as a new curiosity in *Cosmopolitan Magazine* in 1907 (see *Notes & Queries* November 1962, pp.425–6). Some have

tried to identify this phrase as the source of the informal word *batty*, which has the same meaning, but *batty* is attested at a slightly earlier date than the phrase; and attempts to associate it with a William Battie, who wrote an 18th cent. *Treaty on Madness*, and others of the same name or similar, are even less sound. *Early 20th cent.*

> **A E W Mason No Other Tiger 1927**
> *'On this sort of expedition!' Phyllis Harmer exclaimed, looking at Strickland as if he was a natural. 'Dear man, you've got bats in the belfry.'*

> **Stewart Lamont In Good Faith 1989**
> *Some philosophers know a lot about bells and think that everyone who hears ringing noises in their ears must have bats in the belfry.*

like a bat out of hell

with wild speed or frenzy: from the image of bats escaping rapidly and wildly when disturbed. *Early 20th cent.*

> **J Dos Passos Three Soldiers 1921**
> *We went like a bat out of hell along a good state road.*

> **Iain Banks The Crow Road 1993**
> *We were on dipped-beam; the instruments glowed orange in front of the delicious, straight-armed, black-skirted, Doc-shoed, crop-blonde, purse-lipped Verity; my angelic bird of paradise, driving like a bat out of hell.*

See also (as) BLIND as a bat.

bat³ (verb)

not bat an eyelid

originally NAmer to show no reaction, to appear unconcerned. The verb *bat* meaning 'to move (the eyelids)' is unconnected with the other *bat* words; it is probably a variant of *bate* (as in *bated breath*) and dates in this meaning from the 19th cent. It is now used solely in the negative context of the phrase, but in earlier use *bat the eye* meant 'to wink'. *19th cent.*

bate

with bated breath

in a state of great suspense or expectation: also (erroneously, by confusion with the verb *bait*) *with baited breath*. The verb *bate* is a shortening of *abate* meaning 'to lessen': *bated breath* is literally breath that is reduced or held back from emotion. *16th cent.*

> **Shakespeare The Merchant of Venice I.iii.123 (1598)**
> [Shylock to Antonio] *Shall I bend low and, in a bondman's key, | With bated breath and whisp'ring humbleness, | Say this: ...?*

> **Mark Twain The Adventures of Tom Sawyer 1876**
> *Tom began – hesitatingly at first, but as he warmed to his subject his words flowed more and more easily; in a little while every sound ceased but his own voice; every eye fixed itself upon him; with parted lips and bated breath the audience hung upon his words, taking no note of time, rapt in the ghastly fascinations of the tale.*

> **Eleanor Rees Hunter's Harem 1992**
> *For a few moments she imagined the scene as dark-suited managers with grim faces waited with bated breath for the one man who could step in and save the company.*

bath

take a bath

informal to experience a serious financial or political loss. *Late 20th cent.*

> **The Times 1985**
> *It's politics: he's got an election coming up. Mr Fabius (French Prime Minister M Laurent Fabius) doesn't want to take a bath in March and they've got to build up for those elections.*

See also take an EARLY bath.

baton

take up / hand on / pass the baton

to assume or pass on a responsibility or role: from the handing of the baton from one runner to the next in a relay race. *Late 20th cent.*

> **Guardian 1987**
> *Such a coalition would be readier to take up the baton of economic leadership of the western world from the United States.*

> **Ruth Cherrington China's Students 1991**
> *It was left to the capital's campuses to take up the baton.*

> **Daily Mirror 1992**
> *As the Olympic flame died last night, there was every sign that David Coleman might hand on the BBC baton.*

batten

batten down the hatches

to prepare for a difficult time or emergency. A ship's hatches (the means of access to the compartments below decks) have to be covered with tarpaulins held down by battens when rough weather is imminent. Also in the shortened form batten down. Batten is a variant of baton, dating from the 18th cent. in the nautical meaning. *19th cent.*

R L Stevenson *Kidnapped* 1886
'Well,' says I, growing a bit bolder, 'if I'm to choose, I declare I have a right to know what's what, and why you're here, and where my friends are.' 'Wot's wot?' repeated one of the buccaneers, in a deep growl. 'Ah, he'd be a lucky one as knowed that!' 'You'll, perhaps, batten down your hatches till you're spoke to, my friend,' cried Silver truculently to this speaker.

Penelope Fitzgerald *Offshore* 1988
She and Edward would be alone on Grace, and they could batten down and stay in bed for twenty-four hours if they felt like it.

battery

recharge one's batteries

to regain one's energy by resting after a period of exertion. The phrase is attributed to Winston Churchill in a letter of February 1921: 'Subordinate everything in your life to regathering your nervous energy, and recharging your batteries.' *Early 20th cent.*

Janet Tanner *Folly's Child* 1991
She decided to snatch a few more moments of privacy to recharge her batteries in the one place in the whole luxurious house where she was able to relax and feel she was her own person.

battle

battle of the giants

a contest or rivalry between powerful people, countries, or organizations: often in ironic use. Originally with reference to the Battle of Marignano near Milan (September 1515) in which a French army defeated an army of Swiss mercenaries in a fierce contest. The allusion is probably to the so-called Battle of Gods and Giants in Greek myth. According to the poet Hesiod (8th cent. BC), the Giants were the sons of Gaia (Earth) who rebelled against Zeus and the Olympian gods. With the help of Herakles, the gods defeated the Giants, who were buried under volcanoes in various parts of Greece and Italy. *18th cent.*

Thomas Warton *The History of English Poetry* 1774
He is alluding to the stole of Minerva, interwoven with the battle of the giants, and exhibited at Athens in the magnificent Panathenaic festival.

battle royal

a fierce contest or dispute. A metaphor from cockfighting: in a 'battle royal' several birds are made to fight at once. *17th cent.*

John Dryden *The Hind and the Panther* 1687
Though Luther, Zuinglius, Calvin, holy chiefs | Have made a battel Royal of beliefs, | Or, like wild horses, several ways have whirled | The tortured text about the Christian world.

Jack London *The Iron Heel* 1908
Battle royal raged, and the ministers grew red-faced and excited, especially at the moments when Ernest called them romantic philosophers.

New Scientist 1991
A battle royal over who is to fill the current vacuum of leadership in European science planning is now on the cards.

battle stations

readiness for a contest or a challenging undertaking: originally a military term. *Mid 20th cent.*

C S Forester *Good Shepherd* 1955
He should not have brought the men to battle stations at all.

half the battle

a major step in achieving an objective, especially regarded as the most important or challenging part of the undertaking: a metaphor from military activity. *19th cent.*

Edgar Allan Poe *The Business Man* 1840
I got to be well known as a man to be trusted; and this is one-half the battle, let me tell you, in trade.

The Face 1992
I just think women find humour sexy and if you've made a woman laugh you've won half the battle.

See also fight a losing battle *at* LOSE; a running battle *at* RUN.

bay

a Middle English word originally denoting the cry made by hounds in pursuit of their quarry, and hence the encounter when the quarry is caught.

bring somebody/something to bay

to trap or come close to somebody or something being pursued. To *stand at bay* is to be cornered in a pursuit (or, metaphorically, in an argument), like the quarry in a hunt. *16th cent.*

Shakespeare *Richard II* ii.iii.127 (1595)
[Bolingbroke] *You have a son, Aumerle my noble kinsman. | Had you first died and he been thus trod down, | He should have found his uncle Gaunt a father | To rouse his wrongs and chase them to the bay.*

Congreve *Love for Love* 1695
Who would die a martyr to sense in a country where the religion is folly? You may stand at bay for a while; but when the full cry is against you, you won't have fair play for your life.

Dickens *David Copperfield* 1850
There is a sudden change in this fellow, in more respects than the extraordinary one of his speaking the truth ... which assures me that he is brought to bay.

keep/hold somebody/something at bay

to prevent somebody or something from being present or from having an influence. *16th cent.*

---

be

the be-all and end-all

the main purpose or most important feature of something. The locus classicus is Macbeth's soliloquy before the murder of Duncan in Shakespeare's *Macbeth* (1606) i.vii.5, where the context is important: 'If it were done when 'tis done, then 'twere well | It were done quickly. If th'assassination | Could trammel up the consequence, and catch | With his surcease success; that but this blow | Might be the be-all and the end-all, here, | But here upon this bank and shoal of time, | We'd jump the life to come.' Macbeth is saying that he is willing to risk the consequences in the next world as long as there are no unforeseen effects in this world, and so the murder has to be 'the be-all and the end-all' in the sense 'final, not having unexpected ramifications'. This is not quite the modern meaning of the phrase, which became common during the 19th cent. In recent use, the phrase has a positive rather than a limiting sense.

Samuel Butler *Erewhon* 1872
A machine is merely a supplementary limb; this is the be all and end all of machinery. We do not use our own limbs other than as machines; and a leg is only a much better wooden leg than any one can manufacture.

Conan Doyle *The Lost World* 1912
But had the process stopped? Was this gentleman to be taken as the final type – the be-all and end-all of development?

been there, done that

a complacent or world-weary admission that one has done everything there is to do in a particular place. The phrase has been attributed to, or at least associated with, the British film actor Michael Caine, who proposed as his motto 'Been there, done that – It'll certainly be on my tombstone' (as quoted in Elaine Gallagher and Ian MacDonald, *Candidly Caine*, 1990). It also occurs in extended forms such as *been there, done that, got the T-shirt* (with reference to the monotony of package tourism, and with play on the notion that the phrase is itself a T-shirt motto), and in fanciful variations and reversals (see below). *Late 20th cent.*

Sunday Times 1993
We affirm experiences that we haven't had: the-haven't-been-there, haven't-done-that, but-bought-the-T-shirt-anyway phenomenon (wearing trainers when we never run, cycling shorts when we don't even own a bike).

be there for —

to be available to support or comfort a person in need or in distress. *Late 20th cent.*

M Cole *The Ladykiller* 1993
It's because of you, Kate. You were never there for her. You should have dedicated yourself to bringing up your child.

-to-be

prospective, of the future (after a noun, or occasionally as a separate word): used especially to denote personal relationships. *17th cent.*

Shakespeare *Sonnet* lxxxi c1600
Your monument shall be my gentle verse, | Which eyes not yet created shall o'er-read, | And tongues

to be your being shall rehearse | When all the breathers of this world are dead.

Tennyson In Memoriam A.H.H. 1850
I shall be thy mate no more, | Tho' following with an upward mind | The wonders that have come to thee, | Thro' all the secular to-be.

Woman 1991
Mums-to-be only have the right to return to their job if they've worked for the same company for at least two years.

See also be ONESELF; so be it.

bead

draw/get a bead on something
to have one's objective in sight or in mind; originally, to aim a gun at a target. *Bead* is Old English in the now obsolete meaning 'prayer', from which its physical meaning of a small piece of hard material such as amber (originally used to count prayers) was derived. The meaning in the phrase relates to the small metal projection at the front of a gun, used as a sight. *19th cent.*

John William De Forest Playing the Mischief 1875
'Keep your eye peeled,' counseled Pike, seriously. 'You'll need all the sight you've got to draw a bead on her. She suttenly out-dodges and out-squats all the turkeys that ever I hunted.'

Martin Amis Time's Arrow 1991
Each glance, each pair of eyes, even as they narrow in ingenuous appraisal, draws a bead on something inside him, and I sense the heat of fear and shame.

beam

an Old English word in both its main meanings, a heavy strip of wood and a shaft of light. The image in the first phrase below is in fact based on the first of these meanings and not the second.

a beam in one's eye
a fault that one criticizes in others but has even more in oneself: with reference to Matthew 7:3 'And why beholdest thou the mote [= speck of dust] that is in thy brother's eye, but considerest not the beam that is in thine own eye?' *16th cent.*

Shakespeare Love's Labour's Lost IV.iii.159 (1594)
[Biron to the king, then to Longueville] But are you not ashamed ... | All three of you? ... | You

found his mote; the King your mote did see, | But I a beam do find in each of three.

James Fenimore Cooper Deerslayer 1841
'Deerslayer has shown himself a boy ... letting himself fall into their hands like a deer that tumbles into a pit,' growled the old man perceiving as usual the mote in his neighbor's eyes, while he overlooked the beam in his own.

broad in the beam
(said of a person) large at the hips: from the use of *beam* to denote the width of a wooden ship as measured by its longest horizontal timber. *Early 20th cent.*

on the beam
following the right course; correct: with reference to an aircraft's navigation by means of a radio beam. *Mid 20th cent.*

Observer 1948
Hugh Burden, as Barnaby, was right on the beam from the start.

on one's beam-ends
almost without resources, in a desperate position: originally used of a ship that leaned so heavily that its beam-ends were in the water and it was in danger of capsizing. *19th cent.*

Dickens Martin Chuzzlewit 1844
It might become not absolutely lunatic to suspect Mr. Pecksniff of anything so monstrous. In short he laughed the idea down, completely; and Tom was thrown upon his beam-ends again for some other solution.

(way) off (the) beam
greatly mistaken or misconceived: originally with reference to radio signals used in air navigation. *Mid 20th cent.*

Josephine Tey Daughter of Time 1951
'He's away off the beam. Away off.' 'I suspected as much. Let us have the facts.'

bean

full of beans
informal in high spirits, lively and energetic. The phrase originally referred to a healthy horse fed on good beans. *19th cent.*

Robert Smith Surtees Handley Cross 1854
'Ounds, 'osses, and men, are in a glorious state of excitement! Full o' beans and benevolence!

Ludovic Kennedy *On My Way to the Club* 1990
He seemed full of beans though, and after he had given me a rundown on the life cycle of the polyp, three nurses wheeled me across the corridor and into another room.

give somebody beans

informal to scold or punish somebody: also in extended contexts. *19th cent.*

Charles Walcot *Hi-a-wa-tha* 1856
[No-go-miss] *Go in – give him beans!* [Hiawatha] *No: but I'll lick him, only just for greens …* [Minnehaha] *Oh, spare him! – spare him, dear. Don't kill him quite!*

P G Wodehouse *Joy in the Morning* 1946
He wanted to give me beans, but Florence wouldn't let him. She said 'Father you are not to touch him. It was a pure misunderstanding.'

a hill/row of beans

informal, originally NAmer something trivial or of no importance. *Beans* has been in American use in this sense from the early 19th cent., and in this phrase from the 1860s. It is typically used in negative contexts such as *it's not worth a hill of beans*. The phrase became famous from its emotional use in the film *Casablanca* (1942), in which Rick (played by Humphrey Bogart) tells Ilsa (Ingrid Bergman), when he knows they must part, 'it doesn't take much to see that the problems of three little people don't amount to a hill of beans in this crazy world'. The cliché has not driven out all literal use, however: for example, we find an appealing description in Nathaniel Hawthorne's *Mosses From an Old Manse* (1846): 'It was one of the most bewitching sights in the world to observe a hill of beans thrusting aside the soil, or a row of early peas just peeping forth sufficiently to trace a line of delicate green.' *19th cent.*

D H Lawrence *Letter* 1926
I'm forty, and I want, in a good sense, to enjoy my life. Saying my say and seeing other people sup it up doesn't amount to a hill o' beans, as far as I go. I want to waste no time over it. That's why I have an agent.

E Nash *Strawberries and Wine* 1993
Her entire knowledge of what he had to do to earn his crust amounted to not a row of beans.

know how many beans make five

British to be intelligent or well-informed. *18th cent.*

Allan Ramsay *The General Mistake* 1728
And he appears as ane wad guess to think; | Even sae he does, and can exactly shaw | How mony Beans make five, take three awa!

Barry Turner *And the Policeman Smiled* 1991
Paula is living a very bright life with plenty of entertainment and dancing, but she knows how many beans make five!

not have a bean

informal to have no money, to be penniless. *Bean* was used as an informal name for a guinea coin in 19th cent.; the phrase dates from the early 20th cent.

D L Sayers *The Unpleasantness at the Bellona Club* 1928
None of the Fentimans ever had a bean, as I believe one says nowadays.

She 1989
Once you have safely navigated the Full Moon on the 14th – and managed to reassure someone that you'd love them even if they didn't have a bean – then the remainder of this month should be magic time.

See also SPILL the beans.

---

bear[1] (animal)

like a bear with a sore head

very irritable or bad-tempered: also *as cross as a bear with a sore head*, and Grose's *Dictionary of the Vulgar Tongue* (1788) records the form *like a bear with a sore ear*. *19th cent.*

Jane G Austin *Outpost* 1867
'You and I'll go to-morrow and see, anyway,' says Sam, speaking up quick, 'fore I got the chance. 'I'm a-going to see; and, if Harnah'll come too, all the better,' says I, as pleasant as a bear with a sore head.

loaded for bear

informal, NAmer fully prepared for an eventuality, especially an emergency or confrontation. The reference is to hunters having their guns ready for unexpected or sudden appearances of bears. *19th cent.*

Robert W Service *The Spell of the Yukon* 1907
Into the din and the glare, | There stumbled a miner fresh from the creeks, dog-dirty, and loaded for bear.

bear² (verb)

See bear the BRUNT of something; bear FRUIT; bear a GRUDGE; bear the PALM; GRIN and bear it; have one's CROSS to bear.

beard

beard the lion in his den/lair

to challenge or confront somebody on their own ground. The verb *beard* meaning 'seize the beard of', and hence 'confront', dates from Middle English. The notion of daring to grab the lion's 'beard' is also present. *18th cent.*

Smollett *The Regicide* 1749
When the Battle joins! | – Away, Dissembler! – Sooner would'st thou beard | The lion in his rage.

Charles Reade *Hard Cash* 1863
The new client naturally hesitated now: he put on his most fascinating smile, and said: 'Well, Mr. Colls, what do you advise? Is this a moment to beard the lion in his den?'

beat

beat about the bush

to talk about a subject indirectly, without coming to the point: from the practice of beating the bushes to rouse game birds for shooting. Usually used in negative contexts. *16th cent.*

Robert Greene *Pandosto* 1588
Dorastus seeing Fawnia helde him so harde, thought it was vaine so long to beate about the bush: therefore he thought to haue giuen her a fresh charge.

Michael Dobbs *House of Cards* 1989
I shan't beat around the bush, and I shall thank you to be absolutely blunt with me.

beat the bushes

informal, NAmer to search thoroughly: with allusion to the practice of hunters beating down the undergrowth with long sticks to flush out birds and animals. *18th cent.*

Henry Fielding *The History of Tom Jones* 1749
Western began now to inquire into the original rise of this quarrel. To which … Thwackum said surlily, 'I believe the cause is not far off; if you beat the bushes well you may find her.'

beat the clock

to frustrate or counter the effects of the passing of time. The phrase originally referred to time as bringing death, and was trivialized in later use of completing tasks within a limited time available for them. *19th cent.*

Vachel Lindsay *We Cannot Conquer Time* 1912
All our quaint attempts to beat the clock | To tread time down to death with hurrying feet, | Shall slowly end.

Cathy Williams *A French Encounter* 1992
'We wouldn't have to try and beat the clock,' she informed him, looking away, 'if that car of yours wasn't so slow.'

beat it

informal to leave. *Early 20th cent.*

Conan Doyle *The Three Garridebs* 1925
'Help yourselves, gentlemen. Call it a deal and let me beat it.' Holmes laughed. 'We don't do things like that, Mr. Evans. There is no bolt-hole for you in this country.'

K M Peyton *Who, Sir? Me, Sir?* 1983
Common sense told her to beat it while the going was good but loyalty held her, undecided.

beat one's/the meat

informal, originally NAmer (said of a man) to masturbate. *Meat* is the genitals. An early use is by Norman Mailer in his novel *The Naked and the Dead* (1948), set in the Pacific during the Second World War: 'Go beat your meat.' *Mid 20th cent.*

New Musical Express 1992
But may I politely suggest that in future they beat their meat in the privacy of their own studio instead of soiling our evening with such toss?

beat a path to somebody / somebody's door

(said of a large number of people) to flock to see somebody famous or interesting. The phrase *to beat a path* dates from the 16th cent. The expression in its current form has been attributed to the American poet and essayist Ralph Waldo Emerson (1803–82); it does not appear in any of his writings in quite this form but was recollected by Mrs Sarah Yule in her book of reminiscences called *Borrowings*, published in 1889, as having been heard in a lecture given by Emerson: 'If a man write a better book, preach a better sermon, or make a better mouse-trap than his neighbour, tho' he build his house in the woods, the world will make a beaten path to his door.' This squares with a diary entry Emerson made for February 1855, although the all-important reference to the mousetrap is missing: 'If a man ... can make better chairs or knives ... than anybody else, you will find a broad hard-beaten road to his house, though it be in the woods.' *19th cent.*

Dickens *David Copperfield* 1850
I had a good mind to ask an old man, in wire spectacles, who was breaking stones upon the road, to lend me his hammer for a little while, and let me begin to beat a path to Dora out of granite.

— beats all/everything

an expression of amazement or incredulity about some remarkable incident or encounter. *19th cent.*

Scott *Chronicles of the Canongate* 1828
Have you selt [= sold] all off before the fair? This beats all for quick markets!

R M Ballantyne *The Coral Island* 1857
On arriving there we hastened down to the edge of the rocks, and gazed over into the sea, where we observed the pale-green object still distinctly visible, moving its tail slowly to and fro in the water. 'Most remarkable!' said Jack. 'Exceedingly curious,' said I. 'Beats everything!' said Peterkin.

L M Montgomery *Anne of Avonlea* 1909
Beats all how contrary women are.

beat the system

to find a way of evading regulations or procedures. *Mid 20th cent.*

Ian Marsh *Crime* 1992
The reasons given by those who take part in commercial crime rather than straight business tend to stress the pleasure involved in 'trying to beat the system'.

beat somebody to it

to achieve something before somebody else does. *Early 20th cent.*

Gene Stratton Porter *The Girl of the Limberlost* 1909
I am consumed with anxiety to learn if we have made a catch. If we have, we should beat the birds to it.

if you can't beat them, join them

(proverb) it is better to cooperate with rivals and share their advantage, if you cannot outdo them: the form in North America has *if you can't lick them*. Also more colloquially in the form *if you can't beat 'em, join 'em*. *Mid 20th cent.*

Evelyn Anthony *No Enemy but Time* 1987
It wasn't frowned upon for a woman to start talking loud and making a fool of herself. If you can't beat 'em, join 'em, as her father used to say.

it beats me

informal an admission of confusion or bewilderment: I haven't a clue; such-and-such baffles me. *19th cent.*

Lewis Carroll *A Tangled Tale* 1880
As to which I can only say ... it beats me entirely!

to beat all —s

informal the best of its kind. *Late 20th cent.*

Practical PC 1992
At the recent Comdex mega computer show in Las Vegas, a PC screen saver to beat all screen savers was launched by Berkeley Systems.

to beat the band

in a superlative or extreme way, better or more intensely than anything or anybody else: from the notion of drowning out the noise made by a band. Eric Partridge regarded the phrase as a development of the Irish expression *to beat Banaghan* (= tell a marvellous story), which Grose records in 1785 (explaining Banaghan as a minstrel who told wonderful stories), and of the possibly related *beat banagher* (= beat everything) recorded from the mid 19th cent. and possibly connected with the Irish town of Banagher. But these are probably red herrings; the phrase stands on its own feet and needs no such explanation. *19th cent.*

Clyde Fitch *The Cowboy and the Lady* 1899
Don't she beat the band? But – don't be afraid. They ain't going to let her go back the same way.

Jack London *Sea Wolf* 1904
Any jackass gets aboard one [a launch] and thinks he can run it, blowin' his whistle to beat the band and tellin' the rest of the world to look out for him because he's comin' and can't look out for himself.

Jessica Steele *West of Bohemia* 1993
'Thank you for a super time,' she offered sincerely as she waited for the lift to arrive – and felt her heart race to beat the band when all male dark eyes stared down at her.

See also beat somebody at their own GAME; beat one's BREAST; beat the daylights out of somebody at DAYLIGHT; beat the DRUM for something; beaten at the POST; the beaten TRACK; beat a (hasty) RETREAT; beat the PANTS off somebody; MISS a beat.

beautiful

the body beautiful

an ideal of human beauty. The use of *beautiful* for emphasis after a noun originates in *The House Beautiful* in Bunyan's *Pilgrim's Progress* (1678–84), in which *Beautiful* is a name, and is used allusively by 19th cent. writers. *Early 20th cent.*

Hair Flair 1992
For many years the French have firmly believed that regular pummelling is vital to the body beautiful.

beauty

get one's beauty sleep

to go to bed early and sleep well, often with the implication of demanding activity the next day. Traditionally, the sleep one gets before midnight is more restful than that in the small hours. *19th cent.*

Harriet Beecher Stowe My Wife and I 1871
'And now, my dear Eva, have you any more orders, counsels, or commands for the fateful to-morrow?' said I, 'for it waxes late, and you ought to get a beauty sleep tonight.'

beaver

work like a beaver

originally NAmer to work hard and productively: from the industriousness associated with the dam-building activities of beavers in constructing their homes. *18th cent.*

Catharine Sedgwick Home 1835
Harry has worked like a beaver, and with the help of one man and one woman and little Emily, who has done all she could, every thing is ready.

A R Burn Penguin History of Greece 1990
At Athens men, women and children were working like beavers on the walls, using stones from the ruins that lay everywhere.

beck

be at somebody's beck and call

to be constantly ready to respond to somebody's needs or wishes. *Beck* is a Middle English word denoting a nod or other gesture of assent; it was originally a verb and a shortening of *beckon*. Other phrases no longer current include *have at one's beck* and *hang upon the beck of*. *19th cent.*

J S Mill The Subjection of Women 1869
She must always be at the beck and call of somebody, generally of everybody.

bed

and so to bed

used to mark the end of the day's activities. Recent use is influenced by its use at the end of entries in the *Diary* of Samuel Pepys (see the 1666 example below), although the phrase is found earlier. *17th cent.*

Anon Scoggin's Jests 1613
By which meanes, the poore fellow was brought into such a conceit, that he thought himselfe sicke in deede, and so to bed he went.

Pepys Diary 1666
Home, having a great cold: so to bed, drinking butter-ale.

Bette Howell Dandelion Days 1991
A bite to eat, some relaxing television, an hour with Dorothy Wordsworth and so to bed.

a bed of nails

an uncomfortable situation one has to endure: from the board with nails projecting upwards, used by Eastern fakirs for self-mortification. *20th cent.*

a bed of roses

an extremely comfortable or pleasant situation: often used in negative contexts. From the literal use, found for example in Spenser's *Faerie Queene* (1596) II.xii.77: 'Upon a bed of Roses she was layd, | As faint through heat, or dight to pleasant sin.' *17th cent.*

Aphra Behn To Philander 1684
I found thee not, no bed of Roses wou'd discover thee; I saw no print of thy dear shape, nor heard no amorous sigh that cou'd direct me – I ask'd the wood and springs, complain'd and call'd on.

Dickens Oliver Twist 1838
'So-so, Mrs. Mann,' replied the beadle. 'A parochial life is not a bed of roses.'

New Scientist 1991
Clearly, travelling to and from the Garden of England would henceforth be no bed of roses, to mix a metaphor or two.

be in / go to bed with somebody

1 to have sexual intercourse with somebody. *18th cent.*

Henry Fielding *The History of Tom Jones* 1749
He then proceeded to inform her plainly that Jones was in bed with a wench.

M Millar *Soft Talkers* 1957
He's rather sensitive about being caught by the cops in bed with another man's wife.

2 to have a close business relationship with a person or organization, especially when this is regarded as uncomfortable or undesirable. *Late 20th cent.*

Economist 1991
The trouble is that the reform-minded Communists are still in bed with barely reformed Stalinists.

die in one's bed

to die of natural causes, as opposed to a violent death. *17th cent.*

William Bradford *Sundry Reasons for the Removal from Leiden* 1650
He had this blessing added by the Lord to all the rest, to die in his bed, in peace, amongst the midst of his friends.

Mark Twain *A Tramp Abroad* 1889
Martyrdom is the luckiest fate that can befall some people. Louis XVI did not die in his bed, consequently history is very gentle with him.

get out of bed on the wrong side

to be irritable or bad-tempered all day. The notion of sides occurs in several phrases to denote good and bad aspects: *cf* be born on the wrong side of the BLANKET; on the wrong side of the tracks *at* TRACK. In the present phrase, superstitious notions of the (unlucky) left and (favourable) right might also come into play. *19th cent.*

Trollope *The Last Chronicle of Barset* 1867
The Apollos of the world, – I don't mean in outward looks, mamma, – but the Apollos in heart, the men, – and the women too, – who are so full of feeling, so soft-natured, so kind, who never say a cross word, who never get out of bed on the wrong side in the morning, – it so often turns out that they won't wash.

Rachel Elliot *Lover's Charade* 1992
What's wrong Aurora? Did you get out of bed on the wrong side this morning? Or is the strain of running a nightclub finally beginning to get to you?

one has made one's bed and must lie on it

one must accept the unpleasant consequences of one's actions. *19th cent.*

Thackeray *The History of Henry Esmond* 1852
'Tis poor Strephon that has married a heartless jilt and awoke out of that absurd vision of conjugal felicity, which was to last for ever, and is over like any other dream. One and other has made his bed, and so must lie in it, until that final day, when life ends, and they sleep separate.

Samuel Butler *The Way of All Flesh* 1903
I was beginning to leave my protégé to a fate with which I had neither right nor power to meddle ... He had made his bed and he must lie upon it.

would not get out of bed for —

would not even consider something suggested, the implication being that it is inadequate or of no interest. *Late 20th cent.*

Today 1992
The top model turned stuntwoman ... Linda once said she would not get out of bed for less than £10,000. But for almost two million pounds she not only got up, but got to grips with the crumbling guttering on a Paris rooftop.

bedside

a bedside manner

the manner or attitude that a doctor adopts in dealing with patients: also used in other contexts of personal relationships. *Late 20th cent.*

Frances Saunders-Veness *Oh! Sister I Saw the Bells Go Down* 1989
Putting on my best bedside manner, I went to the cheerful locals.

bee

the bee's knees

informal, originally NAmer an outstandingly capable or fine person or thing, originally as a compliment but in more recent use an ironic reference to somebody's own perception of himself or herself. The meaning developed as a reversal of an earlier sense 'something insignificant': *big as a bee's knee*, with the sense 'small or trivial', occurs from the late 18th cent., and Gerard Manley Hopkins in 1870 cited an Irish expression *as weak as a bee's knee*. But *the bee's knees* in the present meaning is not recorded until the 1920s and may not be connected: could *bee's knees* be a corruption of *business*? These phrases gave rise to many fanciful variants based on living creatures, such as *cat's pyjamas*, *gnat's elbows*, *monkey's eyebrows*, and (most recently) *dog's bollocks* (this last also a printers' term for a colon followed by a dash, noted by Eric Partridge). *Early 20th cent.*

> H C Witwer *Fighting Blood* 1923
> *You're the bee's knees, for a fact!*

> What Personal Computer 1993
> *Not only is WinFax Pro the bee's knees, it isn't expensive – you can get it for under £99.*

have a bee in one's bonnet

to be obsessively preoccupied with an idea, opinion, etc. References to 'bees in the head' with similar meaning date from the 16th cent., the notion being of thoughts buzzing around inside like trapped bees. Samuel Colvil's mock poem *Whiggs Supplication* (1681) includes the lines: 'Thou dost interpret Scriptures oddly, | That thou may'st rail upon the Godly: | A Scripturest thou proves, as he was, | In whose fool bonnet-case a bee was.' *19th cent.*

> James Kirke Paulding *Westward Ho!* 1832
> *Mrs. Judith Paddock, the mirror of village gossips, went home with a bee in her bonnet, which buzzed at such a tremendous rate that she was nearly deprived of her wits.*

> G B Shaw *Pygmalion* 1913
> *She's got some silly bee in her bonnet about Eliza.*

beeline

make a beeline for somebody/something

to go rapidly and determinedly in a direct line towards a person or place: from the image of bees returning to the hive. *19th cent.*

> James Hall *Tales of the Border* 1835
> *Early the next morning, our miners had every thing ready for the expedition. The best horse was packed with the tools, and provisions enough for several days. The Indian guide was directed to lead the way. He hesitated for a moment, as if deliberating upon*

the course, and then, having fixed it in his mind, set off on a bee line towards the hidden treasure.

> Mairi Hedderwick *Highland Journey* 1992
> *The car ferry to Arran was full of tourists and, being Friday evening, city commuters who made a determined beeline for the bar before the weekend golf louts took all the elbow room.*

beer

beer and skittles

entertainment and fun. The phrase, and variants of it, also appear in early use as a proverb: *life isn't all beer and skittles* (e.g. in *Tom Brown's Schooldays*: see below). Dickens in *Pickwick Papers* (1837) has the form *porter and skittles*: Sam Weller says 'It's a regular holiday to them – all porter and skittles.' *19th cent.*

> Thomas Hughes *Tom Brown's Schooldays* 1857
> *Well, well, we must bide our time. Life isn't all beer and skittles, but beer and skittles, or something better of the same sort, must form a good part of every Englishman's education.*

beg

beg, borrow, or steal

to acquire something by any available means, whether honest or not: also in the form *beg, borrow, or buy* and other variants. *Beg* and *borrow* occur without a third alternative in the opening of Shakespeare's *The Comedy of Errors* (1594) 1.i.153, where the Duke of Ephesus exhorts the Syracusan merchant Egeon to find a ransom to save his life, 'Try all the friends thou hast in Ephesus; beg thou, or borrow, to make up the sum'. *16th cent.*

> Laurence Sterne *Tristram Shandy* 1760
> *He has taken in, Sir, the whole subject … begging, borrowing, and stealing, as he went along.*

> R L Stevenson *Kidnapped* 1886
> *If I cannae beg, borrow nor steal a boat, I'll make one!*

> Esquire 1991
> *If you don't already have one, beg, borrow or buy a Swiss Army knife – with its corkscrew for wine bottles, bottle-opener for beer, can-opener for tins, knife to cut through the seal on metal whisky bottle-tops …, even a compass for navigating home in the small hours.*

beg the question

to use an unproved assumption as the basis of an argument: originally a (not at all satisfactory) translation of the Latin term *petitio principii*. The sense of *beg* involved here is 'to take for granted', and the thing being taken for granted is 'the question', i.e. the proposition requiring proof. It has also been used to mean 'to avoid the issue', although this meaning overlaps with the first and cannot always be clearly separated from it (as perhaps in the Hume quotation below). In more recent use the phrase is also erroneously understood to mean 'to bring (a question) to mind' or 'to lead one to ask', influenced by the formulaic 'asking' or 'pleading' meaning of *beg* (as in *to beg leave* or *beg pardon*). *16th cent.*

> Locke *An Essay Concerning Human Understanding* 1690
> *I do not ask, whether bodies do so exist, that the motion of one body cannot really be without the motion of another. To determine this either way, is to beg the question for or against a vacuum.*

> David Hume *Enquiry Concerning Human Understanding* 1748
> *But you must confess that the inference is not intuitive; neither is it demonstrative: Of what nature is it, then? To say it is experimental, is begging the question.*

> Henry James *The Ambassadors* 1909
> *He accused himself of being so afraid of what they might do that he sought refuge, to beg the whole question, in a vain fury.*

> S Payne et al *Introduction to Social Administration in Britain* 1990
> *Some definitions of mental illness beg the question of what constitutes normal behaviour.*

come with a begging bowl

to ask for money, especially in a grovelling or obsequious way, in the manner of a beggar holding out a bowl for passers-by to put small change into. The phrase seems to have particular associations with the privatized industries in Britain (especially the railways) seeking subsidies and other support from the government of the day. *Late 20th cent.*

> *Listener* 1977
> *Our industry is always associated with rattling a begging bowl. Some railmen are even embarrassed about going into the pub.*

> *The Times* 2001
> *Railtrack had also decided to pay its shareholders an £88m dividend earlier this month despite 'coming with a begging bowl to Government month after month'.*

go begging

(said of a chance or opportunity) to remain untaken. *16th cent.*

> John Howson *Sermon* 1597
> *Benefices went a begging as Ministers do now.*

> Jack London *The People of the Abyss* 1903
> *There are no jobs going begging through lack of men and women.*

beggar

beggar belief/description

to be so extraordinary or strange as to be barely credible or describable. *Beggar description* is used to exhilarating effect in Shakespeare's description of the arrival of Cleopatra in *Antony and Cleopatra* (1607), as described to Antony by his follower Enobarbus (II.ii.205): 'The barge she sat in, like a burnished throne | Burned on the water … For her own person, | It beggared all description. She did lie | In her pavilion – cloth of gold, of tissue – | O'er-picturing that Venus where we see | The fancy outwork nature.' The phrase became common in free contexts from the mid 18th cent.

> Henry Fielding *The History of Tom Jones* 1749
> *The Behaviour of Jones on this Occasion. His thoughts, his looks, his words, his actions, were such as beggar all description.*

> Smollett *The Adventures of Peregrine Pickle* 1751
> *He was dressed in a coat of white cloth, faced with blue sattin embroidered with silver, of the same piece with his waistcoat; his fine hair hung down his back in ringlets below his waist, and his hat was laced with silver, and garnished with a white feather; but his person beggared all description.*

> John Blake White *The Mysteries of the Castle* 1807
> *Nay – the artifice of these pretendedly devout, oft beggars all belief. I've seen too much of this to be thus easily deceived.*

> Herman Melville *Typee* 1846
> *Who that happened to be at Honolulu during those ten memorable days will ever forget them! The*

spectacle of universal broad-day debauchery, which was then exhibited, beggars description.

beggar on horseback

a poor person who becomes corrupted by the acquisition of wealth: common in various proverbial expressions and also used elliptically. It appears early as a proverb, notably in Shakespeare's *3 Henry VI* (1591) 1.iv.128, where Richard Duke of York berates Queen Margaret (wife of Henry VI) with the words 'It needs not, nor it boots [= profits] thee not, proud Queen, | Unless the adage must be verified | That beggars mounted run their horse to death.' William Cobbett recalls this proverb in his *Political Register* of 1802: 'Our own old saying: "Set a beggar on horse-back, and he'll ride to the devil."' Allusive uses date from the 19th cent.

Saki *Chronicles of Clovis* 1912
'Talk of beggars on horseback,' thought Stoner to himself, as he trotted rapidly along the muddy lanes where he had tramped yesterday as a down-at-heel outcast.

beggars can't be choosers

(proverb) those in need must accept what they are offered. The phrase occurs earliest in the more admonitory form *beggars must/should not be choosers*, being entered this way in John Heywood's collection of 1546. *16th cent.*

Charles Kingsley *Westward Ho!* 1855
'What weapons, Senor?' asked Will again. 'I should have preferred a horse and pistols,' said Don Guzman ... 'they make surer work of it than bodkins; but ... beggars must not be choosers.'

beginner

beginner's luck

the good luck that a beginner at a game or activity is supposed to experience. *19th cent.*

Jack London *White Fang* 1906
His was the luck of the beginner. Born to be a hunter of meat (though he did not know it), he blundered upon meat just outside his own cave-door on his first foray into the world.

beginning

the beginning of the end

the first clear sign that a process is complete or that an objective is about to be achieved. The phrase has been immortalized in more recent times by the speech of Winston Churchill at the Mansion House in London on 10 November 1942, after the British successes at El Alamein in Egypt during the Second World War: 'Now this is not the end. It is not even the beginning of the end. But it is, perhaps, the end of the beginning' (see W S Churchill, *The End of the Beginning* (1943), p.214). *16th cent.*

Shakespeare *A Midsummer Night's Dream* v.i.111 (1595)
To show our simple skill, | That is the true beginning of our end.

J M Barrie *Peter Pan* 1904
Henceforth Wendy knew that she must grow up. You always know after you are two. Two is the beginning of the end.

behind

all behind, like a cow's tail

left behind, or behind in one's work. A modern witticism, sometimes said to be of Irish origin. There is no evidence before the mid 20th cent. (when Eric Partridge listed variants of it in his *Dictionary of Slang*), but C H Rolph, a London policeman and writer on legal topics, in his memoirs *London Particulars* (1980), lists it among the expressions he recalled from his Edwardian childhood, along with 'just what the doctor ordered' and 'are you kidding'.

Independent 1990
The Oscar nominations present no real surprises this year (except, perhaps, for Isabelle Adjani in the Best Actress Category), and the BAFTAs are always too far behind the cow's tail to startle anyone.

Internet Ramblers Website 2005
I just hope I won't be like the cow's tail (always left behind!) and that I don't need oxygen after the 1st mile.

See also behind the times at TIME; PUT something behind one.

bejesus

beat/scare, etc the bejesus out of somebody

to hit or scare somebody very seriously. *Bejesus* is an alteration of *Jesus*: both forms are used as an exclamation. An Anglo-Irish form *bejasus* is also recorded. *Mid 20th cent.*

> Josephine Tey *Brat Farrar* 1949
> *I know men who'd beat the bejasus out of you for that.*

believe

See MAKE believe; seeing is believing *at* SEE.

bell

(as) clear/sound as a bell

completely clear or sound. The version with *sound* is 16th cent., and with *clear* 19th cent.

> Shakespeare *Much Ado About Nothing* III.ii.13 (1598)
> *He hath a heart as sound as a bell, and his tongue is the clapper, for what his heart thinks his tongue speaks.*

> Keats *Letter* 1817
> *I have been writing very hard lately even till an utter incapacity came on, and I feel it now about my head: so you must not mind a little out of the way sayings – though bye the bye were my brain as clear as a bell I think I should have a little propensity thereto.*

> Joseph Conrad *Lord Jim* 1900
> *I could see the line of the horizon before me, as clear as a bell.*

bell the cat

Who will bell the cat? Who is willing to do the difficult or dangerous part of the undertaking everybody is urging? The phrase is based on the fable of the mice and the cat: the mice come up with the clever idea that if the cat were to wear a bell the mice would then get a clear warning every time it came near; but one of the mice then asks, which of them is prepared to put the bell on the cat? There are references to the fable dating from Middle English, notably in the poem *Piers Plowman,* and the phrase occurs earliest in the current form in the 15th cent. The nickname *bell-the-cat* was applied with rose-tinted hindsight by writers in the 17th cent. to Archibald Douglas, fifth earl of Angus (c1449–1513) under James III of Scotland: the story goes that he undertook to 'bell the cat' by causing the downfall of Robert Cochrane and other much-hated royal favourites following the capture and incarceration of the king in Edinburgh Castle in 1482.

> Scott *The Bride of Lammermoor* 1819
> *I say nothing of Miss Ashton; but I assure you a connection with her father will be neither useful nor ornamental, beyond that part of your father's spoils which he may be prevailed upon to disgorge by way of tocher-good [= dowry money] – and take my word for it, you will get more if you have spirit to bell the cat with him in the House of Peers.*

bells and whistles

details; extra features that are attractive but not particularly useful. The phrase is applied typically to machines and gadgets (and originally, in a more literal sense, to fairground organs), and is also used figuratively. *Late 20th cent.*

> *Guardian* 1986
> *One of the features, though, of our legislative process is that a bill gets presented in rather crude form and the bells and whistles have to be added on the hoof as it goes through Parliament.*

> *Practical PC* 1992
> *What might have been first visualised as a basic low cost word processor might have transformed into a full blown all bells and whistles application that has spreadsheets and databases built in, yet, if you're still using the first release, you could be losing out.*

give somebody a bell

informal to telephone somebody. *Late 20th cent.*

> *Outdoor Action* 1992
> *Give them a bell and they'll send you their catalogues.*

ring a bell

to stir the memory or sound familiar. *Mid 20th cent.*

> Margery Allingham *Coroner's Pidgin* 1945
> *'There were always bits about him in the paper at one time.' Campion got up. 'That's where I saw the name, then,' he said wearily. 'It rang only a very faint bell.'*

with bells on

with great panache and success. The phrase is based on the idea of bells and ornaments adding to the excitement or attractiveness of something. *Late 20th cent.*

> *The Times* 1987
> *His advice to would-be winners: 'You just have to work very hard, have a good product and meet the very stiff criteria by showing that it is commercial and has a growing value. I thought I could never get*

*enough information together to win an award, but
in the event we won it with bells on.'*

See also be saved by the bell *at* SAVE.

belle

the belle of the ball

the woman who is most beautiful or admired in
her group, originally at a ball or other grand
occasion. *Belle*, derived from French, is 17th
cent. in English as an adjective and noun. *19th
cent.*

Maria Cummins *Haunted Hearts* 1864
*Whether Polly had sought him or he her, how long
they danced together, and what time the ball broke
up, are matters with which we have nothing to do.
The belle of the ball has gone home, and we have no
motive for outstaying her.*

belly

go belly up

informal to become bankrupt: from the image of a
dead fish or animal floating on its back in the
water. *Mid 20th cent.*

John Steinbeck *The Grapes of Wrath* 1939
*I swear to God I'll wait till you got your back
turned, or you're settin' down, an' I'll knock you
belly-up with a bucket.*

bellyful

have had a/one's bellyful (of something)

to have experienced as much as one can tolerate
of something unpleasant or difficult: in early use
with reference to food or other necessities of life,
and later in unfavourable contexts of things one
would rather be without. *15th cent.*

Shakespeare *Cymbeline* II.i.20 (1610)
*Every jack-slave hath his bellyful of fighting, and I
must go up and down like a cock that nobody can
match.*

William Morris *The Well at the World's End* 1896
*I longed for the play of war and battle. God wot I
have had my bellyful of it since those days!*

below

below stairs

British in the part of a house below ground-floor
level, especially with historical reference to the
servants' quarters in a private house. *16th cent.*

Shakespeare *Much Ado About Nothing* v.ii.10 (1598)
*To have no man come over me – why, shall I always
keep below stairs?*

Frances Hodgson Burnett *The Secret Garden* 1911
*There was no one to see but the servants, and when
their master was away they lived a luxurious life
below stairs.*

belt

belt and braces

a double precaution taken to ensure security:
from the notion of wearing both a belt and braces
to hold up a pair of trousers. *Late 20th cent.*

The Times 1985
*You will probably do well to pay for as much as
possible on your credit cards when abroad. The
delay of anything up to two months in debiting your
account should work in your favour on exchange
rates if other currencies slide against the pound. It is
probably safest to take a belt and braces approach to
changing your money, anyway. Countries like
Greece, for example, regularly have a summer bank
strike.*

Mike Ripley *Angel Hunt* 1991
*It was sealed with Sellotape and staples, a real belt
and braces job.*

(hit somebody) below the belt

(to treat somebody) in a way that is unfair or
violates the rules: from the notion of a boxer
illegally hitting an opponent too low on the
body. *19th cent.*

Jack London *The People of the Abyss* 1903
*To deny us our breakfast after standing for hours!
… It was a cowardly threat, a foul blow, struck
below the belt. We could not strike back, for we were
starving.*

Iain Banks *The Wasp Factory* 1990
*If that last sally was intended to go below the belt, it
failed; the 'better men than you' line was worked out
long ago.*

tighten one's belt

to reduce one's expenditure and live more frugally. When one eats sparingly, one loses weight and clothing needs to be adjusted. *19th cent.*

Kipling *Life's Handicap* 1887
I also was once starved, and tightened my belt on the sharp belly-pinch.

under one's/the belt

1 (said of food or drink) eaten or drunk. *19th cent.*

George Lippard *Paul Ardenheim* 1848
Come, folks, help yourselves! It's the last night of the Old Year, and we'll send the dull old fellow to his grave, with a hearty store of good things under his belt, and a bowl of good liquor to make him sleep easy! Some of the turkey, Parson?

2 (said especially of a task or undertaking) achieved or accomplished and standing to one's credit. *Mid 20th cent.*

John Wain *Strike the Father Dead* 1962
He wanted me to get plenty of Latin and Greek under the belt so that I could be like him.

bend

bend somebody's ear

to pester somebody with talking, especially to get a favour. *Bend one's ear*, recorded earlier (19th cent.), means 'to make an effort to hear something'. *Mid 20th cent.*

Mrs Henry Wood *East Lynne* 1861
She buried her face in her hands and continued speaking: William had to bend his ear to catch the faint whisper.

Penny Junor *Charles and Diana* 1991
It was the most exciting, extraordinary experience he had ever had, and for a long time afterwards he would bend any ear he could find on the subject.

bend one's elbow

informal, NAmer to drink alcohol. *20th cent.*

on bended knee(s)

kneeling, especially in supplication or as a mark of respect: the weak participial form *bended* is now obsolete apart from this phrase. *16th cent.*

Shakespeare *Two Gentlemen of Verona* III.i.228 (1593)
But neither bended knees, pure hands held up, | Sad sighs, deep groans, nor silver-shedding tears | Could penetrate her uncompassionate sire.

Milton *Paradise Lost* vi.195 (1667)
The tenth on bended knee | His massie Spear upstaid.

Edgar Allan Poe *Scenes from 'Politian'* 1835
Thus on my bended knee I answer thee. Sweet Lalage, I love thee – love thee – love thee.

See also **bend over backwards** *at* BACKWARD(S); ROUND the bend.

benefit

give somebody the benefit of the doubt

to accept what somebody says as the truth, or refrain from an adverse judgement of them, where there is no formal proof that they are lying or have done wrong: originally used in judicial contexts. *19th cent.*

Hardy *The Return of the Native* 1878
Forgive you I never can. I don't speak of your lover – I will give you the benefit of the doubt in that matter.

give somebody the benefit of one's experience/judgement, etc

to impose one's views on somebody. The phrase is often used ironically to suggest an unwelcome intrusion. *Early 20th cent.*

Mark Twain *Speeches* 1906
If I had the privilege … of suggesting things to the legislators in my individual capacity, I would so enjoy the opportunity that I would not charge anything for it at all … I would give them the benefit of my wisdom and experience.

Ellis Peters *The Holy Thief* 1993
If the lord abbot agrees, I hope you will stay and give us the benefit of your judgement.

Benjamin

a Benjamin's portion

the largest share: from the biblical account (Genesis 43:34) of Benjamin, the youngest son of the Jewish patriarch Jacob, who received the largest portion of food when he and his brothers were entertained by their long-lost brother Joseph, whom they encountered in Egypt but did not recognize. *18th cent.*

Henry Brooke *The Fool of Quality* 1766
*You shall have your Phœbe restored to you, and she
shall be restored to you with Benjamin's Portion,
even a double Portion!*

bent

bent out of shape
informal, NAmer angry or agitated; also (occasionally) drunk and incapable. *Late 20th cent.*

Guardian 1994
*Sometimes when my mother got bent out of shape,
an acquaintance from a bar or a stranger brought
her home; other times we'd have to go looking for her
or the phone would ring and I'd hear a police
sergeant say: 'We have a Dorothy Pennebaker
Brando here.'*

Independent 1998
*It's the same reason why no one seems to be getting
too bent out of shape about President Clinton. As
long as you're doing your job and not murdering
anybody (although in this town, even that's relative) who cares what your hobbies are?*

Sunday Mirror 2004
*If Portmarnack did not allow black people in what
would we be saying? Anyhow this issue caused a lot
of hassle in my household when I was growing up
and I still get bent out of shape over this topic.*

berserk

go berserk
to become violently or uncontrollably angry:
often used in weakened senses. A *berserk*, or
berserker, was an ancient Scandinavian warrior
who worked himself up into a wild frenzy before
going into battle. *19th cent.*

Charles Kingsley *Hereward the Wake* 1866
*'You cannot go on. The King is at Whichford at this
moment with all his army, half a mile off! Right
across the road to Ely!' Hereward grew Berserk.
'On! men!' shouted he, 'we shall kill a few
Frenchmen apiece before we die!'*

Henry Kingsley *Silcote* 1867
*With her kindly, uncontrollable vivacity, in the
brisk winter air she became more 'berserk' as she
went on.*

berth

give somebody/something a wide berth
to avoid going near somebody or something. In
nautical use a *wide berth* (also *clear berth* and *good
berth*) referred to the sea room needed for ships to
pass hazards or one another without risk of collision. The term dates from the 17th cent., and
figurative examples occur from about 1800 (e.g.
in Scott). *19th cent.*

Dickens *David Copperfield* 1850
*Naturally, we was both of us inclined to give such a
subject a wide berth.*

besetting

a besetting sin
a person's or organization's characteristic fault or
weakness. The expression alludes to Hebrews
12:1 'Let us lay aside every weight, and the sin
which doth so easily beset us.' *18th cent.*

Southey *Joan of Arc* 1795
*Yet retaining still, to punishment | Converted here,
their old besetting sin, | Often impatiently to
quench their thirst | Unquenchable.*

James Fenimore Cooper *Pathfinder* 1840
*Every man has his besetting sin, and matrimony, I
fear, is mine.*

beside
See beside the POINT.

best

the best is the enemy of the good
people or achievements that are good are made to
seem inadequate by those that are even more
outstanding. The phrase is attested earlier (18th
cent.) in French as *le mieux est l'ennemi du bien*,
and in Italian (quoted by Voltaire) as *il meglio e
l'inimico del bene*. An early use in English is by
Archbishop Richard Chenevix Trench in a New
Testament commentary published in 1861: 'The
best is oftentimes the enemy of the good'; and it
occurs from the early 20th cent. in the inverted
form *the good is the enemy of the best*. The notion
goes back further, occurring notably in Shakespeare's *King Lear* (i.iv.326, 1606), where Goneril's husband the Duke of Albany warns that
'striving to better, oft we mar what's well'. The

meaning here is rather of compromising what is satisfactory by aiming at something more ambitious but beyond one's capabilities, i.e. of not letting well alone. Shakespeare conveys a similar sentiment in Sonnet ciii in telling of the hopelessness of describing beauty: 'Were it not sinful, then, striving to mend, | To mar the subject that before was well?' *19th cent.*

the best of British luck

informal an expression of good wishes to somebody who is about to undertake a daunting or unenviable task: also shortened to *the best of British*, and used in fanciful variants such as *the best of Welsh luck. Mid 20th cent.*

C Witting *Driven to Kill* 1961
Here's my P.S.V. [= public service vehicle] badge if you want to take the number – and the best of British luck to you.

for the best

serving one's best interests in the long term. *Middle English*

Chaucer *The Franklin's Tale* (line 886)
I woot wel clerkes wol seyn as hem leste, | By argumentz [= logical reasoning], that al is for the beste.

Shakespeare *3 Henry VI* III.iii.170 (1591)
[Prince Edward] Nay, mark how Louis stamps as he were nettled. I hope all's for the best.

get the best of somebody

to prevail over, or gain an advantage over, somebody, especially in an argument or disagreement. *19th cent.*

Trollope *Phineas Redux* 1874
Phineas Finn and Mr. Bonteen had quarrelled at The Universe. Mr. Bonteen, as far as words went, had got the best of his adversary.

give somebody/something best

to acknowledge or yield to the superiority of somebody or something. *19th cent.*

John Masefield *Everlasting Mercy* 1911
In all the show from birth to rest | I give the poor dumb cattle best.

make the best of it / a bad job

to do the best one can in difficult circumstances. This form is 19th cent. *Make the best of* is recorded from the 17th cent.

Boswell *The Life of Samuel Johnson* 1791
Mrs. Thrale was all for mildness and forgiveness, and, according to the vulgar phrase, 'making the best of a bad bargain'.

Willa Cather *O Pioneers!* 1913
For three years he had been trying to break her spirit. She had a way of making the best of things that seemed to him a sentimental affectation.

Catherine Cookson *The Wingless Bird* 1990
You've got to take what you can in this world and make the best of it.

six of the best

1 corporal punishment, traditionally with six strokes of the cane: formerly a common punishment in boys' schools in the UK. The phrase is now chiefly used figuratively. *Early 20th cent.*

Conan Doyle *The Lost World* 1912
The doctors say that it is all up with the old dear unless some food is got into him, but as he lies in bed with a revolver on his coverlet, and swears he will put six of the best through anyone that comes near him, there's been a bit of a strike among the servingmen.

Wisden Cricket Monthly 1992
Without his moustache, the little spin magician looked more boyish than ever, prompting the thought that unless he cooled down he might benefit from six of the best from the carpet-slipper.

2 in extended use, referring to a selection of six items. *Mid 20th cent.*

Outdoor Action 1992
Paul Traynor outlines six of the best walks around Britain to tempt you off the peaks and into the valleys.

See also one's best BET; best BIB and tucker; the best of all possible worlds *at* WORLD; the best of both/all worlds *at* WORLD; the best thing since sliced BREAD; put one's best FOOT forward; with the best WILL in the world.

bet

all bets are off

informal nobody can know the outcome. *Late 20th cent.*

Independent 1989
Democratic leaders say the fact that the White House remains determined to pursue the capital gains cut suggests that the administration has lost

interest in a steady, bipartisan campaign to reduce the deficit. In that case, they say, all bets are off for co-operation on the budget next year.

one's best bet
the best opportunity or option one has in the circumstances. *Early 20th cent.*

> Alastair MacNeill *Time of the Assassins* 1992
> *My best bet would probably be to fly into one of the neighbouring states and sneak over the border at night.*

don't bet on it / I wouldn't bet on it
informal used to express a reservation or doubt about an assertion or claim. *Early 20th cent.*

> Conan Doyle *The Valley of Fear* 1915
> *'I'll see Reilly the lawyer and take the defense upon myself. Take my word for it that they won't be able to hold you.' 'I wouldn't bet on that.'*

a safe bet
something certain or dependable: originally said of a horse that is expected to win a race. *19th cent.*

> Mark Twain *A Tramp Abroad* 1880
> *Yet it is a very safe bet that two of the three answers would be incorrect every time.*

> Ben Elton *Stark* 1992
> *It's a pretty safe bet that 90 per cent of the mail any particular individual gets will be either dull, depressing or downright disastrous.*

you can bet your boots / bottom dollar / life
you can be quite sure. *19th cent.*

> Mark Twain *A Tramp Abroad* 1880
> *And you bet your bottom dollar, Johnny, it AIN'T just as easy as it is for a cat to have twins!*

---

better

Better, the comparative form used for *good* (which has always lacked inflected forms except in jocular use), dates from Old English (occurring in Alfred and Wyclif). It has formed a natural opening invocation to many proverbs, including *better late than never* (see below), *better safe than sorry* (see SAFE), *better the devil you know* (see DEVIL), and more fanciful admonitions such as *better a small fish than an empty dish* and *better to be an old man's darling than a young man's slave.*

one's better half
one's husband or wife: in earlier use it meant a close friend or intimate, and it was first used by Sidney (see below) in the meaning now current. *16th cent.*

> Sir Philip Sidney *The Countesse of Pembrokes Arcadia* a1586
> *My dear, my better half (said he) I find I must now leave thee.*

> Emily Brontë *Wuthering Heights* 1847
> *No, Heathcliff's a tough young fellow: he looks blooming today. I've just seen him. He's rapidly regaining flesh since he lost his better half.*

> Liz Lochhead *True Confessions and New Clichés* 1985
> *Well, Gillian's always been very independent … Well, we've encouraged that. My Better Half's always maintained, and I agree with him, if they don't want to go to the Church then we won't force them.*

better late than never
(proverb) it is better for something to occur or be done belatedly than not at all. *Middle English*

> Chaucer *The Canon's Yeoman's Tale* (line 1410)
> *They that han been brent, | Allas, kan they nat flee the fires heete? | Ye that it use, I rede ye [= advise you] it leete [= leave it alone], | Lest ye lese al; for bet [= better] than nevere is late.*

> Dickens *Great Expectations* 1861
> *She might have had the politeness to send that message at first, but it's better late than never.*

the better part of something
most or nearly all of something. *16th cent.*

the better to —
in order to do something specified more effectively. *16th cent.*

> Shakespeare *The Merry Wives of Windsor* IV.vi.38 (1597)
> *Her mother had intended, | The better to denote her [= mark her out] to the Doctor – | For they must all be masked and visorèd – | That quaint in green she shall be loose enrobed.*

> Milton *Areopagitica* 1644
> *Lycurgus … sent the poet Thales from Crete to prepare and mollify the Spartan surliness with his smooth songs and odes, the better to plant among them law and civility.*

> Kate Chopin *Awakening* 1899
> *His wife was keenly interested in everything he said, laying down her fork the better to listen, chiming in, taking the words out of his mouth.*

for better or worse

in good and bad circumstances alike; whether good or ill may result. The phrase was given currency by its use in the marriage vows. *Middle English* (in John Gower's *Confessio Amantis*)

Aphra Behn *The Rover* 1677
If thou art for me, child, it must be without the folly, for better for worse.

Byron *Don Juan* 1824
Direct your questions to my neighbour there; he'll answer all for better or for worse.

Nathaniel Hawthorne *The Sister Years* 1842
Whether for better or worse, there will be a probable diminution of the moral influence of wealth, and the sway of an aristocratic class, which, from an era far beyond my memory, has held firmer dominion here than in any other New England town.

K Eric Drexler *Engines of Creation* 1985
For better or for worse, the greatest technological breakthrough in history is still to come.

get/have the better of somebody/something

1 to prevail over, or gain an advantage over, somebody or something. *17th cent.*

Richard Johnson *The Most Famous History of the Seaven Champions of Christendome* 1608
When the wicked Nigromancer Osmond perceiued, that his Magicke spels tooke small effect, and how in despite of his Inchauntments the Christians got the better of the day, he accursed his Art, and banned the houre and time wherein hee first attempted so euill and wicked an enterprise.

Jeremy Collier *A Second Defence of the ... English Stage* 1700
Upon this there follows a noble contest between Pylades and Orestes, who offer'd to die for each other. But before Orestes, who got the better of his friend, came to suffer, he is by good fortune discover'd, and own'd by his Sister Iphigenia; who thereupon contrives their escape.

2 (said of a feeling or attitude) to prevail over a more (or less) generous or positive feeling. *19th cent.*

Herman Melville *Bartleby the Scrivener* 1853
As I walked home in a pensive mood, my vanity got the better of my pity.

go (somebody) one better

to surpass one's own or another's achievement by a small margin: originally with reference to raising a bet in gambling. *19th cent.*

John Oliver Hobbes *The Ambassador* 1898
Do you always like these brutal jokes – this hateful scramble to go one better and be, at any cost, amused?

no better than one should / ought to be

(said of a person) morally weak or sexually promiscuous. *17th cent.*

Henry Fielding *The History of Tom Jones* 1749
For my Lady Bellaston, I darst to say, is no better than she should be.

Samuel Butler *The Way of All Flesh* 1903
He was in some degree consoled by having found out that even his father and mother, whom he had supposed so immaculate, were no better than they should be.

See also against one's better JUDGEMENT; better the DEVIL you know; one's better NATURE; better (to be) SAFE than sorry; have seen/known better days *at* DAY; so MUCH the better.

betting

the betting is (that —)

informal one can be sure (that such-and-such is the case). *Mid 20th cent.*

between

between you and me and the bedpost/gatepost

used about a statement made in confidence. Common in fanciful ad hoc variations. *19th cent.*

Dickens *Nicholas Nickleby* 1839
'Is that my niece's portrait, ma'am?' 'Yes it is, Mr. Nickleby,' said Miss La Creevy, with a very sprightly air, 'and between you and me and the post, Sir, it will be a very nice portrait too, though I say it who am the painter.'

Sabine Baring-Gould *In the Roar of the Sea* 1892
It's a wicked world, and, between you and me and the sugar dissolving at the bottom of my glass, you won't find more rascality anywhere than in my profession.

P G Wodehouse *Damsel in Distress* 1919
Between me and you and the lamp-post, you haven't an earthly.

Economist 1993
Between you and me and that barstool, I can't really tell the difference between their policies and ours.

See also between the DEVIL and the deep blue sea; between a rock and a hard place *at* ROCK[1]; between the sheets *at* SHEET.

betwixt

betwixt and between
having an indeterminate role or identity, neither one thing nor the other. *Betwixt* is a poetic word now mainly confined to the phrase. *19th cent.*

R L Stevenson *Kidnapped* 1886
'And so you're a Jacobite?' said I, as I set meat before him. 'Ay,' said he, beginning to eat. 'And you, by your long face, should be a Whig?' 'Betwixt and between,' said I, not to annoy him.

J Trevithick *Involuntary Unemployment* 1992
Britain's collective bargaining structure lay betwixt and between two polar extremes.

beware

See beware the Greeks bearing gifts *at* GREEK.

beyond

Old English in its physical meanings. Figurative uses based on the meaning 'outside the scope or grasp of' date from the 16th cent.

— is beyond me
informal something is too difficult or obscure for me to understand. *19th cent.*

Jane Austen *Mansfield Park* 1812
'Pray, is she out, or is she not? I am puzzled ...' Edmund, to whom this was chiefly addressed, replied ... 'My cousin is grown up. She has the age and sense of a woman, but the outs and not outs are beyond me.'*

See also the BACK of beyond; beyond the pale *at* PALE[2].

bib

best bib and tucker
one's best clothes. The phrase dates from the 18th cent. and alludes to women's dress of the time: a *bib* was the part of an apron or dress that covered the breast, and a *tucker* was a lace frill worn round the neck.

Robert Smith Surtees *Handley Cross* 1854
Mamma has got on her best bib and tucker, and everything wears a holiday aspect. She is all smiles and serenity.

Esquire 1993
Feel the sweet, fragrant juice gush down your throat, and, if you are not careful, down the front of your best bib and tucker.

stick/poke one's bib in
informal, Australian and NZ to interfere. *Late 20th cent.*

Canberra Times 1984
The doctors should not 'stick their bibs' into negotiations on building workers' wages and conditions.

bickie

big bickies
informal, Australian a lot of money, or something important. Conversely, *small bickies* is a trivial sum, or something of little importance. *Late 20th cent.*

Rosemary McCall *Hearing Loss?* 1992
The sentence ... will not click into sense unless the language is familiar. The same applies if an Australian says 'Don't come the raw prawns on me. Rattle your dags. I'm after big bikkies.'

bid

bid fair
to seem likely to succeed, to offer a good prospect: from the meaning of *bid* 'to offer, to make a bid'. *17th cent.*

Lord Shaftesbury *Characteristics of Men, Manners, Opinions, and Times* 1711
Shou'd physicians endeavour absolutely to allay those ferments of the body, and strike in the humours which discover themselves in such eruptions, they might, instead of making a cure, bid fair perhaps to raise a plague, and turn a spring-ague or an autumn-surfeit into an epidemical malignant fever.

bide

bide one's time
to wait patiently for the right opportunity. *Bide* is Old English in its primary meanings 'to remain in a certain condition' and 'to wait'. The use of *bide*

by (= 'stand by; remain firm to', now replaced by *abide by*) dates from the 15th cent. The transitive meaning survives only in the phrase. *19th cent.*

Trollope *Barchester Towers* 1857
All of which the master perceived; and so also did the mistress. But Mrs Proudie bided her time.

big

give somebody/something the big E
informal, British to reject or dismiss somebody or something roughly. *E* is short for *elbow. Late 20th cent.*

Guardian 1988
A significant minority is temporarily giving expat life the big E and retraining with the aim of going abroad again when prospects improve.

make it big
to be successful. *Late 20th cent.*

Michael Munn *Hollywood Rogues* 1991
Unlike a good many tough guys who made it big in movies, Marvin didn't come from a particularly tough background.

too big for one's boots/breeches
conceited or self-important. *19th cent.*

H G Wells *Kipps* 1905
He's getting too big for 'is britches.

Catherine Cookson *The Rag Nymph* 1992
Well, now that I'm too big for me boots, d'you think me legs'll sprout?

See also big BROTHER; big C *at* C; big CHEESE; big DEAL; big FISH; big GUN; big NOISE; big SHOT; big TIME; big WHEEL; big white CHIEF; get / give somebody a big HAND; top/big BRASS; what's the big IDEA?

bike

get off one's bike
informal, Australian and NZ to lose one's temper. *Mid 20th cent.*

on your bike
1 *informal* a humorous or light-hearted attempt to get somebody to stop being a nuisance and leave. *Late 20th cent.*

Punch 1985
On your bike Jake, I said, this joke has gone far enough, when I caught him taking huge slices from the fridge.

2 *informal* an exhortation to take action. The allusion is to a speech by the Conservative politician Norman Tebbit at the Conservative Party conference in 1981, in which he exhorted the unemployed to go and find work, appealing to the memory of his father who had not rioted but had 'got on his bike and looked for work'. *Late 20th cent.*

Guardian 1985
For eight traumatic months the office argued and battled with the Treasury. We lost. The axe struck. In the event, the hit list went by seniority. Last in first out. For Philip, it was 'on your bike' to some far-flung outpost of Inland Revenue.

bill[1]

Middle English, the primary meaning being 'a written document or note' and hence a list of items of various kinds.

a clean bill of health
a formal assurance that all is well with a person's health or with the working order of a machine, organization, etc. A bill of health, certifying that there was no disease on board, was formerly needed for a ship to leave port, and John Evelyn notes in his memoirs for October 1644: 'Having procur'd a bill of health (without which there is no admission at any towne in Italy) we embarq'd on the 12th.' *Clean bill of health* is recorded from the 19th cent.

Mark Twain *The Innocents Abroad* 1869
Thursday – Anchored off Algiers ... Not permitted to land, though we showed a clean bill of health. They were afraid of Egyptian plague and cholera.

fill/fit the bill
to be suitable for a particular purpose. There are two strands of meaning involved here: in theatrical contexts the phrase refers to a star actor whose name 'fills the bill (i.e. poster)' to the exclusion of other performers; and more generally it means 'to be entirely suitable'. *19th cent.*

Horatio Alger *Cast upon the Breakers* 1896
'Young man,' said the veteran landlord, 'I think you'll do ... You've got a head on your shoulders, you have! I guess you'll fill the bill.'

Jeremy Paxman *Friends in High Places* 1990
Many other jobs get handed out simply because a minister happens to know someone who might fit the bill.

sell somebody a bill of goods
to cheat or swindle somebody. *Early 20th cent.*

top/head the bill
to be the main performer in a show, or the most important attraction. *Early 20th cent.*

P G Wodehouse *Psmith in the City* 1910
When I left the house this morning he was all for cricket … Cricket seems still to be topping the bill.

See also FOOT the bill; PICK up the bill.

bill²

bill and coo
to behave in a sentimentally affectionate way: from the stock image of doves caressing each other's bills. The phrase occurs several times in the novels of Thackeray. *19th cent.*

Thackeray *Vanity Fair* 1848
Bon Dieu, I say, is it not hard that the fateful rush of the great Imperial struggle can't take place without affecting a poor little harmless girl of eighteen, who is occupied in billing and cooing, or working muslin collars in Russell Square?

W S Gilbert *The Gondoliers* 1889
Ever willing | To be wooing, | We were billing, | We were cooing.

billy-o

like billy-o
very much; very intensely The word billy-o is 19th cent., of unknown origin. It occurs only in the phrase. *19th cent.*

Hansard 1992
You know, Mr. Speaker, they would complain like billy-o on the Treasury Bench if we docked their redundancy payments.

bird

Recorded in numerous proverbial expressions from the 15th cent.

the bird has flown
the person one is seeking has gone. The phrase is perhaps associated with the remark of Charles I in the House of Commons in 1642, when he attempted to arrest the Five Members of the Long Parliament (Pym, Hampden, Hazelrigg, Strode, and Holles) and found they had anticipated his purpose and removed themselves: 'I see all the birds are flown.' *16th cent.*

Henry Fielding *The History of Tom Jones* 1749
Perceiving the bird was flown, at least despairing to find him … our hero now blew out his candle, and gently stole back again to his chamber.

Roger Long *Murder in Old Berkshire* 1990
Detective Inspector Anderson, who was in charge of the case, rushed his men to the house only to find the bird had flown, luckily for him only as far as Caversham.

a bird in the hand (is worth two in the bush)
(proverb) something in one's possession is much more valuable than something one still has to acquire. The notion goes back in different forms to the mid 15th cent., and further in the late Latin tag *plus valet in manibus avis unica quam dupla silva* 'a single bird in the hand is worth more than a pair of birds in the wood'.

Bunyan *The Pilgrim's Progress* 1678
That proverb, 'A bird in the hand is worth two in the bush', is of more authority with them than are all the Divine testimonies of the good of the world to come.

Graham Greene *The Honorary Consul* 1973
We have an expression in English – A bird in the hand is worth two in the bush … I would like to live another ten years.

a bird of passage
somebody who is constantly moving from one place to another: originally a term for any migratory bird. *18th cent.*

Fanny Burney *Camilla* 1796
Mrs. Arlbery, casting herself despondingly back the moment she had tasted what he brought her, exclaimed, 'Why this is worst of all! If you can do no better for me, General, than this, tell me, at least, for mercy's sake, when some other regiment will be quartered here?' 'What a cruelty,' said the Major, looking with a sigh towards Camilla, 'to remind your unhappy prey they are but birds of passage!'

John Jones *Dostoevsky* 1983
He has arrived from abroad, yet another bird of passage, 'in the hope of getting a job building our railway bridge'.

the birds and the bees

the facts about sexual reproduction, especially as explained to a child. The two were commonly paired in literary allusion, e.g. by Wilkie Collins in *The Moonstone* (1868): 'The walks were, one and all, solitudes; and the birds and the bees were the only witnesses.' *20th cent.*

New Musical Express 1992
Oi asked Miki from Lush if she would tell me about the birds and the bees but instead she twatted me with a flange pedal.

a bird's-eye view

a broad view of a place from above, or a pictorial representation of this. Also used figuratively: a brief revealing glimpse or comprehending of a situation. *18th cent.*

James Fenimore Cooper The Pioneers 1823
'Get up, you obstinate devils!' cried Richard, catching a bird's-eye view of his situation, applying his whip with new vigour, and unconsciously kicking the stool on which he sat.

Byron Don Juan 1824
A bird's-eye view, too, of that wild, Society; a slight glance thrown on men of every station.

Washington Irving Alhambra 1832
What a morning to mount to the summit of the Tower of Comares, and take a bird's-eye view of Granada and its environs!

Conan Doyle The Lost World 1912
It was a bird's-eye view of creation, as interpreted by science, which, in language always clear and sometimes picturesque, he unfolded before us.

birds of a feather (flock together)

(proverb) people with similar tastes and opinions (tend to seek one another's company). *16th cent.*

Holland transl Livy 1600
As commonly birds of a feather will flye together.

Lewis Carroll Alice's Adventures in Wonderland 1865
'Very true,' said the Duchess: 'flamingoes and mustard both bite. And the moral of that is – "Birds of a feather flock together"'.' 'Only mustard isn't a bird,' Alice remarked.

R Pilcher Flowers in the Rain 1992
She knew that he was mistaken, and they were not birds of a feather, but she was not going to tell him so.

do (one's) bird

informal, British to serve a prison sentence: *bird* meaning 'a period of imprisonment' is a short-

ening of *birdlime*, rhyming slang for 'time' (recorded from the 19th cent.). *Mid 20th cent.*

flip somebody the bird

informal to put up the middle finger as a sign of contempt: *bird* is a slang term associated with various types of gesture, obscurely derived from the phrase *give somebody the bird* (see below). *Late 20th cent.*

Evening Standard 1999
Forgiveably flawed, Honk! is packed with wit, energy and admirable moral purpose. If anyone tells you different, flip them the bird.

give somebody the bird

1 to boo or hiss a performer, originally an actor on stage. To *get the bird* is to be hissed in this way, and is recorded in Hotten's *Slang Dictionary* of 1865. The reference is to the hissing of a 'big bird', i.e. a goose. *19th cent.*
2 to sack or dismiss somebody. *19th cent.*

John Galsworthy The White Monkey 1924
When you were ill, I stole for you. I got the bird for it.

have a bird

informal, NAmer to be shocked or agitated. *Late 20th cent.*

kill two birds with one stone

to achieve two objectives in one course of action. The notion goes back to the Roman poet Ovid (*Ars Amatoria* iii.358: *unus cum gemino calculus hoste perit*). *17th cent.*

Hobbes The Questions Concerning Liberty 1656
T.H. thinks to kill two birds with one stone, and satisfy two arguments with one answer.

Edgar Allan Poe The Literary Life of Thingum Bob Esq 1844
The trade of editor is best: – and if you can be a poet at the same time, – as most of the editors are, by the by, why, you will kill two birds with the one stone.

a little bird told me

used, in various forms, as a teasing refusal to say how one acquired a piece of information or gossip. *18th cent.*

George Eliot Middlemarch 1872
I know all about it. I have a confidential little bird.

Helen Keller The Story of My Life 1901
A little bird had already sung the good news in my ear; but it was doubly pleasant to have it straight from you.

strictly for the birds

informal, originally NAmer trivial or worthless. The phrase originates in US army slang and may refer to the droppings of horses and cattle, which are eaten up by birds. *Mid 20th cent.*

> J D Salinger *Catcher in the Rye* 1951
> *'Since 1888 we have been moulding boys into splendid, clear-thinking young men.' Strictly for the birds.*

See also be an EARLY bird.

birthday

in one's birthday suit

informal naked. In this phrase, *birthday suit* means the suit one was born in, i.e. the bare skin, although it was earlier used to mean a suit worn to celebrate the king's birthday. *19th cent.*

> Today 1992
> *Martinez ... arrived in his birthday suit for a disciplinary meeting at the University of California, Berkeley – as a protest against what he claims is society's 'repression'.*

biscuit

take the biscuit

to be the most remarkable or surprising event or incident. *See also* take the CAKE. *Early 20th cent.*

> P G Wodehouse *Very Good, Jeeves!* 1930
> *Of all the absolutely foul sights I have ever seen, this took the biscuit with ridiculous ease.*

bishop

See as the ACTRESS said to the bishop.

bit¹ (a small piece of something)

a bit of all right

informal somebody or something attractive or pleasing. *19th cent.*

> J D Brayshaw *Slum Silhouettes* 1898
> *She was a nice little bit o' goods. There's her portrait ... A nice little bit of orlright, ain't she?*

> Robert Barnard *Posthumous Papers* 1992
> *He watched the television at night, all night, making remarks like 'That's a bit of all right' at the girls, or 'Kill him' to the wrestlers.*

a bit of fluff/skirt/stuff

a woman regarded sexually. *Early 20th cent.*

> Somerset Maugham *Theatre* 1937
> *It was strangely flattering for a woman to be treated as a little bit of fluff that you just tumbled on to a bed.*

> Shirley Conran *Crimson* 1992
> *Dearest girl, I've told you before, you mustn't let a little bit of fluff spoil your marriage.*

a bit on the side

1 extra money earned separately from one's normal work. *Late 20th cent.*

> Anton Gill *City of Dreams* 1993
> *There was a girl here not long ago, looking for fun, wanting to earn a bit on the side.*

2 a sexual affair, or a person involved in one. *20th cent.*

> She 1989
> *Now had it actually been infidelity – me having watched said movie from the back row of the local Ritzy with my bit on the side at my side – then I would have deserved whatever was coming to me.*

bits and pieces/bobs

miscellaneous small items. *Early 20th cent.*

> Margery Allingham *Hide My Eyes* 1958
> *Give those chaps half an hour in here with their bits and bobs and there's no telling what they might be able to find.*

> Norton York *The Rock File* 1991
> *Some of the tapes we receive arrive on dodgy cassettes, have various bits and pieces of other music on them, and we have to waste time trying to find the relevant bit of the tape.*

do one's bit

to contribute as best one can to a joint effort or cause. *19th cent.*

> Christopher Morley *The Haunted Bookshop* 1919
> *It's quaint to think of old Woodrow ... going over to do his bit among the diplomatic shell-craters.*

to bits

informal completely, utterly (especially in the context of personal feelings, e.g. *thrilled to bits*). *Mid 20th cent.*

See also a bit of ROUGH; a nasty piece/bit of WORK.

bit² (for a horse)

champ at the bit
to show eager impatience: from the literal use with reference to a lively horse pulling on its bit when eager to move. *18th cent.*

get/take/have the bit between one's teeth
to take action in a determined, usually obsessive or wrongheaded, way: a lively horse will grab the bit between its teeth and so make it difficult for the rider to control the reins. *19th cent.*

James Kirke Paulding *The Puritan and His Daughter* 1849
He was exceedingly self-willed, and often took the bit between his teeth, when neither tutor nor proctor could restrain him.

Samuel Butler *The Way of All Flesh* 1903
Ernest was always so outré ... If he was to get the bit between his teeth after he had got ordained and bought his living, he would play more pranks than ever he, Theobald, had done.

Sara Maitland *Three Times Table* 1990
No one, not even Fenna, could actually stand up against Rachel when she had once got the bit between her teeth: she was better at the game of controlling, containing, winning, than anyone else that Maggie knew.

bitch

the bitch goddess
a derogatory term for material success. The phrase was evidently first used by the American philosopher and psychologist William James in a letter of 1906 addressed to H G Wells: 'A symptom of the moral flabbiness born of the exclusive worship of the bitch-goddess success.' *Early 20th cent.*

D H Lawrence *Lady Chatterley's Lover* 1928
He realized now that the bitch-goddess of success had two main appetites: one for flattery, adulation, stroking and tickling such as writers and artists gave her; but the other a grimmer appetite for meat and bones.

bite

bite the big one
informal, NAmer to die. *20th cent.*

bite the dust
(said of a person) to die. The image goes back to the Homeric poems and comes to us via Virgil (see below), and the phrase occurs earliest in the form *bite the ground*. The phrase, for a time a cliché of westerns, is also used in figurative contexts of plans and undertakings that fail. *17th cent.*

Dryden transl Virgil's *Aeneid* 1697
So many Valiant Heros bite the Ground.

R L Stevenson *Treasure Island* 1883
Two had bit the dust, one had fled, four had made good their footing inside our defence.

Joan Smith *A Masculine Ending* 1988
She was determined that the new course would not bite the dust because of a rearguard action by a couple of old fogies like Maurice Webb and Henry Hedger.

bite the hand that feeds one
to offend or harm a supporter or benefactor: also in fanciful variant forms. *18th cent.*

Edmund Burke *Thoughts on the Cause of the Present Discontents* 1770
This ... proposition ... that we set ourselves to bite the hand that feeds us; that with ... insanity we oppose the measures ... whose sole object is our own peace and prosperity.

Samuel Judah *The Buccaneers* 1827
Thou, villain, foul-faithed slave, that would bite the hand that feeds thee.

Willa Cather *O Pioneers!* 1913
Mistress, how can anyone think that? – that I could bite the hand that fed me!

Robert Rankin *The Suburban Book of the Dead* 1993
Don't bite the hand that pulls you out of the shit.

bite one's lip
to dig one's teeth into one's lip as a reflex to control violent emotion. *16th cent.*

Spenser *The Faerie Queene* IV.x.33 (1596)
Yet she was of such grace and vertuous might, | That her commaundment he could not withstand, | But bit his lip for felonous despight.

George Eliot *Middlemarch* 1872
Any stranger ... might have wondered what was the drama between the indignant man of business, and the fine-looking young fellow whose blond complexion was getting rather patchy as he bit his lip with mortification.

Timothy Mo *The Redundancy of Courage* 1991
'I'll do my best,' I said, and then I made her bite her lip in vexation for I said with a smile, 'And I'll tell him you're all in favour, if I may.'

bite one's nails
to nibble at the fingernails, especially in concentration or from nervous excitement: hence *nail-biting* in the sense 'suspenseful'. *16th cent.*

Swift *On Poetry* 1733
Be mindful, when invention fails, | To scratch your head and bite your nails.

Somerset Maugham *Of Human Bondage* 1915
There was a passionate note in her voice which struck Philip. He was biting his nails in his nervousness.

bite off more than one can chew
to agree to a commitment that one cannot then fulfil, or to take on a task that proves to be beyond one. The phrase originates in North America and had passed into British use by the early 20th cent. *19th cent.*

J Beadle *Western Wilds* 1878
You've bit off more'n you can chaw.

G B Shaw *Pygmalion* 1913
Weak people want to marry strong people who do not frighten them too much; and this often leads them to make the mistake we describe metaphorically as 'biting off more than they can chew'.

bite (on) the bullet
to resolve on a difficult or painful undertaking: from the former practice of giving a wounded soldier a bullet to bite on when undergoing surgery without anaesthetic. *19th cent.*

Kipling *The Light that Failed* 1891
Bite on the bullet, old man, and don't let them think you're afraid.

Norman Fowler *Ministers Decide* 1991
My view was that we should bite the bullet, abolish SERPS and encourage substitute private pensions.

bite one's tongue
to restrain oneself with difficulty from speaking. *16th cent.*

Shakespeare *2 Henry VI* i.i.230 (1591)
[York] So York must sit and fret and bite his tongue, | While his own lands are bargained for and sold.

once bitten (twice shy)
(proverb) somebody who has suffered an unpleasant experience will avoid the same circumstances another time: in North America a common form is *once burned twice shy*. The sentiment is much older in other forms than the present proverb, being found for example in John Lyly's *Euphues* (1580): 'It fareth with mee nowe, as with those that haue ben once bitten with the scorpion, who neuer after feele any sting, either of the waspe, or the hornet, or the bee, for I hauing bene pricked with thy falsehoode, shall neuer I hope againe be touched with any other dissembler, flatterer, or fickle friend.' *19th cent.*

Ambrose Bierce *The Fiend's Delight* 1873
'Once bit, twice shy,' is a homely saying, but singularly true. A man who has been swindled will be very cautious the second time, and the third. The fourth time he may be swindled again more easily and completely than before.

Barcroft Boake *Where the Dead Men Lie, and Other Poems* 1897
They yarded him once; but since then | He held to the saying, 'Once bitten, twice shy'.

put the bite on somebody
informal to blackmail somebody or extort money from them. *Mid 20th cent.*

Raymond Chandler *The Big Sleep* 1939
You can put the bite on the peeper and be on your way.

P Chester *Murder Forestalled* 1990
Now the murderer has his hands on the information my client doesn't want made public, and he has put the bite on, too.

take a bite out of something
informal to use or eliminate a large part of a sum of money or other resource. *Late 20th cent.*

The Times 1988
Spending has also held up strongly on company cars where the Chancellor took a severe bite out of the tax advantages, though without ending them altogether.

See also another bite at the CHERRY; bite somebody's HEAD off.

biter

the biter bit

the perpetrator of a foul or wicked deed finds himself all at once the victim. A *biter* is an otherwise obsolete word for a fraudster or swindler. *17th cent.*

Thomas D'Urfey *The Richmond Heiress* 1693
But yet considering the equality, | How oft ye chouce [= chase] *poor women, is't not fit | Once in an age the biter should be bit.*

Dickens *Pickwick Papers* 1837
'Pride, old fellow, pride,' replied Jingle, quite at his ease. 'Wouldn't do – no go – caught a captain, eh? – ha! ha! very good – husband for daughter – biter bit – make it public – not for worlds – look stupid – very!'

Karl Miller *Authors* 1989
A writer is copied by 'someone other' than himself, and that 'someone other' can in a manner of speaking become the writer he copies: the biter bit.

---

bitter

to the bitter end

to the very end of something, no matter what happens. The expression is perhaps influenced by the nautical term *bitter end*, referring to the part of an anchor cable remaining on the deck and attached to the *bitts* (sturdy posts for fastening cables), and by the biblical allusion in Proverbs 5:4 'For the lips of a strange woman drop as an honeycomb, and her mouth is smoother than oil: But her end is bitter as wormwood, sharp as a two-edged sword'. *19th cent.*

Anne Royall *The Tennessean* 1827
My lady would do no sich a thing, for she stood to it, to the bitter end, that she would never laive her mother, poor woman!

Edgar Rice Burroughs *Return of Tarzan* 1913
She had made a bad bargain, but she intended carrying her part loyally to the bitter end.

Graham Greene *Loser Takes All* 1955
A wife ought to believe in her husband to the bitter end.

See also a bitter PILL.

black

(as) black as ink

intensely black. This form is 16th cent. Other forms include *black as a crow* (Middle English), *black as soot* (15th cent.), *black as the devil* (Middle English), and *black as thunder* (19th cent.).

Shakespeare *The Two Gentlemen of Verona* III.i.283 (1593)
[Speed] *What news then in your paper?* [Lance] *The blackest news that ever thou heard'st.* [Speed] *Why, man, how 'black'?* [Lance] *Why, as black as ink.*

Thomas Amory *The Life of John Buncle, Esq.* 1756
On the top of this mountain I saw another large loch that was black as ink in appearance, tho' bright when taken up in a glass.

John Blake White *Foscari* 1806
'Tis news that leads that way – let me be brief. | On coming here, I found my worthy friend, | Black as thunder cloud, when fully charg'd | To vent its fury on the earth.

beat somebody black and blue

to beat somebody so severely that they are covered in bruises: earlier in the form *blak and bla*. *Bla* (derived from Old Norse and surviving in northern dialects) denoted a darker colour than the modern word *blue* (earlier *blew*, derived from French *bleu*) which replaced it in southern English, and was therefore an appropriate word in the context of bruising. *16th cent.*

Shakespeare *The Merry Wives of Windsor* IV.v.105 (1597)
[Mistress Quickly] *Mistress Ford, good heart, is beaten black and blue, that you cannot see a white spot about her.*

Mary Jane Staples *Sergeant Joe* 1992
'Not that I mind 'er pullin' me leg, I'm just thankful you ain't beatin' 'er black an' blue, it upset me when —' The landlady stopped.

be in somebody's black books

to be out of favour with somebody. The book in question was a record of those liable to censure or punishment, and may have had its ultimate origin in the book bound in black that was used to record evidence of scandals in the monasteries before their suppression under Henry VIII in the 1530s. The phrase dates from the 19th cent. in this form.

Wilkie Collins *The Moonstone* 1868
He has been made to feel her temper; he is in her
black books too – and that after having done all he
can to help her, poor fellow!

black box

1 an unspecified or mysterious device: *black* refers
to the obscure nature of the device rather than its
colour. *Early 20th cent.*

Edgar Rice Burroughs *The Beasts of Tarzan* 1914
And presently as he thought there recurred to his
memory the little black box which lay hidden in a
secret receptacle beneath a false top upon the table
where his hand rested.

Guitarist 1992
This, to the outside world, is a little black box,
hidden away in the control cavity at the back of the
guitar.

2 an aircraft's flight recorder. This name dates
from the Second World War, and was originally
used of navigational equipment; it was entered
with this meaning by Eric Partridge in his *Dictionary of RAF Slang* of 1945. *Mid 20th cent.*

a black mark (against somebody)

something that counts against somebody in the
estimation of others: from the practice of putting
a black mark against the name of a miscreant or
wrongdoer in a list of names. *19th cent.*

Disraeli *Sybil* 1845
Cuss you, you old fool, do you think I am to be kept
all day while you are mumbling here? Who's
pushing on there? I see you, Mrs. Page. Won't there
be a black mark against you?

Conan Doyle *Adventure of Wisteria Lodge* 1908
If I didn't know you were a good man, Walters, I
should put a black mark against you for this.

a/the black sheep (of the family)

a bad character, considered as having discredited
a family. The phrase is 18th cent.; the proverb
there's a black sheep in every flock is 19th cent.

Charles Macklin *The Man of the World* 1793
As to ye, my Lady Mac Sycophant, I suppose ye
concluded before ye gave yer consent till this match,
that there would be an end to every thing betwixt ye
and me – Live wee your Constantia, Madam, your
son, and that black sheep there.

Scott *Old Mortality* 1816
The curates, for their own sakes, willingly collect all
these materials for their own regulation in each

parish; they know best the black sheep of the flock. I
have had your picture for three years.

Saki *Chronicles of Clovis* 1912
The youngest boy, Wratislav, who was the black
sheep of a rather greyish family, had as yet made no
marriage at all.

a black spot

1 a disgraceful episode, or a reminder of one. *19th
cent.*

R L Stevenson *Kidnapped* 1886
And that was how I came to enlist, which was a
black spot upon my character at the best of times.

2 a place that is notorious for some danger or
difficulty, especially a length of road that has
been the scene of a high number of accidents.
Early 20th cent.

Today 1992
The accident black spot was Derbyshire where four
people died – three following a multiple smash on
the southbound carriageway of the M1.

3 a weak point in a system or organization. *Mid
20th cent.*

Discovery 1936
The development of newer industries is vital to the
recovery of our distressed areas, which remain the
one black spot in the otherwise remarkable position
of Great Britain.

in the black

in credit, not owing money: from the use of black
figures to show the credit side of an account. *Cf* in
the RED. *Early 20th cent.*

Michael Jefferson *Criminal Law* 1992
What happens when the account is in the black at
the time of presentation but in the red when the bank
honours the withdrawal?

in black and white

1 in extreme contrast; relating to opposed principles. *16th cent.*

Shakespeare *Henry V* II.ii.101 (1599)
'Tis so strange | That though the truth of it stands
off as gross | As black on white, my eye will scarcely
see it.

G K Chesterton *Orthodoxy* 1908
It is true that the historic Church … hates that
combination of two colours which is the feeble
expedient of the philosophers. It hates that evolution
of black into white which is tantamount to a dirty
gray.

2 in print, especially in contrast to the less tangible evidence of something spoken. *17th cent.*

> Bunyan *The Pilgrim's Progress* 1678
> *Thus, I set pen to paper with delight, and quickly had my thoughts in black and white.*

> Hardy *The Mayor of Casterbridge* 1886
> *So come to my house and we will have a solid, staunch tuck-in, and settle terms in black-and-white if you like; though my word's my bond.*

> Laura Martin *Garden of Desire* 1993
> *Perhaps now, now she had finally written it down, could stare at the irretrievable words, written in black and white, she would be able to accept the way things had to be, she would have the strength to return.*

not as black as one is painted
not as bad as one is made out to be. The phrase is 19th cent. in this form; a proverb *the devil is not as black as he is painted*, warning against too ready acceptance of alarming rumours, dates from the 16th cent.

> Edgar Allan Poe *Criticism* 1831
> *But neither are we all brainless, nor is the devil himself so black as he is painted.*

See also this side of / beyond the black STUMP.

blackboard

the blackboard jungle
the education system regarded as a place where the law of the JUNGLE (i.e. chaos) applies. First used as a book title by E Hunter in 1954. Other jungles include the CONCRETE jungle, recorded from the 1960s. *Mid 20th cent.*

> *The Times* 1988
> *The city's [New York's] blackboard jungle of one million children has been deserted by the white middle class, which prefers sending its children to private schools.*

blank

draw a blank
to be unsuccessful in an enquiry, to receive no answer: originally a term for a lottery ticket that did not win a prize. *19th cent.*

> Mark Twain *The $30,000 Bequest* 1906
> *'The chances are just that much increased that I shall catch it this time. I will be shrewd, and buy an*

accident ticket.' And to a dead moral certainty I drew a blank.

firing blanks
informal unsuccessful in various senses of 'shooting', specifically failing to score in ball games, or (said of a man) infertile. *Late 20th cent.*

> *The Times* 1985
> *Predictably, the draw was goalless. Birmingham have been firing blanks for 626 minutes.*

write / give somebody a blank cheque
to allow somebody the freedom to act as they wish, especially in financial matters: originally a bank cheque in which the space for the amount payable is left blank, so that the payee can write in any amount. *Early 20th cent.*

> Saki *Reginald* 1904
> *Unlike the alleged Good Woman of the Bible, I'm not above rubies … She must have been rather a problem at Christmas-time; nothing short of a blank cheque would have fitted the situation.*

blanket

be born on the wrong side of the blanket
to be of illegitimate birth. A good example of a genre of phrases that use 'sides' to denote the right and wrong, or favourable and unfavourable, aspects of a situation: *cf* get out of BED on the wrong side; on the wrong side of the tracks *at* TRACK. *18th cent.*

> Smollett *The Expedition of Humphry Clinker* 1771
> *Thof [= though] my father wan't a gentleman, my mother was an honest woman – I didn't come on the wrong side of the blanket, girl.*

> Liz Lochhead *True Confessions and New Clichés* 1985
> *Of course somebody, Who Shall Be Nameless, would bring up the subject of Burns-And-You-Know-What, and how many of his children were born on The Wrong Side Of The Blanket, What Right Had We to look down on Brown Owl for her shotgun wedding when we were all supposed to look up to Rabbie Burns as Our Big Hero?*

See also WET blanket.

Blarney

have kissed the Blarney Stone
to be articulate and cogent in speech. The expression refers to a stone at Blarney Castle near Cork

in Ireland, which is set in an awkward position in the walls and is said to bestow the gift of eloquent speech on anybody willing to contort themselves in order to kiss it (this involves lying on one's back and bending the head back against a point low down on the inside of a wall; modern-day tourists are given assistance). *Blarney* is a noun (18th cent.) and verb meaning '(to use) flattering talk'. *19th cent.*

blast

a blast from the past
a strong nostalgic reminder of the past, especially a song. *Late 20th cent.*

> Peter Cave *Foxbat* 1979
> *The request is for a real blast from the past – that lovely old Peter, Paul and Mary folk song.*

blaze[1]

like blazes
with great energy or force. The noun *blaze* is Old English in the now obsolete meaning 'torch, firebrand' and in the meaning still current, 'a bright fire or flame'. Several informal phrases use *blaze* in the plural, referring to the 'fires of hell' in Christian belief; and it has been freely used in expressions such as *mad as blazes, what the (blue) blazes, go to blazes* (= hell), etc. The verb meaning 'to burn with a bright flame' dates from Middle English and gave rise to a range of phrasal verbs including *blaze away, blaze out,* and *blaze up. 19th cent.*

> Disraeli *Sybil* 1845
> *'It began at Staleybridge,' said Devilsdust, 'and they have stopped them all; and now they have marched into Manchester ten thousand strong. They pelted the police –.' 'And cheered the red-coats like blazes,' said Mick.*

> Margery Fisher *The Bright Face of Danger* 1986
> *It's black as pitch and blowing like blazes, and any man moving on deck will be washed from Hull to Hackney before he can cast a rope from a pin.*

with guns blazing
very violently or aggressively: originally with literal meaning but now usually figurative. *20th cent.*

> R G Bayly *Patrol* 1989
> *Mike took the initiative, kicked down the door and went in with guns blazing, so to speak, to find – nothing!*

blaze[2]

blaze a trail/way
to show the way for others to follow: originally by marking trees to show a path (see below), now more common in the figurative contexts of innovation or pioneering action that 'leads the way'. The verb is 18th cent. in its original meaning 'to cut a white mark in (trees) by chipping off bark', and is derived from a noun *blaze* (not connected with the more familiar word and associated with a Germanic root *blas* meaning 'bald'), which originally denoted a white spot on the front of a horse's head. *19th cent.*

> Gene Stratton Porter *Freckles* 1904
> *We have just leased two thousand acres of the Limberlost. Many of these trees are of great value. We can't leave our camp, six miles south, for almost a year yet; so we have blazed a trail and strung barbed wires securely round this lease.*

> *Punch* 1992
> *Blazing a trail for the sex guides now commonplace in every newspaper in the country, Punch devised the prophetic At It magazine.*

bleed

The verb is Old English in its intransitive meaning 'to issue blood' and Middle English in its transitive meaning 'to draw blood from'. This later meaning was used as an image for robbery and extortion from the 17th cent., and an intransitive use in the sense 'to lose or be deprived of all one's money' is recorded from the 17th cent. to the 19th cent.

bleed somebody dry/white
to deprive somebody of all their money or resources, especially over a period of time: white refers to the skin colour produced by a major loss of blood and is often identified, especially in literary contexts, as a sign of great fear or cowardice (Lady Macbeth in Shakespeare's *Macbeth* (1606) says to her husband after the murder of Duncan (ii.ii.62) 'My hands are of your colour, but I shame to wear a heart so white'). *19th cent.*

J Lewis May transl Flaubert's *Madame Bovary* 1856
Declaring that it would put him in the most terrible
straits ... and that he was being bled white, he said
he would give her four notes for two hundred and
fifty francs each.

Norman Mailer *Advertisements for Myself* 1959
Stay off the railroads, they bleed ya dry.

one's heart bleeds

one feels great pity or sympathy. The phrase
dates from Middle English and was originally
used (e.g. in Chaucer and Shakespeare) in a
positive way denoting genuine feeling, but it is
now usually ironic or sarcastic in tone and suggestive of sympathy undeserved.

Chaucer *Troilus and Criseyde* IV.12
And on her whiel she [Fortune] *sette up Diomede;*
| For which my herte right now gynneth blede [=
begins to bleed].

Shakespeare *The Winter's Tale* III.iii.51 (1611)
[Antigonus] *Poor wretch, | That for my mother's*
fault art thus exposed | To loss and what may
follow! Weep I cannot, | But my heart bleeds.

Dr Johnson in Boswell's *Life of Samuel Johnson* 1791
When a butcher tells you that his heart bleeds for his
country, he has, in fact, no uneasy feeling.

bless

See not have a PENNY to bless oneself with.

blessing

a blessing in disguise

some consolation or benefit from an otherwise
unfortunate or unpleasant experience. *18th cent.*

Hannah Foster *The Coquette* 1797
Good, when he gives, supremely good, | Not less
when he denies; | E'en crosses from his sovereign
hand, | Are blessings in disguise.

Virginia Woolf *The Voyage Out* 1915
At one time I think she would have lost her senses if
it hadn't been for her garden. The soil was very
much against her – a blessing in disguise.

count one's blessings

to bear in mind the pleasures or advantages one
enjoys, especially in times of trouble or difficulty.
17th cent.

James Shirley *Changes* 1632
What shall I say let me bath here eternally, and
study new Arithmetick, to count our blessings.

a mixed blessing

an advantage or benefit that has some unpleasant
or unwelcome aspects. *Early 20th cent.*

Saki *Reginald in Russia* 1910
Vanessa began to arrive at the conclusion that a
husband who added a roving disposition to a settled
income was a mixed blessing.

Rosemary McCall *Hearing Loss?* 1992
Repetition in everyday conversation can be a mixed
blessing if one is trying to grasp meaning – if only
people would come to the point!

blind

(as) blind as a bat

having poor eyesight: from the traditional but
erroneous belief that bats cannot see and rely on
their hearing. The phrase in this form is recorded
from the 16th cent. Alternative comparisons
include *blind as a beetle* (15th cent.), *blind as a*
mole (16th cent.), and (most oddly of all) *blind*
as an owl (16th cent.).

Herman Melville *Moby Dick* 1851
The next instant, in a jiff, I was blind as a bat – both
eyes out – all befogged and bedeadened with black
foam – the whale's tail looming straight up out of it,
perpendicular in the air, like a marble steeple.

Robert Richardson *The Lazarus Tree* 1992
'Blind as a bat if she takes them out,' Maltravers
commented. 'I'm not,' Tess contradicted. 'I just
don't like wearing glasses.'

a blind alley

a course of action that is unlikely to produce any
results: a blind alley is closed at one end, preventing through access. The metaphor is often
extended with verbs of motion such as *lead* or *go*
(up). *19th cent.*

a blind bit of —

the least —, no — at all. The words most commonly used in this way are *difference* and *notice*.
Mid 20th cent.

Alison Leonard *Gate-crashing the Dream Party* 1990
Vern wandered slowly in front taking not a blind bit
of notice of me, not even when I shouted at the long-
beaked birds and made them flap up into the air
crying like out-of-tune seagulls.

a blind date

a romantic assignation between people who have not met before, or either of the participants. *Early 20th cent.*

blind drunk

completely drunk, so drunk that one cannot see one's way. There is a possible use of the phrase in George Farquhar's comedy *Love and a Bottle*, first performed at Drury Lane in 1698, in which one character declares of another who has commented on his dress that 'This fellow's blind, drunk. I wear a cravat'. The meaning here seems to be 'blind and drunk' rather than 'blind drunk', but it is so close to our phrase as to suggest its evolution. *18th cent.*

John O'Keeffe *Tantara-Rara* 1798
[Toddy] *One bottle wou'd give you such a clear view of this affair, and two bottles wou'd make you see double.* [Sir Ulick] *See double! – Justice shou'd be blind.* [Toddy] *She shou'd be blind drunk.*

the blind leading the blind

a situation in which those who are ignorant or inexperienced are guided by others who are equally or only slightly less so. The allusion is to Matthew 15:14 'Let them alone: they be blind leaders of the blind. And if the blind lead the blind, both shall fall into the ditch.' In this proverbial form the phrase goes back in English to King Alfred (9th cent.), and it is listed in proverb collections of the 16th cent.

Wilkie Collins *The Moonstone* 1868
Mr. Franklin, keeping the ball up on his side, said he had often heard of the blind leading the blind, and now, for the first time, he knew what it meant.

a blind spot

a subject or topic about which one has no knowledge or interest. The expression is based on various technical applications, in particular (1) a spot on the retina of the eye that is insensible to light, and (2) in cricket, a point in front of the batsman on which a falling ball leaves the batsman undecided how to strike it. *19th cent.*

Harper Lee *To Kill a Mockingbird* 1960
Mr. Cunningham's basically a good man ... he just has his blind spots along with the rest of us.

blind somebody with science

to confuse or fool somebody by using technical language they are unlikely to understand. *Mid 20th cent.*

go it blind

informal to act impulsively or recklessly. *19th cent.*

rob/steal somebody blind

informal to rob or cheat somebody ruthlessly. *Late 20th cent.*

Guardian 1986
From the public there is no co-operation at all, not until a maid steals her employer blind or runs off with her husband.

turn a blind eye

to overlook a wrong or transgression or pretend not to notice it: associated with the action of Lord Nelson at the Battle of Copenhagen in 1801, when he put a telescope to his blind eye in order to avoid seeing a signal commanding him to discontinue the action; *turn a Nelson eye* is also recorded. The phrase appears earlier in the form *have a blind eye*. *19th cent.*

Thackeray *The Memoirs of Barry Lyndon* 1856
I always shall consider Phil Purcell as the very best tutor I could have had. His fault was drink, but for that I have always had a blind eye; and he hated my cousin Mick like poison, but I could excuse him that too.

F Mort *Dangerous Sexualities* 1987
Until then, police practice involved turning a blind eye to minor breaches of public decency rather than embarking on lengthy prosecutions.

See also SWEAR blind.

blinder

play a blinder

informal to perform outstandingly well. Used originally in sports, in the sense 'to play an outstandingly good game'. *Mid 20th cent.*

blinding

See effing and blinding *at* EFF.

blink

on the blink

informal (said of a machine) not working properly, faulty. *Blink* here means 'a glimmer or spark', and the physical meaning of *on the blink* is 'about to be extinguished' with reference to a light or spark. *Early 20th cent.*

See also in the blink of an EYE.

blinkers

put blinkers on somebody/something

to suppress a feeling or emotion; to make somebody blind to reality: also in other forms, e.g. *look at life through blinkers*. *Blinkers* on a horse restrict the line of vision to directly ahead, to prevent it from being distracted. *19th cent.*

> George Eliot *Adam Bede* 1859
> *But he's got no notion about buildings: you can so seldom get hold of a man as can turn his brains to more nor one thing; it's just as if they wore blinkers like th' horses, and could see nothing o' one side of 'em.*

> Ian Rankin *Let It Bleed* 1995
> *They probably would go all the way, too, driven by fear and adrenaline. The combination tended to put blinkers on your survival mechanism.*

block

do/lose one's block

Australian, informal to lose one's temper: from the meaning of *block* 'head'. *Early 20th cent.*

> C Drew *Doings of Dave* 1919
> *Did you lose your block last night or what?*

a new kid on the block

a newcomer to a place or group. A block is a group of buildings between streets in an American city. *Late 20th cent.*

> *Guardian* 1987
> *We have the blonde bombshell, in short skirts, high heels, sheer stockings and plunging neckline …*
> *Though she may look like the new kid on the block, we recognise her well. She is Monroe and Madonna; Crepe Suzette and Patsy Kensit; Diana Dors and Susie Kidd; Mandy Rice-Davies and Mandy Smith.*

> Melvyn Bragg *Crystal Rooms* 1993
> *She became a fixture on the small screen, one of a top set of telly celebrities with some columnists talking about her executive future, others predicting a Hollywood career, others just pawing the new kid on the block.*

on the block

to be sold at an auction. *Block* here refers to the stand where formerly slaves stood when being auctioned. *19th cent.*

> David Ross Locke *Divers Views, Opinions, and Prophecies* 1866
> *Her children are free – they are mine, likewise, but I can't sell em on the block, to the highest bidder.*

> *Daily Telegraph* 1992
> *On Wednesday in Paris, the original first manuscript for Ravel's Bolero – probably the most played classical music in the world – goes on the block at Drouot.*

put the blocks on somebody/something

to prevent somebody or something from proceeding: from the use of blocks lodged in front of vehicles' wheels to prevent them from moving. *Late 20th cent.*

> *Liverpool Daily Post* 1990
> *Nigel Roberts … is one of six full Welsh internationals looking to put the blocks on Flintshire's bid for a repeat appearance in the final.*

put/lay one's head on the block

to risk one's life or reputation by a particular course of action: from the process of execution by beheading, in which the condemned person placed their neck over a block. The phrase is 17th cent. in literal senses.

> Thomas Paine *The American Crisis* 1780
> *You stand but on a very tottering foundation. A change of the ministry in England may probably bring your measures into question, and your head to the block.*

> Ray Harrison *Patently Murder* 1991
> *It is not in your nature to put your head on the block; so much I do know.*

See also a CHIP off the old block; KNOCK somebody's block off.

blood

Allusions to blood as a metaphor for feeling and passion are recorded from the 14th cent. and are a common image in the time of Shakespeare (e.g. *King Lear* (1606) IV.ii.63 'Were't my fitness [= proper for me] | To let these hands obey my blood, | They are apt enough to dislocate and tear | Thy flesh and bones'). Most of the phrases based on physical reactions in the blood (*boiling, curdling*, etc) are recorded earlier in intransitive senses with the blood as subject (*the blood boils, curdles*, etc) and later in the now common causative forms beginning with *make*. The phrases based on supposed changes in the blood's temperature (e.g. *in cold blood, make somebody's blood boil*) arise from the medieval belief that the feelings of warmth or chill felt in the face in response to certain emotions were due to a physical change in the blood itself.

after somebody's blood
seeking to punish or take revenge on somebody. As the first quotation shows, the phrase was based originally on the notion of thirsting after a person's blood. *18th cent.*

Charles Leftley *Clavidgo* 1798
Oh! the most savage, horrible thirst after his blood fills me entirely.

Len Deighton *Billion Dollar Brain* 1966
Who gets him out of trouble when the New York office is after his blood?

bad blood
hostility or ill feeling: earlier in the form *ill blood*. The phrase is based on the notion of *breeding bad blood*, which is found in the 17th cent.

John Reynolds *The Triumphs of Gods Revenge* 1635
He will hardly leave her either the will or power to thanke him for his courtesie, and so remounts his horse, and presently gallops home to his Mother, whom he acquaints therewith, but yet conceales it from his Father, whereat she seemes not to be a little joyfull, and yet heartily prayeth to God, that this breed no bad blood in her husband, or prove either an incitation to his choller against her selfe, or a propension of revenge against their Sonne.

Mark Twain *A Tramp Abroad* 1880
I was entitled to these remains, and could have enforced my right; but rather than have bad blood about the matter, I said we would toss up for them.

blood and guts
violent fighting and bloodshed, especially in fictional contexts. Used in the title of a novel, *Blood and Guts in High School*, by American writer Kathy Acker. *Late 20th cent.*

The Times 1985
I'm a blood and guts man myself. I want to go out and smash them. That's my job.

blood and iron
the use of military force as distinct from diplomacy or negotiation: translating German *Blut und Eisen*, a phrase used by the Prussian statesman Otto von Bismarck (1815–98) in a speech in 1886

advocating a militaristic policy and identifying himself as a 'man of blood and iron'. *19th cent.*

G B Shaw *Caesar and Cleopatra* 1901
On the field of Pharsalia the impossible came to pass; the blood and iron ye pin your faith on fell before the spirit of man.

blood and thunder
violent behaviour or activity, especially in fictional contexts. The phrase was sometimes used to describe the sensation novels of the 19th cent. It was also used as an imprecation (e.g. by Byron in *Don Juan* (1824) 'Oh blood and thunder! and oh blood and wounds! These are but vulgar oaths'). *19th cent.*

Nathaniel Hawthorne *Great Stone Face* 1850
Whatever he may be called in history, he was known in camps and on the battle-field under the nickname of Old Blood-and-Thunder.

blood is thicker than water
(proverb) family bonds are stronger than the ties of ordinary friendship. The sentiment occurs in earlier forms; in the current form it is recorded from the 19th cent. and appears in the 1813 edition of John Ray's *English Proverbs*.

Henry James *The American* 1877
He is our seventh cousin, you know, and blood is thicker than water.

—'s blood is up
the person specified is ready for a fight or challenge. *19th cent.*

Byron *Don Juan* 1824
His blood was up: though young, he was a Tartar.

blood on the carpet
a hyperbolic expression for the aftermath of a strong disagreement or reprimand. *Late 20th cent.*

The Times 1985
This year's public expenditure round has been characterized by remarkably few stories of blood on the Chief Secretary's carpet, suggesting either that things have gone reasonably smoothly, or that John MacGregor, who took on the job in September's Cabinet reshuffle, has bludgeoned his victims into silence.

blood, sweat, and tears
hard work or effort needed to achieve something: with allusion to a speech of Winston Churchill's in the House of Commons in May 1940, in which

he warned 'I have nothing to offer but blood, toil, tears, and sweat'. *Mid 20th cent.*

first blood

the first point or advantage gained by one side in a contest: from the literal first drawing of blood in a duel with swords or a boxing match. *19th cent.*

> Scott *Waverley* 1814
> *'Forward, sons of Ivor,' cried their Chief, 'or the Camerons will draw the first blood!'*

freeze somebody's blood

to fill somebody with fear or terror: *cf* make somebody's blood run cold *below. 17th cent.*

> Shakespeare *Hamlet* i.v.16 (1601)
> [Ghost] *I could a tale unfold whose lightest word | Would harrow up thy soul, freeze thy young blood, | Make thy two eyes like stars start from their spheres.*

have blood on one's hands

to be responsible for somebody's death or injury. *19th cent.*

> Oscar Wilde *The Picture of Dorian Gray* 1891
> *He is not the man I am looking for … The man whose life I want must be nearly forty now. This one is little more than a boy. Thank God, I have not got his blood upon my hands.*

in one's blood

part of one's character, innate. *18th cent.*

> Laurence Sterne *A Sentimental Journey* 1768
> *The Bourbon is by no means a cruel race: they may be misled like other people; but there is a mildness in their blood.*

in cold blood

1 in a calm or unagitated state of mind. *16th cent.*

> Shakespeare *Timon of Athens* iii.vi.53 (1609)
> [Alcibiades] *Who cannot condemn rashness in cold blood?*

> Conan Doyle *The Beryl Coronet* 1892
> *Yet when I think of him in cold blood, far away from the glamour of his presence, I am convinced from his cynical speech and the look which I have caught in his eyes that he is one who should be deeply distrusted.*

2 (with reference to violent acts, especially killing) in a calculated or premeditated way: from the ancient notion that blood normally heats with emotion, so that cold blood was a sign of detached calculation (see introduction above). First found in this meaning in a use by Addison

in the *Spectator* in 1711, where he refers to 'killing in cold blood'. *18th cent.*

> Swift *Gulliver's Travels* 1726
> *A soldier is a Yahoo hired to kill in cold blood as many of his own species, who have never offended him, as possibly he can.*

like getting blood out of / from a stone / NAmer turnip

extremely difficult to achieve. The phrase is originally proverbial, dating back in various forms to the 15th cent. and current more recently in the form *you cannot get blood from a stone. 19th cent.*

> Dickens *David Copperfield* 1850
> *'If Mr. Micawber's creditors will not give him time,' said Mrs. Micawber, 'they must take the consequences; and the sooner they bring it to an issue the better. Blood cannot be obtained from a stone, neither can anything on account be obtained at present … from Mr. Micawber.'*

> Somerset Maugham *The Moon and Sixpence* 1919
> *'At all events, you can be forced to support your wife and children … I suppose the law has some protection to offer them.' 'Can the law get blood out of a stone? I haven't any money.'*

make somebody's blood boil

to make somebody very angry: based on the notion of the blood boiling as a sign of strong emotion. *17th cent.*

> John Dunton *A Voyage Round the World* 1691
> *I could hold no longer to hear 'em talk at that lewd rate, my blood boyl'd, my heart trembled, and I hardly had the courage or patience to answer 'em.*

> Byron *Don Juan* 1824
> *It makes my blood boil like the springs of Hecla, to see men let these scoundrel sovereigns break law.*

> Smollett *The Expedition of Humphry Clinker* 1771
> *I call Wilson a rascal, because, if he had been really a gentleman, with honourable intentions, he would have, ere now, appeared in his own character – I must own, my blood boils with indignation when I think of that fellow's presumption.*

make somebody's blood curdle

to revolt or horrify somebody. *18th cent.*

> William Combe *The Justification* 1778
> *Guilt lights the flaming Judgments on the wall | That struck the Assyrian pale, and will appal | The heart that other terrors would disdain, | And make the warm blood curdle in the vein.*

make somebody's blood run cold

to fill somebody with fear or apprehension: *cf* freeze somebody's blood *above*. *18th cent.*

> Henry Fielding *The History of Tom Jones* 1749
> *I protest you have made my blood run cold with the very mentioning the top of that mountain.*

new/fresh blood

1 fresh life or rejuvenating input. *16th cent.*

> Shakespeare *Sonnet xi* c1600
> *And that fresh blood which youngly thou bestow'st | Thou mayst call thine when thou from youth convertest.*

> Dickens *David Copperfield* 1850
> *Some attempts had been made, I noticed, to infuse new blood into this dwindling frame, by repairing the costly old woodwork here and there with common deal.*

2 new members of a group, regarded as bringing it fresh life or strength: from the practice of introducing a new strain in stock breeding. *19th cent.*

> Margaret Fuller *Papers on Literature and Art* 1846
> *What suits Great Britain, with her insular position and consequent need to concentrate and intensify her life, her limited monarchy, and spirit of trade, does not suit a mixed race, continually enriched with new blood from other stocks the most unlike that of our first descent.*

taste blood

to have an early and encouraging success, especially in getting the better of an opponent or competitor: from the notion of animals of prey being stimulated by tasting the blood of their victims. *19th cent.*

> John Neal *Seventy-six* 1823
> *I have no desire to wear a beautiful jacket, or ride a handsome horse – would as soon taste blood in the ranks.*

See also SPIT blood; SWEAT blood.

bloody

bloody/bloodied but unbowed

proud or resolute despite suffering losses or difficulties. *19th cent.*

> W E Henley *Book of Verses* 1888
> *In the fell clutch of circumstance | I have not winced nor cried aloud. | Under the bludgeonings of chance | My head is bloody, but unbowed.*

bloom

the bloom is off the rose

the initial enjoyment or excitement of a situation or experience has gone: also in extended contexts. *Bloom* dates from Middle English in the meaning 'blossom or flower of a plant'; figurative meanings to do with the state of beauty or loveliness are common from the 16th cent. The physical meaning 'fresh glow of the complexion', also used figuratively, is 18th cent.; the phrase is 19th cent.

> Dickens *Hard Times* 1854
> *He had worked his stony way into … Schedule B, and had taken the bloom off the higher branches of mathematics and physical science, French, German, Latin, and Greek.*

blot

blot one's copybook

to make a mistake that spoils one's reputation. A copybook was an exercise book with samples of scripts, in which children practised their writing: an early use of the term is by Shakespeare in *Love's Labour's Lost* (1594) v.ii.42 'Fair as a text B in a copy-book'. The phrase does not occur in allusive uses before the mid 20th cent.

> Dorothy L Sayers *Gaudy Night* 1935
> *Now, it was the College that had blotted its copybook and had called her in as one calls in a specialist.*

> Joan Beech *One WAAF's War* 1989
> *I think at the time the RAF had more volunteers than it could cope with and much weeding out was done, but in his case he blotted his copybook good and proper by doing a bit of unauthorised low flying over a south Devonshire town, frightening all the old ladies.*

a blot on the escutcheon

something that damages a reputation. An escutcheon was the representation of a family's coat of arms, and hence a symbol of its history and reputation. *17th cent.*

> Dryden transl Virgil's *Aeneid* c1690
> *I confess the banishment of Ovid was a blot in his escutcheon.*

> Dickens *A Tale of Two Cities* 1859
> *It was impossible for Monseigneur to dispense with one of these [four] attendants on the chocolate and hold his high place under the admiring Heavens.*

Deep would have been the blot upon his escutcheon if his chocolate had been ignobly waited on by only three men.

Simon Winchester *The Pacific* 1992

Beside the glitter of all the Pacific wealth there are still pockets – becoming ever smaller, the governments and their statisticians insist – where the unhappiness and squalor of the inhabitants remain an insult, a disfiguring blot on the Ocean's otherwise gleaming escutcheon.

a blot on the landscape

an ugly feature that spoils the appearance of a place: also in figurative contexts of anything unsightly or unappealing that spoils an otherwise pleasant scene. The title of Tom Sharpe's novel *Blott on the Landscape* (1975), which satirized the building of motorways as a mark of social progress and featured a character called 'Blott', was a play on the phrase. *19th cent.*

H G Wells *The Time Machine* 1895

And like blots upon the landscape rose the cupolas above the ways to the Under-world.

P G Wodehouse *Jeeves in the Offing* 1960

'And a rousing toodle-oo to you, you young blot on the landscape,' she replied cordially.

blouse

big/great girl's blouse

British, *informal* a silly, over-sensitive, or ineffectual man. The phrase appears to have been invented by the scriptwriters of a television sitcom called *Nearest and Dearest*, broadcast in the 1960s and set in the north of England. The following exchange occurred in an episode of 1969: '[Eli] Go round talking like that, you'll be hearing from our solicitor. [Nellie] He is our solicitor, you big girl's blouse.' The phrase doesn't bear deep analysis and is probably more intuitive than rational. *Mid 20th cent.*

Outdoor Action 1992

I was, I explained, a bit of a big girl's blouse when it came to crumbling ledges, sheer drops, being underwater for unreasonable lengths of time and squeezing into jam jar sized spaces.

blow

be blowed if —

informal an expression of strong conviction about what follows: this form of the past participle is confined to curses and imprecations, which date in various forms from the 18th cent. The underlying meaning is 'to swell or puff up'. There is 18th cent. evidence for the form *blow me up if —*; the current form is 19th cent.

Dickens *Pickwick Papers* 1837

The principal ran to assist Mr. Winkle in mounting. 'T'other side, sir, if you please.' 'Blowed if the gen'lm'n worn't a gettin' up on the wrong side,' whispered a grinning post-boy.

be blown off course

to be forced to change one's plans: a metaphor from sailing. *Late 20th cent.*

Kenneth O Morgan *The People's Peace* 1990

The Wilson years of 1964–70 saw the trauma of the monetary crisis of 1966 and the devaluation of 1967, with the nation 'blown off course' in a mood of some panic.

blow somebody away

1 *informal* to kill or destroy somebody. *Late 20th cent.*

Bernard Cornwell *Crackdown* 1990

If the spics don't blow you away then the Americans will.

2 *informal* to make a strong impression on somebody. *Late 20th cent.*

a blow-by-blow account

a detailed account or description of events as they happened: originally in North American use with reference to boxing commentaries. *Mid 20th cent.*

Jessica Steele *His Woman* 1991

'I've been given the sack,' Leith told her shakily, and, over coffee, gave her a blow-by-blow account.

blow a fuse/gasket

informal to lose one's temper: a metaphor from electrical and mechanical engineering. *Early 20th cent.*

Laura Martin *Garden of Desire* 1993

He raised his eyebrows and gave her a cool stare. 'It was only a suggestion, Robyn; there's no need to blow a fuse.'

blow high, blow low

whatever happens, come what may. The image is of the wind at sea. *19th cent.*

James Fenimore Cooper *The Pioneers* 1823
It's a peeler [= violent storm] without, I can tell you, good woman; but what cares I? blow high or blow low, d'ye see, it's all the same thing to Ben.

blow hot and cold

to vacillate in one's enthusiasm or support for something. The allusion is to a fable of Aesop about a traveller and a satyr who afforded him hospitality: when the traveller blew on his cold hands to warm them and then blew on his hot food to cool it the satyr threw him out because he blew hot and cold with the same breath. *16th cent.*

Erasmus transl Chaloner's *Praise of Folly* 1549
Out of one mouth to blow both hote and colde.

Hardy *Tess of the D'Urbervilles* 1891
I cannot think why you are so tantalizing ... You seem almost like a coquette, upon my life you do ... They blow hot and blow cold, just as you do.

blow somebody's mind

informal to have a strong emotional effect on somebody: originally associated with the effects of hallucinogenic drugs. *Late 20th cent.*

E Nash *Strawberries and Wine* 1993
I mean, when you think about it properly, Johnny, doesn't it just blow your mind?

blow something out of the water

to expose an idea or enterprise as worthless or ill-considered. The image is of firing on a vessel at sea so that it explodes 'out of the water'. The literal and figurative uses both date from the 18th cent.

Frederick Pilon *The Fair American* 1785
[Angelica] Oh, that odious Colonel! it is he who has caus'd all our confusion: I am told that he has declared, he will not leave the house without a wife. [Dreadnought] Say you so? I'll try him. – I'll send him a challenge, and make him eat his words; or he shall blow old Cable out of the water.

blow something sky-high

to destroy something completely: originally in literal senses and later with reference to ideas, proposals, etc. *19th cent.*

Harriet Beecher Stowe *Uncle Tom's Cabin* 1852
Yet our laws positively and utterly forbid any efficient general educational system, and they do it wisely, too; for, just begin and thoroughly educate one generation, and the whole thing would be blown sky high.

blow one's top

to lose one's temper or composure: probably with allusion to the action of oil bursting from a well. *Early 20th cent.*

Machine Knitting Monthly 1992
What with the heat, the fiddly bit and then him, I was ready to blow my top.

blow up in somebody's face

(said especially of somebody's own plan or activity) to go disastrously wrong and affect somebody badly: the image is of a bomb exploding. *Late 20th cent.*

P Chester *Murder Forestalled* 1990
If I'd been arriving at a lot of conclusions that were wrong, then I could be wrong about this too. Not only could be, but would be, and the whole thing would blow up in my face. Worse, maybe Laura's face.

blow with the wind

to act as the circumstances of the time dictate rather than according to any design or principle. References to the wind as a symbolic force driving people along date from Middle English. *17th cent.*

Richard Bentley *Dissertation upon the Epistles of Phalaris* 1699
Persons of a light and desultory temper, that skip about, and are blown with every wind, as grasshoppers are.

See also blow away the cobwebs at COBWEB; blow the GAFF; blow great guns at GUN; blow a HOLE in something; blow the LID off; blow one's own HORN; blow one's own TRUMPET; blow the WHISTLE; give/blow somebody a RASPBERRY; knock/blow somebody's socks off at SOCK[1]; let/blow off STEAM; see how/which way the WIND blows.

blue

a blue-eyed boy

a favourite of somebody in authority. Blue eyes symbolize the appeal and innocence of young children. *Early 20th cent.*

P G Wodehouse *Bill the Conqueror* 1924
If ever there was a blue-eyed boy, you will be it.

James Kirkup *A Poet Could Not But Be Gay* 1991
*I sensed that they approved of him whole-heartedly,
and that by comparison I was no longer the blue-
eyed boy of the family: I did not come up to scratch.*

blue-sky/blue-skies research/thinking

research that does not have any immediate application: from the notion of a blue sky as a place
free from disturbances or difficulties. *Late 20th
cent.*

The Times 1985
*Roberts thinks such plants are possible, but not in
the near future. 'But because new plants can now be
"patented", the big chemical companies are showing an interest. And they can afford some long-term
"blue sky" research,' he says.*

Independent on Sunday 2002
*Lord Birt, former BBC director general, had been
commissioned by Tony Blair to report on transport's long-term future – 'blue skies' thinking.*

do something until one is blue in the face

to persist without having any effect. The image is
of the face turning blue from extreme but fruitless
physical effort. *19th cent.*

Trollope The Small House at Allington 1864
*Then never mention her name to me again. And as
to talking to her, you may talk to her till you're both
blue in the face, if you please.*

Conan Doyle The Poison Belt 1913
*'E can sack me till 'e's blue in the face, but I ain't
going, and that's flat.*

once in a blue moon

very rarely, or (originally) never. To say that the
moon is blue was symbolic of the unlikely, as in
the 16th cent. proverb *If they say the moon is blue,
we must believe that it is true.* The moon looks blue
when it is the second full moon in a month, a
phenomenon that in fact occurs occasionally.
Because of this, the meaning of the phrase has
shifted slightly from 'never' to 'very rarely'. *Once
in a moon* occurs from the 17th cent.; in its current
form the phrase dates from the 19th cent.

Harold Frederic The Damnation of Theron Ware
1896
*When we do have company – that is to say, once in a
blue moon – we display no manners to speak of.*

out of the blue

unexpectedly, without any warning. *The blue*
here is the sky, representing a kind of infinity
(and early uses are often semi-literal). *19th cent.*

R H Dana Two Years Before the Mast 1840
*The stars, too, came out of the blue, one after
another, night after night, unobscured.*

take a blue pencil to something

to correct or censor a piece of writing. A blue
pencil was traditionally used by official censors
in scoring out or changing what others had written. To *blue-pencil* something is to censor it. *19th
cent.*

Kipling Many Inventions 1893
*The blue pencil plunged remorselessly through the
slips.*

Austin Dobson The Last Proof 1913
*Finis at last – the end, the End, the End! | No more
of paragraphs to prune or mend; | No more blue
pencil, with its ruthless line, | To blot the phrase
'particularly fine'.*

talk a blue streak

NAmer, informal to talk at great length. A *blue
streak* is a flash of lightning, fast and bright. *Late
20th cent.*

Donald Goddard et al Trail of the Octopus 1993
*He had a wicked tongue when roused and could talk
a blue streak.*

true blue

genuine: from blue as the colour of constancy and
dependability. The phrase is recorded first in the
17th cent. proverb *true blue will never stain*, based
on the difficulty of obtaining a true blue dye. Blue
was also the colour of the Scottish Presbyterian
Party (as opposed to the royal red), but in more
recent times it has been associated with the British Conservative Party, a *true blue Tory* being a
firm Conservative supporter. *17th cent.*

Scott Redgauntlet 1824
*They are a sturdy set of true-blue Presbyterians,
these burghers of Dumfries; men after your father's
own heart.*

Mark Twain The Adventures of Tom Sawyer 1876
*No, Tom's true-blue, Huck, and he'll come back. He
won't desert.*

the wide/wild blue yonder

the far distance: often used figuratively. After the
title and words of a song by Robert Crawford

(from 'Army Air Corps', 1939): 'Off we go into the wild blue yonder, | Climbing high into the sun.' *Mid 20th cent.*

> Ursula Markham *Hypnosis Regression Therapy* 1991
> *I ... cannot believe that we human beings are simply pawns in some giant chess game being played in the wide blue yonder.*

See also between the DEVIL and the deep blue sea; a bolt from / out of the blue *at* BOLT[1]; in a blue FUNK; out of a CLEAR (blue) sky; scream/yell/cry blue MURDER.

bluff

call somebody's bluff

to challenge somebody to substantiate a suspect or dubious claim or intention, expecting it to be false: from the practice in poker of calling an opponent to show their hand in the expectation that it is not as good as their betting suggests. The noun *bluff* is 18th cent. in its original meaning 'a blinker for a horse'. The verb and noun meanings in relation to poker (which was also itself called *bluff*) are mid 19th cent. The phrase dates from the 19th cent.

blush

Middle English in the meaning 'a look or glance'. The sense 'reddening of the face from shame or embarrassment' is late 16th cent. (Shakespeare *Henry V* (1599) v.ii.232 'Put off your maiden blushes, avouch the thoughts of your heart with the looks of an empress').

at (the) first blush

at the first glance or impression. *16th cent.*

> Stephen Gosson *The Ephemerides of Phialo* 1579
> *I called too minde the replie that Apelles made to a course painter, which brought him a counterfait of his own drawing, requesting his iudgment in the work; Truely, quoth Apelles, hadst thou not tolde me it had bin thine, at the first blush I would haue iudged it to bee doone in haste.*

> Locke *An Essay Concerning Human Understanding* 1690
> *First, all purely identical propositions. These obviously and at first blush appear to contain no instruction in them.*

spare somebody's blushes

to refrain from naming somebody in the context of praise or criticism so as not to embarrass them. *18th cent.*

> Henry Fielding *The History of Tom Jones* 1749
> *As to my concern for what is past, I know you will spare my blushes the repetition.*

> Dickens *Pickwick Papers* 1837
> *I saw her; I loved her; I proposed; she refused me. – 'You love another?' – 'Spare my blushes.'*

board

Old English in the meaning 'a flat piece of cut wood'. Many of the phrases derive from the meaning 'table', which is now obsolete except in special contexts.

above board

legitimate and honest. According to Dr Johnson, the phrase was taken from the gambling tables, where card players cheated by switching cards under the table or 'board' and only hands seen above the table could be trusted. *17th cent.*

> Head & Kirkman *The English Rogue Described* 1668
> *My Master having now had some experience in this way of printing, was resolved to play above board, and get some copy or copies to print, that he might own; which in short time he did, and glad was he to see his name in print, supposing himself now to be some body.*

> George Eliot *Middlemarch* 1872
> *Cheshire was all right – all fair and above board. But there's St. John Long – that's the kind of fellow we call a charlatan, advertising cures in ways nobody knows anything about.*

> *She* 1989
> *A lover is illicit – the whole point of being married, it seems to me, is that everything is above board and clean.*

across the board

applying to everything or everybody. In horse-racing, a bet was displayed 'across the board' when it was put on a horse to win or be placed. Also as a modifier *across-the-board. Mid 20th cent.*

> *New Statesman* 1992
> *In a move more likely to divide the party than unite it, he hinted that the traditional socialist commitment to across-the-board state benefits might be ditched.*

go by the board

to be discarded or abandoned: from the nautical expression *by the board* meaning 'overboard', usually with reference to a fallen mast. *19th cent.*

Dickens *David Copperfield* 1850
How many cups of tea I drank, because Dora made it, I don't know. But, I perfectly remember that I sat swilling tea until my whole nervous system, if I had had any in those days, must have gone by the board.

on board

taking part as one of a group or team: from the (19th cent.) literal meaning 'on a ship, aircraft, or other vehicle'. *Late 20th cent.*

Liverpool Echo 1993
While this would have brought the Tory rebels back on board, it would have left a big question mark over whether Mr Major could continue.

sweep the board

to win all the honours: originally to win everything at cards. *17th cent.*

Pope *The Rape of the Lock* 1711
Spadillio first ... Led off two captive trumps, and swept the board.

take something on board

to give full consideration to a new situation or idea, like loading cargo on a ship. *Late 20th cent.*

Guardian 1984
But rigid sails are no longer outsiders. They form the cutting edge of a new hybrid technology that is serious, important and potentially highly profitable, for it will transform the appearance and the economics of large ships. Anyone who doubts this needs to take on board the disconcerting fact that Japan has just launched a 31,000 ton rigid sail-assisted ship for the Yokohama-Vancouver route, the seventh sail-assisted cargo ship she has brought into service.

boat

be in the same boat

to be involved in or affected by the same circumstances, especially when difficult or dangerous; to share a predicament. *19th cent.*

Dickens *Bleak House* 1853
I also want Ada to know, that if I see her seldom just now, I am looking after her interests as well as my own – we two being in the same boat exactly.

Somerset Maugham *Of Human Bondage* 1915
I'm awfully sorry, old man, but we're all in the same boat. No one thought the war was going to hang on this way.

miss the boat

informal, originally naval slang to act too slowly and so fail to take an opportunity. *Early 20th cent.*

off the boat

newly arrived from another country, used especially with overtones of condescension. *Late 20th cent.*

Len Deighton *Billion Dollar Brain* 1966
The fittings and furnishings inside the old house were old. In America that either means you made it, or you just got off the boat.

push the boat out

British, informal to spend money or celebrate lavishly: probably from the notion of celebrating before setting sail in a ship. *Early 20th cent.*

Barbara Pym *Quartet in Autumn* 1977
'Pushing the boat out, aren't you?' said Norman, with unusual jollity, as Ken topped up his glass.

rock the boat

to speak or act in a way that disturbs a situation or disconcerts other people involved: with allusion to the perilous effect of undue movement by the occupants of a small boat in the water. The phrase may have been given a boost by Frank Loesser's song 'Sit down, you're rocking the boat' from the 1950 musical *Guy and Dolls*. *Mid 20th cent.*

take to the boats

to abandon a failing undertaking abruptly: with allusion to passengers' recourse to the lifeboats in an emergency at sea. *20th cent.*

See also BURN one's boats.

Bob

Bob's your uncle

used to show that something has been or might be easily and quickly achieved. *Bob* is a pet form of the name *Robert*. Whether a particular person of the name lies behind the phrase remains uncertain. Folk etymology has suggested an association with the political nepotism allegedly practised by Lord Salisbury when Prime Minister towards the end of the 19th cent. His family name was Robert Cecil, and he appointed his nephew Arthur Balfour to several jobs for which he was not suited, including chief secretary of Ireland in 1887. Having 'Bob' as your uncle was therefore seen as an advantage. But, as we know, Balfour did well for himself and became Prime Minister himself in due course, which rather robs the story of its point; and our phrase is not recorded until well into the 20th cent., long after the events that are supposed to account for it. (Eric Partridge, in *A Dictionary of Catch Phrases* (1977), identified it as 'since c.1890', but gave no verifiable evidence for this date, and none has come to light since.) Much more compelling is an alternative origin, that *Bob* is not a name at all but a personification (or not even that, since the word requires a capital initial letter to match its typical position at the start of its sentence) of the word *bob* meaning 'satisfactory, in order' (as in *all is bob*). *Mid 20th cent.*

> Ruth Rendell *The Best Man to Die* 1981
> So he hung about in a lonely spot one night, just where the other fellow was due to pass by – and well, Bob's your uncle, as you so succinctly put it.

bodkin

ride/sit bodkin

to travel wedged between two people when there is no proper space for a third person. In Middle English, *bodkin* denoted a small pointed dagger, and the word was later applied to various kinds of needles and large pins. Its figurative meaning 'a person wedged between others' is based on the thinness characteristic of the tools that had the name. *19th cent.*

> Thackeray *Vanity Fair* 1848
> Why pay an extra place? He's too big to travel bodkin between you and me. Let him stay here in the nursery.

body

body and soul

affecting one completely. The pairing of body and soul to represent the physical and spiritual aspects of human existence goes back to Chaucer and becomes more abstracted in later use. *Middle English*

> Marlowe *Dr Faustus* v.106 (1590)
> I, John Faustus of Wittenberg, Doctor, by these presents do give both body and soul to Lucifer, Prince of the East, and his minister Mephistopheles, and furthermore grant unto them … full power to fetch or carry the said John Faustus, body and soul, flesh, blood, or goods, into their habitation wheresoever.

> Kenneth Grahame *The Wind in the Willows* 1903
> As the familiar sound broke forth, the old passion seized on Toad and completely mastered him, body and soul.

keep body and soul together

to manage to stay alive: the form *keep life and soul together* is attested from the late 17th cent. *19th cent.*

> James Fenimore Cooper *Deerslayer* 1841
> You can fish, and knock down the deer, to keep body and soul together.

over my dead body

with my strong disapproval; totally without my consent. Literally, 'only after killing me'. The notion of a person's dead body – i.e. their death – symbolizing total resistance occurs in 19th cent. literature before the phrase in its present form: for example, in Scott's novel *The Black Dwarf* of 1816 ('If you leave Ellieslaw Castle to-night, it shall be by passing over my dead body') and in the following from Harriet Beecher Stowe's *Uncle Tom's Cabin* of 1852: 'I'll give my last drop of blood, but they shall not take you from me. Whoever gets you must walk over my dead body.' *19th cent.*

> Daniel P Thompson *The Green Mountain Boys* 1839
> Here I will remain, and if the enemy enter here, it shall be over my dead body. Nay, not a word, Captain Selden, I will not be denied.

boggle

the mind boggles

an expression of mock bewilderment or ironic speculation about something surprising: the adjectival form *mind-boggling* is recorded from the 1960s. *Boggle* is a 16th cent. word meaning 'to start with fright', used originally with reference to horses. There is a figurative use in Shakespeare's *All's Well That Ends Well* (1603) v.iii.232, where the King of France says to Bertram regarding the ownership of the ring: 'You boggle shrewdly; every feather starts you.' *Mid 20th cent.*

boil

go off the boil
(said of an undertaking or initiative) to become less interesting or exciting. *20th cent.*

> **The East Anglian 1993**
> *Retail sales volumes are also expected to have come off the boil last month after rising strongly over the past quarter.*

it all boils down to —
the essential nature or consequence of something is as specified: from the image of a liquid being reduced or condensed by boiling and evaporation. *19th cent.*

> **Saturday Review 1880**
> *It is surprising to see how much research Mr. S. has sometimes contrived to boil down into a single line.*

> **Harper Lee To Kill a Mockingbird 1960**
> *The only thing we've got is a black man's word against the Ewells'. The evidence boils down to you-did-I-didn't.*

keep the pot boiling
to maintain an activity: used originally in the context of maintaining the means of daily sustenance (as in the quotation): also in 19th cent. use in the form (*help to*) *boil the pot. 19th cent.*

> **Louisa M Alcott Little Women 1868**
> *Those are people whom it's a satisfaction to help, for if they've got genius, it's an honor to be allowed to serve them, and not let it be lost or delayed for want of fuel to keep the pot boiling.*

See also make somebody's BLOOD boil.

bold

(as) bold as brass
arrogantly or brashly confident. Brass as a symbol of hardness and hence insensibility dates from Middle English. A source from the 1780s cites the line 'he died damn'd hard and as bold as brass' as 'an expression commonly used among the vulgar after returning from an execution'. *18th cent.*

> **Dickens The Battle of Life 1846**
> *You're frightened out of your life by a lantern, Clemmy ... But you're as bold as brass in general.*

bolt[1] (projectile)

a bolt from / out of the blue
something totally unexpected, like a thunderbolt descending from a clear blue sky. *19th cent.*

> **Carlyle French Revolution 1837**
> *Arrestment, sudden really as a bolt out of the Blue, has hit strange victims.*

> **G K Chesterton The Innocence of Father Brown 1911**
> *In an instant like a bolt from the blue ... that beautiful and defiant body had been dashed down the open well of the lift to death at the bottom.*

have shot one's bolt
to have done everything one could: with allusion to an arrow fired from a crossbow. The notion of a shot symbolizing an action for which there is only a single chance dates from the 15th cent., although the phrase in its present form is later. *18th cent.*

> **Boswell The Life of Samuel Johnson 1791**
> *I brought on myself his transient anger, by observing that in his tour in Scotland, he once had long and woeful experience of oats being the food of men in Scotland as they were of horses in England. It was a national reflection unworthy of him, and I shot my bolt.*

bolt[2] (the act of bolting)

make a bolt for something
to escape rapidly or suddenly to a place. The phrase is also used in figurative contexts and draws on the image of a bolting horse or other animal. *19th cent.*

> **Edgar Allan Poe King Pest 1835**
> *Having accordingly disposed of what remained of the ale ... they finally made a bolt for the street.*

See also shut the STABLE door after the horse has bolted.

bomb

The figurative meanings are based on the explosive and devastating effects of *bomb* in its primary meaning.

cost/make a bomb
informal to cost or earn a great deal of money. *Mid 20th cent.*

go down a bomb
British, informal to be well received. *Cf* go down like a lead balloon *at* LEAD². *Mid 20th cent.*

> **Liverpool Echo 1993**
> *The Canning Shirt Company … puts transfers and lettering on T-shirts and produces its own designs, including Liverpool logos, which go down a bomb with the tourists.*

go like a bomb
informal to move at great speed, to make rapid progress. *Mid 20th cent.*

---

bombshell

drop a bombshell
to break some devastating news. *Bombshell* is an older word for a bomb, and is here symbolic of an explosive effect. *19th cent.*

> **Dickens Hard Times 1854**
> *Mr Bounderby, red and hot, planted himself in the centre of the path before the horse's head, to explode his bombshell with more effect. 'The Bank's robbed!'*

---

bondi

give somebody bondi
Australian, informal to commit a savage attack on somebody. A *bondi* is a heavy Australian Aboriginal club. *19th cent.*

---

bone

a bone of contention
a subject of prolonged disagreement: used earlier in other forms, e.g. *bone of dissension. 18th cent.*

> **Henry Fielding The History of Tom Jones 1749**
> *Nay, the understandings of this couple were their principal bone of contention, and one great cause of many quarrels, which from time to time arose between them.*

bone idle
utterly or incurably idle. *Bone* is used adverbially as equivalent to *to the bone* (see below), i.e. deeply and fundamentally. The first use seems to be by Thomas Carlyle in a letter of 1836: 'For the last three weeks I have been going what you call bone-idle.' *19th cent.*

> **Edith Nesbitt Jesus in London 1908**
> *And the ones that have lived bone-idle, | If they want Me to hear them pray, | Let them go and work for their livings – | The only honest way!*

close to / near the bone
1 close to the poverty line. *19th cent.*

> **Henry David Thoreau Walden 1854**
> *Moreover, if you are restricted in your range by poverty … you are but confined to the most significant and vital … It is life near the bone where it is sweetest.*

2 (said of a remark, joke, etc) touching on a sensitive matter and likely to cause embarrassment or offence: *cf* close/near to HOME. *Mid 20th cent.*

> **Mick Middles The Smiths 1988**
> *The article wasn't particularly poignant but it did, in places, slide too near to home and too close to the bone.*

cut somebody to the bone
to affect somebody deeply. The image is of a blow or set of bonds that cuts into the victim's flesh, revealing the bone beneath. *19th cent.*

> **Trollope Phineas Redux 1874**
> *You did come to a friend, and though I could not drive out of my heart the demon of jealousy, though I was cut to the very bone, I would have helped you had help been possible.*

cut/pare something to the bone
to reduce something to its bare essentials or minimum. *19th cent.*

> **G B Shaw Letter 1896**
> *I always cut myself to the bone, reading the thing over and over until I have discovered the bits that can't be made to playact anyhow.*

> **The Scotsman 1990**
> *The cost of household goods and services, clothing and footwear all fell as retailers cut prices to the bone in the January sales.*

feel/know something in one's bones
to have a strong intuition about something. *19th cent.*

> **James Fenimore Cooper The Monkins 1835**
> *'We are drifting south'ard, I know,' said Mr. Poke, before he commenced his sight – 'I feel it in my bones.'*

Henry James *The Ambassadors* 1909
But he knew in his bones, our friend did, how almost irresistibly Mrs. Pocock would now be moved to show what she thought of his own.

have a bone to pick with somebody

to have a grievance or disagreement to confront somebody with. In earlier use (from the 16th cent.) *a bone to pick* meant 'a contentious matter to discuss'. *19th cent.*

Hardy *Tess of the D'Urbervilles* 1891
Do Jack Dollop work here? Because I want him! I have a big bone to pick with he, I can assure 'n!

Dogs Today 1992
Dear Father Christmas, I have a bone to pick with you.

make no bones about something

to find no difficulty or objection to something, to have no hesitation about it. The phrase occurs earlier in the form *make no bones at*, and has always been used in negative forms. The earliest published reference to the notion is in the 15th cent. Paston Letters: 'And fond that tyme no bonys in the matere.' It seems to have its origin in an earlier version *find no bones in*, meaning 'to experience no difficulties or problems'. But why bones? It has been thought that this refers to finding unwelcome bones in food, especially in soup, but there are no allusive uses of the phrase that might reinforce such an origin. It depends largely on a line in Skelton's poem *The Tunnying of Elynour Rummyng* (1516), a colourful depiction of the contemporary low life of alehouses and drinkers, in which somebody is said to have 'supped it up at once; | She founde therein no bones'. But does this have any connection with the phrase? Could it not be a fortuitous reference? And most important: how do we get from *finding* bones to *making* them? Other 16th cent. references seem remote from the notion of bones in food. *16th cent.*

Thomas Beard *The Theatre of Gods Judgements* 1597
Divers of the Romane Emperours were so villanous and wretched, as to make no bones of this sinne with their owne sisters, as Caligula, Antoninus, and Commodus: and some with their mothers, as Nero, so much was he given over and transported to all licentiousnesse.

Somerset Maugham *The Moon and Sixpence* 1919
But what the devil does a mentor do when the sinner makes no bones about confessing his sin?

make old bones

to live to an old age: often in negative contexts. *19th cent.*

Somerset Maugham *Of Human Bondage* 1915
The doctor looked at her gravely ... She would not make old bones either.

E V Thompson *Wychwood* 1992
Neither will you ever make old bones if you don't take more care of yourself.

not a — bone in one's body

not showing the slightest sign of the quality mentioned. *20th cent.*

Harpers & Queen 1990
She was so positive, not a negative bone in her body – she had a vision.

point the bone at somebody

Australian, informal to bring about somebody's downfall: from the Aboriginal ritual of pointing a bone at a person as a form of fatal curse. *19th cent.*

to the bone

completely, through and through, with reference to bodily feeling and in figurative contexts: from the image of a wound that is so deep that the bone is exposed, and from the notion of the bones as the seat of feeling. *18th cent.*

William Beckford *Vathek* 1786
The Caliph himself, was greatly inclined to take shelter in the large town of Ghulchissar, the governor of which, came forth to meet him, and tendered every kind of refreshment the place could supply. But, having examined his tablets, he suffered the rain to soak him, almost to the bone, notwithstanding the importunity of his first favourites.

Philip Callow *Van Gogh: A Life* 1990
Dutch to the bone, his ambition was to paint the world realistically.

work (one's fingers/hands) to the bone

to work extremely hard, especially for little reward or gratitude. *18th cent.*

Charles Lloyd *Rosamund Gray* 1795
But Worth, mean and homely, may work to the bone, | While spirits and strength shall decay.

Fanny Burney *The Wanderer* 1814
I do tell my poor husband, we should be mainly happier to work our hands to the bone, ony day of the year, so we did but live by the King's Majesty's

laws, than to make money by being always in a quandary.

Charles Kingsley Westward Ho! 1855
And the poor child took in that new thought like a child, and worked her fingers to the bone for all the old dames in Northam.

See also a BAG of bones; the BARE bones.

---

boo

— wouldn't say boo to a goose
the person named is very shy or reserved. *Bo* is an earlier form of *boo*. *16th cent.*

Thomas Heywood A Woman Killed by Kindness 1607
Theres not one amongst them al can saye, bo to a goose.

Fanny Burney Camilla 1796
'Well, young ladies, what say you to this?' cried he, 'does it hit your fancy? If it does, 'tis your own!' Eugenia asked what he meant. 'Mean? to make a present of it to which ever is the best girl, and can first cry bo! to a goose. Come, don't look disdainfully.'

Baroness Orczy The Scarlet Pimpernel 1905
Our demmed government is all on your side of the business. Old Pitt daren't say boo to a goose.

---

book

bring somebody to book
to bring somebody to justice. The underlying meaning is of making somebody produce evidence or authority to account for their actions. *19th cent.*

Dickens Great Expectations 1861
The late Compeyson … being so determined to bring him to book, I do not think he could have been saved.

by the book
following the rules rigidly: with allusion to consulting a rule book. *16th cent.*

Shakespeare Romeo and Juliet i.v.109 (1596)
[Juliet to Romeo] You kiss by th' book.

M Cole The Ladykiller 1993
The police had been called so everything had to be done by the book.

close/shut the books
to finish trading or business activity for a time: with reference to business accounts. *19th cent.*

in somebody's bad/good books
out of favour (or in favour) with somebody. *Cf* Shakespeare, *Much Ado About Nothing* (1598) I.i.74: '[Messenger to Beatrice] I see, lady, the gentleman [i.e. Benedick] is not in your books. [Beatrice] No. An he were, I would burn my study.' *19th cent.*

Dickens Nicholas Nickleby 1839
I tell you what, Mr. Noggs, if you want to keep in the good books in that quarter, you had better not call her the old lady any more, for I suspect she wouldn't be best pleased to hear you.

Trollope The Prime Minister 1876
I wish I could make out your father more clearly. He is always civil to me, but he has a cold way of looking at me which makes me think I am not in his good books.

in —'s book
in a particular person's judgement or opinion. *Mid 20th cent.*

S Jackman The Davidson Affair 1966
In his book the function of television was to edify, not to entertain.

on the books
included in a list of members, staff, etc. *18th cent.*

George Eliot Middlemarch 1872
There would be the painful necessity at last of disappointing respectable people whose names were on his books.

one for the book
a remarkable event or occasion, worth noting in a diary or book of recollections. *Early 20th cent.*

read somebody like a book
to know somebody's motives and intentions intimately. The image is older than the phrase in its familiar form, e.g. Shakespeare in *Troilus and Cressida* (1602) IV.vii.123 gives Achilles and Hector the following exchange before their single combat: '[Achilles] I will the second time, | As I would buy thee, view thee limb by limb. | [Hector] O, like a book of sport thou'lt read me o'er. | But there's more in me than thou understand'st.' *19th cent.*

D H Lawrence *Sons and Lovers* 1913
Miriam, for her part, boasted that she could read him like a book, could place her finger any minute on the chapter and the line. He, easily taken in, believed that Miriam knew more about him than anyone else.

Michael Frayn *Sweet Dreams* 1976
I can read you like a book – some book I've read six times already.

suit —'s book

to be convenient or suitable for that person. *19th cent.*

Harold Frederic *The Damnation of Theron Ware* 1896
He'd be actually tickled to death if he could nose up some hint of a scandal about her – something that he could pretend to believe, and work for his own advantage to levy blackmail, or get rid of her, or whatever suited his book.

talk like a book

to speak knowledgeably or elegantly. *19th cent.*

R L Stevenson *Treasure Island* 1883
He had good schooling in his young days, and can speak like a book when so minded.

throw the book at somebody

to punish somebody as severely as the law or rules allow: from the meaning 'a book of regulations'. *Mid 20th cent.*

Joseph Heller *Catch-22* 1961
He was formally charged with 'breaking ranks while in formation, felonious assault, indiscriminate behaviour, mopery, high treason, provoking, being a smart guy, listening to classical music, and so on'. In short, they threw the book at him.

Gavin Lyall *The Conduct of Major Maxim* 1982
I'm so far up the creek myself that when they throw the book at me it'll be the whole library.

See also be in somebody's BLACK books; a closed book *at* CLOSE; COOK the books; an OPEN book; take a LEAF out of somebody's book; a turn-up (for the book) *at* TURN.

boom

boom and bust

a period of great prosperity followed by one of severe economic depression. Originally used in the US in the 1940s and by New Labour in the early years of the 21st cent. as a cliché of alleged economic mismanagement. *Boom* in its meaning 'a sudden onset of activity' dates from the late 19th cent., and *bust* meaning 'a sudden collapse or failure' from slightly earlier. *Late 20th cent.*

Guardian 1984
At Mr Sterling's own company he has a group of people with whom he has worked for 15 years or so, and who have succeeded in the difficult task of rehabilitating Town and City, one of the near casualties of the property boom and bust of the middle 1970s.

boot¹

boots and all

informal, originally Australian and NZ completely, including everything. *Mid 20th cent.*

D M Davin *For the Rest of Our Lives* 1947
The next thing he'll do is counter-attack, boots and all.

get / give somebody the boot

informal to be dismissed (or dismiss somebody) from employment. The image is of being physically kicked out of a place. Also in the fanciful extension *get / give somebody the Order of the Boot. 19th cent.*

Rider Haggard *Colonel Quaritch, VC* 1888
There'll be the money to take over the Moat Farm and give that varmint Janter the boot.

put the boot in / into somebody

to attack somebody physically or verbally. *Early 20th cent.*

C J Dennis *Songs of a Sentimental Bloke* 1916
Plunks Tyball through the gizzard wiv 'is sword, 'Ow I ongcored! 'Put in the boot!' I sez. 'Put in the boot.'

seven-league boots

the ability to move or run very fast. The original association is with giants in folk tales and nursery rhymes. The phrase is well attested in physical senses, but it is more common in figurative meanings. *18th cent.*

Coleridge *Shakespeare as Poet* 1814
Every critic… puts on the seven-league boots of self-opinion, and strides at once from an illustrator into a supreme judge.

Scott *Rob Roy* 1817
The inhabitants of the opposite frontier served in her narratives to fill up the parts which ogres and giants with seven-leagued boots occupy in the ordinary nursery tales.

See also (as) TOUGH as old boots; the boot/shoe is on the other FOOT; DIE with one's boots on; HANG up one's boots; one's HEART sinks/falls into one's boots; LICK somebody's boots; you can BET your boots.

boot²

to boot

as well; in addition to other significant things already mentioned. *Boot* in this sense is an Old English word meaning 'profit or advantage'. It survives in modern English only in this phrase, but is found in Shakespeare in other phrases such as *no boot* (= no use) and *make boot* (= take advantage). In a passage from *Henry V* (1599) I.ii.192, the Archbishop of Canterbury compares man's lot with the activities of honey bees: 'Others like merchants venture trade abroad; | Others like soldiers, armèd in their stings, | Make boot upon the summer's velvet buds, | Which pillage they with merry march bring home.' *Boot* (and its variant form *bote*) also occurs in feudal England in compounds denoting a tenant's right to take timber from the estate for repairs and other practical uses, as in *fire-boot, house-boot,* and *hedge-boot.* Old English

Shakespeare *1 Henry IV* III.ii.97 (1596)
[King Henry] *Now, by my sceptre, and my soul to boot, | He hath more worthy interest to the state than thou.*

G B Shaw *Caesar and Cleopatra* 1901
'Lend me your sword and your right arm for this campaign.' 'Ay, and my heart and life to boot.'

bootstrap

pull/drag oneself up by one's (own) bootstraps

to take hold of oneself and put the necessary effort into reforming one's life or improving one's lot. A *bootstrap* is a small strap at the back of a boot for use when pulling the boot over the foot. *Early 20th cent.*

Jack London *Sea Wolf* 1904
It reminded me of the problem of lifting oneself by one's bootstraps. I understood the mechanics of levers; but where was I to get a fulcrum?

booty

shake one's booty

informal to dance vigorously. *Late 20th cent.*

Ben Elton *Stark* 1992
He was strutting up town to shake his booty down to the ground and get down on it like the bitchin' motivatin' groove machine he knew himself to be.

borak

poke borak at somebody

Australian, informal to make fun of somebody. *Borak* is derived from an Aboriginal Australian word that had a strong negative sense 'absolutely not', and was used in the 19th cent. Australian and New Zealand slang to mean 'nonsense'. It may be related to the verb *barrack*, often used in the context of loud shouting and jeering at public meetings. *19th cent.*

born

born-again

newly converted to a cause and inspired by enthusiasm for it: originally with reference to a person's spiritual rebirth as a Christian (*cf* John 3:3 'Jesus answered and said unto him, Verily, verily, I say unto thee, except a man be born again, he cannot see the kingdom of God'). The phrase occurs earlier in the form *to be born again.* *Late 20th cent.*

The Face 1992
I was interested to note that your November cover star Marky Mark is apparently something of a born-again cockney, a fact betrayed perhaps by the self-descriptive rhyming slang on the front of his baseball cap.

born and bred

by birth and upbringing: used after a description or designation of origin to show that a person is typical or representative of a certain place or attribute. The ordinary compositional use of the two words is found in the 14th cent. The sense of *breed* changes over time from the physical meaning (with the phrase often in the more logical order *bred and born*) to the meaning now usually understood, 'to educate and raise'. *17th cent.*

> Head & Kirkman *The English Rogue Described* 1674
> *She seemed to be angry at this Proposal, but I proceeding and telling her that I was a gentleman born and bred, and it may be in all things equal, if not above her friend; she was content to let me kiss her.*

> John Cleland *Memoirs of a Woman of Pleasure* 1748
> *She was really too a gentlewoman born and bred.*

> Dickens *Hard Times* 1854
> *You are not only a lady born and bred, but a devilish sensible woman.*

never in (all) one's born days

never in one's lifetime. *18th cent.*

> Richardson *Pamela* 1741
> *I should not omit one Observation; That Sir Jacob, when they were gone, said, They were pure Company: And Mr. H. He never was so delighted in his born Days.*

> James Fenimore Cooper *The Pioneers* 1823
> *But I am a plain, unlarned man that has … never so much as looked into a book, or larnt a letter of scholarship, in my born days.*

> C Bingham *In Sunshine or in Shadow* 1992
> *Your mother, may God rest her soul, your mother in all her born days never once served a hot meal on a cold plate.*

not born yesterday

not wholly naive or easily fooled. *18th cent.*

> Wilkie Collins *No Name* 1862
> *He took a few turns up and down the room – then suddenly stepped aside to a table in a corner, on which his writing materials were placed. 'I was not born yesterday, ma'am!' said the captain, speaking jocosely to himself. He winked his brown eye, took up his pen, and wrote the answer.*

> Kipling *Kim* 1901
> *'Dost thou know what manner of women we be in this quarter?'… 'Was I born yesterday?'*

not know one is born

to be unaware of one's good fortune. *20th cent.*

> Elvi Rhodes *Cara's Land* 1992
> *People in the country didn't know they were born, he thought.*

there's one born every minute

an expression of dismay or glee at the gullibility of folk: typically used in the context of somebody who has been duped and deceived. The American showman Phineas T Barnum (1810–91) is said to have declared 'there's a sucker born every minute'. *19th cent.*

> Alexander Davidson *The City Share Pushers* 1989
> *Behind their backs, the dealer would call his clients 'suckers', saying: 'There's one born every minute' and, 'They just haven't got a chance!'*

wish one had never been born

to be in such trouble or expectation of punishment that life seems not worth living: *cf* Mark 14:21 'But woe to that man by whom the Son of man is betrayed! Good were it for that man if he had never been born.' *17th cent.*

> Robert Vilvain *An Epitome of Essais* 1654
> *Job … seriously … wished he had never been born.*

> Richardson *Clarissa* 1748
> *To hear the poor man wish he had never been born! To hear him pray to be nothing after death! Good God! how shocking!*

> L M Montgomery *Anne of Green Gables* 1909
> *Five minutes ago I was so miserable I was wishing I'd never been born and now I wouldn't change places with an angel!*

See also be born on the wrong side of the BLANKET; be born with a SILVER spoon (in one's mouth); born in the PURPLE; to the MANNER born.

---

borrow

be living on borrowed time

to have survived beyond expectations or against probability, and be unlikely to survive much longer: also in extended uses. *19th cent.*

borrow trouble

NAmer, informal to attract trouble needlessly. *19th cent.*

> Catharine Sedgwick *A New-England Tale* 1822
> *Sarah, after a little consideration, said, 'I'm a thinking, John, you take on too much; you are a borrowing trouble for Miss Jane. She is a wise, discreet young body, and she may cure Mr. Erskine of his faults.'*

Edgar Rice Burroughs *Tarzan of the Apes* 1912
Maybe we are borrowing trouble. While I do not like the looks of things on board this ship, they may not be so bad after all.

See also borrowed plumes *at* PLUME.

bosom

take somebody to one's bosom
1 to embrace somebody. *18th cent.*

Benjamin Griffin *Injur'd Virtue* 1715
We, Cæsar, say it, and who dares controul? | Stand off, and let me take him to my Bosom: | My Friend! O let me hold thee to my Breast.
2 to marry somebody. *19th cent.*

William Snelling *Tales of the Northwest* 1830
Payton Skah was a husband and a father. As soon as he was reckoned a man, and able to support a family, he had taken to his bosom the young and graceful Tahtokah.

both

have it both ways
to derive advantages from two conflicting standpoints or courses of action: usually in the context of aspiration rather than achievement. *Early 20th cent.*

G B Shaw *Fanny's First Play* 1914
Then I suppose what I did was not evil; or else I was set free for evil as well as good. As father says, you can't have anything both ways at once.

See also CUT both ways.

bothered

See HOT and bothered.

bottle

The meaning underlying the phrases is generally the one associated with alcoholic drink and its attributes, especially in producing false or temporary courage. *No bottle* was a 19th cent. phrase meaning 'useless'.

have/show (a lot of) bottle
informal to show courage or determination. *Mid 20th cent.*

hit / be on the bottle
informal to start drinking alcohol heavily, especially to alleviate distress. The phrase in this form is mid 20th cent. (19th cent. in the form *hit the booze*).

lose one's bottle
informal to lose courage. *Mid 20th cent.*

Sunday Times 1965
It's the worst that could be said about you, that you'd lost your bottle.

bottom

be at the bottom of something
to be the underlying cause or instigation of a complicated or unpleasant situation. *19th cent.*

Maria Edgeworth *Castle Rackrent* 1800
Her diamond cross was, they say, at the bottom of it all; and it was a shame for her, being his wife, not to show more duty, and to have given it up when he condescended to ask so often for such a bit of a trifle in his distresses, especially when he all along made it no secret he married for money.

R L Stevenson *New Arabian Nights* 1882
I appeal to you in this difficulty for information. I must learn what is at the bottom of it all.

be bumping along the bottom
(said of an enterprise or state of affairs) to be at a low point for a time. *Late 20th cent.*

Independent 1989
George Marsh, managing director, said that housebuilding was now 'bumping along the bottom'.

the bottom drops/falls out of something
a venture or situation collapses completely: especially in the phrase *the bottom falls out of the market* = the market or demand for a commodity collapses. *17th cent.*

Mark Twain *The $30,000 Bequest* 1906
The very next day came the historic crash, the record crash, the devastating crash, when the bottom fell out of Wall Street, and the whole body of gilt-edged stocks dropped ninety-five points in five hours.

Economist 1993
Since the bottom fell out of the market for supercars and classic cars, hot-rods have taken over.

get at/to the bottom of something

to establish the true nature or the underlying cause of a difficulty, problem, etc. The notion behind the phrase, as the early uses show, is of reading a story or account 'to the bottom [of the page]', i.e. to the very end, thereby – and only thereby – discovering the cause and circumstances behind it. *18th cent.*

Richardson *Clarissa* 1751
I have just now received a fresh piece of intelligence from my agent honest Joseph Leman. Thou knowest the history of poor Miss Betterton of Nottingham. James Harlowe is plotting to revive the resentments of her family against me. The Harlowes took great pains, some time ago, to endeavour to get to the bottom of that story.

Hardy *The Return of the Native* 1878
Of course I shall get to the bottom of this story at once.

Ann Pilling *Henry's Leg* 1987
He didn't mistrust her exactly, there was just something he couldn't get to the bottom of.

knock the bottom out of something

to cause a venture or idea to collapse; to render something invalid or useless. *19th cent.*

R L Stevenson *The Master of Ballantrae* 1889
Nothing is mine, nothing. This day's news has knocked the bottom out of my life. I have only the name and the shadow of things – only the shadow; there is no substance in my rights.

touch bottom

to have reached the lowest level, especially in difficult circumstances. The image is of sinking in water or a morass. *19th cent.*

Conan Doyle *The Hound of the Baskervilles* 1901
So there is one of our small mysteries cleared up. It is something to have touched bottom anywhere in this bog in which we are floundering.

See also bottom DRAWER; the bottom line *at* LINE[1]; from the bottom of one's HEART; hit/touch rock bottom *at* ROCK[1]; scrape the bottom of the BARREL; you can BET your boots / bottom dollar.

bounce

The image in all the phrases is of a ball or other object being tossed and rebounding, often unpredictably.

bounce back

informal to recover fully after a setback. *Mid 20th cent.*

J D McDonald *Brass Cupcake* 1950
Fictional heroes … can bounce back from a pasting that should have put them in hospital beds.

bounce an idea off somebody

informal to test somebody's reaction to an idea. *Late 20th cent.*

Ski Survey (Ski Club of Great Britain) 1991
It was great working with Rob. We could bounce ideas off each other and share problems.

bounce off the walls

informal to be over-excited or agitated. *Late 20th cent.*

Val McDermid *Dead Beat* 1992
I'd been working and I was wide awake, so rather than go home and bounce off the walls I thought I'd stop off for a coffee.

See also a DEAD cat bounce; the way the ball bounces *at* BALL[1].

---

bound

See (in) DUTY bound; (in) HONOUR bound.

---

bounden

a/one's bounden duty

an obligatory or unavoidable duty. *Bounden* is an archaic past participle of the verb *bind*, surviving only in this phrase. *16th cent.*

William Painter *The Palace of Pleasure* 1567
Ye duety of a chast woman, whose tong ought to be locked, that she speake not but in time and place, and hir feete not straying or wandering, but to keepe hir self within the limits of hir owne house, except it be to serue God, and sometimes to render our bounden duty to them which haue brought vs into light.

Dickens *Pickwick Papers* 1837
Mrs Weller, on a hasty consideration of all the circumstances of the case, considered it her bounden duty to become gradually hysterical.

bounds

out of bounds

beyond a permitted or acceptable boundary or limit: used in physical senses and also figuratively of a person's behaviour. The phrase is 19th cent. in this form (earlier in the form *without one's bounds*).

R L Stevenson *The Strange Case of Dr Jekyll and Mr Hyde* 1886
And at that Mr. Hyde broke out of all bounds, and clubbed him to the earth.

Muriel Spark *The Mandelbaum Gate* 1965
She got into the car and made him drive out of school bounds, miles away.

bow^1 (to bend)

bow and scrape

to behave obsequiously towards somebody in authority. *17th cent.*

J Whitaker *Uzziah* 1646
Have you not known some in a low condition, to bow and scrape?

Bette Howell *Dandelion Days* 1991
That's why I stopped going to the Olde Tyme Dancing with him. Bowing and scraping all night at the class, then effing and blinding all the way home.

bow down in the house of Rimmon

to compromise one's principles for the sake of appearances. The phrase alludes to 2 Kings 5:18, where Naaman seeks permission from Elisha to worship the Syrian deity Rimmon: 'In this thing the Lord pardon thy servant, that when my master goeth into the house of Rimmon to worship there, and he leaneth on my hand, and I bow down myself in the house of Rimmon: when I bow down myself in the house of Rimmon, the Lord pardon thy servant in this thing.' The phrase is 18th cent. in allusive uses (16th cent. in Bible translations).

Charles Kingsley *Westward Ho!* 1855
The worthy parson subsided, – for, after all, Mr. Thomas Leigh paid his tithes regularly enough, – and was content, as he expressed it, to bow his head in the house of Rimmon like Naaman of old, by eating Mr. Leigh's dinners as often as he was invited.

make one's bow

to leave the scene, to depart: originally with reference to actors leaving the stage and later in figurative contexts. *18th cent.*

take a bow

to acknowledge applause or recognition. *20th cent.*

bow^2 (used in archery)

See have a second STRING (to one's bow).

bowl^1 (verb)

be bowled over

to be greatly impressed or overwhelmed: a metaphor, based on the concept of 'falling', from the game of skittles. *19th cent.*

George Meredith *Diana of the Crossways* 1885
Men may be counted on for falling bowled over by a handsome face and pointed tongue.

See also bowl a GOOGLY.

bowl^2 (deep dish)

See a bowl of cherries *at* CHERRY.

bowler

get / be given a bowler hat

informal, in military use to return to civilian life after a period in the army. *Early 20th cent.*

Observer 1959
He [Lord Mountbatten] did not ask for his bowler hat when Mr. Sandys reorganised defence a short time ago.

bows

a (warning) shot across the bows

a warning or criticism that is intended to allay adverse or hostile action: from the literal use of the phrase in naval warfare, a shot across the bows of a ship being intended to make the ship alter course rather than to damage it directly. *19th cent.*

BOX | 102

box

be a box of birds
Australian and NZ, informal to be in good health, happy, etc. *Mid 20th cent.*

> **D M Davin** *For the Rest of Our Lives* 1947
> *Everyone is a box of birds, still celebrating being alive.*

box clever
British, informal to conduct oneself adroitly. *20th cent.*

> **Shirley Conran** *Crimson* 1992
> *Buzz sensed that she had to be careful, she had to box clever, she had to let Adam think she had accepted what he said and would go quietly.*

a box of tricks
informal a clever or ingenious device. *Early 20th cent.*

> **Edward Dyson** *Hello Soldier* 1919
> *We had blown out every clip, | 'N' blooed the hammunition for the little box of tricks.*

> **BBC Good Food** 1991
> *Linda brings along her box of tricks to every session – it holds a tool for most jobs, from opening oysters to piping cream.*

in the box seat
Australian, informal in a favourable position: the reference is to a comfortable seat in a box at the theatre. *20th cent.*

in the same box
in a similar predicament or situation: from the idea of sharing a box at the theatre (or, in some cases, a compartment at a coffee house, which was also called a *box*). *19th cent.*

> **F W Farrar** *Eric, or, Little by Little* 1858
> *'Do let me speak to you sometimes, while I am a new boy, Russell.' 'O yes,' said Russell, laughing, 'as much as ever you like. And as Barker hates me pretty much as he seems inclined to hate you, we are in the same box.'*

> **David Graham Phillips** *Susan Lenox, Her Fall and Rise* 1917
> *You're right, Mr. Burlingham … Miss Sackville ought to share. We're all in the same box.*

in the wrong box
in an awkward or inappropriate situation. In 16th cent. and early 17th cent. usage the phrase was *in a wrong box*; the allusion may be to boxes of medicines and poisons kept by apothecaries. *16th cent.*

> **Dickens** *Oliver Twist* 1838
> *'And I very much question,' added Mr. Bumble, drawing himself up, 'whether the Clerkinwell Sessions will not find themselves in the wrong box before they have done with me.'*

out of the box
Australian, informal exceptionally fine or good: in allusion to the freshness of a new purchase recently removed from its wrapping. Compare the North American phrase *look as if one came out of a bandbox*, meaning 'to look very smart'. *Early 20th cent.*

out of one's box
British, informal affected by alcohol or drugs. *20th cent.*

> **Val McDermid** *Dead Beat* 1992
> *He looked stoned out of his box.*

See also **BLACK** box; Pandora's box *at* **PANDORA**.

Box

Box and Cox
to share a position or amenity and take it in turns to use it, the assumption being that the two people involved never need it at the same time. It was the title of a farce by J M Morton, first staged in 1847, about an unscrupulous landlord who let out the same room to two tenants unbeknown to them, Box (who used it during the day) and Cox (who used it during the night). *19th cent.*

boy

boy meets girl
a phrase summarizing or introducing a romantic encounter: with allusion to plot summaries in which this phrase often features. Used as the title of a novel by B and S Spewack (1936). *Mid 20th cent.*

boys will be boys
(proverb) young men can be expected to be boisterous and irresponsible. The phrase is found earlier in the form *youth will be youth*; *girls will be girls* is recorded earlier (though still 19th cent.) than *boys will be boys*, but is now less common. *19th cent.*

Louisa M Alcott *Little Women* 1868
Boys will be boys, young men must sow their wild oats, and women must not expect miracles.

Esquire 1992
His 'instant portrait' ... was that the client was most likely a starter, could very well be a married man, children off his hands, time on his hands, going back to his own public school days ... and the boys will be boys bit.

one of the boys
a member of a social group of young men. *19th cent.*

C M Yonge *The Daisy Chain* 1856
She opened the hall door, and would have rushed up stairs, but nurse happened to be crossing the hall. 'Miss Ethel! Miss Ethel, you arn't going up with them boots on! I do declare you are just like one of the boys.'

Independent 1989
At the same time she knew that her gender isolated her from the ritualised socialising of other senior officers. You could never, as she said, pretend to be one of the boys in a skirt.

See also jobs for the boys *at* JOB; the old boy NETWORK; separate / sort out the MEN from the boys.

brain

have (got) something on the brain
to be constantly preoccupied with a thought or idea. *19th cent.*

Harold Frederic *The Damnation of Theron Ware* 1896
I can't think of anything else that would make a man spend money like water – just for flowers and bushes. They do get foolish, you know, when they've got marriage on the brain.

Ann Pilling *Henry's Leg* 1987
She was a miner's daughter so she'd got pit disasters on the brain.

pick somebody's brain(s)
to seek information or opinions from a well-informed person. *19th cent.*

Nathaniel Willis *High Life in Europe* 1847
Finding the old landlord smoking his pipe alone under the portico, I lighted a cigar, and sat down to pick his brains of the little information I wanted to fill out the story.

Susan Hill *Gentleman and Ladies* 1968
What a pity you are here only for the day – I could pick your brains very profitably.

See also have SHIT for brains; RACK one's brains.

brake

put a brake on something
to take steps to slow the progress of something that is developing too rapidly: a metaphor from driving vehicles. *Brake* is recorded in figurative use from the 19th cent.; the phrase is late 20th cent.

Betty Rowlands *Finishing Touch* 1991
'Everyone's asking themselves,' she went on before Melissa had a chance to put a brake on her roller-coaster imagination, 'whether there could be a connection between this crime and the Angelica Caroli murder.'

brass

brass monkey weather / brass monkeys
freezing cold: from the expression *cold enough to freeze the balls off a brass monkey.* The origin of *brass monkey* in this context is obscure: one suggestion associates it with the brass rack, supposedly called a *monkey,* on which a ship's cannon balls were stored in the British navy at the time of the Napoleonic Wars. In cold weather, so the story goes, the balls shrank and fell off the plate. The account as told makes no sense historically or logically: there is no evidence that cannon balls were stored in this way (they were in fact kept, much more sensibly, in wooden frames), or that this use of *monkey* was among its many technical meanings, and it is hardly credible that such a process could physically occur, or would be allowed to occur if it could. Curiously, the term *monkey,* though not used in the way just described, did denote a kind of gun or cannon, but the evidence for this is confined to the 17th cent., well before the period in which our phrase came into prominence. In fact the brass monkey image has wider applications beyond freezing balls: other possibilities included *talk the tail off a brass monkey, have the gall of a brass monkey,* and (most interestingly), *hot enough the melt the nose off a brass monkey,* this last the complete antithesis of the current phrase and the earliest recorded use of the brass monkey notion (see below), making it

extremely likely that the ordnance origin is yet another late attempt to rationalize an obscure origin. There may be a connection with the traditional sculptures of three wise monkeys covering their ears, eyes, and mouth respectively to represent the maxim 'Hear no evil, See no evil, Speak no evil', but the original connection probably lies more fancifully with real monkeys, as a source of 1835 seems to suggest: 'He was told to be silent, in a tone of voice which set me shaking like a monkey in frosty weather.' No doubt all these associations became confused over time. *19th cent.*

> Herman Melville *Omoo* 1847
> *Falling to with our hoes again, we worked singly, or together, as occasion required, until 'Nooning Time' came. The period, so called by the planters, embraced about three hours in the middle of the day; during which it was so excessively hot, in this still, brooding valley, shut out from the Trades, and only open toward the leeward side of the island, that labor in the sun was out of the question. To use a hyperbolical phrase of Shorty's, 'It was 'ot enough to melt the nose h'off a brass monkey.'*

> R Connolly *Sunday Morning* 1993
> *It's brass monkeys this winter, the hills as white as Norway, no snow of course, but frost until nine, and log fires every night.*

come/get down to brass tacks
informal to begin to tackle the essentials of a task or the realities of a situation. The origin of this phrase has been the object of much fanciful speculation, of which we might consider four suggestions here: (1) that it is rhyming slang for 'facts' or 'hard facts', (2) that it refers to the tacks used to attach the inner foundation of the sole of a shoe to the upper, which became exposed and caused discomfort when the outer sole wore thin, (3) that it relates to the scraping of weeds and barnacles from the hulls of wooden ships, a task that was not complete until the bolts that fastened the hull were again exposed, and (4) that it refers to brass tacks fixed to the counters of drapers' shops and used to measure out lengths of material being bought. When cloth was measured precisely in this way, instead of by the traditional method of using the length of the arm to gauge a yard approximately, the shopkeepers were indeed 'getting down to brass tacks'. The first (though accepted by Partridge and later editions of Brewer) has all the charac-

teristics of folk etymology, which seeks to rationalize obscure origins; the second is no more persuasive (though entertaining), and the third is unlikely since ships' bolts were generally made of copper and not brass and would hardly be called 'tacks'. The fourth explanation is the most compelling, if a specific origin has to be identified, and the term *brass tacks* is at least recorded in this connection; but it is more likely that the phrase came together from a variety of original applications in the real world. *19th cent.*

> H A Jones *Liars* 1897
> *Come down to brass tacks. What's going to be the end of this?*

> Sinclair Lewis *Our Mr Wrenn* 1914
> *Highbrow sermons that don't come down to brass tacks.*

> T S Eliot *Sweeney Agonistes* 1932
> *That's all the facts when you come to brass tacks: Birth, and copulation, and death.*

not a brass farthing
informal no money at all: also in the phrase *not care a brass farthing* = not care at all. *19th cent.*

> Rider Haggard *King Solomon's Mines* 1885
> *If once they begin to suspect us, our lives will not be worth a brass farthing.*

> Beryl Bainbridge *An Awfully Big Adventure* 1990
> *'Has Mr Potter's friend got money?' she asked …
> 'Not a brass farthing.'*

top/big brass
originally NAmer those in command or authority, especially senior officers in the armed forces. *Brass* refers to the brass or gold insignia worn on officer's uniforms. *19th cent.*

> Boston Herald 1899
> *It was not a big brass general that came; but a man in khaki kit.*

See also have the brass NECK to do something; part brass rags with somebody *at* RAG; where there's MUCK there's brass.

---

brave

brave the elements
to venture out of doors in bad weather. *20th cent.*

a brave new world
an ideal society brought about by social and technological change: from the title of a novel

(1932) by Aldous Huxley about a totalitarian society, itself an ironic use of the words spoken by Miranda in Shakespeare's *The Tempest* (1613) v.i.186: 'How beauteous mankind is! O brave new world | That has such people in't!' Eric Partridge in *Usage and Abusage* (1947) included *brave new world* among a collection of 'vogue words' and described it as 'perhaps as much a cliché as it is a vogue term' and 'a post-war counter, often used ironically rather than optimistically'. *Mid 20th cent.*

> British Medical Journal 1975
> *Three and a half years ago I described my experience of a meeting I attended for briefing on the brave new world of budget holding, the wild card of the recently published NHS Review.*

See also put a brave FACE on something.

---

breach

step into the breach

to take over a role at short notice, especially from somebody who is unexpectedly unable to continue: from military language, in which a breach is a hole made in fortifications during an attack. There are echoes here of the famous line in Shakespeare's *Henry V* (1599), opening the King's exhortation to the English army before the assault on Harfleur (iii.i.1): 'Once more unto the breach, dear friends, once more' (echoed later by Bardolph: 'On, on, on, on, on! To the breach, to the breach!'). To stand in or step into the breach is therefore to face the full force of an attack that has so far proved successful. Also used with some variation, especially in more general senses. *19th cent.*

> Louisa M Alcott Little Women 1868
> *Laurie and his friends gallantly threw themselves into the breach, bought up the bouquets, encamped before the table, and made that corner the liveliest spot in the room.*

> Gene Stratton Porter Freckles 1904
> *Freckles hurried into the breach. 'You must be for blaming it every bit on me.'*

---

bread

the best/greatest thing since sliced bread

informal a new idea or invention of great value: a kind of spoof marketing slogan, with allusion to packets of ready-sliced bread which became common in the 1950s. *Mid 20th cent.*

> John Harvey-Jones Making It Happen 1988
> *Organizations like this are not good at remembering the things you have done well and if ... you are at the bottom of the pile, you will find that you are considered to be alternately either the best thing since sliced bread, or a liability to the organization.*

one's bread and butter

what one lives on, one's livelihood; hence *bread-and-butter* used as a modifier with the meaning 'lucrative'. *18th cent.*

> Richardson Clarissa 1748
> *All this made them secure; and they laughed in their sleeves, to think what a childish way of shewing her resentment, she had found out; Sally throwing out her witticisms, that Mrs. Lovelace was right, however, not to quarrel with her bread and butter.*

> Virginia Woolf The Voyage Out 1915
> *'No, no, Miss Allan; be persuaded you will benefit the world much more by dancing than by writing.' ... 'It's a question of bread and butter,' said Miss Allan calmly.*

a bread-and-butter letter

a letter written by a guest in thanks for hospitality. *Early 20th cent.*

> N Streatfeild Tops and Bottoms 1933
> *Please never write me bread-and-butter letters.*

bread and circuses

entertainments and other benefits bestowed on the people by rulers to win popularity: translating Latin *panem et circenses* (Juvenal *Satires* x.80), referring to the Roman emperors' practice of giving the people grain and gladiatorial shows to ensure popularity. Used as the title of a novel by H P Eden (1914). *Early 20th cent.*

> G B Shaw Man and Superman 1903
> *To hand the country over to riff-raff is national suicide, since riff-raff can neither govern nor will let anyone else govern except the highest bidder of bread and circuses.*

break bread with

to have a meal with somebody, especially in a social context. *Break bread* is an old idiom for eating a meal, and gained currency from its occurrence in the New Testament account of Christ's Last Supper. In Shakespeare's *The Merry Wives of Windsor* (1597) I.iv.146, Mistress

Quickly describes Anne Page as 'an honest maid as ever broke bread'. *16th cent.*

Shakespeare *Timon of Athens* I.ii.48 (1609)
The fellow that sits next him, now parts bread with him, pledges the breath of him in a divided draught, is the readiest man to kill him.

Wilkie Collins *The Woman in White* 1860
'No, no,' she said, earnestly and kindly, 'leave us like a friend; break bread with us once more. Stay here and dine.'

one cannot live by bread alone

(proverb) a person needs spiritual as well as material sustenance: with allusion to Deuteronomy 8:3 (in the Authorized Version of 1611): 'Man doth not live by bread alone, but by every word that proceedeth out of the mouth of the Lord doth man live' (cf Matthew 4:4 'Man shall not live by bread alone'). *19th cent.*

Mark Twain *Speeches* 1906
They say that you cannot live by bread alone, but I can live on compliments. I do not make any pretence that I dislike compliments. The stronger the better, and I can manage to digest them.

J Maitland *Cathedral* 1993
I was so hungry now I could hardly think ... We cannot live by bread alone, but it helps.

cast one's bread upon the waters

to give generously without wishing for an immediate reward: with allusion to Ecclesiastes 11:1 'Cast thy bread upon the waters: for thou shalt find it after many days.' *17th cent.*

James Harrington *The Common-wealth of Oceana* 1656
What Husbands have we hitherto been? What is become of greater Summes? My Lords, if you should thus cast your bread upon the waters, after many daies you would find it: stand not huckling, when you are offer'd Corn and your money again in the mouth of the Sack.

Simon Brett *Cast in Order of Disappearance* 1975
Cast your bread upon the waters, and it will come back buttered.

eat the bread of idleness

literary to take sustenance that one has not worked for: with allusion to Proverbs 31:27 (in the Authorized Version of 1611), which describes the 'virtuous woman' as follows: 'She looketh well to the ways of her household, and eateth not the bread of idleness.' *19th cent.*

Jane Austen *Mansfield Park* 1814
Besides, that would be all recreation and indulgence, without the wholesome alloy of labour, and I do not like to eat the bread of idleness.

have/want one's bread buttered on both sides

to have or want more benefits or advantages than one is entitled to. *19th cent.*

know (on) which side one's bread is buttered

to know where one's advantage lies. *16th cent.*

J Heywood *Proverbs* 1546
I knowe on whiche syde my breade is buttred.

Harriet Beecher Stowe *Uncle Tom's Cabin* 1852
A particular species [of wisdom] much in demand among politicians of all complexions and countries, and vulgarly denominated 'knowing which side the bread is buttered'.

take the bread out of / from somebody's mouth

to deprive somebody of their livelihood by unfair means. *18th cent.*

R H Dana *Two Years Before the Mast* 1840
The next thing to be done is to show to the court and jury that the captain is a poor man, and has a wife and family ... depending upon him for support; that if he is fined, it will only be taking bread from the mouths of the innocent and helpless.

breadline

on the breadline

only just above subsistence level. The *bread line* was originally a line of people waiting to be given bread or other food as charity. *Early 20th cent.*

William Dean Howells *The Impossible* 1910
Now the grande dames are going in for the suffrage, why don't some of them join the Bread Line?

Dundee Courier 1929
My life has been spent among people ... close to the bread line.

break

break a butterfly on a wheel

to destroy something fragile with disproportionate force: *see also* break somebody on the wheel *below. 18th cent.*

Pope *Epistle to Dr Arbuthnot* 1735
*Satire or sense alas! Can Sporus feel? | Who breaks
a butterfly upon a wheel?*

Trollope *The Way We Live Now* 1875
*There isn't much in the book, certainly, as far as I
have looked at it. I should have said that violent
censure or violent praise would be equally thrown
away upon it. One doesn't want to break a butterfly
on the wheel, – especially a friendly butterfly.*

break even
to recoup one's initial outlay or investment; to
balance losses and gains in a transaction. *Early
20th cent.*

break a leg!
a traditional greeting to actors before a performance, used because saying 'good luck' directly is
considered unlucky (like mentioning 'the Scottish play'). The origin of this circumlocution is
obscure: the most common anecdotal explanation is that it stems from the assassination of
Abraham Lincoln at Ford's Theatre in Washington on 14 April 1865. But this is unlikely, because
the expression was not otherwise in use until
several decades after this event. The phrase is
probably related in some way to the German
greeting *Hals und Beinbruch* 'may you break
your neck and your leg', which respects in the
same way a superstition of seeking to ward off
calamity by mentioning it. Other theatrical superstitions are discussed by Steve Roud in *The Penguin Guide to the Superstitions of Britain and Ireland*
(2003), pp.461–3. *20th cent.*

break new/fresh ground
to be innovative, to make pioneering progress.
19th cent.

Conan Doyle *The Sign of Four* 1890
*There are features of interest about this ally. He lifts
the case from the regions of the commonplace. I
fancy that this ally breaks fresh ground in the
annals of crime in this country.*

break somebody on the wheel
to make somebody suffer and break their spirit:
from the literal meaning 'to make somebody
comply by using the wheel' (an instrument of
torture): *see also* break a butterfly on a wheel
above. *19th cent.*

Jack London *The Iron Heel* 1908
*Among them, he said, he had found keen intellects
and brilliant wits, ministers of the Gospel who had*

*been broken because their Christianity was too wide
for any congregation of mammon-worshippers, and
professors who had been broken on the wheel of
university subservience to the ruling class.*

give somebody a break
1 to help somebody with their work to enable
them to rest from it. *Mid 20th cent.*

Mary Jane Staples *The Pearly Queen* 1992
*He'd informed Aunt Edie that to give her a break, he
and Patsy would get the tea later on.*

2 to allow somebody an opportunity; to stop
harassing or creating difficulties for somebody.
Often used in the imperative as a sceptical comment on something said. *Late 20th cent.*

Martin Amis *Money* 1985
*Spank? Give me a break. What kind of a name is
Spank?*

Independent 2001
*I'm stunned to think that anyone would question
the ability of the average Harry Potter fan to concentrate for more than two hours* [on a film ver-
sion]. *Give the kids a break – if it's worth watching,
they'll lap it up.*

have a bad break
to experience bad luck or misfortune: earlier in
the form *make a bad break* = to make a mistake.
19th cent.

make a break (for something)
to head straight for a place, especially by way of
escape; also in the forms *make a break for it* and
make a break for freedom/liberty. The phrase is 19th
cent. in this form; *make a break for it* (with no
direction specified) is early 20th cent.

Mark Twain *Life on the Mississippi* 1883
*I impressed my orders upon my memory ... and
made a straight break for the reef.*

Conan Doyle *The Lost World* 1912
*Their language is more than half signs, and it was
not hard to follow them. So I thought it was time we
made a break for it.*

make a clean break
to detach oneself completely from a situation or
relationship, and make a new start. *Early 20th
cent.*

Willa Cather *Alexander's Bridge* 1912
*It's got to be a clean break, Hilda. I can't see you at
all, anywhere.*

P D James *Death of an Expert Witness* 1979
Gossip has it that his wife had recently left him and he wanted to make a clean break.

See also break the BACK of; break the BANK; break COVER; break somebody's HEART; break the ICE; break LOOSE; break the MOULD; break one's NECK to do something; break RANK(s); break wind *at* WIND[1].

breakfast

have/eat somebody for breakfast
to behave like an unprincipled ogre against whom a normal innocent human being stands no chance. *19th cent.*

W B Churchward *Blackbirding* 1888
Look sharp, or by golly, they will have us for breakfast.

Angela Wells *Viking Magic* 1993
Instinct and an adolescence spent in observation rather than practice told her this was the kind of man who ate little girls like Suzie for breakfast.

See also a dog's breakfast *at* DOG.

breast

beat one's breast
to make a show of grief or sorrow: originally with literal meaning but now symbolic. *Middle English*

Chaucer *Troilus and Criseyde* 1.932
Now bet thi brest, and sey to God of Love, | *'Thy Grace, lord, for now I me repente'.*

Shakespeare *Richard III* II.ii.3 (1593)
[Clarence's young daughter] *Why do you weep so oft, and beat your breast,* | *And cry, 'O Clarence, my unhappy son'?*

C Allmand *The Hundred Years War* 1991
A nation which experienced years of defeat and disaster (as France did in the mid-fourteenth century) beat its breast in self-reproach and accepted war's afflictions.

See also breast the TAPE; make a CLEAN breast (of something).

breath

a breath of fresh air
1 a brief period in the open air, especially after being indoors a long time. *19th cent.*

Bram Stoker *Dracula* 1897
Looking out on this, I felt that I was indeed in prison, and I seemed to want a breath of fresh air, though it were of the night.

Penelope Lively *Passing On* 1990
Why don't we have a pub lunch and a breath of fresh air somewhere pleasant?

2 a person or circumstance that provides a welcome change. *Early 20th cent.*

Mark Twain *Speeches* 1906
In this day and time, when it is the custom to ape and imitate English methods and fashion, it is like a breath of fresh air to stand in the presence of this untainted American citizen.

the breath of life
something one depends on for survival: with allusion to the creation account in Genesis 2:7 'And the Lord God formed man of the dust of the ground, and breathed into his nostrils the breath of life'. The phrase appears in Middle English in Wyclif's translation of the Bible.

Keats *Endymion* 1817
O my love, my breath of life, where art thou?

Liverpool Daily Post 1990
As a life-long Socialist, Baroness Castle admits that politics has been the breath of life to her over the last 50 years.

catch one's breath
to stop breathing momentarily from surprise or strong emotion. *18th cent.*

Hannah Cowley *Albina, Countess Richmond* 1779
Perdition catch thy breath! – | *Knew you, Editha, when you sent me hither,* | *The purport of that villain's tale?*

don't hold your breath
don't expect quick action or results: from the reflex of holding in the breath when anxious or excited about something imminent. *Mid 20th cent.*

Jenny Ashe *Sweet Deceiver* 1993
Don't hold your breath, Miguel, because I'm not going out with you.

give somebody breathing space
to provide somebody with a respite or opportunity to reflect on a situation. *17th cent.*

Thomas Heywood *If You Know Not Me, You Know No Bodie* 1605
[The Queen] *Commit him to the Tower, | Till time affordes vs and our Counsell breathing space. | Whence is that Post?*

hold one's breath
to be in a state of nervous anticipation: originally with the physical meaning of stopping breathing for a few moments when afraid or startled. *19th cent.*

Conan Doyle *The Poison Belt* 1913
A train of coal trucks stood motionless upon the line. We held our breath as the express roared along the same track. The crash was horrible.

in the same breath
done or said at practically the same time as something else. Typically used to refer to actions or statements that come together and are contrasted in character. *17th cent.*

Ninian Paterson *The Fanatick Indulgence* 1683
Give them a power rebellions trump to blow, | In that same breath forbid them to do so.

Charlotte Brontë *Villette* 1853
I assured him plainly I could not agree in this doctrine, and did not see the sense of it; whereupon, with his usual absolutism, he merely requested my silence, and also, in the same breath, denounced my mingled rashness and ignorance.

save one's breath
to desist from saying something unnecessary or unwanted. *19th cent.*

Scott *The Heart of Midlothian* 1818
'Weel, weel, Jeanie,' said Effie, 'I mind a' about the sins o' presumption in the questions – we'll speak nae mair about this matter, and ye may save your breath to say your carritch [= catechism]; and for me, I'll soon hae nae breath to waste on ony body.'

Edgar Rice Burroughs *Tarzan and the Jewels of Opar* 1916
The officer only laughed at the assertion, and advised his prisoner to save his breath for his defense in court.

take somebody's breath away
to overwhelm somebody with emotion or surprise. *19th cent.*

R L Stevenson *Kidnapped* 1886
There was a kind of nobleness in this that took my breath away; if my uncle was certainly a miser, he

was one of that thorough breed that goes near to make the vice respectable.

under one's breath
(said of something spoken) in a whisper; so that nobody can hear. *19th cent.*

Scott *The Antiquary* 1815
But the almoner first recovered his recollection, and, advancing towards Macraw, said under his breath, but with an authoritative tone, 'How dare you approach the Earl's apartment without knocking?'

waste one's breath
to speak to no effect; to be unpersuasive. Often used in negative contexts and in the form *be a waste of breath* (see also save one's breath *above*). Breath features as a medium of speech (as distinct from life) from the 16th cent.

Shakespeare *A Midsummer Night's Dream* III.ii.169 (1595)
Never did mockers waste more idle breath.

Wilkie Collins *The Moonstone* 1868
Being firmly persuaded that the Sergeant was wasting his breath to no purpose on Mrs. Yolland, I sat enjoying the talk between them, much as I have sat, in my time, enjoying a stage play.

breathe

breathe again/freely
to feel relief after the passing of a danger, difficulty, etc. *16th cent.*

Shakespeare *King John* IV.ii.138 (1597)
Bear with me, cousin, for I was amazed [= bewildered] | Under the tide; but now I breathe again | Aloft the flood, and can give audience | To any tongue, speak it of what it will.

breathe down somebody's neck
to be following or watching somebody closely or oppressively. *Mid 20th cent.*

Alice T Ellis *Pillars of Gold* 1993
All my life I've had brothers breathing down my neck, watching my every move, checking on who I'm going out with and what time I'm getting home.

breathe one's last (breath/gasp)
literary or euphemistic to die. *16th cent.*

Shakespeare *3 Henry VI* v.ii.40 (1591)
[Somerset] *Ah, Warwick – Montague hath breathed his last, | And to the latest gasp cried out for Warwick.*

Edmund Burke *Reflections on the Revolution in France* 1790
The absolute monarchy was at an end. It breathed its last, without a groan, without struggle, without convulsion.

Julia Byrne *My Enemy, My Love* 1993
As soon as King Henry had breathed his last the barons had turned on each other like ravening wolves, attacking their neighbours and ripe for every type of lawlessness.

breed

a breed apart
a group of people who are regarded as special in some way or unlike others. *20th cent.*

Alistair Horne *The Price of Glory* 1993
In the eyes of the unhappy infantry, the heavy gunners may have been a breed apart, but beyond them lay one small body of men that seemed to be not even of the same world.

breeze

shoot the breeze
informal to talk or act idly; to relax and have fun. *Late 20th cent.*

Colin Forbes *Whirlpool* 1991
So why do I go on expanding the company instead of putting up my feet and shooting the breeze?

brevity

brevity is the soul of wit
(proverb) wisdom is best expressed concisely. It first appears in the early 17th cent. in Shakespeare's *Hamlet* (1601) ii.ii.91: 'Therefore, since brevity is the soul of wit, | And tediousness the limbs and outward flourishes, | I will be brief.' *Wit* here is used in its older meaning 'wisdom'. Later uses are normally in direct allusion to Shakespeare.

Disraeli *Vivian Grey* 1826
He allowed nothing to influence or corrupt his decisions. His infallible plan for arranging all differences had the merit of being brief; and if brevity be the soul of wit, it certainly was most unreasonable in his subjects to consider his judgments no joke.

brick

bang/knock one's head against / come up against / hit a brick wall
to be frustrated or encounter an insuperable difficulty in an enterprise: *brick wall* as a metaphor for an impenetrable barrier to progress dates from the 19th cent.

Edgar Rice Burroughs *The Warlords of Mars* 1913
I tried my old rushing tactics; but I might as well have rushed a brick wall for all that Solan gave way.

Michelle Magorian *Goodnight Mister Tom* 1983
Although she was terribly fond of the children she found that working with them was like banging her head against a brick wall.

a brick short of a load
informal (said of a person) stupid. There are many variations on this theme: *see also* a SANDWICH short of a picnic. *Late 20th cent.*

Guardian 1988
The clever folk comforted themselves in their plainness by implying that these beautiful people were a few bricks short of a load, not too tightly wrapped, dim, stupid.

come down on somebody like a ton of bricks
to affect or treat somebody with great severity. The phrase is subject to some variation. *Mid 20th cent.*

Graham Greene *Brighton Rock* 1938
If there's any fighting I shall come down like a ton of bricks on both of you.

Amanda Browning *The Stolen Heart* 1992
She felt like crying as dejection hit her like a ton of bricks.

drop a brick
informal to commit a blunder or indiscretion. *Early 20th cent.*

Galsworthy *The White Monkey* 1924
I've got to keep my head shut, or I shall be dropping a brick.

make bricks without straw
to try to achieve an objective without the resources needed. Used with allusion to the account in Exodus (5:6–19) of the Israelite captivity in Egypt, in which the Israelites were required to make bricks for which they had to gather their own straw (an essential ingredient). The meaning has changed: in the biblical account

the Israelites are not required to perform miracles by making the bricks without straw, which is how the phrase has invariably been understood in common usage. In its current meaning the phrase dates from the 19th cent.

> Coleridge *Biographia Literaria* 1817
> *What Hume had demonstratively deduced from this concession concerning cause and effect, will apply with equal and crushing force to all the other eleven categorical forms, and the logical functions corresponding to them. How can we make bricks without straw? Or build without cement?*

> Booker T Washington *Up from Slavery* 1901
> *The task before me did not seem a very encouraging one. It seemed much like making bricks without straw.*

bridge

cross the/that bridge when one comes to it
to deal with a problem or difficulty when it arises. Originally used as a proverb. *19th cent.*

> Longfellow *Journal* 1850
> *Remember the proverb, 'Do not cross the bridge until you come to it.'*

See also BURN one's boats/bridges.

brief

hold no brief for somebody/something
to have no wish to support or defend somebody or something: from the legal meaning of *brief* 'summary of the facts and circumstances of a case'. *Early 20th cent.*

> Ronald Knox *Spiritual Aeneid* 1918
> *When I was at Balliol, we used to adapt the phrase 'I hold no brief for So-and-so'.*

bright

(as) bright as a button
(said of a person) quick and alert: used with play on two meanings of *bright*, 'intelligent' and 'shining'. *19th cent.*

> Nathaniel Hawthorne *Twice-Told Tales* 1837
> *She was a fine smart girl, now wide awake and bright as a button.*

> Margaret Sunley *Fields in the Sun* 1991
> *'She's a canny little thing, as bright as a button,' was his summing up of the maid.*

bright and early
early in the morning, especially as a time to show energy and enthusiasm. *19th cent.*

> Mark Twain *A Tramp Abroad* 1880
> *So tomorrow I'll be up bright and early ... and mosey off to Tennessee.*

bright-eyed and bushy-tailed
lively and eager: from the conventional image of a healthy and spirited squirrel or other animal. Its popularity owed much to its use as a song title by Bob Merrill in 1953, although he may not have coined the phrase. Partridge in his *Dictionary of Slang* (Supplement, 1961) identified the phrase as a Canadian catchphrase, but gave no evidence to support this origin. *Mid 20th cent.*

> Michael Dibdin *Ratking* 1989
> *Every year bright-eyed, bushy-tailed youngsters come from the four corners of the world to study Italian culture and promote peace and international understanding.*

the bright lights
the entertainments and (often false) allure of a large city. *Early 20th cent.*

> James Forbes *The Chorus Lady* 1906
> *I've met more than one doll as has thrown a good man down hard just to get back to the bright lights. They hand out a lot a junk about love for their art, when it's nothin' but a hunch for the excitement.*

> A S Byatt *Still Life* 1988
> *Drifting citywards in her generation, she had really hoped for Paris and bright lights.*

a bright spark
a clever person: often used ironically (especially in the form *some bright spark*) of somebody who has done something questionable or foolish. *20th cent.*

> New Scientist 1991
> *Some bright spark thought Windsor Castle was on fire and called the fire brigade!*

bright young thing
a fashionable and exuberant young person. The phrase took on a special social significance in the 1920s but is found earlier and later with more general reference. *19th cent.*

> R D Blackmore *Lorna Doone* 1869
> *Mr. Faggus gave his mare a wink, and she walked demurely after him, a bright young thing, flowing over with life, yet dropping her soul to a higher one,*

and led by love to anything, as the manner is of
females, when they know what is the best for them.

D H Lawrence *Phoenix* 1928
Show me somebody, then! And she shows me some
guy, or some bright young thing.

Management Today 1991
Of course no bright young thing who wants to
make a quick buck would consider going into the
ministry.

look on the bright side

to be optimistic. In early use also in the form *look*
on the best side. *18th cent.*

Daniel Defoe *Robinson Crusoe* 1719
I learned to look more upon the bright side of my
condition, and less upon the dark side, and to
consider what I enjoyed, rather than what I wanted.

bring

bring the house down

to get tumultuous applause from an audience:
from the notion of the uproar causing the building to collapse. Originally North American (in
the predominant American form *bring down the*
house). *18th cent.*

P H Myers *The King of the Hurons* 1850
He told of their inability to procure food, of their
unwillingness to beg in the great city, of an old
warrior who had sung his death-song in his empty
cabin – and finally 'brought down the house' by a
suddenly drawn picture of the good Henrich
appearing in their midst, with a sleigh-load of yel-
low maize.

Willa Cather *The Song of the Lark* 1915
When she sings, 'Just Before the Battle, Mother,'
she'll bring down the house.

See also bring home the BACON; bring something
HOME to somebody; bring somebody to BOOK;
bring something to light *at* LIGHT[2].

broad

(as) broad as it is long

much the same in all its options or alternatives.
17th cent.

Roger L'Estrange *An Answer to a Letter to a Dissenter*
1687
Whether the Church of England-Men reject the
Roman Catholiques, or the Roman Catholiques

reject the Church of England-Men, 'tis just as broad
as it is long.

Trollope *The Three Clerks* 1858
He wants you to accommodate him with the price of
them. You can either do that, or let him have so
many of your own; it will be as broad as it is long;
and he'll give you his note of hand for the amount.

have broad shoulders

to be capable of dealing with a great deal of work
and responsibility. Broad shoulders, a common
image in literature of the 19th cent., typified
physical strength.

E P Roe *What Can She Do?* 1873
'I've took a liking to you, and I can be a pretty fair
sort of friend if I do work for a livin'.' Mrs. Groody
was good if not grammatical. She had broad
shoulders, that had borne in their day many bur-
dens; her own and others.

in broad daylight

during the daytime, when it is light and one can
be seen: often used in the context of suspicious or
illicit activity. The phrase is 18th cent. in this
form, with earlier use of *broad* in this meaning.

Berkeley *A Treatise Concerning the Principles of*
Human Knowledge 1710
When in broad daylight I open my eyes, it is not in
my power to choose whether I shall see or no.

Christopher Morley *The Haunted Bookshop* 1919
He was eager to know what Weintraub was doing,
but did not dare make any investigations in broad
daylight.

See also broad in the BEAM.

broaden

See broaden one's horizons *at* HORIZON.

broke

go for broke

informal, originally NAmer to make strenuous
efforts, risking everything in the process: based
on the common informal meaning 'having no
money'. *Broke* is an old form of participial adjective from the verb *break*. *Mid 20th cent.*

broken

See a broken REED.

broker

See an HONEST broker.

broom

a new broom

somebody newly appointed to a job or role, and likely to make many changes. The phrase is 18th cent., with allusion to the (16th cent.) proverb *a new broom sweeps clean*.

John Henry Newman *Loss and Gain* 1848
Two great ladies, Mrs. Vice-Chancellor and Mrs. Divinity-Professor can't agree, and have followings respectively: or Vice-Chancellor himself, being a new broom, sweeps all the young masters clean out of the Convocation House, to their great indignation.

A N Wilson *C S Lewis: a Biography* 1990
But there was a new broom coming into the English Faculty at this period. This was the Rawlinson and Bosworth Professor of Anglo-Saxon … His name was J. R. R. Tolkien.

broth

a broth of a boy

informal, chiefly Anglo-Irish a lively young fellow: a 19th cent. metaphor based on the meaning of *broth* 'essence', which is recorded in abstract meanings from the 16th cent.

Byron *Don Juan* 1822
Juan was quite 'a broth of a boy', a thing of impulse and a child of song.

Dogs Today 1992
For an elderly dog, Luke is remarkably virile. He is, as my Irish friends would say, 'a broth of a boy'.

See also too many cooks spoil the broth *at* COOK.

brother

big brother

the State regarded as intrusive in people's lives. Used with allusion to the title of the head of state in George Orwell's novel *Nineteen Eighty-Four* (1949) about a totalitarian regime, which included the constant warning 'Big brother is watching you'. *Big Brother* gained further currency as the title of a voyeuristic 'reality' television programme shown in Britain from 2000, in which viewers continuously watch the behaviour of a group of contestants and vote for those who should be expelled from the group. Derived forms include *big-brotherdom* and *big-brotherly*. *Mid 20th cent.*

Glasgow Herald 1959
One sight of that terrible big-brotherly finger and we will redouble our efforts to find a litter basket.

East Anglian Daily Times 1993
Big Brother will be watching you from the end of this week when spy cameras start to operate in north-east Essex.

The Times 2001
One of the more contentious training issues [at call centres] is using recording equipment – staff resent 'Big Brother' listening in to calls, but some companies insist that it is a valuable way of improving standards.

brow

See by the SWEAT of one's brow.

brown

(as) brown as a berry

(said of a person) having suntanned skin. In early use, the meaning is 'having a dark complexion'. *Middle English*

Chaucer *The Cook's Tale* (line 4368)
A prentys [= apprentice] whilom [= once] dwelled in oure citee, | … Broun as a berye, a propre short felawe.

Sheridan *The School for Scandal* 1777
Here's to the maid with a bosom of snow: now to her that's as brown as a berry.

brown nose

informal an obsequious or sycophantic person: from the repellent image of holding the nose to the anus of the person whose favour is being sought. To *brown-nose* is to curry favour. *Mid 20th cent.*

M Pugh *The Last Place Left* 1969
It was part of the tradition to hate a Highland laird or be a brown-nose.

Melvyn Bragg *Crystal Rooms* 1993
A world which seemed to attract those whom Mark had suspected throughout his life, the penpushers in

the army, the toadies at school, the brown nose specialists.

See also in a brown STUDY.

brownie

brownie point

credit for an achievement, regarded as an imaginary award. The phrase is most probably connected with the notion that points are awarded for achievements to members of the Brownies, the junior section of the Guides; but it has been heavily influenced, especially in recent usage, by the less wholesome activities of the *brown nose. Mid 20th cent.*

> Gill Edwards *Living Magically* 1991
> *We are not awarded extra Brownie points in heaven for living a life full of suffering, nor for one which is dull and dreary.*

brunt

bear the brunt of something

to be the person who bears the main responsibility or consequence of a burden or misfortune: originally with reference to attacks in military engagements. *Brunt* is a Middle English word originally meaning 'a sharp blow or attack'. The meaning in the phrase dates from the 16th cent., and this phrase is now the only use. The form *stand the (first) brunt* is 17th cent.

> Aphra Behn *The Rover* 1677
> *Oh Lord! she's as tall as the St. Christopher in Notre-dame at Paris ... I shall ne'er be able to stand the first Brunt.*

> Thomas Paine *The Rights of Man* 1792
> *As M. de la Fayette, from the experience of what he had seen in America, was better acquainted with the science of civil government ... the brunt of the business fell considerably to his share.*

> Jane Austen *Emma* 1816
> *'Is Miss Woodhouse sure that she would like to hear what we are all thinking of?' 'Oh! no, no' – cried Emma ... – 'Upon no account in the world. It is the very last thing I would stand the brunt of just now.'*

brush

get the brush-off

informal, originally NAmer to be rebuffed or snubbed. *Give somebody the brush-off* is to be the initiator of the snub. The image is of brushing something unwanted off one's clothing, the furniture, etc. *Mid 20th cent.*

See also (as) DAFT as a brush; be tarred with the same brush *at* TAR.

bubble

See BURST somebody's bubble.

buck[1] (a dollar)

make a fast buck

informal to make a quick profit from a dubious transaction or enterprise. The origin of *buck* in this sense is uncertain. *Mid 20th cent.*

> *Weekly Hansard* 1989
> *You will look after the fast buck merchants who are waiting to come in to steal and cheat and to deal in a shoddy, grasping way with bus companies that have been made successful by the local authorities.*

buck[2] (a piece used in poker)

The origin is uncertain, but this is a different word from the one meaning 'dollar' (see above).

the buck stops here / with —

the final responsibility lies with a particular person: said by American President Harry S Truman (1884–1972) in 1952 to be the words printed on a sign on his office desk. *Mid 20th cent.*

> William Tench *Safety is No Accident* 1985
> *The Chief Inspector is, of course, responsible for everything AIB does – the buck stops with him as far as aircraft accident investigation in the UK is concerned.*

pass the buck

to pass to somebody else a responsibility that one should properly take oneself: in poker, the buck was placed before the dealer. *Early 20th cent.*

> Edmund Wilson *Devil Take the Hindmost* 1932
> *He invariably passes the buck to his subordinates.*

> David Freemantle *Profitboss* 1988
> *Isn't it easier to pass the buck to your boss, some staff person or a committee?*

buck³

buck up one's ideas

to make a greater effort; to work harder. The phrase is based on the verb *buck*, describing the action of a horse or mule springing into the air with its feet together and its back curved: this sense is related to the noun *buck* meaning 'a male deer'. *Buck up*, meaning 'to become cheerful' or 'to hurry', is also derived from these words. *20th cent.*

> **Guardian 2003**
> *Education vouchers would introduce a market mechanism that might just persuade some schools to buck their ideas up.*

buck⁴

buck the trend

informal to act contrary to the general tendency or expectation; to be original or innovative. The meaning of *buck* 'to oppose' is an early 20th cent. figurative use of the sense 'to butt against'. *Late 20th cent.*

> **Guardian 1984**
> *Only lead and tin, in fact, have been able to buck the trend, both sustained by their own very special circumstances. Neither market, however, can be viewed as fundamentally strong, especially over the longer term.*

bucket

See a DROP in the ocean / a bucket; KICK the bucket.

Buckley

not have Buckley's (chance)

Australian and NZ, informal to have no chance of succeeding. The name is thought to be that of William Buckley, an escaped convict who lived with Aborigines for many years; but there are alternative suggestions. *19th cent.*

buckram

men in buckram

old use imaginary or non-existent people: with allusion to the 'assailants' (in fact Prince Harry and Poins) of Falstaff in Shakespeare *1 Henry IV*

(1596) II.v.194: '[Falstaff] Two I am sure I have paid – two rogues in buckram suits. I tell thee what, Hal, if I tell thee a lie, spit in my face, call me horse ... Four rogues in buckram let drive at me. [Prince Harry] What, four? Thou saidst but two even now.' *16th cent.*

bud

See NIP something in the bud.

buff

in/to the buff

informal naked. The meaning 'bare skin' dates from the 17th cent. as an extension of meanings designating kinds of skin-coloured clothing and uniform. The phrase dates from the 19th cent. in this form.

> **James Joyce A Portrait of the Artist as a Young Man 1916**
> *My first cousin, Fonsy Davin, was stripped to his buff that day minding cool for the Limericks.*

bug

get / have / be bitten by the bug

to feel a sudden strong enthusiasm for something. *Bug* in the meaning 'enthusiast' dates from the 19th cent. The phrases are mid 20th cent. in their present form.

> **Nevil Shute No Highway 1948**
> *I love being on aerodromes and seeing aeroplanes. It's a sort of bug that gets in you.*

Buggins

Buggins' turn

assignment of a duty on the basis of rotation rather than merit. The phrase is also shortened to *Buggins*, and is based on the typical humdrum type of surname used to represent anybody of no particular importance. It appears in 19th cent. literature, notably as the name of two characters in Trollope: an official in *Framley Parsonage* (1861) and Mrs Buggins in *The Way We Live Now* (1875). The phrase is first used in print during the First World War, in a letter of 1917 from Admiral (later Lord) Fisher: 'I was sorry for Jellicoe superseding Callaghan when the war broke out, but I remembered your old saying, 'Some day the Empire will go down because it is Buggins's turn!' *Early 20th cent.*

> **Winston Churchill** *The Second World War* 1952
> *The departmental view is no doubt opposed to long tenures and the doctrine of 'Buggins's turn' is very powerful.*

> **Julian Critchley** *The Floating Voter* 1993
> *An ironmonger and former captain in the TA, Kevin Malcolm had become, thanks to Buggins, Chairman of the local Chamber of Commerce.*

build

be built on sand
to have no secure foundations: from the parable in Matthew 7:24–7 of the foolish man who built his house on sand contrasted with the wise man who built his on rock. *16th cent.*

> **Ralph Crane** *The Pilgrimes New-yeares-gift* 1625
> *He that to this Soules-Succour lends a hand, | Helpes to remoue this house built vpon Sand, | And sets it on a Rock (his Sauiours Trust) | To the next Worke of comfort he'll be iust.*

> **Trollope** *Phineas Redux* 1874
> *The bitter part of my cup consists in this, – that as he has won what he has deserved, so have we. I complain of no injustice. Our castle was built upon the sand.*

bulge

have/get the bulge on somebody
to have an advantage over somebody: from the meaning of *bulge* 'a part that protrudes', which is closely associated with the verb in its corresponding meaning. *19th cent.*

> **Mark Twain** *A Tramp Abroad* 1880
> *NOW I guess I've got the bulge on you by this time!*

See also be bursting/bulging at the seams *at* SEAM.

bull

like a bull at a gate
hastily and impetuously. *19th cent.*

like a bull in a china shop
extremely clumsy or tactless. *19th cent.*

> **Thackeray** *Vanity Fair* 1848
> *Jos, a clumsy and timid horseman, did not look to advantage in the saddle. 'Look at him, Amelia, dear,*

driving into the parlour window. Such a bull in a china-shop I never saw.'

> **Fiona Pitt-Kethley** *Misfortunes of Nigel* 1991
> *Anthony was always on the phone, rushing about like a bull in a china shop, or lying in bed till twelve with one or other of his girlfriends.*

a red rag to a bull
something that makes a person angry or violent: from the belief that bulls are angered by the colour red, which is the colour of the matador's cape in a bullfight. *19th cent.*

> **Hardy** *The Mayor of Casterbridge* 1886
> *Any suspicion of impropriety was to Elizabeth-Jane like a red rag to a bull.*

take the bull by the horns
to face up to a problem and take decisive action: the image is from a form of bullfighting in which the matador first tires the bull then seizes it by the horns and tries to bring it to the ground. *Cf* Spanish *coger el toro por los cuernos*, French *prendre le taureau par les cornes*. *18th cent.*

> **Isaac Bickerstaff** *Love in a Village* 1763
> *Never exasperate a jealous woman, 'tis taking a mad bull by the horns; – Leave me to manage her.*

> **Scott** *Old Mortality* 1816
> *Now Cuddie, though a brave enough fellow upon the whole, was by no means fond of danger, either for its own sake, or for that of the glory which attends it. In his advance, therefore, he had not, as the phrase goes, taken the bull by the horns, or advanced in front of the enemy's fire.*

> **Henry James** *Confidence* 1880
> *Bernard came straight up to her, with a gallant smile and a greeting. The comparison is a coarse one, but he felt that he was taking the bull by the horns.*

bullet

See BITE (on) the bullet; SWEAT bullets.

bully

bully for —
an (often ironic) expression of congratulations. The sense of *bully* in the phrase is 'admirable, worthy' (17th cent.). In origin it is an adjectival use of a term of endearment common in Shakespeare (e.g. *A Midsummer Night's Dream* (1595)

III.i.8: 'What sayst thou, bully Bottom?'). *19th cent.*

> Gene Stratton Porter *The Girl from the Limberlost* 1909
> *Edith shook hands with all of them ... and went away, gracefully. 'Well bully for her!' said Mrs. Comstock. 'She's a little thoroughbred after all!'*

> Ruth Rendell *The Best Man to Die* 1981
> *'If I'm going to be a real actress I'll have to know what makes people tick. I'm getting quite good at summing people up.' 'Bully for you,' said her father sourly.*

bum

Middle English: probably onomatopoeic or related to *bump*, and not a contraction of *bottom*, which is not recorded in this meaning until a later date.

bums on seats
the audience at a theatre or other place of entertainment, regarded as a source of income. *Late 20th cent.*

> Sasha Stone *Kylie Minogue* 1989
> *I've been offered lots of films just because the producers thought I would put bums on seats.*

give somebody the bum's rush
informal to eject somebody forcibly: from the image of a person being rushed out unceremoniously by the seat of the pants. *Early 20th cent.*

bump

things that go bump in the night
ghosts and supernatural beings: from the traditional association of ghosts (especially poltergeists) with sudden intrusive noises. The phrase is probably derived from the prayer rhyme that includes the lines 'From Ghoulies and Ghosties | And Long Leggetty Beasties | And things that go bump in the night | Good Lord, deliver us'. *Early 20th cent.*

> *Guardian* 1984
> *I used to trot up the wooden hills to Bedfordshire without thought of bogeymen. Now I pull on my pyjamas knowing that the things that go bump in the night are my elbows colliding with the headboard as I try to re-arrange my pillows.*

bumper

bumper-to-bumper
(said of vehicles) close together in heavy traffic. *Mid 20th cent.*

> Nina Bawden *Tortoise by Candlelight* 1989
> *On the road, the cars hooted, bumper to bumper in the week-end crawl to the coast.*

bun

have a bun in the oven
informal to be pregnant. *Mid 20th cent.*

> Nicholas Monsarrat *The Cruel Sea* 1951
> *'I bet you left a bun in the oven, both of you,' said Bennett thickly ... Lockhart explained ... the reference to pregnancy.*

bunch

bunch of fives
a fist, or a blow with the fist: with reference to the fingers and thumb of the human hand. *19th cent.*

> Charles Reade *Hard Cash* 1863
> *'Now look at that bunch of fives,' continued the master; and laid a hand white and soft as a duchess's on the table.*

> Brian Aldiss *Soldier Erect* 1971
> *My regret was that I had not given Wally a bunch of fives in the mush while I had the chance.*

See also the PICK of the bunch.

bundle

A word of Middle English origin, although abstract meanings are relatively recent (19th cent.).

a bundle of fun/laughs
informal a person or thing that is a source of great amusement, enjoyment, etc: *see also* BARREL. *Mid 20th cent.*

drop one's bundle
Australian and NZ, informal to give up hope; to abandon an undertaking. *Bundle* is an old word for 'swag'. *19th cent.*

> P Newton *Wayleggo* 1947
> *My confidence immediately disappeared. However, I could not 'drop my bundle', so into the jungle I went.*

go a bundle on something

British, informal to like or be enthusiastic about: usually in negative contexts. Bundle here means 'a bundle of money' and the phrase originally referred to placing a large bet. Mid 20th cent.

Gavin Lyall The Conduct of Major Maxim 1982
I imagine you've noticed that our dear Prime Minister doesn't exactly go a bundle on us, on any of us?

make a bundle

informal to earn a lot of money: from the image of a bundle or wad of notes. Late 20th cent.

Timothy Mo The Redundancy of Courage 1991
The day of the opening of Danu to the emissions of the outside world, a couple of ancient boats gurgled alongside the wharf, bearing a crowd of stage extras from the outlying, historically malai islands. They were making a bundle of money these days, one way or another.

See also a bag/bundle of nerves at NERVE.

bung

go bung

Australian, informal to die or fail catastrophically. Bung is an Australian Aboriginal word. 19th cent.

bunk

do a bunk

informal to escape hurriedly, especially to avoid an obligation or commitment. The origin of this word bunk (and of the corresponding phrasal verb bunk off which dates from the same time) is unknown: it is probably not connected with the words meaning 'a bed' and 'nonsense'. 19th cent.

G B Shaw Back to Methuselah 1921
If my legs would support me I'd just do a bunk straight for the ship.

burden

See the WHITE man's burden.

burl

give it a burl

Australian, informal to try to do something. From a British dialect word (also birl) meaning 'to spin or twirl'. 20th cent.

C James Charles Charming's Challenges 1981
We're real thrilled You're giving Timbertop a burl, Your Grace.

burn

burn one's boats/bridges

to commit oneself irrevocably to a course of action: a metaphor from military operations, in which an invading army might burn the boats or bridges it had used in the advance so as to preclude retreat and make a successful assault the only option. 19th cent.

James Payn By Proxy 1878
After a severe mental struggle, he had destroyed the will, and so far 'burned his boats'. No retreat lay open to him along the broad straight road of honour.

Edgar Rice Burroughs Son of Tarzan 1915
He had burned his bridges behind him. He must either climb aloft or drop back into the river.

Esquire 1993
He burned his bridges, and, working solely on small-scale projects over which he had total control, descended into drink and drugs.

burn the candle at both ends

1 to spend money extravagantly. In this meaning, the image is of a wasteful use of a candle. 18th cent.

Smollett The Expedition of Humphry Clinker 1771
O Molly! the servants at Bath are devils in garnet. They lite the candle at both ends – Here's nothing but ginketting, and waisting, and thieving, and tricking, and trigging and then they are never content.

Adele Geras The Green Behind the Glass 1989
I thought now was supposed to be the marvellous time, and we're all meant to be living it up, burning the candle at both ends, finding out what we want to do with our lives.

2 to be active at night as well as by day. The image here is of the two ends of the candle representing (symbolically and, when burning, actually) the periods of day and night. 19th cent.

Nathaniel Parker Willis Saratoga 1847
After dinner she mingles in the full-dress crowd once more till tea-time (with perhaps the parenthesis of a drive with a party to the lake), and from tea-time till midnight she is in the same crowd, and goes to bed late to get up again early, and so,

burning her candle at both ends, finds Saratoga enchanting.

Janet Neel *Death of a Partner* 1991
Catherine … was looking a bittie pale; was it just the London air, or had she been burning the candle at both ends?

burn a hole in one's pocket
(said of ready cash) to keep reminding one that it is there to spend, so that it doesn't last long. The phrase is 18th cent. in the current form, but the notion goes back earlier.

Elijah Fenton *Poems on Several Occasions* 1717
The Marriage Earnest-penny lay | And burnt her Pocket, as we say.

Henry James *Confidence* 1880
Bernard's winnings of the previous night were burning a hole, as the phrase is, in his pocket.

burn the midnight oil
to stay up late into the night working or reading. *17th cent.*

Francis Quarles *Emblems* 1635
Wee spend our mid-day sweat, our mid-night oyle; | Wee tyre the night in thought; the day, in toyle.

Trollope *Can You Forgive Her?* 1864
Mr. Palliser always burnt the midnight oil and came to bed with the owls.

slow burn
a growing feeling of anger or annoyance. *Mid 20th cent.*

Josephine Tey *Daughter of Time* 1951
Just a nice polite reasonable Act for him to swallow and like it. I bet he did a slow burn about that one.

Joanna Neil *The Waters of Eden* 1993
He did not look the least bit sorry, Lissa decided irritably. The slow burn of resentment smouldered inside her.

See also burn DAYLIGHT; burn one's fingers *at* FINGER; burn RUBBER; one's ears are burning *at* EAR; have MONEY to burn.

burner

on the back/front burner
informal having a low (or high) priority: from the notion of cooking pots needing less attention when placed at the back of a stove to simmer. *Late 20th cent.*

The Times 1985
Despite the talk of economic reform, there has been a serious neglect of Poland's economic infrastructure, the road and railways, the water and sewage systems, and the social network, the schools and the hospitals. Anything that has not been earmarked directly for export and for earning dollars has been put on the back burner.

burnt

burnt to a cinder/crisp
so burnt as to be ruined or demolished; burnt black. *19th cent.*

Hardy *Far from the Madding Crowd* 1874
'The ladder was against the straw-rick and is burnt to a cinder,' said a spectre-like form in the smoke.

Ray Pickernell *Yanto's Summer* 1988
During the festivities a hastily built bonfire was set alight in the middle of the market place, and an equally hastily assembled replica of the Japanese Emperor was burnt to a cinder on top of it.

buroo

on the buroo/broo
informal, chiefly Scottish and Irish on the dole. *Buroo* (or *broo*) is an informal Scottish and Irish form of *bureau*, used for a Labour Exchange. *Mid 20th cent.*

burr

a burr under/in one's saddle
NAmer a source of constant irritation: the meaning of *burr* here is 'a rough or prickly covering of a fruit or seed'. *20th cent.*

burst

burst a blood vessel
to strain oneself from anger or physical effort. *19th cent.*

Emerson Bennett *Viola* 1852
The moment he saw me, he gave vent to such screams of laughter, that I really began to fear he would burst a blood-vessel and alarm the house.

The Times 2001
In general, a gent removes his hat on coming indoors. That is why the Victorian hall invented the

hatstand. *But modern mores with baseball caps worn back to front and the beret have complicated customs. I should take off your hat indoors. But try not to burst a blood-vessel if younger men have other customs.*

burst somebody's bubble

to dispel a person's illusions or optimism: a bubble was a common image for anything fragile or transitory. *Late 20th cent.*

Dana James *Bay of Rainbows* 1993
She refused to allow his surliness to burst her bubble of well-being.

See also be bursting at the seams *at* SEAM.

Burton

go for a Burton

British, informal to be destroyed or killed: originally with reference to airmen in the Second World War, but now usually in more trivial contexts. The origin of the phrase is uncertain, but a number of anecdotes connect it with Burton-on-Trent in Staffordshire, England, and the celebrated 'Burton ale' produced there. More specifically, it may be based on rhyming slang for *went* (as in *went west* meaning 'was destroyed'); it may relate to the phrase *in the drink* in connection with the shooting down of aircraft out at sea; or it may refer to prewar advertisements for beer, which showed a group of people with one of their number clearly missing – because he (it was invariably he) had *gone for a Burton*, i.e. to get a drink: but how could an obviously enjoyable activity have been the source of such a fatal meaning? Other stories that have arisen to explain the obscure phrase might be of interest: (1) that it refers to the tailors Montague Burton: *going for a Burton* meant getting measured for a suit, the analogy being measurement for a 'wooden overcoat', i.e. a coffin, (2) that an aircraft shot down in flames was called a *burnt 'un*, and (3) that *burton* was a name for various complex devices on board a ship which required a great deal of attention to make them work, so that *gone for a burton* might be an explanation for members of the crew being missing for a lengthy period. *Mid 20th cent.*

Ted Lewis *Get Carter* 1992
The bouncer jumped back to life, but not half as much as he jumped when he turned and saw me
gazing into his eyes from about six inches away. He didn't exactly scream but his blow-wave went for a burton.

bury

bury the hatchet/tomahawk

to settle a disagreement and become reconciled: from the 17th cent. North American Indian practice of burying two hatchets in the ground as a symbol of peace when negotiations to end hostilities were conducted. *18th cent.*

Robert Rogers *Ponteach* 1766
We're glad to see our Brothers here the English. | If honourable Peace be your Desire, | We'd always have the Hatchet buried deep.

Louisa M Alcott *Little Women* 1868
Jenny Snow, a satirical young lady, who had basely twitted Amy … promptly buried the hatchet, and offered to furnish answers to certain appalling sums.

bury one's head in the sand

to refuse to face up to unpleasant or awkward realities: from the practice traditionally attributed to the ostrich of hiding its head in the sand when pursued, believing that if it could not see its pursuers it too must be unseen. The phrase is first found in the 19th cent. in uses that refer directly, in simile form, to the ostrich.

George Sterling *The Play of Everyman* 1917
And will you bury in the sand your head, | To hide the sight of Death's approach, my son? | Lo! he may come to-morrow!

Janet Tanner *Folly's Child* 1991
She was used to his ostrich ways – his ability to bury his head in the sand and shut out the things that displeased or upset him.

bush

the bush telegraph

an informal means of spreading information rapidly: originally with reference to the network of informants in the Australian outback who passed on information about the whereabouts of the police. *19th cent.*

Daily Telegraph 1992
Xan Smiley in Washington senses relief on the Bush telegraph over Kinnock's defeat, but bad vibrations among Clinton's puzzled Democrats.

See also BEAT about the bush.

bushel

hide one's light under a bushel
to keep one's talents and merits hidden: with allusion to Christ's words in the Sermon on the Mount as given in Matthew 5:15 in Tyndale's translation (16th cent.) and in the Authorized Version of 1611: 'Neither do men light a candle, and put it under a bushel, but on a candlestick; and it giveth light unto all that are in the house.' A *bushel* is a measure of capacity for corn and (in the phrase) a vessel containing this measure. *16th cent.*

> Richardson *The History of Sir Charles Grandison* 1753
> *What can a woman do, who is addressed by a man of talents inferior to her own? Must she throw away her talents? Must she hide her light under a bushel, purely to do credit to the man? She cannot pick and choose, as men can.*

> Henry James *The Europeans* 1878
> *Of course with me she will hide her light under a bushel ... I being the bushel!*

business

A Middle English word with two main branches of meaning: 'the state of being busy' (distinguished in modern English by its spelling *busyness*) and 'a person's duty or occupation'.

business as usual
circumstances are normal (especially after an interruption or disruption). *19th cent.*

> Julian Huxley *On Living in a Revolution* 1944
> *The subordination of the profit motive and all ideas of 'business as usual' to the non-economic motive of success in war.*

the business end
the part of a tool or weapon that performs the necessary function: often in humorous use. *19th cent.*

> L M Montgomery *Anne of Green Gables* 1908
> *Mr. Barry came back with Anne, carrying a coil of rope to which was attached a claw-like instrument that had been the business end of a grubbing fork.*

in business
ready to conduct one's work or business operations: originally with reference to commercial operations but also informally in wider application of any activity. *20th cent.*

> Climber and Hillwalker 1991
> *Armed with the right gear and correct information, we were in business.*

make it one's business (to do something)
to take positive steps to do something. *17th cent.*

> Aphra Behn *The Fair Jilt* 1688
> *There was not a man of any quality that came to Antwerp, or pass'd through the city, but made it his business to see the lovely Miranda, who was universally ador'd.*

mean business
to speak or act with serious intent, to be in earnest. *19th cent.*

> Dickens *Little Dorrit* 1857
> *This gentleman, happening also to be the Plaintiff in the Tip case, referred Mr. Plornish to his solicitor, and declined to treat with Mr. Plornish, or even to endure his presence in the yard, unless he appeared there with a twenty-pound note: in which case only, the gentleman would augur from appearances that he meant business, and might be induced to talk to him.*

> Joanna Neil *The Waters of Eden* 1993
> *And you can forget the black looks; I mean business.*

nobody's business
something noteworthy or exceptional; often in the form *like nobody's business* = to an exceptional degree. *19th cent.*

> Louisa M Alcott *Hospital Sketches* 1869
> *At this juncture I took the veil, and what I did behind it is nobody's business; but I maintain that the soldier who cries when his mother says 'Good bye,' is the boy to fight best, and die bravest, when the time comes, or go back to her better than he went.*

> Barbara Whitehead *The Dean It Was That Died* 1991
> *You couldn't trust him, but he could send a ball like nobody's business.*

open for business
able to operate effectively, especially after an interruption: originally with reference to commercial organizations and extended to more generalized contexts. The phrase was a common slogan signifying a return to normal life in the British countryside during the later stages of a foot-and-mouth disease outbreak that affected most of Britain in 2001. *Late 20th cent.*

The Times 1986
Paradise exists and is still open for business in a world of package tours and over-population, on the southern shores of the Mediterranean and a little more than three hours' flying from London.

Keesings Contemporary Archives 1990
The adoption of these principles made it 'more likely that current trends towards market economies and political pluralism will continue', and was a signal to the West that Eastern Europe was now 'open for business'.

The Times 2001
The minister responsible for Rural Britain says that the countryside is open for business, but if he visits his Cotswold weekend retreat he will find the reverse is true.

See also MIND one's own business.

busman

a busman's holiday
a holiday or period of free time that involves the same activity as a person's normal work. In the 19th cent. it was common for working people to be rewarded with outings by coach. The phrase originates in British (and chiefly London) use and has extended to other varieties. In America, folk etymologies have arisen to add extra colour to the more mundane authentic explanation. The most commonly repeated of these associates the phrase with the drivers of early horse-drawn omnibuses, who became so devoted to their horses that they would visit them on their days off to make sure they were being properly looked after. This thick layer of sentimentality gives scant recognition to the realities of city life and of the conditions of working animals at this date. *19th cent.*

bust

See bust a GUT.

busted

a busted flush
informal something that does not meet one's expectations; a failure: a metaphor from poker, where it refers to a sequence of cards (a *flush*) that a player fails to complete and is therefore

'broken'. *Busted* is the past participle of *bust* (= to break), itself a variant of *burst*. Early 20th cent.

Frederick Forsyth The Negotiator 1989
'What the hell do you want to see GM for?' asked Brown. 'He failed. He's a busted flush.'

busy

(as) busy as a bee
extremely busy. Another set simile, *busy as a hen with one chicken* (or *two chickens*), is found from the 16th cent. to the 19th cent. *Middle English*

Chaucer The Merchant's Tale (line 2422)
Lo, whiche sleightes and subtilitees | In wommen been! For ay as bisy as bees | Been they, us sely [= unfortunate] men for to deceyve.

butcher

the butcher, the baker, the candlestick-maker
people of every kind: with allusion to the nursery rhyme *Rub-a-dub-dub*, which is recorded from the late 18th cent. There are several versions, of which the most familiar now is given below. Allusive uses date from the 19th cent.
Rub-a-dub-dub,
Three men in a tub,
And how do you think they got there?
The butcher, the baker,
The candlestick-maker,
They all jumped out of a rotten potato,
'Twas enough to make a man stare.

Robert Browning The Ring and the Book 1842
If wealth, not rank, had been prime object in your thoughts, why not have taken the butcher's son, the boy o' the baker or candlestick-maker?

have/take a butcher's
British, *informal* to take a look: rhyming slang based on *butcher's hook* (= look). *Mid 20th cent.*

Kingsley Amis Take A Girl Like You 1960
Have a butcher's at the News of the World.

butter

look as if butter wouldn't melt in one's mouth
to look deceptively meek or demure. The expression first occurs in print in a work on the French language by John Palsgrave (1530), although he was probably reporting it rather than inventing

it. The symbolism is a little unclear, but the notion of butter staying hard in the mouth is perhaps suggestive of innocent nonchalance concealing something more sinister. *16th cent.*

Charlotte Smith *The Old Manor House* 1793
'Tell me, Betty,' said Monimia tremulously, 'tell me what you know.' 'Why I know – that though he looks as if butter wouldn't melt in his mouth, cheese won't choke him. I can tell you what, Miss, he's slyer than his brother, but not a bitter gooder—What's more, he lets women into his room at night.'

James Joyce *A Portrait of the Artist as a Young Man* 1916
You'd think butter wouldn't melt in your mouth, said Heron. But I'm afraid you're a sly dog.

butterfingers

have / be a butterfingers
to be unable to catch or keep hold of something: from the notion of fingers covered in grease being incapable of gripping or holding. *19th cent.*

Dickens *Pickwick Papers* 1837
At every bad attempt to catch, and every failure to stop the ball, he launched his personal displeasure at the head of the devoted individual in such denunciations as "Ah, ah! Stupid!" – "Now, butter-fingers" – "Muff" – "Humbug" – and so forth – ejaculations which seemed to establish him in the opinion of all around, as a most excellent and undeniable judge of the whole art and mystery of the noble game of cricket.

butterfly

butterflies in one's stomach
an uneasy sensation felt in the stomach as a result of nervousness or apprehension. This gently romantic image is presumably based on the notion that the fluttering of butterflies might produce a similar sensation. *Early 20th cent.*

the butterfly effect
the progressive production of a far-reaching effect by a small and apparently insignificant cause. The phrase is derived from chaos theory as stated by the American mathematician Edward Norton Lorenz (b.1917), who postulated the possibility that the flapping of a butterfly's wings in Brazil could begin a chain of events that eventually led to a tornado developing in Texas. *Late 20th cent.*

button

button one's lip/face
informal to remain silent: from the image of fastening a piece of clothing. *19th cent.*

on the button
with absolute precision; exactly right or at the right time: based on the use of *button* to mean any of various small and precisely placed round parts, e.g. the point of the chin. Cf on the NOSE. *20th cent.*

Martin Amis *Time's Arrow* 1991
The kind of set-up that any sane man would kill for, with her punctual visits and affectionate phone calls, the movies we enjoy together, the fine dining, … plus the exquisitely torpid lovemaking which takes place right on the button every couple of months or so.

press the button
to begin action or set events in train: from the literal use with reference to setting a device, machinery, etc in operation. In the period of cold-war politics after 1945, the phrase became particularly associated with the danger of one side or the other starting a nuclear war, and the apparent logistical ease with which this could be done. The phrase is found in the 19th cent., chiefly in literal senses.

G K Chesterton *The Innocence of Father Brown* 1911
It's some clockwork invention for doing all the housework by machinery. You know the sort of thing: 'Press a Button – A Butler who Never Drinks.' 'Turn a Handle – Ten Housemaids who Never Flirt.'

put one's finger on the button
to identify the salient or apposite point. *20th cent.*

Cathy Williams *A French Encounter* 1992
'Daddy, darling,' Alyssia said, smiling genuinely for the first time since she had stepped foot back on to English soil and kissing him on the tip of his nose, 'in your own cantankerous way, you've put your finger right on the button.'

See also hit/press/push the PANIC button.

buy

buy time

to act in a way that allows one more time to improve one's circumstances: the buying metaphor implies the notion that a price has to be paid. *17th cent.*

Dryden transl Plutarch's *Sertorius* 1690
But he little regarded their censure, and ... told them he must buy time, the most precious of all things to those who go upon great enterprises.

K Eric Drexler *Engines of Creation* 1985
In another tactic for buying time, the leading force can attempt to burn the bridge it built from bulk to molecular technology.

See also buy the FARM; buy a PUP.

buzz

feel / get / give somebody a buzz

to become (or make somebody) excited. Figurative meanings of *buzz* to do with noise and bustle date from the 17th cent.; Addison writing in 1712 claimed that he 'found the whole ... room in a buz of Politicks'. Meanings associated with emotional stimulation and excitement are much more recent, dating from the 20th cent. *Mid 20th cent.*

J Krantz *Scruples* 1978
She walked up Rodeo or down Camden, feeling a sexual buzz as she searched the windows for new merchandise.

by

by and large

generally speaking, on the whole. The phrase was originally a nautical term for the movement of a ship close to the wind (= *by*) and off it (= *large*), making it easier to steer; in early extended use it had a more physical meaning 'everywhere' or 'in all directions'. *17th cent.*

Matthew Stevenson *The Wits Paraphras'd* 1680
To shew his malice by and large, | And save the parish of a charge, | He sends the bastard to the bogs, | To be a breakfast for the dogs.

Harold Frederic *The Damnation of Theron Ware* 1896
They've got their good streaks and their bad streaks, just like the rest of us. Take them by and large,

they're quite on a par with other folks the whole country through.

bygone

let bygones be bygones

to forgive past offences. *Bygone* is a Middle English word, recorded first as an adjective in the meaning 'that has passed' (with reference to time). This is the meaning in Hermione's words at the beginning of Shakespeare's *The Winter's Tale* (1611) I.ii.32: 'This satisfaction | The bygone day proclaimed.' The phrase is 17th cent. in its current form.

Samuel Rutherford *Letter* 1636
Pray ... that byegones betwixt me and my Lord may be byegones.

Somerset Maugham *The Moon and Sixpence* 1919
I want him to come back. If he'll do that we'll let bygones be bygones. After all, we've been married for seventeen years.

C

the big C

informal, euphemistic cancer, regarded as spelt with a capital letter (*see also* CAPITAL). *Late 20th cent.*

> Medau News 1985
> *£150 was raised for the 'BIG C' appeal (Norfolk's cancer research charity) at a … 'get-together'.*

cabbage

See not as GREEN as one is cabbage-looking.

caboodle

the whole (kit and) caboodle

everybody or everything: probably from an obsolete word *boodle* meaning 'lot, large amount', the element *ca-* being an intensive prefix. An alternative suggestion is that it is a corruption of *kit and boodle* meaning 'a collection of equipment', *kit* being a kind of vessel and *boodle* having the meaning just given. (*Boodle* may have been derived from a Dutch word *boedel* meaning 'possession, inheritance'. In 19th cent. American slang, *boodle* also meant 'counterfeit money', but this may well be a different word and it probably does not influence the use in this phrase.) The phrase has had many fanciful variations, sometimes alliterative (e.g. *whole kit and cargo*) and sometimes not (e.g. *whole kit and bilin'*). Francis Grose's *Dictionary of the Vulgar Tongue* (1785) entered the short form *the whole kit* to explain the meaning of *kit*: 'Kit … is also used to express the whole of different commodities; as, Here, take the whole kit; i.e. take all.' *19th cent.*

> Mary Jane Holmes Edna Browning 1872
> *I've no great reason to like that sect, seeing about the only one I ever knew intimately turned out a regular*

hornet, a lucifer match, the very old Harry himself; didn't adorn the profession; was death on Unitarians, and sent the whole caboodle of us to perdition.

cackle

cut the cackle

informal to stop irrelevant talking and make one's point: a metaphor from the noise made by geese and other animals. The use of *cackle* to refer to sounds made by humans is as old as the use relating to animals. *19th cent.*

> Louise & Aylmer Maude transl Tolstoy's War and Peace 1869
> *And why the deuce are we going to fight Bonaparte? … He has stopped Austria's cackle and I fear it will be our turn next.*

Caesar

The Roman general and statesman (100–44 BC).

(like) Caesar's wife

(like) a woman whose position requires that she should be free of any suspicion. The reference is to the account in Plutarch's life of Julius Caesar of Caesar's divorce from his wife Pompeia on the grounds of her association with the notorious libertine Publius Clodius. Clodius was tried for sacrilege after appearing dressed as a woman at the fertility mysteries of Bona Dea in Caesar's house in 62 BC. A proverb *Caesar's wife must be above suspicion* is also recorded in various forms from the 16th cent., notably in Lord North's translation of Plutarch. *19th cent.*

> Richard Penn Smith The Forsaken 1831
> *We know what is due to our station, and the man who marries Miss Morton must be like Cæsar's wife, major, take my word for it.*

> Gavin Lyall The Conduct of Major Maxim 1982
> *And while you're still working at Number 10, a touch of Caesar's wife might be appropriate.*

See also APPEAL to Caesar.

cage

See RATTLE somebody's cage.

cahoots

in cahoots (with somebody)

informal, originally NAmer working or acting in collaboration (with somebody), usually secretly and for an illicit or dishonest purpose: formerly also in the form *in cahoot*. The word *cahoot* may be from French *cahute* meaning 'cabin, hut' or from *cohort*. A verb *cahoot* meaning 'to act in partnership' is also recorded in 19th cent. American use. *19th cent.*

> John William De Forest *Playing the Mischief* 1875
> *He would cheat any body, old or young, gentle or simple, man or woman, saint or sinner, with the same bland greediness and impenitence ... Had he been one of the apostles, he would have played the part of Judas, and got a much better bargain, and never have hanged himself. Had he been one of the converts of the day of Pentecost, he would have gone 'cahoots' with Ananias and Sapphira. In short, he was one of our greatest financial managers and railroaders.*

Cain

The name of the son of Adam and Eve and the murderer of his brother Abel (Genesis 4).

the mark of Cain

the sign of a murderer. The phrase comes from the account in Genesis (4:15), in which God condemned Cain to the life of a fugitive but protected him from harm: 'And the Lord said unto him, Therefore whosoever slayeth Cain, vengeance shall be taken on him sevenfold. And the Lord set a mark upon Cain, lest any finding him should kill him.' *The Mark of Cain* is the title of a melodramatic novel (published in 1886) by the Scottish writer Andrew Lang. *19th cent.*

> Hardy *The Return of the Native* 1878
> *Reddle spreads its lively hues over everything it lights on, and stamps unmistakably, as with the mark of Cain, any person who has handled it half an hour.*

> T G Mahaddie *Hamish: the Story of a Pathfinder* 1989
> *Bennett was the only wartime group commander not to be knighted. We in the Pathfinders who survived, wear this slight like a mark of Cain.*

raise Cain

to cause trouble or conflict: perhaps a euphemism (based on the account in Genesis) for *raise the devil, raise hell*, etc. *19th cent.*

> R L Stevenson *Treasure Island* 1888
> *If I don't have a drain o' rum, Jim, I'll have the horrors ... and if I get the horrors ... I'll raise Cain.*

> Catherine George *Out of the Storm* 1991
> *The gentleman in question was his mother's grandfather, a roistering old sea-dog by the name of Joshua Probert, more inclined to raising Cain than crops.*

cake

cakes and ale

enjoyment and merrymaking. The allusion is to Shakespeare, *Twelfth Night* (1602) II.iii.111, where Sir Toby Belch asks Malvolio, the sanctimonious and self-important steward of Olivia, 'Dost thou think because thou art virtuous there shall be no more cakes and ale?' Cakes and ale were traditional fare for special enjoyment and celebration. The phrase was used as the title of a social satire by Somerset Maugham (1930). *17th cent.*

> Head & Kirkman *The English Rogue Described* 1674
> *The old man treated his mistriss with cakes and ale and such other provision as the place afforded, and after they had sufficiently regaled themselves.*

> Charles Kingsley *Westward Ho!* 1855
> *The good folks of Bideford were trooping home in merry groups, the father with his children, the lover with his sweetheart, to cakes and ale, and flapdragons and mummer's plays, and all the happy sports of Christmas night.*

> Lynne Reid Banks *The L-shaped Room* 1960
> *So supposing you never marry, and if you go on being so fussy you probably never will – are there to be no cakes and ale?*

have one's cake and eat it

to get the benefit from two choices that appear to be mutually exclusive: usually in negative contexts. The phrase originates in the proverb *you can't have your cake and eat it* (earlier and more logically *eat your cake and have it*, the form common in the 19th cent.), which is recorded in John Heywood's collection of proverbs (1546). The first uses as a free phrase are somewhat later. *19th cent.*

Charles Kingsley *Alton Locke* 1850
Have you not neglected our meetings? Have you not picked all the spice out of your poems? And can you expect to eat your cake and keep it too? You must be one thing or the other.

Enoch Powell *Reflections of a Statesman* 1991
We politicians exist to enable the public to have its cake and eat it.

a piece of cake
a task that is very simple or straightforward. Cake is pleasant and enjoyable, and is also easy to cut. The phrase became current in airforce slang during the Second World War, and formed the title of a book about RAF slang (*It's a Piece of Cake, or RAF Slang Made Easy*) by C H Ward-Jackson, published in 1943. *Mid 20th cent.*

> **Ogden Nash** *The Primrose Path* 1936
> *Her picture's in the papers now, | And life's a piece of cake.*

sell/go like hot cakes
to be sold in large quantities. Coffee and hot cakes are offered – usually to specially favoured guests – at various points in the narratives of 19th cent. fiction. *19th cent.*

> **Charles F Briggs** *The Adventures of Harry Franco* 1839
> *Mr. Smith Davis commenced turning over one piece of calico after another, with amazing rapidity … 'You had better buy 'em, Colonel,' said Mr. Lummucks, 'they will sell like hot cakes.'*

> **Guardian** 1989
> *Cards depicting Santa in horribly compromising positions are selling like hot cakes.*

take the cake
to win the honours or first prize. Often used ironically of somebody or something that is remarkable in an unexpected way. The allusion is to cake as the prize in various contests, and in particular the cakewalk, a complex marching dance associated with black people of the southern US. *See also* take the BISCUIT. *19th cent.*

> **Conan Doyle** *The Man with the Twisted Lip* 1891
> *Well, I have been twenty-seven years in the force, but this really takes the cake.*

> **Georgette Heyer** *A Blunt Instrument* 1938
> *I've met some kill-joys in my time, but you fairly take the cake.*

See also the ICING on the cake; a SLICE of the cake.

calends

at/on the Greek calends
never. *Kalendae* (plural) was the name for the first day of the month in the Roman calendar but did not feature in the Greek calendar, and so 'Greek calends' are a fantasy. *17th cent.*

> **Nicholas Billingsley** *A Treasury of Divine Raptures* 1667
> *O may I yield at the Greek Calends (never) | To Satan's laws, but serve the Lord for ever.*

> **Byron** *Don Juan* 1824
> *And tradesmen, with long bills and longer faces, sigh … They and their bills … are left to the Greek kalends of another session.*

calf
See a GOLDEN calf; kill the fatted calf *at* FAT.

call

the call of nature
the need to urinate or defecate. *18th cent.*

> **Laurence Sterne** *Tristram Shandy* 1760
> *Shew me a city so macerated with expectation – who neither eat, or drank, or slept, or prayed, or hearkened to the calls either of religion or nature for seven and twenty days together, who could have held out one day longer.*

> **Sue Seddon** *Travel* 1991
> *A sense of humour is essential, especially when the giggling driver moves the sheltering bus to reveal squatting passengers answering the call of nature.*

call the shots/tune
informal, originally NAmer to have the initiative or be in control. *Call the tune* refers to the (19th cent.) proverb *he who pays the piper calls the tune*; *call the shots* originates in North American use in the 1960s and is based on the practice in target shooting of calling where the shot will strike the target. *Mid 20th cent.*

> **Andrew Walker** *Enemy Territory* 1988
> *In England the daily business of politics is not controlled by the Prime Minister or Westminster: it is Whitehall that calls the tune.*

See also bring/call something to MIND; call somebody's BLUFF; call it a DAY; call somebody names *at* NAME; call off the dogs *at* DOG; call a SPADE a spade; a CLOSE call; too CLOSE to call.

calm

See the calm/lull before the STORM.

camp

have a foot in both camps

to be involved with or sympathetic to both of a pair of rivals, competitors, etc: from the meaning of *camp* 'a group of people who share a particular view'. *Mid 20th cent.*

can

A word going back to Old English in its primary meaning of a vessel for liquids, it has developed other applications reflected in the phrases.

carry the can (back)

to accept the blame or responsibility for something. The phrase is originally forces' slang, and is thought to refer either to the beer can that a soldier was appointed to bring for his fellow soldiers and then carry back when empty (a great responsibility if ever there was one), or to the soil carried away each night from the earth closets in latrines. A connection with the older phrase *carry the cag* (later *keg*) = to be vexed or sullen, recorded by Eric Partridge in *A Dictionary of Slang*, is doubtful. *Early 20th cent.*

> John Braine *Vodi* 1959
> *It's always my fault, everything's my fault. I always carry the bloody can back.*

in the can

1 *informal* achieved: originally used in the cinema industry, referring to completed film stored in circular cans. *Mid 20th cent.*

> New Scientist 1991
> *Looking at the event dispassionately, I realise that I was probably chosen because the film had to be 'in the can' (a technical term we film people use for 'finished') by the end of February.*

2 *informal, originally NAmer* in prison: the analogy is between the sealed container and the enclosed prison cell. *Early 20th cent.*

> Today 1992
> *Riddick Bowe's World Boxing Council belt ended up in the trash can, Mike Tyson ended up in the can, and Lennox Lewis became Britain's first world heavyweight champion without even hitting anyone.*

open (up) a can of worms

informal, originally NAmer to act in a way that can cause unexpected trouble or difficulties. The phrase refers to a container of bait used in fishing. The image is of letting worms or maggots escape and crawl everywhere beyond one's control. *Mid 20th cent.*

> Esquire 1992
> *Premature ejaculation is another can of worms entirely.*

candle

cannot / not fit to hold a candle to somebody

cannot rival or compete with somebody. The phrase was originally used in positive contexts, and draws on the image of an assistant holding a candle for a person to work by. In Shakespeare's *The Merchant of Venice* (1598) II.vi.41, Shylock's daughter Jessica appears dressed as a boy in the company of masquers; when asked to be a torch-bearer she protests, 'What, must I hold a candle to my shames?' In current use the phrase normally appears in negative contexts, the notion being that the subordinate is not worthy even of routine tasks such as this. An older and now obsolete idiom *hold a candle to the devil*, meaning 'to take part in evil schemes', occurs in the (15th cent.) Paston Letters. Uses with *cannot* and other negative words date from the 17th cent., and are common in 19th cent. literature. In the quotation from a dramatic work of 1795 below, the use is negative but the sense is the opposite of the familiar one (the speaker has no need to hold a candle to somebody she herself *can* match) and seems to show how the current meaning emerged. *16th cent.*

> Richard Cumberland First Love 1795
> *Do pr'ythee keep to your own receipt book, and leave me to mine; I know it all, from a lark to a loin of beef, and in the oeconomy of the table woudnt hold a candle to Hannah Glass herself, if she was living and here present.*

> Christopher Morley The Haunted Bookshop 1919
> *Philadelphia girls are amazingly comely ... but none of these can hold a candle to Miss Titania.*

not worth the candle

not justified because of the cost involved. The image is of a candle needed to provide light for an activity, which then does not even produce enough profit to recover the (not insignificant) cost of the candle. The phrase often occurs in the form *the game is not worth the candle* (*cf* French *le jeu ne vaut pas la chandelle*). *17th cent.*

Jeremy Collier A Defence of the Short View 1699
Mr. Congreve would excuse Osmin's Rant, by saying, that most of the incidents of the poem of this scene and the former, were laid to prepare for the violence of these expressions. If it be so, I think the play was not worth the candle.

New Internationalist 1990
Generally it's not worth the candle to try and dodge the revenue authorities.

See also BURN the candle at both ends.

cannon

a loose cannon
a powerful or effective person or thing that can cause harm or damage because nobody is controlling it properly. The image is of a gun running loose on a warship and firing indiscriminately in all directions. *20th cent.*

Daily Mirror 1992
Of course the Palace can't afford to leave her as a loose cannon.

canoe

See PADDLE one's own canoe.

canter

at/in a canter
British at speed or with effortless ease: a metaphor from horseracing, in which a horse can win by such a distance that it does not need to gallop to the finish. *19th cent.*

George Meredith The Ordeal of Richard Feverel 1859
Clare was the name he liked best: nay, he loved it. Doria, too: she shared his own name with him. Away went his heart, not at a canter now, at a gallop, as one who sights the quarry.

canvas

under canvas
1 in a tent or tents; in a camp. *19th cent.*

Virginia Woolf The Voyage Out 1915
I want to go up the river and see the natives in their camps. It's only a matter of ten days under canvas. My husband's done it. One would lie out under the trees at night and be towed down the river by day.
2 (said of a ship) rigged; using sail as distinct from steam power. *19th cent.*

Herman Melville Billy Budd a1891
The indispensable fleet, one wholly under canvas, no steam-power, its innumerable sails and thousands of cannon, everything in short, worked by muscle alone.

cap

cap in hand
acting humbly when asking for a favour; also *cap-in-hand* (adjective). The image is of removing one's hat as a gesture of respect or submission, and may also carry implications of begging. *16th cent.*

Shakespeare Henry V iv.v.18 (1599)
And he that will not follow Bourbon now, | Let him go home and, with his cap in hand | Like a base leno hold the chamber door | Whilst by a slave no gentler than my dog | His fairest daughter is contaminated.

if the cap fits (wear it)
used to suggest that a comment or description might well suit the individual being addressed. It was originally used about a dunce's cap fitting a fool's head, as a reference in Nicholas Breton's satirical poem *The Fooles Cap* (part of *Pasquils Mad-cap*, 1600) shows: 'Where you finde a head fit for this Cappe, either bestowe it vpon him in charity, or send him where he may haue them for his money.' Also (*NAmer*) *if the shoe fits. 18th cent.*

Richardson Clarissa 1751
If indeed thou findest, by the new light darted in upon thee, since thou hast had the honour of conversing with this admirable creature, that the cap fits thy own head, why then, according to the Qui capit rule, e'en take and clap it on: And I will add a string of bells to it, to complete thee for the fore-horse of the idiot team.

Dickens Martin Chuzzlewit 1844
Miss Charity Pecksniff begged with much politeness to be informed whether any of those very low observations were levelled at her; and receiving no more explanatory answer than was conveyed in the

adage 'Those the cap fits, let them wear it,' immediately commenced a somewhat acrimonious and personal retort.

set one's cap at somebody

dated (said of a woman) to pursue a man as a prospective husband. The allusion is to the choice and positioning of caps (formerly a common item of women's clothing) to produce the most attractive and becoming effect. Various idioms based on the same notion are recorded from the 16th cent. and are now mostly obsolete. Cf Goldsmith She Stoops to Conquer (1773): 'Instead of breaking my heart at his indifference, I'll … set my cap to some newer fashion, and look out for some less difficult admirer.' 19th cent.

Jane Austen Sense and Sensibility 1811
'Aye, aye, I see how it will be,' said Sir John, 'I see how it will be. You will be setting your cap at him now, and never think of poor Brandon.' 'That is an expression, Sir John,' said Marianne, warmly, 'which I particularly dislike. I abhor every commonplace phrase by which wit is intended; and "setting one's cap at a man," or "making a conquest," are the most odious of all.'

Thackeray The Virginians 1858
I said people would set their caps at him. If the cap fits you, tant pis! as my papa used to say.

to cap it all

as the last and most troublesome in a series of difficulties or misfortunes: from the meaning of cap 'to exceed or surpass'. The phrase is 19th cent. in the form to cap all.

caper

cut a caper

to skip or dance playfully: from the earliest meaning of caper, 'a playful leap'. There is a famous scene in Shakespeare's Twelfth Night (1602) I.iii.116 where Sir Toby Belch and Sir Andrew Aguecheek are discussing their abilities at dancing: '[Sir Toby] What is thy excellence in a galliard, knight? [Sir Andrew] Faith, I can cut a caper. [Sir Toby] And I can cut the mutton to't … Let me see thee caper. Ha, higher! Ha, ha, excellent!' 17th cent.

capital

make capital out of something

to turn a situation to one's advantage: from the financial meaning. 19th cent.

Harriet Beecher Stowe Uncle Tom's Cabin 1852
Master Sam had a native talent that might, undoubtedly, have raised him to eminence in political life – a talent of making capital out of everything that turned up, to be invested for his own especial praise and glory.

with a capital —

used after a word (and followed by its first letter) to emphasize it: a visualization of the printing convention whereby words are capitalized when they have a special institutional meaning. 19th cent.

Bret Harte Mrs Skaggs's Husbands 1873
My friends think I should have some great aim in life, with a capital A. But I was born a vagabond, and a vagabond I shall probably die.

Andrew Walker Enemy Territory 1988
She could not bring herself to believe in Evil with a capital E, as personified in a spirit-being called Satan or the Devil.

card

Phrases based on playing cards and card games are recorded from the 16th cent.

get one's cards

British, informal to be dismissed from one's employment. The cards are the national insurance card and other official documents that an employer holds during the period of employment (first recorded in this sense in the 1920s). Give somebody their cards is to dismiss somebody or make them redundant. Mid 20th cent.

W J Burley Wycliffe and the Scapegoat 1987
I was going to tell him what he could do with his job but I thought better of it an' I took my cards all polite like.

Amrit Wilson Finding a Voice: Asian Women in Britain 1988
Then she said 'I won't have you answering back, you will be given your cards, you'll be sacked.'

have a card up one's sleeve

to have a secret advantage or stratagem: a metaphor from cheating in card games. Also in extended uses. *19th cent.*

> John Esten Cooke *Henry St John* 1859
> 'Let us hold in, and watch the action of the House of Burgesses. If they proceed to the resolves which become them, they will come to a point, and his Excellency will have to show his hand.' 'Yes, sir,' said St. John, 'and I predict that you'll see a card up his sleeve.'

> John Creighton *Oil on Troubled Waters — Gulf Wars* 1992
> Another card the Iraqis kept up their sleeve was the helicopter gunship.

hold all the cards

to have all the resources or advantages: a metaphor from card games, where the notion is of holding all the cards needed to win a hand. *20th cent.*

> Julian Barnes *A History of the World in 10½ Chapters* 1990
> God holds all the cards and wins all the tricks.

keep/play one's cards close to one's chest

to be secretive about one's plans or intentions. The image is of card players taking particular care to prevent others from seeing their hand. *20th cent.*

> C Lorrimer *Spinning Wheel* 1993
> Perhaps you're just playing your cards close to your chest and the first we'll know about it is your engagement.

on / NAmer in the cards

possible or likely to happen. The phrase occurs in Dickens, Collins, and other 19th cent. writers, and may refer to the chance emergence of particular cards in a card game; but the allusion is also (or chiefly) to tarot cards used in fortune-telling. *19th cent.*

> Wilkie Collins *The Moonstone* 1868
> It's quite on the cards, sir … that you have put the clue into our hands.

play the — card

to use a specified issue for political advantage: from the idea of playing a winning card in a game. The phrase appears to have been coined by Lord Randolph Churchill in 1886 in a letter on the subject of Irish Home Rule: 'I decided some time ago that if the G.O.M. went for Home Rule, the Orange card would be the one to play.' *19th cent.*

> *Financial Times* 1982
> During a tense moment late on Saturday evening when Mr Alexander Haig, the U.S. Secretary of State, and President Leopoldo Galtieri were trying to thrash a way out of the mess, the President is reported to have suddenly threatened to play his Soviet card. Flushed with the unaccustomed acclaim of his people, Gen Galtieri was not bluffing.

> *The Times* 2005
> The Conservative Party may not win this election, but it is winning the argument. Whoever forms the next Government, immigration limits will be on the agenda. This is not about colour. It was Mr Blair who tried to play the race card yesterday.

play one's cards right

to use one's resources or opportunities well, as a card player makes the best use of the cards dealt in a hand. *Early 20th cent.*

> David Graham Phillips *Susan Lenox, Her Fall and Rise* 1917
> 'Seven dollars a week … Couldn't I get – about fifteen – or fourteen? I think I could do on fourteen.' 'Rather! I was talking only of the salary. You'll make a good many times fifteen – if you play your cards right.'

put/lay one's cards on the table

to divulge or declare one's intentions, resources, etc. *19th cent.*

> Robert Browning *The Ring and the Book* 1842
> Come, cards on table; was it true or false?

See also MARK somebody's card; STACK the cards.

---

care

I couldn't care less

informal I am not interested at all, I am quite indifferent. The phrase is originally British from the 1940s; curiously it appears some twenty years later in American use in the form *I could care less*, with the negative omitted. Though roundly condemned as nonsensical by some usage critics, the use fits into a pattern, with the stress on the initial *I*, already represented by *I should be so lucky* and similarly ironic exclamations. *Mid 20th cent.*

not care a straw / two straws / two pins / two hoots

not to care at all. *Straw* was used proverbially from the 13th cent. for something of little value (as in *not worth a straw, it does not matter a straw,* etc) and *pin* from slightly later; *hoot* (possibly not the familiar word) has been used since the late 19th cent. to mean 'the smallest amount'. The phrase goes back in various forms to Middle English.

Chaucer *The Book of the Duchess* (line 718)
Remembre yow of Socrates, | For he ne counted nat thre strees | Of noght that Fortune koude doo.

Spenser *The Faerie Queene* I.v.4 (1590)
Soone after comes the cruell Sarazin, | In woven maile all armed warily, | And sternly lookes at him, who not a pin | Does care for looke of living creatures eye.

Shakespeare *The Winter's Tale* III.ii.109 (1611)
[Hermione] *But yet hear this – mistake me not – no life, | I prize it not a straw.*

Nicholas Breton *The Uncasing of Machivils Instructions to His Sonne* 1613
For be thou poore, what e'er thy preaching be | Thy Parish will not care a pin for thee.

Louisa M Alcott *Little Women* 1868
That's one of your foolish extravagances – sending flowers and things to girls for whom you don't care two pins.

Henry James *An International Episode* 1879
Mrs. Westgate looked at the young girl with sisterly candor. 'I don't care two straws for Mr. Beaumont.'

James Joyce *Ulysses* 1922
Not that I care two straws who he does it with.

take care of something

to deal effectively with something, as a statement expressing completion or satisfaction: developed from other meanings 'to attend to' and 'to look after'. *17th cent.*

John Locke *Toleration* 1692
Let it be granted … that the magistrate understand such washing to be profitable to the curing or preventing of any disease the children are subject unto, and esteem the matter weighty enough to be taken care of by a law.

Mark Twain *The Innocents Abroad* 1869
But they will build no more barricades, they will break no more soldiers' heads with paving-stones. Louis Napoleon has taken care of all that.

career

in full career

at great speed; headlong; with all one's energies engaged: from the meaning of *career* 'a horse's short fast gallop' and originally with the same reference. *17th cent.*

Milton *Sonnets* 1645
How soon hath Time the suttle theef of youth, | Stoln on his wing my three and twentith yeer! | My hasting dayes flie on with full career.

R L Stevenson *Kidnapped* 1886
I began instead to rain kicks and buffets on the door, and to shout out aloud for Mr. Balfour. I was in full career, when I heard the cough right overhead.

carpet

There are two meanings: the current familiar one (a floor covering) and an earlier, originally Middle English meaning that is now obsolete (a table covering).

a magic carpet

a means of travelling in one's imagination: from stories of magic carpets on which people could ride in the air to exotic or fabulous places. *19th cent.*

Kipling *Captains Courageous* 1897
From San Diego to Sixteenth Street, Chicago, let the magic carpet be laid down. Hurry! oh, hurry!

on the carpet

1 (said of a topic or matter) under discussion at a meeting. *Carpet* is used here in its early, and now obsolete, meaning 'covering of the table round which a meeting is held', and the phrase corresponds to the French phrase *sur le tapis*. An early use occurs in the preface to the biographies by Roger North (1653–1734) of his three distinguished brothers, published posthumously in 1742–4, in a sentence that sounds strange or even comical today: 'These three brothers, whose lives are upon the carpet before me.' They were all great-great-nephews of Sir Thomas North, the translator of Plutarch's *Lives of the Noble Grecians and Romans*. *18th cent.*

Charles Lamb *Essays of Elia* 1823
How tenderly you advised an abstemious introduction of literary topics before the lady, with a caution not to be too forward in bringing on the

carpet matters more within the sphere of her intelligence.

Trollope *Doctor Thorne* 1858

The squire, anxious as usual for money, had written to ask what success the doctor had had in negotiating the new loan with Sir Roger. The fact, however, was, that in his visit at Boxall Hill, the doctor had been altogether unable to bring on the carpet the matter of this loan.

2 (said of a person) being reprimanded by a superior or by somebody in authority. The meaning is again predominantly the same as in sense 1 but there is also a notion of the person standing on the carpet (in its modern meaning) in front of those issuing the reprimand. In the early 19th cent., *walk the carpet* was also used of a servant summoned to see the master or mistress. The fact that carpeted rooms were the privilege of those with seniority or authority is also relevant to these senses, and the verb *carpet*, in a corresponding meaning, is recorded from the 1840s. *See also* on the MAT. *19th cent.*

sweep/push something under the carpet
to try to hide a problem or embarrassment, in the hope that it will go unnoticed or be quickly forgotten. *Mid 20th cent.*

carrot

carrot and stick
a combination of a promised reward and threatened punishment as an inducement to do what somebody requires. The phrase is derived from the notion of persuading a donkey to move forward by offering it a carrot but beating it with a stick if it refuses. The figurative use of a dangled carrot as an inducement dates from the 19th cent., and the contrast with a stick from the 1940s. The contrast is often extended in a way that identifies each element with a particular thing (*the carrot of such-and-such* and *the stick of such-and-such*). Also used (with hyphens) as a modifying word as in *carrot-and-stick approach, policy*, etc. *Mid 20th cent.*

David Adamson *Defending the World* 1990
The emphasis generally is on the carrot of incentive rather than the stick of taxes and sharply raised prices.

carry

carry all before one
to be comprehensively victorious, or to win wide support or approval. The image is of a physical body moving with great force and sweeping along everything in its way. *17th cent.*

Dryden transl Plutarch's *Alcibiades* c1690
And now the friends of Alcibiades, carrying all before them at Samos, despatched Pisander to Athens, to attempt a change of government.

carry somebody off their feet
to fill somebody with wild enthusiasm or excitement: often used in passive forms. *19th cent.*

See also carry the CAN; carry the DAY; carry a TORCH for somebody.

cart

in the cart
British, *informal* in difficulty or trouble: a metaphor from the cart formerly used to take convicted criminals to the gallows and for the public exposure of prostitutes. *19th cent.*

Evening Standard 1889
In two races ... Sir George Chetwynd – to use a vulgarism – had been 'put in the cart' by his jockey.

K M Peyton *Who, Sir? Me, Sir?* 1988
If it's just for yourself and you fall off and hurt yourself you can pull out, and nobody's the worse off, but if you're in a team you've got to get round else the whole team is in the cart.

put the cart before the horse
to do things in the wrong or illogical order. The phrase is recorded from Middle English in the form *put the yoke before the ox* (cf French *mettre la charrue devant les boeufs*), and in its current form it occurs occasionally as an admonition introduced by a negative such as *do not. 16th cent.*

George Puttenham *The Art of English Poesie* 1589
Ye have another manner of disordered speach, when ye misplace your words or clauses and set that before which should be behind, & è converso, we call it in English proverbe, the cart before the horse, the Greeks call it Histeron proteron, we name it the preposterous.

Anne Sullivan in Helen Keller's *The Story of My Life* 1901

She makes many mistakes, of course, twists words and phrases, puts the cart before the horse, and gets herself into hopeless tangles of nouns and verbs.

carve

See be carved in (tablets of) STONE.

case

be on / get off somebody's case

to start (or desist from) nagging or finding fault with somebody, or taking them to task: with allusion to law officers being involved in a case. *Late 20th cent.*

Martin Amis *Money* 1985
What does it cost to keep you off my case?

case the joint

to inspect premises furtively with the intention of robbery. *Case* here is the verb meaning 'to enclose in a case' and later 'to strip the case or skin from'; the second is probably the basis of the meaning in the phrase. Shakespeare in *All's Well That Ends Well* (1603) includes the punning line (III.vi.103) 'We'll make you some sport with the fox ere we case him'; and Mrs Hannah Glasse's *The Art of Cookery, Made Plain and Easy* (1747) has the instruction 'Take your hare when it is cased' (*see* first catch your HARE). *Early 20th cent.*

in any case

whatever the other circumstances: *cf* at any RATE; at all events *at* EVENT. *Mid 19th cent.*

on a case-by-case basis

individually; on the basis of the particular circumstances involved: used with reference to judgements and decisions made from instance to instance rather than by application of a general principle. The phrase is commonly heard in political contexts in which the speaker wishes to avoid stating or commenting on a principle. *Late 20th cent.*

See also MEET the case.

cash

See cash in one's chips *at* CHIP.

cast

be cast in a — mould

to have a particular character from birth: a metaphor from sculpture and metal casting. Shakespeare, in *Coriolanus* (1608) v.iii.22, makes Coriolanus refer to his mother Volumnia as 'the honoured mould | Wherein this trunk [i.e. he himself] was framed'. *16th cent.*

A Kingsmill *A Viewe of Mans Estate* a1569
The Sonne of God was well-pleased to be cast in the moulde and simple shape of man.

Malcolm Young *An Inside Job* 1991
I was in danger of being irrevocably cast into the mould of being a 'college man' or academic.

cast the first stone

to be the first to accuse somebody. The allusion is to the biblical account of the woman taken in adultery in the New Testament, John 8:7 'He that is without sin among you, let him first cast a stone at her.' *16th cent.*

John Dunton *A Voyage Round the World* 1691
How base a part then is it to twit any with their former Juvenile Crimes, if they themselves are reform'd; for my own part, I must confess I find enough in my own breast to damp my censuring others, and he that does not, let him fling the first stone.

Dickens *Hard Times* 1854
Thou art not the man to cast the last stone, Stephen, when she is brought so low.

cast something in somebody's teeth

to taunt a person about what they have said or done: also in the obsolete form *cast somebody in the teeth*. The phrase is used by Shakespeare (see below) and appears in Matthew 27:42–3, at the description of the mocking of Christ on the Cross: 'He trusted in God; let him deliver him now, if he will have him: for he said, I am the Son of God. The thieves also, which were crucified with him, cast the same in his teeth.' *16th cent.*

Shakespeare *Julius Caesar* IV.ii.153 (1599)
[Cassius] For Cassius is aweary of the world, | Hated by one he loves, braved by his brother, | Checked like a bondman; all his faults observed, | Set in a notebook, learned and conned by rote, | To cast into my teeth.

cast not/ne'er a clout till May is out

(proverb) an exhortation not to discard winter clothes too soon. *Clout* (related to *cloth*) is an old word for a piece of clothing; the reference to May is to the end of the month and not, as is sometimes thought, to the appearance of spring blossom. *18th cent.*

See also cast somebody ADRIFT; cast one's BREAD upon the waters; cast one's MIND back; throw/ cast in one's LOT.

caste

lose caste

informal to fall in status or prestige. The phrase alludes to the Hindu caste system, in which it is possible to lose rank by certain actions, e.g. by eating unclean food or consorting with a member of a lower caste. *19th cent.*

George Eliot *Middlemarch* 1872
He was a sort of gypsy, rather enjoying the sense of belonging to no class ... That sort of enjoyment had been disturbed when he had felt some new distance between himself and Dorothea ... and his irritation had gone out towards Mr. Casaubon, who had declared beforehand that Will would lose caste. 'I never had any caste,' he would have said, if that prophecy had been uttered to him.

Michael Dibdin *Dirty Tricks* 1991
If I belonged anywhere, it was with these people, the lumpenbourgeoisie, in whose eyes I'd lost caste, fatally and irrevocably.

castle

build castles in the air / in Spain

to have unattainable dreams or ambitions. A castle built in the air is a self-explanatory image in the context of dreaming, but the reference to Spain requires some explanation. This is the older (Middle English) form of the phrase, and corresponds to the French phrase *battre un château en Espagne*. The reference is thought to be to the time of Moorish rule in Spain, when any scheme to build a (Christian) castle would have been highly unrealistic. The current form of the phrase refers to castles in the air, and this dates from the 16th cent.

Margaret Cavendish *The Contract* 1656
His vows to this lady were rather complemental, and loves feignings, than really true, or so authentical to last; he built affections on a wrong foundation, or rather castles in the air, as lovers use to do, which vanish soon away; for where right is not, truth cannot be.

Joseph Conrad *Lord Jim* 1900
And what if something unexpected and wonderful were to come of it? That evening, reposing in a deck-chair under the shade of my own poop awning ... I laid on Jim's behalf the first stone of a castle in Spain.

Enoch Powell *Reflections of a Statesman* 1989
The remarkable thing about political houses built on sand, or castles in the air, is how long they often take to collapse.

cat

the cat has got —'s tongue

a fanciful explanation for a person's silence or refusal to speak: often used as a question (*has the cat got your tongue?*) expressing annoyance when a response is expected, especially from a child. *Early 20th cent.*

Lilian Darcy *A Private Arrangement* 1993
It must have showed ... because his first words to her when they were seated in his red sports car were, 'Cat got your tongue?'

a cat may look at a king/queen

in the right circumstances, even the humblest are on an equal footing with the greatest. *16th cent.*

Robert Greene *Greenes Never Too Late* 1590
A cat may look at a King, and a swain's eye hath as high a reach as a lord's look.

Lewis Carroll *Alice's Adventures in Wonderland* 1865
'Don't be impertinent,' said the King, 'and don't look at me like that!' He got behind Alice as he spoke. 'A cat may look at a king,' said Alice. 'I've read that in some book, but I don't remember where.'

Petronella Pulsford *Lee's Ghost* 1990
She condescends, she condescends. But a cat may look at a queen. A tramp may criticize a prince.

the cat's whiskers / pyjamas / NAmer meow

informal something or somebody outstanding and much admired. See also the bee's knees at BEE. *Early 20th cent.*

Sinclair Lewis *Martin Arrowsmith* 1925
This kid used to think Pa Gottlieb was the cat's pyjamas.

(enough to) make a cat laugh

absurd or ironic: the phrase is connected in its present form with the (19th cent.) fairy tale of *Puss in Boots*, although there is a fortuitous late 16th cent. allusion to animals laughing in delight, and there are references in the early 18th cent. to cats responding verbally to an extraordinary experience. A trace of the eventual idiom can perhaps be seen even earlier in Shakespeare's *The Tempest* (1613) II.ii.86: '[Stephano] Come on your ways. Open your mouth. Here is that which will give language to you, cat. Open your mouth.' *19th cent.*

Hardy *Jude the Obscure* 1895
But, Jude, my dear, you were enough to make a cat laugh! You walked that straight, and held yourself that steady, that one would have thought you were going 'prentice to a judge.

fight like cat and dog

to be constantly arguing or quarrelling. Cats and dogs appear from the 17th cent. as an image of violence and intensity in the context of quarrelling and fighting. John Bunyan, for example, described a squabble between a husband and wife in *The Life and Death of Mr Badman* (1680): 'For their railing, and cursing, and swearing ended not in words: They would fight and fly at each other, and that like cats and dogs.'

Thomas Holcroft *The Adventures of Hugh Trevor* 1794
I have heard you and my mamma say often enough that you both had had your likings; and that you did not like one another; and that that was the reason that you quarrel like cat and dog.

let the cat out of the bag

to reveal a secret carelessly or unwittingly. The cat had diabolical associations from the Middle Ages and is also particularly averse to being confined. Both these images are probably at work here. There is also the suggestion that this phrase is connected with *a pig in a poke* (see buy a PIG in a poke): a person hoodwinked by being sold a cat rather than the much more valuable sucking pig they had paid for would discover the trickery on opening the bag and letting the cat out. But this explanation strains credulity to breaking point, given the cat's aversion to confinement mentioned above. *18th cent.*

Prince Hoare *No Song No Supper* 1792
Well, don't you let the cat out of the bag.

Louisa M Alcott *Little Men* 1871
Mrs. Bhaer cut that most interesting word short off in the middle and began to look over her bills as if afraid she would let the cat out of the bag if she talked any more.

like a cat on a hot tin roof / British on hot bricks

very restless or agitated. John Ray's *Collection of English Proverbs* (1678) includes a reference to 'a cat upon a hot bake-stone'. Captain Marryat's *Mr Midshipman Easy* (1836) refers to a man dancing 'like a bear upon hot plates' with delight. *Cat on a Hot Tin Roof* is well known as the title of a play by Tennessee Williams about emotional and sexual tensions in the deep American South, first performed in 1955. In the dialogue there are several allusions to the phrase, which symbolizes the neurotic and claustrophobic nature of the passions underlying the characters' relationships: in Act I, in an exchange between Margaret and her husband Brick, Margaret declares that she will not take a lover, 'I'm taking no chances. No, I'd rather stay on this hot tin roof.' Brick replies, 'A hot tin roof's 'n uncomfo'table place t' stay on.' *19th cent.*

Mrs Henry Wood *East Lynne* 1861
'Good morning, justice. You had courage to venture up through the snow! What is the matter? you seem excited.' 'Excited!' raved the justice, dancing about the room, first on one leg, then on the other, like a cat upon hot bricks, 'so would you be excited, if your life were worried out, as mine is, over a wicked scamp of a son.'

like the cat that's got/stolen the cream

looking or feeling extremely pleased with oneself. *20th cent.*

Michael Clynes *The White Rose Murder* 1992
He came back an hour later, looking as smug as a cat who'd stolen the cream.

like a scalded cat

in a state of terror or panic. *Mid 20th cent.*

P G Wodehouse *Right Ho, Jeeves!* 1934
Get off the mark ... like a scalded cat, and your public is at a loss.

Amy Myers *Murder at the Masque* 1991
In the supper room Auguste would be running around like a scalded cat, metaphorically if not literally.

like something the cat brought in
informal dishevelled or bedraggled in appearance. Also used in mocking exaggeration and as an ironic or jocular greeting, *Look what the cat brought in. Early 20th cent.*

P Gregory *Fallen Skies* 1993
'Well, look what the cat brought in,' he said. 'Welcome back, Lil.'

not a cat in hell's / cat-in-hell chance
informal no chance at all. The phrase is predominantly 20th cent., but Grose's *Dictionary of the Vulgar Tongue* (1793) includes an entry *no more chance than a cat in hell without claws*: 'said of one who enters into a dispute or quarrel with one greatly above his match'. *18th cent.*

Hansard 1992
I do not want to disappoint the hon. Member for Eastbourne, but the chances of a local income tax are nil, because his party does not have a cat in hell's chance of ever being returned to government.

play cat and mouse with somebody
to tease somebody by alternately encouraging and discouraging them in some course of action. The image is the familiar one of a cat 'playing' with a mouse before killing it. *19th cent.*

George Meredith *The Egoist* 1879
Lætitia was left to think it pleased him to play at cat and mouse. She had not 'hit him to the life,' or she would have marvelled in acknowledging how sincere he was.

Harper Lee *To Kill a Mockingbird* 1960
She had never told on us, had never played cat-and-mouse with us, she was not at all interested in our private lives.

put/set the/a cat among the pigeons
to do or say something that causes great trouble or confusion. The phrase appears in an earlier form in J Stevens' *New Spanish and English Dictionary* of 1706: 'The cat is in the dove-house. They say, when a man is got among the women.' *18th cent.*

Alistair MacLean *Santorini* 1987
If it is your intention to set a cat among the pigeons or let loose an eagle in the dovecote, you don't send a postcard in advance announcing your intentions.

rain cats and dogs
to rain heavily and continuously. There is a 17th cent. reference, in the work of the English playwright Richard Brome (*The City Wit*, 1653), to raining 'dogs and polecats', and 'rain dogs and cats' appears in a number of satirical works called 'travesties' that were written at about this time. There is an occurrence in the work of John Phillips, who wrote a travesty translation of the Roman poet Virgil, called *Maronides*, in 1678: 'Under the branches, wot ye well, | When it rains dogs and cats in Hell, | The shelter'd centaurs roar and yell.' Another instance is in a work called *Cataplus* by Maurice Atkins, published in 1672: 'Neither had he flincht a foot, had fates | Made it rain down dogs and cats; | Though old was body and decrepit.' So when we first come across the phrase in its present form in Jonathan Swift's *Complete Collection of Polite and Ingenious Conversation* (see below), we can be sure that the phrase was already well known, and that Swift or one of his contemporaries did the work of turning it round to make it a little more euphonious to modern ears.

The significance of cats and dogs remains obscure despite many suggestions: a favourite notion of 19th cent. amateur etymologists was that it comes from Greek *kata doxan* meaning 'contrary to belief', i.e. 'inordinate', while others took refuge (via French *catadoupe*) in a Greek word *katadoupoi* (plural) meaning 'waterfall' or 'cataract'. Neither of these explanations can possibly be correct for what is a piece of popular usage. Perhaps heavy rainfall came to be regarded in the same terms as cats and dogs fighting: see fight like cat and dog above. See also rain pitchforks at PITCHFORK. *17th cent.*

Swift *Complete Collection of Polite and Ingenious Conversation* 1738
I know Sir John will go, though he was sure it would rain cats and dogs.

Thomas De Quincy *On Wordsworth's Poetry* 1845
If a man depends for the exuberance of his harvest upon the splendour of the coming summer, we do not excuse him for taking prussic acid because it

rains cats and dogs through the first ten days of April.

Jean Webster *Daddy-Long-Legs* 1912
PS. It's raining cats and dogs tonight. Two puppies and a kitten have just landed on the window-sill.

see how / which way the cat jumps
originally NAmer to await the development of events before making a decision. The cat referred to here is not the animal but a small strip of wood used in tip-cat and similar games, in which the 'cat' is hit at one end to make it spring from the ground and is then struck into the air. *19th cent.*

Scott *Journals* 1826
I would like to be there, were it but to see how the cat jumps.

John Neal *The Down-Easters* 1833
But he knows how the cat jumps, I tell ye – cute as nutmeg – brought up on ten-penny nails, pynted at both eends.

Dennis Kavanagh *Thatcherism and British Politics* 1990
And for the 'trimming' of previous Conservative leaders she borrowed Kipling's words: 'I don't spend a lifetime watching which way the cat jumps.'

that cat won't jump
originally NAmer that idea is unrealistic. This is presumably a development of the previous phrase. *19th cent.*

Emerson Bennett *The Phantom of the Forest* 1868
'I'll do nothing of the kind,' said Blodget, with a savage frown, 'because I don't believe a — word of it myself! No, sir – that cat won't jump! You're lying, and you know it!'

turn cat in pan
to defect to the other side in a dispute. The original (16th cent.) meaning, now obsolete, refers to the process of changing the natural order of things so that they seem the opposite of what they were. It gave way to the current meaning in the 17th cent.

Francis Bacon *Essays* 1601
There is a cunning, which we in England can, the turning of the cat in the pan; which is, when that which a man says to another, he lays it as if another had said it to him.

(when) the cat's away
when controls or restraints are removed; when the person in charge is absent. Shakespeare uses a form of the phrase in *Henry V* with reference to

the danger from Scotland in any conflict with the French (see below); otherwise the phrase in allusive use dates predominantly from the 19th cent., and is an allusion to the proverb *when the cat's away, the mice will play*, which is found from the late 15th cent.

Shakespeare *Henry V* i.ii.172 (1599)
For once the eagle England being in prey, | To her unguarded nest the weasel Scot | Comes sneaking, and so sucks her princely eggs, | Playing the mouse in absence of the cat.

George Meredith *Diana of the Crossways* 1885
Well, it doesn't matter for him, perhaps, but a game of two. ... Oh! it'll be all right. They can't reach London before dusk. And the cat's away.

See also BELL the cat; CURIOSITY killed the cat; a DEAD cat bounce; no/not ROOM to swing a cat.

catch

catch as catch can
a slogan urging people to seize their opportunities. In different forms (e.g. *catch that catch can, catch that catch might, catch that catch may*), the phrase goes back to Middle English; the current form dates from the 18th cent.

Kane O'Hara *Midas: An English Burletta* 1764
There's catch as catch can, hit or miss Luck is all, | And Luck's the best tune of life's Toll lol de roll.

catch it
informal to incur blame or punishment. *19th cent.*

Mrs Gaskell *Mary Barton* 1848
'Let me stay up a little,' pleaded Mary, as her hostess seemed so resolute about seeing her to bed. Her looks won her suit. 'Well, I suppose I mun. I shall catch it down stairs, I know. He'll be in a fidget till you're getten to bed, I know; so you mun be quiet if you are so bent upon staying up.'

Hardy *Tess of the D'Urbervilles* 1891
'You shall catch it for this, my gentleman, when you get home!' burst in female accents from the human heap – those of the unhappy partner of the man whose clumsiness had caused the mishap.

New Scientist 1991
Boy, did I catch it for my remarks about George Orwell's 1984.

catch the sun
1 (said of a place or surface) to be exposed to sunlight or reflect the sun: the notion is probably

of 'capturing' or 'trapping' (hence the term *sun trap*). A 17th cent. drama by Sir William D'Avenant (*The First Days Entertainment at Rutland House*, 1657) conveys this image in a description of streets and buildings that includes the line 'you being fain to lay traps at your windows to catch the sun-beams'. *19th cent.*

> **J R Lowell** *Poetical Works* 1885
> *The buttercup catches the sun in its chalice.*

2 (said of a person) to become slightly sunburned. The meaning is probably as much derived from the one in *catch a cold* or *catch a fever* as from the notion of 'capturing' the sun in the meaning above. A 16th cent. source (Holland's translation of Pliny) writes that people beyond the Ganges 'are caught with the Sun, and begin to be blackish'. The phrase is also found in reverse form, with the sun doing the catching (see below).

> **G & W Grossmith** *Diary of a Nobody* 1892
> *Carrie back. Hoorah! She looks wonderfully well, except that the sun has caught her nose.*

catch a Tartar

to have to deal with somebody who is difficult or troublesome. The Tartars, a group of mainly Mongol and Turkic tribes who established an extensive empire in Central Asia under Genghis Khan in the 13th cent., were notorious for their ferocity and cruelty. *17th cent.*

> **Samuel Butler** *Hudibras* 1663
> *Now thou hast got me for a Tartar, | To make me 'gainst my will take quarter.*

> **Wilkie Collins** *The Moonstone* 1868
> *Betteredge gave me one look at parting, which said, as if in so many words, 'You have caught a Tartar, Mr. Jennings – and the name of him is Bruff.'*

a catch-22 (situation)

an inescapable dilemma: from the novel *Catch-22* by Joseph Heller (1961), set on an imaginary American airbase in the Mediterranean during the Italian campaign of 1943–4. The dilemma underlying the book is expressed at several points and is essentially this: that in order to escape combat duty you have to be crazy but anybody wanting to avoid combat duty must be sane. *Mid 20th cent.*

> *Machine Knitting Monthly* 1992
> *Soon, though, we hit a Catch-22: I could get funding for more equipment if there was a 'group'*

organised, but no village women wanted to be organised if they didn't have machines.

See also catch a COLD; catch one's DEATH; catch/cop/stop a PACKET; catch somebody red-handed *at* RED; get/catch it in the NECK.

cause

make common cause

to cooperate in order to achieve a shared objective. *18th cent.*

> **Adam Smith** *The Wealth of Nations* 1776
> *If … the greater part of the other members are, like himself, persons who either are or ought to be teachers, they are likely to make a common cause, to be all very indulgent to one another, and every man to consent that his neighbour may neglect his duty, provided he himself is allowed to neglect his own.*

> **Gene Stratton Porter** *The Song of the Cardinal* 1915
> *Wild creepers flaunt their red and gold from the treetops, and the bumblebees and humming-birds make common cause in rifling the honey-laden trumpets.*

See also a REBEL without a cause.

caution

throw caution to the winds

to act recklessly or without restraint. *19th cent.*

> **Trollope** *The Last Chronicle of Barset* 1867
> *Lily had cast all such caution to the winds. She had given herself to the man entirely, and had determined that she would sink or swim, stand or fall, live or die, by him and by his truth.*

cave (pronounced **kay**-vee)

keep cave

informal, dated (chiefly in school use) to keep a lookout: from the imperative of Latin *cavere* 'to beware'. *19th cent.*

> **F W Farrar** *Eric, or, Little by Little* 1858
> *'We're making a regular knock-me-down shindy,' said Llewellyn; 'somebody must keep cave.'*

caviar

caviar to the general

something considered too delicate or refined for general appreciation. The locus classicus is

Shakespeare, *Hamlet* (1601) II.ii.439 '[Hamlet to the players] I heard thee speak me a speech once, but it was never acted, or, if it was, not above once; for the play, I remember, pleased not the million. 'Twas caviare to the general.' *General* here means 'the general population', and there is a play on the military meaning in the Saki quotation below. *17th cent.*

> **Trollope *The Duke's Children* 1880**
> *'A man should own his means or should earn them.' 'How many men, sir, do neither?' 'Yes; I know,' said the Duke. 'Such a doctrine nowadays is caviare to the general. One must live as others live around one, I suppose.'*

> **Saki *Reginald* 1904**
> *I became aware that old Colonel Mendoza was essaying to tell his classic story of how he introduced golf into India, and that Reginald was in dangerous proximity. There are occasions when Reginald is caviare to the Colonel.*

Cerberus

See a SOP to Cerberus.

ceremony

stand on/upon ceremony
to act in a formally correct manner. *Stand on* is used in the meaning 'claim respect for' from the late 16th cent. (*cf* stand on one's DIGNITY). *17th cent.*

> **Aphra Behn *The Feign'd Curtizans* 1679**
> *Sir I never stand upon ceremony when there's a woman in the case, – nor knew I 'twas your Sister.*

> **Jane Austen *Sense and Sensibility* 1811**
> *Mrs. Jennings, however, assured him directly, that she should not stand upon ceremony, for they were all cousins, or something like it.*

cess

bad cess to —
Anglo-Irish (as a curse) bad luck to so-and-so. *Cess*, short for *assessment*, was a term (originally 16th cent.) for a special tax (such as the Scottish land tax), and is probably associated with the obligation imposed on Irish households to provide provisions at specially assessed prices for the English lord deputy and his staff. *19th cent.*

> **Frances Hodgson Burnett *Little Lord Fauntleroy* 1886**
> *'Lords, is it?' he heard her say. 'An' the nobility an' gintry. Och! bad cess to them! Lords indade – worse luck.'*

> **Frances Mary Hendry *Quest for a Babe* 1990**
> *An old woman gutting hens told him, 'That's the lass took Marion Aluinn, bad cess to her, up off the shore yesterday! It's maybe for her.'*

chaff

The discarded husks that have been separated from the grain by threshing or winnowing.

an old bird is not caught with chaff
it is hard to fool somebody wise or experienced. *15th cent.* (in Caxton)

separate/sort the wheat from the chaff
to distinguish people or things that are valuable from what is worthless. Symbolic allusions contrasting wheat and chaff date from the time of Chaucer; and in Shakespeare's *The Merchant of Venice* (1598) I.i.116 Bassanio tells Antonio that 'Gratiano speaks an infinite deal of nothing, more than any man in all Venice. His reasons are as two grains of wheat hid in two bushels of chaff.' There are also biblical references, e.g. in the preaching of John the Baptist about the coming of Christ (Matthew 3:12) 'He will … gather his wheat into the garner; but he will burn up the chaff with unquenchable fire.' The phrase dates from the 19th cent. in this form.

> **James Fenimore Cooper *The Pioneers* 1823**
> *How much of this [allegation] is thine own, Richard, and how much comes from others? I would sift the wheat from the chaff.*

chalice

See a poisoned chalice *at* POISON.

chalk

(as) different/like as chalk and cheese
totally different in character, although superficially similar: also in variant phrases comparing the two. Chalk and cheese can be close in outward appearance but are completely different in other ways. The two substances have been proverbial in this way since Middle English. *16th cent.*

Thomas Duffet *Psyche Debauch'd* 1678
Pry'thee stint thy silly talk, | Thou mayest as well turn Cheese to Chalk.

Harold Frederic *The Damnation of Theron Ware* 1896
'But of course – it is all so different!' 'As chalk from cheese!' said Dr. Ledsmar.

chalk and talk
traditional methods of teaching, in which the teacher uses a blackboard (chalk) and addresses the class from the front (talk), as distinct from more progressive interactive methods. *Mid 20th cent.*

(not) by a long chalk
British (not) by a long way: from the practice of using chalk to mark up the points scored in a game. *19th cent.*

Robert Lowell *Antony Brade* 1874
Rabbits ain't alike, – not by a long chalk! Not that sort, at no time o' year, – nary two of 'em, never.

D H Lawrence *Sons and Lovers* 1913
Nothing is as bad as a marriage that's a hopeless failure. Mine was bad enough, God knows, and ought to teach you something; but it might have been worse by a long chalk.

challenge
See physically challenged *at* PHYSICAL.

champ
See champ at the bit *at* BIT².

chance

be in with a chance
to have a good prospect of success or victory: mostly from the 1980s in British use. *20th cent.*

chance one's arm/luck
to try something ambitious or dangerous. The phrase may originate in forces' slang, where 'chancing your arm' meant risking a court martial and the loss of stripes or decorations from the sleeves of a uniform. Eric Partridge, in his *Dictionary of Catch Phrases* (1985 edition, revised by Paul Beale), regarded it as a tailoring phrase that was later taken up by soldiers, but – as so often – he gives no evidence. Other, more fanciful explanations exist: one refers to a 15th cent.

feud between two Irish families, the Ormonds and the Kildares, in which a belligerent, realizing the futility of the squabble, ventured to make peace by thrusting his arm through a hole made in a door; this was 'chancing his arm' because he risked the occupants' hacking it off, although fortunately they shook it and made peace. Apart from historical implausibility, chronology is also against this origin, as the phrase does not occur for another four centuries. *19th cent.*

K M Peyton *Who, Sir? Me, Sir?* 1988
Oh, I'll see you right, gel. Never get anything done in this life if you don't chance your arm.

chance would be a fine thing
there is not much chance of that, welcome though it would be: typically used as a rueful response to some suggestion or fancy. *Early 20th cent.*

Stanley Houghton *Hindle Wakes* 1912
Why didn't you get wed? … There is plenty would have had you. Chance is a fine thing. Happen I wouldn't have wed them.

Maureen Lipman *Thank You for Having Me* 1990
So here I am extolling the worth of twenty minutes' silent meditation as a means of renewing and refreshing your channels … You could use it to combat office harassment (do I hear you say 'Chance would be a fine thing?').

on the (off) chance
just in case the possibility arises. An *off chance* is a 'remote possibility', and the sense of *off* is related to that in (e.g.) *a path off the main road* and in the word *offshoot*. *19th cent.*

R L Stevenson *Weir of Hermiston* 1896
He had no hope to find her; he took the off chance without expectation of result and to relieve his uneasiness.

See also drinking in the last chance saloon *at* LAST¹; not a CAT in hell's chance; not have/ stand the GHOST of a chance; not a hope/chance in HELL; a sporting chance *at* SPORT.

change

change hands
to become the property of a different owner: originally with reference to money, the hand representing the owner who holds it. *17th cent.*

Adam Smith *The Wealth of Nations* 1776

*When property changes hands, when it is trans-
mitted either from the dead to the living, or from the
living to the living, such taxes have frequently been
imposed upon it as necessarily take away some part
of its capital value.*

change the subject

to begin talking about something different during a conversation. *19th cent.*

Dickens *Oliver Twist* 1838

*Upon which the old gentleman, observing Oliver's
colour mounting, changed the subject by asking
whether there had been much of a crowd at the
execution that morning?*

change one's tune

to start behaving in a different way or expressing
different opinions, especially to suit new circumstances: also in the form *speak a different tune*. *16th
cent.*

Thomas Dekker *Northward Hoe* 1607

*Nay Sfoot, then ile change my tune: I may cause
such leaden-heeld rascalls; out of my sight: a knife, a
knife I say: O Maister Allom, if you love a woman,
draw out your knife and undo me, undo me.*

Iris Murdoch *Message to the Planet* 1989

*Her parents were against the match because they
thought Dad was a poor scholar. When they learnt
about the money they soon changed their tune.*

get no change / not get much change out of somebody

to fail to get any information or help from somebody. *19th cent.*

John Buchan *Prester John* 1910

*Still I said nothing. If the man had come to mock me,
he would get no change out of David Crawford.*

have a change of heart

to alter one's feelings or opinions about something. *A Change of Heart* was the title of an early
play by Henry James (1872). *18th cent.*

George Campbell *The Philosophy of Rhetoric* 1776

*Very different is the purpose of the Christian orator.
It is not a momentary, but a permanent effect at
which he aims. It is not an immediate and favourable suffrage, but a thorough change of heart and
disposition, that will satisfy his view.*

John Ruskin *Letter* 1853

*She passes her days in melancholy, and nothing can
help her but an entire change of heart.*

ring the changes

to vary the manner of arranging or doing something: a metaphor from bell-ringing, in which the
changes are the various sequences in which a
peal of bells can be rung. *17th cent.*

John Wilson *Belphegor* 1691

*No (Madam) if the men ring the changes, I know
not why we mayn't shufle, and cast knaves agen?*

See also change/swap horses in midstream *at*
HORSE; change one's MIND.

---

chapter

chapter and verse

precise and verifiable details. The phrase was
originally used with reference to the Bible,
which is organized in chapters and verses, then
to bibliographical references more generally, and
eventually to various types of evidence that support claims, accusations, etc. The phrase is
recorded in literal use from the 17th cent., and
figurative uses are found from the 19th cent.

George Eliot *Middlemarch* 1872

*People say what they like to say, not what they have
chapter and verse for.*

Julian Barnes *Flaubert's Parrot* 1985

*This precise and disheartening indictment was
drawn up by the late Dr Enid Starkie ... Flaubert's
most exhaustive British biographer. The numbers in
her text refer to footnotes in which she spears the
novelist with chapter and verse.*

See also a chapter of accidents *at* ACCIDENT.

---

charge

return to the charge

to renew one's attempt at something: from the
meaning 'a violent rush forwards'. *18th cent.*

Herman Melville *Bartleby* 1853

*His unwonted wordiness inspirited me. I returned
to the charge. 'Well, then, would you like to travel
through the country collecting bills for the merchants? That would improve your health.'*

take charge

to assume authority or custody over others. *Middle English*

charity

charity begins at home
one's first obligations are to one's own family. The phrase is 17th cent. in this form, but the notion goes back to Middle English. John Fletcher's comedy *Wit Without Money* (a1625) contains the line 'I must beat some body, and why not my Master, before a stranger? Charity and beating begins at home.'

> John Dunton *A Voyage Round the World* 1691
> *Nor let any be so unjust to think the Usefulness of this Work is confined to the Author alone (though Charity begins at home) his design being more generous and communicative, and tending to the profit of others as well as himself.*

> Jack London *The Iron Heel* 1908
> *We've paid for our experience in sweat and blood, and we've earned all that's coming to us … Charity begins at home.*

See also (as) COLD as charity.

charm

work/act like a charm
to be surprisingly or amazingly effective: also, in early use, *to a charm*. From the meaning of *charm* 'an act or utterance that is believed to have magic powers'. 19th cent.

> Susan Ferrier *Marriage* 1818
> *Mrs. Douglas here mildly interposed, and soothed down the offended pride of the Highlanders, by attributing Lady Juliana's agitation entirely to surprise. The word operated like a charm; all were ready to admit, that it was a surprising thing when heard for the first time.*

> K Carmichael *Ceremony of Innocence* 1991
> *It's impossible to cry and inhale at the same time. You'd choke. It works like a charm. Some people sing, whistle, talk – that blocks off the crying mechanism too.*

chase

chase the dragon
to take heroin by heating it and inhaling the fumes. The heroin is placed on tin foil and lit with a taper, the fumes forming a pattern on the foil that is said to resemble the tail of a dragon. *Mid 20th cent.*

> Timothy Mo *Sour Sweet* 1982
> *Probably the stuff was now only twenty per cent pure. Still, good enough for 'chasing the dragon' Hong Kong style with match, silver foil, and paper tube, and certainly good enough for the English to dissolve and heat in their tea-spoons and squirt into their veins.*

See also chase rainbows *at* RAINBOW; chase one's own TAIL.

chatter

the chattering classes
the educated sections of society thought of as constantly discussing political and social issues and expressing liberal opinions: usually in depreciatory contexts. *Late 20th cent.*

> *The Times* 1985
> *Despite all the wailing and gnashing of teeth among the chattering classes, the outlook for British broadcasting is actually rather cheery.*

cheap

cheap and cheerful
inexpensive but acceptable or serviceable. *Mid 20th cent.*

> *Independent* 1989
> *And now for something completely different: cheap and cheerful claret.*

cheap and nasty
inexpensive and of poor quality: also in extended uses. *19th cent.*

> Trollope *The Duke's Children* 1880
> *In hunting, as in most other things, cheap and nasty go together. If men don't choose to put their hands in their pockets they had better say so, and give the thing up altogether.*

> Ann Pilling *Henry's Leg* 1987
> *They were cheap and nasty watches, the kind you see on special offer in filling-stations.*

cheap at the price
well worth the price asked. The variant form *cheap at half the price* is counter-intuitive, since the actual price is then greater and not less. What is meant is 'cheap at twice the price', and the form we have is an illogicality, or inversion, of idiom of the kind that language abounds in. There have been attempts to resolve the paradox by regard-

ing the expression as ironic, i.e. making it mean 'excessively priced' (but it is not used that way), and as a trader's cry telling customers that his price is half the normal one and therefore 'cheap' or good value (but this is a rationalization). I prefer to regard the phrase as slightly skewed, as many English idioms are. *19th cent.*

Mark Twain *Roughing It* 1872
To stretch out and go to sleep, even on stony and frozen ground, after pushing a wagon and two horses fifty miles, is a delight so supreme that for the moment it almost seems cheap at the price.

See also DIRT cheap.

cheek

cheek by jowl
close together, side by side. The phrase is recorded in an earlier form *cheek by cheek* from Middle English. *Jowl* is another word for 'cheek', although its use in this meaning is recorded in the phrase at an earlier date than as a single word. *16th cent.*

Shakespeare *A Midsummer Night's Dream* III.ii.339 (1595)
[Lysander] *Now follow, if thou dar'st, to try whose right, | Of thine or mine, is most in Helena.*
[Demetrius] *Follow? Nay, I'll go with thee, cheek by jowl.*

turn the other cheek
to decline to retaliate after being attacked or injured: with allusion to the New Testament accounts of the Sermon on the Mount (Matthew 5:39 'But I say unto you, That ye resist not evil: but whosoever shall smite thee on thy right cheek, turn to him the other also'; *cf* Luke 6:29). *19th cent.*

cheer

The earliest meaning of *cheer* is 'the human face' (as used by Oberon in describing Helena in Shakespeare's *A Midsummer Night's Dream* (1595) III.ii.96 'All fancy-sick she is, and pale of cheer'). From this developed a now obsolete figurative meaning relating to facial expression, and the meaning underlying the phrase, 'disposition, frame of mind'.

be of good cheer
old use to be positive and optimistic, especially at a time of danger or difficulty. The phrase occurs in Shakespeare (see below) and in the Authorized Version of the Bible (1611), e.g. in the account in Matthew 9:2–7 of Christ's curing the man sick of the palsy: 'Jesus seeing their faith said unto the sick of the palsy: Son, be of good cheer; thy sins be forgiven thee.' *Middle English*

Shakespeare *As You Like It* IV.iii.165 (1599)
Be of good cheer, youth. You a man! You lack a man's heart.

three cheers for —
an exhortation to recognize the merits or achievements of somebody or something: used literally to invite those present to cry 'hurrah' three times, and figuratively as a general statement of support. *Three cheers* in its literal meaning is recorded from the 18th cent., and allusive uses from 19th cent. *Two cheers* is occasionally used as an ironic modification implying reluctantly given or qualified enthusiasm, as in the title of a book by E M Forster, *Two Cheers for Democracy* ('there is no occasion to give three'), published in 1951.

Emerson Bennett *Viola* 1852
Away! Away! Away! Three cheers for freedom! And ho for the sunny south!

cheese

a big cheese
informal an important or influential person: first recorded in the meaning 'wealth or fame', and slightly later with reference to individuals. The relevance of cheese in this context is not clear; it may have nothing to do with the familiar word but be an assimilation of a Persian word *chiz* meaning 'thing'. *Early 20th cent.*

Good Housekeeping 1992
With plans to nearly double the number of Disney attractions and hotels in the USA and Japan, the Disney big cheeses are calling this the 'Disney Decade'.

chequered

take the chequered flag
to win: a metaphor from motor racing, in which a chequered flag is used to wave the winner of a race past the finishing line. *20th cent.*

cherry

another bite / two bites at the cherry

more than one chance to succeed in something. *18th cent.*

> Edward Thompson *Trinculo's Trip to the Jubilee* 1770
> *Says I, Beau, you know that I love to be merry, | And our pockets are yet very stout; | Zounds! why should we make then two bites of a cherry, | Shall we coach it within or without?*

a bowl of cherries

a highly enjoyable situation or experience: from the title of a 1931 Lew Brown song, 'Life is just a bowl of cherries'. *Mid 20th cent.*

> Martin Amis *Time's Arrow* 1991
> *Life is no bowl of cherries. It's swings and round-abouts. You win some, you lose some. It evens out. It measures up.*

the cherry on the cake

a pleasing but unnecessary addition to something that is already very pleasant or enjoyable. *Late 20th cent.*

> The Art Newspaper 1992
> *I loathe 'Guernica' because, in the words of another writer, it can be seen as 'the cherry on the great cake of contemporary art'.*

lose one's cherry

informal to lose one's virginity. *Cherry* is used in its slang meaning 'hymen', an extension of uses referring to the lips, which date from the 16th cent. A 19th cent. slang meaning is 'a young girl'. *Early 20th cent.*

> J B Wharton *Squad* 1928
> *'Guess it wuz me turned his head, Mose,' says O'Connors. 'That first night's hike, when he begun to boast o' what a good thing he wuz onto back there an' I told him he wuz too young to lose his cherry. He ain't spoke to me since.'*

Cheshire

See GRIN like a Cheshire cat.

chest

get something off one's chest

to confess or admit to something embarrassing or difficult, especially in order to ease the psycho-logical or emotional burden caused by it. *Early 20th cent.*

> Clyde Fitch *The Truth* 1907
> [Warder] *Now you've got it all 'off your chest'? Tomorrow you'll be all right and ready to forgive again. Shall I call Becky?* [Mrs Lindon] *You're going to accuse her before me?*

> Somerset Maugham *The Moon and Sixpence* 1919
> *'You are a most unmitigated cad.' 'Now that you've got that off your chest, let's go and have dinner.'*

See also keep/play one's cards close to one's chest *at* CARD.

chestnut

an old chestnut

a joke or anecdote, or in recent use simply a topic or issue, that has become tedious from repetition or over-exposure. The phrase is first found in North America in the 19th cent. There have been many explanations of this association, of which the most likely relates to a conversation between two characters called Xavier and Pablo in a melodrama, *The Broken Sword*, first performed at Covent Garden in 1816. Xavier is once again describing his adventures in a cork tree when Pablo interrupts to point out that on previous tellings of the story the tree has been a chestnut.

pull the chestnuts out of the fire

to achieve something difficult on another person's behalf. From the fable of the monkey and the cat, in which a monkey uses the paw of his friend the cat to rake chestnuts out of a fire: the derivation of the word *cat's-paw*, meaning 'tool or dupe'. The phrase is 19th cent. in this form.

> Pall Mall Gazette 1886
> *The Unionists have, indeed, pulled the chestnuts out of the fire for Lord Salisbury.*

chew

chew the fat/rag

informal to make friendly conversation, to chat or gossip. The relevance of *fat* and *rag* is unclear: chewing fat may simply be an allusion to hard chewing, and *red rag* is recorded in US use from the 17th cent. as a slang term for 'tongue'. The first uses appear towards the end of the 19th cent., in a glossary of idioms published in 1891, and slightly earlier in a book about army life that associated the phrase with insubordination in the ranks (J B Patterson, *Life in the Ranks of the British Army in India, and on Board a Troopship*, 1885: 'Persisting to argue the point, or "chew the rag", as it is termed in rank and file phraseology, with some extra intelligent non-commissioned officer.'). There are some turn-of-the-century uses in American sources, which seem to appear from nowhere, and then the 'Taffrail' use in a work set in the Royal Navy at the time of the First World War (see below), which fits better with the earlier history of the phrase. *19th cent.*

> Taffrail *Pincher Martin* 1916
> *D'you think I'm standin' up 'ere 'longside a blackboard chewin' my fat for the good o' my 'ealth, or wot?*

See also chew the CUD.

chicken

be no chicken

1 to be no coward, to act bravely. *18th cent.*

> Henry Fielding *Joseph Andrews* 1742
> *Adams, who was no chicken, and could bear a drubbing as well as any boxing Champion in the Universe, lay still only to watch his opportunity.*

2 to be no longer young. The phrase is 18th cent. in this form. A spring chicken is a young bird of between 11 and 14 weeks, and the phrase *be no spring chicken* is early 20th cent.

> Arthur Murphy *The Old Maid* 1761
> *Recollect, sister, that you are no chicken – you are not now of the age that becomes giddiness and folly.*

> Jeremy Paxman *Friends in High Places* 1990
> *A Broadcasting Standards Council … will be run, under Lord Rees-Mogg, by a bishop, a headmaster, a psychologist, an educationalist, a retired Labour MP and a former television newsreader. None of the figures on any of the regulatory bodies was exactly a spring chicken, and none could be called a radical.*

a chicken-and-egg situation

a situation in which it is difficult to distinguish cause and effect: from the traditional puzzle of which came first, the chicken (to lay the egg) or the egg (to produce the chicken). A variant form *hen-and-egg situation* is also recorded from the 1930s. *Mid 20th cent.*

> A L Rowse *Politics and the Younger Generation* 1931
> *It is the old hen-and-egg argument, that there is no knowing which comes first.*

> C H Rolph *Common Sense about Crime* 1961
> *To argue that there would be no punishment without crime and (ergo) no crime without punishment would be to import the chicken-and-egg sequence into a problem.*

one's chickens come home to roost

past wrong or ill-advised actions will cause one trouble eventually. *19th cent.*

> Nathaniel Parker Willis *Dashes at Life with a Free Pencil* 1845
> *These poems, we may venture to say to you, are chickens of ours that still come home to roost.*

count one's chickens (before they are hatched)

to assume that something will happen or be available before one can be sure about it. The notion appears originally as a proverb (16th cent.) *do not count your chickens until they are hatched*, and the phrase appears in freer allusive form within a century. *17th cent.*

> Samuel Butler *Hudibras* 1664
> *To swallow gudgeons ere they're catch'd, | And count their chickens ere they're hatched.*

running/rushing about like a headless chicken

in a great hurry or panic. A chicken twitches and moves by reflex nervous action after it has been killed by decapitation. *Early 20th cent.*

> E J Dies *Plunger* 1929
> *One man was quoted in the Tribune as saying, 'The old man stood like a rock when other bankers were wringing their hands and flopping about like headless chickens.'*

chief

all chiefs and no Indians

a situation in which there are too many people giving orders and not enough to carry them out: with allusion to traditional stories about native peoples in the American West. *Mid 20th cent.*

big white chief

informal the person in overall charge or authority. A variant form *great white chief* is also recorded. *Mid 20th cent.*

Colin Forbes *Whirlpool* 1991

'Just because I happen to be President of this company I don't play the Great White Chief,' he was fond of saying. 'My door is always open to any employee who has a problem. Night and day I'm available to the folks who work for us.'

chin

keep one's chin up

to remain cheerful in trying circumstances: with allusion to the position of the head, thought of as held up when in good spirits and pointed down when sad or unhappy. Also in the shortened form *chin up* as an encouragement to a person who appears despondent. *Mid 20th cent.*

Michael Falk *Part of the Furniture* 1991

Keep your chin up, girl, we're not lost yet.

stick one's chin out

to show determination or resolve: also in literal or semi-literal uses in which the thrusting forward of the chin is a sign of assertiveness or aggression. *19th cent.*

Seba Smith *May-Day in New York* 1845

'Well, when are you going to pay that rent?' 'When I get it,' says she, sticking her chin out at him, and showing her teeth, like a cat that turns round to fight a dog that's drove her into a corner.

stick one's chin up

to act in a haughty or overbearing manner. *19th cent.*

Trollope *Doctor Thorne* 1858

'Well, what is it?' said Frank, looking rather disgusted. 'What makes you stick your chin up and look in that way?' Frank had hitherto been rather a despot among his sisters.

take it on the chin

to accept criticisms or difficulties bravely or stoically: a metaphor from boxing. *Early 20th cent.*

J P McEvoy *Show Girl* 1928

Jack Milton won't kick in another nickel. And we're going to take it on the chin for five thousand down here this week.

Chinaman

not a Chinaman's chance

NAmer, informal no chance at all. *Chinaman's Chance* is the title of a book by R Thomas (1978). *Early 20th cent.*

chink

a chink in somebody's armour

a weak point in somebody's character or ideas that makes them vulnerable to criticism. *Mid 20th cent.*

N R Hanson *Patterns of Discovery* 1958

Retroductions [= special forms of reasoning] do not always lead to syntheses like those of Newton, Clerk Maxwell, Einstein and Dirac. They sometimes show the first chink in the old armour.

chip

A Middle English word originally referring to small pieces cut off a hard material such as wood or stone. The use referring to a counter in gambling, which underlies several phrases, dates from the 19th cent.

cash/hand/pass in one's chips

informal, originally NAmer to die or give up one's work or life's occupation: a metaphor from gambling, in which players' chips or counters are handed in at the end of a session in exchange for cash. The phrase might therefore be understood as including the notion that life has been a gamble. *19th cent.*

a chip off the old block

a person who takes after one of their parents. The *chip* intended here is a small piece shaved from a block of wood. In the 17th cent. the typical form of the phrase was *chip of the old* (or *same*) *block*. An early use is in a sermon delivered in 1627 by the English bishop and theologian Robert Sanderson, who asked 'Am not I a child of the same Adam, a vessel of the same clay, a chip of the same block, with him?' In the following century, Edmund Burke, commenting on the maiden speech of the Younger Pitt in the House of Commons in 1781, referred to him as 'not merely a chip of the old "block", but the old block itself'. *17th cent.*

John Phillips *Maronides, or Virgil Travesty* 1678
Next him another doubtie Wight | Brave Silvius Aeneas hight, | He, a true chip of the old block, | Like thee, much given to the smock.

L M Montgomery *Anne of Green Gables* 1909
'So this is Stephen's boy … He is very like his father.' 'Everybody says I'm a chip off the old block,' remarked Paul.

Michele Abendstern *I Don't Feel Old* 1990
His grandfather, who taught him songs and ballads and regaled him with tales of his own 'merry' youth when he fought with gamekeepers, clearly saw the young poacher as a chip off the old block.

have a chip on one's shoulder
to be resentful or embittered. The phrase is said to have originated in the US in a strange but well-recorded custom of the 1850s by which a man or boy would issue a challenge by placing a chip of wood on his shoulder: his opponent knocked off the chip as acceptance of the challenge (much like picking up a glove or gauntlet thrown down in the same spirit). A fight then ensued. It is a short conceptual step from this image of the chip as a symbol of bravado to one of hostile resentment. *Not care a chip*, meaning 'not to care at all', appears in the 1860s and may have some connection with our phrase. *19th cent.*

Harper's Magazine 1887
The way that dog went about with a chip on his shoulder … was enough to spoil the sweetest temper.

have had one's chips
to be defeated or eliminated: a metaphor from gambling, the idea presumably being that one has had one's chips and used them or lost them. *Mid 20th cent.*

Hansard 1992
Does not a Ministry of Agriculture, Fisheries and Food report show that production of early potatoes fell considerably, and that meant an increase in price? … Is not this subject wholly appropriate for the Minister, because his Government have had their chips?

when the chips are down
when the critical or decisive moment has been reached: a reference to the placing of bets in gambling. *Mid 20th cent.*

Harper Lee *To Kill a Mockingbird* 1960
Sometimes we have to make the best of things, and the way we conduct ourselves when the chips are down.

choice
See Hobson's choice *at* HOBSON.

chop¹
A 16th cent. word with the primary meaning of the jaw or (often in the plural) the side of the face.

bust one's chops
NAmer, informal to make a great effort. *Late 20th cent.*

chop²
A 15th cent. word meaning 'to barter'.

chop and change
to keep changing one's mind unpredictably. The phrase was first used (from the late 15th cent.) in neutral senses to mean 'to practise trade, to buy and sell'. Tyndale's translation (1525) of Paul's second epistle to the Corinthians (2:17) included the phrase 'choppe and change with the worde of God' (the Authorized Version of 1611 has 'corrupt the word of God'). *16th cent.*

Aphra Behn *A Discovery of New Worlds* (Translator's Preface) 1688
I wish in this and several other things, we had a little more of the Italian and Spanish humour, and did not chop and change our language, as we do our cloths, at the pleasure of every French tailor.

chop logic
to exchange arguments tediously or pedantically. A locus classicus of this phrase occurs in Shakespeare's *Romeo and Juliet* (1596), in the scene in which Juliet incurs her parents' anger for refusing to marry their chosen husband, Paris. Capulet, her father, declares 'is she not proud?', and Juliet replies 'proud can I never be of what I hate [i.e. Romeo, a member of the 'hated' Montagues]'. Capulet protests angrily (III.v.149) 'How, how, how, how – chopped logic? What is this?' *16th cent.*

Henry James *Daisy Miller* 1878
He was angry at finding himself reduced to chopping logic about this young lady.

chop³

The noun form of the verb *chop* meaning 'to cut with a chopper'.

get the chop
to be killed or dismissed or (said of an undertaking) abruptly ended: originally services' slang and in the form *get the chopper*. The image is of cutting things off with blows of a chopper. Other uses of *chop* in this meaning are recorded, e.g. *give somebody the chop, be for the chop*, etc. *Mid 20th cent.*

chop⁴

This word *chop* has nothing to do with the English words of the same spelling, but is derived from Hindi and means 'a seal or stamp'. It was used to denote various kinds of certification of goods in connection with European commerce in the Far East, and acquired the figurative meaning 'something genuine or of high quality'.

not much chop
Australian and NZ, *informal* not very good. *19th cent.*

chord

strike/touch a chord
to say or do something that finds a response in other people's feelings: a metaphor in which the mind is regarded as a musical instrument and its emotions as the strings. *18th cent.*

Shelley *St Irvyne* 1811
'T was then that I contemplated self-destruction; I had almost plunged into the tide of death, had rushed upon the unknown regions of eternity, when the soft sound of a bell from a neighbouring convent, was wafted in the stillness of the night. It struck a chord in unison with my soul; it vibrated on the secret springs of rapture.

James Joyce *A Portrait of the Artist as a Young Man* 1916
His words seemed to have struck some deep chord in his own nature. Had he spoken of himself, of himself as he was or wished to be?

chuck

A 16th cent. word having the primary meaning 'to throw', and used in some idioms as an alternative to *throw* (e.g. *chuck in the sponge*).

chuck it
informal to stop trying; to give up. *19th cent.*

chuck it down
informal to rain heavily. *Late 20th cent.*

Ann Pilling *Henry's Leg* 1987
Outside it was chucking it down and the streets were deserted.

get the chuck
to be dismissed or rejected, especially from a relationship. *19th cent.*

G & W Grossmith *Diary of a Nobody* 1892
If you want the good old truth, I've got the chuck!

give something/somebody the chuck
to dismiss or get rid of somebody or something; to have nothing more to do with them. *19th cent.*

See also throw/chuck one's WEIGHT about/around.

chump

off one's chump
out of one's senses; crazy. The meaning of *chump* 'head' is a figurative extension of the original 18th cent. meaning 'thick chunk of wood cut from timber'. *19th cent.*

G K Chesterton *The Innocence of Father Brown* 1911
Don't you know what psychology means? … Psychology means being off your chump.

cigar

close but no cigar
a good but unsuccessful try; a near miss: a metaphor from US fairground games in which the prize was a cigar. *Late 20th cent.*

Mick Middles *The Smiths* 1988
Nobody risked showering the album with reams of ecstatic praise: 'Close, but no cigar' became the order of the day.

cinder

See BURNT to a cinder.

circle

circle the wagons
to take joint action against a common threat: with allusion to the practice in the American West of forming a defensive circle with the wagons when a wagon train was under attack. *19th cent.*

go/run round in circles
to be frantically active without making any progress. *Mid 20th cent.*

> Thomas Harvey et al *Making an Impact* 1989
> *It would be like taking London's M25 or Washington's beltway, in the hope of getting somewhere; all you would do is go round and round in circles.*

the wheel has turned/come full circle
the cycle of events has taken its course, and justice has been done. The allusion is to Shakespeare, *King Lear* (1606) v.iii.165 '[Edmond] Thou'st spoken right. 'Tis true. The wheel is come full circle. I am here.' Also, in extended use, *come* (or *turn*) *full circle* is 'to return to a former state of affairs'. *17th cent.*

circus

a three-ring/three-ringed circus
a lavish display: from the American practice of holding circuses with three rings giving simultaneous performances. *19th cent.*

> Will Carleton *The Thanksgiving Dance* 1902
> *'There will be a dance tonight at the house of Deacon Adams!'* | *What surprise was in all eyes; how with questions they would work us!* | *'Twouldn't hev rattled folks much more ef we'd hed a three-ring circus.*

> Michael Dobbs *House of Cards* 1989
> *His attempt at a dignified resignation had turned into a three-ring circus.*

See also BREAD and circuses.

civilization

(the end of) civilization as we know it
(the collapse of) social order: often used ironically or humorously. The phrase occurs in the film *Citizen Kane* (1941) and has become a cliché of ironic exaggeration in the cinema and broadcasting. *Mid 20th cent.*

claim

a claim to fame
a reason to be well known: often used ironically or humorously. *18th cent.*

> Jane Brereton *The Dream* 1744
> *Promiscuous throngs the temple croud,* | *And make their claim to fame aloud.* | *From every region there they came,* | *To pay their homage to the Dame.*

> Daily Telegraph 1992
> *Hunt's main claim to fame these days is his two-year term in prison for a particularly nasty libel – he called the Prince Regent 'a fat Adonis of 50'.*

See also LAY claim to something.

clanger
See DROP a clanger.

clap

The meaning reflected in the phrases is an extension (first recorded in the 16th cent.) of the primary meaning 'to strike the hands together' and hence 'to slap in a forceful way' (as in *clap somebody on the back*). In the extended meaning there is the same underlying notion of urgency and promptness, but without the implication of a loud accompanying sound.

clap hold of somebody/something
to take a hold of somebody or something; to seize them. *16th cent.*

clap somebody in jail/irons
to put somebody in prison. *16th cent.*

See also clap/lay/set eyes on something/somebody *at* EYE.

clapper

go/run like the clappers
informal, originally services' slang to move at great speed: also in other contexts involving great speed or force. The word *clapper* here is the striking device: probably that of a bell, although it is sometimes associated with an older sense of the word, a device in a mill that strikes the grain hopper to make the grain move down to the millstones. *Mid 20th cent.*

Esquire 1992
As we move into our twenties and thirties, hormones are no longer racing through the body like the clappers.

class

a class act

an impressive or stylish person or thing: from the adjectival use of *class* to mean 'high-class, excellent', itself an extension of the basic meaning 'a division by grade or quality'. *Late 20th cent.*

Guardian 1989
I doubt that she is much like the real Gertrude Lawrence but she is decidedly a class act.

claw

get/stick one's claws into somebody/something

to gain sinister or manipulative control over a person or thing: the analogy is with a bird of prey. *19th cent.*

Trollope *Framley Parsonage* 1861
The order for foreclosing had gone forth, and the harpies of the law, by their present speed in sticking their claws into the carcase of his property, were atoning to themselves for the delay with which they had hitherto been compelled to approach their prey.

clay

See FEET of clay.

clean

(as) clean as a whistle

absolutely clean or clear. With *clean* as a quasi-adverb, the phrase is often used in the sense 'very effectively, completely'. *19th cent.*

Trollope *Phineas Redux* 1874
He swore to himself that nothing should separate him from Adelaide Palliser ... 'What is a man to do?' he not unnaturally asked his friend Captain Boodle at the club. 'Let her out on the grass for a couple of months,' said Captain Boodle, 'and she'll come up as clean as a whistle. When they get these humours there's nothing like giving them a run.'

clean house

chiefly NAmer to rid an organization of inefficiency or corruption: from the literal meaning 'to do housework'. *Mid 20th cent.*

Scotsman 1990
Mr Perot campaigned with a promise to 'clean house' in Washington and close the yawning shortfall between the US government tax revenues and its spending, expected to reach $327 billion this year.

come clean

informal, originally NAmer to speak frankly, especially by admitting a mistake or wrongdoing, or by confessing the truth after allowing people to be misled: cf make a clean breast (of something) below. *Early 20th cent.*

Daily Mirror 1992
Sellafield finally came clean last night on what happened when plutonium liquid leaked at the heart of the nuclear reprocessing plant.

have clean hands

to be innocent of an illegal or immoral act: with allusion to Psalms 24:3–4 (in the Authorized Version, 1611) 'Who shall ascend into the hill of the Lord? or who shall stand in his holy place? He that hath clean hands, and a pure heart'. Also in the form *keep one's hands clean*. *17th cent.*

Joshua Sylvester transl Du Bartas' *Divine Weeks and Works* 1621
Holde-even the balance, with clean hands, clos'd eyes.

Economist 1993
Though the Bosnian Serbs, headed by the endlessly duplicitous Radovan Karadzic, have behaved worst, no one has clean hands.

make a clean breast (of something)

to own up to a wrongdoing or to perpetuating a lie or misunderstanding: from the notion of the breast as the seat of the human conscience. *18th cent.*

Scots Magazine 1753
He pressed him ... to make a clean breast, and tell him all.

Wilkie Collins *The Moonstone* 1868
Come, come, my girl! ... This is not like yourself. You have got something on your mind. I'm your friend – and I'll stand your friend, even if you have done wrong. Make a clean breast of it, Rosanna – make a clean breast of it!

make a clean sweep

1 to get rid of everything or everybody that's unwanted. *19th cent.*

Dickens *The Mystery of Edwin Drood* 1870

He makes a clean sweep of all untidy accumulations, puts all his drawers in order, and leaves no note or scrap of paper undestroyed, save such memoranda as bear directly on his studies.

2 to win all the prizes in a contest, all the contests in a tournament, all the seats or votes in an election, etc. *19th cent.*

Trollope *The Way We Live Now* 1875

I'll tell you what I'm going to do; and why I'm over here so uncommon sharp. These shares are at a'most nothing now in London. I'll buy every share in the market. I wired for as many as I dar'd, so as not to spoil our own game, and I'll make a clean sweep of every one of them.

Mr Clean

the ideal of the honourable or trustworthy individual, especially a politician or person in authority: one of a number of uses from the late 19th cent. and 20th cent. in which a quality or attribute is personified (compare *Mr Big, Mr Fixit, Mr Right,* etc). *Late 20th cent.*

Independent 1989

The [Indian] *Prime Minister's 'Mr Clean' image of five years ago has all but been destroyed by the scandal.*

See also a clean bill of health *at* BILL[1]; clean up one's ACT; keep one's NOSE clean; show a clean pair of heels *at* HEEL; wipe the SLATE clean.

cleaner

take/send somebody to the cleaners

1 *informal* to defeat an opponent decisively and humiliatingly: from the idea of giving clothes a drastically thorough treatment: *cf* put somebody through the WRINGER. *Mid 20th cent.*

Guardian 1989

His team, World Cup finalists and dotted with household idols, were taken to the cleaners by a bunch of Australian students and farmers in the first Test.

2 *informal* to cheat somebody or rip them off: from the image of stripping them bare or clean. *Mid 20th cent.*

Ideal Home 1991

To avoid being taken to the cleaners, Which? suggested the best way of getting good results was to hire a firm recommended by word of mouth.

clear

(as) clear as day/daylight

easy to see or comprehend. *16th cent.*

Shakespeare 2 Henry VI II.i.110 (1591)

[Gloucester] *In my opinion yet thou seest not well.* [Simpcox] *Yes, master, clear as day, I thank God and Saint Alban.*

clear the air

to relieve tension or hostility by open discussion: from the notion of a thunderstorm clearing sultry conditions in the atmosphere. The literal meaning, referring to the clearing of cloud and mist, dates back to Middle English. *19th cent.*

George Gissing *The Whirlpool* 1897

Hugh Carnaby's position called for no lament; he had a sufficient income of his own, and would now easily overcome his wife's pernicious influence; with or without her, he would break away from a life of corrupting indolence, and somewhere beyond seas 'beat the British drum' – use his superabundant vitality as nature prompted. After all, it promised to clear the air. These explosions were periodic, inevitable, wholesome.

clear the decks

to prepare for action by dealing with any preliminary or awkward matters first: from the literal use, of ships having their decks cleared of unnecessary items and impediments before an engagement at sea. Some early uses are in extended metaphor (as below). *17th cent.*

Thomas Rymer *A Short View of Tragedy* 1692

Our ear shou'd not be hankering after the ryme, when the business should wholly take us up, and fill our head. The words must be all free, independent, and disengag'd, no entanglement of ryme to be in our way. We must clear the decks, and down with the ornaments and trappings in the day of action, and engagement.

in clear

(said of text) in normal language and not in code: translating French *en clair*, used from the 19th cent. *Mid 20th cent.*

Anthony Livesey *Great Battles of World War I* 1989
The Germans were immeasurably helped by the Russian staff practice … of sending radio messages and orders 'in clear' rather than in cypher.

in the clear
free of suspicion, known not to be guilty of any wrongdoing or to be involved in the unpleasant business in question. In earlier (early 20th cent.) uses the phrase meant 'beyond reach' or 'unavailable'. *Mid 20th cent.*

Simon Brett *Murder Unprompted* 1984
Lesley-Jane Decker had been on stage at the time of the shooting, so, unless she had brought in a hired killer, she seemed to be in the clear.

out of a clear (blue) sky
unexpectedly, without any warning: see also out of the BLUE. *19th cent.*

R L Stevenson *Kidnapped* 1886
Indeed, it is one thing to stand the danger of your life, and quite another to run the peril of both life and character. The thing, besides, had come so suddenly, like thunder out of a clear sky, that I was all amazed and helpless.

Economist 1993
Over the past year, many a fund manager has had his confidence shattered as supposedly reliable shares that were the solid core of his portfolio … crashed out of a clear blue sky.

See also (as) clear as a BELL; (as) clear as MUD.

cleft

be caught in a cleft stick
British to be in a situation in which it is impossible to act without adverse consequences: a cleft [= split] stick was used as a kind of holder. In the 18th cent., Jonathan Swift wrote: 'You may … stick your candle in a bottle … or a cleft stick.' The notion in the figurative use is of being held tight and unable to move. *Cleft* is a past participle form of *cleave* meaning 'to split or cut in two'. *See also* CLOVEN. *18th cent.*

Richard Warner transl Plautus' *The Carthaginian* 1772
You're in a cleft stick, pandar – 'Tis his bailiff we told you was the Spartan, and who brought you three hundred Philippeans; and the money is in that purse.

Beatrix Campbell *Wigan Pier Revisited* 1985
Now the local authorities are caught in a cleft stick, hostages to their own political process.

clever

a clever dick
informal an ostentatiously clever person; a know-all. *Dick* is a pet form of the name Richard, and is found from the 16th cent. as an epithet denoting a smart or noteworthy individual, for example in Shakespeare's *Love's Labour's Lost* (1594) v.ii.464: '[Biron] Some carry-tale, some please-man, some slight zany, | Some mumble-news, some tren-cher-knight, some Dick | That smiles his cheek in years, and knows the trick | To make my lady laugh when she's disposed.' (The name *Dick* is chosen here to rhyme with *trick* in the following line.) It is also a founder member of the familiar group of *Tom, Dick, and Harry*. Cf a SMART alec. *19th cent.*

too clever by half
clever or ingenious, especially in an over-subtle or ostentatious way: see also by HALF. *19th cent.*

William Barry *The New Antigone* 1887
I think there is some plan afoot about your drawings and my birthday, though the two things haven't much connection, one would think. It is all the Countess's doing. I wish she would let it alone. She is too clever by half.

Roy Jenkins *Baldwin* 1988
There was also a good ringing pledge in which the ambiguity, although present, was neither obvious nor too clever by half.

click

click one's fingers
to attract attention by, or as though by, making a sharp clicking sound with the thumb and middle finger. *Mid 20th cent.*

Len Deighton *Only When I Larf* 1968
A cigarette girl came past and he clicked his fingers at her and asked for matches.

click into place
to become suddenly clear or obvious, especially in the context of other facts or circumstances: from the notion of a machine part fitting into position, enabling the mechanism to function. *Mid 20th cent.*

Anthony Masters *Traffic* 1991
And above all, what on earth was he doing up here? Then something clicked into place in his mind. Of course!

climb

be climbing the walls
informal to feel frustrated or angry. *Late 20th cent.*

Zzap 64 1992
Hundreds of would-be joystick junkies have been climbing the walls with frustration, as the only compatible datarecorders that have been available lately are of the decidedly dodgy import variety and won't work with many games.

have a mountain to climb
to face a huge task. *20th cent.*

Belfast Telegraph 1990
We might have lost by six goals but got our act together. We gave ourselves a mountain to climb and didn't quite make it.

clip

at a clip
NAmer, informal all at once, at the same time. The meaning of *clip* here is 'a blow or stroke'. *18th cent.*

Robert Munford The Patriots 1798
Ha! damn me, I thought so; yes, yes, honies, you have got it, nine hundred at a clip. Well done, Washington, by God! We'll trim the rascals.

Upton Sinclair The Jungle 1906
Ain't he a daisy, though – blue ribbon at the New York show – eighty-five hundred at a clip! How's that, hey?

clip somebody's wings
to limit somebody's freedom of action: from the literal meaning of cutting back a bird's feathers to prevent it from flying. *16th cent.*

Marlowe The Massacre at Paris xxi.122 (1592)
Away to prison with him! I'll clip his wings | Or e'er he pass my hands. Away with him!

David Lodge Nice Work 1988
There was a time not so long ago when Philip Swallow was for ever swanning around the globe on some conference jaunt or other. Now it seems that the cuts have clipped his wings.

cloak

cloak and dagger
melodramatic or romantic intrigue: with allusion to the disguise afforded by a cloak and the menace represented by a dagger. Originally used in contexts in which cloaks and daggers actually featured, and often therefore with fictional reference. *19th cent.*

Dickens Barnaby Rudge 1840
His servant brought in a very small scrap of dirty paper, tightly sealed in two places, on the inside whereof was inscribed in pretty large text these words. 'A friend. Desiring of a conference. Immediate. Private. Burn it when you've read it.' 'Where in the name of the Gunpowder Plot did you pick up this?' said his master. It was given him by a person then waiting at the door, the man replied. 'With a cloak and dagger?' said Mr. Chester.

clock

hold the clock on something
to time an event or procedure. *20th cent.*

round/around the clock
all day and night; 24 hours. *19th cent.*

Dickens Bleak House 1853
For the cart so hard to draw, is near its journey's end, and drags over stony ground. All round the clock, it labours up the broken steeps, shattered and worn. Not many times can the sun rise, and behold it still upon its weary road.

turn/put back the clock
to return to an earlier state of affairs, especially to regain youth or retrieve a lost opportunity. *19th cent.*

Hardy The Well-Beloved 1897
I'll say nothing then, more than how wonderful it is that a woman should have been able to put back the clock of Time thirty years!

watch the clock
to pay strict attention to one's hours of working, or to one's perceived time limits, so as not to exceed them: this practice is called *clock-watching*. *Mid 20th cent.*

Eleanor Deeping Caring for Elderly Parents 1979
Some visitors never learn how to come and go with grace, and clock-watching, when the time for

departure is drawing near, should be carefully avoided.

clockwork

be as regular as / run like clockwork

to work well and efficiently, according to a fixed routine: the term *clockwork* in its physical meaning dates from the middle of the 17th cent., and by the 18th cent. it was in common use as a metaphor for regularity and order. *18th cent.*

> Richardson *Pamela* 1741
> *It signifies nothing to ask him: he will have his own way. There is no putting him out of his bias. He is a regular piece of clockwork.*

> J B Howe *The British Slave* 1856
> *Don't all the pretty girls run after him? His clothes are all found him; meals as regular as clockwork; and plenty of companions.*

close

behind closed doors

done secretly or furtively: in early use also in the form *with closed doors*. *19th cent.*

> Herman Melville *Pierre* 1852
> *No doubt, Lucy, you will find in the bay scenery some hints for that secret sketch you are so busily occupied with – ere real living sitters do come – and which you so devotedly work at, all alone and behind closed doors.*

> Wilkie Collins *The Haunted Hotel* 1879
> *On the 14th the Directors and their legal advisers met for the reading of the report, with closed doors.*

a close call

a narrow escape; a barely achieved or narrowly missed success. *19th cent.*

> Willa Cather *The Song of the Lark* 1915
> *If old Elmer hadn't played that trick on me, I'd have been in for about fifty thousand. That was a close call.*

a closed book

a subject about which one knows nothing: *cf* an OPEN book. *19th cent.*

> Nathaniel Parker Willis *People I Have Met* 1850
> *To one who is not young – for whom love is a closed book, and who has no ambition in progress – this mere society, without heart or joyousness, is a desert of splendor.*

run somebody close

to come close to equalling another's achievement. *19th cent.*

too close to call

(said of a race or contest) too evenly balanced for the outcome to be predicted. *Late 20th cent.*

> Liverpool Echo & Daily Post 1993
> *Next week's vote on the ordination of women priests could be too close to call, a poll shows today.*

See also close but no CIGAR; close the DOOR on; close one's eyes to *at* EYE; close one's MIND to; close ranks *at* RANK; close to the BONE; close to one's HEART; close to HOME; too close for COMFORT.

closet

come out of the closet

to make a public admission about one's private life, in particular to admit that one is a homosexual. *Closet*, the normal North American word for 'cupboard', symbolizes privacy and secrecy. It occurs in an earlier meaning 'a private room' in the Authorized Version of the Bible (1611) in the context of private prayer, for example at Matthew 6:6 'But thou, when thou prayest, enter into thy closet, and when thou hast shut the door, pray to thy Father which is in secret.' In recent use the phrase has been shortened to a simple phrasal verb *come out*, and even further to produce a transitive sense of the verb *out*, 'to reveal the homosexuality of somebody'. *Mid 20th cent.*

> Mario Puzo *Fools Die* 1978
> *She was coming out of the closet and without words she was telling the world of her bisexuality.*

> Michael Freeland *Kenneth Williams: A Biography* 1990
> *At the same time as not merely coming out of the closet about his sexuality – in fact, by hardly admitting there was a closet there at all – he was also locking so many of his innermost thoughts away.*

cloth

a man of the cloth

a male member of the clergy. Swift (early 18th cent.) used *the cloth* to mean the profession of the clergy; in earlier use a person's cloth was the distinctive uniform or livery of retainers and servants (e.g. *the King's cloth*), and later the clothing worn in a particular walk of life, eventually being applied by metonymy to the profession itself (as in *a man of our cloth*). *19th cent.*

See also CUT one's coat according to one's cloth; CUT from the same cloth.

cloud

be/live in cloud-cuckoo-land
to be in a dream world or have unrealistic ideas or ambitions. *Cloud-cuckoo-land* first appears as a translation of Nephelococcygia, the idealized city of the birds in Aristophanes' comic play *The Birds* (5th cent. BC). There have been many variants of the phrase since the late 19th cent.; in this form the phrase dates from the mid 20th cent.

> *Listener* 1964
> They weigh the evidence and give their judgment in what seems … a cloudcuckooland.

every cloud has a silver lining
(proverb) misfortune can bring some benefits. The concept is older than the phrase, occurring in Shakespeare's *3 Henry VI* (1591) v.iii.13: 'For every cloud engenders not a storm.' *See also* a SILVER lining. *19th cent.*

> George Townsend *The Bohemians* 1861
> Why, what has come upon your sombre face – a smile, as I live! Look, Alice, look! – a cloud with a silver lining!

on cloud nine
informal feeling extremely elated or happy. The phrase is commonly explained as originating in US meteorological terminology, in which cloud types are numbered. *Cloud nine* represents cumulonimbus, a particularly elaborate structure that is susceptible to fantastic imagery: to be on cloud nine is to inhabit a marvellous place. An alternative form *on cloud seven* is no longer used. The imagery suggests a drug-induced euphoria, and the numbers seven and nine are commonly associated with luck or happiness (compare *seventh heaven* and *dressed to the nines*). *Mid 20th cent.*

> Sasha Stone *Kylie Minogue: the Superstar Next Door* 1989
> To me she was, and is, blessed with that wonderful thing that got me so excited about Cliff all those years ago – a unique voice. I recognised it right away, and I was on Cloud Nine.

under a cloud
under suspicion; regarded with (usually temporary) disfavour. Clouds bring rain and cold and cast a shadow, but since they pass in time the attendant circumstances are normally transitory. There may also be a reference here to the passing of the moon behind a cloud, so that it is masked and its light subdued. *16th cent.*

> Charles Gildon *The Post-boy Rob'd of His Mail* 1692
> Nor (continu'd Winter) were these professions made in the sun-shine of a happy state, but when the man was actually under a cloud.

> Joseph Conrad *Lord Jim* 1900
> Her own father had been a white; a high official; one of the brilliantly endowed men … whose careers so often end under a cloud.

See also with one's HEAD in the clouds.

cloven

a cloven hoof
a sign of evil. In pagan mythology the cloven or split hoof of four-footed ruminants was associated with the god Pan; in Christian thought this association was transferred to Satan, who has been depicted as a hybrid being with the torso of a human and the legs and feet of a goat. *Cloven* is a past participle form of *cleave* meaning 'to split or cut in two'. *See also* CLEFT. The phrase is Middle English in the form *cloven foot*.

> Thomas D'Urfey *A Fond Husband* 1677
> Here, prethee read it; 'tis his character; I am sure it looks as if 'twere writ with a cloven hoof. Hah! – what think'st thou?

> P G Wodehouse *The Code of the Woosters* 1938
> It's no use telling me that there are bad aunts and good aunts. At the core, they are all alike. Sooner or later, out pops the cloven hoof.

clover

in clover
enjoying prosperity or pleasant circumstances: with allusion to the feeding of cattle in fields of clover. *17th cent.*

> Abel Boyer *Compleat French Master* 1699
> Do you think to live in clover thus all your lifetime?

Dickens *Hard Times* 1854
She resigned herself with noble fortitude, to lodging,
as one may say, in clover, and feeding on the fat of
the land.

Independent 1989
If Marcos was cynical, he was no more so than the
American foreign policy which kept him in power
and in clover for 20 years.

included in the main name. It was famously
used in the title of *Stalky & Co.* (= Stalky and
his friends), Kipling's story of schoolboy life
(1899). *18th cent.*

Clothes Show 1991
All of us probably envy the ability of Imelda, Ivana,
Diana and co to indulge themselves with a glorious
shopping spree whenever the desire grips them.

club

in the (pudding) club
British, informal pregnant. The origin of the
phrase lies most likely in the bulging pudding-
like appearance of a pregnant woman, rather
than the alternative somewhat far-fetched suggestion that it has to do with all the puddings a
mother will have to make for her child. The
phrase is recorded in Barrère and Leland's *Dic-*
tionary of Slang, Jargon and Cant (1889), but most
of the evidence is from after 1900. *19th cent.*

Liz Lochhead *True Confessions and New Clichés* 1985
A man will tip his hat to you | But never nip your
bum. | Even your ma-in-law will grovel | With
total approval | At the contents of your tum. | Yes,
when you've a bun in the oven | Everything is
apple pie. | I'm a lady-in-waiting, I am | Into
blatant understating | When you're in the club.

join / welcome to the club
a shallow or ironic expression of solidarity with
experiences or attitudes expressed by another
person, as though inviting them to join an association of people in the same position: often used
as a cynical response to another person's account
of their sufferings, as if to say 'You're not the only
one, mate'. *Club* in this meaning dates from earlier in the 20th cent. *Mid 20th cent.*

Frank Kippax *Other People's Blood* 1993
'You're mad,' he said. 'Welcome to the club.'

clutch

See clutch at straws *at* STRAW.

co.

— and co.
and the rest (of a group). The phrase is an extension of its use in the names of businesses (where
co. = company) to represent partners not

coach

drive a coach and horses through something
to make something, especially a measure or proposal, worthless or ineffective. The phrase in this
form is attributed to one Stephen Rice, a 17th
cent. Irish lawyer and judge who reportedly
declared that he would drive a coach and horses
through the Act of Settlement of 1701. Its main
uses remain within the context of political measures and laws. *17th cent.*

New Statesman and Society 1992
What, then, about us in Britain? Unlike in
America, there is no legal or constitutional right
to privacy. But how useful would such a right be
anyway, if an intelligence agency can drive a coach
and horses through it?

coal

coals to Newcastle
something taken or sent to a place that already
has plenty of it. The notion comes from the former role of Newcastle upon Tyne in north-east
England as a centre of the coal industry. *16th cent.*

James Melville *Autobiography* 1583
Salt to Dysart, or colles to Newcastle!

Henry Fielding *The History of Tom Jones* 1749
'I heard you was going to the wars: but I find it was
a mistake.' 'Why do you conclude so?' says Jones.
'Sure, Sir,' answered the barber, 'you are too wise a
man to carry a broken head thither; for that would
be carrying coals to Newcastle.'

R H Dana *Two Years Before the Mast* 1840
The captain offered them fifteen dollars a month,
and one month's pay in advance; but it was like
throwing pearls before swine, or rather, carrying
coals to Newcastle. So long as they had money, they
would not work for fifty dollars a month, and when
their money was gone, they would work for ten.

haul somebody over the coals

to give somebody a severe reprimand: from the literal meaning of dragging a victim over slow-burning coals as a former punishment or form of torture. *18th cent.*

Marryat Peter Simple 1834

Now the first lieutenant was not in the sweetest of tempers, seeing as how the captain had been hauling him over the coals for not carrying on the duty according to his satisfaction.

heap coals of fire (up)on somebody's head

to make somebody who has done you harm feel great remorse by treating them generously: with allusion to St Paul's Epistle to the Romans 12:20 (referring to Proverbs 25:21–22): 'If thine enemy hunger, feed him; if he thirst, give him drink: for in so doing thou shalt heap coals of fire upon his head.' The phrase goes back to Middle English where it appears in Langland's *Piers Plowman*.

John Barton The Art of Rhetorick 1634

[gloss] *Heap coals of fire, for overcome him; Make his bed, for give him ease.*

L M Montgomery Anne of Green Gables 1909

She just carried that sauce and pudding out and brought in some strawberry preserves. She even offered me some, but I couldn't swallow a mouthful. It was like heaping coals of fire on my head.

coast

the coast is clear

there is no danger, or the danger is past: a metaphor from smugglers or invaders watching out for opposition. The phrase occurs figuratively in 16th cent. lyric poetry, sometimes in erotic contexts, such as a poem in a collection dating from the middle of the century now in the Bodleian Library, Oxford (Bodleian MS Ashmole 48: see *Notes & Queries* June 2002, p.197). In these lines the poet is dreaming that his love comes to him in his sleep:

> Then bold was she to stand by me.
> With myrtle and merry chere.
> She vewde the chaumber round abowte.
> She saw the cost was cleare.

Shakespeare also uses the image, e.g. in *1 Henry VI* (1590) I.iv.87 'See the coast cleared, and then we will depart.' Some 16th cent. uses are literal or

semi-literal in meaning, and the transition to a fully figurative use was gradual. *16th cent.*

R L Stevenson Treasure Island 1883

The squire and Gray were busy helping the captain with his bandages; the coast was clear; I made a bolt for it over the stockade and into the thicket of the trees.

coat

See CUT one's coat according to one's cloth.

coat-tails

ride/climb/hang on somebody's coat-tails

to derive benefit, usually undeserved, from another person's success. Other phrases based on a similar image are no longer in use, e.g. *sit on one's own coat-tail* (= to be financially self-dependent). *19th cent.*

Mark Twain Huckleberry Finn 1884

But if only half a man ... shouts 'Lynch him, lynch him!' you're afraid to back down – afraid you'll be found out to be what you are – cowards – and so you raise a yell, and hang yourselves onto that half-a-man's coat tail, and come raging up here, swearing what big things you're going to do.

cobblers

a load of old cobblers

informal a lot of nonsense, utter rubbish. *Cobblers*, rhyming slang for *cobbler's awls* = balls, dates in this sense from the 1930s, and is first used in print in a phrase of this kind (actually, *that's all cobblers*) in the 1950s, although it is undoubtedly earlier in spoken use. An awl is a pointed tool used in leatherwork and shoemaking. *See also* a load of old CODSWALLOP. *Mid 20th cent.*

Julie Burchill in Mail on Sunday 1992

It is odd that those who complain about being censored by PC have become the exact mirror image of those they hate. In the old days, the complaint was 'I'm black, gay or feminist – that's why you won't publish my book.' Now those whose manuscripts are returned to sender say: 'I'm not black, gay or feminist – that's why you won't publish my book.' What never occurs to either camp is the obvious; that the book – or film, or record – might be completely and totally devoid of commercial potential, and that businesses are in business principally to make money. Or simply that the book – or film, or record – might be a load of old cobblers.

cobweb

blow/clear/sweep away the cobwebs

to bring new life or ideas to a situation. The figurative use of *cobweb* in the meaning 'stale or outdated accretion' dates from the 16th cent. *17th cent.*

cock[1] (male fowl)

be cock-a-hoop

to be elated or loudly triumphant. In modern use the phrase has been associated with the male bird, the *hoop* being understood as its crest (*cf* French *huppe* meaning 'crest') and influenced in meaning here by the word *whoop* meaning 'loud cry' (as in *whoops of joy*). But the true origin lies in a different word *cock* meaning 'tap'; this is reflected in a related (16th cent.) form of the phrase *set a cock a hoop*, to remove the tap from a cask and place it on the 'hoop' (though it is not clear exactly what part of the vessel this was) to let the contents run freely, i.e. to drink without restraint. The form *cock-a-hoop* dates from the 17th cent., occurring in Samuel Butler's satirical romance poem *Hudibras* (1663): 'Hudibras … having routed the whole troop, I With victory was cock-a-hoop.'

Francis Kirkman *The Unlucky Citizen* 1673
He permitted me to beat him the first and second games, at which I being cock-a-hoop, brag'd and crow'd like a Dunghil Cock.

Scott *Redgauntlet* 1824
While I speak of this, it is not much amiss to advise thee to correct a little this cock-a-hoop courage of thine.

a cock-and-bull story

a long, rambling and barely believable story or account. The allusion is very probably to some fable; the individual words both have the figurative meaning 'nonsense' in their own right but these are of later date than their use together in the phrase. References to *cock and bull* and *a story of cock and bull* date from the 17th cent., and *cock-and-bull story* itself from the late 18th cent.

When James Murray was compiling the entry for this phrase in the *Oxford English Dictionary*, he posted one of his regular appeals in the periodical *Notes & Queries* (December 1889, p.447) for evidence that antedated the earliest quotation (of 1828) then in his possession. A rush of responses followed exhorting Dr Murray to turn to the final page of Sterne's *Tristram Shandy*, where the story ends with a confused conversation about Walter (the narrator's father) and a bull. The closing words are a punning reference to this as 'a cock and a bull … and one of the best of its kind' (see below: this part was first published in 1767). Murray had been well aware of this evidence and of other evidence of the phrase in its developing stages: what he had wanted was evidence of *cock-and-bull story* in that precise form. In a withering riposte (*Notes & Queries* June 1890, p.494), he rounded on those who had implied his negligence:

I have noticed that people who offer us what we have already, and therefore do not ask for, generally accompany their superfluous gifts with an unnecessary expression of innocent surprise that what they offer 'should have escaped the notice of Dr Murray' … What surprises Dr Murray is that people should rush into print with replies … to his queries without having read them … Cock-and-bull went to press several months ago, and the answers now in N&Q, if they had been ever so intelligent and ever so relevant, would have been of no use to me. Fortunately intelligent and relevant answers were sent direct, one of which carried cock-and-bull story back to 1796. Mr Terry's reference, of the same date [to Grose's Dictionary of the Vulgar Tongue (1796), which included the phrase in a slightly different form, Cock and a Bull Story], … would have been useful as leading up to the modern phrase if it had been sent in time; but the Dictionary cannot stop four months for any word.

In fact there are uses of the phrase in forms close to Sterne's at an earlier date (see below). The published *OED* entry identifies the 1796 use with Dr Charles Burney, whose *Memoirs of the Life and Writings of Metastasio* at last provided the sought-after evidence of the phrase in its developed form: 'Not to tire you with the repetition of all the cock and bull stories which I have formerly told you …' But the story was not quite over. The *Supplement to the OED*, published at the end of the main run of editing in 1933, managed to push the record back one more year, in an *American Gazette* source from 1795. It is a shame, nonetheless, that the Sterne quotation (see below) did not appear anywhere among the evidence for the evolution of the phrase in the *OED* account. The phrase is first found in its present form in the 18th cent.

John Day *Law Trickes* 1608
What a tale of a cock and a bull he tolde my father whilst I made thee and the rest away.

Laurence Sterne *Tristram Shandy* 1767
'Lord!' said my mother, 'What is all the story about?' 'A cock and a bull,' said Yorick, 'and one of the best of its kind I ever heard.'

Byron *Don Juan* 1824
I've heard of stories of a cock and bull; | But visions of an apple and a bee … | Would make us think the moon is at its full.

Somerset Maugham *Of Human Bondage* 1915
'You're a past mistress of the cock-and-bull story,' said Philip. He was vaguely irritated that Mildred still had this passion for telling fibs.

cock of the walk
the dominant member of a group. The *walk* was the area in which a cock bred for fighting was kept and that was fought over between rivals. *19th cent.*

Henry James *The Europeans* 1878
'Seriously, they were glad to see you?' 'Enchanted. It has been the proudest day of my life. Never, never have I been so lionized! I assure you, I was cock of the walk.'

---

cock²

The meanings of the verb are though to be related to COCK¹: the notion of turning or sticking up derives from the position of a cock's neck when crowing.

cock one's ear
to listen attentively for something: with allusion to a dog making its ears erect. Uses of the phrase with *eye* and *nose* are also recorded, and Smollett (1750s) refers to *cocking the eye* as a 'vulgar phrase'. *18th cent.*

John Gay *Pastorals* 1720
Our Lightfoot barks, and cocks his ears.

George Watson *British Literature since 1945* 1991
The new novel, unlike the fictions of Tolkien and Lewis, is stubbornly secular, but with an ear cocked to the supernatural.

cock a snook at somebody
to act with disdain or defiance towards somebody. The physical action suggested by the phrase is of putting a thumb to one's nose and extending or wiggling the fingers in derision. *Cock* here means 'to stick out' or 'to make erect' (as with a *cocked gun*, or a *cocked hat*, one with the brim turned up). *Snook* is used only in this phrase; it may be related to *snout*, a variant that sometimes replaces it in an attempt to make the phrase more comprehensible. A more fruitful connection, however, can be seen in an idiom associated with the word *sight* in its sense to do with surveying and ballistics (as in *drawing a sight*): a slang glossary of 1860 includes the entry '*To take a sight at a person*, a vulgar action employed by street boys to denote incredulity, or contempt for authority, by placing the thumb against the nose and closing all the fingers except the little one, which is agitated in token of derision'. There is a stray use of *cocking a snook* in a diary entry from the end of the 18th cent. ('They cock snooks at one on every occasion'), but usage dates predominantly from a century or so later.

go off at half cock
(said of a plan or undertaking) to begin with inadequate preparation or knowledge and be likely to fail. The image is of firing a pistol with the cock or firing arm pulled partly back and held, as distinct from *full cock*, in which the arm is pulled fully back ready for firing. *At* (or *on*) *full cock* is occasionally found in figurative use, but is not so common as the phrase with *half cock*. *19th cent.*

James Fenimore Cooper *The Deerslayer* 1841
'Alike! Do you call a nigger like a white man, or me like an Indian?' 'You go off at half-cock, and don't hear me out. God made us all, white, black, and red; and, no doubt, had his own wise intentions in colouring us differently.'

Willa Cather *O Pioneers!* 1913
Lou was still the slighter of the two, the quicker and more intelligent, but apt to go off at half-cock.

---

cocked

knock something into a cocked hat
informal to defeat or surpass something completely: a *cocked hat* was a three-cornered hat with the brim permanently turned up, fashion-

able in the 18th cent. and 19th cent. The notion is probably of something being knocked into a strange shape resembling this type of hat, or (as in the quotation below) of a person's head being forced to fit into one. Association with the game of ninepins, in which three of the pins are set up in the form of a triangle, has been suggested but is much more tenuous. *19th cent.*

William Caruthers *The Kentuckian in New York* 1834
Now I wish my head may be knocked into a cocked-hat, if a man had told this to me of the Yorkers in old Kentuck, if I wouldn't have thought he was spinnin long yarns.

Cocker

according to Cocker
with precision; by strict calculation. Edward Cocker (1631–75) was a mathematician who wrote a popular *Arithmetick*. Dickens considered using *According to Cocker* as a title for the novel that was eventually called *Hard Times* (1854), according to his biographer John Forster (*The Life of Dickens*, 1872–4). *19th cent.*

Thomas Moore *The Fudges in England* 1835
As to reasoning – you know, dear, that's now of no use, | People still will their facts and dry figures produce, | As if saving the souls of a Protestant flock were | A thing to be managed 'according to Cocker!'

cockles

warm the cockles of somebody's heart
to give somebody a feeling of pleasure mixed with tenderness. The origin of this enchanting phrase is obscure. It has been thought that the shape of the heart resembles a cockle-shell; the zoological name of the cockle is *cardium*, which means 'heart'. But *cockle* is not otherwise used in this way, as we would expect if this association lay behind the phrase. A more cogent suggestion is that *cockles* is an assimilated form of the medieval Latin name *cochleae* denoting the ventricles of the heart. Early uses have *please* or *rejoice* instead of *warm*. *17th cent.*

Richard Graves *The Spiritual Quixote* 1773
The carriage ... brought them in sight of their village spire, which rose amidst a grove of pines, at the foot of the Cotswold hills: the sight of which,

after near two months absence, rejoiced the very cockles of Jerry's heart.

Rider Haggard *King Solomon's Mines* 1885
To adopt the language of hyperbole, in which all these people seem to indulge, you can tell him that a row is surely good, and warms the cockles of the heart, and that, so far as I am concerned, I'm his boy.

cocoa

I should cocoa!
informal an expression of emphatic agreement, though typically used ironically in a dismissive way, as though to say 'that's nonsense'. Also in the form *coco*. The phrase is probably rhyming slang for *I should say so* or (more closely) *I should hope so*, although the rhyme element is weak and there is no truncation, as there is for example with *butcher's* (*hook*), *plates* (*of meat*), and much rhyming slang. The phrase now has a dated feel, and is normally used to add an ironic period nuance. *Mid 20th cent.*

codswallop

a load of (old) codswallop
informal a lot of nonsense, utter rubbish. The origin of the word *codswallop* is much disputed, but in the end we have to admit that it is unknown, despite ingenious suggestions. The most colourful of these is that it relates to the invention of a special bottle for soft drinks by one Hiram Codd, an improbable name for a native of Bury St Edmunds in Suffolk in the mid 19th cent. The story goes that he invented a special airtight bottle for the soft drinks he manufactured, causing the drink to be derided by beer drinkers as *Codd's wallop, wallop* being a slang name (from the 1930s) for beer. If this is true, we have to explain a gap of nearly a hundred years before the term gained any real currency in the modern sense, and there is no evidence at all of its use in the original meaning thus proposed. The suggestion is, in fact, a load of its namesake. *See also* a load of old COBBLERS. *Mid 20th cent.*

Allan Prior *The Operators* 1966
All that stuff about mutual respect between police and criminal was a load of old codswallop.

coffin

See a NAIL in the coffin of somebody/something.

cog

a cog in the wheel/machine

a minor member of a large or complex organization: with allusion to a cog engaging with other and larger cogs to make a mechanism work. The word *machine* is often qualified as *political machine*, *bureaucratic machine*, etc. *Mid 20th cent.*

> Stephen Spender *World within World* 1951
> *Franz was incapable of becoming a cog in a political machine, and he remained profoundly human.*

coign

coign of vantage

a position enabling one to observe or take action: with allusion to Shakespeare, *Macbeth* (1606) I.vi.7 '[Duncan, describing the nests of house martins] This guest of summer, | The temple-haunting martlet, does approve | By his loved mansionry that the heavens' breath | Smells wooingly here. No jutty, frieze, | Buttress, nor coign of vantage but this bird | Hath made his pendant bed and procreant cradle.' *Coign*, an old spelling of *quoin*, denotes an external cornerstone of a building. The phrase does not appear again until used by Sir Walter Scott in the early 19th cent. *17th cent.*

> Scott *The Bride of Lammermoor* 1819
> *The lands which you now occupy were granted to my remote ancestor for services done with his sword against the English invaders. How they have glided from us by a train of proceedings that seem to be neither sale, nor mortgage, nor adjudication for debt, but a nondescript and entangled mixture of all these rights – how annual-rent has been accumulated upon principal, and no nook or coign of legal advantage left unoccupied, until our interest in our hereditary property seems to have melted away like an icicle in thaw – all this you understand better than I do.*

> George Eliot *Romola* 1863
> *It was near midday, and since the early morning there had been a gradual swarming of the people at every coign of vantage or disadvantage offered by the façades and roofs of the houses, and such spaces of the pavement as were free to the public.*

coil

this mortal coil

literary or humorous the turmoil of life on earth. The allusion is to Hamlet's speech 'To be or not to be' in Shakespeare, *Hamlet* (1601) III.i.69: 'For in that sleep of death what dreams may come | When we have shuffled off this mortal coil | Must give us pause.' *Coil* is a 16th cent. word with the primary meaning 'noisy disturbance' or 'tumult', of unknown origin. The phrase is sometimes used in its original form (i.e. with *shuffle off*), and there are many variants. The speech is often quoted in 18th cent. literary criticism (e.g. by Goldsmith), but genuinely allusive uses in free context date from somewhat later. *17th cent.*

> William Hazlitt *The Spirit of the Age* 1825
> *He is shy, sensitive, the reverse of every thing coarse, vulgar, obtrusive, and common-place. He would fain 'shuffle off this mortal coil', and his spirit clothes itself in the garb of elder time, homelier, but more durable.*

coin

the other side of the coin

an alternative aspect to a situation: with allusion to the obverse, or less important side, of a coin. Also used with a particular coin, such as a halfpenny, specified. *Early 20th cent.*

> *Independent* 1989
> *The rise of ethnic violence throughout the Eastern bloc is unfortunately the other side of the coin to self-determination.*

to coin a phrase

used in this and variant forms to introduce an unusual or ad hoc expression; in modern use (since the mid 20th cent.) typically used ironically to introduce a cliché. *19th cent.*

> Nathaniel Parker Willis *From Saratoga* 1847
> *Before I enter upon the cultivation of grounds, let me lay before the reader my favorite idea of a cottage – not a cottage orné but a cottage insoucieuse, if I may coin a phrase.*

> Michael Dibdin *Dirty Tricks* 1991
> *He was going to have fun if it killed him, to coin a phrase.*

See also PAY somebody in their own coin.

cold

The use of *cold* with reference to lack of emotion or feeling, which underlies many of the phrases, dates from early Middle English and was common by the 16th cent. as a description of a person (*cf* Shakespeare, *Hamlet* (1601) IV.vii.143: 'Therewith fantastic garlands did she [Ophelia] make | Of crow-flowers, nettles, daisies, and long purples, | That liberal shepherds give a grosser name, | But our cold maids do dead men's fingers call them').

(as) cold as charity

extremely cold: with reference to the supposed perfunctory or unfeeling manner in which charities are often administered. *Charity grows cold* (and variants) is recorded from the 16th cent., alluding to Wyclif's translation of Matthew 24:12 'The charite of manye schal wexe coold'. The phrase is 18th cent. in this form.

> Trollope *Can You Forgive Her?* 1864
> *'What's the use of it?' said Lady Glencora. 'There's nothing to see, and the wind is as cold as charity. We are much more comfortable here; are we not?'*

catch (a) cold

to suffer a financial loss or misfortune. *Late 20th cent.*

> Guardian 1984
> *Property and holiday park operator J– W– has joined the lengthy list of smaller companies that have caught a cold in France.*

cold calling

the unsolicited commercial telephoning of individuals in order to sell goods or services: the call is 'cold' in the sense of being unexpected by the person called and not involving any preparation by the caller. A *cold call* is such a call. *Late 20th cent.*

> The Times 1985
> *LHW's attempt to join Liffe began two years ago. That application lapsed after Liffe requested that LHW formally give up 'cold calling' – making unsolicited telephone calls to procure business.*

cold comfort

inadequate consolation for a misfortune. The use of *cold* in the sense 'discouraging, as perceived by the recipient' in connection with words like *comfort, counsel*, etc dates from the 14th cent.; modern use is influenced by *Cold Comfort Farm*, the title of Stella Gibbons' parody (1932) of contemporary novels about rural life. *16th cent.*

> Shakespeare *The Taming of the Shrew* IV.i.28 (1592)
> *Wilt thou make a fire, or shall I complain on thee to our mistress, whose hand – she being now at hand – thou shalt soon feel to thy cold comfort, for being slow in thy hot office.*

> Mary Pix *The Inhumane Cardinal* 1696
> *But Cordelia, whose wisdom far exceeded her years, would return none; only said, she was content to conceal their crime, because they had made love of her, the pretext for it. With this cold comfort, the fryar returns to the impatient prince; who with a diamond had just wrote this distich in the window.*

> Independent 1989
> *Charisma is cold comfort without expert management.*

come in from the cold

informal to be accepted or recognized by a group after a period of rejection or unawareness. The phrase was given wider currency as part of the title of John Le Carré's bleak spy story set in cold-war Berlin, *The Spy Who Came in from the Cold* (1963; also a film by Martin Ritt, 1965). *Mid 20th cent.*

give somebody the cold shoulder

to be deliberately unfriendly towards somebody: the derived verb *cold-shoulder* has the same meaning. The allusion may be to the practice of offering unwanted guests the menials' fare of cold meat from a shoulder of mutton. More probably, it reflects the physical action of turning or hunching the shoulder as a gesture of unwelcome or indifference. This explanation is supported by Sir Walter Scott's uses of the phrase, which appear to be the earliest. The first is in *The Antiquary* (1816): 'Ye may mind that the Countess's dislike didna gang farther at first than just showing o' the cauld shouther – at least it wasna seen farther.' (Scott includes the phrase in a glossary at the end of the book, which suggests that it will have been unfamiliar to his readers. He may well have invented the phrase, or picked it up from local usage.) There is another use in *St Ronan's Well* (1824): 'I cannot tell what to make of him … I must tip him the cold shoulder, or he will be pestering me eternally.' The verbs *show* and *tip* in these examples, and *turn* in others, certainly suggest a physical gesture rather than an offer of food. The phrase became common in 19th cent.

literature (see some examples below), but it now has a somewhat dated tone. *19th cent.*

Dickens *Martin Chuzzlewit* 1844

I'd be your patron, Tom. I'd take you under my protection. Let me see the man who should give the cold shoulder to anybody I chose to protect and patronise.

Charlotte Brontë *The Professor* 1857

All understood the art of speaking fair when a point was to be gained, and could with consummate skill and at a moment's notice turn the cold shoulder the instant civility ceased to be profitable.

Thackeray *The Adventures of Philip* 1862

Tregarvan showed my wife a cold shoulder for a considerable time afterwards, nor were we asked to his tea-parties, I forget for how many seasons.

George Eliot *Middlemarch* 1872

Casaubon has devilish good reasons, you may be sure, for turning the cold shoulder on a young fellow whose bringing-up he paid for.

go/take cold turkey
informal (said of a drug addict) to stop taking drugs abruptly, especially as a method of treatment: with allusion to the goose pimples, resembling the skin of a cold turkey, that a person experiences as a side effect of the treatment. *Early 20th cent.*

have somebody cold
NAmer, informal to have somebody at one's mercy. *Early 20th cent.*

Eddy Shah *Ring of Red Roses* 1992

We had them cold. Sitting targets. With that lot in, screwing it up in their size twelves, they'll all get away.

have/get cold feet
originally NAmer to have doubts or lose confidence about a course of action. *19th cent.*

S Crane *Maggie* 1893

I knew this was the way it would be. They got cold feet.

Os Guinness *Doubt* 1976

Imagine a millionaire who has decided to donate to a charity. He writes out a generous cheque and sends it off. Later he has second thoughts. He gets cold feet and phones his bank manager asking him to stop the cheque.

in the cold light of day/morning
when a situation is considered soberly and objectively. The phrase is based on the idea that one's judgement is likely to be more detached and dependable after a period of reflection when the emotions have become calmer than they tend to be at night. *19th cent.*

Hardy *Jude the Obscure* 1895

I fear I ought not to have run away from that school! Things seem so different in the cold light of morning, don't they?

leave somebody cold
to fail to impress or excite somebody: *cf* French *laisser froid*, German *kalt lassen*. Coldness here implies a lack of emotion, and is derived from the notion that strong emotion warms the body (see the introductory note at BLOOD). *19th cent.*

Matthew Arnold *Essays in Criticism* 1865

It is vain to say that Epictetus is … a better moralist than Jesus, if the warmth, the emotion, of Jesus's answer fires his hearer to the practice of forgiveness of injuries, while the thought in Epictetus's leaves him cold.

(left) out in the cold
ignored or neglected: from the notion of a person being left out of doors with no shelter. *19th cent.*

Somerset Maugham *Of Human Bondage* 1915

I'm disappointed that you didn't add a little Buddhism … And I confess I have a sort of sympathy for Mahomet; I regret that you should have left him out in the cold.

out cold
completely unconscious after a blow or shock. *19th cent.*

Ambrose Bierce *The Fiend's Delight* 1873

No sooner do we pick up a religious weekly than we stumble and sprawl through a bewildering succession of inanities, manufactured expressly to ensnare our simple feet. If we take up a tract we are laid out cold by an apostolic knock straight from the clerical shoulder.

P Falconer *War in High Heels* 1993

She poured champagne and slipped a Mickey Finn into Kattina's glass. With her lesbian lover out cold to the world she searched the houseboat.

pour/throw cold water on something

to disparage or be discouraging about an idea. The image is of the effect caused by cold water being thrown over the body. *19th cent.*

Jane Austen *Emma* 1816

But that would be all over now – Poor fellow! – No more exploring parties to Donwell … Oh! no; there would be a Mrs. Knightley to throw cold water on every thing.

See also in cold BLOOD.

---

collar

feel somebody's collar

to arrest or apprehend somebody. *Mid 20th cent.*

Geoffrey Robertson *Media Law* 1990

Had the editor of 'Private Eye' made impromptu allegations against Goldsmith on prime-time television, the long arm of the criminal law could not have felt his collar.

slip the collar

to escape from restraint or control. The image is of an animal getting loose. *16th cent.*

Hobbes *Leviathan* 1651

For in saying, Divina providentia, which is the same with Dei gratia, though disguised, they deny to have received their authority from the civil state, and slyly slip off the collar of their civil subjection.

---

collision

on a collision course

acting in a way that is likely to cause conflict. The image is of ships, aircraft, or other vehicles heading towards each other with the threat of disastrous consequences. The phrase is also used in literal meanings. *Mid 20th cent.*

New Statesman 1961

The great powers are now headed on a collision course over Berlin.

Eamonn McGrath *The Charnel House* 1990

He sometimes wondered about his own death, but beyond thinking of himself on some long-distance collision course with annihilation, he could not imagine it.

colour

In many phrases the sense of *colour* is a figurative use of the primary meaning; in others the underlying meaning is of *colours* (plural) as 'an identifying badge or flag' in naval and military use.

give/lend colour to something

to make an idea seem more interesting or convincing. *17th cent.*

Delarivière Manley *The Royal Mischief* 1696

Dost thou remember in my Virgin bloom, | When time had scarce lent Colour to my Beauty.

Edgar Rice Burroughs *The Gods of Mars* 1913

My knowledge of their customs lent colour to the belief that he was but being escorted to the audience chamber to have sentence passed upon him.

nail/pin one's colours to the mast

to make one's beliefs or intentions plain, especially in a defiant manner: from the practice of a naval commander nailing up his colours so that they could not be lowered in surrender. *19th cent.*

Robert Bell *The Ladder of Gold* 1850

I retire from the contest, and shall cheerfully give the whole of my influence to that candidate, be he who or what he may, who pledges himself to nail his colours to the mast!

David Lodge *Nice Work* 1988

By living in what their parents called sin, they nailed their colours to the mast of youth revolt, while enjoying the security and mutual support of old-fashioned matrimony.

sail under false colours

to conceal one's true nature or intentions. *18th cent.*

John Henry Newman *Loss and Gain* 1848

Your cap and gown; a university education; the chance of a scholarship, or fellowship. Give up these, and then plead, if you will, and lawfully, that you are quit of your engagement; but don't sail under false colours: don't take the benefit, and break the stipulation.

see the colour of somebody's money

to be given some evidence of a person's willingness to pay for something they have shown an interest in. *18th cent.*

Henry Fielding *The History of Tom Jones* 1749
*Though he hath lived here this many years, I don't
believe there is arrow [= ever] a servant in the house
ever saw the colour of his money.*

show somebody in their / come out in one's true colours

to reveal somebody's (or one's own) true nature or character. *16th cent.*

Shakespeare *2 Henry IV* 11.ii.162 (1597)
*[Prince Harry] How might we see Falstaff bestow
himself tonight in his true colours, and not ourselves be seen?*

with flying colours

with conspicuous success: from the former military practice of a victorious regiment flying its flag in celebration, whereas a defeated army had to lower (or *strike*) its colours. For an early literal use see John Bunyan's *The Holy War* (1682): 'Then did the captains in most warlike manner enter into the town of Mansoul, and marching in with flying colours, they came up to the Recorders house.' *17th cent.*

Jeremy Collier *The Immorality and Profaneness of the English Stage* 1698
*At last Dominick is discover'd to the company,
makes a dishonorable exit, and is push'd off the
stage by the rabble. This is great justice! The poet
takes care to make him first a knave, and then an
example: But his hand is not even. For Lewd Lor-
enzo comes off with flying colours.*

---

column

dodge the column

informal to avoid doing one's work or duty. The meaning here is a military formation of marching soldiers, and the expression dates from the time of the First World War. *Early 20th cent.*

See also FIFTH column.

---

come

as — as they come

informal about as — as one could possibly find. *Early 20th cent.*

P G Wodehouse *Laughing Gas* 1936
*It's his sister Beulah. She was the one who put him
up to it. She's the heavy in the sequence. As tough as
they come.*

L Pemberton *Platinum Coast* 1993
*She's old money and as snooty as they come, while
he's the typical self-made second-generation Italian
who wants to buy himself a piece of class.*

come the —

informal to play a particular role or practise the specified character: often followed by *over* meaning 'in respect of'. *19th cent.*

Dickens *Great Expectations* 1861
*I know what you're a going to say, Pip; stay a bit! I
don't deny that your sister comes the Mogul over
us, now and again. I don't deny that she do throw us
back-falls, and that she do drop down upon us
heavy.*

Sally Heywood *Castle of Desire* 1991
*Don't come the little mother with me ... I don't like
being mothered.*

come into somebody's head/mind

to occur to somebody as a thought: *cf* ENTER somebody's head. The form with *mind* is Middle English, and with *head* 18th cent.

Swift *Gulliver's Travels* 1726
*A fancy came into my head that I would entertain
the King and Queen with an English tune upon this
instrument.*

come off it

informal an exclamation of disbelief at something just said. *Early 20th cent.*

Evelyn Waugh *Put Out More Flags* 1942
*'I don't know what you mean,' she said ... 'Oh,
come off it,' he said. Angela came off it. She began to
weep.*

come / if it comes to that

if that is the case; for that matter: an expression linking a following statement to a preceding one, and usually going one better. It is based on the meaning of *come to* 'to amount to, to be equivalent to'. *Mid 20th cent.*

A N Wilson *C S Lewis: a Biography* 1990
*Lewis ... might have been surprised by the figure he
cut in prose or come to that in life.*

come unstuck/undone

to fail or suffer misfortune. The form with *undone* is 19th cent., and with *unstuck* early 20th cent.

Kipling *Diversity of Creatures* 1911
*'Don't apologise,' said Gilbert, when the paroxysm
ended. 'I'm used to people coming a little – unstuck
in this room.'*

Enoch Powell *Reflections of a Statesman* 1991

So everybody had to go federal – Canada, Australia, South Africa and later on Central Africa and the Caribbean, where it all came unstuck.

come wind, come weather

whatever difficulties might arise (as a profession of resolve). *Wind* and *weather* are linked as symbols of adversity from the 16th cent., but the phrase in its current form is first recorded in the 17th cent.

Bunyan *The Pilgrim's Progress* 1684

Who would true valour see ... | One here will constant be, come wind, come weather.

have it coming (to one)

informal to fully deserve what one is going to suffer: a specific use of *come to* in the meaning 'to be one's deserved experience', attested from the 18th cent. and an extension of much earlier general meanings relating to things (physical and abstract) one receives as one's due. *Early 20th cent.*

Fiona Pitt-Kethley *Sky Ray Lolly* 1992

There were various legends extant about people who'd been expelled for cannabis, abortions and calling the English teacher a cow (brave on a quart of Woodpecker). That pair obviously just had it coming.

not know if one is coming or going

to be confused or dizzy from conflicting pressures or responsibilities. *Early 20th cent.*

New Scientist 1991

Junior education minister William Shelton did not know whether he was coming or going last week when he gave an experimental communications system known as Project Universe its first public airing. Shelton's photograph was fed into the network and transmitted to a scanning device. This reconstituted his image and then sent it back again to the exhibition.

that's where — comes in

a particular person has a role to play in the context mentioned. Probably a metaphor based on stage entrances. *Mid 20th cent.*

WWF News 1990

We needed someone to put the message across and this is where Jane came in – she is a long-time supporter of WWF and now one of our Trustees.

this is where we came in

we are back at the point at which we started. The phrase is used with reference to discussions or arguments that are inconclusive and seem to go round in circles. The origin lies in cinema-going, when films were shown many times over and it was possible to go in and start watching a film at any point, staying on to watch the first part on its next showing up to the point 'where we came in'. *Mid 20th cent.*

Richard Dawkins *The Blind Watchmaker* 1986

This was where we came in. We wanted to know why we, and all other complicated things, exist. And we can now answer that question in general terms.

to come

in the future: often placed after a noun, as in *generations to come. 18th cent.*

Samuel Foote *The Maid of Bath* 1771

Never, never – what, a German dishonour his stock! why Mester Flint, should Mistress Linnet bring you de children for de ten generations to come, they could not be chose de Cannons of Stratsbourg.

J S Mill *The Subjection of Women* 1869

Though the truth may not be felt or generally acknowledged for generations to come, the only school of genuine moral sentiment is society between equals.

what has come over —?

what is the matter with the person named? Also in the form *not know what has come over —. 19th cent.*

Dickens *Nicholas Nickleby* 1839

'What has come over you, my dear, in the name of goodness?' asked Mrs. Nickleby, when they had walked on for some time in silence. 'I was only thinking, mama,' answered Kate.

John Steinbeck *The Grapes of Wrath* 1939

What's come over you, Muley? You wasn't never no run-an'-hide fella. You was mean.

(when you) come to think (of it)

when one considers; on reflection. Also (in the first person) *now I come to think of it. 19th cent.*

Thomas Aldrich *Marjorie Daw* 1873

After breakfast, accordingly, Mr. Bilkins sallied forth with the depressing expectation of finding Mr. O'Rouke without much difficulty. 'Come to think of it,' said the old gentleman to himself, drawing on his white cotton gloves as he walked up Anchor Street, 'I don't want to find him.'

where — is coming from
informal what a person means or intends, regarded as the starting point of a journey. *Late 20th cent.*

The Face 1990
We're trying to bring the knowledge of black history out so that people know where we're coming from and have no reason for prejudice and fear.

See also come the ACID; come apart at the seams *at* SEAM; come CLEAN; come a CROPPER; come down on somebody like a ton of bricks *at* BRICK; come in from the COLD; come of AGE; come the old SOL-DIER; come out/up smelling of roses *at* SMELL; come to GRIEF; come to NOTHING; come up roses *at* ROSE.

comfort

too — for comfort
worryingly or disturbingly as specified. The most common completion is *too close for comfort*, meaning 'alarmingly immediate and threatening' (referring to something undesirable). *19th cent.*

William Gilmore Simms The Partisan 1835
It's well you have me at all, for I've had a narrow chance of it. Swow! but the bullets rung over my ears too close for comfort.

Daily Telegraph 1992
There is only one celebrated instance of a subject's displeasure at an artist's likeness: that of Sir Winston Churchill with his portrait by Graham Sutherland ... It was an 80th-birthday present from past and present members of the Lords and Commons – and apparently far too accurate for comfort.

common

common or garden
of the ordinary or everyday type: from botanical terminology, which dates back to the 17th cent. *19th cent.*

the common touch
the ability to communicate well with ordinary people. The meaning of *common* involved here is essentially the one in *the common people*, i.e. 'characterized by a lack of privilege or special status'

and may be influenced by other senses, e.g. 'belonging to or shared by two or more individuals' as in *make common cause*. The locus classicus is Kipling's poem *If* (see below). Several meanings of *touch* probably shade into one another here: predominant is the sense 'mental or moral sensitivity, responsiveness, or tact' (as in *have a wonderful touch with children*) and 'a distinctive or characteristic manner or quality' (as in *the personal touch*). Some have even identified the use in *a touch of class*, and refer to the Prologue of Act IV of Shakespeare's *Henry V* (1599), which takes place on the eve of the Battle of Agincourt: 'Behold, as may unworthiness define, A little touch of Harry in the night.' *Early 20th cent.*

Kipling If 1910
If you can talk with crowds and keep your virtue, | Or walk with Kings – nor lose the common touch.

Ben Elton Stark 1992
Dixie had a peculiar talent for making many thousands of dollars worth of clothes look like she had bought them at Woolworths. This was her famous common touch.

See also (as) common as MUCK.

company

be/err in good company
to be in the same situation as somebody distinguished or celebrated, especially in the context of error or wrongdoing. *19th cent.*

compare

compare notes
to exchange information about a subject: originally with reference to actual notes made and later used figuratively. The literal and figurative uses overlap and it is often not possible to identify which is meant. *17th cent.*

Richard Fanshawe transl Camoes' Lusiads 1655
Thus He harangu'd: And, with one Voice, the whole | Presence (comparing notes there where they stand) | The matchless courage of the men extol, | Who traverse so much Sea and so much Land.

Kenneth Grahame The Wind in the Willows 1903
We hunger to inquire of each other, to compare notes and assure ourselves that it was all really true, as one by one the scents and sounds and names of

long-forgotten places come gradually back and beckon to us.

comparison

comparisons are odious

it is unreasonable to expect one person or thing to be like another, since circumstances vary: the use in Shakespeare below is a malapropism. There is Middle English evidence in the poetry of John Lydgate: 'Odyous of olde been comparisonis.'

Shakespeare *Much Ado About Nothing* III.v.15 (1598)
[Verges] *Yes, I thank God, I am as honest as any man living that is an old man and no honester than I.* [Dogberry] *Comparisons are odorous. Palabras, neighbour Verges.*

compliment

a back-handed/left-handed compliment

an ambiguous or half-hearted compliment that can easily be mistaken for criticism. A *back-handed* blow was a glancing blow delivered with the arm or with a sword, and the word developed figurative meanings in the 19th cent.: William Godwin's novel *Mandeville* (1817) includes the sentence 'Modesty ... is often the most beggarly and back-handed friend that merit can have'. At about the same time Sir Walter Scott makes a character in *Rob Roy* (1817) declare: 'the creature Morris is sic a cowardly caitiff [= wretch], that to this hour he daurna say that it was Rob took the portmanteau aff him; and troth he's right, for your customhouse and excise cattle are ill liket on a' sides, and Rob might get a back-handed lick at him, before the Board, as they ca't, could help him.' In Dickens' *Hard Times* (1854), the narrator tells us that 'Mr. Bounderby made a back-handed point at Mr. James Harthouse [whom he was introducing] with his thumb'. Despite all this evidence, back-handed compliments do not appear until more recently (20th cent.). *Left-handed* in this context is derived from the widely applied notion of left-handedness as awkward and even 'sinister' (the Latin word for 'left'). A 17th cent. source in the *OED* refers to 'a decayed left-handed bridge over the river [at Chertsey]: I want it mended.' The ultimate origin of the notion, and of the adverse associations of left-handedness, go back to the days of the Roman Republic, when divination by the *haruspices*

involved examining the entrails of animals. If the liver was found to be on the left side of the body, the gods were expressing disfavour and the omens were therefore bad. *Left-handed* in 17th cent. English developed the meaning 'ambiguous' or 'doubtful', and was used with such words as *policy, opinion,* and *wisdom*. The combination *left-handed compliment* first occurs in the mid 19th cent.

James Kirke Paulding *The Dutchman's Fireside* 1831
'Dear cousin,' said Sybrandt, 'how ill you look.' This was what is called rather a left-handed compliment. But Catalina was even with him, for she answered in his very words: 'Dear cousin, how ill you look.'

return the compliment

to respond in the same manner to something said or done: literally to repay a compliment with another, but used figuratively and ironically from an early date. *17th cent.*

Alexander Oldys *The Female Gallant* 1692
The Boobily Knight was strangely surpriz'd to see my Lord at that place, and cou'd hardly salute him, but with a malicious leer, and awkward bow. But my Lord knew how to make his advantage of such an opportunity; and said to him (returning the compliment of hat and cringe), that he was happy to see him there, as well as to hear that Sir Beetlehead was at home: to whom, he desir'd Sir Blunder to lead him the way.

Charles Kingsley *Westward Ho!* 1855
'Here comes a big ship right upon us! Give him all you have left, lads.' They gave him what they had, and hulled him with every shot; but his huge side stood silent as the grave. He had not wherewithal to return the compliment.

conclusion

jump/leap to conclusions

to reach a decision or form an opinion too quickly, without considering all the factors and circumstances that might affect it. *19th cent.*

James Fenimore Cooper *Precaution* 1820
Her own marriage had been so happy, she naturally concluded it the state most likely to insure the happiness of her children; and with Lady Moseley, as with thousands of others, who, averse or unequal to the labours of investigation, jump to conclusions over the long line of connecting reasons.

try conclusions with somebody

to engage in an argument or contest of skills with somebody. *Conclusion* here has the otherwise obsolete meaning 'experiment' (as in *philosophical conclusions*). Shakespeare's Hamlet, in an exchange with his mother Gertrude (*Hamlet* III.iv.179, 1601) makes an apparent allusion to a fable about an ape that tries to imitate escaping birds, with disastrous results: 'Let the birds fly, and, like the famous ape, | To try conclusions in the basket creep, | And break your own neck down.' *17th cent.*

Anon *The Tincker of Turvey* 1630
What he had done, was to try conclusions upon three precepts, which his dying father inioyned him to.

Browning *The Ring and the Book* 1842
Guido would try conclusions with his foe, | Whoe'er the foe was and whate'er the offence.

concrete

be set in concrete

(said of a proposal or idea) to be final and unalterable: often used in negative contexts. *Mid 20th cent.*

Hansard 1992
I do not regard the United Kingdom constitution as set in concrete.

the concrete jungle

inner cities regarded as places of confusion and lawlessness. Coined by Desmond Morris in *The Human Zoo* (1969): 'The city is not a concrete jungle, it is a human zoo.' *Mid 20th cent.*

conduct

conduct unbecoming

behaviour that is shameful or a disgrace to one's position: an elliptical use of the phrase 'conduct unbecoming the character of an Officer' in the Naval Discipline Act of 1860. Some 19th cent. uses may be coincidental. *19th cent.*

John Esten Cooke *Fairfax* 1868
'You think my conduct unbecoming, my lord,' murmured the young lady, 'to treat Mr. Falconbridge with such rudeness and want of ceremony.'

conjure

a name to conjure with

a person who commands respect: with allusion to the practice in magic of invoking a famous name to conjure up a spirit. *Cf* Shakespeare, *Julius Caesar* (1599) I.ii.147: '[Cassius] The fault, dear Brutus, is not in our stars, | But in ourselves, that we are underlings. | Brutus and Caesar: what should be in that 'Caesar'? | Why should that name be sounded more than yours? | Write them together: yours is as fair a name. | Sound them: it doth become the mouth as well. | Weigh them: it is as heavy. Conjure with 'em: | 'Brutus' will start a spirit as soon as 'Caesar'.' *19th cent.*

Montague Summers *A Memoir of Mrs Behn* 1914
For years her name to a new book, a comedy, a poem, an essay from the French, was a word to conjure with for the booksellers.

conspicuous

conspicuous by one's/its absence

only too obviously absent or missing. The expression was listed as a 'hackneyed phrase' by H W Fowler in *Modern English Usage* (1926) and is still often castigated as such. It was coined by Lord John Russell in a speech in 1859: 'Among the defects of the Bill, which were numerous, one provision was conspicuous by its presence, and one by its absence.' Russell later said he owed the expression to a passage of Tacitus (III.76): *praefulgebat Cassius atque Brutus eo ipso quod effigies eorum non visebantur* ('Cassius and Brutus were much more prominent [at a funeral] because their images were not seen'). *19th cent.*

Henry James *An International Episode* 1879
It will have been gathered that the entertainment offered by Lord Lambeth to his American friends had not been graced by the presence of his anxious mother ... The ladies of his immediate family were ... conspicuous by their absence.

conspiracy

a conspiracy of silence

agreement to say nothing about a matter of public concern: attributed by J S Mill in 1865 to the French philosopher Auguste Comte (1798–1857). *19th cent.*

Samuel Butler *The Way of All Flesh* 1903
A conspiracy of silence about things whose truth would be immediately apparent to disinterested enquirers is not only tolerable but righteous on the part of those who profess to be and take money for being par excellence guardians and teachers of truth.

contempt

hold somebody/something in contempt
to despise somebody or something or consider them unworthy of respect: from the legal use of a person who is considered to be in contempt of court because they have disobeyed the court or shown it disrespect. *18th cent.*

Susanna Rowson *Charlotte Temple* 1791
He was one of those men, who, having travelled in their youth, pretend to have contracted a peculiar fondness for every thing foreign, and to hold in contempt the productions of their own country; and this affected partiality extended even to the women.

content

to one's heart's content
as much as one wishes. The phrase in this form dates from 17th cent., but *heart's content* occurs in the meaning 'inward satisfaction' in Shakespeare, e.g. *The Merchant of Venice* (1598) III.iv.42, where Shylock's daughter Jessica takes her leave of Portia with the words 'I wish your ladyship all heart's content.' *17th cent.*

Laurence Sterne *Tristram Shandy* 1760
You have seen enough of my uncle Toby in these, to trace these family likenesses, betwixt the two passions (in case there is one) to your heart's content.

contention

See a BONE of contention.

contest

no contest
a contest or competition in which one participant is certain to be the winner: from the use in boxing to denote a fight that the referee declares void because neither boxer is attempting to fight satisfactorily. *Mid 20th cent.*

John Grant *The Great Unsolved Mysteries of Science* 1990
There is little doubt that the average human being is more intelligent than the average cow – no contest!

contradiction

a contradiction in terms
a statement or proposition containing elements that conflict with each other: originally a term in logic and now in general use of inconsistent or self-contradictory statements. *18th cent.*

Mary Wollstonecraft *A Vindication of the Rights of Woman* 1792
If women are to be made virtuous by authority, which is a contradiction in terms, let them be immured in seraglios and watched with a jealous eye.

convert

convert something to one's own use
old use to steal or appropriate another person's property. *17th cent.*

Congreve *The Mourning Bride* 1697
I've learn'd there are Disorders ripe for Mutiny Among the Troops, who thought to share the Plunder, Which Manuel to his own Use and Avarice Converts.

conviction

have the courage of one's convictions
to act according to one's principles even if these cause difficulties: *cf* French *le courage de son opinion*. The phrase dates from the 19th cent., originally in the form *have the courage of one's opinions*.

Hardy *Jude the Obscure* 1895
But don't press me and criticize me, Jude! Assume that I haven't the courage of my opinions. I know I am a poor miserable creature.

cooee

within cooee of something
within hailing distance of something; close to it. *Cooee* was the cry used as a signal by Australian Aboriginals, and was adopted by the European immigrants. *19th cent.*

cook

cook the books
to falsify financial accounts: from a (17th cent.) meaning of *cook* 'to manipulate or falsify'. *Late 20th cent.*

Michael Dibdin *Dirty Tricks* 1991
When it came to cooking the books, Dennis was in the Raymond Blanc class.

cook somebody's goose
to ruin somebody's plans or thwart their schemes irretrievably. The variant form *do somebody's goose for them* is specified as a 'vulgar phrase' in a mid 19th cent. source, and evidence for the use with *cook* occurs at about this time. One mid 19th cent. source makes play with two metaphors in writing 'To save my bacon I must cook his goose!' *19th cent.*

John Brougham *Metamora* 1859
[Badenough] *Of what shall we accuse him?*
[Worser] *Never fear. We'll cook his goose.*

Virginia Woolf *The Voyage Out* 1915
'It shortens one's life; but I'm afraid, Mrs. Ambrose … we've got to burn the candle at both ends or –'
'You've cooked your goose!' said Helen brightly.

too many cooks spoil the broth
(proverb) a task is badly done if too many people are involved: also used elliptically as *too many cooks*. The sentiment occurs in other forms at a somewhat earlier date. *17th cent.*

B Gerbier *Principles of Building* 1662
When … an undertaking hath been committed to many, it caused but confusion, and therefore it is a saying … Too many cooks spoils [sic] the broth.

Jane Austen *The Watsons* 1804
She professes to keep her own counsel; she says, & truly enough, that 'too many cooks spoil the broth.'

Mark Twain *The Innocents Abroad* 1869
I thought, if five cooks can spoil a broth, what may not five captains do with a pleasure excursion.

cookie

caught with one's hand in the cookie jar
informal, chiefly NAmer exposed as being involved in petty stealing, especially from an employer. *Late 20th cent.*

a smart cookie
informal, chiefly NAmer a canny, quick-thinking person. *Mid 20th cent.*

Good Food 1992
Smart cookies keep their biscuits in a jar.

Elizabeth Oldfield *Sudden Fire* 1993
'And I used to think you were one smart cookie,' Vitor rasped.

the way the cookie crumbles
NAmer, informal how things are or how they turn out. *See also* the way the ball bounces *at* BALL[1]. *Mid 20th cent.*

cool

(as) cool as a cucumber
completely cool or self-assured. The phrase also occurs with *cold* in place of *cool* (see below). *17th cent.*

Beaumont & Fletcher *Cupid's Revenge* 1615
Young maids were as cold as cowcumbers.

John Tatham *The Rump* 1660
Courage as cold as cucumber.

Liz Lochhead *True Confessions and New Clichés* 1985
I didn't know where to look, and that bizzum just sat there cool as a cucumber wolfing down my Celebration Chile Con Carne Surprise.

cool Britannia
a phrase embodying the revival of British pop culture in the 1990s and later associated with the new and revitalized political landscape that people identified – for a time – with the election of a New Labour government in 1997, especially as contrasted with the staleness of the outgoing Conservative government. The phrase first appears in print in 1993, although it had been used in 1967 for the title of a song by the Bonzo Dog Doo Dah Band. It plays on *Rule Britannia*, the title of a patriotic song written to words by James Thomson by Thomas Arne for his masque *Alfred*, first performed in 1740. The slogan rapidly became as hackneyed and tired, and in its own way as ironic, as *back to basics* did under the previous government (*see* BASIC). *Late 20th cent.*

Sunday Times 1993
British pop has always prided itself on its sense of irony and post-modern playfulness. Like displays of pageantry, it's something we do so well unlike those primitive Americans with their earnest rock idols

from the Bruce Springsteen School of Sweat and Sincerity. The children of cool Britannia may not know much about trigonometry, but they do know every art term in the book. On the other hand, your average American rock fan probably thinks dada is somebody you can borrow the car from.

keep/lose one's cool

informal to remain (or fail to remain) calm. *Mid 20th cent.*

Sasha Stone *Kylie Minogue: the Superstar Next Door* 1989
Kylie, said press reports, lost her cool and screamed at the intruders.

See also cool one's heels at HEEL.

coon

a gone coon

NAmer, informal a person or thing that is in dire straits. A *gone coon* was a raccoon being hunted for its fur that had been cornered and was unable to escape. *19th cent.*

Stephen Crane *The Red Badge of Courage* 1895
It's my first and last battle, old boy … Something tells me … I'm a gone coon this first time and – and I w-want you to take these here things – to – my folks.

coop

fly the coop

to escape or elope: from the notion of birds flying to freedom from their cage or 'coop', and influenced by the (18th cent.) slang meaning of *coop*, 'a prison'. *19th cent.*

coot

See (as) BALD as a coot.

cop

An 18th cent. word meaning 'to catch' or 'to steal', of uncertain origin: Damon Runyon in *Guys and Dolls* (1931) refers to a character who 'does a little scrubbing business around a swell apartment hotel … and … cops stationery there'.

cop hold of something

informal to grab or seize something. *Mid 20th cent.*

Ellis Peters *City of Gold and Shadows* 1989
Cop hold of this paddle, and move us in slow.

cop (somebody) one

to hit somebody with a hard blow. *19th cent.*

cop a plea

NAmer, informal to plead guilty as part of a plea bargain with the prosecution. *Early 20th cent.*

S Laws *Darkfall* 1993
Thought I was copping a plea on … diminished responsibility.

it's a fair cop

informal an admission of guilt by an offender who has been caught red-handed (more likely to occur in fiction than in reality). *Early 20th cent.*

Conan Doyle *The Mazarin Stone* 1921
Sam Merton's slow intellect had only gradually appreciated the situation. Now, as the sound of heavy steps came from the stairs outside, he broke silence at last. 'A fair cop!' said he.

not much cop

British, informal not very good. The underlying meaning of *cop* here is 'a catch or acquisition'. *Early 20th cent.*

Punch 1992
If he's a skilled boardroom apparatchik, they say he's not much cop as a coach.

See also catch/cop/stop a PACKET.

copybook

See BLOT one's copybook.

cord

cut the cord

to stop relying on another person and begin to act independently: with allusion to cutting the umbilical cord of a new-born baby. *Mid 20th cent.*

Joanna Neil *The Waters of Eden* 1993
She would cut the cord that bound her to them cleanly and irrevocably.

corn

corn in Egypt

a copious supply. Egypt was an important source of corn in the ancient world. Jacob instructs his sons in Genesis 42:2 'Behold, I have heard that there is corn in Egypt: get you down thither, and buy for us from thence'. *18th cent.*

Thomas Dibdin *The Mouth of the Nile* 1798
[Junk] *I say, we shall come in for our share of pretty girls here, my hearties.* [Pat] *Yes, yes, there's corn in Egypt.*

corner

cut corners
to do something cheaply or quickly by making risky economies: from the literal meaning of going across a corner instead of round it, in order to save time. *19th cent.*

drive somebody into a corner
to force somebody into a position from which there is no escape: originally with physical reference and later in figurative contexts. *16th cent.*

Dickens *Nicholas Nickleby* 1839
Newman had parried these questions as long as he could, but being at length hard pressed and driven into a corner, had gone so far as to admit, that Nicholas was a tutor of great accomplishments, involved in some misfortunes which he was not at liberty to explain, and bearing the name of Johnson.

Trevor Barnes *Taped* 1992
From long experience Blanche knew it was pointless to confront most interviewees, foolish to drive them into a corner.

fight one's corner
to defend one's interests with energy. The phrase is a metaphor from boxing, in which the contestants occupy diagonally opposite corners and receive between rounds any necessary attention from their managers and attendants. *Corner* in this sense dates from the mid 19th cent. *Mid 20th cent.*

The East Anglian 1993
We believe in local democracy and, unlike the Tories, we are prepared to fight our corner for local government.

the four/far corners of the world/earth
distant places: *corner* is used in the sense 'extremity of the earth' from the 16th cent., and Benedick in Shakespeare's *Much Ado About Nothing* (1598) II.iii.98 asks 'Is't possible? Sits the wind in that corner [= is the wind in that direction]?' An alternative form is *the four quarters*, in which the image is of the earth divided into segments,

whereas here it is (more schematically) of a square. A phrase *within the four corners* (of a document), meaning within its scope or coverage, is recorded in the 19th cent. but has not remained in use. *16th cent.*

Shakespeare *The Merchant of Venice* II.vii.39 (1598)
[Morocco] *All the world desires her.* | *From the four corners of the earth they come* | *To kiss this shrine, this mortal breathing saint.*

in somebody's corner
encouraging somebody or giving them support: an image from boxing (*see* fight one's corner *above*). *20th cent.*

(just) round/around the corner
very close or imminent: the phrase is used with reference to place and time from about the same period of the mid 19th cent.

Louisa M Alcott *Work: A Story of Experience* 1873
I confess I once or twice fancied that I caught glimpses of bliss round the corner, as it were; but, before I could decide, the glimpses vanished.

round/around every corner
occurring in many places and at unexpected times. *Early 20th cent.*

A S Byatt *Possession* 1990
He believed he should come across someone who should want his skills – he was an incurable optimist, and imagined a fortunate meeting around every corner.

turn the corner
to begin to recover from a period of difficulty, illness, or hardship. The phrase is recorded in more literal meanings from the 17th cent.: for example an 18th cent. source uses it to refer to somebody who has 'gone away', i.e. has died. *19th cent.*

Mark Twain *A Connecticut Yankee at the Court of King Arthur* 1889
Well, during two weeks and a half we watched by the crib, and in our deep solicitude we were unconscious of any world outside of that sick-room. Then our reward came: the center of the universe turned the corner and began to mend.

See also PAINT somebody into a corner; a TIGHT corner.

corridor

the corridors of power
the highest levels of administration in government, business, or industry: used (but not coined) by C P Snow (1905–80) as the title of a novel (1964) set in Parliament. *Mid 20th cent.*

> Kathryn Tidrick *Empire and the English Character* 1992
> *Whole peoples were now to be regenerated, not by the patient labours of obscure administrators toiling at their life's work in obscure places, but by the brilliant schemes of brilliant people flitting about the corridors of power.*

cost

at all cost(s) / any cost
regardless of the price or difficulties involved: *cf* French *à tout prix* in the same sense. Early uses imply an actual outlay of cash, but the sense of *cost* becomes more generalized in later usage. The form with *any* is 16th cent., and with *all* early 20th cent.

> William Stirling *Julius Caesar* 1637
> *Yet often-times those warie wits have err'd,* | *Who would buy wealth and ease at any cost:* | *Let honesty to profit be preferr'd.*

> Disraeli *Tancred* 1847
> *He had arrived in solitude, and by the working of his own thought, at a certain resolution, which had assumed to his strong and fervent imagination a sacred character, and which he was determined to accomplish at all costs.*

> Somerset Maugham *Of Human Bondage* 1915
> *He still looked upon Christianity as a degrading bondage that must be cast away at any cost.*

cotton wool

wrap/keep somebody in cotton wool
to overprotect somebody. *19th cent.*

> George Eliot *Middlemarch* 1872
> *You have more sense than most, and you haven't been kept in cotton-wool: there may be no occasion for me to say this, but a father trembles for his daughter, and you are all by yourself here.*

couch

a couch potato
informal, originally NAmer an inactive person, especially one who spends a lot of time watching television. *Potato* is a metaphor for a person who is unfit and overweight from lack of exercise, like the corresponding use of *vegetable*. In American use *couch potato* may be associated with the parallel slang term *boob tuber*, with a pun on the second word, for somebody who constantly watches the *boob tube* (i.e. television). *Late 20th cent.*

> Daily Mirror 1992
> *He preferred to play golf, watch videos and settle into the role of couch potato while Fergie did her own thing.*

counsel

a counsel of despair
advice to be followed in extreme circumstances, or if all else has failed. *18th cent.*

> E Jerningham *Faldoni and Teresa* 1773
> *Th' unhappy youth beheld, devoid of fear:* | *See to the grot the faithful maid repair,* | *Prepar'd to act the counsel of despair.* | *With eager arms he strain'd her to his breast,* | *And thus the purpose of his soul express'd.*

a counsel of perfection
advice that is ideal rather than realistic. Originally used in theological contexts and in allusion to Christ's exhortation to the rich man in Matthew 19:21 'Jesus said unto him, If thou wilt be perfect, go and sell that thou hast, and give to the poor, and thou shalt have treasure in heaven.' *17th cent.*

> John Henry Newman *Loss and Gain* 1848
> *Here he was, a young man of twenty-two, professing in an hour's conversation with a friend, what really were the Catholic doctrines and usages, of penance, purgatory, counsels of perfection, mortification of self, and clerical celibacy.*

count

count something on the fingers of one hand
to work out easily how many there are because there are so few: used with reference to things that are unusual or rare. *19th cent.*

Robert Browning *The Ring and the Book* 1842
Why 'twere the easy task | Of hours told on the fingers of one hand, | To reach the Tuscan Frontier.

count (up) to ten

to check oneself before speaking out or losing one's temper: literally, to count to ten under one's breath as a way of restraining oneself. In a letter written in 1817 Thomas Jefferson, third President of the United States, advised 'When angry count 10 before you speak'. *19th cent.*

out / NAmer down for the count

completely unconscious: a metaphor (early 20th cent.) from the knockout in boxing, in which the referee counts in seconds up to ten. *Mid 20th cent.*

Roald Dahl *Matilda* 1989
And there she was, the huge figure of the Headmistress, stretched full-length on her back across the floor, out for the count.

See also count one's blessings *at* BLESSING; count one's chickens *at* CHICKEN; count the pennies *at* PENNY; count SHEEP.

countenance

out of countenance

(so as to be) disagreeably surprised or disconcerted. *16th cent.*

Shakespeare *Love's Labour's Lost* v.ii.614 (1594)
[Biron] *And now forward, for we have put thee in countenance.* [Holofernes] *You have put me out of countenance.*

Dickens *Great Expectations* 1861
Be firm, Herbert … Look the thing in the face. Look into your affairs. Stare them out of countenance.

counter

over the counter

by retail purchase, without the need for special authorization: with reference to a shop counter over which transactions are routinely made. The phrase is commonly used of drugs and medicines that can be bought without a prescription in pharmacies and supermarkets. *19th cent.*

William Larminie *Fand and Other Poems* 1892
And when they sink into quiet, older and wearied at evening, | What the result of their toil, and dreary routine of the day? | Entries in ledgers mostly, and goods sold over the counter.

under the counter

(bought and sold) surreptitiously or illicitly: usually with regard to scarce commodities. *Early 20th cent.*

Aldous Huxley *Jesting Pilate* 1926
One at least of my own novels has to be sold under the counter as though it were whiskey.

country

go/appeal to the country

British (said of the government) to dissolve Parliament and hold a general election. *19th cent.*

Thackeray *The History of Pendennis* 1849
Look at the Whigs appealing to the country, and the Whigs in power! Would you say that the conduct of these men is an act of treason, as the Radicals bawl?

line of country

an area of interest or expertise. The literal meaning is 'an area of terrain' (normally characteristic in some way), which affords a more vivid metaphor than is commonly understood now from such a hackneyed idiom. *19th cent.*

Thomas Hughes *Tom Brown at Oxford* 1861
This sort of thing isn't my line of country at all. So that next time you want to do a bit of gaol-delivery on your own hook, don't ask me to help you.

Alistair MacLean *Santorini* 1987
Anagrams and word puzzles are not in my line of country, sir. I'm no cryptologist.

courage

take one's courage in both hands

to find the courage to do something challenging or frightening. *Early 20th cent.*

See also DUTCH courage; have the courage of one's convictions *at* CONVICTION.

course

run its course

(said of time or events, now especially of an unpleasant or unwelcome experience such as an illness) to continue until it has finished, without the possibility of being stopped or interrupted. The image is of a flowing river. *15th cent.*

Thomas Meriton *Love and War* 1658
Oh, my breath is prov'd an airy substance now, | I wish it were confin'd a longer space | To run its course.

stay the course

to persevere with a dangerous or challenging activity until it is completed. In its current figurative meaning the phrase is a metaphor from horseracing, although in its literal meaning *stay* originally meant 'restrain', and might for example be used (literally) about stemming the flow of a river or (figuratively) about frustrating the working of justice. A character (Lucy Robarts) in Trollope's *Framley Parsonage* (1861) observes that 'there was once a people in some land – and they may be still there for what I know – who thought it sacrilegious to stay the course of a raging fire'. This sense is commoner in 19th cent. literature than the one now current. *19th cent.*

court

pay court to somebody

to flatter or befriend somebody in order to gain their favour. *18th cent.*

Charlotte Lennox *The Female Quixote* 1752
But the Beau, whom she had silenc'd by her reproof, was extremely angry; and, supposing it would mortify her to see him pay court to her cousin, he redoubled his assiduities to Miss Glanville.

See also HOLD court; LAUGH somebody/something out of court.

Coventry

send somebody to Coventry

chiefly British to refuse to talk to somebody or have any dealings with them. The phrase is commonly associated with the treatment of Royalist prisoners during the English Civil War in the 17th cent., as recorded in Lord Clarendon's *Historical Narrative of the Rebellion and Civil Wars in England* (1647): 'At Bromigham a town so generally wicked that it had risen upon small parties of the king's, and killed or taken them prisoners and sent them to Coventry'. The explanation is that the citizens of Coventry, then staunch supporters of the Parliamentarian cause, refused to associate with the Royalist captives sent there, or that sol-

diers' wives were ostracized if they did so. There may be some truth behind the various versions of this story, although allusive uses do not appear until well into the 18th cent., a hundred years or so later, and most of the usage is from the 19th cent., a gap that weakens the link considerably. In 19th cent. use the form of the phrase was more usually *put somebody in Coventry*. *18th cent.*

Fanny Burney *Letter* 1787
I sent his dependence and his building to Coventry, by not seeming to hear him.

Trollope *The Eustace Diamonds* 1873
Lucy was not an enemy, and it was out of the question that she should be treated with real enmity. She might be scolded, and scowled at, and put into a kind of drawing-room Coventry for a time, – so that all kindly intercourse with her should be confined to school-room work and bed-room conferences.

cover

blow somebody's cover

to reveal somebody's secret identity. *Mid 20th cent.*

Peter Cave *Foxbat* 1979
The CIA had little use for a failed agent whose cover was blown.

break cover

to come into the open from a place of hiding: originally with reference to a hunted animal that comes into open ground after concealing itself in undergrowth. *19th cent.*

Scott *Waverley* 1814
A hart of the second year, which was in the same cover with the proper object of their pursuit, chanced to be unharboured first, and broke cover very near where the Lady Emma and her brother were stationed.

Henry Herbert *Sporting Scenes and Sundry Sketches* 1842
I broke cover, and came out. The moment she caught a glimpse of me, she screamed and dropped the trout, and ran.

cover one's back / NAmer ass

to take steps to avoid blame or criticism: from the notion of protecting one's back with clothing or other coverings. *Late 20th cent.*

Accountancy 1992
You can create an organisation culture that says never take chances, always cover your back, always put it in writing, always make sure you've got authority.

cover one's tracks

to conceal evidence of one's past actions: from the practice of concealing the path one has taken, in order to avoid pursuit. *19th cent.*

Conan Doyle *The Sign of Four* 1890
These fellows are sharper than I expected. They seem to have covered their tracks. There has, I fear, been preconcerted management here.

cow

have a cow

NAmer, informal to become angry or excited. *Late 20th cent.*

The Face 1990
Don't have a cow man!

a sacred cow

a person or institution that is granted unreasonable immunity from criticism. The cow is venerated as a sacred animal by Hindus. The term was first used allusively by journalists in the US with reference to a person or piece of writing that is above criticism; the American novelist Upton Sinclair wrote in a work on this theme (*They Call Me Carpenter*) published in 1922: 'It doesn't matter, because I couldn't use the story. Mr. Stebbins is one of our "sacred cows".' *Early 20th cent.*

till the cows come home

for ever, indefinitely: from the former practice of leaving cows out at pasture until they were ready for milking. *16th cent.*

Beaumont & Fletcher *The Scornful Ladie* 1616
Come my braue man of war, trace out thy darling, | And you my learned Councell, set and turne boyes | Kisse till the Cow come home, kisse close, kisse close knaues.

crab

catch a crab

to make a faulty stroke in rowing, in which the oar misses the water or is caught below the surface: probably from the notion of the oar being held by a crab underwater. The Italian phrase *pigliare un granchio*, which translates as 'to catch a crab', refers to blunders in more general terms and is probably not connected. *18th cent.* (recorded in Grose's *Dictionary of the Vulgar Tongue*)

Lewis Carroll *Through the Looking-Glass* 1872
There was something very queer about the water, she thought, as every now and then the oars got fast in it, and would hardly come out again. 'Feather! Feather!' the Sheep cried again, taking more needles. 'You'll be catching a crab directly.'

crack

crack a bottle

to open a bottle of wine and drink it, especially in order to celebrate. *16th cent.*

Shakespeare *2 Henry IV* v.iii.64 (1597)
[Shallow] By the mass, you'll crack a quart together, ha, will you not, Master Bardolph?

Scott *Chronicles of the Canongate* 1827
But, laying aside all considerations of his literary merit, Allan was a good jovial honest fellow, who could crack a bottle with the best.

crack a crib

British criminal slang to break into a house to burgle it. *19th cent.*

Conan Doyle *The Redheaded League* 1891
He'll crack a crib in Scotland one week, and be raising money to build an orphanage in Cornwall the next.

the crack of doom

a thunderclap that heralds the Day of Judgement; hence used allusively of any loud and ominous noise. *Crack* here is used in the meaning 'a loud noise', and *doom* is used in its old sense 'judgement' and the Last Judgement in particular. The locus classicus is Macbeth's appeal to the witches in Shakespeare's *Macbeth* (1606) IV.i.117 'What, will the line [of Banquo's descendants] stretch out to th' crack of doom?', where the image is of relentless continuation right up to the ultimate and universal deadline represented by the Day of Judgement. *17th cent.*

Robert Bell *The Ladder of Gold* 1850
Thus new generations rise and trample down their predecessors who laid the foundations for them; and

thus it has happened from the beginning, and will happen again and again to the crack of doom.

Elizabeth Elgin All the Sweet Promises 1991

If she had polished and dusted till the crack of doom, it would have made no difference.

a fair crack of the whip
a reasonable chance to take part in something or to show what one can do. The image is presumably of the control exercised by a ringmaster in a circus, or by the driver of a horse-drawn vehicle. The phrase is used somewhat differently (and without *fair*) in the James Joyce quotation below. *Early 20th cent.*

James Joyce A Portrait of the Artist as a Young Man 1916

There's a crack of the whip left in me yet, Stephen, old chap, said Mr Dedalus, poking at the dull fire with fierce energy. We're not dead yet, sonny.

have a crack at something
informal to attempt something difficult or challenging, especially something one has not tried before. Used originally with reference to shooting (hence the notion of a 'crack'). *19th cent.*

John Neal Randolph 1823

Murders are things of every day occurrence, here, since the war. Our ears were made familiar, it would seem, with it then – and that, and the wars of Europe, have deluged us with all the banditti and ruffians of the world. Another thing – there was the father, the husband, Frank Omar, and John Omar; all agreed to 'have a crack at him,' as they express it here – so he could not escape you know.

paper over the cracks
to gloss over or explain away differences in order to maintain a semblance of unity or progress. The origin of the expression is attributed to the German statesman Otto von Bismarck (1814–98), who used a corresponding German idiom in a letter dated 14 August 1865: *Wir arbeiten eifrig an Erhaltung des Friedens und Verklebung der Risse im Bau* ('We are working eagerly to preserve the Peace and to cover the cracks in the building'). Among the first uses in English is an article in the 1910 edition of *Encyclopaedia Britannica*, which refers to Bismarck's use of the expression: 'the convention of Gastein, to use Bismarck's phrase, "papered over the cracks".' *Early 20th cent.*

Annual Register 1952

Mr. Bevan agreed to paper over the cracks for the period of the election.

See also the crack of DAWN.

cracked

not all it is cracked up to be
informal not as good or valuable as is generally thought. A *crack* was something excellent or of good quality, a sense reflected in its still current use as a modifying word in contexts such as *a crack regiment*. Also (19th cent.) in the form *be cracked up for*. *19th cent.*

James Hall The Soldier's Bride and Other Tales 1833

The more I hesitated, the less inclination I felt to try the experiment, and I am now convinced that marriage is not the thing it is cracked up to be!

Willa Cather The Song of the Lark 1915

'Bringing up a family is not all it's cracked up to be,' said Mrs. Kronborg with a flicker of irony.

crackers

be/go crackers
informal to be or become mad or angry. There is probably a connection with the use of *cracked* to mean mad or deranged, which dates from the 17th cent. Also *drive somebody crackers. Early 20th cent.*

cracking
See GET cracking.

crackling

a bit of crackling
informal a sexually attractive woman: a metaphor from the word for the cooked skin of a pig. *Crackling* is also used alone as a collective denoting attractive women generally. The phrase was entered in the third edition (1949) of Eric Partridge's *Dictionary of Slang. Mid 20th cent.*

John Mortimer Summer's Lease 1988

In fact his father-in-law had congratulated him on the perfectly splendid bit of crackling Hugh had in his arms in Chancery Lane, and naturally mum was the word.

cradle

from the cradle to the grave

for the entire duration of a person's life. *Cradle* and *grave* occur from an early date as symbols for birth and death. The translators of the Authorized Version of the Bible (1611) wrote in their Preface: 'In the Latin we have been exercised almost from our very cradle.' The phrase occurs in early use in the form *between the cradle and the grave*, and forms part of the title of William Sanderson's *Compleat History of the Life and Raigne of King Charles from his Cradle to his Grave* (1658); an adjectival form *cradle-to-grave* is also recorded. Benjamin Keach wrote in *The Progress of Sin* (1684) 'On those poor babes, they no compassion have; | But hurle them from the cradle to the grave'; here the sense is slightly different. The first recorded use in the form of the phrase now current is by Richard Steele in the *Tatler* No.52 (1709): 'A modest fellow never has a doubt from his cradle to his grave.' In its German equivalent *Von der Wiege bis zum Grabe*, the phrase formed the title of a symphonic poem by Franz Liszt (published in 1881–2). In modern times the phrase has become associated with the development of the welfare state in Britain. Winston Churchill declared in a radio broadcast in 1943 (reported in *The Times* of 22 March) that people 'must rank me and my colleagues as strong partisans of national compulsory insurance for all classes for all purposes from the cradle to the grave'. The National Health Service, set up by the Attlee government in 1948 and funded from taxation, had as its aim 'care from the cradle to the grave'. In June 2005, during a parliamentary debate on the introduction of identity cards in the UK, this slogan was parodied in an attack on the government by the Shadow Home Secretary David Davis (reported in *The Times* of 29 June): 'The party that in 1945 promised that generation welfare from cradle to grave is about to give this generation surveillance from cradle to grave.'

cramp

cramp somebody's style

informal to make it difficult for somebody to act freely or effectively. The phrase is recorded from the first part of the 20th cent., but there is a close use by Charles Lamb in a letter written about a hundred years before: 'I will never write another letter with alternate inks. You cannot imagine how it cramps the flow of the style.' *Early 20th cent.*

> Ernest Cashmore *Black Sportsmen* 1982
> *Bitterness isn't part of my philosophy … I've got no time for it; it cramps your style.*

craw

See in somebody's throat/craw/gizzard *at* STICK[1].

crazy

crazy as/like a fox

NAmer, informal apparently crazy or eccentric, but in a way that conceals shrewdness (hence the comparison to a fox, traditionally noted more for cunning than eccentricity); having method in one's madness (*see* METHOD). The phrase was used as the title of a book by the American humorist S J Perelman, published in 1942. *Mid 20th cent.*

> *Guardian* 1986
> *The State Department's John Whitehead, returning from an effort to beef up support among the wimpish Europeans, speculated that Gadafy might be easing up on terror to save his economy. 'He's crazy, but he's crazy like a fox,' he said.*

creature

creature of habit

a person who follows a fixed routine. *18th cent.*

> Thomas Holcroft *The Adventures of Hugh Trevor* 1794
> *A conviction that man is depraved by nature, and a total forgetfulness that he is merely the creature of habit and accident.*

> Dickens *The Battle of Life* 1846
> *Man's the creature of habit … I had somehow got used to you, Clem; and I found I shouldn't be able to get on without you. So we went and got made man and wife.*

credit

give somebody credit for something

to allow that somebody must have the quality needed in a particular situation. The phrase was used earlier in the slightly different meaning 'to give somebody the chance to fulfil a promise in the future', which is closer to the concrete notion of *credit*. *19th cent.*

> **P D James** *Devices and Desires* 1989
> *Why not give him credit for a simple human weakness; the attraction of eating a good dinner which he hasn't had to cook?*

(give) credit where credit is due
to recognize something as deserving praise. *19th cent.*

> **Dickens** *Martin Chuzzlewit* 1844
> *'The families I've had,' said Mrs. Gamp, 'if all wos knowd, and credit done where credit's doo, would take a week to chris'en at Saint Polge's fontin!'*

creek

be up the creek / up shit creek (without a paddle)
to be in a difficult or dangerous situation (without any means of escape or rescue). *Mid 20th cent.*

> **Joseph Heller** *Catch-22* 1961
> *'Popinjay, is your father a millionaire, or a member of the Senate?' 'No, sir.' 'Then you're up shit creek, Popinjay, without a paddle.' ... 'What does your father do?' 'He's dead, sir.' 'That's very good. You really are up the creek, Popinjay. Is Popinjay your real name?'*

creep

make somebody's flesh creep / give somebody the creeps
to make somebody feel revolted or disgusted. *The creeps* are a feeling caused by a mixture of fear and revulsion, as though things were crawling over one's flesh. *18th cent.*

> **Swift** *Gulliver's Travels* 1726
> *We all three entered the gate of the palace between two rows of guards, armed and dressed after a very antic manner, and something in their countenances that made my flesh creep with a horror I cannot express.*

> **Dickens** *Oliver Twist* 1838
> *He read of men who, lying in their beds at dead of night, had been tempted (so they said) and led on, by their own bad thoughts, to such dreadful bloodshed as it made the flesh creep, and the limbs quail, to think of.*

> **Brian Aldiss** *Frankenstein Unbound* 1991
> *'Mr Bodenland can tell you a story about little children and graves,' Shelley told her. 'It will make your flesh creep!'*

crest

on the crest of a wave
at the peak of success or fame. 'Riding along on the Crest of a Wave' was the title of a rousing song that was especially associated with the Sea Scouts and was from 1936 the anthem of the Scout Association's annual 'Gang Show'. *Mid 20th cent.*

> **G Pearson** *Hooligan* 1983
> *Within not much more than a year, the Boy Scouts had already outstripped the older Boys' Brigade and Church Lads' Brigade movements ... by 1910. By the outbreak of war, with the Boy Scouts riding along on the crest of a wave, the figure stood at 150,000.*

cricket

not cricket
informal not conforming to the accepted rules of behaviour: from the notion that cricket is a byword for competitive courtesy and fair play. *19th cent.*

> **Scotsman** 1990
> *Many argue that ... an appeal by the Crown against too lenient a sentence is simply not cricket.*

crimp

put a crimp in something
informal, chiefly NAmer to thwart a plan or intention. A *crimp* is a wave (in the hair) or fold and the image is of straightness or evenness being disturbed. *19th cent.*

> **Willa Cather** *The Song of the Lark* 1915
> *Your public wanted just about eighty degrees [of effort]; if you gave it more it blew its nose and put a crimp in you.*

crisp

See BURNT to a cinder/crisp.

crocodile

shed/weep crocodile tears

to show false or pretended sorrow, especially hypocritically: from the belief that crocodiles shed tears before attacking or eating their victims. There are many allusions to this legend in literature, and it makes an early appearance in the famous book of travels attributed to Sir John Mandeville (originally written in Anglo-Norman French in about 1356–7, with English versions from later in the 14th cent.). The legend is referred to in the 16th cent. in Spenser's *Faerie Queene* (1596) I.v.18: 'As when a wearie traveller that strayes ... I Doth meet a cruell craftie Crocodile, I Which in false griefe hyding his harmefull guile, I Doth weepe full sore, and sheddeth tender teares'; and in Shakespeare's *Othello* (1604) IV.i.257 Othello responds to Desdemona's tears in the scene with the Venetian ambassador with the rebuke 'O, devil, devil! I If that the earth could teem with woman's tears, I Each drop she falls would prove a crocodile.' The first reference to *crocodile tears* as such is from the 1560s. A famous use in more recent times is by Kipling (see below). *16th cent.*

Alexander Oldys *The Female Gallant* 1692
All this while the plaguy Gypsy sate sobbing and blubbering, and staining with her crocodile tears her handkerchief, which before was as white as innocence.

Kipling *Just So Stories* 1902
'Come hither, Little One,' said the Crocodile, 'for I am the Crocodile,' and he wept crocodile-tears to show it was quite true.

Croesus

See (as) RICH as Croesus.

crook

A 19th cent. Australian slang term meaning 'bad' or 'ill'.

be crook on somebody/something

Australian and NZ, informal to be angry with somebody or about something. *Mid 20th cent.*

F Hardy *Billy Borker Yarns Again* 1967
The landlords are crook on this.

go crook

1 *Australian and NZ, informal* to become ill or (said of a machine) to stop working. *Early 20th cent.*

J Cox *Don't Cry Alone* 1992
You've been a help to me since my old bones went crook, and I'll see you get your dues when the time comes.

2 *Australian and NZ, informal* to lose one's temper. *Early 20th cent.*

H C Baker *I Was Listening* 1978
We rolled him for his overcoat. You ought to've heard him go crook.

cropper

come a cropper

informal to suffer a severe defeat or reversal; originally to have a heavy fall. *Cropper* in this sense is used only in the phrase or in minor variants of it. The phrase first appears in print (in the form *get a cropper*) in a work of 1858 called *Ask Mamma* by R S Surtees, a writer on hunting sports of the Victorian age. It is thought to come from the term *neck and crop*, which was used to refer to a bad fall by a rider in hunting. *Crop* here may be the same as the word for the pouch in a bird's gullet, or it may be a variant of *croup*, the term for a horse's rump. In either case a horse that falls 'neck and crop' does so heavily and comprehensively. *19th cent.*

Trollope *The Way We Live Now* 1875
He had almost fallen in love with Marie when he saw her last, and was inclined to feel the more kindly to her now because of the hard things that were being said about her father. And yet he knew that he must be careful. If 'he came a cropper' in this matter, it would be such an awful cropper!

Somerset Maugham *Of Human Bondage* 1915
He did not know that he had ever done anything but what seemed best to do, and what a cropper he had come!

cross

(as) cross as two sticks

extremely cross or irritable. The phrase is a pun on two meanings of *cross* ('angry' and 'intersecting'). *18th cent.*

Robert Bage *Man As He Is* 1792
You know Mr. Owen ap Jones ap Price, for he was here when you was. He comes a courting to me whether I will or no; and I'm forced to give him my company out of civility, for one can't be rude in one's own house you know. Nothing will say him nay; and it makes me as cross as two sticks.

at cross purposes

(said of two or more people) unwittingly misunderstanding each other or having a different purpose. A game of 'cross purposes', based on unconnected questions and answers, features in entries in the *Diary* of Samuel Pepys, e.g. for 26 December 1666: 'Then to cross purposes, mighty merry; and then to bed.' *17th cent.*

Fanny Burney *Cecilia* 1782
Such, my good young friends, is the moral of your calamities. You have all, in my opinion, been strangely at cross purposes, and trifled, no one knows why, with the first blessings of life.

Charles Lamb *Last Essays of Elia* 1833
Everybody is at cross purposes, yet the effect is so much better than uniformity.

cross one's fingers / keep one's fingers crossed

to trust in one's good fortune and hope for success. The phrase refers to the action of physically crossing one's index finger and second finger as a gesture of hope or optimism. This was also done to ward off retribution that might be incurred from telling an untruth, and in children's games to render a participant immune from capture. The action is a reduced form of the Christian act of making the sign of the cross as an invocation of divine help. Eventually the phrase became used in a purely allusive sense without necessarily involving or implying the actual crossing of the fingers. *Early 20th cent.*

Edward Peple *A Pair of Sixes* 1914
You can't catch me – you can't catch me! ... I've got me fingers crossed! I've got me fingers crossed!

Guardian 1989
At Tonbridge a fellow train man – as BR now prefers to call its conductors – announced: 'This train is bound for London Bridge, fingers crossed.'

cross my heart (and hope to die)

used as a formula asserting the truth or sincerity of something said: from the action of making a small sign of the cross over one's heart, which sometimes accompanies the words. *19th cent.*

Henry Clay Preuss *Fashions and Follies of Washington Life* 1857
[Capt. Smith] *Attended strictly to everything I told you?* [Tom Scott] *Yes indeed, Massy – cross my heart!*

Simon Brett *Murder Unprompted* 1984
Course I will, old boy, course I will. Scout's honour. Cross my heart.

cross somebody's palm with silver

often humorous to pay somebody for a service. Originally used with reference to fortune-telling, when the client would be asked to make a sign of the cross with a silver coin on the palm of the fortune-teller's hand, to ward off harmful spirits rather than as a method of payment. *19th cent.*

Charlotte Brontë *Jane Eyre* 1847
'If you wish me to speak more plainly, show me your palm.' 'And I must cross it with silver, I suppose?' 'To be sure.' I gave her a shilling.

Andrew Taylor *Freelance Death* 1993
Henry raised himself on tiptoe and pranced across the room. 'Cross me palm with silver, duckie,' he crooned ... 'Whereas nowadays we all prefer credit cards.'

cross swords

to come into conflict: a metaphor from duelling or sword-fighting. *19th cent.*

Scott *Old Mortality* 1816
The awe on the insurgents' minds was such, that they gave way before Claverhouse as before a supernatural being, and few men ventured to cross swords with him.

Gardener's World 1991
It seems as if nearly all of us have crossed swords with the dreaded vine weevil.

have one's cross to bear

to have personal troubles to bear like everybody else: from the practice at Roman crucifixions (and Christ's crucifixion in particular) of making a condemned person carry the cross to the place of execution. A figurative use occurs already in the New Testament, where Christ calls on his followers to 'take up the cross', e.g. Matthew 10:38 'And he that taketh not his cross, and followeth after me, is not worthy of me.' References occur in the New Testament translations from Middle English (Wyclif), although the phrase is not recorded in this form until the 1770s. *18th cent.*

Lydia Child *Fact and Fiction* 1846
To these subduing influences, was added the early consciousness of being pointed at as peculiar; of having a cross to bear, a sacred cause to sustain.

Nigel Williams *The Wimbledon Poisoner* 1990
She was a kind of Stakhanovite worker in the field of female suffering, setting new targets for pain, finding each week some new emotional cross to bear.

See also cross the/that BRIDGE when one comes to it; cross the FLOOR; cross somebody's MIND; cross the RUBICON; get one's wires crossed *at* WIRE.

crossfire

be caught in the crossfire
to become inadvertently involved in somebody else's argument: from the notion of being trapped in a position between hostile forces firing at each other. *20th cent.*

Independent 1989
Industry had become an ideological battleground, caught in the left–right crossfire.

crossroads

at a/the crossroads
at a crucial or decisive stage. The image is of several courses of action converging as though at a crossroads, with several choices for further action. *18th cent.*

See also DIRTY work at the crossroads.

crow

as the crow flies
(said of a distance) measured in a direct line as distinct from the course taken by a road. The phrase is said by some to be based on a practice of early navigation at sea: a cage of crows was kept on board and a crow would be released from the top of the mast (hence called the 'crow's nest') in the hope that it would fly directly to land and show the way. But the earliest evidence of the phrase, from the early years of the 19th cent., is distinctly landlocked, as the quotations below show, and we would expect earlier evidence if a naval phrase was familiar enough to have moved into more general currency. Furthermore,

the evidence for the term *crow's nest* (from the early 19th cent.) shows this to be due to its shape and position at the top of the mast, and its primary use was to accommodate a lookout. Whatever the naval practice regarding the crows, it does not seem to have been the origin of our phrase, according to the evidence. *19th cent.*

Scott *Waverley* 1814
'Your horse will carry you there in two hours.' 'I shall hardly give him the trouble; why, the distance must be eighteen miles as the crow flies.'

Dickens *Oliver Twist* 1838
They fired and hit the boy. We cut over the fields at the back with him between us – straight as the crow flies – through hedge and ditch.

eat crow
NAmer, informal to be forced to accept humiliation or defeat. The phrase is presumably based on the unappetizing prospect of eating the flesh of a crow, although the only direct evidence of people being compelled to do this as a punishment consists of apocryphal 19th cent. anecdotes cited in explanation of the phrase. One of these concerns an incident in the British–American war of 1812–14, in which an American soldier strayed into the British lines and, finding no better food, shot a crow, which he was then forced to eat by a British officer who came across the scene. Early uses are associated with newspaper journalism. A contributor to *Notes & Queries* in September 1877 (p.186) who called himself Uneda (one of many such pseudonyms in this source) observed, in a short piece on Americanisms, that 'A newspaper editor, who is obliged by his "party", or other outside influences, to advocate "principles" different from those which he supported a short time before, is said to "eat boiled crow".' This explicit notion of cooking the bird suggests that the punishment was regarded as more than simply spontaneous and a little more than merely fanciful. *Cf* eat DIRT; eat one's HAT; eat HUMBLE pie. *19th cent.*

Mark Twain *Letter* 1884
Warner and Clark are eating their daily crow in the paper.

See also STONE the crows!

crowd

See PASS in a crowd.

crown

crowning glory

a magnificent conclusion or culmination: possibly with allusion to the Latin motto *finis coronat opus* ('the end crowns the work'). Also used humorously with reference to a person's hair, especially when this is extravagantly or showily arranged: see the Joyce quotation. *19th cent.*

> George Eliot *Scenes of Clerical Life* 1858
> *Ample galleries are supported on iron pillars, and in one of them stands the crowning glory, the very clasp or aigrette of Shepperton church-adornment – namely, an organ, not very much out of repair.*

> James Joyce *Ulysses* 1922
> *Gerty's crowning glory was her wealth of wonderful hair. It was dark brown with a natural wave in it.*

cruel

be cruel to be kind

to act harshly towards somebody for their own good. Used with allusion to Shakespeare, *Hamlet* (1601) III.iv.178, where Hamlet justifies his harsh attitude to his mother's marriage to his uncle Claudius with the words 'I must be cruel only to be kind'. As often with references to Shakespeare, allusive uses are first found at a date considerably later than the original use. *17th cent.*

> Henry Oake Pardey *Nature's Nobleman* 1853
> [Maria] *Caroline, that was unkind, cruel of you!*
> [Caroline] *Cruel to be kind, Maria! You are cured.*

crumb

crumbs from somebody's / a rich man's table

an unjustly small share of something contrasted with a large share taken by somebody else: from the New Testament story (Luke 16:21) of the beggar Lazarus, who is described as 'desiring to be fed with the crumbs which fell from the rich man's table'. *19th cent.*

> Mrs Rowson *Charlotte's Daughter* 1828
> *I think it highly disgraceful for one minister of the gospel to be lolling on velvet cushions, rolling in his carriage, and faring sumptuously every day, while many, very many of his poor brethren, labourers in the same vineyard, bowed with poverty, burthened with large families, would, like Lazarus, be glad to feed on the crumbs that fall from the rich man's table.*

> Nursing Times 1992
> *Medicine has a problem – it has a history of sexism and classism. Doctors think nursing is women's work and that the girls will take the crumbs from the medical table.*

crunch

when/if it comes to the crunch

informal when or if decisive action is called for: from the 20th cent. meaning of *crunch* 'crisis, decisive moment'. *Mid 20th cent.*

> Gavin Lyall *The Conduct of Major Maxim* 1982
> *And Harry, for God's sake remember Number 10 when it comes to the crunch. And don't let it come to the crunch, either.*

cruse

a widow's cruse

a modest supply of something that can be made to last a long time. Derived from the story in 1 Kings 17:10–16 of the jar of oil that was miraculously refilled during a drought. *Cruse* is an archaic word for a pot or jar. There are other literary allusions apart from the phrase, e.g. in Thackeray's *Pendennis* (1849): 'I don't envy Pen's feelings (as the phrase is), as he thought of what he had done. He had slept, and the tortoise had won the race. He had marred at its outset what might have been a brilliant career. He had dipped ungenerously into a generous mother's purse, basely and recklessly spilt her little cruse.' *18th cent.*

> Edward Young *Conjectures on Original Composition* 1759
> *An inventive genius may safely stay at home; that, like the widow's cruse, is divinely replenished from within; and affords us a miraculous delight.*

> Edward Bulwer-Lytton *The Last Days of Pompeii* 1834
> *One son alone was spared to her. And she loved him with a melancholy love … And the son died. The reed on which she leaned was broken, the oil was dried up in the widow's cruse.*

crust

See the UPPER crust.

cry

cry for the moon

to want something that cannot be had. The image of the moon as a symbol of the unattainable dates from the 16th cent., e.g. in Shakespeare, *2 Henry VI* (1591) III.i.158 'And doggèd York that reaches at the moon, | Whose overweening arm I have plucked back.' *18th cent.*

Sarah Fielding *The Adventures of David Simple* 1744
He believed he was mad; for no person, in his senses, could ever have enter'd into such a scheme as that of hunting after a real friend; which was just the same thing as little children do, when they cry for the moon.

Oscar Wilde *The Happy Prince* 1888
'Why can't you be like the Happy Prince?' asked a sensible mother of her little boy who was crying for the moon. 'The Happy Prince never dreams of crying for anything.'

cry foul

to complain of an injustice, especially belatedly when other expedients have failed: from the call 'foul' in sports, drawing attention to alleged illegal play. *Mid 20th cent.*

Guardian 1989
Would the West cry foul, and declare that Mr Gorbachev cannot, after all, be trusted to keep his word that the Brezhnev doctrine is dead, and that he will not interfere in the Warsaw Pact countries?

a cry from the heart

a passionate appeal or entreaty: cf French *cri de coeur*. Also *to cry from the heart*, to make such an appeal. *19th cent.*

Thackeray *Catherine* 1839
While his unshorn lips and nose together are performing that mocking, boisterous, Jack-indifferent cry of 'Clo, Clo'; who knows what woful utterances are crying from the heart within?

cry over spilt milk

to express vain regrets for what cannot be recovered or undone: also as a proverb, *(it is) no use crying over spilt milk* (recorded in John Howell's 1659 collection of proverbs in the form *no weeping for shed milk*). *17th cent.*

Frederick Thomas *East and West* 1836
I suppose you have come here now to cry after your spilt milk – to catch the filly after she has gone out of the door that you left open yourself, you nincompoop!

Somerset Maugham *Of Human Bondage* 1915
Why... the futility of regret. It's no good crying over spilt milk, because all the forces of the universe were bent on spilling it.

cry stinking fish

to belittle one's own work or products: from the former practice of street vendors calling out their wares for sale. *17th cent.*

John Dunton *A Voyage Round the World* 1691
Why Reader know, that I do it in hopes that the novelty of the humour will sell my book. I believe Kainophilus is the first author that ever cry'd stinking fish, and therefore I hope that my extravagancy in this affair, will serve as a bait to catch a few silly gudgeons.

for crying out loud

informal, originally NAmer used to express exasperation or annoyance. *Early 20th cent.*

Margery Allingham *Sweet Danger* 1933
Well for crying out loud!... That's a nasty scrape.

Eroica Mildmay *Lucker and Tiffany Peel Out* 1993
Chicago pollution? What are you on about? Perhaps it has just got eczema, for crying out loud.

in full cry

in vigorous pursuit: a metaphor from the baying of hounds in hunting. *17th cent.*

Richard Brome *A Joviall Crew* 1652
I'll single no more. If you'll beg in full cry I am for you.

Boswell *The Life of Samuel Johnson* 1791
Against his Life of Milton, the hounds of Whiggism have opened in full cry.

See also cry WOLF.

cuckoo

a cuckoo in the nest

an unwanted intruder: from the practice of female cuckoos laying eggs in other birds' nests. *19th cent.*

Browning *The Ring and the Book* 1842
No lack of mothers here in Rome ... | The first name-pecking credit-scratching fowl | Would drop her unfledged cuckoo in our nest | To ... give voice at length | And shame the brood.

cucumber

See (as) COOL as a cucumber.

cud

chew the cud

to turn matters over in the mind: from the practice of ruminants re-chewing food they have partly digested. There is some Middle English evidence of allusive uses, and Thomas Cranmer in his *Answer to* [Bishop] *Stephen Gardiner* in 1551 wrote 'as many as haue a trewe faith and beliefe in hym, chawyng theyr cuddes, and perfectely remembryng the same death and passion', but general usage dates predominantly from the 18th cent.

> Henry Fielding *The History of Tom Jones* 1749
> *Allworthy having left her a little while to chew the cud (if I may use that expression) on these first tidings, told her, he had still something more to impart, which he believed would give her pleasure.*

cudgel

An Old English word for a short stick or club used as a weapon.

cudgel one's brain/brains

to force oneself to think hard about something: with allusion to Shakespeare, *Hamlet* (1601) v.i.63 '[First Clown] Cudgel thy brains no more about it.' *17th cent.*

> Colley Cibber *The Rival Fools* 1709
> *Madam, he has been cudgelling his Brains these two hours, to find a present worthy your Ladyships acceptance.*

> Dickens *Oliver Twist* 1838
> *Mr. Gamfield's most sanguine estimate of his finances could not raise them within full five pounds of the desired amount; and, in a species of arithmetical desperation, he was alternately cudgelling his brains and his donkey.*

> Joanna Trollope *The Rector's Wife Described* 1993
> *'I'll think,' Laura said, shutting her eyes. 'I'll cudgel my brains. Cudgel, cudgel.'*

take up the cudgels

to engage vigorously in the support of a person or cause. *17th cent.*

> Head & Kirkman *The English Rogue Described* 1668
> *But so soon as he* [Richard Head] *knew my intention of making his writing a part of (by joyning it to) The Rogue, with some anger he left it, and refused to proceed. He having thus laid down the Cudgels, I then took them up my self, and those loose scribled papers which I had written for his instruction to proceed upon, I viewed over, and after some small correction they serve for the greatest part of this Treatise.*

> Oscar Wilde *A Woman of No Importance* 1893
> *I admired his conduct last night immensely. He took up the cudgels for that pretty prude with wonderful promptitude.*

cue

The meaning underlying the phrases and indeed all uses of the word is the theatrical one, 'the words that serve as a signal to a performer to begin a specific speech or action', which dates from the time of Shakespeare (late 16th cent.). There is a vivid example in the exchanges of the actors in 'Pyramus and Thisbe', the play within the play in *A Midsummer Night's Dream* (v.i.183): '[Bottom] Cursed be thy stones for thus deceiving me. [Theseus] The wall methinks, being sensible, should curse again. [Bottom, to Theseus] No, in truth, sir, he should not. 'Deceiving me' is Thisbe's cue. She is to enter now, and I am to spy her through the wall.'

on cue

at the right moment. *19th cent.*

> David Lodge *Nice Work* 1988
> *As if on cue, a cistern flushed and the door of one of the WC cubicles opened to reveal the emerging figure of George Prendergast, the Personnel Director.*

take one's cue

to act on somebody's suggestion or example. *18th cent.*

> Sarah Fielding *The History of the Countess of Dellwyn* 1759
> *The Captain took his cue; and, after he had expressed a fulsome compliment on the subject of his Lordship's age, the discovery he had before meditated began to stir and bustle within him.*

cuff

off the cuff

spontaneously, without any preparation, especially with reference to public speaking. The underlying idea is of notes hastily written on a shirt cuff, from which a speaker can improvise. Also as a modifying phrase as in *an off-the-cuff observation*. *Mid 20th cent.*

Guitarist 1992

Your solos with Elvis are legendary. Were they completely off the cuff or did you have some idea of what you were going to do?

culture

culture shock

a feeling of psychological and social disorientation caused by confrontation with a new or unfamiliar culture, such as a city-dweller in the countryside or a Londoner in Glasgow. *Mid 20th cent.*

Guardian 1989

With pregnancy things change. Being at home with small babies is an instant culture shock to the young woman of the world.

a culture vulture

a person who enjoys cultural activities. As the word *vulture* implies, the phrase is often used in a depreciatory way implying a lack of discrimination. The expression occurs in the collection of radio pieces by Dylan Thomas published just after his death in 1953 under the title *Quite Early One Morning* (1954): 'See the garrulous others, also, gabbing and garlanded from one nest of culture-vultures to another.' Ogden Nash comes close to it in *Free Wheeling*, which dates from 1931: 'There is a vulture | Who circles above | The carcass of culture.' Earlier combinations of similar meaning include *culture hound* and (more unfavourably) *culture snob*. *Mid 20th cent.*

Country Living 1991

At 6 Frith Street, in the middle of Soho, Hazlitt's is a haven for the saturated culture vulture or worn-out shopper.

cup

in one's cups

drunk, especially with reference to an utterance made while drunk. Use of *cup* in the plural to mean 'a bout of drinking' dates from the 15th cent. The locus classicus for the phrase is the Apocrypha (1 Esdras 3:22): 'And when they are in their cups, they forget their love both to friends and brethren.' The phrase occurs a little earlier in Shakespeare's *Henry V* (1599) IV.vi.43, where the Welsh Captain Fluellen refers to the drunken killing of friends: 'As Alexander killed his friend Cleitus, being in his ales and his cups, so also Harry Monmouth, being in his right wits and his good judgements, turned away the fat knight [Sir John Falstaff].' *16th cent.*

John Bunyan The Life and Death of Mr Badman 1680

Upon a time, a certain drunken fellow boasted in his cups, that there was neither Heaven nor Hell; also he said, He believed, that man had no soul.

not one's cup of tea

not what suits or appeals to one. The phrase dates from the 1930s and was originally used in positive contexts referring to a type of person; the current use is predominantly negative. *Mid 20th cent.*

Nancy Mitford Christmas Pudding 1932

I'm not at all sure I wouldn't rather marry Aunt Loudie. She's even more my cup of tea in many ways.

cupboard

cupboard love

insincere love or affection given as a means of gaining a benefit or advantage, originally food from a cupboard. Also (17th cent.) in the form *cream-pot love*, love given in return for the 'cream'. *18th cent.*

Mrs Humphry Ward Robert Elsmere 1888

The cat looked from one sister to the other, blinking; then with a sudden magnificent spring leaped on to Agnes's lap and curled herself up there. 'Nothing but cupboard love,' said Rose scornfully, in answer to Agnes's laugh; 'she knows you will give her bread and butter and I won't.'

curate

a curate's egg

something that is partly good and partly bad. Based on the caption to a cartoon published in *Punch* in 1895 depicting a curate who, on being given a stale egg by his bishop, assured him 'Parts of it are excellent!' A curate has a junior position in the ecclesiastical hierarchy, and this deference to the much higher office of bishop is understandable. *19th cent.*

Country Living 1991
The Escort has been one of Britain's top-sellers for many years and having tested various examples of the latest in the range I have to give a curate's egg verdict.

curdle

See make somebody's BLOOD curdle.

curiosity

curiosity killed the cat

(proverb) being too inquisitive can get one into trouble. The proverb in this form is surprisingly modern (first appearing in a play of Eugene O'Neill's from 1921), but an older form *care* [in both main senses] *killed the cat* is much older, occurring in Shakespeare. *Early 20th cent.*

Timothy Mo The Redundancy of Courage 1991
There was no one around. The townspeople had learned the hard way that curiosity killed the cat – you stayed indoors if there was trouble.

curl

curl one's lip

to show one's disapproval or disgust: literally, to lift the corner of one's mouth in a sneer. *19th cent.*

James Hogg The Private Memoirs and Confessions of a Justified Sinner 1824
His lip curled with a smile of contempt, which I could hardly brook; and I began to be afraid that the eminence to which I had been destined by him was already fading from my view.

Charlotte Brontë Jane Eyre 1847
In her eagerness she did not observe me at first, but when she did, she curled her lip and moved to another casement.

go out of curl

informal to lose one's energy: from the idea that curly hair is a sign of virility. *Early 20th cent.*

make somebody's hair curl

informal to horrify somebody: *cf* make somebody's HAIR stand on end. *19th cent.*

W S Gilbert The Happy Land 1873
Ah! what dinners one gets down there. There's a certain dish called chops that beats our fairy food into fits; and they've a peculiar kind of nectar known as 'bottled stout', which makes a fairy's hair curl to think of.

Janet Tanner Folly's Child 1991
She'll let the boys do what they like … You ask my brother. The things he could tell you about her would make your hair curl.

current

pass current

to achieve general recognition or validity: originally with reference to coins and banknotes. *18th cent.*

Boswell The Life of Samuel Johnson 1791
Let me add, as a proof of the popularity of his character, that there are copper pieces struck at Birmingham, with his head impressed on them, which pass current as half-pence there, and in the neighbouring parts of the country.

curry

curry favour

to ingratiate oneself with flattery or attention. The phrase is recorded in an older form *curry favel*, which remained in use until the 17th cent.; the form now in use originated in the 16th cent. A *favel*, or *fauvel*, was a chestnut horse, and *curry* is used in its sense of grooming. The name was used in a French Romance called the *Roman de Fauvel* written soon after 1300 by Gervais de Bus, a satire on political and social corruption ridiculed in the adventures of a scheming stallion called Fauvel. As a result, the name became a byword for cunning or duplicity: to *curry Fauvel* (or *Favel*) meant to use flattery to get an advantage. (It may be relevant that in medieval German *den fahlen hengst reiten*, meaning 'to ride the chestnut horse', signified dishonest behaviour.) In

English, *favel* was changed by popular etymology to the more logical *favour* in the 16th cent.

> Spenser *The Faerie Queene* v.v.35 (1596)
> *So from her parting, she thenceforth did labour | By all the meanes she might, to curry favour | With th' Elfin Knight, her Ladies best beloved.*

curtain

behind the curtain
away from the general view. *17th cent.*

> Susannah Centlivre *The Humours of Elections* 1715
> *But come come, Mr. Alderman, there is yet a secret behind the curtain, Pray what cou'd Mr. Tickup, or any of his Friends oblige you with, that is not in my power to have done.*

> Henry Fielding *The History of Tom Jones* 1749
> *Thus stage and scene are by common use grown as familiar to us, when we speak of life in general, as when we confine ourselves to dramatic perform-ances: and when transactions behind the curtain are mentioned, St. James's is more likely to occur to our thoughts than Drury-Lane.*

bring down the curtain on something
to conclude something or bring it to an end: with allusion to the lowering of the curtain at the front of the stage at the end of a theatrical performance. The 20th cent. informal phrase *be curtains (for somebody)* is derived from this. *19th cent.*

> John Todhunter *The Black Cat* 1895 (Preface)
> *Only a 'practical dramatist' could cut the Gordian knot, and at the last moment introduce the erring Mrs. Tremaine, still charming in the garb of a Sister of Mercy, to bring down the curtain upon a tableau of Woman returning to her Duty, and Man to his Morality.*

> Liverpool Daily Post and Echo 1993
> *Yesterday's decision concluded one of the most embarrassing chapters in racing history and brought the curtain down on the 'National That Never Was'.*

custom

See old SPANISH customs.

customer

the customer is always right
dated a customer's wishes should be respected however unusual or awkward they seem: an expression assuring good service in shops, restaurants, etc. *Early 20th cent.*

> Carl Sandburg *Good Morning, America* 1928
> *Behold the proverbs of a people, a nation ... Say it with flowers. Let one hand wash the other. The customer is always right.*

cut

be cut out for/to be something
to be naturally fitted or suited to a particular activity. The image is of cutting out cloth or other material for a particular purpose. *17th cent.*

> P Belon *The Court Secret* 1689
> *All was quiet again, and every body went to make an end of their work in their beds. Thus ended the odd adventures of that cross and ill condition'd night, which had never been cut out for lovers.*

> Claire Rayner *The Meddlers* 1991
> *I was devoted to my own two, you know. But they were my own. I'm not really cut out for adoption. I'm past forty, after all.*

a cut above somebody/something
significantly superior. The underlying meaning is probably that of the style and shape of clothing, hair, etc, although the precise image is unclear. When Charles Lamb wrote in a letter of 1797 'There is much abstruse science in it above my cut', the meaning seems to be 'beyond my under-standing', and the same may be true of the use by a character in Scott's *Heart of Midlothian* (1818): 'Robertson is rather a cut abune me.' *19th cent.*

> George Meredith *The Ordeal of Richard Feverel* 1859
> *This, farmer Blaize well knew, and reckoned con-sequently that here was an animal always to be relied on – a sort of human composition out of dog, horse, and bull, a cut above each of these quadrupeds in usefulness, and costing proportionately more.*

> W H Auden *Dyer's Hand* 1963
> *In New England Protestants of Anglo-Scotch stock consider themselves a cut above Roman Catholics and those of a Latin race.*

cut and dried

completely decided, and not open to further consideration. The phrase also occurs in the 18th cent. and 19th cent. in the form *cut and dry*, and is a metaphor from herbalists' language, cut and dried herbs being those that were prepared for use as distinct from those still growing. (Other associations, with curing meat or seasoning timber, do not fit the circumstances or chronology of the usage.) Early figurative uses were somewhat closer to the literal meaning in implying a lack of originality or spontaneity rather than of opportunities for further thought. The earliest recorded use is of 1710 in a letter to a clergyman describing his sermon as 'ready cut and dry'd'. Later, in 1730, Jonathan Swift wrote in a satirical poem that 'sets of phrases cut and dry, evermore thy tongue supply'. *18th cent.*

John Cleland *Memoirs of a Woman of Pleasure* 1748
She was capable of being made a most agreeable, nay, a most virtuous wife … This presumption her conduct afterwards verified; for presently meeting with a match, that was ready cut and dry for her, with a neighbour's son of her own rank, and a young man of sense and order, who took her as the widow of one lost at sea, … she naturally struck into all the duties of her domestic, with as much simplicity of affection, with as much constancy and regularity, as if she had never swerv'd from a state of undebauch'd innocence from her youth.

George Eliot *Daniel Deronda* 1876
People talk of their motives in a cut and dried way. Every woman is supposed to have the same set of motives, or else to be a monster.

The Face 1990
The movie's message is plain and unequivocal: do drugs and die. The only way to redeem yourself is to check into a rehab clinic, suffer the torments of the damned and make a final public confession of your sins. That's the plot in cut and dried form.

cut and run

to make a speedy and undignified escape. This is a naval metaphor referring to sailors cutting the anchor cable and allowing the ship to run before the wind. *18th cent.*

John O'Keeffe *Wild Oats* 1791
[John Dory] *Why then, the young squire has cut and run.* [Sir George Thunder] *What?* [John] *Got leave to come to you, and the master did not find out*

before yesterday, that instead of making for home he had sheer'd off towards London.

Dickens *Great Expectations* 1861
I treasonably whispered to Joe, 'I hope, Joe, we shan't find them.' And Joe whispered to me, 'I'd give a shilling if they had cut and run, Pip.'

cut and thrust

competitive and stimulating exchange of arguments: a metaphor from duelling and fencing. *18th cent.*

Joseph Neal *Charcoal Sketches* 1838
He may look upon himself as an intellectual 'cut and thrust' – a thinking chopper and stabber.

Herman Melville *Typee* 1846
I felt … like a 'prentice boy who, going to the play in the expectation of being delighted with a cut-and-thrust tragedy, is almost moved to tears of disappointment at the exhibition of a genteel comedy.

cut both ways

to have benefits and disadvantages; (said of an argument) to be equally valid for and against a proposition or point of view. The image is of a sword that has two cutting edges; an early-17th cent. treatise on priestcraft written by one Edmund Hickeringill states that 'fame, like a two-edg'd sword, does cut both ways'. *17th cent.*

William Simms *Richard Hurdis* 1838
'Suppose I had been fortunate – if I was punished by my losses for having played, he who won, I suppose, is punished by his winnings for the same offence. How does your reason answer when it cuts both ways?' 'Even as a two edged sword it doth, my friend; though in the blindness of earth you may not so readily see or believe it.'

Conan Doyle *The Beryl Coronet* 1892
'If his purpose were innocent, why did he not say so?' 'Precisely. And if it were guilty, why did he not invent a lie? His silence appears to me to cut both ways.'

cut one's coat according to one's cloth

to adapt one's life to one's circumstances; to live within one's means. Also in the now obsolete form *cut one's cloth according to one's calling*, and as a proverb (recorded in this form in John Heywood's *Dialogue of Proverbs* of 1546). *16th cent.*

James Harrington *The Commonwealth of Oceana* 1656
There is a saying, that a man must cut his coat

according to his cloth. When I consider what God hath allow'd or furnished unto our present work, I am amazed.

Nicholas Billingsley *A Treasury of Divine Raptures* 1667

Who cuts his Coat according to | His cloth, shall not a begging go.

General Sir William Jackson *Britain's Defence Dilemma* 1990

The period of foreign aid is ending and we must now cut our coat according to our cloth. There is not much cloth. We have to find means of increasing, by £400 million a year, the credit side of our balance of payments.

cut a dash

to look smart or handsome. The underlying meaning of *cut* is the 17th cent. sense 'to perform an action or gesture' (as also in *cut a caper* and *cut a fine figure*). *Dash* is used in the sense 'a showy appearance or display' (*cf* the adjective *dashing*). *19th cent.*

Anne Royall *The Tennessean* 1827

When they were all landed at the bottom, I helped Betsey (who took charge of the baggage) into her carriage first, being determined to cut a dash – our females looked respectable, and might pass better than us.

cut somebody dead

to ignore somebody deliberately. *Dead* here is used as an emphatic adverb qualifying *cut* in its (17th cent.) meaning 'to break off acquaintance with' (as in Jane Austen's *Sense and Sensibility*, where Mr Willoughby tells Elinor of his meeting with Sir John Middleton: 'When he saw who I was … he spoke to me. That he had cut me ever since my marriage, I had seen without surprise or resentment'). *19th cent.*

Frederick Thomas *Clinton Bradshaw* 1835

When I came on board, Miss Penelope spoke to me, and that's all. I thought, at first, she meant to cut me dead. I couldn't rally my spirits, so I laid down in one of the berths.

Fay Weldon *Darcy's Utopia* 1991

And she cut me dead. My own child looked through me with her wide, hazel, dark-fringed eyes and cut me dead.

cut a deal

to make a business arrangement. *Late 20th cent.*

David Mervin *Ronald Reagan and the American Presidency* 1990

To be the president of a trade union is to gain an apprenticeship in negotiating, to develop an instinct for when to 'hang tough' and when to 'cut a deal'.

cut somebody down to size

to expose somebody's excessive self-importance: from the (19th cent.) literal meaning of reducing something to manageable proportions. *Early 20th cent.*

cut a — figure

to appear or present oneself in a particular way. *18th cent.*

Goldsmith *The Good Natur'd Man* 1768

[Croaker] If you were served right, you should have your head stuck up in the pillory. [Lofty] Ay, stick it where you will, for, by the Lord, it cuts but a very poor figure where it sticks at present.

cut from the same cloth

having similar qualities or characteristics. Also in the form (*a man* etc) *of the same cloth*. The reference is to clothing as an indication of a person's profession or line of work and social status. *18th cent.*

Richardson *Pamela* 1741

Mr. Adams being in the House, Mr. B. sent to desire he would dine with us; if it were but in respect to a Gentleman of the same Cloth, who gave us his Company. And with great Modesty he came.

Kazuo Ishiguro *The Remains of the Day* 1989

There existed in those days a true camaraderie in our profession, whatever the small differences in our approach. We were all essentially cut from the same cloth, so to speak.

cut it

1 *informal* to make one's escape, to leave hurriedly. The phrase is derived from a slang meaning of *cut* that is found in other idioms and formerly in expressions such as *cut away, cut off*, etc. The phrase is no longer current. *19th cent.*

Trollope *Doctor Thorne* 1858

'Now, my lady, do you cut it; cut at once,' said Sir Roger, turning hastily round to his better half; and his better half, knowing that the province of a woman is to obey, did cut it.

2 *informal* to be of the required quality: based on *cut the mustard* (see below). *Late 20th cent.*

The Face 1990
*The scientists who brought it into being, at the
Institute of Animal Physiology in 1984, call it 'the
Sheep-like Goat Chimera' … Forlornly comical in
photos, with its gaunt face and fluffy body, no one
else from dusty patent lawyers to impassioned
animal rights activists can resist calling it the
Gheep. And with a name like this, of course, it never
cut it as Bright Promise, or as Horrid Warning.*

cut it out
informal to stop doing something that causes
annoyance: often as an imperative. *Early 20th
cent.*

cut loose
to act independently or without restraint. The
image is of a tied-up animal escaping from its
bonds. *19th cent.*

Harriet Beecher Stowe Uncle Tom's Cabin 1852
*Her husband's suffering and dangers, and the
danger of her child, all blended in her mind, with a
confused and stunning sense of the risk she was
running, in leaving the only home she had ever
known, and cutting loose from the protection of a
friend whom she loved and revered.*

cut one's losses
to abandon an unprofitable or futile activity in
order to avoid further losses or setbacks. A variant form *cut a/the loss* is recorded in early use but
is not now common. *Early 20th cent.*

George Orwell Coming up for Air 1939
*The trouble over Joe aged Father a great deal. To lose
Joe was merely to cut a loss, but it hurt him.*

cut the mustard
informal to meet the necessary standard. *Mustard*
here means 'something outstanding', and the
same underlying metaphor is present in the
phrases *keen as mustard* and *hot stuff*. Much less
likely is a proposed connection with *muster* in the
sense of an army rollcall, aligning our phrase
with *pass muster*: 'cutting' muster would then
suggest 'avoiding or dodging rollcall', which is
the opposite of the meaning to do with excellence
that we have here. The phrase first appears in
print in 1907 in a story called *Heart of the West* by
the American writer O Henry: 'By nature and
doctrines I am addicted to the habit of discovering choice places wherein to feed. So I looked
around and found a proposition that exactly cut
the mustard.' O Henry may even have invented

the phrase, because he applies the metaphor in
other ways elsewhere in his writing. For
example, in *Cabbages and Kings* (1904) he writes
'I'm not headlined in the bills [= given star bill-
ing], but I'm the mustard in the salad dressing
just the same'. In recent use, the phrase has been
used in the shortened allusive form *cut it* (see
above). *Early 20th cent.*

Maeve Binchy Circle of Friends 1991
*Mr Healy was much older than his wife. It was
whispered, Patsy said, that he couldn't cut the
mustard. Eve and Benny spent long hours trying to
work out what this could mean. Mustard came in a
small tin and you mixed it with water. How did you
cut it? Why should you cut it?*

cut no ice
informal to fail to impress; to have no importance
or significance for somebody. *19th cent.*

Clyde Fitch The Climbers 1901
*Business with Dick Sterling became more or less of
a pleasure – but that doesn't cut any ice with me;
he's stolen my money.*

cut somebody off/down in their prime
to end somebody's life or career abruptly at a
time when it is most active and successful. *18th
cent.*

**Thomas Brown Amusements Serious and Comical
1700**
*If you are poor, no body owns you. If rich, you'll
know no body. If you dye young, what pity 'twas
they'll say, that he should be cut off in his prime. If
old, he was e'en past his best.*

cut somebody off without a penny
to disinherit somebody by leaving them out of a
will. Another form of the phrase, now obsolete,
was *cut somebody off with a shilling*. The giving of a
shilling had to be written into the will and this
served as confirmation that the disinheritance
was deliberate and not a result of oversight or
forgetfulness. *18th cent.*

**Frances Sheridan Memoirs of Miss Sidney Bidulph
1761**
*Mr. Vere had four daughters, and it was on this
fortune he chiefly depended to provide for them. The
news of my being cut off with a shilling exceedingly
surprised and exasperated him.*

Thomas Hayden The Killing Frost 1991
*My mother was a Jew. Her family disowned her for
marrying a Gentile. The same thing happened to my*

father. His people were strict Presbyterians. They cut him off without a penny.

the cut of one's jib
the distinctive nature of one's personal appearance: a metaphor from the terminology of sailing ships. A *jib* is a triangular sail set on a stay extending from the top of the foremast to the bow or the bowsprit. *19th cent.*

Francis Parkman *Vassall Morton* 1856
You don't look like a business man. I know a business man, a mile off, by the cut of his jib. I'm a business man myself, and a hard used one at that.

cut a/the rug
to dance energetically, especially to jazz music. *Mid 20th cent.*

Dogs Today 1992
The jazz was hotter than the scorching asparagus soup, and many cut the rug until closing.

cut one's stick
informal to leave abruptly, to be off. The phrase probably refers to the old practice of cutting a walking stick – to aid with the walk and for self-defence – before setting out on a long journey on foot. *19th cent.*

Dickens *The Old Curiosity Shop* 1841
Mr. Chuckster entertained them with theatrical chit-chat and the court circular; and so wound up a brilliant and fascinating conversation which he had maintained alone, and without any assistance whatever, for upwards of three-quarters of an hour. 'And now that the nag has got his wind again,' said Mr. Chuckster rising in a graceful manner, 'I'm afraid I must cut my stick.'

cut one's teeth (on something)
to acquire early experience of or familiarity with an activity: from the literal meaning of a child starting to grow its first teeth. *17th cent.*

Congreve *The Double Dealer* 1694
I'm sure if ever I should have Horns, they would kill me; they would never come kindly, I should dye of 'em, like any child, that were cutting his teeth.

Robert Bird *Sheppard Lee* 1836
Their bones might be made into rings and whistles, for infant democrats to cut their teeth on.

Daily Telegraph 1992
Most young British architects have never seen one of their house designs actually built. In America

and other European countries it is the way they cut their teeth.

the cutting edge (of something)
the pioneering aspect of an enterprise or development, especially in technology. The image is of the edge of a blade cutting through, as symbolic of progress, although the variant form *leading edge*, which is now less common, is an image from aeronautics in which progress is regarded in terms of the front edge of an aircraft wing moving through the air. *Mid 20th cent.*

Kenneth O Morgan *The People's Peace* 1990
The new generation of novelists and playwrights in the 1980s were ... increasingly prone to introspective analysis without a social cutting edge. Successful, Booker Prize-winning women novelists such as Anita Brookner or Penelope Lively, for example, did not reflect the feminist awareness of the time to any marked extent.

cut to the chase
NAmer, informal to get to the point: a metaphor from the silent cinema, in which a film might be edited to make exciting chase scenes feature more prominently. *Early 20th cent.*

cut up rough
informal to behave aggressively or vindictively. A variant form *cut up savage* appears in Thackeray but the phrase is now fixed. *19th cent.*

Wilkie Collins *Man and Wife* 1870
I haven't put that little matter to him yet – about marrying in Scotland, you know. Suppose he cuts up rough with me, if I try him now?

a feeling/atmosphere, etc that one could cut with a knife
a feeling, atmosphere, etc that is so thick or strong as to be almost physical and tangible. *19th cent.*

have one's work cut out
to face a difficult or lengthy task. To *cut out work*, meaning 'to prepare a task or piece of work' and drawing on literal uses in tailoring and dressmaking, is recorded from the 17th cent., but the current phrase in its modern meaning is two centuries later. The notion is perhaps of having difficulty in keeping up with all the work somebody has prepared. *19th cent.*

Dickens *A Christmas Carol* 1843
Old Fezziwig stood out to dance with Mrs. Fezziwig. Top couple too; with a good stiff piece of work

cut out for them; three or four and twenty pair of partners; people who were not to be trifled with; people who would dance, and had no notion of walking.

John Steinbeck *Of Mice and Men* 1937
That Curley got his work cut out for him. Ranch with a bunch of guys on it ain't no place for a girl, specially like her.

make the cut

to come up to the required standard: a term from golf, in which the *cut* is the allocation of players to further rounds of a competition. *Making the cut* means achieving a good enough score to avoid elimination. *Mid 20th cent.*

The East Anglian 1993
If Di Haine's Smooth Escort makes the cut for the Grand National at Aintree tomorrow he could be worth a sporting each-way bet as his trainer has always maintained he was made for the marathon.

See also cut the CACKLE; cut a CAPER; cut corners *at* CORNER; cut the GORDIAN knot; cut the GROUND from under somebody's feet; cut it FINE; cut the KNOT; cut one's own THROAT; cut somebody some SLACK; cut somebody to the QUICK.

cylinder

See firing on all cylinders *at* FIRE.

dab

be a dab (hand) at something

to be expert or skilful at something. *Dab* dates from the 17th cent., when it appears in the *Dictionary of the Canting Crew* (1690s) with the meaning 'one who is skilful or expert at something', but its origin is unknown despite conjectural associations with the adjective *adept* meaning 'highly skilled' (a close meaning, admittedly), with *dapper* meaning 'neat and spruce' (less likely), and with the verb *dab* meaning 'to touch lightly' (much less likely). An American word *dabster*, also meaning 'expert', is also recorded from the 17th cent. *19th cent.*

George Dibdin-Pitt *Susan Hopley* a1855
My master, Count Roccoleoni, and I, mixed with so many of the best English families at Spa and Rome; and as I was fond of the language, I soon got a dab hand at it.

Independent 1989
Martin Cruz Smith is a dab hand at beginnings, as readers of Gorky Park will remember; but he tends to fumble his middle sections, and by the time the climax arrives he's all fingers and thumbs.

dad

Dad's Army

informal enthusiastic but ill-equipped amateurs when up against experienced professionals. The name was originally attached informally to the forces of volunteers raised locally in Britain in 1940 during the early stages of the Second World War. It was originally known as *Local Defence Volunteers*, but at Winston Churchill's suggestion it was renamed *Home Guard*, a term used for local volunteers in America in the 19th cent. and for English Territorial Forces at the beginning of the 19th cent. The affectionate name *Dad's Army* came into use in about 1943. Although the force was disbanded in 1957, the name retains a strong familiarity in British public awareness as the name of a television comedy series broadcast from the 1960s and based on the activities of a Home Guard unit formed by the local bank manager in Walmington-on-Sea, a fictional small town on the south coast of England. *Mid 20th cent.*

Daily Telegraph 1992
To expect the Liberals to control Labour would be like asking Dad's Army to restrain the Mongol Hordes.

daft

(as) daft as a brush

completely crazy; very silly or eccentric. The phrase, a modification of *soft as a brush*, is associated with Ken Platt, a forces entertainer in the Second World War. *Mid 20th cent.*

dag

rattle one's dags

Australian and NZ, informal to hurry. *Dags* are lumps of matted wool entangled with excreta hanging near the tail of a sheep. *Mid 20th cent.*

dagger

(at) daggers drawn

in bitter conflict; at the point of fighting. The phrase is recorded first (16th cent.) in the form *at daggers drawing*, which survived into the first part of the 19th cent.

Thomas Dekker Old Fortunatus 1600
My belly and my purse have beene twentie times at daggers drawing, with parting the little urchins.

Thomas Holcroft The Adventures of Hugh Trevor 1794
This time she was not yet stirring, though it was two o'clock in the afternoon; the next she was engaged with an Italian vender of artificial flowers; the day after the prince and the devil does not know who beside were with her; and so on, till patience and spleen were at daggers drawn.

look daggers at somebody

to glare angrily at somebody. The phrase originates in the form *speak daggers* in Shakespeare, *Hamlet* (1601) III.ii.385, where Hamlet muses on an imminent meeting with his mother Gertrude:

'Let me be cruel, not unnatural. I will speak daggers to her, but use none.' *The Virgin Martyr*, a religious play by Philip Massinger and Thomas Dekker produced in 1622, includes the lines 'And do thine eyes shoot daggers at that man | That brings thee health?' *17th cent.*

Mrs Henry Wood East Lynne 1861
'What is your name?' 'Afy,' replied she, looking daggers at everybody, and sedulously keeping her back turned upon Francis Levison and Otway Bethel.

Beryl Bainbridge An Awfully Big Adventure 1990
She was fiddling with the crochet mats of green wool, flipping them over like pancakes. She flung the fork down, looking daggers at him, and continued.

See also CLOAK and dagger.

daisy

pushing up (the) daisies

informal dead and in one's grave. Earlier (19th cent.) forms include *be under the daisies* and *turn one's toes up to the daisies*. The present form dates from the time of the First World War. *Early 20th cent.*

She 1989
There was some distinctly unladylike wrangling between the grandmothers. 'They were fighting,' says Lucy, 'over the fluffy head of my son, as if his parents were already pushing up daisies!'

See also (as) FRESH as a daisy.

damage

damaged goods

informal a person who is regarded as inadequate or deficient in some way, especially an unmarried woman who is not a virgin. This view of women as commodities to be evaluated in a commercial manner has a period flavour and the phrase is now regarded as offensive, although it is still occasionally used. *Early 20th cent.*

what's the damage?

informal, humorous a coy enquiry about the cost of something: *damage* is recorded in this meaning from the 18th cent., and Byron wrote in 1812 'I will pay the damage [for an engraving]'. *19th cent.*

Harriet Beecher Stowe *Uncle Tom's Cabin* 1852
All the moral and Christian virtues bound in black morocco, complete! ... Well, now, my good fellow, what's the damage, as they say in Kentucky; in short, what's to be paid out for this business? How much are you going to cheat me, now? Out with it!

Damascus

the road to Damascus
a sudden or miraculous revelation, especially one that leads to a change of life. The phrase is derived from the biblical account in the Acts of the Apostles (9:1–20) of the conversion of St Paul (formerly Saul, persecutor of the Christians) in about AD 33, in which he sees a blinding vision of God on the road to Damascus. *19th cent.*

Thomas Hornblower Gill *The Anniversaries* 1838
Thy light not vainly glowed | On that Damascus road.

dammit
See as — as DAMN it / dammit.

damn

Damn has been used as a verb from the 14th cent., occurring in Chaucer and in Wyclif's translation of the Bible. Its use as an expletive dates from the time of Shakespeare, but in most formulaic expressions it no longer has any distinct meaning.

as — as damn it / dammit
British, informal a comparative phrase meaning '— enough to be acceptable or make no difference': typically used with *close*, *near*, and other adjectives indicating near success. The form with *damn it* is 19th cent., and with *dammit* early 20th cent.

be damned if one does and damned if one doesn't
to be liable to criticism whatever one does. *Late 20th cent.*

Guardian 1989
Mrs Aquino now has to decide whether she should be magnanimous in victory or punish those behind the mutiny. She is damned if she does and damned if she doesn't.

damn all
British, informal nothing at all. *Early 20th cent.*

James Joyce *Ulysses* 1922
Proud possessor of damnall.

damn somebody with faint praise
to praise somebody half-heartedly or without much conviction, so that it has the effect of criticism. The locus classicus is Alexander Pope's description of Joseph Addison in *An Epistle to Dr Arbuthnot* (1735): 'Damn with faint praise, assent with civil leer, | And without sneering, teach the rest to sneer; | Willing to wound, and yet afraid to strike, | Just hint a fault, and hesitate dislike.' *18th cent.*

Byron *Don Juan* 1824
But then 't was to the purpose what she spoke: | Like Addison's 'faint praise,' so wont to damn, | Her own but served to set off every joke, | As music chimes in with a melodrame.

I'll be damned if —
informal used to express firm refusal or firm conviction. *19th cent.*

not be worth a damn
to be worthless. *19th cent.*

John Steinbeck *The Grapes of Wrath* 1939
The tires ain't worth a damn, but they're a good size.

not give/care a damn
not to care at all. The phrase is 19th cent. in this form: Goldsmith in the *Citizen of the World* (1760) wrote 'Not that I care three damns what figure I may cut'.

Hardy *Jude the Obscure* 1895
I don't care a damn ... for any provost, warden, principal, fellow, or cursed master of arts in the university!

damnedest

do/try one's damnedest
informal to try one's best to do something: often used as a challenge equivalent to *do your worst*. *19th cent.*

Daniel Thompson *The Green Mountain Boys* 1839
The truth is, Alma, we are poor – poor as Job, when the devil had done his damnedest!

Joseph Conrad *Lord Jim* 1900
Half seriously ... he went on shouting, 'Nothing can touch me! You can do your damnedest.' Somehow the shadowy Cornelius far off there seemed to be the hateful embodiment of all the annoyances and difficulties he had found in his path.

Damocles

See SWORD of Damocles.

Damon

Damon and Pythias

a pair of devoted friends: Damon was a Pythagorean philosopher from Syracuse during the rule of Dionysius I (4th cent. BC). His friend Phintias (which seems to be the proper form of the name) was condemned to death but was allowed to leave Syracuse to settle his affairs, leaving Damon to take his place and risk his own life if Phintias failed to return. He did return, and Dionysius was so moved by this display of loyalty that he let both men go free. Spenser mentions the pair along with other legendary heroes in *The Faerie Queene* (1596): IV.x.27: 'Such were great Hercules and Hyllus deare; ... | Damon and Pythias whom death could not sever; | All these and all that ever had bene tyde, | In bands of friendship there did live for ever.' Allusive uses (as distinct from direct references to the original pair) date from the 18th cent. and proliferate in 19th cent. literature. *18th cent.*

George Colman *Epicoene* 1777
Why, now you are friends. All bitterness between you, I hope, is buried; you shall come forth by and by, Damon and Pythias upon't, and embrace with all the rankness of friendship that can be.

Louisa M Alcott *Little Men* 1871
Nat was devoted to Dan; and all the boys tried to atone to both for former suspicion and neglect ... and Mr. Bhaer was never tired of telling the story of his young Damon and Pythias.

damp

a damp squib

British informal something that turns out to be disappointingly feeble, especially as an anticli-

max. A squib is a firework, which will fail to work properly if damp. *19th cent.*

damper

put a/the damper on something

to have a dulling or deadening influence on something. The earliest (18th cent.) meaning of *damper* is in abstract contexts, typically 'something that damps the spirit'; the technical physical meanings (e.g. a plate controlling the draught in a chimney, a device for holding the strings in a piano) are recorded from the late 18th cent. The phrase is recorded from the 19th cent.

Trollope *Can You Forgive Her?* 1864
Mrs. Greenow shook her head to show that she hardly knew how to answer such a question. Probably it would be so always – but she did not wish to put a damper on the present occasion by making so sad a declaration.

D H Lawrence *Sons and Lovers* 1913
The next day was a work-day, and the thought of it put a damper on the men's spirits.

damsel

a damsel in distress

a young woman in difficulty or danger: with allusion to literary uses in romances about ladies waiting to be rescued, usually by a knight in shining armour (*see* KNIGHT). Damsel in the sense 'a young unmarried woman' has been confined to literary use since the 17th cent. The phrase is found from the 18th cent.

Joseph Addison *Rosamund* 1707
What savage Tiger would not pity | A Damsel so distress'd and pretty!

Goldsmith *The Vicar of Wakefield* 1766
They then travelled on to another adventure. This was against three bloody-minded Satyrs, who were carrying away a damsel in distress.

dance

dance attendance on somebody

to try hard to please somebody by attending to all their needs: the meaning is that underlying the expression *in attendance*. A 19th cent. collection of phrases refers quaintly to 'the ancient custom at weddings, when the bride was expected to dance with every male guest in turn and behave with amiability to all, whatever her personal feeling in the matter' (A Wallace, *Popular Sayings Dissected*, 1894). *16th cent.*

Shakespeare 2 Henry VI I.iii.174 (1591)

[Duke of York] My lord of Somerset will keep me here | Without discharge, money, or furniture, | Till France be won into the Dauphin's hands. | Last time I danced attendance on his will | Till Paris was besieged, famished, and lost.

P Falconer War in High Heels 1993

She found the crew very friendly, and the skipper went out of his way to dance attendance on her. She was invited into the cockpit, and shown the controls, which meant nothing to her. It was as they approached Portugal that the skipper began to hint at what he wanted of her.

dance on somebody's grave

to rejoice in somebody's death. *19th cent.*

Herman Melville Moby Dick 1851

I wonder whether those jolly lads bethink them of what they are dancing over. I'll dance over your grave, I will – that's the bitterest threat of your night-women.

dance to somebody's tune

to do what somebody wants. The phrase is 18th cent. in this form: an older form *dance after somebody's pipe* is attested from the 16th cent. to the 19th cent.

Thomas Holcroft Anna St Ives 1792

And then again what did I say to ee about missee? What did I say? Didn't I as good as tellee witch way she cast a sheepz i? That indeed would a be summut! An you will jig your heels amunk the jerry cum poopz, you might a then dance to some tune.

Rufus Dawes Nix's Mate 1839

I shouldn't like to have such a swim in the tar-kettle as you had the other day – nor toss about either to the tune you danced to in the feather-bed.

lead somebody a (merry) dance

to cause somebody a lot of trouble or worry: *cf* Shakespeare *All's Well That Ends Well* (1603) II.iii.49 '[Lafeu, watching the King of France dance with Helen] Why, he's able to lead her a coranto.' The image is of a leader in a dance guiding others through complicated steps. The phrase in its current form dates from the 19th cent.

Herman Melville Pierre, or the Ambiguities 1852

Now, since we began by talking of a certain young lady that went out riding with a certain youth; and yet find ourselves, after leading such a merry dance, fast by a stage-house window; – this may seem rather irregular sort of writing.

dander

get one's dander up

to lose one's temper. The origin of the word *dander* is obscure, with many theories. It is most probably an American word brought into English dialect use, one of a number of words similar in form meaning either 'dandruff' or (more plausibly) 'the ferment used in making molasses'. The form of the phrase has become fairly fixed, although there has been variation in the past, e.g. by Thackeray in *Pendennis* (1849): 'When my dander is up it's the very thing to urge me on.' Other, less convincing, suggestions are that *dander* is a corruption of *damned anger* (an unlikely combination that does not explain the improbable transition to *nd*) and (more plausibly) of *tander*, a supposed variant of *tinder*: *get one's tinder up* means 'to become inflamed with anger' – which is at least close to the relevant meaning, although the variant is rather wishful thinking than a matter of record. *19th cent.*

William Caruthers The Kentuckian in New York 1834

I was coming down this very street the theatre stands on, at a place they call 'the square,' and I heard two fellers talking as if their dander was up a little; so I walked up and leaned against a lamp-post close by, to listen and see if any fun was going to come of it; presently one of 'em called the other a liar.

dangle

keep somebody dangling

to keep somebody in a state of uncertainty about something: related to the (19th cent.) meaning 'to offer (a hope) enticingly' although in this case it is the person and not the hope that is left to dangle. *19th cent.*

Henry James Washington Square 1881

I have been four times since she came back, and it's terribly awkward work. I can't keep it up indefinitely; she oughtn't to expect that, you know. A woman should never keep a man dangling.

Darby

Darby and Joan

an elderly devoted couple. The expression first appears in a ballad written by Henry Woodfall and published in the *Gentleman's Magazine* in 1735, which includes the following lines: 'Old Darby, with Joan by his side, | You've often regarded with wonder: | He's dropsical, she is sore-eyed, | Yet they're never happy asunder.' There has been much speculation about the identity of the eponymous couple: the prime candidates are John Darby of Bartholomew Close, with whom Woodfall served his apprenticeship, and his wife Joan, described as 'chaste as a picture cut in alabaster', but nothing more is known of them. Henry Fowler (1858–1933), author of *Modern English Usage* and the first edition of the *Concise Oxford Dictionary*, referred to himself and his wife as Darby and Joan in touching occasional verses addressed to her at Christmas and on her birthday; the collection was published in 1931 – when Fowler had become famous – under the title *Rhymes of Darby to Joan*. *18th cent.*

> George Colman *Polly Honeycombe* 1760
> *They squeeze their hard hands to each other, and their old eyes twinkle, and they're as loving as Darby and Joan – especially if Mama has had a cordial or two.*

dark

Dark occurs in several meanings dating from the 17th cent. as a metaphor for secrecy and lack of knowledge: *keep somebody dark* meant to confine them in a room (as in Shakespeare, *All's Well That Ends Well* (1603) IV.i.96 'Till then I'll keep him dark and safely locked'); *keep somebody in the dark* meant to be secretive, and people deprived of information were and still are said to be *in the dark*. Even earlier, from Middle English, is a range of meanings to do with obscurity and difficulty of understanding (*dark speech, dark matters*, etc).

a dark horse

somebody or something that is little known but likely to succeed. The expression was originally used in racing slang to refer to a horse whose form was not known, and later transferred to political candidates, especially in the US. *19th cent.*

> Wilkie Collins *Armadale* 1866
> *The man in this case was rather a 'dark horse', as they say on the turf. He was a certain Captain Manuel, a native of Cuba, and (according to his own account) an ex-officer in the Spanish navy.*

keep something dark

to be discreet or secretive about something. *17th cent.*

> George Moore *Esther Waters* 1894
> *'He does his betting in London now, I suppose?' 'Yes,' said Esther, hesitating – 'when he has any to do. I want him to give it up; but trade is bad in this neighbourhood, leastways with us, and he don't think we could do without it.' 'It's very hard to keep it dark; some one's sure to crab it and bring the police down on you.'*

keep somebody in the dark

to withhold the facts from somebody, to deprive them of information. *18th cent.*

> Mary Wollstonecraft *A Vindication of the Rights of Woman* 1792
> *Tyrants and sensualists are in the right when they endeavour to keep women in the dark, because the former only want slaves, and the latter a play-thing.*

a shot/stab in the dark

a wild guess or attempt: literally an attempt to murder somebody under the cover of darkness, usually in detective stories and sometimes successfully. Also in verb form, *to stab in the dark*. *18th cent.*

> Mercy Otis Warren *The Adulateur* 1773
> *A spirit haughty, sour, implacable, | That bears a deadly enmity to freedom, | But mean and base; who never had a notion | Of generous and manly; who would stab, | Stab in the dark, but what he'd get revenge; | If such a soul is suitable to thy purpose, | 'Tis here.*

> R D Blackmore *Lorna Doone* 1869
> *Now it was my great desire, and my chiefest hope, to come across Carver Doone that night, and settle the score between us; not by any shot in the dark, but by a conflict man to man.*

See also WHISTLE in the dark.

darken

darken somebody's door(s)

to arrive at a person's door as a visitor. The phrase is typically used in negative contexts, and as a warning or prohibition. There are strong implications of unwelcome or menace, the image being of a shadow cast across the door when a visitor stands before it. *18th cent.*

Richardson *Clarissa* 1748
I hope, Sir, said he, to his Father; I hope, Madam, to his Mother; that you will not endeavour to recover a faulty Daughter, by losing an unculpable Son. If ever my sister Clary darkens these doors again, I never will.

dash¹ (verb)

dash it (all)
a mild oath or imprecation: used as a euphemism for *damn. 19th cent.*

Trollope *Phineas Finn* 1869
Phineas was too quick for him, and having seized on to his collar, held to him with all his power. 'Dash it all,' said the man, 'didn't yer see as how I was a-hurrying up to help the gen'leman myself?'

dash² (noun)

See CUT a dash.

date

date rape
rape committed while the victim is on a date with the offender. This is a legally complex issue because the social circumstances confuse the question of consent. *Late 20th cent.*

See also a BLIND date; PASS one's sell-by date.

daunt

nothing daunted
in no way intimidated or disconcerted: normally used qualifying a verb of action. *Nothing* is here used adverbially, a survival from Old English (compare *nothing like, nothing loath*). *Daunt* is a Middle English verb originally meaning 'to overcome', then 'to discourage or dispirit', and is primarily used in the passive or as a participial adjective *daunted. 19th cent.*

Dickens *Oliver Twist* 1838
They dragged Oliver, struggling and shouting, but nothing daunted, into the dust-cellar, and there locked him up.

Davy Jones

go to Davy Jones / Davy Jones's locker
to be drowned at sea. *Davy Jones's locker* is the bottom of the sea, regarded as the resting place of those who have drowned. Davy Jones, the spirit of the sea and sailors' devil, is first mentioned by Tobias Smollett in *The Adventures of Peregrine Pickle* (1751): 'This same Davy Jones, according to the mythology of sailors, is the fiend that presides over all the evil spirits of the deep.' *Davy Jones's locker*, the domain of Davy Jones at the bottom of the sea, is first found in a naval journal of 1803: 'The … seamen would have met a watery grave; or, to use a seaman's phrase, gone to Davy Jones's locker.' The expression *go to Davy Jones* first appears in Herman Melville's *Moby Dick* (see below). The phrase is of obscure origin: among suggestions are that Davy Jones was a pirate or the name of a spirit of the sea, that the two names are corruptions of a West Indian word *duppy* meaning 'devil', and that there is a connection with the biblical name *Jonah*. Jonah, according to the account in the book of the Bible named after him (Jonah 1:17–2:10), was swallowed up by a fish sent by God, spent three days and three nights there, and prayed to God from the belly of the fish. Eventually God ordered the fish to release Jonah, and 'it vomited out Jonah upon the dry land'. So Jonah was saved, which hardly fits with the notion of a place of death from which there was no return. Another occasional variant is *go to Old Davy. 18th cent.*

Herman Melville *Moby Dick* 1851
He got so frightened about his plaguey soul, that he shrinked and sheered away from whales, for fear of after-claps, in case he got stove and went to Davy Jones.

dawn

the crack of dawn
early in the morning. *Crack* is used to mean 'the time taken by the sound of a crack', i.e. a brief moment or instant. *19th cent.*

Daniel Thompson *Gaut Gurley* 1857
With the first crack of dawn the next morning, the loud and startling gallinaceous cachinnation of the droll and wide-awake trapper aroused the woodsmen from their slumbers, and warned them to be up and doing.

Ann Pilling *Henry's Leg* 1987

It had been put out ready for the men from the Refuse Department. They'd be round at the crack of dawn tomorrow, waking everyone up with that big rusty grinder that chewed it all to bits.

See also a FALSE dawn.

---

day

all in a/the day's work

part of what one normally does: often used in resigned acceptance of a difficult or burdensome task. *19th cent.*

Rhoda Broughton *Belinda* 1883

'If I were you,' cries Sarah irreverently, calling after her, 'he should be in still smaller 'fragments' before I had done with him!' Belinda laughs. 'Bah!' she says; 'it is all in the day's work. Perhaps it is better to have too much to do, like me, than too little, like you.'

at the end of the day

informal when one considers everything: often used as a cliché with little substantial meaning. *Late 20th cent.*

Malcolm Young *An Inside Job* 1991

Policing is all about dealing with folk. At the end of the day we must concern ourselves with the practicalities and not philosophies of dealing with everyday problems.

call it a day

to stop work or activity for a time; also, more generally, to cease an activity indefinitely. From the notion of having completed a day's work: the phrase occurs first in the form *call it half a day*. *19th cent.*

Mark Twain *A Connecticut Yankee at the Court of King Arthur* 1889

It would have been best, all round, for Merlin to waive etiquette and quit and call it half a day.

carry/win the day

to be victorious: the (16th cent.) meaning here is 'the day's fighting in battle'. *16th cent.*

Shakespeare *3 Henry VI* II.i.135 (1591)

But all in vain. They had no heart to fight, | And we in them no hope to win the day.

Conan Doyle *A Study in Scarlet* 1887

Amusement and chagrin seemed to be struggling for the mastery, until the former suddenly carried the day, and he burst into a hearty laugh.

day in, day out

continuously or routinely over a long period. *19th cent.*

R L Stevenson *The Master of Ballantrae* 1889

Day in, day out, he would work upon her, sitting by the chimney-side with his finger in his Latin book, and his eyes set upon her face with a kind of pleasant intentness that became the old gentleman very well.

Susan Hill *Gentleman and Ladies* 1968

I would not like to be kept alive by a machine, like a vegetable, day in day out … I would prefer to accept my appointed day.

day of reckoning

a time when misdeeds are punished and the consequences of mistakes have to be addressed: *cf* Byron *Childe Harold's Pilgrimage* (1812) 1.52 'Ah! Spain! how sad will be thy reckoning-day.' In legal use a *day of reckoning* is one on which a debt has to be repaid or an account given of property entrusted to one; it is also used as a euphemism for the Day of Judgement. *18th cent.*

Mary Wollstonecraft *A Vindication of the Rights of Woman* 1792

Gay hopes, or lively emotions, banish reflection till the day of reckoning comes; and come it surely will, to turn the sprightly lover into a surly suspicious tyrant, who contemptuously insults the very weakness he fostered.

Dickens *Nicholas Nickleby* 1838

There will be a day of reckoning sooner or later.

don't give up the day job

a recommendation to stick to what one knows best and not be tempted by attractive but risky alternatives: often jokingly addressed to somebody whose amateur performance in some new activity fails to impress. *Late 20th cent.*

from day one

informal from the very start, *day one* being the first day of an operation or undertaking. *Late 20th cent.*

have had one's/its day

to be no longer useful or fashionable. *19th cent.*

Nathaniel Hawthorne *Earth's Holocaust* 1844
These things of matter, and creations of human
fantasy, are fit for nothing but to be burnt, when
once they have had their day.

have a nice day

a form of farewell originating in North America
in the 1950s and used increasingly in Britain: the
phrase is usually just a token gesture without any
real sincerity on the part of the speaker. *Mid 20th
cent.*

> Robert Fisk *Pity the Nation: Lebanon at War* 1991
> *'That'll be two dollars,' she said. 'Have a nice day.'*
> *She sounded like a clerk at a Manhattan bookstore.*
> *Could this really once have been Palestine?*

have seen/known better days

to experience a decline in one's fortunes. *16th
cent.*

> Shakespeare *As You Like It* II.vii.113 (1599)
> *Under the shade of melancholy boughs, | Lose and*
> *neglect the creeping hours of time, | If ever you*
> *have looked on better days.*

> Shakespeare *Timon of Athens* IV.ii.27 (1609)
> *[Flavius] Wherever we shall meet, for Timon's sake*
> *| Let's yet be fellows. Let's shake our heads and say*
> *| As 'twere a knell unto our master's fortunes, |*
> *'We have seen better days.'*

> Charles Lamb *Rosamund Grey* 1798
> *The old lady loved Rosamund too … Rosamund*
> *was to her at once a child and a servant … They two*
> *lived together. They had once known better days.*
> *The story of Rosamund's parents, their failure, their*
> *folly, and distresses, may be told another time.*

in this day and age

in the present time, nowadays. The phrase is a
hackneyed tautology or, to put it more kindly,
hendiadys (compare *gloom and doom; honestly and
sincerely*, etc) based on the use of *day* meaning
'time or period', which goes back to Middle English. The phrase seems to have been launched by
its use as the title of a 1933 film. *Mid 20th cent.*

> *Guardian* 1984
> *It is totally unacceptable in this day and age to treat*
> *viewers as zombies … The BBC have a duty to*
> *report back to the people who pay their licence fee.*

> Zadie Smith *White Teeth* 2000
> *He's on about tradition again. He's worried about*
> *his sons, you see. Easy for children to go off the rails*
> *in this day and age, you know.*

(just) one of those days

a day of setbacks or misfortunes. The use is
always unfavourable in tone and is an elliptical
form of uses with a continuation, e.g. 'it was one
of those days which do sometimes occur in
March' (Mary Shelley, *Falkner*, 1837), 'one bright
June Sunday – just one of those days that seem
made to put all one's philosophy into confusion'
(Harriet Beecher Stowe, *My Wife and I*, 1871), and
so on. *Mid 20th cent.*

make somebody's day

to provide somebody with an enjoyable or pleasing experience in an otherwise dull or routine
day: often used ironically or sarcastically. Also in
more recent use as an ironic invitation *make my
day* meaning 'excite me; say or do something
interesting'. The phrase achieved notoriety as a
line in the Hollywood film *Sudden Impact* (1983)
in which the hero, played by Clint Eastwood,
pins down a gunman and challenges him with
the words 'Come on, make my day'. Two years
later, probably in conscious allusion to this use,
the American President Ronald Reagan issued a
similar challenge to those urging him to increase
taxes: 'I have my veto pen drawn and ready for
any tax increases that Congress might even think
of sending up. And I have only one thing to say to
the tax increasers. Go ahead – make my day.'
Early 20th cent.

> *Gardener's World* 1991
> *I wish you could have seen those first two lepi-*
> *dopteral visitors. They made my day.*

make a day of it

to spend a whole day celebrating or enjoying
oneself: *see also* make a NIGHT of it. *17th cent.*

> Boswell *The Life of Samuel Johnson* 1791
> *I again begged his advice as to my method of study*
> *at Utrecht. 'Come (said he) let us make a day of it.*
> *Let us go down to Greenwich and dine, and talk of it*
> *there.'*

not —'s day

a day on which a particular person suffers a
series of setbacks or misfortunes. *Late 20th cent.*

> Mike Harding *Walking the Dales* 1989
> *He realised there was no future in it and came round*
> *for a sandwich. They were cheese and onion. Bill*
> *hates cheese and onion sandwiches. It wasn't his*
> *day.*

that will be the day
informal an expression of scepticism about a claim or statement: first recorded in New Zealand slang use. *Mid 20th cent.*

> Catherine Cookson *The Wingless Bird* 1990
> *That'll be the day when you mind your own business.*

See also —'s days are numbered *at* NUMBER; in the COLD light of day; live to fight another day *at* LIVE[1]; a red-letter day *at* RED; one's SALAD days; SAVE the day; (too) LATE in the day.

daylight

beat/shake/scare/frighten the (living) daylights out of somebody
to beat or shake or frighten somebody intensely. *Daylights* here is an 18th cent. slang term for 'eyes', always used in the context of physical violence or threats. Henry Fielding in *Amelia* (1732) makes a character say 'If the lady says such another word to me ... I will darken her daylights'. *19th cent.*

> Charles Hale Hoyt *A Midnight Bell* 1889
> *Dad said if he caught me readin' one of 'em again he'd lick the daylights out of me.*

> Emma Blair *Maggie Jordan* 1990
> *And now there's this Herr Hitler. Folk laugh at him and his funny wee moustache, Mrs Sanderson said, but I don't find him funny at all. Quite the contrary, he scares the living daylights out of me.*

burn daylight
to use artificial light despite there being enough natural light. *16th cent.*

> Shakespeare *Romeo and Juliet* i.iv.43 (1596)
> [Mercutio] *Come, we burn daylight, ho!* [Romeo] *Nay, that's not so.* [Mercutio] *I mean, sir, in delay | We waste our lights in vain, like lamps by day.*

> Charles Lamb *Last Essays of Elia* 1833
> *It beginning to grow a little duskish, Candlemas lustily bawled out for lights, which was opposed by all the Days, who protested against burning daylight.*

daylight robbery
informal extortionate or unashamed overcharging, compared to a robbery committed openly in daylight. The phrase is associated with the (19th cent.) use of *robbery* (unqualified or with

an intensifying word such as *sheer*) in the same meaning. *Early 20th cent.*

> William Boyle *The Mineral Workers* 1910
> [O'Reilly] *Mr. Fogarty, you'll come into the mining with Sir Thomas and the rest? You don't know what you're missing.* [Fogarty] *I'm missing daylight robbery and plunder.* [O'Reilly] *You'd rather sell at honest prices, then?*

see daylight
to begin to understand something that has been obscure. *19th cent.*

> R L Stevenson *The Strange Case of Dr Jekyll and Mr Hyde* 1886
> *These are all very strange circumstances ... but I think I begin to see daylight.*

dead

(as) dead as the/a dodo
no longer living; quite dead. The *dodo* was a large flightless bird of Mauritius that became extinct with the arrival of European settlers. The name is derived from a Portuguese word *duodo* meaning 'fool', and the bird's clumsy movements made it proverbial for stupidity from the 19th cent. *Early 20th cent.*

(as) dead as a doornail
a further simile in the sense 'quite dead'. The reference to *doornail* has given rise to many interesting and colourful explanations, some more plausible than others but all speculative. A doornail was a large nail of the kind used in the Middle Ages and later to form studs in doors. It was symbolic of lifelessness; when hammered into a door it might be 'clinched' or bent over, leaving it 'dead' to further use. It has been used alliteratively with several adjectives beginning with *d* and all denoting different types of human incapacity, including *deaf*, *dour*, and *dumb*, as well as *dead*. Among the more macabre elaborations of the association with death is one that recalls an ancient practice of nailing the skins of malefactors to the doors of churches and barns (*Notes & Queries* November 1936, p.370). *Middle English*

> Shakespeare *2 Henry VI* iv.ix.40 (1591)
> [Cade] *Look on me well – I have eat no meat these five days, yet come thou and thy five men, an if I do not leave you all as dead as a doornail I pray God I may never eat grass more.*

(as) dead as mutton

one of a number of food-based similes in the sense 'quite dead'. The relevance of *mutton*, the meat of sheep, is self-evident. Another (17th cent.) variant *dead as a herring* is now obsolete. *18th cent.*

Isaac Bickerstaffe *The Spoil'd Child* 1792
[Miss Pickle] *O I cou'd listen thus for ever to the charms of love and harmony – but how are we to plan our escape?* [Tagg] *In a low and mean attire muffled up in a great cloak will I await you in this happy spot – but why, my soul, why not this instant fly – thus let me seize my tender bit of lamb – there I think I had her as dead as mutton.*

Somerset Maugham *Of Human Bondage* 1915
I tell you young people that before the nineteenth century is out Wagner will be as dead as mutton. Wagner! I would give all his works for one opera by Donizetti.

be dead meat

informal to be doomed or facing serious trouble: from the literal meaning, 'the meat of a slaughtered animal'. The phrase commonly features as a dire warning in gangster films and thrillers. *19th cent.*

H L Williams *Joaquin* 1865
Drop your belts on the ground, or you're dead meat!

dead and buried

finished or done with: used emphatically to indicate the irrevocable nature of the thing referred to. *17th cent.*

Shakespeare *As You Like It* I.ii.109 (1599)
[Le Beau] *I will tell you the beginning, and if it please your ladyships you may see the end …* [Celia] *Well, the beginning that is dead and buried.*

M Dobbs *House of Cards* 1989
I'm fifty-five and Michael Samuel is forty-eight, which means that he could be in Downing Street for twenty years until I'm dead and buried as a politician.

a dead cat bounce

informal an apparent sign of life in something that is dead or defunct. This bizarre phrase (in which *bounce* is a noun) seems to be based on the notion that even a dead cat will bounce if dropped from a sufficient height (!), and was first used by traders on Wall Street to refer to brief temporary improvements in downward trends. The earliest evidence traced so far is from the 1980s. *Late 20th cent.*

dead from the neck/chin up

informal completely stupid. *Mid 20th cent.*

P G Wodehouse *Stiff Upper Lip* 1963
The sort of dead-from-the-neck-up dumb brick who wouldn't have thought of it.

dead in the water

not able to move or function; completely finished or extinct. The phrase was originally used of ships that were unable to move under their own power. *Late 20th cent.*

Punch 1992
The lady's not for returning. Thatcherism is dead in the water.

the dead of night

the part of the night when it is most dark and quiet: *dead* here means the 'dead period' when there is least activity. *16th cent.*

Shakespeare *Twelfth Night* I.v.260 (1602)
[Viola] *Make me a willow cabin at your gate | And call upon my soul within the house, | Write loyal cantons of contemnèd love, | And sing them loud even in the dead of night.*

the dead of winter

the coldest part of winter. For the meaning of *dead* see the preceding phrase. *16th cent.*

Marlowe *Dr Faustus* xii.11 (1590)
[Duchess] *Were it now summer, as it is January and the dead time of winter, I would desire no better meat than a dish of ripe grapes.*

dead on one's feet

informal exhausted, so one can barely stand up: from (19th cent.) hyperbolic uses of *dead* in similar meanings. *Mid 20th cent.*

John Braine *Life at the Top* 1962
'It doesn't matter who started it now,' I yawned. 'Honestly, I'm dead on my feet, Susan.'

dead to the world

informal oblivious or unaware of one's surroundings. Also, fast asleep. *18th cent.*

Fanny Burney *Evelina* 1778
Dead to the world, and equally insensible to its pleasures or its pains, I long since bid adieu to all joy, and defiance to all sorrow, but what should spring from my Evelina, – sole source, to me, of all earthly felicity.

would not be found/seen/caught dead (doing something)

would not want to be associated with or have anything to do with (the particular action or condition): an expression of rejection. *Early 20th cent.*

See also be a dead RINGER; a dead LETTER; make a dead SET at; over my dead BODY; wait for dead men's shoes *at* SHOE.

deaf

(as) deaf as an adder / a post

totally or very deaf. For the adder as a symbol of deafness see Psalms 58:4 'The deaf adder that stoppeth her ear'. In Britain *deaf-adder* has been a name for the slowworm since the 19th cent. Other, now obsolete, similes include *deaf as a door* and *deaf as a doornail* (*see* DEAD). The form with *adder* is 16th cent., and with *post* 18th cent.

> Sheridan *School for Scandal* 1777
> [Crab] *Miss Letitia Piper, a first cousin of mine, had a Nova Scotia sheep that produced her twins. 'What!' cries the Lady Dowager Dundizzy (who you know is as deaf as a post), 'has Miss Piper had twins?'*

> Ted Hughes *Selected Poems* 1982
> *The deaf adder of appetite.*

fall on deaf ears

to be ignored or unheeded. The notion of ears being deaf in the sense of 'unheeding' is much older than the phrase: see for example Shakespeare, *Titus Andronicus* (1594) II.iii.160 '[Lavinia] Be not obdurate, Open thy deaf ears.' *19th cent.*

> Trollope *Barchester Towers* 1857
> *Shortly after Mr. Harding's resignation, the Jupiter had very clearly shown what ought to be done ... Cassandra was not believed, and even the wisdom of the Jupiter sometimes falls on deaf ears.*

turn a deaf ear

to refuse to listen to what somebody is saying, to ignore them. *17th cent.*

> Benjamin Keach *War with the Devil* 1673
> *What thoughts hast thou of Christ then, sinful Soul, | That thou his Messengers dost thus controul, | And dost to him also turn a deaf ear, | His knocks, his calls, and wooings wilt not hear; | Nor him regard, though he stands at thy door.*

> Garda Langley *Understanding Horses* 1989
> *Horses sometimes suffer depression on going to a new home. They may display their feelings by refusing to eat, and turning a deaf ear to anyone who calls their name.*

See also DIALOGUE of/among/between the deaf.

deal

a big deal

informal something important: often used in negative contexts and (especially as an exclamation) with irony. *Early 20th cent.*

> Amrit Wilson *Finding a Voice: Asian Women in Britain* 1988
> *Parents ... seem to think it is a big deal, a real status symbol to get a Biliti Bor (a bridegroom from England).*

a raw/rough deal

informal, originally NAmer harsh or unfair treatment. *Early 20th cent.*

> Economist 1991
> *A new generation of canny investors who have inherited family fortunes will quickly switch banks if they think they are getting a raw deal.*

a square deal

fair treatment. *Square* here has the meaning 'honest' as used especially in card playing (where *square play* dates from the 16th cent. and *square dealing* from the 17th cent.). *19th cent.*

> Jack London *Theft* 1910
> *The dream of social justice, of fair play and a square deal to everybody. The dreamer – Mr. Knox.*

> Harper Lee *To Kill a Mockingbird* 1960
> *The one place where a man ought to get a square deal is in a courtroom, be he any color of the rainbow.*

death

at death's door

seriously ill and likely to die. Phrases of this kind go back to Middle English; the phrase in its current form goes back to the 16th cent.

> Anon *The Gossips Braule* 1655
> *I am so troubl'd with the winde at my stomack, | That if it were not for the comfort of a little sniffe, | I should be at death's door.*

be the death of somebody

to cause somebody's death: often used in trivial contexts. *16th cent.*

Shakespeare *All's Well That Ends Well* IV.v.8 (1603)
[Countess] *I would a had not known him. It was the death of the most virtuous gentlewoman that ever nature had praise for creating.*

James Kirkup *A Poet Could Not But Be Gay* 1991
My father would not even allow a radio in the house, and when I suggested getting a TV set for him and my mother he adamantly refused, saying that the wireless had been the death of good conversation, and that TV would be the death of the family.

be frightened to death

to be terrified: often used in weakened senses. *18th cent.*

Fanny Burney *Cecilia* 1782
I vow I have sometimes such difficulty to keep awake, that I am frightened to death lest I should be taken with a sudden nap, and affront them all.

Somerset Maugham *The Moon and Sixpence* 1919
I do not know what her hold was on the Captain, but I do not think it was love … At any rate, Captain Nichols was frightened to death of her.

be in at the death

to be a witness of somebody's death or of the demise of something: a metaphor from fox-hunting, when the fox is killed by the hounds. *18th cent.*

catch one's death (of cold)

to catch a severe cold: use of *catch* with reference to diseases and other unpleasant things dates from Middle English. *18th cent.*

Charlotte Smith *Emmeline* 1788
Quite of cold nights this Autumn, when the wind blew, and the sea made a noise so loud and dismal, she has staid there whole hours by herself; only I ventured to disobey her so far as to see that no harm came to her. But three or four times, Ma'am, she remained so long that I concluded she must catch her death.

Dickens *Pickwick Papers* 1837
She would be deserted and reduced to ruin, and I should catch my death of cold in some broker's shop.

die a/the death

to fail or come to an end: from the (16th cent.) literal meaning 'to suffer death'. *19th cent.*

Charles Kingsley *Two Years Ago* 1857
Leave us to draw a cordon sanitaire round the tainted states, and leave the system to die a natural death.

do something to death

to overdo something or perform it excessively. *19th cent.*

like death warmed up / NAmer over

informal, originally services' slang looking pale and ill. *Mid 20th cent.*

Betty Rowlands *Finishing Touch* 1991
I still reckon it was him who killed that girl, alibi or no alibi. And I reckon his wife thinks so too. She's been going around lately looking like death warmed up.

See also DICE with death; a FATE worse than death; FLOG something to death; like GRIM death; a matter of LIFE and death.

debt

pay the debt of/to nature

euphemistic to die: the notion occurs in other forms at an earlier date. *16th cent.*

Thomas Heywood *Troia Britanica* 1606
At Tilbery, the Campe was brauely led | By Elizabeth in person, in whose traine | all Englands Chiualry mustred and met, | Leister meane time to Nature paid his debt.

decent

be decent

informal to be properly dressed and ready to receive a visitor: usually as a coy or jocular enquiry *are you decent?* Ruth Harvey's *Curtain Times* (1949) explained the theatrical origin of the phrase: 'Sometimes, if she knew one of the actors or actresses, she would knock at a door and call "Are you decent?" (That old theatrical phrase startled people who didn't belong to the theatre, but it simply meant "Are you dressed?")' *Mid 20th cent.*

do the decent thing

to act honourably, especially by accepting responsibility for failure or difficulty and resigning from office. *Early 20th cent.*

deck

The primary meaning, a surface area on a ship, developed (from the second half of the 19th cent.) extended meanings denoting other kinds of flat surfaces more generally. The meaning connected with playing cards dates from the late 16th cent.

hit the deck

1 *informal* to fall or throw oneself to the ground, especially to avoid a danger. *Mid 20th cent.*

> Daily Mirror 1992
> *They were firing machine guns into the air. It was like a war zone. We hit the deck and froze – we thought we were going to die.*

2 *informal, services' slang* to land an aircraft. *Mid 20th cent.*

3 *informal* to go to bed. *Mid 20th cent.*

not playing with a full deck

NAmer, informal mentally deficient. *Full deck* here means a complete set of playing cards. *Late 20th cent.*

> Martin Amis Time's Arrow 1991
> *In fact I've had to conclude that I am generally rather slow on the uptake. Possibly even subnormal, or mildly autistic. It may very well be that I'm not playing with a full deck. The cards won't add up for me; the world won't start making sense.*

on deck

NAmer, informal on the scene; ready for action. *19th cent.*

> Gene Stratton Porter The Girl of the Limberlost 1909
> *Lunches and sororities were all I heard her mention, until Tom Levering came on deck; now he is the leading subject.*

See also CLEAR the decks.

deep

dig deep

to use all or much of one's resources to achieve something. *19th cent.*

go (in) off the deep end

informal to give way to anger or other emotion. The metaphor is from diving at a swimming pool, although the image is a lot less clear than that for the next but one phrase under this headword. *Early 20th cent.*

in deep water

in serious trouble. Psalms 69:14 uses the image of deep water to represent difficulty: 'Let me be delivered from them that hate me, and out of the deep waters.' Despite this early (16th cent.) reference point in English, allusive uses are relatively late in date, primarily 19th cent.

> George Eliot Felix Holt 1866
> *'You are then the mother of the unfortunate young man who is in prison?' 'Indeed, I am, sir,' said Mrs Holt, feeling that she was now in deep water.*

jump / dive / be thrown in at the deep end

to face a difficult challenge having had little experience of it: with reference to the deep end of a swimming pool. *Early 20th cent.*

degree

See get the THIRD degree.

dekko

take a dekko

to look at or take note of something. *Dekko* is derived from Hindi *dekho*, the imperative form of *dekhna* meaning 'to look'. *19th cent.*

> Francis Brett Young Portrait of Clare 1927
> *He's promised to look in this evening, just to have a 'dekko' as he calls it, and see that you're all right.*

deliver

deliver the goods

informal to provide what one has promised or what is expected; also, more generally, to meet expectations or requirements. The phrase is also shortened to the absolute form *deliver on* (something promised). *18th cent.*

> John Burgoyne The Lord of the Manor 1781
> [Sir John] *Hussy! how came you by all that money?* [Peggy] *Perfectly honestly – I sold my mistress and myself for it – it is not necessary to deliver the goods, for his honour is provided with a mistress.*

delusion

delusions of grandeur

an excessive opinion of one's own importance. *Early 20th cent.*

The Face 1990
Most MTV Hollywood films are just trailers with delusions of grandeur.

dent

make a dent in something
to have an effect, if only a limited one, on a state of affairs; typically to reduce slightly the scale of a problem or difficulty. *Cf* make a HOLE in something. *Mid 20th cent.*

Anthony Masters *Traffic* 1991
Sakata, with its new car, Glory, had at least made a dent in the numbers of unemployed.

depth

out of / beyond one's depth
not having sufficient ability or comprehension: from the literal meaning of being in water that is too deep to be able to stand in. *17th cent.*

Shakespeare *Henry VIII* iii.ii.362 (1613)
[Wolsey] *I have ventured, | Like little wanton boys that swim on bladders, | This many summers in a sea of glory, | But far beyond my depth; my high-blown pride | At length broke under me.*

derry

have a derry on somebody
Australian and NZ, informal to be prejudiced against somebody: *derry* is probably short for *derry down* (*cf* DOWN on / have a down on somebody). *19th cent.*

S Gore *Holy Smoke* 1968
The Chaldeans ... had a derry on the Christians anyhow, for mucking up all their forecasts, like Daniel did.

design

have a design / designs on something/ somebody
to intend to acquire something, especially surreptitiously or dishonestly; also used of (often unrequited) sexual initiatives towards a person. *Design* in the sense 'underhand scheming' dates from the late 17th cent.: Defoe in *Robinson Crusoe* (1719) refers to 'a faithful servant without passions, sullenness, or designs.' *17th cent.*

Francis Kirkman *The Unlucky Citizen* 1673
I desired him to cause my servant to examine both shop, warehouse, and house, to see if he did not miss any goods, for I began to suspect that our messenger might have had some design upon them, which he might conveniently act whilst he remained in my house.

Jane Austen *Northanger Abbey* 1818
I see that she has had designs on Captain Tilney, which have not succeeded.

deuce

Attested from the mid 17th cent. and probably of German origin. Its first uses were in curses and other exclamations, in which the basic meaning is 'bad luck' or 'mischief' (or 'plague', as in *a deuce on him*). In the 18th cent. the word became personified as an alternative for 'the devil', as in the following phrases and occasionally in others such as *what the deuce* and *deuce-may-care*.

a/the deuce of a —
informal a thing that is especially troublesome or difficult. *19th cent.*

Harriet Beecher Stowe *Uncle Tom's Cabin* 1852
O, yes, to be sure, the question is, – and a deuce of a question it is! How came you in this state of sin and misery?

the deuce to pay
informal imminent trouble. *19th cent.*

W S Gilbert *Iolanthe* 1882
For I'm not so old, and not so plain, | And I'm quite prepared to marry again, | But there'd be the deuce to pay in the Lords | If I fell in love with one of my Wards!

how/what, etc the deuce
used as an intensifying word, equivalent to *how/what*, etc *on earth*? *18th cent.*

David Garrick *Lethe* 1749
[Mrs Tatoo] *Why don't you come along, Mr. Tatoo? What the deuce are you afraid of?*

like the deuce
informal with great speed or intensity. *19th cent.*

F W Thomas *Clinton Bradshaw* 1835
'Bradshaw, you must stir your stumps,' said his friend, as they rode rapidly off: 'the old fellow's running like the deuce.'

device

leave somebody to their own devices

to avoid interfering in somebody's affairs or activity: the sense of *device* 'pleasure or inclination' is current only in the plural, in this phrase and in the phrase *devices and desires* from the Book of Common Prayer. *18th cent.*

> Richardson *The History of Sir Charles Grandison* 1753
> *Lorimer's father, little thinking that his son had connived at the plot formed against his governor, besought him, when he had obtained his liberty, not to leave his son to his own devices.*

> Harper Lee *To Kill a Mockingbird* 1960
> *Calpurnia evidently remembered a rainy Sunday when we were … teacherless. Left to its own devices, the class tied Eunice Ann Simpson to a chair and placed her in the furnace room.*

devil

Devil has been used since Old English, along with the proper name *Satan* and the epithet *Lucifer*, to personify the supreme spirit of evil in opposition to God; it is adapted from the Latin word *diabolus* (Greek *diabolos*) used in more general sense ultimately derived from the Greek verb *diaballein* 'to slander or traduce'. Extended uses relating to other beings and to humans are recorded from an early date, although weakened and playful meanings ('a mischievous or troublesome person') do not appear until the early 17th cent., when Shakespeare, for example, in *Twelfth Night* (II.v.199) makes Sir Toby Belch address his companion Sir Andrew Aguecheek as 'thou most excellent devil of wit'.

better the devil you know (than the devil you don't)

(proverb) it is better to stick with an associate or state of affairs that may not be ideal but is familiar, rather than risk a new situation that might be worse. Related notions, some referring to evil rather than the devil, date from the 16th cent., but the phrase in its current form dates from the 19th cent.

> Trollope *Barchester Towers* 1857
> *'Better the d— you know than the d— you don't know,' is an old saying, and perhaps a true one; but the bishop had not yet realised the truth of it.*

between the devil and the deep blue sea

faced with two equally unwelcome or dangerous courses of action. Early variants include *the devil and the dead sea* and *the devil and the deep sea*. The reference to the sea suggests a nautical origin, and people have pointed to the use of *devil* by sailors as an old name for the seam at the lower end of a ship's hull (the one most difficult to reach, and therefore 'the devil'), making the alignment more plausible. But how can anybody be between a ship's hull and the sea? Even as a choice in allusive senses it does not work very well, and *devil* surely has a more powerful role to play here. The choice implied by the phrase is more likely to be between a bad or wicked fate more generally (the devil) and escape, albeit with the risk of drowning (the sea). Another phrase with a similar meaning, *between Scylla and Charybdis*, is also drawn from the world of seafaring. The phrase is recorded from the 17th cent. The form with *blue* is not found before the 20th cent., which is surprising given that *deep blue sea* occurs otherwise as a fixed expression much earlier.

> Smollett *The Life and Adventures of Sir Launcelot Greaves* 1762
> *The conjurer having no subterfuge left, but a great many particular reasons for avoiding an explanation with the justice, like the man between the devil and the deep sea, of two evils chose the least; and beckoning to the captain, called him by his name.*

the devil is in the detail

(proverb) something apparently harmless or helpful may contain hidden snags when looked at more closely. *Late 20th cent.*

devil-may-care

heedless of authority or convention. *19th cent.*

> Thackeray *A Shabby Genteel Story* 1840
> *He was free of his money; would spend his last guinea for a sensual gratification; would borrow from his neediest friend; had no kind of conscience or remorse left, but believed himself to be a good-natured devil-may-care fellow.*

a/the devil of a —

1 a particularly noteworthy example of its kind. *17th cent.*

> John Dunton *A Voyage Round the World* 1691
> *Whatever thou may'st be for a conjurer, thou art certainly the devil of a poet.*

Jane Austen *Emma* 1816

She has no more heart than a stone to people in general; and the devil of a temper.

2 an inordinate amount or degree of something. *19th cent.*

Dickens *Nicholas Nickleby* 1839

'My life,' said Mr. Mantalini, 'what a demd devil of a time you have been!'

the devil's own —
something particularly troublesome or difficult, or otherwise striking. *19th cent.*

the devil take the hindmost
a proverbial formula asserting one's own claim, priority, etc, often used as an extension of the phrase *every man for himself* (see EVERY). The notion goes back in a slightly different form to the Roman poet Horace (1st cent. AD), who in his *Ars Poetica* ('Art of Poetry') asserted *occupet extremum scabies* 'may the one who is last suffer the itch'. The English phrase first appears in a play (*Philaster, or Love Lies a-Bleeding*) by Shakespeare's contemporaries Beaumont and Fletcher (1620): 'What if ... they run all away, and cry the Devil take the hindmost'. *17th cent.*

the devil to pay
There'll be the devil to pay is a warning of serious trouble to come as a result of something done or happening. The simplest explanation for the phrase lies in the medieval notion of a person making a bargain or pact with Satan, as famously in Goethe's *Faust*. The heavy price (such as Faust's soul) has to be paid in the end. There is an isolated occurrence in a 15th cent. manuscript source quoted in the *Oxford Dictionary of English Proverbs* (third edition, 1970): 'Beit wer be at tome for ay, Than her to serve the devil to pay.' But modern use of the phrase dates from the early 18th cent., when Jonathan Swift used it in *The Journal to Stella* (intimate letters to his friend Esther Johnson, 1711): 'The Earl of Strafford is to go soon to Holland, and let them know what we have been doing; and then there will be the devil and all to pay.' *The devil and all* was an idiom meaning 'a whole lot of work or trouble'. Swift uses it again in the same work: 'This being queen Elisabeth's birthday, we have the devil and all to do among us.' It was also used by Peter Anthony Motteux (1660–1718), translator of Rabelais and Cervantes, and by Oliver Goldsmith (c1730–74).

An early occurrence of the phrase in its current form is in a play by John Breval called *The Play is the Plot*, first performed in London in 1718. It is a comic mythical pastiche and includes a spoof version of the Perseus and Andromeda story, in which Perseus makes an entry with a drawn sword ready to kill the dragon, with the lines: 'In time of publick Danger hence to flee, | Would be a slur to all Knight-Errantry; | I find there is the Devil here to pay, | Would I could see Divine Andromeda.' The devil here is the dragon, and the reference is to slaying the dragon; so it is not quite the modern sense but close enough to be relevant to it. Later in the 18th cent., another dramatist, Charles Coffey, wrote a farce that was actually called *The Devil to Pay*. Needless to say, not everybody has been satisfied with the straightforward origin given above, and attempts have been made, as with so many phrases, to associate this one with the sea. The naval meaning of *devil* (the seam at the lower end of a ship's hull) that we noticed in connection with *the devil and the deep blue sea* surfaces again: to pay the devil was to apply tar to this seam (the verb *pay* is attested in this sense from the 17th cent. and is not the familiar word for giving money). With such an obvious origin at hand, I don't believe this for a moment. *See also* HELL to pay.

Samuel *Foote A Trip to Calais* 1778

Had she had the least suspicion of me, there would have been the devil to pay; we should have all been off in an instant.

give the devil his due
to acknowledge the good points in somebody or something essentially bad or disliked. *16th cent.*

Shakespeare *1 Henry IV* I.ii.117 (1596)

[Prince Harry] Sir John stands to his word, the devil shall have his bargain, for he was never yet a breaker of proverbs: he will give the devil his due.

Aphra Behn *The Rover* 1677

Give the Devil his due, you are a very conscientious Lover: I love a Man that scorns to impose dull Truth and Constancy on a Mistress.

go to the devil
to be damned or ruined: typically used in the imperative as an angry retort or dismissal. *15th cent.*

Thomas Baker *An Act at Oxford* 1704
If you offer, Jew, to marry my mistress, Justice
Bullock and I will issue out our joint warrant, to
force you into the Hundreds of Essex; where you
shall be poyson'd with foggs, agues and damn'd
fulsome air, that you may go to the Devil, and be
smoa'k for hung beef.

how/what, etc the devil
used as an intensifying word, equivalent to *how/*
what, etc *on earth? 16th cent.*

Shakespeare *King John* II.i.134 (1597)
[Austria] *What the devil art thou?* [Bastard] *One*
that will play the devil, sir, with you.

like the devil
informal with great speed or force: often in
unpleasant or unfavourable contexts. The phrase
occurs earlier in the plural form *like devils*, e.g. in
Shakespeare's *Henry V* (1599) III.vii.147: '[The
Constable of France] And then, give them great
meals of beef, and iron and steel, they will eat like
wolves and fight like devils.' *17th cent.*

John Crowne *The English Frier* 1690
Now my daughter was at a play in a box, and young
ranter talks to her, gallants to her coach, follows her
home, all whether she would or no, and there ruffles
my maids, beats my men, breaks my windows, and
runs away like the Devil conjur'd out of a house.

Susannah Centlivre *The Platonick Lady* 1707
She shriek'd out, and drove away like the Devil,
when she saw us engag'd.

play devil's advocate
to take a view in an argument that challenges the
view one actually holds. The *devil's advocate* was a
Vatican official who presented the possible objections to the claims made for a deceased person to
be canonized. *18th cent.*

raise the devil
informal to cause a noisy disturbance: the image is
of such a commotion as to provoke the curiosity
of Satan himself. *18th cent.*

Thomas Baker *The Fine Lady's Airs* 1708
But what crabbed Don's this with the knavish look
of an old plodding conveyancer, whose face and
profession are enough to raise the Devil.

Charles Kingsley *Westward Ho!* 1855
Eustace was one of those impulsive men, with a lack
of moral courage, who dare raise the devil, but never
dare fight him after he has been raised.

speak/talk of the devil
used when a person just spoken of appears unexpectedly: from the proverb *speak* (or *talk*) *of the*
devil and he will surely appear (and many early
variants). Used apologetically by Henry James
(see below), although it had been long in circulation by the time he wrote, and appears in several collections of proverbs from the 17th cent.

Richardson *Clarissa* 1751
Talk of the devil, is an old saying. The lively wretch
has made me a visit, and is but just gone away.

Henry James *Confidence* 1880
Talk of the devil – excuse the adage! Are not those
the ladies in question?

sup/dine with the devil
to have dealings with somebody untrustworthy
or malevolent: from the proverb *he should have a*
long spoon who sups with the devil, which appears
in Chaucer's *Squire's Tale* (line 602): 'Therfore
bihoveth hire [= she needs] a ful long spoon |
That shal ete with a feend.' *Middle English*

James Shirley *The Cardinal* 1653
[Placentia] *Madam, the Cardinal.* [Hernando] *He*
shall sup with the Devil.

Evelyn Anthony *No Enemy but Time* 1987
He'd supped with the devil and no spoon was long
enough.

See also PLAY the devil with; SELL one's soul to the
devil.

dialogue

dialogue of/among/between the deaf
a discussion in which nobody takes much notice
of what the others are saying: *cf* French *dialogue*
des sourds, also used in English contexts. *Late 20th*
cent.

Ann Wroe *Lives, Lies and the Iran-Contra Affair* 1991
The parties continued to keep sitting down together
in hotel rooms across Europe and America,
resuming their dialogue of the deaf.

diamond

diamond cut diamond
British a situation in which a clever or witty person meets another of the same kind. Diamond is
so hard that only another diamond can cut it. *17th*
cent.

Dickens *A Tale of Two Cities* 1859
He was also in the habit of declaiming to Mrs.
Stryver, over his full-bodied wine, on the arts Mrs.
Darnay had once put in practice to 'catch' him, and
on the diamond-cut-diamond arts in himself ...
which had rendered him 'not to be caught'.

John Esten Cooke *Wearing of the Gray* 1867
Then came the tug of war. Stuart must meet
whatever force was brought against him, infantry as
well as cavalry, and match himself with the best
brains of the Federal army in command of them. It
was often 'diamond cut diamond'. In the fields
around Upperville, and everywhere along the road
to Ashby's Gap, raged a war of giants.

See also a ROUGH diamond.

dice

dice with death
to take dangerous risks. The phrase is based on
the gambling sense of *dice* ('to gamble with dice')
and has been used widely during the last fifty
years or so in newspaper reports of motor racing,
in which *dicing* is also used absolutely. *19th cent.*

Edward Bulwer-Lytton *The Last Days of Pompeii*
1834
'To-morrow is, I think, your first essay in the arena.
Well, I am sure you will die bravely!' ... 'Die! No –
I trust my hour is not yet come.' 'He who plays at
dice with death must expect the dog's throw' said
Sosia maliciously.

no dice
informal, originally NAmer of no avail; no use: a
metaphor from gambling. *Mid 20th cent.*

P G Wodehouse *Barmy in Wonderland* 1952
I was around at her bank this morning trying to find
out what her balance was, but no dice. Fanny won't
part.

See also LOAD the dice in favour of / against
somebody.

dickens

how/what, etc the dickens
used as an intensifying word, equivalent to *how/*
what, etc *on earth?* The reference has nothing to do
with the 19th cent. novelist but is a euphemism
for *devil.* The phrase is as old as Shakespeare: in
The Merry Wives of Windsor (1597) III.ii.16, Mistress Page asks the page Robin: 'I cannot tell what

the dickens his name is my husband had of him. –
What do you call your knight's name, sirrah?'
(The reply is 'Sir John Falstaff.') *16th cent.*

dicky bird

not a dicky bird
no information; not a word uttered. A *dicky bird* (a
child's word, dating from the 18th cent., for any
little bird) is rhyming slang for 'word', used primarily in this phrase. *Mid 20th cent.*

Beryl Bainbridge *An Awfully Big Adventure* 1990
I telephoned twice this morning. I couldn't raise a
dicky bird.

dido

cut didoes / be full of didoes
NAmer, informal to do mischief. A *dido* is a prank
or piece of mischief. *19th cent.*

Louisa M Alcott *Little Women* 1868
Mr. Laurie is as full of didoes as usual, and turns
the house upside down frequent; but he heartens up
the girls, and so I let em hev full swing.

die¹ (verb)

be dying to do something
informal to be very eager to do something. *18th*
cent.

Jane Austen *Northanger Abbey* 1818
I am dying to show you my hat.

die hard
(said of habits or attitudes) to take a long time to
change or disappear. In the 18th cent. the phrase
was said to have been a criminals' expression for
resisting death on the gallows at Tyburn in London, but the concept goes deeper, touching on
superstitions about doors and windows at the
time of death. A closed door or window made it
harder for the dying person because the soul was
trapped, as literary allusions show, e.g. in Scott,
Guy Mannering (1815) II.v 'And wha ever heard
of a door being barred when a man was in the
dead-thraw? – how d'ye think the spirit was to
get awa through bolts and bars like these?' *19th*
cent.

Dickens *The Chimes* 1844
Aye, aye! Years ... are like Christians in that
respect. Some of 'em die hard; some of 'em die easy.

This one hasn't many days to run, and is making a fight for it.

die in harness
to die during one's working life. The reference is to a workhorse harnessed to the plough, as symbolic of work: cf Shakespeare, *Macbeth* (1606) v.v.50: '[Macbeth] Blow wind, come wrack, | At least we'll die with harness on our back.' The phrase dates from the 19th cent. in this form.

George Meredith *The Egoist* 1879
Sir Willoughby thought of his promise to Clara. He trifled awhile with young Crossjay, and then sent the boy flying, and wrapped himself in meditation. So shall you see standing many a statue of statesmen who have died in harness for their country.

die in one's shoes
to suffer a sudden or violent death, especially to be executed by hanging. *17th cent.*

die on the vine
to die or disappear before having a chance to develop. *19th cent.*

die with one's boots on
to die while engaged in an activity. *18th cent.* (with earlier references to shoes)

Harold Frederic *The Damnation of Theron Ware* 1896
The money that bought that vote was put up by the smartest and most famous train-gambler between Omaha and 'Frisco, a gentleman who died in his boots and took three sheriff's deputies along with him to Kingdom-Come.

I'd die first
informal used to express strong rejection of a course of action. *18th cent.*

Henry Fielding *The History of Tom Jones* 1749
When I had remained a week under this imprisonment, he made me a visit, and, with the voice of a schoolmaster, or, what is often much the same, of a tyrant, asked me, 'If I would yet comply?' I answered, very stoutly, 'That I would die first.'

never say die
informal an exhortation to keep trying. *19th cent.*

R H Dana *Two Years before the Mast* 1840
Notwithstanding the desolation of the scene, we struck up 'Cheerily ho!' in full chorus. This pleased the mate, who rubbed his hands and cried out – 'That's right, my boys; never say die!'

a — to die for
informal, originally *NAmer* something overwhelmingly beautiful or desirable: now typically used with reference to women and their physical appearance. Also the adjectival form *to-die-for*, as in *a to-die-for outfit*. The phrase is also applied to delicious food, and in an unfortunate distortion of it the British Airways in-flight magazine *High Life* was quoted in 2002 as enticing its passengers with 'chocolate, prune and armagnac cake fit to die from'. *19th cent.*

E N Westcott *David Harum* 1898
Oh! and to 'top off' with, a mince-pie to die for.

She 1989
Ellen Barkin (small of eye and thin of lip), Jamie Lee Curtis (bright-eyed but androgynous), Anjelica Huston (body to die for – unforgiving face), Bette Midler (where do I begin?) uncurled themselves across screens from LA to Llandudno, playing women who were as sexy and salacious as they were ballsy and bloody-minded.

to one's dying day
for the rest of one's life. The phrase appears in Chaucer (*The Wife of Bath's Prologue*, line 507) in the form *to my ending day*: 'Now of my fifthe housbonde wol I telle. | God lete his soule nevere come in helle! | And yet was he to me the mooste shrewe [= greatest rogue]; | That feele I on my ribbes al by rewe [= in a row], | And evere shal, unto myn endyng day.' *17th cent.*

Bunyan *The Pilgrim's Progress* 1678
Some also had been maimed there, and could not, to their dying day, be their own men again.

See also die a/the DEATH; die in one's BED; die in the last DITCH; die like flies *at* FLY.

---

die² (noun)

(as) straight as a die
1 completely honest or straightforward. This is a figurative use of the literal meaning, although it is recorded somewhat earlier. *You'll know me truer than a die* (in this meaning) is found in an 18th cent. ballad. *18th cent.*

Charles Stearns *The Foundling* 1798
You would not conceal any thing now from old spark that's as true as a die – I won't tell tales; burn my whiskers if I do.

Trollope *The Way We Live Now* 1875

'I usually keep engagements when I make them, Mr. Lupton,' said the Duchess. She had been assured by Lord Alfred not a quarter of an hour before that everything was as straight as a die.

2 in an absolutely straight direction. The phrase refers to an engineer's die used in cutting a thread, which must be completely straight to engage effectively with the inside of the rod in which the thread is to be cut. *Smooth as a die* is attested from the 16th cent. (Palsgrave) and *true as a die* from the 18th cent. *19th cent.*

Dickens *Oliver Twist* 1838

Monks drew the little packet from his breast … and tying it to a leaden weight … dropped it into the stream. It fell straight, and true as a die; clove the water with a scarcely audible splash, and was gone.

the die is cast

a crucial and irrevocable decision has been made. The phrase translates the words in Latin (*jacta alea esto* 'let the die be cast') attributed by Suetonius (*Caesar* i.32) to Julius Caesar on crossing the Rubicon into Italy with his army in 49 BC, an act that effectively declared war on the Roman Senate: *see* RUBICON. Other forms, e.g. *the chance is cast*, occur in the 16th cent., and Richard III in Shakespeare's play (1593) declares at the point where he faces defeat and death on Bosworth Field (v.vii.10): 'I have set my life upon a cast, | And I will stand the hazard of the die.' *17th cent.*

Thomas Paine *The American Crisis* 1780

'The struggle,' says Lord Townsend, 'is now a struggle for power; the die is cast.'

M Dobbs *Last Man to Die* 1991

The peoples of Eastern Europe will have exchanged one terror for another. But the die is cast. In politics, as in life, we must move on.

differ

agree to differ

to stop arguing because neither side will yield to the other. *18th cent.*

Robert Bage *Hermsprong* 1796

Before you can set up an undisputed title to an amiable people, you must first learn to agree to differ.

difference

See SPLIT the difference.

different

See different strokes for different folks *at* STROKE.

dig

dig a hole for oneself / dig oneself into a hole

to get oneself into an awkward or dangerous predicament. *Late 20th cent.*

Penny Junor *Charles and Diana* 1991

And on the other burning question that was asked time and time again – whether she will have more children – he said, digging an even deeper hole for himself: 'She'd love a large family because she knows the joys of it.'

dig in one's heels

to refuse to give way on a matter: variants no longer current include *dig in one's feet* and *dig in one's toes*. *Mid 20th cent.*

dig (up) the dirt

to find information that is harmful to the reputation of a public figure: *dirt* in the sense 'scandalous or malicious gossip' dates from the 1920s. *Mid 20th cent.*

Today 1992

The latest revelation that the Home Office trawled through 25-year-old confidential files to try to dig up dirt on Mr Clinton is as outrageous as it is mind-boggling.

See dig somebody in the ribs *at* RIB; dig one's own GRAVE; dig a PIT for somebody.

dignity

beneath/below one's dignity

too trivial or menial a task for one to undertake. Jonathan Swift wrote in a letter in 1711 'I fear I shall be sometimes forced to stoop beneath my dignity, and send to the ale-house for a dinner'. The phrase is often overlaid with irony, and appears in the (informal and usually jocular) Latin form *infra dig(nitatem)*. *18th cent.*

Boswell *The Life of Samuel Johnson* 1791

Soon after the publication of his Dictionary, Garrick being asked by Johnson what people said of it, told him ... it was objected that he cited authorities which were beneath the dignity of such a work, and mentioned Richardson. 'Nay, (said Johnson,) I have done worse than that: I have cited thee, David.'

stand on one's dignity

to demand to be treated with respect. *Stand* is used with *on* in the meaning 'to claim respect for' from the late 16th cent.: *cf* stand on CEREMONY. *19th cent.*

> Mrs Humphry Ward *Robert Elsmere* 1888
> *He looked at her laughing. She laughed too. The infection of his strong sunny presence was irresistible. In London it had been so easy to stand on her dignity, to remember whenever he was friendly that the night before he had been distant. In these green solitudes it was not easy to be anything but natural – the child of the moment!*

dim

See take a dim VIEW of somebody/something.

dime

An American silver coin worth ten cents.

a dime a dozen

NAmer, informal very cheap: hence the adjectival form *dime-a-dozen*. *Mid 20th cent.*

> Daily Telegraph 1992
> *'One thing we don't need in this subcontinent,' Professor Rokeya Kabeer observed, 'is spiritual guidance – we have gurus a dime a dozen.'*

drop the dime on somebody

NAmer, informal to inform on somebody to the police. The image is of an informer making a telephone call to the authorities, which would have cost a dime in the 1960s when the phrase was first used. *Mid 20th cent.*

on a dime

NAmer, informal needing only a very small space: used with reference to manoeuvring a vehicle: *see also* SIXPENCE. *Mid 20th cent.*

diminish

the law of diminishing returns

the economic principle that, after a certain point, increased investment in an enterprise will not produce a significant increase in profit or yield: *diminishing return* is recorded from the early 19th cent. *19th cent.*

> Henry James *Pyramus and Thisbe* 1869
> *He had reached his 'middle years' beset by feelings of literary inadequacy (in the marketplace) and the thought of the years to come, with the prospect of diminishing returns, deeply disturbed him.*

dinkum

fair dinkum

Australian and NZ, informal genuine. The adjectival use of *dinkum* in the meaning 'genuine, honest' dates from the early 20th cent. (as in Edward Dyson's 'all the ways of life, dinkum ways 'n' crook': see below), although *fair dinkum* is late 19th cent. in this meaning and the meaning 'fair play'. It seems to be connected with an English dialect word *dinkum*, which is listed in the *English Dialect Dictionary* published between 1896 and 1905 with the meaning 'a fair share of work'. This meaning is close to the earliest sense of *dinkum* in Australian use, from which the current sense of 'genuine' developed. An origin in Chinese *din gum* meaning 'real gold', used by gold miners when they struck gold, belongs to the realm of folk etymology. *19th cent.*

> Rolf Boldrewood *Robbery Under Arms* 1888
> *It took us an hour's hard dinkum to get neart the peak.*

> Edward Dyson *Hello Soldier* 1919
> *It is thirty moons since I slung me hook | From the job at the hay and corn, | Took me solemn oath, 'n' I straight forsook | All the ways of life, dinkum ways 'n' crook, | 'N' the things on which it was good to look | Since the day when a bloke was born.*

dinner

be done like (a) dinner

chiefly Australian to be defeated or outwitted. *19th cent.*

hand/turn/pass in one's dinner pail

NAmer, informal to die: from the former practice of workmen carrying their dinner in buckets. *Early 20th cent.*

> P G Wodehouse *Frozen Assets* 1964
> *My godfather ... recently turned in his dinner pail and went to reside with the morning stars.*

more — than somebody has had hot dinners

informal more experience of something significant than the other party can have had even of some daily occurrence. *Mid 20th cent.*

Simon Brett *Murder Unprompted* 1984

I've backed more shows than you lot have had hot dinners and I've never seen anything like this.

See also dressed (up) like a dog's dinner *at* DOG.

dint

by dint of something

by means or application of something. *Dint*, now used only in this phrase, derives from an Old English word meaning 'a stroke or blow': an early use, now obsolete, was in the phrase *by dint of sword* = by force of arms. *16th cent.* (in the variant spelling *dent*)

Jane Austen *Emma* 1816

I could not think about you so much without doating on you, faults and all; and by dint of fancying so many errors, have been in love with you ever since you were thirteen at least.

dip

dip one's pen in gall

to write in a malicious or vindictive way: *gall* is an archaic word for 'bile', the bitter fluid secreted by the liver, and was used from the 13th cent. in the figurative meaning 'rancour or bitterness'. A mid 17th cent. source refers to 'the virulencie and gall of our pennes'. *17th cent.*

John Reynolds *The Triumphs of Gods Revenge* 1625

In discretion and love to her honour, she resolves to returne him an answer, when knitting her browes with anger, dipping her pen in gall and vinegar, and setting a sharp edge of contempt and Choller on her resolutions.

dip one's toe(s) in(to) something

to try something cautiously or tentatively: from the literal meaning of putting one's toes into water to test its temperature before committing oneself more fully. *Mid 20th cent.*

See also dip one's WICK.

dirt

Figurative meanings of *dirt* typifying lack of worth or honesty appear early (14th cent.) in its history, applied to people as well as things.

dirt cheap

for practically nothing: the underlying meaning is 'as cheap as dirt'. *19th cent.*

Dickens *Oliver Twist* 1838

Bill was to do this; and Bill was to do that; and Bill was to do it all, dirt cheap, as soon as he got well.

dish the dirt

informal to spread malicious gossip: *dirt* in the meaning 'scandalous or malicious gossip' is recorded from the 1920s, and *dish* is used in the sense 'to serve or provide'. *Mid 20th cent.*

P G Wodehouse *Frozen Assets* 1964

He doesn't think much of you ... He thinks you fall short in the way of dishing the dirt.

do somebody dirt

to harm somebody's reputation maliciously. *19th cent.*

Roald Dahl *Rhyme Stew* 1990

Would you pay a lot | To hear about an evil plot? | Would you, for instance, give your shirt | To know who's going to do you dirt?

eat dirt

to be humiliated or treated ignominiously: *cf* the consolatory proverb *we must eat a peck of dirt before we die* (recorded in various forms from the 17th cent.). *Cf* eat CROW; eat one's HAT; eat HUMBLE pie. *19th cent.*

Meadows Taylor *Confessions of a Thug* 1839

'And yet say, shall I send more money?' 'No,' said I, 'surely not; if he is honest, he will fling it in your servant's face; if he is a rogue, he will keep it, and send word that the stars have changed; in the first case you will eat dirt, in the second you will be cheated, and he will laugh at your beard.'

throw/fling/cast dirt

to use abusive or coarse language. *17th cent.*

Beaumont & Fletcher *Philaster, or Love Lies a-Bleeding* 1620

They will not hear me speak, but fling dirt at me, and call me Tyrant.

treat somebody like dirt

to treat somebody contemptuously or ignominiously. *20th cent.*

> Michael Dibdin *Dirty Tricks* 1991
> *You know what women are like. They'll promise you the earth to get you to come across, then treat you like dirt once they've satisfied their maternal cravings.*

See also DRAG somebody's name through the mud/dirt.

dirty

the dirty end of the stick

informal the unpleasant or dangerous part of a task or undertaking. The image is of a stick used to stir or probe something messy or noxious. *Early 20th cent.*

dirty work at the crossroads

informal dishonest or illicit dealings. The allusion is to the sinister associations of crossroads: as a place where suicides were buried with a stake through the heart (the subject of a discussion in *Notes & Queries* August 1933, p.141), and as a common setting for foul play of various kinds, most famously the story of Oedipus' (unwitting) murder of his father Laius. *Early 20th cent.*

> Agatha Christie *The Adventure of the Christmas Pudding* 1960
> *'Wondered whether you could throw any light on the case. If so, perhaps you'd come round?' 'I will come immediately.' 'Good for you, old boy. Some dirty work at the crossroads – eh?'*

do the dirty (on somebody)

informal to play a mean or underhand trick (on somebody). *Early 20th cent.*

do the dirty work

informal to carry out the required piece of villainy. *19th cent.*

> John William De Forest *Miss Ravenel's Conversion from Secession to Loyalty* 1867
> *Your regiment will be made road-builders, and scavengers, and baggage guards, to do the dirty work of white regiments.*

get one's hands dirty / dirty one's hands

1 to become personally involved in the task in hand, especially hard or manual work. It is primarily a 20th cent. phrase, but there are occasional figurative uses much earlier: for example, among the *Worthies of England* collected by the 17th cent. antiquarian and royal chaplain Thomas Fuller was one who 'rather soyled his fingers, then dirtied his hands in the matter of the Holy Maid of Kent'. *19th cent.*

> Trollope *The Prime Minister* 1876
> *The work was very hard, and what good would come from it? Why should she make her hands dirty, so that even her husband accused her of vulgarity?*

2 to become implicated in dishonest dealings. *Early 20th cent.*

> Conan Doyle *The Valley of Fear* 1915
> *I'll get even with you without needing to dirty my hands.*

play dirty

informal to act dishonestly or maliciously. *Mid 20th cent.*

talk dirty

informal to use coarse or lewd language. *Mid 20th cent.*

> John Steinbeck *Of Mice and Men* 1937
> *Old Susy's a laugh – always crackin' jokes … She never talks dirty, neither.*

See also wash one's dirty LINEN in public.

disappear

See do a disappearing ACT.

disaster

be a recipe for disaster

to be likely to have disastrous consequences. The use of *recipe* in the meaning 'a procedure for achieving something' dates from the 17th cent. *20th cent.*

> Jeremy Paxman *Friends in High Places* 1990
> *He detested the old-style Conservatives. 'The whole squirearchy, old school tie, old boy network was a recipe for disaster.'*

disbelief

suspend one's disbelief

to suppress one's scepticism about a postulated situation in the interests of the developments that might then be based on it, although it is logically implausible in itself: used typically in the context of fictional dramatic situations that call for tolerance of impossible or contradictory circumstances. *Mid 20th cent.*

discretion

discretion is the better part of valour
it is sometimes wiser and more courageous to avoid a conflict or danger and resist the temptation to confront it. The locus classicus is the 16th cent. use by Shakespeare (see below), which was echoed by contemporary dramatists, including Beaumont and Fletcher, but the notion is considerably older and can be found in ancient Greek drama.

> Shakespeare *1 Henry IV* v.iv.118 (1596)
> [Sir John Oldcastle to Prince Harry] *To counterfeit dying when a man thereby liveth is to be no counterfeit, but the true and perfect image of life indeed. The better part of valour is discretion, in the which better part I have saved my life.*

disease

See the REMEDY is worse than the disease.

dish

See dish the DIRT.

dishwater

See (as) DULL as ditchwater/dishwater.

distance

go the distance
to have the stamina to complete a long or arduous task: based on sports terminology. In boxing, *go the distance* means to continue to fight for the full length of the contest (as distinct from being knocked out or having the fight stopped); and *go the distance* (or *route*) in baseball means to pitch for an entire inning. *Mid 20th cent.*

keep somebody at a distance
to avoid friendly or intimate contact with somebody. *17th cent.*

> Richardson *Familiar Letters* 1750
> *I think truly, with you, that Mr. Rushford is a very valuable gentleman; yet he is over-nice, sometimes,*

as to the company I see; and would take upon him a little too much, if I did not keep him at a distance.

keep one's distance
to remain aloof: from the literal meaning, to keep ahead of or away from others. *18th cent.*

> Charles Kingsley *Westward Ho!* 1855
> *They visited the village again next day; and every day for a week or more; but the maiden appeared but rarely, and when she did, kept her distance as haughtily as a queen.*

within spitting distance (of something)
very close: the image is of something close enough to be spat on. The phrase is 19th cent. in the form *spitting range*; but is predominantly 20th cent.

within striking distance (of something)
close enough to be reached or achieved. The expression has been in general use from the 19th cent., but *striking distance* is recorded from the mid 18th cent. as a technical term denoting 'the distance that separates two conductors charged with electricity of different potential' (see the quotation below). *18th cent.*

> Benjamin Franklin *His Invention of the Lightning Rod* 1749
> *And then we see how electrified clouds passing over hills or high buildings at too great a height to strike, may be attracted lower till within their striking distance.*

ditch

die in the last ditch
to die fighting valiantly. The phrase is associated by David Hume with William III of England when he was Stadtholder of Holland (*History of England under the House of Tudor*, 1759: 'There is one certain means by which I can be sure never to see my country's ruin – I will die in the last ditch'), but there is no direct evidence of his use of the phrase. The adjective *last-ditch*, meaning 'as a final effort' (as in *a last-ditch attempt*), is derived from this phrase. *18th cent.*

> William Godwin *St Leon* 1799
> *From this time I saw Bethlem Gabor no more; he died, as he had sworn to do, in the last ditch of his castle.*

Mark Twain *Speeches* 1906
When you had been keeping this sort of thing up two or three hours, ... what did you do? You simply went on until you dropped in the last ditch.

ditchwater

See (as) DULL as ditchwater/dishwater.

dither

all of a dither
in a state of indecision or nervous anxiety. *Dither* is of northern dialect origin. The noun is recorded in the early 19th cent. as a Lancashire word in the local form of the phrase, *aw on o' dither*. It is also attested in the late 19th cent. in a physical technical meaning 'vibration'. A verb form, from which the noun is derived, goes back to the 17th cent. in the meaning 'to quiver or tremble'; a transitive use in the sense 'to bother or confuse' (as in *he's dithered*) appears in the 20th cent.; and in informal Australian use *dithered* also means 'drunk'. *19th cent.*

ditto

say ditto to something
to agree with or approve of something said or proposed. *Ditto* is used in English from the 17th cent. and derived from an Italian word *detto* meaning 'said', which was used with a noun (as in *il detto libro* 'the said book') to avoid the full repetition of something written earlier. *18th cent.*

Edward Bulwer-Lytton *Pelham* 1828
'If, therefore, it be possible to carry off Dawson, after having secured his confession, we must. I think it right to insist more particularly on this point, as you appeared to me rather averse to it this morning.' 'I say ditto to your honour,' returned Job.

dive

take a dive
1 (said of a boxer or footballer) to pretend to be knocked down or made to fall, in order to fool the referee. *Mid 20th cent.*
2 (said of hopes, prices, etc) to fall dramatically. *Late 20th cent.*

divide

divide and rule/conquer
to encourage disagreement among one's opponents in order to prevent them uniting against one: also used in the Latin form *divide et impera*. Wrongly associated from an early date with the Italian statesman and political philosopher Niccolò Machiavelli (1469–1527), the concept occurs in several languages, including French *diviser pour régner* (in Voltaire) and German *entzwei und gebiete*. A source from the late 16th cent. says of Catherine of Medici that she 'set in France, one against the other, that in the mean while she might rule in these divisions'. *17th cent.*

Peter Motteux *The Island Princess* 1699
The Bramins shall foment the Pious mischief; | And when each Party's weaken'd, I'll unmask, | Strike in between, and get the Princess and the Crown. | Revive my hopes! Revive! – Mankind to fool, | Still the great Maxim is; divide and rule.

a house divided against itself
a group or organization that is affected by internal conflict. The phrase alludes to Christ's words in Matthew 12:25: 'Every kingdom divided against itself is brought to desolation; and every city or house divided against itself shall not stand.' *18th cent.*

Thomas Paine *Common Sense* 1776
Some writers have explained the English constitution thus; the king, say they, is one, the people another; the peers are an house in behalf of the king; the commons in behalf of the people; but this hath all the distinctions of an house divided against itself.

dixie

whistle dixie
NAmer, informal to be wasting one's time on fantasies. *Mid 20th cent.*

do

do or die
to persevere in spite of great danger or difficulty. The phrase famously occurs in Burns' battle song *Scots wha hae* (1793): 'Liberty's in every blow! Let us do, or die', and in a different form (*and* not *or*) in Tennyson's *Charge of the Light Brigade* (1854): 'Their's not to make reply, | Their's not to reason

why, | Their's but to do and die: | Into the valley of Death | Rode the six hundred.' *16th cent.*

Spenser *The Faerie Queene* i.i.51 (1596)
Shall I accuse the hidden cruell fate ... | Or the blind God, that doth me thus amate, | For hoped love to winne me certaine hate? | Yet thus perforce he bids me do, or die.

dos and don'ts
the basic rules of conduct or action in a particular situation. *Early 20th cent.*

See also do (one's) BIRD; do one's bit *at* BIT[1]; do the DECENT thing; do the DIRTY on somebody; do somebody a FAVOUR; do one's HOMEWORK; do the honours *at* HONOUR; do one's NUT; do one's own THING; do somebody PROUD; do a RUNNER; do something to DEATH; do the TRICK; have NOTHING to do with somebody/something; MAKE do; NOTHING doing.

dock

in dock
out of action or use because of illness, damage, etc. The phrase refers to ships laid up for repairs, and has been extended to use in connection with people and (more recently) their vehicles. Grose in his *Dictionary of the Vulgar Tongue* (1785) wrote in the entry for *dock*: 'He must go into dock, a sea phrase, signifying that the person spoken of must undergo a salivation.' Variations such as *out of dock* (= just out of hospital) are also recorded. *18th cent.*

Hugh Kelly *The Romance of an Hour* 1774
Well, there's a brave officer laid up for ever in dock. – But death will yellow us all in turn, and so I shall only think of succeeding to the command.

in the dock
being investigated in connection with a crime or wrongdoing: from the use of *dock* for the enclosure where an accused person stands in a court of law. *19th cent.*

Running 1991
Cholesterol is in the dock, accused of being a killer.

doctor

be (just) what the doctor ordered
informal, usually humorous to be exactly what is needed. The phrase is listed among those remem-

bered by C H Rolph in *London Particulars* (1980), his memoirs of an Edwardian childhood, but there is no written evidence before the mid 20th cent.: *see further at* all BEHIND, like a cow's tail.

P G Wodehouse *Nothing Serious* 1950
'You admired my little friend?' 'She is what the doctor ordered.'

Esquire 1993
Three-year-olds give Giotto and Cimabue pretty short shrift. In fact, Alan and I were the only ones to find the old master and pupil just what the doctor ordered.

go for the doctor
Australian and NZ, informal to make a supreme effort. *Mid 20th cent.*

See also doctor's orders *at* ORDER.

dodge
See dodge the COLUMN.

dodo
See (as) DEAD as the/a dodo.

dog
The dog, a domestic and working animal from time immemorial, has been at the centre of numerous idioms, mostly unfavourable or depreciatory in some way. From the 14th cent. it was used widely to refer to various kinds of worthless or cowardly fellows, and it is from this notion that many of the following phrases arise.

call off the dogs
to stop harassing or pursuing somebody. The phrase is derived from hunting, and appears in this form both literally and in extended metaphor (as in the quotation below) in the 18th cent.

Edward Ward *Hudibras Redivivus* 1705
Or who, except by Force, are able | To tame a frantick head-strong Rabble? | So Blood-hounds, when the Scent lies warm, | With threat'ning Yelps the Stag alarm, | Whose Horns cannot his Life defend, | Lest the kind Hunts-man stands his Friend: | Therefore when once you Church-men see, | The Game they hunt in Jeopardy, | Make speedy Haste to shew good Nature, | Call off the Dogs, and save the Creature.

dog-and-pony show

NAmer, informal an elaborate display or show. Late 20th cent.

Photography 1991

There were three soldiers going house-to-house with fifteen photographers and a couple of TV crews; it was what we call a 'dog and pony show'.

dog eat dog

a state of ruthless competition between rivals to succeed: a negation of the (16th cent.) proverb dog does not eat dog. Also as an adjectival phrase dog-eat-dog. 19th cent.

Rider Haggard King Solomon's Mines 1885

My lord, there was one war ... but it was a civil war – dog eat dog.

a dog in the manger

somebody who tries to prevent other people having or using something even though they do not want it themselves. The expression alludes to an old fable about a dog that lay in the horses' manger (feeding trough) to prevent the horses from feeding, although it did not want to eat the food itself. 16th cent.

William Bulleyn A Dialogue Against the Fever Pestilence 1564

Like unto cruell dogges liyng in a maunger, neither eatyng the haye theim selves ne sufferyng the horse to feed thereof hymself.

Defoe Farther Adventures of Robinson Crusoe 1719

The Spaniards would have been satisfied with this, would the other but have let them alone, which, however, they could not find in their Hearts to do long, but like the dog in the manger, they would not eat themselves, and would not let others eat neither.

D H Lawrence Sons and Lovers 1913

'Love's a dog in a manger,' he said. 'And which of us is the dog?' she asked. 'Oh well, you, of course.'

dog it

informal, chiefly NAmer to laze around avoiding work. Early 20th cent.

the dog's bollocks

informal quite the finest thing of its kind: cf the bee's knees at BEE, the cat's whiskers/pyjamas/meow at CAT. Late 20th cent.

The Times Magazine 2002

Any as-yet-undecided sixth-formers attending History in Action may well find themselves swept up as part of this remarkable trend. For fans of historical reenactment, the two-day annual event has to be the dog's impeccably researched, most gloriously presented bollocks.

a dog's breakfast/dinner

British, informal a complete mess or failure: with reference to the jumbled or scrappy nature of a dog's meal. See also dressed (up) like a dog's dinner below. Mid 20th cent.

a dog's life

a dreary and unhappy existence. This and other expressions to do with dogs (dog eat dog, go to the dogs, etc) are based on associations with work and hardship, rather than with the more modern image of dogs as pets that enjoy a comfortable cosseted life. In more recent use the phrase sometimes has this more positive meaning, an interesting example of how the idiom of language can follow the reality of life. 16th cent.

Isaac Bickerstaffe The Plain Dealer 1766

Have a care of the fiddle's end, I say. Gad, I am sure I lead a dog's life with you.

Henry Adams The Education of Henry Adams 1907

A year or two of education as editor satiated most of his appetite for that career as a profession ... Vulgarly speaking, it was a dog's life when it did not succeed, and little better when it did.

the dogs of war

the horrors of war: with allusion to Shakespeare, Julius Caesar (1599) III.i.276 '[Antony] Caesar's spirit, ranging for revenge, ... | Shall in these confines with a monarch's voice | Cry "havoc!" [= give the signal for 'no quarter'] and let slip the dogs of war.' The reference is to hunting dogs released to pursue their quarry. 16th cent.

Henry Fielding The History of Tom Jones 1749

Now the dogs of war being let loose, began to lick their bloody lips; now Victory ... hung hovering in the air; now Fortune ... began to weigh the fates of Tom Jones, his female companion, and Partridge, against the landlord, his wife, and maid.

dog tired

exhausted after hard or prolonged exertion. The image is of a dog wanting to sleep. 19th cent.

Jane Austen Letter 1813

It was 12 before we reached home. We were all dog-tired, but pretty well to-day.

R L Stevenson *Treasure Island* 1883
I was dog-tired when, a little before dawn, the boatswain sounded his pipe, and the crew began to man the capstan-bars.

dressed/dolled (up) / looking like a dog's dinner

smartly or ostentatiously dressed, often for no apparent reason or in a way that causes disapproval or resentment. The reference is ironic, since a dog's meal is symbolic of messiness rather than elegance (*see* a dog's breakfast/dinner *above*). *Mid 20th cent.*

J Wilson *The Suitcase Kid* 1993
Why on earth couldn't your father take some proper photos of you in your own clothes, instead of all dolled up like a dog's dinner?

every dog has its day

good fortune comes to everybody eventually. The locus classicus is Hamlet's words (not quite in the familiar form of the proverb) to Laertes in Shakespeare's play of 1601 (v.i.289): 'Let Hercules himself do what he may, | The cat will mew, and dog will have his day.' But Shakespeare did not invent the phrase; it is found in earlier Elizabethan literature and collections of sayings, notably those of Richard Taverner (1545) and John Heywood (1546). The phrase was used slightly later by Ben Jonson, and in the 18th cent. by Alexander Pope. *16th cent.*

give a dog a bad name

it is difficult to shake off a bad reputation however unjustified it may be. The phrase is derived from the fuller proverb *give a dog a bad name and hang him*, meaning that a dog known for fierceness cannot be trusted and might as well be put down. The proverb is listed in James Kelly's *Complete Collection of Scottish Proverbs* of 1721. *18th cent.*

R H Dana *Two Years before the Mast* 1840
The captain took a dislike to him, thought he was surly, and lazy; and 'if you once give a dog a bad name' – as the sailor-phrase is – 'he may as well jump overboard'.

go to the dogs

informal to decline or deteriorate rapidly: phrases and proverbs based on the notion of giving worthless or rejected food to dogs date from the 16th cent. A more remote explanation refers to the use of Latin *canis* meaning 'dog' as a term for a bad throw of a dice in ancient Rome, three such throws losing the game. *17th cent.*

Smollett *The Adventures of Peregrine Pickle* 1751
All your care is to sit among your companions of the garden, and sing bunting-songs, till you get drunk, leaving your trade at sixes and sevens, and your family to go to the dogs.

in a dog's age

NAmer, informal for a long time.

keep a dog and bark oneself

to employ somebody to do work and then do it oneself, often from lack of trust or obsession with hands-on involvement. Also as a proverb, *why keep a dog and bark yourself?* (and variant forms). *16th cent.*

Brian Melbancke *Philotimus* 1583
It is smal reason you should kepe a dog, and barke your selfe.

Mike Ripley *Angel Touch* 1991
Don't have a dog and bark yourself, dearest. Concentrate on your macramé.

let the dog see the rabbit

to leave somebody to get on with the task they are supposed to do. *Mid 20th cent.*

Enoch Powell *Reflections of a Statesman* 1991
Our task is to bring back the mass-production element into the house-building industry, which can be done only by enabling it largely to work on its own authority for a prospective demand – by 'letting the dog see the rabbit'.

let sleeping dogs lie

to avoid interfering in a situation that is not causing any problems, for fear of causing difficulty oneself. The sentiment appears as a proverb in Chaucer, *Troilus and Criseyde* (III.764): 'It is nought good a slepyng hound to wake', and took its present form in Scott's *Redgauntlet* (1824): 'Take my advice, and speer [= ask] as little about him as he does about you. Best to let sleeping dogs lie.' *19th cent.*

Dickens *David Copperfield* 1850
You and me know what we know, don't we? Let sleeping dogs lie – who wants to rouse 'em? I don't.

David Lodge *Nice Work* 1988
Discussion of Sandra's sex-life could easily stray into the area of his and Marjorie's sex-life, or rather the lack of it, and he would rather not go into that. Let sleeping dogs lie.

like a dog with two tails
extremely pleased or satisfied: from the belief
that a dog wags its tail as a sign of happiness
or pleasure. *Mid 20th cent.*

> Joan Smith *A Masculine Ending* 1988
> *Your husband's been having a busy week ... I heard
> him being interviewed on the news a few minutes
> ago ... Talk about a dog with two tails.*

not a dog's chance
informal no chance at all. *Early 20th cent.*

> John Fowles *The Collector* 1989
> *You don't really stand a dog's chance anyhow.
> You're too pretty. The art of love's your line: not the
> love of art.*

play/turn dog
Australian and NZ, informal to betray or inform on
somebody: from the use of *dog* to mean 'informer'
in North American and Australian usage. *19th
cent.*

put on (the) dog
to put on airs, to act pretentiously. The phrase is
said to come from the popularity in the US in the
19th cent. of lapdogs, which were lavishly pam-
pered and carried as fashion accessories. *19th
cent.*

throw somebody/something to the dogs
to reject somebody or something as worthless:
possibly an echo of Mark 7:27 'Let the children
first be filled: for it is not meet to take the children's bread, and cast it unto the dogs.' *17th cent.*

> Shakespeare *Macbeth* v.iii.49 (1606)
> *Throw physic to the dogs, I'll none of it.*

See also (as) SICK as a dog; the HAIR of the dog;
rain cats and dogs *at* CAT.

dogged

it's dogged as does it
(proverb) perseverance brings success. *Dogged* in
the sense 'stubbornly determined' is based on the
perceived characteristics of certain breeds of
dogs. *19th cent.*

> Trollope *The Last Chronicle of Barset* 1867
> *There was an old lame man from Hoggle End
> leaning on his stick near the door as Mr. Crawley
> went out, and with him was his old lame wife. 'He'll
> pull through yet,' said the old man to his wife;*

*'you'll see else. He'll pull through because he's so
dogged. It's dogged as does it.'*

doggo

lie doggo
to lie low and stay motionless, especially in order
to avoid detection. *Doggo* was first used by
Kipling (*Many Inventions*, 1893: 'I wud lie most
powerful doggo whin I heard a shot') and is
confined to this phrase; it may be associated
with a dog's practice of lying still but alert
when in danger. *19th cent.*

> Somerset Maugham *The Moon and Sixpence* 1919
> *Do you think he's done something that we don't
> know about, and is lying doggo on account of the
> police?*

doghouse

in the doghouse
informal, originally NAmer in disgrace or disfavour. *Doghouse* is the North American word
for a dog's kennel. *Mid 20th cent.*

> *Daily Mirror* 1992
> *Heidi the rottweiler was in the doghouse yesterday
> after she stopped firemen reaching a kitchen blaze.*

dole

on the dole
informal out of work and receiving State benefits.
Dole in this context goes back to Middle English
in the more general sense of 'money or food
given in charity', when it appears in a work by
Caxton: 'a dole to poor people of six shillings'. In
the current specific meaning the word dates from
the early 20th cent., and *on the dole* first appears in
print in the 1920s. *Early 20th cent.*

> Ian Rankin *Strip Jack* 1992
> *I know architects my age, guys I went to college
> with, they've been on the dole for the past dozen
> years.*

dollar

it's dollars to buttons/doughnuts
NAmer, informal it is almost certain: based on the
notion of a fanciful uneven bet in which buttons
and doughnuts are practically worthless. *19th
cent.*

See also the sixty-four thousand dollar question *at* SIXTY; you can BET your bottom dollar.

done

a done deal
a deal or plan that has been finalized. *20th cent.*

done for
1 *informal* doomed to disaster or death. In early use *do* is also used in active forms (e.g. Jane Austen, *Sense and Sensibility* (1811) 'Poor Edward! – he has done for himself completely – shut himself out for ever from all decent society!'). The phrase is 19th cent. in this form.
2 *informal* exhausted, worn out. *Early 19th cent.*

> Jane Austen *Persuasion* 1818
> *Are you going as high as Belmont? Are you going near Camden-place? Because if you are, I shall have no scruple in asking you to take my place, and give Anne your arm to her father's door. She is rather done for this morning, and must not go so far without help.*

done in/up
informal exhausted, worn out. *Early 20th cent.*

> John Steinbeck *The Grapes of Wrath* 1939
> *We can't go, folks ... Sairy's done up. She got to res'. She ain't gonna git acrost that desert alive.*

donkey

donkey work
the tedious or most tiring part of an activity or job: based on the image of the donkey as a patient but much abused work animal. *Early 20th cent.*

> National Review 1920
> *Most of the donkey-work of this preposterous League has fallen on British shoulders.*

(for) donkey's years
for a very long time; for longer than one can remember. An early 19th cent. source uses the phrase in the form *donkey's ears*, showing the phrase to be a pun on *ears* and *years*, alluding to the length of a donkey's ears; in its current form the expression is 20th cent.

> Marina Warner *Indigo* 1992
> *He's been in Paris donkey's years but he's still awfully English.*

talk the hind leg(s) off a donkey
British, informal to talk endlessly and often persuasively. In early use the phrase also occurs with *horse* instead of *donkey*, and it is referred to in this form as an 'old vulgar hyperbole' in an early 19th cent. source. A character (Shand) in Trollope's *John Caldigate* (1879) refers in a conversation to an Australian variant of the phrase with *dog* instead of *donkey*: ' "She had been good-looking at one time, Mrs. Caldigate." "I daresay. Most of them are, I suppose." "And clever. She'd talk the hind-legs off a dog, as we used to say out there." "You had very odd sayings, Mr. Shand." ' *19th cent.*

doodah

all of a doodah
excited or agitated: *doodah* is a nonsense word that comes from the refrain of the American minstrel song 'Camptown Races', by Stephen Foster. *Early 20th cent.*

doom

doom and gloom
a feeling of pessimism or dejection, especially about political or financial prospects: also used in the reverse form *gloom and doom*. The phrase dates in various forms from the cold-war period of nuclear anxiety, and gained a special currency from its prominence in the 1947 stage musical *Finian's Rainbow*, in which a leprechaun named Og utters dire warnings by constantly repeating and inverting the phrase. When a film version of the musical was released in 1968 the phrase took on a new lease of life, originally in the US and later in Britain, and became associated with a succession of grim prospects: economic failure in the 1980s, the future of the planet in the 1990s, and the spread of international terrorism in the first years of the 21st cent. *Mid 20th cent.*

doomsday

till doomsday
for ever or indefinitely: literally 'until the day of judgement' (from the early meaning of *doom* meaning 'judgement'). *Middle English*

Shakespeare *The Comedy of Errors* III.ii.100 (1594) [Dromio of Syracuse] *Marry, sir, she's the kitchen wench, and all grease … I warrant her rags and the tallow in them will burn a Poland winter. If she lives till doomsday, she'll burn a week longer than the whole world.*

door

close/shut the door on/to something

to exclude something as a possibility; to refuse to consider it: for the concept of a door as symbol of opportunity *see* open the/a door to something *below*. A *closed door* (19th cent.) is an obstacle to progress, or an inaccessible avenue of opportunity. *16th cent.*

Thomas Gage *A New Survey of the West India's* 1648 *But this doore of hope was fast shut up.*

John Steinbeck *The Pearl* 1947 *And the beauty of the pearl, winking and glimmering in the light of the little candle, cozened his brain with its beauty … Its warm lucence promised a poultice against illness and a wall against insult. It closed a door on hunger.*

door to door

1 (said of a salesperson) calling at every house on a round. The phrase in this meaning goes back to the 17th cent., when a slang glossary defines *haggler* (in the meaning 'itinerant dealer') as 'one that buys of the country-folks, and sells in the market, and goes from door to door'. In the following century, an Act of Parliament of George II (1744) dealing with public order refers among others to 'all persons going from door to door, or placing themselves in streets, etc'. *16th cent.*

Shakespeare *The Comedy of Errors* IV.iv.40 (1594) *Nay, I bear it [beating] on my shoulders, as a beggar wont her brat, and I think when he hath lamed me I shall beg with it from door to door.*

2 (said of a journey, especially in giving distances) from the very starting-point to the completion. *20th cent.*

a foot/toe in the door

an initial gain or established basis from which further progress can be made. To *have* (or *get*) *a foot in the door* is to become involved, often surreptitiously or insidiously, with an organization or enterprise with a view to further development:

in figurative use first recorded in American sources in the late 1930s. *Mid 20th cent.*

The Rock File 1991 *As the top solicitors are highly regarded in the music business, sometimes this can be another way of getting a foot in the door.*

lay something at somebody's door

to regard somebody as responsible or to blame for something. In early use other words, such as *dish*, were used. The reference to *door* may be associated with the practice of leaving an unwanted illegitimate baby on the doorstep of the putative father. *18th cent.*

Oscar Wilde *The Picture of Dorian Gray* 1891 *His meeting with Adrian Singleton had strangely moved him, and he wondered if the ruin of that young life was really to be laid at his door.*

leave the door open

to allow an opportunity to remain. *19th cent.*

John Neal *Errata, or the Works of Will. Adams* 1823 *While you live, therefore, if there be more than one decent daughter in the family, where you are in love, take care to leave the door open, to back out at – till the last moment.*

open the/a door to something

to make an opportunity for something. The concept of a door as a symbol of opportunity goes back to Middle English: *cf* Wyclif's translation of St Paul's First Letter to the Corinthians 16:9 'A greet dore and euident … is openyd to me' (the Authorized Version of 1611 has 'A great door and effectual is opened unto me'). *Middle English*

Thomas Paine *Common Sense* 1776 *Ye that oppose independence now, ye know not what ye do; ye are opening a door to eternal tyranny, by keeping vacant the seat of government.*

show somebody the door

to order somebody to leave a building, or to dismiss them from employment. *18th cent.*

Fanny Burney *Evelina* 1778 *'Hark ye, Madam,' cried the Captain, 'you'd best not call names, because, d'ye see, if you do, I shall make bold to show you the door.'*

Wilkie Collins *The Moonstone* 1868 *His wife died, and two of his three children died, before the tribunals could make up their minds to show him the door and take no more of his money.*

See also at death's door *at* DEATH; DARKEN somebody's door(s).

doornail

See (as) DEAD as a doornail.

doorstep

on/at one's/the doorstep

immediately or conveniently nearby: *doorstep* is used from the early 20th cent. as a modifying word, e.g. *a doorstep campaign. 19th cent.*

> Conan Doyle *The Six Napoleons* 1914
> It's like my luck! You remember when the stand fell at Doncaster? Well, I was the only journalist in the stand, and my journal the only one that had no account of it, for I was too shaken to write it. And now I'll be too late with a murder done on my own doorstep.

dose

in small doses

a little at a time. *19th cent.*

> Mark Twain *A Tramp Abroad* 1880
> It's awful undermining to the intellect, German is; you want to take it in small doses, or first you know your brains all run together.

like a dose of salts

British, informal very rapidly and efficiently. *19th cent.*

See also a dose of one's own MEDICINE.

dot

dot and carry one

the uneven gait of somebody with a lame or wooden leg; also used as a designation for a person affected in this way. It was originally a teacher's instruction to carry over the tens in arithmetic. *19th cent.*

> Kipling *Gunga Din* 1892
> 'E would dot an' carry one | Till the longest day was done | An' 'e didn't seem to know the use o' fear.

dot the i's and cross the t's

to make sure that all details are correct. The phrase is first recorded in the shorter form *dot the i's* (without reference to the *t's*), and there are earlier (16th cent.) references to checking the dots over the letter *i* as an extreme of fastidiousness in reading manuscripts. *19th cent.*

> *Daily Chronicle* 1896
> He dotted our i's and crossed our t's.

on the dot

informal at precisely the right time or at a precise time specified: the dot is the point on a clock face marking the hour. *Early 20th cent.*

> Frederick Forsyth *The Negotiator* 1989
> He strolled up and down for five minutes then, on the dot of ten, dropped the fat envelope through the letter-box of the apartment-house.

the year dot

informal a time that is too early to remember; a very long time ago. A dot conventionally stands for a number that cannot be specified or determined. *19th cent.*

double

at/on the double

very fast or promptly; literally at a fast pace between walking and running. *19th cent.*

> Kipling *The Madness of Private Ortheris* 1888
> Just as the dusk shut down ... we heard wild shouts from the river ... We set off at the double and found him plunging about wildly through the grass.

double or nothing / British quits

betting odds in which a debt is either cancelled or doubled, depending on the outcome. The phrase is 16th cent. in the form *double or quit.*

> Sir Philip Sidney *The Countesse of Pembrokes Arcadia* a1586
> Nowe lastly, finding Philanax his examinations grow daungerous, I thought to play double or quit.

> Maria Edgeworth *Belinda* 1801
> Sir Philip, there are no women to throw golden apples in my way now, and no children for me to stumble over; I dare you to another trial – double or quit.

See also double DUTCH; a double-edged/two-edged sword/weapon *at* EDGE; double WHAMMY.

doubt

a doubting Thomas
somebody who will only believe something if given explicit proof. The reference is to the account in the New Testament (John 20:24–9) of the apostle Thomas who refused to believe in Christ's resurrection until he was given proof of it when Christ appeared before him. Other forms such as *wavering Thomas* have been in use from the 17th cent. *19th cent.*

> Longfellow *Christus* 1872
> *Like doubting Thomas, you shall lay your hand | Upon these wounds, and you will doubt no more.*

dovecote
See FLUTTER the dovecotes.

down

be down on / have a down on somebody
informal to disapprove of somebody: *have a down on* is of Australian origin. *19th cent.*

> Martin Amis *Time's Arrow* 1991
> *I don't see eye to eye with Tod on all issues. Far from it. For instance, Tod's very down on the pimps ... Where would the poor girls be without their pimps, who shower money on them and ask for nothing in return?*

down and out
destitute; having no resources: a metaphor from boxing, in which a person is regarded as having been hit repeatedly by life and finally knocked out (or at least laid on the floor). Also used from the early 20th cent. in an absolute form *down-and-out* to denote a destitute person. *19th cent.*

down in the mouth
sad or dejected: the image is of a person with the ends of the mouth turned downward in an expression of sadness or dejection. *17th cent.*

> Congreve *The Old Batchelour* 1693
> *[Sir Joseph] Now am I slap-dash down in the mouth, and have not one word to say.*

down on one's luck
having a period of bad luck. Thackeray in *Pendennis* (1849) describes the phrase as his character's 'picturesque expression'. *19th cent.*

> Liz Lochhead *True Confessions and New Clichés* 1985
> *Still, I'd be silly | to think I'm safe | because I earn an honest buck. | The streets these days are full of girls | who're right down on their luck.*

down tools
to stop work abruptly, especially as a form of protest. *19th cent.*

have/mark/put/set somebody/something down as something
to judge somebody in a particular way. *18th cent.*

> Jane Austen *Mansfield Park* 1814
> *She cried bitterly over this reflection when her uncle was gone; and her cousins, on seeing her with red eyes, set her down as a hypocrite.*

See also bring somebody down to EARTH; down at HEEL; down to the GROUND.

downgrade

on the downgrade
deteriorating or in decline. The phrase is predominantly North American, but *downgrade* has been used figuratively in British English since the late 19th cent.

downhill

downhill all the way
1 a trouble-free time of it; an easy ride. *Late 20th cent.*

> Audrey Eyton *The Complete F Plan Diet* 1987
> *By the end of the first week's dieting the scales will start to reveal the true story of your excellent rate of weight loss, and from then on it will be downhill all the way to your ideal weight!*

2 a steady decline in one's fortunes or circumstances. *Late 20th cent.*

> Financial Times 1982
> *The present recession has not been as precipitous as some previous downturns, but it has lasted longer. Last year started off on a reasonably firm note, but business soon began to deteriorate. There was a partial recovery in the latter part of the year, but in 1982 it has been downhill all the way, and many facilities are now running at around 60 or 70 per cent of capacity.*

go downhill
to decline or deteriorate: physical descent is here symbolic of moral decline. There is a single late

18th cent. quotation in the *OED* but the evidence begins mainly in the 19th cent.

George Gissing *New Grub Street* 1891
The paper has been going downhill for the last year; I know of two publishing houses who have withdrawn their advertising from it, and who never send their books for review.

Ben Elton *Stark* 1992
Bullens Creek had started off tiny and tedious and gone downhill from there.

downwardly

See upwardly/downwardly MOBILE.

dozen

a baker's dozen

thirteen: perhaps from the former practice of selling thirteen loaves for twelve to prevent accusations of giving short weight. The extra loaf was common enough to have its own name, *in-bread*. An alternative explanation (first attested in the late 19th cent.) is that certain dealers were entitled to receive thirteen loaves for the price of twelve, the thirteenth providing the profit. An expression *thirteen to the dozen*, referring to types of purchase and payment, is found from the 16th cent.; it probably has a bearing on this phrase and the following one. *16th cent.*

John Fletcher *A Woman Pleas'd* 1620
Two thousand Duckets, ile so pepper him, | And with that money ile turne Gentleman, | Worth a browne Bakers dozen of such Silvio's.

talk nineteen to the dozen

to talk incessantly and very rapidly. The notion is of speaking nineteen words in the time normally taken by twelve, and may well be influenced by *thirteen to the dozen* mentioned above. *18th cent.*

Wilkie Collins *The Moonstone* 1868
I sat enjoying the talk between them ... The great Cuff showed a wonderful patience ... with Mrs. Yolland talking nineteen to the dozen, and placing the most entire confidence in him.

drag

drag one's feet/heels

informal, originally NAmer to act in a deliberately slow or dilatory manner: the phrase is relatively recent, but the notion of tiredness or lethargy making a person drag their feet and an animal drag its tail goes back to the 16th cent. *Mid 20th cent.*

drag somebody's name through the mud/dirt

to ruin somebody's reputation comprehensively. *19th cent.*

Thackeray *Vanity Fair* 1848
'Briggs, you are a fool,' said Miss Crawley: 'Colonel Crawley has dragged the name of Crawley through the mud, Miss Briggs. Marry a drawing-master's daughter, indeed!'

David Belasco *La Belle Russe* 1881
Shake her baby faith in me one jot, peril my place in her childish heart by even so much as a word, and I'll drag their proud name through the dirt and mire of every hell of shame in the kingdom. Heaven have mercy on them!

dragon

sow/plant dragon's teeth

to take action that is intended to settle contention but actually has the effect of bringing it about: from the story of Cadmus, the legendary founder of Thebes. Cadmus reached the site by following the guidance of the Delphic Oracle, but when he sent his companions to fetch water they were killed, to a man, by a dragon that was guarding the spring. Cadmus killed the dragon and on Athena's instructions sowed its teeth in the ground. From this spot a crop of armed men sprang up, who first attacked Cadmus himself until he threw stones in their midst to distract them. They then proceeded to slay one another until only five were left – the ancestors of the ancient Thebans. Milton in his speech called *Areopagitica*, published in 1644, refers to the dragon's teeth of Cadmus as a symbol of something 'vigorously productive' but the phrase is not recorded until later. In the Second World War, *dragon's teeth* was an informal name for spiked anti-tank obstacles placed in the ground. *19th cent.*

Nathaniel Hawthorne *The Scarlet Letter* 1850
Pearl, in the dearth of human playmates, was thrown more upon the visionary throng which she created ... She never created a friend, but seemed always to be sowing broadcast the dragon's teeth,

whence sprung a harvest of armed enemies, against whom she rushed to battle.

tickle the dragon / dragon's tail
informal to undertake a dangerous or hazardous venture. *Mid 20th cent.*

See also CHASE the dragon.

drain

go down the drain
informal to be completely wasted or come to nothing: used especially with reference to money or other resources. *Early 20th cent.*

See also LAUGH like a drain.

drama

make a drama out of something
to magnify or exaggerate the importance of a minor difficulty or setback. The phrase was exploited as the basis of an advertising slogan ('We won't make a drama out of a crisis') by the insurance company Commercial Union in the 1990s, intended to assure its clients of a straightforward approach to settling claims. *19th cent.*

> Ernest Jones *The Student of Padua* 1836
> Let Julian make a drama of his life. It may want kings and queens, daggers and swords, battles and bugles, and machinery.

draught

feel the draught
to become insecure, especially financially. *Early 20th cent.*

> Independent 1989
> Some sectors of the market, however, will take longer to recover than others. The high street shops will feel the draught most keenly.

draw

draw somebody's fire
to divert hostility or criticism away from another target towards oneself. Originally used with reference to gunfire, and then in figurative contexts. *19th cent.*

> Thomas Aldrich *Marjorie Daw, and Other People* 1873
> Van Twiller, haunting the theatre with the persistency of an ex-actor, conducted himself so discreetly

as not to draw the fire of Mademoiselle Olympe's blue eyes.

draw the/a line (in the sand)
to establish a distinction or limit: from the physical act of marking a boundary beyond which movement is forbidden. The phrase is 18th cent.: in recent (mid 20th cent.) use the phrase has become extended more graphically to *draw a line in the sand*, suggesting a more spontaneous or ad hoc arrangement.

> Fanny Burney *Cecilia* 1782
> Where, then, do you draw the line? and what is the boundary beyond which your independence must not step?

> Byron *Don Juan* 1824
> Had Buonaparte won at Waterloo, | It had been firmness; now 't is pertinacity: | Must the event decide between the two? | I leave it to your people of sagacity | To draw the line between the false and true, | If such can e'er be drawn by man's capacity.

> Washington Post 1978
> Notwithstanding the supposed public revulsion toward more federal spending, waste and bureaucracy-building, Congress seems to have gone out of its way to draw a wide line in the sand in front of Carter.

draw a line under something
to regard something, especially a difficult period or sequence of events, as over and done with: a common cliché attending an assortment of political embarrassments in the first years of the 21st cent., normally used by those who want to escape from them. The allusion is to ending a piece of writing with a line drawn across the page. *Late 20th cent.*

> Private Eye 2002
> It really is time to stop harping on about these trivialities, and draw a line under them once and for all!

draw stumps
to stop doing something. The phrase is a metaphor from cricket, in which the stumps are pulled out of the ground at the end of play, and is 19th cent. in literal use.

quick on the draw
quick to react or retaliate: from the use of *draw* to mean 'the removal of a gun from its holster', with reference to stories of gunfighters in the American West. *20th cent.*

Ellen Galford *The Dyke & the Dybbuk* 1993
Between mouthfuls our neighbours take it in turns to interrogate Rainbow. But Goldie, quick on the draw, intervenes. She has her own Stamford Hill street credibility to think of.

See also draw a BEAD on; draw a BLANK; draw the short STRAW; draw a VEIL over something; like pulling/drawing TEETH; the LUCK of the draw.

drawer

bottom drawer
a young woman's collection of clothes and household articles, kept in preparation for her marriage. *19th cent.*

Arnold Bennett *Anna of the Five Towns* 1902
The bride took all the house-linen to her husband … As soon as a girl had passed her fifteenth birthday, she began to sew for the 'bottom drawer'.

out of the top drawer
socially superior; from one of the best families: the top drawer of a chest or cupboard was where the best clothes were kept. *Top-drawer* is used as an adjective with the same meaning. *Early 20th cent.*

drawing

back to the drawing board
we have to start again from scratch: used with reference to a plan or idea that has not succeeded and needs to be totally rethought. Derived from the literal meaning of re-drawing plans or blueprints that have not produced good results, the phrase was used in a cartoon by Peter Arno in the *New Yorker* in 1941, which showed an engineer surveying the wreck of a crashed aircraft, with the caption 'Well, back to the old drawing board'. *20th cent.*

Guardian 1989
Electricity privatisation needs to go back to the drawing board.

on the drawing board
(said of an idea or proposal) at the stage of planning or consideration. *20th cent.*

Barry Turner *And the Policeman Smiled* 1991
Essential services like housing and transport were not even on the drawing board.

dream

in your dreams
said about a hope or ambition that is unlikely to be achieved, except in one's dreams: used typically as a resigned comment on a fanciful suggestion or notion. The phrase is found in Internet newsgroup messages from the 1980s. *Late 20th cent.*

like a dream
in a way that proves to be effortlessly effective or successful: especially in the form *work* (or *go down*) *like a dream. Mid 20th cent.*

Jean Bow *Jane's Journey* 1991
The pudding went down like a dream, in blessed silence, and Christopher and Francis disappeared to brew coffee.

one's wildest dreams
the extremes of one's expectations: used to refer to achievements or outcomes in relation to what might seem likely or reasonable. Something is *beyond one's wildest dreams* when it is outstanding against all expectations, and *in one's wildest dreams* is used in negative contexts to refer to something highly improbable or unlikely. *19th cent.*

Scott *Waverley* 1814
Edward thought he had never, even in his wildest dreams, imagined a figure of such exquisite and interesting loveliness.

dress

all dressed up and nowhere to go
fully prepared for something but not needed for it: from an American song by Silvio Hein and Benjamin Burt, 'When You're All Dressed Up and No Place to Go', which featured in the early Broadway musical *The Beauty Shop* (1913). The phrase was used by the American writer William Allen White in 1916 to describe the Progressive Party after Theodore Roosevelt retired from the presidential race, leaving it without an effective candidate. *Early 20th cent.*

give somebody a dressing down
to reprimand somebody. The expression was originally in the form *give somebody a dressing*, and referred to physical as well as verbal onslaughts. It is a figurative use of the word denoting various

special treatments in crafts and manufacturing processes. To *get a dressing down* is to be reprimanded. *18th cent.*

> Barcroft Henry Boake *Featherstonhaugh* 1897
> *'Confound the fellow!' quoth Featherstonhaugh.* |
> *'Will any man of you come with me* | *And give this Bluecap a dressing-down?'*

See also dressed to KILL; dressed to the nines *at* NINE; dressed (up) like a dog's dinner *at* DOG.

drib

dribs and drabs
small scattered or spasmodic amounts. *Drib* is originally a Scottish word based on *dribble*, meaning 'a small amount', and there is also a verb *drib* meaning 'to fall in drops'; *drab* is a dialect word having much the same meaning chiefly in relation to money, but it has had little currency outside the present phrase. *Dribs and drabs*, however, has never been confined to Scottish use. It first appears in writing in a letter of Ellen Weeton, written in 1809 and published in *Journal of a Governess* (1936–9, reprinted 1969): 'Whether it be better to have a little [news] and often, or a great deal and seldom, I leave to your better judgment to determine. … You may have it in *dribs* and *drabs* if you like it better.' *19th cent.*

drift

get the drift
to grasp the essentials of a situation or explanation without necessarily mastering all the details. *Drift* is a figurative use of the word in its sense 'direction of progress'. In early use also in the form *see the drift*. *18th cent.*

> Scott *Guy Mannering* 1815
> *Mr Protocol accordingly, having required silence, began to read the settlement aloud in a slow, steady, business-like tone. The group around, in whose eyes hope alternately awakened and faded, and who were straining their apprehensions to get at the drift of the testator's meaning through the mist of technical language in which the conveyance had involved it, might have made a study for Hogarth.*

drink

drink like a fish
to drink large amounts: now usually in the context of alcoholic liquor. Also (16th cent.) *drink the ocean dry*. *17th cent.*

> William D'Avenant *The Tempest* 1677
> [Stephano] *May I ask your Grace a question? pray is that hectoring* | *Spark, as you call'd him, flesh or fish?* [Trincalo] *Subject I know not, but he drinks like a fish.*

> Harold Frederic *The Damnation of Theron Ware* 1896
> *That poor creature in there is no more drunk than I am. He's been drinking – yes, drinking like a fish; but it wasn't able to make him drunk.*

See also drink the three outs *at* OUT; DRIVE somebody to drink.

drive

drive somebody to drink
to exasperate or infuriate somebody: the notion is of alcoholic drink as their consolation. *19th cent.*

> Kipling *Stalky & Co* 1899
> *'Pon my sacred Sam, though, it's enough to drive a man to drink, having an animal like Hoof for housemaster.*

what — is driving at
what a person intends or means, especially when this is not immediately clear. *19th cent.*

> Mark Twain *The Innocents Abroad* 1869
> *In that Russian town of Yalta I danced an astonishing sort of dance an hour long … with a very pretty girl, and we talked incessantly, and laughed exhaustingly, and neither one ever knew what the other was driving at.*

See also drive a COACH and horses through something; drive a HARD bargain; drive something HOME.

driver

in the driver's/driving seat
in a position of authority or control. *Early 20th cent.*

> Guardian 1989
> *The bill claimed to be 'putting the patient in the driving seat', but it did not even allow patients to be*

consulted if a hospital decided to opt out of regional health authority control.

drop

at the drop of a hat

informal, originally NAmer without hesitation; promptly. The phrase is probably derived from the former practice of signalling the start of a fight or race by lowering the arm holding a hat. 19th cent.

> George Ade Forty Modern Fables 1901
> Every Single Man in Town was ready to Marry her at the Drop of the Hat.

> Richard Dawkins The Selfish Gene 1989
> This ability of DNA to cut and splice, to jump in and out of chromosomes at the drop of a hat, is one of the more exciting facts that have come to light since the first edition of this book was published.

drop one's aitches

to omit the sound of h at the beginning of a word that is spelt with one. 19th cent.

> G B Shaw Man and Superman 1903
> This man takes more trouble to drop his aitches than ever his father did to pick them up. It's a mark of caste to him.

drop a brick

British, informal to let slip an indiscreet or tactless remark. Early 20th cent.

drop a clanger

British, informal to make an obvious and embarrassing mistake: clanger, i.e. an object that makes a loud clang, is used only in this phrase and underlines the conspicuous nature of the mistake. Mid 20th cent.

> Nicholas Freeling Strike Out Where Not Applicable 1967
> I dropped a monstrous clanger, letting anybody see I wasn't happy, but ... I'm still not happy.

drop dead

1 to die suddenly in the course of ordinary activities: often used as an exclamation to express scornful rejection or dismissal. Mid 20th cent.

> John Osborne Look Back in Anger 1957
> [Jimmy] Let's have that paper, stupid! [Cliff] Why don't you drop dead!

2 used in the form drop-dead to intensify a following adjective describing beauty (especially gorgeous), the sense being that the quality is metaphorically powerful enough to kill: there is a similar, if less fatal, image in stunning. Drop Dead Gorgeous was the title of a 1999 American film comedy set in Minnesota about the jealousies and animosities unleashed by a small-town teenage beauty pageant. Late 20th cent.

drop a hint / hints

to provide a casual clue, for example about one's requirements, intentions, or views, or about some matter not yet made public. The phrase dates from the late 18th cent., but drop is used with a similar meaning ('utter casually') from the 17th cent.: cf Amos 7:16 (in the Authorized Version of the Bible, 1611) 'Prophesy not against Israel, and drop not thy word against the house of Isaac.' 18th cent.

> John Cleland Memoirs of a Woman of Pleasure 1748
> When now fir'd, and on edge, he proceeded to drop hints of his design and views upon me.

drop somebody in it

informal to cause somebody trouble or difficulty: it is generally taken to be a euphemistic substitution for the shit. Mid 20th cent.

> Today 1992
> Despite the appalling business of dropping GMTV in it three weeks before they went on the air, it was far better to make a clean break.

a drop in the ocean / a bucket

something too small or insignificant to have any effect. The phrase occurs with bucket from Middle English, being used in Wyclif's translation of Isaiah 40:15: 'Lo! Jentiles as a drope of a boket' (the Authorized Version of 1611 has 'The nations are as a drop of a bucket'). The image of a drop in the sea or ocean appears from the 16th cent. as the basis of metaphor for being lost or isolated, with a notable use in Shakespeare's The Comedy of Errors (1594) I.ii.35: 'I to the world am like a drop of water | That in the ocean seeks another drop.' The phrase in its present form and meaning dates from the 19th cent.

> Charles Reade The Cloister and the Hearth 1861
> And what is our life? One line in the great story of the Church, whose son and daughter we are; one handful in the sand of time, one drop in the ocean of 'For ever'.

drop somebody a line

to send somebody a brief casual note or letter: *line* means 'a line of writing' and sometimes appears in variant forms, e.g. *drop a few lines. 18th cent.*

Dickens *David Copperfield* 1850

So, put me down for whatever you may consider right, will you be so good? and drop me a line where to forward it.

have the drop on somebody

to have an advantage over somebody: originally to be in a position to attack or fire on an opponent. *19th cent.*

William Simms *Mellichampe* 1836

More than once I had the drop on both of 'em, and could easy enough ha' brought down one or t'other with a wink; but there was no fun in it to think of afterward.

See also be off/drop one's GUARD; drop a BOMB-SHELL; drop somebody/something like a HOT potato; drop names *at* NAME; drop the PILOT.

---

drown

drown one's sorrows

to try to forget or get rid of problems or worries by drinking alcohol. *19th cent.*

Anne Brontë *The Tenant of Wildfell Hall* 1848

In his sober moments, he so bothered his friends with his remorse, and his terrors and woes, that they were obliged, in self-defence, to get him to drown his sorrows in wine, or any more potent beverage that came to hand.

Iain Banks *The Crow Road* 1993

I keep trying to drown my sorrows but they appear to be marginally more buoyant than expanded polystyrene.

like a drowned rat

wet and dishevelled, especially from being out in bad weather. The phrase appears occasionally with *mouse* instead of *rat*, and it is entered in this form in John Ray's *Collection of English Proverbs* (1678 edition). *17th cent.*

Thomas Brerewood *Galfred and Juletta* 1771

Poor Oswald, sous'd like drowned rat.

---

drug

a drug on/in the market

a commodity that is no longer in demand and will not sell: *drug* in this meaning dates from the 16th cent., but the connection with the familiar meaning is unclear and this may be a different word. A theatrical farce of 1760 called *The Way to Keep Him*, by the lawyer and playwright Arthur Murphy (1727–1805), refers to a wife as 'a drug now; mere tar water'. In the 19th cent. the form *drug in the market* was common.

Saki *The Chronicles of Clovis* 1912

All his recent ventures had fallen flat, and flattest of all had gone the wonderful new breakfast food, Pipenta ... It could scarcely be called a drug in the market; people bought drugs, but no one bought Pipenta.

---

drum

beat/bang the drum for/of something

to support or promote something with great enthusiasm or vigour. *20th cent.*

Mike Ripley *Angel Touch* 1991

Mothers Against Drunk Driving, that sort of thing, though usually it's the mums of young daughters who beat the drum. The present Chief Constable is very keen on causes like that.

See also MARCH to a different drum.

---

drunk

(as) drunk as a lord/fiddler

extremely drunk. Similes of this kind go back to Chaucer, who in *The Wife of Bath's Prologue* (line 246) makes the first comparison with an animal in the rather unlikely form of a mouse: the Wife of Bath berates a husband with the charge 'Thou comest hoom as dronken as a mous'. Other animals include fish, rats, sows, and skunks. *Drunk as a lord* first occurs in 17th cent. glossaries, as do *beggar* and *fiddler*. Congreve used *drunk as a fish* in 1700 (see below). More curious is *drunk as a wheelbarrow* (also 17th cent.), which presumably refers to the erratic course wheelbarrows tend to follow however firmly one tries to guide them. Meanwhile some comfort can be derived from proverbs such as *better drunk than drowned*. *17th cent.*

Congreve *The Way of the World* 1700
Why dost thou not speak? Thou art both as drunk and as mute as a fish.

---

dry

(as) dry as dust

extremely dry or uninteresting: often used in the form *dry-as-dust* as a modifying word. *Dryasdust*, with allusion to this phrase, is the name of an imaginary dedicatee of *Ivanhoe* and other works by Sir Walter Scott, and has been used allusively to denote a dull antiquarian or historian. *16th cent.*

Anon *The Faire Maide of Bristow* 1605
The poore deiected Vallenger was heere, | As dry as dust not left a single doyt [= a small Dutch coin].

William James *Varieties of Religious Experience* 1902
How was it ever conceivable ... that a man like Christian Wolff, in whose dry-as-dust head all the learning of the early eighteenth century was concentrated, should have preserved such a baby-like faith in the personal and human character of Nature as to expound her operations as he did in his work on the uses of natural things?

not a dry eye (in the house)

used with reference to an emotionally affecting or sentimental speech, play, film, etc, which has (or might well have) moved everybody watching it to tears. Possibly with allusion to the Scott use below, which appears to be one of the earliest occurrences of the phrase, although in a more literal sense of 'house', which might later have been misunderstood or modified. *19th cent.*

Scott *Waverley* 1814
She ... visited all the places where she had been with my grand-uncle, and caused the carpets to be raised that she might trace the impression of his blood; and if tears could have washed it out, it had not been there now, for there was not a dry eye in the house.

---

duck

duck and dive

to avoid difficulties or criticism by ingenious tactics. *20th cent.*

M Cole *Dangerous Lady* 1992
She was all for a bit of ducking and diving, that's how everyone lived in her estimation.

fine weather for ducks

informal used as a humorous reference to wet weather. *20th cent.*

a lame duck

a person or organization that is weak or incapable: originally used in the context of dealings on the Stock Exchange, where it was applied to defaulters who were unable to meet their financial obligations. More recently, in US politics, the term denotes a president or other official who is unable to stand for re-election, especially during the last months of office before a successor takes over (although the validity of the concept was somewhat undermined in 2000 by the eventful final weeks of the Clinton administration set against the background of the virtually tied election for his successor). *18th cent.*

Richard Cumberland *The Fashionable Lover* 1772
[Colin] *Hold, hold, friend Napthali; you and I munna part; you must keep pace wi' me to Maister Mortimer's.* [Napthali] *To Mr. Mortimer's? Impossible: why I must be at Bank, Sir, I must be at Jonathan's: I've forty bargains to settle. I shall have half the Coffee-house on my back: Wou'd you make me a lame duck?*

(like) a dying duck in thunder / a thunderstorm

looking distressed or forlorn. *18th cent.*

(like) water off a duck's back

easily resisted or ignored: used especially of a criticism or rebuke that fails to impress. *19th cent.*

Trollope *The Prime Minister* 1876
He had often told himself that it was beneath his manliness to be despondent; that he should let such a trouble run from him like water from a duck's back, consoling himself with the reflection that if the girl had such bad taste she could hardly be worthy of him.

play ducks and drakes (with something)

to use money or other resources recklessly: from the game of *duck and drake* (now usually *ducks and drakes*) which involved skimming a stone over the surface of water to make it skip as many times as possible. The game is first recorded in the late 16th cent., and the figurative use of its name from the early 17th cent.

Richard Brome *The Damoiselle* 1653
Let him throw money into the Thames, make ducks and drakes with pieces, Ile do the like.

Wilkie Collins *The Moonstone* 1868
My way in this world had not led me into playing ducks and drakes with my own life, among thieves and murderers in the outlandish places of the earth.

take to something like a duck to water
to take up a new activity with ease. *19th cent.*

Mrs Humphry Ward *Robert Elsmere* 1888
'Do you know,' she went on wistfully, raising her beautiful eyes to her companion, 'after all, he gave me my first violin?' Langham smiled. 'I like that little inconsequence,' he said. 'Then of course I took to it, like a duck to water, and it began to scare him that I loved it so much.'

See also be a sitting duck *at* SIT.

duckling

See an UGLY duckling.

dudgeon

in high dudgeon
in a state of great indignation or resentment. *Dudgeon* is recorded only in the phrase (or variants of it) and is of obscure origin: in its current spelling it is identical in form with an obsolete (14th cent.) word for a kind of wood used to make handles for knives and daggers, but no historical connection has been established with the word used here, which dates from the 16th cent.

Smollett *The Adventures of Peregrine Pickle* 1751
He retired in high dudgeon, threatening to relinquish their society, and branding them with the appellation of apostates from the common cause.

duff

up the duff
British and Australian, *informal* pregnant. The phrase is probably connected with the (19th cent.) word meaning 'pudding' or 'dumpling', and so sharing the imagery of phrases such as *have a bun in the oven* and *in the pudding club*: see BUN and CLUB. *20th cent.*

dull

(as) dull as ditchwater/dishwater
extremely dull or uninteresting: with reference to the stale or dirty water that collects in a ditch. It is

used almost entirely as an element in similes: use with *dull* dates from the 19th cent. but earlier somewhat counter-intuitive comparisons are *digne* (= worthy) *as ditchwater* and *light* (= easy) *as ditchwater*. *Dishwater*, the equally dull-looking water in which dishes have been washed, is occasionally used by substitution; in rapid speech the two words can be indistinguishable. *18th cent.*

See also dull the EDGE of; never a dull MOMENT.

dummy

sell somebody a/the dummy
to deceive an opponent in a sport or game by pretending to pass the ball or appearing to make a move: hence also in figurative contexts. *Early 20th cent.*

dumps

(down) in the dumps
in a gloomy state of mind; despondent. The phrase is first recorded with *down* in Grose's *Dictionary of the Vulgar Tongue* (1785), but *dumps* occurs in this meaning from the 16th cent. (e.g. Shakespeare, *The Taming of the Shrew* (1592) II.i.279 'Why, how now, daughter Katherine – in your dumps?'). *Dumps* is the plural form of *dump* meaning 'a dazed or puzzled state'. Among the more absurd (and unnecessary) 19th cent. explanations (and there are many) is that *dumps* is derived from *Dumops*, the name of a king of Egypt who built a pyramid and then died of melancholy. *16th cent.*

Dickens *Hard Times* 1854
What's the matter? What is young Thomas in the dumps about?

duration

for the duration
for as long as an enterprise or ordeal lasts: typically referring to a war. *Duration* in this sense was first used in the context of the First World War (1914–18), when recruits were officially enlisted 'for four years or the duration of the war'. In 1916, the satirical magazine *Punch* referred flippantly to a lengthy task as likely to take 'three years, or the duration of the war'. The present phrase first appears in general use in

Fraser and Gibbons' *Soldier and Sailor Words* (1925), and it has been widely used in literature set at the time of the Second World War (1939–45). More recently, it has come to mean any lengthy or indeterminate period of time. *Early 20th cent.*

dust

gather/collect dust
to lie unused for a long time. *17th cent.*

> James Shirley *The Dukes Mistris* 1638
> *Every where, | Yet no where to any purpose, we are out | Of use, and like our Engines are laid by | To gather dust.*

not see somebody for dust
to discover that somebody has left abruptly. *20th cent.*

> Julian Barnes *Talking it Over* 1992
> *First ferry and then you won't see us for dust.*

raise / kick up a dust
to cause a disturbance. *17th cent.*

> Berkeley *A Treatise Concerning the Principles of Human Knowledge* 1710
> *Upon the whole, I am inclined to think that the far greater part, if not all, of those difficulties which have hitherto amused philosophers, and blocked up the way to knowledge, are entirely owing to ourselves – that we have first raised a dust and then complain we cannot see.*

shake the dust off one's feet
to leave a place with contempt or disdain: with allusion to Christ's words to his disciples in Matthew 10:14 (in the Authorized Version, 1611) 'And whosoever shall not receive you, nor hear your words, when ye depart out of that house or city, shake off the dust of your feet.' *Middle English* (in Wyclif)

> Stephen Gosson *Playes Confuted in Five Actions* 1582
> *Finding the eares of their hearers stopte with the deafe adder, they beginne to shake the dust fro their shooes against them, and followe the counsell of God him selfe, which biddeth them throwe no pearles to swine.*

throw/cast dust in somebody's eyes
to deceive or mislead somebody by distracting them: the notion is of making an opponent temporarily unable to see: according to Randle Cotgrave's French and English Dictionary (published in 1611, about the time the phrase came into use), the reference is to the leader in a race, 'who to make his fellows aloofe, casteth dust with his heels into their envious eyes'. *17th cent.*

> Colman & Garrick *The Clandestine Marriage* 1766
> [Flower] *Why, my Lord Chief does not go the circuit this time, and my brother Puzzle being in the commission, the cause will come on before him.*
> [Trueman] *Ay, that may do, indeed, if you can but throw dust in the eyes of the defendant's council.*

> W S Gilbert *Iolanthe* 1882
> *I'll never throw dust in a juryman's eyes … Or hoodwink a judge who is not over-wise.*

when the dust settles
when affairs return to normal after a period of change or disturbance. *20th cent.*

> *Independent* 1989
> *As the dust settles on the surprising, but widely approved decision to appoint Claudio Abbado chief conductor of the Berlin Philharmonic Orchestra to replace Karajan, a new round of speculation is about to begin.*

See also (as) DRY as dust; BITE the dust; KISS the dust; turn to (dust and) ashes *at* ASH.

dusty

a dusty answer
an unhelpful or brusque reply: the locus classicus is George Meredith's narrative poem of disillusionment entitled *Modern Love* (1862): 'Ah, what a dusty answer gets the soul | When hot for certainties in this our life!' It is the title of the first novel of Rosamond Lehmann, published in 1927, about a young woman's first emotional involvement. This sense of *dusty*, 'dull or uninteresting', dates from the early 17th cent. and is related to corresponding uses of *dust*, as in *dry as dust*. *19th cent.*

Dutch

The word now used with reference to the Netherlands and their people was formerly used more generally of all people of Germanic stock, and is related to the German word *Deutsch*. It appears in a number of phrases, mostly with derogatory implications; these unfavourable associations may have their origin in the hostility between England and the Dutch during the 17th cent. (see under *Dutch courage* below), although most of the phrases first occur somewhat later and some of them originate in North American use, and the precise underlying notion in the choice of *Dutch* is not always clear.

beat the Dutch
informal, chiefly NAmer to say something remarkable. A variant *beat the Jews* is also used, and both associations are presumably based on stereotypes of garrulity. *18th cent.*

Catharine Sedgwick The Poor Rich Man and the Rich Poor Man 1836
'Yes, so do, Lottie,' said Susan; 'I want to see if my iron is hot.' 'That beats the Dutch,' said Uncle Phil; 'if I had twenty irons in the fire I should let them burn to hear news from Harry.'

do the Dutch (act)
to run away or commit suicide. *Early 20th cent.*

double Dutch
incomprehensible talk. Dutch is a language few people outside the Netherlands can speak. In the 18th cent. the phrase was *High Dutch*. The expression is 19th cent. in this form.

Hardy Jude the Obscure 1896
Then Jude seemed to shake the fumes from his brain, as he stared round upon them. 'You pack of fools!' he cried. 'Which one of you knows whether I have said it or no? It might have been the Ratcatcher's Daughter in double Dutch for all that your besotted heads can tell!'

a Dutch auction
an auction that operates on the basis of decreasing instead of increasing bids: the price starts at a high level and is reduced in stages if no bids are received. *19th cent.*

James Payn By Proxy 1878
Upon this there commenced a Dutch auction of the works in question; Mr. Wardlaw or his wife proposing some preposterous bid, and Nelly insisting on a much smaller and more reasonable figure.

Dutch courage
courage or confidence brought about by drinking alcohol: based on the traditional belief that the Dutch are heavy drinkers. The politician and poet Edmund Waller (1606–87), writing in 1666 about the naval battle of Sole Bay fought between

the English and Dutch the previous year, refers obliquely to this association, confirming its currency at this time: 'The Dutch their wine, and all their brandy lose, | Disarmed of that from which their courage grows.' *19th cent.*

Scott Heart of Midlothian 1818
When a woman wants mischief from you, she always begins by filling you drunk. D—n all Dutch courage. What I do I will do soberly – I'll last the longer for that too.

a Dutch uncle
somebody who criticizes or advises sternly or frankly but kind-heartedly. A contributor to *Notes & Queries* in January 1853 (p.65) noted: 'In some parts of America, when a person has determined to give another a regular lecture, he will often be heard to say, "I will talk to him like a Dutch uncle"; that is, he shall not escape this time.' The expression is perhaps based on the proverbial self-discipline of the Dutch; an alternative suggestion that *Dutch* simply denotes the lack of a blood relationship is not supported by other usage of the word. *19th cent.*

Joseph Neal Charcoal Sketches 1838
'Young people,' interposed a passing official, 'if you keep a cutting didoes, I must talk to you both like a Dutch uncle. Each of you must disperse; I can't allow no insurrection about the premises.'

go Dutch
to pay for oneself as one of a group that incurs a collective expense; to divide the costs equally. Hence a *Dutch treat* is one paid for in this way. *Early 20th cent.*

in Dutch
informal, chiefly NAmer in trouble or disgrace. *Early 20th cent.*

Christopher Morley The Haunted Bookshop 1919
If I don't do anything, something may happen to the girl; if I butt in too soon I'll get in dutch with her.

Dutchman

(or) I'm a Dutchman
used to assert one's conviction (or lack of it) in a preceding statement. *19th cent.*

Dickens Pickwick Papers 1837
'And if he ain't got enough … to make him free of the water company for life,' said Mr. Weller, in

conclusion, 'I'm one Dutchman, and you're another, and that's all about it.'

duty

(in) duty bound

required by one's sense of duty. *18th cent.*

> Smollett *The Expedition of Humphry Clinker* 1771
> *Your insolence to me (said Eastgate) I should have bore with patience, had not you cast the most infamous reflection upon my order, the honour of which I think myself in duty bound to maintain, even at the expence of my heart's blood.*

> Nigel Williams *The Wimbledon Poisoner* 1990
> *But of course, once Mrs Farr Senior had expressed doubts about a woman, it meant Henry was almost duty bound to marry her.*

dye

dyed in the wool

(said of a person, attitudes, etc) thoroughgoing and uncompromising: from the practice of dyeing wool before spinning, in order to give the yarn a more permanent colour. *19th cent.*

> Nathaniel Hawthorne *The Scarlet Letter* 1850
> *He might truly be termed a legitimate son of the revenue system, dyed in the wool, or, rather, born in the purple; since his sire, a Revolutionary colonel, and formerly collector of the port, had created an office for him, and appointed him to fill it.*

dying

See be dying to do something *at* DIE[1]; to one's dying day *at* DIE[1].

eager

an eager beaver

somebody who is unduly zealous in performing obligations or duties and in volunteering for more. What is 'eager' about a beaver? The word is partly chosen for its convenience of sound, but presumably also reflects the animal's fabled industriousness. *Mid 20th cent.*

> Maureen Lipman *Thank You for Having Me* 1990
> *We queued up for our boots, our poles, our skis and met our instructor, Hans, and the rest of the eager beavers in our party.*

ear

The ears are symbolic of listening and attention in many of the phrases, and in others (by a kind of metonymy) represent the individual, rather in the way that *head* also does.

be all ears

to listen closely and with a strong interest in what is being said. In early use the phrase also has the form *all ear. 18th cent.*

> Samuel Low *The Politician Out-witted* 1788
> *Come, Thomas, let's have it. – I'm all ears to hear you.*

> Frederick Douglass *My Bondage and My Freedom* 1855
> *I was all ears, all eyes, whenever the words slave, slavery, dropped from the lips of any white person.*

bring something / collapse about/around one's ears

to cause or suffer great misfortune. *About one's ears* has been a metaphor for disaster from the 17th cent.

> Defoe *Reformation of Manners* 1702
> *Nor let them call him Coward, 'cause he fears | To pull both God and Man about his Ears.*

Byron *Don Juan* 1823
*I have brought this world about my ears, and eke |
The other; that's to say, the clergy – who | Upon my
head have bid their thunders break.*

New Scientist 1991
*Fibre-optic communications, push-button tele-
phones and microcomputers won't stop the country
from literally collapsing around our ears.*

one's ears are burning

one is conscious that one is being talked about.
17th cent.

'W.S.' 1607
*I warrant my Kinsman's talking of me, for my left
eare burnes most tyrannically.*

Beryl Bainbridge *An Awfully Big Adventure* 1990
*'What a lovely thing to do,' he remarked and,
appalled at his patronising tone, told her that her
ears should have been burning on Christmas Day.*

give ear to somebody/something

to listen to somebody or something. The use of *ear*
as symbolic of listening dates from the early 16th
cent. In biblical use (also reflected in the Marlowe
quotation below), the notion is of obeying rather
than simply listening. *16th cent.*

Marlowe *Dr Faustus* xiv.46 (1590)
*The Devil threatened to tear me in pieces if I named
God, to fetch both body and soul if I once gave ear to
divinity.*

give one's ears

to be willing to make any sacrifice to achieve
something. *19th cent.*

Kenneth Grahame *The Wind in the Willows* 1903
*'There's a banquet for you!' observed the Rat, as he
arranged the table. 'I know some animals who
would give their ears to be sitting down to supper
with us to-night!'*

go in (at) one ear and out (at) the other

(said of utterances) to make little impression on a
hearer; to be ignored or quickly forgotten. *16th
cent.*

Arthur Golding *The Sermons of Calvin* 1583
*[A sermon] goes in at the one eare and out at the
other.*

Henry James *Daisy Miller* 1878
*'Well; I hope you know enough!' she said to her
companion, after he had told her the history of the
unhappy Bonnivard. 'I never saw a man that knew*

*so much!' The history of Bonnivard had evidently,
as they say, gone into one ear and out of the other.*

have something coming out of one's ears

to have more of something than one can manage.
20th cent.

Climber and Hill Walker 1991
*This must be the first year when new rock boot
models haven't been coming out of everyone's ears.*

have/gain/win somebody's ear

to have personal access to somebody. *17th cent.*

Milton *L'Allegro* 1639
*That Orpheus self may heave his head | From
golden slumber on a bed | Of heapt Elysian flowres,
and hear | Such streins as would have won the ear |
Of Pluto, to have quite set free | His half regain'd
Eurydice.*

keep an ear / one's ears to the ground

to keep oneself well informed about events that
concern one. The phrase developed from the
practice of literally putting the ears to the ground
to listen for the rumble of horses' hooves and
other sounds in the distance, especially by track-
ers in the American West. It has been frequently
susceptible to cases of (deliberately) absurd
mixed metaphor, as when the Archdeacon of
York George Austin described Robert Runcie,
the former Archbishop of Canterbury, as a
ditherer given to 'sitting on the fence with both
ears nailed to the ground' (as quoted in the *Independent* on 9 September 1996). *19th cent.*

J C Cross *Halloween* 1809
*Hush! hush! be mum! lay your ears to the ground, |
And hark to the Traveller's tread.*

John Dearlove et al *Introduction to British Politics* 1988
*The other party forms the opposition; criticises the
government; keeps its ear to the ground of public
opinion; and stands ready to form a government
should it win the next election.*

listen with half an ear

to give somebody only part of one's attention.
19th cent.

John Anster transl Goethe's *Faust* 1864
*The tune, to which the Stars keep time, you hear, |
You'll catch my whispers with but half an ear.*

make a pig's ear of something

to bungle a task, piece of work, etc. *Mid 20th cent.*

Alice T Ellis *The Clothes in the Wardrobe* 1989
She had enclosed patterns and detailed instructions, and while she hoped, for the sake of appearance at the wedding, that the children's clothes would be properly cut and fitted, she also hoped that between them Cynthia and her dressmaker would have made a pig's ear of the business.

out on one's ear
thrown out of one's home or job with no possibility of returning. *Mid 20th cent.*

Michael Dibdin *Dirty Tricks* 1991
If Clive caught me entertaining a lady friend in the classroom, I would be out on my ear in no time at all.

play it by ear
to use one's instincts and adapt to circumstances in a course of action: from the literal meaning of playing music without using a written score. *Ear* here is used by metonymy for the faculty of hearing and interpreting. *Mid 20th cent.*

up to one's ears in something
informal busily occupied with a task or activity: *see also* up to one's eyes/eyeballs in something *at* EYE. The phrase is 19th cent. in this form; the form *over head and ears* is recorded from the 17th cent.

Edgar Allan Poe *X-ing the Paragrab* 1849
'We must get to press,' said the foreman, who was over head and ears in work.

See also fall on DEAF ears; LEND an ear; make a SILK purse out of a sow's ear; more to something than meets the eye/ear *at* MEET; MUSIC to one's ears; PRICK up one's ears; turn a DEAF ear; WET behind the ears; a word in your shell-like ear *at* SHELL.

early

be an early bird
to rise early in the morning and start one's activities. Used with allusion to the (17th cent.) proverb *the early bird gets the worm*: cf Milton, *Paradise Lost* (1667) iv.642 'Sweet is the breath of morn, her rising sweet, | With charm of earliest Birds.' The phrase is 19th cent. in its allusive form.

Thackeray *The Newcomes* 1854
'You are an early bird,' says Kew. 'I got up myself in a panic before daylight almost, Jack was making a deuce of a row in his room, and fit to blow the door out.'

R L Stevenson *Treasure Island* 1883
Bright and early, to be sure; and it's the early bird, as the saying goes, that gets the rations.

it's / these are early days
it is too soon to be sure of an outcome or expect a result. *16th cent.*

Shakespeare *Troilus and Cressida* iv.iv.180 (1602)
[Ulysses] *No trumpet answers.* [Achilles] *'Tis but early days.*

take an early bath/shower
in sport (originally baseball), to be sent off the field, typically for committing a foul or major infringement: from the bath or shower that players take in the dressing rooms after a game. Also with reference to death and in other humorous figurative uses. *Early 20th cent.*

The New York Times 1929
The Phils bunched three singles for a run in their first inning, then in the second they forged ahead in an outburst which promised Hubbell an early shower.

The Times 1985
Curiosity is a virtue. Boredom is one of the seven deadly sins, in the form of accidie being punished by an early bath in the muddy Styx. We are here for such a short time that we might as well take an interest in everything.

Daily Mirror 1992
He was all set to take an early bath from his marriage to have an affair with soccer writer Suzannah Dwyer.

earn

earn/be worth one's keep
to give a good return on the resources spent on one. *19th cent.*

G B Shaw *Pygmalion* 1915
Regarded in the light of a young woman, she's a fine handsome girl. As a daughter she's not worth her keep; and so I tell you straight.

earner

a nice little earner
British, informal a profitable undertaking, especially one that is not strenuous or demanding. The phrase became familiar in the 1980s from the British television series *Minder*, where it was

much used by the shady dealer Arthur Daley (played by George Cole). *Late 20th cent.*

Economist 1993
At least 400 people have climbed Everest and dozens more are ready with their oxygen tanks. Looking after them is a nice little earner for Nepal, the preferred base.

earth

bring somebody / come back (down) to earth (with a bump/bang)
to make somebody realize, or realize oneself, the realities of a situation after a period of fanciful imagining. *Down to earth* is a common way of describing a person who is practical and realistic in daily life. *19th cent.*

Henry James The American 1877
You seem far away indeed – but you're not in heaven quite yet! Even if you were, however, I should ask you to come down to earth, a moment, to give me a reason, a decent reason, the faintest blush of a reason!

P G Wodehouse Very Good, Jeeves! 1930
I had for some little time been living, as it were, in another world. I now came down to earth with a bang.

cost/charge/pay the earth
to cost, charge, or pay a very large sum of money. *Early 20th cent.*

Susannah James Love Over Gold 1993
Seems ridiculous, really, but I think I've got chicken-pox … What else can it be when you're covered from head to toe in foul little pustules? … And when I think that I paid the earth three days ago to have a facial at that new salon in Sloane Street.

did the earth move for you?
did something wonderful happen to you? The phrase originates in Ernest Hemingway's *For Whom the Bell Tolls* (1940): 'He said, "Maria … I feel as though I wanted to die when I am loving thee." "Oh," she said. "I die each time. Do you not die?" "No. Almost. But did thee feel the earth move?" "Yes. As I died. Put thy arm around me, please."' The context here is a sexual orgasm, and the phrase is typically used with this implication. *Mid 20th cent.*

New Statesman and Society 1992
On one of her adventures, she was in Tokyo having sex with a local man in her flat when a friend rang up asking, 'Did you feel the earth move?'

go to earth
to go into hiding; to disappear. *Early 20th cent.*

Punch 1913
Men who used to go to earth behind evening papers on the entrance of a woman now spring to their feet in platoons without a moment's hesitation.

like nothing on (God's) earth
very strange or unusual. *Early 20th cent.*

Ellen Galford The Dyke & the Dybbuk 1993
Aunt Molly is dressed in an overstuffed pouch of white feathers, with yellow leggings, plastic claws tied around each high-heeled slipper, and a red coxcomb wobbling on her head … Minna purses her lips. 'This, Molly,' she declares, 'is the absolute limit. You look like nothing on God's earth.'

See also the ends of the earth at END; the four/far corners of the world/earth at CORNER; PROMISE the moon/earth; RUN somebody/something to earth.

earthly

not stand an earthly (chance)
British, informal to have no chance at all of success. *Earthly* as an intensifying word dates from the mid 18th cent. The phrase is mid 20th cent. in this form.

Fay Weldon Darcy's Utopia 1991
My falling in love with Julian was nothing to do with me, nothing to do with Julian, but part of the curse put on Bernard that his wife would become the love object of a man more attractive, more wealthy, more intelligent and of a higher status than he, so he didn't stand an earthly.

easy

(as) easy as falling off a log / as pie
informal extremely easy. The image of falling off a log is fairly transparent, and *pie* is based on the (19th cent.) meaning 'something easily achieved'. The phrase is 19th cent. with *log* and early 20th cent. with *pie*.

Ambrose Bierce *The Fiend's Delight* 1873
Gratitude is considerably easier, and vastly more agreeable, than falling off a log, and may be acquired in one easy lesson without a master.

Joseph Conrad *Lord Jim* 1900
It's as easy as falling off a log. Simply nothing to do; two six-shooters in his belt.

Gardener's World 1991
Apple growing made as easy as pie.

Michael Falk *Part of the Furniture* 1991
'It's going to be all right now,' I told her. 'It's going to be all right.' She patted me on the back. 'Easy as pie, wasn't it?' she said. 'Yes, in the end.'

come easy to somebody
(said of a skill or ability) to hold no problems for somebody. *19th cent.*

Harold Frederic *The Damnation of Theron Ware* 1896
It used to come easy to me to be cheerful and resolute and all that; but it's different now.

easy come, easy go
(proverb) money or other acquisitions tend to be used more freely if they have been obtained without any great trouble. The sentiment goes back to the 17th cent. and has parallels from early 15th cent. French. The phrase is 19th cent. in this form.

Harper Lee *To Kill a Mockingbird* 1960
Funny thing, Atticus Finch might've got him off scot free, but wait –? Hell no. You know how they are. Easy come, easy go.

easy does it
informal used as an encouragement to calm down and avoid overreaction. *19th cent.*

Joseph Conrad *Lord Jim* 1900
There's a gentleman wants to get ashore. Up with you, sir. Nearly got carried off to Talcahuano, didn't you? Now's your time; easy does it.

easy on the eye/ear
pleasant to look at or listen to. The expression is mid 20th cent. in this form.

CD Review 1992
The music of The Wizard of Oz is, of course, more familiar to most people, and it's performed well here … my only real grouch was that the children's chorus was far less easy on the ear than that used in Oliver.

go easy on/with somebody
1 to deal leniently with somebody. *19th cent.*
2 to use something economically or indulge in it sparingly. *Mid 20th cent.*

John Steinbeck *The Grapes of Wrath* 1939
Go easy on that there water … That's all there is. This here well's filled in.

have it easy
to enjoy comfortable circumstances. *19th cent.*

Horace Lane *Five Years in State's Prison* 1835
The old saying is, 'one's meat is the other's poison,' but here it is reversed, for the poor old man's poison was my meat, for I had it easy the rest of my imprisonment.

The Face 1992
This generation has it pretty tough. Older people had it easy: they didn't have a problem with sex, they didn't have to wear rubbers so you won't die.

of easy virtue
(said of a woman) sexually promiscuous. The underlying meaning of *easy* is 'compliant, accommodating'. Cf Shakespeare, *Cymbeline* (1610) II.iv.47: '[Posthumus] The stone's too hard to come by. [Giacomo] Not a whit, | Your lady being so easy.' *18th cent.*

Boswell *The Life of Samuel Johnson* 1792
I have often amused myself with thinking how different a place London is to different people … A politician thinks of it merely as the seat of government in its different departments … a dramatick enthusiast, as the grand scene of theatrical entertainments; a man of pleasure, as an assemblage of taverns, and the great emporium for ladies of easy virtue.

take the easy way out
to choose a course of action that saves trouble or expense, while avoiding a better alternative that is more demanding or inconvenient. *Late 20th cent.*

Barry Turner *And the Policeman Smiled* 1991
Deportation was also an option for shifting a problem to another authority. The temptation to take the easy way out was well-nigh irresistible with youngsters who had failed to make their way … who showed their resentment.

take it easy
to relax or remain calm. *19th cent.*

James Joyce *A Portrait of the Artist as a Young Man*
1916
He walked on before them with short nervous steps,
smiling. They tried to keep up with him, smiling
also at his eagerness. – Take it easy like a good
young fellow, said his father. We're not out for the
half mile, are we?

See also (as) easy as ABC; (as) easy as winking *at*
WINK; easier said than done *at* SAY; easy MEAT.

eat

eat somebody alive
to defeat somebody or treat them humiliatingly;
to give somebody a rough time. *19th cent.*

Wilkie Collins *The Moonstone* 1868
'If you wish to inquire for my lady's nephew, you
will please mention him as Mr. Franklin Blake.' She
limped a step nearer to me, and looked as if she could
have eaten me alive. 'Mr. Franklin Blake?' she
repeated after me. 'Murderer Franklin Blake would
be a fitter name for him.'

Betty Rowlands *Finishing Touch* 1991
Here comes your friend. I'd better let her take you
home or she'll eat me alive and spit out the bones.

eat out of somebody's hand
to be under somebody's control, to do everything
they ask: with reference to animals willing to feed
from a human's hand. *Early 20th cent.*

The Face 1990
But the power he's got is scary ... He's got young
black America eating out of his hand, because every
night he takes their culture, and shoves it in
mainstream America's face.

See also eat CROW; eat DIRT; eat one's HAT; eat
one's HEART out; eat HUMBLE pie; eat like a
HORSE; eat SALT with —; eat one's words *at*
WORD; have one's CAKE and eat it; HOUSE and
home.

ebb

at a low ebb
at a low point; in a poor state. The phrase is used
by Shakespeare in a figurative context (*a low ebb of*
linen) in a complicated passage forming part of an
exchange between Prince Harry and Poins in
2 Henry IV (1597) II.i.20, and again in the form
at ebb as one of several sea metaphors in *The*
Tempest (1613) I.ii.438, where Ferdinand tells

Prospero 'Myself am Naples [i.e. have become
King of Naples, as he supposes], | Who with
mine eyes, never since at ebb, beheld | The King
my father wrecked.' *16th cent.*

Thomas Paine *The Rights of Man* 1792
If government be what Mr. Burke describes it, 'a
contrivance of human wisdom' I might ask him, if
wisdom was at such a low ebb in England, that it
was become necessary to import it from Holland
and from Hanover?

ebb and flow
a regular pattern of movement or change, especially in economic fortunes: a metaphor based on
the image of the changing tides. *Ebb* is used figuratively in this way from the 15th cent., and the
phrase dates from the 18th cent. in this form.

echo

applaud/cheer somebody to the echo
to praise somebody enthusiastically. Shakespeare (*Macbeth* v.iii.55) has Macbeth say to the
doctor about Lady Macbeth: 'If thou couldst,
doctor, cast | The water of my land, find her
disease, | And purge it to a sound and pristine
health, | I would applaud thee to the very echo.'
17th cent.

Dickens *The Old Curiosity Shop* 1841
The performance was applauded to the echo.

Belfast Festival 1991
Demidenko himself loves to speak of that memorable
occasion, and its importance for him. Thanks are
due to our audience at that concert – they imme-
diately recognised that this was a new star, and
applauded him to the echo.

eclipse

in eclipse
in a state of obscurity or decline, especially after
being important or prominent. *Eclipse* is used
figuratively with this meaning from the 16th
cent., and the phrase is recorded in the 17th
cent. in the form *in an* (or *my*, etc) *eclipse*.

Richard Braithwait *Panthalia* 1659
Look upon me, I beseech you, not with so con-
temptible an eye; as if I were wholly in my eclipse; or
totally declining.

Phillip E Johnson *Darwin on Trial* 1991
Cuvier's reputation is in eclipse today, but in his time he was known as the Aristotle of biology, the virtual founder of the modern sciences of anatomy and paleontology.

economical

be economical with the truth
to say only what is strictly necessary, especially in answering questions; to be evasive or not completely frank or truthful. In this form the phrase is associated with the 'Spycatcher' trial in New South Wales, Australia in 1986, in which the British government tried to prevent publication of a book by a former employee of MI5. Giving evidence at the trial, Sir Robert Armstrong, then Cabinet Secretary and head of the British Civil Service, referred to a letter cited as evidence in the following terms: 'It contains a misleading impression, not a lie. It was being economical with the truth.' The phrase became popular with the press and was taken up in other contexts; most notably, the junior minister Alan Clark adapted it in giving evidence at the Matrix Churchill trial, when he referred to 'our old friend economical with the actualité'. In earlier centuries, the notion of being sparing or careful with the truth was proposed in a more positive spirit by the statesman and political philosopher Edmund Burke (1729–97), who referred to 'economy of truth, … a sort of temperance, by which a man speaks truth with reason that he may continue to speak it the longer', while Mark Twain (in *Following the Equator*, 1897), wrote that 'Truth is the most valuable thing we have. Let us economize it.' *Late 20th cent.*

Wendy Thompson *Mozart: a Bicentennial Tribute* 1989
Leopold had been forced to come to terms with several disagreeable flaws in his son's character, including his alarming capacity to be 'economical with the truth' when circumstances demanded.

edge

a double-edged/two-edged sword/weapon
a situation or course of action that brings both benefits and difficulties, or has an equal effect in two opposing ways. *17th cent.*

R H Dana *Two Years Before the Mast* 1840
Every circumstance and event was like a two-edged sword, and cut both ways. The length of the voyage, which made us dissatisfied, made the captain, at the same time, feel the necessity of order and strict discipline.

dull the edge of something
to weaken the force or intensity of something, especially an appetite or feeling. The image is of blunting the edge of a knife or sword, reducing its sharpness. *16th cent.*

Gervase Markham *The English Arcadia* 1607
I feele the power of his great authoritie, whereby he abates the overflow of swelling youth, dulles the keene edge of every sharpe piercing eye, make hoarce the sweete sound of the silver voyce.

John Tatham *The Distracted State* 1651
All | Men naturally have an ambition to | Make great their line, and families by succession; | When ours doth blunt the edge of such resolves.

Catharine Sedgwick *A New England Tale* 1852
'I had forgotten,' said Montagu, 'that a boy of two and twenty needs no whetting to his appetite; but sit ye down, and we will dull its edge.'

have an/the edge on/over somebody
to have an advantage over somebody. The phrase dates from the 19th cent. in an obsolete meaning 'to have a grudge against somebody'.

on the edge of one's seat/chair
watching or reading something with great attention and excitement, typically because an element of high suspense is involved: from the notion of a spectator in a theatre or cinema leaning forward in their seat in extreme concentration. *20th cent.*

Esquire 1991
This book [The Day of the Jackal] is particularly clever, for although we know the outcome (de Gaulle was not assassinated), we are on the edge of our seats until the very last page.

set somebody's teeth on edge
to cause somebody annoyance or discomfort: from the physical meaning (which goes back to Middle English) of causing an unpleasant sensation in the teeth. The sense is already transitional in Shakespeare, *1 Henry IV* (1596) III.i.129 'I had rather hear a brazen canstick turned, | Or a dry wheel grate on the axle-tree, | And that would

set my teeth nothing on edge, | Nothing so much as mincing poetry.' *16th cent.*

Henry James *Roderick Hudson* 1876
'Do let us leave this hideous edifice,' she said; 'there are things here that set one's teeth on edge.'

take the edge off something
to reduce the effect or force of something: the phrase is sometimes neutral in context (e.g. one's appetite) and can also refer to something unpleasant. The use of *edge* as a metaphor for power or effectiveness dates from the 16th cent.; *blunt* is used in the same meaning from about the same date and is based on the same image. *17th cent.*

Shakespeare *The Tempest* IV.i.28 (1613)
As I hope | For quiet days, fair issue, and long life | With such love as 'tis now, the murkiest den, | The most opportune place, the strong'st suggestion | Our worser genius can, shall never melt | Mine honour into lust to take away | The edge of that day's celebration.

Henry Fielding *The History of Tom Jones* 1749
Jones, instead of applying himself directly to take off the edge of Mrs. Honour's resentment, as a more experienced gallant would have done, fell to cursing his stars.

See also the ROUGH edge of one's tongue.

edgeways

get a word in edgeways
to manage to say something during a conversation that somebody else is dominating: usually in negative contexts. Early uses refer to words *sliding* in (and out) edgeways. *18th cent.*

Charles Stearns *The Maid of the Groves* 1798
You talk too much, wife – Mr. Treadwell has been here but a moment and you are rattling away and one can't put a word in edgeways.

eff

effing and blinding
using coarse language, swearing: *eff* represents the initial letter of *fuck*, while *blind* is linked to the slang imprecation *blind me* (compare *blimey*). *Mid 20th cent.*

Bette Howell *Dandelion Days* 1991
That's why I stopped going to the Olde Tyme Dancing with him. Bowing and scraping all night at the class, then effing and blinding all the way home.

egg

(as) sure as eggs is eggs
absolutely certain: also in early use in the form *sure as eggs be eggs. 17th cent.*

Thomas Otway *The History and Fall of Caius Marius* 1680
I warrant they came for no goodness. ... 'Twas to seek for Lord Marius, as sure as eggs be eggs.

Richard Graves *The Spiritual Quixote* 1773
Though she is a fine-grown girl, yet, if she lives to Lammas-day next, she will be but fourteen years old, as sure as eggs is eggs.

a bad egg
A wicked or disreputable person. A piece in the *Athenaeum* of 1864 defined a *bad egg* as 'a fellow who had not proved to be as good as his promise', which is a somewhat mild description in terms of typical usage. *19th cent.*

H J Conway *Dred* 1856
Uncle makes it out, that he don't belong to himself, but to this Tom Gordon. There's another bad egg – darn my hide, if I wouldn't sooner belong to the old boy than to him.

go suck an egg
an expression of annoyance or dismissal. *20th cent.*

have egg on one's face
to be made to look foolish by the way things turn out. The image is of yolk stains left on the face after the careless eating of a soft-boiled egg, leaving the eater looking foolish as well as in a mess; or perhaps of having eggs thrown at one. *Mid 20th cent.*

Rugby World and Post 1991
Had they failed, Martin and his men ... would have had enough egg on their faces for a thousand omelettes.

lay an egg
NAmer, informal to fail miserably. *20th cent.*

put/have all one's eggs in one basket

to rely on a single expedient or venture for success. The first uses are in the proverbial form *do not put all your eggs in one basket*. *17th cent.*

> Samuel Palmer *Moral Essays on Proverbs* 1710
> *Don't venture all your eggs in one basket.*

> Mark Twain *The $30,000 Bequest* 1906
> *'It does seem to me that that mine is the place for the whole thirty. What's the objection?' 'All the eggs in one basket – that's the objection.'*

See also a curate's egg *at* CURATE; (kill) the GOOSE that lays the golden egg.

eight

be/have one over the eight

British, informal to have had too much to drink: originally services' slang and based on the notion that eight glasses of beer is the maximum an average man can safely drink. Its first appearance in print is as an entry in Fraser and Gibbons's *Soldier and Sailor Words* (1925), where we find the colourful addition 'the presumption being that an average "moderate" man can safely drink eight glasses of beer'. *Early 20th cent.*

See also the eighth WONDER of the world.

elbow

give somebody the elbow

to dismiss or reject somebody roughly. *20th cent.*

> Petronella Pulsford *Lee's Ghost* 1990
> *I went around being nice to children for a while, being a sort of modern Pied Piper, but I learnt that they're a manipulative lot and crazy for money, literally crazy for it, so I gave them the elbow.*

lift/bend one's elbow

to drink too much alcohol. *19th cent.*

out at (the) elbows

(said of clothing or the person wearing it) worn and ragged, shabby. *17th cent.*

> Shakespeare *Measure for Measure* II.i.58 (1605)
> [Angelo] *Elbow is your name? Why dost thou not speak, Elbow?* [Pompey] *He cannot, sir; he's out at elbow.*

> Jack London *The People of the Abyss* 1903
> *My frayed and out-at-elbows jacket was the badge and advertisement of my class, which was their class.*

up to one's elbows

busily engaged in something: with reference to physical immersion of the arms during washing and other activities. *Cf* Shakespeare, *Julius Caesar* (1599) III.i.107 '[Brutus after Caesar's murder] Stoop, Romans, stoop, and let us bathe our hands in Caesar's blood | Up to the elbows, and besmear our swords.' The phrase dates from the 19th cent. in figurative use.

element

in / out of one's element

enjoying (or lacking) surroundings or circumstances that suit one well; doing (or not doing) what one enjoys or is good at: from the physical sense of *element* 'any of the four substances, air, water, fire, and earth, formerly believed to compose the physical universe'. Figurative uses referring to individuals' personal surroundings are recorded from the late 16th cent. Shakespeare in *The Merry Wives of Windsor* (1597) IV.ii.163 makes Ford depict his wife's 'Aunt of Brentford' (in fact Sir John Falstaff in disguise) in these terms: 'She works by charms, by spells, by th' figure, and such daubery as this is, beyond our element'; and in *Twelfth Night* (1602) III.i.58 the clown Feste points to a hackneyed use by resorting to an absurd use of *welkin* ('the sky or heavens') instead; he addresses Viola, who is presenting herself (disguised as the young man Cesario) for an audience with Olivia: 'Who you are and what you would are out of my welkin – I might say 'element', but the word is over-worn.' Milton has this line in *Paradise Lost* (1667) ii.275: 'Our torments may also in length of time become our elements.' The phrase is 17th cent. in this form.

> Daniel Defoe *Robinson Crusoe* 1719
> *When they came to make boards ... they were quite out of their element.*

elephant

see the elephant

NAmer, informal to gain experience of life and see the world: the elephant is used as a symbol of the unusual and memorable. *19th cent.*

See also a WHITE elephant.

eleventh

at the eleventh hour

at the latest possible time. The origin of the expression lies in the parable in Matthew 20:1–16 (in the Authorized Version, 1611) of the labourers hired at different times during the day: 'When they came that were hired about the eleventh hour, they received every man a penny. But when the first came, they supposed that they should have received more; and they likewise received every man a penny. And when they had received it, they murmured against the goodman of the house.' In modern use there is a doomsday resonance to the phrase, the eleventh hour being the last before the 'reckoning' hour of midnight, and this feeling is perhaps reinforced in people's minds by the circumstances of the armistice that ended hostilities at the end of the First World War: it was signed at 5 a.m. on 11 November 1918 and came into force at 11 a.m., 'at the eleventh hour of the eleventh day of the eleventh month'. *19th cent.*

> **Mary Brunton** *Self-Control* 1811
> *She knew too, that the call might be made effectual even at the 'eleventh hour'; and the bare chance was worth the toil of ages.*

Elysian

the Elysian fields

the home of the blessed after death in Greek mythology (also called Elysium), regarded by Homer and Hesiod as a repose for heroes chosen by the gods for special favour. In later myth Elysium was placed in the underworld, to which Aeneas descended in the sixth book of Virgil's *Aeneid*. *16th cent.*

> **Spenser** *Shepheardes Calender* (November) line 179 (1579)
> *I see thee blessed soule, I see,* | *Walk in Elisian fieldes so free.*

empty

be running on empty

to have no resources or energy left. *20th cent.*

> **Eroica Mildmay** *Lucker and Tiffany Peel Out* 1993
> *'By the way, any chance of room service?' 'Food? Now? You're kidding' … This country is running scared. And we're running on empty.*

empty nest

a home that seems empty after the children have grown up and left and only the parents remain: such a parent is an *empty-nester*. In earlier use, *empty nest* was used to refer to an empty haunt when 'the birds have flown' (i.e. escapees: *see* BIRD). Both images are present in Sir Thomas Morton's *Valiant Expedition of Captain Shrimp* (1632): 'The word, which was given with an alarm, was, "Oh, he's gone, he's gone!" … Their grand leader Captain Shrimp took on most furiously, and tore his clothes for anger, to see the empty nest, and their bird gone.' *Mid 20th cent.*

See also on a full / an empty STOMACH.

end

all ends up

completely, utterly: especially in the context of sporting victories and defeats. *Early 20th cent.*

> **Wisden Cricket Monthly** 1992
> *In the midst of all this came three consecutive balls unlikely to be forgotten as Waqar, steaming in like Larwood, was crashed through the covers by Smith, then beat his man all ends up.*

at the end of the day

when all circumstances are considered; taking everything into account. The phrase is widely regarded as a cliché or meaningless sentence-filler. *Late 20th cent.*

> **Independent** 1989
> *Despite the anger in Hong Kong over Tiananmen, no major company in the colony has pulled out of China. Even Mr Murray, who appeared on television to condemn Peking for its butchery, has since acknowledged that at the end of the day, we have to live with these guys.*

at the end of one's tether / NAmer rope

having come to the end of one's patience, resources, or ability to cope. Earlier phrases now no longer in use, in which *tether* has the figurative use 'range or scope of activity or ability', date from the 16th cent. The notion is of a tied animal that is free to move about as far as its tether will allow it. The phrase is 19th cent. in this form.

Charles Reade *Hard Cash* 1863
*Passion, impatience, pity, and calculation, all drove
her the same road, and led to an extraordinary
scene, so impregnated with the genius of the madhouse – a place where the passions run out to the
very end of their tether – that I feel little able to
describe it; I will try and indicate it.*

come to a bad end
to suffer a bad fate: normally used with overtones
of expectation or even satisfaction that the fate is
thoroughly deserved. *18th cent.*

Joseph Addison *The Drummer* 1716
*[Tinsel] Faith very innocent and very ridiculous!
Well then, I warrant thee, Widow, thou wouldst not
for the World marry a Sabbath-breaker! [Lady]
Truly they generally come to a bad End. I remember
the Conjurer told you, you were short-liv'd.*

Scott *Rob Roy* 1817
*When his eldest son, Archie, came to a bad end, in
that unlucky affair of Sir John Fenwick's, old Hil-
debrand used to hollow out his name as readily as
any of the remaining six, and then complain that he
could not recollect which of his sons had been
hanged.*

end in tears
to have an unpleasant or unhappy outcome. In
early use the phrase implied actual tears; in modern allusive use it typically occurs as a warning
that an apparently normal or interesting situation
will all end in tears. *17th cent.*

Bunyan *The Pilgrim's Progress* 1684
*Oft times their rejoicing ends in tears, and their
sun-shine in a cloud.*

the end is nigh
a formulaic prediction of death or doom, used
especially by religious zealots in sermons and on
placards urging repentance. The phrase does not
occur in this form in translations of the Bible. The
Authorized Version comes close to it in places,
e.g. 1 Peter 4:7 'But the end of all things is at hand:
be ye therefore sober, and watch unto prayer',
whereas the New English Bible has 'The end of
all things is upon us'. *18th cent.*

John Oldmixon *The Governour of Cyprus* 1703
*Go dream of safety, when thy end is nigh, | For Me
– my Soul's so anxious of my Fair, | It ne'er can
rest till I have seen her safe.*

end it (all)
to commit suicide. *19th cent.*

Mary Jane Holmes *Edna Browning* 1872
*She had taken from a shelf, and looked at a bottle of
laudanum, and thought how easy it would be to end
it all, but she dared not do it when she thought
seriously about it.*

the end justifies the means
(proverb) the supposed worthiness of one's purpose can excuse questionable or immoral
methods of achieving it: often used in contexts
suggesting scepticism of the principle. Cf Ovid,
Heroides ii.85 *exitus acta probat* 'the result justifies
one's actions'. The sentiment goes back in English to the 16th cent. The phrase is 18th cent. in
this form.

Scott *The Abbot* 1820
*'Catherine is the betrothed bride of Heaven – these
intimacies cannot be.' 'It is in the cause of Heaven
that I command them to embrace,' said Magdalen,
with the full force of her powerful voice; 'the end,
sister, sanctifies the means we must use.'*

the end of civilization as we know it
the end of a familiar or accepted social order or
way of life: often used ironically to question or
ridicule an exaggerated view of unfavourable
circumstances or setbacks. The phrase is now
regarded as a cliché and is associated with sci-
ence-fiction film dialogues on the theme of attack
from outer space. It is said to have originated in
the film *Citizen Kane* (1941), in which the newspaper tycoon Charles Foster Kane expresses
scepticism about the likelihood of war: 'They
[the leaders of Britain, France, Germany, and
Italy] are too intelligent to embark on a project
which would mean the end of civilization as we
now know it.' *Mid 20th cent.*

Richard Girling *The Best of Sunday Times Travel* 1988
*Two blocks from the hotel is a McDonald's. It was
blown up last year. Now it has two security guards.
They carry rifles and check every car coming into
the parking lot. This must be the end of civilisation
as Americans know it.*

the end of the road/line
the point at which one can make no further progress: possibly influenced by the Dillon and Lau-
der song (1924) 'Keep right on to the end of the
road', although the first evidence of use is somewhat later (1950s). *Mid 20th cent.*

end of story

informal a concluding remark indicating that the speaker has said all there is to say on a subject and discouraging further discussion. *Late 20th cent.*

> **Daily Telegraph 1992**
> *Mr White, incredibly, begins the book with an account of the movie actress Shirley MacLaine visiting Dr Hawking … to ask if he believes in God and he tells her he does not: end of story.*

the end of the world

complete disaster: usually used in negative contexts as reassurance that an apparent misfortune is not as serious as somebody fears. With reference to the ending of the world at doomsday in some beliefs. *Early 20th cent.*

the ends of the earth

the most distant parts of the world: the only survival of a former sense of *end* that goes back to Old English, meaning 'the limits [of a place]' as in *the city's end*. Cf the four corners of the earth *at* CORNER. *19th cent.*

> **Wilkie Collins The Moonstone 1868**
> *My charitable business is an unendurable nuisance to me; and when I see a Ladies' Committee now, I wish myself at the uttermost ends of the earth!*

get/have one's end away

British, *informal* to have sexual intercourse. *Late 20th cent.*

> **Nigel Williams East of Wimbledon 1993**
> *'You can do nothing with Rafiq during Ramadan,' Mr Malik had said. 'He just lies on his bed and thinks about having his end away!'*

keep/hold one's end up

to maintain one's position or perform well in a competition, etc. *19th cent.*

> **Somerset Maugham Of Human Bondage 1915**
> *I believe in God, and I don't believe He minds much about what you do as long as you keep your end up and help a lame dog over a stile when you can.*

make (both) ends meet

to cope financially. An early use is by Thomas Fuller (1608–61) in his biographical work *The History of the Worthies of England* (published posthumously in 1662): 'Worldly wealth he cared not for, desiring onely to make both ends meet.' A few years later the glossary known as *The Dictionary of the Canting Crew* (1690) included

the maxim: 'Tis good to make both ends meet.' The meaning of the phrase is uncertain. Many seek an association in accounting, the 'ends' referring to the beginning and end of the year, during which one's income must last. This view is supported by use of the phrase in an extended form *make the two ends of the year meet* (and in French there is an equivalent phrase *joindre les deux bouts de l'an*), but we do not find this until the 18th cent. It is therefore as likely to be a late extension as an insight into its origin. An alternative suggestion, that it has to do with the amount of material needed to make a piece of clothing reach round the body, so that its 'two ends meet', is no more than speculation, weakened by the absence of any allusions in ordinary usage, as happens with the financial associations. *17th cent.*

> **Eliza Haywood The History of Betsy Thoughtless 1751**
> *He is a hard man, and if it were not for my nursing, we could not make both ends meet, as the saying is; – but he is our landlord, and we dare not disoblige him.*

never/not hear the end of something

to be constantly nagged or reminded about something unpleasant. *19th cent.*

> **Conan Doyle A Study in Scarlet 1887**
> *I wouldn't have the Scotland Yarders know it for the world … I have chaffed them so much that they would never have let me hear the end of it.*

no end of something

informal a large amount of something; more than one can manage. The phrase is also used in the shortened form *no end* in the sense 'immensely'. *17th cent.*

> **James Chamberlaine Manuductio ad Coelum 1681**
> *So that we must this certain truth confess, | That there's no end of all our greediness.*

> **Mark Twain A Tramp Abroad 1880**
> *The stage scenery was ruined, trap-doors were so swollen that they wouldn't work for a week afterward, the fine costumes were spoiled, and no end of minor damages were done by that remarkable storm.*

a/the — to end all —s

a most remarkable example of its kind. *20th cent.*

> **Listener 1964**
> *Looking as far into the technological future as I dare, I would like to describe the invention to end all inventions. I call it the replicator; it is simply a*

duplicating machine. It could make, almost
instantly, an exact copy of anything.

See also at a LOOSE end; at the SHARP end; be at
one's wits' end *at* WIT; be at/on the receiving end
at RECEIVE; the BEGINNING of the end; BURN the
candle at both ends; the DIRTY end of the stick; get
hold of the WRONG end of the stick; go (in) off the
DEEP end; jump in at the DEEP end; make somebody's HAIR stand on end; a MEANS to an end; the
thin end of the WEDGE; to the BITTER end.

endow

be well endowed
to have breasts (if a woman) or genitals (if a man)
of generous proportions: the notion is of a benefit
received by a kind of genetic inheritance or
endowment. *Mid 20th cent.*

enemy

be one's own worst enemy
to behave in a way that harms one's reputation
or earns one discredit. A similar expression,
nobody's enemy but one's own, occurs from the
16th cent.

> Roger Orrery *Mustapha* 1668
> *What sin of mine, oh Heaven! incenses thee? |*
> *Thou mak'st my Son his own worst Enemy.*

> Henry Fielding *The History of Tom Jones* 1749
> *Sophia, when very young, discerned that Tom,*
> *though an idle, thoughtless, rattling rascal, was*
> *nobody's enemy but his own.*

the enemy within
a threat that exists within a nation or organization, as distinct from an external enemy. The
phrase was famously used by Margaret Thatcher
in 1984 in the context of the British miners' strike
of that year, as reported in the *Guardian* of 20 July:
'Mrs Thatcher told Tory MPs that her government had fought the enemy without in the Falk-
lands conflict and now had to face an enemy
within.' At an earlier date (1940), Winston
Churchill had described the BBC as 'an enemy
within the gates, doing more harm than good'.
The phrase has been used as the title of a television drama and a stage play, and of a book by
Robert F Kennedy about the labour movement in
the US, published in 1960. An early use occurs in
John Dryden's tragedy *Amboyna* (1673), III.i: 'I

know not who can be my Enemy within this
Island, except my Rival Harman, and for him, I
truly did relate, what pass'd betwixt us yesterday.' *17th cent.*

> Thomas Holcroft *Anna St Ives* 1792
> *Were it not better with severe but virtuous reso-*
> *lution to repel these flattering and probably*
> *deceitful hopes, than by encouraging them to feed*
> *the canker-worm of peace, and add new force to the*
> *enemy within, who rather stunned than conquered*
> *is every moment ready to revive.*

public enemy number one
somebody who is generally hated as the greatest
threat to a community: originally with reference
to the first on a list of wanted criminals. *Mid 20th
cent.*

> Daily Telegraph 1992
> *Electricity engineers and linesmen on the Orkney*
> *islands went into battle yesterday against their*
> *public enemy number one – the hooded crow.*

enough

enough is as good as a feast
(proverb) one should not look for more than one
needs. The proverb is 15th cent. in this form,
occurring in Thomas Malory's cycle of Arthurian
legends *Le Morte d'Arthur* (c1485): 'Inowghe is as
good as a feste.' The sentiment was much
derided by Charles Lamb in *Last Essays of Elia*
(1833): 'Enough is as good as a feast – not a man,
woman, or child, in ten miles round Guildhall,
who really believes this saying. The inventor of it
did not believe it himself. It was made in revenge
by somebody, who was disappointed of a regale.
It is a vile cold-scrag-of-mutton sophism.'

enough is enough
no more is needed or wanted: originally a statement of satisfaction with what has been achieved,
later an expression of insistence. The phrase
occurs as a maxim and as a free phrase. It is
recorded in John Heywood's *Dialogue of Proverbs*
(1546) and in an anonymous Tudor play called
Tom Tyler, but otherwise most evidence dates
from the 19th cent.

> Washington Irving *The Alhambra* 1832
> *'Let us have up the coffer by all means,' cried the*
> *grasping Alcalde. 'I will descend for no more,' said*
> *the Moor, doggedly. 'Enough is enough for a rea-*
> *sonable man; more is superfluous.'*

enough said

there is no need to say any more on the subject: used in speech to bring a discussion to an end. The phrase is recorded from the 17th cent., and in the informal form *nuff said* from the 19th cent. Hotten's *Dictionary of Slang* (1873) records *N.C.* as an abbreviation of *nuf ced* and associates it with theatre language.

Lodowick Carlell *Arviragus and Philicia* 1639
Who hath yet pleasd all? | Who had that aime, | exprest his wit but small. | Theres enough said, | those that can judge of playes | Will finde as little to dislike, as praise.

Henry Clay Preuss *Fashions and Follies of Washington Life* 1857
[John Sharker] *If you don't hold out your hand to save me – I'm a ruined man!* [Bill Sly] *Squire ... there's my hand. Bill Sly's agreeable – nuff said!*

Mary Jane Holmes *Rose Mather* 1868
'You came from Boston, I b'lieve?' 'Yes, from Boston,' and Rose leaned eagerly forward, while Bill, with his favorite 'Nuff said,' plunged his hand into his pocket, and taking out the picture, passed it to Rose.

See also enough to make the angels weep *at* ANGEL; (enough to) make a CAT laugh.

enter

enter somebody's head

(said of a thought or idea) to occur to somebody: now usually in negative contexts but positive in earlier use. *Cf* COME into somebody's head/mind. *16th cent.*

Thomas D'Urfey *The Intrigues at Versailles* 1697
Nay, if her treachery can't enter into your head, after the story I told you of our late adventure, take it from me, your head, and the brains belonging to it, are in an incureable condition.

Jane Austen *Northanger Abbey* 1818
Guided only by what was simple and probable, it had never entered her head that Mr. Tilney could be married.

envelope

on the back of an envelope

(said of a calculation) made hurriedly or sketchily. The phrase is originally literal in meaning, and occurs in allusive uses. *Early 20th cent.*

M De La Roche *Jalna* 1927
Pushing his plate of cinnamon toast to one side, he jotted them down on the back of an envelope.

push (the edge of) the envelope

to achieve pioneering success, to make progress beyond established limits. The phrase has nothing to do with letters or packets but is derived from the highly specialized terminology of aeronautics. The *envelope* is the line at the edge of a graph that shows the limits of an aircraft's capabilities: to *push the envelope* is to test the aircraft's performance to its utmost. *Late 20th cent.*

Today 1992
But for newcomers it is daunting to stand on the brink of Genghis Khan – one of the runs in China Bowl – and gaze down at unending acres of snow. 'Come on you guys,' exhorts Linda, our daredevil guide, 'Let's get to the edge of the envelope.'

envy

See be GREEN with envy.

equal

first among equals

the senior or most important member of a group: translating Latin *primus inter pares*, which is also used in English contexts. *First among equals* was used as the title of a novel by Jeffrey Archer (1984).

other/all things being equal

assuming other factors are constant in a given set of variables: translating Latin *ceteris paribus* and used in the context of making a choice or drawing a conclusion in which this assumption has to be made. *19th cent.*

Catharine Sedgwick *The Travellers* 1825
Other things being equal, one Englishman is as good as two Frenchmen any day – and that's what every English soldier knows.

err

err on the side of —

to give priority to a specified consideration in following a course of action. The phrase is commonly completed by the word *caution*. To *err on the right* (or *safe*) *side* is to follow a course of action in such a way that any mistake causes the least harm (*see also* be on the SAFE side). *18th cent.*

Richardson *Clarissa* 1748
And, indeed, as thou seldom errest on the favourable side, human nature is so vile a thing, that thou art likely to be right five times in six.

Donald Grant Mitchell *The Lorgnette* 1850
Be sure, my dear Tommy, that if you err, you err upon the safe side; believe me that nothing is more odious than association of one's name with a nursery maid, or a grocer's wife.

to err is human
a justification for human error: in full *to err is human, to forgive divine.* The locus classicus in English is Alexander Pope's *Essay on Criticism* (1711), line 525: 'Good nature and good sense must ever join; | To err is human; to forgive, divine.' However, the phrase, and certainly the sentiment, are a lot older, and can be found in Chaucer and further back in Latin (*humanum est errare*). In the Roman dramatist Plautus (c250–184 BC) the maxim appears in the form *humanum amare est, humanum autem ignoscere est* (*Mercator* II.ii.48 'It is human to love, and human also to forgive'). Cicero in his *Philippics* (polemical speeches against Mark Antony delivered in 44 and 43 BC) expressed the view *cuiusvis hominis est errare; nullius, nisi insipientis, in errore perseverare* ('any man may err, but nobody but a fool will persist in error'), a limit on tolerance of error that is echoed in Chaucer, in the part of the *Canterbury Tales* known as the *Tale of Melibee* (line 1264): 'The proverbe seith that "for to do synne is mannyssh, but certes for to persevere longe in synne is werk of the devel".' The 'divine' aspect first appears in the form 'to repent [is] divine' in the work of Sir Henry Wotton (1568–1639), a diplomat and poet and a close friend of John Donne. We may therefore say that the phrase in its current form dates from the 16th cent.

escutcheon
See a BLOT on the escutcheon.

essence

of the essence
(said especially of time and punctuality) of critical importance, essential. *Essence* here is based on the meaning 'something that embodies the fundamental nature of an idea, characteristic, etc'. *19th cent.*

eternal

eternal triangle
a situation of conflict resulting from the emotional or sexual involvement of two people with a third person. *Early 20th cent.*

Today 1992
Agony aunt Virginia Ironside asks Marje Proops why she ignored her own advice. So it turns out that your eternal triangle wasn't one after all – it was an eternal square.

even

an even break
a fair and reasonable chance. 'Never give a sucker an even break' was a catchphrase associated with the American comedian W C Fields (1880–1946), and was the title of a film in which he starred in 1941. *Break* here draws on its meaning 'a stroke of good luck; an opportunity or chance'. *Early 20th cent.*

Guardian 1989
The rest of the First Division, to twist WC Fields slightly, will be anxious not to give an injury-hit Liverpool an even break.

even Stephen(s)/Steven(s)
a fair chance: arbitrarily based on the alliterative effect of the name. *Early 20th cent.*

get even (with somebody)
to exact revenge (on somebody). *17th cent.*

Anon *Woman's Malice* 1699
Villanes fearing lest too much subjection and submission to her Humours, might make her more bold with him, since he found her advanced to a great pitch of Arrogance, and not having yet digested the Affront she put upon him, in employing him in so base a Negotiation, resolved now to get even with her.

Conan Doyle *The Retired Colourman* 1926
'Now ... suppose that you were shut up in this little room, had not two minutes to live, but wanted to get even with the fiend who was probably mocking at you from the other side of the door. What would you do?' 'Write a message.' 'Exactly.'

on an even keel

(said of an organization, activity, etc) proceeding smoothly and efficiently: from the (16th cent.) literal meaning 'level, not tilting to one side' with reference to ships and nowadays also aircraft. *19th cent.*

event

at all events / in any event

whatever the circumstances: *cf* in any CASE; at any RATE. *17th cent.*

Alexander Garden A Strong Opiniator 1609

For instant greefe, for gladnesse gone, | Believe I nether heat nor coole, | At all events I still am one, | For ought I nether joy nor doole.

Dickens Hard Times 1854

He took the precaution of stepping into a chemist's shop and buying a bottle of the very strongest smelling-salts. 'By George!' said Mr Bounderby, 'if she takes it in the fainting way, I'll have the skin off her nose, at all events!'

ever

it was ever thus/so

things stay the same: a statement of resigned acceptance. *19th cent.*

Edgar Rice Burroughs At the Earth's Core 1914

To him it seemed quite ridiculous to imagine that there was another world far beneath his feet peopled by beings similar to himself, and he laughed uproariously the more he thought upon it. But it was ever thus. That which has never come within the scope of our really pitifully meager world-experience cannot be.

every

every last/single —

used to stress that absolutely every member of a group is included in what is being said. *19th cent.*

R L Stevenson Treasure Island 1883

Captain Smollett rose from his seat, and knocked out the ashes of his pipe in the palm of his left hand. 'Is that all?' he asked. 'Every last word, by thunder!' answered John.

every little helps

(proverb) small amounts can make a difference if there are enough of them. The notion is derived from French, and occurs in English from the 17th cent., notably in the work of William Camden (1551–1623), historian and headmaster of Westminster School (*Remains Concerning Britain*, third edition, 1623): 'Euery thing helpes, quoth the Wren when she pist i' the sea.' The phrase in its current form is first found in the 18th cent.

Richard Cumberland The Jew 1794

I do always do my utmost for my principals: I never spare my pains when business is going; be it ever such a trifle, I am thankful. Every little helps a poor man like me.

Trollope The Last Chronicle of Barset 1867

The bill is out for collection, and must be collected. In times like these we must draw ourselves in a little, you know. Two hundred and fifty pounds isn't a great deal of money, you will say; but every little helps, you know; and, besides, of course we go upon a system.

every man for himself

each individual must look to his or her own safety or interests. The phrase was originally a proverb (as in Chaucer below) but is now typically used with reference to times of crisis or emergency and often with the extension *and the devil take the hindmost* (see DEVIL). *Middle English*

Chaucer The Knight's Tale (line 1182)

At the kynges court, my brother, | Ech man for hymself, ther is noon oother.

Economist 1991

The woman leading the group spots a stand of dead apple trees. Letting out a shriek, she races towards them ... 'They're mine,' she says, wrapping her arms around a clump of morel mushrooms. It is every man for himself in Boyne City's National Mushroom Championship, a race to collect the most morels.

every which way

NAmer, informal randomly or chaotically in every direction. *19th cent.*

Kipling Just So Stories 1902

'Son, son!' said his mother ever so many times, graciously waving her tail, 'now attend to me and remember what I say. A Hedgehog curls himself up into a ball and his prickles stick out every which way at once. By this you may know the Hedgehog.'

See also as every SCHOOLBOY knows; every INCH.

evidence

in evidence
clearly visible or available; conspicuous. *19th cent.*

> Richard Jefferies *Bevis: The Story of a Boy* 1882
> *They could not believe that the two had really spent all the time on an island. This was the eleventh morn since they had left – it could not be: yet there was the raft in evidence.*

evil

put off the evil day/hour
to postpone dealing with an awkward or unpleasant situation for as long as possible. Use of *evil* with designations of time (especially *day* or *hour*) to denote periods of misfortune or disaster goes back to the 14th cent. *17th cent.*

See also the LESSER evil / the lesser of two evils.

exception

the exception that proves the rule
a circumstance or occurrence that by its unusual nature demonstrates the existence of a rule or principle that applies in other cases. The phrase first appears in the guise of a proverb, *the exception proves the rule*, which translates the legal maxim *exceptio probat regulam in casibus non exceptis* 'making an exception confirms the rule in cases for which no exception is made'. The important point behind this legal origin is that *exception* is used here in the sense of a process rather than its result, the crux being the making of an exception and not the exception made, or the discovery of an exception. H W Fowler in *A Dictionary of Modern English Usage* (1926) illustrated this proper meaning with an example probably drawn from his own military service (Fowler served in the First World War despite being well over age): 'Special leave is given for men to be out of barracks tonight till 11 p.m.' This special granting of leave establishes that in other cases the normal deadline applies: it is a genuine case of an exception (i.e. the making of an exception) reinforcing the existence of a rule. The phrase does not properly mean that an exception can be discounted, nor that an exception can only be an exception if there is a rule to be excepted. The distinction has been eroded in modern use

and understanding of the phrase, which has been taken to suggest that any circumstance that does not fit a rule or principle at least shows that the rule applies in the majority of cases: this is at best meaningless and at worst nonsense. *17th cent.*

> John Wilson *The Cheats* 1664
> *If I have shewn the odd practices of two vain persons, pretending to what they were not, I think I have sufficiently justifi'd the brave man, even by this reason, That the exception proves the rule.*

> Wilkie Collins *The Haunted Hotel* 1879
> *To anything fanciful, to anything spiritual, their minds are deaf and blind by nature. Now and then, in the course of centuries, a great genius springs up among them; and he is the exception which proves the rule.*

exhibit

exhibit A
the most important piece of evidence relating to the matter in hand: from the judicial practice of identifying physical items of evidence by a sequence of letters, *exhibit A* being the first, *exhibit B* the second, and so on. In the phrase the assumption seems to be that the first item is also the most important. *Early 20th cent.*

> Robert Rankin *The Book of Ultimate Truths* 1993
> *One married couple ... had come home during the height of the disturbances to discover their teenage daughter being ravished by a young police officer. Exhibit A was expected to be a twenty-one function Swiss Police knife.*

exhibition

make an exhibition of oneself
to appear foolish or ridiculous in public. *19th cent.*

> John Lothrop Motley *Morton's Hope* 1839
> *'Have the kindness to tell me,' said I, 'what particular reason you have for arraying yourself and your dog in such particularly elegant costumes; and for making such an exquisite exhibition of yourself during your promenade?'*

> R L Stevenson *Weir of Hermiston* 1896
> *And at the memory of the blush, she blushed again, and became one general blush burning from head to foot. Was ever anything so indelicate, so forward, done by a girl before? And here she was, making an*

exhibition of herself before the congregation about nothing!

expect

be expecting
informal to be pregnant. The phrase was also used in 19th cent. Anglo-Irish as an ellipsis for 'to be expected to die'. *19th cent.*

> Harper Lee *To Kill a Mockingbird* 1960
> *Early one morning as we were beginning our day's play in the back yard, Jem and I heard something next door … We went to the wire fence to see if there was a puppy – Miss Rachel's rat terrier was expecting.*

England expects
a call to support one's country: from Nelson's flag signal to the fleet at the battle of Trafalgar in 1805, 'England expects that every man will do his duty'. *19th cent.*

> Lewis Carroll *The Hunting of the Snark* 1876
> *For England expects – I forbear to proceed: | 'Tis a maxim tremendous, but trite: | And you'd best be unpacking the things that you need | To rig yourselves out for the fight.*

expect me when you see me
an expression of uncertainty about when one will arrive. *19th cent.*

what can/do you expect?
an expression of resignation about an unwelcome but characteristic event or piece of behaviour. *18th cent.*

> Hannah Foster *The Coquette* 1797
> *Suppose, however, that his views are honorable; yet what can you expect, what can you promise yourself from such a connection?*

expense

See SPARE no expense.

eye

Several figurative uses of *eye* underlie the phrases, notably 'the faculty of seeing', which extends to perception and intelligence more generally, and 'looking or observation' (as in *keep an eye on* and similar phrases).

catch somebody's eye
1 (said of a person or thing) to be suddenly visible or apparent to somebody; to be noticeable or striking. *17th cent.*

> Shakespeare *Troilus and Cressida* III.iii.177 (1602)
> [Ulysses to Achilles] *Then marvel not, thou great and complete man, | That all the Greeks begin to worship Ajax, | Since things in motion sooner catch the eye | Than what not stirs.*

2 (said of a person) to attract somebody's attention deliberately or exchange glances with them, so that they take notice. *19th cent.*

> Henry James *An International Episode* 1879
> *At this point Percy Beaumont certainly looked straight at his kinsman; he tried to catch his eye. But Lord Lambeth would not look at him; his own eyes were better occupied.*

clap/lay/set eyes on something/somebody
to see or look at something or somebody. *Set an eye on* occurs in Chaucer (*The Clerk's Tale*, line 233): 'Upon Grisilde, this povre creature, | Ful ofte sithe [= since] this markys sette his ye'; in its present form the phrase is recorded from the 18th cent. An older version of the phrase, with *lay*, is found at an even earlier date in the (13th cent.) book of devotional advice called *Ancrene Wisse* (or *Ancrene Riwle*): 'Heo lette him leggen eien on hire.' *Clap* is the familiar word for striking the hands in applause or appreciation, used here in its less common group of meanings to do with placing or applying something promptly or quickly (as in *clap hold of*); its use in this phrase dates from the 19th cent.

> John Neal *Randolph* 1823
> *First, there was an essay read, by one of the members; a very substantial, good thing; over which, the best natured gentleman that ever I clapped eyes on, went fairly to sleep, with the happiest countenance in the world.*

> Dickens *Great Expectations* 1861
> *'She* [Miss Havisham]*'s flighty, you know – very flighty – quite flighty enough to pass her days in a sedan chair.' 'Did you ever see her in it, Uncle?' asked Mrs. Joe. 'How could I,' he returned, forced to the admission, 'when I never see her in my life? Never clapped eyes upon her!'*

close/shut one's eyes to something
to ignore something or pretend not to notice it: an early 18th cent. source includes the phrase in the

form 'I cannot shut my Eyes against Manifest Truth'. *18th cent.*

an eye for an eye (and a tooth for a tooth)

retaliation in kind. The phrase is used with allusion to God's commandments to the Israelites on just retribution in Exodus 21:24 (also known as *lex talionis*, the law of retaliation): 'And if any mischief follow, then thou shalt give life for life, Eye for eye, tooth for tooth, hand for hand, foot for foot, Burning for burning, wound for wound, stripe for stripe.' It is found in Bible translations from Middle English, and occurs in the *Cursor Mundi*, a medieval poem on the history and development of mankind.

Charles Johnstone *Chrysal* 1760
What then is this, but a just retaliation? a fulfilling of our law, that says, An eye for an eye, and a tooth for a tooth? And do I not want her wealth to make my settlement happy, in the land of my fore-fathers?

Emily Brontë *Wuthering Heights* 1847
Oh, I owe him so much. On only one condition can I hope to forgive him. It is, if I may take an eye for an eye, a tooth for a tooth; for every wrench of agony return a wrench.

the eye of a needle

a minute opening or space: based on the words of Christ in Matthew 19:24 (in the Authorized Version, 1611) 'And again I say unto you, It is easier for a camel to go through the eye of a needle, than for a rich man to enter into the kingdom of God.' (The New English Bible has *pass through* in place of *go through*.) The translation *eye of a needle* occurs first in Tyndale's translation (1525); *needle's eye* appears in other versions and is the form used allusively in early sources, e.g. Shakespeare, *Richard II* (1595) v.v.17 which refers directly to the passage in Matthew: 'The better sort, | As thoughts of things divine, are intermixed | With scruples, and do set the faith itself | Against the faith, as thus: "Come, little ones", And then again, "It is as hard to come as for a camel | To thread the postern of a small needle's eye".' *16th cent.*

Abraham Cowley *The Guardian* 1650
There's clotted cream in his head in stead of brains; and no more o' that then will compleatly serve to fill the eye of a needle.

G K Chesterton *Orthodoxy* 1908
But if we diminish the camel to his smallest, or open the eye of the needle to its largest – if, in short, we

assume the words of Christ to have meant the very least that they could mean, His words must at the very least mean this – that rich men are not very likely to be morally trustworthy.

the eye of the storm

a brief time or place of peace during a longer period of conflict or violence: literally, the centre point of a storm, round which the storm rages but usually calm in itself (although often misunderstood in the opposite sense). *Eye* has a number of uses denoting various kinds of central points, and the 'eye' of a needle is related to this sense. *19th cent.*

Daily Telegraph 1992
The grand old man of French, even European, socialism with his gaunt profile and livid complexion, calm at the eye of the storm, looking almost like his own ghost.

eyes (out) on stalks

informal staring in extreme curiosity or astonishment. *Mid 20th cent.*

get/keep one's eye in

British to get or keep in practice. *Early 20th cent.*

Kirsty McCallum *Driven by Love* 1993
She found the notes taken from her hand, and a magazine put there instead. 'Read this, Kate. You'll need to get your eye in before we go shopping tomorrow.'

give somebody the (glad) eye

British, informal to look at somebody knowingly, especially in a sexually suggestive way: the meaning of *glad* involved here is 'expressing joy or delight'. *Early 20th cent.*

Douglas Rutherford *A Game of Sudden Death* 1990
There was a jarring of brakes and a cacophony of horn blasts as he squeezed into the gap between the Vauxhall and a black Ford. 'Smile at them,' Patrick told Chris. 'Give them the glad eye.'

a gleam/twinkle in somebody's eye

humorous the beginnings of an idea, especially a child who is likely to be conceived. The phrase was originally used more literally of a look in the eyes revealing excitement or eager anticipation, and came to be used allusively to refer to the thought or idea giving rise to this. *17th cent.*

Thomas Deloney *The Pleasant History of John Winchcomb* 1619
Is it sufficient for their mistrusting natures to take exceptions at a shadow, at a word, at a looke, at a smile, nay at the twinkle of an eye, which neither man nor woman is able to expell?

Daily Telegraph 1992
Anyway, why put a new straitjacket around the economy until recovery is more than a twinkle in the market's eye?

half an eye
less than one's full attention. *16th cent.*

Richard Brome *The Queen and Concubine* a1652
We can spie | Great faults in Noble Coats, with half an eye.

Janet Neel *Death of a Partner* 1991
He could see with half an eye that the kid's aunt was going to be one of the confident, bossy, well-connected women with whom that part of Cambridgeshire was substantially over-provided.

have an eye / eyes for somebody/something
1 to be attracted by or show a definite interest in somebody or something. *17th cent.*

Nicholas Hookes *Amanda* 1653
I have an eye for her that's fair, | An eare for her that sings, | Yet don't I care | For golden haire.
2 to have good knowledge or judgement about a particular subject, or an aptitude for a particular activity. *19th cent.*

have/with an eye for/on/to the main chance
to look out for an opportunity for personal gain or advantage. The *main chance* is a term in the game of hazard for a number from 5 to 8 that a player calls before throwing the dice (the first throw being called the *main*). *17th cent.*

have/keep an/one's eye on something/somebody
to watch something or somebody or monitor their progress. *17th cent.*

Dickens *A Christmas Carol* 1843
The door of Scrooge's counting-house was open that he might keep his eye upon his clerk, who in a dismal little cell beyond, a sort of tank, was copying letters.

have eyes bigger than one's stomach
to take more food than one can manage. *18th cent.*

Swift *Gulliver's Travels* 1726
The Captain understood my raillery very well, and merrily replied with the old English proverb, that he doubted mine eyes were bigger than my belly, for he did not observe my stomach so good, although I had fasted all day.

have eyes in the back of one's head
to be aware of what is going on out of view, especially supposedly or hypothetically when this concerns or threatens one. *19th cent.*

Maria Cummins *The Lamplighter* 1854
So observing was she, and so acute in her judgment, that a report at one time prevailed that Miss Pace had eyes in the back of her head, and two pair of ears.

in the blink/twinkling/wink of an eye
instantly, very rapidly. Originally used with reference to 1 Corinthians 15:52 (in the Authorized Version, 1611): 'In a moment, in the twinkling of an eye, at the last trump: for the trumpet shall sound, and the dead shall be raised incorruptible.' *17th cent.*

Head and Kirkman *The English Rogue Described* 1674
I ran with might and main for some sallad-oyl, a jarr whereof I brought in the twinkling of an eye.

Quinn Wilder *One Shining Summer* 1993
That was Mandy, from pathos to pleasure in the blink of an eye.

keep an eye out/open for something
to be especially watchful for something expected. *19th cent.*

Elizabeth Stoddard *Temple House* 1867
I often see her, on her way to your house. I rather like to keep an eye out for her, on dark nights.

keep one's eyes open/peeled/skinned
to be alert and observant. *Late 20th cent.*

make eyes at somebody
to look at somebody in a lascivious manner. A variant (19th cent.) form *throw one's eyes at* is no longer current. *19th cent.*

Thackeray *The Virginians* 1858
For shame, miss! What would Mr. Lintot say if he saw you making eyes at the captain?

my eye / all my eye and Betty Martin
an expression of scepticism meaning 'complete nonsense'. Of the recorded forms of the phrase only *my eye* is still current and even this sounds dated. The extended form, common in the 19th cent., is now virtually obsolete, although it is maintained in a sort of half-life by continued speculation about its origin. The source of the

name *Betty Martin* is unknown: an 18th cent. writer referred to the expression as a 'sea phrase', which gave rise to the unlikely suggestion, first made by one John Bee (a pseudonym for Badcock) in his sporting glossary *Slang, A Dictionary of the Turf, the Ring, the Chase* (1823) and regularly repeated in issues of *Notes & Queries* throughout the 19th cent. and into the 20th cent., that it is a distortion by British seamen of the words they heard abroad in an invocation to St Martin of Tours: *O mihi, beate Martine*, 'Oh (pray) for me, Blessed Martin'. Such a prayer, however, is otherwise unknown, and the Latin was concocted for the purpose in an excessive fit of folk-etymologizing. A desperate but equally misconceived attempt to salvage this line of inquiry was made in 1914, when Dr L A Waddell proposed in his book *The Phoenician Origins of Britons, Scots, and Anglo-Saxons* that the phrase came from another invocation, *O mihi, Brito Martis*, 'Oh (give help) to me, Brito Martis' (a Cretan goddess whom Waddell linked with Britain through the arrival of Phoenician traders).

As Eric Partridge has noted in a lengthy entry in his *Dictionary of Catch Phrases* (1985 edition, revised by Paul Beale), the phrase originally occurs in the simple form *all my eye*, and the Betty Martin part is a later addition; this evidence is historically incompatible with any notion of the extended version being a corruption of the kind suggested. We might add that the first record in print of the extended version, in Francis Grose's *Classical Dictionary of the Vulgar Tongue* (1785), is in a form that bears little relation to the invocation: *That's my eye Betty Martin*. Partridge thought of Betty Martin as a 'character' of 1770s London life, but conceded that names of this kind are mostly created by spontaneous usage. Another extension, *and Tommy*, makes a brief appearance in the beginning of the 19th cent., reinforcing the conclusion that seeking a clear-cut origin for fanciful names of this kind is a wild-goose chase. A variation no longer current, *all my eye and my elbow*, was used in the 18th cent. *18th cent.*

Hardy A Pair of Blue Eyes 1873
Writing a sermon is very much like playing that game. You take the text. You think, why is it? what is it? and so on. You put that down under 'Generally'. Then you proceed to the First, Secondly, and Thirdly. Papa won't have Fourthlys – says they are all my eye.

one in the eye for somebody
a disappointment or setback for somebody: usually with the implication that their suffering is appropriate or well deserved. The image is of a telling blow aimed at the eye. *Early 20th cent.*

Economist 1991
Advocates of traditional history-teaching welcomed the emphasis on events, people and dates. One in the eye for progressive educationalists, after a hard battle?

open somebody's eyes
to make somebody realize the truth or significance of something, especially when they have been reluctant or unable to acknowledge it previously. Some early uses reflect the notion of a new-born child first opening its eyes and starting to see the world around. To *make somebody open their eyes* has a slightly different meaning 'to make somebody take notice or pay attention' (typically by drawing their attention to something remarkable). *18th cent.*

Mary Robinson Walsingham 1797
Indeed when we look round this wide and eventful scene of sorrow and delusion, how few are there who can thank the author of their being; while thousands, and tens of thousands, lament the hour that first opened their eyes to the miseries of existence.

pass/cast one's eye over something
to read or look at something cursorily, especially in order to check it or give an opinion. *18th cent.*

Mary Scott Nudists May Be Encountered 1991
A note from Mellowes instructed me to cast my eye over the draft, pronto, for inaccuracies.

see eye to eye
to be in full agreement with somebody about something. With possible allusion to the passage on the redemption of the Israelites in Isaiah 52:8: 'Thy watchmen shall lift up the voice; with the voice together shall they sing: for they shall see eye to eye, when the Lord shall bring again Zion.' *19th cent.*

Catharine Sedgwick The Linwoods 1835
Meredith paused. 'We do not see eye to eye,' thought Isabella; but she did not speak, and Meredith proceeded.

up to one's eyes/eyeballs in something
informal busily occupied with a task or activity: *see also* up to one's ears in something *at* EAR. *18th cent.*

Arthur Murphy *Know Your Own Mind* 1778
[Sir John] *My son, Mr. Dashwould, what does he intend?* [Dashwould] *Up to the eyes in love with Lady Bell, and determined to marry her.*

Malcolm Lowry *Ultramarine* 1933
That boy got all poxed up to the eyeballs, voyage before last … Yes, he was poxed all away to hell.

Michael Pearce *The Mamur Zapt and the Right of the Dog* 1991
'There might be some spare cash floating around since it's getting near the end of the year.' He rang back later. 'No chance,' he said. 'They're up to their eyeballs in balance sheets.'

with one's eyes open

fully aware of the difficulties or dangers that a situation or course of action will present. *19th cent.*

Jane Austen *Pride and Prejudice* 1813
Poor Charlotte! it was melancholy to leave her to such society! But she had chosen it with her eyes open; and though evidently regretting that her visitors were to go, she did not seem to ask for compassion.

with an eye to something

having something specified as one's aim or purpose. *See also* have/with an eye for/on/to the main chance *above. 17th cent.*

Francis Bacon *The Wisedome of the Ancients* 1619
This Fable seemes to point at the Leagues and Pacts of Princes, of which more truely the opportunely may be said, that bee they neuer so strongly confirmed with the solemnity and religion of an oath, yet are for the most part of no validitie: insomuch that they are made rather with an eye to reputation, and report and ceremonie; then to faith, security and effect.

with one eye on something

giving part of one's attention to something, while concentrating mainly on something else. *19th cent.*

Dickens *Martin Chuzzlewit* 1844
With a leer of mingled sweetness and slyness; with one eye on the future, one on the bride; and an arch expression in her face, partly spiritual, partly spirituous, and wholly professional and peculiar to her art; Mrs. Gamp rummaged in her pocket again, and took from it a printed card.

See also ALL eyes; a bird's-eye view *at* BIRD; have SQUARE eyes; here's MUD in your eye; HIT some-body in the eye / between the eyes; keep one's eye on the ball *at* BALL[1]; LOOK somebody in the eye(s); LEAP to the eye; MEET somebody's eye; more to something than meets the eye *at* MEET; pull the WOOL over somebody's eyes; turn a BLIND eye; a worm's-eye view *at* WORM.

eyeball

eyeball to eyeball

face to face with somebody, especially in a tense or hostile atmosphere. *Late 20th cent.*

She 1989
The experience may bring you eyeball to eyeball with some of the thoroughly unpleasant aspects of your own personality.

See also give somebody the HAIRY eyeball; up to one's eyes/eyeballs in something *at* EYE.

eyebrow

raise one's eyebrows / an eyebrow

to show doubt or scepticism about something, especially in a restrained or tentative way. To *raise eyebrows* is to cause such a reaction. *19th cent.*

Henry James *The Portrait of a Lady* 1881
But Madame Merle sometimes said things that startled her, made her raise her clear eyebrows at the time and think of the words afterwards.

eye-tooth

give one's eye-teeth for

to be prepared to make any sacrifice in order to achieve or acquire something: the *eye-teeth* are the canine teeth situated below the eyes. *17th cent.*

James Shirley *The Politician* 1655
How his frown | Hath scatter'd 'em like leaves, they fly from him | As nimbly, as their bodyes had no more weight | Then their Petitions; I would give an eye-tooth, | To read but three lines.

face

The primary meaning of the noun, 'the front part of the human head', is the basis for most of the senses underlying the phrases. The main figurative development is the group of senses to do with outward appearance or expression, which arose early in the word's history and is found in Chaucer.

the acceptable face

an aspect of something that is acceptable or attractive, the implication being that there are adverse or unsatisfactory aspects as well. The phrase is based on an earlier use of its opposite by the British Prime Minister Edward Heath in 1973, when he referred to the practices of international corporations in making large pay-offs and exploiting tax loopholes as *the unacceptable face of capitalism*. The phrase rapidly attained a currency in both its positive and its negative forms in extended applications. *Late 20th cent.*

> Guardian 1984
> *There could be between 5,000 and 10,000 young people in Britain forced into caring roles. This is the unacceptable face of care in the community.*

> Today 1992
> *Diana is the acceptable face of the British monarchy – if they lose her services it is a great blow.*

face the music

to confront the unpleasant consequences of one's actions; to accept a reprimand or punishment. The phrase appeared in the 1850s in American use: an article in the *Congressional Globe* in March 1850 warned that 'there should be no skulking or dodging ... every man should "face the music"'. Suggestions as to what music is being faced and where (e.g. a new performer going on stage in a music theatre; a military ordeal or punishment involving a ceremonial band) are no more than

hypothetical and are not based on specific evidence. *19th cent.*

> Harriet Beecher Stowe My Wife and I 1871
> *If, indeed, her engagement were to-day to be declared, I would face the music like a man, walk up to her and present my congratulations in due form.*

get out of somebody's face

NAmer, informal to stop annoying somebody or getting in their way. *20th cent.*

have the (brass) face to do something

to have the nerve or effrontery to do something bold or reckless. *17th cent.*

> Shakespeare Coriolanus IV.vi.122 (1608)
> [Menenius] *If he were putting to my house the brand | That should consume it, I have not the face | To say 'Beseech you, cease.'*

if the face fits

if a particular person is suitable or has the necessary qualifications. *20th cent.*

> The Times 1988
> *If Graham Taylor came back to Watford and they went down, he would be regarded as highly as ever. It's a case of if your face fits.*

in the face of something

1 confronted with a difficulty and having to deal with it. *19th cent.*

> Wilkie Collins The Haunted Hotel 1879
> *In the absence of any such proof, and in the face of the evidence of two eminent physicians, it is impossible to dispute the statement on the certificate that his lordship died a natural death.*

2 despite a contrary factor or consideration. *19th cent.*

> Hardy A Pair of Blue Eyes 1873
> *Loving him in secret had not seemed such thoroughgoing inconstancy as the same love recognized and acted upon in the face of threats.*

in your face

bold or aggressive in manner: often with hyphens as an adjective, and used as an interjection expressing scorn or contempt. *Face* signifies directness and immediacy (as in *look somebody in the face, say something to somebody's face*, etc), and the underlying notion is presumably of a fist shoved threateningly in front of somebody's face. The phrase seems to have its origins in the language of the popular music industry (see the quotation below, from an appropriately named source). *In yer face*, a more aggressive form, became a buzz phrase in the early 1990s, boosted by its role as the title of the theme tune for a Channel 4 television programme, *The Word*. Late 20th cent.

The Face 1992
But then the Mondays, as they insist, have changed. 'Yes Please' isn't about thrills and pills, it's not meant to be consumed through a pumping club sound system, it's altogether on a much mellower tip. Whereas the Mondays were once upfront and in your face, now they've polished up their act, they've sacrificed the power punch of their old menace.

lose face
to be humiliated or personally compromised. *Face* in the meaning 'outward show or appearance' dates from the 14th cent.; the phrase occurs from the 19th cent.

make/pull a face / faces
to have a facial expression of displeasure or dislike. In 16th cent. usage *make faces* meant 'to perform as an actor'. The locus classicus, which develops this meaning, occurs in Shakespeare's *Macbeth* (1606) in the words of Lady Macbeth to her husband after the apparition of Banquo's ghost at the banquet (III.iv. 66): 'Shame itself, | Why do you make such faces? When all's done | You look but on a stool.' But there is an earlier use by Thomas Nashe (see below) which takes the history of the phrase back into the last part of the 16th cent.

Thomas Nashe The Unfortunate Traveller 1594
Another did nothing but winke and make faces. There was a parasite, and he with slapping his hands and thripping his fingers seemed to dance an antike to and fro.

Willa Cather The Song of the Lark 1915
The mention of Harsanyi's name always made him pull a wry face.

off one's face
informal drunk or affected by drugs. *20th cent.*

The Face 1992
No, I go out very rarely now. I wanted to prove it was possible to have a good time without getting off my face.

put a brave/bold/good, etc face on something
to suppress one's fears or anxieties about a situation and try to act confidently. An earlier and now obsolete phrase *show a bold face* dates from the 15th cent.; the phrase in its present form is 19th cent.

William Black A Daughter of Heth 1871
Remorse and misery for all the rest of our years would be the penalty to both of us by your going with me to-night, even though you might put a brave face on the matter, and conceal your anguish.

Virginia Woolf The Voyage Out 1915
For goodness' sake ... one might think you were an old cripple of eighty. If it comes to that, I had an aunt who died of cancer myself, but I put a bold face on it.

save face
to avoid humiliation or embarrassment; to retain people's respect despite a setback or failure. *Early 20th cent.*

Somerset Maugham Of Human Bondage 1915
Then he understood that Mildred had deceived him again. She was not coming back to him. He made an effort to save his face. 'Oh, well, I daresay I shall hear from her. She may have sent a letter to another address.'

set one's face (against something)
to oppose an idea or course of action resolutely. In earlier use *set one's face* was used in positive meanings denoting purpose and direction; the current figurative negative sense dates from the 17th cent. Both meanings are illustrated by passages from the Authorized Version of the Bible (1611): at Genesis 31:21 Jacob 'fled with all that he had; and he rose up and passed over the River, and set his face toward the mount Gilead'; and at Leviticus 20:5 the Lord says to Moses 'Then I will set my face against that man, and against his family, and will cut him off'.

Charles Lamb Essays of Elia 1823
I quarrel with no man's tastes, nor would set my thin face against those excellent things, in their way, jollity and feasting.

show one's face
to appear at a place in person, usually briefly. *16th cent.*

Marlowe Tamburlaine the Great, Part Two v.iii.114 (1587)
Draw, you slaves! | In spite of Death I will go show my face.

Bunyan *The Pilgrim's Progress* 1684

So he said to him, peace be to thee; up, for I have set open the door to thee; come in, for thou art blest. With that he gat up, and went in trembling, and when he was in, he was ashamed to show his face.

Charlotte Brontë *Jane Eyre* 1847

You could not bear me to be raised above you, to have a title, to be received into circles where you dare not show your face, and so you acted the spy and informer, and ruined my prospects for ever.

shut one's face

informal to stop talking, to keep quiet: usually in the imperative. *19th cent.*

Jack London *Sea Wolf* 1904

Get into yer bunks, now, and shut yer faces; I want to get some sleep.

throw something (back) in somebody's face

to reject somebody's idea or proposal in a summary or ungracious manner. The notion of casting something in a person's face occurs in extended metaphor from the early 17th cent., notably by Shakespeare in *Hamlet* (1601) ii.ii.575: 'Am I a coward? | Who calls me villain, breaks my pate across, | Plucks off my beard and blows it in my face, | Tweaks me by th' nose, gives me the lie i'th' throat | As deep as to the lungs? Who does me this?'

Dickens *Nicholas Nickleby* 1839

'But nobody would pay you interest for it either, you know,' returned Arthur, leering at Ralph with all the cunning and slyness he could throw into his face.

Jennifer Taylor *Destined to Love* 1992

He was right, of course; she did owe him the courtesy of an apology, even though he would very likely throw it back in her face.

See also keep a STRAIGHT face; LAUGH in somebody's face; LAUGH on the other side of one's face; not just a PRETTY face; turn one's face to the WALL; WIPE the smile off somebody's face.

fact

the facts of life

information about sexual reproduction and sexual practices, especially as given to children or young people. *19th cent.*

Hardy *Jude the Obscure* 1895

It was that I wanted to be truthful. I couldn't bear deceiving him as to the facts of life. And yet I wasn't truthful, for with a false delicacy I told him too obscurely – Why was I half wiser than my fellow-women? and not entirely wiser! Why didn't I tell him pleasant untruths, instead of half realities?

fade

do/take a fade

informal to run away: based on the notion of 'fading away' or disappearing. *20th cent.*

fail

without fail

without exception or the possibility of compromise: used to strengthen the force of an instruction. *Fail* here is used in its early meaning equivalent to 'failure', which is now obsolete except in this phrase. *18th cent.*

Benjamin Franklin *Autobiography* 1771

Resolve to perform what you ought. Perform without fail what you resolve.

faint

a faint heart

timidity or lack of resolution in an undertaking: from the proverb *a faint heart never won a fair lady* (16th cent., although the sentiment was expressed in other ways from an earlier date). The meaning of *faint* here is 'cowardly, lacking courage', and has survived only in this phrase. It dates from the 17th cent. in allusive use.

not have the faintest

informal to have no idea at all about something. After *faintest* a word such as *idea* or *notion* is implied. *Mid 20th cent.*

William Fox *Willoughby's Phoney War* 1992

'He asked me if I wanted to attest.' 'Funny thing to ask. What does it mean?' 'Haven't the faintest.'

fair

The oldest meanings, which date from Old English, are to do with beauty and colour; the predominant meaning in current use, and the one underlying the phrases, is the one denoting just and honest treatment, which developed in the 14th cent. out of a meaning denoting freedom from (physical and later moral) blemish.

all's fair in love and war

(proverb) an encouragement to be bold in these two allegedly comparable activities, and especially the first. This is a statement about love, as early uses, in assertions such as 'love and war are all one' (17th cent.), make clear. In modern use the proverb often has an extension to cater for a third theme special to the user, such as Michael Foot's assertion (reported in 1986) 'I said on one occasion that all was fair in love, war and parliamentary procedure'. It dates from the 19th cent. in this form.

be fair game

to be a legitimate object for appropriation, attack, ridicule, etc: with reference to game birds that may legally be hunted in the open season. In a use slightly earlier than those recorded for *fair game*, William Cowper in his satirical *Table Talk* (1780) observes that 'a monarch's errors are forbidden game'. *19th cent.*

by fair means or foul

using any methods available, regardless of honesty or integrity. *17th cent.*

Francis Kirkman *The Unlucky Citizen* 1673
I knew that if I should deal with those kind of Gypsies, and they should prove, and I by fair means or foul should be drawn to marry them, that then I should lose my Father for good and all.

Defoe *Captain Singleton* 1720
Finding by our dumb signs to the inhabitants, that there were some people that dwelt at the foot of the mountains, on the other side, before we came to the desert itself, we resolved to furnish our selves with guides, by fair means or foul.

C M Yonge *The Daisy Chain* 1856
By fair means or foul, the commodities were cleared off, and, while the sun-beams faded from the trodden grass, the crowds disappeared, and the vague compliment – 'a very good bazaar,' was exchanged between the lingering sellers and their friends.

fair and square

1 fair(ly) and honest(ly). *17th cent.*

William Wycherley *The Gentleman Dancing-Master* 1673
For you are fair and square in all your dealings, | You never cheat your Doxies with guilt Shillings.

2 exactly or directly; full or squarely. *20th cent.*

Country Living 1991
I mean serious winter puddings, steamed, boiled and baked, sticky, rich and sweet, that sit fair and square on the plate and fill you with a glorious glow of warmth and well-being.

a fair deal

honest and equitable treatment. The name *Fair Deal* was used in the US for a programme of social improvement instituted after the Second World War by President Harry S Truman (1945–53). The phrase also occurs now and then as a variant of *a good* (or *great*) *deal* in the sense 'quite a lot' or 'quite often'. *19th cent.*

fair dos

informal fair and reasonable treatment. *19th cent.*

a fair field and no favour

equal conditions for everybody in a contest. *19th cent.*

Trollope *Phineas Finn* 1869
She desired to taunt him with his old fickleness, and yet to subject herself to no imputation. 'Your right!' she said. 'What gives you any right in the matter?' 'Simply the right of a fair field, and no favour.'

fair's fair

a request for or assertion of fair treatment. *19th cent.*

Garnet Walch *A Little Tin Plate* 1888
Says Jack, 'So I thought; now, fair's fair – | You've to save him, that's what you've to do.'

Barbara Vine *A Fatal Inversion* 1987
'I didn't actually ask you to come.' 'True, but I come, didn't I? I done the work and I'll want paying. Fair's fair.'

fair to middling

reasonably good; tolerable though not outstanding. Both words originally designated the quality of goods: *fair* dates from Middle English in a wide range of applications (some still current) and *middling* – as its name suggests – denoted the second of three grades of quality of a product. The phrase first appears in American literature in the mid 19th cent.

David Ross Locke *Eastern Fruit on Western Dishes* 1875
His countenance, to use a mercantile phrase, was 'fair to middling'. It was undeniably handsome,

though his eye glittered cruelly, something like a frozen mill-pond in winter.

a fair-weather friend
a friend who is unreliable in a time of trouble or difficulty. *18th cent.*

for fair
NAmer, informal completely and wholeheartedly. *Early 20th cent.*

> Jack Kerouac On the Road 1957
> *Then we danced and started on the beer for fair.*

See also a fair CRACK of the whip; fair DINKUM; get / give somebody a fair SHAKE; it's a fair COP.

---

fairy

(away) with the fairies
seemingly mad or crazed. *20th cent.*

> New Musical Express 1992
> *'Well wicked' we say. Not wicked but definitely off with the fairies earlier this week was Alex, bass player and chief hair-shaker from Ned's Atomic Dustbin.*

---

faith

in good faith
with honest or sincere intention. *Good faith* in the sense 'fidelity, loyalty' dates from Middle English, and *in good faith* is also recorded from the same period in the meaning 'really, truth to tell'. The transition to the current meaning occurs in the literature of the 18th cent.

> Ann Radcliffe The Mysteries of Udolpho 1794
> *'That's a plausible scheme, in good faith,' said another with a smile of scorn. 'If I can eat my way through the prison wall, I shall be at liberty!'*

See also PUNIC faith.

---

fall

fall into place
(said of seemingly disparate or obscure information) to begin to seem sensible or coherent. *19th cent.*

> Mrs Humphry Ward Robert Elsmere 1888
> *Examine your synoptic gospels, your Gospel of St. John, your Apocalypse, in the light of these. You have no other chance of understanding them. But so*

examined, they fall into place, become explicable and rational.

fall off (the back of) a lorry
British, informal (said of property) to be acquired dishonestly: based on the traditional excuse made for goods that are suspected of having been stolen. *Mid 20th cent.*

> Guardian 1985
> *If everyone swapped over loads mid-journey, that would give the Tea-leaves another go at it, double opportunity for things to fall from the backs of lorries, like the shiploads of Japanese televisions that do already.*

fall over oneself
to show great eagerness to do something: used earlier in the meaning 'to become confused'. *Early 20th cent.*

> Kylie Tennant Lost Haven 1947
> *Why was it that ... these rich coots with tons of money nearly fell over themselves grabbing at anything they could get free?*

fall short (of) something
to fail to achieve what is required or expected: from military terminology, with reference to a weapon or missile that fails to reach its target. *16th cent.*

> P Belon The Court Secret 1689
> *Whether there was any foul play shew'd to him after this, my Memoirs therein fall short, but it is certain he liv'd not long after that resolution was taken.*

> Byron Don Juan 1821
> *So supernatural was her passion's rise; | For ne'er till now she knew a check'd desire; | Even ye who know what a check'd woman is | ... would much fall short of this.*

take the fall
to accept the blame or responsibility for something, especially in place of the real culprit: a *fall guy* is a person who takes the blame in this way. *See also* take the RAP. *Mid 20th cent.*

> Dashiell Hammett The Maltese Falcon 1930
> *He's not a fall-guy unless he's a cinch to take the fall. Well, to cinch that I've got to know what's what.*

See also bend/fall over backwards *at* BACKWARD(s); be riding for a fall *at* RIDE; come/fall apart at the seams *at* SEAM; come/fall into line *at* LINE¹; fall between two stools *at* STOOL; fall from

GRACE; fall on DEAF ears; fall/land on one's FEET; fall on STONY ground; fall PREY to; fall to the GROUND; fall to —'s LOT.

false

a false dawn
a hopeful sign that proves illusory: from the physical meaning 'light that appears just before sunrise'. *19th cent.*

> **Charlotte Brontë** *Shirley* 1849
> *She looked pretty, meditating thus: but a brighter thing than she was in that apartment – the spirit of youthful hope. According to this flattering prophet, she was to know disappointment, to feel chill no more: she had entered on the dawn of a summer day – no false dawn, but the true spring of morning – and her sun would quickly rise.*

See also PLAY somebody false.

family

the/one's family jewels
informal a man's genitals, regarded as a means of continuing the family. *20th cent.*

> **William Shawcross** *The Shah's Last Ride* 1989
> *Agger was struck by the Pahlavi dogs, particularly the Great Dane, Beno, a vast animal that had a habit of nuzzling people's laps. There go the family jewels, thought Agger to himself more than once.*

in the family way
informal pregnant. The phrase occurs often in 18th cent. literature in the more literal meaning 'in a family environment' (as in *all together in the family way*) or 'as regards a family'; in its special sense the first evidence is predominantly 19th cent.

> **Mrs Gaskell** *Mary Barton* 1849
> *In one o' her letters, poor thing, she ends wi' saying, 'Farewell, Grandad!' wi' a line drawn under grandad, and fra' that an' other hints I knew she were in th' family way; and I said nought, but I screwed up a little money, thinking come Whitsuntide I'd take a holiday and go and see her an' th' little one.*

sell (off) the family silver
to dispose of valuable and irretrievable assets in order to make a short-term profit, typically out of recklessness or desperation, in the manner of the impoverished owners of a large country house. The phrase has been widely used in criticism of the privatization of nationalized industries, most tellingly in a speech given to the Tory Reform Group in 1985 by Lord Stockton (Harold Macmillan, as reported in *The Times* for 9 November): 'First of all the Georgian silver goes, and then all that nice furniture that used to be in the saloon. Then the Canalettos go.' *20th cent.*

famous

famous for fifteen minutes
(said of an obscure or unknown person) achieving a brief period of fame because of some circumstance that catches the public attention for a short time: attributed to a remark made in 1968 by the US artist Andy Warhol, that 'in the future everybody will be world famous for 15 minutes'. The phrase was also the title of a series of BBC radio programmes broadcast in 1988 and concerned with the subsequent fortunes of people who had returned to obscurity after achieving brief fame. *Late 20th cent.*

> **S Hutson** *Heathen* 1993
> *Madame Tussaud's ... sometimes suggest figures I should have here. You know, the 'Famous for fifteen minutes' type. The pop stars, the TV celebrities or sportsmen. I put them in my Warhol Gallery. That's what I call it.*

famous last words
a bold assertion or prediction that might be proved by circumstances to be embarrassingly or perilously wrong: often used as a rejoinder to such an assertion, the implication being that it might prove to be ironically appropriate as final words of the kind attributed to famous people on their deathbeds. Originally in services' use, and recorded in Partridge, *Dictionary of Forces' Slang* (1948). *Mid 20th cent.*

> **Michael Munn** *Hollywood Rogues* 1991
> *Madonna had not even appeared in court with him. Before going to prison he was allowed to go and see her, and she told him, 'I won't divorce you while you're in prison.' Famous last words.*

fancy

The noun *fancy* is derived via Middle English forms *fantsy* and *phant'sy* from the noun *fantasy*.

Fancy has two main strands of meaning which occasionally intertwine: one has to do with thinking and imagining and the other with fondness or liking. The verb dates from the mid 16th cent. and shares these two strands of meaning (which are roughly of the same date), i.e. 'to imagine' and 'to be fond of'. The phrase *fancy oneself* (see below) probably draws on both strands: 'to be fond of or partial to oneself' and therefore 'to think highly of oneself', and 'to imagine oneself ...' (in an elliptical use that leaves the nature of the fancying to the imagination).

fancy oneself
informal to have a high opinion of oneself; to be conceited. In earlier usage one might fancy oneself in love, alone, a paragon of virtue, free from guilt, gifted with second sight, and so on, but in the current informal sense one just fancies oneself, whatever one is. *19th cent.*

Daily Telegraph 1866
He ogles, he 'fancies himself'.

David Lawrence The Chocolate Teapot 1992
Andy (Sharon's twin brother) and Keith (who fancies Sandra) jump on James (who fancies himself) to the accompaniment of loud cheering from everyone else.

fancy one's/somebody's chances
to be confident of a successful outcome to an undertaking. *20th cent.*

tickle somebody's fancy
to excite or interest somebody. *Tickle* here is used in its sense 'to amuse or divert', recorded from the 17th cent. *17th cent.*

Thomas Blount The Academy of Eloquence 1656
Though with some men you are not to jest, or practise capricio's of wit; yet the delivery of the most weighty and important matter, may be carried with such an easie grace, as it may tickle the fancy of the reader, and yield a recreation to the writer.

George Campbell The Philosophy of Rhetoric 1776
Sublimity elevates, beauty charms, wit diverts. The first, as hath been already observed, enraptures, and as it were, dilates the soul; the second diffuseth over it a serene delight; the third tickles the fancy, and throws the spirits into an agreeable vibration.

Dickens Nicholas Nickleby 1839
Newman Noggs did not say that he had hunted up the old furniture they saw, from attic or cellar; or that he had taken in the halfpenny-worth of milk for

tea that stood upon a shelf, or filled the rusty kettle on the hob, or collected the wood-chips from the wharf, or begged the coals. But the notion of Ralph Nickleby having directed it to be done tickled his fancy so much, that he could not refrain from cracking all his ten fingers in succession.

See also TAKE a liking/fancy to.

fantastic
See TRIP the light fantastic.

far

far and away
by a considerable margin. *19th cent.*

far be it from — (to —)
an expression of (often ironic or pretended) reluctance to do or say something that might cause disagreement or offence: in early use also in the form *far be it that — should—. 17th cent.*

Bunyan The Holy War 1682
Far be it, far be it from me to desire to make a war upon you; if ye will but willingly and quietly deliver up your selves unto me.

Jane Austen Pride and Prejudice 1813
Far be it from me ... to resent the behaviour of your daughter. Resignation to inevitable evils is the duty of us all.

a far cry
very unlike, in no way approaching (especially in importance or level of achievement): originally used with reference to places a long way apart, the sense of *cry* being 'calling distance'. In 19th cent. romantic literature we find the expression *a far cry to Lochow*, which Sir Walter Scott described as follows in *A Legend of Montrose* (1819): 'a proverbial expression of the tribe, meaning that their ancient hereditary domains lay beyond the reach of an invading enemy'. *19th cent.*

K Eric Drexler Engines of Creation 1985
This success [with DNA] is a far cry from cloning a whole cell or organism ... but it does show that the hereditary material of these species still survives.

far gone
in a bad state, especially from disease or drunkenness. *16th cent.*

Shakespeare *Richard II* ii.i.185 (1595)
[Duke of York] *O, Richard, York is too far gone with grief, | Or else he never would compare between.*

go too far
to exceed acceptable limits of behaviour, to behave improperly. *18th cent.*

Thomas Amory *The Life of John Buncle, Esq.* 1756
Bellinda soon saw she had gone too far, and did all that could be done to recover him from the fit he was in. She smiled, cried, asked pardon; but 'twas all in vain.

so far so good
used to express provisional satisfaction with the progress of a situation or undertaking in its early stages. *18th cent.*

Richardson *The History of Sir Charles Grandison* 1753
Is not he, are not all my friends, sure of finding me at home, whenever they visit me? So far, so good, said aunt Eleanor.

See also as far as it goes *at* GO.

farm

buy the farm
NAmer, informal to die. The expression originates in US Air Force slang, with specific reference to pilots crashing and dying during combat. The earliest recorded uses are from the 1950s, although the origins probably lie in the Second World War rather than in the (more recent) Korean War. The image of buying a farm and settling down might have been symbolic of retirement from flying, as a kind of metaphor for death. The phrase also occurs in early use in related forms such as *buy the plot* (listed in a glossary of pilots' slang published in *The New York Times* in 1954) and *buy the ranch*, which convey the same image. Alternatively, though much less probably, *buying the farm* might be what the government had to do to recompense a farmer on whose land a military aircraft had crashed: in this sense the pilot *bought the farm* with his life. (For this account, see the journal *American Speech* Vol.XXV for 1955.) But it is surely significant that in its first uses it was often the aircraft and not the pilot that was the subject of the phrase and 'did the buying', which rather undermines both theories. In the 1930s a driver was said to 'buy' an obstacle or hazard when he crashed a car into it, as in *buy the tele-*

graph pole, and in British English *have bought it* also means 'to be killed', in which sense it is found in forces' slang from the time of the First World War. These uses undoubtedly influenced the phrase we are considering here. *Mid 20th cent.*

Kim Newman *The Night Mayor* 1990
I had decided that I wasn't going to wear the arrow suit for Truro Daine. When Daine bought the farm, he left a big hole in the City.

fast

play fast and loose
to behave dishonestly, to say one thing and do another; typically, to trifle with another's emotions. *Fast and loose* was a sleight-of-hand game using a stick and a length of cord, played at fairs. *16th cent.*

Shakespeare *King John* ii.i.168 (1597)
And shall these hands, so lately purged of blood, | So newly joined in love ... | Play fast and loose with faith, so jest with heaven?

pull a fast one
to gain an advantage by deceit or trickery: also in early use in the forms *put over / slip a fast one*, a *fast one* being a trick performed suddenly or rapidly so as to deceive, and perhaps originating in the fast delivery of the ball in cricket. *Early 20th cent.*

Economist 1989
It was soon clear that the Al Fayeds had misled Mr Tebbit, and perhaps pulled a fast one on Mr Rowland.

fat

the fat is in the fire
something done or said is likely to cause trouble: with reference to the spitting effect of cooking fat when it spills over into the flame. In early use (also in the form *all the fat is in the fire*) the meaning was that something had failed irretrievably. *17th cent.*

kill the fatted calf
to celebrate lavishly: from the New Testament story of the prodigal son (Luke 15:11–32), in which the father orders his finest calf to be killed to provide a feast to celebrate his son's repentance and return. *17th cent.*

live off/on the fat of the land

to have a comfortable or luxurious life. In the Old Testament (Genesis 45:18) Pharaoh says to Joseph's brothers 'Ye shall eat the fat of the land'; the meaning of *fat* here, which is otherwise obsolete, is 'the best part' or 'the choicest produce'. The phrase occurs earlier in the form *fat of the soil*. *17th cent.*

> Richardson *The History of Sir Charles Grandison* 1753
> God help me! I never was brought up to anything but to live on the fat of the land, as the saying is.

> Trollope *The Three Clerks* 1857
> I believe he never had a friend, and was known at his club to be the greatest bore that ever came out of Scotland; and yet for thirteen years he has lived on the fat of the land; for five years he has been in Parliament, his wife has gone about in her carriage, and every man in the City has been willing to shake hands with him.

when the fat lady sings

informal when everything is finally over: in full as a proverb, *the opera ain't over till the fat lady sings*, a caution that nothing is finally settled until it's finished. An article published in the *Washington Post* in 1978 claims that the phrase came about as follows: Ralph Carpenter, who was then Texas Tech's sports information director, declared to the press box contingent in Austin, 'The rodeo ain't over till the bull riders ride.' Stirred to top that deep insight, San Antonio sports editor Dan Cook countered with, 'The opera ain't over till the fat lady sings.' The allusion is to the stereotype of the large prima donna singing a final aria before dying or some other dramatic close. But reference to opera seems strange in the context of a popular sport, and in fact the proverb appears two years earlier, in F R and C R Smith's *Southern Words and Sayings* (1976) in the form *Church ain't out 'til the fat lady sings*, which is rather more believable. We can also more readily believe that a shift to the refined world of opera might be made in the broader context of general usage. Yet another version, beginning *the game's not over*, may relate to the practice of hearing a woman singing 'God Bless America' at the end of the World Series baseball games, and in particular Kate Smith, who sang in the 1930s and 1940s and by all accounts fitted the physical description. But this looks like hindsight, since the phrase does not occur this early. Like many phrases for which specific origins are claimed, this one

evidently developed rapidly in different forms, once the notion of the large lady singing took hold on the public imagination. *Late 20th cent.*

> Today 1992
> Three large ladies wearing Viking helmets sang what they called George Bush's swansong outside the White House yesterday. 'We're gathered here to test the hypothesis that it ain't over 'till the fat lady sings,' said Peggy Haine, of the Women of Substance Chorale.

---

fate

a fate worse than death

an unpleasant experience. The expression was originally a euphemism for rape, but is now often used humorously in other contexts. The phrase is 18th cent. in its current form, but the notion is earlier.

> Charles Brockden Brown *Edgar Huntly* 1799
> The only females in the family were my sisters. One of these had been reserved for a fate worse than death; to gratify the innate and insatiable cruelty of savages by suffering all the torments their invention can suggest.

seal somebody's fate

(said of an action, admission, etc) to make unpleasant consequences certain. *17th cent.*

> Elkanah Settle *The Conquest of China by the Tartars* 1676
> But if she prove too tardy in her hate: | If one impression cannot seal thy Fate, | The King shall hear the story of thy Pride, | With some enlargement of my own beside.

See also TEMPT fate.

---

father

the father and mother of a —

(as an intensifying phrase) a particularly large, powerful, formidable, etc example of the thing specified. Originally (as in Bunyan below) a metaphor based on parenthood. In modern use *mother* and *father* is sometimes used alone. In the months preceding the Gulf War of 1991, the Iraqi leader Saddam Hussein promised 'the mother of all battles' (but not the father), and the phrase cropped up again in the more recent war in Iraq which brought about his downfall in 2003. *17th cent.*

Bunyan *The Life and Death of Mr Badman* 1680
*This envy is the very Father and Mother of a great
many hideous and prodigious wickednesses.*

Frances Mary Hendry *Quest for a Babe* 1990
*You've a grip like the father and mother of all
lobsters, Lachlan Cattanach!*

founding father
somebody who founds an organization or institution; originally (as *Founding Father*) a member of the American Constitutional Convention established on independence in 1787. Figurative uses date from the early 20th cent.

how's your father
nonsense or frivolous play; in modern use chiefly with reference to sexual activity. *20th cent.*

like father, like son
a son's character and behaviour are likely to be similar to his father's: compare the Latin tag *qualis pater, talis filius* (= as the father is, so is the son). The corresponding female version *like mother, like daughter* originates in Ezekiel 16:44: 'Every one ... shall use this proverb against thee, saying, As is the mother, so is her daughter.' The phrase is 17th cent. in this form, although the notion goes back to Middle English.

fault

to a fault
to an uncomfortable or excessive degree. *17th cent.*

Jeremy Collier *A Short View of the Immorality of the English Stage* 1698
His Master confesses himself kind to a fault. He owns this Indulgence was a Breach of Justice, and unbecoming the Gravity of an old Man.

favour

do somebody a favour
1 to perform an act of kindness for somebody. The phrase is recorded first in the form *do somebody the favour of* (with the act specified): *cf* Shakespeare, *The Comedy of Errors* (1594) I.i.123: '[Duke to Egeon] And for the sake of them thou sorrow'st for, | Do me the favour to dilate at full | What have befall'n of them and thee till now.' Scott in *The Heart of Midlothian* (1818)

makes a character say 'I have a friend ... who will ... do me so much favour'. *16th cent.*

Marlowe *Dr Faustus* xiii.13 (1590)
We have determined with ourselves that Helen of Greece was the admirablest lady that ever lived. Therefore, Master Doctor, if you will do us that favour as to let us see that peerless dame of Greece, whom all the world admires for majesty, we should think ourselves much beholding unto you.

2 (as *do me a favour*) British, *informal* used as a curt rebuttal of what somebody has just said or done. *Late 20th cent.*

M Cole *Dangerous Lady* 1992
She saw Terry walking towards her and smiled at him ... She ran into his arms for a kiss. 'Hello, Princess!' Maura froze in his arms then pulled away from him. 'Do me a favour, Terry.'

favourite

favourite son
a famous man who is especially respected in his own country or home area: in the US used specifically as a title given to George Washington, and with reference to a presidential candidate who is supported in his home state. *18th cent.*

fear

put the fear of God in/into somebody
to alarm or scare somebody greatly, especially as a deterrent: in early use in the form *rub the fear of God into somebody*. *19th cent.*

Carl Tighe *Gdansk* 1990
Himmler wanted me to dispose once and for all of this type of scientific mischief-making. He himself would put the fear of God into the professors of Königsberg and Breslau; I was to do the same thing in Danzig.

without fear or favour
with complete impartiality. *Early 20th cent.*

feast

feast one's eyes (on somebody/something)
to look appreciatively (at somebody or something). Figurative uses of *feast* are recorded from Middle English, *feast one's ears* appearing in the early 17th cent., e.g. in Shakespeare's *Timon of Athens* (1609) III.vii.33 'Gentlemen, our dinner

will not recompense this long stay. Feast your ears with the music awhile.' *17th cent.*

John Reynolds The Triumphs of Gods Revenge 1623
Now whiles she feasted her eyes on his fresh countenance and faire complexion, he sends his abroad to looke on her plate, rich hangings, and houshold stuffe.

Dickens David Copperfield 1850
He looked at us, as if he could never feast his eyes on us sufficiently. Agnes laughingly put back some scattered locks of his grey hair, that he might see us better.

feast of reason
intellectual conversation: with reference to Alexander Pope's description in *Imitations of Horace* (1733) 11.i of good conversation as 'the feast of reason and the flow of soul'. *18th cent.*

feast or famine
a choice between too much or too little of something. *16th cent.*

Henry Peacham The Garden of Eloquence 1577
Gluttonous feasting, and staruing famine are all one, for both taken the bodie, procure sicknesse, and cause death.

G Holtham et al Oxford Review of Economic Policy 1992
The lumpy nature of demand made it essential that contracts be shared out, to ensure that the competitors were not exposed to the risk of alternating 'feast and famine' in their order books.

a ghost/spectre/skeleton at the feast
a chilling or awkward reminder of something from the past that one would prefer to forget, especially when it spoils an otherwise enjoyable occasion. The phrase alludes, whether consciously or not, to Shakespeare's *Macbeth* (1606) III.iv, where the ghost of Banquo, recently murdered on Macbeth's orders, appears at a feast and drives Macbeth to the point of delirium. The phrase itself, however, does not occur in the play, and the ghost is mentioned specifically only in the stage instructions. There are also echoes of similar dramatic occurrences, such as the arrival of the murdered Commendatore at the banquet to which Don Giovanni invites him in Mozart's opera, and even perhaps the ghostly writing on the wall at the Feast of Belshazzar King of Babylon as described in the Book of Daniel. The phrase in its allusive form dates

from the 19th cent., and the variant with *skeleton* may have its origin in a reference in Plutarch's *Moralia* to the ancient Egyptians' practice of displaying a skeleton at funerary banquets.

Anne Brontë The Tenant of Wildfell Hall 1848
Some of our members protested against this conduct. They did not like to have him sitting there like a skeleton at a feast, instead of contributing his quota to the general amusement, casting a cloud over all, and watching, with greedy eyes, every drop they carried to their lips.

Julia Ward Howe Words for the Hour 1857
Where with hum and confusion scarce tempered by music, | The brilliant assemblage thronged their chief man for his virtue, | Sudden she stood, like a guilty ghost at a banquet.

a movable feast
an event that takes place at different times: with reference to Easter and other Christian festivals that occur on different dates in different years. *19th cent.*

Samuel Lover The Happy Man 1839
In short, as you perceive, my darlin, my drum is like Easter, a sort of moveable feast – then when you've emptied it, turn him up, and you make a seat of him! There my darlin, sit down on that.

Ernest Hemingway Movable Feast a1961
If you are lucky enough to have lived in Paris as a young man, then wherever you go for the rest of your life, it stays with you, for Paris is a movable feast.

feather

a feather in one's cap
a personal achievement or honour. The phrase refers to the former practice of wearing a feather as a mark of honour or distinction, dating back to the award of a crest of three ostrich feathers to the Black Prince after the Battle of Crécy in 1346. It may also relate specifically to the former tribal practice in some countries of adding a feather to the headgear each time an enemy was killed. The phrase is recorded in the *Dictionary of the Canting Crew* (published before 1700) as a mark of a fool, but the allusive meaning changed significantly during the course of the 18th cent. *17th cent.*

William Godwin Things As They Are 1794
Sir, I mean to take care of my own happiness. I do not thank you for your interference. Damn me, if I

think this is any thing else but a trick to put a new feather in your cap at your neighbour's expence.

Kipling *Kim* 1901

And also I will embody your name in my offeecial report when the matter is finally adjudicated. It will be a great feather in your cap.

feather one's (own) nest

to enrich oneself, especially at the expense of others. *16th cent.*

Bunyan *The Life and Death of Mr Badman* 1680

When Mr Badman had well feathered his nest with other mens goods and money, after a little time he breaks.

in fine/high feather

in good health or spirits. Also in early use in variant forms such as *in good feather* and (16th cent.) *of the first feather*. The reference is to a bird's plumage as an indication of its condition. *16th cent.*

Thomas Nashe *Pierce Penniless His Supplication To the Devil* 1592

You shall heare a Caualier of the first feather.

Mark Twain *Life on the Mississippi* 1883

I ascended to the pilot-house in high feather, and very proud to be semi-officially a member of the executive family of so fast and famous a boat.

you could have knocked me down with a feather

informal I was utterly astonished. The earliest use is by Richardson (see below): he has *beat* instead of *knock*, the latter being first attested in this phrase in the 1840s. *18th cent.*

Richardson *Pamela* 1741

I was so confounded at these Words, you might have beat me down with a Feather.

Dickens *Barnaby Rudge* 1841

'Why, if here an't Miss Dolly,' said the handmaid, stooping down to look into her face, 'a giving way to floods of tears. Oh mim! oh sir. Raly it's give me such a turn,' cried the susceptible damsel, pressing her hand upon her side to quell the palpitation of her heart, 'that you might knock me down with a feather.'

See also RUFFLE somebody's feathers; show the WHITE feather; smooth somebody's ruffled feathers *at* RUFFLE.

fed

fed up to the (back) teeth

extremely discontented or bored. *Fed up* occurs as a new slang phrase, often in quotation marks, at the beginning of the 20th cent., and intensifying extensions such as *fed to death* and *fed to the teeth* are recorded from about 1920. The notion is of having eaten as much as one can stand. *Early 20th cent.*

feed

be off one's feed

to have lost one's appetite: originally with reference to animals. *19th cent.*

Charles Reade *Hard Cash* 1863

No, Doctor; I'm off my feed for once: if you had been upstairs and seen my poor sister! Hang the grub; it turns my stomach.

feel

See feel one's AGE; feel somebody's COLLAR; feel the DRAUGHT; feel one's oats *at* OAT; feel the PINCH; feel the PULSE of.

feeler

put out feelers

to test other people's opinions on or reactions to an idea or proposal. The image is of the probing tentacles of an insect. *19th cent.*

James Fenimore Cooper *The Sea Lions* 1849

I wish I had brought an old ensign and a small spar along, to set up the gridiron, in honour of the States. We're beginning to put out our feelers, old Stimson, and shall have 'em on far better bits of territory than this, before the earth has gone round in its track another hundred years.

Clyde Fitch *The City* 1909

Oh, he didn't get far – we were interrupted! He put out a feeler, which was very like a demand, as to what he was going to get out of this election.

feet

back on one's feet

having recovered from an incapacitating illness or injury. *20th cent.*

Dick Francis *Longshot* 1990

It seemed I was going to live: the doctors were cheerful, not cautious. 'Constitution like a horse,' one said. 'We'll have you back on your feet in no time.'

be run/rushed off one's feet

to be so busy that one can hardly keep up. In early use also *rushed off one's legs*. *18th cent.*

George Colman Ygr *Ways and Means* 1788

You must get into a sober family, again, I see. My running-hand will be all I have left for it at last; for I shall be run off my feet, I find, in a fortnight.

fall/land on one's feet

to be successful or happy after overcoming difficulties. The image is probably of a cat or other agile animal landing on its feet after falling from a great height. *19th cent.*

James Kirke Paulding *Madmen All* 1847

The actual and the probable are within every one's reach; but it requires a great genius to overleap the barriers of nature, and land on his feet in the regions of impossibility!

feet first/foremost

(said of a person) recently dead: with reference to removing a corpse in its coffin from a house, etc. *19th cent.*

Susan Gates *The Lock* 1990

They put you in a home. Just give 'em half a chance, they'll whip you in and the only way they let you out of them places is feet first, in a box.

feet of clay

a flaw or weakness in somebody who is considered to be otherwise perfect: with allusion to the biblical account (Daniel 2:33) of a figure that King Nebuchadnezzar of Babylon saw in a dream, which had a head and body of precious metals but feet of iron and clay. When these subsequently collapsed, the whole figure was destroyed. *19th cent.*

Mrs Gaskell *Wives and Daughters* 1866

'I think I've been very weak, Molly,' said Mrs. Hamley, stroking Molly's curls affectionately. 'I've made such an idol of my beautiful Osborne; and he turns out to have feet of clay, not strong enough to stand firm on the ground. And that's the best view of his conduct, too!'

find one's feet

1 (said of a young child or animal) to begin to stand up and walk. *16th cent.*
2 to gain confidence by experience in an undertaking. *17th cent.*

Robert Baron *Pocula Castalia* 1650

Now did he find his feet and gin to move | Upon a wheele of danger.

George Eliot *Middlemarch* 1872

Not that this inward amazement of Dorothea's was anything very exceptional: many souls in their young nudity are tumbled out among incongruities and left to 'find their feet' among them, while their elders go about their business.

have/keep one's feet on the ground

to have a sensible and practical attitude to life. *Mid 20th cent.*

Doremy Vernon *Tiller's Girls* 1988

Suddenly they were wearing expensive clothes on and off stage, taking cabs everywhere, men were showering them with gifts in an attempt just to be seen with them. It was difficult to keep their feet on the ground when they read about themselves in the newspapers.

stand on one's own (two) feet

to rely on one's own resources and act independently. In early use the meaning was also 'to be judged on one's own merits'. *17th cent.*

Defoe *Moll Flanders* 1722

She promis'd to make me easy in my circumstances, and to leave me what she could at her death, secur'd for me separately from my husband, so that if it should come out afterwards, I should be able to stand on my own feet, and procure justice too from him.

take to one's feet

to run away. *18th cent.*

think on one's feet

to be forced to think or decide quickly. *Mid 20th cent.*

Owen Chadwick *Michael Ramsay: A Life* 1991

He discovered an unexpected gift which won boys' respect. He found that he could make a speech – that is, he could think on his feet, and not be at a loss for words.

under somebody's feet

1 *old use* at somebody's mercy: also with *foot*. The image is of being held underfoot. *Old English*

Shakespeare *2 Henry IV* iii.i.58 (1597)
This Percy was the man nearest my soul, | Who like a brother toiled in my affairs, | And laid his love and life under my foot.
2 constantly in somebody's way. *20th cent.*

Ideal Home 1991
If you're fed up with your teenage children getting under your feet in the school holidays, help may be at hand.

vote with one's feet
to express a dissenting opinion by leaving or staying away. *Late 20th cent.*

See also FOOT; CARRY somebody off their feet; DIG in one's heels; DRAG one's feet; KEEP one's feet; SIX feet under; SWEEP somebody off their feet.

fell

in/at one fell swoop
all at once; in a single concentrated effort. The phrase is used with allusion to the words of Macduff on hearing of the murder of his family in Shakespeare's *Macbeth* (1606) iv.iii.220: 'All my pretty ones? | Did you say all? O hell-kite! All? | What, all my pretty chickens and their dam | At one fell swoop?' *Swoop* calls to mind the rapid descent of a bird of prey, such as a falcon, on its unsuspecting victim, and *fell* is an adjective dating from Middle English meaning 'evil, terrible'; it is derived from an Old French word *fel* meaning 'evil', which is also the source of our word *felon*. *17th cent.*

fence

over the fence
Australian and NZ, informal unacceptable or objectionable. *Early 20th cent.*

K S Prichard *Brumby Innes* 1927
It's over the fence Brum, the way you have been carrying on.

rush one's fences
to act hastily or precipitately: a metaphor from steeplechasing, in which a horse that rushes a fence risks falling. *Early 20th cent.*

sit on the fence
to avoid making a decision or expressing an opinion: from the notion of a fence as represent-

ing a boundary between two areas, the areas here representing choices. *19th cent.*

Annals of Cleveland 1830
Now all would-but-dare-not-be-politicians who insist in sitting on the fence, will be amerced a penalty for the same.

See also MEND (one's) fences.

fetch

fetch and carry
to act servilely towards somebody by constantly performing tasks and running errands: originally with reference to dogs retrieving game. *Cf* Shakespeare, *The Two Gentlemen of Verona* (1593) iii.i.273: '[Lance] Here is the catalogue of her conditions. *Imprimis*, she can fetch and carry – why, a horse can do no more. Nay, a horse cannot fetch, but only carry.' *16th cent.*

fettle

in fine/good/high fettle
in a very good state or condition. *Fettle*, meaning 'condition or state', is used only in this group of phrases. It is based on a much earlier (Middle English) verb meaning 'to put in order, to arrange', which in turn derives from a noun *fettle* meaning 'a girdle or belt' (so the notion of girding oneself up comes to mind). Anne Brontë used *fettle up* in her novel *Agnes Grey*, published in 1847: 'So I dusted him a chair, an' fettled up the fire place a bit.' And Mrs Gaskell in *North and South* (1855) makes a character complain that the world 'needs fettling, and who's to fettle it?' This meaning chiefly survives in technical uses such as 'to trim the edges of pottery or metal casts'. *18th cent.*

George Eliot *Middlemarch* 1872
It's a fine thing to come to a man when he's seen into the nature of business: to have the chance of getting a bit of the country into good fettle, as they say, and putting men into the right way with their farming.

few

few and far between
scarce or rare; difficult to find or come by. The image is perhaps of localities, in reality or as shown on a map, or it may be of trees in a wood, as in the quotation from Byron below, or

of visits from angels, as in Thomas Campbell's poem *The Pleasures of Hope* (1799): 'What though my wingèd hours of bliss have been, I Like angel-visits, few and far between.' Jane Austen commented on Campbell's line in *Sanditon* (1817): 'Campbell in his *Pleasures of Hope* has touched the extreme of our Sensations – "Like Angel's visits [*sic*], few & far between." Can you conceive any thing more subduing, more melting, more fraught with the deep sublime than that line?' There is a stray quotation (referring to hedges) from the 17th cent. in the *OED*, but most of the evidence is from the latter part of the 18th cent. or later.

> Byron *Mazeppa* 1819
> *'Twas studded with old sturdy trees, I That bent not to the roughest breeze I Which howls down from Siberia's waste, I And strips the forest in its haste, – I But these were few and far between, I Set thick with shrubs more young and green.*

have had a few
to be slightly drunk. Also in the form *have a few in*. *20th cent.*

> Muriel Spark *The Ballad of Peckham Rye* 1960
> *'Nelly's had a few,' Humphrey said … 'She's a bit shaky on the pins tonight.'*

---

fiddle

The oldest meaning refers to the stringed instrument and dates from early Middle English. Most of the phrases are based on this sense or on the corresponding verb meaning 'to play the fiddle'. In the 17th cent. the noun developed a light-hearted meaning associated with the player of a fiddle, 'one who makes entertainment' and hence 'a jester'. The modern informal meaning 'a dishonest practice' is originally North American and dates from the late 19th cent.

fiddle while Rome burns
to be preoccupied with trivial affairs or entertainment and ignore disastrous events going on around one: from the account given by Suetonius (*Nero* 38) of the great fire that destroyed large parts of Rome in AD 64, during which the emperor Nero is said to have played music and sung. There are direct references to the Nero story from the 17th cent., e.g. in George Daniel's *Trinarchodia* (1649) 'Let Nero fiddle out Rome's

obsequies'; but allusive uses in more generalized contexts date chiefly from the 19th cent.

> James Fenimore Cooper *The Ways of the Hour* 1850
> *This vice is heartless and dangerous when confined to its natural limits, the circles of society; but, when it invades the outer walks of life, and, most of all, when it gets mixed up with the administration of justice, it becomes a tyrant as ruthless and injurious in its way, as he who fiddled while Rome was in flames.*

on the fiddle
British, *informal* involved in dishonest practices. *20th cent.*

> Petronella Pulsford *Lee's Ghost* 1990
> *The rich get richer and the poor get poorer, my accountant's on the fiddle and I'm an overdrawer.*

play second fiddle
to play a secondary or subordinate role to somebody. The allusion is to the first and second violins in an orchestra or chamber group. *Play first fiddle* is attested slightly earlier (late 18th cent.) but is not now in common use. *19th cent.*

> Trollope *The Three Clerks* 1858
> *But he felt that he was forced to play second fiddle before his lady love; and it was Harry Norman's misfortune that though doomed to play second fiddle through life, he could not reconcile himself to that place in the world's orchestra.*

> Peter Lewis *The Fifties* 1978
> *Mao Tse-tung had played second fiddle to Stalin as senior revolutionary but Khrushchev was a different matter.*

See also (as) fit as a fiddle *at* FIT[1].

---

field

be/have a field day
to be or enjoy a spectacular success. A *field day* was a day on which troops were assembled for exercises or for a military display. *19th cent.*

> John Henry Newman *Loss and Gain* 1848
> *He told him of his anxiety to restore Willis to 'the Church of his baptism'; and, not discouraged by Charles's advice to let well alone, and that he might succeed in drawing him from Rome without reclaiming him to Anglicanism, the weather having improved, he asked the two to dinner on one of the later Sundays in Lent. He determined to make a field-day of it; and, with that view, he carefully got*

up some of the most popular works against the Church of Rome.

hold the field

to maintain one's position; to have the upper hand or be winning. *Keep* (or *maintain*) *the field* is recorded from the 17th cent. in the different sense 'to keep up the fight'. The current phrase dates from the 19th cent.

> Mrs Humphry Ward *Robert Elsmere* 1888
> *Lady Aubrey was lying back on the velvet sofa, a little green paroquet that was accustomed to wander tamely about the room perching on her hand. She was holding the field against Lord Rupert and Mr. Addlestone in a three-cornered duel of wits.*

play the field

to exploit several (especially sexual) relationships without making an exclusive commitment. *Mid 20th cent.*

> *Esquire* 1993
> *He gave up playing the field and married a year ago, to a sinewy woman called Cheryl Berkoff.*

take the field

1 (said of an army) to begin a military campaign: the meaning of *field* here is 'an area in which troops are operating'. *17th cent.*

> Aphra Behn *Oroonoko* 1688
> *The Wars came on, the time of taking the field approach'd, and 'twas impossible for the Prince to delay his going at the head of his army.*

2 (said of a sports team) to go out on the pitch for a game. *20th cent.*

See also a FAIR field and no favour; a LEVEL playing field.

fifteen

See FAMOUS for fifteen minutes.

fifth

fifth column

a group within a nation or organization that sympathizes with and works secretly for an enemy or rival. The term originated in 1936 during the Spanish Civil War, when the Nationalist General Mola claimed that an extra 'column' of supporters was present in the city of Madrid, which he was besieging with four columns of troops. *The Fifth Column* is the title of a novel by

Ernest Hemingway (published in 1938) that is set in Madrid during the siege. *Mid 20th cent.*

take the Fifth

in the US, to exercise one's constitutional right to decline to testify in order to avoid incriminating oneself: with allusion to the 'Fifth Amendment', Article V of the US Constitution, passed in 1791, according to which 'no person ... shall be compelled in any criminal case to be a witness against himself ... without due process of law'. *Late 20th cent.*

fig[1] (the fruit)

The word has been used since late Middle English in various expressions (e.g. *a fig for* —!, *not worth a fig*) as symbolic of the insignificant or worthless.

not give/care a fig

to be quite unconcerned. *17th cent.*

> Vanbrugh *The Provok'd Wife* 1697
> *I wou'd not give a fig for a song, that is not full of sin and impudence.*

> Henry James *Confidence* 1880
> *I have given her a choice of Rome or the Nile ... but she tells me she doesn't care a fig where we go.*

not worth a fig

not worth anything, of no value. *16th cent.*

> Alexander Brome *Songs and Other Poems* 1661
> *For surely this Mastiff, though he was big, | And had been lucky at fighting, | Yet he was not qualifi'd worth a fig | And therefore he fell a biting.*

fig[2]

in full fig

smartly or ceremonially dressed for an occasion. This word *fig* is not the fruit but is based on a verb *feague*, itself derived from German *fegen* meaning 'to sweep'. To *feague away* meant 'to set rapidly in motion', and an expression *fig out*, meaning 'to dress up', is recorded from the early 19th cent. *19th cent.*

> Charles Jennings *Now We Are Thirty-something* 1991
> *Church service, guests, parents, binge afterwards in hired accommodation of some kind. Bride will wear something special for the occasion, but not the full fig with veil.*

fight

fight a losing battle
to be bound to fail in spite of all one's efforts. *19th cent.*

> Trollope *Barchester Towers* 1857
> *Why should he give up his enjoyments and his ease, and such dignity as might be allowed to him, to fight a losing battle for a chaplain? The chaplain after all, if successful, would be as great a tyrant as his wife. Why fight at all?*

fight shy of something/somebody
to avoid becoming involved with a person or situation. *18th cent.*

> Mary Robinson *Walsingham* 1797
> *Pure stuff, master; I gets it over by means of a friend, who has as snug a boat as ever crossed the Goodwins: and only, that I mayn't do as I likes, and should fight shy of the penalty, I vou'd set up a varehouse myself, and supply my friends vith sperits of my own importance.*

See also fight FIRE with fire; fight like CAT and dog; fight TOOTH and nail; live to fight another day *at* LIVE[1].

figure

a figure of fun
a person who is often derided or ridiculed. *18th cent.*

> John O'Keeffe *The Positive Man* 1798
> [Stern] *He has put into the Minories to refit, a neat cabin, and a snug berth there. Why sun dazzle my lanthorns! can this be he?* [Enter Grog, fashionably dress'd.] [Bow] *Ha, ha, ha! What a figure of fun!*

fill

fill somebody's shoes/boots
to take over somebody's job or responsibilities. *19th cent.*

> Charlotte Brontë *Jane Eyre* 1847
> *'She is a good hand, I daresay,' said the charwoman. 'Ah! – she understands what she has to do, – nobody better,' rejoined Leah, significantly; 'and it is not every one could fill her shoes: not for all the money she gets.'*

See also fill the bill *at* BILL[1].

final

See the last/final STRAW.

find

finders keepers (losers weepers)
(proverb) somebody who finds something by chance is entitled to keep it, and the former owner will have to accept its loss. The phrase dates from the 19th cent. in this form, and in early use also occurs in the form *findings keepings*. The sentiment, however, is older, expressed in other ways, e.g. 'what a man finds is his own'.

> Edward Eggleston *The Circuit Rider* 1874
> *If I could find the right owner of this money, I'd give it to him; but I take it he's buried in some holler, without nary coffin or grave-stone. I 'low to pay you what I owe you, and take the rest out to Vincennes, or somewheres else, and use it for a nest-egg. 'Finders, keepers,' you know.*

> William Clark Russell *The Wreck of the Grosvenor* 1878
> *'You are to be congratulated on having won the love of a woman whose respect alone would do a man honour.' 'He deserves what he has got,' said the doctor, laughing. 'Findings keepings.'*

find God
to undergo a religious conversion. *18th cent.*

> Henry Baker *Medulla Poetarum Romanorum* 1737
> *Who could know Heav'n, unless that Heav'n bestow'd | The Knowledge? or find God, but Part of God?*

find it in one's heart to do something
to be hard-hearted enough to do something: often in negative contexts. The phrase goes back to Middle English in the form *find in one's heart*.

> William Godwin *Things As They Are* 1794
> *He had been long a stranger to pleasure of every sort, and my artless and untaught remarks appeared to promise him some amusement. In this uncertainty he could not probably find it in his heart to treat with severity my innocent effusions.*

> Dickens *Pickwick Papers* 1837
> *Mr. Pickwick ... caught Arabella in his arms, and declaring that she was a very amiable creature ... said he could never find it in his heart to stand in the way of young people's happiness.*

find one's way

to reach a destination by one's own efforts, and often despite difficulties. Also by extension with reference to things, the implication being that something has passed into another's possession as though by its own efforts, i.e. without human intervention, as a euphemistic description of theft or other suspect acquisition of property. *18th cent.*

> Nathaniel Hawthorne *House of Seven Gables* 1851
> *Beyond all question, he had the blood of a petty huckster in his veins, through whatever channel it may have found its way there.*

See also find one's FEET.

fine

cut/run it/things fine

to leave oneself with very little time to complete a task, reach a destination, etc. *19th cent.*

> Robert Smith Surtees *Handley Cross* 1843
> *Captain Slasher, with a hired barouche and four black screws, all jibbing and pulling different ways – the barouche full of miscellaneous foot cornets in plain clothes (full of creases of course), dashes down East Street, and nearly scatters his cargo over the road, by cutting it fine between Squire Jorum's carriage and the post.*

fine feathers

beautiful clothes: from the proverb *fine feathers make fine birds. 16th cent.*

> Margaret Cavendish *Bell in Campo* 1662
> *He is not one that sets forth to the wars with great resolutions and hopes, and returns with masked fears, and despairs; neither is he like those that take more care, and are more industrious to get gay clothes, and fine feathers, to flaunt in the field, and vapour in their march, than to get usefull and necessary provision.*

> Willa Cather *The Song of the Lark* 1915
> *I was just thinking how tired she looked, plucked of all her fine feathers.*

the finer points

the more detailed or complex aspects of something. *Late 20th cent.*

> P R White *Planning for Public Transport* 1976
> *Many economists expert in the finer points of judging small-time savings, or the effect of taxation in determining net resource costs, have only the haziest idea of costs.*

one's finest hour

one's greatest achievement or moment of glory. The phrase, although of earlier date, is influenced in modern use by the words of Winston Churchill in the House of Commons on 18 June 1940 before the Battle of Britain: 'Let us therefore brace ourselves to that duty, and so bear ourselves that, if the British Commonwealth and its Empire lasts for a thousand years, men will still say, "This was their finest hour".' *19th cent.*

> Emmeline Stuart-Wortley *Sunset at Mola De Gaeta* 1838
> *And still that rich Reflection's boundless blaze, | Wins, fixes, fascinates the admiring gaze! | ... | And casts, as 'twere, his crown from off his brow, | To jewel Earth and Air thus richly now, | And is himself, in this his finest hour.*

fine words

eloquent sentiments and compliments, especially when regarded as inadequate without more substantial support: from the proverb *fine/fair words butter no parsnips* (butter being a traditional garnish for serving parsnips). *17th cent.*

> Thomas Rymer *Reflections on Aristotle's Treatise of Poesie* 1674
> *Studied phrases, a too florid stile, fine words, terms strain'd and remote, and all extraordinary expressions are insupportable to the true Poesie.*

> Jane Austen *Emma* 1816
> *There had been no real affection either in his language or manners. Sighs and fine words had been given in abundance; but she could hardly devise any set of expressions, or fancy any tone of voice, less allied with real love.*

have/get something down to a fine art

to refine one's skill or ability in an activity by experience. The *fine arts* (plural) are those primarily appreciated for their aesthetic qualities, such as painting or sculpture, and in the 1850s John Ruskin in *The Two Paths* defined *fine art* (singular) as 'that in which the hand, the head, and the heart of man go together'. In its plural use the term is not recorded before the middle of the 18th cent., but *fine art* occurs from an earlier date in a looser more compositional sense that generally underlies the present phrase. The phrase itself is found from the 17th cent.

William Lower *The Phoenix in Her Flames* 1639

[Rapinus] *Come sit downe,* | *How long have you professed surgery?* | *I never saw you practise it before.* [Lucinda] *I learnt it from a child.* [Rapinus] *Tis a fine art* | *And well it doth become a Ladies hand* | *Gentlie to touch a wound.*

not to put too fine a point on it

to speak plainly or bluntly: with allusion to the tip of a weapon. The expression is a favourite of Mr Snagsby in Dickens' *Bleak House* (see below). *19th cent.*

Dickens *Bleak House* 1853

'Well, sir,' returns Mr. Snagsby, 'you see my little woman is – not to put too fine a point upon it – inquisitive. She's inquisitive.'

W S Gilbert *Princess Toto* 1876

Don't be angry; but it was generally supposed that you were – in short, dead; and, not to put too fine a point upon it, the Princess is going to marry another Prince – a nice, well-behaved young man – plays the flute, does worsted work, wears goloshes.

one fine day

at some unspecified or random point in a course of events. The phrase is a stock device for introducing an incident or happening that has significant ramifications in the course of a narrative, typically one occurring unexpectedly or after a period that is uneventful. It is famous as the standard English translation of Butterfly's aria *un bel dì vedremo* ('one fine day we'll spy a thread of smoke rising from the sea in the far horizon') in Act II of Puccini's *Madama Butterfly* (1904, text by Giacosa and Illica based on David Belasco's drama of 1900), in which she sings longingly of the return of her lover Pinkerton. *19th cent.*

Maria Edgeworth *Patronage* 1814

One fine day, after dinner, Mrs. Percy proposed, that instead of sitting longer in the house, they should have their dessert of strawberries in some pleasant place in the lawn or wood.

Punch 1992

When the PM sends his personal invitation you can scarcely say: 'Sorry I'm washing my hair.' Not if you really do want to be the Chancellor one fine day.

finger

be all fingers and (all) thumbs

to be clumsy or awkward in handling something delicate or intricate. The phrase occurs earlier in the form *one's fingers are all thumbs*: for example in the works of Sir Thomas More (1550s) we find the admission that 'every fynger shalbe a thombe, and we shall fumble it vp in haste'. John Heywood recorded a similar use in his collection of proverbs of 1546: 'Whan he should get ought, eche fynger is a thumbe.' This use survived into the late 19th cent. but is now obsolete. The English writer and literary scholar Sir Arthur Quiller-Couch (1863–1944) took us a step nearer the current version of the phrase when he wrote in 1899 'I think my fingers must be all thumbs'. The current form seems to be 20th cent.

Independent 1989

Martin Cruz Smith is a dab hand at beginnings, as readers of Gorky Park will remember; but he tends to fumble his middle sections, and by the time the climax arrives he's all fingers and thumbs.

burn one's fingers / get one's fingers burned/ burnt

to suffer as a result of one's own ill-advised efforts or enterprise. The phrase originally implied dangerous or risky meddling, and is now used chiefly in the context of financial undertakings. Early uses show how the phrase arose from the notion of physical touching. *17th cent.*

Lady Mary Wroth *The Countesse of Mountgomeries Urania* 1621

How kind soeuer she might be to him in priuate, had he offerd to touch her publikely, that touch had burnt his fingers.

Robert Montgomery Bird *Sheppard Lee* 1836

If anybody supposes I treated the old woman ill – that I acted dishonestly, and even illegally, in the matter – all I have to say is, that I only did what Abram Skinner the shaver had done a thousand times before me, and what, I have no doubt, other worthy gentlemen of his tribe have done after me. He who rides with the devil must put up with his driving; and he who deals with his nephews must look for something warmer than burnt fingers.

get/pull/take one's finger out

British, informal to stop procrastinating and make a start on what one is supposed to be doing. Mid 20th cent.

give somebody the finger

to raise one's middle finger as an offensive gesture of contempt or irritation. Mid 20th cent.

B Schulberg What Makes Sammy Run? 1941
I must have been a little further gone than I thought, to tell him about my studio troubles with Pancake … 'Let me show you how to give that guy the finger,' he said.

have a finger in every pie

to be involved in very many activities or enterprises. The phrase is often used in a depreciatory way implying unwelcome interference, as also in the earlier (16th cent.) phrase have a finger in the pie meaning 'to be involved' or, more scathingly, 'to be grasping or interfering'. In the opening scene of Shakespeare's Henry VIII (1613), the Duke of Buckingham curses Cardinal Wolsey with the words (1.i.52) 'The devil speed him! No man's pie is freed | From his ambitious finger.' The form of the phrase with every dates from the 19th cent.

Robert Howard The Committee 1665
My Wife is without, together with | The Gentlewoman that is to compound: She will | Needs have a finger in the pie.

Nathaniel Parker Willis Romance of Travel 1840
His seclusion is rendered the more tolerable by the loss of his teeth, which were rudely thrust down his throat by this same Lenzoni (fated to have a finger in every pie) in defence of the attacked party on that occasion.

have/keep one's finger on the pulse

to ensure that one remains aware of the latest developments or trends: a medical metaphor. Late 20th cent.

Martin Amis Money 1985
Nowadays the responsible businessman keeps a finger on the pulse of dependence.

not lay a finger on somebody

to avoid hurting or interfering with somebody. 19th cent.

not lift/move/stir a finger

to avoid making the slightest effort to help. 19th cent.

point the finger

to make a direct accusation against a specific individual or organization: also in the form point the finger of scorn. 18th cent.

John Logan Runnamede 1783
A Baron of the realm, an English chieftain, | Arm'd, and invested with supreme command, | Will never brook dishonour, never bear | The shadow of affront; nor suffer man | To point the finger, or to lift the look | Of scorn against him.

put/lay one's finger on something

to identify the main point or cause of a problem or issue. 19th cent.

John Keble Lectures on Poetry 1844
When … I came to consider Euripides more nearly, many points arose which gave me pause and made me slow to degrade from primary rank a poet who has won such praise: and the chief of them was this, that I think I may venture to say that I have put my finger on a definite source and origin of his poetry.

put the finger on somebody

to inform on a wrongdoer. Early 20th cent.

Kim Newman The Night Mayor 1990
We've got to get out of here … Somebody could have put the finger on us.

snap one's fingers

to make a sharp clicking sound with the fingers, especially in order to demand instant attention. In recent use the image is often merely symbolic, without necessarily implying an actual movement of the hands. 18th cent.

Smollett The Adventures of Peregrine Pickle 1751
To such an unguarded pitch was she provoked, that starting up, she snapt her fingers, in testimony of disdain, and, as she quitted the room, applied her hand to that part which was the last of her that disappeared, inviting the company to kiss it, by one of its coarsest denominations.

Julian Barnes Talking It Over 1992
For a start, have you ever looked at old men, the sort of old men who seduce young women? The roguish high-bummed stride, the fuck-me tan, the effulgent cuff-links, the reek of dry-cleaning. They snap their fingers as if the world is their wine-waiter.

twist/wind/wrap somebody round/around one's little finger

to be easily able to get what one wants from somebody. 19th cent.

Scott *The Bride of Lammermoor* 1819
I see nothing against it but the father or the girl taking a tantrum, and I am told the mother can wind them both round her little finger. Take care not to affront her with any of your Jacobite jargon.

work one's fingers to the bone
to become worn out with hard manual or domestic work. *18th cent.*

John Cleland *Memoirs of a Woman of Pleasure* 1748
I could have made a pleasure of the greatest toil, and work'd my fingers to the bone, with joy, to have supported him.

See also CLICK one's fingers; CROSS one's fingers / keep one's fingers crossed; have one's fingers in the TILL; have GREEN fingers.

fingertip

at one's fingertips
readily available for one to use. *19th cent.*

George Cohan *Broadway Jones* 1912
Well, I believe the plant did show a profit last year. I expect Miss Richards here shortly. She can tell you exactly what it is – she's got it at her finger-tips.

to one's fingertips
completely, utterly. *19th cent.*

Henry James *Guy Domville* 1893
The actor-manager was 'Piccadilly' to his fingertips – a dandy of the 1890's endowed by nature with straight-cut, handsome features and an excellent pair of legs that made him partial to costume pieces.

finish

a fight to the finish
a fight or contest that is continued until one of the parties is completely defeated or destroyed. *Early 20th cent.*

Roi Cooper Megrue *Under Cover* 1914
I know they mean business. This is going to be a fight, Monty, a fight to the finish.

fire

Meanings associated with ardour and passion of feeling, which underlie many of the current phrases, date from late Middle English and are common in the 17th cent. and 18th cent. *Cf* Shakespeare, *Julius Caesar* (1599) I.ii.179 '[Cassius] I

am glad | That my weak words have struck but thus much show | Of fire from Brutus.'

breathe fire
to be very angry. The image is of a fire-breathing dragon, and this image commonly occurs in older literature in extended metaphor. A locus classicus is the biblical description of King Antiochus of Syria in the Book of Maccabees in the Authorized Version (9:7): 'Howbeit he nothing at all ceased from his bragging, but still was filled with pride, breathing out fire in his rage against the Jews.' The use is earlier in graphic descriptions, occurring in the 16th cent. (see below).

John Lyly *Euphuès* 1578
As hee is a terrible God, whose voyce is lyke the rushinge of many waters, so is he a mercifull God whose wordes are as softe as Oyle. Though he breath fire out of his nostrils agaynst sinners, yet is he milde to those that aske forgiuenesse.

catch fire
to become interesting; to take on new life or vigour: from the physical meaning of starting to burn. *18th cent.*

Charles Batteux *A Course of the Belles Letters* 1761
The exordium of the ode should be always bold; for, when the poet snatches his lyre, he is supposed to be forcibly struck with the objects he represents to himself. His imagination catches fire; he sets off like an impetuous torrent, which overflows its banks.

fight fire with fire
to use the same weapons that one's opponents or rivals are using, however underhand or distasteful. *16th cent.*

Shakespeare *King John* v.1.48 (1597)
[Bastard to King John] *Let not the world see fear and sad distrust | Govern the motion of a kingly eye. | Be stirring as the time, be fire with fire; | Threaten the threat'ner, and outface the brow | Of bragging horror.*

Thomas Killigrew *Thomaso* 1664
Not sad, nor much pleas'd; yet I am glad to find Don Harrigo is so neer his cure as to know his disease; I see he'l try to cure fire with fire, the remedy has been often prov'd.

fire and brimstone
a terrible fate or punishment: with allusion to biblical references to the torments of eternal damnation (Genesis 19:24, Psalms 11:6, Revelations 14:10, 20:10, and elsewhere). *Brimstone* is an old

word for 'sulphur', and the combination with *fire* dates from the 16th cent. as a description of the fires of hell. *Fire and brimstone* was formerly also used as a form of imprecation, e.g. by Othello during a violent conversation with Desdemona in Shakespeare's *Othello* (1604) IV.i.231. *17th cent.*

fire in one's/the belly

a strong feeling of determination. *Mid 20th cent.*

firing on all (four) cylinders

in good working order; (said of a person) fit and healthy. *Mid 20th cent.*

go through fire (and water)

to face many dangers and hazards. The phrase dates from the 16th cent. in this form, but the notion goes back to Old English.

Shakespeare *The Merry Wives of Windsor* III.iv.102 (1597)
[Mistress Quickly] *A kind heart he hath. A woman would run through fire and water for such a kind heart.*

in the firing line / line of fire

open to criticism or censure. The expressions are metaphors from military language, but the two terms do not mean quite the same. The *line of fire* is the path along which a bullet or other projectile travels, whereas the *firing line* is a line of armed soldiers firing; but the images are clear in both cases. *19th cent.*

Augustus Thomas *As a Man Thinks* 1911
[Clayton] *Curiosity of that kind in a woman is idle and immoral!* [Elinor] *And in a man?* [Clayton] *A man's on the firing line – a woman's in the commissariat.* [Elinor] *Which is a fine way of saying you have a license for transgression that your wife has not.*

light a fire under somebody

to provoke somebody to action. *20th cent.*

play with fire

to take foolhardy risks. *19th cent.*

Derek Piggott *Gliding Safely* 1990
The remains of the aircraft showed the true potential power of nature ... It was obvious from this that in going into storms we were quite literally playing with fire.

under fire

being strongly criticized, especially from several quarters at once: from the literal meaning of

being within range of an enemy's guns. The phrase is first found in this form in the 19th cent., but figurative use of *fire* in this meaning is slightly earlier (late 18th cent.).

Mark Twain *Sketches New and Old* 1875
She was under fire, now, as usual when the day was done. That is to say, she was being chaffed without mercy, and was enjoying it.

where's the fire?

informal used to express surprise about a person's inclination to hurry or act precipitately. *Early 20th cent.*

Martin Amis *Time's Arrow* 1991
We're up and down those stairs – hey, where's the fire?

See also the FAT is in the fire; HANG fire; pull the chestnuts out of the fire *at* CHESTNUT; SET the world alight / on fire.

---

fireman

See visiting fireman *at* VISIT.

---

firm

be on firm ground

to be sure of one's position in a contest or dispute: from the literal meaning (especially in military contexts) of standing or moving on ground that provides firm support. *19th cent.*

Mrs Gaskell *Wives and Daughters* 1866
'Damn it, Roger! I'm not a child; I won't be treated as such. Leave go I say!' Roger let go; they were now on firm ground, and he did not wish any watchers to think that he was exercising any constraint over his father.

a firm hand

strong control or guidance: from the notion of a firm hand controlling the reins of a horse or the leash of a dog. *19th cent.*

Charlotte Brontë *Villette* 1853
He had stately daughters, too, like himself; these children he reared with a suave, yet a firm hand; they grew up according to inheritance and nurture.

first

at first hand

through personal experience: based on the use of *hand* with the ordinals *first, second*, etc to denote a sequence of persons who experience or possess something. *16th cent.*

first and last

taking everything into account; essentially or most importantly. The phrase occurs in the Authorized Version of the Bible (1611), e.g. at 1 Chronicles 29:29 'Now the acts of David the King, first and last, behold, they are written in the book of Samuel the Seer, and in the book of Nathan the Prophet, and in the book of Gad the Seer.' *The first and last* was common from the 17th cent. in the sense 'the only one'. At the beginning of the banquet scene (III.iv) in Shakespeare's *Macbeth* (1606), Macbeth greets the guests with the words 'You know your own degrees; sit down. At first and last | The hearty welcome.'

first come, first served

(proverb) people will be dealt with in the order in which they arrive, apply, etc. The notion goes back to the time of Chaucer, who draws on a French proverb to the effect that the first comer to the mill gets to grind his corn first (*The Wife of Bath's Prologue*, line 389 'Whoso that first to mille comth, first grynt'). The phrase dates from the 16th cent. in this form.

> Henry Porter *The Two Angrie Women of Abington* 1599
> *How, whose that Nicholas? so first come first serud,*
> *I am for him: how now prouerbe, prouerbe?*

> Scott *A Legend of Montrose* 1819
> *In my camp, all must be upon equality, like the*
> *Knights of the Round Table; and take their places as*
> *soldiers should, upon the principle of – first come,*
> *first served.*

first in, first out

(proverb) goods that were received first are the first to be supplied when a sale is made: used especially as a principle of accounting. Also abbreviated to *FIFO*. *Mid 20th cent.*

first off

informal, originally NAmer as the first point; to begin with. *19th cent.*

> R G Toepfer *Witness* 1966
> *First off, he'd better feed the chickens and slop the pigs.*

first past the post

in elections, the candidate with a simple majority wins: the analogy is with racing, in which the winner is the first to pass the winning post. *Mid 20th cent.*

first thing

early in the morning, as one's first activity: from a more general use in the sense 'the first thing one does, that happens, etc'. *18th cent.*

> Thomas Holcroft *The Road To Ruin* 1792
> *You cheat all day, tremble all night, and act the hypocrite the first thing in the morning.*

first things first

(proverb) everything should be dealt with in due order. *First Things First: Addresses to Young Men* was the title of a book published in 1894. *19th cent.*

first up

first of all; to begin with. *20th cent.*

> New Musical Express 1992
> *First up, they were stopped at the US border for the customary van search and their local driver was found to be in possession of a dozen or so ready-rolled 'recreational' cigarettes.*

from first to last

throughout the course of something, from start to finish. *17th cent.*

> Bunyan *A Book for Boys and Girls* 1686
> *Yea, as for her, the day that she was born, | As loathsome, out of doors, they did her cast; | Naked, and filthy, stinking, and forlorn: | This was her Pedigree from first to last.*

from the (very) first

from the very beginning. The phrase is used in the Authorized Version of the Bible (1611) at the beginning of Luke's Gospel (1:3) 'It seemed good to me also, having had perfect understanding of all things from the very first, to write unto thee in order, most excellent Theophilus.' *17th cent.*

not know the first thing about something

to be completely ignorant or uninformed about something. *19th cent.*

Louisa M Alcott *Hospital Sketches* 1863
Trying to look as if the greater portion of my life had been passed on board boats, but painfully conscious that I don't know the first thing; so sit bolt upright, and stare about me.

of the first order/magnitude

of the most excellent or outstanding kind. *Order* here is used in its meaning 'rank or level'. The image is drawn from astronomy, in which stars of the first order of magnitude are the brightest. *17th cent.*

Aphra Behn *Love Letters From a Noble Man and His Sister* 1685
The Sun at noon is no wonder, but to see as great an Illumination in a Star tho of the first magnitude, we gaze at with admiration.

George Carey *I Believe* 1991
For the Romans, crucifixion was a penalty reserved for criminals and for outcasts. For the first Christians to claim this as the heart of their faith was a scandal of the first order.

there's always a first time / there's a first time for everything

(proverb) used to justify an improbable or unprecedented eventuality. *18th cent.*

J H Ingraham *Blanche Talbot* 1847
Well, you're here now, and there's always a first time, though you've waited till you're pretty old.

Michelle Magorian *Goodnight Mister Tom* 1983
'Ever growed anything afore?' he said, turning to Willie. He shook his head. 'Always a first time.'

See also first among equals *at* EQUAL; first BLOOD; get to first BASE; of the first WATER.

---

fish

a big fish

informal an important or influential person. In 19th cent. literature the expression is also used of desirable male 'catches' sought after by women (as in the extended metaphor from Trollope below). Also *a big fish in a little pond*, a person of importance within his or her immediate sphere of activity but insignificant outside it.

John Pendleton Kennedy *Horse Show Robinson* 1835
This fellow, they say, was cotched cheating with cards one day, when he was playing a game of five shilling loo with the King or the Queen, or some of the dukes or colonels in the guards – for he wa'n't

above any thing rascally. So, it was buzzed about, as you may suppose when a man goes to cheating one of them big fish – and the King gave him his choice to enlist, or go to the hulks; and he, being no fool, listed, as a matter of course.

Trollope *Can You Forgive Her?* 1864
He knew that he had better not follow her. He knew that she was bait with a very visible hook. He knew that he was a big fish for whom these two women were angling. But after all, perhaps it wouldn't do him much harm to be caught.

John R Green *Letter* 1871
They are big fish in a little pond, but one has seen plenty of them shrink ... when they have been plunged into the London 'big water'.

Daily Telegraph 1992
Just how good a choreographer was Bournonville in the first place? ... Was he just a big fish in a very small pool?

fish in troubled waters

to take financial advantage of troubled times or circumstances: based on the proverb *it is good fishing in troubled waters* (because fish proliferate there, if one is prepared to put up with the difficulties). See also pour OIL on troubled waters. *16th cent.*

Richard Braithwaite *A Survey of History* 1638
We shall obserue some, who, though they haue a faire-bet path to walke in, yet will they leaue the tracke, and make the wall or some other high mount their walke. So fates it with these, who had rather fish in troubled waters, then when they are Calme.

Thomas Paine *The American Crisis* 1780
For a thousand reasons, England would be the last country in the world to yield it [obedience] to. She has been treacherous, and we know it. Her character is gone, and we have seen the funeral. Surely she loves to fish in troubled waters, and drink the cup of contention, or she would not now think of mingling her affairs with those of America.

A Short *The Origins of the Vietnam War* 1990
Thus the USSR would be able to fish profitably in the troubled waters of economic chaos.

a fish out of water

a person who is caught in unfamiliar or unsuitable surroundings or circumstances. *17th cent.*

Purchas *Pilgrimage* 1613
The Arabians out of the deserts are as fishes out of the water.

have other/bigger fish to fry

to have other or more important concerns to deal with: often used with dismissive reference to a present unprofitable or troublesome concern. *17th cent.*

like shooting fish in a barrel

easily achieved, especially with reference to picking off victims. *20th cent.*

Derek Robinson *Goshawk Squadron* 1993
> We lost a lot of men. Direct hits on the trenches ... The Jerry observers were looking right down on us. It was murder. Like shooting fish in a barrel.

make fish of one and flesh of the other

Irish to discriminate between people unjustly. *18th cent.*

neither fish, flesh, nor fowl / good red herring

of an indeterminate type or character; hard to classify: also found in other variants. The phrase is recorded from the 16th cent. in John Heywood's collection of proverbs of 1546, and is derived from the ecclesiastical division of food into categories for purposes of fasting and abstinence. *Fish* and *fowl* are regularly paired alliteratively (sometimes with the addition or alternative of *flesh* or *fruit*) in literature of the 17th cent., and provide a rich feast of *f* words representing a variety of things. Shakespeare in *1 Henry IV* (1596) III.iii.127 uses the variant *neither fish nor flesh* (in a conversation in which Sir John Falstaff wittily compares Mistress Quickly to an otter): 'Why? she's neither fish nor flesh; a man knows not where to have her.' A *red herring* (see RED) is a smoked cured herring.

Henry James *Roderick Hudson* 1876
> He had frequent fits of extreme melancholy, in which he declared that he was neither fish nor flesh nor good red herring. He was neither an irresponsibly contemplative nature nor a sturdily practical one.

there are plenty more fish in the sea

(proverb) there are other people in the world to choose from: used especially in the context of a person's romantic prospects. In early use also in the form *there are as good fish in the sea as ever came out of it*. The phrase is 19th cent. in this form, but the notion is recorded from the 16th cent.

See also CRY stinking fish; DRINK like a fish; a pretty KETTLE of fish.

fishing

a fishing expedition

informal, chiefly NAmer an attempt to get information by random enquiry. *Mid 20th cent.*

Accountancy 1992
> There always has to be good reason (which is not defined, but is a sort of distilled wisdom) for undertaking a statutory enquiry; it can't just be a fishing expedition.

fist

make a good/poor, etc fist of/at something

informal to make a creditable (or ineffectual) attempt at something: the image is of the fist as grasping at an objective. *19th cent.*

fit[1] (adjective and verb)

(as) fit as a fiddle/flea

completely healthy and fit. The choice of *fiddle* and *flea* is probably more onomatopoeic than logical, although it is also found in early use in the non-alliterative form *as right as a fiddle*. Attempts to find a rationale for the various versions of the phrase have been forced and contrived to say the least. A fiddle, for example, has to be 'fit' or in peak condition to sound its best, and a flea needs to be fit to perform its astonishing jumps successfully! These underlying notions surely belong more to the realm of desperation than explanation. *17th cent.*

John Fletcher *Women Pleas'd* a1625
> [Bartello] Am I come fit Penurio? [Penurio] As fit as a fiddle. My Master's now abroad about his businesse.

Henry James *The Ambassadors* 1909
> But you're better now; you're safe – I see that for myself ... You're looking, this morning, as fit as a flea.

fit for the gods

perfect of its kind. Originally used with allusion to the words of the assassin Brutus in Shakespeare's *Julius Caesar* (1599) II.i.173 'And, gentle friends, | Let's kill him boldly, but not wrathfully. | Let's carve him as a dish fit for the gods, | Not hew him as a carcass fit for hounds.' *17th cent.*

fit like a glove

(said of clothing) to be a perfect fit. *18th cent.*

Byron *Don Juan* 1824

In her first passion woman loves her lover, | In all the others all she loves is love, | Which grows a habit she can ne'er get over, | And fits her loosely – like an easy glove.

fit to be tied

informal violently angry. The image is of a person so out of control as to need physical restraint. *19th cent.*

Joan Smith *A Masculine Ending* 1988

Daddy's the last person I'd go to for help ... He was fit to be tied when I separated from Hugh, and he seems to blame me for the whole thing.

fit to bust

informal with great effort or determination. The phrase is also used in more explicit extended forms, e.g. *fit to bust a gut. 19th cent.*

Mary Jane Holmes *Millibank* 1871

The affectionate boy could not wait till he reached home before pouring out his tears and grief on her motherly bosom. 'Poor child! I presume he'll cry fit to bust when he sees me,' she said to Mrs. Walter Scott.

Michael Dibdin *Dirty Tricks* 1991

They ganged together round the buffet, whingeing about business, ... exchanging racy stories and tall tales and laughing fit to bust their considerable guts.

See also fill/fit the bill *at* BILL[1].

fit² (noun)

give somebody / have a fit

to greatly shock or startle somebody, or to be extremely shocked or horrified. *19th cent.*

John William De Forest *The Wetherel Affair* 1873

Bless me, where is that paper? Cousin Wetherel would have a fit if I lost it.

in fits

laughing or, in earlier use, weeping uncontrollably. *Fit* in the sense 'a violent outburst', applied chiefly to laughter, tears, etc, dates from the 17th cent.

Henry Fielding *The History of Tom Jones* 1749

Partridge was now summoned, who, being asked what was the Matter, answered, That there was a dreadful Hurricane below Stairs; that Miss Nancy was in Fits; and that the other Sister and the Mother were both crying and lamenting over her.

in/by fits and starts

spasmodically; with occasional bursts of activity: in earlier use in the simpler form *in fits. 17th cent.*

Dryden *The Rival Ladies* 1664

[Rodorick] Cowards have courage when they see not death: | And fearfull hares, that sculk in forms all day, | Yet fight their feeble quarrels by the moonlight. [Manuel] No, light and darkness are but poor distinctions | Of such, whose courage comes by fits and starts.

five

take five

informal, originally N Amer to have a short break or rest. *Five* stands for 'five minutes'. *Early 20th cent.*

fix

fix somebody's wagon

informal to cause somebody's downfall or prevent them from succeeding. *Fix* is used here with strong overtones of its sense 'to take revenge on'. *Mid 20th cent.*

Mario Puzo *Fools Die* 1978

At least he could fix Merlyn's wagon, Ford was beyond his reach. He tried getting her fixed by organizing a campaign of hate mail from fans.

get a fix on somebody/something

to determine the basic nature of somebody or something: from the physical meaning of calculating the position of a ship or aircraft by visual or astronomical observation or from radio or compass bearings. The figurative use may be influenced by the practice of dealers on the London bullion market who determine the price of gold twice a day in a process called a *fix. Mid 20th cent.*

Esquire 1992

Another way to get a fix on people is to identify their heroes.

flag

fly/show the flag / keep the flag flying

to show support for one's country when abroad, especially by promoting its products: originally with reference to ships that flew the ensign when visiting foreign ports. A ship in battle showed its refusal to surrender by keeping its flag hoisted; 'Keep the Old Flag Flying' was the title of a First World War song. Also used in extended contexts with reference to loyalty to a company, organization, etc. *Early 20th cent.*

> Ruth Dudley Edwards *Clubbed to Death* 1993
> *'I only ever go to church when I have to go to funerals ... I suppose you have a family pew in your local?' 'Well, when I'm at home one has to show the flag.'*

put the flags out
to have a public celebration. The phrase is derived from the practice of putting out flags and bunting as part of an outdoor event such as a parade or sports tournament. It is often used ironically to show surprise at an unexpected or overdue response, achievement, etc. Also *the flags are out*, meaning 'the celebrations have started'. *20th cent.*

wrap oneself in the flag
NAmer to make an ostentatious display of patriotism: based on the notion of the flag as a symbol of one's country. *20th cent.*

flagpole

run something up the flagpole
to get initial reactions to a new idea or proposal. *20th cent.*

flame

an old flame
a former admirer or lover. *Flame* is recorded in this meaning from the 17th cent., and the phrase is 19th cent. in this form.

> Thackeray *Vanity Fair* 1848
> *Rebecca instantly stated, that Amelia was engaged to be married – to a Lieutenant Osborne – a very old flame.*

See also SHOOT somebody/something down in flames.

flap

get in a flap
informal to become agitated or panicky: the image is of somebody flapping their arms about in agitation. *Mid 20th cent.*

—'s ears are flapping
the person named is trying hard to overhear something. *Early 20th cent.*

> P G Wodehouse *Carry On, Jeeves!* 1925
> *It was the work of a moment with me to ... dive into a bush ... and stand there with my ears flapping.*

flash

(as) quick as a flash / in a flash
coming very quickly or suddenly, especially with reference to an answer or response. As early uses show, the phrase is short for *quick as a flash of lightning*. *18th cent.*

> Barnabas Bidwell *The Mercenary Match* 1784
> *He dies; as quick as a flash of lightning.*

a flash in the pan
a sudden and short-lived success. The phrase alludes to the firing of the gunpowder in the 'pan' (small hollow) of a musket: on occasions the flint flashed but failed to ignite the charge. The phrase forms part of an extended metaphor at the start of chapter 34 of Dickens' *Bleak House* (1853): ' "Now, what," says Mr. George, "may this be? Is it blank cartridge, or ball? A flash in the pan, or a shot?" An open letter is the subject of the trooper's speculations, and it seems to perplex him mightily.' The verb form *to flash in the pan*, which is recorded earlier (late 18th cent.) in a figurative sense, is no longer current; the noun phrase dates from the 19th cent. in figurative use.

flat

and that's flat
and that is all there is to be said on the matter. In current use the phrase is an expression of determined insistence, but it was used earlier as a simple affirmation of the truth of an assertion, as in Shakespeare's *Love's Labour's Lost* (1594) III.i.102 '[Costard] The boy hath sold him a bargain – a goose, that's flat.' *16th cent.*

> Thomas Betterton *King Henry IV* 1700
> *I'll not march through Coventry with them, that's flat.*

(as) flat as a pancake
completely flat: used in several senses of *flat*. *17th cent.*

John Day *The Blind-Beggar of Bednal-Green* 1659
*Thou speakest all French to me; but off with this
snuffling French Mask, and speak in your English
voyce, or as God sa me I'll beat thy nostrils as flat as
a pancake.*

fall flat
to be a failure or disappointment. Also, to fail in
an obvious or humiliating way. *17th cent.*

flat out
1 *informal* as fast or as hard as possible. The
underlying idea is of a person using their full
strength, and (in the context of speed) there may
be the added notion of an accelerator pedal
pressed flat against the floor of a vehicle being
driven at breakneck speed. *Be flat out for something* is a somewhat dated expression (mainly
mid 20th cent.) denoting determined concentration on achieving an objective. *Mid 20th cent.*
2 *informal* exhausted, worn out. The image is of a
person prostrate after hard work or physical
exertion.

on the flat
on level ground; (in horseracing or greyhound
racing) on an open course without any hurdles or
jumps. *19th cent.*

flat-footed

catch somebody flat-footed
to catch somebody unawares or unprepared. *Mid
20th cent.*

flavour

flavour of the month
a person or thing that is currently fashionable or
popular, but only for a short time: originally as
part of ice-cream marketing in the US in the
1940s, when a particular flavour was promoted
each month. The phrase dates from the late 20th
cent. in extended uses.

Frederick Forsyth *The Negotiator* 1989
*Fact is, the word's out on you, Quinn. Persona non
grata, they're saying at the club. Not the flavour
of the month exactly, especially with your own
people.*

flea

a flea in one's ear
a sharp or humiliating reprimand: usually in the
form *send somebody away with a flea in their ear*. In
Middle English *a flea in one's ear* had the meaning
'something that causes alarm or anxiety' (*cf*
French *avoir la puce à l'oreille*). The phrase is
16th cent. in this sense.

Thomas Shadwell *Epsom-Wells* 1673
*Get you home, you pitiful fellow, or I'll send you
home with a flea in your ear, and you go to that,
thou fumbling fool.*

W S Gilbert *The Gondoliers* 1889
*And if I can catch her I'll pinch her and scratch her,
| And send her away with a flea in her ear.*

See also (as) fit as a fiddle/flea at FIT[1].

flesh

go the way of all flesh
to die: from biblical references to *all flesh* and *all
earth* in the sense of 'human existence'. The dying
words of King David of Israel (1 Kings 2:2) are
given in the Authorized Version (1611) as 'I go
the way of all the earth', and in the Douai translation (probably on the basis of a variant version
of the Latin Vulgate) as 'I enter into the way of all
flesh'. *The Way of All Flesh* is the title of a novel by
Samuel Butler (1835–1902), published posthumously in 1903. *17th cent.*

in the flesh
in bodily form, in person. The phrase dates from
Middle English in the form *in flesh*, and early uses
refer to the Incarnation of Christ.

Thomas Beard *The Theatre of Gods Judgements* 1597
*Although that the sonne of God was not as then yet
manifested in the flesh: yet the power and efficacie of
his death being euerlasting, and from the beginning,
whereof the law with the ceremonies and sacrifices
thereof was as it were a schoolemaister, could not
bee hidden from him.*

Charlotte Brontë *Jane Eyre* 1847
*'My dear master … I am Jane Eyre: I have found
you out – I am come back to you.' 'In truth? – in the
flesh? My living Jane?'*

one's own flesh and blood
one's close relations. *Middle English*

Shakespeare *The Merchant of Venice* II.ii.87 (1598)
[Gobbo] *I'll be sworn, if thou be Lancelot thou art mine own flesh and blood.*

put flesh on (the bones of) something
to give substance or detail to an idea or proposal. *Early 20th cent.*

William Boyle *Family Failing* 1912
Upon my soul, you're clever! Those that know Tom Carragher know that he wouldn't part with a lean beast till he put flesh on her.

See also make somebody's flesh CREEP; one's pound of flesh *at* POUND[1]; PRESS the flesh.

flex

flex one's muscles
to make a show of one's strength or power. *Mid 20th cent.*

Guardian 1972
Pupil power flexes its muscles in London today. The organisers have called on all London secondary school-children to join them in a one-day general strike.

flexible

flexible friend
a credit card: from the advertising slogan for the Access card, with play on the notion that repayment is flexible by virtue of the credit given. *Late 20th cent.*

Daily Mirror 1992
Barclaycard has overtaken Access as Britain's most flexible friend by keeping its annual fee £2 cheaper at £10 and charging lower monthly interest.

flight

in full flight
1 running or escaping at full speed. *19th cent.*

Scott *A Legend of Montrose* 1819
The old Earl of Leven, the covenanting general, was driven out of the field by the impetuous charge of Prince Rupert, and was thirty miles distant, in full flight towards Scotland, when he was overtaken by the news that his party had gained a complete victory.

2 at its peak or height. *Late 20th cent.*

Gardeners' World 1991
The summer bedding season is in full flight now, and to maintain this tapestry of colour, it is advisable to deadhead the flowers as soon as the petals start to fade.

flip

flip one's lid / NAmer wig
informal to become wildly excited or angry: also in the shortened form *flip*. *Mid 20th cent.*

Timothy Mo *The Redundancy of Courage* 1991
Martinho had lost no time in recounting the true details of Osvaldo's moment of weakness, the point at which he'd flipped his lid for the first and last time in his career, that murderous aberration which had been the doom of old friend and new foe alike.

flit

do a (moonlight) flit
informal to depart abruptly (at night), especially in order to avoid an obligation. The noun *flit* is recorded from the 19th cent. and is based on the (Middle English) verb meaning 'to depart, to remove oneself'; *moonlight flitting* is recorded from the 18th cent. in Scottish use. *19th cent.*

Scott *The Heart of Midlothian* 1818
She has left the bones of her mother, and the land of her people, and she is ower the march wi' that son of Belial. – She has made a moonlight flitting of it.

flog

flog a dead horse
to waste one's efforts on a fruitless undertaking or on a matter that has already been settled. The phrase is found from the 19th cent., and occurs earlier in a different form: in a letter of 1770 John Wesley wrote 'we have no need to dispute about a dead horse'.

flog something to death
to pursue a matter or point of view ceaselessly and tediously, so that it loses its effect or value. *19th cent.*

flood

in full flood

talking or acting with great energy: from the literal use describing a river that has swollen and is flowing over its banks: cf in full FLOW. *19th cent.*

> Ouida *Under Two Flags* 1867
> *A tall, fair man, with the limbs of a Hercules, the chest of a prize-fighter, and the face of a Raphael Angel, known in the Household as Seraph, was in the full flood of a story of whist played under difficulties in the Doncaster express.*

floodgate

open the floodgates

1 to release a deluge, especially of heavy rain or tears. Floodgates are used to control a heavy flow of water, especially at the lower level of a canal lock. Early uses are in extended metaphor. *18th cent.*

> William Duff *An Essay on Original Genius* 1767
> *His hypotheses of the position and form of the antediluvian earth, of the causes which produced the universal deluge, occasioned by the opening of the floodgates of Heaven, aided by the bursting asunder of the frame of the earth, ... form altogether such a surprising, ingenious, and at the same time, not improbable system, that we cannot help admiring the whole as the production of an inventive and truly creative Genius.*

> Thackeray *Vanity Fair* 1848
> *How the floodgates were opened and mother and daughter wept, when they were together embracing each other in this sanctuary, may readily be imagined by every reader who possesses the least sentimental turn.*

2 to release strong emotions or feelings. *18th cent.*

> Mary Hays *Memoirs of Emma Courtney* 1796
> *The morality of an uncultivated understanding, is that of custom, not of reason: – break down the feeble barrier, and there is nothing to supply its place – you open the floodgates of infamy and wretchedness. Who can say where the evil may stop?*

> Anne Brontë *The Tenant of Wildfell Hall* 1848
> *I grasped my whip with more determined energy than before – but still forbore to raise it, and rode on in silence, waiting for some more tangible cause of offence, before I opened the floodgates of my soul,*

and poured out the dammed up fury that was foaming and swelling within.

3 to precipitate or be a precedent for a sudden rush of similar unwelcome or undesirable things, such as complaints or legal actions. *20th cent.*

> *Financial Times* 1983
> *They also claimed that they were the victims of discrimination in connection with the payment of compensation ... If the UK claimants eventually succeed it could open the floodgates for similar claims against other governments involving them in tough and expensive renegotiations.*

floor

In the phrases, *floor* is used (except in *take the floor* 2) in the meaning 'part of a legislative or other assembly in which members sit and speak' and in its transferred meaning denoting the people attending a meeting.

cross the floor

British (said of a member of parliament) to join the party opposed to one's present party: from the action of walking across the floor of the House of Commons to sit with the members on the benches on the other side of the central gangway. *20th cent.*

> F Selwyn *Hitler's Englishman* 1987
> *The young Conservative member, whom Beatrice Webb thought the most brilliant man in the House of Commons, crossed the floor to sit as an independent in protest against the use of torture to interrogate Sinn Fein prisoners in 1920.*

from the floor

(said of a speech or question) delivered by an individual attending a meeting and not from the platform. *Mid 20th cent.*

> *Independent* 1988
> *Stephen Bayley, former director of the Design Museum, will chair a debate, taking questions from the floor (many pre-wrapped) and flinging them at a panel of designers, architects, patrons and critics.*

take the floor

1 to stand up at a meeting to make a speech or put a question. *19th cent.*

> Alice Cary *Married, Not Mated* 1856
> *A great excitement pervaded the house when it was read, during which two or three persons took the floor and began speaking at once.*

2 to begin dancing on a dance floor. *19th cent.*

James Hall *The Village Musician* 1833
Often when a dance was ended, he would continue to play on until admonished that his labours were unnecessary; but when a new set took the floor, it was only requisite to give Johnny a smart jog, and off he went again like a machine set in motion.

flotsam

flotsam and jetsam

accumulated odds and ends: from the terms used in maritime law, *flotsam* being a ship's wreckage found floating on the surface of the sea and *jetsam* denoting goods thrown overboard. The phrase dates from the 17th cent. in its physical meaning and from the 19th cent. in figurative senses.

Thomas De Quincey *Notes on Gilfillan's Literary Portraits* 1845
Now, upon this principle of comparison, if we should take any common edition (as the Delphin or the Variorum) of Horace and Lucretius, strictly shaving away all notes, prefaces, editorial absurdities, &c., – all 'flotsam' and 'jetsam' that may have gathered like barnacles about the two weather-beaten hulks, – in that case we ... might then settle the point at once as to which of the two had been the idler man.

flow

go with the flow

to follow the general tendency; to accept what others are doing. *20th cent.*

Pete Silverton & Glen Matlock *I Was a Teenage Sex Pistol* 1990
Most of them just go with the flow, ending up as something like a gas fitter or a policeman.

in full flow

talking or acting with great energy: *cf* in full FLOOD. *19th cent.*

R H Dana *Paul Felton* 1833
Her spirits were in full flow when Paul quitted the room; for it gave animation and cheerfulness to her in all she did, when she thought him near her.

flower

the flower of something

the finest or most perfect example or examples of something: in early use spelt *flour*, the predominant form used until the 14th cent. for all the meanings now divided between *flour* and *flower*. The sense here is not the one now spelt *flower* but the one spelt *flour*, because it denoted the finest part of the wheat. When a distinction in spelling arose during the 16th cent., the association of sense underlying the phrase was transferred to *flower* rather than remaining with *flour*. *Middle English*

Robert Greene *Mamillia* 1583
He was more bound vnto Fortune, which had bestowed vpon him one onely daughter, called Mamillia, of such exquisit perfection and singular beautie, ... as it may suffice for me to say, she was the flower of all Venice.

fluff

See a bit of fluff at BIT[1].

flush

the first flush of something

the early fresh and vigorous stage of something. The underlying meaning of *flush* seems to be 'a surge of emotion', itself a figurative merging of two primary meanings, (1) to do with the flowing or rush of water, and (2) denoting a gentle pink blush, as in *the flush of dawn*. *19th cent.*

Hardy *The Return of the Native* 1878
Now that the first flush of his anger had paled he was disinclined to ascribe to her more than an indiscreet friendship with Wildeve, for there had not appeared in her manner the signs of dishonour.

See also a BUSTED flush.

flutter

flutter the dovecotes

to disturb or unsettle a peaceful community: perhaps with allusion to Shakespeare's *Coriolanus* (1608) v.vi.115 'If you have writ your annals true, 'tis there | That, like an eagle in a dove-cote, I | Fluttered your Volscians in Corioles. | Alone I did it.' *19th cent.*

flutter one's eyelashes

to flirt: from the notion of making one's eyelashes flutter quickly in a conventional show of coyness. *Mid 20th cent.*

Michael Frayn *Sweet Dreams* 1976
You will say yes, won't you, Howard ... If I flutter my eyelashes at you, and promise to bake you one of my apple crumbles?

---

fly

die/drop like flies

to die or collapse in large numbers. *Mid 20th cent.*

Economist 1991
While other retailers are dropping like flies, super-markets are making fat profits.

drink with the flies

Australian and NZ, *informal* to drink by oneself in a bar or other public place. *Early 20th cent.*

D Whittington *Mile Pegs* 1963
'Have a drink?' the larrikin invited. 'Or do you prefer drinking with the flies?'

fly the coop

to succeed in escaping, especially in order to elope. *Early 20th cent.*

fly high

to enjoy great success or prosperity. A *high-flyer* is a person with high ambitions. The phrase dates from the 18th cent. in the related sense 'to reach a high state of activity or feeling'.

a fly in amber

a relic from the past. Amber has been a common medium for preserving the bodies of ancient insects. *19th cent.*

Thomas Aldrich *Marjorie Daw, and Other People* 1873
It was with a thrill of honest pleasure that I came upon this picturesque outcast unexpectedly embalmed, like a fly in amber, in Mr. Keeler's autobiography.

fly in the face of something

to disobey or contradict a directive or belief. *17th cent.*

Jeremy Collier *A Short View of the Immorality of the English Stage* 1698
To disappoint the Stews, is every jot as great a Crime; as to fly in the Face of Nature, and outrage our Parents.

a fly in the ointment

a minor element or aspect that spoils what is otherwise good or enjoyable. The expression alludes to Ecclesiastes 10:1: 'Dead flies cause the ointment of the apothecary to send forth a stinking savour.' *19th cent.*

Catharine Sedgwick *Married or Single?* 1857
Lisle bowed again – not at all as if his head were turned by the 'compliment'; and Alice whispered to Grace, 'The fly in the ointment; how shall we get rid of him?'

fly a kite

to test public opinion on an idea or proposal by trying it out: originally with reference to testing one's credit rating in order to raise capital. The phrase dates from the mid 20th cent. in figurative uses.

fly the nest

(said of a young person) to leave home to set up a home of one's own. *20th cent.*

fly off the handle

to lose one's temper suddenly or unexpectedly: in early use also in the form *go off the handle*. The image is of the head of a hammer becoming detached from the handle while it is being wielded. *19th cent.*

Seba Smith *The Life and Writings of Major Jack Downing* 1833
But the greatest rumpus was at uncle Joshua's; for they said the President must stay there all night. And aunt Keziah was in such a pucker to have every thing nice, I didn't know but she would fly off the handle.

a fly on the wall

an unseen observer of confidential or intimate proceedings: what one would long to be to satisfy one's curiosity about situations involving other people. The phrase took on a whole new meaning with the spread of *fly-on-the-wall* television pro-grammes: a rash of voyeuristic entertainment involving round-the-clock observation of people in their workplace, or volunteers who have been put in stressful or awkward situations. The latter usually involves participation by viewers (the flies on the studio wall, in a sense) who can vote to express their approval or disapproval of this, that, or the other participant. A notable example of the genre is *Big Brother*, one of Chan-nel 4's most popular programmes, based on the phrase in George Orwell's *Nineteen Eighty-Four* (see BROTHER). *Mid 20th cent.*

> Catherine Cookson *The House of Women* 1993
> *Oh, wouldn't I like to be a fly on the wall when you tell her the latest!*

a fly on the wheel

somebody who overestimates their own importance. The phrase is derived from a fable of Aesop's, in which a fly sitting on the axletree of a moving chariot declares 'What a dust I am raising!' It is 19th cent. in its current form, with allusions to the fable from the 16th cent.

give it a fly

informal to make an attempt; to have a go. *Early 20th cent.*

like a blue-arsed fly

informal with frantic energy. A *blue-arsed fly* is a bluebottle, which flies frantically when threatened. The phrase was attributed to the Duke of Edinburgh in a conversation with a press photographer in 1970, as reported in *The Times* of 22 April: 'The Duke of Edinburgh … asked a photographer if he was getting enough pictures … "You have been running around like a blue-arsed fly."' *20th cent.*

on the fly

while continuing with what one is doing; without stopping. *19th cent.*

> Mary Hartwell *A Woman in Armour* 1875
> *It is a historical fact that Bangs married. Whether he caught his bride 'on the fly', or took her in a business way as part pay for his paper, from some overloaded papa, ask me not.*

there are no flies on —

so-and-so is astute and competent: originally used in Australia and the US, the image being of cattle that are so active that flies are unable to settle on them. Early uses in the US refer to honesty and good breeding rather than cleverness. *19th cent.*

— would not hurt/harm a fly

so-and-so is unlikely to cause any trouble or harm. *19th cent.*

> Thackeray *The Adventures of Philip* 1862
> *As for Baynes, I am sure he would not hurt a fly.*

See also fly the FLAG.

flyer

take a flyer

NAmer, informal to take a chance or risk: an extension of the meaning of *flyer* 'a daring or speculative business venture'. *19th cent.*

flying

See with flying colours *at* COLOUR.

Flynn

be in like Flynn

to seize an opportunity. The phrase, which is heavily overlaid with sexual nuance, has been used mostly in America (from the 1940s, especially by servicemen in the Second World War) and Australia. It has been linked to two bearers of the name, one famous and the other less so. The first is Errol Flynn (1909–59), the Australian-born actor noted for playing swashbuckling and playboy roles in Hollywood films as well as leading a private life characterized by heavy drinking and sexual adventure. Flynn himself refers to the phrase in his autobiography *My Wicked, Wicked Ways* (1959), where he relates that 'a new legend was born, and new terms went into the national idiom … A G.I. or Marine or sailor went out at night sparking and the next day he reported to his cronies, who asked him how he made out, and the fellow said, with a sly grin, "I'm in like Flynn."' The other link, favoured by American users of the phrase, is with Ed Flynn, a Democratic Party activist in the 1940s whose promotion of political candidates meant that they were bound to be elected, and so 'in' like Flynn himself. The chronology here is fairly conclusive: the phrase originated in America in political contexts; later it became transferred to the film actor, a more exciting association that has been, not surprisingly, more popular in Australian use. In 1967, a Hollywood spoof film starring James Coburn cashed in on these associations in its modified title *In Like Flint*. The ultimate origin, as suggested by Wentworth and Flexner in their *Dictionary of American Slang* (1960), that it is simply a rhyming extension of *in* (i.e. 'well and truly in'), is much less interesting but highly probable. This view is supported by early occurrences of a compressed form *I'm Flynn*, in which the name goes one step further and actually replaces the adverb it rhymes with. *Mid 20th cent.*

foam

See foam at the MOUTH.

fog

in a fog
confused and uncertain about what to do. *19th cent.*

foggy

not have the foggiest (idea/notion)
British informal to have no idea at all: from the (19th cent.) meaning of *foggy* 'vague, indistinct'. *Early 20th cent.*

David Jones In Parenthesis 1963
Mr. Jenkins seemed not to be existent. But soon he re-appears – he says that no one has the foggiest notion who is where.

fold

return to the fold
to rejoin one's friends or associates after a period of absence or estrangement. The phrase is based on the use of *fold* (literally 'an enclosure for sheep') to mean 'the Christian community'. *19th cent.*

George Horatio Derby Phoenixiana 1856
We have received by the Goliah, an affecting letter from Judge Ames, beseeching us to return to the fold of Democracy from which he is inclined to intimate we have been straying.

follow

follow one's nose
to be guided by one's instincts; to proceed in a direct fashion. An extension of the physical meaning of taking a direct course to a place, the nose being the most forward part of the human body. *17th cent.*

follow suit
to follow another person's example: from the (17th cent.) meaning in cards, 'to play a card of the same suit as the card led'. *Follow suit with somebody*, meaning 'to do the same as somebody',

occurs independently in the 17th cent. based on the meaning 'livery or dress'. *19th cent.*

Dickens A Tale of Two Cities 1859
The emphatic horse, cut short by the whip in a most decided negative, made a decided scramble for it, and the three other horses followed suit.

See also follow in somebody's footsteps *at* FOOT-STEP.

food

food for thought
an idea or proposal that deserves serious consideration. *19th cent.*

food for worms
dead and buried. *Middle English*

Shakespeare 1 Henry IV v.iv.86 (1596)
[Hotspur] *No, Percy, thou art dust,* | *And food for* – [Prince Harry] *For worms, brave Percy.*

fool

be no/nobody's fool
to be astute and unlikely to be deceived or duped. *Early 20th cent.*

fool's gold
something deceptively attractive. *Fool's gold* was a popular name for any yellow metal, especially iron pyrites. *19th cent.*

a fool's paradise
a state of illusory happiness, such as a fool might contemplate. The phrase occurs in the 15th cent. Paston Letters: 'I wold not be in a folis paradyce.'

Colley Cibber The Refusal 1721
[Granger] *Now you see, Witling, your Vanity has brought you into a Fool's Paradise.* [Witling] … *Ha! I wish I had been with you; I am sure you would have thought it Paradise then.*

Richardson Pamela 1741
Well, child, said she, sneeringly, how dost find thyself? – Thou'rt mightily come on of late! – I hear strange reports about thee! – Thou'rt almost got into Fool's Paradise, I doubt! – And wilt find thyself terribly mistaken in a little while, if thou thinkest my brother will disgrace his family to humour thy baby-face!

make a fool of somebody/oneself

to behave or speak in a way that makes some-body (or oneself) look foolish. The phrase dates from the 17th cent. in this form.

Dryden *Amphitryon* 1690
[Jupiter, aside] *I had forgot, and show'd my self a God;* | *This Love can make a Fool of Jupiter.*

more fool —

the person specified is unwise to have acted in such a way. *16th cent.*

Shakespeare *As You Like It* II.iv.14 (1599)
[Touchstone] *Ay, now am I in Ardenne; the more fool I. When I was at home I was in a better place; but travellers must be content.*

Thackeray *Barry Lyndon* 1844
The more great big blundering fool you, for giving the gold piece to him.

play/act the fool

to behave in a deliberately silly or playful way. *Fool* here is used in its sense of court jester. *16th cent.*

Jane Austen *Mansfield Park* 1814
When we meet at breakfast we shall be all in high good-humour at the prospect of acting the fool together with such unanimity.

you could have fooled me

informal an expression of mild doubt or scepti-cism about a claim or assertion: 'I don't believe that.' *20th cent.*

See also SUFFER fools gladly.

---

foot

the boot/shoe is on the other foot

the circumstances have changed and so has the advantage. The phrase has also occurred in other forms in 19th cent. use, e.g. *the boot is on the other* (or *wrong*) *leg. 19th cent.*

William Gilmore Simms *The Wigwam and the Cabin* 1845
' 'Twill be time enough to give the young Chief his answer when he asks the question; and it won't do for us to treat him rudely, when we consider how much we owe him.' But she was of the mind that the boot was on the other leg, – that it was he and not us that owed the debt.

Mary James Holmes *Rose Mather* 1868
The South are only doing what the Thirteen did in '76, trying to shake off the tyrant's yoke. It's the same thing precisely, only the shoe is on the other foot, and pinches mightily.

foot the bill

to accept responsibility for paying a cost, espe-cially a large one: the (verb) meaning of *foot* here is based on a sense to do with adding annota-tions, such as a signature or a total, at the end of a letter, bill, etc, as in Harriet Beecher Stowe, *Uncle Tom's Cabin* (1852): 'The wall-paper was … gar-nished with chalk memorandums, and long sums footed up.' *19th cent.*

get/start off on the right/wrong foot

to make a successful (or unsuccessful) start to an activity, relationship, etc. *Early 20th cent.*

Noel Coward *Present Indicative* 1937
To me a round of applause … even though it be conventional rather than spontaneous, almost always sets my performance off on the right foot.

have one foot in the grave

to be close to death, especially because of old age. *One Foot in the Grave* was the title of a television comedy series shown during the 1990s about a couple coping with early retirement. The phrase is found in the 17th cent., but is used mainly from the 19th cent.

Richard Braithwait *A Commentary upon the Two Tales of … Chaucer* 1615
This Sentence here this Goodwife useth, purposely to withdraw her Husband from intermedling in his own Estate, and absolutely to invest her self in it. As if she should say, You Sir, that have the one Foot in the Grave already, how is it that you incumber your mind so much with things transitory?

Ruth Rendell *The Best Man to Die* 1981
'Of course he's not young,' said Sheila serenely. 'All of thirty-five, I daresay. One foot in the grave and the other on a bar of soap.'

not/never put a foot wrong

to make no mistakes at all. *Mid 20th cent.*

Jeremy Paxman *Friends in High Places* 1990
The system ensures that those who might seem most deserving receive perhaps an Order of the British Empire (OBE) – or a British Empire Medal (BEM) … while a bureaucrat who has successfully worked his way to the top of the civil service without put-

ting a foot wrong will get a knighthood in the Order of the Bath.

put/set one's best foot forward

to make every effort; to do one's best. The phrase first appears in the 17th cent. in this form, but the notion appears earlier in other forms, e.g. in Shakespeare, *Titus Andronicus* (1594) II.iii.192: '[Aaron] Come on, my lords, the better foot before.'

Richard Brome *The Queenes Exchange* 1657
Set the best foot forward, and the best face | You can, my Lord, upon the businesse.

put one's foot down

1 to be firm or insistent. *19th cent.*

James Fenimore Cooper *Satanstoe* 1845
My grandfather had always put his foot down firmly against any connection between relations that were nearer than third cousins.

2 to press hard on the accelerator of a motor vehicle in order to increase its speed. *20th cent.*

put one's foot in it / in one's mouth

informal to make an embarrassing blunder or social gaffe. The phrase has not been well explained hitherto, but must surely be linked to a proverbial expression dating back to the 15th cent. and found (for example) in Tyndale: when food was burnt or otherwise spoiled it was said that 'the Bishop has put his foot in it (or in the pot, etc)'. This expression had other applications, such as this warning to a writer by Milton in 1641: 'I doubt not but they will say, the bishop's foot hath been in your book, for I am sure it is quite spoiled by this just confutation.' The form *put one's foot into it* is recorded in the 18th cent. and 19th cent. The admonition 'You never open your mouth but you put your foot in it' dates from the 19th cent., and is an extension of the phrase rather than an account of its origin (although it coincides with this).

JohnThomas Haines *My Poll and My Partner Joe* 1866
There's some folks speaks wisdom and sense every minute, | Some, when they opens their mouth, always puts their foot in it.

See also FEET; a foot/toe in the DOOR; have a foot in both camps *at* CAMP.

footloose

footloose and fancy-free

free of personal commitments and able to please oneself. *Footloose* meaning 'free to move the feet', i.e. untied, dates from the late 17th cent.; figurative uses are recorded from the 19th cent., and use with *fancy-free* (= free of any affections) from the 20th cent.

Janet Mattinson et al *Marriage Inside Out* 1989
Men propping up the bar over lunch will bewail the loss of earlier freedoms when they were footloose and fancy free.

footsie

play footsie with somebody

informal to have clandestine dealings with somebody: from the literal meaning of flirting with somebody by clandestinely touching their feet with one's own, especially under a table at which both people are sitting. *Footsie* appears in many variants, e.g. *footie, footy*, and in reduplicated forms such as *footie-footie*, from the 1930s. *Mid 20th cent.*

footstep

follow (in) somebody's footsteps

to do what another person has done before, especially by pursuing the same career: also used with *tread* and *walk* instead of *follow*. *16th cent.*

Thomas Beard *The Theatre of Gods Judgements* 1597
After the conquest gotten, he caused solemne thankes to be giuen in all Churches to God for that great deliuerance. I would our moderne Generals and Captaines would learne by this example to follow his footsteps, & not to make their praiers quaffings, and their thanksgiuings carousings, as they vse to doe.

for

be for it

informal, originally services' slang to be in danger of trouble or punishment. *Early 20th cent.*

Robert Moss *The Challenge Book of Brownie Stories* 1988
If that gal gets to the keeper's cottage he'll phone the police an' we'll be for it.

there's/that's — for you

an (often ironic) expression of admiration for or approval of something. The phrase is found in earlier usage pointing out a person or thing of a particular kind without the addition of *for you*, e.g. in Shakespeare, *The Taming of the Shrew* (1592) v.ii.185 '[Petruccio] Why, there's a wench! Come on, and kiss me, Kate. [They kiss.]' This type survives in condescending formulae addressed to a child or subordinate, such as *there's a good boy* or *there's a good chap. 18th cent.*

forbidden

forbidden fruit

something that is extremely alluring but strictly forbidden: with allusion to the fruit forbidden to Adam in the biblical account of the Garden of Eden in Genesis 2:17 'But of the tree of the knowledge of good and evil, thou shalt not eat of it'. Allusive uses date from the 17th cent.

Aphra Behn *The Revenge* 1680
I must confess we all eat of the forbidden Fruit.

Emily Dickinson *Poems, Second Series* 1896
Forbidden fruit a flavor has | That lawful orchards mocks; | How luscious lies the pea within | The pod that Duty locks!

force

forced march

a rapid march by soldiers over a long distance without any pauses. *18th cent.*

William Dunlap *The Archers* 1796
Our troops suffered the rascals to cut to pieces a few hundred men; while the rest, making a glorious change of position, threw themselves, by a forced march, into the castle here.

force somebody's hand

to cause somebody to act precipitately, especially by revealing or threatening to reveal their intentions. *17th cent.*

Aphra Behn *The History of the Nun* 1689
Life could not long support it self, but would either reduce her to Madness, and so render her an hated Object of Scorn to the Censuring World, or force her Hand to commit a Murder upon her self.

force the issue

to compel a decision or course of action to be taken. *Early 20th cent.*

force the pace

to dictate the speed at which something is done: from the literal use of adopting a fast pace in a race in order to tire other competitors. *Mid 20th cent.*

in force

1 in great strength. Also *in great force*. The phrase is Middle English, but is found mainly from the late 17th cent.

Arthur Gorges transl Lucan's *Pharsalia* 1614
Now let the Parthes with Trumpets sounds | Breake out in force beyond their bounds.

2 (said of a law or regulation) valid or having effect. *17th cent.*

Robert Aylett *Divine and Moral Speculations* 1654
Thus Statutes of each Countrey, City, Land, | Which they themselves do call Municipall, | All Laws which now in force with us do stand, | The Common, Civil, Ecclesiasticall.

See also by MAIN force; JOIN forces.

forelock

take time by the forelock

to make good use of an opportunity: with allusion to the personification of Opportunity by Phaedrus, a (1st cent. AD) Roman collector of fables, as *Calvus, comosa fronte, nudo occipitio* 'bald, with a lock of hair at the front and no hair at the back'. *16th cent.*

Thomas D'Urfey *The Fool Turn'd Critick* 1678
And Sir, your Son my Pupil, has instead of Penelope, married as I hear a vast Fortune, a near Kinsman of Franck Amorous, one that fell in Love with him, and he taking time by the forelock this morning married her.

R L Stevenson *Treasure Island* 1883
Now, sir, it's got to come to blows sooner or later; and what I propose is, to take time by the forelock, as the saying is, and come to blows some fine day when they least expect it.

touch/tug one's forelock

to make a gesture that indicates one's social inferiority to another, originally by raising one's hands to one's forehead. *19th cent.*

Charles Reade *Hard Cash* 1863
David called that deserting the ship, and demurred, till Alfred assured him the captain had ordered it. He then submitted directly, touched his forelock to Edward, whom he took for that officer, and went down the ladder; Alfred followed.

fork

Morton's fork
an argument that caters for two contrary possibilities with the same unwelcome conclusion. The 'fork' (i.e. an argument with two prongs) was named after Cardinal John Morton (c1420–1500), who was responsible for collecting taxes under Henry VII. He argued that the rich could afford to pay from their obvious wealth, and the frugal could afford to pay because they must have money put aside. *19th cent.*

with (a) forked tongue
(said of words or speech) spoken dishonestly or deceitfully: with reference to the forked tongue of a snake, an animal proverbial for deception and dishonesty and also taken to represent the devil. *White man speak with forked tongue* became a cliché of Western films of the mid 20th cent. *19th cent.*

Emerson Bennett *The Pioneer's Daughter* 1851
Now mark the result! Brothers, the pale-face spoke with a forked tongue. When the time came for him to go, he went not.

forlorn

a forlorn hope
a desperate hope that persists despite the knowledge that it is unlikely to be fulfilled. The phrase is derived from a Dutch phrase *verloren hoop* meaning 'lost troop', i.e. a band of soldiers who led an attack and were unlikely to survive. This was the original meaning in English; the modern sense is a good example of the workings of folk etymology, by which an expression from another language is assimilated in a form that makes sense in its own terms in the adopting language. The phrase is 17th cent. in this meaning.

form

a matter of form
something that is done as a convention or part of a routine, without any real significance: origin-

ally a legal phrase in the sense 'a point of correct procedure'. *18th cent.*

Henry Fielding *The History of Tom Jones* 1749
The Reader, from what hath been said, may imagine that the reconciliation (if indeed it could be so called) was only matter of form; we shall therefore pass it over, and hasten to what must surely be thought matter of substance.

fort

hold the fort
to take charge while the person normally in charge is absent: a metaphor based on military practice. *19th cent.*

forth

and so forth
and so on, and other things of the same kind. The phrase dates back to Old English in more physical meanings that are no longer current. The now obsolete variant *or so forth* occurs in Shakespeare's *Hamlet* (1601) II.i.61, where Polonius is instructing his man Reynaldo about what to say to get information about Laertes: 'Or perchance | "I saw him enter such a house of sale", | Videlicet, a brothel, or so forth.' In the slightly later *Twelfth Night* (1602) I.v.237, Shakespeare uses the form that is now more familiar, at the point where Olivia is discussing her beauty with Viola (disguised as Cesario): 'I will give out divers schedules of my beauty. It shall be inventoried and every particle and utensil labelled to my will, as, item, two lips, indifferent red; item, two grey eyes, with lids to them; item, one neck, one chin, and so forth.' *16th cent.*

forty

have forty winks
informal to take a short rest or sleep during the day. *19th cent.*

George Eliot *Felix Holt* 1866
Denner, peering and smiling quietly, was about to reply, when she was prevented by the appearance of old Mr Transome, who since his walk had been having 'forty winks' on the sofa in the library, and now came out to look for Harry.

foul

fall/run foul of somebody/something

to come into conflict with somebody or something: from the physical meaning of ships in collision. *16th cent.*

> Congreve *Love For Love* 1695
> [Sir Sampson] *Sleep Quotha! No, why you would not sleep o' your Wedding Night? I'm an older Fellow than you, and don't mean to sleep.* [Ben] *Why there's another Match now, as thof a couple of Privateers were looking for a Prize, and should fall foul of one another. I'm sorry for the Young Man with all my Heart.*

foul one's (own) nest

to act in a way that damages one's own interests: based on the medieval Latin proverb *nidos commaculans inmundus habebitur ales* 'a bird that pollutes its nest may be regarded as unclean', recorded in English from the 13th cent. *Middle English*

> John Crowne *The Married Beau* 1694
> *Was ever such a Coxcomb? I dare not tell this, it will reflect upon all Beaus, and I am loath to foul my own Nest; which is too foul already.*

See also by FAIR means or foul.

four

on all fours (with something)

exactly comparable (to something else). The phrase is now mostly confined to legal contexts, in which it describes exactly analogous cases. The physical meaning on which it is based dates from the 16th cent. and refers to an animal standing or moving on all its four legs: the notion is of things being level and therefore comparable. Up to the 18th cent. the phrase had the form *on all four*, with a word such as *legs* understood. *18th cent.*

> Hardy *The Woodlanders* 1887
> *The paternal longing ran on all fours with her own desire; and yet in forwarding it yesterday she had been on the brink of giving offence.*

See also to the four winds at WIND[1].

fourth

the fourth estate

the press, i.e. journalists: based on the notion of the three estates (the clergy, the nobility, and the commons) traditionally regarded as collectively exercising the political power in the state. In earlier use (late 18th cent.) the term was applied in a jocular ad hoc way to other entities, for example 'the mob'. In the early 19th cent., the essayist William Hazlitt (in *Table Talk*, 1821) referred to William Cobbett, the writer and social reformer, as 'a kind of fourth estate in the politics of this country'. *19th cent.*

fox

See CRAZY as/like a fox.

frame

be in the frame

informal to be under consideration, especially to be suspected or wanted by the police. The image is of a framed portrait being studied, and this also underlies the verb *to frame*, meaning 'to incriminate'. *Mid 20th cent.*

> Janet Neel *Death of a Partner* 1991
> *If Yeo was having it off with Angela Morgan, both he and his missis have to be in the frame.*

Frankenstein

Frankenstein's monster

a creation over which the creator loses control, eventually being destroyed by it. The expression alludes to the novel *Frankenstein* (published in 1818) by Mary Shelley, in which the central character Baron Frankenstein creates a human monster and gives it life. The name of Frankenstein himself is sometimes erroneously used for the creature rather than its creator. *19th cent.*

> Thomas Hood *Odes and Addresses to Great People* 1825
> *The real abstract hero of the age;* | *The staple Stranger of the stage;* | *A Some One made in every man's presumption,* | *Frankenstein's monster – but instinct with gumption.*

free

(as) free as air

completely free, enjoying unrestrained liberty. An early occurrence of the simile in its present form is in the Elizabethan dramatist John Marston's play *What You Will* (1604), and John

Heywood invoked a similar image some seventy years earlier: 'As free as be the byrdes that in the ayre flee.' Reference to birds as symbolic of freedom dates from antiquity. *17th cent.*

for free

at no charge or cost, for nothing: this (mainly North American) use of *for* is called 'pleonastic', i.e. involving more words than are necessary, and is found in other combinations from the beginning of the 20th cent., notably *for fair* and *for real* (see REAL). *Mid 20th cent.*

> Gardeners' World 1991
> *The prudent gardener takes as much care with his produce once picked as when growing, and saves seed in order to obtain plants for free.*

free and easy

marked by informality and lack of restraint: also used with hyphens as an adjective. In early use also in the less euphonious order *easy and free*. *17th cent.*

> Margaret Cavendish The Contract 1656
> *For she having naturally a Majestical Presence, although her Behaviour was easy and free, and a severe Countenance, yet modest and pleasing, and great skill in the Art, keeping her Measures just to the Notes of Musick, moving smoothly, evenly, easily, made her astonish all the Company.*

free, white, and over twenty-one

independent and free to act as one wishes. *Early 20th cent.*

give a free hand/rein to somebody

to allow somebody complete freedom of action. The form with *hand* is 19th cent., and with *rein* mid 20th cent.

it's a free country

used to justify one's actions or express support for the actions of another: often used flippantly or ironically. The phrase is based on common references to the freedoms and responsibilities existing in a 'free country'. *19th cent.*

> Theodor Winthrop John Brent 1862
> *'I don't wish to hear that kind of stuff,' said Brent, turning sternly upon Larrap. 'It's a free country, and I shall say what I blame please,' the fellow said, with a grin.*

make free with something

to use something irresponsibly or without restraint, especially something belonging to another person. *18th cent.*

> Richard Graves The Spiritual Quixote 1773
> *I had a considerable legacy left me by a relation. But, as I had lived very expensively, I was obliged to make free with the principal, and had almost run through it.*

there's no such thing as a free lunch

(proverb) nothing is free; one has to pay for a benefit in some form or other. The phrase is typically used as a cynical comment on the world of business and the ulterior motives that seem to underlie acts of apparent generosity. *Late 20th cent.*

> Daily Mirror 1992
> *When someone else foots the bill there is always a price to pay in the end. As QC George Carman said towards the end of the Mona Bauwens court case earlier this week: 'There's no such thing as a free lunch.'*

freeze

See freeze somebody's BLOOD.

French

excuse/pardon my French

a jocular and not particularly sincere apology after swearing. The form with *excuse* is older, being found in an issue of the American *Harper's Magazine* in 1895. The version with *pardon* dates from the 1930s. The phrase has the ring of forces' slang, and probably owes much to the troops fighting in France in the First World War. *19th cent.*

take French leave

to take leave without permission: from the 18th cent. French custom of leaving a reception without taking one's leave of (= saying farewell to) the host or hostess. Some of the early uses in English are about leave-taking in this sense rather than in the modern sense of unauthorized absence. *18th cent.*

> Smollett The Expedition of Humphry Clinker 1771
> *As for Ditton, after all his courting, and his compliment, he stole away an Irishman's bride, and took a French leave of me and his master.*

fresh

(as) fresh as a daisy
completely fresh. Daisies have been proverbial for freshness since Middle English, possibly on account of their appearance in spring or because their petals open afresh each morning. *Fresh as a rose* occurs in Chaucer, Lydgate, and Spenser. *18th cent.*

> Mary Robinson *Walsingham* 1797
> *At twenty, I fell in love, your honour. The girl was as fresh as a daisy, and had a heart as tender as – your honour's.*

be fresh out of something
1 to have recently arrived from a place. *18th cent.*

> John Cleland *Memoirs of a Woman of Pleasure* 1748
> *My bosom was now bare, and rising in the warmest throbs, presented to his sight and feeling the firm hard-swell of a pair of young breasts, such as may be imagin'd of a girl not sixteen, fresh out of the country, and never before handled.*

2 to have exhausted one's entire supply of something: often used ironically in cases where the supply was non-existent in the first place. *19th cent.*

> Leigh Hunt *A Legend of Florence* 1840
> *Meeting what must be, | Is half commanding it; and in this breath | Of heaven my mind feels duty set erect, | Fresh out of tears.*

> Elizabeth Oldfield *Sudden Fire* 1993
> *'Guess what? We arrived all in one piece,' Ashley said, as she drew the car to a halt outside the stone villa … He reached into the glove compartment. 'Unfortunately I'm fresh out of medals to give you.'*

See also BREAK new/fresh ground; a BREATH of fresh air; new/fresh BLOOD.

friend

a friend at court
a supporter with influence over people in authority: used with historical allusion to political patronage at the royal courts. A medieval proverb recorded in the French romance called *Roman de la rose* appears in its Middle English translation in the form 'For freend in court ay better is | Than peny in purs'. The phrase is found from the 17th cent. in allusive use.

> Dryden *The Wild Gallant* 1669
> *You must get me as much more against to morrow; for then my friend at court is to pay his mercer.*

> Delarivière Manley *The Secret History of Queen Zarah* 1705
> *Away went our new courtier with full expectations of being put in possession of his desires when he came again; he cou'd not forbear smiling to himself to think of the old proverb, that a friend at court was as good as gold in a man's pocket.*

friends in high places
people with influence who are ready to give their support: a 'high place' was in its earliest use a place of worship on high ground, and later symbolic of the upper echelons of society. *19th cent.*

> Mary Coleridge *The King with Two Faces* 1897
> *'If we can do nothing else, we can resist to the death,' said Carl de Geer, his face darkening. 'And then,' said Essen, bowing gracefully over his glass, 'you may be thankful to have one friend in high places.'*

See also a fair-weather friend *at* FAIR; FLEXIBLE friend.

fright

look a fright
(said of a person) to look unsightly or dishevelled. This meaning of *fright* is an extension of an obsolete (17th cent.) sense 'anything that causes terror'. *19th cent.*

> T W Robinson *A Breach of Promise* 1888
> [Achates] *I told them that you had a swelled face like that … Have a swelled face directly! Quick! quick! have a swelled face. They are coming.* [Philip] *I shall look a fright. You fool!*

frighten

put the frighteners on somebody
British, informal to threaten somebody. *Mid 20th cent.*

See also afraid/scared/frightened of one's own SHADOW; beat/shake/scare/frighten the daylights out of *at* DAYLIGHT; be frightened out of one's wits *at* WIT; be frightened to DEATH; frighten the LIFE out of.

frog

have a frog in one's throat
to have a temporarily hoarse voice. *Early 20th cent.*

front

front of house
the parts of a theatre that are accessible to the public, such as the auditorium, foyer, and ticket office: *front of the house* occurs in the early 19th cent. The phrase is mid 20th cent. in this shorter form.

> **Doremy Vernon** *Tiller's Girls* 1988
> *The biggest crime of all was to go round to the front of house or into the street in 'full slap', as stage make-up was called.*

See also on the back/front BURNER.

froth

See foam/froth at the MOUTH.

frozen

See give somebody the frozen MITT.

fruit

bear fruit
to have good results: with allusion to the parable of the sower in Matthew 13:23 (in the Authorized Version, 1611): 'He that received seed into the good ground is he that heareth the word, and understandeth it; which also beareth fruit, and bringeth forth, some an hundredfold, some sixty, some thirty.' The literal use with reference to plants goes back to Old English. *17th cent.*

> **Francis Quarles** *Solomons Recantation* 1645
> *Thus fool'd with vain pursuit | Of blossom'd happinesse that bears no fruit.*

frying pan

out of the frying pan into the fire
free of one difficulty only to encounter another and worse one. The phrase was recorded by John Heywood in his collection of proverbs published in 1546, and there is an early use by Sir Thomas More, 'Lepe they lyke a flounder out of a frying-panne into the fyre.' *16th cent.*

> **Head & Kirkman** *The English Rogue Described* 1668
> *Fearing more danger from without than from within, we prepared for our departure, but having opened the door, we found that we had leapt out of the frying pan into the fire.*

fuck

fuck all
British, coarse slang nothing at all. *Mid 20th cent.*

> **William Fox** *Willoughby's Phoney War* 1991
> *Do try to remember, dear lad, that even odds and sods have to get about – in those miles and miles of deep snow-covered fuck all.*

fudge

fudge factor
an item included in a calculation to take account of an unquantifiable or imponderable factor. *Fudge* is recorded earliest as a dismissive exclamation equivalent to 'stuff and nonsense', then as a verb meaning 'to present facts and figures in a false or misleading way'. The noun meaning 'a deceptive or misleading presentation of facts' is from the late 18th cent., and the sense of a soft creamy sweet from the late 19th cent. *Late 20th cent.*

fuel

add fuel to the fire/flames
to aggravate or intensify an already difficult situation. *16th cent.*

> **Thomas Kyd** *The Spanish Tragedie* 1592
> [Bel-imperia] *But why had I no notice of his ire?*
> [Lorenzo] *That were to adde more fewell to your fire.*

full

full of days/years
old use having reached an old age. The expression *full of days* occurs in Wyclif's translation of Job 42:17 'He diede old, and ful of dais'; the equivalent in the Authorized Version (1611) is 'So Job died, being old and full of days'. *Middle English*

full of oneself

extremely conceited and boastful. *17th cent.*

> Thomas Shadwell *A True Widow* 1679
> *A most admirable coxcomb; he is so full of himself, he ne'r minds another man, and so answers quite from the purpose.*

full steam/speed ahead

(often as an instruction) proceeding with all speed and vigour: from the literal use in the context of steamships and railway locomotives. *19th cent.*

> Conan Doyle *The Sign of Four* 1890
> *'And there is the Aurora,' exclaimed Holmes, 'and going like the devil! Full speed ahead, engineer. Make after that launch with the yellow light.'*

to the full

completely; to the greatest possible degree. *Middle English* (in *Piers Plowman*)

See also (as) full as a GOOG; (at) full PELT; at full STRETCH; go off at half cock *at* COCK²; the full MONTY; full of beans *at* BEAN; full WHACK; in full CRY; in full fig *at* FIG²; in full FLIGHT; in full FLOOD; in full FLOW; in full RIG; in full SWING; not the full QUID; not playing with a full DECK; on a full STOMACH; the wheel has turned/come full CIRCLE.

fullness

the fullness of one's/the heart

the state of being overwhelmed with emotion. *17th cent.*

> David Graham Phillips *Susan Lenox, Her Fall and Rise* 1917
> *She went down the street, turned the first corner, dropped on a doorstep and sobbed and cried, out of the fullness of her heart.*

in the fullness of time

after a certain time has elapsed; eventually: *the fulness of (the) time* was originally used in the Authorized Version of the Bible (1611), e.g. Galatians 4:4 'But when the fulness of the time was come, God sent forth his Son, made of a woman, made under the law.' The phrase dates from the 17th cent. in this form.

fun

for fun / just for the fun of something

for no particular reason; on a whim. *19th cent.*

> Sean Magee *Great Races* 1990
> *He lived in a converted cowshed and was exercised by his owner, who raced his three horses simply for the fun of it.*

fun and games

1 enjoyable or exciting activity: in recent use often with reference to sexual play. *Early 20th cent.*

> Sapper *Bulldog Drummond* 1920
> *We've had lots of fun and games since I last saw you.*

2 (in ironic use) trouble or confusion; a difficult experience. *Late 20th cent.*

> J Porter *Sour Cream* 1966
> *I headed the car in the direction of the coast road. We had the usual fun and games with the local drivers.*

have a bit of fun

informal to have casual sexual relations. The phrase appears in Farmer and Henley's *Slang and Its Analogues* (1893). *19th cent.*

like fun

with energy or enthusiasm, especially with reference to enjoyable activities: *cf* like FURY; like MAD. *19th cent.*

make fun of / poke fun at somebody/something

to make somebody or something an object of amusement or ridicule. The earlier form of the phrase is with *make*, which is found from the 18th cent.

> Charles Stearns *The Wooden Boy* 1798
> *We will contrive some way to make fun of neighbor Hickory – I love to take a fellow, who can't say his soul is his own, and give him a hearty sweat.*

> Mark Twain *The Innocents Abroad* 1869
> *Things I did not like at all yesterday I like very well to-day, now that I am at home, and always hereafter I shall be able to poke fun at the whole gang if the spirit so moves me to do.*

fund

in funds

having an available supply of money. To be *low in funds* is to be short of money. *19th cent.*

Scott *Waverley* 1814
And now, (taking out a morocco case,) let me put you in funds for the campaign.

Thackeray *Catherine* 1839
When flush of cash, he would appear at the coffee-house; when low in funds, the deuce knows into what mystic caves and dens he slunk for food and lodging.

funeral

it's/that's —'s funeral
informal that's so-and-so's fault or responsibility, the implication usually being that they have incurred unwelcome consequences by their own actions and do not deserve any help or support. The phrase is attested earlier (19th cent.) in the form *not —'s funeral* in the sense 'none of so-and-so's business'.

Clyde Fitch *The Woman in the Case* 1904
What's the odds anyway, old girl. It's not your funeral!

funk

in a blue funk
informal terrified or panic-stricken. *Funk* in the sense 'fear or panic' dates from the 18th cent. and is of obscure origin, possibly related to a Flemish word *fonck*. *19th cent.*

Thomas Hughes *Tom Brown's Schooldays* 1857
Hang it, I wish I could take things as you do – but I never can get higher than a joke. Everything's a joke. If I was going to be flogged next minute, I should be in a blue funk, but I couldn't help laughing at it for the life of me.

funny

funny business
suspicious or dishonest behaviour. *19th cent.*

Augustin Daly *Dollars and Sense* 1883
I mean legitimate business. Business – business you know. No funny business.

funny money
money that does not have its normal face value, especially because it is counterfeit or devalued, or because it has been acquired illegally and cannot be used openly: the sense of *funny* is derived from that of *funny business*. *Mid 20th cent.*

Donald Goddard et al *Trail of the Octopus* 1993
Thinking back, Coleman often wonders how many of Hurley's confidential informants in Lebanon were, in fact, paid with funny money.

funny old
strange or remarkable: in earlier use the two words both retained their meanings, whereas in more recent use *old* is used in its depleted sense merely implying affection. *19th cent.*

Thackeray *The Virginians* 1858
A great deal of fine company was at church. There was that funny old duchess, and old Madame Bernstein, with Lady Maria at her side.

funny peculiar / funny ha-ha
used in various ways together or separately to seek or provide clarification between the two principal meanings of the word *funny*. The most familiar use is by Ian Hay in his play of 1936 *The Housemaster*: 'That's funny.' 'What do you mean, funny? Funny-peculiar, or funny ha-ha?' However, the distinction is earlier in American use (see below). *Mid 20th cent.*

Mariel Brady *Genevieve Gertrude* 1928
'I liked that song, myself,' he said, 'even if it isn't classical. It's funny, anyhow.' Genevieve Gertrude raised her hand, 'Do you mean funny peculiar, or funny ha-ha?' she inquired politely. Mr. Kent appeared to swallow his tonsils. His eyes winked very fast. ''Cause,' explained his mentor gravely, 'our teacher don't allow us to say funny when we mean peculiar. It's bad English, you know.'

J Verney *Friday's Tunnel* 1959
John Gubbins leant forward, smiling in a funny-peculiar not funny-ha-ha way.

the funny thing is
used to introduce a remarkable or paradoxical fact. *Early 20th cent.*

Charles Rann Kennedy *The Servant in the House* 1908
Oh, the letters we have had! The funny thing is, for all their fault-finding, they none of them agree with each other!

see the funny side (of something)
to recognize the humorous aspect of an otherwise unpleasant experience or situation. *Early 20th cent.*

James Forbes *The Commuters* 1911
[Sammy] *I beg your pardon, I can't help seeing the funny side of everything.* [Larry] *The man that can see the funny side of this affair, has a ghoulish sense of humor.*

fur

make the fur fly

to cause trouble or an argument: from the physical meaning of animals fighting. Used with some variation. *19th cent.*

> George Lippard *Memoirs of a Preacher* 1849
> *Why you ought to see us in a regular muss! Get out! Don't we make the fur fly!*

furious

give somebody furiously to think

dated to set somebody thinking hard about something: from French *donner furieusement à penser*, and described as a 'paltry borrowing' by H W Fowler in his entry on Gallicisms in *Modern English Usage* (1926). *Early 20th cent.*

furniture

part of the furniture

(usually said of a person) an established or familiar member of a group, organization, etc. *19th cent.*

> Edward P Roe *Opening a Chestnut Burr* 1874
> *Though not a stylish, pretty woman, she was anything but a goodish, commonplace character that he would regard as part of the furniture of the house, useful in its place, but of no more interest than a needful piece of cabinet work.*

furrow

See PLOUGH *a lonely/one's own furrow.*

further

nothing could be further from one's mind/ thoughts

an assertion that one had not been considering a particular thought or idea: often used in jocular or ironic contexts. *19th cent.*

Mary Braddon *Lady Audley's Secret* 1862
He would quietly trot to covert upon a mild-tempered, stout-limbed, bay hack, and keep at a very respectful distance from the hard riders; his horse knowing quite as well as he did, that nothing was further from his thoughts than any desire to be in at the death.

fury

like fury

with great intensity or energy: *cf* like FUN; like MAD. *Fury* is used as a metaphor for the power and energy of natural forces from the 16th cent. *18th cent.*

> Mary Davys *The Accomplish'd Rake* 1727
> *Poor Sir Combish was no sooner relieved than he ran down stairs like fury, ordered his Coach to be got ready that Minute and drove away as fast as Fear and six good Horses could carry him.*

fuse

be on / have a short fuse

informal, originally NAmer to be inclined to lose one's temper easily. *Mid 20th cent.*

> Eleanor Deeping *Caring for Elderly Parents* 1979
> *For some families breakfast can be a time when they are on a very short fuse and tensions abound.*

light a/the fuse

to take action that will have a dramatic effect. *Mid 20th cent.*

> Peter Lewis *The Fifties* 1978
> *And yet in 1953 another keenly awaited publication lit a fuse which eventually would explode many an illusion of carefully tended domestic bliss.*

future

future shock

a state of confusion or disorientation caused by rapid social change or technological progress. The phrase was coined on the analogy of *culture shock* (see CULTURE) by Alvin Toffler in the magazine *Horizon* (1965), where he defined it as 'the dizzying disorientation brought on by the premature arrival of the future'. *Late 20th cent.*

The Times 1988
On the evidence of the week, the post-war British farmer has become a creature inured to the cattle-prod of future shock; not for him the wide-eyed reaction of his Wessex forebears when that proto-type harvester came clanking and steaming into the pages of Hardy's Tess.

gab

the gift of the gab
the ability to speak in an articulate and persuasive way. The noun *gab*, meaning 'idle talk, prattle', is based on the verb meaning 'to chatter' (both 18th cent.). In Scottish use there is an association with *gab* as a variant of *gob* meaning 'mouth' and 'talking', and *gift of the gob* is found in a source from the 1690s. In general use the phrase is attested from the 18th cent.

> William Godwin *Things As They Are* 1794
> *Mr. Tyrrel had recourse to his old friend, to whom he unburthened the tumult of his thoughts. This, cried he, is a new artifice of the fellow to prove his imagined superiority. We know very well that he has the gift of the gab.*

gad

on the gad
old use travelling about, especially in search of pleasure. The noun *gad*, which is used only in the phrase, is based on the (Middle English) verb meaning 'to go from place to place aimlessly' (now used chiefly in *gad about*). *19th cent.*

> Mrs Gaskell *Sylvia's Lovers* 1863
> *Thou might have a bit o' news to tell one after being on the gad all afternoon.*

gaff

blow the gaff
to reveal a secret, especially about something discreditable. *Gaff* is a 19th cent. word meaning 'humbug, nonsense', of uncertain origin. The phrase occurs with *gab* instead of *gaff* in Francis Grose's *Dictionary of the Vulgar Tongue* (1785). *19th cent.*

Marryat *Peter Simple* 1833
One of the French officers, after he was taken prisoner, asked me how we had managed to get the gun up there; but I wasn't going to blow the gaff, so I told him, as a great secret, that we got it up with a kite.

---

gaiety

gaiety of nations
pleasure or enjoyment shared by a large number of people: often used ironically. The expression is derived from Samuel Johnson's assertion, in his *Life of Edmund Smith* (forming part of the *Prefaces to the Works of the English Poets*, 1779–81), that the death of the celebrated actor David Garrick in 1779 had 'eclipsed the gaiety of nations, and impoverished the publick stock of harmless pleasure'. Johnson's memorable phrase was comically echoed by William Hazlitt in his essay *On Actors and Acting* (in the collection called *The Round Table*, 1817): 'What a rich treat to the town, what a feast for the critics, to go and see Betterton, and Booth, and Wilks, and Sandford, and Nokes, and Leigh, and Penkethman, and Bullock, and Estcourt, and Dogget, and Mrs Barry, and Mrs Montfort, and Mrs Oldfield, and Mrs Bracegirdle, and Mrs Cibber, and Cibber himself, the prince of coxcombs, and Macklin, and Quin, and Rich, and Mrs Clive, and Mrs Pritchard, and Mrs Abington, and Weston, and Shuter, and Garrick, and all the rest of those, who "gladdened life, and whose deaths eclipsed the gaiety of nations"!' (Johnson had used the expression 'gladdened life' earlier in the same passage.) *18th cent.*

---

gain

See no PAIN, no gain.

---

gait

go one's (own) gait
to follow one's own course of action: figurative uses of *gait* (literally, 'a manner of walking') are recorded from the 18th cent. In Scottish use *gang one's gait* goes back to late Middle English in a literal meaning. *19th cent.*

Harold Frederic *The Damnation of Theron Ware* 1896
If you let things like that worry you, you'll keep a sore skin all your life. You take my advice and just go ahead your own gait, and let other folks do the worrying.

---

gall

See DIP one's pen in gall; WORMWOOD and gall.

---

gallery

play to the gallery
to act with exaggerated effect, in a way that is calculated to win popular support or approval. The gallery was the highest part of a theatre with the cheapest seats, and the word also denoted the common people who formed the audience in that part of the theatre and were considered as having the poorest tastes. *19th cent.*

Jack London *Theft* 1910
That is Gherst all over. Playing to the gallery. Inducing Knox to make this spectacular exposure on the floor of the House just at the critical time when so many important bills are pending.

---

game

ahead of the game
at a more advanced state of progress than one's competitors in an activity. *Early 20th cent.*

David Belasco *The Girl of the Golden West* 1905
Yet p'raps he was ahead of the game. Ha – I dunno. Oh, say, I just love this conversation with you. I love to hear you talk.

(as) game as Ned Kelly
Australian, informal extremely brave or foolhardy: with reference to the notorious Australian bushranger and cattle thief Ned Kelly (1855–80), who was eventually captured and hanged at Melbourne. *Mid 20th cent.*

beat somebody at their own game
to surpass or outwit somebody by using their own methods. *18th cent.*

Richard Warner transl Plautus' *The Cheat* 1774
O brave! O rare! Charinus the facetious! | At my own game you beat me – But what name | Am I to call this slave by?

the game is up

the plan or plot has been discovered; failure or humiliation is certain. *19th cent.*

> **J G Holman *The Gazette Extraordinary* 1811**
> *As the devil would have it, I somehow grew nervous, and gave the wrong hand for an allemande. From that moment, the game was up – I committed blunder after blunder – at last, my head spun – my heels flew up – down I went – and upset, in my fall, one Duchess, two Countesses and a stiff little Lord of the bed-chamber.*

game over

there is no more to be done; the situation is hopeless. The phrase echoes the message given to the user at the end of a computer game. *Late 20th cent.*

game, set, and match

a complete victory or success: from the use in tennis at the end of the game that secures the winning player victory in the match. *Late 20th cent.*

off/on one's game

playing well (or badly). *19th cent.*

on the game

informal working as a prostitute: in earlier use also in criminals' slang referring to thieving. *Game* has been used in the sense 'amorous play' from the 13th cent.; Shakespeare in *Troilus and Cressida* (1602) IV.vi.64 makes Ulysses say of Cressida that 'these encounterers [= presumptuous people] so glib of tongue | ... wide unclasp the tables of their thoughts | To every ticklish reader, set them down | For sluttish spoils of opportunity | And daughters of the game'. *19th cent.*

> **Ian Rankin *Strip Jack* 2002**
> *Jack smiled. 'You're right, of course, bad for the image having a sister on the game.' 'There are worse forms of prostitution than whoring.' Jack nodded, impressed. 'Very deep, Inspector. Can I use that in one of my speeches?'*

the only game in town

the only thing of its kind worth considering. *20th cent.*

play the game

to behave honourably and according to the accepted rules. *19th cent.*

play —'s game

to act, intentionally or unintentionally, in a way that helps another person, especially a rival, in their plans. Recorded from the 17th cent., but mainly from the 19th cent.

play games with somebody

to treat somebody teasingly or disrespectfully, often playfully but sometimes menacingly. *19th cent.*

> **Harriet Beecher Stowe *The Pearl of Orr's Island* 1862**
> *Oh, pshaw, Mara, you don't know these fellows; they are only playing games with us. If they once catch us, they have no mercy; and for one here's a child that isn't going to be caught.*

what's the/your game?

informal a sceptical or suspicious enquiry: what is going on? what are you scheming? *20th cent.*

> **Tom Stoppard *Rosenkrantz and Guildenstern Are Dead* 1967**
> [Guildenstern] *We are Rosenkrantz and Guildenstern.* [Rosenkrantz] *Never heard of you!* [Guildenstern] *Well, we're nobody special.* [Rosenkrantz] *What's your game?* [Guildenstern] *We've got our instructions.*

See also be FAIR game; GIVE the game/show away; the NAME of the game; TWO can play at that game.

gamut

run the gamut

to experience or take part in the whole range of an activity. *Gamut* is used in figurative meanings from the early 17th cent. It is originally a musical term for a scale or range of notes: a 16th cent. contraction of medieval Latin *gamma ut*, *gamma* being the Greek letter that represented the lowest note in the scale and *ut* the name of the first of six notes forming the hexachord. (The six notes were named after words taken from the Latin hymn to John the Baptist beginning *Ut queant laxis…*) *19th cent.*

> **George Hazelton *Mistress Cochrane* 1900**
> [Duchess of Portsmouth] *But you are at court now. Masking is the first sin at court.* [Nell Gwyn] *Then I'll begin with the first sin and run the gamut.*

gap

stop a gap
to meet an immediate or temporary need: hence a temporary solution is often called a *stopgap*. In its physical sense, stopping a gap was repairing a breach in a wall or hedge; this gave rise to a (now obsolete) proverb *stop two gaps with one bush*, equivalent to 'kill two birds with one stone'. Figurative uses occur from an early date, for example in Shakespeare's *King John* (1597) III.iv.32 '[Constance to King Philip] I will kiss thy detestable bones, | And put my eyeballs in thy vaulty brows, | And ring these fingers with thy household worms, | And stop this gap of breath with fulsome dust, | And be a carrion monster like thyself.' *16th cent.*

garbage

garbage in, garbage out
input of poor quality will produce poor results. The phrase was originally used about computer data, and has rapidly grown into a platitude meaning 'success is proportional to effort and quality of work'. Also abbreviated to *GIGO*. *Late 20th cent.*

garden

cultivate one's garden
to take care of one's own affairs: with allusion to Voltaire, *Candide* (1759) '*Il faut cultiver notre jardin*'. The phrase is mid 20th cent. in allusive uses (other than direct translations of the Voltaire passage).

John Fowles *The Magus* 1988
He lived alone – yes, alone – with a housekeeper, and he cultivated his garden, quite literally, it seemed.

everything in the garden is lovely
informal all is well. *Early 20th cent.*

lead somebody up the garden path
informal to mislead or deceive somebody: also in the form *lead somebody up the garden*. *Early 20th cent.*

Garnet

all Sir Garnet
everything is satisfactory: with allusion to Sir Garnet Wolseley (1813–1913), who conducted successful military expeditions in Egypt and elsewhere. W S Gilbert in *Patience* (1881) refers to 'The genius strategic of Caesar or Hannibal | Skill of Sir Garnet in thrashing a cannibal'. *19th cent.*

gas

all gas and gaiters
1 a satisfactory state of affairs. The phrase was first used by Dickens in *Nicholas Nickleby* (1839), apparently with this meaning, and it was later picked up by P G Wodehouse: see below. The allusion, however, is obscure. *19th cent.*

Dickens *Nicholas Nickleby* 1839
'Aha!' cried the old gentleman, folding his hands, and squeezing them with great force against each other. 'I see her now, I see her now! My love, my life, my bride, my peerless beauty. She is come at last – at last – and all is gas and gaiters!'

P G Wodehouse *Ice in the Bedroom* 1961
She cries 'Oh, Freddie darling!' and flings herself into his arms, and all is gas and gaiters again.

2 self-importance and pomposity, especially with reference to the clergy. The phrase was used as the title of a BBC television comedy series about a bishop and his clergy, broadcast in the 1960s. *Early 20th cent.*

G B Shaw *Adventures of the Black Girl* 1932
Its [the Bible's] one great love poem is the only one that can satisfy a man who is really in love. Shelley's Epipsychidion is, in comparison, literary gas and gaiters.

run out of gas
to lose energy or motivation: literally to run out of fuel, from the American use of *gas* (short for *gasolene*) in a meaning equivalent to British 'petrol'. *Late 20th cent.*

William Safire *Before Fall* 1975
He's too 'up' to sleep – can you sit around with him until he runs out of gas?

step on the gas

to hurry: with reference to pressing down on the accelerator to increase the speed of a vehicle (*cf* put one's FOOT down). *Early 20th cent.*

gasket

blow a gasket

informal to lose one's temper. In an internal-combustion engine, a gasket is a sealing layer between adjoining surfaces; when it 'blows' it breaks, causing the engine to seize up alarmingly and noisily. *20th cent.*

Joan Smith *A Masculine Ending* 1988
Prof. Wylie told Humphrey he'd have to renew Theo's fellowship – can't lose two senior lecturers at once, you know – and Humphrey just about blew a gasket.

gasp

one's/the last gasp

the point at which somebody is about to die or become exhausted: literally, the moment of taking one's final breath. A *last-gasp* action is one done at the last possible moment. *16th cent.*

Shakespeare *As You Like It* II.iii.71 (1599)
[Adam] *Master, go on, and I will follow thee | To the last gasp with truth and loyalty.*

gate

get/be given the gate

NAmer, informal to be dismissed from employment: *cf* show somebody the DOOR. *Early 20th cent.*

P G Wodehouse *Very Good, Jeeves!* 1930
I don't believe there's a female in the world who could see Uncle George fairly often in those waistcoats without feeling that it was due to her better self to give him the gate.

gatepost

See BETWEEN you and me and the bedpost/gatepost.

gauntlet

There are two words involved here. In the first phrase *gauntlet* is derived via French from Latin

gantus and is ultimately of Germanic origin; in the second *gauntlet* is a corruption of *gantlope*, a word derived from Scandinavian and used also in English in its original form.

fling/throw down the gauntlet

to issue a formal challenge. The phrase is derived from the practice in medieval chivalry of issuing a challenge by throwing down one's glove, the challenge being accepted by the person who picked it up (hence *take up the gauntlet*). *Cf* French *jeter le gant*. Recorded from the 17th cent. in figurative use.

run the gauntlet

to be forced to suffer an ordeal or a testing experience in order to achieve an objective: from the former military punishment (known as *the gauntlet*) of being made to run between a file of soldiers armed with sticks. *17th cent.*

John Crowne *Pandion and Amphigenia* 1665
His countenance all the while representing the undaunted constancy wherewith he armed his mind, now he was to run the gauntlet with an invincible Enemy, yet at the same time attiring his looks in such a graceful Majesty, as if this was but his marriage-day with Death.

gear

change gear / move up a gear

to start to act more vigorously or decisively: from the literal changing of gear in a motor vehicle. Recorded from the late 20th cent. in figurative use.

The Times 1977
As Edrich, cutting well, prepared to move up a gear, he was out playing a ball from Michael Buss off his legs to Snow at square leg.

geese

turn geese into swans

to exaggerate the importance of people or events: based on the assumed superiority or greater value of swans as compared with geese. Other forms exist, e.g. *all —'s geese are swans*. *19th cent.*

Edgar Fawcett *The New King Arthur* 1885
For shall not swans be swans, though geese are geese? | And if our swans be geese yet swans are deemed, | The merrier for ourselves that deem them swans.

genie

let the genie out of the bottle

to start a process that one cannot control. To *put the genie back in the bottle* is to put an end to such a process. The phrase alludes to stories from the *Arabian Nights* in which a *genie* (or *jinnee*) is a mischievous or friendly spirit that lives in a lamp (*see* ALADDIN) or bottle and when summoned by the uttering of a formula can take on many forms. *20th cent.*

> Economist 1974
>
> Chairman Mao has formally ordered his revolutionary genie back into the bottle … It sounds like goodbye to all that.

> Today 1992
>
> Now that the genie is out of the bottle, we have to face the fact that the monarchy as we have understood it since Victorian times is virtually over.

gentleman

a gentleman's agreement

an informal agreement based on the honour of the parties involved rather than being legally enforceable. *Early 20th cent.*

> Business 1991
>
> Gone are the days of the one-to-one gentleman's agreement; handsets have replaced handshakes.

a gentleman's gentleman

dated a personal valet. *18th cent.*

> Richard Steele The Lying Lover 1704
>
> Why, madam, the gentleman's gentleman came up to me very civilly, and said his master was in discourse with my Lady he suppos'd.

germ

in germ

in its rudimentary stage; not yet developed. The phrase is based on the meaning of *germ* 'rudiment of an organism' (from Latin *germen* 'seed') which is recorded in figurative use with reference to ideas and concepts from the 16th cent. The meaning relating to microorganisms causing disease developed towards the end of the 19th cent. *19th cent.*

get

be getting at something

informal to imply or hint at something. Often used in the form of a challenge, *what are you getting at?* *19th cent.*

> David Belasco Naughty Anthony 1899
>
> [Cowley] I can quite understand your feeling that way, being the husband. [Chillington] The husband! What are you getting at? What do you refer to when you call me the husband?

be out to get somebody

to want to harm or punish somebody. *Mid 20th cent.*

> Simon Brett Murder Unprompted 1984
>
> Do you know, my psychiatrist spent hour after hour convincing me that it was all in the mind, that nobody really was out to get me, that the world wasn't conspiring against me.

don't get mad, get even

an exhortation to take revenge for a wrong rather than be frustratingly angry. The maxim is attributed to President John F Kennedy (1917–73). *Mid 20th cent.*

get cracking/going/weaving

informal to make a determined start; to start a task with brisk enthusiasm. *Get going* is the earliest version and is found from the 19th cent. *Get cracking* (based on the verb *crack* in its informal 19th cent. meaning 'to move with speed') is recorded from the mid 20th cent. It appears first in Partridge's *Dictionary of Slang* (1937), where it is classed as RAF slang from the 1920s (without specific evidence, but see below on *get weaving*); it was made popular in the novels of Nevil Shute, who also idiosyncratically used a transitive form with a noun as the object of *cracking* (as in *Ruined City*, 1938: 'If I could get this yard cracking again I'd be a very happy man'), which is no longer common. *Get somebody going*, however, remains idiomatic. *Get weaving* is the most recent form. It originates in air force slang of the Second World War (1939–45), and was picked up by Terence Rattigan in his 1942 play *Flare Path*, a tribute to the RAF ('We'd better get weaving, or we'll find this chemist feller has gone to lunch.'). *Weaving* has nothing to do with making cloth, but was based on the use of *weave* in the sense 'to follow an erratic or devious course' in order to avoid enemy fire, a meaning that has spilled into modern usage (e.g. *weave one's way through the traffic*).

Oliver Wendell Holmes *Elsie Venner* 1861
Country-life is apt to be dull; but when it once gets going, it beats the city hollow.

Stella Gibbons *The Matchmaker* 1949
Come on, let's get cracking, we're late now.

get his/hers/theirs, *etc*
informal to be killed: the pronoun implies a noun such as *fate* or *deserts*. *Early 20th cent.*

get it
1 *informal* to be punished or scolded. 'It' is the undefined punishment or retribution. *19th cent.*

John Steinbeck *The Grapes of Wrath* 1939
Pa said, 'I didn' think a that. It ain't right to leave a grave unmounded.' 'Can't he'p it,' said Tom. 'They'd dig 'im right up, an' we'd get it for breakin' the law.'

2 *informal* to answer the door or telephone: normally in spoken use in the future tense as a statement of intention (e.g. *I'll get it*). *Mid 20th cent.*

get it together
informal to become organized or calm (*cf* get one's ACT together), or to start a relationship. *Late 20th cent.*

The Times Literary Supplement 1980
The film seems to miss a trick ... in that these two never get it together, but most voyeurs should be satisfied with what is otherwise on offer.

Fay Weldon *Darcy's Utopia* 1991
When Wendy's father died of lung cancer, he asked Rhoda to move in and presently got it together to marry her, thus putting a stop to Wendy's sudden plan to abandon Dev and move back in with Ken.

get one's own back
to have one's revenge. *Early 20th cent.*

T W H Crosland *Last Poems* 1928
Yet, at the finish – well, we're bidden | To think no thoughts of get-your-own-back | Upon his own effluvious midden!

get somewhere
to make progress or be successful. To *get nowhere* is to achieve nothing despite one's efforts. *19th cent.*

George Gissing *The Odd Women* 1893
Cabs were not to be had; he must either explore the gloom, with risk of getting nowhere at all, or give it up and take a train back.

get-up-and-go
energy and enthusiasm: recorded earlier (late 19th cent.) in the shorter form *get-up*. *Early 20th cent.*

have got it bad/badly
informal to be infatuated or in love. *Early 20th cent.*

how — can you get?
a rhetorical question intended to assert the existence of the named quality in a person or thing. *Mid 20th cent.*

Financial Times 1983
Contractors ... continue to fan the flame of extreme competition by, among other things, encouraging clients to seek the very lowest price by extending tender lists and mixing major contractors with the small fry. This has the effect of reducing their own fees. How daft can you get?

See also be/get REAL; get away with MURDER; get AWAY with you; get the BETTER of; get the DRIFT; get a HANDLE on; get it in the NECK; get one's KIT off; get knotted *at* KNOT; get one's LEG over; get a LIFE; get LOST; get the MESSAGE; get on like a HOUSE on fire; get on somebody's nerves *at* NERVE; get out of somebody's FACE; get one's rocks off *at* ROCK[1]; get the shivers *at* SHIVER; get the SHOW on the road; get under somebody's SKIN; get up somebody's NOSE.

ghost

the ghost in the machine
the mind regarded as a ghost or spirit as distinct from the body, which is the machine. The expression was coined by the philosopher Gilbert Ryle in *The Concept of the Mind* (published in 1949). *Mid 20th cent.*

Godfrey Vesey *Inner and Outer* 1991
The ghost in the machine is, we may say, the machine itself as it appears to itself.

the ghost walks
informal people will be paid their due. The phrase had its origin and chief use in the world of the theatre, and is possibly based on the story of an actor who refused to 'walk on' as Hamlet's ghost

in Shakespeare's play until the actors' salaries were paid. *19th cent.*

give up the ghost

literary to die: in early use also *yield up the ghost.* The phrase is derived from Matthew 27:50 (in the Authorized Version, 1611) 'Jesus, when he had cried again with a loud voice, yielded up the ghost.' Also used humorously of machines that have stopped working. *17th cent.*

Henry More *Philosophicall Poems* 1647
But Autaparnes wox more wan and wo: | He faints, he sinks, ready to give up ghost.

David Lodge *Nice Work* 1988
If it was the battery it must have finally given up the ghost, because there wasn't even the faintest wheeze or whisper from the starter motor.

look as if one has seen a ghost

to look intensely pale from shock or fright: also in variant forms in early use. *18th cent.*

Smollett *The Expedition of Roderick Random* 1748
At that instant a young fellow came out from the place of examination, with a pale countenance, his lip quivering, and his looks as wild as if he had seen a ghost.

not have/stand the ghost of a chance

to have no chance at all. *19th cent.*

Thomas Hughes *Tom Brown's Schooldays* 1857
Williams hadn't the ghost of a chance with Tom at wrestling.

gift

God's (own) gift to —

somebody who is (especially in their own estimation) exactly what the specified group of people wants or needs: often used ironically. *Mid 20th cent.*

Financial Times 1982
In the late 1950s and 1960s ... the Australian property market seemed like God's gift to the investor.

in the gift of —

in so-and-so's power or authority. A variant form *of the gift of* is now obsolete. *17th cent.*

Sir John Vanbrugh *The Relapse* 1697
The largest Boons that Heaven thinks fit to grant, | To Things it has decreed shall crawl on Earth, | Are

in the Gift of Women form'd like you, | Perhaps, when Time shall be no more.

look a gift horse in the mouth

to criticize or look askance at something one has been given. The expression alludes to the proverb *do not look a gift* (or 16th cent. *given*) *horse in the mouth.* At a much earlier date (5th cent. AD) a Latin form of the proverb is found in St Jerome's commentary on St Paul's Epistle to the Ephesians: *noli ... ut vulgare proverbium est equi dentes inspicere donati* 'do not, in the words of the common proverb, look at the teeth of a given horse'. *16th cent.*

See also the gift of the GAB; the gift of tongues *at* TONGUE.

gild

gild the lily

to try to improve or embellish something that is already beautiful. Also in early use *paint the lily.* The phrase originates in Shakespeare's *King John* (1597) IV.ii.11 '[Salisbury] To gild refinèd gold, to paint the lily, | To throw a perfume on the violet, | ... | To seek the beauteous eye of heaven to garnish, | Is wasteful and ridiculous excess.' *16th cent.*

gill

green about/around the gills

looking sickly or unwell. The gills of humans are the flesh under the jaws and ears. The colours more commonly used to suggest illness in early use of the phrase were *white, blue,* and *yellow; red* was used to represent anger, and *rosy about the gills* was occasionally used to denote good health. The phrase in its current form dates from the 19th cent., but references to gills in similar contexts are found from the 17th cent.

gilt

take the gilt off the gingerbread

to make something less attractive by taking away the part that gives it its appeal. Gingerbread was traditionally sold at fairs decorated with gold leaf, and was a common literary symbol of tawdriness. A character (Mr Lovelace) in Richardson's *Clarissa* (1748) compares the world to a fair and calls 'all its joys but tinselled hobby-horses, gilt gingerbread, squeaking trumpets, painted drums, and so forth'. *19th cent.*

Henry J Byron *Cyril's Success* 1871
You have by this time, no doubt, learnt how constant companionship rubs the gilt off your gingerbread husband – gingerbread husband, indeed!

ginger

a ginger group

a pressure group within a political party or other organization, which urges stronger action in pursuit of a cause: *ginger* is used in its (19th cent.) sense 'high spirit, vigour' (*cf* the corresponding verb use as in *to ginger up*). *Early 20th cent.*

gingerbread

See take the GILT off the gingerbread.

gird

gird up one's loins

to muster one's resources and prepare for action. The phrase appears as a common image in the New Testament, and alludes to 1 Kings 18:45–6 (in the Authorized Version, 1611) 'And it came to pass in the mean while, that the heaven was black with clouds and wind, and there was a great rain. And Ahab rode, and went to Jezreel. And the hand of the Lord was on Elijah; and he girded up his loins, and ran before Ahab to the entrance of Jezreel.' The action involved was putting a belt or girdle round the middle of the body to lift loose clothing out of the way for easier movement. A variant form *gird up one's reins* is now obsolete. *17th cent.*

Bunyan *The Pilgrim's Progress* 1678
Then Christian began to gird up his loins, and to address himself to Journey.

girl

all girls together

women enjoying each other's company and support, especially in activities they would not undertake individually. *Mid 20th cent.*

See also PAGE three girl.

give

give and take

1 the process of making mutual concessions and compromises in disputes, negotiations, etc. The association of the verbs *give* and *take* in similar contexts dates from the 16th cent.: cf Shakespeare, *Richard III* (1593) v.iii.6, where Norfolk advises King Richard before Bosworth Field 'We must both give and take, my loving Lord.' *18th cent.*

2 good-natured conversation and exchange of ideas. *19th cent.*

give as good as one gets

to respond with equal effectiveness to attack, criticism, etc: the phrase is recorded earliest in the form *give somebody as good as he brings.* *18th cent.*

give the game/show away

informal to reveal confidential plans or information inadvertently, especially about an intended deception. *Show* here is used in its meaning 'a matter or affair' and *game* is a metaphor for deceit or trickery. *19th cent.*

give it to somebody

informal to reprimand or punish somebody. *19th cent.*

Hardy *Jude the Obscure* 1895
My word – won't he be in a taking! He'll give it to 'ee o' Saturday nights! Whatever it was, he'll say it was a trick – a double one, by the Lord!

give me — (any day)

a statement of strong liking or preference for the thing stated. Cf Shakespeare, *1 Henry IV* (1596) II.v.152: '[Sir John Oldcastle] Call you that backing of your friends? A plague upon such backing! Give me them that will face me.' *16th cent.*

give or take —

allowing for a specified margin of error: also used absolutely without any number specified. *Mid 20th cent.*

Nicholas Freeling *Love in Amsterdam* 1962
'What time would that have been …?' 'Don't know; about a quarter to ten maybe, give or take. Who's dead?' he joked.

give somebody what for

informal to reprimand or punish somebody severely. *19th cent.*

Charles Rann Kennedy *The Idol-Breaker* 1914
I liked the way you give them beltinker, when they first come in. That bit was fine. And the sun rising and all! ... Lord, if I could talk like you, I'd give them what for!

I'll give you/it, etc that
an admission that the person addressed is correct about something, or that the person or thing referred to has some redeeming characteristic, despite one's criticism. *Early 20th cent.*

Michael Falk *Part of the Furniture 1991*
Well at least it's not too far to go to get to work in the morning, I'll give it that.

See *also* give somebody/something BEST; give somebody furiously to think *at* FURIOUS; give one's MIND to; give one's/its NAME to; give somebody a piece of one's MIND; give RISE to something; give somebody up for LOST; give up the GHOST; have / give somebody the WILLIES; not give a DAMN; not give a SHIT; put on / give oneself airs *at* AIR.

gizzard
See stick in somebody's throat/craw/gizzard *at* STICK[1].

glad
give somebody the glad hand
to welcome somebody warmly, especially in an insincere or self-seeking way. *19th cent.*

Conan Doyle *His Last Bow 1917*
'You can give me the glad hand to-night, mister,' he cried. 'I'm bringing home the bacon at last.'

See *also* give somebody the (glad) EYE; in one's glad rags *at* RAG.

glance
at first glance
on first consideration: originally of visual contact but often used figuratively. *17th cent.*

Walter Charleton *The Ephesian and Cimmerian Matrons 1668*
The soldier takes a full view of the distressed Lady, and soon finds his sense had not been deluded by a phantasm, and that she was a real woman, as at first glance he had apprehended her to be.

glassy
(just) the glassy
Australian, informal an excellent person or thing. *Early 20th cent.*

Steele Rudd's *Magazine 1905*
That girl'll do you bad every time; she's the real glassy, an' no mistake.

gleam
See a gleam in somebody's EYE.

glitter
all that glitters/glistens is not gold
(proverb) appearances can be deceptive. The immediate origin of the phrase is in Shakespeare's *The Merchant of Venice* (1598) II.vii.65, where the Prince of Morocco reads the scroll contained in the golden casket that Portia opens: 'All that glisters is not gold; | Often have you heard that told.' But, as is implied here, the saying is much older, and occurs in Chaucer (*The Canon's Yeoman's Tale*, line 962) with a similar rider: 'But al thyng which that shineth as the gold | Nis nat gold, as that I have herd told.' The form *glisters* is replaced in modern use by *glitters* or *glistens*. *16th cent.*

gloom
See DOOM and gloom.

glory
go to glory
euphemistic to die. *19th cent.*

George Eliot *Middlemarch 1872*
The old lady must have been dead a pretty long while – gone to glory without the pain of knowing how poor her daughter was, eh?

in (all) one's glory
in a state of great pride or satisfaction: *glory* in the sense 'splendour or magnificence' dates from the 17th cent. and is often used ironically. The phrase is sometimes used with allusion to Christ's words in the Sermon on the Mount, as given in Matthew 6:28–9 'And why take ye thought for raiment? Consider the lilies of the field, how they grow; they toil not, neither do they spin: And yet

I say unto you, That even Solomon in all his glory was not arrayed like one of these.' *19th cent.*

See also crowning glory *at* CROWN.

glove

fit like a glove
(said of clothes) to be a perfect fit; (in figurative senses) to be entirely suitable. *18th cent.*

Smollett *The Expedition of Humphry Clinker* 1771
I would willingly give him a pair of new shoes, (said he) and half a guinea into the bargain, for the boots, which fitted me like a glove, and I shan't be able to get the fellows of them till the good weather for riding is over.

Willa Cather *The Song of the Lark* 1915
Elsa isn't a part that's particularly suited to Thea's voice at all, as I see her voice. It's over-lyrical for her. She makes it, but there's nothing in it that fits her like a glove, except, maybe, that long duet in the third act.

(when) the gloves are off
(when) the fight, competition, etc is conducted mercilessly or ruthlessly. In current use the allusion is mostly to the more brutal form of fist-fighting with the bare knuckles, but there are earlier uses that suggest an image of removing ordinary gloves in order to get down to business. For example, the New York periodical *The Nation* for May 1892 has the sentence 'The prophets and practitioners of the naturalistic school ... are here handled without gloves.' *19th cent.*

See also HAND *in* glove.

glow

in/of a glow
1 *informal* flushed or sweating. *19th cent.*

Dickens *Our Mutual Friend* 1865
'Sit close to the fire, father, dear, while I cook your breakfast. It's all ready for cooking, and only been waiting for you. You must be frozen.' 'Well Lizzie, I ain't of a glow, that's certain. And my hands seemed nailed through to the sculls. See how dead they are!'
2 in an exceptionally elated or heady state, especially as a result of a success or a bout of conviviality. *19th cent.*

Charles Reade *The Cloister and the Hearth* 1861
Often their sorrows make me weep, sometimes their perversity kindles a little wrath, and their absurdity makes me laugh, and sometimes their flashes of unexpected goodness do set me all of a glow: and I could hug 'em.

glutton

a glutton for punishment
a person who seems eager to take on difficult or unpleasant tasks. *Glutton* is used in the meaning 'one who is devoted to a particular pursuit' from the early 18th cent., and in sporting slang the words *glutton* and *punishment* were used together (though not in the current phrase) from the early 19th cent. *Cf* Kipling, *A Day's Work* (1895): 'He's honest, and a glutton for work.' *Late 20th cent.*

Martin Amis *Time's Arrow* 1991
Opinions of him vary: he is 'incredibly dedicated'; he is 'a glutton for punishment'; he is 'a saint'; he is 'a fucking maniac'.

gnash

gnash one's teeth
to feel or show great anger or anguish, literally by grinding one's teeth together. The phrase alludes to biblical passages, notably Matthew 8:12 'But the children of the kingdom shall be cast out into outer darkness: there shall be weeping and gnashing of teeth.' *16th cent.*

gnat

See STRAIN *at* a gnat.

gnome

the gnomes of Zurich
international bankers and financiers, especially those associated with Swiss banking and regarded as having a sinister influence over the financial sector of national economies. The phrase owes its origin to a speech made by Harold Wilson, British Labour politician and later Prime Minister, reported in Hansard for 12 November 1956: 'All these financiers, all the little gnomes in Zurich and the other financial centres about whom we keep on hearing.' *Mid 20th cent.*

go

(all) the go

informal, dated the height of fashion, the rage: in early use generally without *all. 18th cent.*

> George Colman Ygr *The Heir At Law* 1798
> *Yes, they are quite the dandy; arn't they, mother? – This is all the go, now, they say – cut straight – that's the thing – square waist – wrap over the knee, and all that – slouch is the word now!*

as/so far as it goes

within the limits imposed by circumstances, a person's abilities, etc: used to qualify or restrict the applicability of a statement. *18th cent.*

> George Campbell *The Philosophy of Rhetoric* 1776
> *For my part, nothing can appear more coincident than this, as far as it goes, with the principles which I have endeavoured to establish.*

> Byron *The Blues* 1820
> [Tracy] *You know, my dear friend, that in prose | My talent is decent, as far as it goes; | But in rhyme* – [Inkel] *You're a terrible stick to be sure.*

be all go

informal to be full of activity or hard work. *Late 20th cent.*

don't (even) go there

informal a warning to avoid a subject or topic of conversation. *Late 20th cent.*

from the word go

informal, originally NAmer from the very beginning: with allusion to the instruction 'go' used to start a race, activity, etc. *19th cent.*

> Edward Eggleston *The Hoosier School-Master* 1871
> *Mrs. Means had always suspected him. She seed some mighty suspicious things about him from the word go. She'd allers had her doubts whether he was jist the thing.*

give it a go

informal to make an attempt; to try one's luck in an uncertain venture. *Early 20th cent.*

go all the way (with somebody)

1 *informal* to continue a course of action to its conclusion. The phrase is based on the notion of completing a long journey, and is commonly used with reference to sexual activity leading to full intercourse. *Early 20th cent.*

2 *informal* to agree fully and without any reservation. *Early 20th cent.*

> T L S Sprigge *The Rational Foundations of Ethics* 1990
> *As will be seen later, I do not myself go all the way with the attitudinist theory of ethics.*

go-as-you-please

unrestricted by regulations; free to act. *19th cent.*

> Mark Twain *A Connecticut Yankee at the Court of King Arthur* 1889
> *You see, I had two schemes in my head which were the vastest of all my projects. The one was to overthrow the Catholic Church and set up the Protestant faith on its ruins – not as an Established Church, but a go-as-you-please one.*

go down with (all) guns firing

to offer resistance to the end, although completely beaten or overcome. *20th cent.*

go figure!

NAmer, informal an admission that something cannot be explained. *20th cent.*

> Daily Telegraph 1992
> *He invited … every constitutional party in the Province except the one party which is non-sectarian, which supports the Union, and which is linked to his own governing party in London. As the Americans say, go figure.*

go for it

to seize the chance, to act decisively while the opportunity is offered. *20th cent.*

> Sasha Stone *Kylie Minogue: the Superstar Next Door* 1989
> *You don't just jump between the sheets and say, 'Hey, let's go for it.'*

going, going, gone

humorous something will not be available much longer: from the words that close the bidding on an item at an auction, these being in turn based on the use of *go for* = to be sold for (a stated amount). *18th cent.*

going on (for) —

informal nearly the age or amount specified. *19th cent.*

go it / to it

informal to proceed rapidly or energetically. *19th cent.*

go it alone
informal to act on one's own initiative or without support. *19th cent.*

> **John William De Forest** *Overland* 1871
> *Thus it was evident that the entire brunt of the opening struggle would fall upon Thurstane and his people; that, if there was to be any resistance at all, these five men must commence it, and, for a while at least, 'go it alone'.*

have a go
informal to act with initiative, especially in making an attempt or taking personal action against a thief or attacker: an absolute use of the fuller form *have a go at somebody/something* (see below). *Late 20th cent.*

> **Guardian** 1989
> *Better to have a go and fail than not to have a go at all.*

have a go at somebody/something
1 *informal* to attack somebody, especially to subject them to prolonged or bullying criticism. *19th cent.*

> **R H Froude** *Remains of the Late Richard Hurrell Froude* 1838
> *And now I will have another go at you, about your rule of faith in fundamentals.*

2 *informal* to attempt something difficult or challenging. *19th cent.*

> **Charles Reade** *Hard Cash* 1863
> *You have stumbled on a passage you can't construe. Well, who has not? but we don't shed the briny about it. Here, let me have a go at it.*

3 to make inroads into (food or drink). *20th cent.*

> **New Scientist** 1991
> *He was infallible, kindly and not above having a go at the medicinal whisky.*

have — going for one
informal to enjoy advantages or favourable circumstances: often in the form *have a lot going for one* meaning 'to enjoy many advantages'. *Late 20th cent.*

> **Melvyn Bragg** *Rich* 1989
> *I thought, if you could be Welsh and a Jew, you'd have everything going for you!*

(it's) no go
informal it cannot be done; it is hopeless; a certain action is unsuccessful. The phrase occurs as a running theme throughout Louis MacNeice's poem 'Bagpipe Music' (1937), which begins: 'It's no go the merrygoround, it's no go the rickshaw, | All we want is a limousine and a ticket for the peepshow.' The meaning here is rather 'we do not want ...' *19th cent.*

> **Pilot** 1992
> *I attempted an engine restart – no go.*

make a go of it
informal to make a determined attempt at a task or enterprise. *19th cent.*

on the go
informal constantly or restlessly active. In earlier use the phrase meant 'in a state of decline'. *19th cent.*

what goes around comes around
(proverb) one will have to face the consequences of one's actions in due course. *Late 20th cent.*

who goes there?
used by sentries as a challenge to those approaching. *16th cent.*

> **Shakespeare** *The Taming of the Shrew* I.ii.138 (1592)
> [Grumio] *Master, master, look about you. Who goes there, ha?*

See also all systems go *at* SYSTEM; ANYTHING goes; go APE; go BALLISTIC; go bananas *at* BANANA; go BELLY up; go a BUNDLE on; go down like a lead balloon *at* LEAD²; go halves *at* HALF; go HAYWIRE; going great guns *at* GUN; go one BETTER; go out of one's WAY; go POSTAL; go STRAIGHT; go through the ROOF; go to the dogs *at* DOG; go too FAR; go to PLAN; go to POT; go the way of all FLESH; go WEST; go the whole HOG; LET oneself go.

---

goal

score an own goal
informal to harm one's own interests inadvertently by one's own actions. In football an *own goal* is a goal scored by mistake against one's own side. The phrase is late 20th cent. in figurative use.

> **Daily Telegraph** 1992
> *His admission that Central Office had put a tabloid newspaper in touch with the consultant at the centre of the case was a spectacular own goal.*

goalpost

move the goalposts

to change the rules or objectives of an undertaking or procedure while it is still in progress, especially in order to accommodate unexpected circumstances or difficulties: the implication is usually of unfairness to those involved in implementing the procedure. The goalposts in the metaphor represent the objective aimed at; when moved the goal becomes larger or smaller and correspondingly less or more difficult to hit. Late 20th cent.

Paddy Ashdown Diaries 1997
I think it is important not to beat about the bush so I may as well say bluntly that I feel you have misunderstood us and that the goalposts have moved again.

goat

act/play the (giddy) goat

informal to act foolishly or irresponsibly. In popular folklore goats are regarded as frisky and capricious (a word itself derived from Latin caper = goat); giddy is used in its etymological meaning 'possessed by a god'. 19th cent.

Charles Rann Kennedy The Idol-Breaker 1914
Not me. I'm not going to play the goat in your little seances.

get somebody's goat

informal to annoy or irritate somebody. The allusion is obscure: some relate the phrase to the practice, which is apparently still followed, of putting a goat into the stall of a nervous racehorse to calm it, so that a thief who got (i.e. removed) the goat might profitably bet on the horse then losing. The phrase first appears in print in the work of the American novelist Jack London, who used it in a letter in 1910: 'Honestly, I believe I've got Samuel's goat! He's afraid to come back.' Early 20th cent.

God

God willing

a wish that something will be possible or will happen as planned. The phrase is used earlier in other forms, e.g. if God will. The phrase dates from the 16th cent. in its current form.

Roger Ascham The Scholemaster 1570
I will, God willing, go forwarde orderlie, as I purposed, to instruct Children and yong men, both for learninge and maners.

play God

to have the fate of fellow human beings in one's control and act arrogantly or self-importantly in this role. 20th cent.

The Face 1990
This sort of research, which critics describe as 'playing God', gets even more morally knotty when it comes to gene therapy, with its potential for monitoring and altering human genes to check for and eliminate hereditary diseases.

with God

(said of a dead person, in some religious beliefs) in the afterlife, in heaven. An early use occurs in Shakespeare's Romeo and Juliet (1596), at the point where the Nurse is talking with Lady Capulet about Juliet's age, and observes that her own daughter Susan, who has died, was of the same age (I.iii.21): 'Susan and she – God rest all Christian souls! – | Were of an age. Well, Susan is with God; | She was too good for me.' 16th cent.

See also God helps those who HELP themselves; God's ACRE.

god

little tin god

a pompous or self-important person: first used by Kipling (in Departmental Ditties, 1886), who seems to have been referring to unduly venerated idols in Indian religions. G B Shaw used the form little tin Jesus. 19th cent.

ye gods (and little fishes)

used to express great shock or surprise. The addition of little fishes dates from the 19th cent. in American use; it is unexplained but its divine link in the phrase suggests a biblical reference to the miracle of the loaves and fishes fed to the five thousand (Matthew 14:13–21). 17th cent.

William Prynne Histrio-Mastix 1633
How can we Sweare by Iove, by Mars, by Venus, by Hercules, by the Celestial Gods, or such like Pagan Oathes? How can we exclaime, (as oft we doe in Stage-Plays,) O Iove! O Muses! O Cupid! O Venus! O Neptune! O ye Gods! O Vulcan,

Hercules, Mars, Apollo, Minerva, Castor, Pollux, Lucena, and the like; without a great offence?

Louisa M Alcott *Little Men* 1871
But out of school, – Ye gods and little fishes! how Tommy did carouse!

See also in the LAP of the gods.

---

goddess

See the BITCH goddess.

---

going

be heavy going

to be difficult to deal with or progress. The going is the state of the ground for walking, riding, or driving. *Early 20th cent.*

J B Priestley *Angel Pavement* 1930
He found such books too heavy going and preferred a detective story.

when/while the going is good

when circumstances are favourable. To *make good going* is to make good progress (on land and at sea). In literal uses the phrase dates from the 18th cent., and figurative senses date from the 20th cent.

Defoe *Captain Singleton* 1720
Indeed as the Winds blew fresh at West, as before, we had a smooth Sea, and we found it pretty good going before it, and so taking our smallest Canoe in Tow, we stood in for the Shore with all the Sail we could make.

R H Roberts *In the Shires* 1887
The fences are fair and the going pretty good, although the late rains have made it somewhat heavy.

K M Peyton *Who, Sir? Me, Sir?* 1988
Common sense told her to beat it while the going was good but loyalty held her, undecided.

See also GO.

---

gold

like gold dust

extremely rare or valuable. The phrase was originally used in a more physical sense denoting the stars or anything bright and glittering. *Gold dust* is also a popular name for the plant *Alyssum*

saxatile, which produces a spray of small yellow flowers. Allusive uses date from the 20th cent.

Viz 1998
High quality information in the motor trade is like gold dust – once it has been discovered, no-one wants to share it with anybody.

a/the pot/crock of gold (at the end of the rainbow)

a promised but illusory reward. There are several well-known superstitions connected with rainbows, the most famous being the childhood belief that you can 'cross out' a rainbow by placing two sticks on the ground in the form of a cross or by stamping on its reflection in a patch of oil or water on the ground. Another belief, associated with the Shetland Islands, is that a rainbow over a house presages death. The existence of charms against rainbows further illustrates a belief in their malign properties, but rainbows have also been symbolic of good luck and the promise of good fortune for those who can reach the rainbow's end. The 'crock of gold' represents the reward awaiting anybody who succeeds in this; since, of course, nobody can succeed, the reward is illusory. *20th cent.*

Sally Heywood *Castle of Desire* 1991
You can be sure that whenever you see the crock of gold there'll be some ogre standing guard over it.

See also a HEART of gold; fool's gold *at* FOOL; worth one's WEIGHT in gold.

---

golden

a golden age

a past time of great prosperity or happiness. Classical writers (notably Hesiod and Ovid) described the Golden Age as a time when earlier races of people enjoyed great prosperity and happiness, and freedom from affliction. The successive Silver, Brass, and Iron Ages represented a deterioration from this ideal state. Early uses appear in English translations of Ovid, for example by Arthur Golding in 1567: 'Then sprang up first the golden age, which of it selfe maintainde, | The truth and right of every thing unforst and unconstrainde' (*Metamorphoses* 1.103–4). The term was also applied to the age of Cicero in Roman literature, which was regarded by later critics as the finest period of Latin writing and preceded the Silver Age of the

Augustan writers. The *golden age* of an activity is its period of greatest excellence or refinement. *16th cent.*

> Shakespeare *The Rape of Lucrece* 1594
> *But beauty, in that white entitulèd | From Venus' doves, doth challenge that fair field. | Then virtue claims from beauty beauty's red, | Which virtue gave the golden age to gild | Their silver cheeks, and called it then their shield.*

> Henry Peacham *The Compleat Gentleman* 1622
> *Which time Erasmus calleth, the Golden Age of learning, in regard of so many famously learned men, it produced more then euer heretofore.*

> Scott *Chronicles of the Canongate* 1828
> *If they turned to France in the time of Louis the Fourteenth ... they would find that it was referred to by all Frenchmen as the golden age of the drama there.*

a golden calf
material wealth as an object of excessive veneration: with allusion to the biblical account (Exodus 32) of the golden calf made by Aaron and worshipped by the Israelites during Moses' absence on Mount Sinai. The phrase appears in early Bible translations, and in allusive use from the 18th cent.

> F G Waldron *The Maid of Kent* 1778
> *I think him a most amiable young man; and have often thought it a thousand pities he is not heir to a good fortune; as this idolatrous world of ours, still worshipping a golden calf, would value him much more for inheriting a fund of wealth than virtues.*

the golden goal
in international football (and more recently hockey), the first goal scored in extra time in a match that is part of a knockout competition, in which there has to be a winner and a loser: scoring the golden goal wins that side the match. The first such goal was scored against England by Germany in a European Championship semifinal at Wembley Stadium in 1996. *Late 20th cent.*

a golden handshake
a sum of money paid to an employee on leaving a company, especially through retirement or redundancy. Other expressions based on this use of *golden* include *golden hello* (see below), *golden parachute* (a clause in an executive's contract prescribing a large payment on termination for whatever reason), and *golden retriever* (with

play on the name of the dog: a sum offered to an ex-employee to persuade him or her to return). *Mid 20th cent.*

a golden hello
a payment made to a person who has agreed to join a company as a new employee, often as an added incentive to leave a rival company. *Late 20th cent.*

the golden mean
avoidance of extremes; moderation regarded as an ideal. The phrase translates Latin *aurea mediocritas* (Horace, *Odes* II.x.5); *mediocritas* in this sense does not have the derogatory implications of the English word *mediocrity*. It occurs in Spenser's *Faerie Queene* (1590) II.ii: 'Babes bloudie hands may not be clensd, | the face of golden Meane. Her sisters two Extremities: | strive her to banish cleane', and was also formerly used to mean what is now called the *golden section* (see below). *16th cent.*

> John Dunton *A Voyage Round the World* 1691
> *He indeed, if ever any Master, kept this golden mean, steering exactly betwixt the Rock of one side, and Gulph on t'other.*

the golden section
the division of a line such that the ratio of the smaller part to the larger is the same as the ratio of the larger part to the whole line, a property known to Euclid (4th cent. BC). It has had other names (including *golden mean*), and the current name is based on Latin *section aurea* and German *goldene Schnitt*, in use from the mid 19th cent.

---

gone
See FAR gone; gone with the wind *at* WIND[1].

---

gong

kick the gong around
informal to smoke opium: from a 20th cent. meaning of *gong* 'a narcotic drug'. The phrase is listed in the journal *American Speech* (Vol.XIII) for 1938. *Mid 20th cent.*

> Michael Munn *Hollywood Rogues* 1991
> *Now we have a young swoon actor, the idol of teenagers, caught in a marijuana party – a reefer smoking fest known to the trade as 'kicking the gong around'.*

good

all to the good

generally welcome or advantageous. *To the good* originally denoted profit or gain in accounting. *Mid 20th cent.*

as good as —

practically or very nearly as specified by the following adjective or other word. The phrase is found from late Middle English, and is chiefly used from the 16th cent. *As good as new*, meaning 'in a perfect or very fine condition', occurs from the 17th cent.

John Rainolds *The Overthrow of Stage-Playes* 1599
I made plaine unto you in my former letters by the testimonies of learned men and noble nations; all granted by your selfe, or as good as granted, in that you have either not answered them at all, or unsufficientlie.

Andrew Marvell *Miscellanies and Collections* a1678
I'll hem this shift, | E're thou shalt lack a sail, and lie a drift: | Bring home the old ones; I again will sew, | And darn them up, to be as good as new.

Jane Austen *Northanger Abbey* 1818
Seat, trunk, sword-case, splashing-board, lamps, silver moulding, all you see complete; the iron-work as good as new, or better.

(as) good as gold

very well-behaved: based on the purity of gold and on the alliterative effect. The simile was a favourite of Dickens', who may have invented it, attracted by its alliterative quality. It occurs in *The Old Curiosity Shop* (1841), *A Christmas Carol* (see below), *David Copperfield* (1850), and *Bleak House* (1853). Dickens' friend Wilkie Collins also used it, in *The Moonstone* (1868), as did Charlotte Yonge in *The Daisy Chain* (1856) and Trollope, extensively, in novels published from the 1860s on. Perhaps Dickens picked up the phrase from the old proverb *a friend at court is as good as gold in a man's pocket*, which occurs, for example, in Delarivière Manley's novel *The Secret History of Queen Zarah*, 1705 (see FRIEND). *19th cent.*

Dickens *A Christmas Carol* 1843
'And how did little Tim behave?' asked Mrs. Cratchit … 'As good as gold,' said Bob, 'and better.'

be as good as one's word

to honour a promise or undertaking. *16th cent.*

Thomas Nashe *Strange Newes* 1592
And I deeme he will be as good as his word, for ever yet it hath beene his wont, if he writ but a letter to any friend of his, … straight to give coppies of it abroad in the world.

Shakespeare *2 Henry IV* v.v.83 (1597)
[Shallow] *I beseech you, good Sir John, let me have five hundred of my thousand.* [Sir John] *Sir, I will be as good as my word.*

be good news

to be welcome information. *Early 20th cent.*

Guardian 1989
Bad news for publicans and wine merchants, good news for livers.

be — to the good

to have so much as profit or gain: originally used as a term in accounting. *19th cent.*

Saki *The Chronicles of Clovis* 1912
The aunt picked up thirty-five francs. After that the Brimley Bomefields would have had to have used concerted force to get her away from the tables. When Roger appeared on the scene she was fifty-two francs to the good.

be up to no good

to act suspiciously or threateningly, typically in a clandestine or furtive manner. *19th cent.*

Mary Braddon *Lady Audley's Secret* 1862
I began to think my first thoughts of him might have been right enough after all, and that he couldn't have been up to no good to want to sneak away so precious quiet.

good and —

informal used to add force to a following adjective or adverb: often used with *proper* and *ready*. The combination *good and ready* occurs from the 17th cent. in various meanings, with *good and* serving as a kind of intensifying aside operating on the word *ready*, which carries the main meaning. The phrase is informal in modern use.

Roger Boyle *Parthenissa* 1676
Seeing his Enemies in so good and ready a form, relying on the benefit he had of the Wind, on his Courage, and on his former Success, he resolutely advanced.

the good news … the bad news …

a combination of welcome and unwelcome information, often expressed by the formula *the good news is such-and-such, and the bad news is such-and-*

such, which originated in school humour. It may be preceded by the question 'Do you want the good news or the bad news?' or the statement 'I've got some good news and some bad news …' *Late 20th cent.*

Iain Banks *Complicity* 1993
The good news is I didn't kill your son, in fact he isn't dead at all, but the bad news is he's a multiple murderer.

good oil
Australian, informal reliable information. *Mid 20th cent.*

V C Hall *Dreamtime Justice* 1962
If we could get the 'good oil' from the islanders we might be able to stage a daylight raid.

good Samaritan
somebody who selflessly helps a person in distress. The phrase refers to the New Testament parable of the Good Samaritan (i.e. person from Samaria) who stopped to help a man who had been robbed and lay wounded by the roadside after others had passed him by (Luke 10:30–37; *see also* PASS by on the other side). To Christ's Jewish audience, a Samaritan was an outcast, as we see in the account in John 4:9 of Christ's visit to a Samaritan village: 'Then saith the woman of Samaria unto him, How is it that thou, being a Jew, askest drink of me, which am a woman of Samaria? For the Jews have no dealings with Samaritans.' Also used without *good*. The Samaritans, the charitable counselling organization founded by a London vicar in 1953, drew their name from the biblical account. The phrase dates from the 17th cent. in biblical references, and from the 18th cent. in allusive uses.

Smollett *The Expedition of Roderick Random* 1748
Hodge resembled the Jew more than the good Samaritan, and ordered me to be carried to the house of the parson, whose business it was to practise as well as to preach charity.

Dickens *Martin Chuzzlewit* 1844
He appropriated the rocking-chair to himself, and looked at the prospect, like a good Samaritan waiting for a traveller.

make good
to achieve success; to fulfil a promise or commitment. *Early 20th cent.*

Willa Cather *The Song of the Lark* 1915
'My grandfather Alstrom was a musician, and he made good.' Dr. Archie chuckled. 'Oh, a Swede can make good anywhere, at anything!'

no good to gundy
Australian, informal no good at all. It is probably based on alliterative effect, although there have been attempts to find a definite origin for the word *gundy*, such as an association with a Welsh word meaning 'to steal', an abbreviation of the place name Gundagai in New South Wales, and a link with the American phrase *according to Gunter* meaning 'following the rules' (S J Baker, *The Australian Language*, 1945). None of these suggestions is particularly compelling. *Early 20th cent.*

(that's) a (very) good question
that needs careful consideration: usually said in reply to a telling point made when the person replying needs more time to think of an effective answer. *Early 20th cent.*

too good to be true
so attractive or advantageous as to seem barely credible. Also used to suggest that a person's outstanding reputation might be exaggerated. *16th cent.*

Emanuel Ford *Parismus* 1598
Were it not (quoth she) but that I stande in some doubt hereof (as being too good to be true) I should rest in such happie content by thy newes.

See also be in good COMPANY; be/put somebody on to a good THING; the BEST is the enemy of the good; a good JOB; have a good MIND to do something; in somebody's bad/good books *at* BOOK; in good FAITH; in good TIME; one good TURN deserves another; take something in good PART; throw good MONEY after bad.

---

goods

get/have the goods on somebody
to obtain or possess information about somebody that could be used to their disadvantage. *Early 20th cent.*

See also DELIVER the goods.

goog

(as) full as a goog

Australian, informal very drunk. Goog is an Australian slang word for 'egg'. Mid 20th cent.

Realist 1966
Ginger was bringin' him home in the spring cart, full as a goog, been drinking whisky.

googly

bowl a googly

informal to create a difficult or awkward situation for somebody; to ask an awkward question. In cricket, a googly is a slow ball delivered in such a way that it bounces awkwardly and in an unexpected direction. Figurative uses seem to have developed in Australian services' slang of the First World War, to describe the delivery of bombs. Early 20th cent.

goose

(kill) the goose that lays the golden egg

(to destroy) a valuable source of income (from motives of greed). The phrase is based on the fable of Aesop, in which a man who owns a goose that lays one golden egg a day kills the goose in the expectation of finding a richer supply of gold inside it, but finds nothing. 19th cent.

Isaac Pocock The Robber's Wife 1830
[Rody] We are starving in the midst of plenty, as a man may say, and all for a spoonful of yellow wash, to give the coin a colour. There's our wedge of gold left yet: why not use it? [Drosset] What! kill the goose that lays our golden eggs? melt the ingot that Sawney Macfile has sold over and over, yet always brought back safe?

See also COOK somebody's goose; what's SAUCE for the goose is sauce for the gander; — wouldn't say BOO to a goose.

Gordian

cut the Gordian knot

to solve an intractable problem by an unusual or unexpected method. The phrase is derived from the story of the intricately tied knot encountered by Alexander the Great at Gordium in Phrygia in 333 BC, early in his conquest of Asia. According to legend, the knot had been tied to fix the pole of an ox-cart to the yoke by a peasant named Gordius, who by the prophecy of an oracle became King of Phrygia. The oracle further foretold that whoever untied the knot would become ruler of Asia. Alexander, unwilling to pass on without exploiting this legend but unable to untie the knot by normal means, is said to have cut the knot with his sword (or pulled out the pin that held it together, according to another version), and claimed the title prophesied by the oracle. The information about this incident comes mainly from Arrian (Anabasis of Alexander II.iii) and Plutarch (Alexander 18), both writing several centuries after Alexander's death but using contemporary sources now lost; one of these sources, Aristoboulus, gave the pin-pulling version, and it seems that Ptolemy, a general of Alexander's and later King of Egypt, who also wrote a history of Alexander, did not mention the incident at all. One ancient historian has wisely commented that 'no one can really hope to know what happened at Gordium any more than one can say what song the Sirens sang'. An early allusion in English to this story occurs in Shakespeare's Henry V (1599) I.i.47, where the Archbishop of Canterbury characterizes the King with the words 'Turn him to any cause of policy, | The Gordian knot of it he will unloose'. Gordian knot is also recorded in the sense 'an indissoluble bond'. 16th cent.

Charles Darby Bacchanalia 1680
I could the Gordian knot unty | Of Ecclesiastick Polity.

gorge

The meaning of gorge here, current only in the phrases, is 'the contents of the stomach', which is based on a meaning in falconry 'a meal for a hawk', itself developed from the primary meaning 'the throat, the front of the neck'.

cast the/one's gorge at somebody/something

to dismiss somebody or something with loathing. The phrase is derived from Timon's speech in Shakespeare's Timon of Athens (1609), where he is extolling the power of gold (IV.iii.41): 'This is it | That makes the wappered [= tired] widow wed again. | She whom the spittle house and ulcerous sores | Would cast the gorge at, this embalms and spices | To th' April day again.' 17th cent.

one's gorge rises

one is disgusted or nauseated. The locus classicus is Shakespeare, *Hamlet* (1601) v.i.207, where Hamlet looks on the skull of Yorick: 'He hath borne me on his back a thousand times; and now, how abhorred my imagination is! My gorge rises at it.' *17th cent.*

gory

the gory details

informal, often humorous the explicit or most intimate details of something: originally with reference to accounts or representations of acts of violence and bloodshed. *20th cent.*

> The Times 1985
> He took an extreme right-wing stance, forming a private army and dedicating himself to the feudal traditions of the samurai, a bizarre mixture of beauty and violence. He rehearsed his death a couple of years before in a feature film, the gory details of which we are thankfully spared.

gospel

the gospel truth

something so authoritative as not to be questioned: an extension of a more literal meaning 'the truth contained in the Gospels'. To *take something as gospel* means to accept it in this way. The notion of the Gospels as symbolic of 'absolute' truth goes back to Middle English, and is found in Chaucer's *Troilus and Criseyde* (v.1265): 'Got wot [= knew], I wende [= think], O Lady bright, Criseyde, I That every word was gospel that ye seyde!' The phrase is 18th cent. in its present form.

> Thomas Day The Suicide 1797
> I pity thee, Alphonso! thou art much I Deluded. Plain it is as gospel truth I Can make it: plain as nature's voice can speak, I In every instance, Suicide is guilt.

> William Hazlitt The Spirit of the Age 1825
> He [Byron] says of Mr. Wordsworth's poetry, that 'it is his aversion'. That may be: but whose fault is it? This is the satire of a lord, who is accustomed to have all his whims or dislikes taken for gospel, and who cannot be at the pains to do more than signify his contempt or displeasure.

Gotham

a (wise) man of Gotham

dated a fool. Gotham was a village proverbial for the foolishness of its inhabitants. Its identity is uncertain: it is thought not to be the village of this name in Nottinghamshire, and its use as a nickname for Newcastle and New York is a later (19th cent.) association. There is evidence from the 16th cent., and the expression is listed in the *New Dictionary of the Canting Crew*, published in about 1690.

> Thomas Holcroft Anna St Ives 1792
> Solomon himself, and the seven sages to boot, are but so many men of Gotham, when he is present.

gourd

out of one's gourd

NAmer, informal crazy, out of one's mind: based on the slang meaning of *gourd* meaning 'the head or mind'. *Late 20th cent.*

> New Yorker 1985
> Anybody who lends a billion dollars to Mexico is out of his ever-lovin' gourd.

grab

up for grabs

informal available for anybody to take or win. *Mid 20th cent.*

> Independent 1989
> 'Town cramming' is to be frowned on. This is the process whereby every scrap of green land in a town is up for grabs by development.

grace

The meaning underlying the phrases, 'the state of being favoured', which dates from late Middle English, is no longer current apart from the uses here. The phrase *with good/bad grace* also reflects the other main (and still current) meaning, 'charm or attractiveness (especially of expression or disposition)'.

be in somebody's good graces

to be regarded favourably, to receive approval. *17th cent.*

Philip Ayres *The Revengeful Mistress* 1696
It likewise brought to his memory, the great danger he then was in, not only of losing her favour, but of feeling the effects of her revenge for that fault; as also the difficulty he had to obtain his pardon, and to re-instate himself in her good graces as before.

Jane Austen *Emma* 1816
Mrs. Churchill is not much in my good graces, as you may suspect – but this is quite between our-selves. She is very fond of Frank, and therefore I would not speak ill of her.

fall from grace

to be no longer in favour, especially with a super-ior or a person of influence. The phrase originates in biblical use, in which the meaning is 'to be no longer in divine favour' (i.e. because of one's sins). It occurs in Middle English (in Wyclif), but is predominantly 17th cent. and later.

Galatians 5:4 (Authorized Version of the Bible) 1611
Christ is become of no effect unto you, whosoever of you are justified by the Law: ye are fallen from grace.

Robert Davenport *The City-Night-Cap* 1661
If Verona hath observed any Errours in me, | I well may call for grace to amend them; | But will never fall from grace to befriend you.

James Rusbridger *The Intelligence Game* 1991
That Reagan managed to escape public disgrace was probably only because Americans found it very hard so soon after Nixon to see another president fall from grace.

with good/bad grace

in a manner that is willing and generous (or reluctant and resentful). *18th cent.*

Anthony Ashley Cooper *Characteristicks of Men, Manners, Opinions, Times* 1711
They are forc'd to use odd gestures and contortions. They have a sort of action, and move still, tho with the worst grace imaginable.

grade

make the grade

to reach the expected standard or an acceptable level; to succeed. *20th cent.*

New Scientist 1991
Jupiter is no ordinary planet: it almost made the grade as a star.

grain

There are two main strands of meaning involved here. In most of the phrases the base meaning is 'the texture or pattern of constituent fibres or particles' (as in wood, cloth, etc), but the second phrase relates to the other key meaning 'a seed or fruit of a cereal grass' and related senses. The two strands are interwoven in an interesting way in the phrase *in grain* (see below).

be/go against the grain

to be contrary to one's inclination or natural dis-position. *17th cent.*

Dryden *Amboyna* 1673
Seizing their Factories, I like well enough, it has some savour in't, but for this whorson cutting of throats, it goes a little against the grain, because tis so notoriously known in Christendom, that they have preserv'd ours from being cut by the Spaniards.

a grain of mustard seed

something that is small in itself but can be used to produce something much more significant. Used with allusion to the parable in Matthew 13:31–2: 'The kingdom of heaven is like to a grain of mustard seed, which a man took, and sowed in his field. Which indeed is the least of all seeds: but when it is grown, it is the greatest among herbs, and becometh a tree, so that the birds of the air come and lodge in the branches thereof.' In Palestine the seed of the black mustard (*Brassica nigra*) grew to a great height. Allusive uses date from the 17th cent.

George Mackenzie *Aretina* 1660
All being most ready to signifie their respect to these ladies in the persons of their favorite, seeing most want the means of engaging themselves: from this grain of mustard-seed did grow up that large stalk, whose fruits did thereafter so bite the mouths of all the nation, and by this sparkle was kindled that great fire, which did thereafter both scorch his enemies, and warm his friends.

in grain

downright, thorough, genuine. The phrase is derived from *dyed in the grain*, which refers to colouring with an indelible scarlet dye made from galls of the kermis oak; these were called *grain* because they were formerly taken to be seeds. The same notion lies behind the use of *ingrained*. Middle English

Chaucer *The Tale of Sir Thopas* (line 727)
Sire Thopas wax a doghty swayn [= young gentleman]; | *Whit was his face as payndemayn* [= white bread], | *His lippes rede as rose;* | *His rode* [= complexion] *is lyk scarlet in grayn.*

Shakespeare *The Comedy of Errors* III.ii.108 (1594)
[Dromio of Syracuse] *She sweats a man may go overshoes in the grime of it.* [Antipholus of Syracuse] *That's a fault that water will mend.* [Dromio] *No, sir, 'tis in grain. Noah's flood could not do it.*

See also take something with a pinch/grain of SALT.

grand

a/the grand old man of —
a man who is highly respected in the specified field. *Grand old man* is recorded from the 1850s, and was specifically applied (as *Grand Old Man* and in the abbreviated form *GOM*) in 1882 to William Gladstone (1809–98), who was 73 at the time and went on to win his last election ten years later. *19th cent.*

grandeur
See delusions of grandeur *at* DELUSION.

grandmother

teach one's grandmother to suck eggs
to presume to advise somebody who is already experienced. The phrase first appears in the early 18th cent. in cautionary contexts, and is familiar as a proverb preceded by *do not*. The earliest record in print is from 1707 in John Stevens' translation of the comedies of the Spanish playwright Francisco de Quevedo: 'You would have me teach my grandame to suck eggs.' It occurs a few years later in an exchange given in Swift's *Complete Collection of Polite and Ingenious Conversation* (1738): "I'll mend it, miss" ... "You mend it! Go, teach your grannam to suck eggs."' Other versions of the same notion occur at earlier dates: for example, the 16th cent. scholar Nicholas Udall noted a classical proverb in the English form 'a swine to teach Minerva'. Others based on grandmothers include *groping her ducks* (i.e. to check

them for eggs) and *supping sour milk* (the latter recorded in John Ray's 1670 collection of sayings). There is also, of course, the old adage *you can't teach an old dog new tricks* (*see* TEACH). *18th cent.*

Henry Fielding *The History of Tom Jones* 1749
I remember my old schoolmaster, who was a prodigious great scholar, used often to say, Polly matete cry town is my daskalon. The English of which, he told us, was, that a child may sometimes teach his grandmother to suck eggs. I have lived to a fine purpose truly, if I am to be taught my grammar at this time of day.

grant

take somebody/something for granted
1 to assume something to be true or certain to occur, without seeking proof. *17th cent.*

Bunyan *The Holy War* 1682
What does he but taking it for granted that the Captains were either wounded or dead, he therefore makes at first a stand.
2 to fail to show appreciation for somebody or something. A natural progression from the older meaning. *20th cent.*

The Times 1985
The government is out of political fashion for the moment, and what it has achieved is easily taken for granted.

grape
See SOUR grapes.

grapevine

hear something on the grapevine
to get information unofficially or through rumour. The term *grapevine* (or in full *grapevine telegraph*) originated in America in the 1850s and became popular during the American Civil War to denote unofficial channels of information. There is obviously an implied contrast between the twisted and tangled stems of the vine and the more reliable and direct lines of the electric telegraph. *The Daily Grapevine* was the name of a fictional newspaper in Mark Twain's *The Gilded Age* (1873), a novel set in the postwar period of American adjustment. *Cf* BUSH telegraph. *19th cent.*

grasp

grasp the nettle

to tackle a difficulty with assurance. A nettle is said to sting less painfully when seized tightly than when lightly touched; it takes some nerve to put this piece of folklore to the test. The tradition is reflected in the 'Verses Written on a Window in Scotland' by the English poet Aaron Hill (1685–1750): 'Tender-handed stroke a nettle, | And it stings you for your pains; | Grasp it like a man of mettle, | And it soft as silk remains.' *19th cent.*

> Augustus Thomas *The Witching Hour* 1907
> [Helen] *It's cruel to keep constantly referring to that – that – mistake of Clay's. I want to forget it.* [Jack] *The way to forget it, my dear Helen, is not to guard it as a sensitive spot in your memory, but to grasp it as the wise ones grasp a nettle – crush all its power to harm you in one courageous contact.*

See also clutch/grasp at straws *at* STRAW.

grass

cut the grass from under somebody's feet

to thwart somebody in an intention. *16th cent.*

the grass is (always) greener (on the other side of the fence)

(proverb) life always seems more pleasant in places other than one's own. The concept dates back at least to the 1st cent. AD, and appears for example in Ovid, *Ars Amatoria* 1.349 *fertilior seges est alienis semper in agris* 'the harvest is always more abundant in another's fields', but the first occurrence in English of the current form of the phrase is relatively recent. *19th cent.*

> George Augustus Sala *The Seven Sons of Mammon* 1862
> *The great owners of race-horses, the solid, serious turfites, the substantial, grave-eyed trainers, are seldom seen, and then but for an instant. They have other and weightier business further afield, where the grass is greener, and the throng is not so dense.*

grass roots

the ordinary people, especially (in political contexts) voters. The expression dates from the beginning of the 20th cent., when it was often used in cultural contexts and (with a hyphen) as an adjective, as in *grass-roots values, grass-roots democracy,* etc. The political connotations first

appear in American usage around 1910. *Early 20th cent.*

keep off the grass

a warning not to encroach or take liberties: from the literal use as an instruction to the public in parks and other open spaces. *19th cent.*

> Harriet Ford *The Argyle Case* 1912
> *Here – here. Keep off the grass. This is my busy day.*

not let the grass grow under one's feet

to take prompt action or seize an opportunity. The phrase is found in related forms from the 16th cent., and by the early 17th cent. is established in the current form. Topsell's *Four-footed Beasts*, published in 1607, includes the observation that 'the hare … leaps away again, and letteth no grass grow under his feet'.

> Wilkie Collins *Armadale* 1866
> *The arrangement once made between us, I must do him the justice to say that he showed no disposition to let the grass grow under his feet. He called briskly for pen, ink, and paper.*

put somebody out to grass

to compel somebody to retire. The comparison is with horses and other animals that are left to graze when their useful lives are over. *17th cent.*

grasshopper

See knee-high to a grasshopper *at* KNEE.

grave

(as) still/silent/quiet as the grave

completely quiet or silent. There is a sinister and tragic use in the final act of Shakespeare's *Othello* (1604), at the point where Othello has just strangled Desdemona and is about to be confronted by Iago's wife Emilia, still uncertain about whether Desdemona is completely dead: 'Ha! No more moving. | Still as the grave. Shall she come in? Were't good? | I think she stirs again. No. What's best to do?' *17th cent.*

> Dryden *Troilus and Cressida* 1679
> *By all the gods and by my just revenge, | This Sun shall shine the last for them or us: | These noisy streets or yonder echoing plains | Shall be to morrow silent as the grave.*

dig one's own grave

to bring about one's own ruin or downfall. The phrase is used in a letter of F Scott Fitzgerald written in 1934 (see below), but the image and the phrase itself are considerably older: there is, for example, a powerful image in Samuel Sheppard's *Loves of Amandus and Sophronia* (1650): 'He would fain have slain himself, but wanted fit meanes to accomplish it, and therefore the reprobate wretch, with his own nails, began to tear, and rend the ground, intending to dig his own grave; when (as if sent by some avenging Deity) a crew of ravenous wolves came running upon him, and tearing him all in pieces, buried his loathed body in their hungry mawes.' The reference here to digging one's own grave is of course literal, albeit within extended metaphor. It is difficult to pin down the point of transfer to the current figurative meaning, but allusive uses predominate from the 19th cent.

Elizabeth Barrett Browning *Aurora Leigh* 1856
And hide this letter: let it speak no more | Than I shall, how you tricked poor Marian Erle, | And set her own love digging its own grave | Within her green hope's pretty garden-ground.

F Scott Fitzgerald *Letter* 1934
Of course my apologia is necessarily a whine to some extent; a man digs his own grave and should, presumably, lie in it, and I know that the fault for this goes back to those years, which were really years of self-indulgence ...

somebody is walking over my grave

an expression used when shivering or shuddering involuntarily. It first occurs in a satirical dialogue by Jonathan Swift published as part of his *Complete Collection of Polite and Ingenious Conversation* in 1738, in which a character shudders and declares 'Lord! There's somebody walking over my grave.' It is derived from the popular folklore that one shivers when somebody walks over the site of one's future grave, and has other superstitious associations. One of these is the fear of treading on a tombstone, causing bad luck, as found for example in Coleridge's *The Three Graves* (1798): 'To see a man tread over graves | I hold it no good mark; | 'Tis wicked in the sun and moon, | And bad luck in the dark.' *18th cent.*

George Meredith *The Egoist* 1879
'You are cold, my love? you shivered.' 'I am not cold,' said Clara. 'Some one, I suppose, was walking over my grave.'

take one's secret to the grave

to die without revealing one's secret. This powerful image recalls the related phrase *as silent as the grave* (see above), which is recorded from an earlier date. *19th cent.*

Dickens *Dombey and Son* 1848
She thought how strange and sorrowful it would be, thus to become a grey-haired woman, carrying her secret to the grave, when Florence Dombey was forgotten.

turn in one's grave

(said of a dead person) to be likely to have reacted with horror to something if they were still alive to experience it. Also used in fanciful variants. *19th cent.*

Thackeray *The History of Pendennis* 1849
'He's been there every day, in the most open manner, my dear,' continued Mrs. Speers. 'Enough to make poor Mr. Pendennis turn in his grave,' said Mrs. Wapshot. 'She never liked him, that we know,' says No. 1.

Anne Fine *In Cold Domain* 1995
William's only reason for moving in with Caspar was to set his poor father's corpse spinning in its grave.

See also DANCE on somebody's grave; from the CRADLE to the grave; have one FOOT in the grave.

graven

a graven image

an idol carved from wood or stone and used as an object of false worship: with reference to the second commandment given to Moses according to Exodus 20:4 'Thou shalt not make unto thee any graven image, or any likeness of any thing that is in heaven above, or that is in the earth beneath, or that is in the water under the earth.' *Middle English* (in Wyclif)

gravy

board/ride the gravy train

informal to gain access to a much exploited source of easy money. *Gravy* is used in its informal meaning 'money or other benefits gained easily'. The notion of a gravy train is fanciful, and may be influenced by the image of a *gravy boat*, a dish for serving gravy at a meal. *Mid 20th cent.*

grease

grease somebody's palm

to give somebody a bribe. The phrase is based on the notion of 'grease' (i.e. money put in the hand) helping things to run more smoothly, as in *grease the wheels* below. The phrase now has *palm* as its standard form, but the earliest uses were with *fist* and *hand*. *16th cent.*

Skelton *Magnyfycence* a1529
Wyth golde and grotes they grese my hande, | In stede of ryght that wronge may stande, | And counterfet fredome that is bounde.

Edward Ward *The London Spy* 1698
But the gay curtezan who trades for gold, | That can but grease a palm when she's in bold, | No justice need she dread, or Bridewell fear.

grease the wheels

to take measures to make something (e.g. commerce or government) work more smoothly: a metaphor in which a procedure is compared to a moving vehicle, which runs better when its wheels are well greased. *19th cent.*

See also like (greased) LIGHTNING.

greasy

greasy spoon

informal, originally NAmer a cheap and poor-quality restaurant or café. *Early 20th cent.*

Mike Ripley *Just Another Angel* 1989
I found one of those plastic and formica Little Chefs that were replacing the old greasy spoon eateries and went straight into the Gents.

great

the great and the good

famous and distinguished people collectively. *19th cent.*

Sylvester Judd *Richard Edney and the Governor's Family* 1850
When one is introduced to the great and the good, he instinctively leaves behind his meanness and his littleness.

Jeremy Paxman *Friends in High Places* 1990
When she returned from one of the innumerable meetings and one of her daughters asked who had been present, her usual reply would be, 'Oh, the Great and the Good.'

great and small

all types and sizes: originally used with reference to people, but now more usually of animals or things (as in the lines from Coleridge's *The Rime of the Ancient Mariner* 'He prayeth best, who loveth best | All things both great and small' and the hymn by Cecil Francis Alexander, 'All things bright and beautiful, | All creatures great and small'). The phrase is found in the Middle English romance called *Ipomadon* ('All spake of hym, bothe grete and smalle') and in Coverdale's translation of the Bible (1535). *Middle English*

Thomas Beard *The Theatre of Gods Judgements* 1597
Let every one both great and small learne by these examples to containe themselves within the limits of humanitie.

a great one for —

a person who is fond of or given to a particular activity: based on earlier uses of *great* in the sense 'skilled, accomplished', often followed by *at* or *on*. *Early 20th cent.*

The Artist 1992
I'm a great one for putting a bit of cerulean blue in my green areas, but other painters add other colours, like red.

See also the great OUTDOORS; the great UNWASHED.

Greek

beware/fear the Greeks bearing gifts

(proverb) one should be wary of enemies or rivals appearing to be generous. Used with allusion to the words of the Trojan priest Laocoön in Virgil's Aeneid (ii.49), *timeo Danaos et dona ferentes* ('I fear the Greeks, even when they bring gifts'), warning the Trojans against admitting the huge wooden horse left behind by the Greeks when they had seemingly abandoned the siege of Troy (*see* TROJAN horse). *18th cent.*

Charles Batteux *A Course of the Belles Letters* 1761
Every actor should avoid, in general, whatever appears like art, or studied declamation; as, first, all common place thoughts, and moral sentences,

which are like foreign bodies in the middle of a discourse, that have no connection with any thing else. Thus, instead of saying, We should distrust even gifts when coming from an enemy, he will say, I fear the Greeks even in their bounty.

the Greeks had a word for it

used of something that should not be named or mentioned: with allusion to the Broadway play by Zoe Atkins, first produced in 1929, which featured the goings on among ancient Greek *hetairoi* or prostitutes. *Early 20th cent.*

it is all Greek to me

this is utterly mysterious or incomprehensible to me, like an obscure foreign language. The locus classicus is Shakespeare, *Julius Caesar* (1599) I.ii.278–84 '[Cassius] Did Cicero say anything? [Casca] Ay, he spoke Greek. [Cassius] To what effect? [Casca] Nay, an I tell you that, I'll ne'er look you i'th'face again. But those that understood him smiled at one another, and shook their heads. But for mine own part, it was Greek to me.' The phrase also occurs in a play of about the same time, perhaps a few years later, called *Patient Grissil*, by Shakespeare's contemporary Thomas Dekker (c1572–1632), and there are allusions in other forms in the literature of the day, so it was probably quite widely used by this time. It is derived from a medieval Latin proverb *Graecum est, non potest legi* 'it is Greek; it cannot be read'. *16th cent.*

Jane Barker A Patch-Work Screen for the Ladies 1723
I was a stranger to everybody, and their way of living; and, I believe, my stiff air and awkward mien, made everybody wish to remain a stranger to me. The assemblées, ombre, and basset-tables, were all Greek to me; and I believe my country dialect, to them, was as unintelligible.

Mary Shelley Falkner 1837
We set out on our travels, and went first to Portugal – where I had never been – and do not know a word of Portuguese; and then through Spain – and Spanish is Greek to me.

Christopher Fry The Lady's Not for Burning 1949
I know I am not | A practical person; legal matters and so forth | Are Greek to me, except, of course, | That I understand Greek. | And what may seem nonsensical | To men of affairs like yourselves might not seem so | To me.

See also at/on the Greek CALENDS.

green

(as) green as grass

extremely gullible or naive. *Green* has this meaning from the 15th cent., and is based on the typical colour of unripe fruit and vegetables. The simile plays on the alliteration produced by the association of green with grass, the two words also being related in origin. It makes an early appearance in the work of the medieval cleric John of Trevisa, translator of a universal history (*Polychronicon*) by the Benedictine monk Ranulf Higden. *Middle English*

be green with envy

to be extremely envious. *The green eye* denoting jealousy and envy is found in Shakespeare (*see* the green-eyed monster *below*) and is a figurative use of *green* describing paleness of complexion (as in Shakespeare's *Macbeth* (1606) I.vii.37, where Lady Macbeth berates Macbeth for his doubts about murdering Duncan: 'Was the hope drunk | Wherein you dressed yourself? Hath it slept since? | And wakes it now to look so green and pale | At what it did so freely?').

Henry William Herbert Marmaduke Wyvil 1843
Tush! man, cheer up your love-sick wits! You, Marmaduke Wyvil – you desponding! You, at whose luck all Paris is wild with astonishment, and green with envy!

give somebody the/a green light

to authorize somebody to proceed with a plan, enterprise, etc. The phrase alludes to the green light indicating 'proceed' in a set of traffic signals. To *get the green light* is to receive authorization. *Mid 20th cent.*

Terence Rattigan French without Tears 1937
We had a bottle of wine and got pretty gay, and all the time she was giving me the old green light.

the green-eyed monster

jealousy: with reference to Shakespeare, *Othello* (1604) III.iii.170 '[Iago to Othello] O, beware, my lord, of jealousy. It is the green-eyed monster which doth mock | The meat it feeds on.' At a slightly earlier date Portia in *The Merchant of Venice* (1596) III.ii.110 refers to 'rash-embraced despair, And shudd'ring fear, and green-eyed jealousy.' *17th cent.*

have green fingers

to be an adept and creative gardener. The green fingers are a metaphor for successful growing. *Early 20th cent.*

not as green as one is cabbage-looking

informal more experienced than one appears to be. There is play here on two senses of *green*: (1) referring to the colour of herbs and vegetables, and specifically the cabbage, and (2) 'raw and inexperienced' used with personal reference. *19th cent.*

> **Westminster Gazette 1898**
> *I said I knew 'ow many beans make 5 … and if I wor cabbage-looking I woren't green.*

> **James Joyce Ulysses 1922**
> *Gob, he's not as green as he's cabbagelooking.*

See also green about the gills *at* GILL.

grey

a grey area

a subject or situation, especially in law or morality, that is imprecisely defined or difficult to categorize. The phrase is first recorded in the 1960s as a description of urban areas that are in need of renovation without being categorized as slums. *Late 20th cent.*

grief

come to grief

to fail disastrously; to have an accident. *19th cent.*

> **Mrs Gaskell Wives and Daughters 1866**
> *Molly thought over all that she had heard, as she was dressing and putting on the terrible, over-smart plaid gown in honour of the new arrival. Her unconscious fealty to Osborne was not in the least shaken by his having come to grief at Cambridge.*

give somebody grief

to cause somebody trouble or anxiety. The phrase is derived ultimately from lines in Pope's heroic epistle *Eloisa to Abelard* (1717): 'Then share thy pain, allow that sad relief; | Ah, more than share it, give me all thy grief.' *18th cent.*

> **Richardson Pamela 1741**
> *I know, dear Father and Mother, I must give you both grief and pleasure; and so I will only say, Pray for your Pamela.*

intrude on private grief

to comment on the misfortunes of a rival organization, especially a political party. In the form *not wish to intrude on private grief* the phrase is a flimsy cliché of modern politics. *20th cent.*

grig

(as) merry/lively as a grig

extremely lively or full of fun: *merry grig*, meaning 'an extravagantly lively person', is recorded from the 16th cent., and is common in 17th cent. drama, but the origin of *grig* is obscure. It might have been a corruption of the word *Greek* (*merry Greek* is also recorded), but the relevance of *Greek* is unexplained and it is equally possible that the corruption worked in the opposite direction. *Grig* is also found in the meanings 'young eel' and 'grasshopper or cricket', which are more obviously relevant to the usage in the phrase. The simile dates from the 18th cent.

> **Fanny Burney Camilla 1796**
> *Lionel will find himself a partner, I have no doubt, because he is nothing particular in point of shyness; and as to Camilla, she'll want nothing but to hear the fiddlers to be as merry as a grig.*

grim

like grim death

with great resolve or determination. *Grim* has been used in the context of death since the time of Shakespeare, although the phrase in its current form is considerably later. The image of 'grim death' holding on tight recalls legends of a personified Death calling on his victims, then seizing them or inviting them into his arms as in Matthias Claudius' poem *Der Tod und Das Mädchen* ('Death and the Maiden'), famously taken as a song setting by Franz Schubert in 1817. Death is also represented as the *grim reaper*, a skeletal man shown wearing a hood and carrying a scythe who travels the world to claim his victims. He is a common feature of 19th cent. romantic literature, appearing for example in Mary Fordham's poem *Magnolia Leaves* (1897): 'Here lies a maiden spotless fair, | Whose claim on life for many a year | Seemed sure. But the grim Reaper smiled, | And bending, claimed her for his child.' *19th cent.*

Dickens *David Copperfield* 1850

He had eluded pursuit, and was going to America in a flaxen wig, and whiskers, and such a complete disguise as never you see in all your born days; when the little woman, being in Southampton, met him walking along the street – picked him out with her sharp eye in a moment – ran betwixt his legs to upset him – and held on to him like grim Death.

grin

grin and bear it

to tolerate an unpleasant experience or situation in a stoical way: *grin* here does not have its inoffensive modern meaning, but is based on an older meaning equivalent to a snarl or grimace (of pain or anger) rather than a smile. The principal characteristic was showing the teeth, which is the primary meaning of *grin*. An older form *grin and abide* is recorded in the 18th cent.; and a playful modern variant (from the 1990s) is *grin and bare it*, a phrase beloved of journalists wanting to refer to a fashionable young woman who wears a revealing outfit in public. *19th cent.*

Eaton Stannard Barrett *The Heroine* 1813

I heard a sudden disturbance below; his Lordship exclaiming, 'Oh, what shall I do?' and Jerry crying, 'grin and bear it!'

grin like a Cheshire cat

to smile amiably with a broad fixed grin. References to Cheshire cats and their expressions date from about 1800. The locus classicus is Lewis Carroll's *Alice's Adventures in Wonderland* (1865), in which Alice several times encounters a Cheshire cat that keeps disappearing, starting with its tail and ending with its head, so that its grin is the last part to vanish. But this is not the origin of the phrase, which is found in earlier literature, notably in Thackeray's *The Newcomes* (1854), where there is a reflection on the origin of the phrase: 'Mr. Newcome says to Mr. Pendennis in his droll, humorous way, "That woman grins like a Cheshire cat." Who was the naturalist who first discovered that peculiarity of the cats in Cheshire?' *19th cent.*

grind

grind to a halt

to move or act gradually more slowly until one comes to a complete halt: a metaphor from the slowing down of machinery. *20th cent.*

grindstone

keep one's nose to the grindstone

to keep working hard: based on the notion of a revolving grindstone, a hard round stone that was turned for sharpening knives and tools. (Another explanation – heard in California – is given in Michael Quinion's book of 'language myths' collected under the title *Port Out, Starboard Home* (2004). According to this, the grindstones in a traditional water-powered grist mill had to be set at a precise distance apart, and too close a setting caused overheating. The miller therefore used his nose to check for the slightest smell of burning. This story, though perhaps more entertaining than the usual one, is rejected by Quinion himself, and does not square with the history and forms of the phrase.) The phrase is recorded from the 16th cent. in the form *hold/bring somebody's nose to the grindstone*, i.e. in the context of enforcement or oppression by another rather than of one's own perseverance. It occurs in this form in John Frith's *A Mirrour or Glasse to Know Thyselfe* (1533), the earliest use in print that has so far been traced: 'This Text holdeth their noses so hard to the grindstone, that it clean disfigureth their faces.' It is also listed in John Heywood's collection of proverbs published in 1546. A cartoon of 1650 shows Charles Stuart, the future King Charles II, with his nose held to a grindstone by the Scots. The modern form *keep one's nose to the grindstone*, denoting dedication rather than oppression, first appears in the early 19th cent. The nose is a metaphorical equivalent to the tool being worked on, but the analogy cannot be pressed too far without implying absurd (or at least painful) consequences.

William Painter *The Palace of Pleasure* 1566

Will ye be so mated and dumped, as the shadowe alone of a fonde and inconstant yong man, shall holde your nose to the grindstone, and drawe you at his lust like an Oxe into the stall?

grip

come/get to grips with something

to set about dealing with a problem or difficulty: from the physical meaning 'to grapple or wrestle with somebody'. The phrase is 19th cent. in figurative use and in the form *at grips with*.

Theodore Martin *Aladdin* 1857
But since 'tis stern necessity commands, | Since virtue needs must come to grips with vice, | Banter and whim, as music does in war, | Shall drown the wail and anguish of the fray.

get a grip (on something)

to take control (of a situation). *19th cent.*

get/take a grip on/of oneself

to regain one's composure, to pull oneself together. Typically used in the imperative as an exhortation or encouragement. *19th cent.*

Harry James Smith *Mrs. Bumpstead-Leigh* 1911
Get a grip on yourself, ma, and listen!

Iain Banks *Walking on Glass* 1988
You idiot, Graham told himself, you're looking at this woman as if she was ET. Get a grip of yourself.

lose one's grip

to lose one's composure or one's ability to act effectively. The phrase is a reduction of more specific forms, especially *lose one's grip on life*, meaning 'to die'. *19th cent.*

Dickens *Our Mutual Friend* 1865
The bedroom where the clutching old man had lost his grip on life, was left as he had left it.

Bram Stoker *Dracula* 1897
She was in such an excited state that she seemed to have lost her grip of what German she knew, and mixed it all up with some other language which I did not know at all.

grist

grist to one's mill

something that can be put to good use or profit: *grist* here is related to the verb *grind* and means 'corn for grinding'. It has been used in figurative and proverbial contexts since the 16th cent., and is current now only in this phrase. *Bring grist to one's mill* dates from the 16th cent., and a proverb *all is grist that comes to the mill* from the 17th cent. The allusive form *grist to one's mill* is 19th cent. George Orwell, in his essay *Politics and the English*

Language (1946), called it a 'dying metaphor', along with *ring the changes, toe the line, ride roughshod over, stand shoulder to shoulder*, and several others, which he further explained as 'worn-out metaphors which have lost all evocative power and are merely used because they save people the trouble of inventing phrases for themselves'.

Mrs Humphry Ward *Robert Elsmere* 1888
You and Grey between you call yourselves Liberals, and imagine yourselves reformers, and all the while you are doing nothing but playing into the hands of the Blacks. All this theistic philosophy of yours only means so much grist to their mill in the end.

groove

in the groove

1 *informal* fashionable or trendy. The expression alludes to the groove of a vinyl record, from which music is reproduced. The somewhat dated word *groovy* has the same origin and is used with much the same meaning. *Mid 20th cent.* 2 *informal* alert or in good form, like a sliding component that runs smoothly in its groove. *Mid 20th cent.*

Daily Telegraph 1992
Woosnam lost ground with a 73 and admits that he is 'not in the groove at all'.

gross

by the gross

in large amounts or numbers. *19th cent.*

ground

be thick/thin on the ground

very common (or sparse), on the analogy of fallen leaves or vegetation (or perhaps snow) and usually referring to physical objects. The form *thick on the ground* is the earlier form (18th cent.) by several decades. The first quotation below represents a transitional stage between literal and figurative usage.

Richard Blackmore *Eliza* 1705
While Fairfax strove th'Invader to repel, | Thick on the Ground the slaughter'd Spaniards fell.

William Morris *News From Nowhere* 1891
These houses, though they stood hideously thick on the ground, were roomy and fairly solid in building.

cut the ground from under somebody's feet
to do something that makes somebody's actions or arguments unnecessary or superfluous. *19th cent.*

> Wilkie Collins *Man and Wife* 1870
> *It was impossible to say No: she had fairly cut the ground from under his feet. He shifted his ground. Anything rather than say Yes!*

down to the ground
informal completely; fundamentally: especially *suit somebody down to the ground* = to be entirely suitable for them. The image is of a set of clothes extending down to the wearer's shoes. *19th cent.*

> W S Gilbert *Princess Toto* 1876
> *The life suits me down to the ground. I shall live and die a brigand queen.*

fall to the ground
(said of a plan or undertaking) to fail or be abandoned. *16th cent.*

from the ground up
chiefly NAmer completely; fundamentally: *cf* down to the ground *above*. *19th cent.*

gain ground
to become more popular or successful, especially at the expense of a rival or competitor: originally in military contexts of an army winning actual ground from an enemy (*cf* lose ground *below*). *17th cent.*

> Thomas Otway *The History and Fall of Caius Marius* 1680
> *Consider, Child, my Hopes are all in Thee. | And now Old age gains ground so fast upon me, | 'Mongst all its sad Infirmities, my Fears | For Thee are not the smallest.*

get in on the ground floor
informal to be involved in an enterprise in its early stages: originally used in connection with financial speculations in the US. *19th cent.*

get off / get something off the ground
to begin to make progress in an enterprise: often in negative contexts of failed initiatives. In modern usage the image that immediately comes to mind is of an aircraft taking off, but the notion – if not the phrase in its current form – predates the age of air travel and alludes originally to the flight of birds. William Hazlitt, in his *Lectures on the English Poets* (1818), produces an image in which poetry was invented 'to take the language of the imagination from off the ground, and enable it to spread its wings where it may indulge its own impulses'. *Mid 20th cent.*

> Cherry Gilchrist *The Circle of Nine* 1991
> *I was once invited to a weekend conference of 'rural women' to give a workshop on astrology. It was a dismal, disorganized weekend and a waste of valuable opportunity; everything was left to 'flow', which in practice meant that many events did not even get off the ground.*

go to ground
(said of a person) to go into hiding: from the literal use referring to a fox or other animal that hides in its burrow when under threat. *Mid 20th cent.*

hit the ground running
to begin an activity fully prepared and with all enthusiasm: a metaphor from military activity in which troops are ready for action the moment they land from aircraft, ships, etc. *Mid 20th cent.*

> *Independent* 1989
> *After promising to hit the ground running, people wonder why the President has become the leader of the Slow Is Beautiful Movement.*

hold/keep/maintain/stand one's ground
to defend one's position: originally in physical senses but now usually figurative in meaning. *18th cent.*

lose ground
to become less popular or successful than a rival or competitor (*see* gain ground *above*). *16th cent.*

> Jeremy Collier *A Second Defence ... of the English Stage* 1700
> *Thus those Passions are cherish'd which ought to be check'd, Virtue loses ground, and Reason grows precarious.*

on the ground
in the area where practical work is done, as distinct from planning and theorizing. *20th cent.*

on one's own ground
in a situation involving one's expertise and experience: based on the military meaning with reference to an army fighting on ground with which it is familiar. *19th cent.*

prepare the ground
to do the preliminary work necessary for an enterprise: an image from farming, in which

the ground is prepared for ploughing. 'Preparing the Ground' is the title of a chapter of Mary Braddon's 'sensation' novel *Lady Audley's Secret* (1862). *19th cent.*

> Trollope *The Last Chronicle of Barset* 1867
> *Crosbie might have thought it expedient to send an ambassador down to prepare the ground for him before he should venture again upon the scene himself.*

work/run oneself into the ground
informal to become exhausted from work or exercise. The image is presumably of an early death and burial. *20th cent.*

See also BREAK new/fresh ground; have one's FEET on the ground; RUN somebody/something to earth/ground; SHIFT one's ground.

grove

groves of Academe
the world of academic learning: with allusion to Horace, *Epistles* II.ii.45 *Atque inter silvas Academi quarere verum* 'And to seek the truth among the groves of Academus'. The reference is to the Academia, the grove in Athens named after the Athenian hero Academus, where Plato and other philosophers taught. The phrase was used as the title of a satire on American college life by Mary McCarthy, published in 1952. *19th cent.*

> Herman Melville *The Confidence-Man* 1857
> *Surely, you will not exact those formalities from your old schoolmate – him with whom you have so often sauntered down the groves of Academe, discoursing of the beauty of virtue, and the grace that is in kindliness – and all for so paltry a sum.*

grow

— does not grow on trees
The specified commodity is scarce or valuable: normally used in cautionary contexts, especially of money. An early occurrence is in *Poor Robin's Almanack*, a collection published in London in the 1660s: 'Minc'd Pyes do not grow upon every tree, | But search the Ovens for them, and there they be.' *17th cent.*

> Robert Paltock *The Life and Adventures of Peter Wilkins* 1750
> *I had much ado to persuade them they [fish] did not grow on Trees, which I was then much more*

surprised at, than some time after, that I returned their Visit: But having satisfied them, and given them some possible Hopes they might see one alive next Day, they were very well contented; and we all lay down to Rest.

grudge

bear a grudge
to have a feeling of deep resentment against somebody for something they have done in the past. Other forms, such as *have a grudge at/to*, occur earlier, and the phrase occurs with *nurse*, *pursue*, and other verbs. It dates from the 17th cent. in the current form, and occurs in the Authorized Version of the Bible (1611), in the list of commandments given at Leviticus 19:18: 'Thou shalt not avenge, nor bear any grudge against the children of thy people, but thou shalt love thy neighbour as thyself.'

> Henry James *The Portrait of a Lady* 1881
> *The kindness consisted mainly in trying to make him believe that he had once wounded her greatly and that the event had put him to shame, but that, as she was very generous and he was so ill, she bore him no grudge.*

guard

be off / drop / lower, etc one's guard
to be relaxed and unwary, and vulnerable to an attack or threat. To be *off one's guard* is the opposite of being *on/upon one's guard*, recorded from the 16th cent. in the sense 'in a defensive position'. In Shakespeare's *The Tempest* (1613), Gonzalo warns Alonso, King of Naples, after an intervention by Ariel (II.i.326): 'There was a noise, | That's verily. | 'Tis best we stand upon our guard, | Or that we quit this place.' *17th cent.*

guess

anybody's/anyone's guess
an eventuality or outcome that cannot be estimated or predicted. *Anybody's* and *anyone's* have been used since the mid 19th cent. with other words (e.g. *game*, *race*) to signify similar unpredictability. *Mid 20th cent.*

by guess and by God
by one's own efforts, without help: used originally in nautical language to refer to steering

round hazards without the help of landmarks or a set course. The phrase was used as the title of a book by W G Carr about naval warfare, published in 1931. *Mid 20th cent.*

you/you've guessed it

informal I don't need to tell you, you already know. The phrase is typically used in conversation to introduce a piece of information that the speaker expects the hearer to be well aware of or able to infer easily. *Late 20th cent.*

your guess is as good as mine

informal an admission of ignorance or bewilderment on a particular point. *Mid 20th cent.*

guest

be my guest

an invitation to somebody to do what they wish or intend, usually when this involves the speaker in some way. The phrase is also used retrospectively in the more formulaic sense equivalent to 'you are welcome' or 'don't mention it', as in the 1988 example. *Be My Guest!* is the title of a collection by the British poet Gavin Ewart, published in 1975. *Mid 20th cent.*

> John Mortimer *Summer's Lease* 1988
> 'I think,' Molly said firmly, 'I'd like to have one more look round. By myself this time.' 'Of course. Be my guest.'

gum

up a gum tree

informal in an awkward predicament or difficulty. The phrase first occurs in the early 19th cent. in American and Australian usage in the form *possum up a gum tree* (the tree being the possum's place of refuge), and as the title of a song. In its present form the phrase is mainly confined to British use, and is early 20th cent.

gun

a big gun

informal an important or influential person: often used in the plural and (early 19th cent.) in the form *great guns*. *19th cent.*

blow great guns

(said of the weather) to be wild and windy. *19th cent.*

> R H Dana *Two Years Before the Mast* 1840
> The horizon met the sea in a defined line. A painter could not have painted so clear a sky. There was not a speck upon it. Yet it was blowing great guns from the north-west.

going great guns

working at great speed or with great efficiency. *Early 20th cent.*

jump the gun

to move or act before the proper time: originally used (also in the form *beat the gun*) of a competitor in a race who started before the signal was given. *Mid 20th cent.*

a smoking gun

undisputable evidence of guilt: from the stock image of a killer discovered immediately after the crime and still holding the murder weapon. The phrase became prominent in 2002–3, when UN weapons inspectors were sent to Iraq to investigate and report on the level of illegal weaponry in the country, following suspicions that the regime there still kept supplies of chemical weapons and other so-called 'weapons of mass destruction'. These have never been found. *Late 20th cent.*

> *Guardian* 1984
> The Democratic House Speaker, Mr Tip O'Neill, described the figures, showing that 35 million Americans were below the poverty line in 1983, as 'the smoking gun of Reagan unfairness.'

> *Independent* 2003
> While Mr Baradei said his teams had found nothing to suggest a clandestine nuclear weapons programme in Iraq, Mr Blix offered a series of reasons to suspect evasion on the part of Saddam Hussein. He worried out loud about anthrax and VX gas. About the 6,000 chemical weapons Iraq has not accounted for. About its blocking U-2 spy plane flights. About difficulties in interviewing scientists. At the same time, neither man could offer the Council a 'smoking gun' or anything by way of proof that would help resolve the dilemma facing the international community.

stick to one's guns

informal to refuse to change one's decision, intentions, or opinion despite opposition: based on the notion of continuing to fire one's guns when under fierce attack. *19th cent.*

H D Traill *Recaptured Rhymes* 1882
But the sturdiest ones still stuck to their guns, |
And maintained his legation divine.

top gun

the most important or influential person in a group or community. The image is from gunfighters in the American West, and usage has perhaps been influenced by the release in 1986 of an adventure film called *Top Gun* about gung-ho naval pilots. *20th cent.*

with (all) guns blazing

with indiscriminate or insensitive vigour and determination. *20th cent.*

The Times 1986
Department of Trade investigations come in several shades of seriousness. Politicians code them as white, when they are very discreet, pink, where only the privileged few know what is going on, and red when the inspectors go in publicly with all guns blazing.

See also GO down with all guns firing.

gut

bust a gut

informal to make a stupendous effort. The image is of overexertion or strain producing a hernia or similar physical injury, although the phrase is more often used to refer to mental effort or feats of determination, e.g. in meeting a seemingly impossible deadline. *Early 20th cent.*

guts

hate somebody's guts

to hate or despise somebody with great intensity. *Early 20th cent.*

P D James *Death of an Expert Witness* 1979
He was pretty unpopular with most of the senior staff. But there are always one or two who would have preferred a colleague to a stranger even if they hated his guts.

have somebody's guts for garters

informal to punish or scold somebody severely: typically used as a threat. The phrase first occurs in slightly different forms in dramatic works from the turn of the 16th–17th cent., in Robert Greene's *James the Fourth* (1598) III.ii: 'I'll make garters of thy guts, thou villain', and in Ben

Jonson's *Cynthia's Revels* (1600) IV.iii: 'Sir, I will garter my hose with your guttes.' Other unverified 17th cent. evidence is cited by Partridge in *A Dictionary of Catch Phrases* (second edition, 1985). At this time, when disembowelment was an actual punishment, the threat had a greater air of reality than it does today. Its rhythmic alliteration has no doubt helped to keep it in common use. *16th cent.*

Scott *The Bride of Lammermoor* 1819
The wench has too much sense – and in that belief I drink her health a third time; and, were time and place fitting, I would drink it on bended knees, and he that would not pledge me, I would make his guts garter his stockings.

sweat/work one's guts out

informal to work extremely hard. *Mid 20th cent.*

gutzer

come a gutzer

Australian and NZ, informal to fail dramatically; to 'come a cropper'. Also written as *gutser*: the allusion is to falling on the *gut* or belly. *Early 20th cent.*

gyp

give somebody gyp

British, informal to cause somebody pain or discomfort. *Gyp* is possibly a contraction of *gee-up*, a command to a horse to go faster, which is also attested in dialect use as a noun. The phrase appears in glossaries in the 19th cent., suggesting an early usage in speech, but it does not appear in print until the early 20th cent.

Patrick MacGill *The Brown Brethren* 1917
A cramp in my guts ... Gawd, it isn't 'arf giving me gyp!

habit

be in the habit of / make a habit of doing something

to do a particular thing constantly or repeatedly: used especially in the context of something ill-advised or unwelcome, and (with *make*) often in negative contexts as a caution (e.g. *don't make a habit of it*). *19th cent.*

Sir Joshua Reynolds A Discourse Delivered to the Students of the Royal Academy 1784
However, in justice I cannot quit this Painter without adding, that in the former part of his life, when he was in the habit of having recourse to nature, he was not without a considerable degree of merit, enough to make half the Painters of his country his imitators.

Bayard Taylor Hannah Thurston 1863
At the dinners and evening parties of the English, an intellectual as well as a social propriety is strictly observed, and the man who makes a habit of producing for general inspection, his religious convictions or his moral experiences, is speedily voted a bore.

See also KICK the habit.

hackles

make somebody's hackles rise

to cause somebody to react with anger or indignation: a figurative use of the *hackles* of a cock or dog, feathers or hairs on the neck which are raised when the animal is angered or excited. Also formerly used in the form *somebody's hackles are up*. *19th cent.*

The Times Magazine 2003
Just to read all these businesslike words makes all the hackles of someone with even a modestly earth-maternal instinct rise up, holler and protest.

hail

hail-fellow-well-met

heartily and often excessively informal from the first moment of meeting. The phrase is based on the shorter form *hail-fellow* with similar meaning, i.e. friendly in a way that suggests the greeting 'hail, fellow!' *16th cent.*

Joshua Sylvester transl Du Bartas' Divine Weekes and Workes 1605
There Man and Maister but Hail-fellow is.

Thomas Brown Amusements Serious and Comical 1700
Lantrillou is a kind of a Republick very ill ordered, where all the World are Hail Fellow well met; no distinction of Ranks, no Subordination observed.

Scott Chronicles of the Canongate 1828
I am not such a fool as to desire to be hail-fellow-well-met with these fine folks – I care as little for them as they do for me.

hair

the hair of the dog

a small alcoholic drink taken to cure a hangover: in full *the hair of the dog that bit you*, referring to the belief that the best antidote to the bite of a mad dog is one made from the dog's own hair. The phrase occurs in this original sense in the 16th cent. collection of sayings and proverbs made by John Heywood, but is not common in free text for another century or so.

Edward Ward The Rambling Fuddle-Caps 1705
In order to quench our immod'rate Droughts, | That burnt in our Stomachs, and scorch'd up our Mouths, | We leap'd out of Bed with a strong Appetitus, | To swallow a Hair of the Dog that had bit us.

in somebody's hair

informal persistently annoying somebody or getting in their way. When you finally leave them in peace you are *out of somebody's hair*. *19th cent.*

J H Ingraham Fanny H— or The Hunchback and the Roue 1843
She's a nice good girl, sir ... I'd court her if I dared; but the widder'd soon be in my hair if she 'spected such 'tentions.

keep one's hair on

informal to remain calm and not become excited or angry: usually in the imperative (*keep your hair on!*). This phrase may be connected with the image of the hair reacting to strong emotions such as anger or fear, as in standing on end from fear (see below), and in the hackles of a dog rising when it is angered or excited (*see* HACKLES). *19th cent.*

> George & Weedon Grossmith The Diary of a Nobody 1892
>
> *The last post brought a letter from Lupin in reply to mine ... It ran: 'My dear old Guv., – Keep your hair on. You are on the wrong tack again.'*

let one's hair down

informal to enjoy oneself in a wild or extravagant way: with allusion to the former women's fashion of wearing the hair long and pinning it up in various ways for formal occasions, while letting it hang freely for informality and relaxation. *19th cent.*

make somebody's hair stand on end

to terrify or alarm somebody: based on the physical phenomenon, noted anecdotally by witnesses at executions, by which the hair rises from the scalp and stands almost upright from fear or other strong emotion (the same phenomenon causes goose pimples on other parts of the body). When Hamlet, in Shakespeare's play (1601), sees the ghost of his dead father, the ghost addresses him in this way (i.v.19): 'I could a tale unfold whose lightest word | Would harrow up thy soul, freeze thy young blood, | Make thy two eyes like stars start from their spheres, | Thy knotty and combinèd locks to part, | And each particular hair to stand on end | Like quills upon the fretful porcupine.' *16th cent.*

not turn a hair

to react without concern or emotion: originally used with reference to horses, whose hair becomes ruffled when they are sweating. *18th cent.*

> Jane Austen Northanger Abbey 1818
>
> *'Miss Morland; do but look at my horse; did you ever see an animal so made for speed in your life? ... Three hours and a half indeed coming only three-and-twenty miles! look at that creature, and suppose it possible if you can.' 'He does look very hot to*

be sure.' 'Hot! he had not turned a hair till we came to Walcot Church.'

put hair on somebody's chest

(said especially of food or drink) to toughen somebody or improve their physique: based on the notion of a hairy chest as a sign of masculine strength and fitness. The phrase is typically used in flippant contexts. *20th cent.*

> Tony Harrison Selected Poems 1987
>
> *The Brewery that owns this place supports only the unambiguously 'male' Northern working class spectator sports that suit the image of its butch Brown Ale, that puts hair on your chest, and makes you fight, and when you're legless makes a man of you!*

split hairs

to make oversubtle or pedantic distinctions: also in early use in the form *split a hair, split straws, split words. 17th cent.*

> Richardson Pamela 1741
>
> *Then I have no Notion of that slight Distinction I have so often heard, between forgive and forget, when Persons have a mind to split Hairs, and to distinguish away their Christian Duties by a Word, and say, I must forgive such an Action, but I will never forget it.*

See also get/have somebody by the SHORT and curlies / the short hairs; neither hide nor hair *at* HIDE[2].

hairy

give somebody the hairy eyeball

informal, chiefly NAmer to look at somebody with the eyes narrowed in suspicion or disapproval. The eyeball is 'hairy' from the near meeting of the eyelashes. *Mid 20th cent.*

> W Sonzski Punch Goes Judy 1971
>
> *I was tired of hairy eyeballs from white and black militants who thought I was a liberal jerk.*

hale

hale and hearty

strong and healthy. *Hale* is originally a northern dialect form of an Old English word *hál* meaning 'whole'. It was used alone from the 18th cent. to mean 'having a strong constitution', but from the 19th cent. occurred only with *hearty*, as a form of hendiadys, i.e. the expression of a single idea by two words connected by *and*. The primary meanings of *hearty* arise from the attributes associated with the heart, notably 'courageous' and 'sincere'. The meaning to do with good health dates from the 16th cent. The phrase itself dates from the 18th cent.

> **Miles Peter Andrews *The Reparation* 1784**
> *There, there – I have taken a pretty long ride to-day. What a fine thing it is to be hale and hearty!*

---

half

Half is a Janus-word that can face in two directions at once. The famous adage that an optimist regards a partly filled glass as half full whereas a pessimist regards the same glass as half empty illustrates the point. With a negative word such as *not* or *never*, it can be even more noticeably bidirectional. Historically the tendency with most of the phrases below has been from the negative to the positive and from the neutral to the informal, so that *not half pleased* has changed from meaning 'extremely displeased' to 'extremely pleased'.

— and a half
informal and more: used after a noun to denote its special size or importance. *19th cent.*

> **Eaton Stannard Barrett *My Wife! What Wife?* 1815**
> [Constantia] *Thomas, let no one in, and desire the gentleman to walk up.* [Paddeen] *Ay, a gentleman and a half, and another half to the back of it, Ma'am. The best, handsomest, youngest young man in Europe, Ma'am. – His only fault at all at all, is the ladies.*

by half
by a great deal: normally used after an adjective preceded by *too* (*see also* too CLEVER by half). *17th cent.*

> **Henry Hutton *Follies Anatomie* 1619**
> *Phantastes chaf't t' expresse his raging wit, | Because his stockins did not neately sit; | And strictly askt his man, what as he thought | Concerning 's stockin he had lately bought. | Who said, I think though 'tseeme too straight by half, | Twod fit; but that you are too great ith' Calfe.*

go halves
to share something, especially an expense, (more or less) equally: also in Scottish and Northern English as *go halvers*. *17th cent.*

> **Congreve *Love for Love* 1695**
> [Scandal] *Why, Honour is a publick enemy; and conscience a domestick thief; and he that wou'd secure his pleasure, must pay a tribute to one, and go halves with the t'other.*

half a chance
informal even the slightest opportunity: typically in the form *give somebody half a chance*, as a warning of an unwelcome consequence. *19th cent.*

> **Jonathan Birch *Divine Emblems* 1838**
> *Vain, foolish youth! – to think thy mite of sense | Can cope with such – so consummate in wiles! | … | Those are but grins – that thou mistak'st for smiles! | Thou hast not half a chance! – t'escape unscath'd their paws | Is hopeless – as the captur'd mouse from feline claws.*

half a loaf
something that will serve but is less than one wants: based on the (16th cent.) proverb *half a loaf is better than no bread*. The phrase is 18th cent. in this form.

the half of it
the most important part of something: used mainly in negative contexts in relation to knowledge or information (e.g. *that's not the half of it; you don't know the half of it*). Mid 20th cent.

> **Colin McDowell *A Woman of Style* 1991**
> *That's a woman's lot – forever being prodded and poked and looked up by doctors who are total strangers. Men don't know the half of it.*

half the time
informal, originally NAmer usually, habitually. *19th cent.*

> **James Fenimore Cooper *The Chainbearer* 1845**
> *But roguery is so active, while virtue is so apt to be passive, that in the eternal conflict that is waged between them, that which is gained by the truth and inherent power of the last is, half the time, more than neutralized by the unwearied exertions of the first!*

how the other half lives
the lifestyle of other, especially more wealthy, elements of society. *The other half* means 'the other half of the world', and is found in the

17th cent. saying recorded among George Herbert's *Outlandish Proverbs* (published posthumously in 1640): 'Halfe the world knowes not how the other halfe li[v]es'.

not do things by halves

informal to relish tasks, ideas, suggestions, etc and carry them through with complete enthusiasm. *18th cent.*

> Henry Fielding *The History of Tom Jones* 1749
> *It hath been observed, that Fortune seldom doth things by halves. To say truth, there is no end to her freaks whenever she is disposed to gratify or displease.*

not half

1 *informal* (qualifying an adjective or verb) not nearly, e.g. *not half finished, not half as well. 18th cent.*

> Frances Sheridan *Memoirs of Miss Sidney Bidulph* 1761
> *I will be hanged, said Sir George, if I think you love Faulkland, at least not half as well as he deserves.*

2 *informal* (preceding an adjective or verb) very much, extremely: often used as an interjection denoting a positive reply. In earlier use this had the opposite meaning 'not at all': *not half* can point in either direction, towards either total negation or total affirmation. *18th cent.*

> Richard Cumberland *Amelia* 1771
> [Sir Anthony] *Od's, my Life! Here she comes, and without her Mask: Yes, yes, 'tis she; 'tis Clara. Oh piteous! what a Spectacle. She stares horribly – I don't half like her, and I wish she was not half so fond of me.*

> Thackeray *A Shabby Genteel Story* 1840
> *'Law, Bell,' said Miss Rosalind, 'what a chap that Brandon is! I don't half like him, I do declare!' Than which there can be no greater compliment from a woman to a man. 'No more do I neither,' says Bell. 'The man stares so, and says such things!'*

the other half

informal, originally naval slang a second drink, especially of beer. A half is a half-pint of beer, and the 'other half' is a second half-pint drunk to complete the pint. *Early 20th cent.*

See also go off at half cock *at* COCK²; half the BATTLE; half an EYE; have a (good/great) MIND / half a mind to do something; one's BETTER half; too CLEVER by half.

halfway

a halfway house

a compromise between two extreme propositions or positions: a figurative use of physical meanings denoting buildings, e.g. an inn or hotel halfway through a journey, or a hostel at which former residents of medical or psychiatric institutions can prepare for their return to normal life. The phrase is 19th cent. in figurative use.

> Gerald Massey *Havelock's March* 1861
> *My Rest while toiling up the hill of life! | A Halfway House to Heaven! my noble Wife!*

Hamlet

Hamlet without the prince

an event or occasion at which the expected principal participant is not present: a metaphor based on the absurdity of performing Shakespeare's *Hamlet* without an actor playing the title role. The phrase dates from the early years of the 20th cent., but the notion is older, for example in a letter of Byron dated 26 August 1818: 'My autobiographical essay would resemble the tragedy of Hamlet ..., recited "with the part of Hamlet left out by particular desire".' This may owe its origin to a theatrical story from the 1770s, which tells how the principal actor in a performance of *Hamlet* was unavailable because he had run off with an innkeeper's daughter, leaving the director to announce that the part of Hamlet was 'to be left out, for that night'. *Early 20th cent.*

> *Times Weekly* 1910
> *The Army without Kitchener is like* Hamlet *without the Prince of Denmark.*

hammer

come/go under the hammer

to be offered for sale at an auction: the hammer is the auctioneer's small hammer used to bring the meeting to attention and to signal sales. *19th cent.*

hammer and tongs

with great determination and vigour: with allusion to the tools used by a blacksmith to beat out metal removed from the forge. *17th cent.*

> John Dunton *A Voyage Round the World* 1691
> *So to't I went hammer and tongs, as the vulgar say, and after long and laborious licking, out came this*

beautiful birth, that's just a hop, stride and jump before you.

take a hammering

to be heavily criticized or defeated. *19th cent.*

Rufus Dawes Nix's Mate: an Historical Romance of America 1839

The two master mechanics had looked on during the brief time the contest was going on, and felt rather disposed than otherwise, to see the odious tool of the Governor get a hammering from the enraged tar; but now that the fellow was down and out of wind, they promptly interposed to save him from the drubbing that he would inevitably have received but for their aid.

See also drive/hammer/press/ram something HOME.

---

hand

all hands

everybody involved or needed: normally used in the context of contributing to an effort, and originally with reference to the crew of a ship (often in the form *all hands on deck*). The phrase dates from the 18th cent. in general use.

Phanuel Bacon The Taxes 1757

[Mr Bayes] *There is such spinning going forward, for jackets and trowses – all hands are employ'd.*

H G Wells The Invisible Man 1897

I … threw myself flat behind a counter. In another moment feet went running past and I heard voices shouting, 'All hands to the doors!' asking what was 'up', and giving one another advice how to catch me.

be able to do something with one hand (tied) behind one's back

to be able to do something easily or effortlessly. In recent use the phrase has been applied in negative contexts to mean 'unable to do a job properly because of some incapacity or handicap' (as in the 1993 quotation below). *17th cent.*

Beaumont & Fletcher A King and No King 1619

This Love … begets more mischief than a Wake … He that had seen this brave fellow Charge through a grove of Pikes but t'other day, and look upon him now, will ne'r believe his eyes again: if he continue thus but two days more, a Taylor may beat him with one hand tied behind him.

Art Newspaper 1993

It may well be that for political reasons the Yugoslavs have been fighting the case with at least one hand tied behind their back.

bind/tie somebody hand and foot

to greatly restrict somebody's freedom of action. *19th cent.*

Maria Edgeworth Castle Rackrent 1800

'What is all this?' said my lady, opening the paper in great curiosity – 'It's only a bit of a memorandum of what I think becomes me to do whenever I am able, (says my master); you know my situation, tied hand and foot at the present time being, but that can't last always.'

(from) hand to mouth

with only just enough for one's immediate needs: also used (with hyphens) as an adjective (as in *a hand-to-mouth existence*). Originally used with reference to food being eaten as soon as it is obtained. *16th cent.*

Thomas Tusser Five Hundred Pointes of Good Husbandrie 1573

The wise will spend, or give or lend, yet keepe to have in store, | If fooles may have from hand to mouth, they passe upon no more.

Benjamin Franklin Autobiography 1771

I was pretty diligent; but spent with Ralph a good deal of my Earnings in going to Plays & other Places of Amusement. We had together consum'd all my Pistoles [= gold coins], and now just rubb'd on from hand to mouth.

get / give somebody a big hand

to be applauded (or to applaud somebody) enthusiastically: originally in theatrical contexts. *19th cent.*

get/keep one's hand in

to acquire (or maintain) an expertise in something: the use of *hand in* and *hand out* to denote involvement and non-involvement in an activity goes back to the 15th cent. *Cf* Shakespeare, *Love's Labour's Lost* (1594) IV.i.137 '[Maria] Wide o' the bow hand – i'faith, your hand is out. [Costard] Indeed, a must shoot nearer, or he'll ne'er hit the clout. [Boyet] An if my hand be out, then belike your hand is in.' *18th cent.*

Frederick Reynolds How to Grow Rich 1793

[Clerk] *Please your worship, this poor man is a labourer, and has five children to maintain – But he has been so beaten and bruised by 'Squire Sturdy,*

that he can't work for his family. [Sir Thomas]
Serve him right – Why didn't he get out of his way,
when he knew the 'Squire was so fond of boxing that
he must have practice to keep his hand in.

get one's hands on somebody/something

to catch somebody, or to obtain or acquire use of
something: usually with the implication that the
process is difficult or subject to chance. *19th cent.*

Mark Twain Roughing It 1872

And if ever another man gives a whistle to a child of
mine and I get my hands on him, I will hang him
higher than Haman!

give/lend a (helping) hand

to help somebody in a practical way: in earlier
use, *lend/give/extend*, etc *one's helping hand. 16th*
cent.

Miles Huggarde A Mirrour of Love 1555

If corne be ouergrowen with wede | What would it
helpe that many wordes to spende? | In talking
therof if no man extende | His helping hand the
same wedes out to roote, | The talking therof thou
seest would litle boote.

Shakespeare 1 Henry IV II.v.1 (1596)

[Prince] *Ned, prithee come out of that fat room [=*
vat room] *and lend me thy hand to laugh a little.*

Francis Quarles Divine Poems 1631

There, crooked fraud must helpe, and slie deceit |
Must lend a hand, which by the potent sleight | Of
right-forsaking Bribry must betray | The prize into
our hands, and win the day.

Thomas Paine The American Crisis 1780

I can think no man innocent who has lent his hand
to destroy the country which he did not plant.

Dickens Hard Times 1854

Acquit me of impertinent curiosity, my dear Mrs
Bounderby. I think Tom may be gradually falling
into trouble, and I wish to stretch out a helping
hand to him from the depths of my wicked
experience.

hand in glove

in close collaboration or cooperation. The phrase
is attested earliest in the form *hand and glove* and
in its present form from about 1800, and is based
on the notion of the close fit a glove makes on the
hand. *17th cent.*

Maurice Atkins Cataplus (Minor Burlesques and Travesties) 1672

Yonder come two who now in love | You may
perceive are hand and glove, | But their society
together | Seems too great to last for ever.

Byron Don Juan 1824

Reason ne'er was hand-and-glove | With rhyme.

hand in hand

in close cooperation: based on the primary physical meaning 'each having his or her hand holding the other's'. *Go hand in hand* (17th cent.) is
used of aspects or circumstances that are closely
associated. *16th cent.*

Shakespeare Hamlet I.v.49 (1601)

[Ghost] *O Hamlet, what a falling off was there! – |*
From me, whose love was of that dignity | That it
went hand-in-hand even with the vow | I made to
her in marriage, and to decline | Upon a wretch
whose natural gifts were poor | To those of mine.

the hand of God

supposed divine intervention. The phrase occurs
in translations of the Bible (e.g. Job 2:10 in the
Authorized Version of 1611: 'What? shall we
receive good at the hand of God, and shall we
not receive evil?'), and earlier in Shakespeare's
Richard II (1595), where King Richard is addressing the Earl of Northumberland, one of Boling-
broke's party (III.iii.71): 'We are amazed; and
thus long have we stood | To watch the fearful
bending of thy knee, | Because we thought our-
self thy lawful king. | And if we be, how dare thy
joints forget | To pay their awful duty to our
presence? | If we be not, show us the hand of
God | That hath dismiss'd us from our steward-
ship.' The allusion took on a new meaning in
1986 during the quarter-finals of the football
World Cup when Diego Maradona used his
hand to help him score a goal for Argentina
against England in a match that Argentina
went on to win 2–1. When challenged about the
incident, Maradona is reported to have said that
the goal was 'a little bit of Maradona's head, a
little bit of the hand of God'. *16th cent.*

hand over fist

in large quantities: used especially in the context
of making (or losing) money. The original form of
the phrase was *hand over hand*, which was originally (18th cent.) used in naval language to refer to
rapid climbing of a rope by putting each hand
over the other alternately. This form, together

with the form *hand over fist* (which seems not to have been used in the physical meaning), began to be used figuratively in the following century, initially still in naval contexts (often of one ship pursuing another; and a source of 1880 refers to a heavy squall 'coming up hand over fist') but rapidly spreading into more general use. *19th cent.*

> Alice Cary *The Adopted Daughter: and Other Tales* 1859
> *I shall set up in business for myself; and I tell you what, Harry, I shall make money hand over fist.*

hands down

with ease: used especially of winning or achieving. Originally a horseracing term: if a horse is winning by a large margin the jockey is able to lower his hands and relax his hold on the reins. *19th cent.*

> Harold Frederic *The Damnation of Theron Ware* 1896
> *I'm going to the Assembly for this district, and they ain't nobody can stop me. The boys are just red hot for me. Wish you'd come down, Father Forbes, and address a few words to the meeting – just mention that I'm a candidate, and say I'm bound to win, hands down.*

hands off!

a warning not to touch or interfere with something. *16th cent.*

> Shakespeare *Coriolanus* III.i.180 (1608)
> [Coriolanus] *Hence, old goat!* [Patricians] *We'll surety him.* [Cominius] *Aged sir, hands off.* [Coriolanus] *Hence, rotten thing! or I shall shake thy bones | Out of thy garments.*

hands on/off

involving (or not involving) direct interference and supervision, especially in management of people and projects: also used (with hyphen) as adjectives (as in *a hands-on approach*). Based on the phrase *get one's hands on* (see above). *Late 20th cent.*

> Nigel Williams *The Wimbledon Poisoner* 1990
> *If he had hoped that a row might spur him on to a direct, hands on approach to murdering Elinor, Henry was disappointed.*

a hand's turn

informal a stroke of work: normally used in negative contexts. *19th cent.*

> R H Dana *Two Years Before the Mast* 1840
> *I had the pleasure of helping to get him into the Massachusetts General Hospital ... I went to see him in his ward, and asked him how he got along. 'Oh! first-rate usage, sir; not a hand's turn to do, and all your grub brought to you, sir.'*

have one's hands full

to have plenty to do, to be fully occupied. *15th cent.*

> Malory *Le Morte d'Arthur* c1485
> *Ye shalle haue bothe your handes ful of me.*

> Dekker & Middleton *The Magnificent Entertainment Given to King James* 1604
> *By this time Imagine, that Poets ... and Painters ... had their heads & hands full ... Both of them emulously contending ... with the proprest and brightest Colours of Wit and Art, to set out the beautie of the great Triumphant day.*

have one's hands tied

to be unable to act because of some restriction or hindrance. *19th cent.*

> George Eliot *Middlemarch* 1872
> *The longing was to see Will Ladislaw. She did not know any good that could come of their meeting: she was helpless; her hands had been tied from making up to him for any unfairness in his lot. But her soul thirsted to see him.*

have to / have got to hand it to somebody

informal, originally NAmer to acknowledge a person's achievement. The image is of handing somebody an award. *Early 20th cent.*

> *Harper's Magazine* 1923
> *You've got to hand it to that kid ... He's stood everything and never squealed a yelp. Some young tough, believe me!*

> Julian Barnes *Talking It Over* 1992
> *Still, did you cop the panache? I have to hand it to myself, I really do.*

hold somebody's hand

1 to restrain somebody from hasty or unwise action. Also *hold one's hand* in the sense 'to refrain from action'. *16th cent.*

> Shakespeare *The Merry Wives of Windsor* III.v.98 (1597)
> [Falstaff] *Being thus cramm'd in the basket, a couple of Ford's knaves ... were call'd forth ... they took me on their shoulders; met the jealous knave their master in the door; who ask'd them once or*

twice what they had in their basket. I quak'd for fear
lest the lunatic knave would have search'd it; but
Fate, ordaining he should be a cuckold, held his
hand.

Richard Burton *Tales from the Arabian Nights* 1888
*Then … the lady threw away the sword and said:
'How shall I strike the neck of one I wot not, and
who hath done me no evil? Such deed were not
lawful in my law!' and she held her hand.*
2 to give somebody moral or emotional support.
Mid 20th cent.

J Bentham *Doctor Who: the Early Years* 1986
*With the first Dalek one, for example, I let Richard
Martin, again a new Director, do a few episodes …
and … kind of, held his hand while he eased himself
into the role of Director, which was good experience
for him.*

on hand

1 as one's responsibility; being done. Originally
in the form *take on hand*, 'to accept as one's
responsibility'. *Middle English*

Andrew of Wyntoun *The Original Chronicle* c1420
*This Duncane herd of this tressoune [treason] |
That his eme [kinsman] than [then] tuke on hand.*
2 available; constantly present if needed. *19th
cent.*

Conan Doyle *The Disappearance of Lady Frances
Carfax* 1911
*'What is your London address, Mr. Green?' 'The
Langham Hotel will find me.' 'Then may I recom-
mend that you return there and be on hand in case I
should want you?'*

on somebody's hands

present as a continuing responsibility. *16th cent.*

Thomas Otway *The Souldiers Fortune* 1681
*[Sir David] Prithee do so much as try thy skill,
there may be one drachm of life left in him yet, take
him up to thy chamber, put him into thy own bed,
and try what thou canst do with him; prithee do, if
thou canst but find motion in him, all may be well
yet, I'l go up to my closet in the Garret, and say my
prayers in the mean while. [Lady D] Will ye then
leave this ruine on my hands.*

on the one hand … on the other hand …

used to contrast two propositions or aspects. The
phrase is based on the physical meaning 'a side of
the body', which is extended to direction more
generally. *17th cent.*

John Wilson *Belphegor* 1691
*This, and other accidents, make him incur debts;
and, as other men in like cases, he takes up money to
support his credit; till at last, his ships at sea being
all lost, what with his creditors pressing him on the
one hand, and his wife's uneasiness on the other, he
fairly breaks.*

out of hand

1 done or made immediately, without delay or
without pausing to consider. The phrase in its
earliest uses refers to payment, the notion presumably being that one has the money available
in one's hand ready to pass on. It is now used in a
wide variety of applications, e.g. in the context of
refusals and rejections (to *dismiss something out of
hand* is to reject it without further consideration).
Middle English

John Rastell *Of Gentylnes and Nobilite* c1525
*[Marchaunt to Knight] I am able to bye [buy] now
all the land | That thou hast and pay for it out of
hand.*

Spenser *The Faerie Queene* v.iv.32 (1590)
*But if through stout disdaine of manly mind, | Any
her proud observaunce will withstand, | Uppon
that gibbet, which is there behind, | She causeth
them be hang'd up out of hand; | In which condi-
tion I right now did stand.*
2 not able to be controlled: now used principally
with reference to a person or situation, but in
early use the meaning is rather 'no longer one's
concern' or 'no longer in progress' (see e.g.
Shakespeare, *2 Henry IV* (1597) III.i.103 '[King
Henry to Warwick] I will take your counsel. |
And were these inward [= domestic] wars once
out of hand, | We would, dear lords, unto the
Holy Land'). The phrase is 19th cent. in the current meaning.

Mrs Humphry Ward *Robert Elsmere* 1888
*Lately she has got quite out of hand. She went to
stay with some relations they have in Manchester,
got drawn into the musical set there, took to these
funny gowns, and now she and Catherine are
always half at war.*

put one's hands up

to raise one's hands, especially as a token of
surrender or to show that one is not (any longer)
armed: also as a command *hands up! 19th cent.*

Jack London *The Iron Heel* 1908
*But at that moment, Biedenbach, ever polite and
gentle, said from behind him in a low voice, 'Hands*

up, my young sir.' Young Wickson put his hands up first, then turned to confront Biedenbach, who held a thirty-thirty automatic rifle on him.

the right hand doesn't know what the left hand is doing

there is poor communication between different parts of an organization, leading to inconsistent or contradictory behaviour. *20th cent.*

Penny Junor *Charles and Diana* 1991
The whole set-up had always been curiously amateurish. The right hand never knew what the left was doing.

a safe pair of hands

somebody who is reliable or trustworthy. The phrase originated in the 19th cent. with reference to skill in catching the ball in cricket and other games ('the safest pair of hands in England'). Figurative uses date from the late 20th cent.

Jeremy Paxman *Friends in High Places* 1990
Because of the sensitivity of the subjects under consideration, the highest recommendation in considering who might be suitable to sit on these investigations is the fact that they have a safe pair of hands. Mavericks need not apply.

set/put one's hand to (the plough)

to start working in earnest: with allusion to Luke 9:62 (in the Authorized Version of 1611) 'And Jesus said to them, No man, having put his hand to the plough, and looking back, is fit for the kingdom of God.' The phrase occurs in other forms in earlier Bible translations going back to Wyclif in Middle English.

Henry Peacham *The Garden of Eloquence* 1577
He that putteth his hand to the plough, and looketh backe, is unmeete for the kingdome of God: by looking backe is meant unconstancie or wavering of mind.

take a hand (in something)

to become actively involved (in an activity). The phrase is of American origin and seems to be derived from the language of card games, in which players literally 'take a hand', i.e. a set of cards. *19th cent.*

Mark Twain *The Adventures of Tom Sawyer* 1876
Huck was always willing to take a hand in any enterprise that offered entertainment and required no capital, for he had a troublesome superabundance of that sort of time which is not money.

take something/somebody in hand

1 to undertake a task or responsibility. *Middle English*

2 to embark on the control or reform of a person. *17th cent.*

George Colman Ygr *The Heir at Law* 1798
[Lord Dowlas] *When Dick began to grow as big as a porpus, I got an old friend of mine … to take Dick 'prentice … He's just now out of his time, and I warrant him, as wild and rough as a rock; now, if you doctor – if you would but take him in hand, and soften him a bit … He served his clerkship to an attorney …* [Dr. Pangloss] *An Attorney! – Gentlemen of his profession, my Lord, are very difficult to soften.*

G B Shaw *Pygmalion* 1913
If we were to take this man in hand for three months, he could choose between a seat in the Cabinet and a popular pulpit in Wales.

(take somebody/something) off somebody's hands

to be (or make somebody or something) no longer a person's responsibility. In early use the singular form *hand* is found. *17th cent.*

Thomas Southerne *The Maid's Last Prayer* 1693
[Wishwell at her toilet] *A Woman turn'd of fifty, was ne'er design'd to be lookt upon: I may wash, and patch, and please my self; cheat my hopes, with the dayly expence of plaister, and repairs; No body will take the tenement off my hands.*

Mary Wollstonecraft *A Vindication of the Rights of Woman* 1792
I have then viewed with pleasure a woman nursing her children, and discharging the duties of her station with, perhaps, merely a servant maid to take off her hands the servile part of the household business.

to hand

available, nearby: also *come to hand* in the sense 'to become available'. The notion is of the hand as the principal means of using a tool or implement. *Middle English*

William Hunnis *A Hyve Full of Hunnye* 1578
[narrating Genesis 32:13] *And Iacob there abode that night, and such as came to hand | Hee tooke thereof, and Presents made for Esau t'vnderstand.*

turn one's hand to something

to apply oneself to a task or undertaking, especially one of a practical nature. *17th cent.*

Aphra Behn *The Rover* 1681

[Fetherfool] *We are English, a Nation, I thank God, that stands as little upon Religion as any Nation under the Sun, unless it be in contradiction; and at this time, have so many amongst us, a man knows not which to turn his hand to.*

Hardy *Jude the Obscure* 1895

I shall do something too, of course ... now I can't be useful in the lettering it behoves me to turn my hand to something else.

wait on somebody hand and foot

to attend slavishly to somebody's needs: the phrase occurs earlier in the form *serve somebody foot and hand*. *19th cent.*

Rhoda Broughton *Belinda* 1883

He was looked upon as a genius generally. You should have seen how they all sat at his feet – such feet! – and hung on his words. There was one girl – she was at Girton – who waited on him hand and foot; she always warmed his great-coat for him, and helped him on with his galoshes.

See also be a DAB hand at; caught with one's hand in the COOKIE jar; CHANGE hands; EAT out of somebody's hand; get one's hands DIRTY; give somebody the GLAD hand; have one's fingers/ hand in the TILL; have the WHIP hand; know something like the BACK of one's hand; RUB one's hands; SIT on one's hands; WASH one's hands of.

handle

get a handle on something

informal to get control of a situation or to begin to understand it: the notion is of a handle as the means of getting a physical hold of something. *Late 20th cent.*

handshake

See a GOLDEN handshake.

handsome

handsome is as handsome does

courteous manners and behaviour are more important than appearance. *Handsome* is properly used here in its older meaning 'chivalrous' (and the proverb is recorded earlier with *goodly* instead of *handsome*), although in modern use it is often understood in its meaning relating to good looks. The second use of *handsome* is as an adverb (= in a handsome manner). *17th cent.*

Edward Ward *The London Spy* 1698

Beauty's but Fancy Silly Boys Pursue; | Men Love a Woman that is Just and True; | She's only Handsome that will Handsome do.

Goldsmith *The Vicar of Wakefield* 1766

They are as heaven made them, handsome enough if they be good enough; for handsome is that handsome does.

hang

be hanging over somebody / somebody's head

to be a constant threat. The phrase can be seen as an allusion to the Book of Common Prayer (1552): 'How sore punishment hangeth over your heads', or to the sword of Damocles (see SWORD), although this expression is not found in allusive use until the 18th cent., despite the antiquity of the story itself. *16th cent.*

William Prynne *Histrio-Mastix* 1633

From henceforth therefore, let no Clergy man not onely keepe no taverne or base victualling house, but let him not so much as turne aside into tavernes, but in case of necessity: otherwise canonicall punishments hang over his head who shal attempt to stampe such a brand of infamie upon his order.

Jane Austen *Mansfield Park* 1814

The promised notification was hanging over her head. The postman's knock within the neighbourhood was beginning to bring its daily terrors.

get the hang of something

informal, originally NAmer to learn how to operate or manage something. *19th cent.*

Mark Twain *The Adventures of Tom Sawyer* 1876

They took their lath swords ... struck a fencing attitude, foot to foot, and began a grave, careful combat, 'two up and two down'. Presently Tom said: 'Now if you've got the hang, go it lively!'

hang fire

to be delayed in taking action or in continuing an activity. The term was originally used of a gunpowder-and-flint gun that failed to fire because the charge did not ignite readily. *19th cent.*

Mark Twain *A Tramp Abroad* 1880
We were in bed by ten, for we wanted to be up and away on our tramp homeward with the dawn. I hung fire, but Harris went to sleep at once.

hang one's hat

to settle down to live in a certain place. *19th cent.*

Trollope *The Prime Minister* 1876
Lopez can come in and hang up his hat whenever it pleases him.

Jessica Steele *His Woman* 1991
So, for a start, you can begin by telling me why, when I know as fact that two men at least hang their hat up in your home, you're so intent – the glasses, the schoolmarm hairstyle – on living up to the Miss Frostbite label they've pinned on you here?

hang one's head

to look despondent or ashamed: literally, to lower one's head to avoid eye contact because of one's shame or embarrassment. The phrase goes back to Middle English in literal senses, and figurative uses become common in the 18th cent.

Chaucer *Troilus and Criseyde* III.1079
And therwithal he heng adown the heed, | And fil on knees, and sorwfully he sighte.

Charles Batteux *A Course of the Belles Letters* 1761
Wickedness and villainy are the only things recompensed: they reign in triumph, while virtue, oppressed and persecuted, hangs her head, and mourns in secret.

Thackeray *The Newcomes* 1854
Having been abusing Clive extravagantly, as he did whenever he mentioned his cousin's name, Barnes must needs hang his head when the young fellow came in.

hang in the balance

to be in a critical but uncertain position. The balance is a symbol often associated with a person's fate or fortune (with Fortune typically personified). *18th cent.*

Henry Fielding *The History of Tom Jones* 1749
Now Fortune, taking her scales from her shelf, began to weigh the fates of Tom Jones, his female companion, and Partridge, against the landlord, his wife, and maid; all which hung in exact balance before her.

a hanging offence

a serious mistake or wrongdoing (normally used in negative contexts): from the literal meaning of a crime that carries the death penalty. *20th cent.*

hang in there

informal to persevere in the face of difficulty or opposition. The expression is possibly derived from the boxing ring, where the ropes (or an opponent) can provide a support by which a beleaguered boxer can 'hang in' so as to gain temporary relief. *20th cent.*

Today 1992
Navratilova ... told the crowd that next year will probably be her last year of competing on the tour as a singles player. She will continue as long as possible playing doubles, saying: 'I'll hang in there for as long as I can.'

hang (a) left/right

1 *informal* (in boxing) to hit an opponent decisively with the left (or right) hand. *20th cent.*
2 *informal, originally NAmer* to make a left (or right) turn in a vehicle. *Mid 20th cent.*

Mike Ripley *Just Another Angel* 1989
I almost ran up their exhaust pipe as they turned right off Plumstead Road down the side of a school and into the back streets ... I gave them as long as I dared before cutting up a newsprint lorry and following them. I was just in time to see the Sierra hang a left once over the railway.

hang somebody out to dry

informal, chiefly NAmer to leave somebody in an awkward or vulnerable situation: based on the image of washing left out to dry and flapping aimlessly at the mercy of the wind. A curious but unconnected foretaste of this phrase is found in the *Towneley Mysteries* (15th cent.): 'The dwille [= devil] he hang you highe to dry!' *Late 20th cent.*

Daily Mirror 1992
Allan Lamb, who is at the centre of the ball-tampering row, has been hung out to dry by the game's gutless rulers.

hang tough

NAmer, informal to remain obdurate or firmly resolved. *Late 20th cent.*

William Safire in *The New York Times* 1982
The sympathetic farewell is undiminished: Hang in there vies with Hang tough and Hang loose, and Walk light may cheer up the overweight.

David Mervin *Ronald Reagan and the American Presidency* 1990

As Oliver Wright has remarked, 'to be the president of a trade union is to gain an apprenticeship in negotiating, to develop an instinct for when to "hang tough" and when to "cut a deal".'

hang up one's boots
informal to retire from one's work. *20th cent.*

(I may) be hanged if — is the case
informal used to express determination not to do or allow something: indicating strong or emphatic insistence, or (in early use) conviction. References to hanging as forms of imprecation date from Middle English: *cf* see — hanged first/before *below*. The phrase is 18th cent. in this form.

Isaac Bickerstaff *The Plain Dealer* 1766

[Jerry] *I wish I may be hanged if I ever knew such a woman as you are in my life!*

let it all hang out
informal to be relaxed and uninhibited. *Late 20th cent.*

(one might) as well be hanged for a sheep as a lamb
(proverb) if one is going to be punished for an offence one might as well get the maximum benefit from it; more generally, if one is going to take a risk it might as well be a large one. The phrase is widely used as a colourful dismissal of feeble half-measures, especially when an element of excitement or wrongdoing is involved, and carries a greater frisson than the tame alternative *in for a penny, in for a pound* (see PENNY). It alludes to the former practice of hanging for sheep-stealing, the same penalty being applied regardless of the size or age of the stolen animal. The proverb first appears in the 1678 edition of John Ray's collection of English proverbs. *17th cent.*

not care/give a hang
informal not to care at all. *19th cent.*

Harriet Beecher Stowe *Pink and White Tyranny* 1871

Bob Lennox, with the usual vivacity of Young America, said he didn't 'care a hang who set a ball rolling, if only something was kept stirring'.

see — hanged first/before
informal used to introduce emphatic refusal or rejection: *cf* (I may) be hanged if — is the case *above*. *16th cent.*

Shakespeare *The Taming of the Shrew* II.i.293 (1592)

[Petruccio] *And to conclude, we have 'greed so well together | That upon Sunday is the wedding day.*
[Katherine] *I'll see thee hanged on Sunday first.*
[Gremio] *Hark, Petruccio, she says she'll see thee hanged first.*

Thomas Deloney *The Gentle Craft* 1637

And moreouer, she sayd she scorned to come after you to Islington, saying, she would see you hanged first.

See also hang by a THREAD; hang LOOSE; thereby hangs/lies a TALE.

hangdog

have a hangdog look/expression/face
to look ashamed or dejected. *Hangdog* was originally a noun and was commonly used as a form of depreciatory or abusive address in the sense 'a miserable fellow fit only to be hanged like a dog'. There is a 17th cent. use in the current descriptive meaning by the poet and dramatist Thomas Otway in his comedy *The Cheats of Scapin* (1676, adapted from Molière): 'A thing of mere flesh and blood, and that of the worst sort too, with a squinting meager hang-dog Countenance, that looks as if he always wanted physick for the worms.'

Richard Cumberland *Joanna of Mountfaucon* 1800

Look at his coat, I pray you; look at his badge – I wave all comments on his hang-dog face.

Thackeray *The Newcomes* 1854

His hand was yet on the chamber-door, and Barnes was calling him miscreant and scoundrel within; so no wonder Barnes had a hangdog look.

happy

(as) happy as a sandboy / British Larry / a clam
extremely happy. The exact meaning of *sandboy* is uncertain, although it is sometimes explained as 'a boy who hawks sand for sale'. *Jolly* (or *merry*) *as a sandboy* was used in the 19th cent. to describe somebody who had had too much to drink, and Dickens in *The Old Curiosity Shop* (1841) sets a scene at an inn called the 'Jolly Sandboys', which he describes as 'a small road-side inn ... with a sign, representing three Sandboys increasing their jollity'. Sand was sold for practical uses,

especially for sprinkling on bare floors before sawdust took over this role. *Happy as Larry* is Australian (early 20th cent.) in origin: *Larry* is the pet-name for Lawrence and is sometimes associated with the boxer Larry Foley (1847–1917), although this is doubtful. In the 1840s, the New England lawyer and poet John Godfrey Saxe (1816–87) wrote a sonnet 'To a Clam' which began: 'Inglorious friend! most confident I am | Thy life is one of very little ease; | Albeit men mock thee with their similes | And prate of being "happy as a clam!"'; and the poem's punning conclusion is 'Though thou art tender, yet thy humble bard | Declares, O clam! thy case is shocking hard!' These ironic references to the association of clams with happiness suggest that the notion and the phrase were well established by then, and at about the same time (in 1848) the *Southern Literary Messenger* (Richmond Virginia) declared that the expression *happy as a clam* was 'familiar to everyone'. This American simile is more understandable in its full form *happy as a clam in high water* (or *at high tide*). In these conditions, clams are able to feed and are relatively safe from capture, which has to be done at low tide. The phrases with *sandboy* and *clam* are 19th cent., with *Larry* early 20th cent.

Sydney Grundy *In Honour Bound* 1885
That is all over now. I am as happy as the sandboy in the saying.

P Ling *Flood Water* 1989
'You've been drinking again. I can smell it on you.' 'Yes – I persuaded poor old Eb to take a drop, and it's done him a power of good. He's as happy as a sandboy now.'

happy hunting ground
a pleasant or profitable area of activity: from the traditional English name for the ideal afterworld of Native Americans; also used humorously to mean the heaven that animals, especially domestic pets, go to. The Australian use (1888) below seems to represent an intermediate stage between the literal and allusive uses. *19th cent.*

James Fenimore Cooper *Pathfinder* 1840
'Do the dead of the savages ever walk?' 'Ay, and run too, in their happy hunting-grounds, but nowhere else. A red-skin finishes with the earth, after the breath quits the body. It is not one of his gifts to linger around his wig-wam, when his hour has passed.'

Alpha Crucis *Trucanini's Dirge (A Century of Australian Song)* 1888
With hatchet and flame they drove the game | From our happy hunting grounds, | And ravished and slew, and merciless threw | Our babes to their savage hounds.

Daphne du Maurier *Rebecca* 1938
I ride no more tormented, and both of us are free. Even my faithful Jasper has gone to the happy hunting grounds, and Manderley is no more.

a happy medium
a satisfactory compromise: cf the GOLDEN mean. *18th cent.*

Edward Ward *The History of the Grand Rebellion* 1713
'Twixt Scylla and Caribdis safely steer'd, | And neither Pope or Presbyterian fear'd: | But found, in spite of all their plotting Schemes, | A happy Medium 'twixt the two Extreams.

Jane Austen *Emma* 1816
'No – I have never seen Mr. Elton … is he – is he a tall man?' 'Who shall answer that question?' cried Emma. 'My father would say 'yes,' Mr. Knightley 'no;' and Miss Bates and I that he is just the happy medium.'

See also **many happy returns (of the day)** *at* RETURN.

hard

(as) hard as nails
1 extremely hard, like nails which receive heavy blows. *19th cent.*

Edward Bulwer Lytton *Fables in Song* 1874
Now a metal is iron as hard as nails, | Practical, patient, not easily bored.

2 (said of a person) insensitive and uncompromising. *19th cent.*

George Eliot *Adam Bede* 1859
He'd much ado to speak, poor man, his voice trembled so. And the counsellors, – who look as hard as nails mostly … spared him as much as they could.

G B Shaw *Man and Superman* 1903
[Ann] You are so softhearted! It's queer that you should be so different from Violet. Violet's as hard as nails.

(as) hard as the nether millstone
(said of a person) heartless and uncompromising: with allusion to Job 41:24 (Geneva version, 1560)

'His heart is as strong as a stone, and as hard as the nether millstone.' The Authorized Version (1611) has 'His heart is as firm as a stone; yea, as hard as a piece of the nether millstone.' The nether millstone is the lower of the two stones between which corn is ground. *16th cent.*

be hard put to it (to —)

to find it very difficult to do something specified: *hard* here is an adverb meaning 'with difficulty'. *17th cent.*

> Bunyan *The Pilgrim's Progress* 1678
> *But now, in this Valley of Humiliation, poor Christian was hard put to it; for he had gone but a little way, before he espied a foul fiend coming over the field to meet him.*

drive a hard bargain

to be firm or uncompromising in negotiating a bargain or agreement: *hard* is recorded with *bargain* from the early 17th cent. The phrase is 19th cent. in this form.

> Philip Meadows Taylor *Confessions of a Thug* 1839
> *'And you got them cheap?' said I. 'Yes, they were not dear, Meer Sahib; a man in necessity rarely drives a hard bargain.'*

hard and fast

fixed and unalterable. A *hard-and-fast* limit, line, or *rule* is one that allows no exceptions and is strictly enforced. The phrase was originally nautical, used of a ship that had run aground and could not be moved; figurative uses developed early in its history. *19th cent.*

> Oscar Wilde *The Importance of Being Earnest* 1895
> [Algernon] *Oh! it is absurd to have a hard-and-fast rule about what one should read and what one shouldn't. More than half of modern culture depends on what one shouldn't read.*

hard at it

1 busily working or concentrating on something. *17th cent.*

> Fletcher & Massinger *The Spanish Curat* 1647
> *How fares my studious Pupill? Hard at it still?*

2 fighting or quarrelling. *18th cent.*

> Henry Fielding *The History of Tom Jones* 1749
> *'My Aunt, Sir,' cries Sophia, 'hath very violent Passions, and I can't answer what she may do under their Influence.' 'You can't!' returned the Father, 'and pray who hath been the Occasion of putting her into those violent Passions? Nay, who hath actually*

put her into them? Was not you and she hard at it before I came into the Room?'

a hard case

1 *informal* a person who is beyond reform; a hardened criminal. *19th cent.*

> Edward Eggleston *The Circuit Rider* 1874
> *I had a crony by the name of Lew Goodwin, once. Devilish hard case he was, but good-hearted. Got killed in a fight in Pittsburg.*

2 *Australian, informal* an amusing eccentric. *19th cent.*

> C H Thorp *A Handful of Ausseys* 1919
> *There was a barmaid, quite a hard case and a sport, in one of the hotels.*

a hard nut (to crack)

informal a difficult or intractable problem. *18th cent.*

> John Leigh *Kensington-Gardens* 1720
> [Hackit] *This Matrimony is a hard Nut for my Years to crack: But my Comfort is, there's a good Kernel to be pick'd out of it; – A lusty Portion: And, 'On That alone my Thoughts and Wishes dwell, For when that's got – the Woman's but the Shell'.*

> Kipling *Kim* 1901
> *What am I? Mussalman, Hindu, Jain, or Buddhist? That is a hard nut.*

the hard way

the most difficult way of doing something, often from lack of experience and with the implication that a more straightforward alternative has been eschewed. *Mid 20th cent.*

> *Independent* 1989
> *'I never went to drama school,' he would say without a hint of regret, 'but learnt my craft the hard way.'*

no hard feelings

used to seek or give assurance (depending on the tone of voice and facial expression) that no offence has been intended (or taken) from a disagreement or other difficult exchange of views. *19th cent.*

> Edward Wilkins *Young New York* 1856
> *Good bye, governor – no hard feelings, I hope. If you've any communications for me, you can address me at the club. And about the cheque – make it payable to bearer.*

play hard to get

to put on an air of indifference, especially (in romantic and sexual contexts) in order to appear more desirable or alluring. *Mid 20th cent.*

> **Diana James** *Bay of Rainbows* 1993
> *Polly had recognised then that men could not value a woman who didn't value herself. It had nothing to do with teasing or playing hard to get.*

put the hard word on somebody / give somebody the hard word

Australian and NZ, informal to ask somebody for a favour. *Early 20th cent.*

See also a hard ACT to follow; hard lines *at* LINE[1]; have a hard ROW to hoe; the school of hard knocks *at* KNOCK.

hare

first catch your hare

supposedly the initial instruction in a recipe for making hare soup. The phrase is often associated with *The Art of Cookery, Made Plain and Easy* of Mrs Hannah Glasse, published in 1747, but it was not used by her in quite this form. What she said was more straightforwardly 'Take your hare when it is cased [= skinned]', although she came closer to the mark in her recipe for dressing a carp, where she advises 'First catch your fish'. The phrase in its present form first appears in Thackeray and Mrs Gaskell (see below), and in other works of the 1850s and 1860s. It is used allusively in various contexts to do with fulfilling needs and objectives in which a challenging first step has to be achieved before any progress can be made. *19th cent.*

> **Thackeray** *The Rose and the Ring* 1855
> *'A soldier, Prince, must needs obey his orders: mine are ... to seize wherever I should light upon him – ' 'First catch your hare! ...' exclaimed his Royal Highness.*

> **Mrs Gaskell** *Wives and Daughters* 1866
> *'It would not be like a first marriage, of course; but if you found a sensible agreeable woman of thirty or so, I really think you couldn't do better than take her to manage your home, and so save you either discomfort or wrong.' ... Mr. Gibson had thought of this advice several times since it was given; but it was a case of 'first catch your hare'. Where was the 'sensible and agreeable woman of thirty or so'?*

run with the hare and hunt with the hounds

to remain on good terms with both sides in a dispute; a metaphor from hunting. The phrase is recorded in the 16th cent. collection of sayings and proverbs made by John Heywood. *16th cent.*

start a hare

to raise a controversial topic for discussion: a coursing term dating from the 16th cent. and occurring in Shakespeare's *1 Henry IV* (1596) I.iii.196: '[Hotspur] O, the blood more stirs | To rouse a lion than to start a hare!' The erratic course followed by the hare represents the fortunes of the conversation. The phrase is largely obsolete, but occurs occasionally in print.

See also (as) MAD as a March hare.

harm

out of harm's way

safe from danger. *17th cent.*

> **Samuel Butler** *Hudibras* 1663
> *For in the hurry of a Fray | Tis hard to keep out of harm's way.*

there's no harm in (doing) something

the proposed action will not have any adverse effects and might bring benefits. *18th cent.*

> **Fanny Burney** *Cecilia* 1782
> *I knocked one soft little knock at the door, thinking you might be gone to bed after your journey, merely to ask if it was the right house; but when the servant told me there was a gentleman with you already, I thought there would be no harm in just stepping for a moment up stairs.*

harness

in harness

in one's usual work, surroundings, or routine: the image is of a draught horse harnessed to its load. Occasionally also used in the meaning 'in close association'. *19th cent.*

> **George Meredith** *The Egoist* 1879
> *Sir Willoughby ... wrapped himself in meditation. So shall you see standing many a statue of statesmen who have died in harness for their country.*

harp

harp on the same string

to dwell on a subject at tedious length. The image is of the monotonous playing of a single string of a harp. To *harp on* some theme, meaning to be obsessed with it, occurs in several of Shakespeare's plays, notably in *Hamlet* (1601), where Polonius refers in an aside (II.ii.189) to Hamlet's 'still harping on my daughter', and in *Antony and Cleopatra* (1607) Antony accuses Octavian (III.xiii.144) of being 'proud and disdainful, harping on what I am, | Not what he knew I was'. See also below. *16th cent.*

Shakespeare *Richard III* IV.iv.295 (1593)
[King Richard] *Harp not on that string, madam. That is past.* [Queen Elizabeth] *Harp on it still shall I, till heart-strings break.*

harrow

under the harrow

in a state of great distress or misery: in full *like a toad / like toads under the harrow*. The image is of small animals being caught under the iron teeth of a harrow as it is drawn over the ploughed land to break up lumps of earth. *18th cent.*

Thomas Paine *The American Crisis* 1780
The people of America have for years accustomed themselves to think and speak so freely and contemptuously of English authority, and the inveteracy is so deeply rooted, that a person invested with any authority from that country, and attempting to exercise it here, would have the life of a toad under a harrow.

Harry

See PLAY the devil / Old Harry with something.

hash

make a hash of something

informal to bungle something or do it incompetently: based on the (18th cent.) meaning 'a muddle or jumble', itself a figurative use of the (17th cent.) primary meaning of an improvised meal made from cooked pieces of meat reheated in gravy. *19th cent.*

John Henry Newman *Loss and Gain* 1848
The simple question is, whether I should go to the Bar or the Church. I declare I think I have made vastly too much of it myself. I ought to have begun this way with her; – I ought to have said, 'D'you know, I have serious thoughts of reading law?' I've made a hash of it.

settle somebody's hash

informal, originally NAmer to deal summarily with an opponent, subordinate, rival, etc. *19th cent.*

John Poole *Patrician and Parvenu* 1835
And here's the culprit himself to confess it. But I leave it to you to settle his hash.

See also SLING hash.

haste

more haste, less speed

(proverb) rushing a task can make it more difficult to achieve successfully: *speed* in this context originally had the meaning 'success, fortune' (as in the salutation *good speed*) although it is now generally understood in its predominant current meaning 'the state of moving fast'. A related phrase is *make haste slowly*, an exhortation to act positively but with care and diligence: this translates the Latin motto *festina lente* attributed to the emperor Augustus (Suetonius *Augustus* xxv.4) and dates in its present form from the 18th cent., although the sentiment is expressed earlier in other forms (Chaucer: *he hasteth wel that wisely kan abide*; Dryden: *gently make haste*). *Middle English*

Aphra Behn *The Luckey Chance* 1687
[Sir Feeble to Belmour] *Come Francis, you shall have the Honour of Undressing me for the Encounter, but 'twill be a Sweet one … But is the young Rogue laid, Francis – is she stoln to Bed? What Tricks the young Baggages have to whet a man's Appetite? – A pise [pox] of those Bandstrings – the more Haste the less Speed.*

hasty

See beat/make a hasty RETREAT.

hat

eat one's hat

usually in the form *I'll eat my hat*, an assertion of one's confidence in an outcome, the humiliation supposedly coming into force if the outcome is not as expected. The form *eat old Rowley's hat* (referring to a nickname for Charles II, originally the name of his horse) is mentioned in the *OED*, but no evidence is given for it. *See also* eat CROW; eat DIRT; eat HUMBLE pie. *19th cent.*

> Dickens *Pickwick Papers* 1837
> 'Well, if I knew as little of life as that, I'd eat my hat and swallow the buckle whole,' said the clerical gentleman.

first out of the hat

the first name to be chosen by a random process, or (more generally) the person who gets the first chance at something. *Late 20th cent.*

> Guardian 1984
> The draw was made each evening, so competitors couldn't work out whom they would meet in the next round. They tossed for boats. First out of the hat took the north bank, whichever way the tide was running.

a hat trick

a sequence of three consecutive wins, successes, etc. A *hat trick* was originally a trick performed by a conjuror, typically involving three hats. In the 1870s the phrase is found in a *Cricketing Companion* written by one of the family of Lillywhites: 'Having on one occasion taken six wickets in seven balls, thus performing the hat-trick successfully'. After this the phrase passed rapidly into wider use in similar sporting contexts and into life generally. *19th cent.*

keep something under one's hat

to keep something in your head, i.e. as a secret. *19th cent.*

pass/send the hat round

to collect money from a group of people, especially spontaneously for a special purpose. *19th cent.*

> Trollope *Framley Parsonage* 1861
> Perhaps the joke will be against you, when you are getting up into your pulpit to-morrow, and sending the hat round among the clod-hoppers of Chaldicotes.

pick something out of a hat

to choose something at random. *Mid 20th cent.*

pull something out of the hat

to achieve an unexpected or dramatic success: from a conjuror's traditional trick of making a rabbit appear from an apparently empty hat. *20th cent.*

raise one's hat / take one's hat off to somebody

to acknowledge somebody's ability or achievement: from the practice of doffing one's hat as a sign of respect. *19th cent.*

throw one's hat in/into the ring

to take up a challenge: from the former custom of a contestant throwing his hat into a boxing ring to accept a challenge. *19th cent.*

wear two hats

to have two jobs or perform two functions: from the notion of hats associated with particular occupations, such as the red hat of a cardinal (the earliest recorded association) or the hard hat of a building worker. The phrase also occurs in other forms, such as *wear another hat* meaning 'to perform a second function additional to one's main one', and *under one hat* (see quotation below). *Early 20th cent.*

> Conan Doyle *Through the Magic Door* 1919
> Macaulay's posthumous admiration is all very well, but had they met in life Macaulay would have contrived to unite under one hat nearly everything that Johnson abominated.

See also at the DROP of a hat; HANG one's hat; pull a RABBIT out of the hat; TALK through one's hat.

hatch

down the hatch!

informal an expression of encouragement to drink up. *Mid 20th cent.*

> Malcolm Lowry *Ultramarine* 1933
> 'Well, let's shoot a few whiskies down the hatch, and you'll see three,' I remarked fatuously.

hatches, matches, and dispatches

a newspaper's births, marriages, and deaths columns. *19th cent.*

under the hatches

1 in a depressed or destitute state. *16th cent.*

John Crown *The Countery Wit* 1675

Integrity, Friendship, and Honesty, are so miserably under the hatches, one knows not where to find those poor Creatures.

2 hidden from public knowledge: with reference to a ship's hatches, which gave access to the area below decks. *17th cent.*

R L Stevenson *Treasure Island* 1883

Old Pew ... Where is he now? Well, he's dead now and under hatches.

See also BATTEN down the hatches.

hatchet

do a hatchet job on somebody/something

to criticize somebody or something severely or spitefully: a *hatchet man* is a hired killer (usually with a gun rather than a hatchet), and by extension a vicious or merciless critic. *Mid 20th cent.*

Daily Telegraph 1992

When Laurence Olivier died in 1989, his family closed the door of the study and hid the key ... Now, six months after an American biographer, Donald Spoto, did a hatchet job on Olivier, accusing him of having a homosexual affair with Danny Kaye, the key is to be removed from its resting place.

See also BURY the hatchet.

haul

See haul somebody over the coals *at* COAL.

have

have (got) it in one (to do something)

to have the ability or potential (to do something). *19th cent.*

Conan Doyle *A Study in Scarlet* 1887

I know well that I have it in me to make my name famous. No man lives or has ever lived who has brought the same amount of study and of natural talent to the detection of crime which I have done.

have (got) it in for somebody

to behave in a hostile or vindictive way towards somebody; to seek to harm or punish them. *19th cent.*

Aaron Belford Thompson *Harvest of Thoughts* 1909

Better quit yo' gobblin', turk'y! | People's got it in for you, | Don't you know its nigh Thanksgivin'? | Better hide I tell yo' – sh-o-o!

have (got) it made

informal, originally NAmer to be in a comfortable position; to be sure of success. *Mid 20th cent.*

M Cole *Dangerous Lady* 1992

At your age I already had five children living and not the hope of a decent wage coming. You've got it made if only you'd realise it.

have (got) nothing on somebody/something

informal to be insignificant or negligible in comparison with somebody or something: *see also* have something/nothing on somebody *below*. *Early 20th cent.*

Sylvia Plath *Letter to a Purist* 1956

That grandiose colossus who | Stood astride | The envious assaults of sea | (Essaying, wave by wave, | Tide by tide, | To undo him, perpetually), | Has nothing on you, O my love.

have had it

informal to have failed or be of no use; to have had one's fate decided. The phrase is applied typically to people, machines, etc, with a wide range of meanings, e.g. to have missed one's chance, to have been defeated or killed, to be broken or unusable, to have had enough of something and not wish to continue. The phrase became popular in army and air force slang during the Second World War. *Mid 20th cent.*

L P Hartley *My Fellow Devils* 1951

That was the ghastly moment, coming back to find you gone. Then I did feel I'd had it.

have it away

informal to escape from custody. *Mid 20th cent.*

Kenneth Bulmer *The Professionals* 1983

Jack had it away at the time. More luck than brains ... Half the world's police and Interpol never got near him. Maybe he did have a bit of something – cunning, animal cunning.

have it away/off

British, coarse slang to have sexual intercourse with somebody: the notion seems to be of achieving a prize or award. *Mid 20th cent.*

have it out (with somebody)

to settle a point of contention (with somebody). *19th cent.*

C M Yonge *The Heir of Redclyffe* 1853

'Shall I help you?' said Guy. 'Thank you, but I am not ready yet ... It is of no use to wait for me. Mamma shall have the first turn.' 'Yes, yes, yes; go

and have it out with mamma, next best to Amy herself, as she is run away – eh, Guy?'

have one too many
informal to become slightly drunk, i.e. have one drink too many: the phrase *one too many* is recorded from the 16th cent. in general senses (e.g. Shakespeare, *The Comedy of Errors* (1594) III.i.35 '[Dromio of Syracuse to Dromio of Ephesus] Dost thou conjure for wenches, that thou call'st for such store | When one is one too many? Go, get thee from the door'). *Mid 20th cent.*

have something/nothing on somebody
informal to have information (or no information) that would incriminate or be discreditable to somebody. *Early 20th cent.*

See also have it BOTH ways; have a nice DAY; I have / have I got NEWS for you.

havoc

make/play havoc (with something)
to disrupt or damage something seriously. *Havoc* in this use means 'devastation, destruction', occurring earlier in the command *cry havoc!* given to armies as a signal for looting and seizure of spoil, as in the well-known words of Antony in Shakespeare's *Julius Caesar* (1599) III.i.276: 'Cry "havoc!" and let slip the dogs of war' (*see further* at DOG). A related form of the phrase ('They … despoilled al hir goodes and made hauoke') appears in a 15th cent. work of William Caxton.

Joshua Sylvester transl Du Bartas' *Divine Weekes and Workes* 1605
Sith Famine, Plague, and War (with bloody hand) | Doo all at once make havock of this Land.

Dickens *David Copperfield* 1850
She began to 'help' my mother next morning, and was in and out of the store-closet all day, putting things to rights, and making havoc in the old arrangements.

hawk

watch somebody like a hawk
to keep somebody under constant surveillance, to observe or supervise them closely to ensure they are behaving satisfactorily. *19th cent.*

Charles Reade *Hard Cash* 1863
She told Frank [of her husband's death], and watched him like a hawk. He instantly fell on his knees, and implored her to marry him directly.

hay

hit the hay
informal, originally NAmer to go to bed: *cf* hit the SACK. *Early 20th cent.*

Harriet Ford *The Argyle Case* 1912
Well, Bill, you'd better hit the hay. You've got a ticket for a long dream.

make hay
to make good use of an opportunity while it lasts: a shortening of the (16th cent.) proverb *make hay while the sun shines*, which is listed in John Heywood's collection of proverbs of 1546. Shakespeare alludes to the proverb in *3 Henry VI* (1591), at the point where King Edward addresses Richard, Duke of Gloucester and urges all speed in reaching Coventry to deal with the Earl of Warwick, following the deposition of Henry VI (IV.x.28): 'The sun shines hot; and, if we use delay, | Cold biting winter mars our hoped-for hay.' *16th cent.*

make hay of something
to make a mess or nonsense of something. *19th cent.*

Louisa M Alcott *Little Women* 1868
The luggage has come, and I've been making hay of Amy's Paris finery, trying to find some things I want.

See also a ROLL in the hay.

haywire

go haywire
informal to become erratic or out of control. *Haywire* was originally a North American term for wire used to bundle up bales of hay, and came to symbolize anything improvised or made crudely. A haywire outfit was anything cobbled or patched together from primitive materials, and a person or situation was described as haywire in the sense 'confused' or 'crazy', a meaning that has survived in the use of the phrase, as in Margery Allingham's *Flowers for the Judge* (1936) 'I suppose some wives would have gone haywire by this time' and Evelyn Waugh's *Put Out More*

Flags (1942) 'If anyone so much as mentions concentration camps again, ... I shall go frankly haywire'. *Go haywire* dates in more general meanings from the 1920s in North American use. *Early 20th cent.*

The Times 1945

The compasses acted normally, but over the magnetic pole, where the weather was more favourable, they 'went haywire'.

---

head

bang/knock heads together
to deal summarily with people who are constantly disagreeing or arguing with one another; to make them see sense. *18th cent.*

Boswell The Life of Samuel Johnson 1791 [letter to Johnson]

Without doubt you have read what is called 'The Life of David Hume', written by himself, with the letter from Dr. Adam Smith subjoined to it. Is not this an age of daring effrontery? My friend Mr. Anderson, Professor of Natural Philosophy at Glasgow ... said there was now an excellent opportunity for Dr. Johnson to step forth. I agreed with him that you might knock Hume's and Smith's heads together, and make vain and ostentatious infidelity exceedingly ridiculous.

be on —'s (own) head
to be that person's responsibility or misfortune: also in the admonitory form *on your own head be it* (and variants) in the sense 'you alone must accept the consequences of your actions'. *On one's own head* dates back to the 16th cent. in the meaning 'on one's own initiative'. *Middle English* (in Wyclif)

bite/snap somebody's head off
to reply harshly or angrily to somebody. The phrase is found earlier (18th cent.) with *nose* instead of *head*. *19th cent.*

Charlotte Smith The Old Manor House 1793

'But where did you meet him?' repeated Orlando impatiently. 'Don't bite one's nose off,' said Betty.

Charles Henry Saunders Rosina Meadows 1855

[Jethro] S'pose you won't trade for a box of pills? [Florence] No, sir! [Jethro] But you needn't bite a fellow's head off! You don't know the particular virtue of these pills.

Meredith Evan Harrington 1861

On her way back she passed old Tom's chamber, and his chuckles were audible to her. 'They finished the rum,' said Mrs. Hawkshaw. 'I shall rate [= scold] him for that to-morrow,' said Mrs. Mel. 'Giving that poor beast liquor!' 'Rate Mr. Tom! Oh! Mrs. Harrington! Why, he'll snap your head off for a word.' Mrs. Mel replied that her head would require a great deal of snapping to come off.

come to a head
to reach a climax or crisis. The phrase is probably based on the notion of a boil or abscess forming a head before it breaks, but the figurative meaning is recorded slightly earlier than the physical meaning. A locus classicus occurs at the beginning of Act V of Shakespeare's *The Tempest* (1613), where Prospero tells Ariel 'Now does my project gather to a head'. A few years earlier, Francis Beaumont's play *The Woman Hater* (1607) included the lines 'Heaven, if my | Sins be ripe grown to a head, | And must attend your vengeance: | I beg not to divert my fate, | Or to reprieve a while thy punishment'. *16th cent.*

do somebody's head in
informal to be more than somebody can deal with emotionally or intellectually. *20th cent.*

do something (standing) on one's head
to manage to do something with ease. *19th cent.*

G B Shaw Our Theatre in the Nineties 1896

Of course, Mr Waring does the thing on his head, so to speak; but how can I compliment an actor who has done what he has done on stuff like that?

get/keep one's head down
to lie low, avoiding trouble or concentrating on a task in hand. *20th cent.*

Edward Chisnall Bell in the Tree 1989

De Quincey was more or less in hiding from Edinburgh people to whom he owed large sums of money, so Glasgow, a thriving and blackening metropolis of 365,000 souls, was the ideal place in which to eat your opium and keep your head down.

get one's head round/around something
to succeed in understanding something, especially after initial difficulty or reluctance. *Early 20th cent.*

Julian Barnes *A History of the World in 10½ Chapters* 1990

Will they disappear ... forever wiped out by some killer bug and all that will be left of them is a film in which they're playing their own ancestors? I'm not sure I can get my head round that.

get/have a head start

to secure an initial advantage for oneself: originally with reference to races and other competitions. *19th cent.*

give somebody head

coarse slang to perform oral sex on somebody. *Late 20th cent.*

P Falconer *War in High Heels* 1993
I was dreaming Hedy Lamarr was giving me head.

give somebody their head

to give somebody the chance to act on their own initiative: originally (16th cent.) with reference to allowing a horse to gallop freely by not checking its speed with the reins. The phrase dates from the 18th cent. with reference to people.

Richard Steele *The Tender Husband* 1705
[Pounce] *Not at all, Sir, your Father can't cut you out of one Acre of 1500 a year.* [Humphrey] *What a Fool have I been to give him his Head so long!*

go over somebody's head

to appeal beyond one's immediate superior to somebody at a higher level of responsibility. *See also* over somebody's head *below. 20th cent.*

go to somebody's head

1 (said of alcoholic drink) to make somebody intoxicated or dizzy: also used figuratively with reference to an emotional effect. *19th cent.*

Henry James *Guy Domville* 1893
[stage direction] *Glass in hand, they look at each other, till Round breaks out suddenly as if the wine has begun to go to his head.*
2 (said of fame or success) to make somebody vain or conceited. *Mid 20th cent.*

Agatha Christie *Ten Little Niggers* 1939
He's played God Almighty for a good many months every year. That must go to a man's head eventually.

have a (good) head for something

to have a particular aptitude. *18th cent.*

Phanuel Bacon *The Insignificants* 1757
[Hatband] *But – as to these people – I am afraid you would meet with a hard task to find out any excellencies they had unless you have a very good head for invention.*

have one's head screwed on (the right way)

to be sensible and practical: also *have a good head on one's shoulders. 19th cent.*

Dickens *Bleak House* 1853
Now, it an't necessary to say to a man like you, engaged in your business, which is a business of trust and requires a person to be wide awake and have his senses about him, and his head screwed on tight ... it an't necessary to say to a man like you, that it's the best and wisest way to keep little matters like this quiet.

David Lodge *Nice Work* 1988
'There's no such thing as a free lunch. Who said that?' 'I don't know. Some right-wing economist, I suppose.' 'Had his head screwed on, whoever he was.'

head and shoulders above something/somebody

greatly superior to another thing or person. *19th cent.*

Harold Frederic *The Damnation of Theron Ware* 1896
And your sermon was so head-and-shoulders above all the others!

head over heels

completely or helplessly: typically used about strong feelings, especially love or infatuation. Drawing on the image of a person performing a jubilant or exultant somersault, the original form of the phrase was the more logical *heels over head* (or *heel over head*), which goes back to Middle English. 18th cent. uses include violent contexts in which victims tumble or are hurtled into involuntary somersaults (physical and figurative). The order was reversed, probably unthinkingly and to produce a better balance of syllables, in the first half of the 19th cent., although the older form did not disappear entirely until well into the 20th cent.; a variant form was *head over tip*. Sir Walter Scott, in an early drama based on Goethe called *Goetz of Berlichingen* (1799), gives us the line 'My master threw him head over heels from his horse, his feather-bush was the first thing reached the mire', and at about the same time Fanny Burney in *Camilla* (1796) has a description of a three-year-old child 'jumping and turning head over heels, with the true glee of unspoilt nature'. Thackeray (see below) used the form *head and heels*. Users of a nonsensical variant *head over ears* included G B Shaw in a letter to *The Times* in 1912: 'I plunged in head over ears and … wrote off my 56 years.' Figurative uses are found from the first years of the 19th cent. following on closely from the more euphonious inversion of the phrase.

> M G Lewis *One O'Clock* 1811
> She was but a Peasant like myself, and might have been a peasant still, if by good luck the Count had not rescued her from the giant Hacho, and instantly fallen head over heels in love with her himself.

> Thackeray *Pendennis* 1849
> Thus love makes fools of all of us, big and little; and the curate had tumbled over head and heels in pursuit of it, and Pen had started in the first heat of the mad race.

heads I win, tails you lose

I will win whatever happens: from the tossing of a coin to decide a winner. *19th cent.*

> John Maddison Morton *Box and Cox* 1847
> [Box] *Now then, sir – heads win?* [Cox] *Or tails lose – whichever you prefer.* [Box] *It's the same to me, sir.* [Cox] *Very well, sir. Heads, I win – tails, you lose.*

heads will roll

people will be dismissed or made to resign, especially in the aftermath of a gross failure or political debacle: based on the notion of execution by beheading and in some contexts used in this meaning. Early uses are associated with the rise of Nazi Germany in the 1930s. A newspaper of 1930 reports a speech of Adolf Hitler as follows: 'If our movement is victorious there will be a revolutionary tribunal which will punish the crimes of November 1918. Then decapitated heads will roll in the sand.' *Mid 20th cent.*

> John Birt *The Harder Path* 2002
> Ultra-royalist forces were outraged that the BBC had given Diana a platform at all. I had the chilling sense that a few centuries earlier my head would have rolled for the crime committed.

hold/put a gun/pistol to somebody's head

to compel somebody to act. *19th cent.*

hold up one's head

to maintain one's dignity or self-respect. *16th cent.*

> Dryden *The Kind Keeper* 1680
> [Aldo, aside] *Now cannot I for shame hold up my head, to think what this young Rogue is privy to!*

keep one's head

to remain calm and emotionally controlled in difficult circumstances. *18th cent.*

keep one's head above water

to remain solvent: the image is of avoiding drowning in water by keeping one's head above the surface. *17th cent.*

> John Wilson *The Projectors* 1665
> I have had this design in my head a long time, and made him many a Mortgage, and kept touch with him at his day, meerly to beget an opinion in him that I had great dealings in the world; when yet I have found enough to do, to keep my head above water.

> Mary Wollstonecraft *Maria, or the Wrongs of Woman* 1798
> I found myself once more reduced to beggary … I once more returned to my old occupation; but have not yet been able to get my head above water.

laugh/talk/shout, etc one's head off

to laugh, talk, etc loudly and incessantly. *19th cent.*

> Mrs Gaskell *Wives and Daughters* 1866
> So there are two old horses eating their heads off, while he is constantly talking about money and expense.

lift up one's head

to recover one's dignity or courage, especially after a setback or humiliation: *cf* Judges 8:28 (in the Authorized Version, 1611) 'Thus was Midian subdued before the children of Israel, so that they lifted up their heads no more.' *16th cent.*

lose one's head

1 to be executed by beheading. *Middle English*

> Chaucer *The Knight's Tale* (line 1707)
> Namoore, up peyne of [= on the penalty of] lesynge of youre heed!

> Shakespeare *Richard II* III.ii.138 (1595)
> [Aumerle] *Is Bushy, Green, and the Earl of Wiltshire dead?* [Scrope] *Ay, all of them at Bristol lost their heads.*

2 to panic or behave irrationally. *19th cent.*

Hardy *Tess of the D'Urbervilles* 1891
Tess – don't look at me so – I cannot stand your
looks! There never were such eyes, surely, before
Christianity or since! There – I won't lose my head;
I dare not.

need (to have) one's head examined

to behave foolishly or stupidly: an image based
on the notion that the examination would lead to
a diagnosis of insanity. *Mid 20th cent.*

Eamonn McGrath *The Charnel House* 1990
Any fellow that'd pay a pound a bottle for dirty
water – water that could very well carry typhoid –
should have his head examined.

not make head or tail of something

to be completely unable to understand something: *head or tail* is recorded from the 17th
cent. with the meaning 'something definite,
either one thing or the other'. *17th cent.*

Francis Kirkman *The Unlucky Citizen* 1673
Although we spent much time that night in dis-
coursing on this subject, yet we could find neither
head nor tale in it; wherefore we went to sleep as
well as our cares would let us.

H G Wells *The Invisible Man* 1897
His habit of talking to himself in a low voice grew
steadily upon him, but though Mrs. Hall listened
conscientiously she could make neither head nor tail
of what she heard.

off one's head

informal crazy or foolish. *19th cent.*

John Davidson *The Fleet Street Eclogues* 1893
[Basil] *Twelve notes the bell-voiced midnight*
pealed; | The moon stood still; the wan stars reeled.
[Brian] *Lord! Basil, are you off your head?*

off the top of one's head

without much thought or consideration; impulsively. *Mid 20th cent.*

Colin Dexter *Dead of Jericho* 1981
A bit of bread-and-butter investigation was worth a
good deal more than some of that top-of-the-head
stuff.

on your own head be it

see be on —'s (own) head *above*.

out of one's head

informal high on drugs. *Late 20th cent.*

M Cole *The Ladykiller* 1993
To see that child lying in a cell out of her head on
drugs was like having a knife twisted somewhere in
your bowels.

over somebody's head

1 ignoring or overlooking somebody's prior or
better claim: used especially with reference to
promotion or preferment. The image is of guns
or projectiles being fired in the air over the heads
of people at a target beyond them. *See also* go over
somebody's head *above*. *16th cent.*

Thomas D'Urfey *The Modern Prophets* 1709
I'm an Officer of Merit, and can't brook to have
another put into Employment over my Head.
2 too difficult for somebody to understand. The
image here may be the same as above, with the
added notion of not being able to reach something that other people can reach. *17th cent.*

put heads together

to confer about something. Before the 19th cent.
the normal forms of the phrase are with *lay* or *cast*
instead of *put*. *Middle English*

Chaucer *The Parliament of Fowls* (line 554)
The water-foules han here hedes leid | Togedere,
and of a short avysement [= deliberation], *| Whan*
everych [= every single one] *hadde his large golee*
[= mouthful] *seyd.*

Shakespeare *2 Henry VI* III.i.165 (1591)
[Gloucester] *Ay, all of you have laid your heads*
together – | Myself had notice of your conventicles
– | And all to make away my guiltless life.

James Fenimore Cooper *Deerslayer* 1841
Two or three old women put their heads together,
and it appeared unfavorably to the prospect of
Deerslayer, by their scowling looks and angry
gestures.

put something into somebody's head

to suggest something to somebody. *16th cent.*

George Pettie *A Petite Pallace* 1576
Well, saith shee, do as God shall put in your head, &
of mee make this account, that though you bee the
meanest man in the citie yet will I honour you as if
you were the Emperour.

Shakespeare *Othello* IV.ii 16 (1604)
[Emilia] *I durst, my Lord, to wager, she is honest, |*
Lay down my soul at stake. If you think other, |
Remove your thought; it doth abuse your bosom. |
If any wretch ha' put this in your head, | Let heaven
requite it with the serpent's curse.

rear/raise its (ugly) head

(said of something unwelcome) to become horribly evident; to appear, to the dismay of all around. *18th cent.*

Henry Home *Elements of Criticism* 1762
A flourishing commerce begets opulence; and opulence, inflaming our appetite for pleasure, is commonly vented on luxury, and on every sensual gratification: Selfishness rears its head; becomes fashionable; and, infecting all ranks, extinguishes the amor patriæ, and every spark of public spirit.

stand/turn something on its head

to use an argument to demonstrate the opposite of its original conclusion. *20th cent.*

take it into one's head

to resolve to do something, usually something considered to be unwise or uncharacteristic. *18th cent.*

George Colman *The Deuce is in Him* 1763
[Bell] *He is just returned, but is come home with the strangest conceit that ever filled the brain of a lover. He took it into his head to try my sister's faith by pretending to be maimed and wounded, and has actually visited her this morning in a counterfeit character.*

Dickens *A Christmas Carol* 1843
He takes it into his head to dislike us, and he won't come and dine with us.

talk somebody's head off

to talk incessantly, so that the person listening is too exhausted or bored to reply. *19th cent.*

J G Holland *Sevenoaks: A Story of To-day* 1875
'Come, now!' said he, 'you understand your business, and I understand mine. If you were to take up guns and gutta-percha, I could probably talk your head off, but I don't know anything about these things.'

turn somebody's head

to infatuate or beguile somebody: the phrase occurs earlier with *brain(s)* instead of *head*. *17th cent.*

Dryden *The Kind Keeper* 1680
[Woodall] *Why, you turn my Brains, with talking to me of your Wife's Chamber!*

James Miller *The Coffee House* 1737
[Widow] *Some fluttering Coxcomb or other then has turn'd your Head for you, has he?*

Thomas Hughes *Tom Brown at Oxford* 1861
You have been making serious love to Patty, and have turned the poor girl's head.

turn heads

to attract attention, especially from one's striking appearance. *19th cent.*

Anna Ritchie *Fashion* 1855
[Trueman] *Promise me to call upon the whole circle of your fashionable acquaintants with your own advertisements and in your cook's attire, and I will set you up in business to-morrow. Better turn stomachs than turn heads!*

two heads are better than one

(proverb) one can act more effectively if one listens to advice. The phrase is recorded in its current form in John Heywood's collection of proverbs, published in 1546. It occurs earlier (Middle English, in Gower's *Confessio Amantis*) in the form *two hands are better than one*, and Palsgrave (16th cent.) has the form *two wits are better than one*. *16th cent.*

with one's head in the clouds

in a dreamy or abstracted state of mind. *19th cent.*

Charles Lamb *Essays of Elia* 1823
The man seemed to tread upon air, to taste manna, to walk with his head in the clouds.

Zadie Smith *White Teeth* 2001
Come on, Sam – get it together. Head in the clouds this evening.

See also bang/knock one's head against a BRICK wall; be hanging over somebody/somebody's head *at* HANG; HANG one's head; a HOLE in the head; KNOCK something on the head; not RIGHT in the head; an OLD head on young shoulders; over head and ears (*see* up to one's ears) *at* EAR.

---

headline

hit the headlines

informal to be reported prominently in the newspapers; to achieve notoriety. *Mid 20th cent.*

---

health

come with a (government) health warning

to have hidden dangers or difficulties to which people should be alerted: originally in literal use with reference to the marketing and advertising of tobacco products, and now often used figuratively and in trivial contexts. *20th cent.*

Christine Gilbert *Local Management of Schools* 1990
She joked that the use of performance indicators in education should include a 'government health warning'.

heap

at the top/bottom of the heap
belonging to the most senior (or most junior) part of an organization: also with *pile* instead of *heap*. *20th cent.*

Amrit Wilson *Finding a Voice: Asian Women in Britain* 1988
Asian women are the worst off of all British workers. They are at the bottom of the heap.

strike somebody all of/on a heap
dated, informal to confuse or disconcert somebody: *all on a heap* is recorded in physical meanings from the 16th cent. and occurs in Shakespeare (e.g. *Titus Andronicus* (1594) II.iii.223 '[Martius] Lord Bassianus lies berayed in [= filthy with] blood | All on a heap, like to a slaughtered lamb'). *18th cent.*

Isaac Bickerstaff *The Maid of the Mill* 1765
[Giles] Little Sal ... would fain have had me for a partner, but I said as how I'd go for one I liked better, one that I'd make a partner for life. [Patty] Did you say so? [Giles] Yes, and she was struck all of a heap – she had not a word to throw to a dog.

Scott *Rob Roy* 1817
'Pray, by the by, Mr Jarvie, who may this Mr Robert Campbell be, whom we met with last night?' The interrogatory seemed to strike the honest magistrate, to use the vulgar phrase, 'all of a heap', and instead of answering, he returned the question – 'Whae's Mr Robert Campbell?'

See also heap coals of fire on somebody's head *at* COAL.

hear

be unable to hear oneself think
to be deafened by noise to an extent that makes it difficult to think. *19th cent.*

H W Herbert *The Chevaliers of France* 1853
'Who is that groaning there?' he exclaimed, as a faint acclamation of pain reached his ear, from the old steward, who, sorely bruised and shaken by his fall, was just recovering his senses. 'Par Dieu! I can not hear myself think for the noise. Jump down from your horse, Le Balafré, and cut his throat at once; cut it close under the jaws, down to the back-bone; that will stop his cursed clamor.'

hear hear!
an exclamation of agreement with or support for the words of a speaker in debating or public speaking. The earlier form of the expression, *hear him! hear him!*, makes the origin clear; it is an invocation for others to listen and take note. It is best known as the traditional form of cheering in the British House of Commons, a practice which is recorded from the 17th cent.

heart

Many of the phrases are based on meanings in which *heart* represents the seat of human feelings or attributes, e.g. love (as in *give one's heart to*) and courage (as in *lose heart*). These meanings have often disappeared apart from their use in the phrases.

after one's own heart
sharing one's own attitudes and interests: based on the (otherwise obsolete) meaning 'inclination or purpose'. An early use is in Coverdale's translation (16th cent.) of the Bible (Samuel 13:14) 'The Lord hath sought him out a man after his own heart.'

Thomas Southerne *Sir Anthony Love* 1691
[Sir Anthony] I ... am so far | From imitating you any way, | That when an Elder Brother stood between me and a good Estate, | I made bold to remove him. [Pilgrim] By no violent means. [Sir Anthony] Something before his time. | I had a Joynture too incumber'd me; | But a Physician after my own heart | Eas'd me, and my good Lady-Grandmother.

Edgar Allan Poe *How to Write a Blackwood Article* 1838
'If you wish to write forcibly ... pay minute attention to the sensations.' 'That I certainly will, Mr. Blackwood' ... 'Good! ... I see you are a pupil after my own heart.'

break somebody's heart
to cause somebody deep hurt or sorrow. The notion must be as old as language itself; in Eng-

lish the phrase in its current form appears earliest in Middle English with the *heart* as subject and *break* used intransitively. The phrase occurs several times in the Authorized Version of the Bible (1611), e.g. at Acts 21:13 (where Paul has heard a prophecy of his arrest) 'Then Paul answered, What mean ye to weep and to break mine heart?'

Chaucer *The Knight's Tale* (line 954)
Hym thoughte that his herte wolde breke, | Whan he saugh hem [= saw them] so pitous [= pitiful] and so maat [= dejected].

Shakespeare *Macbeth* IV.iii.211 (1606)
[Malcolm to Macduff, on hearing the news of the murder of Macduff's family] *What, man, ne'er pull your hat upon your brows. | Give sorrow words. The grief that does not speak | Whispers the o'erfraught heart and bids it break.*

Aphra Behn *Love-Letters Between a Noble-Man and His Sister* 1685
By turns the Sister and the Mistress torture; by turns they break his heart, he had this comfort left before, that if Calista were undone, her ruin made way for his Love and happiness with Silvia, but now – he had no prospect left.

Fanny Burney *Cecilia* 1782
O dear! I don't know what I can do! for it will half break my heart, if my dear Miss Beverley should go out of town, and I not see her!

close to one's heart
deeply affecting one emotionally: often used with *lie*. To *lay something (close) to the heart* is an older and now obsolete form of the expression, from which the current phrase is derived. In Shakespeare's *Macbeth* (1606), Lady Macbeth reads a letter from her husband describing the witches' prophecies, the first of which has been fulfilled (I.v.13). The closing greeting of the letter is 'lay it [this news] to thy heart, and farewell'. The image of a fond embrace is also present. The phrase in its more allusive uses dates from the 18th cent.

Defoe *Moll Flanders* 1722
I was sorry to tell him that there was an unhappy circumstance in our case, which lay too close to my heart, and which I knew not how to break to him, that rendered my part of it very miserable, and took from me all the comfort of the rest.

eat one's heart out
to suffer an agony of longing or expectation for something unattainable. The notion of eating

one's heart as a symbol of emotional anguish dates from the 16th cent. The modern exhortation *eat your heart out!* is an encouragement to envy some advantage enjoyed by the speaker or by a third party referred to by the speaker. *19th cent.*

from the (bottom of one's) heart
with complete sincerity or conviction: often with allusion to the Book of Common Prayer (1549) 'If one of the parties ... be content to forgive from the bottom of his heart all that the other hath trespassed against him'. *16th cent.*

Arthur Golding transl Ovid's *Metamorphoses* 1567
Thou standst as dombe and to my wordes no answere can thou give, | But from the bottom of thy heart full sorie sighes dost drive | As tokens of thine inwarde griefe.

have a heart
1 to take courage. *17th cent.*

James Shirley *The Woman of Pleasure* 1637
[Aretina] *What devill? How I tremble.* [Alexander] *Have a heart, Twas a shee devill too, a most insatiate Abominable devill with a taile Thus long.*

2 to be kind or merciful. In modern use often used informally as an exhortation to somebody who is being severe or unreasonable. *19th cent.*

Maria Edgeworth *Belinda* 1801
If you have a heart, you must feel for me – Leave me now – tomorrow you shall hear my whole history – now I am quite exhausted.

Pamela Steel *Guilty Parties* 1990
'But I still don't see how this affects your attitude to having a child of your own.' 'No? Oh Brian, have a heart.'

have one's heart in / put one's heart into something
to be closely involved in or committed to something. *18th cent.*

Fanny Burney *Letter* 1780
I have so little heart in the affair, that I have now again quite dropped it.

Cowper *The Task* 1785
Wolfe, where'er he fought, | Put so much of his heart into his act, | That his example had a magnet's force, | And all were swift to follow whom all loved.

have one's heart in one's mouth

to be greatly excited or anxious: with reference to the supposed leaping of the heart under shock or excitement. *16th cent.*

Joseph Addison *The Drummer* 1716
[Coachman] *This makes one almost afraid of one's own Shadow. As I was walking from the Stable t'other Night without my Lanthorn, I fell a-cross a Beam, that lay in my way, and Faith my Heart was in my Mouth – I thought I had stumbled over a Spirit.*

have one's heart in the right place / somebody's heart is in the right place

to mean well and have good intentions. *18th cent.*

Arthur Murphy *Know Your Own Mind* 1778
[Malvil] *I – I – I am apt to carry my heart at my tongue's end.* [Dashwould] *I knew his heart was not in the right place.*

heart and soul

with great enthusiasm; with one's whole being: normally used adverbially. Shakespeare reverses the normal order in *Henry V* (1599) III.vi.8: 'a man that I love and honour with my soul and my heart'. In its current form the phrase dates from the 17th cent.

Vanbrugh *The False Friend* 1702
[Lopez] *What mighty Matters do you expect, from Boarding a Woman you know is already Heart and Soul engag'd to another?* [Don John] *Why I expect her Heart and Soul shou'd disengage in a Week.*

one's heart misses/skips a beat

one is momentarily afraid or excited. *Early 20th cent.*

David Philips *The Price She Paid* 1912
Then her heart skipped a beat and her skin grew cold and a fog swirled over her brain.

a heart of gold

a generous and noble nature, or the person possessing it. *16th cent.*

Nicholas Udall *Ralph Roister Doister* 1566
[Ralph] *Howe dothe sweete Custance, my heart of gold, tell me how?*

Shakespeare *Henry V* IV.i.44 (1599)
[Pistol] *The King's a bawcock* [= fine fellow] *and a heart-of-gold,* | *A lad of life, an imp of fame.*

heart of oak

a courageous spirit: from the literal meaning, the solid core of wood used for timber. Used with allusion to a sea song celebrating a series of English naval victories of 1759, which includes the lines 'Heart of oak are our ships, Heart of oak are our men'. *17th cent.*

Thomas Shadwell *Epsom Wells* 1673
[Peg] *She loves your honest, true, English Country Gentlemen, and wonders what Ladies can see in foolish London Fellows, to charm 'em so.* [Clodpate] *And so do I, a Company of Spindle-shank Pocky Fellows, that will scarce hold together: I am of your true tuff English heart of Oak, Gudsooks.*

a heart of stone

a ruthless or unfeeling nature. *17th cent.*

Shakespeare *Twelfth Night* III.iv.197 (1602)
[Olivia] *I have said too much unto a heart of stone,* | *And laid mine honour too unchary out.*

hearts and minds

people's feelings and opinions, especially as something to be influenced or won over: used typically in the form *conquer* (or, in modern use, *win over*) *hearts and minds. 17th cent.*

Samuel Pordage *Heroick Stanzas on His Majesties Coronation* 1661
Peace brings him in, Olive his Temples binds, | *And his great virtues conquer hearts and minds.*

Benjamin Thompson transl Kotzebue's *Lovers' Vows* 1801
My father says that we are more indebted to those who form our hearts and minds, than to those who give us mere existence.

Guardian 1989
Downing Street strategists planning their tactics as the battle for hearts and minds over monetary union enters a crucial phase would be wrong, therefore, to assume that Bonn is a natural ally.

one's heart's desire

something one wants passionately. Mainly used from the 18th cent., but the phrase occurs much earlier in the romance *King Alisaunder* (early 14th cent.): 'He hoped to have there of his hertes desyres'. *Middle English*

Marlowe *Dr Faustus* xiii.82 (1590)
[Faustus] *One thing, good servant, let me crave of thee,* | *To glut the longing of my heart's desire:* | *That I might have unto my paramour* | *That heavenly Helen which I saw of late.*

one's heart sinks/falls (into one's boots)

one gets a sudden feeling of despondency or disappointment, typically in reaction to an unexpected event or circumstance. Fanciful references to the heart in various positions of descent date from the 16th cent., and the phrase in its fixed form from the 19th cent.

> Conan Doyle *The Stockbroker's Clerk* 1893
> *I stood for a few minutes with my heart in my boots, wondering whether the whole thing was an elaborate hoax or not.*

> Bette Howell *Dandelion Days* 1991
> *My heart sank into my boots like Granny's lumpy porridge as we made our way to Grindlewood for a day's dusting and polishing.*

heart to heart

confidentially or intimately: originally as a qualifying word, as in a *heart-to-heart talk*. The phrase first appears in absolute form as a noun in the mid 20th cent. *19th cent.*

> Theodore Martin transl Schiller's *William Tell* 1870
> [Stauffacher] *Yet tell me now, I pray, who are the friends,* | *The worthy men, who came along with you?* | *Make me acquainted with them, that we may* | *Speak frankly, man to man, and heart to heart.*

in one's heart of hearts

in one's innermost feelings: originally in the form *heart of heart* (as in Shakespeare, *Hamlet* (1601) III.ii.71 '[Hamlet to Horatio] Give me that man | That is not passion's slave, and I will wear him | In my heart's core, ay, in my heart of heart, | As I do thee'). The form *heart of hearts* is first recorded at the beginning of the 19th cent. *17th cent.*

lose/take heart

to lose (or regain) one's courage or confidence in an undertaking. *Middle English*

lose one's heart

to fall in love with somebody. The phrase is foreshadowed in Act III of Shakespeare's *The Tempest* (1613), at the point where Miranda declares her love for Ferdinand: 'The very instant that I saw you did | My heart fly to your service; there resides | To make me slave to it.' *17th cent.*

> William Wycherley *The Plain Dealer* 1677
> [Novel] *I have an Ambition, I must confess, of losing my heart, before such a fair Enemy as your self, Madam.*

> Sheridan *St Patrick's Day* 1788
> [Doctor] *He says that he has lost his heart to her, and that if you will give him leave to pay his addresses to the young lady, and promise your consent to the union if he should gain her affections, he will on those conditions cure you instantly, without fee or reward.*

not have the heart

to be unable or unwilling to do something particularly cruel or insensitive. The phrase is found in related forms in Middle English sources including the 14th cent. northern poem known as the *Cursor Mundi*. In Shakespeare's *Richard III* (1593), Lady Anne declares before the body of the murdered King Henry VI (I.ii.16): 'Cursèd the blood that let this blood from hence, | Cursèd the heart that had the heart to do it.'

> John Tatham *The Distracted State* 1651
> *'Tis Dark As is the Act I go about; were't light I should not have the heart to kill a Pig.*

> Jane Austen *Mansfield Park* 1814
> *From my soul I do not think she would marry you without love; that is, if there is a girl in the world capable of being uninfluenced by ambition, I can suppose it her; but ask her to love you, and she will never have the heart to refuse.*

set one's heart on something

to be very eager to have or achieve something. *Middle English*

> Chaucer *The Monk's Tale* (line 2742)
> *And eek a sweven [= dream] upon a nyght he mette [= dreamed],* | *Of which he was so proud and eek so fayn [= pleased]* | *That in vengeance he al his herte sette.*

> Jane Austen *Emma* 1816
> *I am very much obliged to you ... If I had set my heart on Mr. Elton's marrying Harriet, it would have been very kind to open my eyes; but at present I only want to keep Harriet to myself. I have done with match-making indeed.*

take something to heart

to be greatly affected or distressed by something said. *Middle English* (in *Cursor Mundi*)

wear one's heart on one's sleeve

to reveal one's feelings or emotions: with allusion to Shakespeare, *Othello* (1604) I.i.64 '[Iago] I will wear my heart upon my sleeve | For daws to peck at. I am not what I am.' The allusive uses are mainly a 19th cent. revival. *17th cent.*

Louisa M Alcott *On Picket Duty, and Other Tales* 1864
Meanwhile, Mr. Bopp, though carrying his heart upon his sleeve, believed his secret buried in the deepest gloom, and enjoyed all the delightful miseries lovers insist upon making for themselves.

See also have a CHANGE of heart; one's heart bleeds *at* BLEED.

heartbeat

a heartbeat away from something
on the verge of something; just a few moments before something is due to happen. *Late 20th cent.*

Guardian 1985
Since Mr Bush is also just a heartbeat away from the presidency without an election – never his forte anyway – his fun was inhibited. Plans for a sea monster to emerge from a Bristol lake to greet him were mucked about by the secret service.

hearth

hearth and home
home and the comforts of home. Use of *hearth* as a symbol of the home dates from Old English, and the coupling of *hearth* and *home* also has an alliterative effect. The symbolism is also found in other languages and goes back to classical antiquity. *19th cent.*

Charlotte Brontë *The Professor* 1857
White necks, carmine lips and cheeks, clusters of bright curls, do not suffice for me without that Promethean spark which will live after the roses and lilies are faded, the burnished hair grown grey. In sunshine, in prosperity, the flowers are very well; but how many wet days are there in life – November seasons of disaster, when a man's hearth and home would be cold indeed, without the clear, cheering gleam of intellect.

James Joyce *A Portrait of the Artist as a Young Man* 1916
And if it be pain for a mother to be parted from her child, for a man to be exiled from hearth and home … O think what pain … it must be for the poor soul to be spurned from the presence of the … loving Creator.

hearty
See HALE and hearty.

heat

In the phrases *heat* is primarily used in its meaning 'intensity of action' (e.g. *in the heat of the battle*), a figurative use which dates from the late 16th cent.

in the heat of the moment
while angry or otherwise emotionally affected. *19th cent.*

G B Shaw *Caesar and Cleopatra* 1901
[Britannus] *Caesar: I ask you to excuse the language that escaped me in the heat of the moment.*

turn the heat on somebody/something
to concentrate criticism or pressure on somebody or something. *Mid 20th cent.*

turn up the heat
to increase criticism or pressure. *Mid 20th cent.*

heather

set the heather on fire
Scottish to cause a stir or disturbance. *19th cent.*

Scott *Rob Roy* 1817
'It's partly that whilk has set the heather on fire e'en now.' 'Heather on fire?' said I. 'I do not understand you.' 'Why,' resumed MacGregor, 'ye ken weel eneugh that women and gear are at the bottom of a' the mischief in this warld.'

heave

heave in sight / into view
to appear in the distance: originally used with reference to ships. The phrase is based on a meaning that is now otherwise obsolete, 'to rise or mount up', with the irregular past tense *hove*; this meaning underlies several nautical phrases. *18th cent.*

James Fenimore Cooper *The Red Rover* 1827–8
'I meant merely to inquire, if you would follow the gentleman you serve to so unseemly and pernicious a place as a gibbet?' … 'If I wouldn't, may I be d—d! After sailing in company for four-and-twenty years, I should be no better than a sneak, to part company, because such a trifle as a gallows hove in sight.'

heave a sigh (of relief)

to show one's sense of relief that a dangerous or unpleasant situation is over or has been averted. *18th cent.*

> Fanny Burney Camilla 1796
> *Sir Hugh, when he had finished the letter, heaved a sigh, and leant his head upon his hand, considering whether or not to let it be seen by Miss Margland; who, however … had so contrived to sit at the table as to read it at the same time with himself.*

heaven

the heavens open

there is a sudden violent downpour of rain. *20th cent.*

> Tom Pow In the Palace of Serpents 1992
> *Then, just as we were tying up the canoe, came the first heavy spats of rain on the leaves and with a roll of thunder the heavens opened.*

heavens to Betsy

informal, originally NAmer an exclamation of surprise or dismay. *Betsy* is a stock American name for a typical woman (and was an affectionate nickname for a pistol, among other things) and the choice here is probably spontaneous. Other forms have arisen, notably *heavens to Murgatroyd*, a catchphrase associated with the Hannah-Barbera cartoon lion Snagglepuss created in 1959, although there are claims that this form of the phrase was in use earlier. *19th cent.*

in seventh heaven

in a state of supreme happiness or rapture. The seventh heaven is the outermost of the series of heavens through which souls advanced according to the Muslim and Talmudic cosmologies; on reaching the seventh heaven the spirit achieved the highest state of eternal bliss. *19th cent.*

move heaven and earth

to make exceptional efforts. *18th cent.*

> Richardson Clarissa 1748
> *For, depend upon it, that some of those, who will not stir to protect me living, will move heaven and earth, to avenge me dead!*

> Jane Austen Mansfield Park 1814
> *But I left no stone unturned. I was ready to move heaven and earth to persuade my sister, and at last I did persuade her.*

smell/stink to (high) heaven

to give off a foul odour: often used figuratively of suspicious or untoward situations. *17th cent.*

> Shakespeare Hamlet III.iii.36 (1601)
> [Claudius] *O, my offence is rank! It smells to heaven. | It hath the primal eldest curse upon't, | A brother's murder.*

See also MANNA from heaven.

heavy

heavy on something

using a lot of something. *20th cent.*

> New Musical Express 1992
> *As far as its lyrics are concerned, 'Creep' is a dark, desperate trawl through unrequited obsession, heavy on self-loathing and personal inadequacy; not an easy song to listen to.*

lie/sit heavy on somebody

to oppress or trouble somebody. *16th cent.*

> Shakespeare Richard III v.v.71 (1593)
> [Ghost of Prince Edward to Richard] *Let me sit heavy on thy soul tomorrow, Prince Edward, son to Henry the Sixth.*

make heavy weather of something

to make a great deal of fuss or difficulty about a simple task or activity: a metaphor based on the difficulties experienced by ships and aircraft in rough weather. *Early 20th cent.*

> Ian Hay The First Hundred Thousand 1915
> *The feckless and muddle-headed, making heavy weather of the simplest tasks.*

> Roy Fisher Poems 1988
> *'Did you have sex?' 'Well – sex was had.' 'Oh God.' 'But – ah – very heavy weather was made of it. Climax wasn't reached.'*

See also be heavy GOING.

heck

a heck of a —

an extremely good, bad, or otherwise noteworthy example of its kind: often used as a vague intensifier. *Heck* is a euphemistic form of *hell*, also used as an exclamation. *Mid 20th cent.*

hedge

hedge one's bets

to cover oneself by supporting both sides, allowing for more than one course of action, etc. In betting, to *hedge* (or, in early use, *hedge in*) *a bet* meant to make a compensating bet on another outcome so as to reduce possible losses on an initial bet; from the early 20th cent. *hedging* was also used of balancing financial risks and investments. *17th cent.*

> George Colman *The Jealous Wife* 1761
> [Sir Harry] *It was proposed, You know, to match Me with Miss Harriot – But She can't take kindly / to me. – When one has made a bad Bet, it is best to hedge off, You know – and so I have e'en swopped Her with Lord Trinket here for his brown Horse Nabob, that He bought of Lord Whistle-jacket, for Fifteen hundred Guineas.*

heel

be well heeled

to have plenty of money, to be well off. The phrase may be connected with the quality of a person's shoes, but there are earlier meanings on which it is ultimately based. In cockfighting, the heels were the spurs fitted to the bird to give it extra capability in the fight, and a cock that was well equipped might be described as *well heeled*. A 17th cent. source noted that 'a sharp heel'd cock, though it be a little false, is much better than the truest cock which hath a dull heel'. By the early 19th cent., the expression had been transferred to the American West in the frontier days, where a gunfighter was *heeled* if he was armed, and *well heeled* if he had a good pair of weapons in his holster. From this meaning it is a short step to the notion of the power of money, and we duly arrive at our modern meaning. *19th cent.*

bring somebody to heel

to make somebody obedient or compliant to one's wishes: based on the use of the phrase *to heel* with reference to a dog that follows close behind the person in charge of it (hence *come/bring/walk*, etc *to heel*). *19th cent.*

> Emily Pfeiffer *The Wynnes of Wynhavod* 1882
> [Murdock] *Take them!* [Trying to force the notes upon Carteret.] [Carteret] *Not I.* [Murdock] *Take them I say … The churl! You will not? Then*

here goes. [Hastily rolling the notes in a paper that he takes from his pocket, and casting them from the window. Aside.] *That brings him to heel again.*

cool/kick one's heels

to be waiting impatiently for somebody or something. *17th cent.*

> Thomas Heywood *The Royal King* 1637
> *Or else he may coole his heeles without if his appetite be hot.*

> Henry Fielding *The History of Tom Jones* 1749
> *Mr. Adderly, which was the name of the other ensign, had sat hitherto kicking his heels and humming a tune, without seeming to listen to the discourse.*

down at heel

in a rundown or shabby condition: from the literal meaning of a shoe that is worn down at its heel. *19th cent.*

> Dickens *Little Dorrit* 1857
> *Wherever he went, this foredoomed Tip appeared to take the prison walls with him, and to set them up in such trade or calling; and to prowl about within their narrow limits in the old slip-shod, purposeless, down-at-heel way.*

kick up one's heels

to have a lively or enjoyable time. *19th cent.*

> Trollope *Phineas Finn* 1869
> *My dear Finn, that makes all the difference. When a man has means of his own he can please himself. Do you marry a wife with money, and then you may kick up your heels, and do as you like about the Colonial Office. When a man hasn't money, of course he must fit himself to the circumstances of a profession.*

rock somebody back on their heels

to surprise or disconcert somebody. *Late 20th cent.*

> Michael Aspel *In Good Company* 1989
> *So I signed, and then she said something that rocked me back on my heels. She said, 'There's only two men I'd commit adultery with right off – you and Frankie Vaughan.'*

show a clean pair of heels

to make good one's escape. *19th cent.*

> Scott *Ivanhoe* 1819
> *'Urge me not with violence, Sir Knight,' said the Jester, keeping at a distance from the impatient*

champion, 'or Folly will show a clean pair of heels, and leave Valour to find out his way through the wood as best he may.'

take to one's heels

to run away or escape. In early use the phrase appears in the form now current and also as *take one's heels* (without *to*). Shakespeare uses both forms in plays of roughly contemporary date: the first in *2 Henry VI* (1591) IV.vii.219 'Heavens and honour be witness that no want of resolution in me, but only my followers' base and ignominious treasons, makes me betake me to my heels' and the second in *The Comedy of Errors* (1594) I.ii.94 'What mean you, sir? For God's sake, hold your hands! Nay, an you will not, sir, I'll take my heels.' *16th cent.*

Congreve *Incognita* 1692
The Assailants, finding their unmanly odds defeated, took to their Heels.

turn on one's heels

to turn round sharply or abruptly. *18th cent.*

Henry Fielding *Amelia* 1752
Instead, therefore, of attempting to follow her, he turned on his Heel, and addressed his Discourse to another Lady.

under the heel of somebody/something

controlled or dominated by an oppressive organization or influence. *19th cent.*

Mark Twain *The Adventures of Tom Sawyer* 1876
And now the minister prayed. A good, generous prayer, it was, and went into details: it pleaded for the … State; for the State officers; for the United States … for Congress; for the President; for the officers of the Government … for the oppressed millions groaning under the heel of European monarchies and Oriental despotisms.

See also Achilles' heel at ACHILLES; DIG in one's heels; DRAG one's feet/heels.

hell

all hell broke / was let loose

there was great confusion or uproar. The locus classicus is Milton, *Paradise Lost* (1667) iv.917, where the Archangel Gabriel says to Satan 'Wherefore with thee | Came not all hell broke loose', but the notion is older (see below). *16th cent.*

Robert Greene *A Quip for an Upstart Courtier* 1592
What a ging [= rabble] was here gathered together, no doubt Hell is broke loose.

Dekker & Massinger *The Virgin Martyr* 1622
[Hircius] But will not you be there sir. [Harpax] No, not for hils of diamonds, the grand Master Who schooles her in the Christian discipline, Abhorres my company; should I be there, You'd thinke all hell broke loose, we shall so quarrell.

come hell or high water

regardless of opposition or difficulties: *hell* and *high water* (= high tide) are recorded from the early 20th cent. as stock symbols for dangers and difficulties, and come from the same range of alliterated imagery as *the devil and the deep blue sea*. The phrase is mid 20th cent. in this form.

Joan Beech *One WAAF's War* 1989
Come Hell or high water, the Met observations had to be made every hour, on the hour, and the show must go on.

for the hell of it

informal just for amusement. *Mid 20th cent.*

a — from hell

the very worst or most troublesome example of its kind that one has experienced: commonly used with reference to everyday life, e.g. *neighbours from hell, holidays from hell*, etc. The phrase has achieved wide currency from its use in titles of voyeuristic television programmes on these subjects. *Early 20th cent.*

Guardian 1984
Peterborough Evening Telegraph columnist John Harper-Tee penned a powerful reminiscence last week of the time he saw a newsreel film of the hydrogen bomb explosion on Christmas Island in 1957: 'An oil painting from hell,' he called it in the course of a piece attacking unilateral disarmers.

get the hell out

informal to leave an unpleasant or awkward situation abruptly. *Early 20th cent.*

give somebody / get hell

to give somebody (or to receive) a severe reprimand. *19th cent.*

go to/through hell and back

to suffer an extremely unpleasant experience. *Early 20th cent.*

R H Davis *Ranson's Folly* 1902
*He had been to hell and back again in twenty
minutes.*

Daily Mirror 1992
*And as a not-particularly-modest Squidgey told her
friend in that most revealing of telephone calls, you
have to have been to Hell and back yourself to know
how to behave nicely with the dying.*

go to hell in a handbasket
informal, chiefly NAmer to deteriorate rapidly. The
phrase occurs earlier in the form *go to heaven in a
handbasket*, and another form, *go to heaven in a
wheelbarrow*, is recorded as early as the 1620s. The
present form of the phrase is probably due as
much to alliterative appeal as to any rational
basis. *Mid 20th cent.*

hell for leather
at full speed: a metaphor from horseriding, in
which leather is used for the reins, saddle, etc.
19th cent.

**Barcroft Boake *Where Dead Men Lie and Other
Poems* 1897**
Hear the loud swell of it [cattle being rounded
up], *mighty pell-mell of it! | Thousands of voices
all blent into one: | See 'hell for leather' now
trooping together, now | Down the long slope of the
range at a run!*

a/one hell of a —
an extremely good, bad, or otherwise noteworthy
example of its kind: also (from early 20th cent.) in
the form *helluva*. *18th cent.*

George Colman Ygr *Ways and Means* 1788
[Sir David] *But let's in, and … quite delight my
Lady with the news: she'll be in a hell of a pucker* [=
a state of agitation]. *A fine fuss with preparations
to-morrow, I warrant: up to the neck in beef, gowns,
ducks, jewels, ribbons, and puff pastry.*

hell on wheels
1 a very unpleasant place. *19th cent.*
2 something or somebody very special. *Mid 20th
cent.*

John Steinbeck *The Grapes of Wrath* 1939
*Her chin shot out. She jumped to her feet. 'You git
away from me, Al Joad. I don' wanta see you no
more.' 'Aw, come on. What's the matter?' 'You
think you're jus' – hell on wheels.' 'Now wait a
minute.' 'You think I got to go out with you. Well, I
don't! I got lots of chances.'*

hell's half acre
NAmer, informal an unpleasant or disreputable
place or region. *19th cent.*

Will Carleton *Farm Festivals* 1881
*O you law-bamboozled fools! You old self-ground
devil's-tools! Do you know you're sowin' ruin out
o' hell's half-acre lot?*

hell to pay
a warning of serious trouble to come. There are
references from the 18th cent. to paying a debt to
hell, and these are essentially variants of the
notion of paying the devil (*see* the DEVIL to
pay). For example, George Huddesford's satirical
poem *Warley* (1778) includes the following lines:
'See the Devil intercepting, | Tries to knock him
off his Steed; | Honest Paul in time has stepp'd
in, | Here's old Hell to pay indeed!'

Edward Thomson *Mary Armistead* 1865
*When daylight comes, there'll be red hell to pay |
For every plank that spans that trifling bridge.*

not a hope/chance in hell
no hope or chance at all: also *not a snowball's
chance in hell*. *Early 20th cent.*

play (merry) hell with something
informal to cause great disruption or damage. *18th
cent.*

H H Brackenridge *Modern Chivalry* 1792
*Hang the devil, said Roderick. I am not afraid of the
devil; I could kick him, and cuff him, and play hell
with him.*

raise hell
to cause trouble or a disturbance. *19th cent.*

Clyde Fitch *The City* 1909
[Hannock] *I guess you realize just as plain as I do
that those very methods in New York, that have
been raising hell with the insurance companies and
all sorts of corporations, aren't a patch on some of
your deals I know of!*

till/until hell freezes over
for ever, or for a very long time. *Early 20th cent.*

William Vaughn Moody *The Great Divide* 1906
[Dutch] *What's eatin' you? She ain't yours yet,
and I guess she won't be, not till hell freezes over.*

hello
See a GOLDEN hello.

help

God helps those who help themselves

(proverb) people who try hard are likely to succeed: the notion of divine approval for those who make their own efforts dates back to classical writers, and appears in French in the form *aidez vous, Dieu vous aidera* (= help yourself, [then] God will help you). *16th cent.*

help the police with their enquiries

to be interviewed by the police as a suspect: a coy euphemism, sometimes shortened to *help the police*. *Mid 20th cent.*

so help me God

used to show that one is sincere and determined: with allusion to the judicial oath taken by witnesses in a lawcourt to 'tell the truth, the whole truth, and nothing but the truth, so help me God': the phrase appears earlier in the form *as God help me* and in other forms. *Middle English*

Chaucer *The Book of the Duchess* (line 550)
But certes, sire, yif that yee | Wolde ought discure [= reveal] *me youre woo* [= woe], *| I wolde, as wys* [= wise] *God helpe me soo, | Amende hyt* [= relieve it], *yif I kan or may.*

Thomas Preston *The Life of Cambises, King of Percia* c1569
Cambises put a Judge to death, that was a good deed: | But to kil the yung Childe was worse to proceed. | To murder his Brother, and then his owne wife: | So help me God and holidom, it is pitie of his life.

hen

(as) rare/scarce as hen's teeth

extremely rare or scarce, since hens do not have teeth. *19th cent.*

Herman Melville *Moby Dick* 1851
'Why, thou monkey,' said a harpooneer to one of these lads, 'we've been cruising now hard upon three years, and thou hast not raised a whale yet. Whales are scarce as hen's teeth whenever thou art up here.'

like a hen with one chicken

fussing over a trivial or unimportant matter. *16th cent.*

John Cleland *Memoirs of a Woman of Pleasure* 1748
These desertions had, however, now so far thinn'd Mrs. Cole's cluck [= clutch], *that she was left with only me, like a hen with one chicken.*

her

her indoors

informal one's wife or girlfriend. The phrase achieved wide currency from its use in the 1980s television series *Minder*, in which the principal character Arthur Daley regularly used this expression to refer to his wife. It was also a jocular tag for Margaret Thatcher when Prime Minister, used by (or put into the mouths of) Cabinet colleagues. *Late 20th cent.*

Guardian 1989
Intrepid Peter Bottomley, former scourge of the dozy British motorist, has not abandoned his life's work just because Her Indoors shunted him from Transport to Northern Ireland.

here

here's one I made earlier

a line made familiar by children's television programmes, especially (from the 1960s) the BBC's *Blue Peter*, in which viewers are shown how to make an object, typically something highly practical using simple household materials, and are finally shown a completed version made in advance. *Late 20th cent.*

here, there, and everywhere

in all directions or places; scattered about. *16th cent.*

Marlowe *Dr Faustus* iv.64 (1590)
If you turn me into anything, let it be in the likeness of a little, pretty, frisking flea, that I may be here and there and everywhere.

here today, gone tomorrow

used to signify a temporary or short-lived occurrence or phenomenon: also (with hyphens) as a qualifying phrase, as in *a here-today-gone-tomorrow celebrity*. *17th cent.*

Mrs Gaskell *Letter* 1838
We are 'here today, & gone tomorrow', as the fat scullion maid said in some extract in Holland's Exercise book.

See also here's looking at you *at* LOOK; here's MUD in your eye.

hero

See go from ZERO to hero.

Herod

out-Herod Herod

to act with great cruelty. The phrase is derived from a line in Shakespeare's *Hamlet* (1601), where Hamlet instructs the players (III.ii.15) 'I would have such a fellow whipped for o'erdoing Termagant. It out-Herods Herod. Pray you avoid it.' Herod was the King of Judaea at the time of the birth of Christ, and ordered the Massacre of the Innocents (boy babies); he was depicted in early miracle plays as a stock figure of a tyrant. 17th cent. uses typically refer directly to Herod; allusive uses in freer contexts become common from the 18th cent.

> Smollett *The Adventures of Peregrine Pickle* 1751
> *Peregrine having eyed the critick some minutes, I fancy (said he) your praise must be ironical, because, in the very two situations you mention, I think I have seen that player out-herod Herod, or, in other words, exceed all his other extravagances.*

herring

See a RED herring.

hewer

hewers of wood and drawers of water

labourers and drudges. The phrase alludes to Joshua 9:21 (in the Authorized Version of 1611) 'And the princes said unto them, Let them live; but let them be hewers of wood and drawers of water unto all the congregation; as the princes had promised them', and it occurs in the 16th cent. in Coverdale's translation of the Bible.

> Smollett *The Adventures of Peregrine Pickle* 1751
> *There are some hewers of wood and drawers of water in this microcosm, who have had forests and fishponds of their own.*

> Charlotte Brontë *Jane Eyre* 1847
> *You hear now how I contradict myself. I, who preached contentment with a humble lot, and justified the vocation even of hewers of wood and*

drawers of water in God's service – I, His ordained minister, almost rave in my restlessness.

hide[1] (verb)

See a hidden AGENDA; hide one's light under a BUSHEL; hide the SALAMI.

hide[2] (noun)

neither hide nor hair

not the least vestige or trace. The words refer to the natural covering of an animal. *Middle English*

hiding

on a hiding to nothing

engaged in an activity that can only end in failure, or in which any outcome will be unfavourable. A *hiding* is a thrashing (on the 'hide'): so the odds reflected in this phrase are at best no gain at all and at worst a beating. *Early 20th cent.*

> A M Binstead *Mop Fair* 1905
> *They will, like the man who was on a hiding to nothing the first time Tom Sayers saw him, 'take it lying down'.*

high

(as) high as a kite

informal, chiefly NAmer extremely drunk or drugged. *High* in the meaning 'intoxicated' dates from the 17th cent., and this phrase from the mid 20th cent.

be for the high jump

to be about to receive a severe reprimand or punishment. Originally used in services' slang of somebody about to be brought before a superior officer on a charge. Fraser and Gibbons in *Soldier and Sailor Words* (1925) records that *high jump* was 'a term used of a man entered on a "Crime sheet", and for trial for a military offence; the suggestion being that the accused would need to jump very high to get over the trouble'. *High jump* also refers to death by hanging. *Early 20th cent.*

high and dry

in a helpless or abandoned situation; lacking resources: originally with reference to ships stranded out of the water. *19th cent.*

Dickens *Martin Chuzzlewit* 1844

'Jest as I'm beginning to come out ... my master deceives me.' 'Deceives you!' cried Tom. 'Swindles me,' retorted Mr. Tapley ... 'Turns his back on ev'ry thing as made his service a creditable one, and leaves me, high and dry, without a leg to stand upon.'

high and low

1 all people of whatever rank. *Middle English*

Chaucer *The Romaunt of the Rose* (line 1252)

And next that daunced [= danced] Curtesye, | That preised [= praised] was of lowe and hye, | For neither proud ne fool was she.

Shakespeare *The Merry Wives of Windsor* II.i.108 (1597)

[Pistol to Ford] He woos both high and low, both rich and poor, | Both young and old, one with another, Ford.

2 everywhere, in every place; in all ways (the meaning in Chaucer below). *Middle English*

Chaucer *Prologue* (line 816)

And that he wolde been oure governour, ... | And we wol reuled been at his devys [at his will] | In heigh and lough.

Head & Kirkman *The English Rogue Described* 1674

Look then further, said mine Host; the Tapster did so, but neither high nor low could he finde this Cup.

high and mighty

arrogant or self-important: originally used in neutral senses to denote high rank, and as an epithet of the Lord in the Book of Common Prayer (1559). *19th cent.*

Jane Austen *Emma* 1816

She was nobody when he married her, barely the daughter of a gentleman; but ever since her being turned into a Churchill she has out-Churchill'd them all in high and mighty claims: but in herself, I assure you, she is an upstart.

high days and holidays

important or special occasions. In the Church calendar, *high days* were important festivals and *holidays* (later distinguished from the secular meaning as *holy days*) were feast days of lesser importance. There is a notable use by Matthew Arnold in *Essays in Criticism* (1865): 'Here, the summer has, even on its highdays and holidays, something mournful.' But he did not invent the phrase (see below). *19th cent.*

Robert Surtees *Handley Cross* 1843

Captain Widowfield was a stout big fellow, as bulky as Jorrocks, and much taller, and being proud of his leg, was wont to adorn his lower man in shorts on high days and holidays.

high jinks

boisterous fun, a lively time. The origins of the phrase lie in various games of fun and chance involving the throwing of dice. Sir Walter Scott in *Guy Mannering* (1815) gives us a description of 'the ancient and now forgotten pastime of High Jinks': 'This game was played in several different ways. Most frequently the dice were thrown by the company, and those upon whom the lot fell were obliged to assume and maintain, for a time, a certain fictitious character, or to repeat a certain number of fescennine [= lewd] verses in a particular order. If they departed from the characters assigned, or if their memory proved treacherous in the repetition, they incurred forfeits, which were either compounded for by swallowing an additional bumper, or by paying a small sum towards the reckoning.' Scott uses the phrase again in his introduction to *Ivanhoe* (1819), where he describes a bout of serious drinking in which the participants take turns determined by 'a species of High Jinks, as it were ... as toasts were given in latter times'. Most of the evidence for this meaning is Scottish, but a similar game features in Thomas Hughes' *Tom Brown's Schooldays* (1857), in an episode where Tom is said to have 'found the eleven at high jinks after supper, Jack Raggles shouting comic songs, and performing feats of strength'. The name occurs in other 19th cent. literature and goes back to the late 17th cent. or earlier, being entered in the *New Dictionary of the Canting Crew*, which was published in the 1690s. There is a obscure use, which antedates any other published usage, in a 17th cent. poetical source, James Scudamore's *Mock Poem upon the Ninth Book of Homer's Odyssey* (in a collection called *Homer à la Mode*): 'Now having thus contriv'd the Plot, | I bad Companions choose by Lot, | (High-jinks, or Fillup) who should be | My Aiders in this Tragedy.' Here, *high jinks* and *fillup* are evidently forms of choice by lot, fitting in with the original gaming meaning of the term. A related sense, referring to a gambler at dice who won by making his opponent drunk, is listed in Francis Grose's *Classical Dictionary of the Vulgar Tongue* (1785). The natural transition to the present more generalized meaning developed during the later part of the 19th cent. In *Tom Brown at Oxford*, Thomas Hughes' 1861 sequel to the *Schooldays*, we hear that 'all sorts of high jinks go on on the grass plot'. *Jinks* is the plural of *jink*, a word originally meaning 'a quick turn that eludes an opponent or pursuer'; to *give the jink* meant to escape in this way, as in Burns' lines *On a Scotch Bard Gone to the West Indies* (1786): 'Come, mourn wi' me! | Our billie's gien us a' a jink, | An' owre the sea!' *19th cent.*

> Somerville & Ross *The Real Charlotte* 1894
> 'Great high jinks they're having upstairs!' she remarked, as the windows and tea-cups rattled from the stamping overhead, and Mr. Beattie cast many an anxious eye towards the ceiling. 'I suppose my young lady's in the thick of it, whatever it is!' ... Mr Lynch was on the point of replying in an appropriate tone of humorous condolence, when the young lady herself appeared on Mr. Corkran's arm, with an expression that at once struck Charlotte as being very unlike high jinks.

a high old time

a highly enjoyable time or experience. *19th cent.*

> Somerville & Ross *The Real Charlotte* 1894
> She was not given to introspection, and could not have said anything in the least interesting about her mental or moral atmosphere ... but she was quite certain ... that ... she was beginning to have what she defined to herself as 'a high old time'.

> Joseph Conrad *Lord Jim* 1900
> I couldn't discover what became of all the trade-goods; there was nothing in the store but rats, having a high old time amongst a litter of brown paper and old sacking.

high, wide, and handsome

informal carefree or flamboyant: associated with an American cowboys' cry at rodeos, 'Ride him, cowboy, high, wide, and handsome'. *Early 20th cent.*

hit the high spots

informal to enjoy city life and its entertainments. *Early 20th cent.*

> Josephine Tey *A Shilling for Candles* 1936
> Two years of hitting the high spots must have educated you to something.

on a high

informal in a state of ecstasy or euphoria, especially one produced by drugs. The noun *high* in this sense dates from the 1950s. *20th cent.*

> Mary Scott *Nudists May Be Encountered* 1991
> Roy concluded, 'Need to have it ratified by the Board. But you can take it as read that you have the contract.' Gillian returned to her office on a high.

on one's high horse

behaving or speaking imperiously or disdainfully: originally in the form *mount/ride the high horse*, i.e. to look down superciliously on others from the height that a large horse offers. *18th cent.*

> Richard Cumberland *The Box-Lobby Challenge* 1794
> You would not trust to my honor, but catching at the very first word blabb'd out by a silly gossip, started forth on your high horse of heroics, and meant to crush me at once in the true tragedy stile of blank verse and revenge.

See also in fine/high FEATHER; RUN high.

hike

take a hike

informal, chiefly NAmer to leave; to go away: usually as an instruction to somebody who is annoying or unwelcome. *20th cent.*

> Hot Press 1990
> Systems topple, statues walk, long-serving political incumbents take a hike in a huge global shake-up.

hill

(as) old/ancient as the hills

extremely old. The phrase is perhaps associated with the biblical passage at Job 15:7 'Art thou the first man that was born? or wast thou made before the hills?' *18th cent.*

> Coleridge *Kubla Khan* 1797
> And there were gardens bright with sinuous rills, | Where blossomed many an incense-bearing tree; | And here were forests ancient as the hills, | Enfolding sunny spots of greenery.

> Susan Ferrier *Marriage* 1818
> Miss Nicky wondered what was to become of the christening cake she had ordered from Perth; it might be as old as the hills before there would be another child born amongst them.

over the hill
informal, originally NAmer past one's prime; too old, especially for a particular activity, job, etc. *Mid 20th cent.*

> Independent 2002
> *Job seekers in their 40s are increasingly excluded from work because employers regard them as 'over the hill', a report warns today.*

up hill and down dale
encountering many obstacles or difficulties during the course of an activity or enterprise. *19th cent.*

> Robert Browning The Ring and the Book 1842
> *So we went prancing up hill and down dale, | In and out of the level and the straight.*

See also a hill of beans *at* BEAN.

hilt

to the hilt
completely. The image is of a knife plunged in so deep that only the hilt or handle can be seen. *17th cent.*

hind

on one's hind legs
standing up, especially in order to speak at a meeting: a humorous extension of the phrase *on one's legs* in the same meaning, which dates from the 17th cent. *19th cent.*

> T W H Crosland Outlook Odes 1902
> *You would like to stand on your hind legs | And address the House on large matters.*

> Nigel Williams The Wimbledon Poisoner 1990
> *The kind of dentist like David Sprott who wasn't afraid to get up on his hind legs at a social gathering and talk, seriously and at length, about teeth.*

See also talk the hind leg(s) off a DONKEY.

hint
See DROP a hint.

hip

shoot from the hip
to react impulsively or aggressively, without much thought or consideration: from the action of a gunfighter in stories of the American West who shoots at an opponent with the gun still in its holster. *20th cent.*

> Louis MacNeice Autumn Journal 1939
> *And reading romances we longed to be grown up, | To shoot from the hip and marry lovely ladies | And smoke cigars and live on claret cup | And lie in bed in the morning.*

hire

hire and fire
informal to take on and dismiss staff: used especially in the context of unstable or fluctuating levels of employment in an organization. *Mid 20th cent.*

> Guardian 1989
> *Allan Martin, sacked as coach to Aberavon's forwards this week, believes that Welsh rugby is becoming too much like football with the current spate of hiring and firing based on league results.*

history

be history
informal, originally NAmer to be in the past and irrelevant; to have no future. *Mid 20th cent.*

make history
to influence the course of events decisively; to be a leading figure in a course of events. *19th cent.*

the rest is history
what follows the events described is already well known; no more need be said. *19th cent.*

> Science 1901
> *Rowland was sent to Europe to study laboratories and purchase apparatus, and the rest is history.*

> Daily Mirror 1992
> *Julie met 36-year-old Grant in a wine bar. She invited him home for a coffee and he set about trying to find out what was wrong with her washing machine. She noticed that he had a cute bum – and the rest is history.*

hit

hit and miss
lacking method or consistency; haphazard: *cf* hit or miss *below. 19th cent.*

Theodore Winthrop *Edwin Brothertoft* 1862
*Major Skerrett departed on his mission. He left
head-quarters a few days before that hit-and-miss
battle of Germantown.*

hit-and-run
originally NAmer used of a traffic incident, or the
driver involved in it, in which a person is hit and
injured and the driver leaves the scene to avoid
responsibility. *Early 20th cent.*

hit somebody in the eye / between the eyes
to make a vivid impact or impression. The phrase
plays on two meanings of the verb *hit*: the physical sense to do with a blow or shot, and the
metaphorical sense 'to affect deeply'. *Early 20th
cent.*

Rachel Crothers *He and She* 1912
*And I'm going to tell you the truth – just as I see it.
If it's good, all right; if it's bad, all right. I'm going
to hit hard – right between the eyes – and I expect
you to take it – like a man.*

hit it off
(said of two people) to like each other, to establish a rapid rapport. *Hit it* is recorded in the same
sense from the mid 17th cent., and the intensifying adverb *off* is added towards the end of the
18th cent., when the meaning tended to be 'to be
successful, to hit the mark' in more general
senses. The current meaning developed in the
early 19th cent.

Fanny Burney *The Wanderer* 1814
*Faith, Madam, I had less to do with her than any of
them. The Demoiselle and I did not hit it off together
at all. I could never get her to speak for the life of me.*

hit or miss
whether one is successful or not; at random: *cf* hit
and miss *above*. *16th cent.*

Shakespeare *Troilus and Cressida* I.iii.377 (1602)
*But hit or miss, | Our project's life this shape of
sense assumes: | Ajax employed plucks down
Achilles' plumes.*

hit the road/trail
informal to set out on a trip: *hit* is recorded in the
informal meaning 'to reach (a place)' from the
16th cent. *Early 20th cent.*

Jack London *Scorn of Women* 1906
*I've got to hit the trail to-night, right away. And
I've got to get my trail clothes. That bearskin
overcoat's too warm. Can't travel in it.*

See also go through / the ROOF; (hit somebody)
below the BELT; hit the BOTTLE; hit the DECK; hit
somebody for SIX; hit the GROUND running; hit
the HAY; hit the headlines *at* HEADLINE; hit HOME;
hit the JACKPOT; hit the MARK; hit the NAIL on the
head; hit the PANIC button; hit/touch rock bottom *at* ROCK[1]; hit the SACK; hit the SPOT; hit the
wrong NOTE.

hitch

hitch one's wagon to a star
to advance one's ambitions by associating oneself
with somebody more successful or powerful:
first used by the American writer Ralph Waldo
Emerson in an essay published in the collection
Society and Solitude (1870). *19th cent.*

hob

play/raise hob
informal, chiefly NAmer to cause great mischief:
hob is a word for an elf or sprite, and *Hob* is a
name for the devil. *19th cent.*

Anne Royall *The Tennessean* 1827
*The orders said how one Bonnypart was married to
his cousin, and that he would make war upon the
country, and pull an old house over their heads, and
play hob, and be the ruination of us all.*

Mary Jane Holmes *Hugh Worthington* 1865
*'Them old maids will raise hob with the boy – nice
little shaver,' thought the kind hearted Jim.*

Hobson

Hobson's choice
1 the choice of taking what is offered, i.e. no
choice at all: with allusion to Thomas Hobson,
an early 17th cent. Cambridge carrier who
insisted on letting his horses out in strict rotation.
17th cent.

Colley Cibber *The Non-Juror* 1718
[Maria] *Can any Woman think herself happy,
that's oblig'd to marry only with a Hobson's
Choice?*

J S Mill *The Subjection of Women* 1869
*Those who attempt to force women into marriage by
closing all other doors against them, lay themselves
open to a similar retort ... It is not a sign of one's*

*thinking the boon one offers very attractive, when
one allows only Hobson's choice, 'that or none'.*
2 *informal* (shortened to *Hobson's*) rhyming slang
for 'voice'. *20th cent.*

hock

in hock (to somebody)

in debt or thrall to another person. From the
literal meaning of roughly the same date: an
object *in hock* is one that has been pawned.
Hock is derived from a Dutch word *hok* meaning
'prison'; the word occurs in English only in the
phrase, where it originally retained the Dutch
meaning. *19th cent.*

> George Henry Jessop *Sam'l of Posen* 1881
> *Philadelphia, June 1, 1854. Mrs. Dalton, In reply to
> your favor, will say that I am pleased to give you the
> loan you ask for, but must ask you to call on me.
> Yours in hock, Isaac Goldstein.*

hog

go the whole hog

informal to do something thoroughly or to its
completion, without reserve or compromise: of
uncertain origin. There are several anecdotal
associations. William Cowper in *The Love of the
World, or Hypocrisy Detected* (1779) told a story
about Muslim divines who supposed that when
Muhammad forbade the eating of a hog he had a
particular part of the animal in mind. Since they
could not know which part of the hog this was,
they felt justified in sharing the hog, i.e. eating the
whole hog, each person taking refuge in the
thought that the part he ate was not the part in
question: 'But for one piece they thought it hard |
From the whole hog to be debarred.' Other, more
straightforward, explanations exist: for example,
butchers in Virginia sold a whole hog more
cheaply than individual cuts, and so 'going the
whole hog' was an attractive proposition. *19th
cent.*

> James Kirke Paulding *Westward Ho!* 1832
> *They gathered together and built the colonel a
> house, but it was a sad falling off from the other;
> being simply constructed of logs, after the manner
> of a primitive settlement; where, there being no
> sawmills, the only resource is to take the whole tree,
> or 'go the whole hog', as they say in 'Old Kentuck'.*

hog the limelight

to seek exclusive attention: originally a theatrical
expression with reference to actors who wanted
major parts. A *limelight* was a stage spotlight, so
called (from the 1820s) because the light was
produced by directing a white flame against a
block of lime; the word has been used figuratively since the mid 19th cent. *Mid 20th cent.*

> *Daily Telegraph* 1992
> *Mr Patten … is brimming with ideas, but in the
> past has been accused of hogging the limelight. A
> Guardian profile said he had 'shown devotion
> beyond the call of duty to self-publicity'.*

hoist

See be hoist with/by one's own PETARD.

hold

hold something against somebody

to let some aspect of a person's past behaviour, or
one of their past deeds, influence one's opinion of
them adversely. *20th cent.*

> Barbara Pym *A Glass of Blessings* 1958
> *At thirty-five he had had too many jobs and his early
> brilliance seemed to have come to nothing. It was
> also held against him that he had not yet married.*

hold court

to be the main object of attention in a gathering of
people: from the central position of the monarch
in a royal court or household. *19th cent.*

> R L Stevenson *Kidnapped* 1886
> *I sat in a dream all morning, only disturbed by the
> passing by of Cluny's scouts and servants coming
> with provisions and reports; for as the coast was at
> that time clear, you might almost say he held court
> openly.*

hold hard

a warning to stop or ease up: originally an
instruction to a rider to pull on the reins to
bring the horse to a stop. *18th cent.*

> George Colman *The Jealous Wife* 1761
> *[Sir Harry] Hold hard! You are all on a wrong
> scent … [Russet] Well! what now? [Sir Harry] It
> was proposed, You know, to match me with Miss
> Harriot – But She can't take kindly to me… and so I
> have e'en swopped her with Lord Trinket here for his
> brown horse Nabob … [Russet] Swopped Her?*

Swopped my daughter for a horse? Zounds, Sir, what d'ye mean?

Dickens *David Copperfield* 1850
'When I was quite a young boy,' said Uriah, 'I got to know what umbleness did, and I took to it. I ate umble pie with an appetite. I stopped at the umble point of my learning, and says I, "Hold hard!" When you offered to teach me Latin, I knew better. "People like to be above you," says father, "keep yourself down." '

hold one's horses
to restrain one's enthusiasm or temper: often used in the imperative. *19th cent.*

Matthews & Jessop *A Gold Mine* 1887
[Mrs Meredith] *I know why you sold your mine. I know to whom you sold it, and the price he paid – the shamefully inadequate price. I would like to apologize for my brother, if I knew how to do it, but – [Woolcot] Stop! Hold your horses! Don't say a word about him! He drove a hard bargain, but – he did more than his bond called for – he's given me a situation.*

hold the line
1 to resist pressure in a difficult situation. The meaning here seems to be derived from the use in team sports, American football in particular, in which *line* is the limit of the field of play; but the phrase is probably influenced by the military sense of a group of soldiers holding their positions when under attack. *19th cent.*

Caroline M Kirkland *Dahcotah* 1849
I left my child in her canoe, and paddled with the others to the shore. As we left her, she turned her eyes towards us, as if anxious to know what we were about to do. The men held the line steadily, and the canoe floated so gently that I began to feel less anxious.

2 (said of or to a telephone caller) to wait during a pause, with the connection open. *Early 20th cent.*

Lewis Orlando Faulkland *Long Distance* 1914
Hullo! Who's this? Frohman's? Well, can you tell me the present whereabouts of a Mrs. J. S. Wright, who was with the Frohman company that played the Prisoner of Zenda at Chicago two years ago? Yes, I'll hold the line. (Under his breath.) You bet your life I will. Hullo! She left the stage in January, 1903, and – What's that?

Daily Telegraph 1992
Now that Nicholas Soames has access to a ministerial Montego, what will happen to Sutton, his old chauffeur? According to Soames's sister, Emma, the admirable Sutton would answer Soames's car phone in the manner of a country butler, asking callers to hold the line while he saw if Sir was in.

hold one's tongue
to remain silent, despite wanting or needing to speak. *Middle English* (in Langland and Gower)

John Hopkins *The Psalms of David* 1562
I held my tonge and spake no word, but kept me close and still, | Yea from good tallke I did refrayne, but sore against my will.

Shakespeare *Macbeth* II.iii.119 (1606)
Why do we hold our tongues, | That most may claim this argument for ours?

hold water
(said of an argument or proposition) to be cogent or convincing. The image is of logic contained in the way that liquid is held in a vessel without leaking, and the phrase is often used with punning allusion (as in the quotation below). *17th cent.*

Dryden *The Wild Gallant* 1669
[Loveby] *I'll tell you Madam, it has upon it a very fair Manor house; from one side you have in prospect an hanging Garden ... In the midst of it you have a Fountain ...* [Constance] *But where lies this Paradise?* [Loveby] *Pox on't; I am thinking to sell it, it has such a villanous unpleasant name; it would have sounded so harsh in a Ladies ear. But for the Fountain, Madam.* [Constance] *The Fountain's a poor excuse, it will not hold water; come the name, the name.*

there is no holding —
so-and-so is determined to act with energy or urgency. *Mid 20th cent.*

P G Wodehouse *Full Moon* 1947
Look at Henry the Eighth ... And Solomon. Once they started marrying, there was no holding them – you just sat back and watched their smoke.

(with) no holds barred
without any restrictions being imposed: from the use in wrestling to denote a contest in which the normal rules are relaxed. The phrase first appears in print in Berrey's and Van den Bark's *American Thesaurus of Slang* (1942). *Mid 20th cent.*

The Times 1958
No holds were barred, so to speak, for the Prince's unorthodox education and his own reputedly emancipated views allowed almost every hypothesis.

See also carry / hold / be left holding the BABY; don't hold your BREATH; get hold of the WRONG end of the stick; hold the CLOCK on; hold the FIELD; hold the FORT; hold one's GROUND; hold somebody's HAND; hold one's NOSE; hold one's OWN; hold one's PEACE; hold the STAGE; hold one's thumbs *at* THUMB; hold somebody/something to RANSOM; hold up one's HEAD; keep/hold somebody/something at BAY.

---

hole

blow a hole in something
to spoil or wreck (a theory or scheme). *20th cent.*

Guardian 1989
My own choice for the single most influential factor would be the decision of the Hungarian Government to subordinate its very clear obligations under an agreement with the GDR to its general duty under the Helsinki Final Act of 1975 – a decision which blew a hole in the sealed frontiers of the GDR, and relegated to the past the comfortable slogans of the last three decades.

a hole in the head
used as a self-evident example of something totally unwanted and to be avoided at all costs: typically in the phrase *need — like a hole in the head. Mid 20th cent.*

J D Salinger *Catcher in the Rye* 1951
Take the Disciples for instance … They were all right after Jesus was dead and all, but while He was alive, they were about as much use to Him as a hole in the head.

a hole in the wall
1 *informal* a small and cramped room or apartment: formerly (in American and British use) with the specific meaning of a place where liquor was sold illegally. Also used (with hyphens) to describe a small-scale business or operation. *19th cent.*

Hazlitt *On the Aristocracy of Letters* 1822
Few persons would pretend to deny that Porson had more Greek than they. It was a question of fact which might be put to the immediate proof, and

could not be gainsaid. But the meanest frequenter of the Cider-cellar or the Hole in the Wall would be inclined, in his own conceit, to dispute the palm of wit or sense with him.

2 *informal* a cash machine built into the wall of a building. *Late 20th cent.*

Guardian 1985
For these transactions it is still necessary to potter down to the nearest hole in the wall or send money by post to be put into your account.

in a hole
in difficulties, especially financial. *19th cent.*

R L Stevenson *New Arabian Nights* 1882
'Show me my signature! Where is my signature?' That was just the question; where was his signature? Leon recognised that he was in a hole.

in the hole
NAmer, informal in debt. *19th cent.*

William C De Mille *Strongheart* 1905
[Thorne] *He'll be six thousand dollars in the hole and as he can't get it, he'll have to leave college.*

Guitarist 1992
With costs like this, even if you take a few days off you're a million quid in the hole!

make a hole in something
to use up a lot of money, resources, etc: *cf* make a DENT in something. *17th cent.*

pick holes in something
to criticize something. *Hole* in the meaning 'flaw or weakness' dates from the 16th cent., and the original form of the phrase appears to be *pick holes in a person's coat. 17th cent.*

Bunyan *The Pilgrim's Progress* 1678
After that they grow cold to public duty, as hearing, reading, godly conference, and the like … Then they begin to pick holes, as we say, in the coats of some of the godly.

Dickens *A Christmas Carol* 1843
Why then, don't stand staring as if you was afraid, woman; who's the wiser? We're not going to pick holes in each other's coats, I suppose?

Virginia Woolf *The Voyage Out* 1915
If I may pick holes in your philosophy, Miss Vinrace, which has its merits, I would point out that a human being is not a set of compartments, but an organism.

See also BURN a hole in one's pocket; a square PEG in a round hole.

holiday

a Roman holiday

enjoyment derived from the suffering of others: with allusion to Byron's description in *Childe Harold's Pilgrimage* (1818) of a gladiator dying in the Roman arena (iv.cxli): 'He reck'd not of the life he lost nor prize, | But where his rude hut by the Danube lay, | There were his young barbarians all at play, | There was their Dacian mother – he, their sire, | Butcher'd to make a Roman holiday.' *19th cent.*

Henry James Daisy Miller 1882
[Reverdy] *You can see very well from this balcony, if you won't go down into the street.* [Mrs Costello] *Down into the street – to be trampled to death? I have no desire to be butchered to make a Roman holiday.*

Edgar Rice Burroughs At the Earth's Core 1914
A short distance before us rose a few low, rocky hills. Toward these our captors urged us, and after a short time led us through a narrow pass into a tiny, circular valley. Here they got down to work, and we were soon convinced that if we were not to die to make a Roman holiday, we were to die for some other purpose.

hollow

The origin of *hollow* as an adverb, as in the first phrase, is obscure. It first occurs in the sense 'with a hollow voice' in the early 17th cent. (e.g. Shakespeare, *Twelfth Night* (1602) III.iv.101 '[Maria] Lo, how hollow the fiend speaks within him [= Malvolio]'), and in its intensifying meaning in the late 17th cent. Its use as an adverb is now confined to the phrases or their variants. The noun is the oldest use of the word, dating from Old English.

beat somebody hollow

to defeat or surpass somebody comprehensively. *18th cent.*

Fanny Burney Evelina 1778
'It would very agreeably remind me of past times,' said she, 'when bowing was in fashion, if the bet was to depend upon the best-made bow.' 'Egad, my Lord!' cried Mr. Coverley, 'there I should beat you hollow, for your Lordship never bows at all.'

in the hollow of one's hand

completely in one's power: *cf* Isaiah 40:12 (in the Authorized Version of 1611) 'Who hath measured the waters in the hollow of his hand, and meted out heaven with the span, and comprehended the dust of the earth in a measure, and weighed the mountains in scales, and the hills in a balance?' *17th cent.*

William Cowper Expostulation a1800
Stand now and judge thyself. – Hast thou incurr'd | His anger who can waste thee with a word, | Who poises and proportions sea and land, | Weighing them in the hollow of his hand.

Hardy The Return of the Native 1878
Eustacia, you have held my happiness in the hollow of your hand, and like a devil you have dashed it down!

ring hollow

to sound false or insincere: with reference to the sound of struck metal. *17th cent.*

Ben Jonson Catiline His Conspiracy 1611
[Cato] *Yet, Marcus Tullius, doe not I beleeve, But Crassus, and this Caesar here ring hollow.* [Cicero] *And would appeare so, if that we durst prove 'hem.*

holy

holier than thou

self-righteously or sanctimoniously virtuous, or professing to be so. *Cf* Isaiah 65:5 (in the Authorized Version of 1611): 'Stand by thyself, come not near to me; for I am holier than thou.' *19th cent.*

Scott Poetical Works a1832
Nay, hear me, brother – I am elder, wiser, | And holier than thou; and age, and wisdom, | And holiness, have peremptory claims, | And will be listen'd to.

Nathaniel Parker Willis Saratoga 1847
The next instance comes from the very heart of holier-than-thou-dom – the exemplary state of Maine.

holy of holies

a specially sacred or sacrosanct place: originally the inner sanctuary of the Jewish temple (*cf* Exodus 26:34 (Wyclif) 'The parti of the tabernacle that is clepid holi of halowes'), and then by extension the inner part of other temples and Christian churches. The phrase is 17th cent. in allusive use.

home

As an adverb *home* used to have a freer role in its meaning 'so as to affect one closely or intimately'; for example in Shakespeare's *Cymbeline* (1610) iii.v.92, Cloten asks Pisanio about Cymbeline's daughter Innogen with the words 'Where is she sir? Come nearer. | No farther halting. Satisfy me home | What is become of her.' This meaning is now largely confined to set phrases.

bring something home to somebody
to make somebody realize the significance or full implications of something. *19th cent.*

> George Meredith *The Ordeal of Richard Feverel* 1859
> *She could make you forget she was a woman, and then bring the fact startlingly home to you. She could read men with one quiver of her half-closed eyelashes.*

close/near to home
(said of a remark, joke, etc) so apposite or direct as to cause embarrassment or offence: *cf* close to / near the BONE. *20th cent.*

come home to somebody
to strike somebody emotionally or intellectually; to reach its mark; to produce a salutary realization in somebody. *18th cent.*

> Fanny Burney *Cecilia* 1782
> *This was an argument that came home to Cecilia, whose deliberation upon it, though silent, was evidently not unfavourable.*

drive/hammer/press/ram something home
to make something understood by constantly repeating it. *18th cent.*

> Aaron Hill *The Snake in the Grass* a1750
> [Poet] *Why, sorrow, she must move: and compassion.* [Genius] *Then she must sing, Mr. Fight-fashion: she must sing ... Bring your Lady to me ... she shall be taught the recitativo dolorosa in a twinkling. She shall learn to hammer home a blunt sentiment, by divisional shakes and fierce nods of her head, in the true time, and tone, of significance.*

hit/strike home
(said of a remark, criticism, etc) to be effective; to convey the intended meaning. *17th cent.*

> Anon *Pasquil's Jestes* 1609
> *At which speech finding his lie hit home, with as much speed as he could, like a lying Gull, gat him away from the company.*

> Dickens *Dombey and Son* 1848
> *His face was turned towards her. By the waning lamp, and at that haggard hour, it looked worn and dejected; and in the utter loneliness surrounding him, there was an appeal to Florence that struck home.*

home and dry
informal completely successful in achieving an objective, especially one that has been demanding: in early Australian use in the variant form *home and dried* and in the fuller form *home and dry and on the pig's back*. An Australian variant still current is *home and hosed*. The allusions are to washing and drying oneself after hard work. *Early 20th cent.*

> Enoch Powell *Reflections of a Statesman* 1991
> *If you can attach the consequences of your own actions (for which you desire to transfer the blame to other people) to somebody who is unpopular already and attribute it to him, you are almost certain to be home and dry.*

a home from home
a place other than one's own home where one feels welcome and comfortable. *19th cent.*

home James
a humorous exhortation to return home promptly: based on the stereotypical instruction, as in a melodrama, to a coachman to drive home with all speed (often in full as *home James, and don't spare the horses*, which was also the title of a 1930s song by Fred Hillebrand). *Early 20th cent.*

make oneself at home
to allow oneself to be relaxed and comfortable, especially in a place belonging to somebody else. *18th cent.*

> J Robinson *The Yorker's Stratagem* 1792
> [Acid] *Mr. Norrard ... I am very proud, I assure you, to see you under my roof: how lucky you was in happening to call here: my good friend, make yourself at home, be perfectly easy about every thing.*

> Dickens *Pickwick Papers* 1837
> *'Sitting for my portrait!' said Mr. Pickwick. 'Having your likeness taken, sir,' replied the stout turnkey. 'We're capital hands at likenesses here. Take 'em in no time, and always exact. Walk in, sir, and make yourself at home.'*

there's no place like home

(proverb) one's own home is where one is happiest. The phrase is fairly recent in its present form but the sentiment can be traced back to the works of the Greek poet Hesiod (7th cent. BC). It occurs in a song entitled *Home, Sweet Home* by J H Payne from the 1820s: 'Be it ever so humble, there's no place like home.' *19th cent.*

Charlotte Brontë *Jane Eyre* 1847
They had lived very little at home for a long while, and were only come now to stay a few weeks on account of their father's death; but they did so like Marsh End and Morton, and all these moors and hills about. They had been in London, and many other grand towns; but they always said there was no place like home.

who's/what's — when he's/she's/it's at home?

informal a humorous or scornful enquiry about the identity of a person or thing. *19th cent.*

J R Planché *King Charming* 1879
[Lord Tinsel] *From great King Charming to your Court I come.* [King Henpeckt] *Who may King Charming be, when he's at home?*

Elizabeth Elgin *All the Sweet Promises* 1991
'*My mentor is the earth mother and my conscience is ruled by karma.*' '*And what's karma, when it's at home?*' *demanded Vi, who knew that consciences were ruled by parish priests.*

See also nothing to WRITE home about.

---

homework

do one's homework

informal to prepare thoroughly for an imminent task or undertaking, so as to be fully ready for the occasion. The comparison is with the work a schoolchild has to do at home in preparation for a coming lesson. *Mid 20th cent.*

Listener 1959
The Soviet reporter had been 'doing his homework' to some effect.

---

honest

(as) honest as the day is long

unfailingly and tirelessly honest. The image is of timeless reliability, comparable to the continuation of time itself. The evidence for this phrase is surprisingly recent; an early use (Erskine Caldwell, *God's Little Acre*, 1933) has *real* in place of *honest* but is used in the explicit context of honesty: 'A real honest-to-God albino?' Shaw asked. 'As real as the day is long.' *Mid 20th cent.*

an honest broker

an impartial mediator: originally used (translating German *der ehrliche Makler*) with reference to the German statesman Otto von Bismarck (1815–98), who advocated a policy of peacemaking in the 1870s. *19th cent.*

Somerset Maugham *The Moon and Sixpence* 1919
He was just a good, dull, honest, plain man. One would admire his excellent qualities, but avoid his company. He was null. He was probably a worthy member of society, a good husband and father, an honest broker; but there was no reason to waste one's time over him.

earn/turn an honest penny

to make an honest living. *19th cent.*

Henry James *Washington Square* 1881
I should like some quiet work – something to turn an honest penny.

honest to God

informal, originally NAmer truly, honestly: also used with hyphens as an adjective. *Early 20th cent.*

Harvey Jerrold O'Higgins *The Dummy* 1914
[Rose] *Honest to God, Mr. Babbing, we had nothin' to do with this game except what they forced on us.*

Elizabeth Elgin *All the Sweet Promises* 1991
If we miss that ferry again I'll shoot myself, honest to God I will.

make an honest woman of somebody

informal to save the reputation of a pregnant woman (or, jocularly, a woman with whom one has a long-standing sexual relationship) by marrying her. There are connotations here of two meanings of *honest*: 'respectable, trustworthy' and the archaic meaning '(said of a woman) chaste'. *17th cent.*

John Wilson *The Cheats* 1664
[Scruple] *But pray Sir, what effect do you conceive, this Conjunction may have, upon the Whore of Babylon?* [Mopus] *Why trulie, that is somewhat uncertain … for my part, I expect, some or other should marrie her up, and make an honest woman of her, or otherwise … she is likelie to get such a Clap, she'll hardly claw it off again in haste.*

Henry Fielding *The History of Tom Jones* 1749
I was made an honest woman then; and if you was to be made an honest woman, I should not be angry.

Adam Smith *The Wealth of Nations* 1776
The banks, they seem to have thought, were in honour bound to supply the deficiency, and to provide them with all the capital which they wanted to trade with.

honour

do/perform the honours

informal to perform a social duty or courtesy, especially serving guests with food or drink. *17th cent.*

Pope transl Horace's *Epistles* I.vi 1737
But if to Pow'r and Place your Passion lye, | If in the Pomp of Life consist the Joy; | Then hire a Slave, or (if you will, a Lord) | To do the Honours, and to give the Word; | Tell at your Levee, as the Crowds approach, | To whom to nod, whom take into your Coach, | Whom honour with your hand.

Scott *Waverley* 1814
The Baron, while he assumed the lower end of the table, insisted that Lady Emily should do the honours of the head, that they might, he said, set a meet example to the young folk.

honour among thieves

a paradoxical form of loyalty that criminals tend to show to each other. Originally as a proverb *there is honour among thieves*, which dates from the 18th cent. in this form but has older origins in related expressions.

F G Waldron *Heigho for a Husband* 1794
Well, Maria, I remember the adage – 'there is honour among thieves;' – therefore, as I would not be thought deficient in a quality the highest glory in, and the very lowest affect, I'll keep my word as far as honestly I can, and go with you to the play.

Mary Shelley *The Fortunes of Perkin Warbeck* 1830
It is common to say that there is honour among thieves and villains. It is not honour; but an acknowledged loss of shame and conscience, and a mutual trust in the instinctive hatred the bad must bear the good, which strongly unites them.

(in) honour bound

morally obliged to do or not to do something. *16th cent.*

Anon *Solyman and Perseda* 1592
[Basilisco] My petty fellow, where hast thou hid thy maister. [Piston] Marrie sir in an Armorours shop, | Where you had not best go to him. [Basilisco] Why so, I am in honour bound to combat him.

hoof

on the hoof

1 by foot or on horseback (the meaning is not always clear). Originally used to denote cattle bought and sold alive for slaughter, and then by extension applied to animals and people on the move. *17th cent.*

Shakespeare *The Merry Wives of Windsor* I.iii.77 (1597)
[Sir John Falstaff] Rogues, hence, avaunt! Vanish like hailstones! Go! | Trudge, plod, away o'th' hoof, seek shelter, pack!

Roger Boyle *Guzman* 1693
Mortal! Why keep'st thou aloof? | Beat it hither on the hoof, | Else though thou wert twice as rich, | Fiends would catch thee by the breech, | And drag thee to grim Charon's cave.

2 spontaneously, without much preparation or thought. *19th cent.*

Andrew Morton *Diana: Her True Story* 1993
Diana, an unwilling international media celebrity, was having to learn on the hoof. There was no training, backup or advice from within the royal system. Everything was piecemeal and haphazard.

under the hoof

oppressed or downtrodden. *19th cent.*

Harriet Beecher Stowe *Uncle Tom's Cabin* 1852
'I'd rather, ten thousand times,' said the woman, 'live in the dirtiest hole at the quarters, than be under your hoof!' 'But you are under my hoof, for all that,' said he, turning upon her, with a savage grin.

hook

by hook or by crook

by any possible means. There are numerous anecdotal explanations of the origin of this phrase, none totally convincing. One account recorded by William Cobbett in the 1820s refers to an old feudal custom by which tenants were entitled to as much firewood as they could cut with a billhook or pull down with a shepherd's crook, which they therefore acquired *by hook or by crook*; this is supported by Gower's (14th cent.) use of *hepe* [= pruning knife] in place of *hook*. The phrase also appears in other Middle English sources, including Wyclif. Two other stories are of interest as examples of easily discounted folk etymology, and these were more regularly repeated than any other phrasal origin (with the possible exception of *setting the Thames on fire* and *raining cats and dogs*) in the queries columns of *Notes & Queries* from the 1850s onwards: (1) in the reign of Charles I two learned judges named Hooke and Crooke were consulted to settle difficult legal problems, so that a decision was reached 'by Hooke or by Crooke' (but the phrase is much older than this), and (2) when Henry II reached the Bay of Waterford in Ireland in 1172, he landed at a place called Crook by a tower called Hook, enabling him to land safely 'by Hook or by Crook' (this was held to be the origin of the phrase in a 17th cent. source).

John Healey *The Discovery of a New World* c1609
There is no variety [= rarity], nor excellent thing of worth in all the world, but they will haue it, by hooke or by crooke, and if they once get it, yee shall sooner get a fart from a dead man, then fetch it back out of their clouches.

drop/go off the hooks
informal, dated to die. Perhaps with reference to meat that is so old it falls from the butchers' hooks. *19th cent.*

Trollope *Phineas Redux* 1874
On taking up the evening paper he at once saw a paragraph stating that the Duke of Omnium's condition to-day was much the same as yesterday; but that he had passed a quiet night ... 'So old Omnium is going off the hooks at last,' said Mr. Maule to a club acquaintance.

get/give somebody the hook
informal to be dismissed (or to dismiss somebody) from a job. *20th cent.*

get one's hooks into something/somebody
informal to get hold of a thing or person, either physically or in other ways, e.g. emotionally. In figurative uses the phrase is typically used of women seeking to gain control of men in various ways. *Hooks* in the slang meaning 'hands or fingers' occurs from the early 19th cent. *Early 20th cent.*

J Potts *Go, Lovely Rose* 1954
Maybe he's eloped with that fat Lang dame. She's been trying to get her hooks into him all winter.

hook it
British, informal to run off; to escape. The phrase is probably influenced by the notion of slinging one's hook (see below). *See also* play HOOKEY. *19th cent.*

Dickens *Bleak House* 1853
'Hook it! Nobody wants you here,' he ses. 'You hook it. You go and tramp,' he ses. 'You move on,' he ses. 'Don't let me ever see you nowheres within forty mile of London, or you'll repent it.'

hook, line, and sinker
informal completely; without any reservations: somebody who accepts a story or excuse in this way is compared to a fish that takes the bait so avidly that it also swallows part of the line and the 'sinker', i.e. the weight attached to the end of the line. *19th cent.*

Harriet Ford *The Argyle Case* 1912
[Joe] Then it was a nibble? [Kayton] No, Joe, a bite. He swallowed it – hook, line and sinker.

Evelyn Waugh *Brideshead Revisited* 1945
I expected you to make mistakes your first year. We all do ... But you, my dear Charles, whether you realize it or not, have gone straight, hook, line and sinker, into the very worst set in the University.

off the hook
1 freed from a difficulty or embarrassment; no longer under suspicion. The reference here and in the following phrase is to a fish caught on, or released from, the hook of a fishing line. *19th cent.*

Trollope *The Small House at Allington* 1864
Eames, when he had got so far as this, on the first perusal of the letter, knew well what was to follow. 'Poor Caudle!' he said to himself; 'he's hooked, and he'll never get himself off the hook again.'

2 (said of a telephone receiver) removed from its base. *Hook* is used here in a different sense, and owes its origin to the design of early telephones, in which the mouthpiece was lifted off a hook when in use and replaced afterwards by means of a hollow metal loop. Modern technology has made this escape from the telephone impossible: a high-pitched whine is transmitted down the line after a short interval. *19th cent.*

William Gillette *How Well George Does It!* 1936
[stage direction] *Idea comes to her. She goes quickly to telephone and takes receiver off the hook.*

David Oates et al *Advice from the Top* 1989
In any crisis, my greatest support is a clean sheet of paper and a pencil and the telephone off the hook.

on the hook

trapped or under somebody's control. *17th cent.*

Congreve *The Double Dealer* 1695
[Mellefont] *Consider I have you on the hook; you will but flounder your self a weary, and be nevertheless my Prisoner.*

sling one's hook

British, informal to leave: in early use also in the form *take one's hook*. Some authorities maintain that the origin is nautical: before a ship could leave harbour its anchor (also called *hook*) had to be raised and secured at the bow. But the phrase is typically used in a casual personal sense that fits ill with the elaborate and formal procedure of a ship leaving for sea. Furthermore, *sling* would be an unusual word to use in this context – unless it is a substitute for *swing*, which makes better sense. An alternative theory connects the phrase with miners leaving their day clothes on hooks before starting work at the coalface, and retrieving them when it was time to leave at the end of the day. Once again it is difficult to see how the hook would be *slung* (or indeed *swung*) in such an arrangement, although the clothes might be. Without early evidence we can only speculate, but the probability is that the phrase arises from a casual and repeated action of some kind that people performed in connection with 'leaving'. Another form of the phrase, which occurs earlier but is now obsolete, is *sling one's daniel*. This is no help in resolving the question of origin, because we do not know what a *daniel* was: perhaps it was some kind of pack, or it might be rhyming slang, although in this case we would expect the association to have survived in folk memory. The phrase is used in a pastoral context in Dryden's translation (1697) of Virgil's third *Eclogue*, but the sense is unclear and the use is probably unrelated to the development of our phrase: 'From rivers drive the kids, and sling your hook; | Anon I'll wash them in the shallow brook.' *19th cent.*

Thomas Bracken *Tom Bracken's Annual* 1896
In brief, a dog of splendid sort, | With such a regal look, | That smaller dogs did as they ought, | Or had to sling their hook.

hookey

play hookey

NAmer, informal to stay away from school without permission, to play truant: *hookey* (or *hooky*) is probably based on *hook it* = to run off. *19th cent.*

hoop

go / put somebody through the hoops

to undergo (or to make somebody undergo) great difficulties: the allusion is probably the same as for the following phrase. *Early 20th cent.*

Hansard 1992
We have all talked about finding a fair local government taxation system. Front Benchers and Back Benchers have been going through the hoops, trying to devise a system that is fair and is always related to ability to pay.

jump through hoops

to follow a complex or difficult procedure in order to get something done: an allusion to the tricks performed by circus animals. *Early 20th cent.*

hoot

not care/give a hoot / two hoots

informal not to care in the least. The connection of *hoot* in this phrase with the cry of the owl is obscure, and this may be a different word. Its core meaning is 'the least amount or particle', and is of North American origin. Apart from a stray use in the late 19th cent., it is invariably used in negative contexts. *Early 20th cent.*

James Forbes *The Traveling Salesman* 1908
[Blake] *Give me a chance, Drury. I've always worked for your best interests. I've never asked a favor – I do so now. I don't give a hoot about myself – but – she's the whole thing to me. I'm begging for the girl I love. Give her a square deal.*

James Joyce *Finnegans Wake* 1939
I did not care three tanker's hoots ... for any feelings.

hop

catch/take somebody on the hop

informal to find somebody unprepared. *Hop* is used here in its meaning 'the act of hopping', the image being of a person caught in a sudden or ungainly movement. *19th cent.*

> Paul Merritt *Hand and Glove* 1874
> [Hand] *We have done our business neatly.* [Glove] *We have – very.* [Hand] *Smartly.* [Glove] *Exceedingly.* [Hand] *Had him on the hop.* [Glove] *We had.*

hop the twig/stick

British, informal to depart or be sent away suddenly; to die: a metaphor from the behaviour of birds in flying off when they sense danger (compare *hop it, hop off,* etc). Recent variations on the theme include *fall off the twig* and *hop the perch.* *18th cent.*

> Mary Robinson *Walsingham* 1797
> *Quiz me, but old stiff-wig came a day after the fair; poor graphy was taken in, kept his bed three days, and hopped the twig on the fourth, queer my nobility.*

> Rachel Anderson *Paper Faces* 1991
> *Dot didn't know what her convalescence was. 'To get you in the pink. For your operation. Like the nice man said. We don't want you hopping the twig.'*

hope

hope against hope

to continue to hope for something that is only remotely possible: based on St Paul's Epistle to the Romans 4:18 (in the Authorized Version of 1611) 'Who against hope believed in hope, that he might become the father of many nations'. *19th cent.*

> Charlotte Brontë *Shirley* 1849
> *Most people have had a period or periods in their lives when they have felt thus forsaken; when, having long hoped against hope, and still seen the day of fruition deferred, their hearts have truly sickened within them.*

hope springs eternal

(proverb) people will always find hope even in the most desperate situations. The locus classicus is Pope's *An Essay on Man* (1734): 'Hope springs eternal in the human breast: | Man never Is, but always To be blest'. However, allusive uses do not appear before the middle of the following century. *18th cent.*

> Dickens *Our Mutual Friend* 1865
> *Having made sure of his watching me, I tempt him on, all over London. One night I go east, another night north … Night after night his disappointment is acute, but hope springs eternal in the scholastic breast, and he follows me again to-morrow.*

horizon

broaden one's horizons

to take on new activities. *Horizon* in the sense 'a limit of thought, action, or experience' dates from the 17th cent. The phrase is recorded from the 19th cent.

> George Gissing *New Grub Street* 1891
> *'Let us have it out, then. You think it was a mistake to spend those months abroad?' 'A mistake from the practical point of view. That vast broadening of my horizon lost me the command of my literary resources.'*

on the horizon

(said of an event) expected to happen shortly: often used in broader metaphors with words such as *appear, surface, loom,* etc. *19th cent.*

> Dickens *David Copperfield* 1850
> *The fair land of promise lately looming on the horizon is again enveloped in impenetrable mists, and for ever withdrawn from the eyes of a drifting wretch whose Doom is sealed!*

horn

blow/toot one's own horn

informal, chiefly NAmer to boast about one's own achievements or abilities: cf blow one's own TRUMPET. *19th cent.*

> George Borrow *Lavengro* 1851
> *He'll have quite enough to do in writing his own lils [Romany, = books], and telling the world how handsome and clever he was … I once heard a wise man say in Brummagem, that 'there is nothing like blowing one's own horn', which I conceive to be much the same thing as writing one's own lil.*

draw/pull in one's horns

to exercise restraint in one's activities or ambitions: the image is of a snail, which draws in the horn-like tentacles on the front of its head when it is threatened. *16th cent.*

Thomas Dilke *The Pretenders* 1698
[Sir Wealthy Plainder] *Alas, alas! in this case there can be no remedy but patience. Now must I forsooth e'en draw in my Horns, sneak off and dance Attendance.*

Henry Fielding *The History of Tom Jones* 1749
The sage pedagogue was contented with the vent which he had already given to his indignation; and, as the vulgar phrase is, immediately drew in his horns. He said, He was sorry he had uttered any thing which might give offence, for that he had never intended it.

on the horn

informal, NAmer on the telephone. *Mid 20th cent.*

on the horns of a dilemma

faced with two equally undesirable alternatives. Philosophical sources of the 16th cent. refer to the 'horned question' or 'horned argument', translations of the scholastic Latin term *argumentum cornutum*, denoting a pair of propositions one of which has to be accepted but either of which results in an opponent's defeat in the argument. (An example of this sophistry is *Morton's fork*: see FORK.) The notion is of a pair of horns representing the two parts of the dilemma: by avoiding one of the horns one runs the risk of being caught on the other. There are references to the concept that are earlier than the phrase in its present form. *19th cent.*

Hardy *A Pair of Blue Eyes* 1873
As was her custom when upon the horns of a dilemma, she walked off by herself among the laurel bushes, and there, standing still and splitting up a leaf without removing it from its stalk, fetched back recollections of Stephen's frequent words in praise of his friend.

hornet

stir up / raise a hornets' nest

to cause trouble or provoke anger. *Nest of hornets* has been used since the 16th cent. as a metaphor for violent opposition or trouble, and the phrase is 18th cent. in its current form.

Richardson *Pamela* 1741
And I did no harm neither, but to myself; for I rais'd a hornet's nest about my ears, that, as far as I know, may have stung to death my reputation.

horse

change/swap horses in midstream

to change one's methods or tactics halfway through an activity. The locus classicus is a speech by Abraham Lincoln in 1864, in which he explained his renomination for President as due less to his own abilities than to a wish by his fellow Republicans 'not to swap horses while crossing the river [*or* stream]'. *19th cent.*

eat like a horse

to eat greedily. The horse has long been regarded as symbolic of strength and industry, and the voracious appetite attributed to it is part of this picture. *Work like a horse* is recorded from the 18th cent., and *eat like a horse* from the previous century.

Thomas Dekker *The Welsh Ambassador* a1632
I could eate like a horse now.

a horse of another / a different colour

a completely different thing. The phrase also appears in early use in the form *a horse of that / the same colour* meaning 'something similar', as in Shakespeare's *Twelfth Night* (1602) II.iii.181: '[Maria] My purpose is indeed a horse of that colour. [Sir Andrew] And your horse now would make him an ass.' *18th cent.*

horses for courses

different people or things suit different needs: from the notion that every racehorse has a particular course on which it performs best. *19th cent.*

straight from the horse's mouth

(said of information) obtained direct from the original source; first-hand: the notion is of the horse as the best possible source for a racing tip. *Early 20th cent.*

wild horses won't/wouldn't drag something out of somebody

nothing would induce somebody to reveal some confidence or secret: with reference to a form of punishment or torture in which a victim was tied to wild horses and dragged or torn apart by them. *19th cent.*

L M Montgomery *Anne of Green Gables* 1909
'Wild horses won't drag the secret from me,'
promised Anne solemnly.' 'How would wild horses
drag a secret from a person anyhow?'

See also a DARK horse; FLOG a dead horse; on one's
HIGH horse; a TROJAN horse.

---

hostage

a hostage to fortune
a commitment that lays one open to the risk of
failure or criticism if it cannot be met or if circumstances change. First used by Francis Bacon
in an essay on marriage (1625), in which he stated
that 'he that hath wife and children, hath given
hostages to fortune; for they are impediments to
great enterprises'. *17th cent.*

> Mary Shelley *The Last Man* 1826
> *The man, says Lord Bacon, who hath wife and*
> *children, has given hostages to fortune. Vain was all*
> *philosophical reasoning – vain all fortitude – vain,*
> *vain, a reliance on probable good. I might heap high*
> *the scale with logic, courage, and resignation – but*
> *let one fear for Idris and our children enter the*
> *opposite one, and, overweighed, it kicked the beam.*

---

hot

Several phrases are based on an early (Old English) figurative meaning denoting ardour and
zeal, and passion of feelings.

be in the hot seat
to have the chief responsibility for an urgent or
dangerous undertaking. *Hot seat* has various
physical applications, notably the electric chair
used for executions in the US, and the ejector seat
in a military aircraft. The use of *hot* to denote
intensity of action in a place dates from the 19th
cent. The phrase is mid 20th cent.

> *Time* 1942
> *We are an entire nation of people who are trying to*
> *wage a war and everyone is trying, himself, to keep*
> *out of the hot seat.*

drop somebody/something like a hot potato
informal to abandon a person or undertaking
suddenly, especially when they become controversial or difficult to handle (rather as a hot
potato is). *Hot potato* is also used by itself to
denote a highly sensitive or controversial political issue. *19th cent.*

Joseph Conrad *Lord Jim* 1900
It was apparently when thus occupied in his shed
that the true perception of his extreme peril dawned
upon him. He dropped the thing – he says – 'like a
hot potato', and walked out hastily.

> *Independent* 2003
> *Police officers are finding their new national uni-*
> *form, which includes a fleece to replace the trad-*
> *itional pullover, has a flaw – it does not keep out the*
> *cold … Paul Tonks, the chairman of the West*
> *Midlands Police Federation, called the uniform*
> *garbage. 'We have just gone through an extremely*
> *cold spell and officers have been bloody freezing.*
> *Other forces have dropped it like a hot potato,*
> *making a mockery of the idea of a national uniform.'*

go/grow/turn hot and cold
to feel uncontrollably agitated or suddenly afraid
or embarrassed. *19th cent.*

> Richardson *The History of Sir Charles Grandison* 1753
> *O Lucy! how my heart flutter'd! The ague-fit came*
> *on again; and I was hot and cold, as before, almost in*
> *the same moment.*

> George Eliot *Adam Bede* 1859
> *It's a strange thing to think of a man as can lift a*
> *chair with his teeth, and walk fifty mile on end,*
> *trembling and turning hot and cold at only a look*
> *from one woman out of all the rest i' the world.*

have the hots for somebody
informal to have a strong sexual desire for somebody: *hots* refers to flushing and similar physical
symptoms. *Mid 20th cent.*

> *The Face* 1990
> *Cynics are betting that the romance is a huge*
> *publicity stunt to help sell the film … Yet a cast*
> *member raises his eyebrows in disbelief when the*
> *quote is repeated. 'I don't know how serious they*
> *are, but Warren and Madonna certainly had the*
> *hots for one another. It was obvious on the set.'*

hot air
empty or meaningless talk. *19th cent.*

> Charles Klein *Maggie Pepper* 1911
> [Jake] *We open a store; I put up the money; you're*
> *the manager, and I'm the treasurer.* [Maggie] *Now,*
> *Jake, it's quite warm enough without you puffing a*
> *lot of hot air into the room.*

hot and bothered
flustered or embarrassed. *Early 20th cent.*

hot off/from the press

newly printed or published: with reference to the use of hot-metal printing, in which newly printed material was indeed 'hot' for a time. The (early 20th cent.) expression *hot news* has the same origin. *19th cent.*

John Minshull *The Merry Dames* 1804

My dear, here – here is my pamphlet hot from the press. Use it at your pleasure in the disposing of its merits.

hot on the heels of somebody

closely pursuing somebody: *cf* in hot pursuit *below*. *19th cent.*

Conan Doyle *The Sign of Four* 1890

'Could we advertise, then, asking for information from wharfingers?' 'Worse and worse! Our men would know that the chase was hot at their heels, and they would be off out of the country.'

hot under the collar

informal angry or irritated. *19th cent.*

in hot pursuit

closely pursuing somebody, especially a wrong-doer: *cf* hot on the heels of somebody *above*. Also in figurative use in the sense 'bent on a certain purpose'. *17th cent.*

William Browne *Britannia's Pastorals* 1616

But rending of her haire, her throbbing brest | Beating with ruthlesse strokes, she onward prest | As an inraged furious Lionesse, | Through uncouth treadings of the wildernesse, | In hot pursuit of her late missed brood.

Richard Ames *The Pleasures of Love and Marriage* 1691

Expose themselves to falls, or guns, or traps, | And twenty other unforeseen mishaps, | All in the hot pursuit of whores and claps.

Dickens *Nicholas Nickleby* 1839

I have been made the instrument of working out this dreadful retribution upon the head of a man who, in the hot pursuit of his bad ends, has persecuted and hunted down his own child to death.

in hot water

in trouble or difficulty. *18th cent.*

Richard Cumberland *First Love* 1795

Billy, Billy, if it is a secret affair, don't meddle or make with it: as sure as can be you'll get into hot water with Sir Miles Mowbray.

make it/things hot for somebody

informal to create trouble or difficulty for somebody. The notion appears much earlier in the related form *make a place too hot to hold somebody* meaning 'to make it difficult for that person to remain there'. *17th cent.*

George Powell *The Imposture Defeated* 1698

You have made Venice too hot to hold you; I never knew you rise in a morning of late, but your Levy was more crowded with Dunns [= creditors] than a rising Favourite's with Solicitors for Preferment.

Maria Sedgwick *The Linwoods* vol 2 1835

'D—n the rebels, I wish I had their bones for firewood.' 'They do their best, sir, to make it hot for the tories,' said Herbert, very good-humouredly.

too hot to handle

informal too awkward, demanding, or notorious to deal with. The phrase is primarily based on the slang meaning of *hot* relating to stolen goods, which dates from the 1920s, but there are sometimes overtones of the more personal sense 'passionate or sexual'. *Mid 20th cent.*

Daily Record (Scotland) 1994

Armed raiders who struck at an Indian restaurant this morning found it too hot to handle. For staff beat them off with curry sauce.

See also BLOW hot and cold; sell like hot cakes *at* CAKE.

---

hour

after / out of hours

outside normal working hours. *19th cent.*

Dickens *Our Mutual Friend* 1865

He then came cherubically flying out without a hat, and embraced her, and handed her in. 'For it's after hours and I am all alone, my dear,' he explained, 'and am having – as I sometimes do when they are all gone – a quiet tea.'

keep good/regular/late hours

to get up and go to bed early or late, or at the same time each day: *hours* is used from the early 17th cent. to denote the time till which a person remains active (*cf* Shakespeare, *Twelfth Night* (1602) I.iii.5 '[Maria] By my troth, Sir Toby, you must come in earlier o' nights. Your cousin, my lady, takes great exceptions to your ill hours.'). *17th cent.*

John Fletcher *The Noble Gentleman* 1647
[Jaques] *Sir this is from* [= contrary to] *your wonted course at home,* | *When did ye there keep such inordinate hours?*

Sir George Etherege *She Wou'd if She Cou'd* 1671
[Sir Oliver, referring to his marriage] *And then the inconvenience of keeping regular hours.*

Congreve *Love for Love* 1695
[Mrs. Foresight] *Husband, will you go to Bed? It's Ten a Clock. Mr. Scandal, your Servant –* [Scandal] *Pox on her, she has interrupted my Design – But I must work her into the Project. You keep early Hours, Madam.*

on the hour
at an exact hour, especially every hour. Also (loosely) in the sense 'constantly, all the time'. *19th cent.*

Ralph Waldo Emerson *Poetry and Imagination* 1876
The poet squanders on the hour an amount of life that would more than furnish the seventy years of the man that stands next him.

Listener 1984
Is there any good reason why we should have news bulletins, local and national, every hour on the hour, chat shows … and wall-to-wall discussion programmes?

the small hours (of the morning)
the period between midnight and dawn. *19th cent.*

Dickens *David Copperfield* 1850
In consideration of the day and hour of my birth, it was declared by the nurse … first, that I was destined to be unlucky in life; and secondly, that I was privileged to see ghosts and spirits; both these gifts inevitably attaching … to all unlucky infants of either gender, born towards the small hours on a Friday night.

the story/subject/person, etc of the hour
the story or event or person that everybody is talking about or that is especially important at a particular time. The phrase emerges from a more general use of *hour* in the sense 'the present time or moment', as in *the business of the hour* = the matter in hand. *17th cent.*

Robert Gould *The Rival Sisters* 1696
[Sebastian] *His guilt has made him pale – come, rouse Antonio,* | *Thou know'st the fatal business of the hour,* | *Therefore prepare.*

John Esten Cooke *Mohun* 1869
I was now going to call on the statesman to express my admiration of his eloquent appeal, and converse upon the exciting topics of the hour.

William Black *A Daughter of Heth* 1871
His narrative of the events of Waterloo had gradually, during many years, become more and more full of personal detail, until the old man at last firmly believed that he himself, in his own proper person, had witnessed the whole of the battle, and been one of the chief heroes of the hour.

till all hours
until very late at night. *Mid 20th cent.*

Jenny Joseph *Persephone* 1986
There's always someone to keep an eye on the kids, and it doesn't seem to bother them having children round and up till all hours. I don't think the children go to bed till the adults do.

within the hour
before an hour has passed. *19th cent.*

Emily Brontë *Wuthering Heights* 1847
My young lady came down dressed for going out, and said she asked to have a ramble on the edge of the moor with me: Mr. Linton had given her leave, if we went only a short distance and were back within the hour.

Young Man 1891
A ride of ten miles within the hour may mean comfort and the capability of doing another twenty easily.

house

get on/along like a house on fire
to do very well and make splendid progress, or (said of two or more people) to take to one another, to have a friendly or successful relationship. The underlying notion is of speed: a house, especially a wooden one or one with a thatched roof, will burn very rapidly. *19th cent.*

Trollope *The Last Chronicle of Barset* 1867
'And now she is dead! I wonder how the bishop will get on without her.' 'Like a house on fire, I should think,' said Johnny. 'Fie, Mr. Eames; you shouldn't speak in such a way on such a subject.'

go (all) round the houses
to go by a long indirect route: normally used figuratively in the sense 'to take a long time to

reach the point; to beat about the bush'. *Mid 20th cent.*

house and home

one's home: an emphatic form with alliterative effect, recorded from an early date. Commonly used in the phrase *eat somebody out of house and home*, in the sense 'to exploit somebody's hospitality'. This phrase owes its origin to Shakespeare's use in 2 *Henry IV* (1597) II.i.75, where Mistress Quickly complains to the Lord Chief Justice about Sir John Falstaff that 'he hath eaten me out of house and home. He hath put all my substance into that fat belly of his'. The notion as a whole dates from Middle English.

Thomas Paine *Common Sense* 1776

I make the sufferers case my own, and I protest, that were I driven from house and home, my property destroyed, and my circumstances ruined, that as man, sensible of injuries, I could never relish the doctrine of reconciliation, or consider myself bound thereby.

Harriet Beecher Stowe *Uncle Tom's Cabin* 1852

Why, laws me, Missis! … other folks hires out der niggers and makes money on 'em! Don't keep sich a tribe eatin' 'em out of house and home.

a house divided

an organization or group that is weakened by internal conflict or disagreement. The phrase is derived from Matthew 12:25, where Christ is replying to the Pharisees' accusation that he had cast out devils by the power of Satan: 'Every kingdom divided against itself is brought to desolation; and every city or house divided against itself shall not stand.' *16th cent.*

Thomas Paine *Common Sense* 1776

Some writers have explained the English constitution thus; the king, say they, is one, the people another; the peers are an house in behalf of the king; the commons in behalf of the people; but this hath all the distinctions of an house divided against itself.

Abraham Lincoln *Speech* 1858

'A house divided against itself cannot stand.' I believe this government cannot endure permanently, half slave and half free.

a house of cards

an insecure or unreliable idea or scheme: literally a flimsy structure made from playing cards that can easily be knocked down. *17th cent.*

Charles Molloy *The Half-Pay Officers* 1720

[Culverin, as Widow coughs] *Ouns, this Cough is worse than an Earthquake; one Shake more, and she falls to Pieces like a House of Cards.*

not give something house room

to refuse to accommodate a person or thing; also, in abstract senses, to refuse to accept or consider something. *18th cent.*

Henry Fielding *The History of Tom Jones* 1749

Let us go directly to yon light. Whether it be a public-house or no, I am sure if they be Christians … they will not refuse a little house-room to persons in our miserable condition.

on the house

without charge: normally used of drinks that are offered free of charge at a public house, hotel, etc. *19th cent.*

put/set one's house in order

to put one's affairs in good order; more generally, to make any changes needed: with allusion to Isaiah's words in 2 Kings 20:1 'Thus saith the Lord, Set thine house in order; for thou shalt die, and not live.' *17th cent.*

Thomas Deloney *The Gentle Craft* 1627

But tell us, hast thou made thy will, and set thy house in order? What if I have not quoth Peachie? Why then quoth Strangwidge, for thy wife and childrens sake go home againe and do it, or else get more aide about thee to preserve thy life.

See also (as) SAFE as houses.

---

housetops

proclaim/shout something from the housetops

to make sure that everybody knows about something: with allusion to Luke 12:3 'That which ye have spoken in the ear in closets shall be proclaimed upon the housetops.' The phrase is 19th cent. in allusive use.

Mark Twain *The $30,000 Bequest and Other Stories* 1906

Whom he loved he loved, and manifested it; whom he didn't love he hated, and published it from the housetops.

how

and how!
informal used as an exclamation of agreement or support: *cf* German *und wie! Early 20th cent.*

Hoyle

according to Hoyle
exactly in accordance with the rules or regulations: with allusion to Edmond Hoyle (1672–1769), a British writer who compiled *Hoyle's Standard Games*, a book of rules for card games. The name rapidly became accepted as a byword for authority. It is mentioned in Henry Fielding's *The History of Tom Jones* (1749): 'I found four gentlemen of the cloth at whist by my fire; – and my Hoyle, sir – my best Hoyle, which cost me a guinea, lying open on the table, with a quantity of porter spilt on one of the most material leaves of the whole book'; and in Byron's *Don Juan* (1824): 'Troy owes to Homer what whist owes to Hoyle.' The allusive use of the phrase dates from the early 20th cent.

hue

hue and cry
a clamour of alarm or protest, an outcry. Historically, a *hue and cry* was from the 16th cent. an alarm raised against a thief or other criminal caught in the act, before the days of public police forces. The phrase is derived from the Anglo-Norman form of the term *hu e cri; hue* could mean the sound of a trumpet or horn as well as the human voice. The word is otherwise obsolete in this sense in English, and the more familiar homophone *hew* is sometimes erroneously substituted for it in our phrase (perhaps influenced by the notion of 'hewing' one's way through obstacles in the chase?).

huff

huff and puff
to complain noisily or talk in a blustering manner: from the physical meaning 'to breathe and blow heavily'. The phrase calls to mind the children's story of the *Three Little Pigs*, in which the wolf famously threatens each of the pigs in turn with the words 'I'll huff and I'll puff and I'll blow your house down.' *Mid 20th cent.*

hum

hum and haw/ha
to hesitate or equivocate. *Hum* is recorded from late Middle English as a pause or hesitation in speech and as a mark of disagreement, and *ha* from the late 16th cent.; in *The Merry Wives of Windsor* (1597) Shakespeare combines them (III.v.128) when Ford utters 'Hum! Ha! Is this a vision? Is this a dream?' *17th cent.*

human

be only human
to have the normal human failings and weaknesses: typically used to excuse a minor lapse or indiscretion. *19th cent.*

Emerson Bennett *The Pioneer's Daughter* 1851
'Rest assured, Colonel, and gentlemen,' said Miller, one of the three that had been out as a scout – 'rest assured, we'll do our best; but don't count too much on us; for we're only human, and the best may fail.'

Barbara Pym *Excellent Women* 1952
'One expects you to behave better than other people,' said Helena, 'and of course you don't.' 'Why should we? We are only human, aren't we, Miss Lathbury?'

humble

eat humble pie
to apologize or concede a point abjectly or submissively. There is play here on several meanings of *humble*: the familiar adjectival meaning and its use in *humble* (or *umble*) *pie*, a name recorded from the 17th cent. for a pie made of *umbles*, the offal of deer and other animals. *Humble pie* was therefore humble fare in yet another sense of the word. Eating is a common metaphor in various forms for frank and contrite admissions of error. *Cf* eat CROW; eat DIRT; eat one's HAT; eat one's words *at* WORD. *19th cent.*

Trollope *The Three Clerks* 1858
He therefore made no recantation to Sir Gregory, ate no humble pie, descended in no degree from his high position – he sat through the day working hard for the service to which he belonged, determined that

at any rate no fault should be found with him in that respect.

hump

get/have the hump

informal to have a fit of sulking or petulance: similarly, to *give somebody the hump* means to annoy them or make them feel resentful. *Hump* in the meaning 'fit of bad temper' dates from the early 18th cent., but the main usage is from the second part of the 19th cent.

> Kipling *Just So Stories* 1902
> *The Camel's hump is an ugly lump | Which well you may see at the Zoo; | But uglier yet is the hump we get | From having too little to do.*

live on one's hump

informal to be able to support oneself: with reference to the ability of a camel to survive for long periods without food or water by drawing on the store of nourishment contained in its hump. *Early 20th cent.*

over the hump

informal past the most difficult phase of an activity: first recorded in criminal slang, in which the *hump* was the halfway point in a prison sentence, so that being *over the hump* meant that the worst part had been served. The core meaning of *hump* is 'the critical point in an activity or undertaking', but the word is now used chiefly in the phrase. *Early 20th cent.*

> Guy Claxton *Being a Teacher* 1989
> *If however I had to single out one particular group of teachers to whom I hope the book will appeal, it is those who have been in the profession for about five to ten years. They are the ones who – as one such teacher put it to me – are over the hump but not over the hill.*

hungry

(as) hungry as a hunter

extremely hungry. The phrase is first recorded in the form *hungry as a huntsman*, drawing on an ancient image of the food-gatherer deserving the fruits of his labours. *17th cent.*

> Frederick Pilon *Barataria* 1785
> [Recorder] *You yourself are my Lord –* [Sancho] *As hungry as a hunter; – therefore, Mr. Recorder, put up your long speech; – and after dinner I'll put*

on my night-cap, and hear you go over the whole of it again with composure.

> Thackeray *The Newcomes* 1854
> *'I've been to look at a horse afterwards at Tattersall's, and I'm as hungry as a hunter, and as tired as a hodman,' says Mr. Newcome, with his hands in his pockets.*

hurry

not — in a hurry

informal to be slow or unwilling to do something specified. The phrase is used with both neutral and judgemental implications. *18th cent.*

> Fanny Burney *Evelina* 1778
> *'Pardie,' cried Madame Duval, 'I sha'n't let you leave me again in a hurry. Why, here we've been in such a fright! – and, all the while, I suppose you've been thinking nothing about the matter.'*

> Samuel Foote *The Commissary* 1785
> [Mrs. Love] *Why then, as my children are young and rebellious, the way to secure and preserve their obedience, will be to marry a man that won't grow old in a hurry.*

hurt

— wouldn't hurt a fly

the person named is very meek and gentle: based on the use of *fly* as a symbol of the trivial or insignificant, which dates from Middle English. *17th cent.*

> Shakespeare *Pericles* xv.127 (1608)
> [Marina] *Believe me, la* [= indeed]. *| I never killed a mouse nor hurt a fly. | I trod once on a worm against my will, | But I wept for it.*

hymn

See SING from the same hymn sheet.

I

See DOT the i's and cross the t's.

ice

be skating on thin ice
to court danger by behaving in an obviously risky manner that cannot be sustained for long. *19th cent.*

> Ralph Waldo Emerson *Essays: First Series* 1841
> *Iron cannot rust, nor beer sour, nor timber rot, nor calicoes go out of fashion, nor money-stocks depreciate, in the few swift moments which the Yankee suffers any one of them to remain in his possession. In skating over thin ice, our safety is in our speed.*

break the ice
to take the first steps in a lengthy or challenging undertaking; in modern use especially to make the first move in a conversation or other social setting, in order to overcome a pervading reserve or formality. The expression is based on the physical meaning of breaking up the frozen surface of a sea or river in order to allow a ship to pass through. An early use of this phrase has recently been pointed out in a letter of the 16th cent. Protestant martyr John Bradford to Cranmer, Latimer, and Ridley, whom he had supposed to be the next in line for execution as heretics under Mary Tudor's suppression of heresy. But it turned out otherwise, and Bradford writes: 'Our dear brother Rogers hath broken the ice valiantly … The next am I, which hourly look for the porter to open me the gates after them, to enter into the desired rest.' *Break the ice* seems a strange idiom to use in the context of being burned at the stake, or perhaps it is a form of bitter irony, suggesting that the phrase was well known at the time. Bradford wrote the letter on 8 February 1555 and he was executed in turn on

1 July. (The details are available in *Notes & Queries* September 2002, pp.323–4.) Otherwise the earliest recorded uses of the phrase are those in Sir Thomas North's translation of Plutarch published as *Lives of the Noble Grecians and Romans* in 1579 ('to be the first to break the ice of the enterprise'), and Shakespeare's *The Taming of the Shrew* (1592), where Tranio responds to Petruccio's advice that the elder daughter (Katherine) must be married before the younger (Bianca) becomes available (I.ii.268): 'And if you break the ice and do this feat, | Achieve the elder, set the younger free | For our access.' *16th cent.*

> Byron *Don Juan* 1823
> *And your cold people are beyond all price, | When once you have broken their confounded ice.*

on ice
in reserve for later use: from the physical meaning of preserving perishable food under refrigeration. *19th cent.*

> Henry James *Roderick Hudson* 1876
> *Giacosa has turned up again, looking as if he had been kept on ice … for her return.*

See also CUT no ice.

iceberg

the tip of the iceberg
the small visible or known part of something much larger, especially something troublesome or problematic. The phrase alludes to the structure of an iceberg, in which a small portion (generally reckoned to be a little over one tenth) appears above the waterline, belying the huge mass lying below it. It is a relatively recent expression, not recorded before the mid 20th cent.

> *Scientific American* 1963
> *This situation is similar to that of poliomyelitis or viral hepatitis, where the cases of illness represent only the tip of the iceberg, with a much larger number of persons carrying the infection and spreading it unknowingly.*

> Michael Green *I Believe in the Holy Spirit* 1985
> *Healings, exorcisms, tongues, prophecy are merely the spectacular tip of the iceberg, the heart of which is a living, loving, believing Christian fellowship.*

icing

the icing on the cake
a desirable but inessential addition to something already successful or excellent, or an unlooked-for bonus. To *put the icing on the cake* is to achieve or obtain this. *Mid 20th cent.*

Paula Marshall *An American Princess* 1993
But for Miss Mates the 'really truly' was the icing on the cake, even if she had more doubts about Sally-Anne's stamina than her missing references.

idea

get ideas (into one's head)
to begin to have overambitious, unrealistic, or otherwise unsuitable thoughts or desires. *19th cent.*

George Eliot *Middlemarch* 1872
There is likely to be another election before long, and by that time Middlemarch will have got more ideas into its head.

give somebody ideas
to cause somebody to have ideas or hopes that might prove difficult to achieve. *18th cent.*

Eliza Haywood *Anti-Pamela* 1741
Yet if we ... consider the number of unfortunate women ... I believe we shall find the miseries these poor creatures undergo ... less owing to their own inclinations, than to the too great indulgence and false tenderness of their parents; who flattering themselves that by breeding them like gentlewomen ... they shall be able to make their fortune by marriage, give them Ideas no way to their advantage.

have no idea
to be completely ignorant or unaware of something: also as an exclamation (*you have no idea!*) used to emphasize a surprising or unexpected fact or circumstance etc. *19th cent.*

Henry James *Confidence* 1880
Bernard, on this occasion, at dinner, failed to make himself particularly agreeable; he ate fast – as if he had no idea what he was eating, and talked little.

that's an idea
informal that is a good thought; that is worth considering: used in response to a good or unexpected suggestion. *19th cent.*

Dion Boucicault *Flying Scud* a1890
[Mo] Look at me; I shall be found out for passing those bills, but I'll swear I'm an innocent party. Let us all be innocent, and leave Chousir in the hole. [Mulligan] That's an idea, and Chousir's only the son of a butcher, so he has no character to lose.

that's the idea
that is the whole point; that is exactly what is meant. Also in weakened senses, simply acknowledging the truth or validity or something said (typically in encouragement or support). *19th cent.*

W S Gilbert *Pirates of Penzance* 1880
[General] And do you mean to say that you would deliberately rob me of these the sole remaining props of my old age, and leave me to go through the remainder of life unfriended, unprotected, and alone? [Pirate King] Well, yes, that's the idea.

Charles Hale Hoyt *A Texas Steer* 1894
[Brander] Gentlemen, I am glad to have you investigate my course to the fullest extent. And if I don't satisfy you, I want you to go back to Texas and steer them all against me. [Gall] That's the idea. Now jolly 'em and put 'em under obligations to you quick.

what's the big idea?
informal (used as a curt response) what do you mean or intend?; what do you think you are doing? *Early 20th cent.*

Christopher Morley *The Haunted Bookshop* 1919
Roger was holding Weintraub's revolver in front of the German's face. 'Look here,' he said, 'what does this mean?' 'It's all a mistake,' said the druggist suavely, though his eyes slid uneasily to and fro. 'I just came in to get some books I left here earlier in the afternoon.' 'With a revolver, eh?' said Roger. 'Speak up, Hindenburg, what's the big idea?'

if

if anything
used to suggest tentatively or tactfully that something is or could be rather the case. *19th cent.*

Harriet Beecher Stowe *Uncle Tom's Cabin* 1852
I don't think my feelings about slavery are peculiar. I find many men who, in their hearts, think of it just as I do. The land groans under it; and, bad as it is for the slave, it is worse, if anything, for the master.

ill

ill at ease
feeling awkward or uneasy: also recorded in the now obsolete form *evil at ease*. The phrase is found in Middle English in the 14th cent. northern poem known as the *Cursor Mundi*.

George Peele *The Love of King David and Fair Bathsabe* 1599
[Ionadab] *Thus it shall be, lie downe vpon thy bed, | Faining thee feuer sicke, and ill at ease, | And when the king shall come to visit thee, | Desire thy sister Thamar may be sent | To dresse some deinties for thy maladie.*

Shakespeare *Othello* III.iii.30 (1604)
[Desdemona] *Why, stay, and hear me speak.*
[Cassio] *Madam, not now: I am very ill at ease, | Unfit for mine own purposes.*

Adelaide Ann Procter *A Lost Chord* 1858
Seated one day at the organ, | I was weary and ill at ease, | And my fingers wandered idly | Over the noisy keys.

take it ill
to resent or take offence at something. *16th cent.*

Shakespeare *Timon of Athens* v.i.88 (1609)
[Timon] *I must needs say you have a little fault ...*
[Poet and Painter] *Beseech your honour | To make it known to us.* [Timon] *You'll take it ill.*

illusion

be under the illusion (that)
to have a mistaken belief (that something is the case). *18th cent.*

George Campbell *The Philosophy of Rhetoric* 1776
Thus unknowingly I may contribute to his relief, when under the strange illusion which makes me fancy, that, instead of giving to another, I am taking to myself.

be under no illusion(s)
to realize what the true situation is, especially when there are difficulties. *19th cent.*

George Eliot *Felix Holt* 1866
Like all youthful creatures, she felt as if the present conditions of choice were final ... It seemed to her that she stood at the first and last parting of the ways. And, in one sense, she was under no illusion. It is only in that freshness of our time that the choice is possible which gives unity to life.

image
See a GRAVEN image.

imagination

not leave much / leave nothing/little to the imagination
to be graphically explicit or revealing, especially (in modern use) with reference to scanty or figure-hugging clothing, or in depicting or describing sexual activity. *19th cent.*

William Hazlitt *The Spirit of the Age* 1825
She is a circumstantial old lady, communicative, scrupulous, leaving nothing to the imagination.

improve

improve the shining hour
make the best use of one's time. The phrase is used with allusion to the song for children entitled *Against Idleness and Mischief* by the English hymn-writer Isaac Watts (1674–1748): 'How doth the little busy bee | Improve each shining hour, | And gather honey all the day | From every opening flower!' Allusive uses date from the 19th cent.

Thackeray *The Newcomes* 1854
Good Lady Walham was for improving the shining hour by reading amusing extracts from her favourite volumes, gentle anecdotes of Chinese and Hottentot converts, and incidents from missionary travel.

in

be in for something
to be about to experience something, usually something unpleasant or unexpected: this meaning developed from an earlier (16th cent.) one in which *be in for* (a period of time) denoted the likely duration of a commitment. To *be in for it* means to be likely to be punished. *19th cent.*

Louisa M Alcott *Little Women* 1868
'Bless me, what's all this?' cried the old lady, with a rap of her cane, as she glanced from the pale young gentleman to the scarlet young lady. 'It's father's friend. I'm so surprised to see you!' stammered Meg, feeling that she was in for a lecture now.

Conan Doyle *The Naval Treaty* 1893
*It was evident to all that I was in for a long illness,
so Joseph was bundled out of this cheery bedroom,
and it was turned into a sick-room for me.*

be in on something
to have a share in or knowledge of something
secret. *Early 20th cent.*

Eugene Walter *The Easiest Way* 1909
*We're partners, aren't we? I ought to be in on any
important transaction like that.*

be/keep in with somebody
to be or remain on friendly terms with somebody.
16th cent.

Richard Edwards *Damon and Pithias* 1571
*I care not who fall, so that I may ryse: As for fine
Aristippus, I wyll keepe in with hym, He is a
shrewde foole to deale withal.*

Dryden *Marriage a la Mode* 1673
[Palamede] *I hate to be disinherited for a younger
brother, which I am sure I shall be if I disobey; and
yet I must keep in with Rhodophil, because I love his
wife.*

the ins and outs
the details and repercussions associated with or
arising from events or situations. *18th cent.*

Laurence Sterne *Tristram Shandy* 1761
*They are nothing but parentheses, and the common
ins and outs incident to the lives of the greatest
ministers of state.*

(there is) nothing/not much/little, etc in it
(there is) no, or very little, difference, advantage,
etc between two things. *19th cent.*

Adam Lindsay Gordon *A Short Rhyme at Random*
a1870
*And as for a tip, why there isn't much in it, | I may
hit the right nail, but first, I declare, | I haven't a
notion what's going to win it | (The Champion I
mean), and what's more I don't care.*

See also be in like FLYNN; HAVE (got) it in for
somebody.

---

inch

every inch
to the utmost degree. It was used as an adverbial
phrase (e.g. in Caxton: 'This man was cursed
every inch') and (from the early 17th cent.) in
the form *every inch a* —, used to emphasize the

worthiness of a name in a particular case. Despite
some 18th cent. occurrences, the phrase was evidently not picked up with any enthusiasm until
the time of the 19th cent. novelists.

Shakespeare *King Lear* IV.v.108 (1606)
[Gloucester] *The trick of that voice I do well
remember. Is't not the King?* [Lear] *Ay, every inch
a king.*

Richard Cumberland *The Box-Lobby Challenge* 1794
*Why aye, there is not one of my name but myself
that knows what patience means. You are a true
Grampus, sister Di, let me tell you, every inch a
Grampus.*

Charlotte Brontë *Shirley* 1849
*That aide-de-camp – Donne, to-wit – narrow as the
line of his shape was compared to the broad bulk of
his principal, contrived, notwithstanding, to look
every inch a curate: all about him was pragmatical
and self-complacent, from his turned-up nose and
elevated chin to his clerical black gaiters, his
somewhat short, strapless trousers, and his squared-
toed shoes.*

give somebody an inch (and they'll take a mile)
(proverb) make a small concession to somebody
(and they are bound to want more): formerly also
with *ell* (an old measure of length equivalent to a
little over a metre) instead of *mile*. *16th cent.*

Charles Goodall transl Juvenal's *Satire 14* (1689)
*Give them an Inch, and they will take an ell, | Blow
you the fire, their greedy passions swell, | They
think they must exceed, or else they can't excel.*

inch by inch
slowly and gradually: used from the 18th cent.
and earlier (17th cent.) in the form *by inches*.

Shakespeare *Cymbeline* v.vi.52 (1610)
[Cymbeline] *O most delicate fiend! | Who is't can
read a woman? Is there more? |* [Cornelius] *More,
sir, and worse. She did confess she had | For you a
mortal mineral, which, being took, | Should by the
minute feed on life, and ling'ring, | By inches waste
you.*

Jane Austen *Emma* 1816
*Emma felt the glory of having schemed successfully.
But it would not do; he had not come to the point ...
'Cautious, very cautious,' thought Emma; 'he
advances inch by inch, and will hazard nothing till
he believes himself secure.'*

not give an inch
to make no concessions at all: originally with physical reference of giving ground. *18th cent.*

> Defoe *Memoirs of a Cavalier* 1720
> *Tilly's Men might be killed and knocked down, but no Man turned his Back, nor would give an Inch of Ground, but as they were wheel'd, or marched, or retreated by their Officers.*

within an inch of something
very nearly at the point of doing or reaching something. See also the next phrase. *19th cent.*

> Henry James *The American* 1877
> *'What is the matter now?' 'The matter now is that I am a man again, and no more a fool than usual. But I came within an inch of taking that girl au serieux.'*

within an inch of one's life
(said especially of violent or vigorous action) done very thoroughly or intensively; (literally) almost to the point of death. *18th cent.*

> Richardson *Clarissa* 1748
> *Their present hardness of heart will be the subject of everlasting remorse to them should you be taken from us – But now it seems (barbarous wretches!) you are to suffer within an inch of your life.*

> George Eliot *Silas Marner* 1861
> *Godfrey was silent for some moments. He would have liked to spring on Dunstan, wrench the whip from his hand, and flog him to within an inch of his life.*

incline

incline one's heart to somebody/something
to be well disposed towards somebody or something: with allusion to the Authorized Version of the Bible (1611), where the phrase is used often, e.g. 1 Kings 8:58 'That he may incline our hearts unto him, to walk in all his ways, and to keep his commandments'. To *incline one's ear* is to listen attentively. *Middle English*

> Chaucer *The Tale of Melibee* (line 1260)
> *Ne ye han nat knowe the wil of youre trewe freends olde and wise, but ye han cast alle hire wordes in an hochepot [mixture], and enclyned youre herte to the moore part and to the gretter nombre.*

Indian

Indian summer
a happy or flourishing period occurring towards the end of a person's life or career: based on the physical meaning 'a period of warm weather in late autumn or early winter' (originally in areas of North America still inhabited by Native Americans, and later by extension in other places). The phrase is 19th cent. in figurative use.

> B P Shillaber *Knitting-Work* 1859
> *The young-old people are those who have, all their lives, kept their feelings young by active sympathy, and love, and kindness; and it is very beautiful to witness such as in this very latest season of life enjoy this Indian summer of the soul.*

influence

under the influence
informal affected by alcohol, drunk. The phrase is elliptical for 'under the influence of liquor', which also appears in the 19th cent.

> Bartley Theodore Campbell *Fairfax* 1879
> *[Mary] Yes, I sent a letter here to Joe, and Wing Lee, failing to find him, and returning somewhat under the influence of liquor, I came myself. Has he received it? Is he in?*

Injun

honest Injun
informal honestly, really: used for emphasis or insistence. *Injun* is an alteration of *Indian* in the (now politically incorrect) sense 'Native American'. *19th cent.*

> Mark Twain *Huckleberry Finn* 1884
> *'Don't you play nothing on me, because I wouldn't on you. Honest injun, now, you ain't a ghost?' 'Honest injun, I ain't,' I says.*

injury

do oneself an injury
to cause oneself physical harm or injury. *19th cent.*

> Trollope *The Last Chronicle of Barset* 1867
> *It is hardly too much to say that in every moment of his life, whether waking or sleeping, he was thinking of the injury that his son was doing him. He had*

almost come to forget the fact that his anger had first been roused by the feeling that his son was about to do himself an injury, – to cut his own throat.

innings

have had a good innings

to have led a full and successful life: a metaphor from cricket, a good innings being one in which a player or side has scored well. *19th cent.*

John Baldwin Buckstone *Jack Sheppard* 1840
Aye, you can't complain, you've had a good innings – you've crack'd all the prime cribs in London – have taken more swag than any cracksman on town, for the last eight years – you've lived like a gentleman all the while – and as your time's up, come away like a Christian.

innocence

in all innocence

without knowing the possible complexities or implications of a situation. *19th cent.*

Dickens *Pickwick Papers* 1837
'Ve may as vell put this bit o' paper into the fire.' 'Wot are you a-doin' on, you lunatic?' said Sam, snatching the paper away, as his parent, in all innocence, stirred the fire preparatory to suiting the action to the word.

inside

know something inside out

to know something well in all its details. *19th cent.*

W S Gilbert *An Old Score* 1870
My good sir, I know you, back view, front view, inside out, and topsy turvy. You're a humbug – you always were a humbug – and you always will be a humbug.

insult

add insult to injury

to act in a way that makes matters worse in a bad situation or when somebody has already been hurt or upset. *18th cent.*

Hugh Kelly *The School for Wives* 1774
[Lees] *Sir, this trifling is adding insult to injury; and shall be resented accordingly. Didn't you come here to give me satisfaction?*

intent

to all intents and purposes

in every important or practical respect; virtually. The phrase is first recorded in an Act of Parliament of Henry VIII in the form *to all intents, constructions, and purposes. Intent* here means 'end or purpose', and the phrase *intents and purposes* is largely tautological. *16th cent.*

Arthur Golding transl Ovid's *Metamorphoses* 1567 [The Story of Semele]
And therefore pray him for to graunt that looke in what degree, | What order, fashion, sort and state he use to companie | With mightie Juno, in the same in euerie poynt and cace, | To all intents and purposes he thee likewise embrace, | And that he also bring with him his bright threeforked mace.

interest

declare an/one's interest

to disclose a personal (typically financial) involvement in a matter that is about to be considered or discussed. *20th cent.*

iron

have many irons in the fire

to have several or too many prospective courses of action to choose from, or to be involved in several or too many activities at once: from the former practice of heating smoothing irons in a fire, ready for pressing clothes. *16th cent.*

John Lyly *Mother Bombie* 1594
[Risio] *Then lets about it speedily, for so many irons in the fire together require a diligent Plummer.*

iron curtain

a political or ideological barrier between nations, especially the one regarded as separating the West from the Communist countries of eastern Europe in the years after the Second World War (the *Iron Curtain*). The term was used from the 18th cent. in a physical sense to mean a safety curtain in a theatre. Figurative uses are recorded from the early 19th cent. (e.g. H G Wells, *Food of Gods* (1904) 'It became evident that Redwood had still imperfectly apprehended the fact that an iron curtain had dropped between him and the outer world'), but modern uses are derived from Winston Churchill's application of the term to the political division of Europe into western and eastern blocs: 'From Stettin, in the Baltic, to Trieste, in the Adriatic, an iron curtain has descended across the Continent.' *19th cent.*

the iron entered into —'s soul
so-and-so was greatly affected by suffering or imprisonment: with allusion to Psalms 105:18. Cranmer (1539) rendered this 'Whose feet they hurt in the stocks: the iron entered into his soul', translating Latin *ferrum pertransiit animam eius,* itself a mistranslation of the Hebrew. The Authorized Version of 1611 translates it correctly 'Whose feet they hurt with fetters: he was laid in iron'. *16th cent.*

> Laurence Sterne A Sentimental Journey 1768
> He was sitting upon the ground upon a little straw, in the furthest corner of his dungeon … As I darkened the little light he had, he lifted up a hopeless eye towards the door … I heard his chains upon his legs, as he turn'd his body … He gave a deep sigh – I saw the iron enter into his soul – I burst into tears – I could not sustain the picture of confinement which my fancy had drawn.

an iron hand/fist in a velvet glove
gentleness and courtesy disguising inner ruthlessness and determination. *19th cent.*

> Frederick W Thomas Clinton Bradshaw, or the Adventures of a Lawyer 1835
> But, understand me, I would cover the iron hand with the velvet glove. Not until it was absolutely necessary, should any pressure be felt, but the soft, persuasive one, that would lead.

> Carlyle Latter-Day Pamphlets 1850
> Soft of speech and manner, yet with an inflexible rigour of command … 'iron hand in a velvet glove', as Napoleon defined it.

> Alexander Woollcott While Rome Burns 1934
> She [Dorothy Parker] is so odd a blend of Little Nell and Lady Macbeth. It is not so much the familiar phenomenon of a hand of steel in a velvet glove as a lacy sleeve with a bottle of vitriol concealed in its folds.

iron out the wrinkles
to eliminate minor difficulties. *Late 20th cent.*

> Independent 1989
> Peter McEnery and Dorothy Tutin play the middle-aged ex-lovers who iron out the wrinkles and get together just in time for the final curtain.

new off the irons
completely new; just made: *irons* here are dies for minting coins. *17th cent.*

> Scott Redgauntlet 1824
> And then, Alan, I thought to turn the ball our own way; and I said that you were a gey sharp birkie [young fellow], just off the irons.

strike while the iron is hot
to act while there is a good opportunity: a metaphor from metalworking, in which the iron is shaped when hot by striking it with the hammer. *16th cent.*

> George Pettie A Petite Pallace 1576
> I perceive by the wanton looks of the Queen, that she is determined to entertain some secret friend, besides the King her husband, and if I flatter not my self, her very countinance towardes me imports some likelyhood of love she bears me: therefore I think it wisdom to strike while the iron is hot, and if it be possible to ease my hart of the grief, which her beauty hath bred me.

See also rule with a ROD of iron.

issue

join/take issue
to disagree or engage in argument on a particular point. *Middle English*

> Samuel Butler Hudibras 1663
> Quoth he, If you'll join issue on't, | I'll give you satisfactory account; | So you will promise, if you lose, | To settle all, and be my spouse.

> Sheridan The School for Scandal 1777
> Her nose and her chin are the only parties likely to join issue.

itch

get/have itchy feet
to have a restless desire for travel or a change of circumstances. *Early 20th cent.*

Los Angeles Times 1920
Some day an itchy foot will give you a desire to travel and see as much as possible of this world before you are hurried into the next.

an itching palm

a greedy or avaricious disposition: with allusion to the words of Brutus to Cassius after the assassination of Caesar in Shakespeare's *Julius Caesar* (1599) IV.ii.62 'Let me tell you, Cassius, you yourself I Are much condemned to have an itching palm, I To sell and mart your offices for gold I To undeservers.' *16th cent.*

ivory

live in an ivory tower

to be immersed in one's own thoughts and writing, aloof and cut off from the real world. The phrase originates in French from the pen of the poet and critic Charles-Augustin Saint-Beuve (1804–69), who used the term *tour d'ivoire* to describe the turret room in which his fellow writer the Comte de Vigny worked and wrote. Saint-Beuve was referring to physical as well as emotional isolation, although the second aspect is usually predominant in the usage that followed. The image of the ivory tower is very old, and very sensual in origin. In the biblical Song of Solomon (7:4), the King of Israel gives a vivid description of his beloved: 'Thy neck is as a tower of ivory; thine eyes like the fishpools in Heshbon, by the gate of Beth-rabbim; thy nose is as the tower of Lebanon which looketh towards Damascus.' This image has pervaded poetic thought for centuries, and was clearly in the mind of William Morris when he described Gudrun in his Chaucerian poem *The Earthly Paradise* (1878–70): 'Her marvellous red lips; round was her chin, I Cloven, and clear-wrought; like an ivory tower I Rose up her neck from love's white-veilèd bower.' Ivory as a symbol of delicate feminine beauty is wonderfully evocative, and the transition of the image to notions of remoteness is imaginative and romantic. It caught the imagination of Henry James, whose novel *The Ivory Tower* was published posthumously, and incomplete, in 1917. References to ivory towers came thick and fast in the work of early 20th cent. writers, including Ezra Pound, H G Wells, and Aldous Huxley. Its continued literary use gave rise to numerous compound forms such as *ivory-towered* and *ivory-towerism*.

Jack

Originally a pet form of the name *John*, derived from the Middle English form *Jankin* (later *Jackin*) and influenced by the French name *Jacques* (which is however related to *James* and not *John*). The name has developed a wide range of meanings denoting types of people and also technical terms for tools and parts of machinery and instruments.

before one can say Jack Robinson

very suddenly or promptly. The original bearer of the name, and the reason one might say it, have never been identified. It was used in a popular song of the early 19th cent., but the phrase is recorded earlier, from the late 18th cent.

> Fanny Burney *Evelina* 1778
> *'Done!' cried Lord Merton; 'I take your odds!' 'Will you?' returned he; 'why then, 'fore George, I'd do it as soon as say Jack Robinson.'*

every man Jack

informal each individual; everybody. *19th cent.*

> Mrs Gaskell *Sylvia's Lovers* 1863
> *We thought as we could come back to our dead fish, as had a boat for a buoy, once we had helped our mate. So off we rowed, every man Jack on us, out o' the black shadow o' th' iceberg, as looked as steady as th' pole-star.*

I'm all right, Jack

an expression of complacent satisfaction with one's own lot and lack of concern for others, often attributed to those who are regarded as having such an outlook. It formed the title of a British comedy film (1959) that caricatured the supposedly narrow self-interest of trade unions in the postwar period. *Early 20th cent.*

> G Pearson *Hooligan* 1983
> *Then, as now, the Conservative Party in the 1950s liked to think of itself as a lonely beacon of*

responsibility in a moral wilderness of couldn't-care-less 'permissiveness' and selfish 'I'm all right Jack' attitudes.

Jack of all trades (and master of none)

somebody who can turn to many different types of work (without being particularly well skilled in any of them). *17th cent.*

Charles Cotton *Burlesque upon Burlesque* (transl Lucian's *Juno and Latona*) 1675
And then thy Son, that hopeful piece, | *Apollo, Jack of all-Trades is:* | *Of many Arts forsooth he's Master,* | *An Archer, Fidler, Poetaster* | *...* | *Nay, he pretends to more then this,* | *He sets up Oracle-shops in Greece,* | *At Delphos, Didyma, and Claros,* | *To each of which he hath a Ware-house* | *Stuff't full of lies, for great and small,* | *To gull poor silly Souls withal.*

Dickens *Great Expectations* 1861
'I am my own engineer, and my own carpenter, and my own plumber, and my own gardener, and my own Jack-of-all-trades,' said Wemmick in acknowledging my compliments.

on one's Jack

British, informal alone. *Mid 20th cent.*

Kingsley Amis *Collected Poems* a1979
Some, their eyes on heavenly mansions, | *Tread the road their fathers trod,* | *Others, whom the Foe hath blinded,* | *Far asunder stray from God.* | *And still others – take old Evans –* | *Anchor on their jack instead;* | *Zion, pro- or non- or anti-,* | *Never got them out of bed.*

jackpot

hit the jackpot

to have great or unexpected success: originally in the context of winning a large prize in a draw or lottery. *Mid 20th cent.*

Kenneth Rexroth *The Dragon and the Unicorn* 1950
I pulled the lever just right and hit the jackpot.

jam

jam on it

British, informal success or good fortune won easily. *Early 20th cent.*

David Michael Jones *In Parenthesis* 1937
Some of yer was born wiv jam on it.

jam tomorrow

the promise of reward at some vaguely defined future time. The locus classicus is Lewis Carroll, *Through the Looking-Glass* (1871): 'The rule is, jam tomorrow and jam yesterday – but never jam today.' *19th cent.*

Rosemary McCall *Hearing Loss?* 1992
Jam yesterday, jam tomorrow, but never jam today.

Jane

plain Jane

a dull or unattractive girl or woman: used as the title of a novel by A P Herbert (1927). The name is originally a feminine form of *John*, derived from Old French *Jehanne* or *Jeanne*. Other feminine forms are *Jean* and *Joan*. *Jane* is used in the phrase because it rhymes with *plain*. In the 1940s the name *Jane* became famous as that of a beautiful and sexually alluring cartoon character in the *Daily Mirror*, in complete contrast to the drab image reflected in the phrase. *19th cent.*

Michael Rophino Lacy *Doing for the Best* 1861
[Stubbs] *Bill 'Awkins mustn't go on no more a calling my daughter plain* Jane. [Bill] *I never called her* plain *Jane.*

James Joyce *Ulysses* 1922
Daughter working the machine in the parlour. Plain Jane, no damn nonsense.

jazz

and all that jazz

informal, often derogatory and other similar things: based on the meaning of *jazz* 'empty talk, nonsense' that developed in the early 20th cent., not long after its first appearances in its main meaning. *Mid 20th cent.*

Fiona Cooper *I Believe in Angels* 1993
The waiter brought two cappuccinos. 'Well, how's it going?' said Alex, after a teaspoon of froth. 'It?' 'Oh, love, life and all that jazz.'

Jekyll

Jekyll and Hyde

a person who shows alternating good and evil characteristics: with allusion to the principal character of R L Stevenson's novella *The Strange Case of Dr Jekyll and Mr Hyde* (published in 1886), who is able to transform himself with a potion into a brutal murderer but eventually loses the ability to revert to his normal self. *19th cent.*

George Robert Sims *The Referee* 1891
Through weary hours I lie awake and toss from side to side, | A genuine Jekyll tortured by a much too real Hyde; | And when at last my drooping lids have shut that Hyde away, | The early milk-cart rattles by and bids the demon stay.

jewel

the jewel in the/somebody's crown
the most beautiful or magnificent part of something. *Jewel* has been used since Middle English to denote a thing or person of great value, and from the 19th cent. *jewels of the crown* was a way of referring to the British colonies, and in particular India. *The Jewel in the Crown* (1966) was the title of the first of four novels by Paul Scott set in India under British rule. In more general use, however, the phrase goes back to the 17th cent.

Joseph Beaumont *Psyche* 1648
Disdain's the highest jewel in my crown: | I who to Heav'n's big sovereign deny'd | To bend my sturdy knee, must not stoop down | To take up vile dust.

Defoe *A Hymn to Peace: Conclusion to the Queen* 1706
Peace is the Basis of Your Glorious Throne, | And Peace, the Brightest Jewel in your Crown.

Frederick Tennyson *The Isles of Greece* 1890
The poor man, losing honour, loses more | Than the big jewel in a crown.

jib

See the CUT of one's jib.

jingbang

the whole jingbang
the whole business or group: of unknown origin, although *jingbang* is recorded in a Banffshire dialect glossary of 1866. The word and its variant *jimbang* (the two forms sounding much the same in speech) occur only in this phrase. There may be a connection with *the whole shebang*, recorded in American use from the 1860s. A *shebang* was originally a simple building of various kinds. *19th cent.*

R L Stevenson *Kidnapped* 1886
The men had a great respect for the chief mate, who was, as they said, 'the only seaman of the whole jing-bang, and none such a bad man when he was sober'.

Job

a Job's comforter
somebody whose attempts to provide comfort or reassurance have the opposite effect: with allusion to the prophet Job's reply to his friends' complaints (Job 16:2) 'I have heard many such things: miserable comforters are ye all.' *18th cent.*

Richardson *Clarissa* 1748
He was willing to hope still, against all probability, that he might recover; and was often asking his sister, if she had not seen people as bad as he was, who, almost to a miracle, when every body gave them over, had got up again? She, shaking her head, told him, she had: But, once saying, that their disorders were of an acute kind, and such as had a Crisis in them, he called her Small-hopes, and Job's Comforter; and bid her say nothing, if she could not say more to the purpose, and what was fitter for a sick man to hear.

job

do a job on somebody
informal to take action to harm somebody. *20th cent.*

Daily Mirror 1992
Matt Hughes the 'Grim Reaper' of ice hockey explained the role he has at Wembley Arena today: 'I go out and do a job on anyone who is giving our top scorers a hard time.'

a good job
a fortunate state of affairs: often followed by a clause with or without *that*. *18th cent.*

Henry Miller & James Baker transl Molière's *The Hypochondriack* 1739
We must absolutely prevent this extravagant Match, which he has got in his Head, and I've thought with my self, it would be a good Job, if we could introduce here a Physician into our Post, to disgust him with his Mr. Purgon, and cry down his Conduct.

jobs for the boys

informal lucrative employment for one's friends or associates. *Mid 20th cent.*

Jeremy Paxman *Friends in High Places* 1990
Margaret Thatcher understood the power of patronage early in her premiership. Her use of it was scarcely unprecedented: 'jobs for the boys', Tory MPs had cried as Harold Wilson infiltrated another trades union general secretary or a congenial academic on to the board of one or another of the great national institutions in his gift.

just the job

informal, originally services' slang exactly what is needed. *Mid 20th cent.*

more than one's job's worth

not worth risking one's job over: used to typify the attitudes of minor officials who insist on applying the rules to the letter. The derived name *jobsworth* has existed since the 1970s as a term for this kind of official. The phrase appeared in print in an advertisement in *The Times* in 1925: 'If you've got "that Kruschen feeling" you can't even *act* misery. So it's more than my job's worth to have it.' *Early 20th cent.*

on the job

1 *informal* hard at work; also, by extension, committing a crime. *19th cent.*

Edward Dyson *Rhymes from the Mines* 1898
That's the boiler at The Bell, mates! Tumble out, Ned, neck and crop – | Never mind your hat and coat, man, we'll be wanted on the job.

2 *informal* having sexual intercourse, typically at a critical or awkward moment. *Early 20th cent.*

Robin Smith *The Encyclopaedia of Sexual Trivia* 1990
In the last year of the nineteenth century the French president, Félix Faure, was enjoying his mistress's favours in a specially designed sex chair when he had a heart attack and died on the job.

See also make the BEST of a bad job.

jockey

jockey for position

to seek to gain an advantage in a contest or competition: originally with reference to horse-racing, in which jockeys manoeuvre against one another for the leading positions. Figurative uses of the verb *jockey* date from the 19th cent., occurring for example in Thackeray's *The Newcomes*

(1854): 'She stood over them in a benedictory attitude, expressing her surprise at an event for which she had been jockeying ever since she set eyes on young Newcome.' The phrase in its developed form is found from the mid 20th cent.

Maria Edgeworth *Patronage* 1814
How could I tell? – so much jockeying goes on in every profession – how could I tell, that a lawyer would be more conscientious than another man?

The Times 1955
In Alberta when there was no jury, congestion was caused by lawyers jockeying for position in order to appear before the right judge.

---

join

joined-up government

efficient government in which the various departments act in harmony: by extension from *joined-up handwriting*. Other combinations are also found, e.g. *joined-up thinking*. *Late 20th cent.*

join forces

to form an alliance; to combine one's efforts with somebody else's: originally in the context of military campaigning. *16th cent.*

John Hall *Poems* 1647
The Sisters sweetly walking hand in hand, | And so entirely twisted that alone | None could be view'd, all were together one; | As twinckling Spangles that together lie, | Joyne forces and make up one Galaxie.

See also join the CLUB; join the (great) MAJORITY.

---

joint

out of joint

disorganized or out of order: from the literal meaning of a bone or joint that has become dislocated. *15th cent.*

Shakespeare *Hamlet* I.v.189 (1601)
[Hamlet to Horatio] *The time is out of joint. O cursèd spite | That ever I was born to set it right!*

John Donne *An Anatomie of the World* a1631
So is the worlds whole frame | Quite out of joynt, almost created lame.

See also CASE the joint.

joke

be no joke

to be a serious matter. *19th cent.*

> **George Eliot** *Middlemarch* 1872
> *It was no joke to have fever in the house. Everybody must be sent to now, not to come to dinner on Thursday.*

> **Daily Telegraph** 1992
> *Dummy corpses dangle aloft, to remind us that Tyburn Tree was no joke.*

the joke is on —

the person named looks foolish after attempting to make somebody else appear so. *19th cent.*

> **William Dean Howells** *A Letter of Introduction* 1892
> *I think you owe Mr. Westgate an apology. The joke's on Uncle Phil, of course; but you ought to see that it's rather embarrassing to Mr. Westgate to find himself the bearer of an empty envelope instead of a letter of introduction.*

joker

the joker in the pack

a person or factor whose effect is unpredictable and that is likely to be troublesome or subversive: from the role of the *joker*, an extra card or one of two extra cards in a standard pack that often has a picture of a jester on its face, as a wild card in many card games. *Late 20th cent.*

> **Michael Dibdin** *Dirty Tricks* 1991
> *Moreover, as the joker in the pack, the only person without a partner, I was a subject of general interest, and to make matters still worse, Lynn Carter had conceived a pallid intellectual crush on me and was always hanging around trying to engage me in conversation.*

Jones

keep up with the Joneses

to compete with one's friends and neighbours, especially in terms of social and material standards. The phrase is derived from a cartoon series called 'Keeping up with the Joneses – by Pop' (a pseudonym of the cartoonist Arthur R Momand), which appeared in the *New York Globe* from 1913 to 1931, on the theme of a family's difficulties in keeping up the same standard of living as its neighbours. The story goes that Momand based the adventures on the real-life happenings of his own neighbours, who were called Smith, but he stopped short of naming the strip after them. *Early 20th cent.*

> **Stewart Lamont** *In Good Faith* 1989
> *The adverts scold us and cajole us and wheedle us and fawn us to keep up with the Joneses.*

journey

See a SABBATH day's journey.

joy

full of the joys of spring

cheerful and lively: often used ironically. *20th cent.*

> **Dogs Today** 1992
> *Taurus (April 21–May 21) You're full of the joys of spring at the moment, so make the most of this harmonious period and get out and about to share your buoyant mood. A black-and-white terrier-type will be coming into your life, which could suggest a more interesting, even hilarious, life-style.*

wish/give somebody joy of something

a (usually ironic) statement of hope that somebody will derive some benefit or satisfaction from something. *16th cent.*

> **Shakespeare** *Much Ado About Nothing* II.i.182 (1598)
> [Benedick] *What fashion will you wear the garland of? …You must wear it one way, for the Prince hath got your Hero.* [Claudio] *I wish him joy of her.*

Judas

a Judas kiss

an act of betrayal by means of an apparently friendly gesture: after Judas Iscariot, the disciple who betrayed Christ when he identified him to the soldiers who came to arrest him in the Garden of Gethsemane (Matthew 26:48–9) 'Now he that betrayed him gave them a sign, saying, Whomsoever I shall kiss, that same is he: hold him fast. And forthwith he came to Jesus, and said, Hail, master; and kissed him.' *Middle English*

> **Margaret Cavendish** *The Presence* 1668
> [Tom] *Nay, they will kiss you.* [Underward] *A Judas-kiss, to betray me.*

George Eliot *The Mill on the Floss* 1860
A woman who was loving and thoughtful for other women, not giving them Judas-kisses with eyes askance.

Liz Lochhead *True Confessions and New Clichés* 1985
Pull the wool | Cock and bull | The crocodile tear, the Judas Kiss | The snake in the grass with ssseductive hiss | Will sink his fangs in your wedded bliss.

judgement

against one's better judgement
used with reference to actions and decisions that disregard a strong intuition that they are unwise or ill-advised. *18th cent.*

Pope *The Works of Shakspear* 1725 [Editor's Preface]
Nay the more modesty with which such a one is endued, the more he is in danger of submitting and conforming to others, against his own better judgment.

Maria Edgeworth *The Absentee* 1812
Why should you force his lordship to pay a compliment contrary to his better judgment, or to extort a smile from him under false pretences?

sit in judgement
to presume to judge other people: usually with implications of unworthiness or hypocrisy. The phrase is an extension of the literal meaning relating to legal judgements. *17th cent.*

John Hall *A Rapture* 1647
Wee'l sit in Judgement, on those Paires that lov'd | In old and latter times, then will we tear | Their Chaplets that did act by slavish fear, | Who cherisht causelesse griefs, and did deny | Cupids prerogative by doubt or sigh.

Scott *Redgauntlet* 1824
My father replied by that famous brocard with which he silences all unacceptable queries, turning in the slightest degree upon the failings of our neighbours – 'If we mend our own faults, Alan, we shall all of us have enough to do, without sitting in judgment upon other folks.'

jugular

go for the jugular
to criticize or attack somebody aggressively or decisively: from the notion of attacking a person fatally in the throat or neck, where the jugular vein runs. *20th cent.*

Marti Caine *A Coward's Chronicles* 1990
Over the past few years a new breed of journalist has evolved – hungry, competitive and aggressive. Unlike the 'old school', the new breed go for the jugular ... Words are put into the mouths of the unwary, and thirty pieces of silver are offered to 'toy-boy' lovers, 'plaything' bimbos and ex-Royal servants.

jump

be jumping up and down
informal to be very angry or excited. Uses become more figurative and less literal in the early 20th cent.

Pauline Phelps *A Telephone Romance* 1905 [front matter]
She must be careful to stand with her body turned toward the audience and only her head toward the left. 'Oh, dear, they've shut us off!' is spoken wildly to the front. She must fairly jump up and down in her excitement.

be one jump ahead of somebody/something
to have an advantage over a rival or threat, or to have preempted them by acting more quickly or more promptly. The expression is also common in fanciful variant forms. *Mid 20th cent.*

Thomas McGrath *A Long Way Outside Yellowstone* 1964
Their business is being human, | And because they travel naked they are fifty jumps ahead of you | And running with all their lights on while half the world is blacked out.

Lindsay Clarke *The Chymical Wedding* 1989
Zachaire was bitten by the gold bug and wandered around Europe, one jump ahead of the plague, seeking to learn from the motley swarm of alchemists to be found in the abbeys and cities.

get/have the jump on somebody
informal to get an advantage over somebody by acting quickly. *Late 20th cent.*

P Chester *Murder Forestalled* 1990
The coppers are going to be mad at me, as it is, if I get the jump on them with Vecchi. At least I'll have to be able to give some reason why I suspected him.

go (and) jump in the lake

informal (usually as an imperative) to go away and stop being a nuisance. *Early 20th cent.*

jump down somebody's throat

1 to be over-eager in one's attentiveness, or (said of a woman) to be only too eager to accept a man's proposal of marriage. *19th cent.*

Trollope *The Small House at Allington* 1864

A girl either is in love or she is not. If she is, she is ready to jump down a man's throat; and that was the case with Lily.

2 to speak to somebody in an angry or hostile way, especially in reply to something they have said. *19th cent.*

Sidney Grundy *A Pair of Spectacles* 1898

The client I spoke to you about – the young man, with the good father – with the indulgent, generous father – who unfortunately got into debt – is not a client at all. I meant myself. [starts back – pause – aside] He doesn't jump down my throat!

jump out of one's skin

to be violently startled by something. In early use one jumped out of one's skin from joy rather than fright. *16th cent.*

Edward Ravenscroft *The Canterbury Guests* 1695

[Greed] *I could e'en jump out of my Skin for joy; now will I Eat often, and give thanks when my Belly's full: For I could never remember to say Grace before Meat, in my Life.*

Joseph Conrad *The Secret Sharer* 1912

I stopped at the open pantry door and spoke to the steward. He was doing something there with his back to me. At the sound of my voice he nearly jumped out of his skin, as the saying is, and incidentally broke a cup.

jump the queue / NAmer line

to obtain an unfair advantage over other people: from the literal meaning of moving in front of other people in a queue in order to receive attention more quickly. *Mid 20th cent.*

Mike Ripley *Just Another Angel* 1989

Then we were staggering into a hospital casualty department and I was grateful Bunny was there – they can be dangerous places on a Friday night. Rayleen helped too, or rather her uniform did, giving us a pseudo-official status which meant we could jump the queue.

jump the rails/track

(said of a train) to leave the track, to be derailed. Also in figurative uses. *19th cent.*

Will Carleton *City Legends* 1890

That time in the shady, flower-breathed grove, | Your hand on my arm, we slowly walked, | My tongue of a sudden fell in love – | Cupid himself! – how I could have talked! | But ere the oration was half begun, | A cow broke through the confounded fences – | Charged on us, with a swinging run | … | And so the words my soul would say, | Were drowned in a loud inglorious 'Whey!' | My word-supply-car jumped the track, | In shunting that wretched milk-train back.

jump ship/boat

to desert an organization, club, team, etc when it is going through a difficult time or is about to collapse: from the literal meaning (said of a crew member) to desert the ship on which one is serving when it puts into a port. *19th cent.*

New Musical Express 1992

There's others who are probably more motivated by fame and hit records and money, which to me doesn't make good music. Billy's been brilliant because we've had him on an album-by-album deal, and he could have jumped ship, but he's been really loyal.

jump to it

informal to make a prompt or enthusiastic start; to act promptly: often used as a peremptory command. *19th cent.*

William Gilmore Simms *Beauchampe* 1842

It'll do her good to tell her that it's very dangerous for her to be thinking about young men from morning to night. It's true you can't say any thing about the danger, for precious little danger she's in; but lord! wouldn't she jump to it if she had a chance.

See also jump the GUN; jump on the BANDWAGON; jump through hoops *at* HOOP; jump to conclusions *at* CONCLUSION.

---

jungle

the law of the jungle

the principle that the strongest and most aggressive people are the ones who succeed, especially in business or political life: an extension of the principle in nature, that the fittest and strongest species outlive the others. A key use is in

Kipling's *Jungle Book* (1894): 'Baloo was teaching him the Law of the Jungle ... Young wolves will only learn as much of the Law of the Jungle as applies to their own pack and tribe.' *19th cent.*

Wilfred Campbell *Poems* 1905
Sunk to the law of the jungle and fen | From the dream of the godlike man, | To learn in the lore of reptile and brute | The cunning of Caliban.

jury

the jury is (still) out (on —)
a certain matter is still being discussed or considered. *Late 20th cent.*

Kenneth O Morgan *The People's Peace* 1990
Prime Ministers from Eden to Wilson left office with their prestige lower than when they had entered Downing Street. On Mrs Thatcher, the jury was still out.

justice

do oneself justice
to achieve the results one is capable of; to show one's talents in the best light. *19th cent.*

W S Gilbert *The Disconcerted Tenor* in *The Bab Ballads* 1898
When distracted with worries in plenty, | And his pulse is a hundred and twenty, | And his fluttering bosom the slave of mistrust is, | A tenor can't do himself justice. | Now observe – [sings a high note] – | You see, I can't do myself justice!

She 1989
Increasingly conscious that her age was held against her, she dyed her grey hair and bought a suit that hangs in the wardrobe beside her jeans and sweaters. 'It's a gesture of faith; that one day my life will be so different it will be an appropriate garment. I did get some interviews but I would be so paralysed I couldn't do myself justice. I'd come out cringing and demoralised.'

do justice to somebody/something
to treat somebody or something fairly or adequately, or show due appreciation: often used as an aside in the form *to do justice to —*. *17th cent.*

Thomas D'Urfey *Bussy D'Ambois* 1691
I know too you loved, and were betroth'd to D'Ambois, | One that, to say truth, was a Man every Inch | Of him: nay, to do him Justice, the

Gentleman | Wanted no parts to recommend him, but that he was poor.

Washington Irving *The Legend of Sleepy Hollow* 1820
I want breath and time to discuss this banquet as it deserves, and am too eager to get on with my story. Happily, Ichabod Crane was not in so great a hurry as his historian, but did ample justice to every dainty.

poetic/poetical justice
an outcome in which vice is punished and virtue rewarded in a manner that is particularly or ironically appropriate. *17th cent.*

John Dennis *Remarks on a Book Entitl'd Prince Arthur* 1696
And it is as certain, that the leaving such a villain, as this Saxon alive, is contrary, not only to common poetical justice, but to the moral of the poem, and to the fable, and to the universality of the action.

rough justice
unfair or unjust treatment; indiscriminate punishment. Used as the title of a novel by C E Montague, published in 1926. *19th cent.*

Roger Boyle *Herod the Great* 1694
My generous Friends, excuse me for one hour, | I'm drawn from hence by Love's Resistless Power. | Mean while, disperse your selves in several ways, | For this rough Justice must a Tempest raise: | And drive into despair the furious Jews, | What ere you learn, let me soon hear the News.

Meredith *Diana of the Crossways* 1885
In either case, she has been badly used. Society is big engine enough to protect itself. I incline with British juries to do rough justice to the victims. She has neither father nor brother ... It wears the look of a cowardly business.

kangaroo

have kangaroos in the/one's top paddock
Australian, informal to be crazy or eccentric: the *top paddock* is the head or mind. *Early 20th cent.*

> Peter Carey *Illywhacker* 1985
> And he was a big man too, and possibly slow-witted
> … He had kangaroos in his top paddock.

a kangaroo court
an illegal or ad hoc court having no authority or legal standing. Although first found in North American sources in the 1850s, the phrase is likely to have some connection with Australia, the land of the kangaroo. Perhaps the term was brought to America by Australian prospectors who joined in the Californian gold rushes of the 1840s and 1850s. The connection is unclear, however, giving rise to much speculation, including the notion that it alludes to the (not widely known) vicious streak in the kangaroo's temperament. This is possible but unlikely, as are attempts to find 'jumping' connections between the courts and kangaroos: for example, that they were concerned with 'claim-jumping'! *19th cent.*

> Harper's Magazine 1895
> The most interesting of these impromptu clubs is the one called in the vernacular the 'Kangaroo Court'. It is found almost entirely in county jails.

keel

See on an EVEN keel.

keen

(as) keen as mustard
British, informal very eager or enthusiastic: based on the strong or 'keen' flavour of mustard as a condiment (and *keenest mustard* occurs at a slightly earlier date than this phrase). The phrase in its current form appears in the collection of sayings called *Paroemiologia* made by William Walker (1659). *17th cent.*

keep

keep one's feet/legs
to avoid falling over, especially on rough or slippery ground. The form with *legs* dates from the 18th cent., and the form with *feet* from the 19th cent.

> John Cleland *Memoirs of a Woman of Pleasure* 1748
> She reconducted me to my own room, where unable to keep my legs, in the agitation I was in, I instantly threw myself down on the bed.

> Edgar Allan Poe *The Narrative of Arthur Gordon Pym of Nantucket* 1837
> The hulk began once more to roll so violently that we could no longer keep our feet.

keep open house
to welcome visitors at any time. *16th cent.*

> Thomas Nash *Pierce Pennilesse* 1592
> Lais, Cleopatra, Helen, if our Clyme hath any such, noble Lord warden of the Wenches & Anglers, I commend them with the rest of our vncleane sisters in Shorditch, the Spittle, Southwarke, Westminster, and Turnbull streete, to the protection of your Portership: hoping you will speedily carry them to hell, there to keepe open house for all yonge deuills that come.

keep (oneself) to oneself
to lead a private or solitary life, to avoid company. *18th cent.*

> Samuel Foote *The Trial of Samuel Foote* 1763
> So that, Gentlemen of the Jury, if you have a mind to keep yourselves to yourselves, and not to suffer any body else to be you but yourselves, and your Lordship does not choose to be in London whilst you are living in Dublin, you will find the prisoner Foote guilty.

you can keep it
informal used to reject something or express a lack of interest in it. *Mid 20th cent.*

you can't keep a good man/woman down
(proverb) anybody who is reasonably competent will be able to overcome setbacks. *20th cent.*

See also be/keep on one's toes *at* TOE; get/start/set/keep the ball rolling *at* BALL[1]; get/keep the SHOW on the road; keep one's eye on the ball *at*

BALL[1]; keep one's HAIR on; keep one's SHIRT on; keep tabs / a TAB on somebody/something; keep/put a tight REIN on somebody/something; keep TRACK of something/somebody; keep something under wraps *at* WRAP; keep up with the Joneses *at* JONES.

kettle

a different / another kettle of fish

informal an entirely different matter: an extension of the following phrase. *Mid 20th cent.*

> Evelyn Waugh *Put Out More Flags* 1942
> *Until now the word 'Colonel' for Basil had connoted an elderly rock-gardener on Barbara's G.P.O. list. This formidable man of his own age was another kettle of fish.*

a pretty/fine kettle of fish

informal a confused or awkward state of affairs. A *kettle of fish* is an old Scottish name for a picnic by a river at which freshly caught salmon were boiled and eaten. Here, a kettle is not the familiar closed container for heating water but an open pot for general cooking over a fire. There is a scene in Sir Walter Scott's novel *St Ronan's Well* (1824) in which a duel is being arranged. The time and place are fixed to ensure the utmost privacy, 'for as the whole company go to the water-side to-day to eat a kettle of fish, there will be no risk of interruption.' Scott further described the nature of this excursion in a note to the text: 'a large caldron is boiled by the side of a salmon river, containing a quantity of water, thickened with salt to the consistence of brine. In this the fish is plunged when taken, and eaten by the company *fronde super viridi* [i.e. on the fresh grass by the river]. This is accounted the best way of eating salmon by those who desire to taste the fish in a state of extreme freshness. Others prefer it after being kept a day or two, when the curd melts into oil, and the fish becomes richer and more luscious.' Figurative uses are known already in the literature of the 18th cent., before Scott wrote, and the phrase is entered in Francis Grose's *Dictionary of the Vulgar Tongue* (1811): 'When a person has perplexed his affairs in general, or any particular business, he is said to have made a fine kettle of fish of it.' Perhaps the practical complications of catching the fish and cooking them on the river bank suggest the notion of a muddle, although Scott makes it all sound

straightforward enough. More likely, the contents of the kettle became messy after cooking or when the meal was finished. See also the preceding phrase. *18th cent.*

> Henry Fielding *The History of Tom Jones* 1749
> *'But there is a fine kettle-of-fish made on't up at our house.' 'What can be the matter, Mr. Western?' said Allworthy. 'O, matter enow of all conscience: my daughter hath fallen in love with your bastard, that's all; but I won't ge her a hapeny, not the twentieth part of a brass varden.'*

See also the POT calling the kettle black.

key

in / out of key

in or not in agreement or harmony: a metaphor from music, the key setting the tonal framework for a piece. *Early 20th cent.*

> Ezra Pound *Epode pour l'Election de son Sepulchre* 1920
> *For three years, out of key with his time, | He strove to resuscitate the dead art | Of poetry.*

kibosh

put the kibosh on something

to put an end to a plan or scheme or, originally, to get the advantage of a person. *Kibosh* is of obscure origin, possibly Yiddish. In early use the typical grammatical object is the person affected rather than the plan; it appears as *ky-bosh*, and in its first recorded appearance (in Dickens' *Sketches by Boz*, 1836) as *kye-bosk*: 'Hoo-roar', ejaculates a pot-boy in a parenthesis, 'put the kye-bosk on her, Mary.' Ten years later, *The Swell's Night Guide* (1846), a glossary of underworld language, noted the meaning '*Kybosh on, to put the*, to turn the tables on any person, to put out of countenance.' In 19th cent. criminal slang *kybosh* meant 'one shilling and sixpence', eighteen old pence, and so the current meaning could have arisen from the notion of paying off a debt, rather like the image implied by *put paid to something*, which means much the same as our phrase. But the early uses, which typically refer to a person, make this development a little awkward. Another explanation related to this one concerns the practice of upping bids at an auction: if a bidder increased a bid to eighteen pence he was said to have *put the kibosh* on the fellow bidders:

but what was so special about this particular sum of money (other than the association with eighteen, which produces a circular argument)? Other suggestions are no more than speculative: that it derives from a Yiddish word *kabas* meaning 'suppress', from a Gaelic phrase *cie báis* (presumably pronounced kai baws) meaning 'cap of death', from a High German word *kiebe* meaning 'carrion', or from a Turkish word (also the origin of English *bosh*) meaning 'nonsense'. There is no evidence of any connection with these words. *19th cent.*

kick

get a kick out of something

to be pleasantly stimulated by an activity. *Kick* in the sense 'a thrill of excitement' dates from the mid 19th cent. and was applied specifically to the effects of alcoholic drinks (a meaning that is still common). The present phrase dates from the early 20th cent.

Daily Express 1928
I was told I should get a kick out of that journey – and I certainly did.

kick oneself

to reprove oneself for a failure or shortcoming, typically in relation to a missed opportunity: often in the form *so-and-so could have kicked (or must be kicking) himself/herself*. *19th cent.*

L P Hartley A Perfect Woman 1955
All the way to Tilecotes he could have kicked himself for not having made the engagement for next week.

kick somebody's ass/butt

to punish or bully somebody aggressively. *See also* kick (some) ass/butt *below*. *Mid 20th cent.*

Len Deighton Spy Story 1974
I'll make sure they kick your ass from sun-up to sack-time.

kick the bucket

informal to die. The phrase first appears in Francis Grose's *Dictionary of the Vulgar Tongue* (1785) and its origins lie in the realms of underworld slang. *Bucket* as used here may not be the familiar word but a word (derived from Old French *buquet*) for a yoke or beam for hanging or carrying things on, including (in dialect use) a slaughtered pig, which was hung by its feet. The view, often found, that the phrase originates in the notion

of a suicide kicking away the bucket on which he stood in order to hang himself, is no more than a guess with no evidence in usage to support it. Later analogous phrases such as *hand in one's dinner pail* (see DINNER) and *hand in one's nosebag* (see NOSEBAG) seem to suggest a more straightforward association, but since these are of a later date they may simply be rationalizations along the lines of folk etymology. *18th cent.*

Matthew Gregory Lewis The Castle Spectre 1798
[Epilogue] *I drew my knife, and in his bosom stuck it; | He fell, you clapped – and then he kicked the bucket! | So perish still the wretch, whose soul can know | Selfish delight, while causing other's woe.*

kick the habit

informal to give up an addictive habit, especially taking drugs. *Kick* here is figurative in the sense 'get rid of'. *Mid 20th cent.*

Saul Bellow Herzog 1964
Between his false teeth (to help him kick the smoking habit, as he had once explained to Herzog) he kept a plastic toothpick.

a kick in the pants / behind / up the arse / up the backside

informal a sharp reminder or stimulus to make an effort: *kick* is used with the meaning 'a blow or setback' from the 17th cent. *Early 20th cent.*

Eugene O'Neill Ah, Wilderness! 1933
Aw, you deserved a kick in the pants … making such a darned slob of yourself.

a kick in the teeth

a sharp rebuff or bitter disappointment. *20th cent.*

kick something into touch

British, *informal* to postpone consideration of an idea or suggestion, or to draw attention away from it. In rugby and other field games, *touch* is the boundary line of the pitch; kicking the ball *into touch* puts it out of play. *20th cent.*

Guardian 1989
There has been a startling 25 per cent rise in the number of single mothers within the past year … Maybe this is all that is needed to re-ignite calls for a review of the welfare benefits which single parents receive – a review actually under way earlier this year, but thankfully kicked into touch by Tony Newton when he took over … as Social Security Secretary.

kick a man when he's down

to behave vindictively towards somebody who has already suffered misfortune. *19th cent.*

Thomas Moore *Tom Crib's Memorial to Congress* 1819

What! Ben, my old hero, is this your renown? Is this the new go [= fashion]? – kick a man when he's down! When the foe has knock'd under, to tread on him then.

kick over the traces

to cast off all restraint or self-control: a metaphor from horse-drawn vehicles. If a horse gets its leg over the traces (the straps by which a cart or other vehicle is attached to the harness), it can kick out more freely. *19th cent.*

kick (some) ass/butt

informal, chiefly NAmer to exert one's authority crudely and aggressively: *kick-ass* is a derivative adjective meaning 'crudely assertive', especially in the context of styles of management. *See also* kick somebody's ass/butt *above. Late 20th cent.*

New Statesman and Society 1992

As the Tory manifesto boasts, there are 18 mini-charters, covering health, public transport, education, local government and so on. It will be up to Waldegrave to 'kick ass' when ministerial colleagues fail to deliver.

kick up a fuss/row

informal to express a strong complaint or disapproval: a figurative use based on the notion of raising a cloud by kicking up dust. *Cf* raise / create / make / kick up a STINK. *19th cent.*

Thomas Dunn English *The Mormons* 1858

I kicked up a fuss, but it didn't do me any good. I moped awhile ... but when he took another and another, I got used to it like, and now I don't care if Timothy Noggs marries the last woman in the place.

Joseph Conrad *Heart of Darkness* 1902

She got in one day and kicked up a row about those miserable rags I picked up in the storeroom to mend my clothes with.

kick somebody upstairs

to promote somebody to an ostensibly higher position where they will be out of the way and less influential in one's own sphere of activity. The notion is first recorded in an embryonic form of the phrase in the work of the Anglican bishop and historian Gilbert Burnet (1643–1715) in a passage citing the Earl of Halifax: 'He had said he had known many kicked down stairs, but he never knew any kicked up stairs before.' *17th cent.*

Joseph Mitchell *A Familiar Letter to Sir Robert Walpole* 1735

Were I, Sir Robert, in your Station, | Great Guardian of the British Nation! | Rather than be, by Poets, teas'd, | I'd give them Places to be pleas'd | ... I'd give them all a Kick up Stairs, | Se Defendendo – on Condition, | They'd promise never to petition, | Nor haunt my Levees, crowd my Door, | Nor plague my busy Servants more.

more kicks than halfpence

inclined to severity rather than kindness. *19th cent.*

Charles Kingsley *Westward Ho!* 1855

I starting up saw armed men and calivers shining in the moonlight, and heard one read in Spanish, with a loud voice, some fool's sermon, after their custom when they hunt the poor Indians, how God had given to St. Peter the dominion of the whole earth, and St. Peter again the Indies to the Catholic king; wherefore, if they would all be baptized and served the Spaniard, they should have some monkey's allowance or other of more kicks than pence.

See also cool/kick one's heels *at* HEEL; kick against the pricks *at* PRICK; kick down the LADDER; kick the GONG around; kick up one's heels *at* HEEL.

---

kid

handle/treat somebody with kid gloves

to treat somebody with great care or special consideration. *19th cent.*

kid's/kids' stuff

informal something extremely simple or straightforward. *Early 20th cent.*

See also a new kid on the BLOCK.

---

kill

be in at the kill

to be present at the decisive or triumphant conclusion of a quest or investigation: a metaphor from hunting. *19th cent.*

dressed to kill

wearing clothes that are intended to make a dramatic impact. *19th cent.*

Keats *Letter to George and Thomas Keats* 1818

One fellow began a song, but an unlucky finger-point from the Gallery sent him off like a shot. One chap was dressed to kill for the King in Bombastes, and he stood at the edge of the scene in the very sweat of anxiety to show himself, but alas the thing was not played.

Joseph Conrad *Lord Jim* 1900

Two nomadic old maids, dressed up to kill, worked acrimoniously through the bill of fare, whispering to each other with faded lips, wooden-faced and bizarre, like two sumptuous scarecrows.

if it kills me/him, etc

informal regardless of any difficulties or dangers (used to denote resolve or determination). *19th cent.*

Charles Reade *The Well-born Workman* 1878

I'll know the truth, if it kills me. I'll never consent to doubt the man I love, no, not for a single hour.

it won't kill you/him, etc

informal there will be no harm in it. *19th cent.*

Noah Bisbee *The History of the Falcos* 1808

Don't be so concerned about him, Miss Columba – it won't kill him, to hang there an hour longer yet – it is not best to take him down, till he has repented of his late conduct.

kill oneself laughing

to laugh uncontrollably: also in the elliptical form *be killing oneself. 19th cent.*

Harriet Beecher Stowe *Oldtown Folks* 1869

Harry insisted upon it, that, after tearing his hair and executing all the other proprieties of despair, he should end by falling on his sword; and he gave us two or three extemporaneous representations of the manner in which he intended to bring out this last scene … We nearly killed ourselves laughing over our tragedy, but still the language thereof was none the less broken-hearted and impassioned.

kill or cure

(said of a procedure or expedient) that will be either effective or catastrophic, with no possibility between these extremes: the image is of a medical remedy either curing the disease or killing the patient. The alignment of the two contrasting notions occurs from the 16th cent.; for example in Shakespeare, *2 Henry VI* (1591) v.i.101, the Duke of York declares: 'That gold must round engird these brows of mine, | Whose smile and frown, like to Achilles' spear,

| Is able with the change to kill and cure.' And Captain John Smith's *History of Virginia* (1624) includes the following reference to the Bermudas: 'Some there were that died presently after they got ashore, it being certainly the quality of that place, either to kill, or cure quickly.' The nonsensical use by Colley Cibber (see below) shows that the expression was a familiar one at the time. *17th cent.*

Richard Ames *An Elegy on the Death of Dr Saffold* 1691

No patient under him long grieving lay; | For was it fever, pox, or calenture, | His drugs could either quickly kill or cure.

Colley Cibber *The Double Gallant* 1707

I tremble at the trial; and yet methinks my fears are vain: But yet to kill or cure 'em once for ever, be just and tell me; are you married?

kill two birds with one stone

to achieve two objectives by means of one action or process. The notion occurs at an earlier date in English in other forms, e.g. Sir John Smythe in 1590 wrote 'to the intent that they might hit two markes at one shoote'; and it can be traced back to Roman antiquity in Ovid's line in *Ars Amatoria* iii.358 *unus cum gemino calculus hoste perit* ('a single shot kills two enemies'). *17th cent.*

Roger Boyle *Mr Anthony* 1690

I could not imagine … which of my two mistresses he was in love with, and therefore, which soever of them he talk'd with, I still, Ingineer like, interpos'd, and made use of my legs to salute, at once, the lady, and kick the rival. 'Tis a new invention of my own, and resembles killing two birds with one stone.

kill somebody with/by kindness

to overwhelm somebody with excessive care or devotion. The phrase is first recorded in the 1550s; the locus classicus is the warning made by Petruccio in Shakespeare's *The Taming of the Shrew* (1592) iv.i.194 'This is a way to kill a wife with kindness, | And thus I'll curb her mad and headstrong humour'; in 1607 there appeared a play by Thomas Heywood with the allusive title *A Woman Killed with Kindness. 16th cent.*

John Wilson *The Cheats* 1664

[Whitebroth] *Go bid my Daughter come hither. 'Tis a good Girle, and will make a good Wife; And I hope, who ever marries her, will be a good Husband to her: – She will deserve it, though I say it.* [Tyro]

Never fear it Sir; If ever I kill her, 'twill be with kindness.

move/close in for the kill

to act decisively to eliminate or deal finally with an opponent, competitor, etc: an image based on the behaviour of predatory animals seeking out their prey. *20th cent.*

See also kill the fatted calf *at* FAT; (kill) the GOOSE that lays the golden egg.

---

killing

make a killing

informal to make a large profit in commerce, especially by trading on the stock exchange. *19th cent.*

David Graham Phillips *Susan Lenox, Her Fall and Rise* 1917
But, as I was saying – one of my gentlemen friends is a lawyer – such a nice fellow – so liberal. Gives me a present of twenty or twenty-five extra, you understand – every time he makes a killing downtown.

---

kilter

in/out of kilter

in (or not in) good working order. *Kilter*, also attested in the form *kelter*, is a dialect word of obscure origin meaning 'frame, order, good condition' (*out of frame* is also recorded in the same sense); it is used only in this phrase. *17th cent.*

William Bradford *Sundry Reasons for the Removal from Leyden* 1650
Hitherto the Indians of these parts had no pieces nor other arms but their bows and arrows, nor of many years after; neither durst they scarce handle a gun, so much were they afraid of them; and the very sight of one (though out of kilter) was a terror unto them.

---

kin

next of kin

the person most closely related to one. *16th cent.*

John Heywood *A Losse by the Devil's Death* 1562
The deuill is dead, who shall his land rightly win, | Thou, for thou by condishin, art next of kin.

Coleridge *The Rime of the Ancient Mariner* 1798
The Bridegroom's doors are opened wide, | And I am next of kin; | The guests are met, the feast is set: | May'st hear the merry din.

See also KITH *and* kin.

---

kind[1] (noun)

nothing of the kind

not at all like the thing mentioned, completely the opposite. *19th cent.*

Dickens *Pickwick Papers* 1837
'Get on your bonnet,' repeated Wardle. 'Do nothing of the kind,' said Jingle.

---

kind[2] (adjective)

take kindly to something

to accept a request or suggestion willingly or with pleasure: originally positive (and in the 17th cent. used in the form *take something kindly*), but now mainly used in negative contexts. *19th cent.*

George Eliot *Middlemarch* 1872
In brief, Lydgate was what is called a successful man. But he died prematurely of diphtheria, and Rosamond afterwards married an elderly and wealthy physician, who took kindly to her four children.

---

king

King Charles's head

an idea one is obsessed with. The expression alludes to Mr Dick in Dickens' *David Copperfield* (1850), whose activities were constantly interrupted by thoughts of the head of King Charles: 'In this condition, he felt more incapable of finishing the Memorial than ever; and the harder he worked at it, the oftener that unlucky head of King Charles the First got into it.' *19th cent.*

king or kaiser

a powerful ruler: the juxtaposition of the two words dates from late Middle English, but its modern allusive use is largely due to its appearances in Sir Walter Scott's poem *The Vision of Don Roderick* (1811): 'And thus it chanced that Valour, peerless knight, | Who ne'er to King or Kaiser veil'd his crest, | Victorious still in bull-feast or in fight, | Since first his limbs with mail he did

invest, | Stoop'd ever to that Anchoret's behest.'
19th cent.

a king's ransom

a huge sum of money, such as might be needed to
ransom a king. *17th cent.*

> **Bunyan A Book for Boys and Girls 1686**
> *One Act of Faith doth bring them to that Flow'r, |*
> *They so long for, that they may eat and live; |*
> *Which to attain is not in others Pow'r, | Tho for it a*
> *King's Ransom they would give.*

See also take the King's SHILLING.

kingdom

come into/to one's kingdom

to achieve success or recognition: with allusion to
the words of the malefactor crucified beside
Christ (Luke 23:42) 'And he said unto Jesus,
Lord, remember me when thou comest into thy
kingdom. And Jesus said unto him, Verily I say
unto thee, To day shalt thou be with me in paradise.' 'I come into my kingdom' is the title of a
chapter of R L Stevenson's *Kidnapped* (1886), in
which the cheating uncle of David Balfour (who
narrates the story) is finally forced to surrender
his inheritance. *19th cent.*

> **Thackeray The Newcomes 1854**
> *Sir Barnes Newcome, Bart., M.P., I need not say, no*
> *longer inhabited the small house which he had*
> *occupied immediately after his marriage; but dwelt*
> *in a much more spacious mansion in Belgravia,*
> *where he entertained his friends. Now that he had*
> *come into his kingdom, I must say that Barnes was*
> *by no means so insufferable as in the days of his*
> *bachelorhood.*

till/until kingdom come

indefinitely, for all time. *Kingdom come* is a name
for the next world, with allusion to the words of
the Lord's Prayer 'Thy kingdom come'. *19th cent.*

to kingdom come

the next world as the destination of somebody
who meets a violent death, e.g. *send/blow somebody to kingdom come*. The phrase is entered in
Francis Grose's *Dictionary of the Vulgar Tongue*
(1785). *18th cent.*

> **Peter Pindar Sir J Banks and the Thieftakers 1789**
> *And if they understood their trade, | His mittimus*
> *would soon be made; | And forty pounds be theirs, a*

*pretty sum, | For sending such a rogue to kingdom
come.*

kiss

kiss and be friends / make up

to become reconciled after a quarrel or disagreement. The form *kiss and be friends* is recorded
much earlier, and appears in Middle English
sources; *kiss and make up* is 20th cent.

> **Fanny Burney Evelina 1778**
> *He'll do you no harm, man! – come, kiss and be*
> *friends!*

> **Kipling Watches of the Night 1888**
> *But Platte was quite right when he said that the joke*
> *had gone too far. The mistrust and the tragedy of it*
> *... are killing the Colonel's Wife, and are making the*
> *Colonel wretched. If either of them read this story,*
> *they can depend upon its being a fairly true account*
> *of the case, and can kiss and make friends.*

kiss and tell

informal to reveal intimate secrets about a relationship with a well-known person, especially to
the press. *17th cent.*

> **Congreve Love for Love 1695**
> *[Miss Pru] Look you here, Madam then, what Mr.*
> *Tattle has giv'n me ... Mr. Tattle is all over sweet,*
> *his Peruke is sweet, and his Gloves are sweet ... He*
> *gave me this Ring for a kiss. [Tattle] O fie Miss, you*
> *must not kiss and tell.*

kiss (somebody's) ass

informal to behave obsequiously. *17th cent.*

> **Anon Pasquils Jests 1609**
> *At last he brought him out of the townes end, to a*
> *poore womans house, that kept a little Iseland curr:*
> *whom shewing vnto this good Goose, Looke you*
> *(quoth he) he lifts vp his taile so high, that you may*
> *kisse his arse if you list.*

> **The Times 1989**
> *Fitzgerald's handwritten comments are also in the*
> *exhibition, along with Hemingway's scrawled note*
> *beneath them: 'Kiss my ass. EH'.*

kiss the dust

to be defeated or forced to submit. *19th cent.*

> **Trollope Last Chronicle of Barset 1867**
> *She had yielded, and had kissed the dust.*

kiss something goodbye
informal to be prepared to lose or forfeit something. *Mid 20th cent.*

Guardian 1984
Kinnock went to Moscow and claimed the Soviets will not aim at Britain if Britain scraps nuclear weapons and kisses goodbye to US missiles. But he did not wave a piece of paper.

kiss of death
an outwardly friendly or well-meant act that brings disastrous consequences: with reference to the kiss of Judas in the Garden of Gethsemane (*see* JUDAS kiss). A well-known use, perhaps the earliest in print, was by Al Smith, who was elected governor of New York State in 1926 and declared that his opponent Ogden Mills had lost because the newspaper publisher William Randolph Hearst 'gave him the kiss of death' by supporting him (as reported in *The New York Times* for 25 October). *Kiss of life*, a term for a kind of mouth-to-mouth resuscitation, was first used in the 1960s. *Early 20th cent.*

Guardian 1985
Fear of possible political repercussions prevents Amnesty from publishing any sort of league table, listing where most prisoners are held, or tortured, or executed. In some countries, they say, it would be the kiss of death for a prisoner, if it became public knowledge that Amnesty was campaigning on his or her behalf.

kiss the rod
to accept punishment willingly: from the former practice of making a child kiss the rod with which it was then beaten. *16th cent.*

Shakespeare The Two Gentlemen of Verona I.ii.59 (1593)
[Julia] *Fie, fie, how wayward is this foolish love | That like a testy babe will scratch the nurse | And presently, all humbled, kiss the rod.*

See also have kissed the BLARNEY Stone; a JUDAS kiss.

kit

get one's kit off
informal to undress or strip, usually to please lecherous onlookers: *kit* meaning 'a set of clothing' is chiefly used, apart from sports contexts, in this phrase. *Late 20th cent.*

New Musical Express 1991
Jane Fonda gets her kit off for the evil Duran Duran in groovy pop-art romp 'Barbarella'.

See also the whole kit and CABOODLE.

kitchen

everything but the kitchen sink
informal practically everything imaginable. The phrase was originally used in forces' slang of the Second World War to describe the weaponry used during intense enemy bombardment. *Mid 20th cent.*

kite

See (as) HIGH as a kite.

kith

kith and kin
one's friends and relations. *Kith* is an Old English word meaning 'one's native land' and hence 'one's friends and neighbours'. It became largely obsolete after the 17th cent., except in the phrase, which dates from the 14th cent. and occurs in *Piers Plowman*. *Kin* also dates from Old English and denotes one's family or relations. *Middle English*

kitten

have kittens
British, informal to be extremely upset or alarmed about something. *Early 20th cent.*

kitty

scoop the kitty
informal to win or achieve everything, to be completely successful: originally in the context of gambling at cards, the kitty being the pool of money staked. *Early 20th cent.*

knee

at one's mother's/father's knee
in early childhood, typically with reference to learning. *19th cent.*

Charlotte Brontë *The Professor* 1857

He learned to read in the old-fashioned way out of a spelling-book at his mother's knee.

G B Shaw *Pygmalion* 1913

[Mrs Pearce] *But there is a certain word I must ask you not to use. The girl used it herself because the bath was too hot. It begins with the same letter as bath. She knows no better: she learnt it at her mother's knee. But she must not hear it from your lips.*

bring somebody/something to their knees

to cause a person or organization to submit or accept defeat or failure: based on earlier uses of *knee* to denote a position of submission, as in *go down on one's knee(s)*. *19th cent.*

Wilkie Collins *Armadale* 1866

His thrice impenetrable armour of habitual suspicion, habitual self-discipline, and habitual reserve, which had never fallen from him in a woman's presence before, fell from him in this woman's presence, and brought him to his knees, a conquered man.

G K Chesterton *Orthodoxy* 1908

The aesthetes touched the last insane limits of language in their eulogy on lovely things. The thistledown made them weep; a burnished beetle brought them to their knees.

knee-high to a grasshopper

(said of a person) very young or small. The phrase is an extension of the simple form *knee-high*, which is recorded from the 18th cent. It is also used with *frog, toad, mosquito*, etc instead of *grasshopper*. *19th cent.*

Charles Reade & Augustin Daly *Griffith Gaunt* 1866

A giant who is so long that it takes two days to see him all in, and a dwarf only knee-high to a grasshopper.

weak at the knees

overcome by fear or anxiety: hence the adjective *weak-kneed* meaning 'faint and weak' or 'feeble, lacking in resolution'. *19th cent.*

T D Sullivan *The Killarney Scare* 1882

What an ease to the minds of the mighty J.P.'s, | Who felt chill at their hearts and grew weak at the knees.

See also on bended knee(s) *at* BEND.

knell

ring/sound the (death) knell of something

to signal the demise of something: from the ringing of a bell as a summons to a funeral. *16th cent.*

Shakespeare *The Merchant of Venice* III.ii.70 (1598)

Tell me where is fancy bred, | Or in the heart or in the head? | How begot, how nourishèd? | ... | It is engendered in the eyes, | With gazing fed; and fancy dies | In the cradle where it lies. | Let us all ring fancy's knell. | I'll begin it: Ding, dong, bell.

knickers

get one's knickers in a twist

British, informal to become extremely agitated or angry. The phrase is modern (20th cent.) in its current form, but the notion of twisted clothing as a metaphor for mental confusion is found in George Eliot's *Romola* (1863): 'Thou hast got thy legs into twisted hose there.'

Michael Dibdin *Dirty Tricks* 1991

I ... greeted Alison with ... genuine pleasure. She appeared disconcerted, even flustered. Hello, I thought, maybe there's something in this for you after all. A woman as socially assured as Alison Kraemer doesn't get her knickers in a twist just because an acquaintance ... asks her how she enjoyed the concert.

knife

before you can say / while you would say knife

informal suddenly or instantly. *19th cent.*

Dion Boucicault *The Jilt* 1885

[Phyllis] *Then Geoff will peel, show in our colours, cherry jacket and cap, and before anyone can say knife, he's up. Don't you hear the murmurs of the crowd? 'They are off, they are off!' Who's ahead? The Irish horse leads! No, the Budleigh colours are at his quarters! See, he can't shake him off!*

James Joyce *Ulysses* 1922

Toss off a glass of brandy neat while you'd say knife.

get/stick one's knife in/into somebody

informal to treat somebody spitefully or vindictively. *19th cent.*

George Douglas *The House with the Green Shutters* 1901
It was his son's disgrace that gave the men he had trodden under foot the first weapon they could use against him. That was why it was more damnable in Gourlay's eyes than the conduct of all the prodigals that ever lived. It had enabled his foes to get their knife into him at last – and they were turning the dagger in the wound.

like a (hot) knife through butter
with great ease; without any resistance. *Mid 20th cent.*

Edgar Rice Burroughs *The Lost Continent* 1955
With our buoyancy generators in commission it would have been a simple thing to enter the water, since then it would have been but a trifling matter of a forty-five degree dive into the base of a huge wave. We should have cut into the water like a hot knife through butter, and have been totally submerged with scarce a jar.

on a knife-edge
in an uncertain or precarious situation or condition, especially one that is evenly balanced between success and failure: a metaphor based on the extended use of *knife edge* to mean 'a ridge of rock' or anything sharp and narrow that one might have to negotiate. *See also* a razor's edge *at* RAZOR. *19th cent.*

Frederick William Orde Ward *Christmas Eve* from *Confessions of a Poet* 1894
The gipsy skulking by the hedge, | The infant in its cot, | The wretch on winter's keen knife-edge, | Have all some resting-spot.

twist/turn the knife
to aggravate or intensify a person's suffering or bad feelings. *19th cent.*

Dickens, Collins, & Fechter *No Thoroughfare* 1867
[Marguerite] (innocently) Have I said anything to distress you? [Obenreise] (bitterly) You have turned the knife in the wound – that's all!

under the knife
undergoing a surgical operation. *18th cent.*

Mary Brunton *Self Control* 1810
She accused herself of having given up her love, her wishes, her hopes and fears, almost her worship, to an idol; and no sooner did this thought occur to the pious mind of Laura, than she became resigned to her loss. She even felt grateful – with such gratitude

as the wretch feels under the knife which amputates the morbid limb.

See also a feeling/atmosphere, etc that one could CUT with a knife; NIGHT of the long knives.

---

knight

a knight in shining armour
a romantic chivalrous hero who comes to the rescue, especially of a damsel in distress (*see* DAMSEL). The concept is an old one and the phrase can be found in literal meanings from the 17th cent., but in allusive uses it is surprisingly recent (1960s) according to the available evidence.

Samuel Holland *Don Zara del Fogo* 1656
His device was a civet-cat disburthening her self a posteriore into the helmet of a knight in shining armour, who held forth his head-piece very handsomly.

Leigh Hunt *Imagination and Fancy* 1844
Bradamante, coming to an inn, hears a great noise, and sees all the people looking up at something in the air; upon which, looking up herself, she sees a knight in shining armour riding towards the sunset upon a creature with variegated wings, and then dipping and disappearing among the hills.

Best 1991
I'm in my 30s now … and a lot of my friends are looking round and saying, 'Why don't you have a family, a husband and a baby?' It's this big disappointment. We've been waiting for the knight in shining armour and then there isn't one. Or if there is, he turns out to be impossible to live with.

a knight of the road
1 *old use* a highwayman: one of a number of jocular phrases (most now obsolete) based on the use of knight in special titles, e.g. *Knight of the Temple, Knight of the Thistle. 17th cent.*

Richard Head *The English Rogue Described* 1665
Come my new and young knight of the road, be ruled by me whose long experience makes me able to command, and my love to you willing to instruct you. Ever lurk or lie in some by-place most advantagious and least suspitious which yields the eye the prospect of the Road so, strictly view the booties, that other mens misfortunes may enrich your condition, and the honest mans loss be your gain.

2 *humorous* a person who travels regularly by road, especially a travelling salesman or a member of a rescue service. *Early 20th cent.*

Today 1992
A lone woman driver says she waited six hours to be rescued by the RAC when her car broke down on a motorway at night. Cold and frightened, Beryl Hayden sat locked inside her Ford Escort on the M25 from 7pm until 1am as traffic roared past. The rescue service, which describes its staff as the 'new knights of the road', boasts women alone should only have to wait 20 minutes.

See also a WHITE knight.

knob

with (brass) knobs on
informal, dated even more so, to an even greater degree: typically used by children in response to an insulting or unwelcome remark, in the form *the same to you with brass knobs on.* The notion is of brass knobs as ornaments to a large bedstead or other piece of furniture, and the phrase is now as old-fashioned as these associations would suggest. *Mid 20th cent.*

Nina Bawden Carrie's War 1988
'We could go down, all the same.' 'Though it'ud be a long way back up.' 'Lazy. Fat, lazy tyke.' 'Fat an' lazy yourself with brass knobs on. Come on, let's go down then, it's not far.'

knock

knock somebody's block off
informal to hit somebody hard, especially in anger: normally used in threats. *Early 20th cent.*

knock somebody dead
to make an overwhelming impression on somebody. *20th cent.*

Hair Flair 1992
There's nothing quite like sexy lingerie to put you in the mood so knock him dead on Valentine's Day with some of this sizzling underwear from the latest Freemans Spring/Summer collection.

knock somebody into (the middle of) next week
informal to hit somebody very hard. *19th cent.*

Charles Augustus Davis Letters of J Downing, Major 1834
The first clip I made was at Amos, – but he dodged it, and I hit one of the editors of the Globe, and knocked him about into the middle of next week.

George Eliot Adam Bede 1859
I believe you would knock me into next week if I were to have a battle with you.

knock it off
informal to stop doing something annoying: usually in the imperative. *19th cent.*

Arthur Joseph Munby Ann Morgan's Love 1896
'Master', she said (for, married though they were, | She kept her old allegiance), 'Master dear, | Ah canna beer this idle life o' yourn! | When will yo knock it off, an' let me be?'

knock on/at the door
to try to gain admittance to a group or organization: used especially of somebody who is well suited or close to success. *20th cent.*

Economist 1991
The third problem is the Security Council, or rather the latterday powers that want permanent seats on it. The five that already have them – America, Britain, China, France and the Soviet Union – are discovering co-operation after years of blocking each other with vetoes. But Germany and Japan, as well as several other not-so-rich but big countries, are knocking on the door.

a knock-on effect
an effect, typically unintended, from an earlier decision or action: a metaphor based on the notion of a series of vehicles hitting each other from behind. *20th cent.*

knock something on the head
to put an abrupt end to something, especially an idea or intention. *16th cent.*

Gabriel Harvey Pierces Supererogation 1593
Titles, and tearmes are but woordes of course: the right fellow, that beareth a braine, can knocke twenty titles on the head, at a stroke.

knock somebody sideways
to have an overwhelming emotional effect on somebody. *Early 20th cent.*

Lynne Reid Banks The L-shaped Room 1960
Everything had happened in the wrong order, and now I had to try to bring my feelings up to counterbalance the overpowering weight of this physical

attraction which had sprung up out of nowhere and knocked me sideways.

the school of hard knocks
difficult or painful experience regarded as a useful process teaching one about life. *Early 20th cent.*

take/get a (hard) knock
to suffer a financial or emotional disappointment or setback: based on the meaning of *knock* 'a setback or rebuff', which dates from the 17th cent. The phrase is found from the 19th cent.

> John William De Forest *Kate Beaumont* 1872
> *It is impossible not to accord some respect to a hearty willingness to give and take hard knocks.*

> Gene Stratton Porter *The Girl of the Limberlost* 1909
> *'She was so anxious to try the world, I thought I'd just let her take a few knocks and see how she liked them.' 'As if she'd ever taken anything but knocks all her life!'*

See also bang/knock one's head against a BRICK wall; bang/knock heads together *at* HEAD; get/lick/knock something into SHAPE; hit/knock somebody for SIX; knock something into a COCKED hat; knock/blow somebody's socks off *at* SOCK[1]; knock spots off *at* SPOT; knock them in the aisles *at* AISLE; touch / knock on WOOD; you could have knocked me down with a FEATHER.

knocker

on the knocker
1 *informal* going from door to door, especially as a salesperson or political canvasser: *knocker* here is a door knocker. *Mid 20th cent.*

> Julian Critchley *The Floating Voter* 1993
> *To go out on the knocker was party activists' jargon for canvassing, a thankless task usually carried out at night with the aid of a failing torch and a broken pencil.*

2 *informal* (said of payment) on credit. The allusion in this and the following sense is obscure, but may have something to do with people knocking on doors to seek payment from occupants. *Mid 20th cent.*

3 *Australian and NZ, informal* (said of payment) made promptly or immediately (*cf* on the NAIL): the opposite of sense 2. *Late 20th cent.*

> Jon Cleary *The Country of Marriage* 1962
> *He checked the quote Sid had given him and wrote out the cheque; it was a bill he had overlooked. Sid was a man who wanted cash on the knocker; not for him the luxury of an overdraft.*

knot

at a rate of knots
informal very fast: a figurative use of *knot* meaning a unit of speed of ships or aircraft. *20th cent.*

cut the knot
1 to sever a connection or relationship, especially marriage or an emotional commitment. The notion brings to mind the image of 'tying the knot' in marriage (see below), although the present phrase is found somewhat earlier. *17th cent.*

> George Wilkins *The Miseries of Inforst Marriage* 1607
> *This hand the which I weare it is halfe hers, | Such power hath faith and troth twixt couples young, | Death onely cuts that knot tide with the tongue.*

> Lady Mary Wroth *The Countesse of Mountgomeries Urania* 1621
> *It is true, I was yours, while I was accounted so by you; but you haue cut the knot, and I am left to ioine the pieces againe in misfortune, and your losse of loue.*

> Edward Moore *Fables for the Ladies* 1756
> *Relentless Death, whose iron sway | Mortals reluctant must obey, | Still of thy pow'r shall I complain? | And thy too partial hand arraign? | When Cupid brings a pair of hearts, | All over stuck with equal darts, | Thy cruel shafts my hopes deride, | And cut the knot, that Hymen ty'd.*

2 to resolve a difficulty, especially in a dramatic or unexpected way. Perhaps used with implicit or subconscious allusion to *cutting the Gordian knot* (see GORDIAN). *18th cent.*

> Sterne *Tristram Shandy* 1760
> *'Tis by the assistance of Almighty God, cried my uncle Toby, looking up, and pressing the palms of his hands close together – 'tis not from our own strength, brother Shandy – a sentinel in a wooden sentry-box, might as well pretend to stand it out against a detachment of fifty men, – we are upheld by the grace and the assistance of the best of Beings. – That is cutting the knot, said my father, instead of untying it.*

get knotted

informal used in the imperative to reject or dismiss somebody in a rude and out-of-hand manner. The significance of *knot* is unclear but it may have its origin in sexual rejection (*cf* tie the knot below). Late 20th cent.

Practical Fishkeeping 1992
That still left equipment, so I pondered which BCA member retailer would be least likely to tell me to get knotted if I telephoned with my hypothetical shopping list.

tie somebody in knots

informal to confuse or bewilder somebody completely: often used reflexively (*tie oneself in knots*). The phrase is probably derived from the acrobatics of contortionists and tumblers. William Barnes' *Poems of Rural Life* (1866) includes this bizarre description: 'We zaw the dancers in a show | Dance up an' down, an' to an' fro, | Upon a rwope, wi' chalky zoles, | So light as magpies up on poles; | An' tumblers, wi' their streaks an' spots, | That all but tied theirzelves in knots.' Figurative uses referring to the heart and other organs of the body can be found from the 16th cent., e.g. in Robert Baron's *Erotopaignion* (1647): 'Dispatch thy ayre-dividing Messenger | With sealed Writs, and summon to appeare, | Hymen, Thalassius, and Raucina too, | The sacred Nuptiall Deities which doe | Tye hearts in knots.'

tie the knot

to marry: originally said of the person who officiates, but now more usually with the couple or one of them as the grammatical subject. *18th cent.*

William Byrd The First Survey in the Dismal Swamp 1729
Marriage is reckoned a lay contract in Carolina, ... and a country justice can tie the fatal knot there, as fast as an archbishop.

know

— as we know it

such-and-such in the form that is familiar today. See also (the end of) CIVILIZATION as we know it. *19th cent.*

John William De Forest The Wetherel Affair 1873
'In short, Mrs. Dinneford, the captivity founded Hebraism', summed up the encyclopedical Count.

'The captivity was the starting-point of the Jewish national faith, as we know it.'

Oscar Wilde The Decay of Lying 1889
The nineteenth century, as we know it, is largely an invention of Balzac.

before one knows it / knows where one is

informal with astonishing speed. *18th cent.*

Fanny Burney Cecilia 1782
Indeed, Miss Beverley, you must be more discreet in future, you will else be ruined before you know where you are.

Anne Brontë The Tenant of Wildfell Hall 1848
But I assure you she is as artful a little hussy as anybody need wish to see; and you'll get entangled in her snares before you know where you are.

be in the know

to be in possession of confidential or exclusive information: based on the use of *know* as a noun meaning 'the fact of knowing', which dates from the 16th cent. (e.g. in Shakespeare, *Hamlet* (1601) v.ii.45 '[Hamlet to Horatio] That on the view and know of these contents, | Without debatement [= deliberation] further more or less, | He should the bearers put to sudden death'). *19th cent.*

G & W Grossmith Diary of a Nobody 1892
I did not pursue the subject further, beyond saying that I should feel glad when ... Lupin would be of age and responsible for his own debts. He answered: 'My dear Guv., I promise you faithfully that I will never speculate with what I have not got. I shall only go on Job Cleanands' tips, and as he is in the "know" it is pretty safe sailing.'

Saki Reginald in Russia 1910
Without more ado Rollo made straight for his trio of enemies, plunged his hand successively into their breast-pockets, and produced three peaches. There was no applause, but no amount of hand-clapping would have given the performer as much pleasure as the silence which greeted his coup. 'Of course, we were in the know,' said the Wrotsley cousin lamely.

for all one knows

as may be possible because one's knowledge is limited. *17th cent.*

John Leanerd The Counterfeits 1679
'Twas pleasant to see ... how the present of a jewel diverted him; and the story of a large stone (which for all I know may be an Indian pebble) that I told him was one of the fam'd jewels of the great Montezuma, seal'd up his inquisitive humour.

Maria Edgeworth *Ormond* 1817
But the difficulty is to baffle the sentinel that is below, and who is walking backward and forward continually, day and night, under the window; and there is another, you see, in a sentry-box, at the door of the yard: and, for all I know, there may be another sentinel at the other side of the wall.

know better than (to —)
to be wise or sensible enough to avoid taking a particular course. *18th cent.*

Hannah Cowley *The Town Before You* 1795
[Lady Horatia] *It is believ'd, Sir, that Mr. Asgill has some regard for her.* [Sir Simon] *I hope not. My nephew, I believe, knows better than to regard such a gill-flirt.*

know what's what
to be knowledgeable or experienced. *16th cent.*

John Ford *The Lovers Melancholy* 1629
Marry what is more then I know? for to know what's what, is to know what's what, and for what's what: but these are foolish figures, and to little purpose.

know who's who
to be acquainted with the people who have power and influence; to know the right people. The phrase occurs much earlier in the more literal meaning 'to be able to distinguish one person from another', e.g. in Chaucer's *The Reeve's Tale* (4300): 'She saugh hem bothe two, | But sikerly she nyste [= did not know] who was who.' The phrase is 18th cent. in this meaning.

Swift *The Journal to Stella* 1713
I showed the Bishop ... at Court, who was who.

not know what hit one
to be killed, attacked, or defeated suddenly or without any warning. *Early 20th cent.*

George Edward Dyson *When the Bell Blew Up* 1898
Still we laboured might and main | Mid the ruins round the boiler where the shattered walls were stacked. | Then his wife discovered Barney, dazed and black, but right as rain; | Said he didn't know what hit him – thought the crack of doom had cracked.

not know what to do with oneself
to be extremely bored or embarrassed. *20th cent.*

not know where / which way to look
to be highly embarrassed by what is happening around one; to be too embarrassed to look somebody in the face. *18th cent.*

Gabriel Odingsells *The Bath Unmask'd* 1725
I am so confounded at your Impudence, I don't know which way to look.

Jane Austen *Mansfield Park* 1814
Fanny, in dismay at such an unprecedented question, did not know which way to look, or how to be prepared for the answer.

there is no knowing
one cannot be sure. *18th cent.*

Thomas Paine *The Age of Reason* 1796
The writer of the book of Deuteronomy ... after telling that Moses went to the top of Pisgah ... tells us that Moses died there in the land of Moab, and that he buried him in a valley in the land of Moab; but as there is no antecedent to the pronoun he, there is no knowing who he was that did bury him.

See also have seen/known better days *at* DAY; know something like the BACK of one's hand; know one's onions *at* ONION; know one's own MIND; know one's PLACE; know the ropes *at* ROPE; know one's STUFF; not know somebody from ADAM.

knuckle
go the knuckle
Australian, informal to fight or punch. *Mid 20th cent.*

J Devanney *By Tropic Sea & Jungle* 1944
I always got on well with the blacks, because I never went the knuckle on them.

near the knuckle
close to the limit of what is decent or acceptable; almost improper or indecent. *19th cent.*

W P Ridge *Minor Dialogues* 1895
I can stand a joke as well as anyone, but whispering's a bit too near the knuckle. If you've got anything to say, say it.

See also RAP somebody's knuckles.

labour

a labour of Hercules
a task calling for great strength or determination: with reference to the twelve labours of Hercules in Greek mythology, which called for (and received) superhuman effort. *Middle English*

> Shakespeare *The Taming of the Shrew* i.ii.252 (1592)
> [Hortensio] *Did you yet ever see Baptista's daughter?* [Tranio] *No, sir, but hear I do that he hath two,* | *The one as famous for a scolding tongue* | *As is the other for beauteous modesty.* [Petruccio] *Sir, sir, the first's for me; let her go by.* [Gremio] *Yea, leave that labour to great Hercules,* | *And let it be more than Alcides' twelve.*

> Emily Brontë *Wuthering Heights* 1847
> *This morning she announced, as a piece of appalling intelligence, that I had actually succeeded in making her hate me! A positive labour of Hercules, I assure you!*

a labour of love
a task done for the pleasure it gives rather than for personal gain: with allusion to St Paul's First Epistle to the Thessalonians 1:3 'Remembering without ceasing your work of faith, and labour of love, and patience of hope in our Lord Jesus Christ'. *17th cent.*

> Richard Graves *The Spiritual Quixote* 1773
> *You must submit to the lowest offices in this labour of love; you must pass through evil report and good report, converse with publicans and sinners, and even with harlots, if there be any prospect of their conversion.*

> J S Mill *Representative Government* 1861
> *It is not sufficiently considered how little there is in most men's ordinary life to give any largeness either to their conceptions or to their sentiments. Their work is a routine; not a labour of love, but of self-interest in the most elementary form, the satisfaction of daily wants.*

labour the point
to discuss or explain a straightforward matter in tedious detail. *18th cent.*

> Pope *Essay on the Life, Writings and Learning of Homer* 1715
> *However, an eager Desire to know something concerning him* [Homer] *has occasion'd Mankind to labour the Point under these Disadvantages, and turn on all Hands to see if there were any thing left which might have the least Appearance of Information.*

ladder

kick down the ladder
to reject or betray people who have helped you to make progress in life, especially if they are possible rivals. The phrase is attributed to a dispatch from Lord Nelson (1794): 'Duncan is, I think, a little altered; there is nothing like kicking down the ladder a man rises by.' But there is a pre-echo of the phrase in Shakespeare's *Julius Caesar* (1599), where Brutus warns (ii.i.21–6) 'But 'tis a common proof | That lowliness is young ambition's ladder, | Whereto the climber-upward turns his face; | But when he once attains the upmost round, | He then unto the ladder turns his back, | Looks in the clouds, scorning the base degrees | By which he did ascend. So Caesar may.' *18th cent.*

> Aaron Leland *The Fatal Error* 1807
> *He'll do as all the great folks do, when they have climbed up, they kick down the ladder; or in plain English, he will hang me for fear I shall drop out the secret.*

> Thackeray *The Book of Snobs* 1848
> *She has struggled so gallantly for polite reputation that she has won it: pitilessly kicking down the ladder as she advanced degree by degree.*

lady

ladies who lunch
women who enjoy an active social life, especially those who are free during the day. The phrase was originally used with reference to the wealthy and fashionable women of Manhattan's East Side in New York, and is sometimes disparagingly and ungenerously applied to women who organize lunches to raise money for charity. *Late 20th cent.*

See also a lady of LEISURE; when the FAT lady sings.

laldie

give it laldie

Scottish, informal to do something with energy or vigour: in Scottish use. *Laldie* (or *laldy*) means 'a thrashing or other punishment'. It may be a child's word or be related to Old English *lael* meaning 'whip'. It is used mainly in *give somebody laldie* (i.e. to punish them), from which the present phrase is derived. *20th cent.*

Don Paterson *Postmodern* 1997
Boy gets haud o' this porno movie, heavy Swedish number, broon-wrapper joab, like ... settles back in the settee ... a' these Swedes gien it laldy on the telly.

lam

do a lam / be on the lam

informal to be on the run from the police. The noun is related to a verb *lam* meaning 'to thrash' (with which *lambaste* is possibly connected) and (from the 19th cent.) 'to run off or escape'. *19th cent.*

Frederick Forsyth *The Negotiator* 1989
I'll come, alone, unarmed, with the stones ... Because I'm on the lam, make it after dark. Say, eight o'clock.

lamb

like a lamb to the slaughter

submissively, like a defenceless victim. The phrase alludes to Isaiah 53:7 (a prophecy of the sufferings of Christ, in the Authorized Version of 1611): 'He was oppressed, and he was afflicted, yet he opened not his mouth: he is brought as a lamb to the slaughter, and as a sheep before her shearers is dumb, so he openeth not his mouth.' *17th cent.*

Smollett *The Adventures of Peregrine Pickle* 1751
The notion of perpetual imprisonment, and the certain ruin they made him believe his cause was threatened with, worked upon his imagination to such a degree, that he suffered himself to be led like a lamb to the slaughter, by this artful band of villains.

lame

See a lame DUCK.

lamp

smell of the lamp

(said of an argument, idea, etc) to be obviously the result of long and arduous work (usually rather than inspiration). *16th cent.*

Robert Herrick *Farewell to Sack* from *Hesperides* 1648
Let my Muse | Faile of thy former helps; and onely use | Her inadult'rate strength: what's done by me | Hereafter, shall smell of the Lamp, not thee.

land

how the land lies

what the real situation is: based on the physical meaning with reference to the main features of a landscape, which was originally in nautical use (compare *the lie of the land*, which dates from the late 17th cent.). The phrase dates from the 19th cent. in figurative use.

in the land of the living

alive. The expression is biblical, e.g. Psalms 52:5 'God shall likewise destroy thee for ever, he shall take thee away, and pluck thee out of thy dwelling place, and root thee out of the land of the living.' Allusive uses appear from the 19th cent.

Edgar Allan Poe *The Mystery of Marie Roget* 1842
Now, though we have no evidence that Marie Roget was in the land of the living after nine o'clock on Sunday, June the twenty-second, we have proof that, up to that hour, she was alive.

the land of Nod

a state of sleep: first used in this sense by Jonathan Swift (in the 1730s) as a pun on *nod* meaning 'to dip the head' and *Nod*, the place to which Cain was banished after killing his brother Abel (Genesis 4:16 'And Cain went out from the presence of the Lord, and dwelt in the land of Nod, on the east of Eden'). *18th cent.*

Herman Melville *Moby Dick* 1851
At last I slid off into a light doze, and had pretty nearly made a good offing towards the land of Nod, when I heard a heavy footfall in the passage, and saw a glimmer of light come into the room from under the door.

live off the land

to make a living from natural produce: the phrase occurs earlier (19th cent.) with *country* instead of *land*. Early 20th cent.

See also fall/land on one's FEET; NO man's land.

landscape

See a BLOT on the landscape.

language

speak the same language

(said of two or more people) to have similar outlooks and attitudes; to understand one another and get on well. *19th cent.*

George Gissing *The Odd Women* 1893
'Tell me, then – is there at this moment any woman living who has a claim upon you, – a moral claim?' 'No such woman exists.' 'But – do we speak the same language?' 'Surely,' he answered, with great earnestness. 'There is no woman to whom I am bound by any kind of obligation.'

lap

The lap has been used to symbolize nurture and security, and as the recipient of good and bad fortune, since the 16th cent. Shakespeare towards the end of *Richard II* (1595) makes the Duchess of York greet her son, the Duke of Aumerle, with the words (v.ii.47) 'Who are the violets [i.e. favourites] now | That strew the green lap of the new-come spring [i.e. at the new royal court]?', and Milton in *Paradise Lost* (1667) has the line (ix.1041) 'Flow'rs were the couch, | Pansies, and violets, and asphodel, | And hyacinth, earth's freshest softest lap.' There are references in 18th cent. literature to the *lap of fortune* and the *lap of freedom*, and *lap of luxury* first appears in the 1780s, bringing about a flurry of colourful usage.

drop/fall in somebody's lap

to come to somebody effortlessly or easily. In modern use (since the mid 19th cent.) the phrase is typically used of something pleasant or welcome, but in earlier occurrences the grammar was reversed, with the person as the subject and the context normally one of falling into an unpleasant or dangerous situation: a 16th cent. legal source given in the *OED* refers to 'clemency to be extended not before they do ... acknow-

ledge themselves to have fallen in the Lapse of the Law'.

William Harrison Ainsworth *Jack Sheppard* 1839
Everything has prospered with him in an extraordinary manner. His business has thriven; legacies have unexpectedly dropped into his lap; and, to crown all, he has made a large fortune by a lucky speculation in South-Sea stock.

drop something in somebody's lap

to give somebody responsibility for a particular problem or task. *Mid 20th cent.*

M Hebden *Mask of Violence* 1970
I'll throw this into Pinow's lap. It's German and high-level, and I don't want to be mixed up in it.

in the lap of the gods

entirely dependent on chance or good luck; beyond human influence or control. The expression is relatively recent in the form now familiar. It occurs earlier as *on the knees of the gods*, echoing lines in Homer's *Iliad* (xvii.514: 'In truth these things lie on the knees of the gods') and *Odyssey* (1.9 in the translation of Butcher and Lang, 1879: 'Howbeit these things surely lie on the knees of the gods, whether he shall return or not'). In a letter of 10 April 1922, D H Lawrence wrote as follows about a planned journey to New Mexico: 'I shall be fulfilling my real desire to approach America from the west, over the Pacific. I hope I shall arrive in Taos with ten cents left in my pocket – ten cents left to me in the world, even. Knees of the Gods.' This was perhaps a conscious echo of the fortunes of Odysseus. *19th cent.*

Henry James *The Other House* 1896
She's a poor little lamb of sacrifice. They were at her again, when I came away, with the ribbons and garlands, but there was apparently much more to come, and I couldn't answer for it that a single sneeze wouldn't again lay everything low! ... It's in the lap of the gods. I couldn't wait.

in the lap of luxury

in an environment of great comfort or ease. The phrase first appears towards the end of the 18th cent., followed shortly by a use in Maria Edgeworth's *Moral Tales for Young People* (1802) and colourful uses by Shelley and Byron (see below). Later it was to be a favourite expression of Dickens' and Thackeray's.

Samuel Jackson Pratt *Soliloquies of a Highwayman* from *Miscellanies* 1785
What piles of wealth, | What loads of riches glitter through each street? | How thick the toys of fashion crowd the eye! | The lap of luxury can hold no more.

Thomas Day *The Suicide* 1797
While yet in tender youth, thou tak'st | From him, the sole support he ever knew. | From the gay lap of luxury and ease, | Thou send'st him, unprepared, to drink the dregs | Of poverty and shame.

Shelley *St Irvyne* 1811
Ah! that eventful existence whose fate had dragged the heir of a wealthy potentate in Germany from the lap of luxury and indulgence, to become a vile associate of viler bandits, in the wild and trackless deserts of the Alps.

Byron *The Bride of Abydos* 1813
And Woman, more than Man, when Death or Woe, | Or even Disgrace, would lay her lover low, | Sunk in the lap of Luxury will shame – | Away suspicion! – not Zuleika's name!

Dickens *Hard Times* 1854
'Perhaps some people may ... like to hear, in his own unpolished way, what Josiah Bounderby ... has gone through. But you must confess that you were born in the lap of luxury, yourself. Come, ma'am, you know you were born in the lap of luxury.' 'I do not, sir,' returned Mrs Sparsit with a shake of her head, 'deny it.'

in the 19th cent., often in the form *large as life and twice as natural. 19th cent.*

William loor *Independence* 1805
So, here we are, as large as life. I am, at all events, entitled to one merit – that of being punctual.

William Gilmore Simms *Border Beagles* 1840
I reckon you didn't read the newspapers. It was all there – all put down as large as life.

Charlotte Brontë *Villette* 1853
'Dr. and Mrs. Bretton were at M. de Bassompierre's this evening?' 'Ay, ay! as large as life.'

have it large
informal to go out and have a good time; to live it up, typically by drinking alcohol or taking recreational drugs. To *give it large* is to applaud loudly and excitedly at a show or rock concert. Late 20th cent.

The Times 1993
It's 11pm, 12 minutes before transmission. A comic is warming up the elite night-lifers, exhorting them to 'give it large'.

larger than life
disproportionately large or important. *19th cent.*

Henry James *The Portrait of a Lady* 1881
I don't make professions any more than I make paper flowers or flouncey lampshades – I don't know how. My lampshades would be sure to take fire, my roses and my fibs to be larger than life.

lares

lares and penates
the home. The lares and penates were the protective gods of the ancient Roman household, and came to symbolize the home itself. *18th cent.*

Gilbert West *Stowe* 1732
Two Buildings rise ... | Of These, a Shelter from the scorching Rays, | One in the Garden spreads its rustick Base: | One in the Park, an habitable Frame, | The Household Lares, and Penates claim.

large

(as) large as life
(said of a person) conspicuously or obviously present. The phrase was originally used with literal meaning of a portrait or other work of art that was life-size; figurative uses developed

lark

up with the lark
up very early in the morning: an image based on the dawn singing of the skylark, often in flight 'up' high in the sky. *16th cent.*

Shakespeare *Richard III* v.v.10 (1593)
[King Richard] *Stir with the lark to-morrow, gentle Norfolk.* [Norfolk] *I warrant you, my lord.*

Dekker & Webster *Westward Hoe* 1607
[Justiniano] *Sir, your vulgar and foure-peny-pen-men ... may keepe their beds, and lie at their pleasure: But we that edifie in private, and traffick by wholesale, must be up with the lark.*

Larry

See (as) HAPPY as a sandboy / Larry / a clam.

last[1] (final)

be the last word

1 to be the definitive statement or treatment of a subject. *19th cent.*

Conan Doyle *The Bruce Partington Plans* 1908
As to Holmes, he returned refreshed to his monograph upon the Polyphonic Motets of Lassus, which has since been printed for private circulation, and is said by experts to be the last word upon the subject.

2 to be the most up-to-date or fashionable example of something. *Early 20th cent.*

Saki *The Chronicles of Clovis* 1912
Filboid Studge had become a household word, but Dullamy wisely realized that it was not necessarily the last word in breakfast dietary; its supremacy would be challenged as soon as some yet more unpalatable food should be put on the market.

(drinking) in the last chance saloon

informal given one last chance to do what is expected of one: based on the fanciful name of a saloon or bar. *Mid 20th cent.*

Tom Clark *Jazz for Jack* 1949
scribbling these notes on a Saturday night in the last chance saloon of life.

have/say the last word

to make the final statement or decision about something. *16th cent.*

J Philpot *Examinations and Writings* 1555
My Lord of Lincoln … said that thou wert a frantic fellow, and a man that will have the last word.

Locke *An Essay Concerning Human Understanding* 1690
The Schools having made disputation the touchstone of men's abilities, and the criterion of knowledge, adjudged victory to him that kept the field: and he that had the last word was concluded to have the better of the argument, if not of the cause.

if it's the last thing I do

informal used as an emphatic assertion of one's intention. *Early 20th cent.*

last but not least

last to be mentioned or considered but not the least important: often used as a fairly meaningless concluding remark. The locus classicus is from Shakespeare's *Julius Caesar* (1599) III.i.186, where Mark Antony greets the conspirators after Caesar's assassination: 'Let each man render me his bloody hand. | First, Marcus Brutus, will I shake with you; | Next, Caius Cassius, do I take your hand; | Now, Decius Brutus, yours; now yours, Metellus; | Yours, Cinna; and, my valiant Casca, yours; | Though last, not least in love, yours, good Trebonius.' *16th cent.*

Boswell *The Life of Samuel Johnson* 1791
That excellent place of publick amusement, Vauxhall Gardens … is peculiarly adapted to the taste of the English nation; there being a mixture of curious shew – gay exhibition – musick, vocal and instrumental, not too refined for the general ear – for all which only a shilling is paid; and, though last, not least, good eating and drinking for those who choose to purchase that regale.

last thing

1 as the final action, especially before going to bed: also *the last thing, last thing at night. 19th cent.*

Mary Pix *The Deceiver Deceived* 1698
[Ariana] *Why truly, Beatrice, I always say my Prayers for his Eyes restoration the last thing I do, that is, just when I am falling asleep.*

Wilkie Collins *The Moonstone* 1868
My daughter had seen Miss Rachel put the Diamond in the drawer of the cabinet, the last thing at night. She had gone in with Miss Rachel's cup of tea, at eight the next morning, and had found the drawer open and empty.

2 the least likely thing. *19th cent.*

Jane Austen *Northanger Abbey* 1818
I am very sorry if I have offended him. It was the last thing I would willingly have done.

to the last

until the very end: recorded earlier in the now obsolete meaning 'to the utmost'. *17th cent.*

Dryden *All for Love* 1678
My fortune jades me to the last; and death, | Like a great man, takes state, and makes me wait | For my admittance.

See also BREATHE one's last (breath/gasp); die in the last DITCH; FAMOUS last words; one's/the last GASP; the last of the Mohicans *at* MOHICAN; the last STRAW; on one's/its last legs *at* LEG.

---

last[2] (shoemaker's model)

stick to one's last

to confine oneself to what one knows and not pass judgements outside one's competence. A *last* is a model of the human foot, on which a shoemaker places a shoe or boot for shaping or repairing it. The phrase is derived from the proverb *let the cobbler stick to his last*, translating the Latin maxim *ne supra crepidam sutor iudicaret; quod et ipsum proverbium venit* 'the cobbler should not judge beyond his sandal – a saying that has become a proverb' (in Pliny's *Natural History* xxxv.85). The context in which Pliny wrote these lines was a discussion of a painting by the Greek painter Apelles (4th cent. BC), who pronounced the maxim to silence those who in his view criticized his work without having the knowledge to do so. Erasmus recorded this in the form *ne sutor ultra crepidam*, and it is as a translation of this that the phrase came into English in the 16th cent.

Shakespeare *Romeo and Juliet* i.ii.37 (1596)
[Peter, the servingman] *Find them out whose names are written here? It is written that the shoemaker should meddle with his yard and the tailor with his last, the fisher with his pencil and the painter with his nets.*

H H Brackenridge *Modern Chivalry* 1792
After all, it comes to the old proverb at last, Ne sutor ultra crepidam, | *Let the cobbler stick to his last; a sentiment we are about more to illustrate in the sequel of this work.*

Baynard Rush Hall *Something for Every Body* 1846
Aye! these profound and learned gentlemen say – 'Blockhead! your skull is too thick, you do not understand us – we are too deep for your sounding-line – stick to your last.'

late

(too) late in the day / NAmer game
at a late stage in an activity or undertaking, especially when this is too late to be of use. *18th cent.*

John Donne *In Memory of Doctor Donne* 1633
It was his Fate (I know't) to be envy'd | *As much by Clerkes, as lay men magnifi'd;* | *And why? but 'cause he came late in the day.*

Jane Austen *Emma* 1816
It was rather too late in the day to set about being simple-minded and ignorant.

See also the late UNPLEASANTNESS.

laugh

be laughing
informal to be in a fortunate or comfortable situation. *Mid 20th cent.*

Autocar and Motor 1990
If next year's Mondeos all prove as durable as this, Ford will be laughing.

don't make me laugh
informal used to reject a suggestion with contempt. *Late 20th cent.*

Rachel Anderson *Paper Faces* 1991
Your old man a hero? Don't make me laugh! Your Dad couldn't have knocked the skin off a rice pudding.

for a laugh / for laughs
for spontaneous fun or amusement. *19th cent.*

Herman Melville *Redburn: His First Voyage* 1849
Once Jackson himself ... told a truly funny story, but with a grave face; when, not knowing how he meant it, whether for a laugh or otherwise, they all sat still, waiting what to do, and looking perplexed enough.

good for a laugh
likely to cause amusement though not much else. *Late 20th cent.*

have/get the last laugh
to be proved right or be ultimately successful in spite of others' earlier doubts. *Early 20th cent.*

Theodore Dreiser *Sister Carrie* 1900
But Carrie ... courtesied sweetly again and answered: 'I am yours truly.' It was a trivial thing to say, and yet something in the way she did it caught the audience, which laughed heartily ... The comedian also liked it ... 'I thought your name was Smith,' he returned, endeavouring to get the last laugh.

laugh in somebody's face
to show one's contempt for somebody by laughing openly at them. The phrase has also been extended to cover abstract entities, e.g. *laugh in the face of danger* (or *death*). *17th cent.*

Congreve *The Way of the World* 1700
Prithee fill me the glass, | *Till it laugh in my face,* | *With ale that is potent and mellow;* | *He that*

whines for a lass, | Is an ignorant ass, | For a bumper has not its fellow.

the laugh is on —

a person who seemed to be on top has been made to look foolish. *Early 20th cent.*

G B Shaw *Man and Superman* 1903
[Violet] *Do you mean to work? Do you want to spoil our marriage?* [Hector] *Well, I don't mean to let marriage spoil my character. Your friend Mr Tanner has got the laugh on me a bit already about that.*

laugh like a drain

British, informal to laugh loudly or coarsely. *Mid 20th cent.*

a laugh a minute

very funny or entertaining: normally used ironically. *20th cent.*

laugh on the other side of one's face/mouth

to be made to look foolish after showing superiority or self-satisfaction. *19th cent.*

George Eliot *Adam Bede* 1859
Let it alone, Ben Cranage. You'll mayhap be making such a slip yourself some day; you'll laugh o' th' other side o' your mouth then.

laugh somebody/something out of court

to dismiss somebody or something as ridiculous. The allusion is to a legal case that is dismissed out of hand. *Early 20th cent.*

Conan Doyle *The Hound of the Baskervilles* 1901
'Surely we have a case.' 'Not a shadow of one – only surmise and conjecture. We should be laughed out of court if we came with such a story and such evidence.'

laugh oneself silly/sick

to laugh uncontrollably. *18th cent.*

Fanny Burney *The Wanderer* 1814
This harangue ... soon broke up the party: Miss Sycamore, indeed, only hummed, rather louder than usual, a favourite passage of a favourite air; and the Miss Crawleys nearly laughed themselves sick.

laugh somebody/something to scorn

to ridicule somebody or something. Used with allusion to biblical usage, including Job 12:4: 'I am as one mocked of his neighbour, who calleth upon God, and he answereth him: the just upright man is laughed to scorn.' *Middle English*

Shakespeare *Venus and Adonis* 1593
Even as the sun with purple-coloured face | Had ta'en his last leave of the weeping morn, | Rose-cheeked Adonis hied him to the chase; | Hunting he loved, but love he laughed to scorn.

laugh up one's sleeve

to show restrained or hidden amusement at the misfortune or discomfort of a rival: used earlier in the form *laugh in one's sleeve*. *16th cent.*

John Reynolds *The Triumphs of Gods Revenge* 1635
But our wretched Ursina ... laughes in her sleeve for joy, to have thus happily bereaved Sanctifiore of his life, who so lately and so treacherously had bereaved her of her honour and chastity.

no laughing matter

something very serious: also in early variant forms, e.g. *no laughing game*. *16th cent.*

Richard Whitford *A Werke for Householders* 1530
It [confession] is no laughynge game.

John Healey *The Discoverie of a New World* 1607
The houses of this town (fair though it be) have none of them any foundation ... Had not we rather give honest burial to the harmless stones, then tear them out of their graves? Hold ye content my friends, this is no laughing matter.

play something for laughs

to try to cause amusement, especially from a serious situation. *Early 20th cent.*

New Statesman and Society 1992
He works the same trick in Pygmalion. What emerges in Howard Davies' production is a Shaw played for laughs, dressed to impress, and similarly short on ideas.

See also be crying/laughing all the way to the BANK; enough to make a CAT laugh; laugh one's HEAD off.

laurel

The phrases allude to the laurel awarded as a crown to the victor in a contest.

look to one's laurels

to take care that one's position is not lost to a rival. *19th cent.*

Francis Jeffrey Waverly from *Contributions to the Edinburgh Review* 1844
This at least we will venture to say, that if it be indeed the work of an author hitherto unknown, Mr. Scott would do well to look to his laurels, and to rouse himself for a sturdier competition than any he has yet had to encounter!

rest on one's laurels

to become complacent or uninspired in the wake of previous successes or achievements. *19th cent.*

Henry James *The Ambassadors* 1903
Didn't she just wish to assure him that ... he was absolutely not to worry any more, was only to rest on his laurels and continue generously to help her?

lavender

lay something up in lavender

to keep something carefully for use in the future: in early use with reference to people 'put out of the way' by being imprisoned or kidnapped. *17th cent.*

Edward Ravenscroft *Scaramouch* 1677
[Pancrace, angry at his son Octavio's intention to marry Aurelia] *I'l harken to nothing ... I'l lay him up in Lavender.* [Plautino, aside] *His fears make him require sweeting.* [to Pancrace] *Sir I am glad to see you safe return'd.*

Scott *Kenilworth* 1821
I promise you, Master Foster hath interest enough to lay you up in lavender in the Castle at Oxford, or to get your legs made acquainted with the town-stocks.

law

be a law unto oneself

to be idiosyncratic or unconventional. Originally (17th cent.) used with allusion to St Paul's Epistle to the Romans 2:14 (in the Authorized Version, 1611), and in the sense 'following one's own conscience': 'For when the Gentiles, which have not the law, do by nature the things contained in the law, these, having not the law, are a law unto themselves.' The sense changed from matters of conscience to matters of whim and fancy in the 19th cent.

Laurence Sterne *Tristram Shandy* 1760
In the darkest doubts it shall ... give the state he lives in, a better security for his behaviour than all

the causes and restrictions put together, which lawmakers are forced to multiply: – 'Forced,' I say, as things stand; human laws not being a matter of original choice, but of pure necessity, brought in to fence against the mischievous effects of those consciences which are no law unto themselves.

Nathaniel Hawthorne *The Scarlet Letter* 1850
It was as if she had been made afresh, out of new elements, and must perforce be permitted to live her own life, and be a law unto herself, without her eccentricities being reckoned to her for a crime.

lay down the law

to issue orders or assert one's opinions in a domineering or forceful manner. *18th cent.*

Pope *An Imitation of the Sixth Satire of the Seventh Book of Horace* 1738
Our Courtier walks from dish to dish, | Tastes for his Friend of Fowl and Fish; | Tells all their names, lays down the law, | 'Que ça est bon! Ah gouter ça!'

Scott *Chronicles of the Canongate* 1828
Ye saw how quietly he behaved after I had laid down the law – I'll never believe the lady is in any risk from him.

take the law into one's own hands

to take action on one's own account to right a wrong or have revenge, instead of deferring to a legal authority. *19th cent.*

Dickens *David Copperfield* 1850
But you'll excuse me if I say, sir, that there are neither slaves nor slave-drivers in this country, and that people are not allowed to take the law into their own hands. If they do, it is more to their own peril, I believe, than to other people's.

take somebody to law

to begin legal proceedings against somebody. *19th cent.*

John Barr *Crack Between Mrs Scandal And Mrs Envy* from *Poems and Songs, Descriptive and Satirical* 1861
She's driving the neebors distracted, | They're threat'nin' to tak her to law, | But she squeals aye the louder and louder, | It's done by the way o' a thraw.

there's no law against —

an assertion of one's right to take a particular course of action, usually when under criticism. *17th cent.*

John Crown *The Country Wit* 1674
There's no Law against owning ones own name.

G B Shaw *Man and Superman* 1903

Those who go to the racecourses can stay away from them and go to the classical concerts instead if they like: there is no law against it.

See also the law of the JUNGLE; the law of the Medes and Persians *at* MEDE.

---

lay

lay claim to something

to claim something formally, to assert one's right to it. *16th cent.*

Shakespeare *The Comedy of Errors* III.ii.84 (1594)

[Antipholus of Syracuse] *What claim lays she to thee?* [Dromio of Syracuse] *Marry, sir, such claim as you would lay to your horse; and she would have me as a beast – not that, I being a beast, she would have me, but that she, being a very beastly creature, lays claim to me.*

lay a/the ghost

to eliminate or be rid of a serious anxiety or fear: from the literal meaning 'to prevent a spirit from walking' (*cf* Shakespeare, *Romeo and Juliet* (1596) II.i.26 '[Mercutio] 'Twould anger him | To raise a spirit in his mistress' circle | Of some strange nature, letting it there stand | Till she had laid it and conjured it down'). In early use also with *devil* or *spirit* instead of *ghost*, and from the 17th cent. in figurative use.

Samuel Butler *Hudibras* 1663

For though his Topicks, frail and weak, | Could ne'er amount above a Freak: | He still maintain'd 'em, like his Faults, | Against the desperat'st Assaults; | And back'd their feeble want of Sense | With greater Heat and Confidence: | ... | Yet when his Profit moderated, | The fury of his Heat abated: | For nothing but his Interest | Could lay his Devil of Contest.

lay somebody low

to knock or bring somebody down. *Middle English*

Chaucer *The Manciple's Tale* (line 222)

She shal be cleped [= called] his wenche or his lemman [= mistress]. | And, God it woot, myn owene deere brother, | Men leyn that oon [= one] as lowe as lith that oother.

lay something on thick / with a trowel

to overemphasize or greatly exaggerate something. The allusion is to applying a coat of paint or plaster, and the form *with a trowel* (i.e. a builder's trowel) is derived from Celia's ambivalent compliment to Touchstone in Shakespeare's *As You Like It* (1599) I.ii.99 'Well said. That was laid on with a trowel.' *16th cent.*

lay something to rest

to dispel or eliminate anxieties about something: from the euphemistic use in relation to burial of the dead, which dates from late Middle English. *19th cent.*

Mark Twain *The Adventures of Tom Sawyer* 1876

Mutiny was effectually laid to rest for the moment.

See also burn/lay RUBBER; clap/lay/set eyes on *at* EYE; lay something at somebody's DOOR; lay down the LAW; lay it on the line *at* LINE[1]; lay something on the TABLE; lay SIEGE to somebody; lay something up in LAVENDER; set/lay STORE by something.

---

lead[1] (verb)

lead somebody astray

to encourage somebody to behave badly, or to delude them in some way: recorded earlier in the physical meaning 'to divert somebody from the right path or route'. *18th cent.*

Mary Wollstonecraft *A Vindication of the Rights of Woman* 1792

It has also been asserted, by some naturalists, that men do not attain their full growth and strength till thirty; but that women arrive at maturity by twenty. I apprehend that they reason on false ground, led astray by the male prejudice, which deems beauty the perfection of woman – mere beauty of features and complexion ... whilst male beauty is allowed to have some connection with the mind. Strength of body, and that character of countenance, which the French term a physionomie, women do not acquire before thirty, any more than men.

Edward Fairfax *Godfrey of Bulloigne* 1600

The blowes were mortall which he gave or lent, | For whom he hit he slew, else by his side | Laid low on earth.

Jane Austen *Mansfield Park* 1814
Miss Crawford, in spite of some amiable sensations, and much personal kindness had ... still shewn a mind led astray and bewildered, and without any suspicion of being so ... She might love, but she did not deserve Edmund by any other sentiment.

lead somebody by the nose
to control somebody by deception: with allusion to Shakespeare, *Othello* (1604) I.iii.393 '[Iago] The Moor is of a free and open nature, I That thinks men honest that but seem to be so, I And will as tenderly be led by th' nose I As asses are.' *17th cent.*

Francis Bacon *Essays (Of Suitors)* 1601
In suits which a man doth not well understand, it is good to refer them to some friend of trust and judgment, that may report, whether he may deal in them with honor: but let him choose well his referendaries, for else he may be led by the nose.

lead from the front
to involve oneself actively in an undertaking in which one is directing others. *20th cent.*

lead with the chin
informal to speak or act in a way that invites retaliation: originally boxing slang, referring to a contestant who leaves his chin unprotected and is therefore likely to be hit. *Mid 20th cent.*

Fiona Cooper *Jay Loves Lucy* 1991
Each business meeting put a spark of challenge in her green eyes. She led with the chin and got her own way most of the time.

See also lead somebody a (merry) DANCE; lead somebody up the GARDEN path.

---

lead² (the metal)

go down / NAmer over like a lead balloon
informal to be a complete failure: used especially of suggestions, jokes, etc made in public. The image is of a balloon made of lead plummeting to the ground. *Cf* go down a BOMB. *Late 20th cent.*

Today 1992
John Major's tub-thumping speech at the Guildhall on Monday night went down in the City like a lead balloon. It smacked of deja vu.

lead in one's pencil
informal male vigour, especially sexual: there is an obvious analogy and word play with *penis*,

which is also related to *pencil* in being derived from Latin *penicillus* 'little brush', a diminutive of *penis* meaning 'tail'. *Mid 20th cent.*

Simon Brett *Cast in Order of Disappearance* 1975
Steenie was putting the show on, and he'd got a thing going with this bint Veronica. Always put it about a bit, Steenie. Had a lot of lead in his pencil, that boy.

swing the lead
informal, originally services' slang to neglect one's work by making excuses; to malinger. *Lead* here refers to the weight at the end of a line used to determine the depth of water; swinging the lead would distort the reading. *Early 20th cent.*

---

leaf

shake/tremble like a leaf
to shake or tremble from fear or anxiety. *17th cent.*

Benjamin Keach *The Glorious Lover* 1679
My very Name is frightful unto all, I Who trembling fly, if I upon them fall. I ... I See how they faint, and shrink, and shreek for fear, I If of my coming once they do but hear: I They quiver all, and like a Leaf do shake, I And dare not stand when I approaches make.

take a leaf out of somebody's book
to follow somebody's example in a specific matter. *19th cent.*

John Howard Payne *The Fall of Algiers* 1825
[Algernon] Instruct me then; how can the threatening danger be averted? [Timothy] By doing as I shall direct; or in other words, by taking a leaf out of my book. [He tears a leaf from his note-book, and delivers it to Algernon.]

Thomas Hughes *Tom Brown at Oxford* 1861
It is a great pity that some of our instructors in more important matters ... will not take a leaf out of the same book.

turn over a new leaf
to decide to improve one's behaviour or way of life: from the former practice of making a pupil who had spoilt a page of a copybook turn over the page and write out the exercise again. *16th cent.*

Richard Braithwait *A Comment upon the Wife of Bathes Tale* 1615
She puts him to his Book-Oath, but he will neither take it, nor her by his goodwill. He must now turn

over a new Leaf, and act another fresh Scene of Sorrow.

leak

have/take a leak
informal, originally NAmer to urinate. *Mid 20th cent.*

Robinson Jeffers *Collected Poetry* a1938
Uh? Who's drunk? | I was drunk this afternoon, but let me go take a leak, | We'll see who's drunk.

Graham Greene *Travels with my Aunt* 1969
All these hours of standing without taking a leak.

See also SPRING a leak.

lean

See bend/fall/lean over backwards *at* BACK-WARD(S).

leap

by/in leaps and bounds
with great speed and rapid progress. Now used typically in complimentary senses, although the use by Dryden (see below) implies excess rather than achievement. *17th cent.*

Dryden *The Art of Poetry (The Epic)* a1700
Yet sometimes artless poets ... | Puffed with vain pride, presume they understand, | And boldly take the trumpet in their hand: | Their fustian muse each accident confounds; | Nor can she fly, but rise by leaps and bounds, | Till, their small stock of learning quickly spent, | Their poem dies for want of nourishment.

Pope transl Homer's *Iliad* 1720
High o'er the surging Tide, by Leaps and Bounds, | He wades, and mounts; the parted Wave resounds.

a leap in the dark
a difficult or hazardous action undertaken without knowing the likely outcome. The phrase seems to owe its origin to the last words attributed to the philosopher Thomas Hobbes in 1679: 'I am about to take my last voyage, a great leap in the dark.' It was given a substantial boost when it was used in a speech by Lord Derby in 1867 during the debate on the Parliamentary Reform Bill, which proposed major changes to the electoral franchise: 'No doubt we are making a great experiment, and "taking a leap in the dark".' Also, in more recent use, 'a wild guess'. *17th cent.*

John Dunton *A Voyage Round the World* 1691
He had found a hole to creep out of the World at, and was going to take a long leap in the dark he cou'd not tell whither.

Mark Corner *Does God Exist?* 1991
Faith ... is a deliberate defiance of what reason says, a leap into the dark that accepts that which it claims is 'absurd' or 'paradoxical'.

leap to the eye
to be clearly visible or apparent. Hookes' use (see below) is not quite in the current sense, although it foreshadows it. *17th cent.*

Nicholas Hookes *Amanda* 1653
Joy ... like your Conserves, with more choice delight | Feeds all the humours of the appetite, | Playes with a curious palate, and from thence | Leaps to the eye, then to another sense, | So doth enrich the soul.

George Douglas Brown *The House with Green Shutters* 1901
The fields are not similar as pancakes; they have their difference; each leaps to the eye with a remembered and peculiar charm.

Michael Field *The Accuser* 1911
[Herod] Prove me this love of which there is no proof, | Prove me my children's love! That they love you | Leaps to the eye.

lease

a new lease of / NAmer on life
a renewed period of healthy activity, strength, or usefulness: a metaphor from property law. The notion of *life* as a leasehold occurs in Shakespeare's 2 *Henry VI* (1591) IV.ix.5: '[Cade] These five days have I hid me in these woods and durst not peep out ... But now am I so hungry that if I might have a lease of my life for a thousand years, I could stay no longer.' *17th cent.*

Thomas Randolph *Hey for Honestie, Down with Knavery* (transl Aristophanes' *Plutus*) 1651
[Old Woman] How do you think I can endure to lie alone, when so many sprights are walking? How shall I keep off the nightmare, or defend my self against the temptations of an incubus? [Chremylus] Alas good relique of antiquity! pay thy fine and take a new lease of lust.

John Crown *The Destruction of Jerusalem by Titus Vespasian* 1677
[Phraates] *I wou'd not a new Lease of life refuse, | Cou'd I the deed obtain by any Art.*

leash

strain at the leash

to be eager to start a task or activity. The image is of a dog pulling at its leash in an effort to get away. *19th cent.*

Edith Nesbit *Songs of Love and Empire* 1898
Like an angry sun, like a splendid star, | War gleams down the long years' track; | They strain at the leash, the dogs of war, | And who shall hold them back?

least

least said, soonest mended

(proverb) a difficulty or disagreement can best be resolved by avoiding discussion of it. The expression dates from the 18th cent. in this form (usually *least said is soonest mended*), but the notion dates from the 15th cent. and is recorded in John Heywood's *Two Hundred Epigrammes* (1555): 'Lyttle sayde, soone amended.'

James Cobb *The Strangers at Home* 1786
[Regnalto] *Wretch! what have you to say in defence of yourself?* [Aldobrand] *Nothing good Signor Regnalto – Least said is soonest mended.*

not (in) the least

not at all: typically used as a polite but emphatic denial or rejection. *18th cent.*

Swift *Gulliver's Travels* 1726
I am not in the least provoked at the sight of a lawyer, a pick-pocket, a colonel ... a politician, a whore-master, a physician ... a traitor, or the like; this is all according to the due course of things: but when I behold a lump of deformity and diseases both in body and mind, smitten with pride, it immediately breaks all the measures of my patience.

not least

especially, in particular. *18th cent.*

Dr Johnson in Boswell's *Life of Samuel Johnson* 1791
The supreme power has, in all ages, paid some attention to the voice of the people; and that voice does not least deserve to be heard, when it calls out

for mercy. There is now a very general desire that Dodd's life should be spared.

to say the least (of it)

to put it mildly: used with reference to a disapproving statement that could be expressed more strongly if one wished. *19th cent.*

Wilkie Collins *No Name* 1862
Her doubt was confirmed as a certainty; and the result, which might be expected to take place towards the end of the summer, was, at her age and with her constitutional peculiarities, a subject for serious future anxiety, to say the least of it.

leave

leave much / a lot to be desired

to be very unsatisfactory. Also recorded in the form *leave little to be desired* (and earlier *leave nothing to wish*) with the opposite sense. *19th cent.*

Harold Frederic *The Damnation of Theron Ware* 1896
They admitted freely that, by the light of his example, their own husbands and sons left much to be desired.

leave somebody standing

informal to surpass somebody spectacularly. *Early 20th cent.*

Henry Newbolt *Poems New and Old* 1921
He's leading them straight for Blackmoor Gate, | And he's setting a pounding pace! | We're running him now on a breast-high scent, | But he leaves us standing still; | When we swing round by Westland Pound | He's far up Challacombe Hill.

Marti Caine *A Coward's Chronicles* 1990
If I stretch my imagination, I can admit to feeling a little tired lately, but put that down to the ageing process. I still have an abundance of energy that leaves my contemporaries standing.

leave something to chance

to take a risk that something will work out well without ensuring that it does. Also *leave nothing to chance* 'to make every effort to avoid failure or disappointment'. *17th cent.*

Sir Arthur Gorges transl Lucan's *Pharsalia* 1614
Lest that confusions murdrous might | Shold wrong the work that they would right: | For if this rage to chance were left, | Thy life (O King) might so be reft.

Charles Duffett *The Spanish Rogue* 1674
Some way their bus'ness shall my own advance, |
I'll follow them, and leave the rest to chance.

Eliza Haywood *The History of Miss Betsy Thoughtless*
1751
At first, she thought of going to the painter, and
bribe him to take a copy of it for her use; – 'but then,'
said she, 'a copy taken from a copy goes still farther
from the original; – besides, he may betray me, or he
may not have time to do it, and I would leave
nothing to chance.'

Frances Brooke *The History of Emily Montague* 1769
You see them just turn the turf once lightly over,
and, without manuring the ground, or even
breaking the clods of earth, throw in the seed in the
same careless manner, and leave the event to chance,
without troubling themselves further till it is fit to
reap.

take leave of one's senses
to act foolishly; to be crazy: often in the form of a
question (*have you taken leave of your senses?*) put
to somebody who has acted in an extraordinary
manner. *19th cent.*

John Blake White *The Mysteries of the Castle* 1807
The scoundrel has taken leave of his senses! What
can this confusion mean?

Dickens *David Copperfield* 1850
'Copperfield,' he said at length, in a breathless voice,
'have you taken leave of your senses?' 'I have taken
leave of you,' said I, wresting my hand away. 'You
dog, I'll know no more of you.'

See also be left at the POST; carry / hold / be left
holding the BABY; leave somebody COLD; leave no
STONE unturned; leave WELL alone; take FRENCH
leave.

leech

like a leech
clingingly or obsequiously close to somebody:
from the action of leeches in clinging to the
skin of a person or animal to suck blood. *18th
cent.*

Congreve *The Way of the World* 1700
[Lady Wishfort (to Mrs. Marwood)] *Oh, don't*
leave me destitute in this perplexity! – no, stick to
me, my good genius. [Mrs. Fainall] *I tell you,*
madam, you are abused. – Stick to you! ay, like a

leech, to suck your best blood – she'll drop off when
she's full.

leeway

make up (the) leeway
to recover from a shortcoming in performance
due to lost or wasted time: a nautical metaphor
based on the leeway, or amount of deviation, by
which a ship drifted or was blown from its
course. *19th cent.*

R L Stevenson *Kidnapped* 1886
Though I was clumsy enough and (not being firm
on my sealegs) sometimes fell with what I was
bringing them, both Mr. Riach and the captain were
singularly patient. I could not but fancy they were
making up leeway with their consciences, and that
they would scarce have been so good with me if they
had not been worse with Ransome.

left

have two left feet
to move clumsily or awkwardly: often used of an
inept (usually male) dancer. *Early 20th cent.*

left, right, and centre
everywhere, in every direction. *20th cent.*

Paul Muldoon *Lunch with Pancho Villa* from *Mules*
1977
Look, son. Just look around you. | People are get-
ting themselves killed | Left, right and centre |
While you do what? Write rondeaux?

See also HANG a left.

left-handed
See a back-handed/left-handed COMPLIMENT.

leg

feel/find one's legs
to remain standing or walking, especially after a
period of incapacity (*cf* Shakespeare, 2 *Henry VI*
(1591) II.i.150 '[Simpcox] Alas, master, I am not
able even to stand alone. | You go about to
torture me in vain. (*Enter a Beadle with whips.*)
[Gloucester] Well, sirrah, we must have you find
your legs. | (*To the Beadle*) Whip him till he leap
over that same stool'). *16th cent.*

Dickens *The Cricket on the Hearth* 1845
Two months and three da-ays! Vaccinated just six weeks ago-o! Took very fine-ly! Considered, by the doctor, a remarkably beautiful chi-ild! Equal to the general run of children at five months o-old! Takes notice, in a way quite won-der-ful! May seem impossible to you, but feels his legs al-ready!

get one's leg over
informal to have sexual intercourse: the phrase is modern in its present form, although there are earlier references to the physical manoeuvre involved. A *leg-over* (attested from the 1970s) is an act of sexual intercourse. *Late 20th cent.*

Esquire 1993
The Oxford of the late Sixties was going through the heady delights of the sexual revolution. Anyone who didn't get his leg over and smoke a few joints wasn't in it as a normal human being.

have the legs of somebody/something
to outdo somebody in speed or stamina. *19th cent.*

not have a leg to stand on
to lack the least support or basis for one's position, especially in a controversy. *19th cent.*

Charles Lamb *Last Essays of Elia* 1833
But the fashion of jokes, with all other things, passes away; as did the transient mode [the fashion for pink stockings] which had so favoured us. The ankles of our fair friends in a few weeks began to reassume their whiteness, and left us scarce a leg to stand upon.

on one's/its last legs
near the end of one's resources or of a thing's useful existence; on the verge of failure or exhaustion. The original meaning was 'near to death'. The expression occurs several times in the works of John Dryden. *17th cent.*

Dryden *The Kind Keeper* 1680
Sir; Debauchery is upon its last Legs in England: witty men began the Fashion; and, now the Fops are got into't, 'tis time to leave it.

shake a leg
1 *informal* to dance freely. *18th cent.*

Edward Thompson *The Syrens* 1776
[George] Since I could crack a biscuit, the wind never piped such a reel to my understanding. [Frank] It is shaking a leg to a rum tune.

Burns *Kilmarnock* 1786
I'll laugh an' sing, an' shake my leg, | As lang's I dow!

2 *informal* to hurry up; to be prompt; to get up briskly in the morning. *20th cent.*

show a leg
British, *informal* to get out of bed; to start doing something useful. *19th cent.*

Conan Doyle *The Sign of Four* 1890
He tapped at the winder – about three it would be. 'Show a leg, matey,' says he: 'time to turn out guard.'

stretch one's legs
to go for a short walk, especially after a period of inactivity. In earlier use *stretching the legs* meant walking briskly but now it usually suggests a casual stroll. The phrase dates from the 17th cent., and the sense weakens during the 18th cent.

John Dunton *A Voyage Round the World* 1691
This divine cottage is situated some leagues from the temple; so that the Holy Man with crab-tree truncheon sets out with the sun, and stretcheth his legs with a good handsom walk.

Richard Cumberland *The Natural Son* 1785
With your leave, I'll stretch my legs awhile; I have been so long in the saddle, that, except two or three tumbles and a roll by the way, I have scarce felt my feet these three days.

Wilkie Collins *The Woman in White* 1860
My mind is more easy than it was; and I am going out to stretch my big legs with a sunny little summer walk.

See also BREAK a leg!; KEEP one's feet/legs; on one's HIND legs; PULL somebody's leg.

legend

a legend in one's lifetime
a person of great fame and achievement, comparable to the heroes of legend. The phrase was first used by Lytton Strachey in *Eminent Victorians* (1918), where he wrote of Florence Nightingale that 'she was a legend in her lifetime, and she knew it'. In the 1970s the phrase was given an ironic twist in the form *a legend in one's own lunchtime*, initially with reference to Clifford Makins, former sports editor of the *Observer*. *Early 20th cent.*

legit

on the legit

informal honest; within the law. *Legit* is short for *legitimate* (in the meaning 'legal'), and has been in use from the end of the 19th cent. *Mid 20th cent.*

leisure

at one's leisure

at a time that suits one; when one feels like it. *At leisure*, meaning 'having time to spare, without urgency', dates from Middle English, occurring in the *Cursor Mundi* (a long northern poem on man's spiritual development, *c*1300) and in Chaucer. Note also Byron's maxim in *Don Juan* (1823): 'Men love in haste, but they detest at leisure', and the more specific warning against hasty action contained in the proverb *marry at haste and repent at leisure* (recorded in this form from the 17th cent.). *15th cent.*

> Shakespeare *Venus and Adonis* 1593
> *A thousand kisses buys my heart from me; | And pay them at thy leisure, one by one.*

a lady/woman/man/gentleman/person of leisure

a person who has private means and does not have to work for a living. *19th cent.*

> Epes Sargent *What's to be Done* 1842
> *Her dress was extremely plain, and, from the rapidity of her movements, it was evident that she was not a young lady of leisure.*

> Oliver Wendell Holmes *The Bunker-Hill Battle* from *Complete Poems* 1912
> *Every woman's heart grew bigger when we saw his manly figure, | With the banyan buckled round it, standing up so straight and tall; | Like a gentleman of leisure who is strolling out for pleasure, | Through the storm of shells and cannon-shot he walked around the wall.*

lemon

the answer's a lemon

informal used to show that there is no satisfactory or useful answer to a question. *Lemon* has been used since the early 20th cent. in American slang to mean anything useless or disappointing, and may be connected with the lemon as an image

that appears, usually denoting failure, in gambling machines. *Early 20th cent.*

> Nicholas Freeling *Tsing-Boum* 1969
> *One makes requests through official channels and the answer is a lemon.*

hand somebody a lemon

informal to pass off something fake as the genuine article; to swindle somebody. *Early 20th cent.*

lend

lend an ear / one's ears

to listen to somebody with attention and sympathy: *lend a deaf ear*, meaning 'to refuse to listen', occurs in Middle English, predating the phrase in its current form. The phrase is often used with conscious or subconscious allusion to the famous opening line of Antony's speech at the funeral of Caesar in Shakespeare's *Julius Caesar* (1599) III.ii.74: 'Friends, Romans, countrymen, lend me your ears.' The phrase occurs elsewhere in Shakespeare, e.g. in *1 Henry IV* (1596) I.iii.216: '[Worcester] You start away, | And lend no ear unto my purposes.' *16th cent.*

> Milton *Paradise Regained* 1671
> *To sage Philosophy next lend thine ear.*

lend one's name to something

1 to agree to support an idea or enterprise publicly. *19th cent.*

> Arthur Hugh Clough ed. Dryden's transl of Plutarch's *Life of Galba* 1864
> *He overthrew Nero rather by his fame and repute in the world than by actual force and power … To him the title was offered, and by him it was accepted; and simply lending his name to Vindex's attempt, he gave to what had been called rebellion before, the name of a civil war.*

2 one thing lends its name to another when the second thing takes the name of the first. *19th cent.*

See also give/lend a (helping) HAND.

less

in less than no time

informal very quickly. *19th cent.*

> Lewis Carroll *Alice's Adventures in Wonderland* 1865
> *The Queen's argument was that, if something wasn't done about it in less than no time, she'd have everybody executed, all round.*

lesser

the lesser evil / the lesser of two evils

the less harmful or unsatisfactory of two bad choices: originally (in Chaucer and elsewhere) as a proverb *choose the lesser of two harms/evils*, etc. The notion goes back to classical writers (e.g. Cicero *De Officiis* iii.29 *minima de malis* '[choose] the least of evils'). *Middle English*

> Thomas Paine *The Rights of Man* 1792
> *After this, another William, descended from the same stock, and claiming from the same origin, gained possession; and of the two evils, James and William, the nation preferred what it thought the least; since, from circumstances, it must take one.*

let

let alone —

even disregarding some other person or thing that might be mentioned; not to mention them. There is a significant use by Maria Edgeworth in her historical novel (one of the earliest of the genre) *Castle Rackrent* (1800): 'Now it was that the world was to see what was in Sir Patrick [O'Shaughlin]. On coming into the estate, he gave the finest entertainment ever was heard of in the country – not a man could stand after supper but Sir Patrick himself, who could sit out the best man in Ireland, let alone the three kingdoms itself.' In a glossary note we find the comment '*Let alone*, in this sentence, means put out of the consideration. This phrase *let alone*, which is now used as the imperative of a verb, may in time become a conjunction, and may exercise the ingenuity of some future etymologist.' The phrase is developed from the notion of letting or leaving somebody alone, in the sense 'not to bother with them or have dealings with them'. *Let* and *leave* were interchangeable in this context. A character in Richardson's epistolary novel *The History of Sir Charles Grandison* (1753) observes 'I was about to ask a question – but 'tis better let alone'. Jane Austen, in a letter of 1816, remarks that 'we shall have no bed in the house … for Charles himself – let alone Henry'. *19th cent.*

let somebody down gently

to give somebody unwelcome news or information in a way that will avoid upset or humiliation:

in early use with *easily* or *easy* instead of *gently*. *18th cent.*

> Richardson *Clarissa* 1751
> [author's footnote] *Joy, let me here observe … is not absolutely inconsistent with Melancholy; a soft gentle Joy, not a rapid, not a rampant Joy, however; but such a Joy, as shall lift her temporarily out of her soothing Melancholy, and then let her down gently into it again.*

> Mrs Gaskell *North and South* 1855
> *I am losing hope sadly about Frederick; he is letting us down gently, but I can see that Mr. Lennox himself has no hope of hunting up the witnesses under years and years of time.*

let something drop/fall

to reveal a secret or confidence inadvertently or casually. *18th cent.*

> Henry Fielding *Love in Several Masques* 1728
> [Catchit] *There's a terrible Scene of Mischief going forwards. Mr. Malvil, has been taxing me about Mr. Merital, and so, I let drop a few Words, and so, he has taken a Fit of Jealousie, and so see the Consequence.*

> Fanny Burney *The Wanderer* 1814
> *'I don't well know,' he said, 'what class to put you in; but if you are really a virtuous woman, to be sure I ought to ask your pardon for that little hint I let drop; and, moreover, if I asked it upon my knees, I can't say I should think it would be overmuch, for affronting a virtuous woman, without cause.'*

let oneself go

1 to behave or speak openly and without restraint; to enjoy oneself thoroughly. *19th cent.*

> Henry James *The American* 1877
> *'I can't talk of her rationally. I admire her too much.' 'Talk of her as you can,' rejoined Newman. 'Let yourself go.'*

2 to develop untidy or slovenly habits and neglect one's appearance. *Early 20th cent.*

> Susan Hill *Gentleman and Ladies* 1968
> *The previous afternoon, she had set her hair on small rollers. She intended to give the best possible impression. They should not think her a woman who had let herself go. And so many did. Dorothea's hips must be all of forty-four inches.*

let it drop/rest

to say or do nothing more about a particular matter. *16th cent.*

Shakespeare *The Taming of the Shrew* III.i.54 (1592)
[Bianca] *I must believe my master, else, I promise you, I should be arguing still upon that doubt. But let it rest.*

let it go/pass

to dismiss a thought from one's mind; to ignore a remark or comment. *16th cent.*

Shakespeare *The Merry Wives of Windsor* I.iv.13 (1597)
[Quickly] *His worst fault is that he is given to prayer; he is something peevish that way – but nobody but has his fault. But let that pass.*

Boswell *The Life of Samuel Johnson* 1791
Next morning, while we were at breakfast, Johnson gave a very earnest recommendation of what he himself practised with the utmost conscientiousness: I mean a strict attention to truth, even in the most minute particulars. 'Accustom your children (said he) constantly to this; if a thing happened at one window, and they, when relating it, say that it happened at another, do not let it pass, but instantly check them; you do not know where deviation from truth will end.'

without let or hindrance

without any obstruction or impediment (as a legal phrase): *let* as used here survives as a term in tennis and badminton for a ball or shuttlecock that touches the top of the net in a service, but is otherwise obsolete except in legal phrase. *19th cent.*

Henry David Thoreau *Civil Disobedience* 1849
I could not but smile to see how industriously they locked the door on my meditations, which followed them out again without let or hindrance, and they were really all that was dangerous.

See also let off STEAM; let RIP; let something SLIP.

---

letter

a dead letter

1 a law or regulation that is no longer enforced: in the New Testament epistles the 'letter' of the old Mosaic law is called 'dead' and is contrasted to the living 'spirit' of the new law (e.g. St Paul's Epistle to the Romans 7:6 'But now we are delivered from the law, that being dead wherein we were held; that we should serve in newness of spirit, and not in the oldness of the letter'). *17th cent.*

R Fletcher *Ex Otio Negotium* 1656
Hence let the Law be canoniz'd no better | Than a meer corps of words, a bare dead letter.

Thomas Paine *The Age of Reason* 1796
The only sect that has not persecuted are the Quakers; and the only reason that can be given for it is, that they are rather Deists than Christians. They do not believe much about Jesus Christ, and they call the scriptures a dead letter.

2 a letter or packet that cannot be delivered because the address is unknown or the recipients untraceable; a dead-letter office is the department of a post office that deals with such letters and returns them to their senders. *18th cent.*

Maria Edgeworth *The Absentee* 1812
So I took it for granted that it found its way to the dead-letter office, or was sticking up across a pane in the … post-master's window at Huntingdon, for the whole town to see, and it a love-letter.

Herman Melville *Bartleby* 1853
Bartleby had been a subordinate clerk in the Dead Letter Office at Washington … Dead letters! does it not sound like dead men? Conceive a man by nature and misfortune prone to a pallid hopelessness, can any business seem more fitted to heighten it than that of continually handling these dead letters, and assorting them for the flames?

a man/woman of letters

a scholar or writer. *17th cent.*

Congreve *The Double Dealer* 1694
But I'm the more amazed, to find you a woman of letters, and not write! Bless me! how can Mellefont believe you love him?

to the letter

literally or in detail: also *according to the letter*. To *the letter of the law*, meaning 'according to a strict legal interpretation', occurs from the 16th cent.

Lewis Wager *The Life and Repentance of Mary Magdalene* a1562
That they judge nothyng in Christ aryght: | To the letter of the law so fast I do them bynde, | That of the spirite they have no maner of light.

Robert Bage *Man As He Is* 1792
Then Sir, for the future, I request that you will learn precision in your duty, and obey me according to the letter.

Henry James *The Portrait of a Lady* 1881
And there were directions of his which she liked to think she obeyed to the letter. Perhaps, as regards

some of them, it was because her doing so appeared to reduce them to the absurd.

level

be level pegging
to be on equal terms in a contest or competition: from the use of pegs moved round a board marked with rows of holes to keep the score in a game of cribbage. *Early 20th cent.*

do one's level best
to do one's very best. The phrase dates from the 19th cent. Forms with *levelest* and *level worst* are also recorded in North American use.

Mark Twain *A Tramp Abroad* 1880
'Confound it, I don't seem to understand this thing, no way; however, I'll tackle her again.' He fetched another acorn, and done his level best to see what become of it, but he couldn't.

a level playing field
a situation in which everybody involved has the same opportunity of succeeding: from the notion of a playing field being level to afford the same conditions to both sides in a game played on it. This and the verb form of the phrase, *to level the playing field*, are found from the late 20th cent.

S J Berwin et al *Competition and Business Regulation in the Single Market* 1992
One of the objectives of the company law harmonisation programme is to remove such obstructions and create a level playing field in corporate management structures.

on the level
informal honest or genuine: used earlier with the meaning 'modest in aim or ambition'. *18th cent.*

Sir Joshua Reynolds *A Discourse Delivered to the Students of the Royal Academy* 1790
The Caracci, it is acknowledged, adopted the mechanical part with sufficient success. But the divine part which addresses itself to the imagination as possessed by Michael Angelo or Tibaldi, was beyond their grasp: they formed, however, a most respectable school, a style more on the level, and calculated to please a greater number.

Clyde Fitch *The City* 1909
The public would put George Rand in the Roosevelt class with a vengeance, wouldn't they! – if they were on to this one piece of manipulation ... And he pretends to think his methods are on the level.

liberty

take liberties (with somebody/something)
1 to go beyond recognized limits in one's dealings with somebody, especially by being excessively familiar towards them. *18th cent.*

John Cleland *Memoirs of a Woman of Pleasure* 1748
I had seen him taking the last liberties with my servant-wench.

Joanna Baillie *The Siege* 1798
[Countess] *You see, good Sir, I take great liberties with the Baron, as, I doubt not, with the privilege of a brother, you yourself sometimes do.*
2 to take risks with something. *19th cent.*

Conan Doyle *The Empty House* 1903
On the other hand, if all the world was convinced that I was dead they would take liberties, these men, they would soon lay themselves open, and sooner or later I could destroy them.

take the liberty
to undertake something without explicit permission or authority: often followed by *of doing something* or *to do something*. *17th cent.*

Francis Bacon *Essays (Of Friendship)* 1601
Augustus raised Agrippa ... to that height, as when he consulted with Maecenas, about the marriage of his daughter Julia, Maecenas took the liberty to tell him, that he must either marry his daughter to Agrippa, or take away his life; there was no third way, he had made him so great.

licence

a licence to print money
a commercial enterprise that makes a great deal of income with little effort. *20th cent.*

Independent 1989
If speed is of the essence – and all marketing surveys say it is – then the microwave is the manufacturers' version of the licence to print money.

lick

at a lick
1 all at once; at a stroke. *17th cent.*

John Wilson *A Song of Thanksgiving* a1667
Even as those three renowned ones, in furnace seven times fired, | Were safe preserved. Flesh and bones, skin, hair, and cloathes unseared: | The smoak

devouring at a lick all them (and all entire) | *Which in their malice were so quick, to cast them in the fire.*

Mary Jane Holmes *Edna Browning* 1872

When Roy asked where her kin lived, the old man answered, 'Oh, in forty places ... You'd better let her run a spell whilst you hunt up t'other one; two gals at a lick is too much.'

2 at a fast speed or pace: also with *lick* qualified by *great, full,* etc: based on a dialect meaning 'a spurt or burst of speed in racing'. *19th cent.*

a lick and a promise
something done hastily and without the expected thoroughness, especially a wash: in earlier use as *lick* (without *promise*) meaning 'a dab of paint' or 'a quick wash'. *19th cent.*

lick somebody's boots/arse
to behave obsequiously towards somebody, typically in humiliation or to seek favour. *19th cent.*

Mark Twain *Huckleberry Finn* 1884

And then think of me! It would get all around, that Huck Finn helped a nigger to get his freedom; and if I was to ever see anybody from that town again, I'd be ready to get down and lick his boots for shame.

Esquire 1992

He has told colleagues in the force in South Africa ... that he is ready 'to lick your arse in Church Square on a Sunday, if I can't solve it in two days'.

lick one's lips/chops
to be eagerly looking forward to something: originally with reference to food. *16th cent.*

George Chapman *May-day* 1611

[Lodovico] Be bold and carelesse, and stand not santring [= sauntering] a far off, as I have seen you, like a dog in a firme-typot, that licks his chops and wags his tail.

lick one's wounds
to withdraw to recover after a defeat or humiliation. The image is of an animal withdrawing and licking its wounds after a fight with a rival or with another animal. *17th cent.*

Dryden *All for Love* 1678

[Antony] We can conquer, | *You see, without your aid.* | *We have dislodged their troops;* | *They look on us at distance, and, like curs* | *'Scaped from the lion's paws, they bay far off.* | *And lick their wounds, and faintly threaten war.*

See also get/lick/knock something/somebody into SHAPE; if you can't lick them, join them (*see* if you can't beat them, join them) *at* BEAT.

lid

Lid has existed in figurative use with reference to containing or releasing only since the early 20th cent. The image is of things being forced into or released from a sealed container, and the phrase is often extended to form part of a broader metaphor.

blow the lid off
informal to remove all control or restraint from a situation: also in numerous variant forms *the lid is off, with the lid off,* etc. *Early 20th cent.*

P Chester *Murder Forestalled* 1990

Somebody told you that Vecchi and the girl were at the Regal Arms. You gave instructions that I would be the one to blow the lid off.

keep a/the lid on something
1 *informal* to prevent a situation from getting out of control. *Late 20th cent.*

A Rogers & M Keith *Hollow Promises?* 1991

The government in 1989 had to appoint a special transport minister for Docklands (Mr Portillo) to keep the lid on the widespread anger of developers about the lack of transport to Docklands.

2 *informal* to keep something secret. *Late 20th cent.*

Today 1992

In fact, the Princess of Wales – a woman Selina is often compared with – must wish she was able to keep the lid on her private life as tightly as Selina has. There are no talkative friends or 'Squidgy' tapes lurking in Selina's background.

put a/the lid on something
informal to bring something to a conclusion or stop; to repress or clamp down on an activity. *Early 20th cent.*

Daily Telegraph 1992

The new job has changed Kenyon in other ways, too. His sense of humour was always a feature of the critics' circuit; I treasure a bulging mental file of his roguish observations on fellow critics and luminaries in the music trade. His new responsibilities have put the lid on this ... he has taken up fluent corporation-speak surprisingly quickly.

put the (tin) lid on something

British, *informal* to be the final act or circumstance that makes a situation intolerable. *Late 20th cent.*

M Cole *The Ladykiller* 1993

Out on the pavement, an elderly woman with a small sausage dog gave him a filthy look. He sighed again. That put the tin lid on it as far as Patrick Kelly was concerned. The old bird thought he was a nonce.

take/lift the lid off / lift the lid on something

informal to reveal unwelcome information about a person or thing. *Late 20th cent.*

See also FLIP one's lid.

---

lie[1] (verb)

as/so far as in me lies

to the extent that I am capable or have authority. The phrase is 18th cent. in this form, but many earlier variants exist, e.g. with *much* instead of *far*.

Hume *Enquiry Concerning Human Understanding* 1748

Your deliberations, which of right should be directed to questions of public good, and the interest of the commonwealth, are diverted to the disquisitions of speculative philosophy; and these ... enquiries, take place of your more familiar but more useful occupations. But so far as in me lies, I will prevent this abuse.

let something lie

to allow a difficult or unwelcome situation to continue. *19th cent.*

R L Stevenson *Kidnapped* 1886

When a friend that likes you very well has passed over an offence without a word, you would be blithe to let it lie, instead of making it a stick to break his back with.

lie in state

(said of a distinguished person recently dead) to be laid out in a public place before burial. *18th cent.*

Robert Hunter *Androboros* 1714

[Solemn] *When is he to be Interr'd?* [Tom of Bedlam] *This Ev'ning, but is to lie in State here till then.*

Charlotte Brontë *Jane Eyre* 1847

Mr. Reed had been dead nine years: it was in this chamber he breathed his last; here he lay in state; hence his coffin was borne by the undertaker's men.

lie low

to act discreetly and avoid being noticed: based on literal uses which go back to Middle English. The phrase is 19th cent. in figurative use.

Mark Twain *Life on the Mississippi* 1883

They know all that can be known of their abstruse science; and so, since they conceive that they can fetter and handcuff that river and boss him, it is but wisdom for the unscientific man to keep still, lie low, and wait till they do it.

take something lying down

to accept something unpleasant or unwelcome without protesting: normally used in negative contexts or questions. The image is of lying on the ground while being beaten or assaulted. *19th cent.*

Edward George Dyson *Khaki Verse* 1919

We fairly felt their bullets play | *Among our hair for half a day.* | *...* | *They pass you with a vicious hiss* | *That makes you duck; but, hit or miss,* | *It isn't in the Sultan's skin* | *To shift Australia's cheerful grin.* | *My oath, old man, though we were prone,* | *We didn't take it lying down.*

See also how the LAND lies; let sleeping dogs lie *at* DOG.

---

lie[2] (noun and verb)

give the lie to something

to show that something is not true or not the case as was previously thought. In earlier use the meaning was commonly 'to accuse somebody openly of lying' (as in an exchange between Ariel and Stefano in Shakespeare's *The Tempest* (1613) III.ii.77: '[Ariel] Thou liest. [Stefano] ... Give me the lie another time'); but in more recent use the subject is typically a fact or circumstance. *16th cent.*

Shakespeare *As You Like It* III.ii.377 (1599)

[Orlando] *Fair youth, I would I could make thee believe I love.* [Rosalind] *Me believe it! You may as soon make her that you love believe it, which I warrant she is apter to do than to confess she does. That is one of the points in the which women still give the lie to their consciences.*

I tell / am telling a lie / that's a lie

informal an expression used to correct a statement one has just made and immediately realizes to be mistaken. *17th cent.*

John Davies *Lamia the Witch* from *Wittes Pilgrimage* c1605
But I can prove | Where thou thy Chastitie did'st vulnerate: | O no, I lie, thou stil didst keep it sound | But others gave, and it receav'd the wound.

George Colman *The Battle of Hexham* 1790
[Gregory] *I'll warrant we'll find such snug delicious beds of dry leaves –* [it rains hard] *s'bud, no, I lie – it rains like all the dogs and cats in the kingdom; there won't be a dry twig left large enough to shelter a cock-chaffer.*

live a lie

to live a life that conceals one's true nature or past. *18th cent.*

Charles Robert Maturin *Melmoth the Wanderer* 1820
'But to me, and to all the community, you seemed to be resigned to the monastic life.' 'I seemed a lie – I lived a lie – I was a lie – I ask pardon of my last moments for speaking the truth – I presume they neither can refuse me, or discredit my words – I hated the monastic life.'

See also lie through one's TEETH; NAIL a lie.

---

life

beat/knock the life out of somebody

informal to beat somebody severely. *19th cent.*

be the life and soul of the party

to be in a lively mood and keep everybody around one entertained. *Life* and *soul* occur together with the meaning 'soul or essence' from the 18th cent., and *life of the party* (without *soul*) is also recorded from this date: the present phrase is therefore a variant of earlier forms. *19th cent.*

Charlotte Brontë *Jane Eyre* 1847
For, after all, Mr. Rochester, and – because closely connected with him – Miss Ingram, were the life and soul of the party. If he was absent from the room an hour, a perceptible dulness seemed to steal over the spirits of his guests; and his reentrance was sure to give a fresh impulse to the vivacity of conversation.

(do) anything for a quiet life

to acquiesce in other people's wishes if that leaves one undisturbed. *Anything for a Quiet Life* is the title of a play by Thomas Middleton (c1621). *17th cent.*

Edward Ravenscroft *The English Lawyer* 1678
[Polla] *Now, you Fustilugs, who am I now?*
[Ignoramus] *Any body for a quiet life.*

Delarivière Manley *The Adventures of Rivella* 1714
Some Persons … thought he yielded to his Lady's Importunities only for a quiet Life.

George Colman *The Jealous Wife* 1761
I must live in Peace – Patience is the best Remedy – Any thing for a quiet Life! and so on.

Dickens *Pickwick Papers* 1837
'I know the gentleman 'll put that ere charge into somebody afore he's done,' growled the long man. 'Well, well – I don't mind,' said poor Winkle, turning his gunstock uppermost; – 'there.' 'Anythin' for a quiet life,' said Mr. Weller; and on they went again.

for dear/one's life

as though one's life were at stake: used in the context of daring or urgent actions. *19th cent.*

Mark Twain *A Tramp Abroad* 1880
The fiddlers under the eaves of the stage sawed away for dear life, with the cold overflow spouting down the backs of their necks.

for the life of me

informal no matter how hard I try: in earlier use with *heart* instead of *life* (cf Shakespeare, *The Taming of the Shrew* (1592) 1.ii.38 '[Petruccio] Good Hortensio, I bade the rascal knock upon your gate, | And could not get him for my heart to do it'). *19th cent.*

Herman Melville *Typee* 1846
For the life of me, I could not understand why a woman should not have as much right to enter a canoe as a man.

frighten/scare the life out of somebody

informal to terrify somebody. *Early 20th cent.*

Gene Stratton Porter *Freckles* 1904
Seems that her father has taught her to shoot … The spunky little thing followed them right out into the west road, spitting lead like hail, and clipping all around the heads and heels of them … Scared the life near out of me body with the fear that she'd drop one of them.

get a life

informal, originally N Amer to start to enjoy life and do interesting things: normally used as an admonition to somebody who is not making the best of their opportunities or who is doing something deemed tedious or pointless by the speaker. An early use in print was in a caricature in the *Washington Post* in 1983: 'Gross me out, I mean, Valley Girls was, like, ohmigod, it was last year, fer sure! I mean, get a life! Say what?' *Late 20th cent.*

> Pilot 1992
> *They're people who go around airports and air-shows collecting the 'tail numbers' on aeroplanes ... the really sophisticated ones use little pocket memo recorders instead of notebooks. All attempts to explain just why anyone would want to do this failed. 'You tell those guys they should get a life!' he roared, still not entirely convinced that it wasn't all some Limey hoax.*

life and limb

one's life and physical faculties. *17th cent.*

> Locke *Essay Concerning Civil Government* 1690
> *They may repulse the present attempt, but must not revenge past violences. For it is natural for us to defend life and limb.*

life in the fast lane

an exciting or ambitious lifestyle: with reference to the outer lane of a motorway, intended for the fastest traffic. *Late 20th cent.*

> Stuart Cosgrove *Hampden Babylon* 1991
> *Now at his lowest ebb, Marinello can reflect on life in the fast lane. His house was re-possessed. His marriage has collapsed ... He claims he has lost over £250,000 in his life and at the age of 40 is forced to survive on state benefits of £63.*

a matter of life and death / a life-and-death matter

a matter of crucial importance: originally in the literal context of a person being on trial for a capital offence. *17th cent.*

> Bunyan *The Holy War* 1682
> *You the Gentlemen of the Jury being impannelled for our Lord the King to serve here in a matter of life and death, have heard the trials of each of these men the prisoners at the Bar.*

> James Fenimore Cooper *The Pioneers* 1823
> *'I bethought me of your flimsy things,' cried Natty, throwing loose the folds of a covering of buckskin*

that he carried on his arm, and wrapping her form in it ... 'now follow, for it's a matter of life and death to us all.'

not on your life

informal used to express complete refusal or rejection. The phrase is a shortening of earlier fuller admonitory forms such as *stir/speak/tarry/fail not on your life. See also* not on your NELLY. *18th cent.*

> Thomas Holcroft *The School for Arrogance* 1791
> [Edmund] *The Count your brother? – My sister, my family, must be informed.* [Lydia] *Not on your life, Edmund. So implacable are his enemies, that my father informs me an Exempt, bribed by them, has followed him to England.*

see life

to gain wide experience of the world: based on the use of *life* to mean 'the active part of human experience', which dates from the middle of the 17th cent. *18th cent.*

> Boswell *The Life of Samuel Johnson* 1791
> *But he produced one work this year ... This was 'The Life Of Richard Savage', a man, of whom it is difficult to speak impartially, without wondering that he was for some time the intimate companion of Johnson; for his character was marked by profligacy, insolence, and ingratitude: yet, as he undoubtedly had a warm and vigorous, though unregulated mind, had seen life in all its varieties.*

take one's life in one's (own) hands

to do something that risks death. *19th cent.*

> Mark Twain *The Prince and the Pauper* 1881
> *Then ... mind the little beast for me while I take my life in my hands and make what success I may toward mounting the big one.*

this is the life

an expression of satisfaction with one's present circumstances or experiences. *Early 20th cent.*

> Roi Cooper Megrue *Under Cover* 1914
> [Nora] *It's wrong to go to bed so early. It can't be much after two.* [Singing] *Oh, this is the life.*

to the life

(said of a copy or representation) portraying the original subject exactly. *17th cent.*

> Aphra Behn *The Rover* 1677
> *Oh that our Nokes, or Tony Lee could show | A Fop but half so much to th' Life as you.*

to save one's life
even if one's life were at stake: used in negative contexts of things one is incapable of undertaking or unwilling to undertake. The phrase was a favourite of Trollope's and occurs in several forms in his writing, e.g. in *Can You Forgive Her?* (1864): 'Had it been to save my life I could not have written the letter.' *19th cent.*

> Hardy *Far from the Madding Crowd* 1874
> She said in the same breath that it would be ungenerous not to marry Boldwood, and that she couldn't do it to save her life.

See also (as) LARGE as life; the facts of life *at* FACT; larger than life *at* LARGE; a new LEASE of life; WALK of life; within an INCH of one's life.

lifeline

throw a lifeline to somebody
to offer somebody a means of escaping from an awkward situation. The phrase is based on the meaning 'a line for preserving life', e.g. one thrown to save a drowning person. *Lifeline* has other meanings: an essential route for communication and supplies; and the mark on the hand that is regarded as important in palmistry. These meanings have also given rise to figurative uses. *19th cent.*

> Willa Cather *The Song of the Lark* 1915
> I remember when I first heard you in Pittsburg, long ago. It was a life-line you threw me.

lifetime

the — of a lifetime
an exceptionally enjoyable or worthwhile experience, the implication being that it will only occur once in a person's life. *Early 20th cent.*

> Jack London *Son of the Wolf* 1915
> 'Twas the anchor-ice comin' up. To the right, to the lift, as far as iver a man cud see, the water was covered with the same. An' like so much porridge it was, slickin' along the bark of the canoe, stickin' like glue to the paddle … 'Twas the sight of a lifetime.

lift

See lift up one's HEAD; not lift a FINGER.

light¹ (adjective)

(as) light as a feather
extremely light; having very little weight. A feather, as well as being one of the lightest things imaginable, is associated with flight. *16th cent.*

> James Shirley *The Wedding* 1626
> Light as a feather, hanging will never kill you.

be light on something
to have only a little of something. *20th cent.*

> Nicola Malizia et al *Malta: the Hurricane Years 1940–41* 1987
> I chased him west along the south coast of the island and closed off Gozo. He went into the drink well out to sea off the island, by which time I was light on fuel and out of ammo.

be light on one's feet
to move deftly and nimbly. *19th cent.*

> George Meredith *The Ordeal of Richard Feverel* 1859
> Blue eyes – just what I like! And such a little impudent nose, and red lips, pouting – the very thing I like! And her hair? darkish, I think – say, brown. And so saucy, and light on her feet.

make light of something
1 to disparage or mock something. *16th cent.*

> Francis Bacon *Essays (Of Seeming Wise)* 1612
> Some, whatsoever is beyond their reach, will seem to despise, or make light of it, as impertinent [= irrelevant] or curious [= arcane]; and so would have their ignorance seem judgment.

2 to treat something as unimportant, or discount it as trivial: *cf* make LITTLE of something. *19th cent.*

> Mark Twain *What Is Man? And Other Essays* 1906
> He made light of the wound, but he died of it in a few days.

make light work of something
to achieve a task or objective with ease. *19th cent.*

> Helen Hunt Jackson *Twin Lakes* 1896
> We'll fly with a sail all swelling, | And make light work of the miles!

light² (verb and noun)

according to one's lights
in terms of, or measured by, one's own standards or opinions: based on the (16th cent.) plural

meaning 'facts or pieces of information'. *19th cent.*

Henry James *Confidence* 1880
You will be rather surprised, perhaps, at my having selected her as the partner of a life-time; but we manage these matters according to our lights. I am very much in love with her, and I hold that an excellent reason.

bring something to light
to disclose or reveal information: *cf* Job 28:11 (in the Authorized Version of 1611) 'He bindeth the floods from overflowing; and the thing that is hid bringeth he forth to light.' *16th cent.*

Shakespeare *Much Ado About Nothing* v.i.226 (1598)
[Borachio] *What your wisdoms could not discover, these shallow fools have brought to light, who in the night overheard me confessing to this man how Don John your brother incensed me to slander the Lady Hero.*

come to light
(said especially of information) to be revealed or made known: in early use in the form *come in light*. *Middle English*

Shakespeare *The Merchant of Venice* II.ii.74 (1598)
[Lancelot] *Give me your blessing. Truth will come to light; murder cannot be hid long – a man's son may, but in the end truth will out.*

Goldsmith *Elegy on the Death of a Mad Dog* 1766
But soon a wonder came to light, | That showed the rogues they lied; | The man recovered from the bite, | The dog it was that died.

go out like a light
to fall asleep or lose consciousness immediately or suddenly. *Mid 20th cent.*

Ellis Peters *City of Gold and Shadows* 1989
Something hit me on the back of the head, here, and I went out like a light. I remember dropping. I never felt the ground hit me.

in the light of / NAmer in light of something
1 in the nature or character of something. *18th cent.*

Hume *Enquiry Concerning Human Understanding* 1748
The other species of philosophers considers man in the light of a reasonable rather than an active being, and endeavours to form his understanding more than cultivate his manners.

2 with the insight or information provided by something. *19th cent.*

Henry James *Roderick Hudson* 1876
And in the light of your late interview, what do you make of your young lady?

the light of one's life
the person one most loves or is especially devoted to. *19th cent.*

Ben Jonson *The Gypsies Metamorphos'd* 1640
[the Patrico] *An old mans wife, | Is the light of his life, | A young one is but his shade.*

Ralph Waldo Emerson *Essays: Second Series* 1844
It takes a good deal of time to eat or to sleep, or to earn a hundred dollars, and a very little time to entertain a hope and an insight which becomes the light of our life.

punch somebody's lights out
to beat somebody up. *Lights* here is used primarily in the meaning 'eyes', although the sense 'lungs of a slaughtered animal' (which is based on *light* meaning 'having little weight') may also be involved. *20th cent.*

The Times 1988
Penalties for violence have risen by more than 90 per cent over the past 10 years. It is not a question of spontaneity: 'When you have somebody on your team whose sole purpose is to punch somebody's lights out, it's a tactic,' said one team manager. 'It has become a bit of a problem.'

see the light
1 (said of writing, literature, music, etc; also *see the light of day*) to be presented or published. *17th cent.*

Dryden *The Kind Keeper* 1680 [front matter]
The same Fortune once happen'd to Moliere, on the occasion of his Tartuffe; which notwithstanding afterwards has seen the light, in a Country more Bigot than ours, and is accounted amongst the best Pieces of that Poet.

Boswell *The Life of Samuel Johnson* 1791
He this year resumed his scheme of giving an edition of Shakspeare with notes ... He promised his work should be published before Christmas, 1757. Yet nine years elapsed before it saw the light.

2 to understand something suddenly. *19th cent.*

Hardy *Jude the Obscure* 1895
I can't help being as I am, I am convinced I am right – that I see the light at last. But oh, how to profit by it!

3 to undergo a religious conversion, especially to Christianity. *Early 20th cent.*

P Ling *Flood Water* 1993
'Maybe Ernest will come round. He might see the light and be received into the Faith.' 'He'll never do that. He's been brought up strictly, he goes to synagogue.'

stand/be in somebody's light
to be in somebody's way, preventing them from making progress: from the literal meaning 'to prevent somebody from using or enjoying the light'. To *stand in one's own light*, in the figurative meaning 'to be a hindrance to oneself', was a common phrase in the 16th cent. and 17th cent.

John Heywood *Works* 1562
Plentie is no deintie, ye see not your owne ease. I see, ye can not see the wood for trees. Your lips hang in your light, but this poore man sees ... how blindly ye stand in your owne light.

Lyly *Euphues* 1579
Heere ye may beholde gentlemen, how lewdly wit standeth in his owne lyght.

Mark Twain *The $30,000 Bequest and Other Stories* 1906
A man who cannot learn stands in his own light.

throw/cast/shed light on something
to explain or clarify something obscure or complex. The image is of a light shining on a scene and clarifying it. *16th cent.*

Edward Young *The Complaint, or Night Thoughts on Life* 1742
The scene thou seest attests the truth I sing, | And every star sheds light upon thy Creed.

See also hide one's light under a BUSHEL; in the COLD light of day; light at the end of the TUNNEL; light a FIRE under somebody; light a/the FUSE.

lightning

lightning never strikes (the same place) twice
the same disaster or misfortune does not visit an individual more than once. *19th cent.*

Peter Hamilton Myers *The Prisoner of the Border* 1857
'Golly, massa, look at that!' he exclaimed, springing suddenly aside, and pointing at the cannon ball they had so narrowly escaped, and which now lay harmless beside them. 'Let us get away from here.' 'Never fear, Brom. Sit down on it, if you wish to be quite safe. Lightning never strikes twice in the same place, nor cannon balls either, I presume.'

like (greased) lightning
with great speed. The phrase *like lightning* dates from the 18th cent., and from the 19th cent. with *greased*.

Henry Fielding *The History of Tom Jones* 1749
Grimalkin, who, though the youngest of the feline family ... and though inferior in strength, is equal in fierceness to the noble tiger himself, when a little mouse ... escapes from her clutches for a while ... flies like lightning on her prey.

Trollope *The Eustace Diamonds* 1873
The superintendent, who intended to be consolatory to Lizzie, expressed his opinion that it was very hard to know what a young woman was. 'They looks as soft as butter, and they're as sly as foxes, and as quick, as quick, – as quick as greased lightning, my lady.'

like[1] (verb and noun)

like it or not
regardless of what one thinks or wants; willy-nilly. A shortening of *whether you* (or *we, they,* etc) *like it or not. 19th cent.*

Mrs Gaskell *Wives and Daughters* 1866
'I will tell you where I think you have been in fault, Clare, if you like to know.' Like it or not, the plain-speaking was coming now. 'You have spoilt that girl of yours till she does not know her own mind.'

the likes of —
informal people or things that are similar to the one specified. Normally used in depreciatory ways: in early use in the form *the like of. 17th cent.*

Hobbes *Leviathan* 1651
From desire ariseth the thought of some means we have seen produce the like of that which we aim at; and from the thought of that, the thought of means to that mean.

H G Wells *The Invisible Man* 1897
'Invisible, eigh?' said Huxter … 'Who ever heard the likes of that?'

Frederick Pilon *The Deaf Lover* 1780
[Young Wrongward] *What, then, you have neither brought nor received a letter here to-day?* [Betsy] *Lord! Sir, who'd trust the likes of me with a letter?*

See also like it or LUMP it; not like the LOOK of something.

like² (preposition)
See like FATHER, like son.

like³ (adjective)
(as) like as two peas (in a pod)
identical; indistinguishable, in the way that, for most people, one pea is from another. The notion occurs in John Lyly's *Euphues* (1580): 'As lyke as one pease is to an other.' *Pease* is the earlier form of the word, *pea* arising from the mistaking of *pease* for a plural. *16th cent.*

Fanny Burney *Evelina* 1778
'I thought, at the time,' said Mr. Branghton, 'that three shillings was an exorbitant price for a place in the gallery.' … 'Why it's as like the twelvepenny gallery at Drury-lane,' cried the son, 'as two peas are to one another. I never knew father so bit before.'

likely
a likely story
used ironically to express doubt about what somebody has said or claimed. *18th cent.*

Henry Fielding *The History of Tom Jones* 1749
Susan could not help endeavouring to quiet the concern which her mistress seemed to be under … by swearing heartily she saw Jones leap out from her bed. The landlady fell into a violent rage at these words. 'A likely story, truly,' cried she, 'that a woman should cry out, and endeavour to expose herself, if that was the case!'

liking
to one's liking
pleasing, satisfactory; what one wants: recorded earlier in the form *at/after one's liking*. *16th cent.*

Shakespeare *All's Well That Ends Well* I.i.147 (1603)
[Paroles] *Besides, virginity is peevish, proud, idle, made of self-love – which is the most inhibited sin in the canon. Keep it not, you cannot choose but lose by't … Away with't.* [Helen] *How might one do, sir, to lose it to her own liking?*

See also TAKE a liking to somebody/something.

lily
See GILD the lily.

limb
out on a limb
in an exposed and unsupported position: originally in American use. The meaning here is 'a branch of a tree', the idea being that a position at the end of the branch leaves one exposed and vulnerable. *19th cent.*

tear somebody limb from limb
to savage somebody brutally: literally, to dismember somebody. *16th cent.*

Thomas Nashe *Nashes Lenten Stuffe* 1599
Hee will … tear him limbe from limbe, but hee will extract some capitall confession from him.

limit
be the limit
informal to be the extreme of what is reasonable; to be exasperating or intolerable. *Early 20th cent.*

Samuel Mathewson Baylis *In the Name of the King* from *At the Sign of the Beaver* 1907
Of all the mangy curs | That ever were whelped in this King-cursed land to bark at a man and run, | You're the limit, dead right!

over the limit
having exceeded a permitted maximum: in current use usually with reference to the legal limit of alcohol in the blood allowed to a person who is driving a motor vehicle. *Late 20th cent.*

Best 1991
Can you be breathalysed in your own home? My boyfriend drank too much the other night and was followed home in his car by the police. He's just got inside the house when they knocked on the door and asked to breath-test him. He was over the limit and will now lose his licence.

line[1] (noun)

The meaning in many of the phrases is the military one referring to a formation of soldiers abreast.

be/get/step out of line

to act in an unusual or inappropriate way. *Mid 20th cent.*

Hilda Doolittle *Collected Poems* a1944

So the first – it is written, will be the twisted or the tortured individuals, out of line, out of step with world so-called progress.

Don Hedley *World Energy* 1986

Although Mexico was not an OPEC member in November 1984 it cut exports in line with OPEC reductions to help maintain prices and has generally taken care not to step out of line.

the bottom line

the most significant point, especially the main criterion that determines whether something is convincing or viable: a metaphor from accounting, in which the bottom line is the last line of figures in a financial report that shows the profit or loss. *Late 20th cent.*

Wedding and Home 1990

The bottom line to consider when tasting wine is whether or not you actually like it.

come/fall into line

to conform with accepted opinions or principles of behaviour: a metaphor from military formation. *19th cent.*

John Keble *Lectures on Poetry* 1841

All this admirably falls into line with the passages from the Prometheus before quoted, on which I argued that Aeschylus, beyond doubt a follower of Pythagoras, rejected both the extravagances of Epicurus and the doctrines of fatalism.

Jack London *The Iron Heel* 1908

Day by day unions and more unions voted their support to the socialists, until even Ernest laughed when the Undertakers' Assistants and the Chicken Pickers fell into line.

get a line on something/somebody

informal to get some basic information about something. *19th cent.*

William Gillette & Arthur Conan Doyle *Sherlock Holmes* 1899

I knew you was on some rum lay – squatting down in this place for over a year; but I never could seem to – get a line on you.

hard lines

bad luck or ill fortune, especially when suffered through no fault of one's own. Early uses (e.g. by Scott, below) suggest a nautical origin, although *lines* may simply denote fate or fortune as marked off by a line, as in Psalms 16:6 (in the Authorized Version, 1611): 'The lines are fallen unto me in pleasant places; yea, I have a goodly heritage.' A newspaper use from 1865 reinforces the link between this meaning and our phrase: 'The poor Pope's lines seem just now to have fallen in most unpleasant places, and are indeed hard lines.' *19th cent.*

Scott *Redgauntlet* 1824

The old seaman paused a moment. 'It is hard lines for me,' he said, 'to leave your honour in tribulation.'

lay/put it on the line

to state one's view on a matter clearly and unequivocally. The phrase was first used in the meaning 'to pay a debt', and the sense of *line* here is probably that connected with accounting (as in *bottom line*). *Mid 20th cent.*

take a — line on something

to have a particular opinion about something, or a certain policy towards it. *Mid 20th cent.*

The Art Newspaper 1993

Gardiner takes a curiously prudish line on the emotional mainsprings of Epstein's art by denying or glossing over the disturbing sexual elements in his pre-1914 work, including 'Rock Drill'.

See also DRAW the/a line (in the sand); DRAW a line under something; the END of the road/line; HOLD the line; the line of least RESISTANCE; SHOOT a line; TOE the line.

line[2] (verb)

line one's pockets

to make a profit by unfair or illicit means. In earlier use the phrase appears as *line one's coat/breeches*, etc. *17th cent.*

Shakespeare *Othello* 1.i.53 (1604)

[Iago] *Others there are | Who, trimmed in forms and visages of duty, | Keep yet their hearts attending on themselves, | And, throwing but shows of service on their lords, | Do well thrive by 'em, and when they have lined their coats, | Do themselves homage.*

Charles Kingsley *Westward Ho!* 1855

That cunning old Drake! how he has contrived to line his own pockets, even though he had to keep the whole fleet waiting for him.

---

linen

wash one's dirty linen in public

to discuss discreditable personal matters openly. *19th cent.*

Trollope *The Way We Live Now* 1875

What disappointed ambition there might be among conservative candidates was never known to the public. Those gentlemen do not wash their dirty linen in public.

Oscar Wilde *The Importance of Being Earnest* 1895

The amount of women in London who flirt with their own husbands is perfectly scandalous. It looks so bad. It is simply washing one's clean linen in public.

---

lion

a lion in the way

a danger, especially one invented as an excuse for inaction: with allusion to Proverbs 26:13 'The slothful man saith, There is a lion in the way; a lion is in the streets.' *17th cent.*

Milton *Of Reformation Touching Church-Discipline in England* 1641

They fear'd not the bug-bear danger nor the lion in the way that the sluggish and timorous politician thinks he sees.

Catharine Sedgwick *Clarence* 1830

I have thought over and over again what I told you the day we parted. I am right – it is all fudge – there is no lion in the way.

Tennyson *The Holy Grail* 1869

Lancelot shouted, 'Stay me not! | I have been the sluggard, and I ride apace, | For now there is a lion in the way.' | So vanish'd.

the lion's den

a situation of great danger or difficulty: with allusion to the prophet Daniel, who according to the biblical account (Daniel 6:16–22) was thrown into a den of lions by King Darius of Persia but was protected by an angel sent by God. The phrase occurs early in extended metaphor, e.g. in Dryden's *The Spanish Fryar* (1681): 'What bull dare bellow, or, what sheep dares bleat, | Within the lion's den?' *17th cent.*

Thomas Betterton *The Amorous Widow* 1706

[Cuningham] *Pox on her old mouldy chops: | She's for engrossing all to her self. | How she thrust her niece in before her. | I'll in, and try to beckon her into the garden, if you'll interpose, shou'd the Aunt miss her, and follow us.* [Love] *'Sdeath! Wouldst have me run into the lion's den, | Just when I have scap'd his paw!*

Scott *Waverley* 1814

'And how do you, being an Englishman,' said the Knight, 'protect your life and property here, when one of your nation cannot obtain a single night's lodging, or a draught of water, were he thirsty?' 'Marry, noble sir,' answered the Franklin, 'use, as they say, will make a man live in a lion's den; and as I settled here in a quiet time, and have never given cause of offence, I am respected by my neighbours, and even, as you see, by our forayers from England.'

the lion's mouth

a place of great danger. The phrase, which is found in Middle English, was originally used with biblical allusion to Psalms 22:21 'Save me from the lion's mouth: for thou hast heard me from the horns of the unicorns', and to 2 Timothy 4:17 where Paul declares 'Notwithstanding the Lord stood with me, and strengthened me ... and I was delivered out of the mouth of the lion'. However, in more recent usage the image·is rather of the traditional circus act in which the tamer puts his head into the mouth of a trained lion.

William Mountford *The Life and Death of Doctor Faustus* 1697

I am Wrath; I had neither Father nor Mother, but leap'd out of a Lion's Mouth when I was scarce an Hour old.

Henry Fielding *Rape upon Rape* 1730

Asking your Worship's Pardon, I don't care to run my Finger into the Lion's Mouth. I would not willingly have to do with any Limb of the Law.

the lion's share

the largest part of something shared. *18th cent.*

Edmund Burke *Reflections on the Revolution in France* 1790
Where the letting of their land was by rent, I could not discover that their agreements with their farmers were oppressive; nor when they were in partnership with the farmer, as often was the case, have I heard that they had taken the lion's share. The proportions seemed not inequitable.

throw somebody to the lions

to leave somebody at the mercy of their enemies or harshest critics. The allusion is to the religious persecutions of the Roman Empire, when Christians were herded into the arenas of amphitheatres to be savaged by lions. *Cf* throw somebody to the wolves *at* WOLF. *20th cent.*

The Times 1985
'Mahogany and rosewood were fashionable, while black and gilt, as well as looking a little like burnished bronze, were being used on grandiloquent furniture in France. So he and his followers produced things like your table.' 'If you ask me, Mr Smith and his friends should have been thrown to the lions.'

---

lip

hang on somebody's lips

to listen to somebody attentively, or eagerly await their word or command. *17th cent.*

John Oldham *Satyrs upon the Jesuits* 1679
Strait count him Holy, Vertuous, Good, Devout, Chast, Gentle, Meek, a Saint, a God, who not? Make Fate hang on his Lips, nor Heaven have Pow'r to Predestinate without his leave.

pass somebody's lips

to be spoken by somebody. *16th cent.*

Richardson *Pamela* 1740
And I promise you, that I will never let your Name pass my Lips, but with Reverence and Gratitude.

pay lip service to something

to acknowledge or support something in words without acting on it. *17th cent.* .

Christopher Smart *The Parables of Jesus Christ* 1768
With words and mouths this froward race | Adore me, and approach my face, | And their lip-service they devote, | While all their hearts are far remote.

| *But all that worship is in vain, | Which for your Maker you would feign.*

See also BITE one's lip; CURL one's lip; LICK one's lips; my lips are sealed *at* SEAL; a STIFF upper lip.

---

list

enter the lists

to issue a challenge or take part in a contest: from the meaning of *lists* 'a place or scene of competition', in particular the enclosure in which medieval knights jousted. *17th cent.*

---

little

quite the little —

an especially noteworthy example of a quality or attribute: normally used ironically or condescendingly. *19th cent.*

Keats *Letter* 1819
Mr Lewis went a few morning<s> ago to town with Mrs Brawne they talked about me – and I heard that Mr L said a thing I am not at all contented with – Says he 'O, he is quite the little Poet' now this is abominable – you might as well say Buonaparte is quite the little Soldier.

make little of something

1 to treat something as unimportant: *cf* make light of something *at* LIGHT[1]. *17th cent.*

Thomas Southerne *The Wives Excuse* 1692
I see you make little of the matter, to hide it from my fears; | And there indeed you're kind: but 'tis in vain | To think of concealing from me, what you intend.

Byron *Don Juan* 1824
She also had no passion for confession; Perhaps she had nothing to confess:– no matter, Whate'er the cause, the church made little of it.

2 to fail to tackle a task satisfactorily or make a go of it. *19th cent.*

Dickens *David Copperfield* 1850
He was a sort of town traveller for a number of miscellaneous houses, now; but made little or nothing of it, I am afraid.

live[1] (verb, rhymes with *give*)

be (the) living proof (of something)

to demonstrate the truth or validity of something by one's existence or by one's characteristics or qualities. *19th cent.*

> Dickens *Hard Times* 1854
> *I shall have the satisfaction of causing you to be strictly educated; and you will be a living proof to all who come into communication with you, of the advantages of the training you will receive.*

live and breathe something

to be completely absorbed or preoccupied by an activity or pursuit. *20th cent.*

live and learn

(proverb) one can always learn from experience: normally used in the context of a surprising or unexpected experience or piece of information. Explicit correlation between living and learning occurs from the 16th cent., sometimes in the admonitory form *we live to learn*. The phrase dates from the late 16th cent. in its current form.

> John Pomfret *The Sceptical Muse* 1699
> *Thus from the time we first begin to know | We live and learn, but not the wiser grow; | We seldom use our liberty aright, | No Judge of things by Universal Light.*

> Henry Fielding *The History of Tom Jones* 1749
> *I should not have lived so many years, and have taught school so long, without being able to distinguish between fas et nefas: but it seems we are all to live and learn.*

live and let live

(proverb) to tolerate other people's views and behaviour so that one's own might be tolerated in turn. The maxim is entered in a book of Scottish proverbs by David Fergusson (1648), and in John Ray's *Collection of English Proverbs* of 1678. *17th cent.*

> Smollett *The Life and Adventures of Sir Launcelot Greaves* 1761
> *For my peart, measter, I knows nothing amiss of the doctor – he's a quiet sort of an inoffensive man ... You knows, master, one must live, and let live, as the saying is.*

live from / out of a suitcase

to be constantly changing one's address or travelling from one place to another. *Mid 20th cent.*

live in the past

to be nostalgic for earlier times or cling to outdated attitudes. *Late 20th cent.*

live it up

informal to enjoy an extravagant lifestyle. *20th cent.*

> Lawrence Ferlinghetti *Pictures of the Gone World* 1955
> *dancing and going swimming in rivers on picnics in the middle of the summer and just generally 'living it up'*

live one's own life

to be independent and choose one's own career and lifestyle. *19th cent.*

> Nathaniel Hawthorne *The Scarlet Letter* 1850
> *It was as if she had been made afresh, out of new elements, and must perforce be permitted to live her own life, and be a law unto herself, without her eccentricities being reckoned to her for a crime.*

live rough

to live in the open or in improvised shelters, especially from being homeless. In earlier use, the meaning was rather 'to live a hard and reckless life'. *19th cent.*

> Dickens *Great Expectations* 1861
> *Yes, Pip, dear boy, I've made a gentleman on you! It's me wot has done it! I swore that time, sure as ever I earned a guinea, that guinea should go to you. I swore arterwards, sure as ever I spec'lated and got rich, you should get rich. I lived rough, that you should live smooth.*

> R L Stevenson *Treasure Island* 1883
> *Here it is about gentlemen of fortune. They lives rough, and they risk swinging, but they eat and drink like fighting-cocks, and when a cruise is done, why, it's hundreds of pounds instead of hundreds of farthings in their pockets.*

live to fight another day

to survive a defeat or setback with the possibility of better fortune in the future. *18th cent.*

> Frederick Pilon *The Fair American* 1785
> *Were I by Trade | A fighting blade, | This maxim shou'd | With me hold good, | That he who fights, and runs away, | May live to fight another day.*

live to tell the tale

to be able to tell others about a dangerous experience one has survived. The phrase occurs in Shakespeare in a different form, as *live to tell it,* e.g. in *Romeo and Juliet* (1596) 1.i.221 '[Romeo] She hath forsworn to love, and in that vow do I live dead that live to tell it now.' *18th cent.*

Pope transl Homer's *Iliad* 1715
All Troy must perish, if their arms prevail, | Nor shall a Trojan live to tell the tale.

Edgar Allan Poe *Hans Phaal* 1835
I had no hope that either cat or kittens would ever live to tell the tale of their misfortune.

live with oneself
to retain one's dignity or self-respect: usually in negative contexts or questions. *Late 20th cent.*

Cathy Williams *A French Encounter* 1992
I couldn't live with myself if I sent someone on their way with an outfit that made them look awful.

the living image of something/somebody
an exact copy or representation of something or somebody. *19th cent.*

Wilkie Collins *The Woman in White* 1860
There stood Miss Fairlie, a white figure, alone in the moonlight; in her attitude, in the turn of her head, in her complexion, in the shape of her face, the living image, at that distance and under those circumstances, of the woman in white!

where one lives
informal, chiefly NAmer in a place or way that affects or hurts one most deeply. *19th cent.*

J G Holland *Miss Gilbert's Career* 1860
When that little wife of mine says, 'Tom, you're a good feller, God bless you,' it goes right in where I live. Well, it does!

within living memory
at a past time within the lifetime of people now living. *19th cent.*

Hardy *Jude the Obscure* 1895
This ancient track ran east and west for many miles, and down almost to within living memory had been used for driving flocks and herds to fairs and markets. But it was now neglected and overgrown.

See also be living on borrowed time *at* BORROW; live by one's wits *at* WIT; live in SIN; live a lie *at* LIE²; live off the FAT of the land; live off the LAND; live over the SHOP.

live² (adjective, rhymes with *hive*)

be a live wire
informal to be full of energy and enthusiasm, or wildly excited. The image is of an electric current passing through a wire. *Early 20th cent.*

Jack London *Theft* 1910
[Hubbard] *But don't forget that this Knox is a live wire. Somebody might get stung.*

lively
See (as) merry/lively as a GRIG.

living
See LIVE¹; OWE somebody a living.

load

get a load of something
to pay attention to something surprising. *Early 20th cent.*

load the dice in favour of / against somebody
to prearrange all the elements of a situation to somebody's advantage or disadvantage: loaded dice were weighted with lead in order to make them fall in a certain way. *18th cent.*

Smollett *The Adventures of Ferdinand Count Fathom* 1753
Upon a little recollection he plainly perceived he had fallen a sacrifice to the confederacy he had refused to join; and did not at all doubt, that the dice were loaded for his destruction.

Upton Sinclair *Jungle* 1906
That they were in jail was no disgrace to them, for the game had never been fair, the dice were loaded. They were swindlers and thieves of pennies and dimes, and they had been trapped and put out of the way by the swindlers and thieves of millions of dollars.

take a/the load off one's feet
informal to sit or lie down, especially after lengthy or tedious exertion. *Mid 20th cent.*

take a load off somebody's mind
to relieve somebody of a great worry or responsibility: *load* in the meaning 'burden of affliction or responsibility' dates from the 16th cent., often associated in early use with the heart rather than the mind (e.g. Shakespeare 2 *Henry VI* (1591)

III.i.157: '[Gloucester] Sharp Buckingham unburdens with his tongue | The envious load that lies upon his heart'). *Cf* a WEIGHT off somebody's mind. *19th cent.*

> **Dickens *David Copperfield* 1850**
> *'Uriah Heep is a great relief to me,' said Mr. Wickfield, in the same dull voice. 'It's a load off my mind, Trotwood, to have such a partner.'*

See also loaded for bear *at* BEAR¹.

---

loaf

use one's loaf
informal to think intelligently or sensibly about something: *loaf*, a shortening of *loaf of bread*, which is rhyming slang for *head*, is recorded in this sense from the 1920s, originally in services' slang, and the phrase first appears in the late 1930s. *Mid 20th cent.*

See also HALF a loaf.

---

loath

nothing loath
perfectly willing to fall in with a proposal. *Loath* (also spelt *loth*) is derived from an Old English word *lath* meaning 'hostile', and is related to *loathe*. In Middle English, *nothing loth* meant 'liking well' in a more positive sense.

> **Gower *Confessio Amantis* c1383**
> *And sche, which was him nothing loth, | Welcomede him into that lond, | And softe tok him be the hond, | And doun thei seten bothe same.*

> **Milton *Paradise Lost* ix.1039 (1667)**
> *Her hand he seis'd, and to a shadie bank, | Thick overhead with verdant roof imbowr'd | He led her nothing loath.*

> **Scott *Waverley* 1814**
> *She appeared, indeed, in full splendour in her father's pew upon the Sunday when he attended service for the last time at the old parish church, upon which occasion, at the request of his uncle and Aunt Rachel, he was induced (nothing loth, if the truth must be told) to present himself in full uniform.*

lock

lock horns
to engage in an argument or dispute: a metaphor based on the action of cattle entangling their horns when fighting head on. *19th cent.*

> **David Ross Locke *Swinging Round the Circle* 1867**
> *Wood he go through with it? Wood he lock horns with Wade and Summer, and dare the wrath uv Thad Stevens?*

> **Willa Cather *The Song of the Lark* 1915**
> *You were fumbling and awkward. Since then you've come into your personality. You were always locking horns with it before.*

lock, stock, and barrel
wholly or completely. The phrase is based on the constituent parts that make up a flintlock gun: the lock was the firing mechanism, perhaps so called because it resembled the lock of a door. It is curious, perhaps, that guns of this type had been in use for several centuries before providing us with our phrase. The earliest use we know of is in a letter written by Sir Walter Scott in 1817: 'Like the Highlandman's gun, she wants stock, lock, and barrel, to put her into repair.' The phrase was commonly used about this time to refer to the complete parts of the gun. *19th cent.*

> **Bram Stoker *Dracula* 1897**
> *It be all fool-talk, lock, stock, and barrel; that's what it be, an' nowt else.*

under lock and key
locked up and secure. *Lock* and *key* (or in early use in the reverse order) occur together from early Middle English to denote persons or things kept in security. *Under a lock* is recorded from the 15th cent.

> **Gower *Confessio Amantis* c1383**
> *To kepe hir bodi nyht and day, | Sche hath a wardein redi ay, | ... | Which under lock and under keie, | That noman mai it stele aweie, | Hath al the Tresor underfonge [= received] | That unto love mai belonge.*

> **Sir William D'Avenant *The Wits* 1636**
> *[Engine] Draw out the Chest within, that's big enough | To hold you: it were dangerous to have | My Ladies Guardian to find you Sir! [Elder Pallatine] How! layd up like a brush'd Gowne, under lock | And key! By this good light, not I!*

locker

See go to Davy Jones's locker *at* DAVY JONES; a SHOT in the locker.

log

See (as) EASY as falling off a log; SLEEP like a log.

loggerhead

at loggerheads

in quarrelsome disagreement: *loggerhead* is an archaic word for a dunce or fool, literally meaning 'a head made of a *logger* [= block of wood]' and hence 'a person with a disproportionately large head'. The word occurs in Shakespeare, *Love's Labour's Lost* (1594) IV.iii.202 '[Biron to Costard] Ah, you whoreson loggerhead, you were born to do me shame.' The phrase occurs in the 17th cent. in the form *to loggerheads*; it dates from the 19th cent. in this form.

loin

See GIRD up one's loins.

loiter

loiter with intent

to wait around at a place with the intention of committing a crime. *Loitering with Intent* is the title of a novel by Muriel Spark (1981). *19th cent.*

H V Esmond *One Summer's Day* 1901
[Hoddesden] *Don't answer me, sir! What are you doing here?* [Seth] *'Ow am I to tell you if I don't answer?* [Hoddesden] *Quite right! I apologize. I'll have you locked up for loitering with intent to commit a felony.*

Esquire 1993
Piccadilly Circus is the traditional haunt of bus-loads of Day-Glo-rucksacked European school-children loitering with intent to spend their last tenner on a Sex Pistols T-shirt.

Lombard Street

all Lombard Street to a China orange

informal a near certainty, expressed as the long odds of the wealth of Lombard Street, London's mercantile centre, pitted against something trifling. There are other forms of comparison, e.g. in the 18th cent. we find *all Lombard Street to an eggshell.*

J Palgrave Simpson *Daddy Hardacre* 1857
[Hardacre] *Now, that's just your mistake. The proper use o' money is to save it up, and take proper care on't.* [Enter Jobling] [Jobling] *Mr. Hardacre said that – Lombard Street to a China orange.* [Hardacre] *You're right, Muster Jobling. I always like to gi' the young folks good moral advice.*

lonesome

by/on one's lonesome

informal completely alone. *19th cent.*

Conan Doyle *His Last Bow* 1917
Well, I guess you'll have to fix me up also. I'm not staying in this gol-darned country all on my lonesome.

long

(as) long as your arm

extremely long (in various senses). An extension of the notion in the phrase *at arm's length* as symbolizing a significant or safe distance: *see* ARM. *19th cent.*

James Fenimore Cooper *Redskins* 1846
Leases as long as my arm, I calcerlate?

Helen Keller *The Story of My Life* 1901
The crane is a large and strong bird. His wings are as long as my arm, and his bill is as long as my foot. He eats little fishes, and other small animals. Father says he can fly nearly all day without stopping.

in the long run/term

over a longer period of time; in due course: in earlier use (17th cent.) in the form *at the long run.* *18th cent.*

Adam Smith *Wealth of Nations* 1776
In the long-run, therefore, the operations of this bank increased the real distress of the country which it meant to relieve.

the long and the short (of it)

the gist or outline of something; the upshot. The phrase also occurs in early use in the reverse form the *short and the long*, for example in Shakespeare's *The Merry Wives of Windsor* (1597) where Nim, one of the followers of Sir John

Falstaff, tells Master Page about Falstaff (II.i.126) 'He loves your wife. There's the short and the long.' In *Henry V* (1599) we find (III.iii.61) 'the brief and the long'. Further back, in Middle English, there occur equivalent adverbial phrases such as 'to say longly or short'. The phrase dates from the 16th cent. in its modern form.

Charles Sackville My Opinion a1706
I'd make this the long and the short of the story: | The fools might be Whigs, none but knaves should be Tories.

long in the tooth

past one's best days: from the fact that the teeth appear longer in old age because of gum recession, and originally used with reference to horses. *19th cent.*

Thackeray The History of Henry Esmond 1852
His cousin was now of more than middle age, and had nobody's word but her own for the beauty which she said she once possessed. She was lean, and yellow, and long in the tooth.

not be long for this world

(as a euphemism) to be near death: first used by Byron ('I cannot be long for this world') in a letter addressed to John Murray in September 1822. *19th cent.*

George Eliot Middlemarch 1872
He can't be long for this world, my dear; I wouldn't hasten his end, but what with asthma and that inward complaint, let us hope there is something better for him in another.

See also (not) by a long CHALK; (not) by a long SHOT.

longbow

draw the longbow

literary to make exaggerated claims: based on the prowess associated with skilful use of the longbow in medieval England. The phrase dates from the 17th cent. but occurs mainly in 19th cent. literary use.

R H Dana Two Years Before the Mast 1840
He had, of course, been in all parts of the world, and was remarkable for drawing a long bow. His yarns frequently stretched through a watch, and kept all hands awake.

look

be looking for trouble

to act in a way that is likely to cause conflict or difficulty, usually intentionally: *cf* be asking for trouble at ASK. *Early 20th cent.*

Jack London White Fang 1906
The effect on White Fang was to give him a greater faith in himself, and a greater pride. He walked less softly among the grown dogs; his attitude toward them was less compromising. Not that he went out of his way looking for trouble.

here's looking at you

used as a toast in drinking: from the film *Casablanca* (1942), in which Rick (played by Humphrey Bogart) addresses Ilse (played by Ingrid Bergman) with the words 'Here's looking at you, kid'. *Mid 20th cent.*

Martin Amis Money 1985
My father inhaled richly and rose to his feet. He slapped a hand on the cocktail console. He said explanatorily, 'Pink champagne. Well, it's not every day, is it? Come on Vron! ... Here's looking at you, my love.'

look down one's nose at somebody/something

to regard somebody or something with disdain. *Early 20th cent.*

look somebody in the eye(s)/face

to face somebody confidently or defiantly. The form with *face* is 16th cent., with *eye* mid 20th cent.

Shakespeare Romeo and Juliet III.v.162 (1596)
[Capulet] Hang thee, young baggage, disobedient wretch! | I tell thee what: get thee to church o' Thursday, | Or never after look me in the face.

look lively/aware

to act promptly; to start work. *19th cent.*

Samuel Lover The Hall Porter 1839
[Mrs Best] Stop, miss, stop your snivelling, or you'll have an ugly nose, too; it's beginning to get red, already. Mop up your eyes there, and look lively. The brisket's at the door, and I can wait no longer.

Kenneth Grahame The Wind in the Willows 1903
The Badger bade the other two set a table on its legs again ... 'I want some grub, I do,' he said, in that

rather common way he had of speaking. 'Stir your stumps, Toad, and look lively!'

look the other way

to ignore an incident of wrongdoing. *19th cent.*

Henry James *The American* 1877
I don't take an 'intellectual pleasure' in her pro-spective adventures. I don't in the least want to see her going down hill. I had rather look the other way.

look sharp

to act promptly: normally used as an instruction. *18th cent.*

Joseph Trapp transl Virgil's *Eclogues* 1731
[Menalcas] And when I cry'd, Now whither runs That Thief? | Look sharp there, Tityrus, and count thy Flock; | You skulk'd behind a Bush, and slunk away.

not like the look of something

to be suspicious of something. *19th cent.*

Lewis Carroll *Alice's Adventures in Wonderland* 1865
The baby grunted again, and Alice looked very anxiously into its face to see what was the matter with it. There could be no doubt that it had a very turn-up nose, much more like a snout than a real nose: also its eyes were getting extremely small for a baby: altogether Alice did not like the look of the thing at all.

See also look daggers at somebody *at* DAGGER; look on the BRIGHT side; look the PART.

---

lookout

be on the lookout

to be alert to danger or other contingencies: in 19th cent. use also with *upon* instead of *on*. *18th cent.*

Henry Fielding *The History of Tom Jones* 1749
The lady ... was on her side contriving how to give the captain proper encouragement, without appearing too forward; for she was a strict observer of all rules of decorum. In this, however, she easily succeeded; for as the captain was always on the look-out, no glance, gesture, or word escaped him.

be on the lookout for somebody/something

to watch out for somebody or something. *19th cent.*

Jane Austen *Emma* 1816
You are afraid of giving me trouble; but I assure you, my dear Jane, the Campbells can hardly be

more interested about you than I am. I shall write to Mrs. Partridge in a day or two, and shall give her a strict charge to be on the look-out for any thing eligible.

---

loop

loop the loop

(said of an aircraft or its pilot) to complete a manoeuvre involving a complete vertical circle in the air in which the aircraft flies upside down at the top of the circle. *Early 20th cent.*

Tom Kettle *Poems and Parodies* 1916
But I hit one ball a wallop like a kick of a Spanish bull | ... | It looped the loop like Pégoud in parabolic curves; | It was salve to my wounded feelings and balm to my ruffled nerves.

throw/knock somebody for a loop

informal to surprise or disconcert somebody completely: from *loop* meaning 'a curved vertical course described by a vehicle or aircraft'. *Early 20th cent.*

Arthur Stringer *Shadowed Victory* 1943
And when a raider with a boyish voice Sang out, | 'We'll knock von Runstedt for a loop!' | A laugh went round the forward-looking ranks.

---

loose

at/on a loose end / NAmer at loose ends

having nothing to do for a short time; bored or unoccupied. The literal meaning of *loose end* here is 'a length of string or cord left hanging or unattached'; as early as the 16th cent. it developed figurative uses denoting uncompleted or unexplained details. *19th cent.*

R H Dana *Two Years Before the Mast* 1840
'Well, poor George is gone! His cruise is up soon! He knew his work, and did his duty, and was a good shipmate.' Then usually follows some allusion to another world, for sailors are almost all believers; but their notions and opinions are unfixed and at loose ends.

Saki *The Chronicles of Clovis* 1912
I found a military Johnny hanging round on a loose end at the club, and took him home to lunch once or twice.

break loose
to escape from restraint or confinement. *Middle English*

> **Locke An Essay Concerning Human Understanding 1690**
> *If to break loose from the conduct of reason, and to want that restraint of examination and judgment which keeps us from choosing or doing the worse, be liberty, true liberty, madmen and fools are the only freemen.*

hang/stay loose
informal, originally NAmer to take a light-hearted attitude; to be relaxed. *Late 20th cent.*

See also a loose CANNON.

lorry
See FALL off the back of a lorry.

lose

fight a losing battle
to engage in a struggle that is bound to end in failure. *19th cent.*

> **Trollope Barchester Towers 1857**
> *As he went on stammering and floundering, he saw that his wife's eye was fixed sternly on him. Why should he encounter such evil for a man whom he loved so slightly as Mr. Slope? Why should he give up his enjoyments and his ease, and such dignity as might be allowed to him, to fight a losing battle for a chaplain? ... From that moment he determined to fling Mr. Slope to the winds.*

lose one's mind / *informal* marbles
to become insane or deranged. *Lose one's mind* dates from Middle English. *Marbles* in the sense 'mental faculties' dates from the early 20th cent. in expressions such as *have all one's marbles* and *with some of one's marbles missing,* and occurs in the present phrase from the mid 20th cent.

> **Chaucer The Book of the Duchess (line 551)**
> *For he had wel nygh lost hys mynde, | Thogh Pan, that men clepeth god of kynde* [= that men call the god of nature], *| Were for hys sorwes never so wroth.*

lose sleep over something
to worry or fret about something, literally so much that one is kept awake at night: normally used in negative contexts. *Mid 20th cent.*

> **Daily Telegraph 1992**
> *I'm not saying I lose sleep about it, but the prospect of making a howler in front of millions of people is a worry.*

lose one's/the way
to lose one's sense of purpose or understanding of one's objectives in an undertaking: a figurative use of the meaning 'to become lost on a journey', which appears in the 16th cent. (Palsgrave, *Lesclarcissement* (1530): 'I wander, as one dothe that hath lost his waye'). *17th cent.*

> **Shakespeare King John iv.iii.141 (1597)**
> *I am amazed, methinks, and lose my way | Among the thorns and dangers of this world.*

See also have lost the PLOT; keep/lose TRACK of something/somebody; lose one's BALANCE; lose FACE; lose one's GRIP; lose GROUND; lose one's HEAD; lose one's HEART; lose one's NERVE; lose one's PATIENCE; lose one's RAG; lose one's SHIRT; lose SIGHT of; lose one's TEMPER; lose one's TOUCH.

loser

be on to a loser
informal to be involved in an activity that is bound to fail: *loser* here means 'a losing bet' and hence 'a failure'. *20th cent.*

> **Punch 1992**
> *I carelessly accepted an invitation to debate with Mrs Williams on the future of social democracy etc on the radio. Mrs Williams was at the time the most popular woman in the world, after Mother Teresa, and it occurred to me, rather too late, that I was on to a loser here.*

lost

all is not lost
there is still hope of success, despite many difficulties or setbacks. The locus classicus is Milton, *Paradise Lost* (1667) i.105 'What though the field be lost? All is not lost'; but the quotation from Beaumont and Fletcher below predates it. *17th cent.*

> **Beaumont & Fletcher Loves Cure 1647**
> [Vitelli] *Come on, | All is not lost yet: You shall buy me deerer | Before you have me: keep off.*
> [Clara] *Feare me not | ... my sword | For this time*

knowes thee onely for a friend, | *And to all else I turne the point of it.*

be lost for words

to be unable to speak or reply, especially from astonishment or emotion. *20th cent.*

be lost on somebody

to go unnoticed or unappreciated by somebody; to have no effect on them. *17th cent.*

Shakespeare *The Tempest* IV.i.190 (1613)
[Prospero] *A devil, a born devil, on whose nature* | *Nurture can never stick; on whom my pains,* | *Humanely taken, all, all lost, quite lost.*

Aphra Behn *The False Count* 1682
[Clara] *Carlos, though young, gay, hansome, witty, rich; I hate as much as you the old Francisco; for since I cannot marry my Antonio, both Youth and Beauty are but lost on me, and Age decrepid wou'd be equal torment.*

get lost

informal, originally NAmer to go away: usually as an intemperate command to somebody to leave one in peace. *Mid 20th cent.*

Janet Tanner *Folly's Child* 1991
I'm a bitch, she thought sometimes. I use Nick shamelessly and I don't like myself for it. But he's got no one to blame but himself. He allows me to do it. If I were a man I'd tell me to get lost.

give somebody up for lost

to acknowledge that somebody has not survived or will not return. *19th cent.*

Edgar Allan Poe *Narrative of Arthur Gordon Pym of Nantucket* 1837
The cook stood with an axe, striking each victim on the head as he was forced over the side of the vessel by the other mutineers. In this manner twenty-two perished, and Augustus had given himself up for lost, expecting every moment his own turn to come next.

See also be lost in the SHUFFLE; a lost SOUL.

lot

The underlying meaning relates to the casting and drawing of lots, and the resulting outcome.

fall to —'s lot

to become a particular person's responsibility. *16th cent.*

Robert Parry *Moderatus* 1595
Then (quoth Florida) let the proposition be: Whether outward beauty, or inward bountie deserveth most praise, or is of greatest force to procure love. The theme being given, it fell to Cornelius lot to be the orator, who was of a very sharp and quick wit.

throw/cast in one's lot with somebody

to join forces or ally oneself with a person or group: *cf* Proverbs 1:14 'Cast in thy lot among us; let us all have one purse' [where *lot* = a division of plunder]. *16th cent.*

John Bunyan *The Pilgrim's Progress* 1678
Well, neighbour Obstinate, said Pliable ... I begin to come to a point; I intend to go along with this good man, and to cast in my lot with him.

love

There are many maxims and idioms associated with love, as one might expect and hope. The best known is the surviving proverb *love is blind*, but love has also been lawless (in Chaucer and Dryden), full of fear (also in Chaucer), jealous (in Shakespeare's *Venus and Adonis*), and without reason (in *A Midsummer Night's Dream*). She laughs at locksmiths (*Venus and Adonis* once more), lasts as long as there is money (in Caxton), locks no cupboards, and makes a wit of the fool (in Burton's *Anatomy of Melancholy*).

love is blind

(proverb) love can prevent us from thinking clearly. Chaucer included this advice in *The Merchant's Tale* (line 1593) 'For love is blynd alday, and may nat see'. There is a playful use in Shakespeare's *The Two Gentlemen of Verona* (1593) in an exchange between Valentine and his clownish servant Speed (II.i.67): '[Valentine] I have loved her ever since I saw her, and still I see her beautiful. [Speed] If you love her you cannot see her. [Valentine] Why? [Speed] Because love is blind.' *Middle English*

make love (to somebody)

1 to woo or behave romantically towards somebody: an older meaning found in literature up to the early 20th cent. *16th cent.*

Spenser *The Faerie Queene* II.ii.17 (1596)
He that made love unto the eldest Dame, | *Was hight [= called] Sir Huddibras, an hardy man* | *Yet not so good of deedes, as great of name.*

2 to have sexual intercourse (with somebody): now the usual meaning. *Mid 20th cent.*

not for love or money
informal not at all; not in any circumstances. *16th cent.*

there's little / not much love lost between them
they (two people mentioned) openly or obviously dislike each other heartily. The underlying idea in current use (attested from the 17th cent. but not dominant until the 19th cent.) is that there is no love to spare because none exists; in earlier use the notion was the reverse of this, that there is indeed much love and none of it is wasted. This older meaning survived to the 19th cent. but has been driven out by the other. Correspondence in the journal *Notes & Queries* from the 1860s onwards shows the confusion caused by this meaning shift, different contributors taking opposing sides on the basis of the contrary interpretations that can be made of it. *16th cent.*

See also for the love of MIKE.

low

the lowest of the low
the most inferior members of a society, group, etc. *Early 20th cent.*

G B Shaw *Androcles and the Lion* 1916
[Megaera] *Everybody knows that the Christians are the very lowest of the low.*

lower

See raise/lower one's sights *at* SIGHT.

luck

as luck would have it
used to express the fortuitous nature of an occurrence: in early use also in the form *as good/ill luck would have it*, depending on whether the event referred to was favourable or not. In Shakespeare's *The Merry Wives of Windsor* (1597) Falstaff declares (III.v.77) 'As good luck would have it, comes in one Mistress Page, gives intelligence of Ford's approach'. However, some editions read 'As God would have it ...' *17th cent.*

one's luck is in/out
one has good (or bad) luck in a situation. *19th cent.*

the luck of the draw
something dependent on chance and beyond one's control. *Late 20th cent.*

Ruth Rendell *The Best Man to Die* 1981
He went to the door where the sunshine showed off his elegant figure and absence of paunch to best advantage. 'All a matter of metabolism,' he said airily. 'Some have it rapid.' He looked back at Wexford. 'Others slow. The luck of the draw.'

make one's own luck
to be successful by using one's abilities and taking one's opportunities. *20th cent.*

no such luck
an admission of regret: in early use also qualified by *good*. *19th cent.*

Dickens *Hard Times* 1854
'Tom, love, I am telling Mr Harthouse that he never saw you abroad.' 'No such luck, sir,' said Tom.

push one's luck
to try to achieve even better luck than one has already had, often at the risk of ending one's run of good fortune. *Early 20th cent.*

ride one's luck
to rely on a period of good fortune without taking risks. *20th cent.*

try one's luck (at something)
to attempt something risky or challenging. *18th cent.*

Report on the Manuscripts of the Duke of Buccleuch (Historical MSS Commission) 1741
We shall go to Jamaica ... and try our luck once more.

you never know your luck
used as optimistic encouragement in an undertaking of doubtful outcome. *19th cent.*

See also DOWN on one's luck.

lucky

you'll/they'll, etc be lucky / I should be so lucky
informal used as an expression of doubt or uncertainty about an outcome. *20th cent.*

Ronald Bergan *Dustin Hoffman* 1991
*Dustin seemed to need his shrink sessions more
than ever. He had first gone to a psychotherapist
because he felt he was a failure, and now he was
going to help him cope with success. All actors
should be so lucky!*

lull

See the calm/lull before the STORM.

lump

like it or lump it
you must put up with something whether you
like it or not, *lump* here meaning 'to take in a
lump', i.e. as a whole. Also in the form *if you* (or
they, etc) *don't like it you* (or *they*, etc) *can lump it.*
19th cent.

John Neal *Rachel Dyer* 1828
*I will say that much, afore I stop, Mr. Sheriff Berry,
an' (dropping his voice) if you dont like it, you may
lump it ... Who cares for you?*

Trollope *The Way We Live Now* 1875
*I shall ask him for a horse as I would any one else,
and if he does not like it, he may lump it.*

Somerset Maugham *Of Human Bondage* 1915
*Well, what I always say is, people must take me as
they find me, and if they don't like it they can lump
it.*

a lump in the throat
a dry feeling in the throat caused by emotion.
19th cent.

Louisa M Alcott *Little Women* 1868
*As the tears streamed fast down poor Jo's cheeks, she
stretched out her hand in a helpless sort of way, as if
groping in the dark, and Laurie took it in his,
whispering, as well as he could, with a lump in his
throat – 'I'm here. Hold on to me, Jo, dear!'*

lunch

do lunch
informal to meet a friend or colleague for lunch.
Late 20th cent.

out to lunch
informal, originally NAmer crazy or out of touch
with reality. *Mid 20th cent.*

P Darvill-Evans *Deceit* 1993
*'But, Doctor ... this ... thing's completely hat-
stand, isn't it?' 'I beg your pardon? Hatstand?' The
Doctor clutched his own hat protectively. 'Bonkers.
Barmy. Out of its tree. Round the bend, out to
lunch. You know.'*

See also ladies who lunch *at* LADY; there's no such
thing as a FREE lunch.

lurch

leave somebody in the lurch
to leave somebody in a vulnerable or difficult
situation when they are dependent on one's help
or support. *Lurch* was originally the name of a
game, and then a term for a high score in this
game, leaving other players at a disadvantage: to
save the lurch meant to prevent an opponent from
achieving such a score. The meaning 'discomfit-
ure' or 'awkward situation' is recorded from the
16th cent. but is now obsolete except in the
phrase. *16th cent.*

Henry Fielding *The History of Tom Jones* 1749
*Indeed, I look upon the vulgar observation, 'That
the devil often deserts his friends, and leaves them in
the lurch,' to be a great abuse on that gentleman's
character.*

lyrical

See WAX lyrical.

McCoy

the real McCoy

a person or thing that is genuine or authentic; the real thing. The expression was used by R L Stevenson in the form *real Mackay* in a letter of 1883, and the likelihood is that he had whisky in mind, since the distillers G Mackay were promoting their brand as 'the real Mackay' in the 1870s, perhaps (though not necessarily) alluding to a phrase already in use. The phrase then crossed the Atlantic and appears in the 1920s in different forms, *McKie* and *McCoy*, as a description of good whisky obtained from Canada. So the likelihood is that the phrase was imported from Scotland along with the whisky. Hugh MacDiarmid used it in a poem in Scots of 1926 (see below). But the story doesn't end there. Not surprisingly, numerous McCoys have been wheeled out in an attempt to link the phrase to a particular individual. The front runner among these is a boxing champion active in the 1890s called Kid McCoy. According to this story a man in a bar challenged McCoy's identity, whereupon the boxer knocked him down, proving the point and evoking the comment that this was indeed the 'real McCoy'. But this account – even if it is genuine – is more likely to be a later association than the true origin of the phrase, which is much more probably connected with the quality of whisky than with the outcome of bar brawls. *19th cent.*

> Hugh MacDiarmid *A Drunk Man Looks at a Thistle* 1926
> Forbye, the stuffie's no' the real Mackay. | The sun's sel' aince, as sune as ye began it, | Riz in your vera saul: but what keeks in | Noo is in truth the vilest 'saxpenny planet'. (Besides, the whisky isn't the real MacKay. Once, the sun itself rose in your very soul when you began it: but what peeps in now is the vilest 'sixpenny planet'.)

mad

(as) mad as a hatter

this version of the phrase reminds us immediately of the hatter in Lewis Carroll's *Alice's Adventures in Wonderland* (1865): ' "In that direction," the Cat said, waving its right paw round, "lives a Hatter: and in that direction," waving the other paw, "lives a March Hare. Visit either you like: they're both mad." ' But this is not the first use, although it must have given the phrase a boost. We find it earlier in Thomas Haliburton's satirical work *The Clockmaker* (published anonymously in London in 1837) and in Thomas Hughes' *Tom Brown's Schooldays* (1857), which predated *Alice* by some eight years. The comparison seems to be connected with an old belief that hat-making could cause mercury poisoning because of the nitrate fumes given off in the manufacture of felt. It is possible, despite the mercury link, that the author of *Alice* (the scholar Charles Dodgson) had an Oxford character in mind, since Hughes, a contemporary of Dodgson with Oxford connections, makes the same comparison: 'He's a very good fellow, but as mad as a hatter.' This character is sometimes identified with a certain furniture dealer called Theophilus Carter, who was doubly entitled to the epithet 'Mad Hatter' on account of his eccentric ideas and his habit of wearing a tall top hat. But, as so often, we cannot be sure that he was not a later association with a phrase that already existed. *19th cent.*

> G K Chesterton *Orthodoxy* 1908
> A flippant person has asked why we say, 'As mad as a hatter'. A more flippant person might answer that a hatter is mad because he has to measure the human head.

(as) mad as a March hare

completely mad. *March hare* refers to the frisky behaviour of hares in the mating season in March: this comparison is one of the earliest for madness. In its full form we first encounter it in the time of Henry VIII, when Thomas More wrote 'as mad not as a march hare, but as a madde dogge'. Two centuries earlier Chaucer made the association with hares in *The Friar's Tale* (line 1327): 'For thogh this Somonour [= summoner] wood were [= was mad] as an hare, | To telle his harlotrye [= wickedness] I wol nat spare.' *16th cent.*

like mad

with great energy or enthusiasm: literally, like a person who is mad. *17th cent.*

Aphra Behn *The Rover* 1677
[stage direction] *They fight, the Spaniards join with Antonio, Blunt laying on* [= dealing blows] *like mad.*

madding

far from the madding crowd

in a secluded place away from the turmoil of the world. The phrase alludes to a line in Gray's *Elegy Written in a Country Churchyard* (1751), 'Far from the madding crowd's ignoble strife, | Their sober wishes never learned to stray', although there are earlier uses of the combination *madding crowd*. *Madding* (from the verb *mad*) means 'frenzied', and is chiefly poetical in use. The phrase was used by Thomas Hardy as the title of a novel published in 1874. *18th cent.*

Henry Jones *Poems on Several Occasions* 1749
Her favour'd sons from 'midst the madding crowd, | Her sons select with gentle hand she drew, | Secreted timely from th'austere and proud, | Their fame wide-spreading, tho' their numbers few.

madness

that way madness lies

a proposed course of action is bound to lead to disaster: with reference to Lear's words in Shakespeare's *King Lear* (1606) III.iv.21 'O Regan, Goneril, Your old kind father, whose frank heart gave all – O, that way madness lies. Let me shun that. No more of that.' *17th cent.*

Bram Stoker *Dracula* 1897
Strange that it never struck me that the very next house might be the Count's hiding-place! Goodness knows that we had enough clues … The bundle of letters relating to the purchase of the house were with the typescript. Oh, if we had only had them earlier we might have saved poor Lucy! Stop; that way madness lies!

magic

See a magic CARPET.

magnitude

See of the FIRST order/magnitude.

main

The use of *main* as an epithet of power and strength derives from Old English.

by main force

by use of physical strength. *16th cent.*

Shakespeare *2 Henry VI* I.i.208 (1591)
[Salisbury] *Then let's away, and look unto the main.* [Warwick] *Unto the main? O, father, Maine is lost! | That Maine which by main force Warwick did win, | And would have kept so long as breath did last! | Main chance, father, you meant – but I meant Maine, | Which I will win from France or else be slain.*

in the main

mostly; for the most part. *17th cent.*

Congreve *The Way of the World* 1700
We hit off a little wit now and then, but no animosity. – The falling-out of wits is like the falling out of lovers: – we agree in the main, like treble and bass.

with might and main

with all one's strength or power. The phrase occurs in Middle English lyrics and ballads from the 12th cent. on, and in the northern poem of c1300 called *Cursor Mundi*.

majority

join the (great) majority

a euphemism meaning 'to die'. *The majority*, or *the great majority*, are the dead. The phrase first appears in English in Edward Young's drama *The Revenge*, produced at Drury Lane in 1721: 'Life is the desert, life the solitude. Death joins us to the great majority.' The image, however, goes back to Roman literature, where it appears in the simpler form (without *great*) in Petronius' *Satyricon* (1st cent. AD) xliii.5: *abiit ad plures. 18th cent.*

Lewis Carroll *Sylvie and Bruno Concluded* 1893
I pushed open the little wicket-gate and slowly took my way among the solemn memorials of the quiet dead, thinking of the many who had, during the past

year, disappeared from the place, and had gone to 'join the majority'.

See also the SILENT majority.

---

make

be the making of somebody

to bring about somebody's success or good fortune: *making* in the sense 'advancement, success' dates from the 15th cent., and the phrase in this form from the 17th cent.

Joseph Harris *Love's a Lottery* 1699
I am very well known, Sir, all about that end of the town; and a pretty woman will be the making of me.

have the makings of something

to have the right qualities to become a particular kind of person or thing. *17th cent.*

Shakespeare *Henry VIII* iv.i.89 (1613)
She had all the royal makings of a queen.

in the making

in the process of being produced or developed. *17th cent.*

Milton *Areopagitica* 1644
Where there is much desire to learn, there of necessity will be much arguing, much writing, many opinions; for opinion in good men is but knowledge in the making.

make believe

to pretend or feign something: often followed by a *that* clause, and in earlier use by a verb with *to* (see the Dickens quotation below). *17th cent.*

William Clark *The Grand Tryal* 1685
For who, say they, shall ever us perswade, | Or make believe that thou a soul hast made, | A something, which doth after death exist.

Fanny Burney *Camilla* 1796
Why, when they're cleaning out his room, if they happen but to sweep away a bit of paper as big as my hand, he'll make believe they've done him as much mischief as if they'd stole a thousand pound.

Dickens *Barnaby Rudge* 1840
He watches all the time I sleep, and when I shut my eyes, and make-believe to slumber, he practises new learning softly; but he keeps his eye on me the while, and if he sees me laugh, though never so little, stops directly.

make do

to manage with inadequate or improvised resources. The 20th cent. use is anticipated by Edith Wharton in *Greater Inclination* (1899): 'She had ... accepted it [marriage] as a provisional compensation, – she had made it "do".' *Early 20th cent.*

Phillip E Johnson *Darwin on Trial* 1991
Orthodox genetic theory insists that no such guiding principle for mutation exists, so creatures have to make do with whatever blind nature happens to provide.

make or break/mar

to be the decisive factor in determining whether a person or thing is successful or not: the form *make or mar* is the earlier. The phrase occurs in Middle English in John Lydgate's *Assembly of Gods* (c1420): 'Neptunus, that dothe bothe make & marre'.

John Heywood *Of Making and Marryng* from *Works* 1562
Make or mar I wyll, so saist thou euer: | But thou doost euer marre, thou makst neuer.

Shakespeare *A Midsummer Night's Dream* i.ii.33 (1595)
[Bottom] The raging rocks | And shivering shocks | Shall break the locks | Of prison gates, | And Phibus' car | Shall shine from far, | And make and mar | The foolish Fates.

of one's own making

(said of a misfortune or difficulty) brought about by one's own actions or behaviour. *17th cent.*

Dryden transl Ovid's *Metamorphoses* c1699
But man a slave of his own making lives; | The fool denies himself what nature gives.

on the make

1 *informal* intent on or preoccupied with financial or social advancement, especially by unscrupulous means. *19th cent.*

Ambrose Bierce *The Fiend's Delight* 1873
Some time ago we courted her, but finding she was 'on the make', threw her off.

James Barrie *What Every Woman Knows* 1908
There are few more impressive sights in the world than a Scotsman on the make.

2 *informal* in search of a sexual partner or sexual adventure. *20th cent.*

Catherine Cookson *The Rag Nymph* 1992
That was on a Saturday night when the gents came down for their pickings. Anyway, I've been thinkin' about her. She's not up to much, is she, if she takes a bairn like that 'un with her when she's on the make?

put the make on somebody
informal, chiefly NAmer to make sexual advances towards somebody. *Late 20th cent.*

Sandra Gilbert *Blood Pressure* 1988
Don't listen to her, she's jealous, he said. Can't you see she's just another single lady trying to put the make on me?

See also make a BEELINE for; make the CUT; make a DAY of it; make somebody's DAY; make HAY; make a NIGHT of it; make up one's MIND; make WAY for somebody/something.

malice

with malice aforethought
with the intention of committing a violent crime. *Malice* is used in the legal sense 'wrongful intention', and the phrase translates the Anglo-French legal term *malice prepense*, referring to the requirement that malice be established as a factor in a killing for it to constitute murder. The translated version of the phrase appears in the form *malice forethought* in Acts of Parliament of the reign of Charles II. *Malice Aforethought* was the title of a celebrated psychological thriller by the British crime writer Francis Iles (pseudonym of Anthony Berkeley Cox) published in 1931, in which a doctor administers poison to his wife over a period. *17th cent.*

Smollett *The Adventures of Ferdinand Count Fathom* 1753
The company endeavoured to appease this citizen, by representing that his misfortune was no other than a common inflammation; nor was it owing to malice aforethought, but entirely to the precipitate passion of an incensed young man, who, by the bye, acted in his own defence.

mammon

the mammon of unrighteousness
material wealth or possessions, especially when ill-gotten. With reference to Luke 16:9 (Authorized Version, 1611), in the context of Christ's warning that no man can serve two masters: 'And I say unto you, Make to yourselves friends of the mammon of unrighteousness; that, when ye fail, they may receive you into everlasting habitations' (see also Matthew 6:24 'Ye cannot serve God and mammon'). *Mammon* was used from the 14th cent. to personify wealth in its bad aspects and is derived from a Hebrew word *mamon* meaning 'money, riches'. *17th cent.*

man

as — as the next man
no less — than anybody else. *19th cent.*

William Tappan Thomas *Major Jones's Sketches of Travel* 1848
I like a good song as well as anybody, and have got jest as good a ear for musick as the next man, but I hain't got no notion of hearin twenty or thirty men and wimmin all singin together, in a perfect harrycane of noisy discord, so a body can't tell whether they're singin 'Hail Columbia' or 'Old Hundred'.

a man about town
a worldly and socially active man. *18th cent.*

Eliza Haywood *Jenny and Jemmy Jessamy* 1753
In the first place he is a young heir, lately come to the possession of an estate sufficient to support a coach and six; in the next he is handsome, well made, has as genteel an address as any man about town; lastly, he is allow'd to have wit, honour, and good nature, and his name is Jessamy.

man and boy
for the whole of a man's life from childhood. The locus classicus is Shakespeare, *Hamlet* (1601) v.i.158 '[First Clown at Yorick's grave] I have been sexton here, man and boy, thirty years', although the expression is found earlier (see below). The Scottish poet William Dunbar used the expression (early 16th cent.) in the form *baith man and lad*. *16th cent.*

Anon *A Warning to Fair Women* 1599
[Browne] Hearke ye, my friend, Are not you seruant vnto mistres Drurie? [Roger] Yes indeed forsooth, for fault of a better, I haue seru'd her (man and boy) this seuen yeeres.

Washington Irving *The Sketch Book (Stratford-on-Avon)* 1819–20
In the course of my rambles I met with the gray-headed sexton, Edmonds, and accompanied him

home to get the key of the church. He had lived in Stratford, man and boy, for eighty years, and seemed still to consider himself a vigorous man.

a man for all seasons

a man who can adapt himself to any situation or set of circumstances. The phrase was first used by Robert Whittington in 1520 with reference to Sir Thomas More (1478–1535), the English politician and scholar who served Henry VIII. Whittington was rendering the Latin of Erasmus, who said (in the preface to *Encomium Moriae* ('In Praise of Folly') 1509) that More played *omnium horarum hominem* 'a man of all hours'. The epithet was used by Robert Bolt as the title of a play (1960) and later film about More's life. *16th cent.*

the man in the moon

an imaginary or fantastic person; or, in more recent use, a person who has little knowledge or experience of the real world. The name has been used since the 14th cent., and is based on an imagined form resembling a human face on the surface of a full moon. *No more than the man in the moon* is recorded as a form of emphatic negative from the 16th cent., and generalized allusive uses date from the 17th cent.

Congreve *Love for Love* 1695
[Foresight] *But what do you know of my Wife, Sir Sampson?* [Sir Sampson] *Thy Wife is a Constellation of Vertues; she's the Moon, and thou art the Man in the Moon: Nay, she is more Illustrious than the Moon; for she has her Chastity without her Inconstancy.*

a man of God

a clergyman or holy person. The phrase appears in Middle English (in Wyclif), and *godes man* is recorded in Old English.

Cotton Mather *A City Helped of the Lord* 1702
He was a man of prayer, which was indeed a ready way to become a man of God. He would say, 'That prayer was the principal part of a minister's work; 'twas by this, that he was to carry on the rest.'

the man of the moment

a man who is particularly important or distinguished at a particular time. *19th cent.*

Nathaniel Hawthorne *Mr Higginbotham's Catastrophe* 1834
Dominicus, in his vanity of heart, forgot his intended precautions, and mounting on the town pump, announced himself as the bearer of the

authentic intelligence which had caused so wonderful a sensation. He immediately became the great man of the moment.

a man of straw

1 a counterfeit person or thing, especially a sham argument or adversary, set up only in order to be easily countered: the comparison is with an effigy stuffed with straw. *16th cent.*

William Wycherley *The Country Wife* 1675
[Horner] *I will not be your drudge by day, to squire your wife about, and be your man of straw, or scarecrow only to Pyes and Jays; that would be nibbling at your forbidden fruit.*

2 a morally or financially unreliable person. *19th cent.*

Dickens *Pickwick Papers* 1837
'But the costs, my dear sir, the costs of all this,' reasoned the attorney, when he had recovered from his momentary surprise. 'If the defendant be a man of straw, who is to pay the costs, sir?'

the man on the Clapham omnibus

the average or typical person: after the district of southwest London. The phrase is attributed to Lord Bowen, an English judge who is reported as using it in 1903 to characterize the ordinary citizen and his attitudes as a member of a jury. *Early 20th cent.*

Penny Junor *Charles and Diana* 1991
Another instance of Charles's outspokenness was his attack on the proposed Paternoster Square development. This turned him into a hero of the silent majority. He discovered ... that his was not a voice in the wilderness; instead, he was speaking for the man on the Clapham omnibus.

man's best friend

an affectionate term for a dog. *20th cent.*

a man's man

a man who is more at home in the company of other men than he is with women. The expression was first used by George Du Maurier (1834–96) in *The Martian* (a story about school life published posthumously in 1897) 'He had been essentially a man's man hitherto, in spite of his gay light love for lovely women; a good comrade par excellence, a frolicsome chum, a rollicking boon-companion, a jolly pal!' *19th cent.*

Herman Melville *Israel Potter* 1855
Franklin was not less a lady's man, than a man's man, a wise man, and an old man.

man to man

1 (said of meetings, confrontations, etc) involving two men directly. *16th cent.*

John Grange *The Golden Aphroditis* 1577
He minded was in such a place, at such an houre of suche a day, to incounter with him personally, man to man in the defence of his Lady.

2 (said of remarks, opinions, etc) direct and frank, as might be the case when one person addresses another directly. *19th cent.*

James Fenimore Cooper *Deerslayer* 1841
Harkee, Master Deerslayer, since we are on the subject, we may as well open our minds to each other in a man-to-man way.

to a man

involving everybody, without exception. *18th cent.*

John Gay *The Beggar's Opera* 1728
[Crook-Finger'd Jack] *Where shall we find such another Set of Practical Philosophers, who to a Man are above the Fear of Death?*

See also MEN; be one's OWN man/woman; EVERY man for himself; every man / everybody has a/ their PRICE; the man in the STREET; a man of the CLOTH; a man/woman of letters *at* LETTER; a man/woman of the WORLD.

manna

manna from heaven

a sudden and unexpected source of benefit or wealth. In the biblical account of the Exodus (Exodus 16), *manna* (derived from a Hebrew word *mān*) was food miraculously supplied to the Israelites in their journey through the wilderness. In English from the 13th cent. the word developed a figurative meaning denoting spiritual God-given nourishment. In the closing moments of Shakespeare's *The Merchant of Venice* (1598: v.i.293), Lorenzo thanks Portia and Nerissa (who has just told Lorenzo that he and Jessica will inherit Shylock's wealth) with the words: 'Fair ladies, you drop manna in the way | Of starvèd people.' The phrase in its current form dates from the 16th cent.

Austin Saker *Narbonus* 1580
Fidelia, for so was the Gentlewoman nominated, reached him the wing of a Partrich, & laid it before him, which he so gratefully accepted, & thankefully received, as if it had bin Manna sent from Heaven.

Richardson *The History of Sir Charles Grandison* 1753
Pure Love is, perhaps, to lovers as the manna of heaven was to the Israelites.

George Eliot *Felix Holt* 1866
Annette was one of those angelic-faced helpless women who take all things as manna from heaven: the good image of the well-beloved Saint John wished her to stay with him, and there was nothing else that she wished for except the unattainable.

manner

in a manner of speaking

in one sense; so to speak. *Manner of speaking* in the sense 'form or style of expression' dates from the 16th cent., and the phrase with *in* from the later part of the 19th cent.

to the manner born

accustomed to a particular way of life or position from birth or as if from birth: with reference to Shakespeare, *Hamlet* (1601) 1.iv.16 '[Horatio] Is it a custom? [Hamlet] Ay, marry is't, | And to my mind, though I am native here | And to the manner born, it is a custom | More honoured in the breach than the observance.' *17th cent.*

Edgar Allan Poe *Some Words with a Mummy* 1845
But you, Mr. Gliddon – and you, Silk – who have travelled and resided in Egypt until one might imagine you to the manner born – you ... whom I have always been led to regard as the firm friend of the mummies – I really did anticipate more gentlemanly conduct from you.

manse

daughter/son of the manse

the daughter or son of a Protestant, especially a Presbyterian minister. *Manse* here means 'a residence of the clergy'. *19th cent.*

Lord Neaves *Songs and Verses* 1875
O! law is a trade that's not easy to learn, | And a good many failures we daily discern; | But, touching this matter, I'm anxious to mention | A fact I've observed, that may claim some attention: | If you look round the Bar you will see at a glance | Not a few of the foremost are Sons of the Manse.

many

be (one) too many for somebody
to confuse or outwit somebody. *17th cent.*

Defoe *Colonel Jack* 1723
And indeed, this was the most Prudent step she cou'd take, or, as we may say, the only step she had left to take: But I was too many for her here too, my Intelligence about her was too good, for her to Conceal such an Affair from me.

many's the time
such-and-such occurs or has occurred often. *18th cent.*

Henry Fielding *The History of Tom Jones* 1749
'How,' says Jones, starting up, 'do you know my Sophia?' 'Do I! ay marry,' cries the landlady; 'many's the time hath she lain in this house.'

See also HAVE *one too many.*

map

all over the map
informal, originally NAmer completely disorganized. *20th cent.*

off the map
in an insignificant position; of no account. *Early 20th cent.*

Ford Madox Ford *Poems Written on Active Service* 1918
'Cheerio: you'll be back in a month' – 'You'll have driven the Huns off the map.'

Brian Aldiss *A Tupolev Too Far* 1993
'And whereabouts are you from?' Alice asked, rather sharply. 'Oh, you won't have heard of it. A place in Nebraska. Just a hick town, I guess. Right off the map.'

put something on the map
to give something prominence or importance. *Early 20th cent.*

wipe something off the map
to obliterate something completely. *Early 20th cent.*

marble

See LOSE *one's mind/marbles.*

march

get one's / give somebody their marching orders
to be summarily expelled or dismissed (or to dismiss somebody summarily), especially from a job: a metaphor from military language. *Mid 20th cent.*

Daily Telegraph 1992
When tax inspectors sat on high stools and wrote with quills, the sober ranges of Somerset House were an apt location for them. In the age of the computer, they would be better off in Croydon or Nottingham. The incoming government should give them their marching orders.

march to (the beat of) a different tune/drum/trumpet
to differ from most people in one's attitudes or habits. The image is of a marching band, in which the tune determines the pace and manner of the movement. An individual marching to a different tune would be very conspicuous. *20th cent.*

steal a march on somebody
to outdo or outwit somebody without their realizing it until too late: originally in military contexts of an army advancing secretly while the enemy are resting. *18th cent.*

Charles Macklin *The Man of the World* 1781
Why you stole a march on me this morning – gave me the slip … tho' I never wanted your assistance more in my life.

March

See (as) MAD *as a March hare.*

mare

a mare's nest
a false discovery, illusion, or deliberate hoax: based on the notion of a *mare's nest* (or *horse nest*, now obsolete, recorded from the late 16th cent.) as a symbol of the fantastic or imaginary. *17th cent.*

marine

tell that to the (horse) marines
an indignant expression of disbelief in what somebody has said. In 1823 Byron noted the

'old saying' (as he called it) 'That will do for the marines, but the sailors won't believe it', and this fuller version (alluding to the traditional contempt of the Navy for the Marines) is recorded in slightly differing forms elsewhere in the early 19th cent. The variant form *horse marines* adds an element of fantasy to the saying, referring to an imaginary cavalry corps and based on the fantastic notion of horse soldiers serving on a ship. The origin of the expression is said to be associated with the English court of Charles II. When Samuel Pepys mentioned his belief in flying fish he received support for their existence from an officer of the Marine Corps; the King believed him and declared that only the marines had the experience and knowledge of far places to be able to provide such evidence. Anybody who doubted a similar story in future should first 'tell it to the marines'. *19th cent.*

Thackeray *Pendennis* 1849
Colonel, you are a queer feller. No man could have supposed, from your manners, that you had tasted anything stronger than tea all night, and yet you forget things in the morning. Come, come, – tell that to the marines, my friend, – we won't have it at any price.

Trollope *The Small House at Allington* 1864
Is it reasonable to suppose that a creature such as she, used to domestic comforts all her life, should have gone off in this way, at dinner-time, taking with her my property and all her jewels, and that nobody should have instigated her; nobody assisted her! Is that a story to tell to such a man as me! You may tell it to the marines!

---

mark

be quick/slow off the mark
to react or respond promptly (or slowly) to a suggestion or piece of information: the image is of a competitor in athletics at the start of a race. Other forms, such as *get off the mark* and *be the first off the mark*, are also attested. *Early 20th cent.*

C Day Lewis *A Time to Dance* a1972
But look, balanced superbly, quick off the mark | Swooping like centre three-quarter whose impetus storms a gap ... M'Intosh touched her down.

hit the mark
to reach the right conclusion; to guess correctly. The image is of hitting a target with an arrow or

other weapon. The phrase occurs frequently in extended metaphor in literary contexts (as in Shakespeare, *Love's Labour's Lost* (1594) IV.i.127: '[Maria] A mark marvellous well shot, for they both did hit it!'). *See also* hit the NAIL on the head. *16th cent.*

Philip Sidney *The Countesse of Pembrokes Arcadia* a1586
Your wisdom would assuredly determine, how the mark were hit, not whether the bow were of ewe or no, wherein you shot.

Bunyan *The Pilgrim's Progress* 1684
[James] There is not always Grace where there is the fear of Hell; yet to be sure there is no Grace where there is no fear of God. [Greatheart] Well said, James, Thou hast hit the Mark, for the fear of God is the beginning of Wisdom; and to be sure they that want the beginning, have neither middle, nor end.

leave/make its mark
to have an important or lasting effect on a person or thing. *19th cent.*

Wilkie Collins *The Haunted Hotel* 1879
There stood the adventuress whose character had left its mark on society all over Europe ... inconceivably transformed into a timid, shrinking woman!

make one's mark
to succeed in life and become famous. *19th cent.*

Henry James *Washington Square* 1881
Even at the age of twenty-seven Austin Sloper had made his mark sufficiently to mitigate the anomaly of his having been chosen among a dozen suitors by a young woman of high fashion, who had ten thousand dollars of income and the most charming eyes in the island of Manhattan.

mark somebody's card
to give somebody useful information: from the practice in horseracing, in which a tipster will mark a punter's racecard to show the favoured runners. *Late 20th cent.*

mark time
to hang about or spend time on routine activities until something more important or challenging turns up: from the military meaning of soldiers marching on the spot without moving forward. *19th cent.*

Conan Doyle *Through the Magic Door* 1919
A pre-eminently good novel must always advance and never mark time. 'Ivanhoe' never halts for an instant.

near / close to the mark
not far from the truth: *mark* here and in the next phrase is used in its meaning 'a goal or target'. *18th cent.*

off / wide of the mark
not accurate or appropriate. *17th cent.*

Fanny Burney *Cecilia* 1782
'Why this is talking quite wide of the mark,' said Mr. Hobson, 'to suppose a young lady of fortunes would marry a man with a bob jerom (= a wig with the hair caught into a bunch at the back).'

up to the mark
meeting the required standard: *mark* here is used in its meaning 'a rating or assessment of merits'. *19th cent.*

Dickens *Great Expectations* 1861
We drank all the wine, and Mr. Pumblechook pledged himself over and over again to keep Joseph up to the mark (I don't know what mark), and to render me efficient and constant service (I don't know what service).

See also a BLACK mark; the mark of CAIN; mark with a WHITE stone.

market

be in the market for —
to be interested in buying a particular thing: also in figurative contexts. *19th cent.*

Cornelius Mathews *The Politician* 1840
You, my most sagacious and supple sir, make a traffic in the credulity of the world; set your follies out for sale; call about you gaping chapmen, who are in the market for a ranting demagogue, in sound mouthing condition!

on the market
available for people to buy: occurs earlier (18th cent.) in the form *in the market* (see be in the market for — above) *19th cent.*

play the market
to speculate on the Stock Exchange. *Mid 20th cent.*

See also a DRUG on the market.

marriage

a marriage of convenience
a marriage contracted for some advantage rather than for love: a translation (first used by the English essayist and politician Joseph Addison in 1711) of the French phrase *mariage de convenance*, this form also being used in English contexts from the middle of the 19th cent. Often used figuratively in modern use. *18th cent.*

Mary Brunton *Self Control* 1810
His generous nature revolted from suffering his sister to feel herself a mere pensioner on his bounty, or to seek dear-bought independence in a marriage of convenience, a sort of bargain upon which he looked with double aversion, since he had himself felt the power of an exclusive attachment.

Independent 1989
So where is the catch? Does a marriage of convenience between sport and television come with a promise to love, honour and obey?

marrow

to the marrow (of one's bones)
through and through; completely. *19th cent.*

Edgar Allan Poe *William Wilson* 1839
'Gentlemen,' he said, in a low, distinct, and never-to-be-forgotten whisper which thrilled to the very marrow of my bones, 'Gentlemen, I make no apology for this behaviour, because in thus behaving, I am but fulfilling a duty.'

marry

marry money
to marry a wealthy husband or wife. *19th cent.*

Hardy *The Mayor of Casterbridge* 1886
Henchard ... no longer envied Farfrae his bargain. He had married money, but nothing more.

master

See SERVE two masters.

mat

go to the mat
to engage in a fight or argument. The *mat* here is that used to cover the floor in gymnastics and wrestling. *Early 20th cent.*

on the mat

receiving a formal reprimand from a superior: from military terminology, the *mat* being that on the orderly room floor on which a soldier stood to face an accusation from a commanding officer. *See also* on the CARPET. The phrase dates from the early 20th cent. in extended use: the military term is late 19th cent.

Idris Davies *Free Discipline* 1946
O we shall cherish Freedom – you can bet your shirt on that – | Till our masters are our errand boys, and the Head is on the mat.

match

meet one's match

to face one's equal in a contest, especially after a long period of success against weaker opponents: the phrase is recorded earlier (from the 14th cent.) in the form *find one's match*. *17th cent.*

Congreve *The Way of the World* 1700
Why this wench is the passe-partout, a very master-key to everybody's strong-box … Well, Mr. Fainall, you have met with your match.

See also the whole shooting match *at* SHOOT.

Matilda

waltzing Matilda

Australian, informal carrying a pack of possessions on one's travels, like an itinerant. *Matilda* is an Australian slang name for 'swag', and its use in this expression was given special currency by the song 'Waltzing Matilda' by A B Paterson (1864–1941). *19th cent.*

matter

as a matter of fact

in truth, actually. The phrase is recorded earlier in the form *in (the) matter of fact*; and *matter of fact* has been used in law from the 16th cent. to denote what is attested in fact as opposed to opinion and conjecture. Since the late 19th cent. it has been used as a link phrase with reduced meaning simply emphasizing the force of the statement that follows, correcting a previous statement, and so on. *18th cent.*

Edmund Burke *Reflections on the Revolution in France* 1790
They endeavor to prove that the ancient charter, the Magna Charta of King John, was connected with another positive charter from Henry I, and that both the one and the other were nothing more than a reaffirmance of the still more ancient standing law of the kingdom. In the matter of fact, for the greater part these authors appear to be in the right.

Jerome K Jerome *Three Men in a Boat* 1889
'Why, who told you I caught the trout!' was the surprised query … 'As a matter of fact, you are quite right. I did catch it. But fancy your guessing it like that.'

for that matter

as far as that is concerned: also (18th cent.) in the form *for the matter of that*. In more recent use the expression introduces a further point that, despite appearing to be an afterthought, is as important as one already mentioned. *16th cent.*

Sir Philip Sidney *The Countesse of Pembrokes Arcadia* a1586
Yong man … you use but a point of skill, by confessing the manifest smaller fault, to be beleeved hereafter in the deniall of the greater. But for that matter, all passeth to one end, and hereafter we shal have leisure by torments to seke the truth, if the love of truth it selfe will not bring you unto it.

Aphra Behn *The Rover* 1677
[Belvile] A pox upon him, he's our Banker, and has all our Cash about him, and if he fail we are all broke. [Frederick] Oh let him alone for that matter, he's of a damn'd stingy Quality, that will secure our Stock.

Jane Austen *Pride and Prejudice* 1813
'What an excellent father you have, girls!' said she, when the door was shut. 'I do not know how you will ever make him amends for his kindness; or me either, for that matter.'

See also a matter of FORM; a matter of LIFE and death.

Matthew

the Matthew principle/effect

the principle that those who already have will be given more. The expression was coined by the US sociologist Robert K Merton (born 1910) and is based on a passage in Matthew 25:29 'Unto every one that hath shall be given, and he shall have abundance; but from him that hath not shall be taken away even that which he hath.' *Late 20th cent.*

---

max

to the max

to the utmost extent: *max* as a shortening of *maximum* is recorded from the late 19th cent., originally in the context of maximum scores at certain colleges in the US. *Late 20th cent.*

> The Face 1992
> *When you've developed a habit that's hard to break, when you've pissed your best mates off to the max, something's got to give, right?*

---

may

be that as it may

whether that is true or not: used to emphasize the intrinsic validity of a statement. Recorded earlier (e.g. in Shakespeare) in the form *be it as it may*. *19th cent.*

> Washington Irving The Legend of Sleepy Hollow 1820
> *In the bosom of one of those spacious coves ... there lies a small market-town ... which by some is called Greensburgh, but which is more generally and properly known by the name of Tarry Town. This name was given, we are told, in former days, by the good housewives of the adjacent country, from the inveterate propensity of their husbands to linger about the village tavern on market days. Be that as it may, I do not vouch for the fact, but merely advert to it, for the sake of being precise and authentic.*

---

maybe

and I don't mean maybe

an expression intensifying the force of a statement or assertion: originally used in jazz slang. *Early 20th cent.*

---

meal

make a meal of something

to deal with something in an unduly laborious or inefficient way. *19th cent.*

---

mean^1 (verb)

I mean to say

an expression introducing an emphatic assertion, and often used as a meaningless filler or link phrase. The phrase is based on such expressions as *do you mean to say* and *you don't mean to say*, which are used with the notion 'is that really the case?' *18th cent.*

> Thomas Holcroft Human Happiness or, The Sceptic 1783
> *Twas in the latter end of spring, | My heart was light as Wood-lark's wing; | My health was good, my spirits better, | My mind without a single fetter; | By cares nor crosses was I teaz'd, | Nor spleen, nor passion, on me seiz'd: | I mean to say, I felt, just then, | What happiness is call'd, by men.*

> Mary Braddon Lady Audley's Secret 1862
> *Was he eccentric – I mean to say, peculiar in his habits, like your cousin?*

---

mean^2 (adjective)

no mean —

a very good example of a particular thing, especially a quality or achievement. The locus classicus is St Paul's assertion in Acts 21:39 that he was a Jew of Tarsus and 'a citizen of no mean city'; at a slightly earlier date (1596) than this quotation from the Authorized Version of the Bible (1611), Shakespeare in *The Merchant of Venice* (1598) 1.ii.7 makes Portia's attendant Nerissa say that 'It is no mean happiness ... to be seated in the mean'. See also the Milton quotation below. There is an allusion to St Paul's phrase in the title *No Mean City* of a notorious novel by Alexander McArthur about Glasgow published in 1935, dealing with crime and violence in the Gorbals of the 1930s. *16th cent.*

> Milton Areopagitica 1644
> *I suppose them, as at the beginning of no mean endeavour, not little altered and moved inwardly in their minds: some with doubt of what will be the success, others with fear of what will be the censure.*

---

mean^3 (noun)

See the GOLDEN mean.

meaning

not know the meaning of the word

to act habitually in a way that is contrary to that implied by the word in question. *19th cent.*

> Henry William Herbert *The Brothers* 1835
> *I have seen sights of horror a thousand and a thousand times, – on the field, on the scaffold, in fire, and on the sea, – but never did I know the meaning of the word FEAR till then.*

means

a means to an end

something that achieves a useful purpose without having much value in itself. The phrase is recorded from the 17th cent. in philosophical contexts, and became popularized in the 19th cent. *17th cent.*

> Hobbes *Leviathan* 1651
> *For when we say one power is subject to another power, the meaning either is that he which hath the one is subject to him that hath the other; or that the one power is to the other as the means to the end.*

> Robert Bell *The Ladder of Gold* 1850
> *Men who regard money as a means to an end, seeking in other sources the true satisfaction of life, seldom grow rich.*

measure

for good measure

in addition to what is chiefly necessary or relevant. *Good measure* ensures an adequate or proper supply of a commodity in return for the price asked. *19th cent.*

> Mark Twain *Life on the Mississippi* 1883
> *It is the equivalent of the thirteenth roll in a 'baker's dozen'. It is something thrown in, gratis, for good measure.*

get/take/have the measure of something/somebody

to become familiar with the character or abilities of a person or thing. *19th cent.*

> Henry James *The American* 1877
> *To begin with, she had a very plain face and she was entirely without illusions as to her appearance. She had taken its measure to a hair's breadth, she knew the worst and the best, she had accepted herself.*

in some measure

to a certain extent, partly. Also *in great measure* in the sense 'to a large extent, mostly'. *16th cent.*

> Shakespeare *2 Henry IV* I.i.139 (1597)
> [Northumberland] *In poison there is physic; and these news, | Having been well, that would have made me sick, | Being sick, have in some measure made me well.*

> Mary Shelley *Frankenstein* 1818
> *Two days passed in this manner before he was able to speak; and I often feared that his sufferings had deprived him of understanding. When he had in some measure recovered, I removed him to my own cabin, and attended on him as much as my duty would permit.*

made to measure

made or organized to suit a particular person or purpose: originally with reference to suits and other clothing, and then in extended and figurative contexts. *19th cent.*

> Ambrose Bierce *A Jack-at-all-Views* 1909
> *Strange man! how odd to see you, smug and spruce, | There at Chicago, burrowed in a Chair, | Not made to measure and a deal too loose, | And see you lift your little arm and swear | Democracy shall be no more!*

measure one's length

(said of a person) to lie or fall flat. *16th cent.*

> Shakespeare *A Midsummer Night's Dream* III.iii.17 (1595)
> [Demetrius] *Faintness constraineth me | To measure out my length on this cold bed.*

meat

In some phrases the underlying meaning is the old and more general one 'food, nourishment', which survives otherwise only in dialect use.

be meat and drink to somebody

1 *British, informal* be a source of great enjoyment or support to somebody. *16th cent.*

> Shakespeare *As You Like It* v.i.10 (1599)
> [Touchstone] *It is meat and drink to me to see a clown. By my troth, we that have good wits have much to answer for.*

Dickens *Hard Times* 1854
First of all, you see our smoke. That's meat and drink to us. It's the healthiest thing in the world in all respects, and particularly for the lungs.

2 British, informal to be quite routine for somebody. *16th cent.*

Shakespeare *The Merry Wives of Windsor* i.i.274 (1597)
[Slender] *Why do your dogs bark so? Be there bears i' th' town?* [Anne] *I think there are, sir. I heard them talked of.* [Slender] *I love the sport well – but I shall as soon quarrel at it as any man in England. You are afraid if you see the bear loose, are you not?* [Anne] *Ay, indeed, sir.* [Slender] *That's meat and drink to me now.*

easy meat
a person or animal that can easily be overcome or outwitted. *19th cent.*

meat and potatoes
chiefly NAmer basic or everyday needs or concerns. *Mid 20th cent.*

John Steinbeck *The Grapes of Wrath* 1939
I been scrabblin' over this here State tryin' to work hard enough and move fast enough to get meat an' potatoes for me an' my wife an' my kids.

New Musical Express 1992
Satanic and necrophiliac obsessions, the meat and potatoes of death-metal, don't so much take a back seat as miss the bus altogether thankfully.

See also be DEAD meat.

medal

the reverse of the medal
the contrary view of a matter; the other side of the question to the one considered so far: *cf* the other side of the COIN. *17th cent.*

John Evelyn *Diary* 1641
The medaill was reversing, and our calamities were but yet in their infancy.

Harold Frederic *The Damnation of Theron Ware* 1896
But to me, do you know, there is an enormous fascination in celibacy. You forget that I know the reverse of the medal. I know how the mind can be cramped, the nerves harassed, the ambitions spoiled and rotted, the whole existence darkened and belittled, by – by the other thing.

Mede

the law of the Medes and Persians
an unalterable rule or circumstance. The phrase refers to Daniel 6:8, in which the leading men of the kingdom appeal to King Darius to 'establish the decree, and sign the writing, that it be not changed, according to the law of the Medes and Persians, which altereth not' (see also 6:12, 6:15). It appears in Middle English in Wyclif's translation, and allusive uses date from the 17th cent.

Richard Bernard *The Isle of Man* 1627
Old man, the Law of the King allowes thee not the benefit of the clergie, for the reward of sin is death, this is his Maiesties decree unchangeable, as the Law of the Medes and Persians.

Charlotte Brontë *Jane Eyre* 1847
I don't doubt myself: I know what my aim is, what my motives are; and at this moment I pass a law, unalterable as that of the Medes and Persians, that both are right.

medicine

a dose/taste of one's own medicine
unpleasant treatment of the kind that one has often meted out to others. *Medicine* has been used figuratively to mean 'something disagreeable one has to accept' from the middle of the 19th cent. There are punning allusions in some 19th cent. literature. *19th cent.*

Sydney Grundy *A Fool's Paradise* 1899
[Sir Peter] *Your husband complained of his medicine. I thought I'd test it; so I took a dose.* [Beatrice] *You took it?* [Sir Peter] *Yes.* [Philip] *A doctor take a dose of his own medicine!*

Gene Stratton Porter *The Girl of the Limberlost* 1909
There is nothing in all this world so good for people as taking a dose of their own medicine.

meek

(as) meek as a lamb
extremely meek or gentle. The expression occurs in Middle English, in the religious poems of John Lydgate (c1370–1449).

meet

meet the case

to be suitable or adequate. *19th cent.*

Wilkie Collins *The Moonstone* 1868
If, on the other hand, he stood in urgent need of realizing a large sum by a given time, then Lady Verinder's Will would exactly meet the case, and would preserve her daughter from falling into a scoundrel's hands.

meet one's eye/ear

to become visible or audible: *cf* Milton, *Il Penseroso* (1632) line 120 'Of Forests, and inchantments drear, | Where more is meant then meets the ear'. *See also* more (to something) than meets the eye/ear *below. 17th cent.*

Aphra Behn *The Rover* 1677
I wonder how you learnt to love so easily, I had a thousand charms to meet my eyes and ears, e'er I cou'd yield.

meet somebody's eye/eyes/gaze

to look at somebody in the face. *17th cent.*

Congreve *The Mourning Bride* 1677
[King] Ha! seize the Mute; Alonzo, follow him. | Entring he met my Eyes, and started back, | Frighted.

D H Lawrence *Sons and Lovers* 1913
He courted her now like a lover. Often, when he grew hot, she put his face from her, held it between her hands, and looked in his eyes. He could not meet her gaze. Her dark eyes, full of love, earnest and searching, made him turn away.

meet somebody halfway

to come to a compromise agreement with somebody. *See also* meet trouble halfway *below. 16th cent.*

meet one's maker

to die: sometimes used facetiously. *19th cent.*

Isaac Williams *From the Altar* 1849
To that unearthly stillness, more intense, | Where man must meet his Maker, and be known, | Commune and answer with his God alone, | Of judgment, and of sorrow, and of sin.

meet trouble/danger halfway

to expect trouble needlessly and take unnecessary action against it. The notion is that if one stayed put the trouble would not arrive, although in some 19th cent. usage the sense is more 'to face up to trouble or danger'. *See also* meet somebody halfway *above. 19th cent.*

Dickens *Great Expectations* 1861
He was not disposed to be passive or resigned, as I understood it, but he had the notion of meeting danger halfway. When it came upon him he confronted it, but it must come before he troubled himself.

L M Montgomery *Anne of Green Gables* 1909
Doesn't Mr. Allan preach magnificent sermons? Mrs. Lynde says … the first thing we know some city church will gobble him up … But I don't see the use of meeting trouble halfway, do you, Marilla? I think it would be better just to enjoy Mr. Allan while we have him.

more (to something) than meets the eye/ear

more than is immediately obvious or apparent. The phrase is attested with *eye*, with some variation, from the mid 19th cent. and is now the more common use, but it occurs much earlier with *ear* in Milton (*see* meet one's eye/ear *above*). *17th cent.*

George Eliot *Silas Marner* 1861
'Come, come, let us go and sit down … and have no more lifting. You might hurt yourself, child. You'd need have somebody to work for you – and my arm isn't over strong.' Silas uttered the last sentence slowly, as if it implied more than met the ear.

Walter Colton *The Discovery of Gold in California* 1908
Bob's story is only one of a thousand like it in California, and has a deeper philosophy in it than meets the eye.

See also make ends meet *at* END; meet one's MATCH; meet one's WATERLOO.

meeting

a meeting of minds

an understanding or agreement between people arising from common attitudes and ways of thinking. *19th cent.*

J N Pomeroy *Treatise on Equity Jurisprudence* 1883
There is a mutual mistake – that is, where there has been a meeting of minds – an agreement actually entered into – but the contract, deed, settlement, or other settlement, or other instrument, in its written form, does not express what was really intended.

megillah

the whole megillah
a long rambling story. The phrase alludes to the length of the *Megillah*, a name for each book or 'roll' (Hebrew *megillah* = roll) of the Jewish scriptures (the Song of Solomon, Ruth, Lamentations, Ecclesiastes, and Esther), which are read in the synagogue on appointed days. In more recent usage, the phrase has taken on a more generalized meaning 'everything involved or to be expected'. *Mid 20th cent.*

melting pot

throw something in the melting pot
to bring people or things together to make something new out of them, just as metals in their molten state can be formed into new and original creations. The term *melting pot* dates from the 16th cent. in its physical sense. Figurative uses proliferate from the 19th cent., although John Dryden had used it as an image in describing the language of Shakespeare in the Preface to his adaptation of *Troilus and Cressida* (1679): 'If Shakespeare were stript of all the bombast in his passions, and dress'd in the most vulgar words, we should find the beauties of his thoughts remaining; if his embroideries were burnt down, there would still be silver at the bottom of the melting-pot.' It was used as the title of a play on Jewish themes by Israel Zangwill (1908), which portrayed America as 'the great Melting-Pot where all the races of Europe are melting and re-forming'. The term was deplored by George Orwell in his essay *Politics and the English Language* (1946) as a 'lump of verbal refuse', along with *Achilles' heel, acid test, hotbed,* and other expressions.

Nathaniel Parker Willis *Dashes at Life with a Free Pencil* 1845
Of the inspired males Mr. Poe only took up the copperplate five – Byrant, Halleck, Longfellow, Sprague, and Dana. These, as having their portraits engraved in the frontispiece of Griswold's 'Poets and Poetry of America,' were taken to represent the country's poetry, and dropped into the melting-pot accordingly.

memory

have a memory like a sieve
informal to be very forgetful: the image is of a sieve being unable to hold its contents because it is full of holes. There is a slightly different sense, of retaining only what is useful or convenient in the mind, in the quotation below. *18th cent.*

Frances Sheridan *The Dupe* 1764
Your memory is prodigiously like a sieve; | Your interest it preserves, like weighty grains, | But promises are chaff, it ne'er retains.

if memory serves (me) (right)
if I remember correctly. *18th cent.*

Alexander Hamilton in *Federalist Papers* (US) 1788
The Earl of Chesterfield (if my memory serves me right), in a letter to his court, intimates that his success in an important negotiation must depend on his obtaining a major's commission for one of those deputies.

take a trip/walk down memory lane
to enjoy oneself thinking about pleasant past experiences. *A trip down memory lane* is occasionally used to introduce a collection of reminiscences, and *Down Memory Lane* is the title of a compilation of short comedy films by the US film producer Mack Sennett (1949). *Mid 20th cent.*

men

men in suits
senior businessmen or executives, who wear dark suits to a man: used to emphasize the faceless or characterless nature of business at executive level, and the indistinguishability of those involved in it. This facelessness has been further emphasized since the 1970s by the use of *suit* by itself as a form of metonymy (substitution of an attribute for the thing it represents) for 'a man in a suit', with the same meaning. *20th cent.*

Jean Bow *Jane's Journey* 1991
Jane asked for an overdraft, the bank manager (slogan: 'We Like to Say "Yes" '), a pompous Dad's Army look-alike, after conferring with some nasty men in suits who turned their backs to her, had shown her the door.

men in white coats
doctors and hospital staff: from the traditional use of white coats by medical personnel. Usually

in humorous use but with a tinge of menace, especially in the stereotypical image of the mentally ill being borne off by such people. *20th cent.*

Mike Ripley *Just Another Angel* 1989
I patted Armstrong's stubbly radiator and promised him a good clean-out. A pensioner walking his dog on the other side of the street quickened his pace, obviously not wanting to be there when the men in white coats came for me.

separate / sort out the men from the boys
(said of a task or responsibility etc) to be challenging or difficult enough to call for maturity or strength of character. *Late 20th cent.*

Bernard Bergonzi *Exploding English* 1990
Any damn fool ... could think of questions; it was answers that separated the men from the boys.

See also MAN; TWELVE good men and true.

---

mend

mend (one's) fences
to make one's peace with somebody. The allusion is to keeping fences in good repair to remain on friendly terms with one's neighbours (hence the proverb *good fences make good neighbours,* a sentiment recorded from the 17th cent. and quoted in Robert Frost's poem 'Mending Wall' of 1914). Used in the 19th cent. in the US in this form and with *look after* instead of *mend* of congressmen returning home to renew contact with their voters. *19th cent.*

mend one's pace
to speed up, to go faster. A common phrase in literature of the 16th cent. and early 17th cent. The most familiar use is probably in Shakespeare, *Hamlet* (1601) v.i.64 '[First Clown at the grave] Cudgel thy brains no more about it, for your dull ass will not mend his pace with beating'. *16th cent.*

Spenser *The Faerie Queene* IV.vii.22 (1596)
She looking backe espies that griesly wight [= fellow] | Approching nigh, she gins [= begins] to mend her pace, | And makes her feare a spur to hast her flight.

Bunyan *The Pilgrim's Progress* 1678
[Pliable] *Well, my good companion, glad am I to hear of these things: come on, let us mend our pace.*
[Christian] *I cannot go so fast as I would, by reason of this burden that is on my back.*

on the mend
informal recovering from an illness or injury. The phrase is attributed to the poet Coleridge in Mrs Sandford's 1802 memoir of Thomas Poole and his circle, which included Coleridge and Wordsworth: Coleridge is said to have declared that his health 'has been on the mend ever since Poole left town'. The phrase has been extended to other contexts, such as the recovery of broken-down machines and of bad situations. *19th cent.*

Charlotte Yonge *The Heir of Redclyffe* 1853
'Poor Morville,' wrote Maurice, 'had been carried ashore at Corfu, in the stupor of a second attack of fever. He had been in extreme danger for some time, and though now on the mend, was still unable to give any account of himself.'

D H Lawrence *Sons and Lovers* 1913
The weeks passed. Morel, almost against hope, grew better. He had a fine constitution, so that, once on the mend, he went straight forward to recovery.

See also mend one's ways *at* WAY.

---

mention

be mentioned in dispatches
to be commended for an act of courage or bravery: originally in the context of military action, in which a soldier's name is entered in official dispatches for acts of special bravery in the front line. *Early 20th cent.*

Henry Newbolt *Poems New and Old* 1921 [introductory material]
Thirty-five Old Cliftonian officers served in the campaign of 1897 on the Indian Frontier, of whom twenty-two were mentioned in despatches, and six recommended for the Distinguished Service Order.

---

mercy

be thankful/grateful for small mercies
to be glad of minor benefits in an otherwise unpleasant or troublesome situation. Among early users of the phrase was Sir Walter Scott in *The Heart of Midlothian* (1818): '"Ye are thankfu' for sma' mercies, then," said Mrs Howden, with a toss of her head.' *19th cent.*

---

merry

See (as) merry as a GRIG; lead somebody a merry DANCE; play merry HELL with.

mess

See sell something for a mess of POTTAGE.

message

get the message
informal to understand the import of something said or written: often used in response to another's insistence or harassment about a particular matter. *Late 20th cent.*

send the wrong message
to imply something unwelcome or ill-advised: often used in the context of actions by those in authority that might be justified in themselves but run the risk of encouraging excessively tolerant attitudes. Also *send the right message* (in the opposite sense). *Cf* send the wrong signal(s) *at* SIGNAL. *Late 20th cent.*

messenger

shoot/kill the messenger
to regard the bringer of bad news as responsible for what has happened: based on the notion of the thanklessness of bearing ill tidings as a feature of dramatic situations, especially in tragedy (e.g. Sophocles, *Antigone* 'No man loves the messenger of ill'). Often used in the form *don't shoot the messenger*. *18th cent.*

> Roger Boyle, Earl of Orrery *King Saul* 1703
> [Abishai] *I must obey, tho' I believe I err,* | *Liking the News to kill the Messenger.*

> Scott *Old Mortality* 1816
> *'At least send a trumpet and flag of truce, summoning them to lay down their weapons and disperse,' said Lord Evandale ... 'Well,' said Claverhouse, 'and who the devil do you think would carry a summons to these headstrong and desperate fanatics? They acknowledge no laws of war. Their leaders, who have been all most active in the murder of the Archbishop of St Andrews, fight with a rope round their necks, and are likely to kill the messenger.'*

method

method in one's madness
sense or logic underlying apparently foolish or crazy behaviour: with reference to Shakespeare,

Hamlet (1601) II.ii.208 '[Polonius] Though this be madness, yet there is method in't.' *17th cent.*

> Henry James *Roderick Hudson* 1876
> *One might still have said, if one had been disposed to be didactic at any hazard, that there was a method in his madness, that his moral energy had its sleeping and its waking hours, and that, in a cause that pleased it, it was capable of rising with the dawn.*

mettle

on one's mettle
ready to act in a difficult or challenging situation. *Mettle* is originally a variant spelling of *metal* that from the 16th cent. developed figurative meanings, obscuring its identity and making it seem a separate word. The meaning underlying the phrase is 'courage or spirit'. *18th cent.*

> Robert Fergusson *Leith Races* 1773
> *Ere servant maids had wont to rise* | *To seeth [= boil] the breakfast kettle,* | *Ilk dame her brawest ribbons tries,* | *To put her on her mettle,* | *Wi' wiles some silly chiel [= fellow] to trap,* | *(And troth he's fain [= and in truth he's keen] to get her).*

Mexican

Mexican overdrive
the practice of coasting downhill in a motor vehicle, with the engine disengaged: based on the negative image of Mexico in the US, where the expression is mainly used. *Late 20th cent.*

a Mexican wave
a wavelike movement made by a large number of people, especially spectators in a sports stadium, in which adjacent files of people stand up in successive unison and raise their arms, each file sitting down again while the next stands up and performs the same movement. It is so called because it was first generally observed during the football World Cup finals held in Mexico in 1986. *Late 20th cent.*

> Maureen Lipman *Thank You for Having Me* 1990
> *When we drew level the six of us did a protracted and violent Mexican wave, screaming at the tops of our lungs and behaving like the thugs we are.*

mickey

take the mickey (out of somebody)
informal to tease or ridicule somebody unkindly
or persistently. The origin of the phrase is uncertain; *Mick(e)y* is a pet name for *Michael* and may
here be connected with *Mickey Bliss*, rhyming
slang for *piss* (*cf* take the PISS, recorded from
about the same date). An alternative suggestion,
that *mickey* is a shortening of *micturition*, a formal
and technical word for 'urination', is no more
than an ingenious fabrication. *Mid 20th cent.*

microscope

come under the microscope
to be scrutinized or examined in detail: a metaphor from scientific examination using a microscope. *19th cent.*

> Oscar Wilde *The Picture of Dorian Gray* 1891
> *I will not bare my soul to their shallow, prying eyes.*
> *My heart shall never be put under their microscope.*

Midas

the Midas touch
the talent for making money out of any activity
one turns one's hand to: with allusion to Midas,
King of ancient Phrygia in Asia Minor (now
Turkey), who was famed in Greek legend for
turning anything he touched into gold. The
phrase is 19th cent. in this form, but references
to the concept are recorded from the 17th cent.

> Robert W Service *Ballads of a Cheechako* 1909
> *So twenty years, with their hopes and fears and*
> *smiles and tears and such, | Went by and left me*
> *long bereft of hope of the Midas touch.*

middle

the middle of nowhere
a remote or isolated place. *Mid 20th cent.*

steer/take a middle course
to adopt a moderate policy or procedure, avoiding extremes. *17th cent.*

> Dryden *All for Love* 1678 [Preface]
> *I have therefore steered the middle course; and have*
> *drawn the character of Antony as favourably as*
> *Plutarch, Appian, and Dion Cassius would give me*
> *leave.*

midnight

See BURN the midnight oil.

midstream

in midstream
during the course of a process or activity. *19th
cent.*

> Henry James *The Ambassadors* 1903
> *He had walked many miles and didn't know he was*
> *tired; but he still knew he was amused, and even*
> *that, though he had been alone all day, he had never*
> *yet so struck himself as engaged with others and in*
> *midstream of his drama.*

See also change/swap horses in midstream *at*
HORSE.

might

might is right
(proverb) those who are powerful can act as they
wish, without having to give a moral justification
for their actions. The notion was well known in
classical antiquity: for example, Plato in *The
Republic* has Thrasymachus declare that 'justice
is nothing other than the interest of the stronger'.
In English the contrast between *might* and *right*
dates from Middle English: a 14th cent. political
song includes the admonition 'For might is right,
the land is lawless', and Thomas Heywood's 16th
cent. collection of phrases and proverbs contains
the warning 'We see many times might over-
cometh right'. *Middle English*

> Samuel Nicolson *Acolastus* 1600
> *O manners, times, O world-declyning daies! Where*
> *might is right, and men do what they please.*

> Herman Melville *Moby Dick* 1851
> (Whale Song) *Oh, the rare old Whale, mid storm*
> *and gale | In his ocean home will be | A giant in*
> *might, where might is right, | And King of the*
> *boundless sea.*

See also with might and MAIN.

Mike

for the love of Mike
informal used as an exclamation of impatience or
exasperation: *Mike* is a 19th cent. pet name for an
Irishman. *Early 20th cent.*

James Joyce *Ulysses* 1922
O move over your big carcass out of that for the love of Mike listen to him the winds that waft my sighs to thee so well.

mile

be miles away
informal to be lost in thought and inattentive. The image is of physical distance making communication impossible. *19th cent.*

> Wilkie Collins *No Name* 1862
> *'Mrs. Wragge is not deaf,' explained the captain. 'She's only a little slow. Constitutionally torpid – if I may use the expression. I am merely loud with her ... as a necessary stimulant to her ideas. Shout at her – and her mind comes up to time. Speak to her – and she drifts miles way from you directly.*

go the extra mile
to try especially hard to achieve something or do it well. The phrase may ultimately be derived from the account of Christ's Sermon on the Mount (Matthew 5:41 in the Authorized Version of the Bible, 1611): 'And whosoever shall compel thee to go a mile, go with him twain' (in the New English Bible this is translated 'If a man in authority makes you go one mile, go with him two'). Its popularity was probably boosted by its occurrence in a revue song by Joyce Grenfell entitled 'All We Ask Is Kindness' (1957): 'Working like a beaver | Always with a smile | Ready to take the rough and smooth | To go the extra mile.' The phrase has also been attributed to the American President George Bush (senior) in the context of efforts to secure a peaceful solution to the crisis in the Middle East preceding the Gulf War of 1991. *20th cent.*

a mile a minute
informal extremely fast or vigorously. *Mid 20th cent.*

miles from anywhere
informal in a remote or isolated place: also *forty miles*, *a hundred miles*, etc, and in the humorous form *miles from nowhere*. *Early 20th cent.*

> Saki *The Chronicles of Clovis* 1912
> *Towards the finish, however, we must have held rather too independent a line, for we lost the hounds, and found ourselves plodding aimlessly along miles away from anywhere.*

run a mile
informal to recoil in fear or disgust from something: literally, to take refuge by running away as far as one can. *Mid 20th cent.*

see/tell/spot something a mile off
informal to recognize clearly something suspicious or unwelcome: also used occasionally with other verbs of perception, e.g. *smell*. *19th cent.*

> Charlotte Brontë *The Professor* 1857
> *We have fine noses for abuses; we scent a scoundrel a mile off.*

> Ernest Hemingway *In Our Time* 1924
> *The Hungarians were backing their wagon out of an alley ... How did you know they were wops when you bumped them? Wops, said Boyle, I can tell wops a mile off.*

stand/stick out a mile
informal to be blatantly obvious. *Mid 20th cent.*

> Evelyn Waugh *Scoop* 1933
> *'Have you noticed it?' 'Yes ... it sticks out a mile.'*

milk

milk and honey
wealth and prosperity: with allusion to the biblical reference to the Promised Land in Exodus 3:8 as 'flowing with milk and honey'. *Middle English* (in Wyclif)

> Bunyan *The Pilgrim's Progress* 1687
> *Then said Christian, Ah! my friend, the sorrows of death hath compassed me about; I shall not see the land that flows with milk and honey.*

milk-and-water
weak or insipid: the image is of milk diluted with water. *Milk and water* was used at an earlier date (16th cent.) to denote a bluish-white colour and a cloth of this colour. *18th cent.*

> William Godwin *Things as They Are* 1795
> *You are a prisoner at present, and I believe all your life will remain so. Thanks to the milk-and-water softness of your former master!*

> Byron *Don Juan* 1824
> *And one good action in the midst of crimes | Is 'quite refreshing', in the affected phrase | Of these ambrosial, Pharisaic times, | With all their pretty milk-and-water ways.*

the milk in the coconut
informal, originally NAmer something puzzling or mysterious, like how the milk got into the coconut. *19th cent.*

> Henry Esmond *The Law Divine* 1922
> [Bill] *Do you think there's anything in it?* [Ted] *He had her latchkey and he wanted to stick to it – That looks as if there was some milk in the cocoanut, don't it?*

the milk of human kindness
concern for the welfare of others. The phrase is typically used in ironic or mocking contexts, as in the original use in Shakespeare's *Macbeth* (1606) I.v.18, where Lady Macbeth doubts her husband's resolve: 'Yet do I fear thy nature. | It is too full o'th' milk of human kindness | To catch the nearest way.' *17th cent.*

> Smollett *The Adventures of Ferdinand Count Fathom* 1753
> *The Count's mother … abounded with 'the milk of human kindness', which flowed plentifully among her fellow-creatures; and to every son of Mars who cultivated her favour, she liberally dispensed her smiles, in order to sweeten the toils and dangers of the field.*

> Mary Wollstonecraft *A Vindication of the Rights of Woman* 1792
> *And when a question of humanity is agitated he may dip a sop in the milk of human kindness, to silence Cerberus.*

See also CRY over spilt milk.

mill

go through / put somebody through the mill
to undergo (or make somebody undergo) a difficult or unpleasant experience. The image is of grain being ground as it passes through the milling process. *19th cent.*

> R H Dana *Two Years Before the Mast* 1840
> *I've been through the mill, ground, and bolted, and come out a regular-built-down-east johnny-cake, good when it's hot, but when it's cold, sour and indigestible; – and you'll find me so!*

run of the mill
routine or commonplace: with reference to the smooth and predictable running of a mill, or to the material as it is produced by a mill and before sorting for quality. In the early 20th cent. *run of*

the kiln and *run of the mine* were also used. *Run of the mill* first appears in print around 1930. *Early 20th cent.*

million

gone a million
Australian, informal badly affected or smitten by something; completely overcome. *Early 20th cent.*

> A Wright *Breed Holds Good* 1918
> *He was 'gone a million', meaning he was in love with Dorrie.*

look/feel like a million dollars
to look or feel extremely attractive or in good health. *Early 20th cent.*

> P G Wodehouse *Carry On, Jeeves!* 1925
> *It was one of those topping mornings, and I had just climbed out from under the cold shower feeling like a million dollars.*

a million miles from something
completely different from or unlike something. *Not a million miles (away* or *removed) from* is used as a kind of litotes (emphatic statement by denial of the opposite) to denote resemblance or similarity. *Early 20th cent.*

> Henry James *The Golden Bowl* 1904
> *She knew more and more – every lapsing minute taught her – how he might by a single rightness make her cease to watch him; that rightness, a million miles removed from the queer actual, falling so short, which would consist of his breaking out to her diviningly, indulgently, with the last happy inconsequence.*

> Financial Times 1982
> *It is perhaps indicative that his warmest words, apart from those reserved for President Sadat of Egypt, for a foreign head of state are for Joe Clark, briefly Canadian Prime Minister in 1979–80 and a man from a background not a million miles away from Mr Carter's own.*

See also THANKS a million.

millstone

a millstone round one's neck
a severe burden or responsibility. The phrase was originally used with allusion to Christ's words in Matthew 18:6 'But whoso shall offend one of these little ones which believe in me, it were

better for him that a millstone were hanged about his neck, and that he were drowned in the depth of the sea.' *18th cent.*

Smollett *The Adventures of an Atom* 1769
He declared, that not a man should be sent to the continent, nor a subsidy granted to any greedy, mercenary, freebooting Tartar; and threatened, that if any corrupt minister should dare to form such a connexion, he would hang it about his neck, like a millstone, to sink him to perdition.

William Hazlitt *Lectures on the English Poets* 1818
No other style of poetry has succeeded, or seems likely to succeed, in the present day. The public taste hangs like a millstone round the neck of all original genius that does not conform to established and exclusive models.

See also (as) HARD as the nether millstone.

mince

not mince words/matters
to express one's opinion honestly and frankly, especially when this is unfavourable. In early use the form was *mince it*; e.g. in Shakespeare's *Henry V* (1599) King Harry declares to Catherine, daughter of the King of France (v.ii.127) 'I know no ways to mince it in love, but directly to say, "I love you"', and in *Antony and Cleopatra* (1607) i.ii.98 Antony says to a messenger 'Speak to me home [= plainly]. Mince not the general tongue'. *Not mince words* is found from the 19th cent.

Hardy *Jude the Obscure* 1895
I know it was not your fault; but those women friends of yours gave you bad advice. If they hadn't, or you hadn't taken it, we should at this moment have been free from a bond which, not to mince matters, galls both of us devilishly.

mincemeat

make mincemeat of somebody
informal to defeat somebody soundly and conclusively in a contest, argument, etc. *17th cent.*

Charles Reade *The Cloister and the Hearth* 1861
'In Heaven's name, what ill did I ever to ye; what harsh word cast back, for all you have flung on me, a desolate stranger in your cruel town?' ... They stared at this novelty, resistance; and ere they could recover and make mincemeat of her, she put her

pitcher quietly down, and threw her coarse apron over her head, and stood there grieving, her short-lived spirit oozing fast.

mind

bear/keep something in mind
to think about something at the appropriate time and not forget it. *Middle English*

Chaucer *The Man of Law's Tale* (line 1127)
In the olde Romayn geestes [= Roman histories] *may men fynde | Maurices lyf; I bere it noght in mynde.*

be in / NAmer of/on two minds
to be undecided about something: the phrase occurs earlier (18th cent.) in the form *be of many/diverse minds*. *19th cent.*

Keats *Letter* 1819
It is a wretched business. I do not know the rights of it – but what I do know would I am sure affect you so much that I am in two Minds whether I will tell you any thing about it.

L M Montgomery *Anne of Green Gables* 1909
Anne was of two minds whether to have her cry out then and there, or wait till she was safely in her own white room at home.

be of one mind
(said of two or more people) to have the same opinion on a matter, to be in agreement. *15th cent.*

Richard Sherry *A Treatise of the Figures of Grammer* 1555
But he that loveth the authours of peace when he hath the victorie, forsooth declareth that he had rather not to fight, the [= than] *to be victor. And of this I can beare Marcellus witnes. For as alwaies of peace, euen like of warre also, were we of one mind.*

Shakespeare *All's Well That Ends Well* ii.i.236 (1603)
He and his physicians | Are of a mind: he, that they cannot help him; | They, that they cannot help.

bring/call something to mind
to remember something, or (said of an occurrence, encounter, etc) to cause one to remember something. *Middle English*

Milton *Areopagitica* 1644
Next to His last testament, who bequeathed love and peace to His disciples, I cannot call to mind where I have read or heard words more mild and peaceful.

Shakespeare *Henry VIII* II.iv.32 (1613)
Sir, call to mind | That I have been your wife in this
obedience | Upward of twenty years, and have been
blest With many children by you.

Bunyan *The Pilgrim's Progress* 1678
Your saying that he is a pretty man, brings to my
mind what I have observed in the work of the
painter, whose pictures show best at a distance, but,
very near, more unpleasing.

cast one's mind back
to think back to an earlier time or experience.
Early 20th cent.

Conan Doyle *Through the Magic Door* 1919
Go down and stand by the huge granite sarcopha-
gus in the dim light of the crypt of St. Paul's, and in
the hush of that austere spot, cast back your mind to
the days when little England alone stood firm
against the greatest army that the world has ever
known.

change one's mind
to come to a different conclusion or opinion from
before. *16th cent.*

Shakespeare *The Two Gentlemen of Verona* III.ii.59
(1593)
[The Duke] You are already love's firm votary,
And cannot soon revolt, and change your mind.

Tennyson *Dora* 1842
'My girl, I love you well; | But if you speak with
him that was my son, | Or change a word with her
he calls his wife, | My home is none of yours. My
will is law.' | And Dora promised, being meek. She
thought, | It cannot be: my uncle's mind will
change!

close/shut one's mind to something
to refuse to consider or think about something
unpleasant or unwelcome. *19th cent.*

Frederick Tennyson *The Isles of Greece* 1890
And pity for the pains I cannot heal | Hath shut my
mind to deeds I cannot share, | And made me deaf
to any sound but sighs.

come/spring to mind
to be thought of suddenly or unexpectedly. The
form with *come* occurs in the Middle English
poem *Piers Plowman*.

cross somebody's mind
(said of a thought) to occur to somebody. *18th
cent.*

Ann Radcliffe *A Sicilian Romance* 1790
The astonishment of Cornelia for some moment
surpassed expression; at length a gleam of recol-
lection crossed her mind, and she too well under-
stood the scene before her.

give one's mind to something
to devote oneself to a particular task or activity.
The phrase is recorded earlier (16th cent.) in the
meaning 'to indulge in or become addicted to (a
bad habit)'; it dates from the 19th cent. in the
current meaning.

give somebody a piece of one's mind
to tell somebody frankly what one thinks about
them or their behaviour, especially in a sternly
disapproving way: the phrase occurs earlier with
tell, unfold, etc instead of *give*. *16th cent.*

John Wilson *The Projectors* 1665
[Mrs Gotam] O that these men must do all things
by themselves, and never advise with their wives till
it be too late – But I'll make my gentleman know a
piece of my mind before I have done with him.

have a (good/great) mind / half a mind to do something
to be inclined to do something unexpected or
controversial. The unqualified form, which goes
back to Middle English, is more neutral in implication and is now dated. The fuller forms *half a
mind* and *a good mind* are found from the 18th
cent.

Henry Fielding *Shamela* 1741
He bid me get out of the Room for a saucy Baggage,
and said he had a good mind to spit in my face.

have a mind of one's own
to think and behave in an independent way. *19th
cent.*

James Hall *The Harpe's Head* 1833
Mrs. Lee had a mind of her own; her sensibilities
were acute, and her ambition great; and as she
carefully improved every opportunity for gaining
information, she became as intelligent as a lady
could well be without the interesting aids above
mentioned.

have something on one's mind
to be preoccupied with something, especially a
concern or anxiety. *19th cent.*

Jane Austen *Mansfield Park* 1814
'But, Fanny,' he presently added, 'in order to have a
comfortable walk, something more is necessary than

merely pacing this gravel together. You must talk to me. I know you have something on your mind.'

in one's mind's eye

in one's imagination. The use dates from Middle English, although the locus classicus is Hamlet's line in Shakespeare's *Hamlet* (1601), where he describes a mental vision of his father (I.ii.184, just before Horatio tells him of the appearance of the ghost): 'My father – methinks I see my father. [Horatio] O, where, my lord? [Hamlet] In my mind's eye, Horatio.' *Middle English*

know one's own mind

to be confident about one's decisions. *19th cent.*

> Jane Austen *Northanger Abbey* 1818
> *And as to most matters, to say the truth, there are not many that I know my own mind about.*

make up one's mind

to reach a decision: *make up* is used in the meaning 'to reach (some resolve)' from the 16th cent. and occurs in Shakespeare, but the phrase in its modern form is later. *19th cent.*

mind over matter

determination to overcome physical problems or challenges. *19th cent.*

> Adah Isaacs Menken *Infelicia* 1873
> *The leaf may be torn, and traces of tears, that fell as prayers went up, may dim the holy copy, but its fair, sharp, and delicate outlines will only gleam the stronger, and prove the lesson of life, that poor, down-trodden humanity has been studying for ages and ages – the eternal triumph of mind over matter!*

mind one's own business

to refrain from interfering in other people's concerns. *17th cent.*

> John Dunton *A Voyage Round the World* 1691
> *Those who dare be so presumptuous, we shall meet with 'em in the next Chapter, and perhaps more severely in other places, if they don't mend their Manners, and mind their own Business.*

mind the shop/store

to take charge for a time, especially while those normally in charge are absent for a short time. *Mid 20th cent.*

mind your backs

a warning to people to keep out of the way of somebody who wants to get past, especially with a heavy or bulky load. *20th cent.*

> K M Peyton *Who, Sir? Me, Sir?* 1988
> *'Mind yer backs! Mind yer backs!' An extremely large horse was towing Mrs Bean down the ramp. It slithered on to the road, looked round for the nearest tuft of grass and made straight for it, pulling Mr Bean after it.*

not pay somebody any mind / pay no mind to somebody

to take no notice of somebody who is being tiresome or unpleasant. *Early 20th cent.*

out of one's mind

insane: also (in weakened senses) foolish or unwise. *Middle English*

> Chaucer *The Pardoner's Tale* (line 494)
> *Senec [= Seneca] seith a good word doutelees; | He seith he kan no difference fynde | Bitwix a man that is out of his mynde | And a man that is dronkelewe [= addicted to drink].*

put somebody in mind of something

to remind somebody of something, to make them think of it. In early use the sense was of deliberate reminding, but in more recent use the notion has been rather of incidental or fortuitous association of thoughts. *16th cent.*

> Francis Bacon *Essays* 1601
> *I find the generals commonly in their hortatives, put men in mind of their wives and children.*

put one's mind to something

to devote one's attention to a particular task or problem. *19th cent.*

> William Dean Howells *A Foregone Conclusion* 1875
> *'Have you hit upon that new explosive yet, which is to utilize your breech-loading cannon?' ... 'No, ... I have not touched the cannon since that day you saw it at my house; and as for other things, I have not been able to put my mind to them.'*

speak/say one's mind

to speak frankly and honestly. *16th cent.*

> Brian Melbancke *Philotimus* 1583
> *And why I doe complaine, giue eare, & say your mind.*

> Shakespeare *As You Like It* II.vii.59 (1599)
> *[Jaques] Give me leave | To speak my mind, and I will through and through | Cleanse the foul body of th'infected world, if they will patiently receive my medicine.*

See also have/keep an OPEN mind; LOSE one's mind; mind one's Ps and Qs *at* P; OPEN one's mind; READ somebody's mind.

minor

in a minor key
(said of speech or writing) involving restraint or understatement: a metaphor from music, in which works written in a minor key tend to be more subdued or melancholy. *19th cent.*

> Henry James *Roderick Hudson* 1876
> *Roderick's humor, for the time, was pitched in a minor key; he was lazy, listless, and melancholy, but he had never been more friendly and kindly and appealingly submissive.*

mint

in mint condition
in perfect condition as if new: literally, like a newly minted coin or postage stamp. *Early 20th cent.*

> Iris Murdoch *Flight from the Enchanter* 1956
> *Volumes were not arranged in any particular order, nor were they stamped or catalogued. She examined several shelves. The books were chaotic, but in mint condition, since reading was not a popular activity at Ringenhall.*

mirror

(it's) all done with mirrors
used with reference to an apparently amazing or inexplicable occurrence or achievement. The allusion is to illusion, the use of mirrors and other devices by conjurors to deceive their audiences. The phrase was used by Noel Coward in *Private Lives* (1933), and *They Do It With Mirrors* was the title of a murder mystery by Agatha Christie, published in 1952. *Mid 20th cent.*

> *New Musical Express* 1992
> *To rock diehards, The Orb may well represent the unauthentic, trivial voice of the faceless 'It's all done with mirrors' culture. But they're wrong. This is a music of extreme gravity and import.*

mischief

do somebody/oneself a mischief
to cause somebody (or oneself) an injury. *Middle English*

> Chaucer *The Legend of Good Women* (line 2331)
> *And yit this false thef | Hath don this lady yit a more myschef, | For fere lest she shulde his shame crye, | And don hym openly a vileyne* [= bring shame on him].

with a mischief
with great force or determination: now said typically of untoward or unwelcome happenings, but originally used in more neutral contexts. *Cf* with a VENGEANCE. *16th cent.*

> William Painter *The Palace of Pleasure* 1566
> *Lette them alone with a mischief, to keepe companie with beggers.*

> Philip Massinger *The City-Madam* 1658
> [Lacie] *How like you this Exordium?* [Plenty] *Too modest, with a mischief!*

misery

put somebody/something out of their/its misery
1 typically, to kill a badly injured animal in order to end its suffering: *misery* occurs in dialect use from about the same time in the meaning 'physical pain'. *17th cent.*

> Thomas Betterton *The Counterfeit Bridegroom* 1677
> *Now I am past all hopes, I shall be kill'd for being my own pimp – pox on him, he's poor, consequently desperate, and undoubtedly he'l cut my throat, that he may be hang'd, and be out of his misery.*

2 to relieve somebody of extreme anxiety or curiosity by telling them what they are waiting to know. *19th cent.*

> Trollope *Phineas Finn* 1869
> *I venture to send you a line to put you out of your misery; – for you were very miserable when you were so good as to come here yesterday. Your dear little boy is safe from me; – and, what is more to the purpose, so are you and your husband.*

miss

give something a miss
British, informal to decide not to do something. *Early 20th cent.*

Muriel Gray *The First Fifty* 1991
However, winter would transform it into something perilous in the extreme, even with crampons and an axe, and I'd give it a miss during that season unless you're an experienced mountaineer.

miss a beat
to hesitate or falter. *Not miss a beat*, in contrast, means 'to act effectively and promptly'. The metaphor is from music. *Cf* one's HEART misses/skips a beat. *Early 20th cent.*

a miss is as good as a mile
(proverb) if one fails it hardly matters how close one came to success. The oddity of the current form is due to its being a shortening of the full form *an inch in a miss is as good as an ell* (an obsolete unit of length equal to about four feet). *17th cent.*

not miss much
to be vigilant and notice everything that happens around one. *20th cent.*

not miss a trick
informal to lose no opportunity of taking advantage of a situation: *trick* here is used in its meaning 'a round of play in cards, as a unit of scoring'. *Early 20th cent.*

Sinclair Lewis *Babbitt* 1922
'I'll bet … you were a bad old egg when you were a kid!' 'Well, I wasn't so slow!' 'I bet you weren't! I'll bet you didn't miss many tricks!'

See also miss the BOAT.

mission

mission creep
the gradual escalation of the role and objectives of a military force in an area of conflict, e.g. from peace-keeping to active combat. The phrase is now forever linked with criticism of the conduct of coalition wars in Afghanistan and Iraq in 2002–3, which regarded the commitment as uncontrollably open-ended. Also in extended and figurative use, with reference to a similar widening of the aims, role, or activities of an organization. *Late 20th cent.*

Guardian 2003
'Mission creep' became a byword for the lack of defined goals during the allied forces' attack on Afghanistan with critics warning the Americans they faced being sucked into a Vietnam-style civil war unless they stopped their mission creeping into other regions.

mistake

and no mistake
used to emphasize the certainty of something one has just said; without any doubt. *19th cent.*

Hardy *A Pair of Blue Eyes* 1873
Those two youngsters had a near run for it, and no mistake!

make no mistake (about it)
do not doubt it: used for emphatic insistence or to preclude doubt about something said. *19th cent.*

William Clark Russell *The Wreck of the Grosvenor* 1878
No flesh an' blood o' mine as I had any kind o' feeling for should set foot on board ship without fust having a row with me. Make no mistake. I'm talkin' o' females, Miss. I say the sea ain't a fit place for women and gells.

G B Shaw *Pygmalion* 1913
[Mrs Higgins] You certainly are a pretty pair of babies, playing with your live doll. [Higgins] Playing! The hardest job I ever tackled: make no mistake about that, mother.

there's no mistaking —
a particular person or thing is very easy to recognize. *19th cent.*

mite
See a widow's mite *at* WIDOW.

mitt

A mitt was originally a kind of glove that left the ends of the fingers uncovered for better dexterity: the word is an 18th cent. shortening of *mitten*. From the 19th cent. it developed the informal meaning 'a hand or fist'. James Joyce says of a character in *Dubliners* (1914) that 'he was also handy with the mits', meaning he could defend himself.

get one's mitts on something
informal to obtain something, especially in a grasping or dubious way. Often used humorously. *20th cent.*

Ski Survey 1991
These are the contenders, the hardy perennials of quality skiing for discerning Brits, the so-called top resorts which tour operators will tell you they could sell twenty times over if only they could get their mitts on more beds.

Internet website 2003
Get your mitts on some Stadium mustard. Order a case today!

give somebody the frozen mitt
informal to be deliberately unfriendly towards somebody: the image is of a reluctant handshake. *Early 20th cent.*

mix

mix and match
to form a set or collection of similar or complementary things by taking them from various sources. *Mid 20th cent.*

See also a mixed BLESSING.

mixture

the mixture as before
the same treatment received or given again: with allusion to instructions formerly put on a repeated medical prescription. *19th cent.*

James Kenney *Turn out!* 1812
[Somerville] *You have often been a sharer in my gaiety: now, if you have nothing better to do, we'll for a few moments mingle our sorrows.* [Forage] *We have mingled nothing else lately, sir. It will be only, as the apothecary says, the mixture as before.*

mobile

upwardly/downwardly mobile
improving (or losing) one's social status; advancing (or declining) in personal circumstances. *Mid 20th cent.*

David Lodge *Nice Work* 1988
It is an upwardly mobile street of nineteenth-century terraced cottages, where houseproud middle-class owners rub shoulders with less tidy and less affluent working-class occupiers.

mocker

put the mocker(s) on somebody/something
to ruin or bring misfortune to somebody or something. The origin of the word *mockers* is uncertain; it may be a modification, influenced by the verb *mock* meaning 'to deride or ridicule', of a Yiddish word *makeh* meaning 'a boil or sore' and also (more relevantly) 'a plague'. *Early 20th cent.*

Bookseller 1993
According to numerous crime sources, the reason that Hoover never pursued organised crime after the late '30s was that the mob, in the shape of Meyer Lansky no less, had the mockers on him because of evidence of his homosexuality.

mockery

make a mockery of something
to undermine the worth or use of something or make it seem absurd or futile. In earlier use the phrase also has the simpler sense 'to mock'. To *become a mockery* is to seem ridiculous. In the developed sense of the phrase, *mockery* is used in its (16th cent.) meaning 'a person or occasion that deserves ridicule'. *19th cent.*

Washington Irving *Sketch Book* 1819
Few pageants can be more stately and frigid than an English funeral in town. It is made up of show and gloomy parade: mourning carriages, mourning horses, mourning plumes, and hireling mourners, who make a mockery of grief.

Henry James *The Portrait of a Lady* 1881
Her mind, assailed by visions, was in a state of extraordinary activity, and her visions might as well come to her there, where she sat up to meet them, as on her pillow, to make a mockery of rest.

Mohican

the last of the Mohicans
the sole survivor of a particular race or kind, especially a noble or much admired one. From the title of a novel by James Fenimore Cooper (1789–1851), one of a series about a lone woodsman and adventurer of the American West called Natty Bumppo and known variously as Leatherstocking, Deerslayer, Hawkeye, and Pathfinder. *19th Cent.*

Boston Transcript 1832
We have seen the last of the Mohigans and the last of the cocked-hats, and we pray that we may be able to say, on the morrow we have seen the last of the snow-storms.

Elizabeth Stoddard *The Morgesons* 1862
I don't want to brag, but you won't find a soul in Surrey to come here, and live, as I have lived. You will have to take a Paddy; the Paddies are spreading, the old housekeeping race is going. Hepsey and I are the last of the Mohicans, and Hepsey is failing.

molehill

See make a MOUNTAIN out of a molehill.

moment

at this moment in time
now, at the current time. One of the best known and most persistent verbose circumlocutions from the 1970s, which continues to cause irritation to purists. *Late 20th cent.*

Guardian 1989
The prince ... proffered a modern translation of Hamlet's 'To be, or not to be'. It ran: 'Well, frankly, the problem as I see it at this moment in time is whether I should just lie down under all this hassle – I mean, let's face it – know what I mean?'

the moment of truth
a moment of testing or crisis on the outcome of which everything depends: originally the final sword thrust in a bullfight (Spanish *el momento de la verdad*). The phrase is mid 20th cent. in extended use.

have one's/its moments
to experience short or periodic moments of success. The phrase is a shortening of fuller expressions with *of*, (e.g. *moments of satisfaction*), as in the first examples below. *19th cent.*

James Fenimore Cooper *The Monikins* 1835
That journey would always be remembered as one of the pleasantest events of my life; for, while it had its perils and its disagreeables, it had also its moments of extreme satisfaction.

Oscar Wilde *The Picture of Dorian Gray* 1891
Soul and body, body and soul – how mysterious they were! There was animalism in the soul, and the body had its moments of spirituality.

Robinson Jeffers *Moments of Glory* a1962
They have their moments, and if one loved them they ought to die in those moments: but who could love them?

never a dull moment
there is always some excitement or interest. *19th cent.*

Jerome K Jerome *Three Men in a Boat* 1889
Of all experiences in connection with towing, the most exciting is being towed by girls ... There is never a dull moment in the boat while girls are towing it.

money

be in the money
informal to have a lot of money, especially from an unexpected piece of good fortune. *Early 20th cent.*

for my money
as far as I am concerned; as my choice or opinion. *16th cent.*

Shakespeare *Much Ado About Nothing* II.iii.59 (1598)
[Benedick, awaiting the start of a song] *Now divine air! Now is his soul ravished. Is it not strange that sheep's guts should hale souls out of men's bodies? Well, a horn for my money, when all's done.*

have money to burn
to have enough money to be able to spend lavishly or carelessly. *19th cent.*

money for jam / old rope
informal remuneration gained easily or for little effort: originally used in services' slang, where jam and old rope were both common commodities. *Early 20th cent.*

Evelyn Waugh *Put Out More Flags* 1942
At the moment there were no mortars and he was given instead a light and easily manageable counterfeit of wood which was slung on the back of his haversack, relieving him of a rifle. At present it was money for old rope.

put (one's) money on something
to have confidence in an outcome. *Mid 20th cent.*

put one's money where one's mouth is
originally NAmer to support one's opinions by action. *Mid 20th cent.*

throw good money after bad

to try to recover one's losses in an ill-advised plan or scheme by putting more money into it in the hope of eventual success. The phrase is reminiscent of Gresham's Law, named after the Elizabethan financier Thomas Gresham (1519–79), which states that 'bad money drives out good', i.e. if a debased currency exists side by side with a currency of higher intrinsic value, the latter will tend to be exported. *17th cent.*

> Thomas Paine *The American Crisis* 1780
> *If you cast your eyes on the people of England, what have they to console themselves with for the millions expended? Or, what encouragement is there left to continue throwing good money after bad? America can carry on the war for ten years longer, and all the charges of government included, for less than you can defray the charges of war and government for one year.*

throw money at something

to spend large amounts of money in an attempt to resolve a problem or difficulty. *20th cent.*

See also BURN a hole in one's pocket; not for LOVE or money; see the COLOUR of somebody's money.

---

monkey

(as) artful/clever/mischievous as a wagonload/load of monkeys

informal extremely clever or mischievous. *Early 20th cent.*

> H V Esmond *Billy's Little Love Affair* 1904
> [Mrs Herring] *Lady D's as cute as a wagon load of monkeys, and thanks to Jane's stupidity, she's forewarned fore-armed.*

have a monkey on one's back

The image of a clinging monkey symbolizing unwelcome burdens has various applications, and from the 1930s *monkey* has been common as a slang word for 'drug addiction'.
1 to be angry. *19th cent.*
2 *informal* to be addicted to or dependent on drugs. *Mid 20th cent.*

make a monkey (out) of somebody

informal to make somebody look foolish or ridiculous. To *make a monkey of oneself* is, correspondingly, to appear foolish from one's own actions. *18th cent.*

> Arthur Murphy *The School for Guardians* 1767
> [Lovibond] *I thought it a pity you should lose any more time, and so now you may go and bow, and kneel, and make a monkey of yourself before some other window.*

> Liz Lochhead *True Confessions and New Clichés* 1985
> *Begging your pardon, Sir, but some of those alleged artists that get feted on BBC Two could paint no better than a monkey in the zoo. If they ask me Sir, they're just trying to make a monkey out of you.*

monkey business

mischievous or underhand activity: from the proverbial playfulness of monkeys. *19th cent.*

> Clyde Fitch *The Climbers* 1901
> [Edward Warden] *How long will you give me?*
> [Miss Godesby] *Oh, come, I can't have any monkey business! You must get me my security today.*

not give a monkey's

informal to be unconcerned about something or indifferent to it: sometimes more crudely completed with words such as *toss, fuck,* etc. *Mid 20th cent.*

> David Lodge *Nice Work* 1988
> *'I'm afraid it's a non-starter, Brian,' said Wilcox. 'Stuart Baxter didn't think so,' said Everthorpe, fluffing out his sideboards with the back of his hand.' 'I don't give a monkey's what Stuart Baxter thinks,' said Wilcox.*

See also SPANK the monkey.

---

monster

See Frankenstein's monster *at* FRANKENSTEIN; the green-eyed monster *at* GREEN.

---

month

a month of Sundays

a very long or seemingly endless period of time: probably with allusion to the traditional lack of activity or entertainment on Sundays when religious restrictions had some social force, shops were closed, etc. *19th cent.*

> Henry Clay Preuss *Fashions and Follies of Washington Life* 1857
> [Sharpsteel] *Yes, Captain, but there is another old adage which says, 'there is a time when forbearance ceases to be a virtue'.* [Capt. Jack Smith] *True, sir;*

and that time happens once in a 'month of Sundays'.

Kipling *Just So Stories* 1902
Painted Jaguar was sitting on the banks of the turbid Amazon sucking prickles out of his paws and saying to himself – 'Can't curl, but can swim – Slow-Solid, that's him! Curls up, but can't swim – Stickly-Prickly, that's him!' – 'He'll never forget that this month of Sundays,' said Stickly-Prickly.

See also FLAVOUR of the month.

monty

the full monty
everything needed or wanted; the whole lot. In recent use (see below) in the sense 'total nudity', especially in striptease. The origin of the expression is obscure: most of the explanations offered look like associations rather than true sources, while others are absurdly far-fetched. Here are some of the more colourful examples: (1) it is a corruption of 'the full amount'; (2) it is a reference to a complete set of clothes available from the British chain of outfitters named Montague Burton; (3) it is derived from *monte*, the Spanish word for 'mountain', used as the name of a card game played in Mexico and California in the 19th cent., and extended in Australian and New Zealand slang (as *monte* or from the mid 20th cent. *monty*) to mean 'a certainty'; (4) it meant breaking the bank at the casino at Monte Carlo; (5) it is associated with Field Marshal Montgomery, whose nickname was indeed *Monty*, and specifically with his practice of eating a full breakfast when campaigning in North Africa in the Second World War: this account belongs firmly in the 'far-fetched' category, as does (6) a connection with *full Monte* as a mark of quality for sheepskins packed in Montevideo, the capital city of Uruguay.

Few of these accounts can be squared with the much later first appearance of the phrase. The use of a capital initial (*Monty*) in early uses in print might suggest an origin in a name (as in 2 and 5 above). The most likely explanation is that it was a fanciful invention of the early 1990s around which folk etymologies rapidly accumulated (rather in the manner of OK and posh). The tailoring origin appears in a novel by John Le Carré called *The Tailor of Panama*, published in 1996, in

which a tailor hears the phrase used by a customer and comments 'It must be twenty years since I heard that expression … Bless my soul. The full Monty. My goodness me.' (Needless to say, a folk memory in a fictional context is worthless.) A year later the phrase achieved a special currency – which intensified speculation about its origin – from its use as the title of a British film, directed by Peter Cattaneo and released in 1997, about a group of unemployed Sheffield steelworkers who try to raise money by putting on a male striptease act and attracting a large audience with a promise of total nudity, or 'the full monty'.

People claim to have heard the expression – in its more general meaning – as far back as the 1950s, but there is no verifiable evidence before the late 1980s. Then, it is mentioned in a guide to the language of the British television soap opera *Coronation Street* (Jeffrey Miller, *Street Talk*, 1986), so presumably it was used a significant number of times in the broadcasts up to that time. Others attribute it to the comedian and scriptwriter Ben Elton, but it is much more likely that he picked it up from existing usage. *Late 20th cent.*

The Times 1±986
Miller has collected a genuinely interesting (and entertaining) fistful of Street lingo, much of it very old in origin. It's good to know that 'fratchy' is 'quarrelsome', 'clarty' is 'dirty', a 'sough' is a 'drain', and that 'the full monty' is 'everything included'. Producers of Call My Bluff will be using the book for years to come.

Wisden Cricket Monthly 1992
Admittedly, Bicknell began the current campaign sluggishly as he experimented with an abbreviated approach, then reverted to the full Monty in the B&H quarterfinal against Lancashire to help set up a notable victory.

moon

bark at/against the moon
to make a loud fuss to no effect: with allusion to the proverbial reaction of dogs to a full moon. *17th cent.*

Edward Ward *Poems on Divers Subjects* 1706
They shew their Teeth, tho' destitute of Pow'r, | And sit like Mungrils barking at the Moon, | In hopes to fetch the Lofty Being down.

cry/ask for the moon

to seek what is unattainable. The notion of the moon as a symbol of the unreachable goes back to the time of Shakespeare (e.g. 2 *Henry VI* (1591) III.i.158 'And doggèd York that reaches at the moon, | Whose overweening arm I have plucked back'). The phrase is 19th cent. in this form.

Mortimer Collins *Poetical Works* 1886
This world's his nursery: well we know his tune – | A baby-giant, crying for the moon.

many moons ago/gone by

informal a long time ago. Also *ere many moons*, in the sense 'before very long'. *17th cent.*

Shakespeare *Antony and Cleopatra* III.xii.6 (1607)
[Dolabella] *Caesar, 'tis his schoolmaster; | An argument that he is plucked, when hither | He sends so poor a pinion of his wing, | Which had superfluous kings for messengers | Not many moons gone by.*

Andrew Shiels *The Witch of Westcot* 1831
But when I hunted in the snow, | Once, many many moons ago; I chased one moose – I chased him long, | But he was like the torrent strong.

W A Mackay *By Trench and Trail* 1918
No one will rejoice more than Oscar Dhu to see the demon rum utterly destroyed in Canada ere many moons.

over the moon

informal extremely pleased, delighted: originally with allusion to the nursery rhyme beginning 'Hey diddle diddle, | The cat and the fiddle, | The cow jumped over the moon'. Early uses are more directly allusive in extended metaphor, e.g. 'ready to jump over the moon in delight' (and see the quotation below). *18th cent.*

Boswell *The Life of Samuel Johnson* 1791
If all this had happened to me, I should have had a couple of fellows with long poles walking before me, to knock down every body that stood in the way. Consider, if all this had happened to Cibber or Quin, they'd have jumped over the moon.

See also once in a BLUE moon; PROMISE the moon/earth.

moonlight

See do a moonlight FLIT.

morning

morning, noon, and night

informal round the clock; continuously. *19th cent.*

Washington Irving *Sketch Book* 1819
During the time of the fair … the late quiet streets of Little Britain are overrun with an irruption of strange figures and faces; every tavern is a scene of rout and revel. The fiddle and the song are heard from the tap-room, morning, noon, and night.

mortal

See this mortal COIL.

Morton

See Morton's FORK.

most

for the most part

in most cases or respects; mainly: use of *most* signifying degree and qualifying a singular noun survives only with *part*. *Middle English*

Lord Berners transl Froissart's *Chronicles* 1523
For the most partye he hymselfe was with the kyng at Turney.

Shakespeare *As You Like It* III.ii. 399 (1599)
At which time would I, being but a moonish youth, grieve, be effeminate, changeable, longing and liking, proud, fantastical, apish, shallow, inconstant, full of tears, full of smiles; for every passion something, and for no passion truly anything, as boys and women are for the most part cattle of this colour.

mote

a mote in somebody's eye

a fault that one criticizes in others but has even more in oneself: *see* a BEAM in one's eye. *Middle English*

mothballs

in mothballs

in a state of temporary disuse: from the practice of applying a moth repellent (such as mothballs made from naphthalene) to stored clothes and furnishings. *Mid 20th cent.*

Today 1992
The dress Pretty Woman Julia Roberts ordered for her cancelled wedding to Brat Packer Kiefer Sutherland could end up being auctioned off for charity. The £5,500 creation is currently in moth-balls in a warehouse in downtown Los Angeles.

mother

some mothers do 'ave 'em
used to suggest a person's ineptitude or incompetence: somewhat dated but revived in the 1970s as the title of a television comedy programme about a bungling disaster-prone man in his early thirties. *Early 20th cent.*

> Elizabeth Ferrars *Cup & Hip* 1975
> *'Some mothers do have 'em', she said drily. 'Do you think that bright idea of yours would make Helen feel better?'*

See also the FATHER and mother of a —.

motion

go through the motions
to imitate the physical movements involved in an activity; in later use, to carry out an activity half-heartedly or mechanically; to do the minimum necessary. *19th cent.*

> Scott *Old Mortality* 1816
> *She pressed her handkerchief to her face, sobbed with great vehemence, and either wept, or managed, as Halliday might have said, to go through the motions wonderfully well.*

> Rita Dove *Mother Love* 1995
> *It's too late for apologies though you go through the motions.*

motley

wear motley
to fool about, to play the fool. *Motley* is the multi-coloured costume worn by jesters from Elizabethan times, when characters in plays of Shakespeare make humorous and punning allusions to it: Jaques in Shakespeare's *As You Like It* (1599) II.vii.34 says 'A fool, a fool! I met a fool i'th' forest, | A motley fool ... O noble fool, | A worthy fool – motley's the only wear', and in *Twelfth Night* (1600) I.v.52 Feste says to Olivia 'Lady, "Cucullus non facit monachum"; that's as

much to say as I wear not motley in my brain.' *17th cent.*

> Scott *Ivanhoe* 1819
> *'I am rich enough to reward them from mine own wealth,' answered Cedric. 'And some,' said Wamba, 'have been wise enough to reward themselves; they do not march off empty-handed altogether. We do not all wear motley.'*

mould

break the mould
to do something original; to bring about fundamental changes to an established system or procedure: from the practice of casting metal in a mould, then breaking the mould so that no more identical copies of particular artefacts could be produced. Hence the expression *they broke the mould*, used admiringly with reference to people regarded as having unique or special qualities or characteristics. The phrase became familiar in Britain in the 1980s, when founders of the Social Democrats saw their cause, in Roy Jenkins' words (in a speech made in June 1980), as 'breaking the out-of-date mould of British politics'. *16th cent.*

> Shakespeare *King Lear* III.ii.8 (1606)
> [Lear] *Thou all-shaking thunder, | Strike flat the thick rotundity o'th' world, | Crack nature's moulds, all germens* [= seeds] *spill at once | That makes ingrateful man.*

cast/made in / of the same mould
having the same form or character: a metaphor from casting artefacts (see the previous phrase). *16th cent.*

> John Dickenson *Greene in Conceipt* 1598
> *Noting more exactly one of her company, whose lewde and dissolute life was commonly known, he began knauishly to suspect, that ech of her other mates were likewise of the same mould.*

> Richard Braithwait *Nature's Embassie* 1621
> *How artfull thou, and gracefull too by birth, | A King, yet shewes that thou art made of earth, | Not glorying in thy greatnesse, but would seeme, | Made of the same mould other men haue bene.*

> Swift *Ode to Sir William Temple* 1689
> *Shall I believe a Spirit so divine | Was cast in the same Mold with mine?*

George Farquhar *The Inconstant* 1702
A Dutch Man is thick, a Dutch Woman is squab, a Dutch Horse is round, a Dutch Dog is short, a Dutch Ship is broad bottom'd; and, in short, one wou'd swear the whole products of the Country were cast in the same Mold with their Cheeses.

mountain

if the mountain won't go to Mohammed (Mohammed must go to the mountain)
(proverb) if one side in a negotiation or dispute will not concede a point, the other side will have to compromise or there will be deadlock: based on the story (told in English by Francis Bacon in his *Essays*, 1625) that Mohammed, when challenged to prove his worth as a prophet, summoned Mount Safa to come to him. When the mountain did not move, Mohammed went to the mountain, thanking God for his mercy in sparing him from being crushed had he granted the prayer and made the mountain move. *17th cent.*

M G Lewis *The Monk* 1796
It being absolutely necessary for every fashionable convent to have him for its confessor, the nuns are in consequence obliged to visit him at the abbey; since, when the mountain will not come to Mahomet, Mahomet must needs go to the mountain.

make a mountain out of a molehill
to exaggerate the importance of something trivial or unimportant: with allusion to the smallness of molehills. The phrase is first recorded in the *Book of Martyrs* by John Foxe (1570).

move mountains
to make huge efforts or achieve great results: often used in the context of the power of faith, with particular reference to St Paul's first letter to the Corinthians 13:2 ('And though I have the gift of prophecy, and understand all mysteries, and all knowledge; and though I have all faith, so that I could remove mountains, and have not charity, I am nothing'). *18th cent.*

Robert Munford *The Candidates* 1798
Yes, damn it, you all promise mighty fair, but the devil a bit do you perform; there's Strutabout, now, he'll promise to move mountains. He'll make the rivers navigable, and bring the tide over the tops of the hills, for a vote.

Robert Browning *The Ring and the Book* 1842
There is but one way to brow-beat this world, I Dumb-founder doubt, and repay scorn in kind, – I To go on trusting, namely till faith move Mountains.

mouth

all mouth and (no) trousers
(said of a person) all talk and no action: also shortened to *all mouth*. The phrase is typically used by women about men, but there is some dispute about whether the phrase should include the negative *no*. Without it, *mouth and trousers* makes good sense in denoting verbal and sexual arrogance respectively, but what is the explanation of *no trousers*? Perhaps it just arises from confusion (or false analogy) with such phrases as *all talk and no action, all spin and no substance*, and so on, which are now common. *All mouth and trousers* (no *no*), was a frequently heard snub to cocky men in the BBC comedy series *Last of the Summer Wine*. *Mid 20th cent.*

Simon Armitage *Zoom!* 1989
He knew his son was all mouth and trousers I but fair is fair, and family is family.

by word of mouth
by using spoken language as distinct from writing or print; orally. *By mouth* is recorded in the same meaning from Middle English but gave way to the current form around 1600. In Shakespeare's *Julius Caesar* (1599), a servant delivering a message from Octavian to Mark Antony stops short when he sees the body of the murdered Caesar: 'He … bid me say to you by word of mouth – (*seeing the body*) O Caesar!'; and in *Twelfth Night* (1601) III.iv.187, Sir Toby Belch tells Sir Andrew: 'I will deliver his [Cesario's, i.e. Viola's] challenge by word of mouth.' *16th cent.*

Hobbes *Leviathan* 1651
Whether these laws were then written, or not written, but dictated to the people by Moses, after his forty days being with God in the Mount, by word of mouth, is not expressed in the text.

foam/froth at the mouth
to be extremely or uncontrollably angry. The image is of a fit or seizure, when saliva oozes from the mouth. *17th cent.*

Congreve *The Old Batchelour* 1693
*Ha, ha; 'Twill be a pleasant Cheat. – I'll plague
Heart-well when I see him. Prithee, Frank, let's
teaze him; make him fret till he foam at the Mouth,
and disgorge his Matrimonial Oath with Interest. –
Come, thou'rt so musty.*

John Neal *Seventy-six* 1823
*Arnauld arose; and but for me, would have struck
my father. 'That, in my own house!' cried he, black
in the face with passion, and frothing at the mouth.*

make somebody's mouth water
to be very desirable or alluring: with reference to
the flow of saliva in the mouth when anticipating
food. Figurative uses are recorded from a date
not much later than that of the literal use, and
there are pornographic undertones in some uses.
17th cent.

Charles Cotton *Virgile Travestie* from *Scarronides*
1667
*Aeneas in his misty cloak, | Heard every word
Queen Dido spoke. | Her hony-words made his
mouth water, | And he e'en twitter'd to be at her.*

John Crown *The Married Beau* 1694
*[Thomback] 'Tis Shittlecock, and he has got a
Madam with him. – He's kissing. He makes my
mouth water. Who is she?*

put words into somebody's mouth
1 to tell somebody what to say. The locus classicus is God's words to Moses in Exodus 4:14–15,
in angry response to Moses' complaint about his
own lack of eloquence: 'Is not Aaron the Levite
thy brother? I know that he can speak well. And
also, behold, he cometh forth to meet thee: and
when he seeth thee, he will be glad in his heart.
And thou shalt speak unto him, and put words in
his mouth: and I will be with thy mouth, and with
his mouth, and will teach you what ye shall do.'
Middle English (in Wyclif)
2 to attribute an opinion to somebody when they
have not in fact expressed it. *18th cent.*

Roger Boyle *King Saul* 1703
*David may be truly said in this excellent author's
lines, as well as his own, to speak like the man after
God's own heart, and has more grateful acknow-
ledgments payd here to his high deserts than some
modernists who have put their words into his
mouth, and made him cease to be either King or
Psalmist.*

shut/close one's mouth
to stop speaking, to be silent: often in the imperative. *Middle English* (in Gower)

Shakespeare *King Lear* v.iii.145 (1606)
*[Albany to Goneril] Shut your mouth, dame, | Or
with this paper shall I stopple it.*

take the words (right) out of somebody's mouth
to anticipate what another person is about to say.
16th cent.

Shakespeare *Henry V* iv.vii.40 (1599)
*[Fluellen to Gower, who has objected to the
likening of King Henry to Alexander the Great
in the matter of violent rage] It is not well done,
mark you now, to take the tales out of my mouth ere
it is made an end and finished. I speak but in the
figures and comparisons of it.*

See also a bad/bitter/nasty TASTE in one's mouth;
DOWN in the mouth; SHOOT one's mouth off;
straight from the horse's mouth *at* HORSE;
WATCH one's mouth.

mouthful

give somebody a mouthful
informal to speak angrily. *20th cent.*

Hanif Kureishi *The Buddha of Suburbia* 1990
*Jeeta, who had heard everything, rushed over ...
And she gave Anwar a mouthful. I'd never heard
her speak like this before. She was fearless.*

say a mouthful
informal, chiefly NAmer to say something important or interesting. *Early 20th cent.*

Carl Sandburg *Slabs of the Sunburnt West* 1922
*You said it. You said a mouthful. We're all a lot of
damn fourflushers* [= bluffers].

movable
See a movable FEAST.

move

get a move on
informal to hurry up: originally in the form *get a
move on oneself. 19th cent.*

make a move
to set off or begin to act. To *make the first move* is to
take the initiative in a group. *19th cent.*

Disraeli *Vivian Grey* 1826
In a few minutes, the Archduke, bowing to his circle, made a move, and regained the side of a Saxon lady, from whose interesting company he had been disturbed by the arrival of Prince Salvinski – an individual of whose long stories and dull romances the Archduke had, from experience, a particular dread.

Louisa M Alcott *Little Women* 1868
Jo saw her mistake; but, fearing to make the matter worse, suddenly remembered that it was for her to make the first move toward departure, and did so with an abruptness that left three people with half-finished sentences in their mouths.

make a move on / put the moves on somebody
informal to make sexual advances. *20th cent.*

Will Self *My Idea of Fun* 1993
The next day we companionably photocopied the notes together. I had got up early that morning and done my best to make myself look presentable. I still had no thought – for obvious reasons – of making any move on her but I felt it would be enough if she wasn't repelled by me. She wasn't.

move with the times
to keep up with modern fashions and opinions. *Mid 20th cent.*

Business 1991
Kleinwort recalls the aluminium war of the late 1950s. 'I think that's when American methods started to be applied and the whole atmosphere became less smooth, less gentlemanly; a wave of toughness started to hit the City. I regret some of the changes, but I think you've got to accept them and move with the times, however unfortunate that may be.'

See also change GEAR / move up a gear; move the goalposts *at* GOALPOST; move HEAVEN and earth; move mountains *at* MOUNTAIN; not move a MUSCLE; the SPIRIT moves one.

mover

a mover and shaker
a person of power and influence, who can get things done. The phrase is often used in the plural, with allusion to the English poet Arthur O'Shaughnessy's lines ('Ode', 1874) 'We are the music makers, | We are the dreamers of dreams | ... | We are the movers and shakers | Of the world for ever, it seems.' *19th cent.*

much

not up to much
informal not very important or noteworthy. *19th cent.*

W S Gilbert *Princess Toto* 1876
You're just the sort of man we want up here, for, between ourselves, our Brigands are not up to much.

so much the better/worse
it is better (or worse) for the reason just given. *19th cent.*

Emily Brontë *Wuthering Heights* 1847
I have not broken your heart – you have broken it; and in breaking it, you have broken mine. So much the worse for me, that I am strong.

See also (there is) nothing/not much IN it.

muchness

much of a muchness
(said of two things) very close in appearance, value, etc; difficult to distinguish. The noun *muchness* is now otherwise obsolete in its original meaning 'large size', which dates from Middle English. The phrase is first known from Sir John Vanbrugh's comedy *The Provok'd Husband* (1728), completed by Colley Cibber): '[Manly] I hope ... you and your good woman agree still? [Moody] Ay, ay; much of a muchness.' For many people the locus classicus is in the words of the dormouse in *Alice's Adventures in Wonderland* (see below). *18th cent.*

Fanny Burney *Camilla* 1796
'I take it, then,' he said, 'that was what stinted your growth so, Miss? for, I take it, you're not much above the dwarf as they shew at Exeter Change? Much of a muchness, I guess.'

Lewis Carroll *Alice's Adventures in Wonderland* 1865
The Dormouse ... woke up again with a little shriek, and went on: ' – that begins with an M, such as mouse-traps, and the moon, and memory, and muchness – you know you say things are "much of a muchness?" – did you ever see such a thing as a drawing of a muchness?' 'Really, now you ask me,' said Alice, very much confused, 'I don't think – ' 'Then you shouldn't talk,' said the Hatter.

muck

(as) common as muck
British, informal socially inferior. 20th cent.

Punch 1992
I'm as common as muck, me. But I gotta lotta posh friends. An' when we get together at me chateau in France, like, we all 'ave a bit of a party.

make a muck of something
British, informal to bungle a task. Early 20th cent.

where there's muck there's brass/money
(proverb) there is often wealth in parts of the country that are dirty and ugly. The phrase is first recorded in the form muck and money go together (and similar variants), and is entered in John Ray's English Proverbs of 1678. The form with brass is 20th cent. 17th cent.

mud

(as) clear as mud
informal very obscure or difficult to understand. 19th cent.

Lord Neaves Songs and Verses 1875
Now Darwin proves as clear as mud, | That, endless ages ere the Flood, | The Coming Man's primeval form | Was simply an Ascidian worm.

fling/sling/throw mud
to make scandalous accusations: with allusion to the proverb throw dirt (or mud) enough, and some will stick. 18th cent.

Horace Walpole Anecdotes of Painting in England 1762
Never did two angry men of their abilities throw mud with less dexterity.

here's mud in your eye
informal a humorous drinking toast originating in the armed services and probably associated with the mud of the trenches in the First World War. Early 20th cent.

—'s name is mud
so-and-so has caused offence and is in disgrace. The phrase is American in origin, recorded from the 1820s, and may be associated with an obsolete (18th cent.) meaning of mud = a fool. It became associated by a form of folk etymology (rather as OK became associated with 'Old Kinderhook', the American presidential candidate of 1840)

with a certain Dr Samuel Mudd, a country doctor who in 1865 treated an injury sustained by the escaping assassin of Abraham Lincoln. Dr Mudd informed the police and was promptly arrested and imprisoned himself for complicity. The chronology of the evidence makes this story impossible (quite apart from its inherent improbability) as the source; nor (if further argument is needed) is the phrase recorded with the spelling mudd, which we would surely expect at some stage in its development. 19th cent.

New Orleans Lantern 1887
Zeller wants to be Recorder … but his name is mud.

See also DRAG somebody's name through the mud.

muddy

muddy the waters
to confuse the issue by introducing complications or irrelevancies. Muddy is used figuratively in the sense 'to confuse or obscure' at an earlier date than literal uses, and it occurs in extended metaphor in Shakespeare's All's Well That Ends Well (1603) v.ii.4: 'I have ere now, sir, been better known to you, when I have held familiarity with fresher clothes. But I am now, sir, muddied in Fortune's mood, and smell somewhat strong of her strong displeasure.' 20th cent.

Enoch Powell Reflections of a Statesman 1991
I know as a politician that when you are doing something naughty, nothing is more effective than to muddy the waters with complication. What you fear most is an opponent who will point to a few simple but undeniable facts.

mug

a mug's game
British, informal a foolish or risky course of action: based on the (19th cent.) word mug meaning 'a fool', still much used informally. Early 20th cent.

G B Shaw The Apple Cart 1930
[Magnus] So I have not upset the apple cart after all, Mr Nicobar. [Nicobar] You can upset it as soon as you like for all I care. I am going out of politics. Politics is a mug's game.

mullock

poke mullock at somebody

Australian and NZ, informal to make fun of somebody, to deride them: based on a dialect word mullock meaning 'rubbish, refuse matter', and used in Australia with specific reference to waste or discarded material in mining. Early 20th cent.

> J Truran Where Plain Begins 1933
> Silas ... was engaged ... in what he would have called 'pokin mullock' at Crispin's daughter.

multitude

cover a multitude of sins

to conceal a wide range of difficulties or shortcomings. Used with allusion to the first epistle of Peter 4:8 (in the Authorized Version, 1611) 'And above all things have fervent charity among yourselves: for charity shall cover the multitude of sins.' 17th cent.

> Aphra Behn The Revenge 1680
> I must confess we all eat of the forbidden Fruit; and for my own part, though I am, as they say, a Bawd that covers a multitude of sins, yet I trust I am none of the wicked that go to Steeple-houses with profane Organs in 'em.

mum

This word mum has nothing to do with the familiar name for 'mother', but is a representation (dating from Middle English) of the inarticulate sound made when the lips are closed to avoid speaking. It occurs as an interjection from an early date: in Shakespeare's King Lear (1606) I.iv.179, the Fool sings 'Mum, mum. | He that keeps not crust nor crumb, | Weary of all, shall want some', and in 2 Henry VI (1591) I.ii.98, mum means 'secrecy' (in a passage where the speaker addresses himself): 'Seal up your lips and give no words but mum; | The business asketh silent secrecy.' A verb form, meaning 'to make silent', is recorded from the late 14th cent.

keep mum

to remain silent. The phrase is recorded from the 16th cent. in the forms stand mum and play mum and in other variants; keep mum is found from the 19th cent.

> John Heywood A Play of Love 1534
> Then wyst [= knew] I well the nody [= that nobody] must cum | To do as he dyd or stande and play mum.

> Mark Twain The Gilded Age 1873
> Well you can't cure it, you know, but you can prevent it. How? Turnips! that's it! Turnips and water! Nothing like it in the world, old McDowells says, just fill yourself up two or three times a day, and you can snap your fingers at the plague. Sh! Keep mum, but just you confine yourself to that diet and you're all right.

mum's the word

used as a warning to keep quiet and not let slip a secret or confidence. 18th cent.

> Ebenezer Cooke The Maryland Muse 1731
> Now, having told o'th' greatest Villain, | You can't expect me to go still on; | And other Rebels Names bespatter, | So Mum's the Word about this Matter.

> Robert Browning The Ring and the Book 1842
> Were it not simple Christian charity | To warn the priest be on his guard, – save him | Assured death, save yourself from causing it? | I meet him in the street. Give me a glove, | A ring to show for token! Mum's the word!

murder

get away with murder

to do whatever one wishes, however outrageous, without being punished or having to face the consequences. Early 20th cent.

> Allen Ginsberg Collected Poems a1980
> I don't like the Crown's Official Secrets Act | You can get away with murder in the Government that's a fact.

murder will out

murder will always be discovered in the end. See also TRUTH will out. Middle English

> Chaucer The Nun's Priest's Tale (line 4242)
> Mordre wol out; that se we day by day.

scream/yell/cry blue murder

to protest loudly and noisily: blue has been used as symbolic of disease and harm from the 18th cent., and murder as an exclamation of horror (originally with real force but later in more trivial use) from the late 15th cent. Blue murder is entered with the explanation 'a desperate or alarming cry' in Hotten's Dictionary of Slang of 1859. The phrase dates from the 19th cent. in the current form.

Murphy

Murphy's law

the principle that if anything can go wrong it will (see ANYTHING): also called *Sod's law* (see SOD). It is said to have been coined by a Californian aviation project manager named George Nichols in 1949 and is called *Murphy's law* after Nichols' colleague, Captain E Murphy. Murphy is said to have pronounced, in the course of an experiment, that if an aircraft part can be installed incorrectly somebody will do it eventually, although other versions of the story place the emphasis on Murphy's associates, and some even question Murphy's existence: a kind of folk etymology in reverse. Awareness of the natural perverseness of life is, of course, much older than all this. *Mid 20th cent.*

Celia Brayfield *The Prince* 1990
Thanks to the operation of Murphy's Law relating to parents, they were coming downstairs hand-in-hand just as Jo's mother walked in the door.

muscle

not move a muscle

to keep completely still, especially under emotional stress or provocation: also with reference to the face, denoting a calm or controlled expression. *19th cent.*

Mary Brunton *Self-Control* 1811
Mrs Herbert received all her mother's reprimands in silence, without moving a muscle, without announcing, by the slightest change of colour, that the sarcasm had reached further than her ear.

Dickens *Martin Chuzzlewit* 1844
'I am glad to see you, sir,' observed the major, shaking hands with Martin, and not moving a muscle of his face. 'You are pretty bright, I hope?'
See also FLEX one's muscles.

mushroom

like mushrooms

(said of things increasing in number) rapidly and in great numbers: with allusion to the rapid appearance of mushrooms in the wild overnight. *19th cent.*

Louisa M Alcott *Little Women* 1868
Almost before she knew where she was, Jo found herself married and settled at Plumfield. Then a family of six or seven boys sprung up like mushrooms, and flourished surprisingly.

music

music to one's ears

something one is very pleased to hear: used especially of good news or other welcome information. *18th cent.*

John & Charles Wesley *On the Conversion of a Common Harlot* from *Hymns and Sacred Poems* 1739
Dead she was, but now's alive: | Loud repeat the glorious sound, | Lost she was, but now is found! | This through ages all along, | This be still the joyous song, | Wide diffused o'er earth abroad, | Music in the ears of God.

William Combe *The Diaboliad* 1777
On earth he made my Hell; and have not I, | As Satan's Queen, a right to make him fry? | What music to my ears, to hear him yell.

Dickens *Nicholas Nickleby* 1839
The ground seemed elastic under their feet; the sheep-bells were music to their ears; and exhilarated by exercise, and stimulated by hope, they pushed onwards with the strength of lions.

mustard

See CUT the mustard; a GRAIN of mustard seed.

muster

pass muster

to bear scrutiny; to reach an acceptable standard: originally a military term (with the earlier form *pass the musters*) meaning 'to undergo a muster or review without censure'. *16th cent.*

Dryden *Marriage a la Mode* 1673
Come, read your works: twenty to one half of 'em will not pass muster neither.

mutton

mutton dressed as lamb

a middle-aged or elderly woman who tries to look much younger. *19th cent.*

> Charles Dibdin *A Collection of Songs* 1814
> *So since for strange sights I to town took my range, | 'Faith I zeed sights in plenty, and all of them strange; | I zeed folks roll in riches, who pleasure ne'er knew, | ... | Time and oft drest lamb-fashion I zeed an old ewe.*

> Kipling *The Day's Work* 1898
> *Look at young Davies makin' an ass of himself over mutton-dressed-as-lamb old enough to be his mother!*

> Reginald Hill *A Clubbable Woman* 1987
> *I meant she was, well, always showing herself off, you know, putting on the style. Mutton dressed as lamb.*

See also (as) DEAD as mutton.

n

to the nth degree

to the utmost: based on *n* as an indefinite number in mathematics. *19th cent.*

---

nail

hit the nail on the head

to make an exactly apposite remark; to make the right response. *16th cent.*

> Bunyan *The Holy War* 1682
> *Now I think if we shall tempt them to pride, that may do something; and if we tempt them to wantonness, that may help. But in my mind, if we could drive them into desperation, that would knock the nail on the head.*

a nail in the coffin of somebody/something

a step towards the destruction or disappearance of somebody or something. *18th cent.*

nail a lie

to reveal something as a falsehood. *19th cent.*

> Belasco & De Mille *The Wife* 1887
> *That little she-devil will spread this rumor from one end of Washington to the other. Gray must nail the lie at once.*

on the nail

(said of payment) made immediately: *on* (or *upon*) *the nail* was originally used with more general meaning in the sense 'immediately, straight away'. The relevance of *nail* here is uncertain, but it seems likely to be in the same sense area as in *hit the nail on the head* (see above) and *right on the nail* (see below) in which the image is one of accuracy and concentration of effort. *16th cent.*

> Philemon Holland transl Livy 1600
> [He] *paid the whole debt downe right on the naile, unto the creditour.*

right on the nail

completely precise or accurate. *19th cent.*

Hector Macneill *Town Fashions* 1810
[Friend] *Perhaps our joint exertions may succeed;* | *Point out the tares, and I'll attempt to weed.* [Author] *All is against us! – every tongue will rail!* – | *Who likes the hammer hit right on the nail* | *That comes against him with resistless force?*

M Wandor et al *Tales I Tell My Mother* 1978
Screwy sort of argument – I mean, what she was really saying was half right on the nail, and half like a whirlpool that sucks everything into it.

See also (as) HARD as nails; nail one's colours to the mast *at* COLOUR.

naked

the naked truth

the plain facts, without any attempt to hide their unpleasantness: *see also* the UNVARNISHED truth. The notion was known in Latin as *nuda veritas*, which appears in the work of the poet Horace (1st cent. BC). *The Naked Truth* was the title of a British film released in 1957. *16th cent.*

Shakespeare *Love's Labour's Lost* v.i.703 (1594)
[Armado] *The naked truth of it is, I have no shirt. I go woolward for penance.*

name

call somebody names

to insult somebody verbally. In Shakespeare's *Richard III* (1593) Richard, Duke of Gloucester (the future king) challenges Queen Margaret, the widow of Henry VI (i.iii.234) with the words 'I cry thee mercy then, for I did think | That thou hadst called me all these bitter names', to which she replies 'Why so I did, but looked for no reply.' *16th cent.*

John Ford *The Fancies Chast and Noble* 1638
He pinched me, called me names, most filthy names.

Boswell *The Life of Samuel Johnson* 1791
'You do not think, then, Dr. Johnson, that there was much argument in the case.' Johnson said, he did not think there was. 'Why truly, (said the King,) when once it comes to calling names, argument is pretty well at an end.'

drop names

to refer ostentatiously to well-known people as one's friends or associates. In early use, names drop (from the lips) rather than being dropped, and the implication is more of casual utterance than pretension. Overtones of disapproval appear in 20th cent. use, when *name-drop* and *name-dropping* are common derivative forms. *19th cent.*

Jane Austen *Persuasion* 1818
He certainly knew what was right, nor could she fix on any one article of moral duty evidently transgressed; but yet she would have been afraid to answer for his conduct. She distrusted the past, if not the present. The names which occasionally dropt of former associates, the allusions to former practices and pursuits, suggested suspicions not favourable of what he had been.

Mary Jane Holmes *Cousin Maude and Rosamond* 1860
'My only boy is over the sea – my only daughter is selfish and cold, and all the day I'm listening in vain for some one to call me father.' 'Father!' The name dropped involuntarily from the lips of Maude De Vere, standing without the door.

Guardian 1984
McCormack's book is an excellent read, even if it is illuminating in a completely different way to the one he intended. Its readability owes much to the author's failure to follow one of his own strictures. Don't name-drop, he insists, but it is the names McCormack drops and the anecdotes of the famous and fabled which make his book entertaining at least. An early name he drops is that of Richard Nixon ... Somehow, I would have thought that Nixon and McCormack might have had much in common.

give it a name

informal what would you like to drink? The notion of identifying one's choice is taken further with an added dash of irony in the form *name your poison* (see POISON). *19th cent.*

Dickens *Hard Times* 1854
'What thall it be, Thquire, while you wait? Thall it be Therry? Give it a name, Thquire!' said Mr Sleary, with hospitable ease. 'Nothing for me, I thank you,' said Mr Gradgrind.

J B Priestley *Festival at Farbridge* 1951
What are you drinking? Give it a name, chaps – there's everything here.

give one's/its name to something
to be the source of a name with which something is associated. *17th cent.*

have somebody's name/number on it
to be designed or intended for a particular person. The expression was originally applied to bullets and shells in the First World War, as a soldier's fatalistic acceptance of death if a bullet 'had his name (or number) on it', and it has since become common in extended applications of any sinister or unpleasant fate or outcome that one cannot avoid. *Early 20th cent.*

in all but name
having the form or character of something without being called by its name. *19th cent.*

Edgar Allan Poe *William Wilson* 1839
Thenceforward my voice was a household law; and at an age when few children have abandoned their leading-strings, I was left to the guidance of my own will, and became, in all but name, the master of my own actions.

J E Neale *Queen Elizabeth* 1934
In all but name the Papacy was at war with Elizabeth.

in name only
in outward form but not in reality: used in particular of a marriage that has not been consummated. *17th cent.*

Archbishop Bramhall cited by Hobbes in *A Treatise on Liberty and Necessity* 1654
We have learned in the rudiments of logic, that conjugates are sometimes in name only, and not in deed.

make a name for oneself
to acquire a certain reputation. *19th cent.*

Trollope *Can You Forgive Her?* 1864
I feel sure that he would make a name for himself in Parliament.

name and shame
to identify and name people who have done wrong, in order to shame them into improving their behaviour (or, in tabloid journalism, in order to sell newspapers). *Late 20th cent.*

Guardian 1995
Those who cultivate moral confusion for profit should understand this: we will name their names and shame them as they deserve to be shamed.

the name of the game
informal the main point to note or recognize in some activity. *Late 20th cent.*

Michael Falk *Part of the Furniture* 1991
It was a matter of discovering which day centres offered what services – where I could go, for example, to have a shower or clean my clothes, or maybe have a cheap meal. Survival was the name of the game and I was managing to do just that.

name names
to identify people, especially in the context of blame for wrongdoing. *17th cent.*

Vanbrugh *The Relapse* 1697
Don't press me then to name names; for that I have sworn I won't do.

Smollett *The Expedition of Humphry Clinker* 1771
Writing is all a lottery – I have been a loser by the works of the greatest men of the age. I could mention particulars, and name names; but don't choose it.

name no names
to avoid identifying people involved in an activity or incident. *18th cent.*

Fanny Burney *Journal* 1792
She desired he would name no names, but merely mention that some ladies had been frightened.

Dickens *David Copperfield* 1850
She named no names, she said; let them the cap fitted, wear it.

no names, no pack drill
(proverb) people who are not named cannot be blamed or punished: *pack drill* is a military punishment involving a lengthy period of marching up and down in full kit. *Early 20th cent.*

The Times 2002
On inspection, the problems a smart card might solve evaporate one by one. My more flamboyant colleagues (no names, no pack drill) nonetheless urged that we intervene not just before breakfast, lunch and dinner, but before the rest of the world adopted smart cards so that British industry could seize the market.

or my name is not —
(with the speaker's actual name added) used to emphasize one's belief in the truth of a statement. *19th cent.*

Dickens *Pickwick Papers* 1837
'Whenever I meet that Jingle again, wherever it is,' said Mr. Pickwick ... 'I'll inflict personal chas-

tisement on him, in addition to the exposure he so richly merits. I will, or my name is not Pickwick.'

put a name to somebody/something
to identify somebody or something, or remember what they are called. *19th cent.*

> Dickens Bleak House 1853
> *'This is not a time,' says Mr. Bogsby, 'to haggle about money,' though he looks something sharply after it, over the counter; 'give your orders, you two gentlemen, and you're welcome to whatever you put a name to.' Thus entreated, the two gentlemen (Mr. Weevle especially) put names to so many things, that in course of time they find it difficult to put a name to anything quite distinctly.*

to one's name
in one's possession; giving one a right to something. *19th cent.*

> Dickens Pickwick Papers 1837
> *Sam's two hundred pounds stood transferred to his name, and Wilkins Flasher, Esquire, having been paid his commission, dropped the money carelessly into his coat pocket, and lounged back to his office.*

what's in a name
the name for a thing does not affect its character or value: with allusion to Shakespeare, *Romeo and Juliet* (1596) II.i.85 '[Juliet to Romeo] What's in a name? That which we call a rose I By any other word would smell as sweet.' *16th cent.*

> Bonnell Thornton The Battle of the Wigs 1768
> *What's in a name? That which we call a Wig, I By any other name would look as big.*

> J R Planché Once upon a Time There Were Two Kings 1879
> *[Princess] My name is Carpillona. [King] What a queer one! [Princess] What's in a name? Yours, sir, is Periwigulus, But can that make you any more ridiculous?*

you name it
informal anything you can think of: originally as part of advertising slogans of the type *you name it, we've got it. Mid 20th cent.*

> Dogs Today 1992
> *I scuttled to the corner and crouched, trembling and moaning ... Then I stood and drooped everything; my head, ears, tail. You name it, I drooped it! 'I don't want a temperament like that,' the woman said.*

See also DRAG somebody's name through the mud/dirt; —'s name is MUD; take somebody's name in VAIN.

nap^1 (verb)

catch somebody napping
(said of an event or incident) to happen to somebody when they are unprepared or inattentive: a figurative use of the verb *nap* meaning 'to take a short sleep', in early use with *take* instead of *catch*. *16th cent.*

> Shakespeare Love's Labour's Lost IV.iii.128 (1594)
> *[Longueville] You may look pale, but I should blush, I know, I To be o'erheard and taken napping so.*

nap^2 (noun)

go nap
to risk everything in a single venture: a metaphor from the card game called *nap* (short for *Napoleon*), in which *going nap* means taking all five tricks in a hand. *19th cent.*

> T W H Crosland The Five Notions 1903
> *Never go nap on an army mule, 'cause he'll skip! skip! skip!*

not go nap on somebody/something
Australian, informal to dislike or care little for somebody or something: an extension of the previous phrase. *Early 20th cent.*

> Kia Ora Coo-ee 1918
> *Talking of souvenirs, I don't go nap on any of the ordinary kind which lose interest after they have been looked at once or twice.*

nasty
See a bitter/bad/nasty TASTE in the mouth; a nasty piece of WORK; something nasty in the WOODSHED.

nation

one nation
a socially united nation: often (with hyphen) as an adjectival phrase, as in *one-nation politics, Conservatism*, etc. *One Nation* was the title of a pamphlet published by the Conservative Party shortly before their return to power in 1951. This

alluded to Disraeli's ideal of social union as advocated in his novel *Sybil, or the Two Nations*, published in 1845, in which social division is deprecated as follows: 'Two nations; between whom there is no intercourse and no sympathy; who are as ignorant of each other's habits, thoughts, and feelings as if they were dwellers in different zones, or inhabitants of different planets; who are formed by a different breeding, are fed by a different food, are ordered by different manners, and are not governed by the same laws … The Rich and the Poor.' The ideal of a united nation influenced the social policies of the Conservative administration in the 1950s, and it became prominent again as a slogan in the 1990s, following the Thatcherite policies of the previous decade which opponents regarded as socially divisive. *19th cent.*

native

go native

when living abroad or in an unfamiliar environment, to adopt the way of life of the local people. *Early 20th cent.*

Kipling *Kim* 1901
Kim did not sweep the board with his reminiscences; for St. Xavier's looks down on boys who 'go native altogether'.

nature

one's better nature

the side of one's character that tends to generosity and tolerance. *19th cent.*

R H Dana *Two Years Before the Mast* 1840
It was almost the first time that I had been positively alone – free from the sense that human beings were at my elbow, if not talking with me – since I had left home. My better nature returned strong upon me. Everything was in accordance with my state of feeling, and I experienced a glow of pleasure at finding that what of poetry and romance I ever had in me, had not been entirely deadened by the laborious and frittering life I had led.

get/go back to nature

to return to a simple way of life without dependence on machines and other features of modern life; hence the (early 20th cent.) adjectival phrase *back-to-nature*, often used in a depreciatory man-

ner. The phrase dates from the 18th cent., although the modern connotations were not always present in the early uses.

Mary Wollstonecraft *A Vindication of the Rights of Woman* 1792
Rousseau's observations, it is proper to remark, were made in a country where the art of pleasing was refined only to extract the grossness of vice. He did not go back to nature, or his ruling appetite disturbed the operations of reason, else he would not have drawn these crude inferences.

in the nature of things

because of the way things are; inevitably. *17th cent.*

Locke *An Essay Concerning Human Understanding* 1690
If we should inquire a little further, to see what it is that occasions men to make several combinations of simple ideas into distinct, and, as it were, settled modes, and neglect others, which in the nature of things themselves, have as much an aptness to be combined and make distinct ideas, we shall find the reason of it to be the end of language.

in a/the state of nature

1 in an uncivilized or undomesticated state. The phrase owes its currency in large measure to Locke's use (see below) referring to the condition of humankind before the development of organized society. *17th cent.*

Locke *An Essay Concerning Civil Government* 1690
And thus, in the state of Nature, one man comes by a power over another, but yet no absolute or arbitrary power to use a criminal, when he has got him in his hands, according to the passionate heats or boundless extravagancy of his own will.

Darwin *The Descent of Man* 1871
Domesticated animals vary more than those in a state of nature.

2 (in Christian thought) in a morally bad and unrepentant state. *17th cent.*

An [sic] Collins *Divine Songs and Meditacions* 1653
As all men in the state of nature be, | And have been ever since mans wofull fall, | Who was created first, from bondage free, | Untill by sinn he thrust himself in thrall.

3 completely naked. *18th cent.*

John Cleland *Memoirs of a Woman of Pleasure* 1748
The cooling air, as I stood in this state of nature, join'd to the desire I had of bathing first, enabled me

to put him off, and tranquillize him, with the remark, that a little suspense would only set a keener edge on the pleasure.

the nature of the beast
the unalterable character of something. *17th cent.*

Defoe *A New Yeares Gift for the Late Rapparees: A Satyr* 1691
Art can do much, but here all Art's in vain; | Knock out your Teeth, and add a clog and chain, | The Nature of the Beast will still remain.

See also the CALL of nature.

navel

contemplate one's navel
to concentrate on one's own interests and pre-occupations, especially at the expense of broader considerations; to waste time in self-absorption. The phrase was used by Eugene O'Neill in *Days Without End* (1933) with *regard* instead of *contemplate*. *Mid 20th cent.*

Eddie Gibbs *I Believe in Church Growth* 1992
By this means the church is preserved from 'analysis paralysis', with the church curtailing its activities and returning its plans to cold storage while it contemplates its navel. The church should resist the temptation to merely tick over.

near

one's nearest and dearest
one's closest relatives and friends. The expression was used ironically at an early date, originally in adjectival form: *cf* Shakespeare, *1 Henry IV* (1596) III.ii.123 '[Henry to Prince Harry] Why Harry, do I tell thee of my foes, | Which art my near'st and dearest enemy?' The transition to absolute use as a noun phrase occurs during the 18th cent. and 19th cent.

Dryden *Don Sebastian, King of Portugal* 1690
All these require your timous assistance; shall I say they beg it? No, they claim it of you, by all the nearest and dearest tyes of these three P's self-pre-servation, our property, and our prophet.

Richardson *The History of Sir Charles Grandison* 1753
He very gratefully thank'd his sister for her care, as a man would do for one the nearest and dearest to him.

Scott *Ivanhoe* 1819
While all mourned and honoured the dead, thou hast lived to merit our hate and execration – lived to unite thyself with the vile tyrant who murdered thy nearest and dearest.

so near and yet so far
unattainable despite being close or immediate: also used with regretful reference to an achieve-ment narrowly missed. *18th cent.*

Tennyson *In Memoriam A.H.H.* 1850
He thrids the labyrinth of the mind, | He reads the secret of the star, | He seems so near and yet so far.

Hardy *Tess of the D'Urbervilles* 1891
Sleep, however, he could not – so near her, yet so far from her – and he continually lifted the window-blind and regarded the backs of the opposite houses and wondered behind which of the sashes she reposed at that moment.

neat

See (as) clean/neat as a new PIN.

necessary

a necessary evil
something unpleasant or unwelcome that one has to put up with because of the benefits it might bring. *16th cent.*

W Baldwin *A Treatise of Morall Phylosophie* 1547
A woman is a necessary euyll.

Henry Carey *Poems on Several Occasions* 1729
O Ladies, Ladies! marry whilst you may; | Consider you grow older ev'ry day! | A Husband is a necessary evil; | But chalk and coals, and oatmeal, are the Devil.

neck

break one's neck to do something
to take great risks in order to achieve something difficult or challenging. *19th cent.*

Reginald Heber *Blue-beard* a1826
He is now on the staircase. – Oh, would it might crumble – | I'd break my own neck to ensure him a tumble!

get/catch it in the neck
to be severely rebuked or punished. *Early 20th cent.*

Margaret Drabble *The Radiant Way* 1988
Ivan usually managed to deliver her some back-
handed compliment, whereas Charles always got it
in the neck.

have the (brass/barefaced) neck to do something

to have the nerve or cheek to do something the
speaker disapproves of: *neck* is used here in its
old meaning 'impudence, cheek', which is based
on the notion of stiffening the neck as a sign of
obstinacy (perhaps instead of bowing it in submission): *cf* Coverdale's translation (1535) of 2
Kings 17:14 'They … hardened their necks,
according to the hardneck of their fathers.' *Neck*
in this meaning is recorded in dialect glossaries
from the end of the 19th cent., and phrases such
as *have the barefaced neck* appear from the 1930s.
Mid 20th cent.

John Francombe *Stone Cold* 1990
It must be important for her to have driven all the
way up north and bluff her way into his house. He
glanced up at her almost respectfully as he poured
himself some tea. If she had the nerve, the sheer
bloody brass neck, to do that, then maybe he'd give
her a few minutes.

neck and neck

keeping abreast in a race or contest: originally
(late 18th cent.) with reference to horses staying
level in horseracing. The expression occurs from
the 19th cent. in figurative use.

James Ewell Heath *Whigs and Democrats* 1839
I have ascertained that the other parts of the district
will be about equally divided, or, as the sportsmen
say, neck and neck, between the candidates, – so
that, in fact, you may be said to have the issue of the
day's contest in your own hands.

Mark Twain *Life on the Mississippi* 1883
Two red-hot steamboats raging along, neck-and-
neck, straining every nerve that is to say, every rivet
in the boilers – quaking and shaking and groaning
from stem to stern, spouting white steam from the
pipes, pouring black smoke from the chimneys,
raining down sparks, parting the river into long
breaks of hissing foam – this is sport that makes a
body's very liver curl with enjoyment. A horse-race
is pretty tame and colorless in comparison.

a neck of the woods

a particular geographical area or locality: often
used in the form *this* (or *the same*) *neck of the woods.*

A *neck of the woods* in late 18th cent. and 19th cent.
US usage denoted a settlement in remote or
wooded country, and was based on the (16th
cent.) meaning of *neck* 'a narrow piece of land
with water on each side'. *19th cent.*

neck or nothing

used to express determination to risk everything
in a venture. *17th cent.*

Anon *Ovidius Exulans* 1673
No I protest that were a low thing, Alas! I still cry
Neck or nothing.

Byron *Don Juan* 1824
First one or two, then five, six, and a dozen, | Came
mounting quickly up, for it was now | All neck or
nothing, as, like pitch or rosin, | Flame was sho-
wer'd forth above.

stick one's neck out

informal to expose oneself to danger or criticism
by speaking or acting boldly. *Early 20th cent.*

talk/speak through (the back of) one's neck

informal to talk nonsense. *19th cent.*

up to one's neck in something

informal very busy or involved in something.
Early 20th cent.

win by a neck

to come first by a small margin in a contest: a
metaphor from racing, in which a *neck* is a measure denoting a small lead. *19th cent.*

Laman Blanchard *Poetical Works* 1876
Lay odds on the Ladies! 'Tis said | You may find it a
capital spec.; | Though man may have won by a
head, | 'Tis woman who wins by a neck.

needle

a needle in a haystack

something that is difficult to find because it is
hidden in a mass of other things. The notion is
much older with other imagery, e.g. *a needle in a*
meadow (early 16th cent.); the forms *a bottle* [=
bundle] *of hay* (from late 16th cent.) and *a truss of*
hay (18th cent.) mark a transition to the current
form, which is achieved by the 19th cent.

Charles Kingsley *Westward Ho!* 1855
'We'll find him for you, if he's in the fleet. We'll
squeeze it out of our prisoners somehow. Eh,
Hawkins? I thought all the captains had promised
to send you news if they heard of him.' 'Ay, but it's

ill looking for a needle in a haystack. But I shall find him.'

See also (as) SHARP as a needle.

needs

An archaic adverbial form of *need*, with the meaning 'necessarily'.

must needs do something
must inevitably do something; cannot avoid it. *Middle English*

> Shakespeare *The Merchant of Venice* iv.i.202 (1598)
> *This strict court of Venice | Must needs give sentence 'gainst the merchant there.*

needs must (when the devil drives)
one must occasionally do things one would prefer not to. There is ellipsis of *one* at the beginning of the phrase. *Middle English* (in Lydgate)

> Shakespeare *All's Well That Ends Well* i.iii.30 (1603)
> [Lavatch] *I am driven on by the flesh, and he must needs go that the devil drives.*

> R L Stevenson *The Master of Ballantrae* 1889
> *Needs must when the devil drives. The truth is we are within easy walk of the place, and I will show it to you to-morrow.*

nelly

not on your nelly/nellie
informal in no circumstances; certainly not: based on *not on your life* (see LIFE), *nelly* being short for *Nelly Duff*, rhyming slang for *puff* (= breath of life). *Mid 20th cent.*

sitting by Nelly/Nellie
informal learning a new job by watching somebody who is more experienced. The phrase has been especially popular in the mill towns of the north of England, where the name *Nelly* typically represents a clever or dependable young woman who can show the ropes to a newcomer. The appearance of the name in old music hall songs of the early 20th cent. ('Nellie Dean' and so on) probably gave the idea a strong boost. Further back in time, *Nelly* has similar associations of humble origins and occupations: for example, Nell Gwyn the mistress of Charles II (whose dying words, 'let not poor Nelly starve', have resonated down the centuries), and Little Nell in Dickens' *The Old Curiosity Shop* (1841). The

phrase first appears in print in the 1960s. *Mid 20th cent.*

nerve

a bag/bundle of nerves
informal an extremely nervous or agitated person. *20th cent.*

get on somebody's nerves
to begin to irritate or distress somebody. *19th cent.*

> Oscar Wilde *The Picture of Dorian Gray* 1891
> *It is very tragic, of course, but you must not get yourself mixed up in it. I see by The Standard that she was seventeen. I should have thought she was almost younger than that. She looked such a child, and seemed to know so little about acting. Dorian, you mustn't let this thing get on your nerves.*

have/need nerves of steel
to show or need great composure and not be easily upset. *19th cent.*

> Browning *Martin Relph* 1879
> *'Tis an ugly job, though, all the same ... to have to deal | With a case of the kind, when a woman's in fault: | We soldiers need nerves of steel!*

live on one's nerves / one's nerve ends
to live an emotionally demanding life. *Mid 20th cent.*

lose one's nerve
to become uneasy or overcautious about something one was previously determined about. The phrase is recorded earlier, and perhaps fortuitously, in the context of caring for wool, *nerve* here meaning 'texture'. *19th cent.*

> Charles Kingsley *Westward Ho!* 1855
> *Hit or not hit, the steersman lost his nerve, and shrank from the coming shock.*

strain every nerve
to make a great physical effort: *nerve* here is used in its archaic meaning 'a sinew or tendon'. *Cf* Shakespeare, *Cymbeline* (1610) iii.iii.94: '[Belarius] The princely blood flows in his cheek, he sweats, | Strains his young nerves, and puts himself in posture | That acts my words.' The phrase is 18th cent. in this form.

Pope *Odyssey* xii.256 (1725)
Strain ev'ry nerve, and bid the vessel fly. If from yon
justling rocks and wavy war Jove safety grants; he
grants it to your care.

touch a raw nerve

to cause somebody to react by mentioning a
sensitive matter, often unintentionally. *Mid 20th*
cent.

See also a WAR of nerves.

Nessus

Nessus' shirt / shirt of Nessus

an inescapable cause of misfortune or suffering:
from the story of the centaur Nessus, whom
Hercules killed for attempting to rape his wife
Deianeira. Before he died, he persuaded Deianeira to make a potion from his blood and smear
it on Hercules' shirt; if Hercules wore the shirt it
would make him love her. Many years later,
when jealous of another woman, she sent Hercules the shirt; but the potion was deadly poison
and caused Hercules to die in agony, unable to
remove the tunic without pulling off lumps of his
own flesh. *17th cent.*

Shakespeare *Antony and Cleopatra* iv.xii.43 (1607)
[Antony] *The shirt of Nessus is upon me. Teach*
me, Alcides, thou mine ancestor, thy rage.

nest

See EMPTY nest; FEATHER one's (own) nest; a
mare's nest *at* MARE.

net

slip/fall through the net

to escape or elude a carefully set up system of
entrapment; to evade detection. *Early 20th cent.*

G B Shaw *Mrs Warren's Profession* 1902
Nothing can really shake the confidence of the
public in the Lord Chamberlain's department except
a remorseless and unbowdlerized narration of the
licentious fictions which slip through its net.

See also SURF the Net.

nettle

See GRASP the nettle.

network

the old boy network

the system of favouritism and preferment operating among people of a similar social (usually
privileged) background, especially among former pupils of public schools. *Mid 20th cent.*

Jeremy Paxman *Friends in High Places* 1990
When Clark had to hire someone to become chief
executive of the new regulatory authority, the
Treasury gave him a list of nine admirals, seventeen
generals and six air marshals and told him they'd be
disappointed if he didn't find the right chap among
them. Clark preferred the old boy network, and
settled on an old pal from the Ministry of Infor-
mation, Robert Fraser.

never

never-never land

an imaginary ideal place: in current use often
understood as a land from which one 'never'
comes back. Also used with allusion to *Never*
Land (or *Never Never Land*), an ideal country in
J M Barrie's *Peter Pan* (published in 1904); but the
expression goes back earlier with reference to the
Australian outback, in particular the unpopu-
lated northern part of Queensland, and was the
subtitle of a play called *The Moment of Death* by
Israel Zangwill produced four years before Barrie's story. *19th cent.*

Barcroft Boake *Where the Dead Men Lie and Other*
Poems 1897
'Tis a song of the Never Never land | Set to the tune
of a scorching gale | On the sandhills red, | When
the grasses dead | Loudly rustle, and bow the head
| To the breath of its dusty hail.

See also never say die *at* DIE[1].

new

a new one on —

an idea or suggestion that somebody has not
heard before. The phrase dates from the 19th
cent., but is chiefly found in the 20th cent.

Upton Sinclair *The Jungle* 1906
'I work in the stockyards – at least I did until the
other day. It's in my clothes.' 'That's a new one on
me,' said the newcomer. 'I thought I'd been up

against 'em all. What are you in for?' 'I hit my boss.'

See also a new / different / whole new ball game *at* BALL[1]; a new BROOM; a new kid on the BLOCK; new off the irons *at* IRON; new WINE in old bottles; turn over a new LEAF.

news

be good/bad news
informal to be a welcome (or unwelcome) circumstance or discovery: an extension of the literal meaning with regard to information received. *Early 20th cent.*

I have / have I got news for you
used to introduce a piece of information that will surprise or impress the hearer, and arising from the more neutral sense 'I have something to tell you'. In the form *Have I* …, the phrase gained further currency as the title of a satirical television quiz show about current affairs, broadcast from 1990. *18th cent.*

> H B Dudley *The Woodman* 1791
> [Medley] *But come, I've news for you! – Have you heard of the strange gentleman just come on the forest?*

> Michael Field *The Father's Tragedy* 1885
> [Ramorgny] *Then have I news for you. The Bishop of St. Andrews died last night.*

> W S Gilbert *Foggerty's Fairy* 1903
> [Walkinshaw] *Don't be too sure; I have news for you. Delia Spiff, your late fiancée, arrived from Melbourne yesterday.*

that is news to me
informal I had not heard that before (with reference to information). *19th cent.*

> James Fenimore Cooper *The Pioneers* 1823
> *But I did not know that the patient was a son of Leather-stocking: it is news to me, to hear that Natty had a wife.*

See also the GOOD news … the bad news ….

next

the boy/girl next door
an image of an approachable and amiable young person suitable for a casual romantic relationship. *Mid 20th cent.*

in next to no time
very quickly. *Mid 20th cent.*

next in line
immediately below a particular person in a hierarchy, or next to receive a benefit, award, etc or suffer a certain treatment. *20th cent.*

> *Guardian* 1989
> *Twenty-seven people were arrested when the police finally got the camp back under control in the early evening. The confrontation took place at the Chi Ma Wan island detention centre, which houses those believed to be next in line for deportation.*

nibs

his nibs
used humorously or belittlingly of a self-important person or a person in authority: occasionally also *her nibs. Nibs* in this sense is used only in the phrase and is of obscure origin; *nib* is listed as a slang term for a gentleman in the Australian James H Vaux's collection of criminal slang *Vocabulary of the Flash Language* (1812), and this use may be connected. An earlier form *nabs*, which was used in a similar way from the late 18th cent., may suggest a straightforward vowel change. *19th cent.*

> Bret Harte *Condensed Novels and Other Stories* 1867
> *Why, you see, after touching your hat, you should have touched him lightly with your forefinger in his waistcoat, so, and asked 'How's his nibs?'*

nice

nice one
informal used to express admiration for an adroit move. The phrase became popular in the advertising slogan *nice one, Cyril* (used to advertise bread), which also formed a chant of football crowds when the Tottenham Hotspur player Cyril Knowles was on the pitch. *20th cent.*

nice try
used to express ironic sympathy over another's failed ploy. *Late 20th cent.*

> *Today* 1992
> *Some have tried to explain away this usage as being a play on the French 'angle', which supposedly sounds like 'anglais'. Nice try, but the French have no such word as 'angle'.*

nice work if you can get it

an envious comment on another's good fortune in having a lucrative occupation or way of life that is pleasant and undemanding: with allusion to the title of a song by Ira Gershwin containing the lines 'Holding hands at midnight | 'Neath a starry sky, | Nice work if you can get it, | And you can get it if you try' (from *Damsel in Distress*, 1937). *Mid 20th cent.*

See also have a nice DAY.

nicety

to a nicety

as well or as completely as possible. *18th cent.*

> **Defoe Roxana 1724**
> *He was especially employ'd, and order'd to haunt him as a Ghost; that he should scarce let him be ever out of his Sight; he perform'd this to a Nicety, and fail'd not to give me a perfect Journal of all his Motions, from Day to Day.*

nick

The phrases use *nick* in different senses, but they are the same word, the one originally meaning 'a notch or groove', which is recorded from the 15th cent. From this sense developed the meaning 'a score or count', e.g. in a game or in keeping a tally, and then 'a precise point or moment' in this activity. The other meaning involved here, 'a state or condition', is relatively recent.

in good/bad nick

British, informal in good (or bad) condition: originally in dialect use. *Early 20th cent.*

in the nick of time

at the last possible moment; just before it would be too late. *In* or *at the* (*very*) *nick* dates from the 16th cent. in the meaning 'at the decisive moment' (with reference to people arriving, etc); from the mid 17th cent. it was followed by *of* to denote the precise moment of something happening, with *opportunity* and *time* as the two principal collocates. Addison commented on this use in the *Tatler* in 1710. *17th cent.*

> **Head & Kirkman The English Rogue Described 1674**
> *Glad was I that it should come into my head to ramble into the Country at that nick of time, for my extraordinary familiarity with them might have raised a suspition to the endangering of my person.*

> **Jeremy Collier A Second Defence 1700**
> *Menelaus likewise designing to Murther Andromache and her Son Molossus, is disappointed in his Barbarity by Peleus, who comes in the nick of time to the rescue of the Innocent.*

> **Charles Kingsley Westward Ho! 1855**
> *Those two, I believe, were going to murder the old man in the hammock, if we had not come in the nick of time. What have you done with them?*

nickel

accept/take a wooden nickel

NAmer, informal to be fooled or swindled: based on the image of a wooden nickel as representing something worthless. *Early 20th cent.*

nigger

a nigger in the woodpile

informal, originally NAmer a hidden or unknown person or thing that is likely to cause trouble. The phrase originates in North America and appears in early use in the form *nigger in the fence*. The phrase is now considered to be offensive. *19th cent.*

> **Barnard & Burgess The County Fair 1889**
> *Well, I might have known there was a nigger in the woodpile somewhere.*

night

make a night of it

to spend the night celebrating or enjoying oneself: *see also* make a DAY of it. *17th cent.*

> **Dekker & Webster Northward Hoe 1607**
> [Bellamont] *Come since we must stay: wele be mery, chamberlaine call in the musick, bid the Tapsters & maids come vp and dance, what weel make a night of it.*

night of the long knives

a treacherous betrayal or ruthless action: originally with reference to the massacre of British chieftains by the Saxon Hengist in 472, and to the murder on 29–30 June 1934, on Hitler's orders and with help from Himmler and the SS, of Ernst Röhm and Kurt von Schleicher and other members of the SA (*Sturmabteilung*, or storm troopers), after which the assassins were presented with daggers inscribed by Himmler. In more recent times, the phrase has been applied to political acts of comparable ruthlessness, albeit carried out without physical violence as far as one is aware: most notably to the action of the British Prime Minister Harold Macmillan in sacking one third of his Cabinet on a single day in July 1962. *Mid 20th cent.*

---

nine

The exact relevance of *nine*, as distinct from any other number, is not always clear, but its choice is likely to be due in many cases to its status as the highest number written (in arabic numerals) as a single figure, and to its proximity to the round number ten, as in *nine times out of ten* below.

dressed (up) to the nines
dressed up very smartly or elaborately. *To the nine(s)*, first used by Burns ('Thou paints auld Nature to the nines' in *Pastoral Poetry*, 1790s), originally had the more general meaning 'to perfection', and was first used with the specific application to dress in the 1850s, when it is recorded in Hotten's *Dictionary of Slang* (1859). The philologist and etymologist Walter Skeat (in *Notes & Queries* January 1903, p.34) sought an origin in 'dressed up to the neyen [= eyes, also a variant of *nine*]', which makes better sense than the suggestion has been credited with. Nonetheless, this can only be regarded as (admittedly superior) speculation, although it is a lot more compelling than another suggestion that has appeared in print. This relates the phrase to the famed smartness of a regiment (the 99th Foot Soldiers) of the British Army in the 1850s. Other regiments aspired to emulate them and so be dressed in a manner equal 'to the nines'. This explanation is about as forced and contrived as it could possibly be; it is also chronologically invalid, since the phrase occurs much earlier, and appears to be a typical example of folk etymology that attempts find historical contexts for phrases of obscure origin. *19th cent.*

Trollope *The Eustace Diamonds* 1873
There's Smiler about town as bold as brass, and dressed to the nines.

a nine days' wonder
a short-lived sensation: based on the proverbial figure of nine days, found from the time of Chaucer (see below) and in early books of proverbs, as the likely duration of a novelty. There are joking references to the phrase in Shakespeare: for example, in *3 Henry VI* (1591) III.ii.113 (in an exchange between King Edward, George of Clarence, and Richard of Gloucester about marriage) '[King] You'd think it strange if I should marry her. [George] To who, my lord? [King] Why, Clarence, to myself. [Richard] That would be ten days' wonder at the least. [George] That's a day longer than a wonder lasts.' And in *As You Like It* (1599) III.ii.170 Rosalind tells Celia 'I was seven of the nine days out of the wonder before you came.' *16th cent.*

Chaucer *Troilus and Criseyde* IV.588
For whan men han wel cryd, than wol they rowne [= whisper, i.e. quieten down]; | Ek [= also] wonder last but nyne nyght nevere in towne.

Samuel Rowlands *The Famous Historie of Guy Earl of Warwicke* 1607
With hasty journey he is homeward bound. | Leaving the vulgar to the nine days wonder: | Arriving safely on the English ground, | Posting to her, suppos'd too long asunder.

nine times out of ten
nearly always. *18th cent.*

Sheridan *The Critic* 1781
Love! – Oh nothing so easy; for it is a received point among poets, that where history gives you a good heroic out-line for a play, you may fill up with a little love at your own discretion; in doing which, nine times out of ten, you only make up a deficiency in the private history of the times.

G K Chesterton *The Innocence of Father Brown* 1911
Why do these idiots always assume that the only person who hates the wife's lover is the wife's husband? Nine times out of ten the person who most hates the wife's lover is the wife.

nine to five
a daily routine of office work, conventionally beginning at nine o'clock in the morning and ending at five o'clock in the afternoon: normally used (often with hyphens as an adjectival phrase) with overtones of tedium and drudgery. Hence a *nine-to-fiver* is a drudge who works typical office hours, no more and (usually) no less. *Mid 20th cent.*

Caterer & Hotelkeeper 1991
As for sociable hours, I would not be in this trade if I expected to work nine to five, Monday to Friday.

See also on CLOUD nine.

ninepence

(as) fine/right as ninepence
extremely fine; in perfect condition. The phrase is commonly associated with the former practice of giving silver ninepenny pieces as love tokens. The phrase is recorded in the collection of proverbs published by the royal historiographer James Howell in 1659. It has largely fallen out of use, perhaps hastened on its way by the introduction of decimal coinage in Britain in 1971. *17th cent.*

no more than ninepence in the shilling
1 *informal* not having much money; not well off. *19th cent.*

Trollope *The Eustace Diamonds* 1873
The Greystocks were all people who wanted money. For them there was never more than ninepence in a shilling, if so much.

2 *informal, dated* lacking intelligence or common sense; not bright or clever. The phrase is based on pre-decimalization British currency, in which a shilling consisted of twelve pence: the sum of ninepence was therefore only three quarters of the full amount. *Mid 20th cent.*

J B Priestley *Festival at Farbridge* 1951
Poor woman can't help it if she's got a husband who's – yer know, lad – ninepence in the shilling, a bit barmy.

ninepin

go down / drop / fall / tumble like ninepins
to fall ill or die in large numbers: based on the image of all the pins being bowled over in a game of ninepins. Figurative uses are attested from an early date in the history of the word. *17th cent.*

nineteen

See talk nineteen to the DOZEN.

nip

nip something in the bud
to put an early stop to an activity, before it becomes established. A metaphor from the practice of removing the buds of plants to reduce their growth, and in early use often in the context of

feelings and passions. The phrase emerges in Elizabethan drama from the 1560s on, first in the forms *nip in the head* and *nip in the blade*, and Shakespeare in 2 *Henry VI* (1591) III.i.89 has York tell King Henry 'Cold news for me, for I had hope of France, | As firmly as I hope for fertile England. | Thus are my blossoms blasted in the bud.' The earliest recorded occurrences of the phrase in the form now familiar are in plays of Fletcher and Dekker from the first decade of the 17th cent.

Lady Mary Wroth *The Countesse of Mountgomeries Urania* 1621
And all this was but melancholy, and truely that is enough to spoil any, so strangely it grows upon one, and so pleasing is the snare, as till it hath ruind one ... This I have found and smarted with it; leave it then, and nip it in the bud, lest it blow to overthrow your life and happiness.

Dickens *Pickwick Papers* 1837
After great consternation had been excited in the mind of Mrs. Cluppins, by an attempt on the part of Tommy to recount how he had been cross-examined regarding the cupboard then in action, (which was fortunately nipped in the bud by his imbibing half a glass of the old crusted 'the wrong way', and thereby endangering his life for some seconds,) the party walked forth, in quest of a Hampstead stage.

nit

keep nit
Australian, informal to keep watch as an accomplice to a crime: probably a variant of *keep nix*, used with the same meaning, *nix* being attested as a warning signal that somebody is approaching. *Early 20th cent.*

Truth 1903
She was aided in securing patrons by a bludger, who ... kept 'nit' for the traps so that Amy could walk freely when she got on her beat.

no

the noes have it
there is a majority against a proposal. The formula is first recorded in the diaries of Thomas Burton, a member of Cromwell's Parliament in the 1650s: 'A member stood up and said, that the Noes in the former question had it.' *Cf* the ayes have it *at* AYE. *17th cent.*

a no-go area

an area of activity that is not allowed to a particular person or group: an extension of the physical meaning of a prohibited or restricted area or district, which gained currency from its use in the context of social divisions in Northern Ireland. *Late 20th cent.*

no man's land

an area of thought or activity that has an ill-defined or anomalous character: a figurative use of the physical meanings 'an unoccupied area between two opposing armies' and earlier 'a piece of ground without an owner'. *19th cent.*

> Harold Frederic *The Damnation of Theron Ware* 1896
>
> *So the truth remains always the truth, even though you give a charter to ten hundred thousand separate numskulls to examine it by the light of their private judgment, and report that it is as many different varieties of something else. But of course that whole question of private judgment versus authority is No-Man's-Land for us.*

no sooner said than done

dealt with immediately and promptly. *18th cent.*

> Anon *The London Bully* 1683
>
> *He gave order to the Usher to fetch immediately some Rods, for he was resolved to have him punished very solemnly; no sooner said than done; the poor Carrot-pated Boy was whipt with so much rigour, that in fortnights time it was not possible for him to sit directly upon his Bum.*

not/never take no for an answer

to persevere in spite of initial rejection or refusal: often used as an exhortation. *19th cent.*

> Wilkie Collins *The Moonstone* 1868
>
> *Mr. Godfrey, after taking leave of my lady, in a most sympathizing manner, left a farewell message for Miss Rachel, the terms of which made it clear to my mind that he had not taken No for an answer, and that he meant to put the marriage question to her once more, at the next opportunity.*

nobody

See be no/nobody's FOOL; nobody's BUSINESS.

nod

be on nodding terms / have a nodding acquaintance with somebody

to know somebody slightly. The image is of nodding the head as a nominal greeting on a casual encounter. The phrase is subject to variation. *19th cent.*

> Hardy *The Mayor of Casterbridge* 1886
>
> *Elizabeth-Jane had perceived from Henchard's manner that in assenting to dance she had made a mistake of some kind. In her simplicity she did not know what it was, till a hint from a nodding acquaintance enlightened her.*

> Graham Greene *The Honorary Consul* 1973
>
> *He knew nobody there by more than sight – at best a nodding acquaintance.*

get / give somebody/something the nod

to receive (or give) authority for an action: based on an older (16th cent.) meaning of *nod* denoting assent or approval. *Mid 20th cent.*

a nod's as good as a wink

a clear hint or warning does not need to be elaborated or laboured: a shortening of the (18th cent.) proverb *a nod's as good as a wink to a blind horse. 19th cent.*

> George Lovell *Look Before You Leap* 1888
>
> *Why I let him in, miss. Don't be frightened. He is in the next room, only waiting a nod from you to come in. I won't ask you to answer, miss; but if you don't say no, a nod is as good as a wink, and I shall understand.*

on the nod

without a formal discussion or vote. To *nod something through* is to approve it in this way. *19th cent.*

> George Moore *Esther Waters* 1894
>
> *He had heard something that was good enough for him. He didn't suppose the guv'nor would take him on the nod, but he had a nice watch which ought to be good for three ten.*

noise

a big noise

informal an important or influential person, especially one who makes his or her presence felt. *Early 20th cent.*

James Joyce *Come-all-ye* a1941
*I shook claws with all the hammers and bowed to
blonde and brune, | The mistress made a signal and
the mujik called the tune. | Madamina read a
message from the Big Noise of her State | After
which we crowed in unison: That Turco's talking
straight!*

make a noise
to make a fuss, especially as a means of attracting
attention or publicity. *17th cent.*

> Bernard Mandeville *The Lyon in Love* from Aesop
> Dress'd 1704
> *Besides she lov'd a fierce gallant, | Says he, they
> have ask'd my consent; | If now I make a Noise
> about it, | Who knows but they may do't without it.*

none

See be none the wiser *at* WISE; none the WORSE for
something.

nonsense

make (a) nonsense of something
to make something seem worthless or ridiculous.
Mid 20th cent.

nook

every nook and cranny
everywhere possible, especially as representing
the coverage or penetration of an exhaustive
search. *19th cent.*

> William Morris *The Well at the World's End* 1896
> *Cloudless was the day, and the air clean and sweet,
> and every nook and cranny was clear to behold from
> where they stood.*

noose

put one's head in a noose
to put oneself into a vulnerable position or bring
about one's own downfall: originally with reference to incriminating oneself in a capital offence,
risking one's own execution. *19th cent.*

> Henry James *The American* 1877
> *In a general way I don't see why a widow should
> ever marry again. She has gained the benefits of
> matrimony – freedom and consideration – and she*

has got rid of the drawbacks. Why should she put
her head into the noose again?

nose

be unable to see further than (the end of) one's nose
to be limited to immediate consequences in making decisions or judgements; to lack good judgement and forethought. *19th cent.*

> Nathaniel Hawthorne *The Scarlet Letter* 1850
> *I saw my own prospect of retaining office to be better
> than those of my Democratic brethren. But who can
> see an inch into futurity, beyond his nose? My head
> was the first that fell!*

count noses
to count the number of people voting or belonging to an organization, party, etc. *17th cent.*

> Defoe *A New Discoverie of an Old Intreague* 1705
> *And to make up the show with men of sense comes
> common sergeant for an evidence; with we's, and
> they's, with us's, and suppose's tells how in Com-
> mon-Hall he counted noses.*

cut off one's nose to spite one's face
to act in a way that harms oneself in one's eagerness to have revenge on somebody else. The
phrase occurs in many variants, originally as a
proverb in the form *he that biteth his nose off,
shameth his face*. The phrase appears as *cut off
one's nose to be revenged of one's face* in Grose's
Dictionary of the Vulgar Tongue (1788). *16th cent.*

> R L Stevenson *The Master of Ballantrae* 1889
> *The public disgrace of his arrival … rankled in his
> bones; he was in that humour when a man – in the
> words of the old adage – will cut off his nose to spite
> his face; and he must make himself a public spectacle
> in the hopes that some of the disgrace might spatter
> on my lord.*

get up somebody's nose
informal to be a continuing cause of irritation or
annoyance to somebody. *Mid 20th cent.*

give somebody a bloody nose
informal to defeat somebody decisively: literally,
to get the better of them in a fight, leaving them
bruised and bleeding. A *bloody nose* is such a
defeat or punishment. *18th cent.*

Henry Fielding *The History of Tom Jones* 1749
This matter … was no other than a quarrel between
Master Blifil and Tom Jones, the consequence of
which had been a bloody nose to the former; for
though Master Blifil, notwithstanding he was the
younger, was in size above the other's match, yet
Tom was much his superior at the noble art of
boxing.

Christopher Morley *Parnassus on Wheels* 1917
I was mad at both men for behaving like schoolboys.
I was mad at Andrew for being so unreasonable, yet
in a way I admired him for it; I was mad at Mifflin
for giving Andrew a bloody nose, and yet I appre-
ciated the spirit in which it was done.

hold one's nose
to distance oneself from a source of distaste or
displeasure: from the literal meaning of squeezing the nostrils to keep out an unpleasant smell.
19th cent.

keep one's nose clean
informal to avoid trouble: possibly with allusion
to keeping one's nose out of a glass, i.e. to avoid
drinking alcohol, a meaning of the phrase in
services' slang. *19th cent.*

Lantern (New Orleans) 1887
There's worse fellows than you looking for it, and if
you only keep your nose clean, we'll let you have it.

keep one's nose out of something
to refrain from interfering in somebody else's
affairs. The nose here, as in other phrases, is
symbolic of (generally unwelcome) curiosity
and prying. *19th cent.*

Maria Edgeworth *The Absentee* 1812
'Keep your nose out of the kitchen, young man, if
you please,' said the agent's cook shutting the door
in lord Colambre's face. – 'There's the way to the
office, if you've money to pay, up the back stairs.'

on the nose
1 *informal, NAmer* precisely, exactly: *cf* on the
BUTTON. *Mid 20th cent.*

John Parker *The Joker's Wild: Biography of Jack*
Nicholson 1991
'That is the greatest script I have ever read. I think
Fellini wrote it.' 'Are you serious?' Nicholson
replied. 'You really understand it?' 'Understand
every single word,' said Fonda. 'It's right on the
nose.'
2 *Australian and NZ, informal* bad-smelling, offensive. *Mid 20th cent.*

Barry Humphries *Bazza Pulls It Off* 1971
Excuse I not shakin' hands sport but me mits are
pretty much on the nose.
3 (said of payment) immediate. *Mid 20th cent.*

M Cole *The Ladykiller* 1993
Now how about I take you to a doctor I know in
Swiss Cottage. Payment on the nose and no ques-
tions asked. How's that?

pay through the nose
to pay an exorbitant amount. The phrase is commonly associated with the so-called 'nose tax'
imposed by the Danes in Ireland, non-payment
of which was punished by having the nose slit;
but it is hard to explain the gap of several centuries between these historical circumstances and
the earliest uses of the phrase, which is first
found in 1672 in Andrew Marvell's mock-biblical
prose work *The Rehearsal Transpros'd* ('Made
them pay for it most unconscionably and through
the nose'). *17th cent.*

Thomas Brown *A Ballad on the Times* 1698
We pay through the nose, | For subjecting of Foes;
| But, for all our expences, | Get nothing but
blows.

Fanny Burney *Cecilia* 1782
As to a lady, let her be worth never so much, she's a
mere nobody, as one may say, till she can get herself
a husband, being she knows nothing of business,
and is made to pay for everything through the nose.

poke/thrust one's nose into something
to interfere in somebody else's affairs: literally to
thrust one's face into a place out of curiosity or to
make one's presence known. *17th cent.*

Thomas D'Urfey *The Rise and Fall of Massaniello*
1700
How comes it now good Mrs. Sprat, | You are so
impudent of late? | T' endeavour to forestall my
wares, | And thrust your nose in my affairs, |
What is't you would be at?

put somebody's nose out of joint
informal to offend or disconcert somebody; to
displace somebody from a position of regard or
affection. *16th cent.*

Francis Kirkman *The Unlucky Citizen* 1673
My mother being dead, it was not two months
before my father was re-married, and then was my
nose out of joynt, for although my father by his
marriage imbettered himself, and leaving off his

trade became a gentleman, yet I was miserable and more a slave than ever.

thumb one's nose

to show disrespect or contempt: literally by putting the thumb against the end of the nose and extending the fingers. Also in variant forms. *19th cent.*

> Edgar Allan Poe *Never Bet the Devil Your Head* 1841
> *Then, applying his thumb to his nose, he thought proper to make an indescribable movement with the rest of his fingers.*

> James Whitcomb Riley *Complete Works* 1916
> *And he thumbed his nose at the old gray mare, | And hid hisse'f in the house somewhere.*

turn up one's nose (at somebody/something)

to toss one's head back in anger or contempt; more generally, to reject something with studied superciliousness. *19th cent.*

> Byron *Don Juan* 1819
> *The Senhor Don Alfonso stood confused; | Antonia bustles round the ransacked room, | And, turning up her nose, with looks abused | Her master, and his myrmidons.*

> Robert B Brough *Camaralzaman and Badoura* 1848
> *Though suitors approach her again and again, | She turns up her nose at each Jack man.*

under somebody's nose

(said especially of wrongdoing) committed in open defiance of a person present or nearby. *16th cent.*

> John Heywood *Woorkes* 1562
> *All folke thought them not onely to lyther [= too wicked], | To lynger bothe in one house togyther. | But also dwellyng ny (= nigh) under their wyngs, | Under their noses, they might convey thinges, | Suche as were neither to heavie nor to whot [= hot]. | More in a month then [= than] they their maister got | In a whole yere.*

win by a nose

to win by a small margin. The image is from horseracing, in which the horse's nose is a measure of short distance. *Early 20th cent.*

with one's nose in the air

acting with haughty arrogance. *17th cent.*

> William Wycherley *The Gentleman Dancing-Master* 1673
> *And your Spanish hose, and your nose in the air, make you look like a great grisled long Irish greyhound, reaching a crust off from a high shelf, ha, ha, ha.*

> Mark Twain *The Adventures of Tom Sawyer* 1876
> *He carried his exploits to her immediate vicinity; came war-whooping around, snatched a boy's cap, hurled it to the roof of the school-house, broke through a group of boys, tumbling them in every direction, and fell sprawling, himself, under Becky's nose, almost upsetting her – and she turned, with her nose in the air, and he heard her say. 'Mf! some people think they're mighty smart – always showing off!'*

See also (as) PLAIN as day / as the nose on your face; FOLLOW one's nose; keep one's nose to the GRINDSTONE; lead somebody by the nose *at* LEAD[1]; RUB somebody's nose in something.

---

nosebag

hand in one's nosebag

informal to die: a humorous metaphor from horsebreeding. *20th cent.*

---

not

See not in my back YARD; not HALF; not (in) the LEAST; not LEAST.

---

note

hit/strike the wrong note

to act or speak in an inappropriate or inapposite way. *19th cent.*

> Henry James *The Europeans* 1878
> *The Baroness turned her smile toward him, and she instantly felt that she had been observed to be fibbing. She had struck a false note. But who were these people to whom such fibbing was not pleasing?*

strike/sound a — note / a note of —

to introduce into a conversation or situation a tone or atmosphere of the kind described. *19th cent.*

> Dickens *Bleak House* 1853
> *As they ascend the dim stairs ... Mr. Bucket mentions that he has the key of the outer door in his pocket, and that there is no need to ring. For a man so expert in most things of that kind, Bucket takes time to open the door, and makes some noise too. It may be that he sounds a note of preparation.*

take note (of something)
to pay attention (to something). *16th cent.*

Shakespeare *The Merchant of Venice* v.i.120 (1598)
[Portia] *Go in, Nerissa. | Give order to my ser-*
vants that they take | No note at all of our being
absent hence; | Nor you, Lorenzo; Jessica, nor you.

nothing

be (as) nothing (compared) to something
to be unimportant or trivial compared with
something else. *18th cent.*

Adam Smith *The Wealth of Nations* 1776
Those who consider the blood of the people as
nothing in comparison with the revenue of the
prince, may perhaps approve of this method of
levying taxes.

come to nothing
(said of a plan or course of action) to fail; to have
no good result. *16th cent.*

Henry Chettle *The Forrest of Fancy* 1579
Were he never so subtle witted or indued with never
so great abundance, one way or other al [= all] wold
quickly go to wrack, & come to nothing.

Jane Austen *Mansfield Park* 1814
Mrs. Norris began to look about her, and wonder
that his falling in love with Julia had come to
nothing.

have nothing on
1 to be wearing no clothes, to be naked. *18th cent.*

Daniel Defoe *Robinson Crusoe* 1719
Then I called a council, that is to say, in my
thoughts, whether I should take back the raft, but
this appeared impracticable; so I resolved to go as
before, when the tide was down: and I did so, only
that I stripped before I went from my hut, having
nothing on but a checkered shirt and a pair of linen
drawers, and a pair of pumps on my feet.

2 *informal* to be free of commitments. *Early 20th
cent.*

have nothing on —
1 to be noticeably inferior to a particular person
or thing. *Early 20th cent.*

2 *see* HAVE something/nothing on somebody.

have nothing to do with somebody/some-
thing
1 (said of a person) to avoid any dealings with a
particular person or thing. *17th cent.*

Shakespeare *King Lear* ii.ii.32 (1606)
[Oswald to Kent] *Away. I have nothing to do with*
thee. [Kent] *Draw, you rascal.*

2 (said of a matter) to have no connection with a
particular person or thing. *17th cent.*

Locke *Essay Concerning Human Knowledge* 1690
This source of ideas every man has wholly in him-
self; and though it be not sense, as having nothing to
do with external objects, yet it is very like it, and
might properly enough be called internal sense.

3 (said of a matter) to be no concern of a particular person, to be aware of their business. *20th cent.*

Alice T Ellis *Pillars of Gold* 1993
In a way you're right, I suppose. If she's dead
somewhere else, it's got nothing to do with us, but if
she's dead on our doorstep, we ought to do
something.

make/think nothing of something
in current use generally with *think*, although *make*
is the older form.

1 to despise or belittle something. *17th cent.*

2 to be undaunted by a task or activity that might
generally be regarded as daunting or challenging: often followed by a verbal noun in -*ing*.
17th cent.

Cotton Mather *Of Beelzebub and His Plots* 1693
He was a very puny man, yet he had often done
things beyond the strength of a giant. A gun of
about seven foot barrel, and so heavy that strong
men could not steadily hold it out with both hands;
there were several testimonies … that he made
nothing of taking up such a gun behind the lock
with but one hand, and holding it out like a pistol at
arms-end.

nothing doing
informal nothing much is happening or likely to
happen: also used in declining to accept or agree
to something. A development from earlier uses of
be doing with reference to business being conducted. *19th cent.*

R H Dana *Two Years Before the Mast* 1840
Several times, in the course of the night, I got up,
determined to go on deck; but the silence which
showed that there was nothing doing … kept me
back.

nothing if not —
above all; very definitely the type of person or
thing described. *17th cent.*

Shakespeare *Othello* II.i.122 (1604)
[Iago to Desdemona] *O, gentle lady, do not put me to't,* | *For I am nothing if not critical.*

nothing less than

entirely, completely; quite equal to. In earlier use the phrase also had the virtually opposite meaning 'far from being', with *nothing* more closely attached to the preceding statement than to the following *less*, as in *they expected nothing less than* [*they expected*] *an attack*; this use is no longer current. *16th cent.*

Shakespeare *1 Henry VI* II.v.100 (1590)
[Richard] *But yet methinks my father's execution* | *Was nothing less than bloody tyranny.*

stop/stick at nothing

to be prepared to take any action, however wrong or dishonest, to achieve one's ends; to act unscrupulously. *17th cent.*

Aphra Behn *Love-Letters Between a Noble-Man and His Sister* 1687
No, she would on to all the revenges her youth and beauty were capable of taking, and stick at nothing that led to that interest.

sweet nothings

humorous affectionate or sentimental exchanges whispered between lovers. *Early 20th cent.*

Marti Caine *A Coward's Chronicles* 1990
The bed was comfortable and so large you had to shout sweet nothings.

(there is) nothing (else) for it (but)

there is no alternative to a risky or desperate course of action proposed. *18th cent.*

Laurence Sterne *Tristram Shandy* 1760
As I perceived the commissary of the post-office would have his six livres four sous, I had nothing else for it, but to say some smart thing upon the occasion, worth the money.

(there is) nothing to it

informal it is very easy or straightforward. *Mid 20th cent.*

to say nothing of —

without even mentioning (another case in point): used rhetorically to draw attention to a further point in an argument by seeming to dismiss it. *Mid 20th cent.*

Robert Crawford *The Savage and the City in the Work of T S Eliot* 1990
And until we set in order our own crazy economic and financial systems, to say nothing of our philosophy of life, can we be sure that our helping hands to the barbarian and the savage will be any more desirable than the embrace of the leper?

you ain't seen nothing yet

there are many more exciting things to come: an alteration of the Al Jolson song 'You ain't heard nothing yet' (1919; also featured in the film *The Jazz Singer*, 1927). Popularized (with *seen*) by Ronald Reagan during his successful campaign for re-election to the American presidency in 1984. *Early 20th cent.*

See also like nothing on (God's) EARTH; nothing daunted *at* DAUNT; nothing LOATH; nothing to WRITE home about; not leave much / leave nothing to the IMAGINATION; (there is) nothing IN it.

notice

at short / a moment's notice

with little or no warning. *18th cent.*

Ann Radcliffe *The Italian* 1797
Yet he gave orders, that preparation should be made for his setting out at a moment's notice.

Jane Austen *Emma* 1816
Your inexperience really amuses me! A situation such as you deserve, and your friends would require for you, is no everyday occurrence, is not obtained at a moment's notice.

put somebody on notice / serve notice on somebody

to warn somebody of something (usually unpleasant or unwelcome) that is likely to affect them: an extension of the meaning relating to formal notification of a requirement to perform an obligation. *19th cent.*

Disraeli *Sybil* 1845
'I think one of the greatest grievances the people have,' said Caroline, 'is the beaks serving notice on Chaffing Jack to shut up the Temple on Sunday nights.'

take notice

to consider a matter or give one's attention to it. *See also* SIT up (and take notice). *16th cent.*

Shakespeare *Henry VIII* i.i.101 (1613)
[Norfolk to Buckingham] *Like it your Grace, |
The state takes notice of the private difference |
Betwixt you and the Cardinal.*

now

now or never
used to express urgency. *16th cent.*

Shakespeare *2 Henry VI* iii.i.331 (1591)
[York] *Now, York, or never, steel thy fearful
thoughts.*

nowhere

See the MIDDLE of nowhere.

nudge

a nudge and a wink
a gesture of coy or covert encouragement: in
literal use, a nudge or slight dig in the side
accompanying a winking of the eye as a signal
of covert or conspiratorial association. *20th cent.*

Fiona Pitt-Kethley *Misfortunes of Nigel* 1991
*He wrote to Eleanor. He got her address from his
editor, who handed it to him with a nudge and a
wink. 'Sounds like a bit of a raver from her stories,'
he said.*

nudge nudge
used as a coy or humorous reference to sexual
innuendo in a statement just made: popularized
by its use (in the form *nudge, nudge, wink wink, say
no more*) in the British television comedy programme *Monty Python's Flying Circus*, first broadcast in the late 1960s. *Late 20th cent.*

New Musical Express 1992
*Lesley still has to deal with idiot boy hecklers:
'Women cannot express their sexuality freely in any
area of life, especially in popular music. Basically,
because yer average gig-goer is still stuck in the
'wink wink, nudge nudge' mentality of the '70s.*

See also dig/nudge/poke somebody in the ribs *at*
RIB.

nuff

See ENOUGH said.

nuisance

make a nuisance of oneself
to behave in a way that annoys people or causes
trouble. *19th cent.*

Louisa M Alcott *Hospital Sketches* 1869
*If John had been a gentlemanly creature, with
refined tastes, he would have elevated his feet, and
made a nuisance of himself by indulging in a 'weed'.*

John Steinbeck *The Grapes of Wrath* 1939
*For a long time he won't have nothin' to say to
nobody. Just walks aroun' like he don't see nothin'
an' he prays some. Took 'im two years to come out of
it, an' then he ain't the same. Sort of wild. Made a
damn nuisance of hisself.*

number

by numbers
following instructions in a mechanical or
unimaginative way. An early use of the phrase
was in *paint by numbers* = paint on a prepared
canvas on which the choice of colours is indicated
by numbers, but more recent use has been in the
context of education and the whole debate about
standards and 'dumbing down'. *Late 20th cent.*

Tim Brighouse et al *Managing the National Curriculum* 1991
*The last thing we want is teaching by numbers,
reducing learning to a series of mechanistic measured units.*

—'s days are numbered
a particular person or thing is not likely to survive for long: based on an older notion of human
beings' days being numbered, i.e. their lives
being limited to a preordained length. *19th cent.*

R L Stevenson *The Strange Case of Dr Jekyll and Mr
Hyde* 1886
*My life is shaken to its roots; sleep has left me; the
deadliest terror sits by me at all hours of the day and
night; I feel that my days are numbered, and that I
must die.*

do/lay a number on somebody
NAmer, informal, especially Black slang to criticize
or humiliate somebody openly. *Mid 20th cent.*

have somebody's number
to understand somebody's real motives or intentions. *19th cent.*

Dickens *Bleak House* 1853
Whenever a person proclaims to you 'In worldly matters I'm a child,' you consider that that person is only a-crying off from being held accountable, and that you have got that person's number, and it's Number One.

one's number is up
one is doomed: based on the notion of a person being chosen at random to perform some unpleasant task when their number is drawn. *19th cent.*

Somerset Maugham *Of Human Bondage* 1915
In the examination room Philip was seized with panic, and failed to give right answers to questions from a sudden fear that they might be wrong. He knew he was ploughed and did not even trouble to go up to the building the next day to see whether his number was up.

take care of / look after number one
to put one's own interests first: based on *number one* = the first person, i.e. oneself. *18th cent.*

Mrs Hannah Cowley *A Day in Turkey* 1792
[Paulina] Oh, Peter, how could we run away, and leave our father? [Peter] Why, we only took care of number one, and we have a right to do that all the world over.

Dickens *Oliver Twist* 1838
It's your object to take care of number one – meaning yourself.

without number
too many to know the number; innumerable. *17th cent.*

Hobbes *Leviathan* 1651
But they that venture to reason of His nature, from these attributes of honour, losing their understanding in the very first attempt, fall from one inconvenience into another, without end and without number.

See also a BACK number; have somebody's NAME/ number on it; public ENEMY number one.

---

nut

In some phrases *nut* is used in its slang meaning 'the head', which dates from the mid 19th cent.

do one's nut
informal to become suddenly angry: in early use also *do the nut. Early 20th cent.*

the nuts and bolts
the basic practical issues of a situation. *Late 20th cent.*

David Oates & Derek Ezra *Advice from the Top* 1989
Sir Adrian Cadbury is not one of those who subscribes to the popular theory that a truly professional manager can take over the helm of any type of business with only a superficial knowledge of the nuts and bolts.

off one's nut
informal out of one's mind; crazy: also entered in a slang glossary of 1860 in the sense 'drunk'. *19th cent.*

Kipling *Limits and Renewals* 1928
If I pull the string of the shower-bath in the papers … Castorley might go off his veray parfit gentil nut.

a tough/hard nut to crack
informal a difficult problem to solve or person to deal with: *tough nut* in the sense of a difficult or obstinate person dates from the middle of the 19th cent. *Late 20th cent.*

Bill Millin *Invasion* 1991
I had a very deep feeling that the attack on the village by the Black Watch was not going to be successful due to the fact that the enemy were well dug in and were determined to hold on to this position. It was a tough nut to crack.

See also take/use a SLEDGEHAMMER to crack a nut.

---

nuts

be nuts about / *British* on somebody/something
informal to be very keen on or enthusiastic about somebody or something. The phrase first appears in slang glossaries compiled about the turn of the 18th–19th cent.: Francis Grose's *Classical Dictionary of the Vulgar Tongue* (1785) and James H Vaux's *Vocabulary of the Flash Language* (the work of a criminal deported to Australia, published there as an appendix to memoirs in 1812). *18th cent.*

J R Planché *Polly Connor* from *Songs and Poems* 1881
Pretty girl was Polly Connor, | When first I met her years ago; | I was awful 'spoons' upon her, | She was nuts on me, I know.

John Steinbeck *Of Mice and Men* 1937
'We gonna have a little place,' Lennie explained patiently. 'We gonna have a house an' a garden and

a place for alfalfa, an' that alfalfa is for the rabbits, an' I take a sack and get it all fulla alfalfa and then I take it to the rabbits.' She asked, 'What makes you so nuts about rabbits?'

not be able to do something for nuts

informal to be completely inept at doing something. *Nuts* are a stereotype for anything trivial or worthless. *See also* not be able to do something for TOFFEE. *19th cent.*

> Conan Doyle *The Missing Three-Quarter* 1904
> *He's a fine place-kick, it's true, but then he has no judgment, and he can't sprint for nuts.*

nutshell

in a nutshell

in a few words; in essence. The nutshell has been symbolic of smallness from an early date: in Shakespeare's *Hamlet* (1601) Hamlet tells Rosencrantz (II.ii.256) 'O God, I could be bounded in a nutshell and count myself a king of infinite space, were it not that I have bad dreams.' *19th cent.*

> Wilkie Collins *The Haunted Hotel* 1879
> *She held up her hand for silence, and finished the second tumbler of maraschino punch. 'I am a living enigma – and you want to know the right reading of me,' she said. 'Here is the reading, as your English phrase goes, in a nutshell.'*

nutty

(as) nutty as a fruitcake

informal utterly crazy: *nutty* in the meaning 'crazy' dates from the late 19th cent. (compare *nuts, off one's nut*, etc). *Mid 20th cent.*

> *Climber and Hillwalker* 1991
> *He visited Nepal in 1984 to attempt the traverse of Makalu … They had been above 8000 metres for several days and Steve recalls being as 'nutty as a fruit-cake'.*

oar

rest on one's oars

to lessen one's efforts; to relax. The image is of rowers leaning on their oars, thereby bringing the blades out of the water. *18th cent.*

> Caroline M Kirkland *Forest Life* 1850
> *In truth I, who am obliged almost to rest on my oars, look at John's rapid progress with a feeling akin to envy.*

stick/poke/put one's oar in

to interfere, especially by giving an opinion that is not asked for: originally in the form *put one's oar in another man's boat*, which explains the allusion more fully. Transitional uses with *concerns, business*, etc replacing *boat* date from the early 18th cent. The phrase is 18th cent. in its current forms.

> Charles Coffey *The Devil to Pay* 1731
> *I will govern my own House without your putting in an oar.*

> W H Ireland *All the Blocks* 1807
> *So tacitly will I the Satire heed; | And merely put my oar in, when there's need.*

> Dickens *Pickwick Papers* 1837
> *You've hit it. The gen'l'm'n as wrote it wos a tellin' all about the misfortun' in a proper vay, and then my father comes a lookin' over him, and complicates the whole concern by puttin' his oar in.*

oat

feel one's oats

NAmer, informal to feel full of energy; to be full of oneself. The image is of a horse feeding; the expression had disapproving overtones in early use, which have since largely disappeared. *19th cent.*

Herman Melville *Bartleby* 1853
*I verily believe that buttoning himself up in so
downy and blanketlike a coat had a pernicious effect
upon him – upon the same principle that too much
oats are bad for horses. In fact, precisely as a rash,
restive horse is said to feel his oats, so Turkey felt his
coat. It made him insolent. He was a man whom
prosperity harmed.*

get/have one's oats
British, *informal* to have sexual intercourse. *Early
20th cent.*

off one's oats
informal having no appetite for food. *19th cent.*

sow one's wild oats
to enjoy the excesses of youth, before settling
down to a steady life: with allusion to mischief
caused by the wild oat, which differs from the
cultivated variety and harms it if they are mixed.
The image of sowing seeds has obvious sexual
connotations, and the futility of sowing worthless or even harmful types of seed is also strongly
present as a notion. *16th cent.*

Thomas Newton *Lemnie's Touchstone of Complexions*
1576
*That wilfull and vnruly age, which lacketh rypenes
and discretion, and (as wee saye) hath not sowed all
theyr wyeld oates.*

James Shirley *The Constant Maid* 1640
*[Close] Of wild oats; I heard you had much | To
sow still.*

object

be no object
(usually said of a cost or expense) to present no
problem; to be no limiting factor in reaching a
decision: often with the verb suppressed, e.g.
money no object. 18th cent.

Edmund Burke *Reflections on the Revolution in France*
1798
*With them it is a sufficient motive to destroy an old
scheme of things because it is an old one. As to the
new, they are in no sort of fear with regard to the
duration of a building run up in haste, because
duration is no object to those who think little or
nothing has been done before their time, and who
place all their hopes in discovery.*

Occam

Occam's razor
a scientific principle that explanations should
include as little reference as possible to things
that are not known for certain (Latin *entia non
sunt multiplicanda praeter necessitatem*, literally
'things should not be multiplied beyond what
is necessary'): named after the English scholastic
philosopher William of Ockham (Latinized as
Occam; 1285–1349) with whom this maxim was
associated, although it does not appear in this
form in any of his extant writing and there is a
gap of several centuries before its first recorded
occurrences. *19th cent.*

Sir William Hamilton *Lectures on Metaphysics* 1837
*This is the law of parcimony, which forbids, without
necessity, the multiplication of entities … where a
known impotence can account for the effect. We are,
therefore, entitled to apply Occam's razor to this
theory of causality.*

occasion
See RISE to the occasion.

odd

odd one/man out
somebody or something that differs in some
respect from all the others in a set or group; an
exception to the general rule: originally used of a
method of picking one person from a group for a
certain role, forfeit, etc. *19th cent.*

Philip James Bailey *The Age* 1858
Ten million men toss; he's the odd man out.

odds

ask no odds
NAmer, informal to seek no favours. *17th cent.*

John Ford *Love's Sacrifice* 1633
*[Duke] I see th'art arm'd; prepare, I craue no odds,
| Greater then is the iustice of my cause.*

Emerson Bennett *Kate Clarendon* 1848
*'Set me free, is all I ask,' growled Moody. 'And thou
wilt seek my aid no more!' returned Luther. 'I never
did seek it,' grumbled Moody; 'and once free again, I
will ask no odds of any.'*

at odds with somebody/something

in disagreement or at variance with somebody or something. In early (16th cent.) use *at odds* also meant 'different, unequal'. *Odds* is used in the sense 'dissension, disagreement' and is now chiefly confined in this meaning to the phrase, but *cf* Shakespeare, *Othello* (1604) II.iii.85, where Iago tells Othello of the brawl between Cassio and Roderigo: 'I cannot speak | Any beginning to this peevish odds, | And would in action glorious I had lost | Those legs that brought me to a part of it.' *16th cent.*

Nahum Tate *Cuckolds-Haven* 1685
[Security] *The Farmer is ever at odds with the weather, sometimes the Clouds are barren, their Harvests are too thin; sometimes the Season is too fruitful, and Corn will bear no Price.*

Laurence Sterne *Tristram Shandy* 1765
This is not a distinction without a difference. It is not like the affair of an old hat cocked – and a cocked old hat, about which your reverences have so often been at odds with one another – but there is a difference here in the nature of things.

by all odds

NAmer by a long way. *19th cent.*

Herman Melville *Moby Dick* 1851
For not only are whalemen as a body unexempt from that ignorance and superstitiousness hereditary to all sailors; but of all sailors, they are by all odds the most directly brought into contact with whatever is appallingly astonishing in the sea; face to face they not only eye its greatest marvels, but, hand to jaw, give battle to them.

give/lay odds

to be sure that something is the case: in betting, giving or laying odds denotes odds that are favourable to the person making the bet. *16th cent.*

Shakespeare *2 Henry IV* v.v.103 (1597)
[Prince John] *I will lay odds that, ere this year expire, | We bear our civil swords and native fire | As far as France.*

it is/makes no odds

it does not matter, it makes no difference. *17th cent.*

Shakespeare *Timon of Athens* I.ii.59 (1609)
Here's that which is too weak to be a sinner: | Honest water, which ne'er left man i' th' mire. | This and my food are equals; there's no odds.

odds and ends

miscellaneous items and remnants. The phrase is perhaps based on *odd ends*, which is recorded in the same sense at an earlier date. *End* here is used in its meaning 'a remnant or piece cut off'. *18th cent.*

John Galt *Annals of the Parish* 1821
Hers, however, was but a harmless vanity; and, poor woman, she needed all manner of graces to set her out, for she was made up of odds and ends, and had but one good eye, the other being blind, and just like a blue bead.

odds and sods

informal in services' slang, men attached to a battalion for miscellaneous duties; now used generally as a variant of *odds and ends*. *Mid 20th cent.*

Roger Garfitt *The Hooded Gods* 1989
These are the odds and sods among the gods, the other ranks, the omnipresences, teamen, charmen, male midwives.

over the odds

more than is right, fair, or acceptable. *Early 20th cent.*

Kingsley Amis *A Reunion* 1979
Thirty years ago | Jim had been Sergeant Woods, | The chap you did well to know | If you wanted some over-the-odds | Bit of kit, travel warrant, repair.

shout the odds

informal to speak loudly and in an opinionated manner: originally services' slang. *Early 20th cent.*

D M Jones *The Dream of Private Clitus* 1974
Some say he was born shouting the odds, in full parade kit, with a pacing-stick under his cherubic little arm.

what's the odds?

1 what difference does it make? *19th cent.*

Dickens *Oliver Twist* 1838
'Look here!' said the Dodger, drawing forth a handful of shillings and half-pence. 'Here's a jolly life! What's the odds where it comes from?'

2 what is the likelihood (of such-and-such happening)? *20th cent.*

odour

be in good/bad odour with somebody

to be in (or out of) somebody's favour. *19th cent.*

R L Stevenson *Kidnapped* 1886
*I saw four travellers come into view … The third
was a servant, and wore some part of his clothes in
tartan, which showed that his master was of a
Highland family, and either an outlaw or else in
singular good odour with the Government, since the
wearing of tartan was against the Act.*

the odour of sanctity
an atmosphere of sanctimoniousness: originally a
state of holiness, translating French *odeur de sain-
teté*, and based on the medieval belief that the
bodies of holy persons gave off a sweet odour
when they died. *17th cent.*

Anon *Eve Revived* 1684
*It was only a Relique filled with Blessed Bran, being
the same which a certain Hermite was used to make
his Bread of, who Lived near Lyons in a great Odour
of Sanctity.*

James Joyce *A Portrait of the Artist as a Young Man*
1916
*His very body had waxed old in lowly service of the
Lord – in tending the fire upon the altar, in bearing
tidings secretly, in waiting upon worldlings, in
striking swiftly when bidden – and yet had
remained ungraced by aught of saintly or of prelatic
beauty. Nay, his very soul had waxed old in that
service without growing towards light and beauty
or spreading abroad a sweet odour of her sanctity.*

off

badly/well off
in poor (or good) circumstances. These are now
the most common uses (along with comparatives
and superlatives *better, best, worse, worst*, etc) of *off*
in a sense that formerly had many more adverb
collocates (e.g. *sadly off, miserably off, how are you
off?*, etc). In modern use the sense is predominantly financial, and the phrase is equivalent to
'poor' or 'wealthy', but in 18th cent. and 19th
cent. use the sense applied to social conditions
more generally. *18th cent.*

Ann Radcliffe *The Romance of the Forest* 1791
*'Let us be gone,' said the ruffian, 'and have no more
of this nonsense; you may think yourself well off it's
no worse.'*

Jane Austen *Emma* 1816
*As for objects of interest, objects for the affections …
the want of which is really the great evil to be
avoided in not marrying, I shall be very well off,*

*with all the children of a sister I love so much, to
care about.*

off and on / on and off
from time to time; intermittently: *off and on* is the
earlier form, its reverse not being attested until
the middle of the 19th cent. *16th cent.*

Samuel Rowlands *A Merry Fooles Bolts* 1614
*At last a Fly lights on his Maisters nose: | Wherat
he chafes, and sayes, you had best be gone, | But
still the Flye playd with him off, and on.*

Henry Neville *Plato Redivivus* 1681
*A bloody War ensued, for almost forty years, off and
on.*

offence
See a hanging offence *at* HANG.

office

good offices
a beneficial service or action carried out for
another person: used earlier in the singular,
this being the oldest meaning of *office*, analogous
to that of the Latin source *officium*. *17th cent.*

Richard Belling *A Sixthe Booke to the Countesse of
Pembrokes Arcadia* 1624
*Thus I lay, deerly purchasing the little ease of my
bodie with the affliction of my minde, untill mine
eares like faithfull servants, desirous to end this
dissension between their Master and himselfe,
caus'd all the powers of my mind to joine in
attentivenes: and mine eies, loath to be out-gone in
such good offices, did look that way from whence the
noise came.*

Swift *Gulliver's Travels* 1726
*He ordered his coach to wait at a distance, and
desired I would give him an hour's audience; which
I readily consented to, on account of his quality and
personal merits, as well as the many good offices he
had done me during my solicitations at court.*

official

and that's official
informal used as an end-of-sentence tag in conversation and informal writing to add authority
to a statement or assertion. *Mid 20th cent.*

Best 1991
Ten per cent of Britons profess to eating meat only rarely and nearly 50 per cent agreed that they eat much less than they used to. And that's official according to recent figures from the National Health Survey.

offing

in the offing
likely to happen in the near future; imminent. The *offing* in nautical language is the part of the deep sea visible from the shore or anchoring ground. The earliest evidence of a figurative use is in a letter of Josiah Wedgwood written in 1779, where the phrase refers to the more distant future ('but that is at present in the offing'). Some 19th cent. uses refer to spatial location rather than time (as in the 1823 quotation below) and are therefore intermediate in sense between the nautical meaning and the current one; the first uses that are clearly of the current meaning date from the turn of the 19th–20th cent. *18th cent.*

James Fenimore Cooper *The Pioneers* 1823
As he was sheering nearer, every stretch he made towards the house, I could do no better than to let your honor know that the chap was in the offing.

H V Esmond *The Law Divine* 1922
[Ted] (He gives a squeal of delight as he sees the table) *Pop! there's fizz in the offing.*

oil

no oil painting
British, informal (usually said of a person) physically plain or unattractive. *Mid 20th cent.*

J B Priestley *Angel Pavement* 1930
'Member him, Edna? – teeth sticking out a yard, and all cross-eyed ... Still, we can't all be oil paintings.

oil and water
two people or things that do not mix well together. *19th cent.*

Edgar Allan Poe *Criticism* 1831
Now, had this court of inquiry been in possession of even the shadow of the philosophy of Verse, they would have had no trouble in reconciling this oil and water of the eye and ear, by merely scanning the passage without reference to lines ... continuously.

oil the wheels
to improve progress and efficiency; to make things work more smoothly. The phrase is often used in extended metaphor, as in the second quotation below. *18th cent.*

Barnabas Bidwell *The Mercenary Match* 1784
[Major Shapely] *For gold does any thing, and every thing;* | *It makes the Lawyer plead, the Parson preach,* | *The Merchant trade, the Doctor tend the sick,* | *And Politicians oil the wheels of state.*

Lydia M Child *Hobomok* 1824
Recreation is no doubt good to oil the wheels as we travel along a rugged road; but a wise man will do as Jonathan, who only tasted a little honey on the end of his rod.

pour oil on troubled waters
to try to bring calm to a troubled situation. E Cobham Brewer, the editor of *A Dictionary of Phrase and Fable*, wrote in one of his regular contributions to the journal *Notes & Queries* (October 1884, p.307): 'I have myself had more letters on the subject than any other.' The origin of the phrase, as recorded by Brewer in *Phrase and Fable*, lies in the physical phenomenon whereby stormy waves subside when oil is poured on them. The practice was a topic of discussion by the Royal Society in 1774, leading some to postulate that this gave rise to the phrase, or at least that the origin of the phrase must be later than the discussion. But similar maritime phenomena are recorded at much earlier dates: for example, the Roman scholar and natural historian Pliny (1st cent. AD) wrote that 'all seas are made calm and still with oil' (*Natural History* ii.103). The phrase also occurs in an earlier form *pour oil on the waves*, and is commonly associated with a story about St Aidan in the writings of the early English historian Bede: Aidan encountered a young priest who was escorting a maiden to be the bride of King Oswy, and gave the priest a cruse of oil to pour on the waves if the sea became rough. There was indeed a storm and the priest made good use of the oil, as he had been told. A similar story is told in a modified form about St Nicholas, the 4th cent. Bishop of Myra. *See also* FISH in troubled waters. *19th cent.*

Charles Kingsley *Westward Ho!* 1855
He could hear voices high in dispute; Parsons as usual, blustering; Mr. Leigh peevishly deprecating,

and Campian, who was really the sweetest-natured of men, trying to pour oil on the troubled waters. See also BURN the midnight oil.

---

old

for old times' sake
as an acknowledgement of pleasant shared experiences (see the old days/times below).

of the old school
having traditional values or attitudes; old-fashioned. 18th cent.

Maria Edgeworth Belinda 1801
I am of the old school, and though I could dispense with the description of Miss Harriet Byron's worked chairs and fine china, yet I own, I like to hear something of the preparation for a marriage, as well as of the mere wedding.

the old days/times
former times, especially when regarded nostalgically or as significantly different from the present. Often qualified by good or bad, and in the phrase for old times' sake (see above). 17th cent.

Francis Bacon Essays 1601
They that reverence too much old times, are but a scorn to the new.

Jane Austen Emma 1816
He saw no fault in the room ... It was long enough, broad enough, handsome enough. It would hold the very number for comfort. They ought to have balls there at least every fortnight through the winter. Why had not Miss Woodhouse revived the former good old days of the room? – She who could do any thing in Highbury!

old enough to be —'s father
considerably older than the person concerned: usually with the implication that a supposed romantic relationship is unlikely or inappropriate. 18th cent.

Sheridan The School for Scandal 1777
[Charles Surface] Why, look'ee, Joseph, I hope I shall never deliberately do a dishonourable action; but if a pretty woman was purposely to throw herself in my way – and that pretty woman married to a man old enough to be her father – [Joseph Surface] Well! [Charles Surface] Why, I believe I should be obliged to borrow a little of your morality, that's all.

an old head on young shoulders
a young person who has the knowledge and experience of a much older one. The notion occurs famously in Shakespeare's The Merchant of Venice (1598), where the Duke reads Bellario's letter introducing Balthasar (Portia in disguise, IV.i.160): 'I beseech you let his lack of years be no impediment to let him lack a reverend estimation, for I never knew so young a body with so old a head.' In 20th cent. literature the phrase formed the motto, along with the crème de la crème, of Muriel Spark's progressive Edinburgh schoolmistress Jean Brodie: 'The Brodie set was left to their secret life as it had been six years ago in their childhood. "I am putting old heads on your young shoulders," Miss Brodie had told them at that time, "and all my pupils are the crème de la crème."' (The Prime of Miss Jean Brodie, 1961). 16th cent.

H Smith Preparative for Marriage 1591
It is not good grafting of an olde head upon young shoulders.

Dickens The Cricket on the Hearth 1845
Its chirp was such a welcome to me! It seemed so full of promise and encouragement. It seemed to say, you would be kind and gentle with me, and would not expect (I had a fear of that, John, then) to find an old head on the shoulders of your foolish little wife.

an old one
a well-known and much repeated joke, excuse, etc. 19th cent.

National Police Gazette (US) 1881
The gold brick swindle is an old one but it crops up constantly ... The bar, or brick as it is called ... is really of base metal. One corner, however, is of gold.

the old school tie
class distinction or favour: based on the notion of the tie of a public school as a symbol of social privilege. Mid 20th cent.

Ted Hughes Lupercal 1960
Predictably, Parliament | Squared against the motion. As soon | Let the old school tie be rent | Off their necks, and give thanks, as see gone | No shame but a monument – | Trafalgar not better known.

See also (as) old as the hills at HILL; come the old SOLDIER; make old bones at BONE; the old ADAM; the old boy NETWORK; old SPANISH customs/practices; an old wives' tale at WIFE; PLAY the devil / Old Harry with something.

olive

hold out an olive branch

to make an offer or gesture of conciliation or goodwill to an enemy or rival: with allusion to the piece of an olive branch brought to Noah by a dove as a sign that God's anger had abated and that it was safe to leave the Ark, in the biblical account (Genesis 8:11) of the Flood. References to the olive branch as an emblem of peace date from the 14th cent.; a notable 16th cent. example is in Shakespeare, *3 Henry VI* (1591) IV.vii.34: '[George of Clarence] No Warwick, thou art worthy of the sway, | To whom the heav'ns in thy nativity | Adjudged an olive branch and laurel crown, | As likely to be blest in peace and war.' 17th cent. and 18th cent. literature is full of references to peaceable people with olive branches in their hands or in their mouths (the latter in more direct reference to the biblical origin: *beak* is sometimes incongruously used); but the phrase in its current form, with *offer*, *hold out*, etc, dates from the turn of the 18th–19th cent. *18th cent.*

> Henry Brooke *The Fool of Quality* 1766
> You must therefore promise me to carry a token to her also, as an olive branch of that peace which I want to be made between us.

> Jane Austen *Pride and Prejudice* 1813
> As a clergyman, moreover, I feel it my duty to promote and establish the blessing of peace in all families within the reach of my influence; and on these grounds I flatter myself that my present overtures of goodwill are highly commendable, and that the circumstance of my being next in the entail of Longbourn estate will be kindly overlooked on your side, and not lead you to reject the offered olive-branch.

on

be on about something

informal to be talking or behaving in an odd or unexpected way in some particular respect that invites enquiry: often in the form *what are you on about?* *Early 20th cent.*

> Marsha Rowe *So Very English* 1990
> What the bloody hell did you go an' marry me for if you wanted to go to London? You don't know what the hell you're on about, you've no idea at all.

be on at somebody

informal to nag somebody or complain incessantly to them. *Mid 20th cent.*

> Pete Silverton & Glen Matlock *I Was a Teenage Sex Pistol* 1990
> He was always on at me to become a cab driver or something. Just in case the music didn't work out.

be on to somebody

informal to have good evidence about some illicit proceeding or about somebody's intentions, especially when they are up to no good. *19th cent.*

> Stephen Crane *Blue Hotel* 1899
> The cowboy looked with admiration upon the Easterner. 'You were straight,' he said, 'You were on to that there Dutchman.'

be on to something

informal to be close to an important discovery. *19th cent.*

it's not on

informal that is not a practical or acceptable proposition. *Mid 20th cent.*

> Today 1992
> There was a stunned silence as fair-haired Watson's three elderly victims watched him being led away to start his surprise sentence. Pressure groups last night backed the judge's crackdown. A spokesman said: 'At last we have seen some action. Attacks on our old people are simply not on.'

on it

Australian, informal having a lot to drink. *Early 20th cent.*

> Truth 1908
> People who have ... been 'on it', next morning are fined 'five shillings'.

on side

supporting or contributing to the effort of a team, organization, etc. *Late 20th cent.*

> J Cartwright *Masai Dreaming* 1993
> As far as he is concerned, nobody cares how accurate our portrayal of Claudia's love life is. He cites Out of Africa. But Karen Blixen did not end up in Auschwitz, I reply. We are not making a documentary – get him on side if you can. Fifteen thousand for the research.

you're on

informal used to accept a bet or challenge. *Mid 20th cent.*

Sara Maitland *Three Times Table* 1990
'I'm only not divorced because I was never married. I have a delightful little bastard who can chaperone a long-delayed revenge match.' 'You're on.' She opened the door of the car and climbed out ... He beat her easily at chess the following week.

See also OFF and on / on and off.

---

once

(every) once in a while
from time to time; occasionally. *18th cent.*

Hannah Foster *The Coquette* 1797
It seems to me that love must stagnate, if it have not a light breeze of discord once in a while to keep it in motion.

Herman Melville *Moby Dick* 1851
Every once in a while Peleg came hobbling out of his whalebone den, roaring at the men down the hatchways, roaring up to the riggers at the mast-head, and then concluded by roaring back into his wigwam.

once a —, always a —
used to imply the permanence of (usually unfavourable) human characteristics. Famous published examples include 'Once a Jacobin always a Jacobin' (title of an article by Coleridge, 1821), 'Once a gentleman, and always a gentleman' (Dickens, *Little Dorrit*, 1857), 'Once a Catholic, always a Catholic' (in Angus Wilson, *The Wrong Set*, 1949: alluded to in the play-title *Once a Catholic* by Mary O'Malley, 1971). *18th cent.*

Dr Johnson in Boswell's *Life of Samuel Johnson* 1791
He said, foppery was never cured; it was the bad stamina of the mind, which, like those of the body, were never rectified: once a coxcomb always a coxcomb.

once (and) for all
for the final or only time; conclusively. *16th cent.*

Shakespeare *Richard II* II.ii.148 (1595)
[Green] Farewell at once – for once, for all, and ever.

once and future
used to denote a person, institution, etc that is secure and established: with allusion to the Arthurian tetralogy *The Once and Future King* (1958) by T H White, itself drawing its title from Sir Thomas Malory's *Le Morte d'Arthur* (c1485), which (xxi.7) contains a reference to the epitaph on Arthur's tomb: *Hic iacet Arthurus, rex quondam rexque futurus* 'Here lies Arthur, former king and future king'. *Mid 20th cent.*

Maureen Lipman *Thank You for Having Me* 1990
Jack sighed and glanced sideways, briefly, into the Cortina where Prince Charles and Princess Diana stared ahead obliviously, on their way to who knows where. Before he could speak, the lights changed and out of innate respect Jack remained stationary, waiting for his once and future King to go first.

once in a lifetime
(said of an opportunity or special pleasure) occurring very rarely and therefore to be made the most of. *19th cent.*

Nathaniel Hawthorne *The Scarlet Letter* 1850
It was, moreover, a separate and insulated event, to occur but once in her lifetime, and to meet which, therefore, reckless of economy, she might call up the vital strength that would have sufficed for many quiet years.

once upon a time
a formula used to introduce a story set in the remote or nebulous past, especially a fairy story or fable: also used allusively in more general contexts of former situations or circumstances regarded nostalgically. *16th cent.*

George Peele *Old Wives' Tale* 1595
Once upon a time, there was a king or a lord, or a duke.

See also once bitten (twice shy) at BITE.

---

one

be all one (to somebody)
to be a matter of indifference (to somebody). *One* is used in the sense 'the same, not different', and the phrase therefore corresponds closely to *all the same* (see SAME). *17th cent.*

William Warner *A Continuance of Albions England* 1606
Doe dandle, knock it on the head, | All one to me alive or dead.

Alexander Brome *Songs and Other Poems* 1661
Either love or say you will not, | For love or scorn's all one to me.

Jane Austen *Northanger Abbey* 1818
'It will never do. We set out a great deal too late. We had much better put it off till another day, and turn round.' 'It is all one to me,' replied Thorpe rather

angrily; and instantly turning his horse, they were on their way back to Bath.

get something in one

informal to find the right answer or solution at the first attempt: with allusion to scoring a hole in one in golf. *Mid 20th cent.*

Mike Ripley *Angel Hunt* 1991
We were in a small courtyard into which had been crammed half a dozen hutches and garden-shed-type constructions. There was also a ten-foot square pen of some sort like a small corral, made out of odd bits of timber, and in one corner, a pile of what was unmistakably manure. 'It's a frigging zoo,' I said. 'Got it in one,' said Prentice smugly.

one to/on one

involving two parties or groups coming into direct contact or opposition: an extension of the use (mid 20th cent.) in team sports to denote the balance of attacking and defending players. *One on one* is more common in American use. *Late 20th cent.*

Tom Pow *In the Palace of Serpents* 1992
I wanted to meet Peruvians and speak to them one to one.

one-stop

involving a single action, approach, etc: originally with reference to a shop that provides all a customer's needs in a particular line of goods. *Mid 20th cent.*

the one that got away

something desirable but elusive. The reference is to the proverbial excuse made by a fisherman for his failure to return home with a better catch: there was indeed a sizeable fish, which proved too large and swift to land. The phrase was later used of a person who has managed to escape capture or danger and, more facetiously, of an eligible bachelor who has remained unattached. *Early 20th cent.*

Robert Lefever *How to Combat Alcoholism & Addiction* 1988
It may appear paradoxical but the compulsive gambler may get the biggest adrenalin surge from the biggest loss and, like the proverbial fisherman, may boast of the 'one that got away'.

you are a one

a teasing way of calling a person unusual, oddly mannered, mildly impertinent, etc. *19th cent.*

George Lander adapting Dickens' *Bleak House* 1888
He is a one – er, I can tell you. He's all over the shop, he is.

D H Lawrence *Sons and Lovers* 1913
'Your mester's got hurt,' he said. 'Eh, dear me! … And what's he done this time?' 'I don't know for sure, but it's 'is leg somewhere' … 'Eh, dear, what a one he is! There's not five minutes of peace, I'll be hanged if there is! His thumb's nearly better, and now – '

See also be/have one over the EIGHT; in/at one FELL swoop; one for the ROAD; public ENEMY number one; rolled into one *at* ROLL; take care of / look after NUMBER one.

---

oneself

be oneself

to act naturally and avoid affectation. *19th cent.*

Oscar Wilde *Lady Windermere's Fan* 1892
[Lord Darlington] *You said once you would make no compromise with things. Make none now. Be brave! Be yourself!* [Lady Windermere] *I am afraid of being myself! Let me think! Let me wait!*

---

onion

know one's onions

informal to be well informed about a subject. The origin of the expression is unknown. It has been associated with the English lexicographer Charles T Onions, the last surviving editor of the original *Oxford English Dictionary* who wrote its very last entries (including *zyxst*, an obsolete form of *sixth*, and *zyxt*, a dialect form of the verb *see*); but if this were the case we would expect the first uses to be British whereas they are in fact American, from the 1920s. In any case Onions, for all his erudition, was hardly a household name. A simpler and more appealing explanation is that *onions* is short for *onion rings*, rhyming slang for 'things'. The phrase belongs to a set of food-related expressions, others including *know one's oats, oil, apples,* and *eggs,* as well as the more general word *stuff.* The journal *American Speech* recorded the forms with *onions* and *stuff* in 1927: '*Know your onions* or *know your stuff*, have grasp of your subjects.' *Early 20th cent.*

Liverpool Echo & Daily Post 1993
French student Frederique Mace knows her onions after spending a week on work experience at Asda's superstore in Wallasey. Frederique, 18, is among a group of teenagers from Lorient in Brittany doing temporary jobs at offices, schools and shops across Wirral.

open

for openers
as a start, to begin with. *Late 20th cent.*

CD Review 1992
The BBC Scottish SO under their conductor-in-chief Jerzy Maksymiuk are firmly in charge of accompaniments for the Hyperion project, and for openers the gifted Piers Lane ... has the spotlight.

have/keep an open mind
to be receptive to new ideas or suggestions: somebody who does this is called *open-minded*. *18th cent.*

Charles Johnstone Chrysal 1760
I therefore immediately became a Schemer, and entered into every project which my own brain could invent, or artful imposition suggest to me, blindly, wilfully giving up the serenity of an open mind, for the vain appearance of mysterious consequence and design.

Bram Stoker Dracula 1897
I have tried to keep an open mind; and it is not the ordinary things of life that could close it, but the strange things, the extraordinary things, the things that make one doubt if they be mad or sane.

in/into the open
into public view or knowledge; no longer secret. *Mid 20th cent.*

open-and-shut
easily settled; conclusive. Used especially of an argument or legal case that is so straightforward that one opens it and immediately closes it. *19th cent.*

an open book
a person or thing that is easy to understand. The notion behind the phrase is clear from the use as a simile seen in the Burroughs quotation below. Cf a closed book *at* CLOSE. *19th cent.*

Dickens The Haunted Man 1847
When she asked him whether they should go home now, to where the old man and her husband were, and he readily replied 'yes' – being anxious in that regard – he put his arm through hers, and walked beside her; not as if he were the wise and learned man to whom the wonders of nature were an open book, and hers were the uninstructed mind, but as if their two positions were reversed, and he knew nothing, and she all.

Edgar Rice Burroughs The Lost Continent a1950
'We are lost!' was written as plainly upon Taylor's face as though his features were the printed words upon an open book.

open one's/somebody's mind
1 to reveal one's thoughts and opinions with frankness. *17th cent.*

James Mabbe The Spanish Bawd 1631 [argument]
Melibea, after some exchange of words, opens her mind to Celestina; telling her how fervently she was falne in love with Calisto.

Fanny Burney Evelina 1778
'Well, then, Miss Anville,' said the Captain, turning to me, 'do you and Molly go into another room, and stay there till Mrs. Duval has opened her mind to us.'

Wilkie Collins No Name 1862
Something in his look and manner took her memory back to the first night at Aldborough, when she had opened her mind to him in the darkening solitude.
2 to be receptive, or make somebody receptive, to ideas and suggestions. *18th cent.*

Addison in Spectator 1712
We are obliged to devotion for the noblest buildings, that have adorned the several countries of the world. It is this that has set men at work on temples and publick places of worship, not only that they might, by the magnificence of the building, invite the Deity to reside within it, but that such stupendous works might, at the same time, open the mind to vast conceptions.

open sesame
a means of gaining access to something that is normally inaccessible: with reference to the magical command used by Ali Baba to open the door of the robbers' den in the folk tale *Ali Baba and the Forty Thieves* from the *Arabian Nights*. *19th cent.*

Scott Waverley 1814
'That cannot be. You cannot be to them Vich Ian Vohr; and these three magic words,' said he, half smiling, 'are the only Open Sesame to their feelings and sympathies.'

See also open the floodgates *at* FLOODGATE; with one's eyes open *at* EYE; with open arms *at* ARM.

opportunity

opportunity knocks
there is a strong chance of success but one has to seize it: a shortening of the (mid 20th cent.) proverb *opportunity knocks but once* (or *opportunity never knocks twice*), which occurs earlier with *fortune* or *fate* instead of *opportunity. Late 20th cent.*

Thomas Harvey et al Making an Impact 1989
Opportunity knocks: When I talk about positions and opportunities for pictures I don't suggest that you can plan them all. Part of the presenter's role is to watch for good photo opportunities as they arise spontaneously in the course of events.

option

keep/leave one's options open
to avoid committing oneself or making a definite choice. *Late 20th cent.*

Independent 1989
The play, because it wants its bread buttered on both sides, keeps its options open until the end on the issue of whether she is genuinely taken in by her husband's lie or whether her insistence that the girl stay the weekend, her broody concern for the future of the fictitious baby ... are just ways of stoking up Jacques's embarrassment.

orange
See all LOMBARD STREET to a China orange.

orbit

into orbit
informal into a state of intense activity or excitement. The metaphor came into prominence when the first artificial satellites began to be sent into the earth's orbit in the 1950s, the figurative uses appearing almost simultaneously with the literal ones. *Mid 20th cent.*

Hanif Kureishi The Buddha of Suburbia 1990
Ted said he'd go fishing if he needed therapy. Anything too technical might catapult him into orbit again.

order

doctor's orders
instructions from a doctor forming part of medical treatment, typically with regard to diet or situations to be avoided: in figurative use of instructions more generally that one has to follow, often used as a convenient excuse for inaction or rest. *19th cent.*

Clyde Fitch The Climbers 1901
I heard Trotter casually observe he'd been obliged to give up smoking entirely – doctor's orders!

in order
1 in the normal or correct sequence. *Middle English*

Shakespeare As You Like It v.iv.86 (1599)
[Jaques] *Can you nominate in order now the degrees of the lie?* [Touchstone] *O sir, we quarrel in print, by the book, as you have books for good manners. I will name you the degrees. The first, the Retort Courteous; the second, the Quip Modest; the third, the Reply Churlish; the fourth, the Reproof Valiant; the fifth, the Countercheck Quarrelsome; the sixth, the Lie with Circumstance; the seventh, the Lie Direct.*
2 (said of parts, arrangements, etc) correctly positioned or organized. *Middle English*

Shakespeare 3 Henry VI i.ii.69 (1591)
[Edward] *I hear their drums. Let's set our men in order,* | *And issue forth and bid them battle straight.*
3 (said of behaviour or actions) acceptable or appropriate. *Middle English*

orders are orders
instructions must be obeyed. The phrase is also found in the affectedly ungrammatical form *orders is orders*, influenced by its use as the title of a 1933 film produced by Michael Balcon, set in an army barracks (renamed *Orders are Orders* in a remake of 1954). *19th cent.*

Herman Melville Pierre 1852
'My business is pressing. I must see Mr. Stanly.' 'I am sorry, sir, but orders are orders: I am his particular servant here – the one that sees his silver

every holyday. I can't disobey him. May I shut the door, sir? for as it is, I can not admit you.'

out of order

1 not in the normal or correct sequence. *16th cent.*

Hobbes *Leviathan* 1651
Men were fain to apply their fingers of one or both hands to those things they desired to keep account of; and that thence it proceeded that now our numeral words are but ten, in any nation, and in some but five, and then they begin again. And he that can tell ten, if he recite them out of order, will lose himself, and not know when he has done.

2 (said of behaviour) not acceptable. *16th cent.*

John Bale *Johan Baptystes preachynge* c1550
I wyll therfor change to a lyfe, I hope, moch better. No man so wycked, nor so farre out of order, As I wretche have bene in murther, rape and thefte.

3 (said of a machine or device) not working properly: developed from such uses as in *bad/ good*, etc *order* which date from the 16th cent.; in 19th cent. literature *in good order* was also used as a humorous euphemism for 'drunk'. *17th cent.*

Milton *Psalm 82* 1648
They know not nor will understand, | In darkness they walk on, | The Earths foundations all are mov'd | And out of order gon.

See also a TALL order.

---

other

See how the other HALF lives; the other HALF.

---

out

be out for something / to do something

to have something as one's purpose or intention. *19th cent.*

H G Wells *The War of the Worlds* 1898
Farmers were out to defend their cattle-sheds, granaries, and ripening root crops with arms in their hands.

drink the three outs

old use to become very drunk. There have been various explanations of what the 'three outs' might be, including this from a 17th cent. source entitled *Woe to Drunkards*: 'Stay and drinke the three outs first that is, wit out of the head, money out of the purse, ale out of the pot.' *17th cent.*

out and about

going about one's normal outdoor activities, especially after confinement due to illness or injury. *19th cent.*

Mrs Gaskell *Sylvia's Lovers* 1863
He was out and about by the earliest dawn, working all day long with might and main.

out and away

by a long way; considerably. *19th cent.*

R L Stevenson *Treasure Island* 1883
'Who's the best shot?' asked the captain. 'Mr. Trelawney, out and away,' said I. 'Mr. Trelawney, will you please pick me off one of these men, sir?'

out with —

an exhortation to be rid of somebody or something. *19th cent.*

G B Shaw *Shaw on Theatre* 1919
Out with the lot of them, then: let us cut the cackle and come to the 'osses.

out with it

used to encourage somebody to say what they have to say, especially when they are being hesitant or inarticulate. *17th cent.*

Dryden *All for Love* 1678
[Antony] *Here, here it lies; a lump of lead by day, | And, in my short, distracted, nightly slumbers, | The hag that rides my dreams.* [Ventidius] *Out with it; give it vent.*

John Armstrong *Miscellanies* 1770
Out with it – Speak – the worst at once.

Dickens *Hard Times* 1854
Now, let me hear what it's all about. As it's not that, let me hear what it is. What have you got to say? Out with it, lad!

take/carry one out of oneself

to provide one with an enjoyable and unexpected diversion. The form with *carry* is no longer common. *19th cent.*

Jane Austen *Persuasion* 1818
A submissive spirit might be patient, a strong understanding would supply resolution, but here was something more; here was that elasticity of mind, that disposition to be comforted, that power of turning readily from evil to good, and of finding employment which carried her out of herself, which was from nature alone.

Somerset Maugham *The Moon and Sixpence* 1919
Love is absorbing; it takes the lover out of himself.

See also HAVE it out (with somebody); in/out of POCKET; out at (the) elbows *at* ELBOW; out-Herod HEROD; out of BOUNDS; out of HAND; out of ORDER; out of the QUESTION; out of sorts *at* SORT; out of this WORLD; out to LUNCH; three strikes and you're out *at* STRIKE.

outdoors

the great outdoors
the open air; life in the countryside: *outdoors* occurs from the mid 19th cent. in the meaning 'open outdoor spaces'. *Mid 20th cent.*

Esquire 1991
The stainless steel hip-flask is perfect for taking a little home comfort with you into the great outdoors.

outside

at the outside
at the most, as the maximum. *19th cent.*

Rider Haggard She 1887
How near to or how far from sunset we might be, neither of us had the faintest notion; all we did know was that when at last the light came it would not endure more than a couple of minutes at the outside, so that we must be prepared to meet it.

get outside of something
informal to have something to eat or drink. *19th cent.*

D Arrowsmith in Big Game of North America 1890
My wife said she knew, from his full stomach and his sneaking look, that he [a raccoon] *was outside of her pet turkey.*

on the outside looking in
(said of a person) excluded from a group or organization. *Late 20th cent.*

Alison Leonard Gate-crashing the Dream Party 1990
People used to tell their dreams, lurid ones, sexy ones, when we were crammed into the locker-rooms during wet breaks. All about running for trains they couldn't catch or being sat on by scaly monsters, and they got hold of books that told you that it meant Sex. It always meant Sex. I used to listen and wish I'd got something to offer. I was on the outside looking in.

over

be all over somebody
to behave over-attentively or obsequiously towards somebody. Perhaps the notion is of kissing a person's body all over as a sign of affection; or it may be of 'running' all over them, as in the first quotation below. *19th cent.*

Harriet Beecher Stowe We and Our Neighbors 1875
You can keep servants if you don't follow them up, and insist on it that they shall do their duty. Let them run all over you and live like mistresses, and you can keep them. For my part, I like to change – new brooms always sweep clean.

E Pugh Harry the Cockney 1912
The worst of women is ... they never leave you alone ... They're all over you.

over and done with
finished and unalterable: *over* in the meaning 'finished, dealt with' dates from the 17th cent. *19th cent.*

Kipling The Gate of the Hundred Sorrows 1888
Sometimes when I first came to the Gate, I used to feel sorry for it; but that's all over and done with long ago, and I draw my sixty rupees fresh and fresh every month, and am quite happy.

See also over the MOON; over the TOP.

overboard

go overboard
informal to be excessive in one's enthusiasm or behaviour: based on the image of a person leaping over the side of a ship. *Mid 20th cent.*

Dogs Today 1992
Leo (July 24–Aug 23): A happier period is ahead, rather than of late, and you're in for some high times with plenty of hilarity. Don't go overboard with it, or your owner won't thank you.

throw something overboard
to reject or discard something. *17th cent.*

overdrive
See MEXICAN overdrive.

over-egg

over-egg the pudding/cake

to make something more elaborate than necessary: the notion is of too much egg being put into a mixture, making it too rich and difficult to cook satisfactorily. *19th cent.*

Daily Telegraph 1961
Mr Foot seems to have been ill served by his seconder, Mr Will Griffiths ... who is reported to have made the mistake of 'over-egging the pudding'.

overplay

overplay one's hand

to act over-confidently, risking one's chances of success: a metaphor from card-playing. *Mid 20th cent.*

Guardian 1989
Noriega ... declared last weekend that his forces were in 'a state of war' with the US. 'That was his biggest blunder,' Mr Goldman said. 'He badly overplayed his hand.'

overstep

overstep the mark

to go beyond acceptable levels of behaviour: the image is of a runner placing a foot ahead of the starting mark, thereby incurring a penalty. *19th cent.*

Disraeli Vivian Grey 1826
The chief of Reisenburg has, in his eagerness to gain his grand ducal crown, somewhat overstepped the mark.

owe

owe somebody a living

to bear a responsibility for sustaining somebody or providing for them: normally used in negative contexts of situations in which people expect society in general to provide for them. *Early 20th cent.*

Edgar Rice Burroughs The Jungle Tales of Tarzan 1916
If Tarzan felt that the world owed him a living he also realized that it was for him to collect it.

owe somebody one

informal to owe somebody a favour: also used ironically of intended revenge. *19th cent.*

Thackeray The Adventures of Philip 1862
Thank you, I owe you one. You're a most valuable man, Chesham, and a credit to your father and mother.

own

behave as if/though one owns/owned the place

to act in an arrogant or self-important manner. *Early 20th cent.*

Edward Peple A Pair of Sixes 1914
For a week he's been swaggering around here as if he owned the place. Drinks my whiskey – smokes my best cigars – and then he's always with her!

be one's own man/woman/person

to be in control of one's own affairs and in a position to act independently. The phrase occurs earliest, in Chaucer (see below), with reference to a woman, and the first occurrence in a male context is not for another two centuries. *Middle English*

Chaucer Troilus and Criseyde II.750
I am myn owene womman, wel at ese – | *I thank it God – as after myn estat* [= as befits my station in life].

James Mabbe The Spanish Bawd 1631
[Sempronio] *You know full well, that he that serues another, is not his own man.*

Congreve The Way of the World 1700
[Waitwell] *For now, I remember me, I'm married, and can't be my own man again.*

come into its/one's own

to become useful or effective. *Early 20th cent.*

Timothy Thomas Fortune Dreams of Life 1905
His noble brow | *Unwrinkled was; his eagle eye* | *No more was blurred with mystery.* | *Reason had come into its own,* | *And this in all his acts was shown.*

get one's own back

to have one's revenge. *Early 20th cent.*

Robinson Jeffers Collected Poetry 1928–38
He smiled painfully and Hildis saw | *His tongue glitter in the lamplight, moistening his lips. 'I got my own back,' he said. 'More than my own.'*

hold one's own

to maintain one's position when under attack; to meet hostility or competition resolutely. *16th cent.*

> Shakespeare 2 Henry IV III.ii.202 (1597)
> [Shallow] *And is Jane Nightwork alive?* [Falstaff] *She lives, Master Shallow ...* [Shallow] *By the mass, I could anger her to th' heart. She was then a bona-roba* [= prostitute]. *Doth she hold her own well?*

oyster

the world is one's oyster

one has many opportunities: the locus classicus is contained in the exchange between Sir John Falstaff and Pistol in Shakespeare, *The Merry Wives of Windsor* (1597) II.ii.4 '[Sir John] I will not lend thee a penny ... [Pistol] Why then, the world's mine oyster, which I with sword will open.' There is a long gap in usage of the phrase until the early 19th cent. *16th cent.*

> Upton Sinclair Jungle 1906
> *He was the child of his parents' youth and joy; he grew up like the conjurer's rosebush, and all the world was his oyster.*

P

mind one's Ps and Qs

informal to behave discreetly and avoid causing offence. The phrase may be based on the notion of *p* and *q* as confusable letters needing special care when learning to write: *learning one's p's and q's* is recorded in the 19th cent., but the allusive phrase is of an earlier date. The first record of the phrase in print in its current form is in a work called *Who's the Dupe?* by the 18th cent. dramatist Hannah Cowley, first performed in 1779. There we find the warning 'You must mind your P's and Q's with him, I can tell you'. The phrase appears also in the form *peas* and *cues*: this may represent some kind of wordplay, since *cue* is entered in Johnson's *Dictionary* as a representation of the letter Q. (A use of *P and Q* to mean 'of prime quality' is recorded in the *English Dialect Dictionary* for Shropshire and Herefordshire in the mid 19th cent., and appears in print in the form *pee and kew* much earlier in a source of 1612 in the *OED*; but there doesn't seem to be any historical or semantic link between this use and the more familiar 18th cent. one.)

More colourful but purely speculative suggestions have been made about the origin of the phrase: (1) that it is connected with 18th cent. hairstyles, and was based on the notion of 'minding your *toupées* [artificial locks of hair] and your *queues* [pigtails]'; (2) that it relates to an ancient custom of hanging a slate behind the door of an alehouse to record a customer's credit, a P or a Q being chalked on it according to whether a pint or a quart had been drunk; (3) that it is based on an admonition to children to mind their manners by always saying *P[lease]* and *[than]K YOU*, i.e. by minding their P's and KYOU's. Kipling, in *Just So Stories* (*How the Alphabet Was Made*, 1902), offered an even more appealing explanation in his account of how a necklace was made from the alphabet: 'P and Q are missing. They were lost, a long time ago, in a great war, – and the tribe mended the necklace with the dried rattles of a rattlesnake, but no one ever found P and Q. That is how the saying began, "You must mind your P's and Q's".' The true, if less colourful, explanation probably lies simply in the alliterative quality of the letters, which have often been chosen as attractive-sounding representatives of the alphabet. The phrase now sounds a little quaint and distinctly dated. *18th cent.*

Francis Gentleman The Pantheonites 1773
Plague on his P's, Q's and turtle too; I had not swallowed above two mouthfuls, before my throat was burnt to a cinder.

Henry James Washington Square 1881
He sent for her to the library, and he there informed her that he hoped very much that, as regarded this affair of Catherine's, she would mind her p's and q's. 'I don't know what you mean by such an expression,' said his sister. 'You speak as if I were learning the alphabet.' 'The alphabet of common sense is something you will never learn,' the doctor permitted himself to respond.

W H Auden Homage to Clio 1960
Artemis, | Aphrodite, are Major Powers and all wise | Castellans will mind their p's and q's.

pace

go the pace
to travel or move at great speed. *19th cent.*

J Lewis May transl Flaubert's Madame Bovary 1856
What is it he's got, the old fellow? He coughs enough to bring the house down, and I'm very much afraid he'll soon be needing a wooden suit more than a flannel waistcoat. He didn't half go the pace in his young days!

keep pace with somebody/something
to manage to conduct one's affairs, perform tasks, etc, at the same rate as somebody or something. The expression is used by Hermia in Shakespeare's *A Midsummer Night's Dream* (1595) III.iii.33: 'I can no further crawl, no further go. My legs can keep no pace with my desires.' There are other uses from about this date, some probably earlier than Shakespeare's (see examples below). *16th cent.*

Brian Melbanke Philotimus 1582
When hemp will not spring in a fertile ground never tilled, it will not grow and flourish in a dried heath: since he could not keep pace, when his legs were lithe and leenie, and his horse & footecloth at his command, how can he outrun his fellows, when his limmes are all lamed, though you lend him a crutch to lean upon?

Edward Guilpin Skilaetheia 1598
Thys leaden-heeled passion is too dull, | To keep pace with this Satyre-footed gull.

off the pace
behind the leader or leaders in a race or contest. *20th cent.*

the pace of life
the speed or intensity with which one conducts one's life: hence also *a change of pace* and other related phrases. *18th cent.*

John Gay The Captives 1724
[Astarbe] Tell me, Sophernes, does not slav'ry's yoke | Gall more and more through ev'ry pace of life? | I am a slave, like you.

Mrs Humphry Ward Robert Elsmere 1888
Langham would walk home in a state of feeling he did not care to analyse, but which certainly quickened the pace of life a good deal.

put somebody/something through their paces
to test somebody by making them demonstrate their abilities: originally used in the context of training horses (*see also* show one's paces *below*). *18th cent.*

Goldsmith The Vicar of Wakefield 1766
I had, in the usual forms, when I came to the fair, put my horse through all his paces; but for some time had no bidders. At last a chapman approached, and, after he had for a good while examined the horse round, finding him blind of one eye, would have nothing to say to him.

set the pace
to control the speed at which a race is run or an activity progresses. *19th cent.*

Edward Harrigan Reilly and the Four Hundred 1890
[Lavinia] Yes, there's danger in the slums. [Emiline] Slumming is an English fad. [Lavinia] Dear old England! [Percy] Ah! [Emile] Our British cousins set the pace.

Upton Sinclair *Jungle* 1906
He plays like one possessed by ... a whole horde of demons. You can feel them in the air round about him, capering frenetically; with their invisible feet they set the pace, and the hair of the leader of the orchestra rises on end, and his eyeballs start from their sockets, as he toils to keep up with them.

show one's paces

to demonstrate what one can do: used originally of horses (*see also* put somebody/something through their paces *above*). *19th cent.*

Harriet Beecher Stowe *Uncle Tom's Cabin* 1852
He seized Tom by the jaw, and pulled open his mouth to inspect his teeth; made him strip up his sleeve, to show his muscle; turned him round, made him jump and spring to show his paces.

George Eliot *Felix Holt* 1866
He had heard that Philip Debarry's courier was often busy in the town, and it seemed especially likely that he would be seen there when the Market was to be agitated by politics, and the new candidate was to show his paces.

stand/stay the pace

to be able to maintain the same (usually extreme) speed or rate of activity as others. *19th cent.*

Saki *Reginald* 1904
I bundled her up on to her pony, and gave her a lead towards home as fast as I cared to go. What with the wet and the unusual responsibility, her abridged costume did not stand the pace particularly well, and she got quite querulous when I shouted back that I had no pins with me – and no string.

pack

go to the pack

Australian and NZ, informal to deteriorate or go into decline. The allusion is probably to the main pack in a group of animals, as distinct from the leaders. *Early 20th cent.*

A Wright *A Colt from the Country* 1922
Expects to win the Cup with Western Chief. If he don't he's gone to the pack sure.

pack one's bags

to prepare to leave a place, especially one's home. *Mid 20th cent.*

pack them in

informal (said of entertainment) to attract a large audience. *Mid 20th cent.*

Today 1992
Eubank has got where he is by aggravating public and opponents alike to the point that all they want to see is the object of their dislike brought down with a bump. It is a sad truth that nice guys don't pack them in. Poor Michael Watson was never as big a draw as Eubank or that other thoroughly disagreeable middleweight Nigel Benn.

pack it in/up

informal, originally services' slang to stop what one is doing, especially an arduous or tedious task or an unsuccessful attempt: also as an instruction to somebody to stop doing something annoying. *Mid 20th cent.*

pack a punch

1 to be capable of hitting hard. *Mid 20th cent.*

Andy Martin *Walking on Water* 1991
A wave 10 feet high and 500 feet long can pack a punch of 400,000 pounds per linear foot of its crest.

2 to be impressive or effective. *Mid 20th cent.*

BBC Good Food 1991
At last! takeaway sandwiches with flavour that packs a punch! Marks & Spencer's American-style sandwich range includes Pastrami on Rye with a dynamic edge of American mustard and crunchy dill pickle.

send somebody packing

to dismiss somebody summarily or with a reprimand. To *pack oneself*, meaning 'to take oneself off, to leave', dates from the turn of the 16th cent. *16th cent.*

Shakespeare *1 Henry IV* II.v.300 (1596)
[Sir John] *What doth gravity out of his bed at midnight? Shall I give him his answer?* [Prince Harry] *Prithee do, Jack.* [Sir John] *Faith, and I'll send him packing.*

See also no names, no pack drill *at* NAME.

packet

catch/cop/stop a packet

informal to be killed or wounded in action: from the First World War forces' slang sense of *packet* 'a bullet or shell'. The phrase is entered in Fraser and Gibbons' *Soldier and Sailor Words* (1925). *Early 20th cent.*

cost a packet
informal to be very expensive: *packet* is short for 'a packet of money' (or 'notes', etc). *Early 20th cent.*

paddle

paddle one's own canoe
to be independent and self-reliant: a phrase common in 19th cent. literature but now largely fallen out of use. *19th cent.*

> William Gilmore Simms *Mellichampe: A Legend of the Santee* 1836
> *Every man paddle his own canoe, says I; and, if I has an enemy, I shouldn't like to stand by and let another man dig at his throat to spile my sport, neither would you, I reckon.*

page

page three girl
a sexually attractive young woman of the kind that appears topless in photographs in tabloid newspapers. Page three is the page on which these photographs have appeared in the British newspaper the *Sun* since the 1970s. *Late 20th cent.*

paid

put paid to something
to bring something to an abrupt end; to thwart or subvert a plan or intention. *Early 20th cent.*

pain

be at (great) pains to do something
to make a special effort or take special care to do something: in early use in the form *at the pains*. *18th cent.*

> Boswell *The Life of Samuel Johnson* 1791
> *The particulars of this conversation I have been at great pains to collect with the utmost authenticity, from Dr. Johnson's own detail to myself.*

be a pain in the neck/arse/ass/backside, etc
informal to be a nuisance or source of annoyance: originally in the form *give somebody a pain in the neck*, and later reduced to just *be a pain*. *Early 20th cent.*

no pain, no gain
one has to suffer in order to achieve success or improvement. The notion goes back to the 16th cent., and the English poet Robert Herrick wrote in his collection *Hesperides* (1648): 'No paines, no gaines. | If little labour, little are our gaines: | Mans fortunes are according to his paines.' *17th cent.*

take pains
to make special efforts or take special care. *16th cent.*

> Shakespeare *Much Ado About Nothing* II.iii.238 (1598)
> [Benedick] *Fair Beatrice, I thank you for your pains.* [Beatrice] *I took no more pains for those thanks than you take pains to thank me. If it had been painful, I would not have come.*

paint

like watching paint dry
(said of an activity) slow and tedious. *Late 20th cent.*

> The Times 1985
> *The match which clinched it for them was more like an interminable final round of the World Rolling Maul and Protracted Scrummaging championship. The Midlands were slightly more ambitious – they must have tried to run the ball at least three times. London's approach had a thrill-factor approximate to that gained when watching paint dry.*

painting the Forth Bridge
a task that continues indefinitely, because by the time the end is reached it has to be started from the beginning again. The metaphor is derived from the customary maintenance of the steel rail bridge over the Firth of Forth in Scotland, which has a painted surface equivalent to 135 acres and famously needs continuous renewal from end to end (although since 1993 it has not received this). *19th cent.*

paint somebody into a corner
to treat somebody in a way that leaves them no scope for escape or manoeuvre. To *paint oneself into a corner* is to put oneself in this position. *Late 20th cent.*

> Guardian 1989
> *'He is the sort who goes on TV to say what his members want without taking into account the effect on the public,' said one union official. 'Mrs Thatcher will love him. She will be able to paint him*

into a corner as she has not been able to do with his predecessors.'

Daily Mail 1992
Curious as well – and disquieting – that the Chancellor continues to paint himself into a corner by emphasising that even in a realignment of other currencies in the ERM, devaluation of the pound would be wrong and self-defeating.

paint the town red
informal, originally N Amer to go out and celebrate extravagantly. *19th cent.*

William Gill Adonis 1884
[Girls] *Lovers all away I cast, Mr. Right has come at last.* [Adonis] *If some one don't hold me down, red I soon shall paint the town.*

painting
See no OIL painting.

pair

a pair of hands
a person regarded as a contributor to work: *see also* a safe pair of hands *at* HAND. *17th cent.*

Robert Johnson The Worlde 1630
Her enemies brought ten hundred thousand paire of hands to pull downe the wals of Ierusalem.

Edward Ravenscroft The Canterbury Guests 1695
Who e'er it was, they thought | One pair of heels worth two pair of hands; they ran for't, | As if the Devil drove 'em.

See also another pair of shoes *at* SHOE.

pale¹ (verb)

pale into insignificance
to seem unimportant or trivial when something else of much greater importance is considered. *19th cent.*

Sidney Lanier Tiger-Lilies 1867
Lighter of heart, Mrs. Parven had instinctively bent herself to hospitable deeds, had assembled her dusky handmaidens, had bustled up-stairs and down-stairs and in the kitchen, had removed the wreck of furniture, had restored order out of chaos, had, in short, issued commands whose multitude made Napoleon's feat of three thousand despatches in an hour sink into pale insignificance.

Edgar Rice Burroughs The Warlord of Mars 1913
The cheers that had rung out for me paled into insignificance beside those which thundered through the vast edifice now, for she whom the nobles carried was Dejah Thoris, beloved Princess of Helium.

pale² (noun)

beyond the pale
violating the normal social conventions or standards of behaviour. A *pale* was an upright post or stake (Latin *palus*) forming part of a fence, and from the 15th cent. the word denoted an enclosed area, so that the area *beyond the pale* was a wild part outside the fence that enclosed civilization. The term *English Pale* was used historically to mean any of several regions under English jurisdiction that shared boundaries with other regions, notably Calais in France and parts of Ireland and Scotland, but our phrase is more probably connected with the general meaning than with any particular (and much earlier) application of it. The same applies to the term *Pale of Settlement* used to translate the Russian term *čerta osedlosti* 'boundary of settlement', which referred to the specified territories to which the Jews of Russia and Poland were confined from 1791 to 1917: the English term is not recorded until the 1890s (and even then mainly in generic rather than formal reference), well after the generic use of *beyond the pale* had become established. In early use *without* (or *outside*) *the pale* meant outside the jurisdiction or control (for example, of the Church). Sir Walter Scott uses the phrase in this sense in his novel *A Legend of Montrose* (1819): 'The Prelatists and Presbyterians of the more violent kind became as illiberal as the Papists, and would scarcely allow the possibility of salvation beyond the pale of their respective churches.' Uses such as *beyond the pale of reason, of the law, of society, of pity*, etc from the 17th cent. onwards give way to absolute uses of *beyond the pale*, in the current meaning, during the 19th cent.; the Dickens quotation below marks the transition, and the use by Mrs Wood is one of the earliest in the fully developed form of the phrase without the addition of a qualifying 'of —'. *Beyond the Pale* is the title of a story by Kipling (1888). *19th cent.*

Dickens *Pickwick Papers* 1837
I look upon you, Sir, as a man who has placed himself beyond the pale of society, by his most audacious, disgraceful, and abominable public conduct. I view you, Sir, personally or politically, in no other light but as a most unparalleled and unmitigated viper.

Mrs Henry Wood *East Lynne* 1861
'I wish you happiness, Isabel.' 'Thank you,' she returned, in a sarcastic tone, though her throat beat and her lips quivered. 'You are premature in your congratulations, Captain Levison.' 'Am I? Keep my good wishes, then, till the right man comes. I am beyond the pale myself, and dare not think of entering the happy state,' he added, in a pointed tone.

palm

The two main meanings, the concave part of the human hand and the tropical tree or a leaf from it, are essentially the same word: the tree was so named because its leaf was thought to resemble an open hand in shape.

bear the palm
to win a great prize or victory. The palm was a traditional symbol of triumph or victory and appears as such in Middle English sources, notably in Chaucer's *Second Nun's Tale* (line 240): 'The Angel seyde, "God liketh thy requeste, | And bothe with the palm of martirdom | Ye shullen [= shall] come unto his blisful feste [= feast]."' *17th cent.*

Nathaniel Lee *The Princess Of Cleve* 1689
The Soldiers love him, and he bears the Palm | Already from the Marshals of the Field.

Charles Batteux *A Course of the Belles Letters* 1761
In accidental constructions, and old terms new drest, but, which still preserve the air of antiquity, La Fontaine indisputably bears the palm in this part of fable.

Mary Robinson *Walsingham* 1797
So prepossessing are the graces of form and feature, that from every little circle she bore away the palm of victory, while the mild, intelligent, and unassuming Penelope was often scarcely noticed.

have somebody/something in the palm of one's hand
to control a person or thing completely. *19th cent.*

William Blake *Auguries of Innocence* 1803
To see a World in a Grain of Sand | And a Heaven in a Wild Flower, | Hold Infinity in the palm of your hand | And Eternity in an hour.

read somebody's palm
to tell somebody's fortune by studying the lines on the palms of their hands. A famous instance, though not including our phrase as such, occurs in Charlotte Brontë's *Jane Eyre* (1847): 'She told me to hold out my hand. I did. She approached her face to the palm, and pored over it without touching it. "It is too fine," said she. "I can make nothing of such a hand as that; almost without lines: besides, what is in a palm? Destiny is not written there."' *19th cent.*

See also CROSS somebody's palm with silver; GREASE somebody's palm.

pan

go down the pan
informal to fail or end in disaster. The reference is to a lavatory pan. *Mid 20th cent.*

Maitland *Cathedral* 1993
The damage was done as far as my faith was concerned … That Christmas Eve night confirmed my worst fears, it was like a kind of 'royal flush' … all three kings – Pa, Santa and the King of Kings – all down the pan together.

pancake
See (as) FLAT as a pancake.

Pandora

a Pandora's box
a situation or process that once begun can cause great trouble. In Greek mythology Pandora was the first mortal woman, described by the poet Hesiod as 'a beautiful evil'. She received gifts from all the gods (hence her name, which means 'all-gifted'): Zeus's gift was a box (or, in earlier versions, a jar), which she – or her husband, Epimetheus – unwisely opened, releasing all human troubles to spread over the world (or, in another version of the myth, causing all the gods' blessings to escape and be lost for ever, apart from hope). *16th cent.*

Sir Thomas Browne A Letter to a Friend 1672
And if Asia, Africa, and America should bring in their list [of diseases], Pandoras Box would swell, and there must be a strange pathology.

Richardson Clarissa 1751
The Lord, Jack! What a world of mischief, at this rate, must Miss Rawlins know! – What a Pandora's box must her bosom be! – Yet, had I nothing that was more worthy of my attention to regard, I would engage to open it, and make my uses of the discovery.

panic

hit/press/push the panic button
to panic or overreact in the face of difficulty or danger: a panic button is a switch for operating or stopping a device in an emergency. *Mid 20th cent.*

She 1989
Fifty is a toughie. 'The very thought of it makes me want to press the panic button, crawl under the bed and call for HRT,' says one friend.

panic buying
the buying, especially by the general public, of large quantities of a commodity that is likely to become scarce. Used especially in the context of fuel shortages. *Late 20th cent.*

Economist 1991
Shops in Manila have been stripped bare in panic buying, there have been runs on banks, and the government has advised city-folk to grow vegetables in their gardens and to stop ironing clothes to save energy.

pants

beat/bore/scare, etc the pants off somebody
informal used as an intensifying phrase: to beat somebody decisively, or to make somebody extremely scared, bored, etc. *Mid 20th cent.*

Evelyn Waugh A Handful of Dust 1934
She bores my pants off, but she's a good trier.

catch somebody with their pants down
informal, originally NAmer to discover somebody in an embarrassing situation, especially a sexually compromising one: see also catch somebody with their TROUSERS down. *Mid 20th cent.*

Economist 1993
Now, over the smoking issue, the World Bank's directors (says one of them) have been 'caught with our pants down; and it's so bloody embarrassing'.

in/wearing short pants
still a young boy, wearing short trousers as boys regularly did before the age of about 9 or 10. Also in British use in the form *in short trousers. 20th cent.*

Catherine Cookson My Beloved Son 1992
It was more than five years since she had seen him and she was saying he hadn't changed. He imagined for a moment that he was still in short pants, until she turned to him and added, 'What I mean is, I would have still recognised you.'

See also by the SEAT of one's pants.

paper

be unable to argue/fight, etc one's way out of a paper bag
to be utterly inept at arguing, fighting, etc. *Mid 20th cent.*

Daily Mirror 1992
Harrison Ford is terrified of losing his superstar touch. The Hollywood tough-guy, whose new movie Patriot Games opens next month, admits: 'Every morning I ask myself: "I wonder if I'm going to be able to act today?" Sometimes I arrive on the set knowing I couldn't act my way out of a paper bag.'

not worth the paper it is printed on
(said of a document, undertaking, etc) having no value at all: originally and still chiefly in the context of paper money. *19th cent.*

Mark Twain The Innocents Abroad 1869
A year ago, when Italy saw utter ruin staring her in the face and her greenbacks hardly worth the paper they were printed on, her Parliament ventured upon a coup de main that would have appalled the stoutest of her statesmen under less desperate circumstances.

on paper
in writing or print; in theory as distinct from practice. *18th cent.*

Benjamin Franklin Autobiography 1771
I ask'd what Terms were to be offer'd the Owners of the Waggons; and I was desir'd to put on Paper the Terms that appear'd to me necessary. This I did, and they were agreed to.

Thomas Paine *Common Sense* 1776
Pray what is it that Britain can do, whose power will be wholly on paper, should a civil tumult break out the very day after reconciliation?

a paper tiger

a person, power, etc, that appears to be or is portrayed as being strong or threatening, but is actually ineffectual: a translation of a phrase used by the Chinese leader Mao Zedong (1893–1976) with reference to America and other 'reactionaries' in 1946. *Mid 20th cent.*

Peter Lewis *The Fifties* 1978
Why didn't Khrushchev go ahead and provoke the war? That was only the first occasion that Chairman Khrushchev reminded Chairman Mao that the paper tiger had nuclear teeth.

See also paper over the cracks *at* CRACK.

par

From Latin *par* meaning 'equal'. There are two applications underlying the phrases: the commercial meaning 'equality of value' (in exchange rates, share values, etc), and the use in golf to denote the average score calculated for a particular hole, based on the number of strokes a first-class player would normally expect to make. In some uses the two strands overlap conceptually.

above par

better or more valuable than average. *18th cent.*

Laurence Sterne *Tristram Shandy* 1761
We really expect too much – and for the livre or two above par for your suppers and bed – at the most they are but one shilling and ninepence half-penny.

Coleridge *Biographia Literaria* 1817
For a school-boy of that age, I was above par in English versification, and had already produced two or three compositions which, I may venture to say, without reference to my age, were somewhat above mediocrity.

below par

1 less good or valuable than average. *18th cent.*

Swift *Gulliver's Travels* 1726
He represented to the Emperor the low condition of his treasury; that he was forced to take up money at great discount; that exchequer bills would not circulate under nine per cent below par; that in short I had cost his Majesty above a million and a half of

sprugs (their greatest gold coin, about the bigness of a spangle).

2 (said of a person) suffering bad health. *18th cent.*

Samuel Butler *The Way of All Flesh* 1903
The wear and tear of the last three years had told on him, and though not actually ill he was overworked, below par, and unfit for any further burden.

on a par (with something)

having the same status or value as something. *18th cent.*

Frances Reynolds *An Enquiry Concerning the Principles of Taste* 1785
Witness the exterior artificial appearance of humanity in a neighbouring nation, which probably is on a par with the most uncultivated rustic.

par for the course

what is normal or to be expected in a particular situation: a metaphor from golf (see above). *Mid 20th cent.*

Michael Falk *Part of the Furniture* 1991
I came upon an advertisement for a receptionist to work at a local authority office building, not too far from my new home. It seemed about par for the course, so I applied, was interviewed and then offered the job.

up to par

reaching the expected or desired level or standard. Typically used facetiously of one's health or general disposition. *19th cent.*

Harriet Beecher Stowe *Pink and White Tyranny* 1871
'Hang it all!' said John, with a great flounce as he turned over on the sofa. 'I'm not up to par this morning.'

parade

rain on somebody's parade

informal, chiefly NAmer to spoil another person's success or enjoyment. *Late 20th cent.*

Independent on Sunday 2002
Choosing to eliminate sensation in the penis doesn't automatically strike me as the most intelligent or democratic approach to 'better sex' but I don't want to rain on Durex's parade. If something feels better, it feels better … and if Performa gives some men a confidence boost then that is great.

paradise

See a fool's paradise *at* FOOL.

parcel

part and parcel
an essential or inseparable part of something: the phrase occurs in the early 15th cent. in the form *parcel and part*, and early uses are mainly in legal and other formal contexts referring to clauses of contracts and bills. *Parcel* is used as an emphasizer in its old meaning 'a constituent part' (as in *a parcel of land*). *16th cent.*

> Henricus Agrippa von Nettesheim *Of the Vanitie and vncertaintie of Arts* 1530
> *Whiche thinge we will nowe declare to be true, ranginge thorow euery part and parcel.*

pass the parcel
(said of a group of people) to keep passing the initiative or responsibility from one person to another, so that no action is taken. Based on a children's party game in which a parcel with several layers of wrapping is passed round while music plays; each time the music stops the child holding the parcel is allowed to remove some of the wrapping until eventually a prize is revealed. *20th cent.*

pardon

See excuse/pardon my FRENCH.

pare

See cut/pare something to the BONE.

parenthesis

in parenthesis
as an aside or afterthought. *19th cent.*

> W S Gilbert *The Gondoliers* 1889
> *Take a pair of sparkling eyes ... | Take a figure trimly planned ... | Take a dainty little hand, | Fringed with dainty fingerettes, | Press it – in parenthesis; – Ah, take all these, you lucky man – | Take and keep them if you can!*

part

look the part
to have a physical appearance appropriate to a particular role or function: originally in the context of play-acting. *19th cent.*

> Jane Austen *Mansfield Park* 1814
> *Amelia should be a small, light, girlish, skipping figure. It is fit for Miss Crawford, and Miss Crawford only. She looks the part, and I am persuaded will do it admirably.*

a man of (many) parts
a man who displays a wide range of abilities or talents. The underlying meaning is 'an actor's role in a play': *cf* Jaques's speech in Shakespeare's *As You Like It* (1599) II.vii.142 'All the world's a stage, | And all the men and women merely players. | They have their exits and their entrances, | And one man in his time plays many parts, | His acts being seven ages.' *A Man of Many Parts* was used as the title of a poem by the US poet James Whitcomb Riley (1849–1916), which has the opening lines: 'It was a man of many parts, | Who in his coffer mind | Had stored the Classics and the Arts | And Sciences combined.' *17th cent.*

> Philip Massinger *The City-Madam* 1658
> *Call him in. You shall first know him, then admire him | For a man of many parts, and those parts rare ones.*

part company
1 (said of two or more people) to separate or stop associating, especially after a disagreement. *Middle English*

> Chaucer *The Nun's Priest's Tale* (line 2993)
> *Wherfore they mosten of necessitee, | As for that nyght, departen compaignye; | And ech of hem gooth to his hostelrye, | And took his loggyng as it wolde falle.*

2 to disagree with somebody or have a different opinion from them. *19th cent.*

> Washington Irving *Christmas Day* 1820
> *Every thing went on lamely and irregularly until they came to a chorus beginning 'Now let us sing with one accord,' which seemed to be a signal for parting company: all became discord and confusion.*

take something in good part
to accept something modest or disappointing without taking offence when it is offered in a

generous spirit: now generally with reference to a criticism or other adverse remark. *16th cent.*

Shakespeare *The Comedy of Errors* III.i.27 (1594)
[Balthasar] *Small cheer and great welcome makes a merry feast.* [Antipholus of Ephesus] *Ay, to a niggardly host and more sparing guest.* | *But though my cates* [= provisions] *be mean, take them in good part.*

Francis Bacon *Essays* (Of Great Place) 1601
Embrace and invite helps, and advices, touching the execution of thy place; and do not drive away such, as bring thee information, as meddlers; but accept of them in good part.

See also for the MOST part; part and PARCEL; part brass rags with *at* RAG.

parting

the parting of the ways

the point at which people must separate or at which a decision must be made: based on the literal meaning 'a place at which a road divides', with particular reference to the passage in Ezekiel (21:21) in which the King of Babylon is said to have 'stood at the parting of the way, at the head of the two ways'. The phrase is 19th cent. in allusive use.

Henry James *The Ambassadors* 1903
He's at the parting of the ways. He can come into the business now – he can't come later.

party

the party's over

informal a period of good fortune or enjoyment has come to an end. Also used with some irony about the demise or disappearance of familiar names and institutions. The phrase appears in two popular songs from the mid 20th cent.: in Noel Coward's 'The Party's Over Now' from *Words and Music* (1932) and 'The Party's Over' from the musical comedy *Bells Are Ringing* (1956) by Comden and Green, with music by Jule Styne. When the British Prime Minister Harold Macmillan (later Lord Stockton) resigned in 1963, the BBC's satirical show *That Was the Week That Was* featured the song, sung by William Rushton in a quavering voice imitating Macmillan. *Mid 20th cent.*

Evelyn Waugh *Scoop* 1938
'The party's over,' said Bannister ... 'We all want a rest ... From tomorrow onwards for the next six years I shall get a daily pile of bumf from the Ministry of Mines.'

pass

come to a pretty pass

(said of events or circumstances) to reach an unwelcome or unfortunate state: based on the (16th cent.) meaning of *pass* 'a position in a state of affairs', which is normally qualified in some way (e.g. Shakespeare *The Taming of the Shrew* (1592) v.ii.124 '[Widow] Lord, let me never have a cause to sigh | Till I be brought to such a silly pass'). *18th cent.*

Richardson *Clarissa* 1748
To what a pretty pass, nevertheless, have I brought myself! – Had Cæsar been such a fool, he had never passed the Rubicon.

Richard Cumberland *The West Indian* 1771
A fine case, truly, in a free country; a pretty pass things are come to, if a man is to be assaulted in his own house.

Harriet Beecher Stowe *Uncle Tom's Cabin* 1852
Things have got to a pretty pass, if a woman can't give a warm supper and a bed to poor, starving creatures, just because they are slaves, and have been abused and oppressed all their lives, poor things!

head/cut somebody/something off at the pass

to forestall somebody's intentions at a critical moment. The phrase is probably derived from the stock line often heard in Western films of the 1940s and 1950s. *Mid 20th cent.*

pass by on the other side

to disregard or avoid a responsibility: with allusion to the parable of the Good Samaritan (*see* GOOD), in which the Priest and Levite ignore the man attacked by robbers and pass him by on the other side of the road (Luke 10:31–32). *19th cent.*

Kipling *Miss Youghals Sais* 1888
Strickland was in the Police, and people did not understand him; so they said he was a doubtful sort of man, and passed by on the other side.

pass in a crowd

to be inconspicuous: also in 19th cent. use in the form *pass muster in a crowd*. The notion is of going unnoticed among other people by being acceptably good but not exceptional. *18th cent.*

> Dickens *The Battle of Life* 1846
> 'Which makes it the more probable that she may be tired of his idea,' calmly pursued the client, 'and not indisposed to exchange it for the newer one of another lover, who ... might perhaps pass muster in a crowd with Mr. Alfred himself.'

pass one's sell-by date

(said typically of a person or institution) to become worn out or no longer useful. The phrase owes its origin to the commercial practice introduced in Britain in the early 1970s of stamping or marking perishable goods with the latest date by which they may be sold. It was apparently newspaper journalists who first spotted the copy potential of the phrase, though not until well into the 1980s: in 1987 a headline in the *Daily Telegraph* referred dismissively to 'Socialism: the package that's passed its sell-by date.' *Late 20th cent.*

sell the pass

to betray one's friends or allies. *Pass* here is used in its meaning 'a narrow passage through hills or mountains', which forms an objective in military fighting. By giving information about the location of a pass, a traitor can enable the enemy to 'turn the pass' and outflank a defending force. In 19th cent. sources it is often described as an Irish expression connected with betraying one's friends to the authorities. *19th cent.*

> Charles G Halpine *Baked Meats of the Funeral* 1866
> There can be produced neither oral nor written evidence against any member of the Provisional Government, even supposing (as has never yet happened) that some 'A' should wish to prove a traitor, or, as they say in Ireland, 'to sell the pass'.

See also pass the buck *at* BUCK²; pass one's EYE over something; pass the HAT round; pass somebody's lips *at* LIP; pass MUSTER; pass the TIME of day; take up / hand on / pass the BATON.

passage

passage of/at arms

an exchange of blows; a fight or quarrel. The underlying meaning of *passage*, 'something that

passes, i.e. an event or occurrence', is now obsolete except in senses to do with people's dealings with one another, either by negotiation or, as here, by fighting. *19th cent.*

> Charles Kingsley *Westward Ho!* 1855
> If she wished for a passage of arms in her own honour, she could easily enough compass one: not that she would do it for worlds!

work one's passage

to receive free passage on a ship in exchange for work done during the voyage. *18th cent.*

> Edward Dorrington *The Hermit* 1727
> He sees ... hay-makers, going to work, ... and resolves to make one of their Number, and work his passage up to London.

See also RITE of passage.

---

past

not put it past — (to —)

to regard a person as quite capable of doing something foolish or rash, or to declare one's lack of surprise that they might do it. Gerard Manley Hopkins in the 1870s refers to the expression as being of Irish origin. *19th cent.*

past it

informal incompetent or useless from old age: *it* refers to 'one's prime'. *19th cent.*

> Dickens *The Chimes* 1844
> 'Tis harder than you think for gentlefolks to grow up decent, commonly decent, in such a place. That I growed up a man and not a brute, says something for me – as I was then. As I am now, there's nothing can be said for me or done for me. I'm past it.

---

pasture

put somebody out to pasture

to make somebody retire, especially late in life or after many years of work or service: with allusion to the treatment of farm animals that are put out to graze when their useful life is over. *Early 20th cent.*

> George Ade *The Sultan of Sulu* 1902
> The Datto Mandi is a warlike gentleman who holds forth on the other side of the island. About a month ago I needed a new batch of wives. I turned the former assortment out to pasture, then I went over

to Parang and stampeded seven of Mandi's lovely nieces. This annoyed Mandi.

pat¹ (adjective)

have something off pat
to be able to say or do something entirely from memory: from the (17th cent.) meaning of *pat* 'exactly suitable or apposite; ready for the occasion' (*cf* Shakespeare, *Hamlet* (1601) III.iii.73, where Hamlet contemplates killing Claudius at prayer: 'Now might I do it pat, now he is praying, | And now I'll do it, and so he goes to heaven.') *Early 20th cent.*

> Somerset Maugham *Of Human Bondage* 1915
> *Others find the examinations too hard for them ... they forget as soon as they come into the forbidding buildings of the Conjoint Board the knowledge which before they had so pat.*

pat² (verb and noun)

pat somebody on the back
to congratulate or praise somebody: *a pat on the back* (early 19th cent.) is an expression of praise or congratulation. *19th cent.*

> Somerset Maugham *Of Human Bondage* 1915
> *Philip felt a little inclined to pat himself on the back for his skill in managing the business.*

pat³

on one's pat
Australian, informal on one's own, alone: rhyming slang based on *Pat Malone* = alone. The full form is also used. *Early 20th cent.*

> *Troppo Tribune* 1943
> *The truck is gorn – I'm on me flamin' pat.*

patch

a good/bad patch
a period of favourable or adverse circumstances or luck. The phrase marks the most common use of *patch* in the meaning 'a short period of time characterized in some way', although there are other variants, such as *sticky*. The first recorded use, by P G Wodehouse, is with *good* (see below). *Early 20th cent.*

> P G Wodehouse *The Heart of a Goof* 1926
> *How like life it all was! ... We strike a good patch and are beginning to think pretty well of ourselves, and along comes a George Parsloe.*

not a patch on somebody/something
nowhere near as good as somebody or something. *19th cent.*

> Charles Reade *Hard Cash* 1863
> *I lost my rudder at sea once, and had to ship a makeshift: but it was a curs't complicated thing; not a patch upon yours, Mr. Fullalove.*

See also a PURPLE patch.

path

See lead somebody up the GARDEN path; the line/path of least RESISTANCE.

patience

lose one's patience
to become openly impatient. *17th cent.*

> James Mabbe transl Aleman's *Guzman d'Alfarache* 1622
> *How had they almost made me to lose my patience, and my judgement!*

patter

the patter of tiny/little feet
the sound of a young child, signifying its presence; often used to refer to the birth of a new baby. *19th cent.*

> Longfellow *Tales of a Wayside Inn* 1863
> *I hear in the chamber above me | The patter of little feet, | The sound of a door that is opened, | And voices soft and sweet.*

pause

give somebody pause (for thought)
to cause somebody to hesitate or reflect before acting. *17th cent.*

> Shakespeare *Hamlet* III.i.70 (1601)
> *For in that sleep of death what dreams may come | When we have shuffled off this mortal coil | Must give us pause.*

pave

pave the way for something
to create the circumstances or environment that will enable something to happen or exist. *16th cent.*

Thomas Paine *Paine Opposes the Execution of Louis XVI* 1792
The history of monarchy in France was a system pregnant with crimes and murders, cancelling all natural ties, even those by which brothers are united. We know how often they have assassinated each other to pave a way to power.

pay

it always pays to —
doing the specified thing is worth the expense or effort. *19th cent.*

not if you paid me
under no circumstances: used to express outright refusal of an offer, invitation, suggestion, etc. *19th cent.*

Conan Doyle *The Hound of the Baskervilles* 1901
Look at Sir Charles's death! That was bad enough, for all that the coroner said. Look at the noises on the moor at night. There's not a man would cross it after sundown if he was paid for it.

pay as you go
used of a service in which payments are made according to the level of use, instead of paying a bill in arrears: in recent use applied in particular to tariffs for mobile telephones. *Late 20th cent.*

Credit Management 1992
Telecom Gold requires a PC and a suitable modem (which many offices will have anyway) and costs are by subscription (£40 plus £5.50 a month) with services billed on a 'pay as you go' basis.

pay somebody in their own coin
to treat somebody as they treat others, usually harshly or unjustly. *Coin* here is in its figurative use based on the meaning 'money in circulation'. First known to have been used by Sir Walter Ralegh (1554–1618) in his *Apologia*: 'For us to defend our selves and pay them with their owne Coyne'. *17th cent.*

Charles Cotton *Scarronides* 1667
If thou in the exploit wilt joyn, | Shall pay him back in his own coin, | And bring him back by our contriving, | Since he's so goodly, dead, or living.

pay the piper
to finance an undertaking: used especially to imply the rights and expectations that this brings. A shortening of the (17th cent.) proverb *they that dance must pay the piper* (or *fiddler*), now more familiar in its later (19th cent.) reverse form *he who pays the piper calls the tune*. *17th cent.*

Thomas Flatman *Heraclitus Ridens* 1681
After all this Dance he has led the Nation, he must at last come to pay the Piper himself.

pay one's respects
to make a short courtesy visit to somebody: the use of *pay* in the sense 'to bestow (a benefit)' dates from the late 16th cent. (e.g. 'not paying me a welcome' in Shakespeare, *A Midsummer Night's Dream* (1595) v.i.99). *18th cent.*

Swift *Gulliver's Travels* 1726
There are few persons of distinction, or merchants, or seamen, who dwell in the maritime parts, but what can hold conversation in both tongues; as I found some weeks after, when I went to pay my respects to the Emperor of Blefuscu, which in the midst of great misfortunes, through the malice of my enemies, proved a very happy adventure to me.

pay one's/its way
(said of a person or undertaking) to earn enough money to cover the costs involved, without incurring a debt. *19th cent.*

Herman Melville *Moby Dick* 1851
In this world, shipmates, sin that pays its way can travel freely and without a passport; whereas Virtue, if a pauper, is stopped at all frontiers.

you pays your money and you takes your choice
there is little to choose between the available alternatives. This form of words, making jocular use of dialect verb forms, first appeared as a joke line in *Punch* in 1846: 'Which *is* the Prime Minister?' … 'Which ever you please, my little dear. You pays your money, and you takes your choice.' *19th cent.*

Mark Twain *Huckleberry Finn* 1884
Here's your opposition line! here's your two sets o' heirs to old Peter Wilks – and you pays your money and you takes your choice!

See also pay COURT to somebody; pay the DEBT of/ to nature; pay through the NOSE.

pea

See (as) like as two peas (in a pod) *at* LIKE³.

peace

at peace

1 in a state of calm or tranquillity. *Middle English*

Shakespeare *Julius Caesar* II.ii.1 (1599)
[Caesar] *Nor heaven nor earth have been at peace tonight.* | *Thrice hath Calpurnia in her sleep cried out,* | *'Help, ho! They murder Caesar!'*

2 *euphemistic* dead. The development of this sense, which is a special use of the preceding sense, can be seen in Shakespeare's ironic use of the phrase in *Macbeth* (1606) IV.iii.180, where Ross is reluctant to tell Macduff of the murder of his wife and children: '[Macduff] How does my wife? [Ross] Why, well. [Macduff] And all my children? [Ross] Well, too. [Macduff] The tyrant has not battered at their peace? [Ross] No, they were well at peace when I did leave 'em.' The irony lies in the fact that the audience already knows of the death of Macduff's family. The image is often linked to that of sleeping, as in the Congreve quotation below. *17th cent.*

Congreve *The Mourning Bride* 1697
[Almeria] *Anselmo sleeps, and is at Peace; last Night* | *The silent Tomb receiv'd the good Old King;* | *He and his Sorrows now are safely lodg'd* | *Within its cold, but hospitable Bosom.*

hold/keep one's peace

to remain silent about a confidential or sensitive matter: the locus classicus is the invocation to any objector in the marriage ceremony in the Book of Common Prayer (1552): 'Let him now speak, or else hereafter for ever hold his peace.' *15th cent.*

Shakespeare *The Two Gentlemen of Verona* v.ii.18 (1593)
[Thurio] *How likes she my discourse?* [Proteus] *Ill, when you talk of war.* [Thurio] *But well when I discourse of love and peace.* [Julia, aside] *But better indeed when you hold your peace.*

keep the peace

to avoid causing a public disturbance. *15th cent.*

Shakespeare *Romeo and Juliet* I.ii.1 (1596)
[Capulet] *But Montague is bound as well as I,* | *In penalty alike, and 'tis not hard, I think,* | *For men so old as we to keep the peace.*

See also no peace/rest for the WICKED.

peach

a peach of a —

a beautiful or very fine example of something: based on the figurative meaning of *peach*, which dates from the 18th cent. (The use is ironic in the 1911 example below.) *Early 20th cent.*

James Forbes *The Commuters* 1911
She's all right, but I'm in wrong. I've had a peach of a day.

John Steinbeck *The Grapes of Wrath* 1939
We seen a wreck this mornin' … Big car. Big Cad' … Hit a truck. Folded the radiator right back into the driver. Must a been doin' ninety. Steerin' wheel went right on through the guy an' lef' him a-wigglin' like a frog on a hook. Peach of a car. A honey. You can have her for peanuts now.

peaches and cream

used to describe a facial complexion of soft creamy skin with pale and downy pink cheeks. *Early 20th cent.*

pear

go pear-shaped

informal (said of an idea or undertaking) to go wrong; to fail. The phrase is said to have its origin in RAF slang, referring to the shape of an aircraft that has crashed nose-first, but the meaning is transparent regardless of its history. In recent times *pear-shaped* has been used as a management term to describe organizations that vary in the extent of personnel at different levels, and this use may well have some bearing on the phrase. *20th cent.*

pearl

cast/throw pearls before swine

to give precious things to people who do not appreciate them: with allusion to the account of the Sermon on the Mount in Matthew 7:6 'Give not that which is holy unto the dogs, neither cast ye your pearls before swine, lest they trample them under their feet, and turn again and rend you.' *Middle English* (in Wyclif)

pearly

pearly whites
informal the teeth: so called from their white colour as conventionally represented in advertising, cartoon films (often with a visible glint), and suchlike. *20th cent.*

pebble

not the only pebble on the beach
(said of a person, especially in romantic contexts) not the only person who is available or suitable: with allusion to the title of an 1896 song 'You're Not the Only Pebble on the Beach'. The sentiment recurs in the song itself: 'Let the maiden understand | That she's not the only pebble on the beach!' The phrase is also used as an admonition against self-congratulatory complacency. *19th cent.*

John Oliver Hobbes *The Ambassador* 1898
[Yolande] *I live for Art. Marriage is like a good pie spoilt in the baking … [Katie] Why, Yolande, how you do act! I sh' think you'd be ashamed! [Yolande] Get along! He's not the only pebble on the beach!*

pecker

keep one's pecker up
informal to be in good spirits: often used as an exhortation to somebody who is despondent. *Pecker* here probably refers to the beak or bill of a bird, whereas its familiarity in 20th cent. American English as a slang word for 'penis' gives the phrase a rather different construction when used on that side of the Atlantic. *19th cent.*

George Moore *Esther Waters* 1894
You mustn't give way like that, old girl. You must keep yer pecker up. You're dead beat … You've been walking about all night, no wonder. You must come and have some breakfast with us.

Joseph Conrad *Lord Jim* 1900
He had every facility given him to remain under lock and key, with a chair, a table, a mattress in a corner, and a litter of fallen plaster on the floor, in an irrational state of funk, and keeping up his pecker with such tonics as Mariani dispensed.

pee

pee oneself laughing
informal to laugh uncontrollably: *pee* is a euphemism for *piss* (being its initial letter), and the image is of laughing to the point at which one urinates in one's clothes (especially when drunk, presumably). *Mid 20th cent.*

peg

off the peg
(said of clothes) sold in a ready-made form, as distinct from being specially tailored to the buyer. *Off the Peg* is the title of a poem by Louis MacNeice, published in 1966, in which our memories, especially of tunes, are compared to clothes. The poem opens with the words 'The same tunes hang on pegs in the cloakrooms of the mind | That fitted us ten or twenty or thirty years ago', and concludes 'Each tune, each cloak, if matched to weather and mood, wears well | And off the peg means made to measure now.' *Early 20th cent.*

a peg on which to hang something
an idea or circumstance used as the basis or starting point of an argument or discussion. *19th cent.*

Kipling *Pig* 1888
Nafferton cast about for a peg whereon to hang his earnestness.

G B Shaw *Man and Superman* 1903
[The Devil] *Yes; and this civilization! what is it, after all? [Don Juan] After all, an excellent peg to hang your cynical commonplaces on.*

a square peg in a round hole
somebody who is placed in a situation that does not suit them or their abilities. *19th cent.*

Somerset Maugham *The Moon and Sixpence* 1919
In England and France he was the square peg in the round hole, but here the holes were any sort of shape, and no sort of peg was quite amiss.

take somebody down a peg or two
to reveal somebody as being less important or capable than they imagine themselves to be: based on the image of a vertical series of pegs symbolizing a person's social or intellectual status. Variant forms of the phrase are also recorded from an early date. *17th cent.*

Thomas Hearne *Remarks and Collections* 1707
You'll bring me down a peg lower in my conceit.

See also be LEVEL pegging.

Pelion

pile/heap Pelion on Ossa

to add more problems or difficulties to an already difficult situation. Pelion and Ossa are two mountains in Thessaly in northern Greece; in Greek mythology the giants Otus and Ephialtes tried to pile these mountains on Olympus in order to reach the gods and overthrow them. The phrase occurs occasionally in the form *Ossa on Pelion*, which is less euphonious but strictly more accurate in its allusion to Virgil, *Georgics* I.281 *imponere Pelio Ossam*, which is the source of the English phrase. *16th cent.*

---

pelt

(at) full pelt

with great speed or force. *Pelt* is used in the (19th cent.) sense 'moving at a vigorous pace'. *19th cent.*

Charles Reade *Hard Cash* 1863
He was on the look out for the robber, and, as Alfred came round the corner full pelt, darted at the reins with a husky remonstrance, and Alfred cut into him with the whip.

---

pen

put/set pen to paper

to start writing. *17th cent.*

Locke *An Essay Concerning Human Understanding* 1690
If it seems too much to thee, thou must blame the subject; for when I put pen to paper, I thought all I should have to say on this matter would have been contained in one sheet of paper; but the further I went the larger prospect I had.

See also DIP one's pen in gall; with a STROKE of the pen.

---

penny

count / watch / NAmer pinch the pennies

to be careful or cautious about how much one spends. *Early 20th cent.*

in for a penny (in for a pound)

(proverb) once begun, an undertaking needs complete commitment: literally, if you are going to spend money, spend whatever it takes to achieve success. *17th cent.*

E Ravenscroft *Canterbury Guests* 1695
It concerns you to ... prove what you speak ... In for a penny, in for a pound.

Mrs Gaskell *Mary Barton* 1849
'Oh, Job, speak! tell me all!' 'In for a penny, in for a pound,' thought Job. 'Happen one prayer will do for the sum total. Any rate, I must go on now.'

not have a penny to bless oneself with

to be impoverished or destitute: the allusion is either to the representation of a cross on former English silver pennies or to the former practice of crossing oneself, or another person's palm, with a piece of silver to bring good luck. The phrase is recorded in John Heywood's collection of proverbs and sayings (1562). *16th cent.*

Thomas Brown *Amusements Serious and Comical* 1700
One idle day I ventur'd into one of these Gaming-Houses ... Some that had lost were swearing, and damning themselves, and the Devil's Bones, that had left them never a penny to bless their heads with.

pennies from heaven

an unexpected financial reward or benefit; a windfall: from the title of a 1936 film which included a song of the same name with lyrics by Johnny Burke and sung by Bing Crosby. The song included the words 'Every time it rains, it rains | Pennies from heaven.' *Mid 20th cent.*

the penny drops

the true meaning or explanation becomes apparent: with allusion to coin-operated machines that worked when a penny was put into a slot and dropped into the mechanism. *Mid 20th cent.*

a penny for your thoughts

used to attract somebody's attention when they appear to be lost in thought: also in the form *a penny for them*. *16th cent.*

penny wise (and pound foolish)

(proverb) if one is too cautious about spending small sums, one may end up having to pay much larger ones in due course: *see also* take care of the pennies (and the pounds will take care of themselves) *below*. *17th cent*.

Francis Bacon *Essays* 1601
Be not penny-wise; riches have wings, and sometimes they fly away of themselves, sometimes they must be set flying, to bring in more.

Topsell *The Historie of Four-footed Beastes* 1607
If by couetousnesse or negligence, one withdraw from them their ordinary foode, he shall be penny wise, and pound foolish.

a pretty penny

informal a considerable sum of money gained or lost. *18th cent*.

Frederick Pilon *The Deaf Lover* 1780
Well, my master cheats his ward, and I cheat my master, for he has never seen this picture (pulls out a miniature) *nor the letter that came with it yet – if these ar'n't mock diamonds round it, it will bring a pretty penny – let me see now.*

put in one's pennyworth

informal to contribute to a conversation or discussion. The use of *pennyworth* to denote a substantial or worthwhile act or achievement dates from the 16th cent., an early application being in the context of revenge. An early use with reference to speaking, though not of the phrase itself, occurs in Shakespeare's *The Merchant of Venice* (1598) 1.ii.68: '[Nerissa] What say you then to Falconbridge, the young baron of England? [Portia] You know I say nothing to him, for he understands not me, nor I him: he hath neither Latin, French, nor Italian, and you will come into the court and swear that I have a poor pennyworth in the English.' *20th cent*.

spend a penny

to use the lavatory; to urinate: with allusion to coin-operated locks on the doors of public lavatories, which were opened by putting a penny in the slot. The phrase does not appear in print until the 1940s, by which time public conveniences charging a penny had been a feature of London life for about a century. There is a coincidental use of the phrase, not in the specific meaning it now has, in Dickens' *Dombey and Son* (1848): 'The young Toodles, victims of a pious fraud, were deluded into repairing in a body to a chandler's shop in the neighbourhood, for the ostensible purpose of spending a penny.' *Mid 20th cent*.

Jack Caplan *Memories of the Gorbals* 1991
He would then leave the kitchen and find the WC directly opposite the front door; just a WC, no bath, no wash-hand basin, no toilet-paper, no mod-cons; if he did wish to 'spend a penny', well, yesterday's newspaper was cut neatly into 6 inch squares and nailed on to a convenient wall.

take care of the pennies (and the pounds will take care of themselves)

(proverb) an exhortation to be frugal: the sentiment effectively contradicts that implied by *penny wise and pound foolish* (see above). *18th cent*.

turn up like a bad penny

(said of an unwelcome person or thing) to reappear constantly: also as a proverb *a bad penny always turns up* (and variants). A *bad penny* is a counterfeit coin that is not wanted and therefore passes rapidly from one person to another. The phrase dates from the 18th cent. in the form *bad pence*.

two/ten a penny

informal very common and having little value: based on the literal use relating to price. *19th cent*.

Benjamin Webster *Caught in a Trap* 1844
[Goguenard] *If we of the Fronde had not whopped the Queen's party yesterday, these delicacies ... these attentions, would have been devoted to them sordid cabbage growers! Another plum.* [Fan] *Two a penny, sir.* [Goguenard] *But we have scattered them like dust before the wind.*

Doremy Vernon *Tiller's Girls* 1988
A few were unfortunate, they fell in love with Russians. Wasn't there something wrong with Russia at any time? Anyway, they would fall in love with these Counts who were ten a penny and even pay for their drinks.

See also earn/turn an HONEST penny; not have two coins/pennies to RUB together.

---

perch

knock/take somebody off their perch

to cause somebody to lose an important position or status. *19th cent*.

Scott *Chronicles of the Canongate* 1827
'My eyes!' muttered Seelencooper, 'this cockerel crows gallant, to come from a Scotch roost; but I would know well enough how to fetch the youngster off the perch.'

perish

perish the thought

used to dismiss an idea or suggestion as absurd or intolerable: the only modern survival of the use of *perish* in imprecations, dating from the 16th cent. *18th cent.*

> Mary Robinson *Walsingham* 1797
> 'Sir Sidney Aubrey deserves that you should think kindly of him: his virtues, the generosity of his nature, should interest you by congeniality, and place you beyond the reach of obligation you must remain with us; you must be the friend, the associate of this noble, this accomplished kinsman.' 'Perish the thought!' exclaimed I. 'Under all the horrors of approaching events, this spot would be a scene of torture, which my fortitude would shrink at.'

person

See be one's OWN man/woman/person.

perspective

in / out of perspective

reflecting the right priorities; correctly assessing the importance or relevance of something: a metaphor from the (17th cent.) use referring to the correct or incorrect proportions in the visual arts. *17th cent.*

> Robert Aylet *David's Troubles Remembered* 1638
> They always with the times are discontent, | Still blaming States and Churches government, | Kings, Nobles, Judges, Priests and Rulers all, | Without respect within their censure fall; | Whose faults are greater in perspective shown, | But all must cover'd be that are their own.

petard

be hoist with/by one's own petard

to be the victim of one's own scheming or trickery. From Shakespeare, *Hamlet* (1601) III.iv.185 (from additional passages in the second Quarto): 'Let it work, | For 'tis the sport to have the engineer | Hoised with his own petard.' *Hoised* or *hoist* is the past participle of an old verb *hoise* meaning 'to raise aloft' (on which the noun *hoist* is based), and *petar* or *petard* is a small bomb used for blowing doors and gates in; so the phrase literally means 'blown up by one's own bomb'. *17th cent.*

phoenix

See rise like a phoenix from the ashes *at* ASH.

phut

go phut

informal to break or break down. *Phut* is partly an imitation of the sound of a gun or of a machine breaking down, but the first recorded use, by Kipling in 1888, suggests a possible connection with a Hindi word *phatna* meaning 'to split or burst'. *19th cent.*

physical

get physical

1 *informal* to resort to force or violence. *Late 20th cent.*
2 *informal* to have amorous or sexual relations. *Late 20th cent.*

> Nigel Williams *They Came from SW19* 1992
> I had so far managed to avoid being kissed by the old bat, but I had the strong feeling that, by the end of the day, she and I were going to be getting physical.

physically challenged

(said of a person) physically disabled or handicapped: a 'politically correct' euphemistic alternative used by those who consider the traditional terms to be depreciatory or insulting. *Late 20th cent.*

> *Toronto Star* 2002
> According to a study released in the spring, 55 per cent of physically challenged people make an average of four trips a year.

physician

physician, heal thyself

(proverb) an exhortation to attend to one's own faults before finding fault with others: with allusion to a passage in Luke 4:23 in which Christ returns to his home town of Nazareth 'And he said unto them, Ye will surely say unto me this proverb, Physician, heal thyself: whatsoever we have heard done in Capernaum, do also here in thy country.' The proverb appears in forms close to the current one from the 16th cent., or in the

Latin form *medice, cura teipsum*, as in Shakespeare's *2 Henry VI* (1591) II.i.57, where Cardinal Beaufort warns the Duke of Gloucester, who is Lord Protector, 'Medice, teipsum – I Protector, see to't well; protect yourself.'

pick

pick and choose

to pick only the best or most suitable from a number of alternatives: normally used disapprovingly with implications of excessive fastidiousness. In early use also in the form *pick and cull.* *17th cent.*

Byron *Don Juan* 1824
My similes are gather'd in a heap, I So pick and choose – perhaps you'll be content I With a carved lady on a monument.

pick something clean

to remove the flesh from the bones of a carcass. *18th cent.*

Swift *Gulliver's Travels* 1726
I had only one misfortune, that the rats on board carried away one of my sheep; I found her bones in a hole, picked clean from the flesh.

the pick of the bunch

the very best of a number of people or things. *Early 20th cent.*

H V Esmond *The Law Divine* 1922
[Claudia] *You're rather a dear, aren't you? And it's high time you got another hat.* [Kate] *You might spare me one of your superfluous ones.* [Claudia] *Come round any old time and you can have your pick of the bunch.*

Today 1992
Five condoms were sold for more than £80,000 yesterday even though they were well past their sell-by date. The condoms, sold at London auctioneers Christie's, dated from the 19th century. The pick of the bunch was printed with an erotic scene, complete with a vital silk drawstring.

pick up the bill/tab

NAmer, informal to agree to pay the bill, especially for a group of people of which one is a member. *Mid 20th cent.*

Independent 1989
Normally, developers paying a barrister to represent them at an inquiry must pick up the tab.

pick up the pieces

informal to resume a normal life after a setback or disaster. The metaphor is anticipated by Dickens in *Our Mutual Friend* (1865): 'In her communication with her friend by letter, she was silent on this theme, and principally dilated on the backslidings of her bad child, who every day grew worse and worse. "You wicked old boy," Miss Wren would say to him, with a menacing forefinger, "you'll force me to run away from you, after all, you will; and then you'll shake to bits, and there'll be nobody to pick up the pieces!"' *Early 20th cent.*

Henry James *The Ambassadors* 1903
This at least I shall have got out of the damned Old World: that I shall have picked up the pieces into which it has caused you to crumble.

See also pick somebody's brain(s) *at* BRAIN; pick holes in something *at* HOLE; pick up the THREAD.

picnic

no picnic

a difficult or unpleasant task or experience: based on the (early 19th cent.) use of *picnic* in the sense 'something enjoyable or exciting'. *19th cent.*

Kipling *Wee Willie Winkie* 1888
I got my 'ead chipped like a egg; I've got pneumonia too, an' my guts is all out o' order. 'Taint no bloomin' picnic in those parts I can tell you.

See also a SANDWICH short of a picnic.

picture

be/look a picture

to be very beautiful. *19th cent.*

G & W Grossmith *Diary of a Nobody* 1892
Carrie looked a picture, wearing the dress she wore at the Mansion House.

every picture tells a story

(proverb) one can draw conclusions from what one sees. The phrase occurs in a slightly different form in the opening pages of Charlotte Brontë's *Jane Eyre* (1847), where Jane is describing her delight in finding a quiet spot to read her book, *Bewick's History of British Birds*, in which 'each picture told a story: mysterious often to my undeveloped understanding and imperfect feelings, yet ever profoundly interesting'. The current form was reinforced by its use as an advertising slogan for 'kidney pills' in the 1920s, which accompanied a picture of a person bent over with back pain and unable to stand upright. *19th cent.*

get the picture
to grasp the essentials of a situation. *Mid 20th cent.*

David Lawrence *The Chocolate Teapot* 1992
Then again there's the 'right-I-warned-you-off-to-the-Head's-study' sort and the 'I'll-pretend-I-didn't-hear-that' sort. Do you get the picture?

in the picture
fully informed and up to date about a situation: in this and similar phrases, *picture* is used in its meaning 'a mental image or idea'. Often in the form *put somebody in the picture* in the sense 'to give them the necessary information'. *Early 20th cent.*

John Betjeman *Executive* 1958
And how did I acquire her [a speedboat]? *Well to tell you about that* | *And to put you in the picture I must wear my other hat.*

one picture is worth ten thousand words
(proverb) it is often easier to show something than to describe it. *Early 20th cent.*

R Haydn *Journal of Edwin Carp* 1954
'One picture speaks louder than ten thousand words.' Mr Bovey repeated the adage this morning ... when he handed me my finished portrait.

out of the picture
no longer involved in something. *Early 20th cent.*

Augustus Thomas *The Earl of Pawtucket* 1903
And Fordyce, père will kindly continue to keep out of the picture.

a/the picture of something
the very epitome of a quality or state. An early use of the expression is in Lyly's prose romance *Euphues* (1580): 'Behold England, where Camilla was born, the flower of courtesy, the picture of comelyness.' *16th cent.*

Wilkie Collins *The Woman in White* 1860
Louis ... surprised me inexpressibly, by declaring that my sister's foreign husband was dressed superbly, and looked the picture of prosperity.

pie

(as) nice/sweet as pie
very pleasant or agreeable. *19th cent.*

a piece/slice of the pie
a share in the profits or rewards. *Late 20th cent.*

Scotland on Sunday 1993
Even the Stones anthem Satisfaction, usually seen as a critique of consumerism, can be read without irony, as the cry of a man who wants a bigger slice of the pie.

pie in the sky
an illusory hope or prospect of future happiness; misplaced optimism. The words come from the refrain of a 1911 American song promoted by the movement known as IWW (Industrial Workers of the World) parodying a Salvation Army hymn that promised the virtuous their reward in heaven. In the parody, workers are ironically exhorted to 'Work and pray, live on hay, | You'll get pie in the sky when you die'. *Early 20th cent.*

See also as EASY as falling off a log / as pie; eat HUMBLE pie; have a FINGER in every pie.

piece

all of a piece (with something)
consistent or compatible (with something). *17th cent.*

Locke *An Essay Concerning Human Understanding* 1690
But in the future part of this Discourse, designing to raise an edifice uniform and consistent with itself ... I hope to erect it on such a basis that I shall not need to shore it up with props and buttresses ... or at least, if mine prove a castle in the air, I will endeavour it shall be all of a piece and hang together.

George Eliot *Middlemarch* 1872
'My dear Chettam, it won't lead to anything, you know,' said Mr. Brooke ... 'It's all of a piece with Casaubon's oddity.'

go to pieces
to lose control of oneself from stress, shock, or anger: *to pieces* occurs earlier in figurative meanings relating to loss of control or cohesion. *19th cent.*

Joseph Conrad *The Secret Sharer* 1912
Those two old chaps ran the ship. Devil only knows what the skipper wasn't afraid of (all his nerve went to pieces altogether in that hellish spell of bad weather we had).

in one piece
unharmed, without being injured or damaged. *Early 20th cent.*

Harper Lee *To Kill a Mockingbird* 1960
I made a secret reconnaissance of Jem. He seemed to be all in one piece, but he had a queer look on his face.

pick/pull/tear somebody/something to pieces
to criticize somebody or something ruthlessly. *17th cent.*

Henry Fielding *The History of Tom Jones* 1749
He well knew the hatred which all her neighbours, and even her own sisters, bore her, and how ready they would all be to tear her to pieces.

a piece of ass/tail
informal a young woman regarded sexually: *piece of flesh* and other forms denoting people are attested from the 16th cent. (e.g. Shakespeare, *Cymbeline* (1610) IV.ii.128 'Then why should we be tender | To let [= sensitive about letting] an arrogant piece of flesh threat us'). James Joyce in *Ulysses* (1922) uses *piece of goods*. *Mid 20th cent.*

Guardian 1988
She [Carly Simon] had numerous advantages. Musical skills aside, she was, in James Taylor's expressive phrase, 'a damn fine piece of ass'. She made an album called Spoiled Girl in 1985, and the title carried a ring of authenticity. If she hadn't made it as a singer, there would have been no cause for panic.

say one's piece
to state one's opinion; to say what one has to say: based on the meaning of *piece* 'a passage to be recited'. *19th cent.*

take something to pieces
to dismantle something, to separate it into its parts. *18th cent.*

Mary Wollstonecraft *A Vindication of the Rights of Woman* 1792
Every one who sees her will say, There is a modest and discreet girl; but while you are near her, your eyes and affections wander all over her person, so that you cannot withdraw them; and you would

conclude, that every part of her dress, simple as it seems, was only put in its proper order to be taken to pieces by the imagination.

See also give somebody a piece of one's MIND; a nasty/filthy piece of WORK; a piece of the ACTION; a piece of CAKE.

pierce

pierce somebody's heart/soul
to affect somebody emotionally; to move them deeply, as though with the thrust of a weapon. The phrase is an extension into broader metaphor of figurative uses of *wound, hurt, injure,* and similar words. *16th cent.*

Shakespeare *3 Henry VI* III.i.38 (1591)
[King Henry] *Her sighs will make a batt'ry in his breast, | Her tears will pierce into a marble heart.*

Jane Austen *Persuasion* 1818
I can listen no longer in silence. I must speak to you by such means as are within my reach. You pierce my soul. I am half agony, half hope. Tell me not that I am too late, that such precious feelings are gone for ever.

pig

buy a pig in a poke
to buy or accept something without checking it first or establishing its value: perhaps from the practice of putting a cat into a *poke* (= bag) and passing it off as a sucking pig: *see* let the CAT out of the bag. *16th cent.*

in a pig's eye
informal, chiefly Australian and NAmer used to express contemptuous disbelief in something said. *19th cent.*

make a pig of oneself
informal to eat excessively or greedily. *20th cent.*

Guitarist 1992
In fact it's the same show, still sponsored by us, but this time there's also percussion, synthesisers, PA and recording equipment to try and buy. In other words, fire up the Transit, shove every member of the band inside, come down and make thorough, absolute pigs of yourselves.

make a pig's ear of something
informal to make a mess of something; to bungle a task or undertaking. The pig's ear is regarded as

the least valuable part of the animal when slaughtered (*cf* make a SILK purse out of a sow's ear). *Mid 20th cent.*

pig/piggy in the middle
a person who is caught in an awkward situation between two others who are in disagreement or conflict: based on the children's game in which two players throw a ball back and forth to one another while a third player standing between them tries to intercept it (and changes places with the thrower if successful). *Mid 20th cent.*

pigs might fly
a scornful expression of scepticism about the likelihood of something suggested. The notion is found in the obsolete (17th cent.) proverb *pigs fly in the air with their tails forward*, which redoubles the absurdity, and in other fanciful allusions. It first appears in print in a 1616 edition of a dictionary for young people originally written by John Withals with additions by other contributors. *19th cent.*

> Lewis Carroll *Alice's Adventures in Wonderland* 1865
> *'I've a right to think,' said Alice sharply … 'Just about as much right,' said the Duchess, 'as pigs have to fly.'*

stare/gape like a stuck pig
old use to stare incessantly: a *stuck pig* is one that has been stabbed and would therefore stare out in its distress. Also *bleed* and *squeal like a stuck pig*. *17th cent.*

> Thomas D'Urfey *The Comical History of Don Quixote* 1696
> *Young Robin so pleas'd her, | That when she came home, | She gap'd like a stuck pig, and star'd like a mome.*

> Dickens *Great Expectations* 1861
> *'Now perhaps you'll mention what's the matter' said my sister, out of breath, 'you staring great stuck pig.'*

sweat like a pig
informal to sweat profusely. *20th cent.*

> Julian Barnes *A History of the World in 10½ Chapters* 1990
> *Bloody weather. Bloody hot all the time. Sweating like a pig, comme un porco.*

pigeon

be —'s pigeon/pidgin
to be that person's particular business or concern. *Pidgin* is a Chinese corruption of the English word *business* (as also in *pidgin English*); this form occurs in the first uses (as in the Kipling quotation below), but in later use it has been assimilated to the familiar English word *pigeon*. *Early 20th cent.*

> Kipling *Traffics and Discoveries* 1904
> *'What about their musketry average?' I went on. 'Not my pidgin,' said Bayley.*

pike

come down the pike
NAmer, informal to appear on the scene: a *pike* (short for *turnpike*) is a highway in American English. *Mid 20th cent.*

pikestaff

(as) plain as a pikestaff
completely plain or evident: originally (early 16th cent.) in the form *plain as a packstaff*, a 'plain' flat-topped pedlar's staff on which a pack could be placed when resting. The form with *pikestaff* appears from the late 16th cent., and both forms continued in use to the end of the 17th cent. (occurring in Dryden), from which point *packstaff* disappeared. *Cf* as PLAIN as day / as the nose on your face. *16th cent.*

pile

make a/one's pile
to become wealthy: *pile* in the meaning 'accumulated wealth', usually in the form *pile(s) of wealth, money*, etc, dates from the early 17th cent. *19th cent.*

> Conan Doyle *The Noble Bachelor* 1892
> *Frank wouldn't throw up his hand, though; so he followed me there, and he saw me without pa knowing anything about it … Frank said that he would go and make his pile, too, and never come back to claim me until he had as much as pa.*

pile on the agony

to exaggerate the effects of a bad situation: in 19th cent. use also with *up* instead of *on*, and in 20th cent. use in the informal form *pile it on*. *19th cent.*

Mark Twain *The Innocents Abroad* 1869
I tried to imagine the music in full blast, the leader of the orchestra beating time, and the 'versatile' So-and-so … charging around the stage and piling the agony mountains high – but I could not do it with such a 'house' as that.

pill

a bitter pill (to swallow)

a difficult situation to accept: *pill* in the sense of something unpleasant that has to be accepted dates from the 16th cent. *18th cent.*

Charles Johnson *The Wife's Relief* 1712
[Horatio] *Lookee, Sir – these are your only Conditions; you must sign this instrument for 500ol. payable to me or my order, if I save you; and I'll countersign this to pay the same value to your heirs, if I do not –* [Sir Tristrum] *'Tis a bitter Pill – but I will know what Method you take first.*

Jane Austen *Mansfield Park* 1814
Mrs. Rushworth will be very angry. It will be a bitter pill to her; that is, like other bitter pills, it will have two moments' ill flavour, and then be swallowed and forgotten.

sugar/sweeten the pill

to make an unpleasant situation or obligation seem more acceptable: also (17th cent.) in the form *gild the pill*. *17th cent.*

Thomas Goffe *The Careles Shepherdess* 1656
Still you | Doe gild the Pill, you'd have me take, but I | Assure you Sir my heart is none of mine.

Samuel Foote *The Commissary* 1765
My house is a perfect academy, such a throng of fencers, dancers, riders, musicians, – but, however, to sweeten the pill, I have a fellow-feeling for recommending the teachers.

pillar

from pillar to post

from one place or situation to another, usually with connotations of difficulty or harassment. In early uses of the phrase, which goes back to Middle English, *pillar* and *post* are the other way round; the present form, recorded from the 16th cent., is probably due to euphony and to the frequent presence earlier in the sentence of the verb *tossed*, which would produce awkwardness if *post* were to come next. But there are examples of the order *post to pillar* well into the 19th cent. The phrase is thought to be a metaphor from the bouncing and rebounding of the ball in real tennis, and was discussed by Sir James Murray during his editing of the *Oxford English Dictionary*, in *Notes and Queries* December 1905, p. 528. Murray commented as follows: 'The original form of this expression was *from post to pillar*. Of twenty-two quotations between 1420 (Lydgate) and 1700 now before me, seventeen have the original and five the later form, three of the latter being in verse, and having *post* riming with *tost*, *tossed*, which was apparently the *fons et origo* of the transposition … May I throw out the conjecture … that the game in which there was a chance of something being tossed from post to pillar was tennis?'

Fletcher & Shakespeare *The Two Noble Kinsmen* III.v.117 (a1616)
And dainty Duke, whose doughty dismal fame | from Dis to Daedalus, from post to pillar, | Is blown abroad.

Peter Anthony Motteux *The Amorous Miser* 1705
[Diego] *A Dragoon!* [Octavio] *Yes, and a pretty Gentleman; but is now coming home with a Design to hang up his Arms in his Father's Hall with the Trophies of his Ancestors, having an Aversion to starving and being drub'd from Pillar to Post by a handly* [= handful?] *of foul ugly Rogues call'd Hussars.*

Hardy *Jude the Obscure* 1895
No man had ever suffered more inconvenience from his own charity, Christian or heathen, than Phillotson had done in letting Sue go. He had been knocked about from pillar to post at the hands of the virtuous almost beyond endurance.

a pillar of society / the establishment

a person or institution much respected for their integrity and sense of social responsibility. The figurative use of *pillar* as a support for the institutions of the State is much older in freer contexts, going back into Middle English especially with reference to the Church. *19th cent.*

William Hazlitt *The Spirit of the Age* 1825
In the words of a contemporary writer, 'Reason is the queen of the moral world, the soul of the uni-

verse, the lamp of human life, the pillar of society, the foundation of law, the beacon of nations, the golden chain let down from heaven, which links all accountable and all intelligent natures in one common system.'

pilot

drop the pilot

to dispense with a trusted leader or adviser. The image is of a ship's pilot leaving the scene after guiding a ship through a channel or into harbour, made famous by the scene of Kaiser Wilhelm II of Germany dismissing Otto von Bismarck as depicted by John Tenniel in a *Punch* cartoon of 1890. The phrase dates from the early 20th cent. in allusive use.

The Times 1990
Mrs Thatcher will seek to re-establish her position in her closing address to the Scottish Conservative Party conference in Aberdeen today ... Mr Kenneth Baker, the Tory chairman, told Conservative MPs to cease their 'idle speculation' about the leadership and concentrate their fire on Labour. As the Tories headed for clearer waters, they should not, must not and would not 'drop the pilot'.

pin

(as) clean/neat as a new pin

extremely clean or neat. *18th cent.*

Peter Pindar Anticipation 1812
Thus, from the ashes of my good old inn, | Another rises, neat as a new pin.

R L Stevenson Treasure Island 1883
To me he was unweariedly kind; and always glad to see me in the galley, which he kept as clean as a new pin; the dishes hanging up burnished, and his parrot in a cage in one corner.

one could hear a pin drop

the silence and sense of expectation is or was intense. *19th cent.*

Henry James The Turn of the Screw 1898
My insistence turned him from me and kept him once more at his window in a silence during which, between us, you might have heard a pin drop.

for two pins I would —

used to express one's strong (and often petulant) inclination to do a particular thing. *Pins* as sym-

bolic of the trivial or least significant thing occurs also in the phrase *not care a pin / two pins / a row of pins for something. 19th cent.*

Charles Reade The Cloister and the Hearth 1861
My poor soul, hope not to escape their sight! The only way is not to think of them; for if you do, it poisons your cup. For two pins I'd run and leave thee. Art pleasant company in sooth.

The Times 2003
To prove that I know what's socially chic, I am off to buy some ribbed leggings for a woman with saddle-bag thighs, a box of Belgian chocolates for a girl who is trying to stick to the Cambridge diet and a bottle of after-shave for a man with a beard. For two pins I would also buy one of those jigsaws that don't have a picture on the lid, but throughout the whole of my life I have never met anybody who has been nasty enough to me to deserve that.

on pins and needles

in a state of suspense or agitation. *Pins and needles* is popularly used for the pricking sensation in the fingers or limbs when recovering from numbness. *19th cent.*

Harold Frederic The Damnation of Theron Ware 1896
I was too green before. I took the thing seriously, and I let every mean-fisted curmudgeon and crazy fanatic worry me, and keep me on pins and needles. I don't do that any more. I've taken a new measure of life.

pin one's ears back

1 to prepare oneself for swift action; to act with determination and resolve. *19th cent.*

Herman Melville Redburn: His First Voyage 1849
However, they lay in their bunks smoking, and kept talking on some time in this strain, and advising me as soon as ever I got home to pin my ears back, so as not to hold the wind, and sail straight away into the interior of the country.

2 *informal* to listen attentively; to be vigilant. *Mid 20th cent.*

Philippa Wiat The Child Bride 1990
Someone, sometime, bore an infant on the wrong side of the blanket! The lady Anne is a Mowbray all right, so 'tis plain from which side of the family this lass comes. That being so, I must watch my step and keep my ears pinned back.

stick pins into somebody

to incite or harass somebody to action. *19th cent.*

Henry James *The Portrait of a Lady* 1881
Isabel presently found herself in the singular situation of defending the British constitution against her aunt; Mrs. Touchett having formed the habit of sticking pins into this venerable instrument.

See also nail/pin one's colours to the mast *at* COLOUR.

pinch

at / NAmer in a pinch
in an emergency or in extreme circumstances. The phrase occurs in this sense in Caxton's *Book of Feats of Arms* (1489): 'Corageously at a pynche [he] shal renne upon hem'. *Be at a pinch* meant 'to be at a critical juncture', as in John Bunyan's *The Holy War* (1682): 'But Diabolus did not count that in this expedition of his, these doubters would prove his principal men, for their manhood had been tried before, also the Mansoulians had put them to the worst, only he did bring them to multiply a number, and to help if need was at a pinch.' *15th cent.*

Thomas Dekker *The Ravens Almanacke* 1609
Devout father, to make a rehearsall of my sins is folly ... And sir therefore I confesse heere that my belly is bigge, and your sweete surgerie hath wrought it, so either you must bestirre your wits to helpe now at a pinch, or else your discredit will be as great as my dishonour.

feel the pinch
to be pressured or stressed; to suffer difficulties. In modern use, the typical meaning is to be short of money, especially with reference to somebody who is normally quite comfortably off. *Pinch* is used as a metaphor representing hardship as pain, a use that dates from the early 17th cent. (e.g. Shakespeare, *King Lear* (1606) II.ii.384 '[Lear] Rather I abjure all roofs, and choose ... I To wage against the enmity o'th' air I Necessity's sharp pinch'). *19th cent.*

Thackeray *The Adventures of Philip* 1862
Have you ever felt the pinch of poverty? In many cases it is like the dentist's chair, more dreadful in the contemplation than in the actual suffering.

George Eliot *Middlemarch* 1872
This uncommonly pretty woman – this young lady with the highest personal attractions – was likely to feel the pinch of trouble – to find herself involved in circumstances beyond her control.

See also take something with a pinch of SALT.

pineapple

the rough end of the pineapple
Australian and NZ, informal harsh or unfair treatment. *Mid 20th cent.*

Sydney Morning Herald 1976
Waffling witnesses, even those of lofty social standing, were given short shrift, if not the rough end of the pineapple.

pink

in the pink
in good health or condition: an elliptical use in which *of condition* (or *health*) is omitted. Other uses of *pink* in this meaning (e.g. *the pink of perfection, fashion, taste*, etc) are recorded from the late 16th cent.; this figurative use is a synonym for the corresponding meaning of *flower*, and there is also a play on *pink* as the hue of a good complexion. The substitution is pointed to as a novelty in Shakespeare, *Romeo and Juliet* (1596) II.iii.54 '[Mercutio] Nay, I am the very pink of courtesy. [Romeo] Pink for flower. [Mercutio] Right.' *19th cent.*

pip^1 (noun)

give somebody the pip
dated, informal to cause somebody to be irritated or dejected: *pip* here is not the familiar word but a disease of poultry. The phrase is recorded in Farmer and Henley's *Slang and Its Analogues* (1890–1904). *19th cent.*

H V Esmond *The Law Divine* 1922
Personally I don't think it matters much whose latch-key a fellow's got, as long as he's got somebody's. It's being without one at all that gives one the pip.

squeeze somebody until the pips squeak
to obtain the maximum amount of money from somebody: first used by the British politician Sir Eric Geddes in 1918 with reference to the reparations exacted from Germany after the First World War: 'The Germans, if this Government is returned, are going to pay every penny; they are going to be squeezed as a lemon is squeezed – until the pips squeak.' The same phrase was used

by Denis Healey, Labour Chancellor of the Exchequer, in 1973, referring to plans to increase taxation for high earners. *Early 20th cent.*

Guardian 1985
Sir Keith's squeeze is making the educational pips squeak even louder. The teaching unions are girding themselves for a campaign of non-cooperation with the new curriculum reforms.

pip² (verb)

pip somebody at/to the post
to beat somebody at the very last minute, especially in a race or competition: the *post* is the finishing post in a race. The underlying meaning of *pip* is 'to hit with a shot' and hence 'to defeat'; it is based on the noun in the sense 'a small ball or shot'. In the late 19th cent. to *pip* somebody meant to reject or 'blackball' them in an election. *Early 20th cent.*

pipe

put that in your pipe and smoke it
you will just have to accept the situation whether you like it or not. The image is of filling a pipe with tobacco: the phrase remains current despite the decline in pipe-smoking as a popular activity, and has always been commonly addressed to people (for example, women) who have never been strongly associated with either pipes or tobacco. *19th cent.*

Thackeray The History of Pendennis 1849
If you ask me no questions, perhaps I'll tell you no lies, Captain Strong – put that in your pipe and smoke it, my boy.

pipeline

in the pipeline
informal in the process of being produced, developed, delivered, etc. An early figurative use of *pipeline* occurs in Aldous Huxley's *Crome Yellow* (1921) about a group of intellectuals meeting at a country house, in which one of the characters asks 'Have you ever read my little book, *Pipe-Lines to the Infinite*?' *Mid 20th cent.*

piping

piping hot
(said especially of food): hot and well cooked. *Piping* is from the verb *pipe* meaning 'to play on a pipe', and refers to the sizzling sound of very hot food when removed from the oven. *Middle English*

Chaucer The Miller's Tale (line 3379)
He sente hire [= her] pyment [= spiced wine], meeth [= mead], and spiced ale, | And wafres [= cakes], pipyng hoot out of the gleede [= fire].

piss

piss in/against the wind
to waste one's time on a fruitless adventure or undertaking: based on the (17th cent.) proverb (said to be of Italian origin) *he who pisses against the wind wets his shirt* (i.e. achieves nothing useful). *17th cent.*

take the piss (out of somebody)
British, informal to make fun of somebody. There may well be a connection here with *take the mickey* (*see* MICKEY), which is often explained as rhyming slang based on *Mickey Bliss* (= 'piss'). Another explanation relates the phrase to *piss-proud*, a slang expression first recorded in Francis Grose's *Dictionary of the Vulgar Tongue* (1788 edition), which describes an erection of the penis that occurs during sleep and remains on waking up (supposedly caused by a full bladder, and there is play on two meanings of *proud*, the familiar one and 'upright'). Taking the piss out of this situation therefore makes good sense in terms of the current meaning. But the chronology poses a problem with this explanation, since our expression does not appear until the 1940s. *Mid 20th cent.*

Douglas Dunn The Happier Life 1972
They form the wasted days, that treacherous silt, | That to remember truly takes the piss | As much as alcohol or cannabis.

See also shit/piss or get off the POT.

pissed

(as) pissed as a newt/fart
informal very drunk. *Newt* is one of several members of the animal world that are proverbially

associated with drunkenness (others are *coot*, *mouse*, and *parrot*), and the reasons for these choices are obscure. The suggestions for *newt* include the 'tightness' of its skin (which stretches credibility) and its capacity as an amphibian to immerse itself in liquid as a drunk might do (a little more convincing: compare *drunk as a fish*). *Mid 20th cent.*

> R Mason *The World of Suzie Wong* 1957
> *Christ, I'm pissed. I'm pissed as a newt.*

pissed off

informal fed up or irritated. *Mid 20th cent.*

> Lorenzo Thomas *Chances Are Few* 1979
> *While spirits pout, we others spot and fade | Spinning with fortune like unspooling film | Unleashing great comedians and pissed-off heroes.*

> *Guardian* 1989
> *'I am sorry about this,' begins the driver's voice. 'There's a train stopped in front of us. The driver's left it and no one knows where he's gone. And we can't move till someone finds him.' This excuse is met by a low moan crawling through the carriages. 'I'm sorry!' goes the disembodied voice; 'I'm as pissed off about this as you are. I want to get home too.'*

pit

be the pits

informal, originally NAmer to be the worst possible or the worst of its kind: a shortening of *armpits*, denoting body odour and hence unpleasantness generally. *Mid 20th cent.*

> David Lawrence *The Chocolate Teapot* 1992
> *Some of the people who became the greatest successes in the Bible were the weediest failures in the eyes of other people at the time. Take Gideon, for example ... Gideon describes himself as a member of the weakest group in his tribe and as 'the least important member' of his family! In other words Gideon was the pits in his own eyes.*

dig a pit for somebody

to set a trap (in figurative senses) for somebody: based on a (16th cent.) proverb *dig a pit for another and fall into it oneself*, itself derived from Old Testament images, e.g. Psalms 7:15 'He made a pit, and digged it, and is fallen into the ditch which he made.' *16th cent.*

the pit of one's stomach

one's inner feelings. The *pit* is the small depression near the stomach and below the ribs, and this region is regarded as the seat of one's fears and anxieties. In some uses there is overlap between the physical and allusive meaning. *19th cent.*

> Scott *Guy Mannering* 1815
> *Meg stood her ground against this tremendous volley of superlatives, which Sampson hawked up from the pit of his stomach, and hurled at her in thunder.*

> Dickens *David Copperfield* 1850
> *It was in vain to take refuge in gruffness of speech. I spoke from the pit of my stomach for the rest of the journey, but I felt completely extinguished, and dreadfully young.*

See also pit one's wits against somebody/something at WIT.

pitch

make a pitch for something

to try to secure an agreement or benefit: based on the meaning of *pitch* 'a persuasive way of speaking' (as in *sales pitch*). *20th cent.*

> *Observer* 1991
> *Replacement by hardliners gave Bakatin an instant liberal image, which he reinforces by criticising the use of military force in the Baltic republics. He calls himself 'a radical centrist' and is a good-looking grandfather of 53. He makes a pitch for the women's vote, remarking that most other male politicians think the best way to make women's lives easier would be to invent a lighter pneumatic drill.*

queer somebody's pitch

to spoil somebody's chances of doing something well or successfully. *Pitch* here refers to the site used by a street vendor or travelling performer, and *queer* is used in its meaning 'to spoil or interfere in something'. We can imagine that competing traders found ways of making life difficult for neighbouring stallholders, although we can only guess now at exactly how this was done. The phrase makes an early appearance in *Swell's Night Guide* (1846), and seems to have passed into theatrical vocabulary judging by a collection of reminiscences published in 1886: 'The smoke and fumes of "blue fire" which had been used to illuminate the fight came up through the chinks of the stage, fit to choke a dozen Macbeths, and – pardon the little bit of professional slang – poor Jamie's "pitch" was "queered" with a vengeance.' *19th cent.*

pitchfork

rain pitchforks
to rain heavily. The phrase draws on the image of pitchforks as long thin streaks like heavy rain: an early use refers to raining pitchforks 'tines downwards'. See also rain cats and dogs *at* CAT. *19th cent.*

pity

(the) more's the pity
used to express regret or disappointment. *16th cent.*

John Fletcher *Loves Pilgrimage* a1625
But now the pillars that bare | Up this blessed Town in that regular debate, and | Scambling, are dead, the more's the pity.

Delarivière Manley *The New Atalantis* 1709
But, the more's the pity (poor Gentlewoman) 'twas not her luck. The Rogue wou'd not Marry her; because he knew her Father wou'd not give her a Groat with him, but bespoke her very fair.

Charlotte Brontë *Jane Eyre* 1847
'Is all the soot washed from my face?' he asked, turning it towards her. 'Alas! yes: the more's the pity! Nothing could be more becoming to your complexion than that ruffian's rouge.'

place

all over the place
informal in a state of confusion or chaos; completely muddled. *Early 20th cent.*

Harold Pinter *The Birthday Party* 1959
Why is it that before you do a job you're all over the place, and when you're doing the job you're as cool as a whistle?

be going places
informal, originally NAmer to be on the way to success. *Mid 20th cent.*

Clothes Show 1991
Jonathon Morris is a young man going places ... He's about to pop up in all sorts of other places – and sporting a groovy new haircut.

in another place
British in the House of Lords: used by members of the House of Commons. First used by Edmund Burke in a speech of 1789: 'The present minister, he understood, had been called "a heaven-born minister" in another place.' The point of such euphemisms is to avoid the awkwardness of direct reference in matters associated with rivalry and disagreement: compare the use of *the other place* by members of Oxford University when referring to Cambridge, and vice versa. *18th cent.*

know one's place
to be aware of one's position and appropriate behaviour. *17th cent.*

Shakespeare *Twelfth Night* II.v.52 (1602)
[Malvolio] *Telling them I know my place, as I would they should do theirs.*

a place in the sun
a position of advantage or privilege. The phrase appears originally in French in the *Pensées* of Pascal (1623–62): *Ce chien est à moi, disaient ces pauvres enfants; c'est là ma place au soleil; voilà le commencement et l'image de l'usurpation de la terre.* A translation of 1688 renders this as follows: 'This Dog is mine, said those poor Children; that's my place in the Sun. This is the beginning and Image of the Usurpation of all the Earth.' Modern use of the phrase owes its origin to a use in a speech by the German Chancellor Bernhard von Bülow, referring to German ambitions in East Asia, as reported in *The Times* in 1897: 'We desire to throw no one into the shade, but we also demand our own place in the sun-light.' *17th cent.*

put somebody in their place
to remind somebody of their position; to deflate their arrogance or presumption with a rebuff. *19th cent.*

R L Stevenson *Weir of Hermiston* 1896
In the long vague dialogues she held in her mind, often with imaginary, often with unrealised interlocutors, Archie, if he were referred to at all, came in for savage handling. He was described as 'looking like a stork,' 'staring like a caulf,' 'a face like a ghaist's.' 'Do you call that manners?' she said; or, 'I soon put him in his place.'

D H Lawrence *Sons and Lovers* 1913
Mrs. Morel usually quarrelled with her lace woman, sympathised with her fruit man ... laughed with the fish man – who was a scamp but so droll –

put the linoleum man in his place, was cold with the odd-wares man, and only went to the crockery man when she was driven – or drawn by the cornflowers on a little dish; then she was coldly polite.

plain

(as) plain as day / as the nose on your face

completely plain or evident. There is an early ironic use by Shakespeare in *The Two Gentlemen of Verona* (1593) II.i.128 '[Speed] O jest unseen, inscrutable, invisible | As a nose on a man's face or a weathercock on a steeple.' *Cf* (as) plain as a PIKESTAFF. *Plain as day* dates from the 17th cent. and uses proliferate in 19th cent. literature.

Nathaniel Lee *Theodosius* 1680
Though plain as day I see my own destruction, | Yet to my death, and oh, let all the Gods | Bear Witness! I swear I will adore thee.

plan

go to plan

(said of an undertaking) to proceed as intended or expected. *Mid 20th cent.*

Louis MacNeice *Autumn Journal* 1939
Everything is going to plan; | They want the crest of this hill for anti-aircraft, | The guns will take the view | And searchlights probe the heavens for bacilli | With narrow wands of blue.

See also plan B *at* B.

planet

on another planet

informal completely out of touch with earthly reality, like an alien from another planet: typically used of somebody who appears to have no grasp of the circumstances of ordinary life and makes suggestions or expresses opinions that are totally unrealistic or inappropriate. The phrase appears in other forms, e.g. *What/which planet are you living on?* *Late 20th cent.*

Hull Daily Mail 2003
So first off – gay bishops. What's wrong with having a gay bloke as a bishop? All these idiots in the Church of England who would rather pretend there's no such thing as a clergyman who likes the fellas – what planet are they living on? I'm sure

men have been doing it with other men since the beginning of time, and so what?

plank

walk the plank

to lose one's position or livelihood; to face death or disaster. The expression alludes to the former practice attributed (chiefly in 19th cent. literature) to pirates of making prisoners walk blindfold to their deaths along a plank extending from the side of the ship over the sea. *19th cent.*

Lydia Child *Letters From New York* 1843
But they, who thus drove him 'to walk the plank', made cool, deliberate preparations to take life, and with inventive cruelty sought to add every bitter drop that could be added to the dreadful cup of vengeance.

Sydney Dobell *The Roman* 1850
Walking the plank | Of life o'er the abyss, we fear to glance | Or upward to the stars, or downward to the grave.

See also (as) THICK as two short planks.

plate

hand/give somebody something on a plate

to give something without the recipient having to make any great effort: *cf* on a SILVER platter. *Early 20th cent.*

on one's plate

as one's responsibility to be dealt with or worked on, like food to be eaten. *Early 20th cent.*

play

make a play for somebody/something

to take positive action to try to obtain somebody or something. *Early 20th cent.*

Winchell Smith *The Fortune Hunter* 1909
[Harry] *Good! I knew it. And you made a play for Lockwood's daughter, eh?* [Nat] *Certainly not! You're forgetting your instructions. I allowed her to make a play for me.*

make great play of/with something

to emphasize or exploit the advantages or importance of something for one's own purposes. *Mid 20th cent.*

Country Living 1991
Here, on an acre formerly abounding in thistles and docks, we have woven our own covert of windbreaks and fuchsia bushes and make great play of raising cabbages where cabbages – or at least, where sweetcorn, courgettes and petits pois – were hardly intended to grow.

play both ends against the middle
to support both sides of a case or argument; to avoid a commitment or definitive judgement in a matter. *Late 20th cent.*

Mario Puzo *Fools Die* 1978
He was trying to play both ends against the middle, doing his friend the favor and yet trying to warn the reader off the book with an ambiguous quote.

play by the rules
to follow assiduously the proper conventions of action or behaviour. *20th cent.*

New Musical Express 1992
It's a truly revolutionary music. It's departed from the old form and structures. It isn't playing by the rules, it's sometimes beautiful, sometimes energising, sometimes soothing and often funny in its own way.

play the devil / Old Harry with something
to cause widespread damage or disruption, typically to something vulnerable or complex. In early use the phrase appears in the shorter form *play the devil*. *Old Harry* has been a familiar nickname for the devil since the 18th cent. *16th cent.*

Shakespeare *King John* ii.i.135 (1597)
[Austria] *What the devil art thou?* [Bastard] *One that will play the devil, sir, with you, | An a may catch your hide and you alone … | I'll smoke your skin-coat an I catch you right.*

James Fenimore Cooper *Deerslayer* 1841
This being up two nights de suite … plays the devil with a man's faculties!

play fair
to obey the rules and act honestly: also *play somebody fair*. *Middle English*

Shakespeare *Measure for Measure* iii.i.142 (1605)
[Isabella] *Heaven shield my mother played my father fair.*

play somebody false
to deceive somebody or treat them dishonestly. *Play false* occurs in Lyly's *Euphues,* and among the first uses with a grammatical object (*play somebody false*) are several occurrences in plays of Shakespeare from the 1590s (*The Comedy of Errors,* 1594) onwards. Especially touching is the exchange between Miranda and Ferdinand, while playing at chess, in *The Tempest* (1613) v.i.174: '[Miranda] Sweet lord, you play me false. [Ferdinand] No, my dearest love, I would not for the world. [Miranda] Yes, for a score of kingdoms you should wrangle | An I would call it fair play.' *16th cent.*

play for time
to procrastinate or make excuses in order to gain time for oneself. *Early 20th cent.*

play a/one's hunch
to act on the basis of one's instinct or gut feeling. *20th cent.*

Krome Barratt *Logic and Design* 1989
The conscious use of analogy, metaphor, playing a hunch, brainstorming, sheer chance, trial and error or heuristics are the stuff of the think tank, where lively minds, well versed in vertical thinking, strike imaginative sparks one from another.

play into somebody's hands
to act in a way that gives an opponent or rival an advantage. *18th cent.*

Edgar Rice Burroughs *Tarzan and the Jewels of Opar* 1916
Pulling on his boots and buckling his cartridge belt and revolver about his hips he stepped to the flap of his tent and looked out. There was no sentry before the entrance to the prisoner's tent! What could it mean? Fate was indeed playing into his hands.

play it cool
informal to give an impression of nonchalance. *Mid 20th cent.*

Woman 1991
I was one of those people who used to be sort of potty about someone and then go off them within two weeks. With Simon, it was different. I played it cool.

play (it) safe / play for safety
to act cautiously and avoid risks. *Early 20th cent.*

See also act/play the (giddy) GOAT; keep/play one's cards close to one's chest *at* CARD; make/play HAVOC with; not playing with a full DECK; play one's ACE; play ball *at* BALL[1]; play a BLINDER; play one's cards right *at* CARD; play ducks and drakes with *at* DUCK; play FAST and loose; play the FIELD; play the FOOL; play the GAME; play GOD; play HARD to get; play HOOKEY; play it by EAR; play the MARKET; play (merry) HELL with; play POSSUM; play to the GALLERY; play with FIRE.

playing field

See a LEVEL playing field.

please

as — as you please

informal used to emphasize the exceptional degree to which a person or thing has a particular quality or attribute. *19th cent.*

Henry James *Confidence* 1880
Gordon Wright and his wife were out of town, but Bernard went into the country, as boldly as you please, to inform them of his little project and take a long leave of them.

pleased

See (as) pleased as PUNCH.

pleasure

at Her/His Majesty's pleasure

British (as a euphemism) detained in prison. *19th cent.*

Hardy *Far from the Madding Crowd* 1874
'Is that you, Laban?' said Gabriel. 'Yes – 'tis come. He's not to die. 'Tis confinement during Her Majesty's pleasure.'

have the pleasure of something

used in formulas introducing a polite request: especially *may I have the pleasure of — ?* Early uses are more literal in sense, and we can discern a development of formulaic uses in the 18th cent. and 19th cent. *17th cent.*

Aphra Behn *The Rover* 1677
I'll neither ask nor give a vow, tho I could be content to turn Gipsy, and become a Left-hand Bridegroom, to have the pleasure of working that great miracle of making a maid a mother.

Swift *Gulliver's Travels* 1726
The Maids of Honor often invited Glumdalclitch to their apartments, and desired she would bring me

along with her, on purpose to have the pleasure of seeing and touching me.

Jane Austen *Emma* 1816
There, it is done. I have the pleasure, madam ... of restoring your spectacles, healed for the present.

A S Byatt *Possession* 1990
May I hope that you too enjoyed our talk – and may I have the pleasure of calling on you. I know you live very quietly, but I would be very quiet – I only want to discuss Dante and Shakespeare and Wordsworth and Coleridge and Goethe and Schiller and Webster and Ford and Sir Thomas Browne et hoc genus omne.

(it was / has been) a/my pleasure

used as a polite reply to an expression of thanks. *19th cent.*

Henry James *The Portrait of a Lady* 1881
'He said very little about you, but I spoke of you a good deal.' Isabel waited. At the mention of Mr. Goodwood's name she had turned a little pale. 'I'm very sorry you did that,' she observed at last. 'It was a pleasure to me, and I liked the way he listened.'

pledge

sign/take the pledge

originally N Amer to make a formal undertaking to abstain from drinking alcohol: with allusion to formal abstinence agreements made by members of temperance societies such as the Band of Hope. *19th cent.*

Harold Frederic *The Damnation of Theron Ware* 1896
Now discipline is an important element in the machinery here. Coming to take the pledge implies that you have been drunk and are now ashamed.

plight

plight one's troth

to make a solemn promise, especially of marriage. *Plight* means 'to give as a pledge' and is related to the noun meaning 'a situation of danger'; *troth*, related to *truth*, means 'honesty' and was used in oaths. Both words are archaic and in modern use are confined to the marriage vows. *Middle English*

Chaucer *The Wife of Bath's Tale* (line 1009)
'Plight me thy trouthe heere in myn hand,' quod she, | 'The nexte thyng that I requere thee, | Thou shalt it do, if it lye in thy myght.'

plot

Used in the phrases in its meaning 'the sequence of events of a story'.

have lost the plot
to be no longer au fait with what is happening; to have lost contact with reality. *Late 20th cent.*

> *Bath Chronicle* 1999
> We have come to expect Labour and Liberal Democrat councillors to talk a lot of nonsense about traffic, but it becomes worrying when the officers advising them seem to have lost the plot as well.

the plot thickens
the situation has developed and become more complex or interesting. The analogy, in which *thicken* is used as a metaphor within a metaphor, is with the development of a literary or dramatic plot. The phrase first occurs in Act III of *The Rehearsal*, a drama by George Villiers, Second Duke of Buckingham, produced in 1672: '[Thimble] Brave Pretty-man, it is at length reveal'd, | That he is not thy Sire who thee conceal'd. [Bayes] Lo' you now, there he's off again. [Johnson] Admirably done i'faith. [Bayes] Ay, now the Plot thickens very much upon us.' *17th cent.*

> John Dunton *A Voyage Round the World* 1691
> Tis a great deal to me, and a very considerable part of my Life, for as you'll find the plot thickens apace, and the hinge of all my future fortunes is just upon turning.

plough

plough a lonely / one's own furrow
to follow an independent or isolated course of action. *Early 20th cent.*

> *Economist* 1991
> But Mr Yeltsin himself has been unable to give the miners public support because their strike threatens Russia's stubborn attempts to plough its lonely furrow of economic reform.

plough the sand
dated to work fruitlessly. *16th cent.*

See also set/put one's HAND to the plough.

plug

See PULL the plug on something.

plum

have a plum in one's mouth
to speak with a low rich-sounding voice, typically associated with an affected superior or upper-class accent. *20th cent.*

> *The Times* 1985
> Officers who had come up through the ranks shared a distaste for the sort of Sandhurst product they called a 'Rupert' – 'a few silly young officers who talk with a bag full of plums in their mouth', growled an old quartermaster, adding 'well, they can't help how they speak'.

plumb

out of plumb
not quite vertical (with reference to something that should be). *Plumb*, used from the 14th cent. and derived from Latin *plumbum* meaning 'lead', is the weight at the end of a line used to determine the true vertical. Also (19th cent.) *off plumb*. *19th cent.*

> Frederic S Cozzens *The Sparrowgrass Papers* 1856
> He from that Tuscan city had come, | Where a tower is built all out of – plumb!

plumb the depths
1 to examine or investigate the obscure or concealed details of something: from testing or measuring the depth of the ocean. *19th cent.*

> Matthew Arnold *Merope* 1858
> Much is there which the sea | Conceals from man, who cannot plumb its depths.

2 to reach the extremes of an unpleasant or bad condition: also in humorous or trivialized use. *20th cent.*

plume

borrowed plumes
finery that is not one's own, or to which one is not entitled: with allusion to the fable of the jackdaw that borrows the peacock's plumes. *16th cent.*

> Spenser *The Faerie Queene* v.iii.20 (1596)
> He could no longer beare, but forth issewed, | And to the boaster said; Thou losell base, | That hast

with borrowed plumes thyselfe endewed, | And others worth with leasings doest deface, | When they are all restor'd, thou shalt rest in disgrace.

plunge

take the plunge
informal to take a decisive first step in a course of action, especially in spite of doubts or after lengthy consideration: based on the image of diving into water. *19th cent.*

> Thackeray *Pendennis* 1848
> *The poor boy had taken the plunge. Trembling with passionate emotion, ... his voice almost choking with feeling, poor Pen had said those words which he could withhold no more, and flung himself and his whole store of love, and admiration, and ardour, at the feet of this mature beauty.*

plus

plus-minus
South African, informal approximately; more or less. *20th cent.*

poach

poach on somebody's preserve(s)/territory
to encroach on or interfere in somebody's sphere of activity. *19th cent.*

> Oscar Wilde *The Picture of Dorian Gray* 1891
> *The masses feel that drunkenness, stupidity, and immorality should be their own special property, and that if any one of us makes an ass of himself he is poaching on their preserves.*

poacher

poacher turned gamekeeper
a person who turns from attacking or threatening something to defending or protecting it. The proverb *an old poacher makes the best gamekeeper* is recorded from the 17th cent., and the notion occurs as early as Chaucer's *Physician's Tale* (lines 83–5): 'A theef of venysoun, that hath forlaft [= forsaken] | His likerousnesse [= greedy ways] and al his olde craft, | Kan kepe a forest best of any man'. *Mid 20th cent.*

pocket

have deep pockets
informal to enjoy great wealth. *20th cent.*

> *Evening Standard* 2002
> *Top lot is an extraordinary Queen Anne giltwood mirror, one and a half metres high, with elaborately moulded and incised decoration in the form of a family coat of arms, shells, flowers and scrolls ... If you have a manor house and deep pockets, this is the purchase for you.*

in / out of pocket
having made a gain (or loss) in a transaction, especially a small or trivial one. *Out of pocket* occurs in the 17th cent. in a now obsolete meaning 'having no money'. *18th cent.*

> Dickens *Hard Times* 1854
> *I wish these fellows had tried to rob me when I was at his time of life. They would have been out of pocket, if they had invested eighteenpence in the job; I can tell 'em that.*

in somebody's pocket
closely involved with somebody or constantly in their company: now often with the implication of financial dependence and control, although the notion of being in a pocket originally denoted close location rather than financial involvement. Also *live in one another's pockets* = to have a mutual financial dependence. *19th cent.*

put one's hand in one's pocket
to pay for something from one's own resources. The implication is usually of constant calls on one's assets. *17th cent.*

> Edward Ravenscroft *Dame Dobson* 1684
> *Nay, don't put your hand in your pocket, I'le have no reward till you are satisfied I have deserv'd it, when the business is over.*

> Isaac Bickerstaffe *The Maid of the Mill* 1765
> *Lord what is it to you, if his honor has a mind to give me a trifle? Do pray gentleman, put your hand in your pocket.*

> Thackeray *The Adventures of Philip* 1862
> *A man who takes your money is naturally offended if you remonstrate; you wound his sense of delicacy by protesting against his putting his hand in your pocket.*

See also line one's pockets at LINE².

poetic

See poetic/poetical JUSTICE.

point

beside the point

irrelevant. In current use the phrase is normally used with reference to comments and observations, but in earlier use it is the speaker who is said to be *beside the point*. *17th cent.*

John Ford *The Fancies Chast and Noble* 1638
[Livio] *If the Marquesse | Hath utter'd one unchaste, one wanton syllable, | Provoking thy contempt: not all the flatteries | Of his assurance to our hopes of rising, | Can or shall slave our soules.* [Castamela] *Indeed not so Sir, | You are beside the point, most gentle Signior, | Ile be no more your ward, no longer chamber'd, | Nor mew'd up to the lure of your Devotion.*

Phanuel Bacon *The Oculist* 1757
[Oculist] *But, Mr Try, if I may presume to be so inquisitive – Has your Honour fix'd upon any place in particular?* [Mr Try] *You are quite beside the point, Sir – Let the place be what it will – I have no objection, provided the salary and perquisites are pretty tolerable.*

Hardy *The Return of the Native* 1878
'She is getting old, and her life is lonely, and I am her only son.' 'She has Thomasin.' 'Thomasin is not her daughter; and if she were that would not excuse me. But this is beside the point. I have made up my mind to go to her, and all I wish to ask you is whether you will do your best to help me.'

make a point of something

to take particular care to do something, or to attach importance to it: *cf* French *faire un point de*. *18th cent.*

David Garrick *High Life Below Stairs* 1759
I'll be with you in the evening, if possible; though, hark ye, there is a Bill depending in our House, which the Ministry make a point of our attending.

Jane Austen *Pride and Prejudice* 1813
When my niece Georgiana went to Ramsgate last summer, I made a point of her having two men-servants go with her.

point of no return

the stage in a journey or undertaking at which it is necessary or more practical to continue to its conclusion rather than to turn back or give up. Also used generally to refer to any critical point beyond which certain (usually unwelcome) consequences are bound to result. *Mid 20th cent.*

Sun 2000
Let's hope George can rediscover the strength to continue the battle. But there are others who need to stay strong, too. Friends and barmen who may be tempted to cheer him up with a drink. If they really want to help him, they must keep temptation at bay. After all, who would want to give Bestie the drink that takes him past the point of no return?

score points off somebody

to make a show of superiority over somebody in an argument or dispute. *Mid 20th cent.*

stretch/strain a point

to distort the rules slightly to accommodate a particular need or circumstance; to go beyond one's normal limits. *16th cent.*

take somebody's point

to concede the validity or truth of a particular point that somebody makes, while disagreeing with them on the issue more generally. *19th cent.*

Henry James *The Ambassadors* 1903
'You say there are two? An attachment to them both then would, I suppose, almost necessarily be innocent.' Our friend took the point, but he had his clue. 'Mayn't he be still in the stage of not quite knowing which of them, mother or daughter, he likes best?'

up to a point

to a certain extent but not completely: often used as a polite way of disagreeing. The form *up to a certain point* is recorded from the early 19th cent., and in *Don Juan* (1824) Byron makes a pun on the meanings of *point* (XIII.lxxx–lxxxi): 'For good society | Is no less famed for tolerance than piety, – | That is, up to a certain point; which point | Forms the most difficult in punctuation.' *19th cent.*

Hardy *A Pair of Blue Eyes* 1873
Stephen, do you not think that if marriages against a parent's consent are ever justifiable, they are when young people have been favoured up to a point, as we have, and then have had that favour suddenly withdrawn?

Evelyn Waugh *Scoop* 1938
Mr Salter's side of the conversation was limited to expressions of assent. When Lord Copper was right,

he said, 'Definitely, Lord Copper'; when he was wrong, 'Up to a point'.

win on points

to emerge successful, especially in a disagreement or dispute, by achieving a number of effective gains and advantages rather than by a single decisive action or argument: a metaphor from boxing, in which a contestant can win by being awarded a higher number of points by the judges, without achieving a knockout. Also *lose on points*, to be unsuccessful when an opponent wins in this way. *Mid 20th cent.*

> The Times 1987
> *We end up with the ludicrous suggestion that, although Labour lost badly at the polls, it won on points, as if the two are somehow equally worthy.*

See also point the BONE at somebody; point the FINGER.

point-blank

ask/tell, etc somebody point-blank

to ask or tell somebody something directly and without warning: from the physical meaning of firing a gun or shot directly at the target and at close range. The origin of the phrase probably lies in the notion of 'pointing at the blank', i.e. the blank centre of the target, with analogies in *cutthroat*, *break-neck*, and other compounds. A postulated direct French source *point blanc* (= white spot) is not otherwise known to exist. *16th cent.*

poison

a poisoned chalice

a responsibility or reward that is given as a benefit but is likely to bring trouble or misfortune to the person to whom it is given. With allusion to the words of Macbeth before the murder of Duncan in Shakespeare's *Macbeth* (1606) I.vii.11: 'This even-handed justice | Commends th'ingredience [= contents] of our poisoned chalice | To our own lips.' *17th cent.*

name your poison / what's your poison?

humorous say what you would you like to drink: *poison* as a humorous name for alcoholic drink dates from the early 18th cent. in North American use. See also give it a NAME. *Early 20th cent.*

James Joyce *Dubliners* 1914
Just as they were naming their poisons who should come in but Higgins!

poke

take a poke at somebody

informal to hit or attack somebody. *Mid 20th cent.*

See also dig/nudge/poke somebody in the ribs *at* RIB; make FUN of / poke fun at somebody/something; poke one's NOSE into something; stick/poke one's BIB in; stick/poke/put one's OAR in.

pole

be poles apart

to have nothing in common; to disagree fundamentally. The *poles* are the North and South Pole at the extremities of the earth. *Early 20th cent.*

> Penny Junor *Charles and Diana* 1991
> *She was quite out of her depth and, frankly, bored. Her own friends were poles apart from his. They were young, rich and ambitious, typical Hooray Henries, with Sloane Ranger girlfriends.*

in pole position

in a position of advantage. In motor racing, the *pole position* is the position on the inside of the front row of the starting grid, which gives an advantage at the first bend; it is awarded to the driver who has achieved the fastest time in a practice or qualifying session. The phrase is borrowed from horseracing: the *pole* is the fence on the inside of the course, where horses have an advantage at bends over those further out from the fence. *Late 20th cent.*

> Guardian 1985
> *The US will be a debtor to the tune of, perhaps, $100 billion. The Japanese will be creditors to the tune of, perhaps, $125 billion. And we will be second with, say, a bit under $100 billion. Our brief reign in pole position will be over.*

up the pole

informal, dated in trouble or difficulty, especially pregnant but unmarried. *19th cent.*

political

politically correct

(said especially of language) respecting sensitivities and avoiding causing offence, e.g. to minorities. The two words have been used together at least since the 18th cent., but it was in the late 20th cent. that they acquired the status of a fixed expression with special connotations to do with acceptability of usage; the term itself has, however, acquired unfavourable overtones of manipulative sociolinguistic dogmatism.

Guardian 1986
Inner London Schools are trying to stamp out the First XI mentality by stopping inter-school football matches. Cricket is seemingly all but extinct within the state system. Rugby cannot be mentioned within politically correct society. Now even the egg-and-spoon race has been banned from a Bristol infants school because it is too competitive. There must be no winners and no losers in our schools today. And, in a novel twist which Lewis Carroll didn't think of when he pioneered this approach, not even any prizes either.

politics

play politics
originally NAmer to act from motives of political advantage rather than on the basis of principle. *19th cent.*

Henry Adams The Education of Henry Adams 1907
Principles had better be left aside; values were enough. Adams knew that he could never learn to play politics in so masterly a fashion as this: his education and his nervous system equally forbade it.

pomp

pomp and circumstance
solemn ceremonial formality. With allusion to Othello's words in Shakespeare's *Othello* (1604) III.iii.359: 'O, farewell, | Farewell the neighing steed and the shrill trump, | The spirit-stirring drum, th'ear-piercing fife, | The royal banner, and all quality, | Pride, pomp, and circumstance of glorious war!' 'Pomp and circumstance' was the title given by Sir Edward Elgar to a set of five marches for symphony orchestra, of which the trio section of the first became, in a slightly altered form and with words by A C Benson, the finale ('Land of Hope and Glory') of the *Coronation Ode* of 1902. *Circumstance* is archaic in this meaning except in the phrase. Allusive uses date from the end of the 18th cent.

Sheridan The School for Scandal 1777
Farewell all quality of high renown, | Pride, pomp, and circumstance of glorious town! | Farewell! your revels I partake no more, | And Lady Teazle's occupation's o'er!

pony

See on shanks's mare/pony *at* SHANKS.

poor

(as) poor as a church mouse / as church mice
extremely poor: from the notion of a church mouse being particularly unfortunate because scraps of food are not normally left around in a church. *18th cent.*

poor little rich girl/boy
a young person who is wealthy but dissatisfied: often used ironically or mockingly. 'Poor Little Rich Girl' is the title of a 1925 song by Noel Coward. Also used (with hyphens) as a qualifying phrase, as in *poor-little-rich-girl stuff*. *Early 20th cent.*

Karl Miller Authors 1989
Ronald Fraser had no love for horses. The poor little rich boy was looked after by a second mother in the person of strict Ilse, from Germany.

a/the poor man's —
a cheaper and less attractive or less fashionable alternative to something valuable but costly. The phrase occurs from the 17th cent. in the names of plants and herbs, e.g. *poor man's remedy* as a name for wild valerian and *poor man's orange* denoting a kind of grapefruit. In 19th cent. Australia and the US, *poor man's diggings* referred to inferior alluvial gold deposits that needed less capital investment to develop. These uses passed imperceptibly into the more whimsical use that is now familiar: in 1854 Herman Melville wrote that housewives called a cup of cold rainwater a 'poor man's egg'. *19th cent.*

Byron Don Juan 1824
From thence to Holland's Hague and Helvoetsluys, | That water-land of Dutchmen and of ditches, | Where juniper expresses its best juice, | The poor man's sparkling substitute for riches. | Senates and sages have condemn'd its use – | But to deny the mob a cordial, which is | Too often all the clothing,

meat, or fuel, | Good government has left them, seems but cruel.

G B Shaw *Pygmalion* 1913
[Doolittle] *I met the boy at the corner of Long Acre and Endell Street.* [Higgins] *Public house. Yes?* [Doolittle] *The poor man's club, Governor: why shouldn't I?*

a poor relation
a member of a group that is considered to be inferior to or less important than all the others: also applied to amenities, institutions, etc. *19th cent.*

See also take a dim/poor VIEW of.

pop

Some of the uses here are of the verb in its meaning 'to put suddenly or abruptly', which is used in physical and abstract senses. You can pop a cake in the oven as well as popping something down in a notebook. There is some evidence that in 18th cent. usage the physical action was a little more substantial than is normally implied today. Fanny Burney, for example, in *Evelina* (1788), included the rather odd remark 'when he had shooked me till he was tired, and I felt all over like a jelly, without saying never a word, he takes and pops me into the ditch!'

have/take a pop at somebody
informal to attack or criticize somebody. *Pop* here is 'a blow or stroke'. *20th cent.*

New Musical Express 1991
Ugly Kid Joe are likeable, fun assholes … They even take a pop at Donald Trump on 'Panhandlin' Prince', although doubtless they'll change sides when the money starts to roll in.

pop goes the weasel
a catchline taken from the 19th cent. rhyme beginning with these two verses:

Half a pound of tuppenny rice,
Half a pound of treacle.
That's the way the money goes,
Pop goes the weasel.

Up and down the City Road,
In and out the Eagle,
That's the way the money goes,
Pop goes the weasel.

The verses appeared, with the same refrain, in all sorts of different versions. *Pop* here means 'to pawn', though what exactly a weasel was in this context remains unclear; some people think it is a slang term for a tailor's iron. The Eagle was a tavern and music hall in the City Road in East London, whose customers might well have needed to pawn a thing or two to pay for their drinking, although it takes some believing that they would part with the tools of their own trade. The first reference in print to the song is in a newspaper notice of 1854 from the publishers Boosey and Sons: 'The new country dance "Pop goes the weasel", introduced by her Majesty Queen Victoria.' *19th cent.*

Robert Smith Surtees *Handley Cross* 1854
'Pop goes the weasel again!' exclaimed Mr. Jorrocks, straddling and working his arms, as if he were riding. He then resumed his reading.

pop one's clogs
British, informal to die. The meaning of this phrase, which is perhaps an elaboration of *pop off*, is obscure. If *pop* means 'to pawn' (as in *pop goes the weasel* above), it might be explained as pawning one's shoes before death, when there is no further need for them (but why *clogs*?). The phrase does not appear to go back before the 1970s. *Late 20th cent.*

Chris Kelly *The Forest of the Night* 1991
'I had a horse once, "Cheerful Charlie",' Jos said to no one in particular … 'Died on the public weighbridge … just went on his knees and popped his clogs. Funny thing.'

pop the question
British, informal to propose marriage. *18th cent.*

Richardson *The History of Sir Charles Grandison* 1753
You had nothing to do, but bridle and make stiff courtesies to him, with your hands before you – Plagued with his doubts and with your own diffidences; afraid he would now, and now, and now, pop out the question; which he had not the courage to put.

poppy

a tall poppy
informal, chiefly Australian a successful or distinguished person: with allusion to the legend that Tarquinius Superbus, the semi-legendary last king of Rome, demonstrated how to deal with

opponents by lopping the heads off poppies growing in a field. *Early 20th cent.*

> H L Nielsen *Voice of the People* 1901
> The 'tall poppies' were the ones it was desired to retrench, but fear was expressed that, as usual, retrenchment might start at the bottom of the ladder, and hardly touch those at the top at all.

port

any port in a storm
(proverb) any refuge is welcome in desperate circumstances: a metaphor from seafaring. *18th cent.*

> John Cleland *Memoirs of a Woman of Pleasure* 1748
> I feel pretty sensibly that it was going by the right door, and knocking desperately at the wrong one … I told him of it: 'Pooh,' says he, my dear, 'any port in a storm.'

See also a WIFE in every port.

position
See JOCKEY for position.

possessed

like one/somebody possessed
with great violence or fury: formerly also in the form *like all possessed*. The allusion is to being possessed by the devil or an evil spirit. *18th cent.*

possum

play possum
informal to pretend to be asleep or unconscious, especially to avoid a danger or threat. *Possum* is a shortened form of *opossum*, an American marsupial animal that feigns death when attacked (unrelated to the Australian marsupial of the same name). *19th cent.*

> Rider Haggard *She* 1887
> What happened to Job after that I am sure I do not know, but my own impression is that he lay still upon the corpse of his deceased assailant, 'playing possum' as the Americans say.

post

beaten at the post
defeated or outwitted at the last moment or by a narrow margin: a metaphor from racing (*see* pip somebody at the post *at* PIP²). *20th cent.*

> Scotsman 1993
> The threat of further redundancies is hanging over the UIE offshore construction yard in Clydebank after it failed to win a vital 40 million order from BP. The yard was beaten at the post by Trafalgar House in Middlesbrough for the order to build an 8,000 ton integrated deck.

be left at the post
to be unable to compete: a metaphor from racing, the *post* being the starting post. *Mid 20th cent.*

keep somebody posted
to keep somebody informed about a developing situation: the expression is originally North American, and probably relates to the meaning of *post* used in accounting, 'to enter items in a ledger'. In early use the phrase often appeared in the form *posted up*. *19th cent.*

> Mark Twain *Life on the Mississippi* 1883
> That's where the benefit of the bank comes in. There is water enough in 103 now, yet there may not be by the time we get there, but the bank will keep us posted all along.

See also (as) DEAF as an adder / a post; FIRST past the post; from PILLAR to post; pip somebody at the post *at* PIP².

postal

go postal
informal to go on a violent spree; to kill people indiscriminately. Also used in the weakened sense 'to fly into a rage'. The phrase owes its origin to reports of postal workers in the US running amok and killing colleagues. *Late 20th cent.*

> Evening Standard 1998
> I photocopied the article then slid it under his door accompanied by a note which said: 'Dear Graydon, Glad to see you got as far as the first room on your trip to London. Better luck next time. Regards, Toby.' He went postal. 'Frankly, you're just not a good enough friend to make that kind of crack,' he

said, anger pulsing through his face like an electrical current.

pot

go to pot
to deteriorate or collapse, especially from neglect. The image is of meat being cut to pieces to go in the pot for cooking. The phrase occurs in early use (16th cent.) in the form *go to the pot*; the present form without *the* is recorded from the 17th cent.

Head & Kirkman *The English Rogue Described* 1674
The evidence was so clear against him that he was likely to be cast, and then he was sure to go to pot, for he had been singed on the fist already, and the Judge who was to try him was very severe on that account.

keep the pot boiling
to maintain an activity, especially at a vigorous level. *19th cent.*

Louisa M Alcott *Little Women* 1868
Those are people whom it's a satisfaction to help, for if they've got genius, it's an honor to be allowed to serve them, and not let it be lost or delayed for want of fuel to keep the pot boiling.

the pot calling the kettle black
one person criticizing another for faults they both have. *18th cent.*

put somebody's pot on
Australian and NZ, *informal* to inform on somebody. *19th cent.*

Bell's Life in Sydney 1864
The police are, of course, severely censured by everybody for 'neglect of duty', and they, in turn, 'put the pot on' magistrates for the mischievous leniency they show.

shit/piss or get off the pot
informal get on with something or let others do it. *Mid 20th cent.*

See also a/the pot/crock of GOLD (at the end of the rainbow).

potato

small potatoes
informal of little or no importance. In this form the phrase is of North American origin and dates from the 1830s, but the notion is anticipated in slightly different forms in the 18th cent., for example by Coleridge, who wrote in a letter of 1797 that 'the London literati appear to me to be very much like little potatoes, that is no great things'. Also in the extended form *small potatoes and few in the hill. 19th cent.*

Baynard Rush Hall *Something for Everybody* 1846
These parasites teach that because he is now become so big and grand, the ordinary maxims and rules that answered in his earlier days, and which are well enough for small folks and Christian pilgrims, are 'small potatoes' in his case; and that Uncle Sam, like John Bull, should have a code of laws for his own use.

See also a COUCH potato; drop somebody/something like a HOT potato.

pot-luck

take pot-luck
to accept whatever food or hospitality is available: *pot-luck* dates from the 16th cent. and means literally 'whatever happens to be in the cooking pot' (as in the examples below). *18th cent.*

Richard Graves *The Spiritual Quixote* 1773
As Wildgoose, he supposed, had not dined, he should be very welcome to take pot-luck with him.

Scott *Chronicles of the Canongate* 1828
I hope Mr Lawford will take pot-luck with us, for it is just his own hour; and indeed we had something rather better than ordinary for this poor lady – lamb and spinage, and a veal Florentine.

pottage

sell something for a mess of pottage
to obtain something trivial or unimportant at the expense of something much more valuable: from the biblical account (Genesis 25:29–34) of the famished Esau selling his birthright to his brother Jacob in return for some simple food. *Mess* is an old word for a portion of food, and *pottage* is a thick stew of meat and vegetables: *mess of pottage* occurs in the 16th cent. in connection with the story of Esau; the phrase used in the Authorized Version (1611) is 'pottage of lentils' but *mess of pottage* is the form found in Bunyan (see below). In its current form the phrase dates from the 17th cent.

Bunyan *The Pilgrim's Progress* 1678
[Hope] *Why art thou so tart, my brother? Esau sold his birthright, and that for a mess of pottage, and that birthright was his greatest jewel; and if he, why might not Little-faith do so too?*

pound¹ (noun)

one's pound of flesh

all that one is entitled to, however questionable it might be morally to claim this. The allusion is to Shakespeare's *The Merchant of Venice* (1598) IV.i.98, in which the usurer Shylock claims his surety of a pound of Antonio's flesh when Antonio is unable to repay his debt ('The pound of flesh which I demand of him is dearly bought. 'Tis mine, and I will have it'). The situation is saved by the clever advocacy of Portia, who warns Shylock against spilling one drop of Antonio's blood, since his blood is not part of the surety. Allusive uses free of the specific context of Shakespeare's drama date from the 19th cent.

Catharine Sedgwick *Clarence* 1830
Gerald threw down the note; 'the sycophantic, selfish rascal!' he exclaimed, 'yes, pay him, my dear mother – if it were the pound of flesh, I would pay him.'

Willa Cather *The Song of the Lark* 1915
'Now, sir,' the Captain turned to him, 'you don't want to sell anything. You must be under the impression that I'm one of these damned New England sharks that get their pound of flesh off the widow and orphan. If you're a little short, sign a note and I'll write a check.'

pound² (verb)

take a pounding

to be heavily or overwhelmingly defeated. The image is of bombardment from heavy artillery. *Early 20th cent.*

pour

See it never rains but it pours *at* RAIN; pour COLD water on something; pour OIL on troubled waters.

powder

keep one's powder dry

to remain alert and be ready to take action when needed. The allusion is to the words attributed in various forms to the English soldier and statesman Oliver Cromwell (1599–1658) when his army was about to cross a river: 'Put your trust in God, my boys, and keep your powder [= gunpowder] dry.' *19th cent.*

powder one's nose

(said of a woman) to visit the bathroom or lavatory. *Powder room* is a (now somewhat dated) name for a toilet in a large department store or hotel. *Early 20th cent.*

power

do somebody/something a power of good

to be very helpful or beneficial: *power* is used in its meaning 'a lot, a great deal'. *18th cent.*

Thomas Gray *Correspondence* 1770
It will do you a power of good one way or other.

more power to your elbow

an expression of approval or support for somebody. *19th cent.*

the power behind the throne

a person who exerts great influence over a ruler or government without having any formal authority. The notion, though not the phrase as such, occurs in a speech of the Elder Pitt in 1770: 'There is something within the court greater than the King himself.' *19th cent.*

Mark Twain *Life on the Mississippi* 1883
Every captain of the lot was formally ordered to immediately discharge his outsiders and take association pilots in their stead. And who was it that had the dashing presumption to do that? Alas! it came from a power behind the throne that was greater than the throne itself. It was the underwriters!

power dressing

dressing in a way that emphasizes one's position or importance, and gives an impression of authority and efficiency. The term is particularly associated with the attitudes and ambitions of the 1980s and with the increased awareness of women as a force in the world of business. *Late 20th cent.*

Daily Mail 1999
Mrs Clinton needs all the help she can get. Her strong feminist views have not stopped the ambitious lawyer from paying a great deal of attention to her appearance including one complete makeover of her image when her husband's political career took off in the Eighties. Out went the thick-framed glasses and sensible shoes suited to a law school academic and in came blonde highlights and power dressing.

the powers that be

the people in authority: with allusion to St Paul's Epistle to the Romans 13:1. The expression appears in Tyndale's translation (1525) and in the Authorized Version of 1611: 'Let every soul be subject unto the higher powers. For there is no power but of God: the powers that be are ordained of God.'

practical

for practical purposes

as far as real needs or circumstances are concerned. *19th cent.*

Edgar Allan Poe *Eureka* 1848
Although this intended definition is, in fact, no definition of the Universe of stars, we may accept it, with some mental reservation, as a definition (rigorous enough for all practical purposes) of the Universe proper – that is to say, of the Universe of space.

practice

practice makes perfect

(proverb) regular practice can make one proficient in something. *16th cent.*

See also old SPANISH customs/practices.

practise

practise what one preaches

to behave in a way that is consistent with what one expects of others. *19th cent.*

Charles Kingsley *Westward Ho!* 1855
He could say with honest pride, as Raleigh did afterwards when he returned from his Guiana voyage, that no Indian woman had ever been the worse for any man of his. He had preached on this

point month after month, and practised what he preached; and now his pride was sorely hurt.

prawn

See come the RAW prawn.

prayer

not have a prayer

informal to have no chance of success. *Mid 20th cent.*

Guardian 1989
Whether the men of the Eighties want to risk their ageing bodies against such threats, only the Nineties will reveal. Boxing White Hopes like Cooney do not have a prayer of toppling Tyson.

preach

preach to the converted

to waste one's efforts advocating or recommending something to those who already favour it. *19th cent.*

precious

precious little/few

not very many: *precious* as an intensifying adverb is largely confined to these uses. *19th cent.*

Mark Twain *The Innocents Abroad* 1869
Yet who really knows the story of Abelard and Heloise? Precious few people. The names are perfectly familiar to everybody, and that is about all.

pregnant

a pregnant silence/pause

a meaningful or significant silence: *pregnant* in this meaning dates from the 15th cent. *19th cent.*

Henry James *Roderick Hudson* 1876
Miss Garland rose and turned to rejoin her companions, commenting these admissions with a pregnant silence. 'Poor Miss Light!' she said at last, simply.

premium

at a premium

rare or difficult to obtain and therefore valuable or expensive: from the financial meaning 'at a value higher than par' (the opposite of *at a discount*). *19th cent.*

Dickens *Martin Chuzzlewit* 1844
In less than four-and-twenty hours the scanty tavern accommodation was at a premium.

put/place a premium on something
to attach particular importance or value to something. *Early 20th cent.*

presence

presence of mind
the ability to retain one's self-possession and act calmly in an emergency or difficult situation. *17th cent.*

William Congreve *Incognita* 1692
It required no less wit and presence of mind than she was endowed with so to acquit her self on the suddain.

Jane Austen *Emma* 1816
He is a most charming young man. Ever since the service he rendered Jane at Weymouth, when they were out in that party on the water, and she, by the sudden whirling round of something or other among the sails, would have been dashed into the sea at once, and actually was all but gone, if he had not, with the greatest presence of mind, caught hold of her habit – (I can never think of it without trembling!).

present

all present and correct
everybody accounted for, nobody missing or absent. *20th cent.*

Malcolm Hamer *Sudden Death* 1991
She looked as delightful as ever, trimly turned out in cream trousers and a bright red sweater and with the bumps all present and correct and in the right places.

present company excepted
apart from the people present: used to exclude the hearers of a spoken generalization, especially when it is critical or unfavourable. *The present company*, in various forms, was a favourite phrase of Dickens'. *17th cent.*

Charles Gildon *The Post-boy Rob'd of His Mail* 1692
The Follies of all men, except those of the present company, afford wonder, and laughter, but those are plac'd too nigh to be distinguish'd.

Dickens *Bleak House* 1853
Everybody, it appears, the present company excepted, has plotted against Mrs. Snagsby's peace.

(there is) no time like the present
an exhortation to act promptly. The sentiment occurs somewhat earlier in other forms. *17th cent.*

Richard Cumberland *First Love* 1795
No time like the present, therefore I'll charitably leave you together – which is a good-natur'd way of making you perfectly disagreeable to each other.

Charlotte Brontë *Jane Eyre* 1847
I rose, opened the piano, and entreated him, for the love of heaven, to give me a song. He said I was a capricious witch, and that he would rather sing another time; but I averred that no time was like the present.

press

press the flesh
informal, chiefly NAmer to shake hands. *Early 20th cent.*

The Times 1987
Candidates should stick by the side of the celebrity to ensure inclusion in any photos or TV clips. Neither celebrity nor candidate should carry anything except a pen. Their hands should be free to press flesh, sign autographs, accept gifts or pick up babies (up to age two) or pets (up to spaniel).

See also be pushed/pressed for TIME; drive/hammer/press/ram something HOME.

pretty

(as) pretty as a picture
extremely pretty or attractive: applied in various ways to women, gardens, scenery, etc. The comparison is first recorded in dialect use in the first years of the 20th cent., along with *pretty as paint*, *pretty as a speckled pup*, and others. *19th cent.*

Augustin Daly *The Lottery of Love* 1888
By gorm! you were pretty as a picture, then, and I came precious near falling right down heels over head in love with you.

Edith Wharton *Ethan Frome* 1911
She sat down on the tree-trunk in the sun and he sat down beside her. 'You were as pretty as a picture in that pink hat,' he said. She laughed with pleasure.

not just a pretty face
clever as well as attractive: used with reference to a woman to counter traditional male stereotypes. *20th cent.*

Daily Telegraph 1992
In this film, the plot comes by postcard. But Voyager is more than just a pretty face; one would expect no less from Volker Schlondorff.

sitting pretty
enjoying comfortable circumstances or advantages. *Early 20th cent.*

Roald Dahl *Matilda* 1989
And who's finished up the better off? Me, of course. I'm sitting pretty in a nice house with a successful businessman and you're left slaving away teaching a lot of nasty little children the ABC.

See also come to a pretty PASS; a pretty PENNY.

prey

fall prey to something
to be defeated or overcome by something. *19th cent.*

Jane Austen *Pride and Prejudice* 1813
Though she did not suppose Lydia to be deliberately engaging in an elopement without the intention of marriage, she had no difficulty in believing that neither her virtue nor her understanding would preserve her from falling an easy prey.

price

at any price
regardless of the cost or sacrifice. *17th cent.*

Richard Brome *The Northern Lasse* 1632
Oh that I could at any price or penance now redeeme one day! Never was hasty match sooner repented.

Edmund Burke *Reflections on the Revolution in France* 1790
These gentlemen deal in regeneration; but at any price I should hardly yield my rigid fibers to be regenerated by them, nor begin, in my grand climacteric, to squall in their new accents or to stammer, in my second cradle, the elemental sounds of their barbarous metaphysics.

every man / everybody has a/their price
money can always be used to persuade people. *18th cent.*

Thomas Paine *The Rights of Man* 1792
What are the present Governments of Europe but a scene of iniquity and oppression? What is that of England? Do not its own inhabitants say it is a market where every man has his price, and where corruption is common traffic at the expense of a deluded people?

a price on —'s head
a reward offered for the capture or death of a wanted person. *17th cent.*

William Clark *The Grand Tryal* 1685
Against me God his Ban has issued, | Proscrib'd me, set a price upon my head.

Scott *Waverley* 1814
The generous, the courteous, the noble-minded Adventurer, was then a fugitive, with a price upon his head.

price oneself out of the market
to offer one's goods or services at prices that are higher than those of one's competitors without offering any greater value, thereby making the competitors more attractive to customers. *Mid 20th cent.*

what price —?
what value or significance does — have? The expression is often used of something that has lost its value or is likely to lose it. *19th cent.*

James Joyce *A Portrait of the Artist as a Young Man* 1916
Mr W. S. Gilbert ... speaks of the billiard sharp who is condemned to play: 'On a cloth untrue With a twisted cue And elliptical billiard balls.' He means a ball having the form of the ellipsoid ... Moynihan leaned down towards Stephen's ear and murmured: 'What price ellipsoidal balls! Chase me, ladies, I'm in the cavalry!'

prick

kick against the pricks
to harm oneself in a futile attempt to oppose or resist something: based on the image of a beast of burden kicking when goaded or spurred, with particular reference to the words spoken to Saul on the road to Damascus (Acts 9:5) 'I am Jesus

whom thou persecutest. It is hard for thee to kick against the pricks.' *Middle English* (in Wyclif)

a pricking in one's thumbs

an uneasy premonition or foreboding: with allusion to Shakespeare, *Macbeth* (1606) IV.i.61 '[Second Witch on the arrival of Macbeth] By the pricking of my thumbs, | Something wicked this way comes.' *17th cent.*

prick (up) one's ears

to start to listen when something catches one's attention: from the literal use of a dog or horse that puts its ears erect in alertness. *17th cent.*

> Shakespeare *The Tempest* IV.i.176 (1613)
> [Ariel] *Then I beat my tabor, | At which like unbacked* [= unridden] *colts they pricked their ears, | Advanced their eyelids, lifted up their noses | As they smelt music.*

pride

one's pride and joy

a person or thing that one is especially proud of or devoted to. Both words occur separately in their concrete meaning 'a source of pride (or joy)' from Middle English (e.g. in Wyclif). *19th cent.*

> Wilkie Collins *The Haunted Hotel* 1879
> *'Will the day never come,' he pleaded, 'when the privilege of protecting you may be mine? when you will be the pride and joy of my life, as long as my life lasts?' He pressed her hand gently.*

pride goes before a fall

(proverb) excessive pride and self-importance is likely to bring about one's humiliation or downfall. The sentiment is biblical (Proverbs 16:18 'Pride goeth before destruction, and a haughty spirit before a fall') and it occurs in English from the 14th cent., the form *pride will* (or *must*) *have a fall* being usual in the 18th cent.

pride of place

the highest or best position. The phrase was originally a term in falconry, denoting a high position the bird occupies before making its swoop, as we see in Shakespeare, *Macbeth* (1605) II.iv.12 '[Old Man to Ross] On Tuesday last | A falcon, tow'ring in her pride of place, | Was by a mousing owl hawked at and killed.' Uses in free contexts date from the 19th cent.

> Browning *The Ring and the Book* 1842
> *Took her wrongs – | And not once, but so long as patience served – | To the town's top, jurisdiction's pride of place, | To the Archbishop and the Governor.*

See also swallow one's pride *at* SWALLOW².

prime

prime the pump

to provide the initial (often financial) support needed to get an enterprise under way. From the literal use, to put a small amount of water into a pump in order to make it start: hence also *pump-priming*. *Mid 20th cent.*

> Mario Puzo *Fools Die* 1978
> *He, Lieverman, would throw in the pump-priming cash, the development money.*

primrose

the primrose path

a life of ease and pleasure, especially one ending in disaster: with allusion to Shakespeare, *Hamlet* (1601) I.iii.50 '[Ophelia to Laertes] Do not, as some ungracious pastors do, | Show me the steep and thorny way to heaven | Whilst like a puffed and reckless libertine | Himself the primrose path of dalliance treads.' *17th cent.*

prince

prince charming

an ideal suitor: named after the hero of the fairy tale *Cinderella*, an 18th cent. translation of *Cendrillon* by Charles Perrault (1628–1703). *19th cent.*

> Oscar Wilde *The Picture of Dorian Gray* 1891
> *She was thinking of Prince Charming, and, that she might think of him all the more, she did not talk of him, but prattled on about the ship in which Jim was going to sail.*

prisoner

a prisoner of conscience

a person who is imprisoned for their political or religious beliefs. The term was first used by Amnesty International in the early 1960s. *Mid 20th cent.*

take no prisoners
to be ruthless or uncompromising in one's dealings with others. The image is of the treatment of enemies in warfare, killing one's opponents rather than letting them live. *20th cent.*

problem

have a problem with something
to find a proposition or notion unacceptable or objectionable; to take issue with something. *Late 20th cent.*

Procrustean

a Procrustean bed/remedy
a means of enforcing conformity: after Procrustes, a robber in Greek mythology who tied his victims to a bed, making them fit if they were the wrong size by either stretching them or cutting bits off. *19th cent.*

Edgar Allan Poe *Criticism* 1831
Here is a trochaic line: 'See the / delicate-footed / rain-deer'. The prosodies – that is to say the most considerate of them – would here decide that 'delicate' is a dactyl used in place of a trochee ... Others ... would insist upon a Procrustean adjustment, thus 'del'cate', an adjustment recommended to all such words as silvery, murmuring, etc ... whenever they find themselves in trochaic predicament.

prodigal

a prodigal son
a repentant spendthrift or libertine: with allusion to the biblical story (Luke 15) of the ne'er-do-well younger son who repents and returns home to be welcomed with great celebration by his father. *See also* kill the fatted calf at FAT. *16th cent.*

Shakespeare *The Winter's Tale* IV.iii.96 (1611)
[Autolycus] I know this man well. He hath been since an ape-bearer, then a process-server – a bailiff – then he compassed the motion of the Prodigal Son, and married a tinker's wife within a mile where my land and living lies, and having flown over many knavish professions, he settled only in rogue. Some call him Autolycus.

production

make a production of something
to do something with excessive fuss or show. *Mid 20th cent.*

Kate Kingston *A Warning of Magic* 1993
But there was nothing she could do about it, short of giving him an explanation for the presence of Richard's car outside her flat. And why should she make a production of it? Even if he cared, he probably wouldn't believe her.

profession

the oldest profession
prostitution. Kipling referred to it as 'the most ancient profession in the world' in 'On the City Wall' (*In Black and White*, 1888). *19th cent.*

prolong
See prolong the AGONY.

promise

promise the moon/earth
to make extravagant and unrealistic promises. *19th cent.*

Disraeli *Lothair* 1870
They had been married several years and she treated him as a darling spoiled child. When he cried for the moon, it was promised him immediately; however irrational his proposition, she always assented to it.

promises, promises
a sceptical or ironic reaction on hearing another person's intentions. *20th cent.*

Guardian 1985
In the past few weeks the Government has ... held out the possibility of freehold rights for qualified Africans in 'white' South Africa. 'Promises, promises,' said a senior Progressive Federal Party MP, Dr Alex Boraine, shortly after President PW Botha had opened the first full session of the country's new tricameral Parliament. 'How many times have we heard before that the Government is moving away from "unnecessary" discrimination?'

proof

the proof of the pudding is in the eating

(proverb) the real value or effectiveness of something can only be determined from use or experience of it, and not from appearances or claims made. The notion goes back to the 14th cent.: *proof* here is used in the meaning 'an operation designed to establish a fact or truth; a test'. In its current form the expression dates from the 17th cent. An alternative phrase, *the proof is in the pudding*, though sometimes found, makes no sense.

Edward Ward *The Rambling Fuddle-Caps* 1706
I hope, like the cook, you'll not turn painter-stainer; | If you do, notwithstanding your huffing and prating, | The proof of the pudding shall be in the eating.

prop

prop up the bar

to spend many hours in a pub drinking. *Mid 20th cent.*

Listener 1965
He was to be seen almost every night propping up the left end of the bar in the Wheatsheaf.

pro

the pros and cons

the factors in favour of and against a suggestion or proposal: from Latin *pro* 'for' and *contra* 'against'. *17th cent.*

Thomas Holcroft *He's Much to Blame* 1798
I assure you, I am for pros and cons and whys and wherefores. Your Aristotles, and Platos, and Senecas, and Catos are my delight! I honor their precepts, venerate their cogitations, and adore the length of their beards!

J S Mill *Representative Government* 1861
I believe, however, that in this case there is in general, among those who have yet heard of the proposition, no other hostility to it than the natural and healthy distrust attaching to all novelties which have not been sufficiently canvassed to make generally manifest all the pros and cons of the question.

protest

under protest

reluctantly and after stating one's objections. *19th cent.*

Wilkie Collins *The Woman in White* 1860
There is really no need to threaten me. Shattered by my miserable health and my family troubles, I am incapable of resistance. If you insist, you take your unjust advantage of me; and I give way immediately. I will endeavour to remember what I can (under protest), and to write what I can (also under protest).

proud

do somebody proud

to treat somebody very well, or give them cause for pride or gratification. *19th cent.*

Trollope *The Last Chronicle of Barset* 1867
When she suggested that it might be expedient for the sake of the family that she should come back to Mr. Bangles for further information at a subsequent period, he very politely assured her that she would 'do him proud', whenever she might please to call in Hook Court.

proven

not proven

neither proved nor disproved; not capable of proof: from the judicial verdict in Scots law, when there is not enough evidence to establish either guilt or innocence. *18th cent.*

providence

See TEMPT fate/providence.

prune

prunes and prisms

(said of speech) prim and affected. Used with allusion to the words of Mrs General in Dickens' *Little Dorrit* (1857): 'Father is rather vulgar, my dear … Papa … gives a pretty form to the lips. Papa, potatoes, poultry, prunes and prism, are all very good for the lips: especially prunes and prism. You will find it serviceable in the formation of a demeanour, if you sometimes say to yourself in company or on entering a room,

"Papa, potatoes, poultry, prunes, and prism, prunes and prism".' *19th cent.*

> **John William De Forest** *Playing the Mischief* 1875
> *How could I know all about Congressional rules, and decorums, and prunes and prisms? It would be very hard in you to make me suffer for your mistakes.*

> **L M Montgomery** *Anne of Avonlea* 1909
> *Dora's nose was straight, Davy's a positive snub; Dora had a 'prunes and prisms' mouth, Davy's was all smiles; and besides, he had a dimple in one cheek and none in the other, which gave him a dear, comical, lopsided look when he laughed.*

public

go public
1 to form a public company. *Mid 20th cent.*

> **David Oates et al** *Advice from the Top* 1989
> *Conran had launched a business empire that was eventually to employ thirty-three thousand people ... His empire mushroomed across Britain, France and the USA. It went public in 1981.*

2 to reveal information in the press or other public media. *Late 20th cent.*

> **A Hall** *The Kobra Manifesto* 1976
> *The girl's fever ... had either driven or panicked Kobra into the open and in seizing the Boeing they'd gone public.*

in the public eye
well known to the general public from the press, broadcasting, etc. *17th cent.*

> **Shakespeare** *Antony and Cleopatra* III.vi.11 (1607)
> [Caesar] *Unto her | He gave the stablishment of Egypt; made her | Of lower Syria, Cyprus, Lydia, | Absolute queen.* [Maecenas] *This in the public eye?* [Caesar] *I' th' common showplace, where they exercise.*

See also public ENEMY number one.

publish

publish and be damned
an expression of defiance in the face of public exposure for impropriety: the words are attributed to the Duke of Wellington when replying to a blackmail threat to publish gossip about the relationship with his mistress Harriet Wilson. *19th cent.*

> **John Steinbeck** *Of Mice and Men* 1937
> *Old Candy was watching her, fascinated ... 'We'd tell,' he said quietly. 'We'd tell about you framin' Crooks.' 'Tell an' be damned,' she cried. 'Nobody'd listen to you.'*

publish or perish
a slogan emphasizing the importance to academic institutions of publishing their research material in order to retain financial support. *20th cent.*

> **Bernard Bergonzi** *Exploding English* 1990
> *Despite the contempt expressed in the past for the American principle of 'publish or perish', British universities are more and more looking at volume of publication – otherwise, 'performance indicators' – as a sign of virtue.*

pudding

See in the (pudding) CLUB; the PROOF of the pudding is in the eating.

puff

in all one's puff
British, informal in one's entire life: based on the meaning of puff 'breath (of life)'. *Early 20th cent.*

> **James Joyce** *Ulysses* 1922
> *You never saw the like of it in all your born puff.*

pull

pull somebody's leg
to deceive or tease somebody playfully. The origin of the phrase is unclear: it may have something to do with the idea of tripping somebody and making them fall by pulling their legs from under them. Another theory has to do with the way public hangings were carried out in former times. Friends of the condemned man were said to have pulled his legs when dangling from the rope to speed up the process of asphyxiation and shorten his suffering. In Thomas Hood's poem 'The Last Man' the hangman, left alone in the wood, contemplates suicide but desists, crying out 'In vain my fancy begs, | For there is not another soul alive | In the world to pull my legs.' But this is hardly a matter to be associated with mild deception and teasing. *19th cent.*

pull the other one/leg (it's got bells on)

informal a sceptical reaction to being teased, or to something that sounds implausible. *Mid 20th cent.*

Scuba World 1991
There is no doubt that swordfish have succeeded in piercing the bottom planking of boats, but if any were ever sunk in this way is unknown. Even so, if you see the 'sail' of a sailfish, or the 'sword' of a swordfish coming straight towards you, it might be wise to take avoiding action. Just think what your insurers would say: 'Sunk by a swordfish. Pull the other one.'

pull out all the stops

to do everything possible to achieve a result or effect: pulling out all the stops of an organ produces a full and thrilling sound. Also in variant forms such as *pull out more stops*, etc. The phrase is predominantly 20th cent. in use, although Matthew Arnold refers in an essay published in the 1860s to one who 'tries to pull out a few more stops in that ... somewhat narrow-toned organ, the modern Englishman'. Figurative references to organ stops date from the 16th cent. *Early 20th cent.*

Glasgow Herald 1994
The Vienna negotiations over the proposed partition of Bosnian territory and the Muslim demand for access to the Adriatic sea coast controlled by Croats are seen as a vital preliminary to the resumption of the Geneva conference. This coincides with the beginning of Greece's six-month presidency of the European Union, giving rise to speculation that Athens, as a traditional ally of Serbia, will pull out the stops to broker a breakthrough agreement.

pull the plug on something

informal to put an end to an activity or operation. The phrase originally referred to the literal pulling of a plug to empty a lavatory pan in old systems, but in modern use the notion is probably a more general one, either of emptying liquid from a container or of breaking an electrical connection, i.e. pulling a plug in a different sense. *Late 20th cent.*

Irish News 2001
The loss-making ITV Digital may not even be around come the end of the year, let alone by 2003 – and ITV is coming under increasing pressure to pull the plug on the channel.

pull one's punches

to be cautious or restrained in one's criticism or reactions: typically used in negative contexts. From the literal meaning referring to ineffective punching in boxing. *Mid 20th cent.*

Liverpool Echo 2002
For the past few years, Californian design expert Ann Maurice has proved that she doesn't pull her punches. Sometimes she has laughed at what people have created in their homes, at other times she has ripped down items without asking what the owners think.

pull rank (on somebody)

to assert one's authority (over somebody) when persuasion fails. *Early 20th cent.*

pull strings / NAmer wires

to make use of one's contacts and influence in order to achieve something: the image in this and the following phrase is of the manipulation of a puppet. *Mid 20th cent.*

pull the strings

to be in control of events or activities: with allusion to pulling the strings of a puppet to make it dance or move. The image is occasionally expressed in a more explicit metaphor (as in the quotation below). *19th cent.*

Wilkie Collins The Woman in White 1860
What are we (I ask) but puppets in a show-box? Oh, omnipotent Destiny, pull our strings gently! Dance us mercifully off our miserable little stage!

pull together

(said of two or more people) to cooperate to achieve a common goal. *18th cent.*

Wordsworth The Waggoner 1805
A word from me was like a charm; | Ye pulled together with one mind; | And your huge burthen, safe from harm, | Moved like a vessel in the wind!

pull oneself together

to recover one's composure after losing control. *19th cent.*

Kate Chopin The Awakening 1899
'One of these days,' she said, 'I'm going to pull myself together for a while and think – try to determine what character of a woman I am, for, candidly, I don't know. By all the codes which I am acquainted with, I am a devilishly wicked specimen of the sex. But some way I can't convince myself that I am. I must think about it.'

pull one's weight

to do one's full share of work: literally in rowing, to pull the oars in proportion to one's own weight, hence contributing appropriately to the team effort. *19th cent.*

See also draw/pull in one's horns *at* HORN; like pulling TEETH; make/pull a FACE; pull a FAST one; pull a RABBIT out of the hat; pull one's socks up *at* SOCK[1]; pull the WOOL over somebody's eyes.

---

pulp

beat/smash somebody to a pulp

to beat somebody severely: from the use with reference to paper-making and similar processes in which materials are reduced to a soft pulp. *20th cent.*

Maeve Binchy *Circle of Friends* 1991

'Listen, I'll go in tomorrow and kick the shit out of the fellows who did it.' 'No, no, Jack, please. That would make it worse.' 'Not if I beat them to a pulp it won't. They won't try anything again.'

---

pulse

feel the pulse of something

to gauge the underlying opinions or sentiments of a group of people in a particular matter: a metaphor from medical usage, in which feeling a person's pulse determines their heart rate. *17th cent.*

Henry James *The American* 1877

She was evidently versed in the current domestic history; she was placed where she could feel the pulse of the house.

---

pump

pump iron

informal to exercise using weights. *Late 20th cent.*

Guardian 1984

Today's clear-eyed, pink-cheeked beauty munches fibre, drinks Perrier, pumps iron and chants mantras. She has glowing skin, regular motions, hard muscles and no anxiety.

punch

beat somebody to the punch

to forestall somebody or act before they do: a metaphor from boxing. The phrase is mid 20th cent. in figurative use (the use in boxing is early 20th cent.).

J Curtis *Conjure Me* 1993

In the store cupboard, he found a can of beef stew and dumped it in a saucepan to heat. He ate it with some biscuits, getting it down fast, his face close to the plate, his fork-hand hooking round to beat illness to the punch.

punch above one's weight

to perform or contribute in excess of one's reputation or supposed abilities: another metaphor from boxing, in which competitors are classed according to their body weights. *20th cent.*

Economist 1993

He has made a string of good speeches, written – unlike those of most ministers – mainly by himself … He has eloquently explained why Britain should and can still 'punch above its weight'.

punch the clock

informal to clock in or out for work: from the practice of inserting a card into a machine to record the time of entry and exit (also called *punch in/out*). *Early 20th cent.*

roll with the punches

to adapt to unexpected circumstances, especially problems and setbacks: from the movement of a boxer in rolling his body to avoid or lessen the force of his opponent's blows. *Mid 20th cent.*

She 1989

I have decided to give myself time. After all, time is really what this is all about – whether it is friend or enemy, whether to roll with its punches or fight back.

See also PACK a punch; PULL one's punches; punch somebody's lights out *at* LIGHT[2].

Punch

(as) pleased as Punch

extremely pleased or satisfied. The simile alludes to Mr Punch in 'Punch and Judy', who is traditionally depicted with a self-satisfied grin on his face. The name *Punch* is a shortening of *Punchinello*, the (17th cent.) name of a character in a puppet show of Italian origin. Also occasionally *as proud as Punch. 19th cent.*

> Mrs Gaskell *Mary Barton* 1849
> *Well! grandfather came home as proud as Punch, and pulled the bottle out of his pocket.*

> Dickens *Hard Times* 1854
> *'When Sissy got into the school here,' he pursued, 'her father was as pleased as Punch.'*

Punic

Punic faith

the violation of trust; treachery. The phrase translates Latin *punica fides*. It literally means 'Phoenician faith' and refers to Carthage, a city founded by Phoenicians and the enemy of Rome over several centuries: Rome defeated Carthage in several wars and finally destroyed the city in 146 BC. *17th cent.*

punt

take/have a punt at something

informal, chiefly Australian and NZ to attempt something; to have a go. *Punt* here is the word for a kick of a ball, typically done quickly with the ball dropped from the hands without hitting the ground. *Mid 20th cent.*

> *Sydney Morning Herald* 1969
> *Melbourne … selectors have 'taken a punt' in naming 20-year-old Russell Collingwood as centre half-forward.*

pup

buy / sell somebody a pup

British, informal to be cheated, or to cheat somebody, by buying or selling something worthless or useless. This is another example of a 'deceit' idiom based on the value of animals (*cf* buy a PIG in a poke, let the CAT out of the bag). *Early 20th cent.*

purdah

in purdah

in a state of seclusion or isolation from other people. In Hindi and Urdu a *parda* is a screen or veil behind which women are concealed from the eyes of strangers in traditional Hindu and Muslim societies. The phrase dates from the early 20th cent. in extended use.

pure

(as) pure as the driven snow

completely pure, like white snow driven into smooth drifts or undulations. The American actress Tallulah Bankhead (1903–68) was famously quoted as adapting the phrase in describing herself with the words 'I'm as pure as the driven slush'. *Mid 20th cent.*

pure and simple

that and nothing else. Originally used in more literal senses and with grammatical mobility; now typically placed after the person or thing referred to. *17th cent.*

> William Leighton *Vertue Triumphant* 1603
> *Establish such decrees as may us leade, | To know the path of perfect good to treade. | The last is pure and simple policie; | By which the subiects do their fortunes shroud.*

> Oscar Wilde *The Importance of Being Earnest* 1895
> *[Jack] I have always pretended to have a younger brother of the name of Ernest, who lives in the Albany, and gets into the most dreadful scrapes. That, my dear Algy, is the whole truth pure and simple. [Algernon] The truth is rarely pure and never simple. Modern life would be very tedious if it were either, and modern literature a complete impossibility!*

See also the real SIMON Pure.

purler

come/go a purler

informal to fall heavily or headlong. *Purler* is derived from a verb *purl* meaning 'to upset or overturn'. *Early 20th cent.*

> *New Scientist* 1991
> *Beware of fine writing, chaps. You can come a terrible purler.*

purple

born in/to the purple

born into a ruling family or into the aristocracy: *purple* has been associated with the dress of royalty since Byzantine times, its exclusiveness probably due to the high cost of the purple dye. The children of ruling emperors were known as *Porphyrogenitus* (or *Porphyrogenita* if female), meaning 'born of the purple', because they were born in a room (called 'Porphyra', from *porphyros* = purple) that was adorned with purple decoration. *18th cent.*

> Jabez Hughes *Claudian* a1731
> *And may Maria fruitfully increase, | And bring a young Honorius forth with Ease, | In Purple born, to press his Grandsire's Knees.*

a purple patch
a florid or elaborate passage in a piece of literature. The phrase translates *purpureus pannus* from the Roman poet Horace (1st cent. BC), in *De Arte Poetica* 14: *Inceptis gravibus plerumque et magna professis, | Purpureus, late qui splendeat, unus et alter | Adsuitur pannus* ('To weighty undertakings and those that claim great objects, is often sewn on here and there a purple patch of one kind or another that makes a fine show far and wide'). *19th cent.*

> Henry Ellison *Stones from the Quarry* 1875
> *Must I tag on some 'purple patch'; thereby | Get Shakspear to eke out my penury, | And lace my threadbare jacket with his gold!*

> Somerset Maugham *Of Human Bondage* 1915
> *'Who was Ruskin anyway?' asked Flanagan. 'He was one of the great Victorians. He was a master of English style.' 'Ruskin's style – a thing of shreds and purple patches,' said Lawson.*

---

purpose

accidentally on purpose
informal, usually humorous in a way that appears to be accidental but is in fact deliberate. *18th cent.*

> Defoe *Augusta Triumphans* 1728
> *There are sharpers of different stations and denominations ... Under pretence of taking a bottle, or spending an evening gayly, they draw their cull to the tavern, where they sit not long before the Devil's bones or books are found accidentally on purpose, by the help of which they strip my gentleman in an instant, and then generously lend him his own money.*

> Disraeli *Sybil* 1845
> *Lord de Mowbray advancing, was met accidentally on purpose by Mr Tadpole, who seemed anxious to push forward to Lord Marney.*

purse

hold the purse strings
to have financial control of an organization or enterprise. There are other variations in the phrase (see below), which is based on the image of a purse with a drawstring to close it. *19th cent.*

> Henry James *Roderick Hudson* 1876
> *The prince has been an orphan from his third year; he has therefore had a long minority and made no inroads upon his fortune. Besides, he is very prudent and orderly; I am only afraid that some day he will pull the purse-strings too tight.*

See also make a SILK purse out of a sow's ear.

---

pursuit
See in HOT pursuit.

---

push

at a push
British, informal in extreme circumstances; in an emergency. The phrase is listed in the *Dictionary of the Canting Crew*, published at the end of the 17th cent.

come to the push
to reach a point where action is needed. *Push* is used here in its meaning 'concerted attack or effort'. *17th cent.*

> Francis Bacon *The Wisedome of the Ancients* 1619
> *For most men, before it come to the push, can acutely prie into and discerne their enemies estate.*

give somebody / get the push
informal to dismiss somebody (or be dismissed) from a job; to reject somebody (or be rejected). *19th cent.*

push at/against an open door
to find support or approval in an unexpected quarter or against expectations. *20th cent.*

> British Medical Journal 1978
> *Purchasers and providers recognise that sharing of information can contribute to the shared aim of improving health care. There is no reason why the same approach could not be adopted here. If the National Health Service Management Executive was to tackle this issue it might find that it was pushing at an open door.*

when push comes to shove

informal, originally NAmer when action is called for or a difficulty must be faced: often used loosely for general emphasis. The notion is of having to shove if mere pushing is ineffective, and is probably based on what goes on in ball games. *Mid 20th cent.*

> **Daily Mirror 1996**
> *Geri also claims to be 'desperately worried' about a single European currency. 'Britain was the first to break away from the Roman Empire,' she says. 'When push comes to shove, the pounds, the dollars and deutschmarks can't be equal. They can't all be at the same standard.'*

See also be pushed/pressed for TIME; push the BOAT out; pushing up (the) daisies *at* DAISY; push one's LUCK.

---

put

not know where to put oneself

to feel extremely awkward or embarrassed. *20th cent.*

> **Tom Stoppard Rosencrantz and Guildenstern Are Dead 1966**
> [Guildenstern] *What about our evasions?*
> [Rosencrantz] *Oh, our evasions were lovely. 'Were you sent for?' he says. 'My lord, we were sent for'. I didn't know where to put myself.*

put something behind one

to forget a bad experience or mistake and look to the future. *19th cent.*

> **Mrs Gaskell North and South 1855**
> *But we will not talk of that any more, if you please. It is done – my sin is sinned. I have now to put it behind me, and be truthful for evermore, if I can.*

put it/something about

1 to spread a piece of news or gossip. *18th cent.*
2 *informal* to be sexually promiscuous. The first recorded use is in a letter written by Byron in January 1817, in which he refers to his brief affair with Claire Clairmont (the stepsister of Mary Shelley) who has given birth to a daughter. Byron excuses himself as follows: 'I never loved nor pretended to love her – but a man is a man – & if a girl of eighteen comes prancing to you at all hours – there is but one way – the suite of all this is that she was with child … Whether this impregnation took place before I left England

or since – I do not know – the (carnal) connection had commenced previously to my setting out – but by or about this time she has – or is about to produce. – The next question is is the brat *mine*? – I have reason to think so … This comes of 'putting it about' (as Jackson calls it) & be damned to it – and thus people come into the world.' *19th cent.*

put it to somebody

to submit an assertion or question for consideration: often followed by a *that* clause. *17th cent.*

> **Edward Howard The Six Days Adventure 1671**
> [Frankman] *Marry do I, and dare swear it before your Tribunal | Of Love too, if you please. – How Madam! Command my love? [Crispina] I put it to you as a Supposition, Sir.*

> **Richardson Clarissa 1748**
> *Once more, however, I will put it to you, – Are you determin'd to brave your papa's displeasure?*

> **Kipling A Friend's Friend 1888**
> *All the women wanted him turned out, and all the men wanted him kicked. The worst of it was, that every one said it was my fault. Now, I put it to you, how on earth could I have known that this innocent, fluffy T. G. would break out in this disgusting manner?*

put one over on somebody

informal to trick or deceive somebody: a variant form with *across* instead of *over on* is recorded from about the same date but is now less common. *Early 20th cent.*

put something to bed

informal to make the final preparations for printing and publishing a newspaper or book: with allusion to settling a child or sick person for the night. *Mid 20th cent.*

> **Monica Dickens My Turn to Make Tea 1951**
> *We went to press, or, as we liked to say in our nonchalant Fleet Street jargon, we put the paper to bed.*

put up or shut up

informal, chiefly NAmer to justify oneself or keep silent: usually in the imperative. There are two images at work here: one is of physically putting up (i.e. raising) one's fists in readiness to fight, and the other is of putting up (i.e. paying) money in making a bet or bid. *19th cent.*

stay put

informal to remain in the same position or situation. The phrase is originally North American and is described in Bartlett's *Dictionary of Americanisms* (1848) as a 'vulgar expression'. *19th cent.*

> Louisa M Alcott *Hospital Sketches* 1863
>
> *A second and saner phantom, 'all in white', came to the rescue, in the likeness of a big Prussian, who spoke no English, but divined the crisis, and put an end to it, by bundling the lively monoped into his bed, like a baby, with an authoritative command to 'stay put', which received added weight from being delivered in an odd conglomeration of French and German.*

> Willa Cather *Alexander's Bridge* 1912
>
> *You've got to hang about for me, you know. I can't even let you go home again. You must stay put, now that I have you back. You're the realest thing I have.*

See also keep/put a tight REIN on somebody/something; not put it PAST — (to —); put BACKBONE into somebody; put one's best FOOT forward; put the boot in / into somebody *at* BOOT[1]; put a brave FACE on something; put one's FINGER on something; put the FINGER on somebody; put one's FOOT down; put one's FOOT in it; put one's hands up *at* HAND; put one's MIND to something; put out feelers *at* FEELER; put the screws on somebody *at* SCREW; put a sock in it *at* SOCK[1]; put TWO and two together; put the wind up somebody *at* WIND[1]; put somebody WISE; put words into somebody's MOUTH; set/lay/put STORE by something.

putty

be (like) putty in somebody's hands

to be easily influenced or manipulated by somebody. *Mid 20th cent.*

> P D James *Devices and Desires* 1989
>
> *Father can be remarkably obstinate when he thinks he knows what he wants and Mother is putty in his hands.*

Pyrrhic

a Pyrrhic victory

a victory won at such a great cost that it brings no benefit to the victor. The phrase alludes to the battle fought between Pyrrhus of Epirus and a Roman army at Asculum in 279 BC, in which Pyrrhus was victorious but lost so much of his army that he could not take advantage of his success. *19th cent.*

QT

See on the QT *at* on the QUIET.

quantity

See an UNKNOWN quantity.

quart

get/fit a quart into a pint pot
to attempt to accommodate something large in too small a space; also in extended uses, to attempt an impossible task. *19th cent.*

Daily News 1896
What he might describe in homely phrase as putting a quart into a pint pot.

quarter

give no quarter
to show no mercy or clemency; to offer no terms. The phrase originates in the treatment of prisoners, *quarter* being used in the sense 'an exemption from being put to death'. The relation of this sense to the physical meanings is obscure, although it may be connected with the notion of quarters as accommodation for prisoners. This meaning, and related meanings to do with parts of a town or city, arose from the concept of a place divided into zones or regions, originally conceived in terms of the compass (hence the four-fold notion). The term was also applied to the parts of an army camp. A phrase that is perhaps related, *keep good quarters with somebody*, occurs in Shakespeare's *The Comedy of Errors* (1594) II.i.107, where Adriana, wife of Antipholus of Ephesus, tells her sister about a man who 'promised me a chain. | Would that alone o' love he would detain, | So he would keep fair quarter with his bed.' *17th cent.*

See also a BAD quarter of an hour.

queen

See take the (King's/Queen's) SHILLING.

Queensberry

the Queensberry Rules
the basic rules of behaviour: a generalized use with allusion to the code of rules for boxing drawn up in 1867 under the sponsorship of the eighth Marquess of Queensberry. First used figuratively by G B Shaw in 1895: 'There the contest was in the presence of a court, with measured ground and due formality – under Queensberry rules, so to speak.' *19th cent.*

queer

in Queer Street
in difficulties, especially financial ones. *Queer Street* is recorded from the early 19th cent. as a place where difficulties or troubles of various kinds abound; financial contexts became predominant in the 20th cent. *19th cent.*

Dickens Pickwick Papers 1837
I don't wish to say anything that might appear egotistical, gentlemen, but I'm very glad, for your own sakes, that you came to me: that's all. If you had gone to any low member of the profession, it's my firm conviction, and I assure you of it as a fact, that you would have found yourselves in Queer Street before this.

See also queer somebody's PITCH.

question

be a question of time
to be bound to happen eventually. *19th cent.*

Wilkie Collins The Moonstone 1868
At your age, and with your attractions, is it possible for you to sentence yourself to a single life? Trust my knowledge of the world – nothing is less possible. It is merely a question of time.

the — in question
the person or thing being considered or talked about. *17th cent.*

Shakespeare Cymbeline I.i.34 (1610)
His father | Was called Sicilius ... | And had, besides this gentleman in question, | Two other

sons who in the wars o' th' time | Died with their swords in hand.

out of the question

not to be considered or permitted; impossible: originally used in the meaning 'irrelevant to the issue'. *18th cent.*

Fanny Burney Evelina 1778

As to consulting you, my dear, it was out of all question, because, you know, young ladies hearts and hands are always to be given with reluctance.

Jane Austen Northanger Abbey 1818

But do not insist upon my being very agreeable, for my heart, you know, will be some forty miles off. And as for dancing, do not mention it, I beg; that is quite out of the question.

See also the sixty-four thousand dollar question *at* SIXTY.

be quids in

informal to be financially secure or advantaged; to have gained in a deal or made a large profit. *Early 20th cent.*

Which Mortgage 1991

Borrowers are bombarded with all types of special schemes, designed to save them money. But many borrowers choose an appealing discount deal as the sole criterion when they take out a loan. And yet this does not automatically mean they will be quids in.

not the full quid

Australian and NZ, *informal* intellectually deficient. *Mid 20th cent.*

G Dutton Andy 1968

Yer mad. I don't think yer got the full quid.

---

quick

cut somebody to the quick

to make somebody feel deeply hurt or upset. The *quick* is an area of tender or sensitive flesh such as that beneath the nails of the hands and feet. Other phrases, such as *touch* and *sting to the quick*, are recorded from the 16th cent., and Fanny Burney wrote in a letter of October 1793 'I could not deeply consider the situation of these venerable men, without feeling for them to the quick.' *17th cent.*

Mary Wollstonecraft A Vindication of the Rights of Woman 1792

Tell me, ye who have studied the human mind, is it not a strange way to fix principles by showing young people that they are seldom stable? And how can they be fortified by habits when they are proved to be fallacious by example? Why is the ardour of youth thus to be damped, and the luxuriancy of fancy cut to the quick?

See also (as) quick as a FLASH; be quick off the MARK; quick on the DRAW.

---

quid

A slang term of uncertain origin for a pound sterling (originally a sovereign or guinea).

quiet

(as) quiet as a mouse/lamb

extremely quiet or gentle. The form with *mouse* is derived from an earlier (late 16th cent.) phrase *speak like a mouse in cheese* meaning 'to speak very softly'. *19th cent.*

Emily Brontë Wuthering Heights 1847

Cathy ran to me instead of Linton, and knelt down and put her burning cheek on my lap, weeping aloud. Her cousin had shrunk into a corner of the settle, as quiet as a mouse, congratulating himself, I dare say, that the correction had lighted on another than him.

W H Auden Homage to Clio 1960

Henry Adams | Was mortally afraid of Madams: | In a disorderly house | He sat quiet as a mouse.

on the quiet

secretly; without anybody knowing: also shortened to *on the QT* (or *qt*). *19th cent.*

George Augustus Sala The Seven Sons of Mammon 1862

If he'd only promise to drop in sometimes of a Sunday, and take a bit of dinner on the quiet at my little place at Forest Hill, I'd write his name off my ledger to-morrow.

See also (as) still/silent/quiet as the GRAVE; (do) anything for a quiet LIFE.

quits

Based on the adjective *quit* meaning 'free (of a person or thing)'. The suffix *-s* is not fully explained, but may be influenced by the Latin word *quitus* (or *quittus*) meaning 'discharged' formerly entered on receipts to denote a payment made.

call it quits

1 to acknowledge that terms are now even and that neither side has an advantage. The phrase dates from the 17th cent. in the form *cry quits*.

Aphra Behn *The City Heiress* 1682
These are your Tory rogues, your Tantivie roysters; but we shall cry quits with you, rascals, erelong.

2 to call a halt to an activity, especially after partially completing it. *19th cent.*

Emerson Bennett *Wild Scenes on the Frontiers* 1859
Oh, no, Kelser – I don't want to take anything up; and so I beg you won't say nothing to him. Come! let's take a drink all round, and call it quits.

The Face 1992
As 12-ounce cans of vegetables bounce off the side of my car, one of them smashing my rearview mirror and another sailing with surprising accuracy through my open car window and striking me on the shoulder, I decide to call it quits for the night and return in daylight.

quiver

an arrow in the quiver

one among a range of resources or possibilities. Also in other forms, e.g. *more than one arrow in the quiver*. *19th cent.*

Mark Twain *Life on the Mississippi* 1883
He was uncertain as to when she might get her trip, but thought it might be to-morrow or maybe next day. This would not answer at all; so we had to give up the novelty of sailing down the river on a farm. We had one more arrow in our quiver: a Vicksburg packet, the Gold Dust, was to leave at 5 P.M.

qui vive

on the qui vive

alert and attentive. French *qui vive?*, meaning 'long live who?', was originally a challenge made by a sentry to an approaching individual to declare their allegiance. *18th cent.*

George Eliot *Middlemarch* 1872
When he was under an irritating impression of this kind he would go about for days with a defiant look, the colour changing in his transparent skin as if he were on the qui vive, watching for something which he had to dart upon.

quote

quote ... unquote

used to indicate in speech that something the speaker is saying is derived from the words of somebody else and does not necessarily form the speaker's own opinion. *Mid 20th cent.*

S Ransome *The Deadly Miss Ashley* 1950
She says, quote, 'What girl wouldn't?' unquote.

R

the three Rs

reading, writing, and arithmetic, the three essential features of a basic education. Of these, only *reading* properly begins with an *r*; *writing* begins with the sound of *r*, whereas *arithmetic* has *r* only in its second syllable and the phrase therefore humorously assumes a shortened pronunciation (*'rithmetic*); in fact the words often appear as *reading*, *riting*, and *rithmetic* in early 19th cent. sources. The phrase is occasionally extended in use to other sets of words beginning, or made to begin, with an *r*. *19th cent.*

> Caroline M Kirkland *Forest Life* 1850
> When we have had only a taste of the sweetness of 'book-learning', we shall no longer content ourselves with 'the three Rs, readin', ritin' and 'rethmetic', but view them as only the stepping-stones to things far more delightful.

rabbit

breed like rabbits

informal (said of people) to have many children: typically used humorously or disapprovingly. *19th cent.*

> Mark Twain *The Prince and the Pauper* 1881
> 'Another new claimant of the crown!' cried the officer. 'Verily they breed like rabbits to-day. Seize the rascal, men, and see ye keep him fast while I convey this precious paper within and send it to the king.' He hurried away, leaving the prisoner in the grip of the halberdiers.

pull a rabbit out of the hat

to achieve a spectacular success against all probability or expectations. The image is of the traditional conjurors' trick of making a rabbit appear from an apparently empty top hat. *Mid 20th cent.*

> Agatha Christie *Sad Cypress* 1940
> 'You want me, I see, to be the conjurer. To take out of the empty hat rabbit after rabbit.' 'You can put it that way if you like.'

race

be in the race

informal, chiefly Australian and NZ to have good prospects of success. *Early 20th cent.*

> Worker 1904
> It's emu dung, and not too bad in place | Of 'bacca, when you're stony broke | And graft's not in the race.

a race against time

a need to act rapidly in order to achieve an undertaking against a deadline. *19th cent.*

> Susan Fenimore Cooper *Elinor Wyllys* 1846
> Troops of men of all ages were hurrying over the side-walks of Broadway, usually enlivened by the gay dresses and bright faces of the ladies. There were young men running a race against time, carrying lists in their hands with an impossible number of visits to be paid during the day.

rack

at rack and manger

having plenty; not wanting for anything. The allusion is to the provision of hay in a *rack* and *manger* in a stable. The phrase goes back to Middle English, where it appears in the works of John Wyclif.

go to rack and ruin

to suffer from deterioration or neglect. *Rack* (also spelt *wrack* and related to *wreck*) means 'destruction' or 'ruin' and in early use occurs alone, e.g. Milton *Paradise Lost* (1667) xi.821 'A world devote to universal rack'. *16th cent.*

> Mary Wollstonecraft *Maria or the Wrongs of Woman* 1798
> My plan ... was to take a house, and let out lodgings; and all went on well, till my husband got acquainted with an impudent slut, who chose to live on other people's means – and then all went to rack and ruin. He ran in debt to buy her fine clothes, such clothes as I never thought of wearing myself.

on the rack

under great mental or emotional stress: based on the image of being tortured on the rack, an instrument formerly used for stretching the victim's body. In Shakespeare's *The Merchant of Venice* (1598) III.ii.25 Bassanio appeals to Portia, whom he loves, with the words 'Let me choose, | For as I am, I live upon the rack.' And in *Othello* (1604) III.iii.340, Othello tells Iago 'Thou hast set me on the rack. | I swear 'tis better to be much abused | Than but to know't a little.' *16th cent.*

rack one's brains

to try hard to remember something. *Rack* here means 'test or strain severely'; a 16th cent. source contains an exhortation 'Rack not thy wit to win by wicked ways'. See also CUDGEL one's brain/brains. *17th cent.*

> John Cleland *Memoirs of a Woman of Pleasure* 1748
> But watch'd, and overlook'd as I was, how to come at it, was the point, and that to all appearance, an invincible one: not that I did not rack my brains and invention how at once to elude my mother's vigilance, and procure myself the satisfaction of my impetuous curiosity.

raft

a (whole) raft of —

a large number or collection of things. *Raft* is a variant form of *raff* meaning 'a large number or collection', most familiar in modern use as an element in *riff-raff*. *19th cent.*

> James Kirke Paulding *Westward Ho!* 1832
> I wish I may be forced to pass the 'old sycamore root' up-stream twice a day, if I'd give the Mississippi Navigator for a whole raft of such creturs.

rag

(from) rags to riches

progressing from extreme poverty to great wealth, especially in a remarkable way: *rags-to-riches* is used as an adjectival phrase. *Mid 20th cent.*

> *Art Newspaper* 1992
> The story seemed to have everything to meet the commercial demands of Hollywood. There was a rags to riches tale about the son of immigrants who went to parties with the rich and famous, a recognisable name, and even a dead body.

in one's glad rags

informal, originally NAmer in one's best clothes; in formal dress. *Early 20th cent.*

lose one's rag

informal to lose one's temper: earlier in the form *get one's rag out*, and other expressions in which *rag* is symbolic of temper. *Mid 20th cent.*

> Robert Rankin *The Suburban Book of the Dead* 1993
> 'Hello?' shouted Balberith. 'Someone answer me or I'm gonna lose my rag.'

on the rag

NAmer, informal (said of a woman) menstruating: a *rag* here is a sanitary towel. *Late 20th cent.*

part brass rags with somebody

to break off a friendship after a quarrel. The phrase is said to be of nautical origin: sailors would keep the rags they used to clean the ship's brass in shared jars; when two sailors got on bad terms for any reason, the owner of the jar might throw out the other's rags. *19th cent.*

rag, tag, and bobtail

the rabble or riff-raff. The expression occurs in various forms (also *ragtag and bobtail* and *tag, rag, and bobtail*); *rag* and *tag* denote ragged clothes, and a *bobtail* is a dog or horse that has had its tail cut short. *17th cent.*

> Smollett *The Life and Adventures of Sir Launcelot Greaves* 1762
> Mr Gobble, thanks be to God, can defy the whole world to prove that he ever said an uncivil word, or did a rude thing to a gentleman, knowing him to be a person of fortune. Indeed, as to your poor gentry and riff-raff, your tag, rag, and bobtail, or such vulgar scoundrelly people, he has always behaved like a magistrate, and treated them with the rigger of authority.

See also CHEW the fat/rag; a RED rag to a bull.

rage

all the rage

informal very popular or fashionable: based on the use of *the rage* meaning 'a short-lived fad or craze'. *19th cent.*

> Thomas Haynes Bayly *Parliamentary Letters* 1818
> Works of all kinds shall issue from the press, | To tell the world the virtues you possess; | Enumerating all you've done and said, | And giving us

your life before you're dead; | *Your 'beauties' then*
shall grace some hot-press'd page | *(Selected*
beauties now are all the rage).

ragged

run somebody ragged
informal, chiefly NAmer to exhaust somebody by
making them work hard. *Early 20th cent.*

rail

go off / run off / leave the rails
informal to start behaving erratically or unpredictably: based on the image of a train leaving the
track and careering off out of control. Conversely,
to *be* or *stay on the rails* is to act sensibly and with
self-control. *19th cent.*

John Buchan *Greenmantle* 1916
*It was the best story, the clearest and the fullest, I
had ever got of any bit of the war. He told me just
how and why and when Turkey had left the rails.*

Rosemary Conley *Rosemary Conley's Inch Loss Plan*
1990
*Please try and be really strong tonight and don't
cheat at all. You have done so well to get to this
point, it is vital that you stay on the rails until the
first weighing and measuring day.*

Frank Kippax *Other People's Blood* 1993
*Jessica put on a grave expression. 'There are some
traditions, I will admit. If I did marry Parr, and had
two little children and made a lovely home, I'd be
allowed to run off the rails a bit, so long I was
discreet. Once a woman's done the social bit, she's
allowed to take a lover, as a right.'*

See also RIDE the rails.

rain

(come) rain or shine
whatever the conditions or circumstances: literally, whether it is raining or fine. *17th cent.*

it never rains but it pours
(proverb) troubles and difficulties all seem to
come together. *18th cent.*

Thomas Holcroft *The Adventures of Hugh Trevor*
1794
*The very next day I received a note from the bishop,
inviting me to partake of a family dinner, with him
and his niece. So it is! And so true is the proverb: it*

*never rains but it pours! Good fortune absolutely
persecuted me! Honours fell so thick at my feet that
I had not time to stoop and pick them up!*

See also (as) RIGHT as rain; rain cats and dogs *at*
CAT; rain on somebody's PARADE; rain pitchforks
at PITCHFORK; rain stair-rods *at* STAIR.

rainbow

chase rainbows / a rainbow
to have illusory ambitions; to pursue unachiev-
able goals. A *rainbow-chaser* is somebody who
does this. *Cf* a/the pot/crock of GOLD at the
end of the rainbow. *19th cent.*

Donald Grant Mitchell *Dream Life: A Fable of the
Seasons* 1851
*I shall leave you here in the middle of your first foray
into the world of sentiment, with those wicked blue
eyes chasing rainbows over your heart, and those
little feet walking every day into your affections.*

raincheck

take a raincheck (on something)
NAmer, informal to decline an offer or invitation,
with the intention of taking it up later. Based on
the US practice of giving a ticket, called a *rain-
check*, to spectators at a rained-off sporting event,
allowing them a refund or admission at a future
date. *Mid 20th cent.*

Pamela Hansford Johnson *The Humbler Creation*
1959
*Westlake said, 'I'll take a rain-check. Be back.'
Maurice, not certain of this idiom which he vaguely
knew to be American, watched him go. 'Has he had
enough?' he asked Kate ... 'I should make a guess
that he has to have a drink.'*

Philippa Davies *Status: What It is and How to Achieve
It* 1991
*Although meetings are not always called to decide
upon definite action – the purpose may be, for
instance, to do a 'raincheck' on the progress of a
project – everyone involved should have a clear idea
of the meeting's objective(s) and an active contribution to make.*

rainy

save/keep something for/against a rainy day

to keep money or some other resource in reserve for a time of need: probably derived from the practice of outdoor labourers who depended on the weather for their livelihood putting money aside to cover rainy days when there was no work. *16th cent.*

Anon *The Life and Death of Mrs Mary Frith* 1662
I held very good correspondence now also with those grandees of this function of thievery, the blades and hacks of the highway; who having heard from their inferiour tribe this repute of my equitable dealing, did deposite in my hands some of their coine against a rainy day.

raise

raise the roof

to make a din; (said especially of an audience, congregation, etc in a large building) to make a great noise of singing or clapping and cheering a performer: also said of the person or people being cheered. The image is of huge waves of sound rising to the roof and lifting it from the building. *Early 20th cent.*

Christopher Morley *The Haunted Bookshop* 1919
Aubrey remembered something having been said about the old terrier sleeping in the kitchen. He felt sure Bock would not let any German in at night without raising the roof. Probably the best way would be to watch the front of the shop.

See also play/raise HOB; raise CAIN; raise the DEVIL; raise a DUST; raise one's eyebrows *at* EYEBROW; raise one's HAT to somebody; raise HELL; raise the STANDARD; raise the wind *at* WIND¹; rear/raise its (ugly) HEAD.

rake¹ (tool)

(as) thin/lean as a rake

extremely thin. The phrase refers to the slender handle of a rake, and occurs earlier in the form *lean as a rake*. *Middle English*

Chaucer *Prologue* (line 287)
A clerk ther was of Oxenford also, | That unto logyk hadde [= had studied logic] longe ygo. | As leene was his hors as is a rake, | And he nas nat [= was not] right [= very] fat, I undertake.

Spenser *The Faerie Queene* ii.xi.22 (1596)
As pale and wan as ashes was his looke, | His bodie leane and meagre as a rake.

rake over the (old) coals / the ashes

to revive memories of an unpleasant experience or one that is best forgotten. The image is of raking ashes or dying embers in order to make them flare up again. Figurative uses date from the 20th cent.

Today 1992
Wilkinson ... was unwilling to get drawn into a slanging match yesterday. 'I do not see the point in raking over old coals,' he said philosophically.

rake² (dissolute person)

a rake's progress

a gradual deterioration into dissipation: with reference to *The Rake's Progress*, a series of eight engravings by William Hogarth (1697–1764) which depict the descent of a spendthrift young heir from his wealthy inheritance to despair and madness. There are various references to these pictures in contemporary literature: in Oliver Goldsmith's *She Stoops to Conquer* (1773), Squire Hardcastle lists some of the contents of his house, which his visitor the young Marlow mistakenly believes to be an inn; these include 'a set of prints too. What think you of the rake's progress for your own apartment?' The theme provided the subject of a drama by Leman Rede (1833) and an opera by Stravinsky, first performed in Venice in 1951, with a libretto by W H Auden and Chester Kallman. Most allusive uses date from the turn of the 20th cent., but Thackeray used the phrase as a chapter heading in *The History of Pendennis* (1849) and also in *The Virginians* (1858). *19th cent.*

ram

See drive/hammer/press/ram something HOME; force/ram something down somebody's THROAT.

rank

break rank(s)

to abandon or fail to maintain loyalty or solidarity: based on the notion of soldiers falling out of line in a battle formation. To *be* or *stand out of rank*, recorded from the 17th cent. but no longer current, had a similar meaning. Figurative uses appear in the 19th cent., although the phrase is found in military contexts from the 17th cent.

Thackeray *The Adventures of Philip* 1862
Men are poltroons and run. Men maraud, break ranks, are guilty of meanness, cowardice, shabby plunder.

close ranks

to unite in mutual support. The image is of soldiers making a close formation (i.e. the opposite of the previous phrase). Apart from a stray 17th cent. use of *close files* (by the English jurist John Selden in 1649: 'The Barons and Clergy suddenly close their files, and like a stone wall stood firm to each other'), figurative uses do not emerge until the 19th cent.

Maria Edgeworth *Tales of Fashionable Life* 1809
With difficulty I mounted my horse, and escaped from the closing ranks of my persecutors. At night I gave directions to have the gates kept shut, and ordered the porter not to admit any body at his peril.

James Fenimore Cooper *Pathfinder* 1840
Cheer up, my brave friend, and trust to a father's knowledge of womankind. Mabel half loves you already, and a fortnight's intercourse and kindness, down among the islands yonder, will close ranks with the other half. The girl as much as told me this herself, last night.

rise from/through the ranks

to start in a junior or subordinate position and work one's way to the top by one's own efforts or abilities: originally used in the context of military promotion. *19th cent.*

Maria Edgeworth *Patronage* 1814
John Clay is a man just risen from the ranks … lately promoted from being a manufacturer's son, to be a subaltern in good company.

Oscar Wilde *The Importance of Being Earnest* 1895
[Lady Bracknell] Who was your father? He was evidently a man of some wealth. Was he born in what the Radical papers call the purple of commerce, or did he rise from the ranks of aristocracy?

See also PULL rank.

ransom

The meaning of *ransom* in the first phrase relates not to a sum of money but to the process of ransoming. This is the oldest sense, dating from Middle English; it fell out of use after the 16th cent., and was revived largely by Sir Walter Scott in the 19th cent. Modern use of the word is mostly confined to the phrase.

hold somebody/something to ransom

1 to kidnap somebody and demand money for their release. *19th cent.*

Scott *Ivanhoe* 1819
Here, Jew, step forth. – Look at that holy Father Aymer, Prior of the rich Abbey of Jorvaulx, and tell us at what ransom we should hold him? – Thou knowest the income of his convent, I warrant thee.

Horatio Alger *Cast upon the Breakers* 1893
'I suppose you would like to know why we brought you here.' 'I would very much.' 'We propose to hold you for ransom.' 'But why should you? I am only a poor boy.' 'You are the friend of Jefferson Pettigrew. He is a rich man. If he wants you back he must pay a round sum.'

2 to threaten a person, country, or organization with some harmful action unless they agree to certain terms. A notable use in the late 20th cent. was in connection with the activities of trade unions in taking industrial action that was regarded as 'holding the country to ransom'. *Mid 20th cent.*

Beatrix Campbell *Wigan Pier Revisited* 1985
At a stroke, claimant became synonymous with criminal. The campaign crossed class boundaries and created an apparent unity of interest between taxpayers and workers held to ransom by skivers supported by a soft state.

See also a king's ransom at KING.

rap

Rap in the sense 'rebuke or criticism' dates from the 18th cent.; the sense reflected in the phrases emerges via an early 20th cent. meaning 'a criminal accusation'.

beat the rap

informal to escape punishment for wrongdoing. *Early 20th cent.*

rap somebody's knuckles / somebody on/ over the knuckles

to criticize or rebuke somebody mildly: used earlier with *fingers* instead of *knuckles*. *18th cent.*

Benjamin Franklin *The Way to Wealth* 1757
Experience keeps a dear school, but fools will learn in no other ... However, remember this, They that will not be counselled, cannot be helped; and further, that, If you will not hear Reason, she will surely rap your knuckles.

take the rap

to accept the blame for a mistake or wrongdoing, especially when others are equally or more to blame. *Mid 20th cent.*

Kim Newman *The Night Mayor* 1990
This team could have persuaded the Pope to confess that Judas Iscariot had been framed by George Washington, and that Jesus H. Christ had let Huey, Dewey and Louie take the rap for the St Valentine's Day Massacre.

rare

See (as) rare as hen's teeth *at* HEN.

raspberry

give/blow somebody a raspberry

to make a rude sound by blowing noisily with one's tongue between one's lips, in imitation of breaking wind: based on *raspberry tart*, rhyming slang for *fart*. Also, in extended senses, to express explicit or undisguised contempt. *Early 20th cent.*

Independent 1989
The winners ... will collect only around £5,000 less than the £30,000 total prize money that was on offer for the sub-continent's 1987 World Cup, which is doubtless why Australia and the West Indies were eventually persuaded to join the party after originally blowing it a loud raspberry.

rat

rats deserting a sinking ship

a rush to leave an organization or undertaking that is about to fail or collapse. The phrase is based on the traditional belief that rats on a ship know if it is about to sink and will jump overboard. *19th cent.*

Edward Payson Roe *What Can She Do?* 1873
The maid had no regrets at departure, and went away with something of the satisfaction of a rat leaving a sinking ship.

H D Traill *Shaftesbury* 1886
A subtle note of ironical compassion, as of a rat who was leaving the sinking ship, for a rat who has ineptly selected the same moment for joining it.

See also SMELL a rat.

rate

at any rate

by any means; in any case; whatever the other circumstances: *cf* in any CASE; at all events *at* EVENT. *17th cent.*

Locke *An Essay Concerning Human Understanding* 1690
Hence it comes that, at any rate, we desire to be rid of the present evil, which we are apt to think nothing absent can equal.

Thomas Paine *The American Crisis* 1780
In this natural view of things, your lordship stands in a very critical situation: your whole character is now staked upon your laurels; if they wither, you wither with them; if they flourish, you cannot live long to look at them; and at any rate, the black account hereafter is not far off.

See also at a rate of knots *at* KNOT.

ration

come up with / be given the rations

informal (said of an award or benefit) to be given automatically and not on the basis of individual merit: originally in services' slang, used deprecatingly of military decorations that were regarded as undeserved. *Early 20th cent.*

rattle

rattle somebody's cage

to annoy or irritate somebody: with allusion to rattling the cage of an animal at a zoo, causing it to become angry or excited. *20th cent.*

See also rattle one's SABRE; THROW one's rattle/toys out of the pram.

raw

catch/get/hit/touch somebody on the raw

to disconcert somebody by referring to a sensitive matter. *19th cent.*

Epes Sargent *Fleetwood, or the Stain of Birth* 1856
Do you read the Scorpion? Capital paper! Full of fun! Has hits at every body – touches people on the raw in fine style – that's a fact.

Wilkie Collins *The Moonstone* 1868
Sergeant Cuff had hit me on the raw, and, though I did look down upon him with contempt, the tender place still tingled for all that. The end of it was that I perversely led him back to the subject of her ladyship's letter.

come the raw prawn
Australian, informal to use deception; to misrepresent a situation. *Raw prawn* means 'an act of deception'. *Mid 20th cent.*

Guardian 2003
So, because one eccentric Australian TV star still uses the anachronistic crikey, we all do … Such assumptions are typically British, but jeez, we don't expect them in a Guardian leader. By the way, for future reference, it's not the Northern Territories, but Territory; the vast area that lies between the cities and the outback is known as 'the country'; Australians attend the theatre in similar numbers to sporting events; and koalas are marsupials, not bears (OK, the tired Qantas ads don't help). But to suggest Tony picked up the expression during one of his sojourns in Australia is truly coming the raw prawn.

in the raw
1 in a natural or crude state; (said of a person) uneducated and ignorant. *19th cent.*

Joseph Neal *Charcoal Sketches* 1838
Lamps is lamps, and moons is moons, in a business pint of view, but practically they ain't much if the wicks ain't afire. When the luminaries are, as I may say, in the raw, it's bad for me.

Economist 1991
Most prominent among the effects singled out for blame is the hostile takeover, both in America and in Britain. It is easy to understand why, for the hostile takeover brings with it a language and an atmosphere of conflict that sounds destructive and sometimes is. It exposes capitalism in the raw.
2 (said of a person) naked: *raw* in the sense 'exposed flesh' dates from the early 19th cent. *Mid 20th cent.*

ray

(little) ray of sunshine
informal somebody or something that brings a person affection and happiness: often used ironically. Early uses are found in extended metaphor, as in the 1864 quotation below. *19th cent.*

Maria Cummins *Haunted Heart* 1864
But the winter of poor Angie's life had not yet made a spring for her. All was cold, hard, dark in the soil of her stricken heart. No seed of hope had sprouted there, no ray of sunshine, melting the winter snow, had diffused its moisture through the dry crust that enshrouded her soul in gloom.

Theodore Dreiser *Sister Carrie* 1900
Hurstwood could not keep his eyes from Carrie. She seemed the one ray of sunshine in all his trouble.

razor

a razor's edge
a critical situation: cf Dryden *The Hind and the Panther* (1687) iii.688 'You have ground the persecuting knife | And set it to a razor edge on life.' The phrase was used as the title of a novel by Somerset Maugham, published in 1944. *See also* on a knife-edge at KNIFE. *17th cent.*

Chapman transl Homer's *Iliad* x.150 (1611)
Now on the eager razors edge, for life or death we stand.

See also Occam's razor at OCCAM.

reach
See reach for the stars at STAR.

read

read between the lines
to seek or discern a hidden or implicit meaning in something spoken or written. *19th cent.*

George William Bagby *What I Did With My Fifty Millions* 1874
People have been so delighted with the extravaganzas of Moses Adams that they have demanded the publication of his lucubrations in an enduring book form. It seems never to have occurred to them that in laughing at Moses's follies they are laughing at their own. De te fabula narratur. Those who read between the lines (as the French say) detect in all

Moses's phantasies a lurking satire on the disposition made by poor old Virginia of her 'fifty millions' on internal improvements.

Hardy Tess of the D'Urbervilles 1891
That very night she began an appealing letter to Clare, concealing from him her hardships and assuring him of her undying affection. Any one who had been in a position to read between the lines would have seen that at the back of her great love was some monstrous fear – almost a desperation – as to some secret contingencies which were not disclosed.

read somebody's mind
to deduce or realize what somebody is thinking from knowledge of them or from their present demeanour: a particular use of the verb *read* in the sense 'to discern the nature or character of (somebody or something) from visible signs', as in Shakespeare's *The Winter's Tale* (1611) III.iii.73, where an old shepherd sees a baby and declares 'What have we here? Mercy on's, a bairn! A very pretty bairn. A boy or a child, I wonder? A pretty one, a very pretty one. Sure some scape [= moral transgression]. Though I am not bookish, yet I can read 'waiting-gentlewoman' in the scape.' *See also* read somebody like a BOOK. *18th cent.*

Colley Cibber Love in a Riddle 1729
At one short view, I read your mind, and person! | Which equally have given surprise, and wonder!

Maria Edgeworth The Absentee 1812
'Don't look so like a chafed lion; others may perhaps read your countenance, as well as I do.' 'None can read my mind so well,' replied he.

read my lips
pay attention to what I am saying: with allusion to the visual interpretation of a speaker's words by deaf people. The phrase has attained a special currency in recent years from its use by the American President George Bush during an election campaign in 1988, when he made the pledge: 'Read my lips: no new taxes'. *Late 20th cent.*

D J Enright Daughters of Earth: Valediction 1972
Into your roomy ear I speak, | Your lofty eye will read my lips.

take something as read
to assume that something is correct without further discussion: originally with reference to the minutes of a meeting when accepted without amendment at the next meeting. *19th cent.*

you wouldn't read about it
Australian and NZ, informal an expression of extreme doubt or incredulity. *Mid 20th cent.*

J Cleary Just Let Me Be 1950
Everything I backed ran like a no-hoper. Four certs I had, and the bludgers were so far back the ambulance nearly had to bring 'em home. You wouldn't read about it.

See also read somebody like a BOOK; read the RIOT act.

ready

at the ready
available for use or action: originally with reference to a firearm ready for firing. *19th cent.*

J M Barrie Peter Pan 1904
Now he crawled forward like a snake; and again, erect, he darted across a space on which the moonlight played, one finger on his lip and his dagger at the ready.

ready for the off
informal about to leave. *20th cent.*

Treasure Hunting 1991
At the start of the event, one whole side was full of detector users ready for the off!

ready to roll
informal about to start moving: from the rolling movement of wheels. *Mid 20th cent.*

Mike Ripley Just Another Angel 1989
That night, it was Kümmel, a fresh packet of Gold Flake and about forty quid (thirty drinking money, ten in another pocket for emergency taxi home or suchlike) and dressed in my Who Bears Wins sweatshirt and long brown leather jacket, I was ready to roll.

real

be/get real
to be realistic; to stop deluding oneself: normally used in the form of peremptory advice. The phrase originates in (mid 20th cent.) US college slang, where it had the meaning 'be honest, tell the truth'. *Late 20th cent.*

Golf Monthly 1991
Wayne Levi is the best player in America? Get real. But, but, he did win four tournaments.

for real

informal sincere or genuine, often dangerously or alarmingly so; in earnest. On this use of *for*, see for FREE. *Mid 20th cent.*

> **Economist 1991**
> But the film's British audience had its mind on other matters. 'Was the horse killed for real?' they wanted to know after one scene.

See also the real MCCOY; the real SIMON Pure.

---

reap

reap the harvest/fruits/crop of something

to experience the consequences of one's own actions or decisions. *16th cent.*

> **Spenser The Faerie Queene I.iv.47 (1590)**
> At last when perils all I weened [= thought] past, | And hop'd to reape the crop of all my care, | Into new woes unweeting [= unknowing] I was cast.

you reap what you sow

(proverb) actions bring unavoidable consequences: with reference to St Paul's letter to the Galatians 6:7 'Be not deceived; God is not mocked. For whatsoever a man soweth, that shall he also reap.' In English, the notion goes back to the 10th cent., and the phrase appears in Middle English translations of the Bible.

---

rear

See rear/raise its (ugly) HEAD.

---

reason

for reasons best known to himself/herself, etc

(said of another's actions, decisions, etc) for reasons or motives that seem to the speaker strange or inexplicable. *17th cent.*

> **William Chillingworth The Religion of Protestants 1638**
> Yet it hath pleased God (for Reasons best known to himselfe) not to allow us this convenience.

it stands to reason

it is logical or reasonable: used to introduce an assertion or conclusion on which the speaker expects to receive general agreement. In 16th cent. and 17th cent. use also in the form *stand with reason. 17th cent.*

> **Philemon Holland transl Xenophon's Cyropaedia 1632**
> It standeth to good reason, that they who repose mutuall trust one in another, will joyntly sticke to it.

> **Richardson Pamela 1741**
> What are the Rules I am to observe from this awful Lecture? Why, these: ... That Rakes cannot have a greater Encouragement to attempt a marry'd Lady's Virtue, than her slight Opinion of her Husband. To be sure, this stands to Reason, and is a fine Lesson.

> **Dickens Oliver Twist 1838**
> When a man's his own enemy, it's only because he's too much his own friend; not because he's careful for everybody but himself ... That stands to reason.

see / listen to reason

to be willing to accept advice or be reasonable. *16th cent.*

> **Shakespeare 1 Henry IV I.iii.182 (1596)**
> [Poins] If he fight longer than he sees reason, I'll forswear arms.

theirs/ours not to reason why

it is not their (or our) place to question authority, however perverse, unreasonable, or mistaken it seems to be. The phrase quotes Tennyson's *The Charge of the Light Brigade* (1854), which describes the suicidal British charge towards the enemy guns at the Battle of Balaclava during the Crimean War: 'Forward the Light Brigade! | Was there a man dismay'd? | Not tho' the soldier knew | Some one had blunder'd: | Their's not to make reply, | Their's not to reason why, | Their's but to do or die: | Into the valley of Death | Rode the six hundred.' *19th cent.*

within reason

within reasonable limits. The phrase occurs earlier (16th cent.) in the form *within the bounds* (or *confines*, etc) *of reason*, and in Shakespeare's *Othello* (1604) IV.ii.223, Roderigo comes very close to the modern use of the phrase when he asks Iago whether he can really hope to possess Desdemona: 'Well, what is it? Is it within reason and compass?'

> **Harriet A Jacobs Incidents in the Life of a Slave Girl 1861**
> 'But it is another woman I want to bring,' said Peter. 'She is in great distress, too, and you shall be

paid any thing within reason, if you'll stop and take her.'

rebel

a rebel without a cause

a young person who is dissatisfied with life and society but does not have a particular aim to pursue: from the title of a film released in 1955 starring James Dean as a rebellious young teenager. The film, and Dean himself (who was killed shortly afterwards in a car crash that was strangely reminiscent of the film's climax), became icons of 1950s youth culture. *Mid 20th cent.*

Financial Times 1982
Unlike the rebel without a cause who stares down at him from the wall, Phil's anger has specific roots in his domestic life and a glowering sense of frustration.

rebound

on the rebound

in an emotionally unsettled state resulting from a broken relationship or other personal disappointment. The image is of a ball or other object bouncing back uncontrollably. Also in the 19th cent. in the form *in the rebound;* and a similar phrase *by rebound* is recorded in more general figurative senses in the 17th cent. and 18th cent.

George Eliot *Middlemarch* 1872
Resistance to unjust dispraise had mingled with her feeling for him from the very first, and now in the rebound of her heart after her anguish the resistance was stronger than ever.

receive

be at/on the receiving end of something

to be the unfortunate person who bears the brunt of an unpleasant or harmful action: based on the notion of being fired on, or of being the recipient of an unpleasant message. *Mid 20th cent.*

Rosalie Ash *Calypso's Island* 1993
She'd found herself on the receiving end of a great deal of teasing about her impromptu topless dip in the sea and her valiant rescuer, and she'd fenced it as calmly as she could.

recharge

See recharge one's batteries *at* BATTERY.

reckon

to be reckoned with

of some importance or influence. *19th cent.*

Henry James *Washington Square* 1881
The year that had elapsed since her brother's death reminded her of that happy time, because, although Catherine, in growing older, had become a person to be reckoned with, yet her society was a very different thing, as Mrs. Penniman said, from that of a tank of cold water.

record

beat/break the record

to surpass all previously recorded performances, especially in sporting events. The phrase is also common in extended uses in the sense 'to be the best or most noteworthy example known.' *19th cent.*

George Gissing *The Whirlpool* 1897
It must break the record for a neat houserobbery, don't you think? And they'll never be caught – I'll bet you anything you like they won't. The job was planned weeks ago; that woman came into the house with no other purpose.

for the record

to be regarded or reported as official. Often used in a weakened sense, 'to add to the list of facts or information.' *Mid 20th cent.*

Guardian 1989
Funny how religion is creeping into the environment debate. Here's Mrs Thatcher ... 'Like the Garden of Eden to Adam and Eve anything which is given free is rarely valued.' Vox Pope. And, just for the record, here's the Pope's first pronouncement on the environment. 'It is manifestly unjust that a privileged few should continue to accumulate excess goods ... while masses of people are living in conditions of misery.'

a matter of record

something that can be verified from formal records. The phrase, and its variant *thing of record,* is first found in parliamentary rolls from the reign of Henry VI. *15th cent.*

off the record

not for publication or recording officially. The phrase is mid 20th cent. in this form and meaning; to be *struck off the record* (19th cent.) is to be deleted from an official record of proceedings, as in a lawcourt.

Charles Reade *Hard Cash* 1863
Judgment was entered for the plaintiff; and the defendant's ingenious plea struck off the record.

Harold Ickes *Secret Diary* 1933
He met and answered every question, although in some instances his answers were off the record.

on (the) record

officially recorded or published, or intended for official publication. *On the record* (with *the*) is much more recent, and has stronger implications for the nature of the information concerned, than *off the record*. To *go on record* or *put on record* (both early 20th cent.) is to make an official statement. *16th cent.*

Shakespeare *Richard III* v.vi.65 (1593)
If we be conquered, let men conquer us, | And not these bastard Bretons, whom our fathers | Have in their own land beaten, bobbed, and thumped, | And in record left them the heirs of shame.

Dekker *The Witch of Edmonton* a1632
And shall I then for my part | Unfile the sacred oath set on record | In Heaven's Book?

Henry Fielding *The History of Tom Jones* 1749
She then delivered her cousin the letter with the proposals of marriage, which, if the reader hath a desire to see, he will find already on record in the XVth book of this history.

put/set the record straight

to correct a mistake or misapprehension. *Mid 20th cent.*

Trevor Barnes *Taped* 1993
Dexter saw Lancaster's eyes flicker as he registered the implications of what Blanche had just told him. 'It must have been terrible when she told you about Nicola's affair with Parkin. I want to give you a chance to put the record straight. Tell me what really happened.'

red

(as) red as (a) beetroot

extremely red, especially red in the face from embarrassment. *19th cent.*

Dickens *Our Mutual Friend* 1865
Bella soaped his face and rubbed his face, and soaped his hands and rubbed his hands, and splashed him and rinsed him and towelled him, until he was as red as beetroot, even to his very ears.

better dead than red

destruction in a nuclear war would be preferable to submission to communism: a common slogan during the arms race of the cold-war period. The colour red has been associated (via its connotations of blood and violence) with revolution and communism since 1848, when revolutionaries in France proclaimed the Second French Republic as the 'Red Republic', and the red flag has been a symbol of communist and socialist parties from the same date. *Mid 20th cent.*

catch somebody red-handed

to catch somebody in the very act of wrongdoing or criminal activity. The phrase is derived from the earlier (16th cent.) use of *with the red hand* in the sense 'with clear evidence of guilt', alluding to the bloodstained hands of a murderer. The word *red-handed* seems to have been first used (as a single word) in this meaning by Sir Walter Scott (see below), and it predates more literal uses referring to those discovered in an act of violence. *19th cent.*

Scott *Ivanhoe* 1819
There are enough of outlaws in this forest to resent my protecting the deer. I did but tie one fellow, who was taken redhanded and in the fact, to the horns of a wild stag, which gored him to death in five minutes.

in the red

in debt, owing money: from the use of red figures to show the debit side of an account. Cf in the BLACK. *Early 20th cent.*

a red herring

an irrelevant distraction, especially one intended to divert attention from the matter at hand. A red herring was a smoked herring that had turned red in the curing process. Its strong smell was commonly used in training dogs to follow a scent, because a red herring dragged across the main trail tested the dogs' ability to resist a false scent. *19th cent.*

Conan Doyle *The Adventure of the Priory School* 1904
If you are telegraphing home, Mr. Huxtable, it would be well to allow the people in your neigh-

bourhood to imagine that the inquiry is still going on in Liverpool, or wherever else that red herring led your pack.

red in tooth and claw

involving violence and bloodshed: with allusion to Tennyson's poem *In Memoriam A.H.H.* (1850) canto 56 'Man ... | Who trusted God was love indeed | And love Creation's final law – | Though Nature, red in tooth and claw | With ravine, shrieked against his creed.' *19th cent.*

a red-letter day

a day that has been specially memorable or enjoyable: from the practice of marking special feast days in red letters on Church calendars. A similar origin accounts for our word *rubric*, meaning 'a rule or instruction'. It comes from the Latin word *ruber* meaning 'red': a rubric was originally an entry or heading in a book, and it came to be used for a special instruction printed in a book of the liturgy. *18th cent.*

> Fanny Burney *Cecilia* 1782
> '*Why you know, ma'am,' answered Mrs. Belfield, 'To-day is a red-letter day, so that's the reason of it.' 'A red-letter day?' 'Good lack, madam, why have not you heard that my son is turned book-keeper?'*

red-light district

the part of a town or city in which prostitution and other commercial sexual activity is centred: from the use of a red light as a sign outside a brothel. *Early 20th cent.*

a red rag to a bull

an action or statement that is likely to make somebody angry or violent. The phrase is derived from the traditional belief that bulls are infuriated by the colour red, which is the colour of a bullfighter's cape. There is an early reference to the notion in John Lyly's *Euphues* (1580): 'He that commeth before an elephant will not weare bright colours, nor he that commeth to a bul red.' In its developed form the phrase dates from the 19th cent.

> Mark Twain *A Tramp Abroad* 1880
> *And then there is painting. What a red rag is to a bull, Turner's 'Slave Ship' was to me, before I studied art. Mr. Ruskin is educated in art up to a point where that picture throws him into as mad an ecstasy of pleasure as it used to throw me into one of rage, last year, when I was ignorant.*

reds under the bed

informal communists or communist sympathizers obsessively regarded as a hidden and harmful influence in society. *Late 20th cent.*

> Economist 1983
> *It is difficult to establish whether Mr Manley's Cuban infatuation was no more than that, or whether by the end of the 1970s there were reds under beds and, if so, how many and at whose invitation.*

see red

informal to be extremely angry. The image is the same as in *a red rag to a bull* above. *Early 20th cent.*

See also PAINT the town red.

---

redress

See redress the BALANCE.

---

reduce

in reduced circumstances

in a state of poverty, having been wealthy in the past. *19th cent.*

> Dickens *Pickwick Papers* 1837
> *A low tap was heard at the room door. Mr. Bob Sawyer looked expressively at his friend, and bade the tapper come in; whereupon a dirty slipshod girl in black cotton stockings, who might have passed for the neglected daughter of a superannuated dustman in very reduced circumstances, thrust in her head.*

reduce somebody to the ranks

to deprive somebody of their rank or status as a punishment: originally in military contexts, with reference to the demotion of a non-commissioned officer. *19th cent.*

> Scott *Waverley* 1814
> *And so Timms was shot, and I was reduced to the ranks.*

---

reed

a broken reed

a person who is no longer capable or effective, and can no longer be relied on. The phrase alludes to Isaiah 36:6, where Sennacherib of Assyria mocks King Hezekiah for his alliance with the Egyptian pharaoh with the words 'Lo, thou trustest in the staff of this broken reed, on

Egypt; whereon if a man lean, it will go into his hand, and pierce it.' *16th cent.*

Smollett *The Adventures of Peregrine Pickle* 1751
This new adviser, who (though a courtier) was a rival of the other, gave our adventurer to understand, that he had been leaning upon a broken reed; that his professed patron was a man of a shattered fortune and decayed interest.

refer

refer to drawer
a formula used by a bank to inform the payee of a cheque that payment has not been made, normally because of inadequate funds in the payer's (the *drawer*'s) account. *Early 20th cent.*

reference

always verify your references
(proverb) an exhortation to be sure of one's facts before speaking out. The expression is particularly associated with M J Routh (1755–1854), President of Magdalen College, Oxford, although the phrase is not recorded in print until about half a century after his death. *Early 20th cent.*

rein

keep/put a tight rein on somebody/something
to control somebody or something firmly, especially expenditure or extravagant behaviour: a metaphor from horseriding, in which the reins are held tight to control a lively or newly trained horse. *18th cent.*

John O'Keeffe *The Highland Reel* 1789
[Laird of Rausey] *You'll marry Jenny?* [Sandy] *If she will honor me.* [Laird of Rausey] *It is an honor, if you knew all. Here's an hundred pounds with her; don't ask why I give you this – she's wild and vulgar, but keep a tight rein, and you – may reclaim her.*

Catharine Maria Sedgwick *Redwood* 1824
Two of the brethren agreed to go and talk to Betty on the subject, and make her promise that she would put a tight rein on her tongue.

Mrs Gaskell *Ruth* 1853
If my father had thought me extravagant, he would have kept me in with a tight rein.

Seba Smith *My Thirty Years out of the Senate* 1859
He says he means to keep a tight rein over Taylor, and not let him do much.

take up the reins
to assume control. *18th cent.*

Clara Reeve *The Progress of Romance* 1785
It is a book that speaks to the heart, and engages that in its behalf, and when reflexion comes afterwards, and reason takes up the reins, we discover that it is dangerous and improper for those for whose use it is chiefly intended, for young persons.

See also give a FREE hand/rein to somebody.

reinvent

reinvent oneself
(said especially of a famous person or celebrity) to change one's appearance or character, especially in order to revive a flagging image or reputation. *Late 20th cent.*

The Face 1990
Alma Cogan was a British plain Jane who reinvented herself via extravagant frocks and bouffants to become a massive Fifties singing star.

reinvent the wheel
to waste time and effort devising something that already exists, or in some other fruitless activity. *20th cent.*

Judith Waters & Lester Ray *Environmental Scanning and Business Strategy* 1989
In any case, if a writer has managed to put some key point rather well, why not both give him the credit for doing so, and at the same time avoid struggling to reinvent the wheel?

relief

on relief
chiefly NAmer receiving state benefits: *relief* in the sense 'financial aid to those in need' dates from the 16th cent. *Mid 20th cent.*

relieve

relieve oneself
to urinate or defecate: from the notion of 'relieving oneself' of a burden or responsibility. *Mid 20th cent.*

relieve one's feelings

to speak plainly from a feeling of anger or disappointment. *19th cent.*

Jane Austen *Emma* 1816
Emma heard him almost immediately afterwards say to himself, over a newspaper ... 'Hum! just the trifling, silly fellow I took him for.' She had half a mind to resent; but an instant's observation convinced her that it was really said only to relieve his own feelings, and not meant to provoke; and therefore she let it pass.

relieve somebody of something

informal, euphemistic to deprive somebody of something by stealing it: a euphemism based on the (17th cent.) meaning 'to release somebody from a burden or responsibility.' *Mid 20th cent.*

religion

get religion

informal, originally NAmer to be converted, especially suddenly or dramatically, to a zealous religious belief. *18th cent.*

James Hall *Legends of the West* 1832
Tom 'got religion' at a camp-meeting, and for a while was quite a reformed man. Then he relapsed a little.

remain

it remains to be seen

something is still uncertain or unknown. *18th cent.*

Scott *Waverley* 1814
I am actually in the land of military and romantic adventures, and it only remains to be seen what will be my own share in them.

remedy

the remedy is worse than the disease

action taken to deal with a situation produces an even worse outcome. *16th cent.*

James Howell *Dodona's Grove* 1640
Prince Rocalino replied, that touching his first proposition, for an army to goe with him, the remedy would be farre worse than the disease, though there should bee tumults in Druina.

rent

rent-a —

informal used to refer to people or things easily acquired for some transitory purpose. The most common application is in *rent-a-mob*, denoting public demonstrations in which most of the participants were specially brought in by interested parties. Based on the names of car-rental firms and similar businesses, dating from the early 20th cent. The phrase is late 20th cent in extended use.

Sounds 1990
Friday marks the start of a new music programme as Channel 4 turns its hand to dance. A mix of 'live' performances, the ubiquitous rent-a-crowd dancers and this week Norman Cook explains how police recently raided his bar-b-q believing it to be an illegal rave.

reputation

live up to one's reputation

to behave in the way that people might expect from common knowledge. *20th cent.*

Publishers' Weekly 1971
Los Angeles ... more than lives up to its reputation as a low-profile, seemingly endless sprawl with no center.

residence

— in residence

(said of a writer, artist, musician, etc) serving in a regular capacity in a place, such as a college or gallery, and available to give classes, lectures, etc. Often incorporated into an official title such as *artist-in-residence* or *poet-in-residence*. The meaning of *residence* in association with posts requiring the incumbent to live in the place of tenure dates from late Middle English in ecclesiastical contexts, and developed secular applications towards the end of the 16th cent. *Mid 20th cent.*

Margaret Drabble *The Radiant Way* 1988
In a renovated Georgian terrace house less than a quarter of a mile from the Civic Centre, actors, actresses, arts officers, leisure officers, artists-in-residence, playwright-in-residence, and a visiting jazz musician gathered together to laugh, to sing, to eat spinach salad and green bean salad and mackerel pate and wholemeal bread and curried brown rice.

resistance

the line/path of least resistance
the course of action that is easiest to follow or affords fewest difficulties. Originally a term in military artillery denoting the shortest distance between the surface of the ground and an explosive charge buried below it, used as a factor in calculating the strength of the charge. *19th cent.*

> Bram Stoker *Dracula* 1897
> *I shall fix some things she like not – garlic and a crucifix – and so seal up the door of the tomb. She is young as Un-Dead, and will heed. Moreover, these are only to prevent her coming out; they may not prevail on her wanting to get in; for then the Un-Dead is desperate, and must find the line of least resistance, whatsoever it may be.*

resort

The meaning underlying the phrases, 'something that one has recourse to', dates from Middle English and is found in Chaucer. The two phrases sometimes overlap somewhat in meaning.

a last resort
a final expedient, when everything else has been tried without success. Typically as a parenthetic phrase *as a last resort*. *18th cent.*

> John Gay *The Beggars' Opera* 1728
> [Macheath] *I beg you, gentlemen, act with conduct and discretion. A pistol is your last resort.*

> Richardson *Clarissa* 1748
> *I shewed him the Letter she wrote, and left behind her for me, with an intention, no doubt, absolutely to break my heart, or to provoke me to hang, drown, or shoot myself; to say nothing of a multitude of declarations from her, defying his power, and imputing all that looked like Love in her behaviour to me, to the persecution and rejection of her friends; which made her think of me but as a last resort.*

> Herman Melville *Bartleby* 1853
> *The landlord's energetic, summary disposition had led him to adopt a procedure which I do not think I would have decided upon myself; and yet, as a last resort, under such peculiar circumstances, it seemed the only plan.*

in the last resort
regardless of whatever else happens; in the end: a translation of French *en dernier ressort*, used originally to denote a court of law from which there is no appeal. *17th cent.*

> William Temple *Essays* 1672
> *All government is a restraint upon liberty; and under all, the dominion is equally absolute, where it is in the last resort.*

respect

be no respecter of persons
to regard or treat everybody in the same way, regardless of their position: with reference to Acts 10:34 'Then Peter opened his mouth, and said, Of a truth I perceive that God is no respecter of persons.' *17th cent.*

> Washington Irving *Bracebridge Hall* 1822
> *The latter, however, was no respecter of persons, but rather seemed to exult in having such important antagonists.*

> James Fenimore Cooper *The Pioneers* 1823
> *The law, gentlemen, is no respecter of persons in a free country.*

with respect to something
concerning, having regard for, or in relation to something. *17th cent.*

> Locke *An Essay Concerning Human Understanding* 1690
> *But ... it may be worth while to consider them [these maxims] with respect to other parts of our knowledge, and examine more particularly to what purposes they serve, and to what not.*

See also PAY one's respects.

rest

give something/it a rest
informal to stop doing something or referring to a subject that has become annoying or tedious: often used in the imperative or as an exhortation. *Mid 20th cent.*

> J B Priestley *Daylight on Saturday* 1943
> *I'm a bit tired of hearing about him today. So let's give him a rest.*

rest one's case
to have provided all the arguments and evidence needed in support of a point of view: based on

the legal use, with reference to the presentation of a case in court. *Early 20th cent.*

See also no peace/rest for the WICKED; the rest is HISTORY; rest on one's laurels *at* LAUREL; rest on one's oars *at* OAR.

retreat

beat/make a (hasty) retreat
to leave unceremoniously in order to avoid discovery or some other awkward or unpleasant situation. *19th cent.*

> Charlotte Brontë *Jane Eyre* 1847
> *The new servants that had been hired from Millcote, were bustling about everywhere. Threading this chaos, I at last reached the larder; there I took possession of a cold chicken, a roll of bread, some tarts, a plate or two and a knife and fork: with this booty I made a hasty retreat.*

> Darwin *The Descent of Man* 1871
> *The baboons in return rolled so many stones down the mountain, some as large as a man's head, that the attackers had to beat a hasty retreat.*

return

by return of post
(with reference to a postal reply) by the next available post in the opposite direction: originally, with the return of the messenger or courier who brought the original missive (*cf* French *par retour du courrier*). *18th cent.*

> Charlotte Smith *Emmeline* 1788
> *I have reason to believe Miss Mowbray has no dislike to this proposal; and hope to hear from your Lordship thereon by return of post.*

> Jane Austen *Northanger Abbey* 1818
> *Mr. and Mrs. Morland, relying on the discretion of the friends to whom they had already entrusted their daughter, felt no doubt of the propriety of an acquaintance which had been formed under their eye, and sent therefore by return of post their ready consent to her visit in Gloucestershire.*

many happy returns (of the day)
a formula of congratulations on a person's birthday: the wish is that the day will 'return' many times, i.e. that the recipient will have a long life. *18th cent.*

> Charles Lamb *Essays* 1823
> *The compliments of the season to my worthy masters, and a merry first of April to us all! Many happy returns of this day to you.*

See also return to the FOLD.

reverse

reverse the charges
to arrange for the recipient of a telephone call to be charged for it instead of the caller. *Early 20th cent.*

See also the reverse of the MEDAL.

rewrite

rewrite history
to present past facts in a way that suits a present purpose. *19th cent.*

> Oscar Wilde *The Critic as Artist* 1891
> *Gilbert, you treat the world as if it were a crystal ball. You hold it in your hand, and reverse it to please a wilful fancy. You do nothing but rewrite history.*

rhyme

no rhyme or reason
no logical explanation or rationale (cf French *ni rime ni raison*). *Rhyme* is used in its meaning denoting the correspondence of sounds in words, producing harmony and euphony, and is coupled with *reason* (originally in the form *against all rhyme and reason*) from about 1500. In its current form the phrase dates from the 17th cent.

> Thomas Rawlins *Tunbridge Wells* 1678
> *Some more such flights (good Servant) as we walk, for your discourse before was neither Rhime, nor reason.*

rib

dig/nudge/poke somebody in the ribs
to alert or warn somebody, literally by prodding them in the side with one's hand or elbow. *19th cent.*

> Rider Haggard *She* 1887
> *'Old fellow,' said Leo ... 'We seem to have tumbled into clover. I hope that you have made the most of*

your opportunities. By Jove, what a pair of arms she has got!' I nudged him in the ribs to make him keep quiet, for I caught sight of a gleam from Ayesha's veiled eyes.

rich

(as) rich as Croesus

extremely rich, like King Croesus of Lydia, an ancient kingdom in Asia Minor (now Turkey). In the Greek sources, Croesus was proverbial for his wealth (6th cent. BC). The phrase is recorded in a 16th cent. collection of epigrams.

> Richardson Pamela 1741
> Your Papa, in his humourous Manner, mentions his large possessions and riches: But, indeed, were he as rich as Croesus, he should not have my consent, if he has no greater merit.

> Thackeray The History of Pendennis 1849
> 'If he had a good coat, you fancied he was as rich as Crazes.' 'As Croesus,' said Mr. Bowles.

a bit rich

(said of a remark or criticism) somewhat ironic or impudent in view of the person making it: based on the (17th cent.) use of rich to mean 'amusing, entertaining' and hence 'outrageous.' Mid 20th cent.

rid

be/get rid of something

to free oneself of something unwanted: to be well rid of somebody or something is to benefit from having rid oneself of a troublesome person or thing. 15th cent.

> Shakespeare Julius Caesar III.ii.71 (1599)
> [First Plebeian] This Caesar was a tyrant. [Third Plebeian] Nay, that's certain. We are blessed that Rome is rid of him.

riddance

good riddance

an expression of satisfaction or relief that a person or thing has gone: used earlier in other forms, e.g. fair riddance, happy riddance. Also used in the extended form good riddance to bad rubbish. 17th cent.

> Shakespeare Troilus and Cressida II.i.121 (1602)
> [Thersites] I will see you hanged like clodpolls ere I come any more to your tents. I will keep where there is wit stirring, and leave the faction of fools. [Patroclus] A good riddance.

> Dickens Dombey and Son 1848
> 'A good riddance of bad rubbish!' said that wrathful old lady. 'Get along with you, or I'll have you carried out!'

riddle

talk/speak in riddles

to use ambiguous or confusing language. 19th cent.

> Nathaniel Hawthorne The Scarlet Letter 1850
> 'I know not what to say – the disease is what I seem to know, yet know it not.' 'You speak in riddles, learned sir,' said the pale minister, glancing aside out of the window.

ride

(along) for the ride

informal wanting to be involved in something without having to contribute to it or accept any responsibility. Mid 20th cent.

> Pete Silverton & Glen Matlock I Was a Teenage Sex Pistol 1990
> It never seemed to enter their minds that someone might like to buy a pair of trousers from Sex and a shirt from somewhere else. You had to buy everything from them ... I thought the Sex stuff was a bit weird but not so weird that I didn't want to get involved with it. It was interesting. I was along for the ride.

be riding for a fall

informal to act in a reckless way that invites failure or disaster: a metaphor from horseriding. 19th cent.

> Conan Doyle Wisteria Lodge 1908
> Holmes shrugged his shoulders as we walked away together. 'I can't make the man out. He seems to be riding for a fall. Well, as he says, we must each try our own way and see what comes of it.'

an easy/rough ride

a pleasant (or unpleasant) experience. An easy ride was a journey that could be done comfortably within a certain time; a *rough ride* was an uncomfortable ride over bumpy ground. *Mid 20th cent.*

let something ride
informal to allow an activity to continue without intervening. *Mid 20th cent.*

> **P Chester Murder Forestalled 1990**
> *'Any visitors?' 'No ... doctor's orders ... She needs plenty of rest and quiet.' 'How about the police? They'll want to see her for sure.' 'Far as I can find out they've let it ride for the moment. They probably figure the public wouldn't like them very much if they dragged a sick girl from her bed.'*

ride high
to be successful. The image is of a distinguished or powerful person riding on a magnificent horse or in a grand vehicle. *19th cent.*

ride off into the sunset
informal to complete an undertaking or adventure with a successful and happy conclusion: from the conventional ending of some Western films, in which the triumphant hero is seen riding (usually alone) towards the horizon at sunset. *20th cent.*

> **Spare Rib 1989**
> *La Negra Angustias is the stirring tale of a black woman who survives the vicissitudes of being young, female and attractive, to follow her father's example and lead a band of rebels. She falls in love, but soon realises that her political role is more important, and ends up riding off into the sunset with her troops to join Zapata.*

ride the rails
informal, chiefly NAmer to travel by rail, especially illegally. *Mid 20th cent.*

— rides again
informal there are renewed signs of a particular phenomenon, especially in a new or unexpected form and when this is unwelcome or controversial: from the title of a 1939 film, *Destry Rides Again. Mid 20th cent.*

ride shotgun
to travel in the passenger seat of a vehicle: with reference to the armed guard who sat with the driver on a stagecoach in the American West. *Mid 20th cent.*

> **Guardian 1989**
> *A suited smart alec, riding shotgun on rugby union's suddenly careering shamateur bandwagon, this week told a group of British international*

players that they should soon be able to charge £1,500 for a solitary interview.

take somebody for a ride
informal to deceive somebody, especially for financial gain. *Early 20th cent.*

See also ride BODKIN; ride on somebody's COAT-TAILS; ride ROUGHSHOD over somebody.

rig

in full rig
wearing formal or ceremonial dress: a metaphor from seafaring. *19th cent.*

right

In the simile-based idioms (*as right as rain*, etc) there is considerable play on two major strands of meaning, which both date back to Old English: the mostly obsolete meaning 'straight, direct' (as in Dryden's 'make room for the Italian poets, the descendants of Virgil in a right line') and the current predominant meanings 'correct' and 'just, morally good'.

(as) right as rain
(said of a person) completely well, especially after illness or injury. This particular comparison, though the most familiar today, arose – comparatively recently – towards the end of the 19th cent., superseding older forms. The choice of *rain* may be partly due to its alliterative effect, although it is sometimes explained in terms of the beneficial effect rain has on growth. The other strand of meaning ('straight, direct': see above) offers a more tangible – and more convincing – evolution, for rain, while embodying no particularly vivid sense of health or well-being, does indeed fall in straight lines. This association is greatly reinforced by the existence of an older form *right as a line* in 16th cent. sources: in Thomas Preston's tragedy *The Life of Cambises King of Percia* (c1569), for example, the King declares: 'I have dispatched him, down he dooth fall, | As right as a line his hart I have hit.' A few years later, we find a more figurative use in George Chapman's comedy *May-Day* (1611), where the following exchange occurs: 'Thou maist see this boy is no shred of a Taylor, | Is he not right of my looke and spirit. | Right as a line, yfaith.' There was evidently much play in these expressions on

the two meanings of *right*. Such wordplay is a common feature of the development of idioms, and so the substitution of *rain* for *line* is quite understandable. The notion of things being straight and upright is present in other, now obsolete, comparisons: *right as a gun, right as my leg* (common in 17th cent. drama), and *right as a trivet* (see the following phrase). *19th cent.*

Somerville & Ross *The Real Charlotte* 1894

If only this infernal Fitzpatrick girl would have stayed with her cads in Dublin everything would have been as right as rain.

(as) right as a trivet

completely satisfactory; in good health or condition. A *trivet* is an iron tripod placed over a fire for pots and other cooking utensils, thus affording the image of a stable and level object. The locus classicus belongs to Dickens (see below), who was evidently fond of the phrase since he used it several times in later works, including *Martin Chuzzlewit* and *Our Mutual Friend*; but he probably did not invent the phrase, since it is found two years before Dickens' first use, in Thomas Hood's *Dead Robbery* (1835). Later in the century, it occurs several times in the works of Trollope. *19th cent.*

Dickens *Pickwick Papers* 1837

'And this,' said Mr. Pickwick, looking up, 'is the Angel! We alight here, Sam. But some caution is necessary. Order a private room, and do not mention my name. You understand.' 'Right as a trivet, sir,' replied Mr. Weller, with a wink of intelligence.

bang to rights

informal (said of a criminal) caught red-handed. The phrase was used as the title of a book on prison life by Frank Norman (1958). *Early 20th cent.*

Guardian 1987

George Davis, the man freed from prison in the 1970s following a massive campaign, was gaoled for 18 months with nine suspended yesterday after being caught 'bang to rights'. Southwark Crown Court heard that Davis and a second man, John Gravell, were trapped in the mail carriage of a train travelling from Brighton to Victoria. Police found Davis holding the van door shut while Gravell was cutting open three mail bags.

not right in the head

slightly crazy or eccentric. *Right in one's wits* is found in the 17th cent., and the current form of the phrase dates from the 18th cent. Jamieson's *Etymological Dictionary of the Scottish Language* of 1808 has an entry for the Scottish form *richt*: *no richt*, insane; and a Northamptonshire glossary of 1854 includes the example 'He's not right in his head'.

Fanny Burney *Camilla* 1796

'Well, my dear,' cried she, 'this is one of the most miraculous adventures I've met with yet; as sure as you're alive that man that stares so is not right in the head! for else what should he run away for, all in such a hurry, after looking at us so particular for nothing?'

put/set somebody right

to correct somebody's mistaken impression or wrong information about something: in earlier use, to make somebody well or good-tempered. *17th cent.*

Aphra Behn *The Debauchee* 1677

I have that rare quality, – the more I drink the soberer I am, 'tis a miracle to me now that, – therefore give me some wine, to set me right, that I may look thus gravely on my uncle.

Congreve *Love for Love* 1695

Who's that, that's out of his Way? – I am Truth, and can set him right – Hearkee, Friend, the straight Road is the worst way you can go.

right enough

informal for sure, certainly. *19th cent.*

Charles Reade *Hard Cash* 1863

I thought they had broken prison; but 'twas no business of mine: they paid for the bread right enough.

a right one

informal a perverse or difficult person. *Mid 20th cent.*

Kathleen Dayus *Where There's Life* 1991

However, she wasn't so pleased with the harmonium. 'We ain't 'avin' that contraption in the 'ouse. We ain't got no room fer it,' she told Dad. Dad scowled at Mum when one of the removal men said to him, 'Yow've got a right one theea mate. I know what I'd do if she was my missus.'

see — (all) right

1 *informal* to ensure that a particular person is duly compensated or rewarded for a favour done or for trouble they have taken. *Mid 20th cent.*
2 *informal* to protect the welfare of somebody in one's care or charge. *Mid 20th cent.*

she's/she'll be right

Australian and NZ, informal everything will be well: used as an expression of (usually unfounded or over-optimistic) reassurance. *Mid 20th cent.*

(somewhere) to the right of Genghis Khan

extremely right-wing or reactionary: with allusion to the Mongol leader (*c*1162–1227) who conquered territory from the Black Sea to the Pacific and ruled his empire efficiently but brutally (at least by reputation). *Late 20th cent.*

Sky 1989
Baroness Phillips is director of the Association For The Prevention Of Theft From Shops. 'My leftie grandchildren think I'm to the right of Genghis Khan, but I really believe that you have to show people you can't do this sort of thing and get away with it,' she says.

See also (as) fine/right as NINEPENCE; be/get/ keep on the right SIDE of somebody; on the right SIDE of.

Riley

the life of Riley/Reilly

informal a pleasant and carefree existence: perhaps based on a 1919 song by H Pease which includes the lines 'My name is Kelly, Michael Kelly, | But I'm living the life of Reilly just the same', although it is more likely that Pease was drawing on a phrase already in use. Others seek an American origin in songs written towards the end of the 19th cent. and using the name Reilly (or Riley) or O'Reilly, but none of these match the phrase and they are largely irrelevant, since we are dealing with a common name that is likely to arise in any Irish context. *Early 20th cent.*

Independent 1992
A 22-year-old conman who lived the life of Reilly for a month in a Merseyside hotel after telling the management he was Everton's latest signing has been jailed for four months.

Rimmon

See bow down in the house of Rimmon *at* BOW[1].

---

ring[1] (verb)

ring down/up the curtain

to mark the end (or beginning) of an activity or undertaking: with allusion to the ringing of a bell in a theatre as a signal to raise the stage curtain at the beginning of a performance or to lower it at the end. *Early 20th cent.*

S Kaye-Smith John Galsworthy 1916
Thus the curtain rings down on Irene Forsyte, crushed under the heel of prosperity.

ring in somebody's ears/head

to linger with affection or nostalgia in the memory, like a melodious sound still heard in the ear after it has ceased. *16th cent.*

Shakespeare Romeo and Juliet II.ii.74 (1596)
[Friar Laurence to Romeo] *Thy old groans yet ring in mine ancient ears. | Lo, here upon thy cheek the stain doth sit | Of an old tear that is not washed off yet.*

See also ring a BELL; ring the changes *at* CHANGE; ring the (death) KNELL of.

---

ring[2] (noun)

hold the ring

to be the impartial monitor of a disagreement or dispute: a metaphor from boxing, in which the referee 'holds [i.e. has charge of] the ring.' *Early 20th cent.*

run rings round somebody

to surpass or outwit somebody with great ease. The image is of a child or animal running in circles around somebody to amuse or pester them. *19th cent.*

See also throw one's HAT in/into the ring.

---

ringer

be a dead ringer (for somebody)

informal to look exactly like somebody else, or to resemble them closely in some way. In American slang, a *ringer* was a horse or other racing competitor that was fraudulently substituted for another at the last moment in order to fix the result. At the end of the 19th cent., it appears in sporting contexts in figurative senses, and uses in free context occur around 1900, including this one by George Ade in *More Fables* (1900): 'Bob ... was a Ringer for a United States Senator, all except the White Coat.' *19th cent.*

riot

read the riot act

to issue a stern warning. The Riot Act was passed under George I in 1715 at the time of the Jacobite riots, when there was a serious threat to the position of the new king; the threat was fomented by meetings of Stuart supporters and brought to fruition in the rebellions of 1715 and 1745. The Act sought to prevent seditious meetings by pre-scribing that a group of twelve or more people who assembled for an unlawful purpose could be arrested if they refused to disperse after a formal warning. The Act was repealed in 1967. *19th cent.*

> Henry David Thoreau *Walden* 1854
> *To do things 'railroad fashion' is now the byword; and it is worth the while to be warned so often and so sincerely by any power to get off its track. There is no stopping to read the riot act, no firing over the heads of the mob, in this case.*

run riot

to act or function wildly or without restraint: used originally (and in the form *hunt riot*) of hunting hounds that had lost the scent. *16th cent.*

> Thomas Beard *The Theatre of Gods Judgements* 1597
> *Thus many men run riot, by assuming to them-selves too much libertie, and breake the bounds of civill honesty.*

rip

let rip

informal to act or speak without restraint: based on the meaning 'to rush headlong', and used earlier in the form *let it* (or *her*, etc) *rip* = to allow somebody or something to go ahead unchecked. *19th cent.*

> R L Stevenson *Treasure Island* 1883
> *When I'm in Parlyment, and riding in my coach, I don't want none of these sea-lawyers in the cabin a-coming home, unlooked for, like the devil at prayers. Wait is what I say; but when the time comes, why let her rip!*

rip into somebody

informal, originally Australian and NZ to criticize somebody fiercely. *Mid 20th cent.*

> Malcolm Hamer *Sudden Death* 1991
> *What's wrong with Oliver Moreton? He ripped into me just now for going into the PGA caravan.*

rise

get a rise

informal to have an erection of the penis. *Mid 20th cent.*

get/take a rise out of somebody

informal to provoke somebody to an annoyed reaction by teasing them: a metaphor from ang-ling, in which a *rise* is the movement of a fish to the surface of the water to take the bait (*cf* rise to the BAIT). *19th cent.*

> Thackeray *Catherine* 1840
> *'Do I remember her?' said the ensign; 'do I remember whisky? Sure I do, and the snivelling sneak her husband, and the stout old lady her mother-in-law, and the dirty one-eyed ruffian who sold me the parson's hat, that had so nearly brought me into trouble. O but it was a rare rise we got out of them chaps, and the old landlady that's hanged too!'*

give rise to something

to be the origin or cause of something. *17th cent.*

> Lord Shaftesbury *An Inquiry Concerning Virtue, or Merit* 1699
> *Thus have we consider'd the self-passions ... They are original to that which we call selfishness, and give rise to that sordid disposition of which we have already spoken.*

> Sheridan *The School for Scandal* 1777
> *Very trifling circumstances have often given rise to the most ingenious tales.*

rise and shine

informal, originally services' slang to get out of bed promptly and begin the day's activities. Often used in the imperative, the phrase also covers more generalized situations involving the need for prompt action. *Early 20th cent.*

> Ellen Galford *The Dyke and the Dybbuk* 1993
> *If I hadn't chucked away the rulebook shortly after Johannes Gutenburg invented printing, this would be the proper time for me to rise and shine.*

rise to the occasion

to be capable of an exceptional effort or performance in a difficult situation or emergency. *19th cent.*

> Henry James *Roderick Hudson* 1876
> *I knew there were vulgar people of that way of feeling, but I didn't expect it of you. Make an effort, Mr. Mallet; rise to the occasion.*

See also rise from the ashes *at* ASH; rise to the BAIT; —'S STAR is rising.

rite

rite of passage

a ritual associated with a person's change of status in life, such as reaching adulthood, marriage, etc: translating French *rite de passage*, a term coined in 1909 (in the plural, as the title of an ethnographic study) by the French sociologist and folklorist Arnold van Gennep (1873–1957). *Early 20th cent.*

ritz

put on the ritz

informal to put on a show of glamour and luxury: a back-formation from the adjective *ritzy* meaning 'opulent', itself based on *Ritz*, the name of a chain of hotels noted for their opulence. *Puttin' on the Ritz* was the title of a film directed by Edward Sloman (1930), for which Irving Berlin wrote a similarly titled song. *Early 20th cent.*

> Press Association 1994
> *Not all British men are slobs when it comes to putting on the ritz – some have proved 'it's not what you wear but the way that you wear it'.*

river

sell somebody down the river

to betray somebody for one's own gain or advantage: with reference to the practice of slave-owners on the Mississippi in America selling unwanted or troublesome domestic slaves to owners further down the river in Louisiana, where conditions were much harsher. *19th cent.*

> Harriet Beecher Stowe *Uncle Tom's Cabin* 1852
> *What's the use o' talents and them things, if you can't get the use on 'em yourself? Why, all the use they make on't is to get round you. I've had one or two of these fellers, and I jest sold 'em down river. I knew I'd got to lose 'em, first or last, if I didn't.*

road

down the road

informal, chiefly NAmer in the future. *Mid 20th cent.*

> Rugby World and Post 1992
> *One game later, Probyn and his mates were back in their rightful position and flankers, nursing and cursing their unfamiliar bruises, were back in theirs. A few years down the road and along come the fitness men with their clipboards and stopwatches.*

in / out of somebody's road

informal in (or out of) somebody's way; being (or not being) a nuisance to them. *Out of the road* occurs earlier with the general meaning 'inappropriate' (as in *it would not be out of the road if …*). *19th cent.*

one for the road

informal a last alcoholic drink before setting off on a journey. *Mid 20th cent.*

> Ruth Rendell *The Best Man to Die* 1981
> *George Carter dipped his hand into his pocket and brought out some small silver. 'One for the road then, Jack?' Charlie looked at the little coins. 'What's that? Your missus's housekeeping?' George flushed. He wasn't married; Charlie knew he wasn't married.*

on the road

travelling or touring, especially on business. *17th cent.*

> Defoe *Robinson Crusoe* 1719
> *So that we were in all six of us, and five servants, besides my man Friday, who was too much a stranger to be capable of supplying the place of a servant on the road.*

road pricing

the practice of charging motorists for the use of certain busy roads, to raise extra revenue or to reduce congestion. *Mid 20th cent.*

a road to nowhere

a futile or fruitless course or action. *Mid 20th cent.*

> Guardian Weekly 1970
> *People on foot on a hot road walking from nowhere to nowhere.*

Daily Telegraph 1992
The return of socialism would be the 'road to nowhere, a dead end' at a time when economic recovery was around the corner.

the rule of the road
the fixed procedure for the movement of traffic on a designated side of the road in each direction. *19th cent.*

Hardy *The Mayor of Casterbridge* 1886
According to the strict rule of the road it appeared that Henchard's man was most in the wrong; he therefore attempted to back into the High Street. In doing this the near hind-wheel rose against the churchyard wall, and the whole mountainous load went over.

take (to) the road
to set out on a journey, especially a long one. *19th cent.*

Kipling *Kim* 1901
Kim considered the benevolent yellow face wrinkle by wrinkle. 'It is less than three days since we took road together, and it is as though it were a hundred years.'

See also all roads lead to ROME; the END of the road; HIT the road; the road to DAMASCUS.

roar

be roaring drunk
to be extremely and noisily drunk. *17th cent.*

Thomas Otway *Friendship in Fashion* 1678
He came where I was last night roaring drunk: swore dam him, he had bin with my Lord such a one, and had swallow'd three quarts of Champaigne for his share.

do / carry on a roaring trade/business
to succeed in selling one's goods or services in large numbers; to be highly successful in commerce. *18th cent.*

John O'Keeffe *Fontainebleu* 1785
The British Lion is my sign; | A roaring trade I drive on; | Right English usage, – neat French wine | A landlady may thrive on.

Christopher Morley *The Haunted Bookshop* 1919
The Milwaukee Lunch did a roaring business among the sensation seekers who came to view the ruins of the bookshop.

roast
See rule the roast *at* RULE the roost.

rob

rob Peter to pay Paul
to take money or assets from one source to pay another; to pay off a debt by incurring another. The phrase probably derives generally from the association of the two saints, who share the same feast day on 29 July; more specific connections have been claimed, but all are significantly later than the earliest uses. The phrase goes back to Middle English, where it is found in the works of John Wyclif: 'Lord, hou schulde God approve that thou robbe Petur, and gif this robbere to Poule in the name of Christ?'

Robin

a round Robin
a written petition or protest having several signatories, with the signatures arranged in a circle so that the first to sign could not be identified. The phrase has a nautical origin; it was used by sailors at sea who were anxious to prevent reprisals against individuals when they made group complaints. Robin may be derived from the personal name, or it may be a corruption of the French word *ruban* meaning 'ribbon': in 18th cent. France, petitions were put on a ribbon and the ends were joined, forming a *rond ruban*. The term has also been used to describe a sporting tournament in which each team plays all the others. In more recent use it may denote a letter or document that is sent to several recipients simultaneously or in succession, originally (and chiefly in American use) with the idea that each recipient might add a comment before passing it on to the next. *18th cent.*

Charles Johnstone *Chrysal* 1760
Though it is but just to comfort you, with an account of the return which he met for his kindness, which was no less than a round-robin to the lords of the admiralty, for his refusing to let them go ashore, and spend their money, in the same manner, the next time they came in.

Mrs Gaskell *North and South* 1855
Miss Hale, I had a round-robin from some of my men – I suspect in Higgins' handwriting – stating

their wish to work for me, if ever I was in a position to employ men again on my own behalf. That was good, wasn't it?

round Robin Hood's barn

by a circuitous or roundabout route. The expression alludes to the semi-historical figure of English folklore, Robin Hood, a 13th cent. outlaw who lived in Sherwood Forest in Nottinghamshire and was said to rob the rich to give to the poor. He was rapidly celebrated as a figure of heroism and romance, and songs and ballads were written round his name. His barn, where he stored all his booty, was presumably in an out-of-the-way place, so that travelling round it involved a considerable detour. The phrase emerges as a piece of 19th cent. romantic nostalgia: it originated in dialect and local use, and is recorded in *Notes & Queries* for June 1878, p.486. It also appears at about the same time in American contexts and is well established in figurative meanings to do with rambling conversations and suchlike. *19th cent.*

Seba Smith *My Thirty Years out of the Senate* 1859
Mr. Chairman, we seem to be going all round Robin Hood's barn, but I don't see as we are anywhere near coming to the point.

---

rock¹ (noun)

between a rock and a hard place

informal, originally NAmer faced with two equally unwelcome alternatives; in a dilemma. The phrase is recorded in local use in the US in the early years of the 20th cent., in the meaning 'bankrupt', and is perhaps modelled on *between Scylla and Charybdis* (see SCYLLA), although the correspondence between a 'hard place' and a whirlpool (Charybdis) is difficult to envisage. *Early 20th cent.*

John Buchan *The Courts of the Morning* 1929
There was a woman we had with us and she got away. The Indians must have helped her, and they cut the bridge behind her, and the next morning the whole Indian outfit did a bunk. After that we were between a rock and a hard place.

get one's rocks off

informal to have a sexual orgasm: based on *rocks* as a slang term for the testes. *Mid 20th cent.*

G V Higgins *A City on a Hill* 1975
I've been reduced to dressing up in order to get my rocks off.

S Hutson *Captives* 1992
From the sitting room he could still hear Plummer speaking. 'You used to go out with Jim Scott, didn't you?' Hitch asked. She nodded slowly. 'I'll bet he'll miss you inside,' said Hitch. 'Only his right hand for company when he used to have you to get his rocks off.'

hit/touch rock bottom

to experience a low point in one's fortunes. The original physical meaning of *rock bottom* is 'bedrock', from which arose the sense of 'lowest possible' with reference to prices, rates, and suchlike, in which *rock* is effectively an intensifier. The present phrase with its overtones of misfortune (equivalent to the figurative use of *nadir*) dates from the mid 20th cent.

H Edib *The Clown and His Daughter* 1935
By the time she had touched the rock-bottom of misery she had also reached a decision.

on the rocks

1 (said of an undertaking or relationship, a person's fortunes, etc) in great difficulty and likely to fail: with allusion to a ship foundering on rocks in the sea (as in the extended metaphor in the quotation below). *17th cent.*

John Reynolds *The Triumphs of Gods Revenge* 1623
She forsakes the helme that might have steered her to the port of happinesse, and safetie; and so fills the sayles of her resolutions with the winde of despayre, which threaten no lesse then to split the barke of her life on the rocks of her destruction and death.

2 *informal* (said of an alcoholic drink) served over ice cubes. *Mid 20th cent.*

---

rock² (verb)

See rock the BOAT.

---

rocker

off one's rocker

informal eccentric or crazy: with allusion to coming adrift from the rocker of a cradle or rocking chair. *19th cent.*

P G Wodehouse *The Inimitable Jeeves* 1923
'His Grace ... had exhibited a renewal of the symptoms which have been causing the family so

much concern. I could not leave him immediately. Hence my unpunctuality, which I trust has not discommoded you.' 'Oh, not at all. So the Duke is off his rocker, what?' 'The expression which you use is not precisely the one I should have employed myself with reference to the head of perhaps the noblest family in England, but there is no doubt that cerebral excitement does, as you suggest, exist in no small degree.'

---

rod

make a rod for one's own back
to do something that will cause oneself trouble later. The phrase occurs earlier (15th cent.) in the form *make a rod for oneself*. *16th cent.*

Thomas Blague *A Schole of Wise Conceytes* 1569
What time as trees had their proper language, a countryman came into the woode and required a handle for his Axe, they graunted his requeste. When he had well mended his axe, he began to cut downe the trees: then the wood al too late repented his gentlenesse, and was full sory that he had made a rod for his owne tayle.

rule with a rod of iron
to be ruthlessly tyrannical or authoritarian. The phrase alludes to Revelations 2:27 (in the Authorized Version, 1611): 'And he shall rule them with a rod of iron; as the vessels of a potter shall they be broken to shivers.' It first appears in Bible translations from the 15th cent., but principal usage dates from 18th cent. and 19th cent. literature.

Defoe *Colonel Jack* 1722
But that it is owing to the brutallity, and obstinate temper of the Negroes, who cannot be mannag'd by kindness, and courtisy; but must be rul'd with a rod of iron, beaten with scorpions, as the Scripture calls it; and must be used as they do use them, or they would rise and murther all their masters.

spare the rod
to be over-lenient. The phrase is based on the proverb *spare the rod and spoil the child*, an old maxim that children should not be treated leniently: *and* here implies a consequence. The sentiment occurs earlier in other forms, notably in the Bible, Proverbs 13:24 'He that spareth his rod, hateth his son.' The same advice occurs in the homilies of the Anglo-Saxon monk Aelfric

(c1000): 'Se the sparath his gyrde [= stick], he hatath his cild.'

Caroline Kirkland *The Fountain and the Bottle* 1850
They sent him to school every winter, and charged the master not to spare the rod if it was needed to make him a good boy.

a rod in pickle
the threat of punishment. The present form replaces older (16th cent.) forms *rod in lye* (= detergent) and *rod in piss*. All these liquids are preservatives signifying the keeping of things for later use. *17th cent.*

B Spenser *Vox Civitatis* 1625
I feare God hath worse rods in pickell for you.

See also KISS the rod.

Roland

a Roland for an Oliver
a blow for a blow; tit for tat: from the names of two knights (paladins) of Charlemagne, whose exploits always matched each other and were celebrated in the medieval French *Chanson de Roland*. According to one account, the two met in combat and fought for several days without result. There is a reference to them in Shakespeare's *1 Henry VI* (1590) I.iii.9, where the Duke of Alençon recalls, after a French defeat, that 'Froissart, a countryman of ours, records | England all Olivers and Rolands bred | During the time Edward the Third did reign'. References to Roland and Oliver date from the 14th cent., e.g. in Chaucer's *Book of the Duchess* (line 1123): 'The traytor that betraysed Troye, | Or the false Genelloun [= Ganelon], | He that purchased the tresoun | Of Rowland and of Olyver.'

Smollett *The Life and Adventures of Sir Launcelot Greaves* 1762
To be sure, Sir, (said he) they thought you as great a nincompoop as your squire – trim tram, like master, like man; – but I hope as how you will give them a Rowland for their Oliver.

Scott *The Antiquary* 1815
I promise you he gave my termagant kinsman a quid pro quo – a Rowland for his Oliver, as the vulgar say, alluding to the two celebrated Paladins of Charlemagne.

roll

be rolling drunk

to be extremely drunk and staggering about. *19th cent.*

Hardy *The Return of the Native* 1878

A small apple tree ... grew just inside the gate, the only one which throve in the garden, by reason of the lightness of the soil; and among the fallen apples on the ground beneath were wasps rolling drunk with the juice.

be rolling in money / in it

informal to be very wealthy. Also in the shortened form *be rolling*. The image is of physically rolling in something comfortable or luxurious; the figurative use of *roll* with reference to wealth dates from the 16th cent. *18th cent.*

Fanny Burney *Cecilia* 1782

Oh Miss Beverley, how happy are you! able to stay where you please, – rich, – rolling in wealth which you do not want, – of which had we but one year's income only, all this misery would be over, and we might stay in our dear, dear country!

on a roll

informal enjoying a run of success or good fortune. The image is of a moving vehicle rapidly gaining momentum. *Late 20th cent.*

Mike Ripley *Angel Hunt* 1991

'Do you know how much a cat pelt is worth in some parts of Europe? ... And even if they really are fakes – synthetic fur –' she was on a roll now – 'it's made from petrochemicals and they're non-biodegradable and therefore damaging to the environment.'

rolled into one

(said especially of qualities or attributes) combined in one person or thing. *19th cent.*

Lewis Carroll *Sylvie and Bruno* 1889

'What a beautiful fact! But how is it proved?'
'Thus,' replied Arthur, with all the gravity of ten Professors rolled into one.

a rolling stone

a person who is constantly on the move and elusive: with allusion to the (16th cent.) proverb *a rolling stone gathers no moss*, i.e. a person who does not settle down will not acquire wealth or social status. The notion dates back to classical antiquity, and becomes caught up with the legend of Sisyphus, who was famously punished by the gods of the underworld for defying Death by being made to roll a huge stone up a hill, the stone constantly rolling down again just as it was about to reach the top. *17th cent.*

Thackeray *The Memoirs of Barry Lyndon* 1856

I have served in Spain and in Piedmont; but I have been a rolling stone, my good fellow. Play – play has been my ruin!

a roll in the hay

informal frivolous or casual sexual intercourse. *Mid 20th cent.*

The Face 1992

They hadn't waited all these years for one quick roll in the hay.

roll of honour

a list of people who have made great achievements, originally in war but also in sport and other areas of activity. *18th cent.*

Defoe *Jure Divino, a Satyr* 1706

Be Thou the Maiden Subject of my Pen; | Agent of Justice, first of wisest Men. | Fancy him, Satyr, of that Hero-Race, | That in our Roll of Honour still takes Place.

roll one's own

informal to do something independently or without any help: from the literal use with reference to making one's own cigarettes with papers and loose tobacco. *Mid 20th cent.*

New Statesman 1992

Betty Boothroyd herself makes one of those up-beat speeches that roll their own psychology.

roll up one's sleeves

to start in earnest on an activity. The image is of preparing for a fight or a lengthy piece of physical work. *19th cent.*

William Caruthers *The Kentuckian in New York* 1834

Now, thinks I, we'll see some sport; so I rolled up my sleeves, and held my arms both stretched out to keep back the crowd.

D H Lawrence *Pansies* 1929

Then I am willing to fight, I will roll my sleeves up | And start in.

See also have people rolling in the aisles *at* AISLE; roll with the punches *at* PUNCH.

Rome

all roads lead to Rome

(proverb) different ideas and courses of action can have the same result: translating medieval Latin *mille vie ducunt hominem per secula Romam* 'a thousand roads lead a man for ever to Rome.' *Middle English*

> Chaucer *A Treatise on the Astrolabe* Prologue (line 40)
> *Right as diverse pathes leden diverse folk the righte way to Rome.*

Rome was not built in a day

(proverb) a complex task or undertaking will take a long time to complete: normally used as a warning against impatience. The proverb derives from medieval French *Rome ne fut pas faite toute en un jour*. It is found in the *Adages* of the Dutch humanist scholar Erasmus (*c*1467–1536) and in John Heywood's *Dialogue of Proverbs* (1546). *16th cent.*

> John Grange *The Golden Aphroditis* 1577
> *Alpha Omega lykyng well this ready deriuation, so aptly alluded with an unfayned similitude, with brydeled lippes answeared, Rome was not buylded in one day, wherewith N.O. helde him as content for that tyme.*

when in Rome (do as the Romans do)

(proverb) people should accommodate themselves to the manners and practices prevailing in the place where they are living at the time. The proverb is based on medieval Latin (*si fueris Romae, Romano vivito more; si fueris alibi, vivito sicut ibi* 'If you are in Rome, live by the Roman custom; if you are elsewhere, live by the custom of that place') and is attributed to the 4th cent. Saint Ambrose of Milan. *15th cent.*

> R Taverner transl *Erasmus' Adages* 1552
> *That which is commonly in euery mans mouth in England Whan you art at Rome, do as they do at Rome.*

roof

go through / hit the roof

1 *informal, originally services' slang* to lose one's temper, to be greatly angered by something. The phrase makes an early appearance in Fraser and Gibbons' *Soldier and Sailor Words* (1925). *Early 20th cent.*

> J P McEvoy *Show Girl* 1928
> *Milton gave me a couple of drinks early in the evening out of his flask and Jimmy hit the roof.*

2 (said of prices, costs, etc) to escalate to a very high level: *roof* has been used as an alternative to *ceiling* to denote an upper limit of this kind from the 15th cent. *Mid 20th cent.*

> Daily Mirror 1992
> *The first day's publication of the photos produced an incredible increase in sales of 482,118 more than the same day the week before. The second day went through the roof with a whopping 573,604. But wait for it. Day three, when the Mirror published the whole Fergie holiday snaps album, went up even more – by 583,647.*

the roof falls in

a disaster or catastrophic failure happens; everything goes wrong. *19th cent.*

> Mark Twain *The Innocents Abroad* 1869
> *I wasted so much time praying that the roof would fall in on these dispiriting flunkeys that I had but little left to bestow upon palace and pictures.*

See also RAISE the roof.

rooftop

shout something from the rooftops

to make something publicly known in a conspicuous and prominent way, especially when it has been kept secret hitherto: with allusion to Luke 12:3 'Therefore whatsoever ye have spoken in darkness shall be heard in the light; and that which ye have spoken in the ear in closets shall be proclaimed upon the housetops.' *20th cent.*

> Economist 1976
> *The typical manager's standard of living has taken a caning recently. He knows it, even the chancellor admits it, and here is the British Institute of Management with a salary survey to prove it. And, though the BIM does not shout this from the rooftops, to provide a very simple answer to it: change employers.*

room

in a smoke-filled room

(said especially of political negotiations and decisions) made by a small group of people in private meetings, rather than by a public or democratic process: first used in a report in a Washington newspaper in 1920 about the selection of Warren Harding of Ohio as the Republican candidate in the forthcoming presidential election. *Early 20th cent.*

Financial Times 1982
What actually happened is that, once again, the handful of rather old men who sit in the smoke-filled rooms in which the late Mayor Daley of Chicago was at home and who habitually determine the course of Japanese politics asserted themselves.

no/not room to swing a cat

hardly any room at all: used to describe a small and confined space. *Cat* here is sometimes understood in its literal meaning of swinging a real cat by its tail; or it may be short for *cat-o'-nine-tails*, i.e. a whip with nine lashes, which makes for a more realistic image. The phrase is described as a 'vulgar saying' in a 17th cent. source. *17th cent.*

Smollett The Expedition of Humphry Clinker 1771
Now mark the contrast at London – I am pent up in frowzy lodgings, where there is not room enough to swing a cat; and I breathe the steams of endless putrefaction.

Dickens David Copperfield 1850
The glory of lodging over this structure would have compensated him, I dare say, for many inconveniences; but, as there were really few to bear, beyond the compound of flavours I have already mentioned, and perhaps the want of a little more elbow-room, he was perfectly charmed with his accommodation. Mrs. Crupp had indignantly assured him that there wasn't room to swing a cat there; but, as Mr. Dick justly observed to me, sitting down on the foot of the bed, nursing his leg, 'You know, Trotwood, I don't want to swing a cat. I never do swing a cat. Therefore, what does that signify to me?'

room at the top

an opening for advancement to the highest levels of a profession or organization. The phrase has been attributed to the US politician and renowned orator Daniel Webster (1782–1852), whose maxims included 'there is always room at the top'. The phrase was used as the title of a novel by John Braine (1957; made into a film in the following year) about bourgeois values and aspirations in the postwar period. Its hero Joe Lampton is told 'You're the sort of man we want. There's always room at the top.' *Early 20th cent.*

George Orwell The English People 1947
The masses ... know it is not true that 'there's plenty of room at the top'.

---

roost

See RULE the roost.

---

root

root and branch

thoroughly or completely. The phrase originates as a metaphor for the total destruction at the end of the world in the Old Testament (Malachi 4:1 'The day that cometh shall burn them up, saith the Lord of hosts, that it shall leave them neither root not branch'). In the 17th cent., it was applied to a petition (known as the *root-and-branch petition*) laid before the English Parliament in 1641 for the total abolition of episcopal Church government. The image is of a tree being felled and its roots destroyed to prevent its regrowth. The phrase first occurs in adverbial use in the mid 17th cent.

Bunyan The Holy War 1682
For I received but now by the post from my Lord Lucifer, (and he useth to have good intelligence) That your old King Shaddai, is raising of an army to come against you, to destroy you root and branch.

put down roots

to settle down to life in a particular place: the image (in this and *take root* below) is of a plant sending its roots down into the ground in order to establish itself. *Mid 20th cent.*

James Kirkup A Poet Could Not But Be Gay 1991
The desire to put down roots is a recognition of human rootlessness.

strike at the root of something

have a profound or devastating effect on something, especially an established institution: *cf* Matthew 3:10 (the preaching of John the Baptist) 'And now also the axe is laid unto the root of the trees: therefore every tree which bringeth not forth good fruit is hewn down, and cast into the fire.' *16th cent.*

take root

to become fixed or established (see *put down roots* above): in literal use (often of the vine in biblical allusions) from the 15th cent. *17th cent.*

Locke A *Third Letter Concerning Toleration* 1692
The Christian religion by this means takes root in that country and spreads itself, but does not suddenly grow the strongest.

rope

give somebody / let somebody have enough rope

allow somebody enough freedom of action and they will cause their own downfall: a shortening of the (17th cent.) proverb *give a man rope enough and he will hang himself* (and variants), with play on the figurative meaning of *rope* meaning 'licence, leeway'.

Hardy *Far from the Madding Crowd* 1874
These middle-aged men have been pulling her over the coals for pride and vanity … but I say, let her have rope enough.

know the ropes

to be well informed about the procedures involved in a task or undertaking: a metaphor from the days of sailing ships, when sailors had to be thoroughly familiar with the workings of a ship's rigging and handling the ropes (see the 1840 quotation below). An extended use in the context of being streetwise in London life is noted in a slang dictionary of 1874. *19th cent.*

R H Dana *Two Years Before the Mast* 1840
In the midst of this conversation the captain appeared; and we winded the boat round, shoved her down, and prepared to go off. The captain, who had been on the coast before and 'knew the ropes', took the steering oar, and we went off in the same way as the other boat.

on the ropes

in a desperate situation; close to defeat or humiliation. In boxing, a losing fighter might be forced back on the ropes at the side of the ring by his opponent; the phrase is recorded in this literal context from the early 19th cent. *Early 20th cent.*

Birmingham Post 1999
Mr Hague looked wounded when his words were thrown back at him. Mr Maude laughed, but only in the sick way someone does when they know they are the butt of the joke. The Tories were on the ropes and Mr Brown was merciless.

a rope of sand

something that offers an illusion of security or support. *17th cent.*

Richardson *The History of Sir Charles Grandison* 1753
Bad people will indeed find out bad people, and confederate with them, in order to keep one another in countenance; but they are bound together by a rope of sand; while trust, confidence, love, sympathy, and a reciprocation of beneficent actions, twist a cord which ties good men to good men, and cannot be easily broken.

See also MONEY for jam / old rope.

rose

Used in a number of phrases as a symbol of the pleasant or enchanting; and in *under the rose* as a symbol of secrecy.

come up roses

informal to develop or progress in a pleasing way. *See also* come out/up smelling of roses *at* SMELL. *Mid 20th cent.*

Punch 1992
How long will it be before one of our major political parties has the guts to campaign against the European Community in its present form, rather than sticking their collective heads in the merde and pretending that everything's coming up roses?

everything's / it's all roses

informal the situation is very pleasing; all is going well. *Late 20th cent.*

M2 Presswire 2002
China Southern Airlines had a banner year in '01 – operating 365,000 flight hours, with more than 208,000 takeoffs/landings and carried a whopping 19 million passengers! Of course not everything was roses and pink champagne. 'The impact of the September 11th terrorist attacks in New York City reverberated – like cascading waves in a pond – around the world and China was no less affected by the impact.'

not all roses

informal not completely acceptable or pleasing. *19th cent.*

Graham Greene *Brighton Rock* 1938
An impulse of pity made her say: 'It's not all that good, Maisie.' She tried to destroy the appearance of her own happiness. 'Sometimes he's bad to me. Oh, I can tell you,' she urged, 'it's not all roses.'

roses all the way

informal very pleasant or agreeable: with allusion to Browning's line (see the quotation below). *19th cent.*

Browning The *Patriot* (Men and Women) 1855
It was roses, roses, all the way, | *With myrtle mixed in my path like mad.*

there is no rose without a thorn

(proverb) an apparently pleasant or ideal state of affairs will present some difficult aspect or drawback. The phrase goes back to Middle English, and is found in the work of John Lydgate (mid 15th cent.). Shakespeare refers to the image in *1 Henry VI* (1590) II.iv.69, during an exchange between Somerset and Richard Plantagenet which takes place beside a rose briar. Richard invites them both to pluck a white rose, which they both do. Later in the exchange Richard asks 'Hath not thy rose a canker, Somerset?', whereupon Somerset replies 'Hath not thy rose a thorn, Plantagenet?'; and the same pairing of thorn and canker occurs in Sonnet xxxv: 'No more be grieved at that which thou hast done: | Roses have thorns, and silver fountains mud. | Clouds and eclipses stain both moon and sun, | And loathsome canker lives in sweetest bud.' The phrase appears also in allusive and altered versions, and the image of a rose without a thorn has been a common poetical device for referring to a loved one.

George Eliot *Adam Bede* 1859
Mrs Poyser would probably have brought her rejoinder to a further climax, if every one's attention had not at this moment been called to the other end of the table, where the lyrism, which had at first only manifested itself by David's sotto voce performance of 'My love's a rose without a thorn', had gradually assumed a rather deafening and complex character.

under the rose

in confidence or secrecy: corresponding to Latin *sub rosa*, German *unter der rose*. The rose as a symbol of secrecy is found throughout medieval Europe and earlier. In classical antiquity there was a story that Cupid gave a rose to Harpocrates, the god associated with secrets (identified with Egyptian Horus), in gratitude for his discretion about his and his mother's (Venus's) adventures. The English version of the phrase was used in 1546 in state papers of the reign of Henry VIII, and was followed by an explanation

of its meaning, which suggests that it was then unfamiliar. *16th cent.*

John Dunton *A Voyage Round the World* 1691
Besides, under the rose, he's a pretty author himself, has done several curious things that I cou'd name, and which I'll assure you have taken very well.

See also a BED of roses; come out/up smelling of roses *at* SMELL; (stop and) SMELL the roses.

---

rot

The phrases draw on the image of rot slowly eating into wood or other hard materials (usually from within) and destroying them: this figurative use of *rot* originated in cricket commentaries, as a metaphor for a rapid loss of wickets suffered by one side.

the rot sets in

there is an unaccountable succession of failures or disasters. *19th cent.*

stop the rot

to put an end to a succession of failures or disasters. *Early 20th cent.*

Westminster Gazette 1901
It is to be hoped that something can be done (as cricketers say) to 'stop the rot'.

---

rotten

a rotten apple

somebody who is a bad lot, and likely to corrupt others. The image is of a single bad apple in a pile or barrel, making all the others go rotten too. There is also play on the word *rotten* in its meaning 'morally corrupt', which dates from the time of Chaucer. The notion of a rotten apple as something worthless (or worse than worthless) is found in Caxton, towards the end of the 15th cent.: 'The sones of a traytour whiche ben not worthe a roten apple.'

Shakespeare The *Merchant of Venice* I.iii.100 (1598)
The devil can cite Scripture for his purpose. | *An evil soul producing holy witness* | *Is like a villain with a smiling cheek,* | *A goodly apple rotten at the heart.*

Iris Murdoch The *Message to the Planet* 1989
I'm awful, I'm dreadful, I'm a drab, a slut, a bitch, a rotten apple.

something is rotten in the state of Denmark
there is something wrong or untoward: used as
an indication of deep social or moral decadence
and also in more trivial or facetious contexts. The
phrase originates in the observation of the soldier
Marcellus after the appearance of the ghost of
Hamlet's father in Shakespeare's *Hamlet* (1601)
I.iv.67. *17th cent.*

rough

a bit of rough
informal sexual activity with a crude or unsophisticated man, regarded as appealing. *20th cent.*

rough and ready
1 (said of a method or procedure) crudely or
hastily conceived. *19th cent.*

> Hardy *Far from the Madding Crowd* 1874
> *When a dozen men are ready to speak tenderly to
> you, and give the admiration you deserve without
> adding the warning you need, it stands to reason
> that my poor rough-and-ready mixture of praise
> and blame cannot convey much pleasure.*

2 (said of a person) uncouth or unsophisticated.
19th cent.

> Dickens *David Copperfield* 1850
> *I'm obleeged to you, sir, for your welcoming manner
> of me. I'm rough, sir, but I'm ready – least ways, I
> hope I'm ready, you unnerstand.*

rough around the edges
generally sound but with a few minor imperfec-
tions. *20th cent.*

a rough diamond
a person with good feelings but crude manners.
A *rough diamond* is one in its natural state, before
it has been cut and polished; the phrase appears
as a simile (as in the quotation below) from the
17th cent. and in direct figurative use from the
19th cent.

> John Fletcher *A Wife for a Month* 1624
> *But who shall work her Sir, | For on my conscience
> she is very honest, | And will be hard to cut as a
> rough diamond.*

> Trollope *Dr Thorne* 1858
> *Well, about Louis; a very bad sort of fellow; isn't he?
> Drinks – eh? I knew his father a little. He was a
> rough diamond, too.*

the rough edge/side of one's tongue
harsh words; a scolding. *19th cent.*

a rough passage
a difficult time or experience. *Mid 20th cent.*

> Guardian 1989
> *The Government is to amend the Environment
> Protection Bill and is expecting a rough passage
> through the Lords where a select committee is
> already examining the NCC's scientific base.*

sleep rough
to sleep in the open or in an uncomfortable or
makeshift place. *19th cent.*

take the rough with the smooth
to accept life's difficulties along with its pleasures; to take what comes. *Rough* in the sense 'the
unpleasant or unwelcome part of something' –
contrasted with the *smooth* or pleasant side – is
well attested from the 17th cent., and appears
earlier in Middle English in the text *Beryn*: 'Take
yeur part as it comyth, of roughe and eke of
smooth.' Towards the end of the 18th cent.,
Mary Wollstonecraft contrasted *rough* and *smooth*
in corresponding meanings in *The Wrongs of
Woman* (1798): 'Every woman, and especially a
lady, could not go through rough and smooth, as
she had done, to earn a little bread.' *One must take
the rough with the smooth* appears as the subtitle of
a poem called 'Woman's Rights' in the series
Verses New and Old (1865) by Arthur Joseph
Munby (1828–1910). *19th cent.*

> James Cross *The False Friend* 1809
> *I've ta'en cruises many, in squalls and fair weather!
> | Been loving on shore boys, and dauntless at sea; |
> Made my mind up to take rough and smooth both
> together, | Set sail fair or foul, for 'twas all one to
> me!*

See also CUT up rough; rough JUSTICE.

roughshod

ride roughshod over somebody
to disregard the feelings or wishes of others in
promoting one's own. A horse is roughshod
when its shoes have the heads of nails projecting,
in order to give it a better grip on surfaced roads.
19th cent.

> Dickens *The Old Curiosity Shop* 1841
> *Mr. Swiveller was so much confounded by the
> single gentleman riding roughshod over him at this*

rate, that he stood looking at him almost as hard as he had looked at Miss Sally.

round

go/make the round(s)

to go from place to place or be passed from person to person. *17th cent.*

> Anon *Choice Novels and Amorous Tales* c1652
> *He was seen to come thither, but he begins to go the round about Aleria's house, faigning to plant nets to catch birds, and to hunt wild beasts.*

in the round

1 (said of a sculpture) made as a free-standing piece and not attached to a background. *19th cent.*
2 (said of a theatre or theatrical performance) with the stage raised and the audience placed all round it. *Mid 20th cent.*

> *New Statesman and Society* 1992
> *The business of importing dramatic madness to Broadmoor was embarked on with enormous misgivings … Performing King Lear in the round meant making eye-contact with members of the audience, some of whom may have really been embroiled in mayhem the actors were merely playing at.*

3 (figuratively) solid, three-dimensional; considered from all angles. *20th cent.*

> Jean Bow *Jane's Journey* 1991
> *The only memorable 'in the round' person she met was her host's eighty-year-old mother, quick, intelligent and agile with, moreover, a sense of humour.*

round the bend/twist

informal eccentric or crazy. The phrase is first recorded as naval slang: *Round the Bend* was the title of a novel by Nevil Shute (1951). *20th cent.*

> Harper Lee *To Kill a Mockingbird* 1960
> *Why, Atticus said he went round the bend at the University. Said he tried to shoot the president.*

See also a square PEG in a round hole.

row

have a hard/rough row to hoe

to face a difficult task or experience. *19th cent.*

> Henry James *Roderick Hudson* 1876
> *It was very certain to Rowland's mind that if she had given him up she had by no means ceased to care for him passionately, and that, to exhaust her charity for his weaknesses, Roderick would have, as the phrase is, a long row to hoe.*

in a row

in succession, one after another. The literal spatial use of people or things situated or arranged in a line goes back to Chaucer (14th cent.), but the abstract use in relation to time rather than space is relatively recent and appears first in American use, whereas British use favoured the idiom — *times running* (see RUN). *19th cent.*

> Mark Twain *Life on the Mississippi* 1883
> *Town like this don't have fires often enough – a fellow strikes so many dull weeks in a row that he gets discouraged.*

royal

no royal road

no easy way to achieving something, especially to gaining knowledge: with allusion to the remark attributed to the Alexandrian mathematician Euclid (4th cent. BC), that 'there is no royal short cut to geometry', supposedly in reply to King Ptolemy I who wanted the study of geometry to be made easier. *18th cent.*

> William Hazlitt *The Round Table* 1817
> *Iago had to pass through a different ordeal: he had no appliances and means to boot; no royal road to the completion of his tragedy.*

rub

not have two coins/pennies to rub together

informal to be impoverished or destitute. Also used figuratively in other contexts. *Early 20th cent.*

> Celia Brayfield *The Prince* 1990
> *Colin Lambert hasn't got two grey cells to rub together and will say anything to get his name in this column.*

> *Evening Standard* 1992
> *Mirabita's father died in 1989. 'It was Christmas Eve and the kids and I were gutted,' he said after the hearing. 'I never got on with my mother and she walked out us in 1990. We didn't have two pennies to rub together.'*

rub one's hands

to show eager expectation of something pleasant or interesting, literally by rubbing one's hands against each other. *18th cent.*

Scott *Waverley* 1814
The wily agent listened with apprehension when he found Waverley was still in a state of proscription – was somewhat comforted by learning that he had passport – rubbed his hands with glee when he mentioned the amount of his present fortune – opened huge eyes when he heard the brilliancy of his future expectations.

rub somebody's nose in something

informal to cause somebody particular embarrassment by dwelling on some unwelcome topic, such as a mistake or unpleasant experience. The phrase is most likely derived from the practice of rubbing the noses of household pets in their messes when inappropriately deposited, as part of their house-training. *Mid 20th cent.*

Kim Newman *Bad Dreams* 1990
Judi had always tried to rub his nose in parts of his life he just wanted to let lie there and be profitable. He was glad he had got rid of her.

rub shoulders / NAmer elbows

to associate with other people or mix socially with them. *19th cent.*

John Brougham *The Game of Life* 1856
I have played the Game of Life boldly, and have lost! The world is wide enough for me to live in, without rubbing shoulders against any here!

Conan Doyle *Through the Magic Door* 1919
You who have sat with me before upon the green settee are familiar with the upper shelf, with the tattered Macaulay, the dapper Gibbon, the drab Boswell, the olive-green Scott, the pied Borrow, and all the goodly company who rub shoulders yonder.

rub somebody (up) the wrong way

to irritate or displease somebody: now normally with *up*, although *rub somebody the wrong way* and *rub the hair the wrong way* are also recorded in the 19th cent. The image is of rubbing an animal's fur against the direction in which it naturally lies. *19th cent.*

Helen Keller *The Story of My Life* 1901
I appreciate the kind things Mr. Anagnos has said about Helen and me; but his extravagant way of saying them rubs me the wrong way.

there's/here's the rub

that is the crucial point or difficulty. The phrase originates in Shakespeare's *Hamlet* (1601), where Hamlet's soliloquy 'To be, or not to be' continues (III.i.67) 'To die, to sleep. | To sleep, perchance to dream. Ay, there's the rub, | For in that sleep of death what dreams may come | When we have shuffled off this mortal coil | Must give us pause.' *Rub* is used in its meaning 'obstacle or difficulty'. In the 18th cent., Oliver Goldsmith described the phrase as 'a vulgarism beneath the dignity of Hamlet's character' (*On Metaphors*, 1763).

Richard Steele in the *Spectator* 1712
But her relations are not intimates with mine. Ah! There's the rub!

James Fenimore Cooper *The Pioneers* 1823
'There was one part, though, which might have been left out, or something else put in; but then, I s'pose that, as it was a written discourse, it is not so easily altered, as where a minister preaches without notes.' 'Ay! there's the rub,' … cried the landlady.

See also rub SALT in somebody's wound.

---

rubber

burn / NAmer lay rubber

informal to drive or travel at great speed. The phrase alludes to the heating of road tyres at high speeds, and is based on the collective use of *rubber* denoting the tyres of a motor vehicle. *Late 20th cent.*

Evening Standard 1993
Who gives a monkey's these days how fast you can go from nought to 60? Our customer is not the sort of guy who sits at the traffic lights in Park Lane and gives it a couple of thousand revs so he can burn rubber and leave everyone else behind. People who buy our cars want to know how fast it'll go from 50 to 70 in fifth gear.

Rubicon

cross the Rubicon

to commit oneself irrevocably to a course of action, especially a daring or challenging one: with allusion to Julius Caesar's crossing of the Rubicon with his army in 49 BC. The Rubicon was a stream that marked the boundary between Cisalpine Gaul, of which Caesar was proconsul (provincial governor), and Italy. By crossing the boundary with his army, Caesar was invading Italy and precipitating a civil war with the Roman Senate, supported by Pompey, whom Caesar eventually defeated. *See also* the die is cast at DIE². *17th cent.*

> Dryden *The Conquest of Granada* 1672
> *This noyse may chill your Blood, but mine it warms: | We have already past the Rubicon.*

ruffle

ruffle somebody's feathers
to annoy or upset somebody: with allusion to the practice of birds in ruffling their feathers as a sign of anger. Figurative uses date from the 19th cent.

> Dickens *David Copperfield* 1850
> *Dora's aunts soon agreed to regard my aunt as an eccentric and somewhat masculine lady, with a strong understanding; and although my aunt occasionally ruffled the feathers of Dora's aunts, by expressing heretical opinions on various points of ceremony, she loved me too well not to sacrifice some of her little peculiarities to the general harmony.*

smooth somebody's ruffled feathers
to soothe or console somebody who has been angered or upset. *17th cent.*

rug

pull the rug from under somebody's feet
to take action to undermine somebody's position or intentions, especially by suddenly withdrawing one's support. *Mid 20th cent.*

> *Today* 1992
> *As Britain's jobless total nudges three million, insurance companies are pulling the rug from under thousands of homebuyers.*

See also CUT a/the rug.

rule

as a rule
generally speaking; for the most part. *19th cent.*

> Dickens *David Copperfield* 1850
> *'In the course of the week,' said Miss Clarissa, 'we shall be happy to see Mr. Copperfield to tea. Our hour is half-past six.' I bowed again. 'Twice in the*

week,' said Miss Clarissa, 'but, as a rule, not oftener.'

a rule of thumb
a practical method or principle based on experience, rather than a precise or technical one. The phrase dates from the 17th cent. and is probably connected with the use of the thumb as a rough guide in measuring length. A more specific origin has been suggested in the supposed practice of brewers checking the temperature of a fermenting brew by dipping a thumb in it, but this does not have much to commend it as a method, since the thumb is not particularly sensitive to small variations in heat (unlike the elbow, traditionally used to gauge the temperature of bathwater). The phrase has also become curiously entangled with wife-beating, a practice more common in the 18th cent. than it is today, and then widely regarded as permissible within limits. What these limits were is unclear, but they allegedly included a rule that was attributed to Sir Francis Buller, a brilliant lawyer who became the youngest barrister to be appointed a judge in Britain (at the age of 32), that a husband may beat his wife, so long as 'the stick with which he administers the castigation is not thicker than his thumb'. Edward Foss, in his *Biographical Dictionary of the Judges of England* (1864), threw doubt on the authenticity of this pronouncement ('no substantial evidence has been found that he ever expressed so ungallant an opinion'), but it was the subject of a caricature by James Gillray, which carried the caption 'Judge Thumb' and showed him carrying two bundles of 'thumbsticks' – 'for family correction: warranted lawful'. The phrase is also used (often with hyphens) adjectivally, as in *a rule-of-thumb calculation, method*, etc.

> William Hope *The Compleat Fencing-master* 1692
> *What he doth, he doth by rule of thumb, and not by art.*

rule the roost
to be in complete authority or control; to lord it over others, usually implying the sort of disdainful pride conventionally attributed to a cockerel keeping a roost of hens in order. The predominant form for four centuries up to the end of the 19th cent. was *rule the roast*, presumably in the sense of presiding over a feast or banquet; this was the only version of the phrase entered in the first edition of the *Oxford English Dictionary*, the

version with *roost* being added in the *Supplement to the OED* in 1982 with evidence from the mid 18th cent. onwards. This version, which had become the exclusive form by the early 20th cent., has greater immediacy, although 'ruling the roast' might now conjure up a picture from the world of suburban barbecues.

Thomas Watson *The Hecatompathia* 1582
I will enforce my selfe to live content, | Till so my thoughts have fed upon delay, | That Reason rule the roast and love relent.

Charles Aleyn *The History of Henry the Seventh* 1638
And there the king whose right they did so boast | Must be content to fit, and rule the roast.

Trollope *Barchester Towers* 1857
He [Dr Proudie] was biding his time, and patiently looking forward to the days when he himself would sit authoritative at some board, and talk and direct, and rule the roast, while lesser stars sat round and obeyed, as he had so well accustomed himself to do.

— rules, OK
an expression of great enthusiasm or support for something: such-and-such is a great or fine thing. The phrase originated in the 1970s in graffiti and captions, where it is still regularly encountered; it is also used ironically to express contempt or disapproval. *Late 20th cent.*

Guardian 1986
The work force has shrunk by 20 per cent without a single enforced redundancy. Productivity is up, up and away. Commercial considerations rule, OK.

Julian Critchley *The Floating Voter* 1993
He had changed but not bathed, and the new slogan on his T-shirt, 'Maggie rules, OK' did not compensate for the stench of the great unwashed.

run the rule over something
to check something quickly for its accuracy or suitability: in earlier use in criminals' slang of a thief feeling a victim's pockets for their contents. *19th cent.*

See also rule with a ROD of iron; WORK to rule.

rumour

rumour has it
there is a rumour: usually followed by a *that* clause. *Early 20th cent.*

Edgar Rice Burroughs *The Gods of Mars* 1913
Where they visited they wrought the most horrible atrocities, and when they left carried away with them firearms and ammunition, and young girls as prisoners. These latter, the rumour had it, they sacrificed to some terrible god in an orgy which ended in the eating of their victims.

run

give somebody the run-around
informal to cause somebody trouble or inconvenience by prevaricating or behaving evasively. *Early 20th cent.*

(go) take a running jump
informal to go away and leave somebody alone: often used as an angry or impolite instruction or dismissal. Also used in the extended form *take a running jump at oneself*. *Early 20th cent.*

have a (good) run for one's money
to get good value from one's expenditure. To *give somebody a run for their money* is to offer them a substantial challenge (often without money as such being involved). The phrases probably originate in racing terminology, referring to a horse that has run well despite not being placed, or they may allude to a fairground ride or other form of public entertainment. *19th cent.*

Denman Thompson *Our New Minister* 1903
[Strong] *I hear Mrs. Bartlett is an excellent cook.* [Skeezicks] *Aces up! no exercise gallop there, you get a run for your money, every time, I can tell you those.* [Strong] *You have an odd way of expressing yourself.*

Richard Harding Davis *The Dictator* 1904
I gave him a run for his money. He got the run, I got the money.

D H Lawrence *Sons and Lovers* 1913
'You wouldn't be long in breaking your neck at a hurdle race!' she said. 'So long as I get a good run for my money! Will you?' 'Nay; you may settle that atween you.'

in / out of the running
having a good (or poor) chance of being chosen for a post, award, etc. In horseracing, the *running* is the action of a horse in moving round the course. *19th cent.*

make a run for it
to attempt to escape: in early use in the form *make a run of it. 19th cent.*

make / take up the running
to take the initiative or determine the rate of progress in an enterprise; more literally, to take the lead and set the pace in a running race. In early use the phrase sometimes appears within extended metaphor. *19th cent.*

Dickens *Our Mutual Friend* 1865
This man that we have received our information from, has got a start, and if he don't meet with a check he may make the running and come in first.

run dry
(said of a supply) to be used up: based on the literal use in relation to sources of water. *17th cent.*

run high
(said of feelings and emotions) to be strongly or forcibly shown. The metaphor is drawn from two main images: the sea when its waves are high and its currents strong, and the high temperature reached by a fever. *17th cent.*

Jeremy Collier *A Defence of the Short View* 1699
Now when passions runs high, disappointment rises with them, and good humour grows more precarious.

R H Dana *Two Years Before the Mast* 1840
We had no chronometer, and had been drifting about so long that we had nearly lost our reckoning … For these various reasons, the excitement in our little community was running high.

run into the sand/sands
(said of an undertaking or enterprise) to peter out; to come to nothing. *Mid 20th cent.*

Economist 1978
Khrushchev … attempted to decentralise planning by giving powers to regional councils. He even tried to loosen the Soviet Union's control over eastern Europe. A brave attempt, but it failed: all Khrushchev's reforms ran into the sands.

a running battle/fight
a fight or dispute that continues for a considerable time in successive stages. The form *running fight* is recorded from the 17th cent. and *running battle* from the 19th cent. The phrase was originally used with reference to a military engagement that continued in successive locations, as distinct from a pitched battle.

Joseph Harris *The City Bride* 1696
But Fortune favouring, and the wind springing a fresh gale, we got clear off and try'd to make a running fight.

Dickens *The Battle of Life* 1846
Snitchey and Craggs had a snug little office on the old Battle-Ground, where they drove a snug little business, and fought a great many small pitched battles for a great many contending parties. Though it could hardly be said of these conflicts that they were running fights – for in truth they generally proceeded at a snail's pace.

run off at the mouth
informal, chiefly N Amer to talk incessant nonsense. *Early 20th cent.*

Joanna Neil *The Waters of Eden* 1993
It seems to me that Adam has had far too much to say for himself. That never used to be a fault of his, running off at the mouth.

run somebody/something to earth/ground
to find a well-hidden person or thing after a long search: with allusion to the hunting of foxes and other animals, in which the quarry seeks refuge in its underground earth or burrow, pursued by the hounds. *19th cent.*

Charles Kingsley *Westward Ho!* 1855
Whereon by a sudden impulse, the young lady took plenty of coca, her weapons and her feathers, started on his trail, and ran him to earth just as he was unveiling the precious mystery.

— times running
a certain number of times in succession. *See also* in a ROW. *18th cent.*

Goldsmith *The Vicar of Wakefield* 1766
I threw deuce-ace five times running.

Dickens *The Haunted Man* 1847
'Let me think,' said the old man. 'For how many Christmas times running, have I sat in my warm place, and never had to come out in the cold night air; and have made good cheer … Is it twenty, William?'

(try to) run before one can walk
to try to do something difficult or ambitious without being sufficiently familiar with the basic techniques or principles involved: an extension of the proverb *one must walk before one can run*

(and variants), which is recorded explicitly from the 17th cent. and in sentiment from the 14th cent. *Early 20th cent.*

See also be as regular as / run like CLOCKWORK; be run off one's FEET; cut/run it/things FINE; fall/run FOUL of; go/run to SEED; run somebody CLOSE; run the GAUNTLET; run its COURSE; run a MILE; run of the MILL; run out of STEAM; run rings round somebody/something *at* RING²; run RIOT; run with the ball *at* BALL¹; run with the HARE and hunt with the hounds; work/run oneself into the GROUND.

---

runner

do a runner
British, informal to run away or abscond, especially from custody or supervision, or to have an adulterous affair. *Late 20th cent.*

> **Julian Barnes** *Talking It Over* 1992
> *She was twenty-eight, I discovered; her parents (mother French, father English) had separated some years previously when Pater had done a runner with a bimbo.*

---

run-up

in the run-up to something
during the period leading to a significant occasion or event. The phrase first appeared in this meaning in British newspapers during the 1960s. It is a figurative use drawn from various physical meanings in sports and games, notably the bowler's approach to the crease in delivering the ball in cricket. *Mid 20th cent.*

> **Guardian 1984**
> *George Rallis, the outgoing New Democracy Prime Minister, made an early concession of defeat and appeared on television together with Mr Papandreou to ensure that public excitement stayed within bounds. Greece, which had been unable to accept Papandreou's challenge in the run-up to the 1967 coup, had become more mature.*

---

rush

a rush of blood (to the head)
a sudden thrill or feeling of excitement. *19th cent.*

> **Hardy** *The Return of the Native* 1878
> *Till this moment he had not met her eye since the morning of his marriage, when she had been loitering in the church, and had startled him by lifting her veil and coming forward to sign the register as witness. Yet why the sight of him should have instigated that sudden rush of blood she could not tell.*

See also give somebody the bum's rush *at* BUM; rush one's fences *at* FENCE.

---

rut

in a rut
following a tedious invariable routine: based on the notion of a vehicle's wheel travelling constantly in the same rut in the ground. The phrase also occurs in various other forms such as *get out of the rut*, etc. *19th cent.*

> **Somerset Maugham** *The Moon and Sixpence* 1919
> *When he was appointed Registrar at Thomas's I hadn't a chance of getting on the staff. I should have had to become a G.P., and you know what likelihood there is for a G.P. ever to get out of the common rut.*

sabbath

a sabbath day's journey

a short journey. In the New Testament (Acts 1:12) the Mount of Olives is described as being *a sabbath day's journey* from Jerusalem (in the Authorized Version, 1611). This was a little over one kilometre and referred to the distance a Jew was allowed to travel in order to attend a place of worship, corresponding to the distance between the people and the Ark during the Hebrews' period in the wilderness (see Joshua 3:4).

> Richard Polwhele *Epistle to Dr Downman* 1794
> *A sabbath-day's journey, at least, had we rumbled,*
> | *Ere a word to my wife or my children I grumbled.*

sabre

rattle one's sabre

to put on a show of force or aggression in order to intimidate an opponent, without intending a real attack. The sabre was a sword with a broad curved blade, used in cavalry fighting. The derivative form *sabre-rattling* is also found. Figurative uses date from the early 20th cent.

sack

get the sack

to be dismissed from one's job: to *give somebody the sack* is to dismiss them. The phrase is derived from French *donner le sac* (= bag), probably with allusion to the former practice of workmen carrying a bag of tools around with them and taking them away on leaving. The phrase is recorded from the 16th cent. with *bag* instead of *sack*, and in an older more neutral meaning 'to leave suddenly.' *19th cent.*

> Kipling *The Gate of the Hundred Sorrows* 1888
> *There was ten of us met at the Gate when the place was first opened. Me, and two Baboos from a*

Government Office somewhere in Anarkulli, but they got the sack and couldn't pay (no man who has to work in the daylight can do the Black Smoke for any length of time straight on).

hit the sack

informal to go to bed: *cf* hit the HAY. *Mid 20th cent.*

> Imamu Baraka *Preface to a Twenty Volume Suicide Note* 1961
> *Watched television for a while. Read the | paper, then hit the sack.*

sackcloth

in sackcloth and ashes

showing a public display of mourning or repentance. Wearing sackcloth and smearing ashes on one's head are mentioned in the Bible as marks of lamentation and penitence (e.g. Esther 4:1 'Mordecai rent his clothes, and put on sackcloth with ashes, and went out into the midst of the city'; Matthew 11:21 'Woe unto thee, Chorazin! woe unto thee, Bethsaida! for if the mighty works, which were done in you, had been done in Tyre and Sidon, they would have repented long ago in sackcloth and ashes'). *16th cent.*

> Thomas Heywood *A Funeral Elegie Upon ... King James* 1625
> *By humane power, I never heard or read | Sackcloth and ashes could revive the dead.*

sacred

See a sacred cow.

saddle

be in the saddle

to be in control or authority; literally, to be the rider of a horse. *17th cent.*

> John Hind *Lysimachus and Varrona* 1604
> *Do thy vertues increase like the pace of a Crab, who creepeth backward? Hast thou in the cradle bin continent, and wilt thou in the saddle be impudent?*

> Henry James *Roderick Hudson* 1876
> *'If you have work to do, don't wait to feel like it; set to work and you will feel like it.' 'Set to work and produce abortions!' cried Roderick with ire. 'Preach that to others. Production with me must be either pleasure or nothing. As I said just now, I must*

either stay in the saddle or not go at all. I won't do second-rate work.'

safe

(as) safe as houses
completely safe: based on the notion of the permanence of buildings, at least in relation to other physical aspects of everyday existence. *Safe as churches* and *safe as the bank* are also found in the 19th cent. In early use the meaning was rather to do with certainty than with safety in the physical sense (as in the quotation below). *19th cent.*

> Hardy *Far from the Madding Crowd* 1874
> *'Say he's wanted to meet mistress near church-hatch tomorrow morning at ten,' said Oak, in a whisper. 'That he must come without fail, and wear his best clothes.' 'The clothes will floor us as safe as houses!' said Coggan. 'It can't be helped,' said Oak. 'Tell her.'*

be on the safe side
to allow a margin of error in one's calculations or expectations. *19th cent.*

> Jane Austen *Sense and Sensibility* 1811
> *Whether he had asked her pardon for his intrusion on first coming into the room, he could not recollect; but, determining to be on the safe side, he made his apology in form, as soon as he could say any thing, after taking a chair.*

better (to be) safe than sorry
(proverb) it is better to take extra precautions to prevent a bad situation than to risk regret later. *19th cent.*

> Samuel Lover *Rory O'More* 1837
> *'Jist countin' them, – is there any harm in that?' said the tinker: 'it's better to be sure than sorry.'*

safe sex
sexual relations in which the couple take precautions to prevent the spread of sexually transmitted diseases, especially the HIV virus. *Late 20th cent.*

> Will Self *My Idea of Fun* 1993
> *I screwed around the crowd, all kinds of people, fat and thin, young and old, male and female. I performed cunnilingus, sodomy, intercrural sex and even safe sex – long before it became fashionable.*

See also a safe BET; a safe pair of hands *at* HAND.

safety

there's safety in numbers
(proverb) one derives support and comfort from being with other people who might share one's concerns or intentions. The notion can be found in a slightly different form in the Bible (Proverbs 11:14 'In the multitude of counsellors there is safety'). The phrase dates from the 19th cent. in its current form.

> Jane Austen *Emma* 1816
> *They were just approaching the house where lived Mrs. and Miss Bates. She determined to call upon them and seek safety in numbers. There was always sufficient reason for such an attention; Mrs. and Miss Bates loved to be called on.*

sail

sail close to / near the wind
to take risks in an enterprise or business activity, especially by operating close to the limits of what is legally or morally acceptable: a metaphor from nautical language, in which to sail close to the wind is to take the closest possible course to the direction from which the wind is blowing. *19th cent.*

> Hardy *The Mayor of Casterbridge* 1886
> *'She had already married another – maybe?' Henchard seemed to think it would be sailing too near the wind to descend further into particulars, and he answered 'Yes.'*

See also take the wind out of somebody's sails *at* WIND[1].

sake

for God's/heaven's sake
used as an exclamation of protest, impatience, or frustration: *for God's sake* occurs in Middle English in running text, and from the 16th cent. as a distinct imprecation; *for heaven's sake* first appears in the 18th cent.

> Shakespeare *The Taming of the Shrew* Induction ii.1 (1592)
> [Sly] *For God's sake, a pot of small ale!*

Benjamin Franklin *Dialogue between Franklin and Gout* 1780
[Franklin] *Oh! Oh! – for Heaven's sake leave me; and I promise faithfully never more to play at chess, but to take exercise daily, and live temperately.*

See also for OLD times' sake.

---

salad

one's salad days

a time of youthful inexperience or indiscretion. The phrase comes from Shakespeare's *Antony and Cleopatra* (1607). Cleopatra is reflecting with her attendant Charmian on her former love affair with Julius Caesar (I.v.72): 'My salad days, | When I was green in judgement, cold in blood, | To say as I said then.' *Salad Days* was the title of a 1954 London musical about a magic piano that makes everybody dance, by Julian Slade and Dorothy Reynolds. Allusive uses do not appear until the 19th cent.

Alice Cary *The Bishop's Son* 1867
'Will you just tell me what you were in love with, when you were in love?' 'That was in my salad days, and I beg you will never speak of it again; if I were to fall in love now, I should know what it was with, and you are a man, with sense and judgment, and in the full maturity of all your powers.'

Dylan Thomas *Under Milk Wood* 1954
[Gossamer Beynon] *I don't care if he is common,* [second voice] *she whispers to her salad-day deep self,* [Gossamer Beynon] *I want to gobble him up. I don't care if he does drop his aitches.*

---

salami

hide the salami

informal, originally NAmer to have sexual intercourse. *Salami* is a slang word for the penis, which is 'hidden' in the act of penetration during intercourse. *Late 20th cent.*

Sunday Times 1994
If you want to argue realism, older men should be sleeping with older people. If it's fantasy we're after, I want to see Keanu Reeves playing hide the salami with Uma Thurman. And I want it now!

---

saloon

See (drinking) in the last chance saloon *at* LAST[1].

---

salt

eat salt with —

to be a person's guest. References to salt as representative of hospitality go back to Middle English, and a proverb recorded from the 16th cent. advises 'trust no man unless thou hast first eaten a bushel of salt with him.' *16th cent.*

John Lyly *Euphues* 1578
Why diddest thou leave Athens the nourse of wisdome to inhabite Naples the nourisher of wantonnesse? Had it not bene better for thee to have eaten salt with the Philosophers in Greece, then sugar with the courtiers of Italy?

put salt on somebody's tail

to capture somebody: based on the advice traditionally given to children to put salt on the tail of a bird in order to catch it. *17th cent.*

rub salt in somebody's wound

to make somebody's unpleasant or painful experience even worse, especially by adding a further hurtful remark. *Mid 20th cent.*

Robinson Jeffers *At the Birth of an Age* 1938
Did you believe in me once, that you rub salt in my wound?

Pamela Bennetts *Topaz* 1988
'Did you know the marquis was getting married again?' He didn't want to rub salt into her wounds. He just wanted to warn her how hopeless her case was.

the salt of the earth

a person or group who shows kindness and support for others: with allusion to Matthew 5:13 'Ye are the salt of the earth: but if the salt have lost his savour, wherewith shall it be salted?' *Middle English*

Chaucer *The Summoner's Tale* (line 2196)
Ye been the salt of the erthe and the savour [= delight].

sit above the salt

to have an exalted place: with allusion to the position of guests at a dinner table in the days when a huge salt cellar stood in the middle of the table. The more distinguished guests sat 'above the salt', i.e. between the salt cellar and the head of the table, while guests of inferior status sat 'below the salt.' *16th cent.*

Joseph Hall *Virgidemiarum* 1598
Secondly, that he doe, on no default, | Ever presume to sit above the salt.

take something with a pinch/grain of salt

to regard a claim or assertion with a degree of scepticism: also in modern Latin *cum grano salis*. A pinch of salt can improve the flavour of something to eat or make it more palatable. *17th cent.*

worth one's salt

good at one's work; capable and efficient. The phrase is said to be derived from the practice of paying a special sum of money to Roman soldiers to buy salt; the English word *salary* is based on Latin *salarium* 'money for buying salt' (from *sal* = salt). *19th cent.*

R L Stevenson *Treasure Island* 1883
It did all our hearts good to see him spit in his hand, knit his brows, and make the blade sing through the air. It was plain from every line of his body that our new hand was worth his salt.

See also like a DOSE of salts.

Samaritan

See GOOD Samaritan.

same

all/just the same

in spite of what has been said or done; nonetheless; even so. *19th cent.*

Jane Austen *Mansfield Park* 1814
You have been five years with us, and my sister always meant to take you when Mr. Norris died. But you must come up and tack on my patterns all the same.

all the same to —

informal making no difference to a person; of no concern to them. The phrase appears commonly in the formula *if it's all the same to you* in the sense 'if you have no objection' (and is often used ironically). *18th cent.*

James Cobb *English Readings* 1787
Nay, if you like it, I'll take t'other side of the question – 'tis all the same to me – I'll engage to speak on any thing for a quarter of an hour at least – what say you to that, old gentleman?

Dickens *Pickwick Papers* 1837
I should perfer your givin' me a answer to my question, if it's all the same to you.

by the same token

applying the same argument or principle (in a different case); for the same reason: *token* itself has little precise meaning here. *15th cent.*

one and the same

(used as an emphatic form) the very same person or thing: corresponding to Latin *unus et idem. 16th cent.*

Shakespeare *Love's Labour's Lost* I.ii.3 (1594)
[Armado] *Boy, what sign is it when a man of great spirit grows melancholy?* [Mote] *A great sign, sir, that he will look sad.* [Armado] *Why, sadness is one and the selfsame thing, dear imp.* [Mote] *No, no, O Lord, sir, no.* [Armado] *How canst thou part sadness and melancholy, my tender juvenal?*

the same again

informal another of the same kind as before: often as a question, by way of an offer of another drink. *Mid 20th cent.*

Gavin Lyall *The Conduct of Major Maxim* 1982
George grunted and finished his sherry. 'Thank God: now I can have a real drink. What about you? Same again?'

the same but/only different

informal the same in important respects but differing in others; identical with some exceptions. The qualification in the second part of the phrase varies considerably from one context to another and typically conveys the main emphasis of the expression. *Mid 20th cent.*

Karl Miller *Authors* 1989
Amis and Larkin are the same but different. The poem and novel I have attributed to them respectively can also, for certain purposes, be attributed to them both.

same difference

informal essentially the same; no real difference despite appearances: often used to counter an assertion of some subtle or pedantic distinction. *Mid 20th cent.*

G Roberts *The Highest Science* 1993
'Call me old fashioned, but I think brains belong in heads, not in tanks.' 'It's not a brain, and that's not a tank,' Sheldukher replied evenly. 'Same difference,' the Doctor said casually.

same here
informal an expression of agreement or involvement in what has been said. *19th cent.*

> Brougham & Dickens *Dombey and Son* 1885
> [Florence] *Well, good morning, Mr. Toots.*
> [Susan] *The same here, Mr. Aspen-leaf.*

> Conan Doyle *The Lost World* 1912
> *'I suppose, now, when you went into that room there was no such notion in your head – what?' 'No thought of it.' 'The same here. No thought of it.'*

sand

the sands are running out
the available or permitted time is nearly over: with allusion to the sand of an hourglass. Also in the fuller form *the sands of time* (or *life*, etc) *are running out*. *16th cent.*

> Shakespeare *Pericles* xxii.1 (1608)
> [Gower] *Now our sands are almost run;* | *More a little, and then dumb.*

See also be built on sand *at* BUILD; BURY one's head in the sand; a ROPE of sand; RUN into the sand.

sandboy

See (as) HAPPY as a sandboy.

sandwich

a sandwich / two sandwiches short of a picnic
informal (said of a person) stupid or crazy. Variants on the theme of trivial incompleteness include *a brick short of a load* (see BRICK), *several currants short of a bun*, and *a slice short of a full loaf*. *Late 20th cent.*

> Esquire 1993
> *It will not surprise those who have driven one to know that the Metro is a stunningly good car. Having read that, the rest of you probably now think that the author is a sandwich short of a picnic.*

sardine

like sardines
very tight and crowded, like the sardines in a tin. *19th cent.*

> Bartley Theodore Campbell *The Galley Slave* 1879
> *Here we are in Paris a whole month, sealed up like sardines, afraid to show ourselves for fear that awful scandal should leak out.*

> Mary Gervaise *The Distance Enchanted* 1983
> *Susan Breeze … tried to wriggle away from her portly neighbour, whose big fur collar had been tickling her neck for the last half-hour. Vaguely she wondered who had coined the phrase 'packed like sardines'. Sardines, she thought, travelled in luxury compared with human beings forced to use the railways at Christmas time.*

sauce

what's sauce for the goose is sauce for the gander
(proverb) something appropriate in one case should also be appropriate in a similar case. Originally in the sense 'what is suitable for a man is also suitable for a woman', the phrase appears in collections of proverbs from the 17th cent.

> Byron *Don Juan* 1824
> *But there's another little thing, I own,* | *Which you should perpetrate some summer's day,* | *And set the other half of earth to rights;* | *You have freed the blacks – now pray shut up the whites.* | *Shut up the bald-coot bully Alexander!* | *Ship off the Holy Three to Senegal;* | *Teach them that 'sauce for goose is sauce for gander,'* | *And ask them how they like to be in thrall?*

saucer

have/with eyes like saucers
to be staring in wonder or amazement: an old comparison dating from the 14th cent. or earlier. The phrase dates from the 16th cent. in its current form.

> Dryden *The Wild Gallant* 1663
> *We met three or four hugeous ugly devils, with eyes like saucers.*

> Charles Reade *The Cloister and the Hearth* 1861
> *Whist! whisper! that little darling is listening to every word, and eyes like saucers.*

sausage

not a sausage

British, informal nothing at all. *Mid 20th cent.*

D M Greenwood *Unholy Ghosts* 1991
'The school is about a quarter of a mile from the Rectory. You didn't see anything else on your return home?' 'Not a sausage.' In his spare time Spruce climbed rocks in Wales and Scotland. He felt much the same sensation now as he searched around for a fresh foothold.

save

be saved by the bell

to escape a dangerous or unpleasant predicament by a timely intervention at the last moment: often used as an exclamation expressing relief at an unexpected escape from difficulty. The image is drawn from the world of boxing, in which a contestant is saved from being counted out if the bell marking the end of the round intervenes before the count is finished. Another theory sometimes canvassed connects the phrase with the burial of corpses in former times, when there was a greater danger than there is today of mistakenly interring somebody who was still alive. To prevent this, so the theory goes, a string was tied to the arm of the corpse and connected to a bell above ground, so that any victim who turned out to be still living could alert those above ground and so be 'saved by the bell'. This account is pure invention, aimed – like many stories about phrases – at providing more colour to an otherwise routine explanation. *Mid 20th cent.*

Jean Evans *A Dangerous Diagnosis* 1993
Her breath caught in her throat as he stared at her and her pulse-rate accelerated. Someone tapped at the door, and a spasm flickered across his features as she released her breath in a tiny hissing sound. 'Saved by the bell, I think,' he murmured wryly. She did need rescuing, though not for the reason he imagined.

save the day

to find a solution to a problem or difficulty, especially at the last moment. The phrase originates in the context of military engagements, in which 'the day' was the day's fighting and its outcome. *19th cent.*

George Chesney *The Battle of Dorking* 1871
I have also a dim recollection of seeing the Life Guards trot past the front, and push on towards the town – a last desperate attempt to save the day – before we left the field.

Edgar Rice Burroughs *The Warlord of Mars* 1913
'Where is Salensus Oll? He alone may revive the flagging courage of our warriors. He alone may save the day for Okar. Where is Salensus Oll?' The nobles stepped back from about the dead body of their ruler, and one of them pointed to the grinning corpse.

save one's skin/neck

to escape from danger or difficulty, especially by avoiding injury: see also save one's BACON. *17th cent.*

John Phillips *Maronides* 1678
He soon fix'd wings unto his back, | And thither fled to save his Neck: | Th' amazed Birds their tayls beshite, | They take him for some monstrous Kite.

See also save one's BACON; save one's BREATH; save FACE; SCRIMP and save; to save one's LIFE.

say

easier/sooner said than done

a suggestion or idea is theoretically attractive but impractical or difficult to implement. In Middle English the notion occurs in the form *better said than done*. An early occurrence of the phrase in its current form is in Thomas Heywood's (16th cent.) collection of phrases and proverbs.

have something/nothing to say for oneself

to be able (or unable) to justify or excuse one's actions, behaviour, etc: often used in the form of a question in the context of a reprimand or imminent punishment. *18th cent.*

Richard Graves *The Spiritual Quixote* 1773
As soon as young Newland had ... surveyed Wildgoose's face, half-shaved (which he took for a disguise); 'Well, you rascal,' says he ... 'What have you to say for yourself, guilty or not guilty?' 'Ah,' says Wildgoose ... 'I am but too guilty.'

that/it goes without saying

that is too obvious or familiar to need mentioning: translating French *ça va sans dire* and used with reference to things that are regarded by the speaker as common knowledge or a matter of course. *19th cent.*

Lewis Carroll *Sylvie and Bruno* 1889
'There is also a restless young woman in the case,'
Lady Muriel added. 'That goes without saying, my
child,' said her father. 'Women are always restless!'

that is to say
in other words: used (as a fuller form of *that is*) to
introduce a further explanation of something just
said. The phrase occurs in Middle English (see
Chaucer, below).

Chaucer *Prologue* (line 181)
A fissh that is waterlees [= out of water] – | *That*
is to seyn, a monk out of his cloystre.

there is no saying
one cannot be certain about something. *19th cent.*

Jane Austen *Mansfield Park* 1814
I never spent so happy a summer … there is no
saying what it may lead to.

when all is said and done
once everything has been taken into consideration: *cf* in the final ANALYSIS. *16th cent.*

you can say that again
informal an exclamation of agreement with or
approval for something just said. *Mid 20th cent.*

Eve Merriam *The Nixon Poems* 1970
It's a free country said the man swinging an ax-
handle at his neighbor | *You can say that again said*
the neighbor swung against and swinging back.

you don't say
informal used to express (often ironic or sarcastic)
surprise at something just said: used earlier in the
form *you don't say so. 17th cent.*

Thomas Southerne *Oroonoko* 1696
[Welldon] *Therefore I must own to you, that I am*
marry'd already. [Widow Lackitt] *Marry'd! you*
don't say so I hope! How have you the conscience to
tell me such a thing to my face!

Jane Austen *Northanger Abbey* 1818
'Look at that young lady with the white beads round
her head,' whispered Catherine, detaching her friend
from James. 'It is Mr. Tilney's sister.' 'Oh!
Heavens! You don't say so! Let me look at her this
moment.'

See also say/give the WORD; to say NOTHING of; —
wouldn't say BOO to a goose.

scald

like a scalded cat
extremely suddenly or rapidly. The image is of a
cat's reaction to being scalded, and a proverb *a*
scalded cat fears cold water is found in literature
from the 16th cent. The present phrase originated
in Air Force slang of the Second World War,
when rapid raids by light fighter-bombers were
described as *scalded-cat raids.* In modern use it is
often used of fast-moving vehicles. *Mid 20th cent.*

Autocar and Motor 1990
After Brundle's Jaguar took off like a scalded cat, it
was Mass who hunted it down, and soon engaged it
in a lurid battle.

scale¹ (weighing apparatus)

throw something into the scale
to take some particular point into account when
assessing a situation. *18th cent.*

Henry Fielding *The History of Tom Jones* 1749
And now both scales being reduced to a pretty even
balance, her love to her mistress being thrown into
the scale of her integrity, made that rather pre-
ponderate.

tip/turn the scales at —
to weigh the specified amount. *16th cent.*

Shakespeare *2 Henry IV* II.iv.256 (1597)
The weight of a hair will turn the scales between
their avoirdupois.

See also tip the scales/balance *at* TIP¹.

scale² (covering membrane)

the scales fall from somebody's eyes
somebody is no longer deceived; somebody suddenly realizes the truth of a situation: with allusion to the description of St Paul's regaining his
sight in Acts 9:18 'And immediately there fell
from his eyes as it had been scales: and he
received sight forthwith.' *18th cent.*

Defoe *Hymn to the Mob* 1715
But if the scales fall off thy eyes | *And heavenly*
light again thy soul supplies, | *Let all the engines of*
deceit stand clear, | *Nothing's so fatal but they*
ought to fear

scarce

make oneself scarce

informal to leave abruptly; to stay out of the way. *19th cent.*

> John Banim *The Chaunt of the Cholera* 1831
> But, they'll see a few more of us, day after day, | Ere we make ourselves scarce for them – that's what I say!

See also (as) rare/scarce as hen's teeth *at* HEN.

scare

See beat/shake/scare/frighten the (living) day-lights out of *at* DAYLIGHT.

scene

appear/come on the scene

to become involved in an enterprise or activity: more literally, to arrive at a place, especially where something significant is happening. The metaphorical use of *scene* in the sense 'the theatre of life' dates from the 17th cent. *19th cent.*

> Dickens *Great Expectations* 1861
> There appeared upon the scene – say at the races, or the public balls, or anywhere else you like – a certain man who made love to Miss Havisham.

behind the scenes

out of public view; in secret: in a theatre, the area 'behind the scenes' lies behind the stage out of view of the audience. The transition from literal to figurative usage is well caught in the quotation below. *18th cent.*

> Boswell *The Life of Samuel Johnson* 1791
> The play went off tolerably, till it came to the conclusion, when … the Heroine … was to be strangled upon the stage, and was to speak two lines with the bow-string round her neck … The audience cried out 'Murder! Murder!' She several times attempted to speak; but in vain. At last she was obliged to go off the stage alive … This passage was afterwards struck out, and she was carried off to be put to death behind the scenes.

a change of scene/scenery

somewhere new to live or stay, especially as a refreshing change. *18th cent.*

> Jane Austen *Pride and Prejudice* 1813
> Poor Jane! I am sorry for her, because, with her disposition, she may not get over it immediately … But do you think she would be prevailed on to go back with us? Change of scene might be of service – and perhaps a little relief from home may be as useful as anything.

not somebody's scene

informal not what somebody is interested in or able to take part in: here, the meaning of *scene* is transferred from the place where an activity or pursuit is followed to the activity itself. *Mid 20th cent.*

> Celia Brayfield *The Prince* 1990
> What's the matter with you, Sel – you know Lorna can't play that kind of part. A nympho barfly shacked up with a prizefighter – that's not her scene.

set the scene

to describe the place or circumstances in which something has happened or is about to happen: a metaphor from theatrical terminology, in which *setting the scene* means 'preparing the stage for the next part of the action.' *18th cent.*

scent

follow/pursue the scent

to follow clues to reach an objective: from the literal sense in foxhunting. *17th cent.*

> Lewis Theobald *Richard II* 1720
> This is Confed'racy! Does his Ambition Follow the Scent of Blood so hot already?

put/throw somebody off the scent

to mislead somebody in pursuit of a goal or objective. *19th cent.*

> Frances Hodgson Burnett *The Secret Garden* 1911
> Him an' Miss Mary thinks it's best plan to do a bit o' groanin' an' frettin' now an' then to throw folk off th' scent.

schedule

according to schedule

following a plan or intention. *Early 20th cent.*

> O Henry *Rolling Stones* 1906
> Tuesday, the day set for the revolution, came around according to schedule.

SCHEME | 636

scheme

the best-laid schemes/plans

plans that go wrong, despite careful planning:
with allusion to Robert Burns's line in 'To a
Mouse' (1785) 'The best-laid schemes o' Mice
an' Men | Gang aft a-gley'. The reference in
the poem is to the destruction of the fieldmouse's
nest by the plough. *18th cent.*

> Susan Ferrier *Marriage* 1818
> *But alas! the insecurity of even the best laid schemes
> of human foresight! Lady Juliana was in the midst
> of arrangements for endless pleasures, when she
> received accounts of the death of her now almost
> forgotten husband.*

the scheme of things

the way thing are organized; the circumstances
one is faced with. *19th cent.*

> Saki *Reginald in Russia* 1910
> *He reviled and railed at fate and the general scheme
> of things, he pitied himself with a strong, deep pity
> too poignant for tears, he condemned every one with
> whom he had ever come in contact to endless and
> abnormal punishments.*

school

a school of thought

a particular philosophy or way of thinking. *19th
cent.*

> J S Mill *Utilitarianism* 1863
> *Nor is there any school of thought which refuses to
> admit that the influence of actions on happiness is a
> most material and even predominant consideration
> in many of the details of morals, however unwilling
> to acknowledge it as the fundamental principle of
> morality, and the source of moral obligation.*

See also of the OLD school; the OLD school tie; the
school of hard knocks *at* KNOCK.

schoolboy

(as) every schoolboy knows

used to introduce a piece of supposedly common
knowledge. A famous use is by the historian
Lord Macaulay in an article in the *Edinburgh
Review* of 1840: 'Every schoolboy knows who
imprisoned Montezuma, and who strangled Ata-
hualpa.' Whether or not this was true in Macaulay's day, it certainly isn't today, although what

facts might reasonably be substituted to make
reasonable sense of the phrase must be left to the
reader's imagination. The notion of the schoolchild as a repository of basic knowledge is however older than Macaulay: the 17th cent. English
theologian Jeremy Taylor used the phrase 'every
schoolboy knows it', and in the 1720s Jonathan
Swift described a commonplace piece of knowledge as 'what every schoolboy knows'. The
phrase in its current form dates from the end of
the 18th cent.

> Hugh Blair *Lectures on Rhetoric and Belles Lettres* 1783
> *The common example of this, is that noted passage
> in Cicero which every schoolboy knows: 'Facinus est
> vincire civem Romanum; scelus verberare, prope
> parricidium, necare; quid dicam in crucem tollere.'*
> *['It is a crime to put a Roman citizen in bonds: it is
> the height of guilt to scourge him; little less than
> parricide to put him to death. What name then shall
> I give to crucifying him?']*

> Scott *Rob Roy* 1817
> *Mons Meg ... figures frequently in public accounts
> of the time, where we find charges for grease to
> grease Meg's mouth withal, (to increase, as every
> schoolboy knows, the loudness of her report).*

science

See BLIND somebody with science.

score

go over / have a few over the score

informal, chiefly Scottish to drink heavily. *18th cent.*

know the score

informal to be well informed about what is happening or what the facts are: the meaning of *score*
here is 'the crux of a matter', and is derived from
the sense in games and sports. *Mid 20th cent.*

> Thomas Hayden *The Killing Frost* 1991
> *Durkin replied with a broad conspiratorial wink,
> and slurred, 'We know the score, don't we, Alec?'
> Alec was appalled; he swore under his breath. No
> one, not even his uncle, knew that he was attached to
> Military Intelligence.*

on that/this score

for that reason; as far as that is concerned: *on the
score of* meaning 'for that reason' dates from the
17th cent. and is based on a figurative use of *score*

in the meaning used in game and sports. *17th cent.*

Susanna Centlivre *The Perjur'd Husband* 1700
[Bassino] *Armando, Thou'rt a Friend, and on that score | I must desire you to repair to Turin, | With all the speed you can, to bear these letters | To our great Prince.*

settle/pay a score / old scores
to take revenge for past wrongs one has suffered. The expression is based on the use of *score* denoting a debt accumulated by a series of tallies. A tally was a length of wood, on which debts were recorded by *scoring* (in the sense 'cutting' that is still in use) a series of grooves or nicks. Paying a debt recorded in this way was correspondingly known as *settling* (or *paying*) *the score*. The meaning shifted from this straightforward one to the notion of getting one's own back or having revenge. *18th cent.*

Henry Fielding *The History of Tom Jones* 1749
'Some of your officers,' quoth the landlord, 'will find there is a devil, to their shame, I believe. I don't question but he'll pay off some old scores upon my account. Here was one quartered upon me half a year, who had the conscience to take up one of my best beds, though he hardly spent a shilling a day in the house.'

See also score an own GOAL; score points off somebody *at* POINT.

---

scorn
See LAUGH somebody/something to scorn.

---

scot

to get off scot-free
to escape an obligation or punishment. The expression has nothing to do with Scotland or any stereotypes connected with the Scots (despite the occasional use of a variant *scotch-free* in the 16th cent. and a pun in Shakespeare mentioned below), but dates back to the Middle Ages, when people paid a *scot* or local tax: the word is originally Scandinavian and means 'payment'. The system, known as *scot and lot*, required that individuals pay in full according to their wealth. Shakespeare introduces a pun on *scot* and *Scot* towards the end of *1 Henry IV* (1596): after the death of Hotspur (v.iv.113) Prince Harry gives a

short epitaph over the body, then discovers Sir John Falstaff who has been hiding from Hotspur and now admits that ' 'twas time to counterfeit [= put on a disguise], or that hot termagant Scot [i.e. Hotspur] had paid me, scot and lot too'. The expression *scot-free* appears early, in the 13th cent., in a literal meaning 'free from the obligation to pay a scot'. Figurative uses do not start to come until the 17th cent., according to the available evidence. In the 1660s, for example, the Oxford antiquarian and historian Anthony Wood wrote that 'Oxford escaped scot free of the plague'. Other suggestions include an association with the word *scotch* meaning 'to cut a notch in' and then 'to crush', which survives in modern use in the figurative meaning of *scotching* (= refuting) a rumour. According to this account debts were 'scotched', i.e. rubbed off the slate on which they were recorded, leaving the debtor *scot(ch) free*; but there is no convincing connection here either in the word forms (we would expect to find a form *scotch-free* somewhere along the line) or in the sense development. *17th cent.*

Anon *The London Jilt* 1683
As for my part I remain'd peaceably sitting, and was studying of the means to make him pay for this disorder, for tho' he asked me a thousand pardons which I willingly granted him in appearance, I was loath to let him come off at so cheap a rate as to let him go scot-free.

---

scout

scout's honour
used as an expression of good faith. The expression, contained in Baden-Powell's 1908 handbook *Scouting for Boys*, was originally the pledge by which a member of the Scouts promised to obey the Scout law. *Early 20th cent.*

Catherine George *Out of the Storm* 1991
'I'm sorry, Dr Vaughan. For getting the wrong end of the stick, I mean. It was pretty far-fetched, really.' He smiled slowly. 'Not that much, you know! But you needn't lose any sleep over it, I promise – scout's honour.' Leonora smiled faintly. 'Were you a boy scout?'

scrape

See bow and scrape *at* BOW[1]; scrape (an) ACQUAINTANCE with somebody; scrape (the bottom of) the BARREL.

scratch

from scratch

from the very beginning. In sports and competitions, the *scratch* was a line marking the starting point for all the competitors except those who had been awarded an advantage or handicap, who were allowed to start further ahead. *See also* up to scratch *below. Mid 20th cent.*

> R G Bayly *Patrol* 1989
> *It was the first time I had seen a ship built from scratch and it was quite an experience to watch the steel plates being cut by their ingenious machine.*

scratch a — and find a —

(proverb) if you look more closely at somebody or something you will see their true nature: from the notion of scratching the surface of a precious metal to ensure that it is genuine. The original form of the proverb was *scratch a Russian and you'll find a Tartar*, which was attributed in French to Napoleon. G B Shaw wrote in *St Joan* (1924) 'Scratch an Englishman, and find a Protestant.' *See also* scratch the surface *below. 19th cent.*

> Mrs Humphry Ward *Robert Elsmere* 1888
> *'Didn't I tell ye?' the gasfitter's snarling friend said to him. 'Scratch him and you find the parson. These upper-class folk, when they come among us poor ones, always seem to me just hunting for souls, as those Injuns he was talking about last week hunt for scalps. They can't get to heaven without a certain number of 'em slung about 'em.'*

scratch one's head

informal to feel puzzled or confused, or to be searching for a solution to a difficulty: literally, to scratch the top of one's head as a gesture indicating this feeling. *18th cent.*

> Smollett *The Expedition of Roderick Random* 1748
> *When lights were brought, the occasion of all this disturbance soon appeared; which was no other than our fellow lodger, whom we found lying on the floor scratching his head, with a look testifying the utmost astonishment, at the concourse of apparitions that surrounded him.*

> Emerson Bennett *The Border Rover* 1857
> *The old trapper eyed me sharply for a while, as if he thought I might be playing upon his credulity; and then, apparently satisfied of my sincerity, he scratched his head and looked puzzled.*

scratch the surface

1 to investigate something more deeply or thoroughly. *19th cent.*

> Olive Schreiner *The Story of an African Farm* 1883
> *The innocent are accused, and the accuser triumphs. If you will take the trouble to scratch the surface anywhere, you will see under the skin a sentient being writhing in impotent anguish.*

2 to deal with a matter inadequately or superficially. The phrase is typically used in negative contexts to suggest that there is much more to a situation than has so far been explored; it also appears in the form *scratch the surface* (of something seemingly routine or uninteresting) *and* ... (something of greater interest will become apparent). *Early 20th cent.*

up to scratch

informal reaching a satisfactory or acceptable standard or level: originally in the form *up to the scratch*. The reference is to the line marking the starting point or operative point in various sports: Dickens associates it specifically with boxing (see below). *Cf* up to SNUFF. *19th cent.*

> Dickens *Hard Times* 1854
> *The third gentleman now stepped forth. A mighty man at cutting and drying, he was; a government officer; in his way (and in most other people's too), a professed pugilist; always in training, always with a system to force down the general throat like a bolus, always to be heard of at the bar of his little Public-office, ready to fight all England. To continue in fistic phraseology, he had a genius for coming up to the scratch, wherever and whatever it was, and proving himself an ugly customer.*

> Trollope *The Eustace Diamonds* 1873
> *I'm not going to marry a whole family; and the less I have of this kind of thing the more likely it is that I shall come up to scratch when the time is up.*

you scratch my back and I'll scratch yours

if you will support me or do me a favour I will do the same for you: often used with depreciatory overtones to denote devious or underhand cooperation between people. Hence also *back-*

scratcher (noun), *back-scratching* (adjective). *18th cent.*

> Edward Ward *All Men Mad* 1707
> *Scratch me, says one, and I'll scratch thee.*

screw

have a screw loose
(said of a person) to be eccentric or slightly crazy: based on the notion of a faulty component in a machine. In 19th cent. use (notably in Dickens: see below) the phrase also refers to incomplete or unreliable arrangements. *19th cent.*

> Dickens *Pickwick Papers* 1837
> *My uncle was confirmed in his original impression that something dark and mysterious was going forward, or, as he always said himself, that 'there was a screw loose somewhere'.*

put the screws on somebody / tighten the screw(s)
to apply psychological pressure on somebody to do what one wants: from the use of thumbscrews as instruments of torture. To *tighten the screw(s) is to increase the psychological pressure applied.* Screw has been used in the singular and plural in this figurative sense from the 17th cent. *19th cent.*

a turn of the screw
an intensification of a feeling or emotion that is already strongly felt: literally, a turning of the screw in an instrument of physical torture. Often used with allusion to the ghost story by Henry James with this title (1898). *19th cent.*

> Harold Frederic *The Damnation of Theron Ware* 1896
> *With another turn of the screw, they sold the piano she had brought with her from home, and cut themselves down to the bare necessities of life, neither receiving company nor going out.*

See also have one's HEAD screwed on (the right way).

scrimp

scrimp and save
to save what little one has; to be poor and thrifty. *Scrimp* is derived from a chiefly Scots adjective *scrimp* meaning 'scant, meagre'. Both the verb and the adjective date from the 18th cent., and are perhaps of Scandinavian origin; the associ-

ation with *save* is recorded from the middle of the 19th cent.

> Walter C Smith *Hilda Saint-Wife* 1902
> *I scrimp and save, and, at times, I am almost weary of life;* | *It would have been better for him had he married a managing wife.*

scruff

by the scruff of one's/its neck/collar
(held or seized) roughly by the back of the neck: used figuratively with reference to seizing opportunities, challenges, etc. *Scruff* is an altered form of *scuff*, a dialect word for the nape of the neck. *19th cent.*

> Wilkie Collins *No Name* 1862
> *These London Men ... are not to be trifled with by louts. They have got Frank by the scruff of the neck — he can't wriggle himself free.*

Scylla

between Scylla and Charybdis
faced with two dangers or unwelcome choices, in which avoiding the one forces one against the other: with allusion to the rock named *Scylla* and the whirlpool named *Charybdis*, which were located (in Homer's *Odyssey*) on each side of the straits of Messina between Italy and Sicily, so that ships passing through could keep clear of one only by approaching dangerously close to the other. *16th cent.*

> Robert Greene *Gwydonius* 1584
> *Ah Gwydonius (quoth he) what folly hast thou committed by this thy fearefull flight, what carefull calamitie is like to insue of this thy cowardise in avoyding Scylla thou art falne into Charibdis.*

sea

(all) at sea
completely lost or bewildered: a metaphor based on the notion of a ship that is out of sight of land and has lost its bearings. *18th cent.*

a sea change
a radical or far-reaching change. The phrase quotes the song 'Full Fathom Five' in Shakespeare's *The Tempest* (1613), where Ariel sings of Ferdinand's dead father (I.ii.403):

Full fathom five thy father lies.
Of his bones are coral made;
Those are pearls that were his eyes;
Nothing of him that doth fade
But doth suffer a sea-change
Into something rich and strange.
Sea-nymphs hourly ring his knell.

Here the meaning is literal, 'a change worked by the sea', because Ferdinand's father was drowned at sea. Shakespeare's use is specific to the situation and usage in physical senses since then has largely been confined, apart from direct quotations of Ariel's song, to literary and poetic imagery of the sea itself changing in various ways (as in the Mary Braddon quotation below, included more for its charm than its direct relevance). We see a gradual transition to figurative allusive uses during the 19th cent., over two hundred years after Shakespeare. *17th cent.*

Mary Braddon Lady Audley's Secret 1862
Lucy Audley's clear blue eyes dilated as she fixed them suddenly on the young barrister. The winter sunlight, gleaming full upon her face from a side window, lit up the azure of those beautiful eyes, till their colour seemed to flicker and tremble betwixt blue and green, as the opal tints of the sea change upon a summer's day.

Mrs Humphry Ward Robert Elsmere 1888
Here all that in London had been oppressive in the August heat suffered 'a sea change', and became so much matter for physical delight.

seal

my/his/her, etc lips are sealed
I (or he/she, etc) can be trusted to keep a secret or confidence. *19th cent.*

Frederick Douglass My Bondage and My Freedom 1855
Listening to complaints, however groundless, Barney must stand, hat in hand, lips sealed, never answering a word. He must make no reply, no explanation; the judgment of the master must be deemed infallible.

P G Wodehouse Ice in the Bedroom 1961
Her lips ... shall be sealed, if necessary with Scotch tape.

put/set the seal on something
to confirm an arrangement: from the former practice of pressing a personal wax seal on a letter or other document as a mark of its authenticity. *17th cent.*

Shakespeare Hamlet iii.iv.60 (1601)
[Hamlet to Gertrude, pointing to a portrait of his father] *A combination and a form indeed | Where every god did seem to set his seal | To give the world assurance of a man. | This was your husband.*

set/put one's seal to something
to give one's personal approval or endorsement of something: see the preceding phrase. *16th cent.*

seam

be bursting/bulging at the seams
to be full to the point of overflowing: said of a room, building, or locality, and also in figurative contexts. The image is of the *seams* or lines of stitching where pieces of fabric are joined together, which are likely to split if put under pressure. *Mid 20th cent.*

Louis MacNeice Dreams in Middle Age 1966
Our lives are bursting at the seams | With petty detail.

come/fall apart at the seams
to fail disastrously; to be completely ruined: see the preceding phrase. *Mid 20th cent.*

season
See a MAN for all seasons.

seat

by the seat of one's pants
informal, originally services' slang using instinct and experience and trusting a little to luck, rather than applying logic or technical knowledge. The phrase was originally used in the context of controlling an aircraft or vehicle, and this image is often preserved in the extended metaphor of more recent usage. *Mid 20th cent.*

Guardian 1989
What is the Government up to? Alas, it is flying by the seat of its pants. This student loans scheme has degenerated into open shambles.

See also be in the HOT seat.

second

a second childhood
a person's old age, regarded as a return to a childlike state. *17th cent.*

> Aphra Behn *Oroonoko* 1688
> *At this character, his old heart, like an extinguished brand, most apt to take fire, felt new sparks of love, and began to kindle; and now grown to his second childhood, longed with impatience to behold this gay thing, with whom, alas! he could but innocently play.*

second nature
what one does instinctively or by habit: originally as a proverb *habit* (or *usage*) *is second nature. 16th cent.*

> John Dickenson *Greene in Conceit* 1598
> *Boldnesse bred by use grewe so absolute, in being dissolute, that it seemed in hir a second nature.*

second sight
the supposed ability to discern what is invisible, or to imagine what is unknown or secret. *17th cent.*

second thoughts
a change of opinion after further thinking; reservations or doubts about an earlier opinion. Also *on second thoughts*, used to introduce a doubt or reservation about an opinion or decision just expressed; and in formulas of reassurance such as *do not give it a second thought* meaning 'do not worry about that.' *17th cent.*

> Emily Brontë *Wuthering Heights* 1847
> *The gardeners and coachman were there; but Linton was with them. They had already entered the court. Heathcliff, on second thoughts, resolved to avoid a struggle against the three underlings; he seized the poker, smashed the lock from the inner door, and made his escape as they tramped in.*

second to none
not bettered by any other; incomparable. The notion goes back to Middle English; Chaucer in *Troilus and Criseyde* (v.836) describes Troilus as 'in his tyme, in no degree secounde'. A Latin form *nulli secundus* appears later (19th cent.) in English contexts. *16th cent.*

> Shakespeare *The Comedy of Errors* v.i.7 (1594)
> [Second Merchant] *How is the man esteemed here in the city?* [Angelo] *Of very reverend reputation, sir,* | *Of credit infinite, highly beloved,* | *Second to none that lives here in the city.*

See also play second FIDDLE.

secret

in (on) the secret
one of a small number of people sharing private or confidential information: also *be let into the secret* = to be admitted to this number. *17th cent.*

section
See the GOLDEN section.

see

be seeing things
to be having hallucinations; to imagine things: often used in jocular or trivialized contexts. *Early 20th cent.*

> D Rutherford *Return Load* 1977
> *Was I seeing things or was that Sally driving your truck?*

(I'll) be seeing you
informal a formula of farewell: also in more recent use *I'll see you*, often shortened to *see you. Mid 20th cent.*

see somebody coming
informal to realize that a particular person is gullible and easily tricked or swindled: usually in forms such as *they must have seen you coming* = they tricked you with little difficulty. *Mid 20th cent.*

see something coming
informal to be all too well aware of an imminent danger or difficulty: also in extended form *see something coming a mile off. Mid 20th cent.*

seeing is believing
(proverb) one is more ready to believe something one has seen for oneself: often used as an encouragement to action rather than reliance on words and promises. *17th cent.*

> Nahum Tate *Cuckolds-Haven* 1685
> *I ask thy pardon and am sorry for thy friend with all my heart – But, Sirrah, seeing is believing, shew me your sermon-book, produce your shorthand-book, quickly I say.*

see a man about a dog

informal used as an evasive or euphemistic excuse for leaving, especially for some secret purpose that one cannot admit to. The expression came into use in the late part of the 19th cent., and became a useful standby in America during the Prohibition years of the 1920s, when there was a special reason for needing to leave suddenly: to get a drink. (Although others are not hard to imagine, seeking out a mistress, for example.) The earliest known use is in a play called *Flying Scud* written in the 1860s by the popular and prolific Irish dramatist Dion Boucicault (1820–90). The context makes the point of the phrase fairly clear in this case, i.e. the speaker wants to escape from an awkward predicament that arises unexpectedly: '[Quail] I have just heard that the bill I discounted for you bearing Lord Woodbie's name, is a forgery. I give you twelve hours to find the money, and provide for it. [Mo Davis, looking at watch] Excuse me, Mr. Quail, I can't stop; I've got to see a man about a dog. I forgot all about it till just now.' *19th cent.*

see somebody/something through

to continue to give support to a person or undertaking until it is completed. *19th cent.*

see one's way (clear) to something

to agree to perform a special favour or request. *18th cent.*

see you later (alligator)

informal a light-hearted or jocular formula of farewell: a shortening of *I'll see you later*. The rhyming addition of *alligator* is derived from a 1957 song containing the words 'See you later, alligator, | After 'while, crocodile, | Can't you see you're in my way, now, | Don't you know you cramp my style?'; hence the common response *in a while, crocodile*. *19th cent.*

Mrs Henry Wood *East Lynne* 1861
I cannot stay to hear now, William. I will see you later, madame.

Bartley Theodore Campbell *My Partner* 1879
[Major Britt] Virtue kindles strength. (Touching his heart) See you later. (Exits pompously).

Clyde Fitch *Her Own Way* 1903
See you later! I'll go and take a squint at auntie.

James Joyce *Ulysses* 1922
Tooraloo, Lenehan said, see you later. He followed M'Coy out across the tiny square of Crampton Court.

what you see is what you get

informal, originally NAmer something displayed or advertised represents exactly what is on offer: used as an assurance of straightforwardness. An advertisement in the *Washington Post* in 1955 assured its readers 'The complete G.E. kitchen is in the price of the home ... No extras – what you see is what you get!' Also shortened to *wysiwyg* (pronounced **wiz**-i-wig), used especially in computing to denote a system that can reproduce data as hard copy in the same format as it appears on the screen. *Mid 20th cent.*

Rachel Elliot *Winter Challenge* 1993
'How do you manage to contain two such totally different women inside one body?' ... She gave a careless shrug. 'What you see is what you get.' 'Oh, no.' He shook his head decisively. 'What I see is a beautiful, desirable woman. What I get – is a cold, unwelcoming ice-maiden.'

when you've seen one, you've seen them all

informal used to refer to the sameness or predictability of certain people or things. *19th cent.*

See also have seen better days *at* DAY; see — (all) RIGHT; see the BACK of; see EYE to eye; see REASON; you ain't seen NOTHING yet.

---

seed

go/run to seed

to deteriorate, especially to become unattractive by being shabby or careless about one's appearance: literally (said of a vegetable plant), to develop seed after flowering and therefore be unfit for eating. *17th cent.*

John Dunton *A Voyage Round the World* 1691
Let Bow-steeple, and Salisbury steeple, and Grantham steeple run to seed as far as they will, and give the very clouds a glyster, or rather suppositor, – I say Graffham steeple is Graffham steeple still – and there's an end on't.

See also sow the seed(s) of something *at* SOW².

seize

seize the day

to make the most of one's present opportunities; to live for the moment. The phrase translates Latin *carpe diem* from Horace, *Odes* I.xi.7: *Dum loquimur, fugerit invida | Aetas: carpe diem, quam minimum credula postero* ('While we are talking, envious time is fleeing: seize the day, trust not in the future'). The English phrase was used as the title of a novel on humanist themes by Saul Bellow (1956). *19th cent.*

> Browning *Rabbi Ben Ezra* 1864
> *Thou, to whom fools propound, | When the wine make its round, | 'Since life fleets, all is change; the Past gone, seize to-day!'*

> G W H Griffin *Shylock* 1874
> *Oh, bosh! don't bandy words, because | My father's out, let's seize the day, and go!*

sell

sell somebody/something short

to undervalue or underestimate a person or thing. *Sell short* in financial markets means 'to sell stocks one does not own, in the hope of buying them more cheaply before the expected time of sale.' *19th cent.*

> Mark Twain *The Innocents Abroad* 1869
> *Taking advantage of the inflated market, many of our shrewdest operators are selling short.*

> Henry Pluckrose *What is Happening in our Primary Schools* 1987
> *They contained articles by a variety of writers (including politicians, and teachers) each of whom had one common aim and purpose – to show that progressive methods in both primary and secondary schools were 'selling children short'.*

sell one's soul / oneself (to the devil)

to take any steps, even when wrong or sinful, to achieve one's purpose: with allusion to the story of Faust, who made a contract with the devil (in the form of Mephistopheles) by which Faust was granted his desires in this life at the expense of the damnation of his soul for eternity after death. The story forms the basis of plays by Marlowe and Goethe. *16th cent.*

See also buy / sell somebody a pup; sell somebody a bill of goods *at* BILL[1]; sell somebody down the

river; sell somebody a/the DUMMY; sell like hot cakes *at* CAKE; sell the PASS.

send

See send somebody packing *at* PACK; send somebody to COVENTRY.

sense

bring somebody to their senses

to make somebody realize that they have been thinking or behaving foolishly. *18th cent.*

> John Gay *The Beggar's Opera* 1765
> [Lockit] *And so, after all this mischief, I must stay here to be entertain'd with your catterwauling, Mistress Puss! – Out of my sight, wanton strumpet! you shall fast and mortify yourself into reason, with now and then a little handsome discipline to bring you to your senses.*

come to one's senses

1 to recover consciousness. *17th cent.*

> Peter Anthony Motteux *The Novelty* 1697
> [Cynthio] *So it may – But what have you done with my Spaniard?* [Mezzetin] *Sir, he's come to his Senses: The Dose which I pour'd into his Glass never works above a quarter of an Hour.*

> Washington Irving *Legends of the Alhambra* 1832
> *Tio Nicolo did not come to his senses until long after sunrise, when he found himself at the bottom of a deep ravine, his mule grazing beside him, and his panniers of snow completely melted.*

2 to realize that one has been foolish and must think or behave more sensibly. Also *see sense. 19th cent.*

> Alice Cary *The Bishop's Son* 1867
> *'Bless my heart, I hope you are not going crazy too!' says Mrs. Fairfax. 'On the contrary, I think I am just coming to my senses,' says Mrs. Whiteflock. 'And as regards Samuel, I never saw a nicer man about a house in my life, and I've lived with a good many.'*

make sense

to be logically valid; to contain valid meaning: originally with reference to words and utterances, and later in extended use of people and their opinions or actions with the meaning 'to be reasonable or understandable.' *17th cent.*

Head & Kirkman *The English Rogue Described* 1674
They spake Latine, and then Spanish, of all which he understood not so much as to make sense, and therefore answered them in French which none of them understood.

George Campbell *The Philosophy of Rhetoric* 1776
Wherefore then, it may be asked, is this denominated one sentence, and not several? For this reason, that though the preceding words, when you have reached any of the stops above mentioned, will make sense, and may be construed separately, the same cannot be said of the words which follow.

G B Shaw *Back to Methuselah* 1921
She spoke to me without any introduction, like any improper female ... Improper female doesn't make sense.

make sense of something/somebody
to find a meaning in words, actions, or phenomena; to be able to explain them. In early use with *on* instead of *of*. *17th cent.*

Jeremy Collier *A Defence of the Short View* 1699
But this expression I shall leave with the reader, and give him some time to make sense on't.

Maria Edgeworth *Belinda* 1801
These were my lady's own words – I shall never forget them – They struck and astonished me, ma'am, so much, I stood like one stupified, and then left the room to think them over again by myself, and make sense of them if I could.

Stephen Hawking *Black Holes and Baby Universes* 1993
I have used examples from relativity and quantum mechanics to show the problems one faces when one tries to make sense of the universe.

See also take LEAVE of one's senses.

---

separate

go (one's) separate ways
to part; to leave by different routes; in extended use, to end a friendship or a business or romantic association. *18th cent.*

Gabriel Odingsells *The Bath Unmask'd* 1725
Don't you loiter here any longer then. It wou'd not be amiss, for you to go separate ways to cut off Observation.

Scott *Rob Roy* 1817
'Good night, ma'am, and remember the law is not to be trifled with.' And we rode on our separate ways.

John Esten Cooke *Henry St John* 1859
'I am glad to reciprocate your Excellency's desire, that in future we go separate ways,' he said with courtly calmness; 'I did not seek your Excellency formerly, you sought me; and now I depart, careless of your Excellency's hatred or regard.'

John Bedford *The Titron Madness* 1984
She had grown up in a cold, almost emotionally empty vacuum. If only they had fought, screamed at one another, gone their separate ways, even had lovers.

See also separate the MEN from the boys; separate the SHEEP from the goats; separate the wheat from the CHAFF.

---

serve

serve somebody right
to be the fate or punishment that somebody deserves: often in the form *it serves you* (or *him, her,* etc) *right*, as an expression of satisfaction at a well-deserved come-uppance. In early use the phrase commonly appears in the passive form *be rightly served*, in the sense 'to have had one's just deserts'. These idiomatic uses are based on the more general meaning, 'to treat somebody fairly or appropriately.' *16th cent.*

Bunyan *The Life and Death of Mr Badman* 1680
Truly I think that his Master served him right; for in doing as he did, he shewed him plainly, as he said, that he had not so much government of himself as his horse had of himself.

Congreve *The Old Batchelour* 1693
Hang me, if I pity you; you are right enough serv'd.

serve one's time
1 to complete the normal period of service in an official position, apprenticeship, etc. *16th cent.*
2 (also *serve time*) to serve a prison sentence. *19th cent.*

serve two masters
to obey two superiors whose principles or requirements conflict with one another: with allusion to Christ's warning in the Sermon on the Mount against serving two masters, God and Mammon, as told in Matthew 6:24 'No man can serve two masters: for either he will hate the one, and love the other; or else he will hold to the one, and despise the other. Ye cannot serve God and mammon.' *17th cent.*

Hobbes *Leviathan* 1651
If the Apostle had meant we should be subject both to our own princes and also to the Pope, he had taught us a doctrine which Christ himself hath told us is impossible, namely, to serve two masters.

See also if MEMORY serves (me) (right); serve the/somebody's TURN.

service

be at —'s service
to be available to a particular person when required. At your service is used as a polite response when called on, as it is by Malvolio in reply to Olivia in Shakespeare's *Twelfth Night* (see below). *17th cent.*

Shakespeare *Twelfth Night* I.v.289 (1602)
[Olivia] *What ho, Malvolio.* [Malvolio] *Here, madam, at your service.*

be of service to somebody
to help or be of use to somebody. *18th cent.*

sesame

See OPEN sesame.

set

all set (on something / to do something)
fully prepared for an activity. The expression refers to athletes at the start of a track event, at which the starter gives the instruction *Get set!* At this point the athletes raise their bodies and put the weight on their hands and front foot; the muscles are 'set' when they are tensed and rigid. However, the phrase is much older than this in wider applications, in which *set* means 'prepared, in place' more generally. To be *all set on* a purpose is to be determined about it. *17th cent.*

John Reynolds *The Triumphs of Gods Revenge* 1622
She cannot erect her eyes to heaven, she is all set on revenge.

Anon *The Dutch Rogue* 1683
When they were all set, they began to dance and make a great noise, which at length, though hardly, awakened Ambrose.

Mrs Gaskell *Mary Barton* 1849
After breakfast, we were all set to walk in procession, and a time it took to put us in order, two and

two, and the petition, as was yards long, carried by th' foremost pairs.

make a dead set at somebody
to try hard to win the attention or affections of somebody. In criminal slang a *dead set* was a determined scheme to rob or defraud, and the phrase took on a more general meaning of a concerted assault, physical or verbal. The term was later used of a hunting dog standing still with its muzzle pointing towards the prey. *19th cent.*

Byron *Don Juan* 1823
I'd rather not say what might be related | Of her exploits, for this were ticklish ground; | Besides there might be falsehood in what's stated: | Her late performance had been a dead set | At Lord Augustus Fitz-Plantagenet.

set in one's ways
reluctant to change one's opinions or habits. The use of *set* in the meaning 'fixed or settled' in relation to feelings and attitudes dates from the 17th cent., and the phrase is found from the 19th cent.

Harriet Beecher Stowe *Dred* 1856
Well, Nina, to tell you the truth, sister Anne is a little bit conventional – a little set in her ways; but, after all, a large-hearted, warm-hearted woman. You would like each other, I know.

John Steinbeck *The Grapes of Wrath* 1939
'Didn' John never have no fambly?' 'Well, yes, he did, an' that'll show you the kind a fella he is – set in his ways. Pa tells about it. Uncle John, he had a young wife. Married four months.'

set little / much / a great deal by something
to consider something to be of little (or great) value or worth. *17th cent.*

set one's teeth
to be determined or resolute: from the action of clenching one's teeth as a gesture of resolution. The quotation below is from King Harry's speech 'Once more unto the breach …' before the siege of Harfleur. *16th cent.*

Shakespeare *Henry V* III.i.15 (1599)
Now set the teeth and stretch the nostril wide, | Hold hard the breath, and bend up every spirit | To his full height.

set to work

to start in earnest on a task or enterprise. Also in the transitive form *set somebody to work*, in the sense 'to give somebody work to do.' *17th cent.*

Milton *Comus* 1637
Wherefore did Nature powre her bounties forth | ...
| And set to work millions of spinning worms, |
That in their green shops weave the smooth-hair'd
silk | To deck her Sons.

set the world alight / on fire / British set the Thames on fire

to cause great excitement or interest. The phrase is typically used in negative contexts about dependable-but-dull people who will 'never set the world (or Thames) on fire'. This colourful image calls to mind the Greek legend of Phaethon – although it is probably not a conscious source of the modern phrase. Phaethon, son of the sun god Helios, was granted the favour of driving his father's fire-chariot for a day. Alas Phaethon was unable to keep the horses under control and they bolted, threatening to set the world on fire; only Zeus's intervention with a timely thunderbolt saved the day. The myth of Phaethon was the subject of an opera by the French baroque composer Lully (*Phaëton*, 1683), and (allusively) of a novel by Angus Wilson entitled *Setting the World on Fire* (1980).

During the 19th cent., amateur etymologists repeated a belief that the origin of the *Thames* version lay not in the natural explanation but in the term *temse*, a sift used in brewing: a lazy worker, it is said, would never 'set the temse on fire' (see e.g. *Notes & Queries* March 1865, p.239). This is about as far-fetched as one can get, but the conviction with which this account was rediscovered and put forward – again and again – is remarkable. An early (18th cent.) use extends the phrase with the addition 'though he lives near the Bridge', significantly reinforcing the physical image of the river at an early stage in the history of the expression, which is also recorded in this form in the third edition (1796) of Grose's *Dictionary of the Vulgar Tongue*. A corresponding reference to the Rhine in place of the Thames is recorded from the 17th cent. The expression was a favourite of Anthony Trollope, who used it several times in *The Three Clerks* (1857), *Framley Parsonage* (1861), *The Small House at Allington* (1864), and *The Eustace Diamonds* (1872). *18th cent.*

Frederick Reynolds *Fortune's Fool* 1796
She sent Ap-Hazard a love-letter – he shew'd it me;
and may I never set the Thames on fire, if I don't
think she is now in his cabin.

Jane Austen *Persuasion* 1818
The baronet will never set the Thames on fire, but
there seems no harm in him.

See also be carved/set/written in STONE; clap/lay/set eyes on *at* EYE; put/set PEN to paper; set one's FACE (against something); set one's HAND to (the plough); set one's HEART on something; set out one's STALL; set the PACE; set the SCENE; set the STAGE for something; set STORE by; set somebody's teeth on EDGE; set the wheels in motion *at* WHEEL.

---

settle

See settle accounts with somebody *at* ACCOUNT; settle a SCORE; settle somebody's HASH.

---

seven

See in seventh HEAVEN; seven-league boots *at* BOOT[1].

---

shade

put somebody/something in the shade

(said of a person, achievement, etc) to be so remarkable or significant as to cause another to look less significant or interesting. The image of *shade*, or absence of light, as a metaphor for obscurity goes back to the 17th cent. *19th cent.*

Ralph Waldo Emerson *Essays* 1841
Ordinarily every body in society reminds us of
somewhat else or of some other person. Character,
reality, reminds you of nothing else. It takes place of
the whole creation. The man must be so much that
he must make all circumstances indifferent – put all
means into the shade. This all great men are and do.

shades of —

used to draw attention to a person or thing that a particular circumstance reminds one of: *shade* here is used in its meaning 'ghost' or 'dead spirit.' *19th cent.*

Charles Lamb *Essays and Sketches* 1822
*Let that domicile for groundling rogues and base
earth-kissing varlets envy thy preferment, not seldom fated to be the wanton baiting-house, the
temporary retreat, of poet and of patriot. Shades of
Bastwick and of Prynne hover over thee. Defoe is
there, and more greatly daring Shebbeare. From
their (little more elevated) stations they look down
with recognitions.*

shadow

afraid/scared/frightened of one's own shadow
extremely nervous or timorous. *16th cent.*

Aphra Behn *The Lucky Mistake* 1689
*At other times Vernole was the most tame and
passive Man in the World, and one who was afraid
of his own shadow in the Night.*

be a shadow of one's former self
to be greatly diminished in size or strength, especially from age, illness, exhaustion, etc. *Shadow*
has been used as a metaphor for enfeeblement or
emaciation from the 16th cent. *18th cent.*

Eliza Fenwick *Secresy* 1795
*Sir Thomas Barlowe loved this young man as a son;
and, to receive him scarcely a shadow of his former
self, will create distressing emotions.*

wear oneself / be worn to a shadow
to become exhausted from overwork. *18th cent.*

Smollett *The Adventures of Ferdinand Count Fathom*
1753
*The poor afflicted orphan, worn to a shadow with
self-consuming anguish, eager to find some lowly
retreat, where she could breathe out her soul in
peace, and terrified at the frantic behaviour of
Renaldo, communicated to Fathom her desire of
removing.*

shaft

get / give somebody the shaft
NAmer, informal to be treated (or to treat somebody) unfairly or slightingly: probably based on
the use of *shaft* meaning 'the human leg', the
image being of kicking a rejected person away.
Mid 20th cent.

shaggy

a shaggy-dog story
a protracted joke or story dependent for its
humorous effect on the pointlessness or irrele-
vance of the conclusion. The expression probably
arose from the fact that a shaggy dog was a
common subject for stories of this kind. Apocryphal but entertaining anecdotes have been
put forward to explain the origin more precisely
and more colourfully. These mostly centre on lost
dogs whose owners advertise for their recovery
in the newspapers. Various responses follow: all
dogs of the area that fit the description are
rounded up and the shaggiest is chosen, a reader
takes pity on the owner and proceeds to replace
the dog with one that is even shaggier, and so on.
Shaggy-dog stories indeed. A collection of
shaggy-dog stories was published in 1946
under that title, one of the first uses in print.
Mid 20th cent.

shake

get / give somebody a fair shake
informal, chiefly NAmer to treat somebody fairly or
justly. *Shake* here refers to a throw of the dice, and
the image is symbolic of the chance of luck and
fate. *19th cent.*

in two shakes (of a lamb's tail)
informal very shortly or quickly: also *in a couple of
shakes, in three shakes,* and other variants. *19th cent.*

R L Stevenson *Treasure Island* 1883
*We held a council in the cabin. 'Sir,' said the cap-
tain, 'if I risk another order, the whole ship'll come
about our ears by the run. You see, sir, here it is. I
get a rough answer, do I not? Well, if I speak back,
pikes will be going in two shakes; if I don't Silver
will see there's something under that, and the
game's up. Now, we've only one man to rely on.'*

more than one can shake a stick at
informal a considerable number. The expression
was first used in America in the early part of the
19th cent., but the choice of words is not readily
explained. It probably doesn't need to be: *shaking
a stick* simply means pointing a stick, and that is
what anybody might do in counting. There is no
need to look further. The first known use in print
is from the *Lancaster Journal* in Pennsylvania in
1818: 'We have in Lancaster as many Taverns as

you can shake a stick at.' Taverns – or any large buildings – are things we might well want to point physically at, and so are moving things such as vehicles and animals (which have also been mentioned in this context). In current use the expression is invariably couched in the form *more — than you can shake a stick at. 19th cent.*

no great shakes

informal of little importance or consequence: perhaps with allusion to the shaking of dice in games. *19th cent.*

> Mrs Gaskell *Ruth* 1853
> *Ay, I remember; and I remember a bit more than you want me to remember, I reckon. It were King Solomon as spoke them words, and it were King Solomon's son that were King Rehoboam, and no great shakes either. I can remember what is said on him.*

shake one's head

to move one's head from side to side to indicate disagreement or refusal. *Middle English*

shake in one's shoes/boots

informal to tremble with fear or apprehension: an extension of the use of *shake* in the context of emotion, which dates from Middle English. *19th cent.*

> Charles Kingsley *Westward Ho!* 1855
> *In spite of all your swearing and bullying, you know you are now shaking in your shoes for fear. So you had much better hold your tongue, give me a drink of cider, and leave ill alone, lest you make it worse.*

See also shake the DUST off one's feet; shake a LEG.

shanks

on shanks's mare/pony

walking, on foot. *Shank* originally denoted the tibia in the leg, and later the leg itself. In Scottish use it is also a verb: to *shank it* is to go by foot and to *shank somebody* is to march them off (often to somewhere unpleasant). In Scott's novel *The Antiquary* (1816) a character declares 'some say ye should baith be shankit aff till Edinburgh Castle', although here the prospect is more attractive. In early uses *mare* and *nag* are used instead of *pony*, which first appears in this context in the 19th cent. *Shank* is sometimes spelt with a capital initial, regarding the word as a

name, a personification of the owner of the pony who provides it when none other is available. *18th cent.*

> Samuel Bishop *The Horseman* 1796
> *No – trust me – no! I'd rather, soft and fair, | Kick up a Ten-toe Trot; and ride on Shanks's Mare.*

shape

get/lick/knock something/somebody into shape

to get a thing or person into the right condition forcefully or with determination. The notion of licking (originally people, later things and situations) into shape seems to be derived from an old belief that bear cubs are born as shapeless lumps and need to be licked into their proper shape by their mothers. This notion was known to the Arab philosopher and physician Avicenna (980–1037), and there are references to it in Middle English sources. Later, George Chapman's comedy *The Widow's Tears* (1612) alludes to it in the line 'He has not licked his whelp into full shape yet'. To *get oneself into shape*, or *get into shape*, is to take exercise to improve one's fitness. *17th cent.*

> John Fletcher *The Mad Lover* a1625
> *Nor wrote you so, that one's part was to lick | The other into shape, nor did one stick | The others cold inventions with such wit, | As served like spice, to make them quick and fit.*

> George Eliot *Felix Holt* 1866
> *The Rector was quite satisfied. He had talked himself into thinking that he should like to give Sherlock a few useful hints, look up his own earlier sermons, and benefit the Curate by his criticism, when the argument had been got into shape.*

in / out of shape

in good (or poor) physical condition. In early use, the reference was rather to a person's moral or psychological state. The image is of a physical object twisted out of its proper form. *17th cent.*

> Henry More *Philosophical Poems* 1647
> *Nor stopt he here, but told me all her guise | How law-lesse quite and out of shape she's grown | Affecting still wilde contrarieties, | Averse from what for good all others own.*

the shape of things to come

the likely course of events in the future: with allusion to the title of a novel by H G Wells (1933). *Mid 20th cent.*

take shape

(said of an idea or plan) to develop a definite or distinctive form: originally with physical reference to things being gradually perceived by the eye. *18th cent.*

> Matthew Green *The Spleen* 1737
> *Virtue, in charming dress array'd, | Calling the passions to her aid, | When moral scenes just action join, | Takes shape, and shews her face divine.*

> Mark Twain *The Adventures of Tom Sawyer* 1876
> *A sort of undefined longing crept upon them. This took dim shape, presently – it was budding homesickness.*

---

share

share and share alike

to share things equally or fairly: in early use in the form *share and share like*. *16th cent.*

> Richard Edwards *Damon and Pithias* 1571
> *Farewell cocke, before the Colier againe doo us seeke, | Let us into the Courte to parte the spoyle, share and share like.*

> Defoe *The Life ... of the Famous Captain Singleton* 1720
> *When we had brought all our purchase together, we had in the whole three pound and a half of gold to a man, share and share alike, according to such a weight and scale as our ingenious Cutler made for us to weigh it by.*

---

sharp

(as) sharp as a needle

extremely astute or clever. *17th cent.*

> Thomas Middleton *The Famelie of Love* 1608
> *Then sir she has a certaine thing called tunge, ten times more sharp then a needle, and that at the least displeasure, a man must have shotte quite through him.*

> Shakespeare *Cymbeline* I.iii.19 (1610)
> [Innogen] *I would have broke mine eye-strings, cracked them, but | To look upon him till the diminution | Of space had pointed him sharp as my needle.*

at the sharp end

informal involved in the most active, difficult, or dangerous aspects of a situation or undertaking. There is more than one image at work here: the humorous use of *sharp end* for the bow of a ship (originally in services' slang of the 1940s) is also recorded in the form *at the sharp end* to mean 'well forward, to the front'. The phrase is also surely influenced by the notion of the 'sharp' working end of a tool or instrument. *Late 20th cent.*

have a sharp tongue

to tend to speak in a caustic or bad-tempered manner. *17th cent.*

> Margaret Cavendish *Matrimonial Trouble* 1662
> *You have a sharp tongue when spight moves it; but let me hear no more of these words, but do as I command you.*

See also LOOK sharp.

---

she

who's she – the cat's mother?

used as a rebuke, especially to a child, who refers to another person with the personal pronoun *she* instead of more politely by her name: also in variant forms. The idea behind the phrase appears in the 1890s, but the phrase in its current form is from the second decade of the 20th cent. It is a typical example of a spontaneous creation that defies any attempt to explain its origins. *Early 20th cent.*

---

shed

See throw/cast/shed light on *at* LIGHT[2].

---

sheep

cast/throw/make sheep's eyes at somebody

to cast wistful or longing amorous glances at somebody: presumably from the soulful look that can be discerned in a sheep's eyes. *16th cent.*

> Sir Philip Sidney *The Countesse of Pembrokes Arcadia* a1586
> *Mopsa throwing a great number of sheeps eyes vpon me.*

> John Phillips *Maronides* 1672
> *Cast your sheep's eyes on yonder lad | In coat of yellow flannel clad, | Mounted upon a Hobby horse.*

Smollett *The Expedition of Roderick Random* 1748
There was a young lady in the room – a fine buxom
wench, i' faith! and she threw so many sheep's eyes
at a certain person, whom I shall not name, that my
heart went knock, knock, knock, like a fulling mill.

count sheep

to count sheep jumping over a fence in one's
imagination, as a way of helping oneself to fall
asleep. The notion is attested in other forms from
the 1850s. *Early 20th cent.*

separate the sheep from the goats

to identify and distinguish between the superior
and inferior members of a group. The phrase
alludes to the description of the Last Judgement
in Matthew 25:32 'And before him shall be
gathered all nations: and he shall separate them
one from another, as a shepherd divideth his
sheep from the goats. And he shall set the
sheep on his right hand, but the goats on the
left.' *17th cent.*

Locke *An Essay Concerning Human Understanding*
1690
We in vain pretend to range things into sorts, and
dispose them into certain classes under names, by
their real essences, that are so far from our discovery
or comprehension. A blind man may as soon sort
things by their colours, and he that has lost his smell
as well distinguish a lily and a rose by their odours,
as by those internal constitutions which he knows
not. He that thinks he can distinguish sheep and
goats by their real essences, that are unknown to
him.

See also a/the BLACK sheep (of the family).

sheet

between the sheets

used in allusion to illicit or clandestine sexual
activity. *17th cent.*

Shakespeare *Othello* II.i.379 (1604)
[Iago] *I hate the Moor,* | *And it is thought abroad*
that 'twixt my sheets | *He has done my office.*

Alexander Radcliffe *Ovid Travestie* 1696
Dream of you as soon as I'm in Bed; | *You tickle*
me, and cry, Do'st like it Saff [= Sappho]? | *Oh*
wonderous well! and then methinks I laugh. |
Sometimes we mingle Legs, and Arms, and Thighs;
| *Sometimes between the sheets, methinks does rise.*

come down in sheets

informal to rain heavily. *18th cent.*

Henry Baker *Medulla Poetarum Romanorum* 1737
Mean time the sky descends in sheets of rain: |
You'd think all Heav'n were pouring on the Main.

three sheets in the wind

informal very drunk. In nautical language in the
days of sailing ships, if the *sheets* (ropes holding
the sails in position) were allowed to hang freely,
the ship would wander off course and career in
all directions. The image was originally of a
drunken sailor staggering about after heavy
drinking during a spell of shore leave. *19th cent.*

R H Dana *Two Years Before the Mast* 1840
He talked a great deal about propriety and steadi-
ness, and gave good advice to the youngsters and
Kanakas, but seldom went up to the town, without
coming down 'three sheets in the wind'.

shelf

off the shelf

available immediately from existing stock, without needing a special order. *Mid 20th cent.*

on the shelf

1 *informal* in a state of inactivity or disuse. The
image is of a book or other useful object remaining on a shelf unused. There is a stray citation
from the 16th cent. (not quite in the current form
or sense) in the *OED*, but otherwise usage dates
predominantly from the 18th cent.

Sarah Fielding *The History of the Countess of Dellwyn*
1759
Now Plato and Aristotle might moulder on the
shelf, all their precepts forgotten.

2 *informal* (said of a woman) unmarried and now
too old for marriage. *19th cent.*

shell

come out of one's shell

to become less shy or reserved: also, in opposite
meaning, *retreat into one's shell*. The image is of a
snail or tortoise, which withdraws its head into
its shell when threatened. *19th cent.*

Hardy *A Pair of Blue Eyes* 1873
How she must have laughed at him inwardly! He
absolutely writhed as he thought of the confession
she had wrung from him on the boat in the darkness

of night. The one conception which had sustained his dignity when drawn out of his shell on that occasion – that of her charming ignorance of all such matters – how absurd it was!

(a word) in your shell-like ear

a quiet word or whisper in private. The image of the ear as a shell goes back to Keats, who wrote in an ode of 1817: 'Had I a man's fair form, then might my sighs I Be echoed swiftly through that ivory shell, I Thine ear and find thy gentle heart; so well I Would passion arm me for the enterprise.' It was a common image of 19th cent. romantic literature: 'her white shell-like ears' (George Eliot, *Adam Bede*, 1859); 'her ears tiny and shell-like (Charles Reade, *Hard Cash*, 1863); 'the white shell-like sinuosities of her little ear' (Hardy, *Far from the Madding Crowd*, 1874); and Rider Haggard's 'She' describes herself in this way: 'Tell me, am I not beautiful? ... Take me feature by feature, forgetting not my form, and my hands and feet, and my hair, and the whiteness of my skin, and then tell me truly hast thou ever known a woman who in aught, ay, in one little portion of her beauty, in the curve of an eyelash even, or the modelling of a shell-like ear, is justified to hold a light before my loveliness?' (*She*, 1887). Such an image is inevitably vulnerable to humorous treatment, as in P G Wodehouse's 'Gourmet's Love Song' (in *Punch* 1902): 'So, Effie, turn that shell-like ear, I Nor to my sighing close it.' *Shell-like ear* is reduced to *shell-like*, and the phrase occurred in this form in the 1960s radio comedy series *Round the Horne*. See also have a WORD in somebody's ear. *19th cent.*

Thomas Hood *Bianca's Dream* 1827
This, with more tender logic of the kind, I He pour'd into her small and shell-like ear, I That timidly against his lips inclined.

W S Gilbert *To Phoebe* from *The Bab Ballads* 1898
Sentences so fiercely flaming I In your tiny shell-like ear, I I should always be exclaiming I If I loved you, Phoebe, dear.

shift

make shift

to get by with limited means or resources. *Shift* is used here as a noun in its meaning 'a measure or expedient forced by circumstances', which is

reflected also in the adjective *makeshift* meaning 'crudely improvised.' *16th cent.*

shift for oneself

to manage by oneself or without help, especially in less than ideal circumstances; to rely on one's own efforts. The verb *shift* here means 'to manage or cope', which dates from Middle English and chiefly survives in this phrase. *16th cent.*

shift one's ground

to change one's position or standpoint in an argument or discussion: literally, to move from the position at which one is standing (the predominant meaning before the 19th cent.). In Shakespeare's *Hamlet* (1601), there is a play on the literal and figurative meanings of the phrase when Hamlet and his comrades swear an oath to secrecy after the appearance of the ghost of Hamlet's father (I.v.158): '[Horatio] Swear the oath, my lord. [Ghost (under the stage)] Swear. (They swear.) [Hamlet] Hic et ubique? Then we'll shift our ground. – Come hither, gentlemen, and lay your hands again upon my sword. Never to speak of this that you have heard, Swear by my sword.' *17th cent.*

Edward Ravenscroft *King Edgar and Alfreda* 1677
Quickly let's shift our ground, I Or rather quit me here, that we may not I Be surpriz'd together.

Mary Brunton *Self-Control* 1811
By the use of ambiguous terms, by ingenious sophistry, by dexterously shifting from the ground of controversy, she could baffle, and perplex, and confound her opponents.

shift oneself

British, informal to take action; to hurry up: often used in the imperative. *17th cent.*

Thomas D'Urfey *Trick for Trick* 1678
Sirrah, no more of your French shruggs, I advise you. I If you are Lowsie, shift your self.

shilling

take the (King's/Queen's) shilling

to enlist in the army: from the former practice of giving new recruits a shilling on signing up. *18th cent.*

Ouida *Under Two Flags* 1867
He ... finally, working his passage home again, took the Queen's shilling in Dublin, and was drafted into a light cavalry regiment.

shine

take the shine off something/somebody

to spoil the allure or excitement of something or somebody, especially by surpassing them. The image is of the shine fading on a pair of shoes or a piece of furniture. *19th cent.*

Charles Augustus Davis *Letters of J Downing* 1834
I got a letter from Zekel Bigelow t'other day, who I see is pretty busy now in Wall-street, and will soon take the shine off the most of the Brokers there.

take a shine to somebody/something

to develop an immediate liking for somebody or something. The phrase is based on a group of meanings of *shine* to do with conviviality and commotion, which are sometimes related to *shindy* and regarded apart from the main meanings of the word. *19th cent.*

John William De Forest *Kate Beaumont* 1872
He met up with her last sale-day, an' took an awful shine to her. Talks like he was goin' to marry her. Mebbe he will.

shingle

hang out one's shingle

NAmer to start practising one's profession. A *shingle* was a square piece of wood, originally a roof tile and later a board; here, it is a sign or notice board. *19th cent.*

Frederick W Thomas *Clinton Bradshaw* 1835
Be admitted to the practice of the law, when the court sits, and let us open shop together – hang out our shingle on the outer wall. You and I, Kentuck, against the field.

ship

ships that pass in the night

people who meet once by chance and hardly notice each other: with reference to lines in Longfellow's *Tales of a Wayside Inn* (Part 3, 1874) 'Ships that pass in the night, and speak each other in passing; | Only a signal shown and a distant voice in the darkness; | So on the ocean of life we pass and speak one another, | Only a look and a voice; then darkness again and a silence.' Oscar Wilde's lines about an encounter in the *Ballad of Reading Gaol* (1898) are reminiscent: 'Like two doomed ships that pass in storm | We had

crossed each other's way: | But we made no sign, we said no word, | We had no word to say.' *19th cent.*

spoil the ship for a ha'porth of tar

to ruin something for want of a little more effort or expense: originally as a proverb *do not spoil the ship for a ha'porth of tar*. *Ship* has come about as a dialect pronunciation of *sheep*, the original point of the proverb. Tar was used to protect injured or sore skin of sheep from flies, and hence a lack of tar caused suffering or death. Early uses of the proverb have *hog* as well as *sheep* and *lose* instead of *spoil*, and it is entered in this form in John Ray's *Collection of English Proverbs* (1670): 'Ne'er lose a hog for a half-penny-worth of tarre.' In modern use the phrase is often reinterpreted as referring to the use of tar to make a ship watertight. *17th cent.*

when one's ship comes in / comes home

when one makes one's fortune: with allusion to merchant ships returning to their home port laden with valuable cargo. Another version of the phrase is *when one's boat comes in*, which is no doubt influenced by the refrain to a northern dandling song *The Little Fishy* (which exists in various regional forms): 'Dance to your daddy, | My little babby, | Dance to your daddy, my little lamb; | You shall have a fishy | In a little dishy, | You shall have a fishy when the boat comes in.' *19th cent.*

Alice Cary *The Bishop's Son* 1867
Sam, do you know any good fellow that would spade my garden for me some leisure morning? If you do, see that he does it, will you? and when my ship comes in, he shall be remembered!

See also rats deserting a sinking ship *at* RAT; run a TIGHT ship.

shipshape

shipshape and Bristol fashion

tidy and in good order: with reference to Bristol in the west of England, a major port in the days of the British Empire and renowned for its efficient organization. *19th cent.*

Scott *Chronicles of the Canongate* 1828
When we set out on the jolly voyage of life, what a brave fleet there is around us, as stretching our fresh canvass to the breeze, all 'shipshape and Bristol

fashion', *pennons flying, music playing, cheering each other as we pass.*

shirt

bet/put one's shirt on something
informal to bet all the money one has on something. *19th cent.*

keep one's shirt on
informal, originally NAmer to remain calm and not lose one's temper: typically used in the imperative. *See also* get SHIRTY. *19th cent.*

Augustus Thomas *Arizona* 1899
Well, keep your shirt on, Tony. Ain't anybody kickin'.

Frank Dumont *The Cuban Spy* 1915
[Phelim] *But you might be a cruiser, a blockade runner, or a sort of a pirate.* [Valdez] *Sir! I will not brook an insult.* [Phelim] *Keep your shirt on! I said you looked it. If the cap fits you you can wear it.*

lose one's shirt
informal to lose all one has, especially by gambling. *Mid 20th cent.*

the shirt off one's back
informal somebody's last remaining possessions, used especially in negative and implied contexts, e.g. *to give* (or *take*) *the shirt off one's back.* The notion goes back to Middle English and is found in Chaucer (*The Wife of Bath's Tale*, line 1186): 'Whoso that halt hym payd of [= is satisfied with] his poverte, | I holde hym riche, al [= even if] hadde he nat a sherte.' The phrase in its current form dates from the 17th cent.

Laurence Sterne *Tristram Shandy* 1761
I would give the shirt off my back to be burnt into tinder, were it only to satisfy one feverish enquirer, how many sparks at one good stroke, a good flint and steel could strike into the tail of it.

shirtsleeves

in one's shirtsleeves
wearing a shirt without a jacket over it. *18th cent.*

Kate Chopin *No-Account Creole* 1894
'Excuse me one minute,' Pierre added, remembering that he was in his shirtsleeves and rising to reach for his coat, which hung upon a peg near by.

shirty

get shirty
informal to be bad-tempered or irritable. The connection with shirts may seem obscure, but it is related to other phrases of the same kind: *get somebody's shirt out*, meaning 'to make them lose their temper' and the more familiar *keep one's shirt on* (*see* SHIRT), meaning 'to remain calm'. The underlying notion is presumably of taking off one's shirt in readiness for a fight. *19th cent.*

H V Esmond *Billy's Little Love Affair* 1903
You always were a jolly good sort and all that, don't get shirty when Jack's wire startled me into thinking you were dead.

shit

be in the shit
coarse slang to be in serious trouble or difficulty. *Mid 20th cent.*

be scared/bored shitless
coarse slang to be completely terrified or thoroughly bored. *Mid 20th cent.*

Lawrence Durrell *Spirit of Place* 1936
Yes this war is worrying. Of course we're scared shitless because if there's any place Benito wants more than Ethiopia it's Corfu. He smashed up the town with bombs in 1925, and had to be chased out by the British.

be shitting bricks
coarse slang to be in a state of great anxiety or alarm: *see also* shit oneself *below. Mid 20th cent.*

have shit for brains
coarse slang to be stupid or foolish. *Shit-for-brains* is a term of general abuse. *Mid 20th cent.*

Independent 1992
Another letter reads: 'Hey, shit-for-brains, you are such a loser ... there is no room on this planet for flaming liberal faggots like you.'

not give/care a shit
coarse slang not to care at all: a stronger form of *not give/care a damn* (see DAMN). *Early 20th cent.*

James Joyce *Ulysses* 1922
He's a whitearsed bugger. I don't give a shit for him.

not know shit from Shinola
coarse slang to be completely innocent or unaware: from Shinola, the trade name of an American brand of boot polish. *Mid 20th cent.*

> Independent 1992
> *Every first-time movie-maker I meet doesn't know shit from Shinola – you're all constipated. I'm here to get you off the pot and running.*

shit oneself
coarse slang to be overcome by fear: literally to be so terrified that one loses control of one's bowels. *See also* be shitting bricks *above. Mid 20th cent.*

when the shit hits the fan
coarse slang when the serious problems begin, or when a disaster or misfortune becomes generally known. A graphic if somewhat repulsive image of a rapidly rotating fan scattering excrement thrown at it. *Mid 20th cent.*

> The Times 1988
> *There was a shocked silence. Finally one of them said: 'But surely you no longer represent him?' Lantz no longer did; but to them it was unthinkable that an agent would suggest a director who was not his client. 'But I'm still a fan,' he told them and added, 'it's a unique case of the fan hitting the shit.' Now it was his turn to be discreet. He would not divulge the name of the director.*

See also be up the CREEK / up shit creek (without a paddle); shit/piss or get off the POT.

shiver

get the shivers
to feel nervous or fearful. Something *gives one the shivers* when it has this effect. The image is of the physical reaction to a fever or fright. *19th cent.*

> Charles Kemble Plot and Counterplot 1808
> *I was almost frighten'd out of my wits when I recognized him; – don't you remember offering me your smelling bottle, and asking what ailed me? I told you I had the shivers, and so I had.*

> Mrs Henry Wood East Lynne 1861
> *I don't defend Dick Hare, I hate him too much for that, but if his father had treated him differently, Dick might have been different. Well, let's talk of something else; the subject invariably gives me the shivers.*

shiver my timbers
a sailor's oath. It is normally found only in fiction, notably in R L Stevenson's seafaring romance *Treasure Island* (1883), where it is a characteristic utterance of the old sea dog Long John Silver. But an earlier use is by Captain Marryat in another sea story, *Jacob Faithful* (1834): 'I won't thrash you Tom. Shiver my timbers if I do.' The words presumably invoke the notion of a shipwreck, in which the timbers of the ship are *shivered* (i.e. splintered) on the rocks. *19th cent.*

shock

a short, sharp shock
a brief period of severe punitive conditions intended as a deterrent, especially to young offenders. In recent times, the phrase was used most famously as a slogan of tough action on law and order at the 1979 Conservative Party conference by the Home Secretary William Whitelaw; during the 1980s regimes of tough military-style discipline were imposed on young people convicted of crimes, achieving limited success and attracting much criticism. The phrase can be traced back to the description of an execution in Act I of W S Gilbert's *The Mikado* (1885): 'Awaiting the sensation of a short, sharp shock, | From a cheap and chippy chopper on a big black block.' It dates from the mid 20th cent. in its current use.

See also FUTURE shock.

shoe

another pair of shoes
informal, dated a different matter entirely; something quite different. *19th cent.*

> Dickens Great Expectations 1861
> *My gentleman must have horses, Pip! Horses to ride, and horses to drive, and horses for his servant to ride and drive as well. Shall colonists have their horses (and blood 'uns, if you please, good Lord!) and not my London gentleman? No, no. We'll show 'em another pair of shoes than that, Pip, won't us?*

be in —'s shoes
to be in another person's situation or position: also *step into —'s shoes* in the sense 'to take over a position previously held by that person.' *18th cent.*

know/feel where the shoe pinches

to recognize the cause or source of a difficulty that others are unaware of: said to be based on a Roman proverb *nemo scit praeter me ubi me soccus premat* 'no one knows better than me where the shoe pinches me'. The sentiment is found in Chaucer's *The Merchant's Tale* (line 1553) 'But I woot [= know] best where wryngeth [= squeezes] me my sho', and comes a little closer to the modern form in the works of the Scottish poet and priest William Dunbar (c1460–c1513): 'Thow knawis best quhair [= where] bindis the thi scho.' *16th cent.*

wait for dead men's shoes

to be waiting to take over somebody's position or possessions when they die, retire, etc. The implication is of a futile wait, and the phrase appears in a fuller form as a proverb, *he goes barefoot that waits for dead men's shoes*. It appears in this form in John Heywood's collection of proverbs of 1546. *16th cent.*

See also the boot/shoe is on the other FOOT; if the shoe fits *at* if the CAP fits.

---

shoestring

on a shoestring

with barely adequate means or resources: a shoestring is symbolic of cheap improvised materials. *Early 20th cent.*

Jack Black *You Can't Win* 1926
The new owners had no bankroll, just opened up on a shoestring.

---

shoot

shoot somebody/something down in flames

to destroy an idea or argument completely, or to make somebody appear ridiculous: a metaphor from aerial warfare, in which an aircraft that is shot down is liable to burst into flames as it descends. *Mid 20th cent.*

M O'Brine *Mills* 1969
She, herself, had been a little shocked by his answer, but had secretly enjoyed seeing Eileen shot down in flames. In her job she had to deal with all kinds, but it was the Eileen Sangsters who tried her patience to the hilt.

shoot oneself in the foot

informal to act in a way that inadvertently damages one's cause or reputation or spoils one's chances. In the citation below, which is from the *OED* and the earliest use on record, the phrase is part of an extended metaphor comparing the art of writing to the use and care of guns. *Mid 20th cent.*

W Howells *Mankind in the Making* 1959
Certain common useful phrases can be dangerous ... Like guns, they will do the right thing in the right hands, but they are loaded, and ordinary citizens without Ph.D.'s are not the only ones who have accidents with them. Many a specialist has shot himself in the foot when he thought he was only cleaning a paragraph.

shoot a line

informal to talk boastfully or with pretentious exaggeration. The phrase has an obscure origin but is probably a metaphor from theatrical language, referring to excessively loud or overemotional declamation of an actor's lines on stage. An alternative suggestion, that it originates in soldiers of the First World War deliberately wounding themselves in order to escape further duty, lacks evidence and is unlikely in view of the much later date from which general usage is found. *Mid 20th cent.*

Noel Coward *Blithe Spirit* 1942
The whole thing's a put up job – I must say, though, she shoots a more original line than they generally do.

shoot one's mouth off

informal to talk loudly and arrogantly: in early use in the form *shoot off one's mouth*. *19th cent.*

N P Langford *Vigilante Days* 1890
Why, you fool; there you go, shooting off your mouth to me the first thing. Didn't I caution you not to tell any one?

the whole shooting match

informal everything, the whole lot: an extension of the 19th cent. phrase *the whole shoot*, i.e. all the people and equipment taking part in a shooting party. *Late 20th cent.*

Guardian 1986
Think what it must have been like for Rover salesmen to have been trying to sell cars against a background of (well-founded) rumours that the Government is trying to sell off the whole shooting

match to a rival company which may well discontinue the range you are planning to buy in favour of its own.

See also shoot the BREEZE; shoot from the HIP.

shop

all over the shop
informal everywhere; all over the place, especially in a careless or untidy mess. The phrase originates in boxing slang, where a contestant who treats his opponent roughly is said to 'knock him all over the shop'. Cf all over the PLACE; all over the SHOW. 19th cent.

live/sleep over the shop
to live at the place of one's work: originally with reference to shopkeepers who had rooms above their shops. 19th cent.

Nathaniel Parker Willis Saratoga 1847
As we said above, this is a true republic. A young man whose appearance is four-story-housy, can very well afford to let a few people know that he sleeps over the shop.

talk shop
to discuss affairs connected with one's work, especially in a tedious or obsessive way in social contexts and at other unsuitable times: based on a somewhat wider (19th cent.) use of shop as symbolic of one's particular work or business. 19th cent.

Kipling A Germ-Destroyer 1888
His guest did not bore the Viceroy. On the contrary, he amused him. … The Viceroy was pleased with Mellish because he did not talk 'shop'.

short

be caught/taken short
informal to need to urinate or defecate, especially at an awkward time or in difficult circumstances. In earlier use, to take short meant 'to catch at a disadvantage.' 19th cent.

bring/pull somebody up short
to make somebody stop or pause abruptly in what they are doing. 19th cent.

get/have somebody by the short and curlies / the short hairs
informal to gain control over somebody or have them totally at one's mercy: with allusion to the

pubic hair and to grabbing somebody by the genitals. The phrase is 19th cent. with short hairs and mid 20th cent. with short and curlies.

Kipling Wee Willie Winkie 1888
Then they'll rush in, and then we've got 'em by the short hairs!

in short order
chiefly NAmer immediately or summarily. 19th cent.

in the short run/term
over a short period of time; within the immediate future. 19th cent.

make short work of something
to achieve or complete a task or piece of work quickly and easily. 16th cent.

Shakespeare Romeo and Juliet II.v.35 (1596)
[Friar Laurence] Come, come with me, and we will make short work, | For, by your leaves, you shall not stay alone | Till Holy Church incorporate two in one.

short and sweet
brief and reasonably pleasant: now often used ironically of experiences that are unexpectedly brief. 16th cent.

Margaret Tyler The Mirrour of Princely Deedes and Knighthood 1578
The whole discourse in respect of the ende not unnecessary, for the varietie & continuall shift of fresh matter very delightfull, in ye speaches short & sweet, wise in sentence, and wary in provision of contrary accidents.

the short end of the stick
the less satisfactory or less advantageous part in a bargain or deal. The origin is obscure and the literal sense is not immediately clear, although associations with casting lots (see draw the short STRAW) are probable. 20th cent.

See also a BRICK short of a load; give somebody short SHRIFT; a SANDWICH short of a picnic; a short, sharp SHOCK.

shot

be/get shot of something/somebody
to be (or get) rid of something or somebody: based on an obsolete meaning of shoot 'to escape or avoid': cf the earlier form be/get shut of somebody/something (see SHUT). 19th cent.

a big shot
informal an important or influential person: in early use with *great* instead of *big*. *19th cent.*

give something one's best shot
to try one's hardest to succeed in a task or undertaking. *20th cent.*

like a shot
informal with great speed and eagerness. *19th cent.*

(not) by a long shot
informal (not) by a long way. *19th cent.*

> Mark Twain *Life on the Mississippi* 1883
> *Yes, I do recognize it now. It is the most wonderful thing I ever heard of; by a long shot the most wonderful – and unexpected.*

a shot in the arm
informal a badly needed boost or stimulus to an enterprise: from the medical meaning, an injection in the arm. *Early 20th cent.*

a shot in the locker
something kept in reserve for later use: often used in negative contexts. A figurative use of the meaning in naval warfare, in which a *locker* was a chest or compartment used for storing ammunition. *19th cent.*

> Thackeray *Vanity Fair* 1848
> *'I've always been accustomed to travel like a gentleman,' George said, 'and, damme, my wife shall travel like a lady. As long as there's a shot in the locker, she shall want for nothing,' said the generous fellow, quite pleased with himself for his magnificence of spirit.*

> L M Montgomery *Anne of Avonlea* 1909
> *'There's just one more thing, Marilla,' said Anne, with the air of producing the last shot in her locker.*

shot to pieces/hell
informal (said of an idea, plan, etc) savagely criticized or ridiculed: a figurative use of the military sense. *Mid 20th cent.*

See also CALL the shots; a shot in the DARK; a (warning) shot across the BOWS.

shotgun

a shotgun wedding/marriage
a marriage forced on the couple, typically by the bride's parents when the bride is pregnant. *Early 20th cent.*

> Sinclair Lewis *Elmer Gantry* 1927
> *There were, in those parts and those days, not infrequent ceremonies known as 'shotgun weddings'.*

See also RIDE shotgun.

shoulder

be on somebody's shoulder
to watch or supervise somebody closely. *20th cent.*

cry/weep on somebody's shoulder
to tell all one's troubles to a sympathetic listener: hence *a shoulder to cry on* is somebody who will sympathize with another's problems or difficulties. *Mid 20th cent.*

look over one's shoulder
to watch warily for a threat or danger. *20th cent.*

put one's shoulder to something / to the wheel
to make a determined effort, especially in a cooperative undertaking. The allusion is to extricating a cart that has become bogged down in mud, achieved by applying the shoulder to its wheels. *17th cent.*

> Andrew Marvell *An Account of the Growth of Popery* 1677
> *If it had hitherto seemed to go up-hill, there was a greater cause to put the whole shoulder to it.*

> R L Stevenson *The Strange Case of Dr Jekyll and Mr Hyde* 1886
> *'It turns me cold to think of this creature stealing like a thief to Harry's bedside; poor Harry, what a wakening! And the danger of it! for if this Hyde suspects the existence of the will, he may grow impatient to inherit. Ah, I must put my shoulder to the wheel – if Jekyll will but let me,' he added, 'if Jekyll will only let me.'*

shoulder to shoulder
1 side by side: originally used with reference to soldiers standing in formation. *16th cent.*

Sir Philip Sidney *The Countesse of Pembrokes Arcadia* a1586

But when they drew nere, Argalus horse being hot, prest in with his head: which Amphialus perceiving, knowing if he gave him his side, it shoulde bee to his disadvauntage, prest in also with him, so as both the horses & men met shoulder to shoulder, so as the horses (hurt as much with the striking, as being striken) tumbled down to the earth, daungerously to their maisters, but that they by strength nimble, & by use skilfull, in the falling shunned the harme of the fall, and without more respite, drewe out their swordes with a gallant braverie.

2 acting or working together to achieve a common purpose. *19th cent.*

straight from the shoulder
(said of a criticism, rebuke, etc) delivered bluntly and frankly: based on the literal use with reference to blows delivered with the fists. *19th cent.*

See also give somebody the COLD shoulder; have a CHIP on one's shoulder; an OLD head on young shoulders; RUB shoulders.

shout

all over bar the shouting
(said of a challenge, competition, etc) virtually won or achieved: probably with reference to the cheers of the crowd at the end of a game or spectacle, or to the objections of an audience disputing the result of a boxing match. *19th cent.*

in with a shout
having a good chance of achieving something. *Shout* here means 'a hope of success', and probably relates to the colloquial meaning 'a mention or greeting.' *20th cent.*

shout the odds
informal to talk in a loud and opinionated way: from the practice of bookmakers calling out the odds to punters at a racecourse. *Early 20th cent.*

shove

See when PUSH comes to shove.

show

In many of these phrases *show* is used in its noun sense 'an elaborate display or entertainment', recorded from the 16th cent., and the derived

(18th cent.) sense 'a matter or affair' (as in *give the show away* (see GIVE)).

all over the show
everywhere; all over the place, especially untidily. *Cf* all over the PLACE; all over the SHOP. *Mid 20th cent.*

get/keep the show on the road
to start (or continue) activity on a plan or enterprise. The image is of a travelling circus or group of theatrical performers. *Mid 20th cent.*

the only show in town
informal the only thing of any importance or value. *20th cent.*

show one's hand/cards
to disclose one's intentions, resources, etc. The phrase is a metaphor from card-playing: *cf* put one's cards on the table *at* CARD. *19th cent.*

Wilkie Collins *The Moonstone* 1868
My father saw that the one chance for him was to show his hand: he admitted, at once, that he wanted the papers. The Colonel asked for a day to consider his answer.

the show must go on
activities must continue however adverse the circumstances: originally with reference to a circus or other actual 'show' that has to take place whatever the difficulties to avoid loss of the company's reputation and income. *Mid 20th cent.*

Roy Dunlop *In All Directions* 1986
The first flight was scheduled for the last week in January, and as luck would have it there was a wild prairie blizzard blowing across western Canada at just the wrong time. But, as they say in the entertainment field, the show must go on.

a show of hands
a vote by raising the hands to indicate assent or dissent. *18th cent.*

steal the show
informal to receive most of the attention or admiration: originally of an actor or other performer, and by extension with reference to social gatherings or other public events. *Mid 20th cent.*

See also fly/show the FLAG; GIVE the game/show away; show a clean pair of heels *at* HEEL; show somebody the DOOR; show one's FACE; show somebody in their true colours *at* COLOUR;

show a LEG; show one's paces *at* PACE; show one's TEETH.

shred

of shreds and patches
made of miscellaneous scraps. In Shakespeare's play *Hamlet* (1601), in an exchange with his mother, Hamlet refers (III.iv.87–93) to his uncle King Claudius as 'A murderer and a villain, … a vice of kings, … A cutpurse of the empire and the rule, … A king of shreds and patches'. The reference is partly to the representation of Vice in the old mystery plays, who was dressed up as a travesty of a king in multicoloured rags. The allusive use comes via Act I of Gilbert and Sullivan's *The Mikado* (1885), in which Nanki-Poo, in the famous 'wandering minstrel' song, calls himself 'a thing of shreds and patches.' *19th cent.*

> Ralph Waldo Emerson *Representative Men* 1850
> *Here is the world, sound as a nut, perfect, not the smallest piece of chaos left, never a stitch nor an end, not a mark of haste, or botching, or second thought; but the theory of the world is a thing of shreds and patches.*

shrift

give somebody short shrift
to deal cursorily or peremptorily with somebody. To *get short shrift* is to be dealt with in this way. *Shrift* is an old word meaning 'penance' or 'confession' (in religious contexts), and *short shrift* was a brief period of time allowed to a criminal to make his confession to a priest before execution. In Shakespeare's *Richard III* (1593) Lord Hastings is warned (III.iv.95) 'Make a short shrift; he [Gloucester] longs to see your head.' *19th cent.*

> Saki *Reginald in Russia* 1910
> *'I'm certain a fox was shot or trapped in Lady Widden's woods the very day before we drew them.'* *'Major, if any one tried that game on in my woods they'd get short shrift,' said Mrs. Hoopington.*

shuffle

be/get lost in the shuffle
informal, chiefly NAmer to be overlooked or forgotten in a confused situation: a metaphor from card games. *Mid 20th cent.*

shuffle the cards
to manipulate affairs: with allusion to the shuffling of playing cards to produce a random or unpredictable order. *16th cent.*

> Thomas Churchyard *A Myrrour For Man* 1552
> *Playn dealing gets prayse, the world so began,* | *Now couzning and craft, is crept into man.* | *And all our new knacks, are cards finely shuffled,* | *That coms from their hands, whose faces are muffled.*

shut

be/get shut of somebody/something
to be (or get) rid of a person or thing: based on an obsolete meaning 'to be relieved or freed from (a burden)': *cf* be/get SHOT of something/somebody. *16th cent.*

> Thomas Nashe *Have with You to Saffron-Walden* 1596
> *Doo what I can, I shall not be shut of him.*

> John Steinbeck *The Grapes of Wrath* 1939
> *Grampa waved his hand back and forth. 'Once a fella's a preacher, he's always a preacher. That's somepin you can't get shut of.'*

shut up shop
1 to close one's business premises for the day or for a longer period. *16th cent.*

> Richard Brathwaite *A Survey of History* 1638
> *There is another morall too which ariseth naturally from that cinnamon-nested bird; and without much criticisme might be applyed to a pen-feathred citizen; who having now (as hee thinks) sufficient wealth, has shut up shop, and bid adue to his trade.*

2 to break off from an activity or bring it to a close. *17th cent.*

See also close/shut the DOOR on/to something; close/shut one's eyes to something *at* EYE; close/shut one's MIND to something; shut one's MOUTH; shut the STABLE door after the horse has bolted.

shutter

put up the shutters
to close one's business for the day or permanently. *19th cent.*

> Dickens *Oliver Twist* 1838
> *The undertaker had just put up the shutters of his shop, and was making some entries in his day-book*

by the light of a most appropriate dismal candle, when Mr. Bumble entered.

shy

have a shy at something

to make an attempt at something; to have a shot. This is the noun now mostly familiar as a fairground word; its original meaning is 'a quick throw of a stone', and so the use in the phrase is comparable to that of *shot*. *19th cent.*

sick

The two main strands of meaning, 'ill' and 'disgusted', often overlap in the phrases.

(as) sick as a dog/cat

informal extremely sick, typically to the point of constant vomiting. Other animals are also invoked in the simile from time to time. The earliest use is with *dog*, probably because of the unfavourable associations that animal had from an early date (*see* DOG). Cats do not come into the picture until the early 19th cent.: perhaps the fact that cats are rather more clean in their habits than dogs, and tend to be rather more discreetly sick, has kept them in the background in this animal imagery. The sense can also be 'thoroughly dejected or disappointed', as with (*as*) *sick as a parrot* below. *17th cent.*

> John Crowne *Sir Courtly Nice* 1685
> *Beast, Clown, Fool, Rascal. Pox take him – what shall I do with him? it goes against my stomach horribly to fight such a Beast. If his filthy Sword shou'd touch me, 'twou'd make me as sick as a Dog.*

> Susan Ferrier *Marriage* 1818
> *I rested very ill; my bed was very uncomfortable; and Sir Sampson's as sick as a cat – humph!*

(as) sick as a parrot

British, informal thoroughly dejected or disappointed, the opposite of *in seventh heaven* or *over the moon*. This comparison differs in meaning from (*as*) *sick as a dog/cat* above, which refers to physical illness. It was particularly associated during the 1970s and 1980s with the satirical magazine *Private Eye*. *Late 20th cent.*

> *Private Eye* 1979
> *The Moggatollah admitted frankly that he was 'sick as a parrot' at the way events had been unfolding.*

> *The Times* 2002
> *We were gutted. The heads were down, the boys were sick as parrots, and there didn't seem much to play for. The news that Scotland had been red-carded in its bid to stage the Euro 2008 football championships broke an hour before Question Time and cast a pall over the proceedings.*

be worried sick

informal to be extremely worried; literally, to be worried enough to become ill. *Mid 20th cent.*

> John Le Carré *Call for the Dead* 1961
> *'You look worried sick,' said Mendel. 'I am.' There was a pause. Mendel said: 'It's the devil you don't know that gets you.'*

make one (feel) sick

to give one a feeling of intense annoyance or disgust. *19th cent.*

> Charlotte Brontë *Jane Eyre* 1847
> *I am glad you are no relation of mine: I will never call you aunt again as long as I live. I will never come to see you when I am grown up; and if any one asks me how I liked you, and how you treated me, I will say the very thought of you makes me sick, and that you treated me with miserable cruelty.*

sick and tired of / sick of the sight of / sick to death of something

informal thoroughly fed up with something, and wanting to have no more of it. *18th cent.*

> Fanny Burney *Cecilia* 1782
> *'You are, at least, then, fond of the society of your friends?' 'O no! to be worn out by seeing always the same faces – one is sick to death of friends; nothing makes one so melancholy.'*

the sick man (of —)

a country that is much less prosperous or successful than its neighbours: originally applied to the Sultan of Turkey, and then to Turkey as a country in relation to Europe and by extension to other countries. *19th cent.*

sick to/at one's stomach

thoroughly upset or disgusted: in early use with *in* and *to* rather than *at*. *17th cent.*

side

be/get/keep on the right side of somebody

to earn somebody's favour or goodwill: to *get on the wrong side* is to fall out of favour or incur their displeasure. *19th cent.*

> Harriet Jacobs *Incidents in the Life of a Slave Girl* 1861
> *Their knowledge of my precarious situation placed me in their power; and I felt that it was important for me to keep on the right side of them, till, by dint of labor and economy, I could make a home for my children.*

let the side down

to disappoint or fail one's friends or colleagues, especially by failing to live up to the standards expected of one. A metaphor from team sports, in which individuals are expected to give their full support to the side. *Mid 20th cent.*

on the right side of —

(with reference to a person's age) less than a significant stated number (usually a multiple of ten or other round number); younger than the specified age. To be *on the wrong side of* that number is to be older. *18th cent.*

> Defoe *Reformation of Manners* 1702
> *On the wrong side of eighty let him whore, | He always was, and will be, lewd and poor.*

> Jane Austen *Sense and Sensibility* 1811
> *His appearance, however, was not unpleasing, in spite of his being, in the opinion of Marianne and Margaret, an absolute old bachelor, for he was on the wrong side of five-and-thirty.*

on the side

1 as something separate from one's normal occupation or activity, usually with the implication of something illicit or disreputable. *19th cent.*

> Theodore Dreiser *Sister Carrie* 1900
> *'By George, I won't stand that!' thought the thespian. 'I'm not going to have my work cut up by some one else. Either she quits that when I do my turn or I quit.' 'Why,' … said the manager, 'That's what she's supposed to do. You needn't pay any attention to that.' 'But she ruins my work.' 'No, she don't,' returned the former, soothingly. 'It's only a little fun on the side.'*

2 as an additional item in a meal: literally, *on the side* of the plate (or the table) apart from the main dishes. *19th cent.*

3 secretly, especially with reference to sexual infidelity. *Early 20th cent.*

> Willa Cather *The Song of the Lark* 1915
> *From your cradle, as I once told you, you've been 'doing it' on the side, living your own life, admitting to yourself things that would horrify him. You've always deceived him to the extent of letting him think you different from what you are.*

on the — side

somewhat as described by the adjective: normally used in unfavourable contexts, e.g. *on the mean side* = tending to be mean, *on the loud side* = rather loud. *18th cent.*

> Swift *Gulliver's Travels* 1726
> *I would never marry after threescore, but live in an hospitable manner, yet still on the saving side.*

take sides / take a side

to give one's support to one side in a dispute or argument: normally used with connotations of unfairness or partiality. *18th cent.*

> Francis Coventry *The History of Pompey the Little* 1750
> *They soon began to take sides in the dispute, 'till at length it became one universal Scene of Wrangle.*

> Nathaniel Hawthorne *The Scarlet Letter* 1850
> *It may appear singular, and, indeed, not a little ludicrous, that an affair of this kind, which, in later days, would have been referred to no higher jurisdiction than that of the selectmen of the town, should then have been a question publicly discussed, and on which statesmen of eminence took sides.*

See also a bit on the side *at* BIT[1]; the other side of the COIN.

sideline

on/from the sidelines

from the standpoint of somebody observing an event or process and not participating in it: from the lines marking the boundaries of a sports pitch, where trainers and other non-players stand. *Mid 20th cent.*

sideways

See KNOCK somebody sideways.

siege

lay siege to somebody

to pursue or criticize somebody relentlessly or with determination until they yield: a metaphor based on the military sense of besieging a town or stronghold until it is forced to surrender. *16th cent.*

Shakespeare *The Merry Wives of Windsor* II.ii.226 (1597)
[Ford to Sir John Falstaff] *There is money. Spend it, spend it; spend more; spend all I have; only give me so much of your time in exchange of it as to lay an amiable siege to the honesty of this Ford's wife. Use your art of wooing, win her to consent to you.*

sieve

See have a MEMORY like a sieve.

sigh

See HEAVE a sigh (of relief).

sight

at first sight

when first viewed or thought of, before full or proper consideration. The phrase dates from Middle English in the straightforward sense 'when seeing (or seen) for the first time', as in Shakespeare's *As You Like It* (1599) III.v.83 'Who ever loved who loved not at first sight?' Uses implying that fuller consideration would improve awareness are considerably later. *17th cent.*

Hobbes *Leviathan* 1651
Likewise if a popular or aristocratical Common-wealth subdue an enemy's country, and govern the same by a president, procurator, or other magistrate, this may seem perhaps, at first sight, to be a democratical or aristocratical government. But it is not so.

Swift *Gulliver's Travels* 1726
I would not have dwelt so long upon a circumstance, that perhaps at first sight may appear not very momentous, if I had not thought it necessary to justify my character in point of cleanliness to the world.

in/within one's sights

(said of an objective or aim) within one's capabilities or expectations; nearly achieved: with allusion to the sights of a gun. *Mid 20th cent.*

lose sight of something/somebody

1 to be no longer able to see a person or thing. *17th cent.*

William Bradford *Bradford and Winslow's Journal* 1622
As we went to view the place, one said he thought he saw an Indian house among the trees; so went up to see. And here we and the shallop [small boat] lost sight one of another till night.

2 to be no longer aware of or attending to a matter. *18th cent.*

Thomas Paine *The Age of Reason* 1796
It is an idea I have never lost sight of, that all our knowledge of science is derived from the revolutions (exhibited to our eye and from thence to our understanding) which those several planets or worlds of which our system is composed make in their circuit round the Sun.

out of sight, out of mind

(proverb) one soon forgets about a person or thing that is no longer present or visible. *15th cent.*

Robert Greene *Gwydonius* 1584
Which things considered, supposing yt Castania had cast him off, & that she plaid, out of sight out of mind ... he presented her with this Letter.

raise/lower one's sights

to increase (or reduce) one's ambitions or aspirations: with allusion to raising or lowering the sights of a gun according to the target aimed at. *Mid 20th cent.*

set one's sights on something

to aim to achieve or acquire something. *Mid 20th cent.*

a sight for sore eyes

a person or thing whose appearance or arrival is an occasion for joy or relief. *19th cent.*

Dickens *David Copperfield* 1850
'Well, the sight of me is good for sore eyes, as the Scotch say,' replied Steerforth, 'and so is the sight of you, Daisy, in full bloom. How are you, my Bacchanal?'

See also HEAVE in sight.

sign

signed, sealed, and delivered

completed or agreed: originally with reference to official documents, which received the signatures and seals of the parties involved and were then delivered to the appropriate authority. Originally *signed and sealed*, used in the preambles to Acts of Parliament. *15th cent.*

a sign of the times

something that is typical or especially characteristic of the period to which it belongs. The phrase is used in translations (including Tyndale, 1525, and the Authorized Version, 1611) of Matthew 16:3 'O ye hypocrites, ye can discern the face of the sky; but can ye not discern the signs of the times'; but the allusion here is purely physical. Uses in the modern sociological sense date from the first part of the 19th cent.

Edgar Allan Poe *Marginalia* 1849
The increase, within a few years, of the magazine literature, is by no means to be regarded as indicating what some critics would suppose it to indicate – a downward tendency in American taste or in American letters. It is but a sign of the times, an indication of an era in which men are forced upon the curt, the condensed, the well-digested in place of the voluminous.

sign on the dotted line

to make a legal agreement: with allusion to the line of dots on a document, marking the place where signatures are entered. *Early 20th cent.*

Raymond Hitchcock *Fighting Cancer: a Personal Story* 1989
I was back to that school chapel with the chaplain doing his Goddest to get me to sign on the dotted line and hand over my soul.

signal

send the wrong signal(s)

to give the wrong impression from one's manner or mode of expression: in particular, to appear to be undermining what is generally acceptable or approved of. The phrase is used especially in the context of statements and actions of those in authority and the likely interpretation of them by those regarded as vulnerable or impressionable, e.g. young people. Also *send the right signals*

(in the opposite sense). *Cf* send the wrong MESSAGE. *Late 20th cent.*

Guardian 1984
The President was delaying the defence cuts ahead of the talks between Mr Shultz and Mr Gromyko, because of concern that cutting Pentagon spending now would send the Russians the wrong signals about America's determination to stay with its arms build-up if necessary.

silence

silence is golden

(proverb) the wisest course is often to say nothing: in full *speech is silvern, but silence is golden*. *19th cent.*

Thomas Carlyle in *Fraser's Magazine* 1832
Out of silence comes thy strength. Speech is silvern, silence is golden.

silent

the silent majority

the majority of people who do not assert their views, and are generally regarded as moderate in outlook: the implication is that only those holding extreme views make them known, while moderate views are likely to go unexpressed and so unheard. The phrase dates in rather more neutral senses from the second half of the 19th cent., but its modern political connotations are much associated with the aspirations of President Richard Nixon in appealing to the *silent majority* of Middle America in speeches in the late 1960s. *19th cent.*

See also (as) still/silent/quiet as the GRAVE.

silk

make a silk purse out of a sow's ear

to make something fine or beautiful from poor materials. The phrase is first attested as a proverb from the early 16th cent. in the form *none can make goodly silke of a gotes flece*; the version with *silk purse* appears in the second half of the same century, and is recorded in a collection of proverbs made by William Walker in 1672 (with the amusing addition '… a scholar of a blockhead'). *16th cent.*

George Colman Ygr *The Heir At Law* 1798
*I wish you could learn him to follow my example,
and be a little genteel: – but there's no making a silk
purse out of a sow's ear, they say.*

D H Lawrence *The Rainbow* 1915
*You can't make a silk purse out of a sow's ear, as he
told his mother very early, with regard to himself.*

take silk
to become a Queen's (or King's) Counsel: from
the silk gown that QCs wear. *19th cent.*

Trollope *The Prime Minister* 1876
*Mr Wharton was and had for a great many years
been a barrister practising in the Equity Courts …
He had begun his practice early, and had worked in
a stuff gown till he was nearly sixty … He would
take his silk as an honour for his declining years, so
that he might become a bencher at his Inn.*

silly

the silly season
British a period of six to eight weeks in August
and September when there tends to be a shortage
of important news. Many legislative bodies are in
recess and the news and broadcasting media
resort to more trivial stories. *19th cent.*

silver

be born with a silver spoon (in one's mouth)
to be a member of a wealthy family or a privileged class: with allusion to the practice of god-
parents making a child a present of a silver
spoon. *19th cent.*

Dickens *David Copperfield* 1850
*I was much impressed by the extremely comfortable
and satisfied manner in which Mr. Waterbrook
delivered himself of this little word 'Yes,' every now
and then. There was wonderful expression in it. It
completely conveyed the idea of a man who had been
born, not to say with a silver spoon, but with a
scaling ladder, and had gone on mounting all the
heights of life one after another, until now he looked,
from the top of the fortifications, with the eye of a
philosopher and a patron, on the people down in the
trenches.*

have a silver tongue
to be very eloquent or persuasive: also *be silver-
tongued*. *18th cent.*

Richardson *Clarissa* 1748
*Did you not bewitch my grandfather? Could any
thing be pleasing to him, that you did not say or do?
How did he use to hang, till he slabber'd again, poor
doting old man! on your silver tongue!*

Charles Kingsley *Westward Ho!* 1855
*Ah, my silver-tongued scholar! and are you, then,
the poet? or have you been drawing on the inex-
haustible bank of your friend Raleigh, or my cousin
Sidney?*

on a silver platter
(said of something given or sought) involving no
effort on the part of the recipient, achieved with
great ease: from the use of a small silver tray by a
butler or waiter in presenting things. *19th cent.*

a silver lining
a hopeful sign or aspect in an otherwise bad or
gloomy situation: from the proverb *every cloud
has a silver lining* (see CLOUD). The physical image
is alluded to at an early date in Milton's *Comus*
(1634) i.93: 'Was I deceiv'd, or did a sable cloud /
Turn forth her silver lining on the night? / I did
not err, there does a sable cloud / Turn forth her
silver lining on the night / And casts a gleam
over this tufted Grove.' *19th cent.*

Thomas Bailey Aldrich *Daisy's Necklace* 1857
*The cloud which had fallen on her seemed to have no
silver lining; all was cold, black and sunless.*

the silver screen
films or the cinema industry: with allusion to the
silver coating given to early cinema screens to
increase definition of the image. *Early 20th cent.*

Simon

the real Simon Pure
the real or authentic person or thing in question:
from the name of a character in Susannah Centlivre's play *A Bold Stroke for a Wife* (1718), who is
described as a 'quaking preacher'. He is imper-
sonated by another character for part of the
action until he returns and establishes his true
identity as the real Simon Pure. *18th cent.*

John O'Keiffe *Wild Oats* 1792
*Somebody called Harry – zounds, if the real Simon
Pure, that is, should be arrived, I'm in a pure way.*

Scott *Guy Mannering* 1815
*A young seafaring man came forward. – 'Here,'
proceeded the counsellor, 'is the real Simon Pure –*

here's Godfrey Bertram Hewit, arrived last night from Antigua via Liverpool, mate of a West Indian, and in a fair way of doing well in the world, although he came somewhat irregularly into it.'

Mark Twain *The Innocents Abroad* 1869

It grew dark, and they put candles on the tables – candles set in bright, new, brazen candlesticks. And soon the bell – a genuine, simon-pure bell – rang, and we were invited to 'the saloon'.

sin

for one's sins

chiefly humorous as a punishment or penance: used with reference to an unpleasant or arduous experience. *19th cent.*

Mark Twain *The Prince and the Pauper* 1881

He restored the pretty things to their several places, and soon was cracking nuts, and feeling almost naturally happy for the first time since God for his sins had made him a prince.

like sin

with great force or intensity. Typically used with *hate* and other words expressing strong hostile emotion, but also used more generally as an intensifying word. *19th cent.*

Harriet Beecher Stowe *Uncle Tom's Cabin* 1852

Them stupid ones, as doesn't care whar they go, and shifless, drunken ones, as don't care for nothin', they'll stick by, and like as not be rather pleased to be toted round; but these yer prime fellers, they hates it like sin.

live in sin

now chiefly humorous to live together and have sexual relations without being married. *19th cent.*

William Barry *The New Antigone* 1887

'Do you mean, my poor sister,' he said in the same calm voice, like that of a physician at the bedside of a patient, 'that you are living in sin?'

sing

all-singing all-dancing

equipped with a large number of clever or showy features: originally used with reference to elaborate or spectacular stage shows and now often depreciatory. In the early days of sound cinema in the 1920s, musicals were often advertised with formulas such as *all talking, all singing, all dancing*.

The phrase became popular during the growth of computer technology from the 1980s on, usually from the mouths or pens (or keyboards) of lay people who were either dazzled by it or interested in promoting it. *Late 20th cent.*

Guardian 1984

Holmes [a new police database] *... should provide our detectives with unrivalled facilities when dealing with crimes such as homicides and serious sexual offences ... It's the all-singing all-dancing act.*

sing another / a different tune/song

to change one's attitude or standpoint on a matter. The phrase goes back in related forms to Middle English, in Gower's *Confessio Amantis*: 'Now schalt thou singe an other song.'

Charles Gildon *The Post-boy Rob'd of His Mail* 1692

A happy Man, (said Grave) content with his present Fortune; And yet perhaps, before the revolving year comes about, (pursu'd Winter) he may sing another Tune.

Jane Austen *Persuasion* 1818

'Ah! my dear,' said the Admiral, 'when he has got a wife, he will sing a different tune.'

sing for one's supper

to do work in order to earn a reward or favour. The allusion is to the (originally 18th cent.) nursery rhyme *Tommy Tucker*: 'Little Tommy Tucker | Sings for his Supper: | What shall we give him? | White bread and butter.' *19th cent.*

Washington Irving *Legends of the Alhambra* 1832

He sought the mansion of the padre. Alas, it was above the class of houses accessible to a strolling student like himself. The worthy padre had no sympathy with him; he had never been Estudiante sopista, obliged to sing for his supper.

sing from the same hymn sheet

(said of a group of people) to express the same views or objectives in public, especially when they are supposed to be cooperating with one another; to be seen to agree. The phrase in its present form is fairly recent, but it has older origins in variant forms such as *sing the same song* and *sing the same tune*. For example, Robert Browning's blank-verse tragedy *Luria* (published in 1846 as part of the collection called *Bells and Pomegranates*) contains the lines 'Priests, greybeards, Braccios, women, boys and spies, | All in one tale, each singing the same song, | How thou must house, and live at bed and board.' *Late 20th cent.*

The Times 1989
The March issue of Bar News makes a particular point of stressing the importance which the Bar attaches to ensuring that, and I quote, 'everyone sings from the same hymnsheet'. Well, I do not have a hymnsheet. I can assure you that my mind is not closed.

Hansard 1992
For the past year or so, all hon. Members except my hon. Friends on the Front Bench have sung from the same hymn book about decommissioning. This year, I am delighted that my hon. Friends have at least found the same page of the hymn book.

singe

singe one's wings
to suffer harm or damage as a result of a risky venture. The allusion is to moths, which risk getting their wings singed from the heat when they fly close to a strong light. *19th cent.*

Henry Adams The Education of Henry Adams 1907
Seneca closed the vast circle of his knowledge by learning that a friend in power was a friend lost – a fact very much worth insisting upon – while the gray-headed moth that had fluttered through many moth-administrations and had singed his wings more or less in them all … acquired an instinct of self-preservation that kept him to the north side of La Fayette Square.

sink

a sinking feeling
an uncomfortable feeling in the stomach, caused by the realization or expectation that something unpleasant is about to happen. *19th cent.*

George Moore Esther Waters 1894
When the news that Ben Jonson had broken down at the bushes came in his Lordship had drunk a magnum of champagne, and memory of this champagne inspired a telling description of the sinking feeling consequent on the loss of a wager, and the natural inclination of a man to turn to drink to counteract it.

sink or swim
to succeed or fail according to one's own efforts and achievements: in early use in the form *float or sink. Middle English*

Chaucer The Complaint unto Pity (line 110)
For wel I wot [= know] *although I wake or wynke* [= sleep], | *Ye rekke* [= care] *not whether I flete or synke.*

Shakespeare I Henry IV I.iii.192 (1596)
[Hotspur] *If he fall in, good night, or sink or swim!*
See also everything but the KITCHEN sink.

siren

a siren song/call/voice
the allure afforded by something that is excitingly dangerous or harmful: with reference to the sirens, women of the sea who in Homer's *Odyssey* lured sailors to their deaths by the beauty of their singing. *16th cent.*

Alexander Garden The Theatre of Scotish Kings (Constantine III) c1600
A simple, and too Credulous a King, | Brought to beleeve, a siren Song too soone: | Which losses large, unto his Bands did bring.

George Granville, Baron Lansdowne Works 1736
How was the Scene forlorn, and how despis'd, | When Timon, without Musick, moraliz'd? | Shakespeare's Sublime in vain entic'd the Throng, | Without the Aid of Purcel's Siren Song.

sit

be a sitting duck
to be a prominent or vulnerable target: a metaphor from the sport of shooting. Also in 19th cent. use in the form *sitting bird.*

sit at —'s feet
to be a particular person's follower or pupil. *16th cent.*

Trollope The Three Clerks 1857
It was quite manifest that Alaric had not sat at the feet of Undy Scott without profiting by the lessons which he had heard. 'With what face,' continued he, 'can you pretend to be more honest than your neighbours?'

sit easy/heavy on the stomach
(said of food) to be easy (or difficult) to digest. *18th cent.*

Charles Gayler *Love of a Prince* c1860
[Baron] *You have no idea, my dear Lieutenant, how extremely heavy bon-bons are!* [Count Gustave] *Heavy on the stomach?*

sit on one's hands
to do nothing, to remain inactive. *Early 20th cent.*

sit on somebody's tail
to monitor or harass somebody oppressively: in particular, to drive very close to a vehicle in front, especially while waiting to overtake it. *20th cent.*

Alistair MacLean *Santorini* 1987
'You've come a long way in a short time.' 'Needs must when the devil drives. And he's sitting on my tail right now.'

sit tight
to stay resolutely where one is; to refuse to move or take any action. *18th cent.*

Kipling *Kim* 1901
Hurree Babu reached for the pipe, and sucked it till it guggled again. 'Now I will speak vernacular. You sit tight, Mister O'Hara. It concerns the pedigree of a white stallion.'

sit up (and take notice)
to become suddenly attracted to or interested in something and start paying attention to it, especially after being previously unconcerned. *19th cent.*

See also sit in JUDGEMENT; sit on the FENCE.

six

at sixes and sevens
in a state of confusion: originally in the form *set* (or *stand*) *on six and seven*, meaning 'to gamble all one's possessions'. This form appears in Chaucer (see below) and other Middle English sources. In gamblers' jargon, *sixes and sevens* are the two highest values of dice (perhaps a corruption of French *cinque* and *sice*, since there is no seven on a dice). Betting everything on the high numbers alone could end in disaster. An alternative suggestion, that the phrase is connected with careless or confused use of an abacus, has no substance. By the time of Shakespeare the form of the phrase has become *at six and seven*, as we find in Shakespeare's *Richard II* (1595), where the Duke of York speaks of the urgency of the situation (II.ii.122): 'I should to Pleshey too, but time will not permit. | All is uneven, | And every-

thing is left at six and seven.' The current form with plurals, *at sixes and sevens*, first appears in Francis Grose's *Dictionary of the Vulgar Tongue* (1786).

Two other stories are no more than red herrings, but they provide interesting insights into the workings of folk etymology. One is based on a passage in Job (5:19) in the Authorized Version of the Bible (1611), where Job is addressed by Eliphaz the Temanite: 'He [God] shall deliver thee in six troubles: yea, in seven there shall no evil touch thee.' The New English Bible makes this more intelligible as follows: 'You may meet disaster six times, and he will save you; seven times, and no harm shall touch you.' But the connection between this (surely) reassuring use of numbers and the notion of confusion and chaos is difficult to sustain. The other story, even more entertaining but no more probable for that, concerns the medieval trade guilds or livery companies, and in particular a dispute between the Merchant Taylors Company (of tailors) and the Skinners Company (of fur traders). The two companies had a common interest, and both wanted precedence in ranking. In 1484 the Lord Mayor of London, Sir Robert Billesden, settled the dispute by assigning the sixth and seventh positions to the two guilds, to alternate between them in successive years. By this judgement, the story goes, the two companies were to remain 'at sixes and sevens' with each other. This is, needless to say, no account of origin, which the facts show to be much earlier, but rather an attempt to assign an origin to circumstances that fortuitously coincide with some of the features of an expression already in use (in this case, the numbers six and seven).

Chaucer *Troilus and Criseyde* IV.622
Lat nat [= let not] this wrecched wo thyn herte gnawe, | But manly sette the world on six and sevene; | And if thow deye a martyr, go to hevene!

Nathaniel Hawthorne *Mr Higginbotham's Catastrophe* 1834
The coach rumbled up to the piazza of the tavern, followed by a thousand people; for if any man had been minding his own business till then, he now left it at sixes and sevens, to hear the news.

hit/knock somebody for six
to harm or defeat somebody profoundly, or to disturb them emotionally: with allusion to a hit to

the boundary in cricket, scoring six runs. *Early 20th cent.*

six feet under

informal dead and buried: with allusion to the normal depth of a grave. *Mid 20th cent.*

six of one and half a dozen of the other

a choice between two very similar or equally attractive alternatives. *19th cent.*

> Wilkie Collins *The Moonstone* 1868
> *I got the new coat as cheap as I could, and I went through all the rest of it as cheap as I could. We were not a happy couple, and not a miserable couple. We were six of one and half a dozen of the other.*

See also six of the BEST.

sixpence

on a sixpence

in a very small space: used especially with reference to the capacity of vehicles to turn in a very tight circle. A sixpence was the smallest coin in Britain's pre-decimal currency. *20th cent.*

> *Pilot* 1992
> *The nose then has to be hauled well up to break the descent rather than the aeroplane. If you get it right the Beaver stops on a sixpence.*

sixty

the sixty-four (thousand) dollar question

the critical question or decision: from the question winning a prize of sixty-four dollars in a US radio quiz show. *Mid 20th cent.*

> J C Polkinghorne *The Quantum World* 1984
> *The sixty-four thousand dollar question is this: as the electrons arrive one by one at the detector, which slit have they come through?*

size

one size fits all

informal used in various ways, usually disparagingly, to denote a standard procedure, institution, etc that is inflexible and meant to cater for all eventualities: based on clothing manufactured in a single size for all customers. *Late 20th cent.*

> *Sunday Times* 1990
> *More sophisticated clients will want more focused services. They will want help over the long haul*

rather than a quick fix. They will want to deal with clever people who concentrate on them rather than being presented with low-level, one-size-fits-all solutions.

that's (about) the size of it

informal that is essentially correct: typically used to express agreement with another person's assessment of a situation. *19th cent.*

> R L Stevenson *Treasure Island* 1883
> *I began dimly to understand. 'You mean all's lost?' I asked. 'Ay, by gum, I do!' he answered. 'Ship gone, neck gone – that's the size of it.'*

skate

get/put one's skates on

informal to hurry up: in early 20th cent. services' slang also used in the sense 'to (clear off and) avoid duty.' *19th cent.*

> Dickens *David Copperfield* 1850
> *I felt the words of my lessons slipping off, not one by one, or line by line, but by the entire page; I tried to lay hold of them; but they seemed, if I may so express it, to have put skates on, and to skim away from me with a smoothness there was no checking.*

See also be skating on thin ICE.

skeleton

a skeleton in the cupboard / NAmer closet

a closely guarded secret that might cause shame, especially in a family's past. The phrase first appears in literary use by Thackeray in the mid 19th cent. (see below), but it is thought to have been in use earlier. *19th cent.*

> Thackeray *The Virginians* 1858
> *A hundred years ago, people of the great world were not so strait-laced as they are now, when everybody is good, pure, moral, modest; when there is no skeleton in anybody's closet.*

See also a ghost/spectre/skeleton at the FEAST.

skid

The meanings (usually in plural uses) underlying the phrases are those denoting runners or rollers of various kinds used to move large vehicles or objects.

hit the skids
informal to experience a precipitate defeat or downfall. *Early 20th cent.*

on the skids
informal (said of an operation or enterprise) failing or deteriorating rapidly. Also (said of a person) facing downfall or ruin. *Early 20th cent.*

P Lowe *The Origins of the Korean War* 1989
Earlier in the conversation MacArthur discounted suggestions that Walt Butterworth would assume responsibility for dealing with a treaty. Butterworth was 'on the skids', having been made a scapegoat by Acheson for the bankruptcy of American policy in China.

put the skids under somebody
1 *informal, originally NAmer* to bring about somebody's downfall. *Early 20th cent.*
2 *informal* to make somebody hurry. *Late 20th cent.*

---

skin

be skin and bone
to be extremely thin or emaciated. The expression occurs in Middle English, and is entered in John Heywood's *Two Hundred Epigrammes* (1555): 'And yet art thou skyn and bone.'

Smollett *The Adventures of Ferdinand Count Fathom* 1753
'Flesh' cried she … 'none of your names, Mr Yellow chaps. What! I warrant you have an antipathy to flesh, because you yourself are nothing but skin and bone. I suppose you are some poor starv'd journeyman taylor come from France, where you have been … living upon rye-bread and soup maigre, and now you come over like a walking atomy … and so forsooth, you … pretend to find fault with a surloin of roast beef.'

Charlotte Brontë *Jane Eyre* 1847
Meantime, Mr. Rochester affirmed I was wearing him to skin and bone, and threatened awful vengeance for my present conduct at some period fast coming.

by the skin of one's teeth
by a narrow margin, only just. Originally a literal translation of Job 19:20, rendered in the Authorized Version of 1611 as: 'My bone cleaveth to my skin and to my flesh, and I am escaped with the skin of my teeth.' *16th cent.*

Susan Fenimore Cooper *Elinor Wyllys* 1846
He had understood that the plaintiff … claimed to have just escaped drowning, by the skin of his teeth, when picked up on the coast of Africa.

get under somebody's skin
1 *informal* to annoy or upset somebody, especially persistently. Also, to become an obsession to somebody. In this last sense, 'I've got you under my skin' is the title of a song by Cole Porter (1936). *19th cent.*

Willa Cather *The Song of the Lark* 1915
'How could you fall for a mouse-trap like Pink Alden, Archie?' Dr. Archie laughed as he began to carve. 'Pink seems to get under your skin. He's not worth talking about.'

2 *informal* to understand somebody's feelings; to sympathize with somebody. *Mid 20th cent.*

Faith Baldwin *Innocent Bystander* 1933
Jimmy worked out a series of single-policy investments for her, finally. And that was all there was to it, unless you count her following him to the door and her soft-spoken good-bye. 'I did get you here, didn't I – under any pretext?' He replied, irritated, 'If it was a pretext we'll forget it.' That pleased her, she had got under his skin, he had at least admitted something. She said, soothingly: 'Of course it wasn't – entirely. Business and pleasure, a delightful combination.'

have a thick skin
to be indifferent or unresponsive to criticism: with reference to the tough hide of an animal. To *have a thin skin* is to be sensitive to criticism. Also *thick-skinned* (adjective) and (up to the 19th cent.) *thickskin* (as a noun meaning 'a dull or stupid person'). *16th cent.*

Shakespeare *The Merry Wives of Windsor* IV.v.1 (1597)
[Host] What wouldst thou have, boor? What, thickskin? Speake, breathe, discuss.

Henry James *Roderick Hudson* 1876
'The way you treated Christina Light. I call that grossly obtuse.' 'Obtuse?' Rowland repeated, frowning. 'Thick-skinned, beneath your good fortune.'

it's no skin off my nose / NAmer back / NAmer ass
informal it doesn't affect me or make any difference to me. *Early 20th cent.*

there's more than one way to skin a cat

(proverb) there is more than one way of achieving what one wants. The current phrase is one of a number of fanciful proverbs arising in the mid 19th cent. and based on the violent treatment of cats and dogs, e.g. *there are more ways of killing a cat than choking it with cream* (or *killing a dog than choking it with butter*). The earliest form on record is *more ways to kill a dog than hanging*, which appears in the edition of John Ray's *English Proverbs* published in 1678. *19th cent.*

> Mark Twain *A Connecticut Yankee at the Court of King Arthur* 1889
> Then the Church came to the front, with an ax to grind; and she was wise, subtle, and knew more than one way to skin a cat – or a nation; she invented 'divine right of things', and propped it all around, brick by brick.

under the skin

beneath outward appearances; fundamentally: originally used by Kipling (in *The Seven Seas*, 1896) in the phrase *sisters under the skin*, i.e. women with common interests. *19th cent.*

> Olive Schreiner *The Story of an African Farm* 1883
> The innocent are accused, and the accuser triumphs. If you will take the trouble to scratch the surface anywhere, you will see under the skin a sentient being writhing in impotent anguish.

See also JUMP out of one's skin; SAVE one's skin.

---

skirt

See a BIT of fluff/skirt/stuff.

---

skull

out of one's skull

informal crazy or deranged; out of one's mind. *Mid 20th cent.*

> *Liverpool Echo* 1993
> In the completed and highly recommended movie Branagh does look totally out of his skull in that scene.

---

sky

the sky's the limit

informal, originally NAmer there is virtually no limit to what can be achieved, won, earned, etc. *Early 20th cent.*

> W R Burnett *Vanity Row* 1952
> If there's ever anything we can do for you … You know. Sky's the limit, as people say.

praise somebody to the skies

to praise somebody very highly: in early use with *extol* instead of *praise*. *17th cent.*

> John Marston *Jacke Drums Entertainment* 1601
> Last day thy praise extold him to the skies.

> Lewis Carroll *The Hunting of the Snark* 1876
> The Bellman himself they all praised to the skies – | Such a carriage, such ease and such grace! | Such solemnity, too! One could see he was wise, | The moment one looked in his face!

See also out of a CLEAR blue sky.

---

slack

The phrases are based on the meaning to do with loose or spare lengths of rope: figurative uses date from the early 20th cent.

cut/give somebody some slack

NAmer, informal, especially Black slang to show somebody some consideration; to give them a chance. *Mid 20th cent.*

> M F Jackmon in Jones & Neal *Black Fire* 1969
> Say, baby, light'n up on me – gimme some slack.

take/pick up the slack

to use up spare resources or use resources more effectively or economically: literally, to tighten a length of rope so that it becomes taut and therefore stronger. *Mid 20th cent.*

> *Daily Telegraph* 1992
> In the bad times the market for second and retirement homes disappeared, and the local market can't take up the slack.

---

slap

have/take a slap at something

informal to make a determined attempt at something. *Slap* here is equivalent to *smack*, meaning 'a blow or hit': *see* have/take a SMACK at something.

a slap in the face/eye

a sharp or unexpected rebuff or insult: used with reference to words or actions. *19th cent.*

> Henry James *Confidence* 1880
> Lovelock, also, whom Bernard saw every day, appeared to think that destiny had given him a slap

in the face, for he had not enjoyed the satisfaction of a last interview with Miss Evers.

G B Shaw *The Philanderer* 1898
Her going away is a downright slap in the face for these people.

a slap on the back

a hearty expression of friendship or congratulation, sometimes by actual performance of the action but often used allusively. To *slap somebody on the back* is to congratulate them. *19th cent.*

Edgar Allan Poe *The Narrative of Arthur Gordon Pym of Nantucket* 1837
On the second of July the mate came below drunk as usual, and in an excessively good-humor. He came to Augustus's berth, and, giving him a slap on the back, asked him if he thought he could behave himself if he let him loose.

a slap on the wrist

a mild rebuke or punishment. *Early 20th cent.*

slate

on the/one's slate

British, informal on credit, to be paid for at a later date. Debts incurred at retailers were formerly chalked up on slates on the wall. *Early 20th cent.*

wipe the slate clean

to expunge an unfavourable or tarnished record; to begin again without any debts or wrongdoings to one's name. A *clean slate* is accordingly an untarnished record, or one from which unfavourable features have been removed. *19th cent.*

Bram Stoker *Dracula* 1897
I believe we forgot everything, except, of course, personal fear, and it seemed to wipe the slate clean and give us a fresh start.

sledgehammer

take/use a sledgehammer to crack a nut

to use excessive or disproportionate means to achieve something relatively simple or straightforward. The phrase also occurs in early use in the form *use a sledgehammer to kill a gnat*. *19th cent.*

L C Judson *Sages and Heroes of the American Revolution* 1851
He at once became the nucleus around which a band of patriots gathered and formed a nut too hard to be cracked by the sledgehammer of monarchy.

Independent 1989
The principle of proportionality – do not use a sledgehammer to crack a nut – is straightforward logic.

sleep

be able to do something in one's sleep

to be able to perform a task with great ease, especially from having performed it so often in the past. *Mid 20th cent.*

James Russell *Underground* 1989
Keeping night-watch is the easiest job in the world. So easy you can do it in your sleep. You have to give yourself things to do, to keep yourself awake.

sleep around

informal to have casual sexual relations with several partners; to be sexually promiscuous. *Early 20th cent.*

Aldous Huxley *Point Counter Point* 1928
'Sleeping around' – that was how he had heard a young American girl describe the amorous side of the ideal life, as lived in Hollywood.

sleep easy

to have no worries or feelings of guilt. *19th cent.*

Hardy *The Mayor of Casterbridge* 1886
I have never opened the safe at all as yet; for I keep ma papers at the bank, to sleep easy o' nights.

Conan Doyle *The Five Orange Pips* 1891
You can understand that this register and diary may implicate some of the first men in the South, and that there may be many who will not sleep easy at night until it is recovered.

sleep like a log/top

to sleep very soundly. The comparison with a log is presumably based on its stillness; the other is harder to explain but probably has something to do with the motionless appearance of a top – and its mesmeric associations – when spinning. Both forms occur from the 17th cent.

Fletcher & Shakespeare *The Two Noble Kinsmen* III.iv.26 (a1616)
O for a prick now, like a nightingale, | To put my breast against. I shall sleep like a top else.

G K Chesterton *The Innocence of Father Brown* 1911
Royce, anyhow, was not so drunk as that, or he would be sleeping like a log by now.

the sleep of the just

deep sleep, typically enjoyed by those with a clear conscience. *19th cent.*

> **Browning *The Ring and the Book* 1842**
> *They sank | By the way-side, in some shelter meant for beasts, | And now lay heaped together, nuzzling swine, | Each wrapped in bloody cloak, each grasping still | His unwiped weapon, sleeping all the same | The sleep o' the just.*

sleep tight

sleep well and peacefully. The phrase is typically used as an affectionate and reassuring goodnight wish to a child at bedtime and has virtually no grammatical variation. It is sometimes extended in fanciful ways, for example *Goodnight, sleep tight, mind the bugs don't bite*. The use of *tight* (halfway between adjective and adverb in function) is probably due as much to the rhyming effect with *goodnight* as to any precision of meaning, and we find it used again as a simple intensifying word in *sit tight* and *hold tight*. *Tight* here is an assuring word, suggesting security, and the combination *tight asleep* is found in 19th cent. literature. So attempts to find an explanation for our phrase in the tightness of bedclothes (to prevent them sagging? to keep the bugs out?) and other aspects of the bedding are largely futile. A physical explanation, if we need one at all, is more likely to be found in the sleeper, with eyes tight shut, than in the bed slept on. *19th cent.*

sleep with one eye open

to sleep lightly in order to remain vigilant and be ready for any emergency or difficulty. *19th cent.*

> **Nathaniel Hawthorne *The House of the Seven Gables* 1851**
> *A cautious man is proverbially said to sleep with one eye open. That may be wisdom. But not with both; for this were heedlessness!*

See also let sleeping dogs lie *at* DOG; live/sleep over the SHOP; LOSE sleep over something; sleep ROUGH.

sleeve

up one's sleeve

(said of an idea, resource, etc) kept secretly aside in case it is needed in the future: originally with reference to a handkerchief kept in one's sleeve (*in one's sleeve* being an early variant form), but in recent use the image may be that of a conjuror keeping an egg, watch, card, or other small object up his sleeve in order to produce it as if by magic, or of a gambler cheating at cards by having one or more concealed up his sleeve. *16th cent.*

> **George Puttenham *The Arte of English Poesie* 1589**
> *To have a journey or sicknesse in his sleeve, thereby to shake of other importunities of greater consequence.*

> **Henry James *The Ambassadors* 1903**
> *The interruption left Miss Gostrey time, before the subsequent hush, to express as a sharp finality her sense of the moral of all their talk. 'I knew you had something up your sleeve!'*

See also an ACE up one's sleeve; have a CARD up one's sleeve; LAUGH up one's sleeve; ROLL up one's sleeves; wear one's HEART on one's sleeve.

sleigh

take somebody for a sleigh ride

informal to cheat or mislead somebody. The phrase is based on a US slang meaning of *sleigh ride* 'a hoax or false story', and *taking a sleigh ride* also refers to the effects of taking hallucinogenic drugs, which doubtless influences the use and understanding of our phrase. *Mid 20th cent.*

sleight

sleight of hand

an adroit piece of deception: literally, skilful use of the hands in conjuring or juggling. The physical sense dates from Middle English, and the first figurative evidence from the 16th cent.

> **Thomas Churchyard *Sir Simon Burleis Tragedy* 1593**
> *The dreadfull Duke did drive a wondrous drift | To worke his will, with slipperie sleight of hand: | And sought to give King Richards friends a lift, | For whom he did prepare a secret band.*

> **George Chapman *Batrachomyomachia* 1624**
> *And without Truth, all's only sleight of hand, | Or our Law-learning, in a Forraine Land.*

> **Aphra Behn *Oroonoko* 1688**
> *He is bred to all the little arts and cunning they are capable of; to all the legerdemain tricks and sleight-of-hand, whereby he imposes upon the rabble; and is both a doctor in physic and divinity: and by these tricks makes the sick believe he sometimes eases their pains, by drawing from the afflicted part little serpents, or odd flies, or worms, or any strange thing.*

slice

a slice of the cake

a share in the proceeds or profits: the image is the common one (dating from the 18th cent.) of a cake, representing assets or gains, being cut up and shared. *Cake* is sometimes qualified in some way, as in *the national cake, the labour cake*, etc. *Mid 20th cent.*

See also the best/greatest thing since sliced BREAD; a piece/share/slice of the ACTION.

slide

let something slide

to allow a situation to deteriorate through carelessness or negligence: also, in earlier use, with the more neutral meaning 'to let something take its course'. A common phrase, occurring in Shakespeare and elsewhere, was *let the world slide* = let events take their natural course. The modern meaning is always depreciatory. *Middle English*

Chaucer *The Clerk's Tale* (line 82)
I blame hym thus: that he considered noght | In tyme comynge what myghte hym betyde, | But in his lust present was al his thoght, | As for to hauke and hunte on every syde. | Wel ny [= well nigh] alle othere cures [= cares] leet he slyde.

Shakespeare *The Taming of the Shrew* Induction i.3 (1592)
[Sly] Y'are a baggage. The Slys are no rogues. Look in the chronicles – we came in with Richard Conqueror. Therefore, paucas pallabras, let the world slide.

sling

sling hash

NAmer, informal to serve food in a café or diner. *Hash* is cooked and reheated meat or other food of a kind served in cheap eating places called *hash joints*, and a *hash-slinger* is a name for a waiter or waitress in one of these. *Sling* is used in the sense 'to pass round' with reference to drinks and dishes from the late 19th cent. and *hash-slinger* is also found then, although the phrase *sling hash* itself is a little later (early 20th cent.).

Gold Hill News (Nevada) 1868
The nice young man of Washoe may or may not be some kind of a clerk, a hash-slinger, or a check-guerrilla.

O Henry *The Four Million* 1906
I'm going back there and ask her to marry me. I guess she won't want to sling hash any more when she sees the pile of dust I've got.

Observer 1995
His descriptions of the petty tyrant managers who bust his chops at the slightest provocation, the would-be actors and actresses (He: 'I'm an actor'. She: 'Oh, which restaurant?'), who may sling hash but consider bussing their own tables beneath them.

slings and arrows

unfavourable circumstances or factors: with allusion to the words of Hamlet's soliloquy in Shakespeare's *Hamlet* (1601) III.i.60 'Whether 'tis nobler in the mind to suffer | The slings and arrows of outrageous fortune, | Or to take arms against a sea of troubles, | And, by opposing, end them.' *17th cent.*

Oliver Goldsmith *On Metaphor* 1763
If the metaphors were reduced to painting, we should find it a very difficult task ... to represent with any propriety outrageous Fortune using her slings and arrows, between which, indeed, there is no sort of analogy in nature. Neither can any figure be more ridiculously absurd than that of a man taking arms against a sea, exclusive of the incongruous medley of slings, arrows, and seas, justled within the compass of one reflection.

Maria Edgeworth *The Absentee* 1812
Mrs. Dareville ... gave full scope to all the malice of mockery ... Her slings and arrows, numerous as they were and outrageous, were directed against such petty objects, and the mischief was so quick ... that, felt but not seen, it is scarcely possible to register the hits, or to describe the nature of the wounds.

See also put/have somebody's ass in a sling at ASS²; sling one's HOOK.

slip

give somebody the slip

to succeed in eluding somebody; to escape unperceived. *16th cent.*

John Bunyan The Pilgrim's Progress 1678

Thou hast done in this, according to the proverb, 'Changed a bad for a worse'; but it is ordinary for those that have professed themselves his servants, after a while to give him the slip, and return again to me. Do thou so too, and all shall be well.

let something slip

1 to allow time or an opportunity to pass without making use of it. Also in fuller form *let something slip through one's fingers/grasp. 16th cent.*

Milton Comus 1634

List, Lady, be not coy, and be not cozened | With that same vaunted name Virginity; | Beauty is Nature's coin, must not be hoarded, | But must be current, and the good thereof | Consists in mutual and partaken bliss, | Unsavory in th' enjoyment of itself. | If you let slip time, like a neglected rose | It withers on the stalk with languished head.

Thomas Paine Common Sense 1776

The present time, likewise, is that peculiar time, which never happens to a nation but once, viz., the time of forming itself into a government. Most nations have let slip the opportunity, and by that means have been compelled to receive laws from their conquerors, instead of making laws for themselves.

2 to reveal something secret or confidential inadvertently. The image is of letting words slip from the mouth (or tongue, etc): see the Tennyson quotation below. *18th cent.*

John Armstrong The Forced Marriage 1770

This noble Count, proud of his ancient blood, | Had two young daughters. The eldest Julia, | Some time had lived confined for an attempt | To steal a marriage with a youth whose family, | Tho' not obscure, he thought no match for his. | Now grown impatient of his jealous cares, | It pleased him in my favour to let slip | Some distant hints, which with a ranc'rous joy | My father snatched; he pressed me eagerly | To seize th' occasion.

Edgar Allan Poe How to Write a Blackwood Article 1838

Turn up your nose at things in general, and when you let slip any thing a little too absurd, you need not be at the trouble of scratching it out, but just add a footnote.

Tennyson The Marriage of Geraint 1859

I will not let his name | Slip from my lips if I can help it.

a slip of a girl/boy

a young and small girl or boy. *Slip* is recorded in this meaning from the 16th cent.: a translation of Virgil's *Aeneid* published in 1582 refers to 'the slip Ascanius' (the son of Aeneas). This use, without a complement introduced by *of*, continues until the 19th cent. (and occurs in Sir Walter Scott) but is now largely obsolete. Its form with *of* occurs earliest with *boy*, although *girl* (or another female equivalent such as *daughter*) is more usual. The meaning of *slip* in these uses is developed from its primary (15th cent.) meaning 'a twig or off-shoot.' *17th cent.*

a slip of the pen/tongue

a casual or minor error in writing or speaking. The form with *pen* dates from the 17th cent. and with *tongue* from the 18th cent.

Byron Don Juan 1824

He slumber'd; yet she thought, at least she said | (The heart will slip, even as the tongue and pen), | He had pronounced her name – but she forgot | That at this moment Juan knew it not.

there's many a slip

(proverb) things can go wrong at any stage, even (or especially) right at the end: in full *there's many a slip 'twixt cup and lip*. The sentiment is much older than the first appearances of the proverb in its present form. *19th cent.*

Hardy Far from the Madding Crowd 1874

'Pray don't speak of it, sir,' said Oak, hastily. 'We don't know what may happen. So many upsets may befall 'ee. There's many a slip, as they say – and I would advise you – I know you'll pardon me this once – not to be too sure.'

See also slip through the NET; slip on a BANANA skin.

slippery

the slippery slope

a process or course of action that will inevitably lead to trouble or disaster. *Mid 20th cent.*

Independent 1989

Sponsorship is the slippery slope towards the erosion of editorial independence.

slow

slow but sure

(proverb) needing or taking a long time but achieving the required purpose in the end: in full *slow but sure* (or *slow and steady*) *wins the race*, the underlying meaning of *sure* here being 'sure-footed, treading securely'. The earliest form is *slow and sure*, in which the two adjectives are complementary rather than contrastive; and the adverbial form *slowly and* (or *but*) *surely* is also common. *Slow but sure* makes an early appearance in the proverb *God's mill grinds slow but sure*, recorded in the *Outlandish Proverbs* of George Herbert published posthumously in 1640. *17th cent.*

> Thomas Paine *The American Crisis* 1780
> *Immediately after the battle of Germantown, the probability of Burgoyne's defeat gave a new policy to affairs in Pennsylvania, and it was judged most consistent with the general safety of America, to wait the issue of the northern campaign. Slow and sure is sound work.*

> Dickens *Great Expectations* 1861
> *I was slow to gain strength, but I did slowly and surely become less weak, and Joe stayed with me, and I fancied I was little Pip again.*

smack

have/take a smack at something

informal to make a determined attempt at something: based on the meaning of *smack* 'a blow or hit' in cricket or other ball games. *See also* have/take a SLAP at something. *19th cent.*

a smack in the eye/face

informal a rebuke or insult. *19th cent.*

> Arthur Pinero *The Second Mrs Tanqueray* 1895
> *Of course, it's my duty, as an old friend, to give you a good talking to ... but really I've found one gets so many smacks in the face through interfering in matrimonial squabbles that I've determined to drop it.*

small

it's a small world

(proverb) used to express surprise at a coincidence, especially an unexpected encounter with an acquaintance. *19th cent.*

> Henry Esmond *One Summer's Day* 1901
> [Chiara] *It's a small world, Captain Rudyard.*
> [Dick] *You've not forgotten me.* [Chiara] *Not much! Wasn't it good of me not to speak to you before all your fine friends?*

the small hours

the early hours of the morning after midnight: so called from the low or 'small' numbers from one o'clock onwards. *19th cent.*

> George Eliot *Middlemarch* 1872
> *That night after twelve o'clock Mary Garth relieved the watch in Mr. Featherstone's room, and sat there alone through the small hours.*

small is beautiful

something small can be just as good as – or even better than – a larger version of it: used as a slogan by conservationists and picked up by advertisers. The phrase was popularized as the title of a book by the Oxford-educated German economist and writer E F Schumacher (1911–77) published in 1973. The book bore the subtitle *A Study of Economics as if People Mattered*, and it became a benchmark of the New Age movement. *Late 20th cent.*

> *She* 1989
> *For an international movement that still rates 'small is beautiful' as one of the most glorious clichés of the 20th century, the Earth Summit is quite improbably big.*

the small print

the more detailed provisions of a contract or other legal document, often appearing obscurely in small print and likely to cause trouble in the future by being disregarded or overlooked. There are early references in the literal sense to print so small as to be difficult to read, but usage with the modern implication of deception or at least concealment is more recent. *Mid 20th cent.*

> *Independent* 1989
> *Legal expenses insurance generally tends to be full of small print and exclusions.*

See also no/small/little WONDER; small potatoes *at* POTATO; SWEAT the small stuff.

smart

(as) smart as paint

extremely clever or quick-witted. The simile plays on the meanings of *smart*: a coat of new paint is a good way of smartening up a room or building fairly readily. *19th cent.*

R L Stevenson *Treasure Island* 1883
Now, Hawkins, you do me justice with the cap'n. You're a lad, you are, but you're as smart as paint. I see that when you first came in.

get smart
informal, chiefly NAmer to be cheeky or impertinent. *Mid 20th cent.*

John Steinbeck *The Grapes of Wrath* 1939
'Joe, is this the fella that hit you?' The dazed man stared sickly at Casy. 'Don't look like him.' 'It was me, all right,' Casy said. 'You got smart with the wrong fella.'

look smart
informal to act quickly or promptly. Typically used in the imperative, and extended to *look smart about it!* 18th cent.

Colley Cibber *Love Makes a Man* 1701
I would have you change your Taylor, and dress a little more en Cavalier: Lay by your Book, and take out your Snuff-box, Cock, and look smart, hah!

Roald Dahl *Matilda* 1989
'Where is Bruce Bogtrotter?' A hand shot up among the seated children. 'Come up here!' the Trunchbull shouted. 'And look smart about it!' An eleven-year-old boy who was decidedly large and round stood up and waddled briskly forward. He climbed up on to the platform.

a smart alec(k)
informal, originally NAmer somebody who is ostentatiously and irritatingly clever or knowledgeable; a know-all. Was there an original Alec who was smart? It is unlikely, although G L Cohen, in *Studies in Slang* (1985), has sought to identify him with Alex Hoag, a New York thief of the 1840s who took enormous risks but bought his way out of trouble by having paid accomplices within the police department. But in that case, why don't we sometimes hear of a smart *alex*? (In the earliest evidence, which dates from the 1860s onwards, the forms found are *Aleck* and *Alick*, with capital initials, and *Alec* makes its appearance after the turn of the century.) It makes a good story but the identification can be no more than speculative. Lower-case forms are recorded from the 1930s. *Cf* a CLEVER dick. *19th cent.*

J H Beadle *The Undeveloped West* 1873
I had the pleasure of seeing at least a score of 'smart Alecks' relieved of their surplus catch.

James Forbes *The Traveling Salesman* 1908
Ain't you the cute little smart Alec? That joke was old when my grandfather wuz alive!

smell

come out/up smelling of roses/violets
to survive a difficult situation or process with some credit. The image is clear from the fuller form of the phrase, which begins *fall in a dungheap* (or *the shit*) *and come* .... A related expression, *everything's coming up roses* meaning 'everything has turned out well' (*see* come up roses *at* ROSE), draws on the same image. *Mid 20th cent.*

Financial Times 1983
Said one employee at the factory: 'He's made a harsh decision. From his view it's probably right, but I don't think he should come out smelling of roses. He's paid to take the knocks.'

Fiona Pitt-Kethley *Misfortunes of Nigel* 1991
What he really needed to come out of this marriage smelling of roses was a lucky accident. Then Gina could become a beautiful memory.

smell blood
to discover a vulnerable point in an opponent or rival, and prepare to attack. The image is of an animal that is able to find a wounded prey from the smell of its blood. *19th cent.*

Rider Haggard *King Solomon's Mines* 1885
Are your senses awake, Isanusis – can ye smell blood, can ye purge the land of the wicked ones who compass evil against the king and against their neighbors?

smell a rat
informal to begin to suspect a trick or deception. The image is of a cat knowing a rat is present from its smell without being able to see it. *16th cent.*

Thomas Heywood *A Mayden-head Well Lost* 1634
I like not this: I smell a rat.

(stop and) smell the roses
informal, originally NAmer to enjoy life's transitory pleasures. *Mid 20th cent.*

Washington Post 1957
Don't worry, don't hurry. You're only on this earth for a visit so stop and smell the flowers.

See also smell of the LAMP.

smile

come up smiling
informal to emerge cheerfully from a difficult experience or misfortune: originally used of a boxer ready to start a new round after being worsted in a previous one. *19th cent.*

Mark Twain *The Adventures of Huckleberry Finn* 1884
We didn't cook none of the pies in the washpan, afraid the solder would melt; but Uncle Silas he had a noble brass warming-pan which he thought considerable of ... and we snaked her out, private, and took her down there, but she failed on the first pies, because we didn't know how, but she come up smiling on the last one.

See also WIPE the smile off somebody's face.

smoke

go up in smoke
1 *informal* (said of a plan or undertaking) to come to nothing; to be abandoned. *Mid 20th cent.*

Daily Mirror 1992
A polo sponsorship deal won by Major Ron Ferguson has gone up in smoke – only weeks after Fergie's topless snaps were revealed. Tobacco company Davidoff Cigarettes is dropping its £30,000 cash backing for Major Ron's Royal Berkshire Polo Club and supporting its rivals Cowdray Park instead.

2 *informal* to lose one's temper. *Mid 20th cent.*

Mary Gervaise *The Distance Enchanted* 1993
I hope the chemist will send up the things tonight ... Matron will go up in smoke if he doesn't.

smoke and mirrors
an elaborate and misleading explanation: with allusion to the use of smoke and mirrors by a conjuror. *20th cent.*

Keesings Contemporary Archives 1992
The Democratic chairman of the House of Representatives budget committee, Leon E. Panetta, described the package as 'gimmickry' and accused the administration of using 'smoke and mirrors' in order to finance its tax cuts and spending initiatives.

smoke like a chimney
to smoke tobacco heavily. *19th cent.*

Louisa M Alcott *Hospital Sketches* 1869
If John had been a gentlemanly creature, with refined tastes, he would have elevated his feet, and made a nuisance of himself by indulging in a 'weed'; but being only an uncultivated youth, with a rustic regard for pure air and womankind in general, he kept his head uppermost, and talked like a man, instead of smoking like a chimney.

there's no smoke without fire
(proverb) a rumour or report usually has some basis in fact. The notion occurs earlier in (13th cent.) French: *nul feu est sens fumee ne fumee sens feu* ('no fire is without smoke, and no smoke is without fire'), and is found in English in various forms from the 15th cent. *No smoke but some fire* occurs in the 17th cent., and the current form dates from the 19th cent.

Dickens *Hard Times* 1854
Nor could any such spectator fail to know ... that these men, through their very delusions, showed great qualities, susceptible of being turned to the happiest and best account; and that to pretend (on the strength of sweeping axioms, howsoever cut and dried) that they went astray wholly without cause, and of their own irrational wills, was to pretend that there could be smoke without fire.

watch my smoke
NAmer, informal a boast of prompt and quick action: probably with reference to the smoke or dust raised by rapid movement or activity. *Early 20th cent.*

P G Wodehouse *Meet Mr Mulliner* 1927
'You are a curate, eh?' 'At present. But,' said Augustine, tapping his companion on the chest, 'just watch my smoke.'

See also a smoking GUN.

smooth

See smooth somebody's ruffled feathers *at* RUFFLE.

snake

a snake in one's bosom

a friend or protégé(e) who betrays a benefactor: from the notion of a woman nursing a poisonous snake in her bosom. The phrase is also found with *adder* and *viper* instead of *snake*, and the concept can be found as a symbol of treachery as early as Cicero in the 1st cent. BC (*Oratio de Haruspicum Responsis* xxiv.50: in Latin *in sinu viperam habere*). In English the notion dates from Middle English, and the phrase occurs in its developed form by the 17th cent.

Chaucer *The Merchant's Tale* (line 1786)
O servant traytour, false hoomly hewe, | *Lyk to the naddre* [= adder, serpent] *in bosom sly untrewe,* | *God shilde us alle from youre aqueyntaunce!*

Shakespeare *2 Henry VI* III.i.343 (1591)
[York] *I fear me you but warm the starvèd snake,* | *Who, cherished in your breasts, will sting your hearts.*

Charles Gildon *The Post-boy Rob'd of his Mail* 1692
This Gentleman's Wisdom, (said Temple) like that of most young men, is bought at his own expence. Young, or old, (return'd Winter) we often, by our Unskilfulness in men, cherish a snake in our bosom.

Boswell *The Life of Samuel Johnson* 1791
There lurks, perhaps, in every human heart a desire of distinction, which inclines every man first to hope, and then to believe, that nature has given him something peculiar to himself ... Every desire is a viper in the bosom, who, while he was chill, was harmless; but when warmth gave him strength, exerted it in poison.

a snake in the grass

a secretly untrustworthy or treacherous person: ultimately from Virgil, *Eclogues* III.93: *latet anguis in herba* ('a snake is lurking in the grass'). An earlier version of the same idea, now obsolete, was *a pad* [= toad] *in the straw*. The current phrase is the title of a work by Charles Leslie (1697). *17th cent.*

Wilkie Collins *The Moonstone* 1868
In plain English, I didn't at all relish the notion of helping his inquiries, when those inquiries took him (in the capacity of snake in the grass) among my fellow-servants.

snap

in a snap

very quickly, in a moment: based on the meaning of *snap* 'a sudden or quick movement' (also the basis of the name of the card game). *18th cent.*

Alexander Ross *Helenore* 1768
An' now the fead [= feud] *is softn'd ... The face o' things is alter'd in a snap.*

Anna Sewell *Black Beauty* 1877
One day he was at this game, and did not know that the master was in the next field; but he was there, watching what was going on: over the hedge he jumped in a snap, and catching Dick by the arm, he gave him such a box on the ear as made him roar with the pain and surprise.

snap out of it

informal to shake off a bad mood, to stop being miserable or sulky: often used in the imperative. In the early 20th cent. *snap* was used more freely in meanings denoting sudden or prompt changes of position or behaviour, occurring in the form *snap into* as well as *snap out of*. *Early 20th cent.*

David Lodge *Nice Work* 1988
'Essentially it's the idea that unconsciously we all long for death, for non-being, because being is so painful.' 'I often feel like that at five o'clock in the morning,' said Wilcox. 'But I snap out of it when I get up.'

See also bite/snap somebody's HEAD off; snap one's fingers *at* FINGER.

snappy

look / make it snappy

informal to act quickly or promptly. *Snappy* (a derivative of *snap*) has several meanings to do with neatness and conciseness; the one involved here is predominantly the 19th cent. meaning 'sudden, instantaneous', but it is also influenced by some of the other meanings. *Early 20th cent.*

Robert Kelly *The Loom* 1975
Make it snappy – I have | *a fantasy scheduled for* | *eleven.*

sneeze

not to be sneezed at

worth considering or taking seriously. The expression is now always used in negative contexts, but *sneeze at* was formerly also used positively with the meaning 'to despise or disregard.' *18th cent.*

> **George Colman Ygr *The Heir At Law* 1798**
> *Well, come, two hundred pounds, now a days, are not to be sneezed at, consider how consoling it is, my dear Miss, to think that with good management, it may be a matter of two years before you are left without a penny in the whole wide world.*

> **Rider Haggard *King Solomon's Mines* 1885**
> *'Sir Henry,' said I, 'this is the most liberal offer I ever had, and one not to be sneezed at by a poor hunter and trader. But the job is the biggest I ever came across, and I must take time to think it over.'*

snook

See cock a snook at somebody *at* COCK².

snow

See (as) PURE as the driven snow.

snowball

See not a snowball's chance in hell *at* not a hope/chance in HELL.

snuff

up to snuff

informal meeting the required standard. The phrase originates in the early 19th cent., when snuff-taking was common. It referred originally to people's wits or intelligence, and rapidly broadened into the more general meaning 'up to standard, satisfactory'. In more recent use it often means 'in good health'. *Cf* up to SCRATCH. *19th cent.*

> **Trollope *Doctor Thorne* 1858**
> *'Why, you see, I haven't exactly popped to her yet; but I have been doing the civil; and if she's up to snuff, as I take her to be, she knows very well what I'm after by this time.' Up to snuff! Mary Thorne, his Mary, up to snuff! To snuff too of such a very disagreeable description!*

> **John Mortimer *Summer's Lease* 1988**
> *She and Carlo were staying a night, possibly two nights, because Carlo hadn't felt up to snuff all the summer (here young Carlo groaned wearily and*

leant against a wall in confirmation of his feeling considerably below snuff).

snug

(as) snug as a bug (in a rug)

humorous very comfortable: also in early use in other rhyming or alliterative forms, e.g. *as snug as a bee in a box. 18th cent.*

> **Thomas Bracken *His Majesty's Throne* 1886**
> *The poor little colleen fell head over heels in love wid me, and I didn't know what to do … bekays I'm a married man, an' Molly is mighty jealous, so she is. Be the hokey she made me as snug as a bug in a rug, an sure enuff I was begining to get fond of her whin his Majesty discovered our saycrit, an' thin ther' was the devil to pay.*

so

so be it

used to express resigned or reluctant acceptance of an event or situation: originally a translation of *Amen* used to conclude a prayer. *Be* here is the subjunctive form of the verb. *16th cent.*

> **Robert Greene *Menaphon* 1589**
> *If they be so wise quoth Menaphon, they shew but their mother witts; for what sparkes they have of inconstancie, they drawe from their female fosterers, as the Sea dooth ebbes and tides from the Moone. So be it sir answered Pesana, then no doubt your mother was made of a Weather cocke, that brought foorth such a wavering companion.*

See also and so FORTH.

soap

no soap

informal, chiefly NAmer there is no chance of a particular thing happening: used to announce unwillingness to comply. The origin may lie in a nonsense passage said to have been devised as a memory test by the English actor and playwright Samuel Foote (1720–77), given in Maria Edgeworth's collection of lessons for children called *Harry and Lucy Concluded* (1825): 'Harry observed how much more easy he found it to learn lines which he understood, than to get by heart lists of names … Their father said he would, if they liked it, try the experiment, by repeating for them some sentences of droll nonsense, which were put together by Mr Foote, a humorous writer, for the purpose of trying the memory of a man, who boasted that he could learn any thing by rote, on once hearing it ... Harry's power of attention, which he had prepared himself to exert to the utmost, was set completely at defiance, when his father, as fast as he could utter the words, repeated the following nonsense, abruptly beginning with – "So she went into the garden to cut a cabbage-leaf to make an apple-pie; and at the same time a great she-bear coming up the street, pops its head into the shop. 'What, no soap?' So he died, and she very imprudently married the barber; and there were present the Picninnies, and the Joblillies, and the Garyulies, and the grand Panjandrum himself, with the little round button at top; and they all fell to playing the game of catch as catch can, till the gun powder ran out at the heels of their boots."' *Early 20th cent.*

not know — from a bar of soap
Australian, informal to be completely unacquainted with a person. *Early 20th cent.*

> Simon Brett *Murder Unprompted* 1984
> *Whereas Charles Paris, who knew that he had given one of the best performances of his career in The Hooded Owl, was a name that the punters wouldn't know from a bar of soap.*

sober

(as) sober as a judge
completely sober. An alternative form *as grave as a judge* is recorded in the 17th cent. *18th cent.*

> Henry Fielding *Don Quixote in England* 1734
> *Oons, Sir! do you say that I am drunk? I say, Sir, that I am as sober as a Judge; and if any Man says that I am drunk, Sir, he's a Liar, and a Son of a Whore. My Dear, an't I – sober now?*

sock¹ (noun)

knock/blow somebody's socks off
informal to impress or overwhelm somebody greatly. To *knock the socks off somebody* also means 'to defeat or trounce somebody.' *19th cent.*

pull one's socks up
informal to make a determined effort to improve or reform. The image is of smartening one's appearance and avoiding sloppiness. Early use

around the turn of the 19th–20th cent. appears from the printed evidence to have been more trivial in tone and less admonitory than it is now. *19th cent.*

> H F McClelland *Jack and the Beanstalk* 1893
> *Pull up your socks! I'll see naught goes wrong with you.*

put a sock in it
British, informal to stop talking, especially when one has been talking tediously or at length: often used in the imperative. The notion is of a sock or mute being put in the end of a musical instrument to soften or deaden the sound it produces. *Early 20th cent.*

> J B Priestley *The Good Companions* 1929
> *Two or three members of his audience laughed, but a young man in a green cloth cap was very annoyed. 'Oh, put a sock in it,' he said to the ripe gentleman, who immediately and very loudly asked him what he meant by it.*

sock² (verb)

sock it to somebody
informal, chiefly NAmer to speak or act forcefully or impressively: literally, to deliver an effective blow in a fight. *Sock it to me* became a popular catchphrase in the late 1960s as a result of its use in a weekly American television comedy show called *Rowan and Martin's Laugh-in*, but the phrase is a lot older, and can be traced back to the 1860s, the time of the American Civil War. There is an obvious connection with *sock* = hit, and the context that suggests itself is a ball game of some kind. To *give somebody sock*, meaning to thrash them, dates from about the same time. *19th cent.*

> John William De Forest *Kate Beaumont* 1872
> *'I want to make him miserable,' she continued. 'I've no objection,' observed Bent, lighting a cigar, and watching her through the smoke. 'Sock it to him.'*

sod

Sod's law
the principle that if anything can go wrong, it will (*see* ANYTHING): also called *Murphy's law* (*see* MURPHY). *Sod* is abbreviated from *Sodomite* and has been widely used since the 19th cent. as a (now relatively mild) term of abuse and swear

word. In the phrase it is personified. Late 20th
cent.

Financial Times 1985
Since pen first hit paper (or rather finger hit
microprocessor) the weather outside my window
has changed from the soggy gloom that inspired
those first thoughts to the sort of crisp clear iciness
that I suggested was never seen in London. Sod's
law, of course. But I still reckon New York is a great
place to be in winter.

soft

(as) soft as butter

easily swayed or persuaded. The phrase plays on
two meanings of *soft*: the physical meaning and
the figurative meaning 'readily influenced, compliant.' *18th cent.*

Smollett The Expedition of Humphry Clinker 1771
She is a poor good-natured simpleton, as soft as
butter, and as easily melted – not that she's a fool.

be soft on somebody/something

1 *informal, originally NAmer* to have amorous feelings towards somebody. *19th cent.*

A R Calhoun The Color Guard 1870
I know Sam Roberts has allus been soft on me, an'
I've been soft on him; you'd be soft on him, too, Miss
Gurusha, if you was me. Sam is the best felloh.
2 to treat somebody or something leniently. *19th*
cent.

have a soft spot for somebody

to have feelings of affection or sentimental weakness towards somebody: originally *have a soft spot*
in one's heart (or *head*). *17th cent.*

C M Yonge Dynevor Terrace 1857
Jane has a soft spot in her heart, and will not think
true love is confined within the rank that keeps a
gig.
See also a soft TOUCH.

soldier

come the old soldier (over somebody)

informal to use one's age and experience to take
advantage of others or to avoid one's responsibilities. First uses in literature are in Sir Walter
Scott (see below) and Thomas Hughes, *Tom*
Brown at Oxford (1861). The phrase was evidently
familiar in the services, despite its disparaging

overtones, in the early years of the 20th cent.:
Fraser and Gibbons record it in their *Soldier and*
Sailor Words (1925). *Old soldier*, in the sense of a
person who is experienced or affects to be so in a
world-weary or exploitative way, is a use dating
from the 18th cent. *19th cent.*

Scott St Ronan's Well 1824
Were it not that I think he has scarce the impudence
to propose such a thing to succeed, curse me but I
should think he was coming the old soldier over me,
and keeping up his game.

some

and then some

informal, chiefly NAmer and more besides. *Early*
20th cent.

something

make something of —

to make good use of something; to use it effectively. *19th cent.*

Jane Austen Mansfield Park 1814
We cannot have two Agathas, and we must have one
Cottager's wife; and I am sure I set her the example
of moderation myself in being satisfied with the old
Butler. If the part is trifling she will have more
credit in making something of it.

make something of oneself/somebody

to succeed in life, or help somebody to succeed.
18th cent.

Fanny Burney Evelina 1778
She told them that she had it in her head to make
something of me.

something tells me

I have a certain impression or feeling: typically
followed by a clause with or without *that*. *16th*
cent.

Shakespeare The Merchant of Venice III.ii.4 (1598)
[Portia to Bassanio] I pray you tarry. Pause a day
or two | Before you hazard, for in choosing wrong |
I lose your company. Therefore forbear a while. |
There's something tells me – but it is not love – | I
would not lose you.

son

son of —

humorous a derivative or later version of something well known: from its common use as the title of a sequel to a book or film, e.g. *Son of Tarzan* (1929), *Son of Kong* (1934). *Early 20th cent.*

son of a bitch

informal a term of abuse used of a man. Now most common in the US, and in spellings such as *sonofabitch, sonuvabitch*, etc. The expression is occasionally found in the double plural form *sons of bitches*. There is a similar notion in more compositional form in Shakespeare's *King Lear* (1606) II.ii.21, where the Earl of Kent describes Goneril's steward Oswald as 'one that ... art nothing but the composition of a knave, beggar, coward, pander [= pimp], and the son and heir of a mongrel bitch'. *18th cent.*

> John Shirley *The Triumph of Wit* 1707
> *There stands Jack Ketch, that Son of a Bitch, that owes us all a grudge.*

> Byron *Letter* 1818
> *The Son of a Bitch [Southey] on his return from Switzerland two years ago – said that Shelley and I 'had formed a League of Incest and practised our precepts with &c' – he lied like a rascal.*

son of a gun

informal an affectionate term for a man or boy: originally applied to baby boys born at sea, who were accommodated near the midship guns. *18th cent.*

> Samuel Derrick *A Collection of Original Poems* 1755
> *Heavy port makes us sad, | Champagne makes us mad, | And geneva drives folks into heinous-sin; | But no harm was e'er done, | By that son of a gun, | Who walks off with his skinful of Dennison.*

song

for a song

informal for very little cost: from the practice of selling old songs cheaply at fairs. Shakespeare in *All's Well That Ends Well* (1603) III.ii.9 uses *song* in the meaning 'trivial amount' when he makes the clown Lavatch say to the Countess 'I know a man that had this trick of melancholy sold a goodly manner for a song.' *17th cent.*

give/make a song and dance (about something)

to make a great fuss about something straightforward or simple. *19th cent.*

on (full) song

doing well; being successful: chiefly used in commercial contexts and in journalism. *Mid 20th cent.*

sop

a sop to Cerberus

something offered to placate or propitiate somebody whose help one needs: with allusion to the three-headed dog named Cerberus who guarded the entrance to Hades in Greek mythology. Aeneas on his descent to Hades, as described by Virgil in the *Aeneid* (vi.417), is told to give Cerberus a specially drugged cake. There are references to Cerberus as the guardian of Hades in English earlier than the emergence of the phrase in the form given: for example, in Chaucer's *The Monk's Tale* (line 3292): 'He [Hercules] drow out Cerberus, the hound of helle.' The phrase occurs regularly in 17th cent. drama in the original context, and from this use a figurative and allusive use developed, as in Congreve below. *17th cent.*

> Congreve *Love for Love* I.iv.17 (1695)
> *Bid Trapland come in. If I can give that Cerberus a sop, I shall be at rest for one day.*

sorcerer

a sorcerer's apprentice

a person who is unable to put a stop to a process they have been responsible for starting. *The Sorcerer's Apprentice* is the name of a symphonic poem (in French *l'Apprenti sorcier*) by Paul Dukas (1865–1935), itself based on a ballad of Goethe (*Der Zauberlehrling*, 1797). In the story, a sorcerer leaves his apprentice to mind his workshop and returns to find that the apprentice has uttered all sorts of spells to which he does not know the countermanding instruction, causing chaos. A cartoon version of the story, with Dukas's music and Mickey Mouse as the apprentice, formed a particularly memorable part of Walt Disney's film *Fantasia* (1940). *Mid 20th cent.*

sore

a sore point
a point or issue that is contentious: the words occur earlier (16th cent.) by chance in the meaning 'a cause of pain or distress.' *19th cent.*

> George Eliot *Middlemarch* 1872
> *The affair of the chaplaincy remained a sore point in his memory as a case in which this petty medium of Middlemarch had been too strong for him.*

stand/stick out like a sore thumb
(especially of something ugly or unwelcome) to be glaringly obvious. *Mid 20th cent.*

See also a SIGHT for sore eyes.

sorrow

more in sorrow than anger
(said especially of actions) undertaken because one is sad or regretful about something rather than angry: with allusion to Shakespeare, *Hamlet* (1601) I.ii.229, where Horatio tells Hamlet that the ghost of Hamlet's father had 'a countenance more in sorrow than in anger'. Allusive uses date from the 18th cent. and feature noticeably in the work of women writers: Fanny Burney (1752–1840, see below), Sarah Fielding (1710–68, sister of Henry Fielding), and Mrs Ann Radcliffe (1764–1823).

> Fanny Burney *Cecilia* 1782
> *Fixing his eyes upon Cecilia, with an expression more in sorrow than in anger, after contemplating her some time in silence, he exclaimed, 'Ah lovely, but perishable flower! how long will that ingenuous countenance, wearing, because wanting no disguise, look responsive of the whiteness of the region within?'*

See also DROWN one's sorrows.

sort

The earliest (13th cent.) sense in English relates to a person's fate or fortune in life. It is derived from Latin *sors*, which had the same meaning, originally denoting a wooden piece used for drawing lots. Chaucer used it to mean 'destiny' or 'fate' more generally, but by this time another strand of meaning had developed, 'a kind or type', and this is found in Chaucer too (in *The Cook's Tale*, line 4381): '[He] gadered hym a meynee [= company] of his sort, | To hoppe and synge and maken swich [= such] disport.'

it takes all sorts
(proverb) people have different characters and behave and act differently: in full *it takes all sorts to make a world*. *17th cent.*

not a bad sort
quite a good or worthy person: the use of *sort* with a qualifying word dates from the 16th cent. *19th cent.*

out of sorts
not in good health or spirits; not feeling well. The sense of *sort* here is uncertain. It could plausibly refer to printers' type, which was organized or 'sorted' into compartments called *sorts* according to the typeface; but this sense is not recorded for some fifty years after the first recorded occurrence (in 1621) of the phrase, and we would expect *out of sorts* to be used first in a printing context if it were the true origin. In fact the opposite seems to be the case: in the 1780s the American Benjamin Franklin, who was a printer and publisher as well as a statesman and diplomat, used our phrase in a punning way in a printing context, which suggests that the phrase already existed in its own right: 'The founts, too, must be very scanty, or strangely out of sorts.' Another possibility is that it originates in card games, in which a deck that was not properly shuffled was said to be 'out of sort'. But there is no evidence that the phrase was used in this way. *17th cent.*

> Humphrey Mill *A Night's Search* 1640
> *Thus long she liv'd, through guile she many won | To serve her ends, and so they were undone, | But yet at last, she growing out of sorts, | To feed the streame, and keep her Venus sports.*

> Thomas Rymer *A Short View of Tragedy* 1692
> *Who would thrust into a crowd to hear what Mr. Iago, Roderigo, or Cassio, is like to say? From a Venetian Senate, or a Roman Senate one might expect great matters: But their Poet was out of sorts; he had it not for them; the Senators must be no wiser than other folk.*

See also separate / sort out the MEN from the boys.

soul

Underlying many of the phrases given here is the image of the soul (often coupled with the heart: see HEART and soul) as the seat of the emotions and human nature, which goes back to Old English. The sense of *soul* referring to an individual human being (chiefly in enumeration or with an emotive adjective attached) is common from Middle English, and occurs in Chaucer (*The Parliament of Fowls*, line 33: 'This bok of which I make mencioun ... Chapitres sevene it hadde, of hevene and helle | And erthe, and soules that therinne dwelle'), and in Coverdale.

bare / lay bare one's soul
to reveal one's true feelings. *19th cent.*

> James Fenimore Cooper *The Bravo* 1831
> *He has laid bare his soul to me, as one whose feet were in the grave; and, though offending, like all born of woman, towards his God, he is guiltless as respects the state.*

have no soul
to be lacking in fine feelings or understanding. *17th cent.*

> Dryden *Cleomenes, the Spartan Hero* 1692
> *Alas! Ptolomy has no Soul, | 'Tis what he wants, I love in Cleomenes.*

a lost soul
a person who is unable to cope with the difficulties of life: a figurative use of the sense referring to a person damned in the afterlife. *19th cent.*

> Kate Chopin *The Awakening* 1899
> *I've been working like a machine, and feeling like a lost soul. There was nothing interesting.*

not able to call one's soul one's own
totally dependent on or controlled by somebody else. *16th cent.*

See also be the LIFE and soul of the party; BREVITY is the soul of wit; SELL one's soul.

sound

See (as) clear/sound as a BELL.

soup

in the soup
informal, originally NAmer in serious difficulty or trouble. *19th cent.*

sour

sour grapes
an attitude of disparagement towards something that another person possesses or has achieved when one cannot attain it oneself. From the fable (attributed to Aesop) of the fox who desires a bunch of grapes but rejects them as sour-looking when he finds he cannot reach them. *18th cent.*

> Arthur Murphy *The Way To Keep Him* 1760
> *She stands watering at the mouth, and a pretty fellow that, says she. – Ay, ay, gaze on, says I, gaze on; – I see what you would be at: – You'd be glad to have me, – You'd be glad to have me! – But sour grapes, my dear! I'll go home and cherish my own lovely Wanton.*

SOW[1] (female pig, rhymes with *cow*)

have the right/wrong sow by the ear
(proverb) to have understood a situation correctly (or incorrectly). *16th cent.*

See also make a SILK purse out of a sow's ear.

SOW[2] (verb, rhymes with *so*)

sow the seed(s) of something
to start a process that will eventually develop into something much larger or more worthwhile. The figurative use of *seed* in the sense of the hidden or latent start of a process of development dates from Old English; early uses of this phrase are romantic in tone and often refer explicitly to love as the flower that will blossom from the seed (see the Chaucer quotation below). *Middle English*

> Chaucer *The Romaunt of the Rose* (line 1617)
> *For Venus sone, daun [= Dan = Sir] Cupido, | Hath sowen there of love the seed.*

See also sow one's wild oats *at* OAT.

space

watch this space
an instruction to watch out for developments in a situation or process: literally, to keep looking in the advertising pages of a newspaper or magazine for further information to be posted there. *Early 20th cent.*

spade

call a spade a spade
to speak frankly or bluntly: literally, to call something by its proper name. The use of *spade* is based on a mistranslation of an analogous phrase in Plutarch's *Apophthegmata*. Plutarch (1st–2nd cent. AD) used the Greek word *skaphe* meaning 'bowl' or 'basin', which Erasmus evidently confused with *skapheion*, derived from *skaphein* meaning 'to dig', turning it into Latin as *ligo* meaning 'mattock'; this in turn was translated by the dramatist and scholar Nicholas Udall (1542) into English as 'spade'. In an essay of Lucian of Samosata (Syrian Greek, 2nd cent. AD), the phrase appears in the fuller form 'to call a fig a fig and a bowl a bowl'; presumably there is a connection intended here between the fruit and its receptacle. In antiquity the phrase was used to characterize the bluntness of the Macedonians as compared with the refinement of the Greeks of the city-states. The English phrase has come into disfavour, especially in America, because of its real or imagined association with the racial sense of *spade* (which, as it happens, is based on an entirely different word, the card suit *spades*); but it is still common in British use. *16th cent.*

> Stephen Gosson The Ephemerides of Phialo 1579
> *The pardon he craves is for his simplicitie, which hath beene somewhat homely brought up like a rude Macedon, and taught to call a spade, a spade without any glosing.*

spades

in spades
informal, originally NAmer in the extreme; to a high degree: an odd phrase derived from the status of spades as the highest rank in bridge and other card games. *Early 20th cent.*

Spanish

old Spanish customs/practices
questionable or unorthodox working practices that have long been established. The phrase was prominently used in the 1980s with reference to practices of the Fleet Street print unions. The relevance of Spain is unclear, although it may have something to do with the *mañana* reputation of procrastination popularly associated with that country. *Mid 20th cent.*

spank

spank the monkey
informal to masturbate: usually with male reference, although *monkey* is a slang term for both the male and the female genital organs. *Spank* here refers to stimulation with the hand. *Late 20th cent.*

spanner

throw/put a spanner in the works
informal to halt or wreck a plan, process, etc by a mischievous or damaging intervention. The phrase occurs earlier (1920s) with *monkey wrench* instead of *spanner*, and this form is reflected in the title of a novel by Edward Abbey (*The Monkey Wrench Gang*, 1974), with reference to acts of industrial sabotage. *Mid 20th cent.*

spare

(and) to spare
more than is needed; left over. *18th cent.*

> Thomas Betterton The Amorous Widow 1706
> *No, no, I have my belly full, I thank you, and some to spare.*

go spare
1 *informal* to become extremely angry or distraught. *Mid 20th cent.*
2 *informal* to remain unused or not needed. *Mid 20th cent.*

spare no expense
to pay whatever is needed. *Spare no cost* appears in the preamble to an Act of Parliament of Henry VII of England (1491); otherwise the evidence comes predominantly from the literature of the 19th cent.

> Maria Edgeworth Tales of Fashionable Life 1809
> *My foster-brother's cause, or, as it was now generally called, Lord Glenthorn's cause, came on to be tried. I spared no expense, I spared no exertions.*

See also spare somebody's blushes *at* BLUSH; spare the ROD.

spark

sparks (will) fly

there is (or will be) excited discussion or activity. *Early 20th cent.*

strike sparks (off each other / one another)

(said of two or more people) to stimulate one another's imagination or activity when working together. *19th cent.*

> Harold Frederic *The Damnation of Theron Ware* 1896
> *He searched his brain now for some clever quip that would strike sparks from the adamantine mood which for the moment it was her whim to assume.*

speak

speak well for somebody/something

to show somebody or something in a favourable light. *19th cent.*

> Richard Cumberland *A Hint to Husbands* 1806
> *It speaks well for your candour, worthy sir; | And by the same rule I must plead my humour | For having married, though you all prefer | A life of singleness and liberty.*

speak as one finds

to make judgements on the basis of personal experience. *16th cent.*

> Shakespeare *The Taming of the Shrew* II.i.66 (1592)
> [Petruccio] *I see you do not mean to part with her, | Or else you like not of my company.* [Baptista] *Mistake me not, I speak but as I find. | Whence are you, sir? What may I call your name?*

speak for oneself

to give an opinion as one's own or speak on one's own behalf. *Speak for yourself* is a common rejoinder used by somebody addressing another whose opinion or attitude they do not subscribe to or feel included by. *18th cent.*

> Charles Johnstone *Chrysal* 1760
> *I laid out nothing but what I thought necessary, and I charged nothing but what I laid out: I mean not to arraign the conduct of others; I only speak for myself.*

speak in/with tongues

to be inspired by religious fervour to speak in a language one does not know. The practice, called *glossolalia* and now associated with charismatic

forms of Christianity, is attributed to the apostles in Acts (e.g. 10:46, 19:6; *cf* Paul's first letter to the Corinthians 12:30). *See also* the gift of tongues *at* TONGUE. *16th cent.*

speak volumes

(said of a sign, gesture, circumstance, etc) to be as significant or informative as many words would be. *Volume* is used here in its sense of 'a large book.' *19th cent.*

> Herman Melville *Typee* 1846
> *A regular system of polygamy exists among the islanders, but of a most extraordinary nature, – a plurality of husbands, instead of wives; and this solitary fact speaks volumes for the gentle disposition of the male population.*

See also speak one's MIND; speak of the DEVIL; speak the same LANGUAGE.

spec

on spec

informal in the hope of success, without any firm plan; trusting to chance. *Spec* is a shortening of *speculation* dating from the late 18th cent. in North American use and the early 19th cent. in British use. *19th cent.*

> Dickens *Pickwick Papers* 1837
> *'And of them Dodson and Foggs, as does these sort o' things on spec,' continued Mr. Weller, 'as well as for the other kind and gen'rous people o' the same purfession, as sets people by the ears, free gratis for nothin'.'*

spectre

See a ghost/spectre/skeleton at the FEAST.

speed

up to speed

1 performing at the required rate or standard: originally in physical senses with reference to a sporting animal or a vehicle. *19th cent.*
2 fully briefed or informed on a subject or issue. *Late 20th cent.*

> Herald Express (Torquay) 1999
> *A spokesman for the Police Federation … said: 'The officers have been notified of their reinstatement. The force will be looking at where the best place for them will be and there will be training to be con-*

sidered to bring them up to speed with current legislation.'

See also FULL steam/speed ahead; more HASTE, less speed.

spell

under a/—'s spell
infatuated or greatly influenced by a person or thing, as if under a magic spell. *17th cent.*

Mary Pix *The Innocent Mistress* 1697
O' my Conscience, this charming little Beauclair has me under a Spell, and I shall meet with nothing but Disappointments till I submit to her.

Joseph Conrad *Lord Jim* 1900
The cutter could be seen in the falling darkness under the spell of tide and wind, that for a moment held her bound, and tossing abreast of the ship.

spend
See spend a PENNY.

spick

spick and span
spotlessly clean and tidy; neat and spruce. A shortening of *spick-and-span new*, recorded from the 16th cent. This in turn was an extension of *span-new*, itself derived from Old Norse *spán-nyr* meaning 'chip new'; *spick* is from Dutch *spik-splinternieuw*, literally 'splinter new.' *17th cent.*

Ben Jonson *The Magnetick Lady* 1640
There's nothing vexes me, but that he has staind | My new white sattin Doublet; and bespatter'd | My spick and span silke Stockings, o' the day | They were drawne on.

Head & Kirkman *The English Rogue Described* 1674
He had found him the cunningest knave that ever he met with. These are new tricks indeed, spick and span new, piping hot.

Wilkie Collins *Armadale* 1866
Oh dear, dear! there was the same spick-and-span reception-room for me to wait in, with the neat conservatory beyond, which I saw again and again and again at every other house I went to afterwards.

spike

spike somebody's guns
to take action to thwart somebody's plans or intentions: from the (17th cent.) practice of driving a metal spike through the touch-hole of a captured enemy cannon to make it useless. *19th cent.*

spill

spill the beans
informal to divulge information carelessly or indiscreetly. *Early 20th cent.*

spill one's guts
informal to divulge everything one knows; to confess completely. *Early 20th cent.*

See also CRY over spilt milk.

spin
See spin a YARN.

spirit

be with somebody in spirit
to be thinking about somebody, especially at some important moment, though not present with them. *19th cent.*

Charlotte Brontë *Shirley* 1849
Have you been with me in spirit when I did not see you? Have you entered into my day-dreams, and beheld my brain labouring at its scheme of a future?

enter into the spirit of something
to commit oneself wholeheartedly to an activity. *18th cent.*

Swift *Gulliver's Travels* 1726
I introduced Didymus and Eustathius to Homer, and prevailed on him to treat them better than perhaps they deserved; for he soon found they wanted a genius to enter into the spirit of a poet.

out of spirits
in a gloomy or depressed state. Also *in spirits* = in a cheerful frame of mind. *18th cent.*

Henry Fielding *Amelia* 1752
All the other company assembled at table as usual, where poor Booth was the only person out of spirits. This was imputed by all present to a wrong cause; nay, Miss Mathews herself either could not, or

would not, suspect that there was any thing deeper than the despair of being speedily discharged, that lay heavy on his mind.

the spirit is willing (but the flesh is weak)

one has good principles and good intentions but is vulnerable to human weakness and temptation: with allusion to the words of Christ in the Garden of Gethsemane when he returned from prayer to find his disciples sleeping (Matthew 26:41 'Watch and pray, that ye enter not into temptation: the spirit indeed is willing, but the flesh is weak'). *17th cent.*

the spirit moves (one)

one feels stimulated to do something, especially something important or worthwhile: adopted by the Quakers to refer to the promptings of the Holy Spirit. *17th cent.*

---

spit

be the (dead/very) spit / spitting image of somebody/something

informal to be an exact likeness of a person or thing. The seemingly obscure connection with spitting seems to lie in the bizarre notion that one person could be spat from the mouth of another identical person. There is 17th cent. evidence for the use of the verb *spit* in this meaning, as recorded in a miscellany of sayings and customs called *Wonders Worth Hearing* collected by Nicholas Breton and published in about 1602: 'Two girls, ... the one as like an owl, the other as like an urchin, as if they had been spit out of the mouths of them.' *Spitting image* (early 20th cent.) is a corruption via *spitten image* (early 20th cent., with *spitten picture* from late 19th cent.) of *spit and image* (which dates from the late 19th cent. and also occurs slightly earlier (mid 19th cent.) in the form *spit and fetch*); a form *spit image* (early 20th cent.) is also found. An alternative suggestion, that *spit* is a contraction of *spirit*, in the meaning 'essence or essential character', is an unnecessary and unconvincing piece of rationalization; to have any credibility it would need to be reflected in the forms in which the phrase is used, but no such evidence exists. *19th cent.*

spit and polish

extreme attention to cleanliness and orderliness: with allusion to the use of spit instead of polish to clean boots in the armed services. *19th cent.*

spit and sawdust

(said of a bar or pub) very basic and lacking in comforts: from the former practice of covering the floor of a bar with sawdust into which customers spat. Also used adjectivally, as in *a spit-and-sawdust pub*. *Mid 20th cent.*

spit blood/venom, etc

to express extreme or violent anger. The notion of spitting out noxious and poisonous substances as symbols of violent utterance goes back to Chaucer, whose Pardoner declares in his Prologue (line 421) 'Thus quyte [= have revenge on] I folk that doon us displesances [= make trouble for us]; | Thus spitte I out venym under hewe [= pretence] | Of hoolynesse, to semen [= seem] hooly and trewe.' A 16th cent. source has the line 'Herein they ... spitte oute the poyson of theyr hatred', and there are many colourful references in 17th cent. and 18th cent. literature to spitting out fire and poison. Spitting blood has another connotation of course: as a symptom of disease. A character in Henry Fielding's novel *Amelia* (1752) describes certain injuries he has received and includes among the consequences that 'it caused me to spit blood, and was attended with a fever, and other bad symptoms'. Surprisingly, though, *spitting blood* does not appear in its figurative meaning until the middle of the 20th cent. Meanwhile another strand of meaning appears: in Australian slang from the start of the century, to *spit chips* (early 20th cent.) is to have a raging thirst, and the same sense seems to underlie the more recent variant *spit feathers* (another image of dryness, presumably), although both phrases are often taken, in British use at least and probably mistakenly, to mean the same as *spit blood*, i.e. to be violently angry. This is a good example of a process of linguistic monopoly, whereby a well-established and dominant meaning makes it difficult for other meanings to retain their separate identity without being subsumed into the main one. *Middle English*

spit in the eye/face of somebody/something

to regard something or somebody with contempt or scorn: figurative uses of *spit* in meanings to do with expressing contempt date from the 16th cent. *17th cent.*

spit it out

to admit or confess something with reluctance or difficulty. *19th cent.*

Mrs Gaskell *North and South* 1855
And now dunnot talk to me, but just read out th'
chapter. I'm easier in my mind for having spit it
out; but I want some thoughts of the world that's far
away to take the weary taste of it out o' my mouth.

G W H Griffin *Shylock* 1874
What is your plaint, come, spit it out at once, | This
Christian owes you two-pun-ten?

See also not TRUST somebody as far as one can
throw them / spit; spit into/against the wind *at*
WIND[1].

splash

make a splash
to attract attention or cause a sensation. *19th cent.*

William Dimond *The Sea-side Story* 1801
Then let's agree, like souls of glee, | To share this
scene of gaiety; | To make a splash, to cut a dash.

spleen

See VENT one's spleen on somebody.

split

split the difference
to reach an agreement between two amounts by
taking the average of the two: referred to as a
'vulgar phrase' in a speech by William Pitt the
Elder (1708–78). *18th cent.*

Annual Register 1771
The disagreement … is now amicably settled, by the
splitting the difference between his surveyor's
estimate and that taken by the surveyor for the
executors.

split one's sides / oneself / NAmer a gut
to be overcome by laughter: *split oneself* is the
form that occurs earliest. *17th cent.*

Matthew Stevenson *The Wit's Paraphrased* 1680
When he to me did recommend | All things, but
most his Trojan friend, | I split my sides, and only
said | My Dear, well you shall be Obey'd.

Dickens *Martin Chuzzlewit* 1844
Mr. Jonas was infinitely amused: protesting that he
had seldom seen him better company in all his life,
and that he was enough to make a man split his sides
with laughing.

split the vote
(said of two or more candidates in an election) to
offer similar policies so that votes are split
between them, allowing another candidate to
win. *19th cent.*

See also split hairs *at* HAIR.

spoil

spoilt for choice
offered so many choices that it is difficult to
decide. *Mid 20th cent.*

Alex Nisbett *The Technique of the Sound Studio* 1962
At a radio organization such as the BBC it is easy to
feel spoilt for choice.

See also spoil the SHIP for a ha'porth of tar; too
many cooks spoil the broth *at* COOK.

spoke

put a spoke in somebody's wheel
to prevent somebody's plans from succeeding.
The phrase is said to refer to the spoke or pin put
through a hole in a solid cartwheel to slow it
down when going downhill, and one 17th cent.
source refers to the devil as putting a spoke in
somebody's *cart*. But *spoke* may be a misunderstanding of the Dutch word *spaak* (meaning 'bar'
or 'stave') used in the Dutch form of the phrase.
17th cent.

Fletcher *The Mad Lover* 1617
A thousand cuckolds shall that husband be, | That
marries thee, thou art so mischievous. | Ile put a
spoke among your wheels.

sponge

See THROW in the towel / throw in/up the
sponge.

spoon

make a spoon or spoil a horn
to be resolved to achieve something, whether this
is a success or a failure: from the former Scottish
practice of making spoons out of the horns of
cattle. *19th cent.*

win the wooden spoon
to come last in a race or contest. A wooden spoon
was formerly given to the candidate who came

last in the mathematical tripos examination at Cambridge. *19th cent.*

> **Byron *Don Juan* 1821**
> *Sure my invention must be down at zero, | And I grown one of many 'wooden spoons' | Of verse (the name with which we Cantabs please | To dub the last of honours in degrees).*

See also GREASY spoon.

sport

make sport of/at somebody/something
old use to ridicule a person or thing. *16th cent.*

> **Shakespeare *The Merry Wives of Windsor* III.iii.144 (1597)**
> [Ford to Page, Caius, and Evans] *Pray you come near. If I suspect without cause, why then, make sport at me; then let me be your jest – I deserve it.*

a sporting chance
a reasonable chance of success: originally with reference to the uncertainty associated with the outcome of a sporting event. *19th cent.*

> **Conan Doyle *The Lost World* 1912**
> *'There were powers abroad in earlier days which no courage and no mechanism of his could have met. What could his sling, his throwing-stick, or his arrow avail him against such forces as have been loose tonight? Even with a modern rifle it would be all odds on the monster.' 'I think I should back my little friend,' said Lord John, caressing his Express. 'But the beast would certainly have a good sporting chance.'*

the sport of kings
horse racing and hunting: with reference to the associations of royalty with these sports. The earliest uses referred to war-making. *18th cent.*

spot

hit the spot
informal (said especially of food and drink) to be just what is needed. *19th cent.*

in a (bad/tight) spot
informal experiencing trouble or difficulty. *Early 20th cent.*

knock spots off somebody/something
informal to be or perform very much better than somebody or something. Although of American

origin, the expression has now largely passed to British use: it may allude to the 'spots' or pips on a playing card, which had to be knocked out in a pistol-shooting competition. *19th cent.*

> **John William De Forest *Mrs Ravenel's Conversion* 1867**
> *'What do you think? They ain't going to attack the fort, be they?' Then calling his homespun pomposity to his aid, he added, with a show of bravado, 'I can't see it. They know better. We can knock spots out of 'em.'*

put somebody on the spot
1 *informal* to put somebody in an embarrassing or difficult position, especially by expecting them to make an immediate decision or answer when they may not be ready to do so: from earlier uses of *on the spot* meaning 'lacking the opportunity to move' and so 'immediately.' *Early 20th cent.*

2 *informal, chiefly NAmer* to arrange to murder somebody: chiefly in criminal slang. *Early 20th cent.*

See also a BLIND spot.

spout

up the spout
1 *informal* no longer working or usable; spoilt or ruined. The phrase was originally used to refer to things that were pawned or pledged, and a person was *up the spout* when in debt or in arrears with a payment (as in the Trollope quotation below): a *spout* was a kind of lift formerly used in pawnbrokers' shops. *19th cent.*

> **Trollope *The Three Clerks* 1857**
> *'I shall be up the spout altogether if you don't do something to help me.' 'But you are so unpunctual, Mr. Tudor.' 'Oh d—it! you'll make me sick if you say that again. What else do you live by but that? But I positively must have some money from you to-day. If not, I am done for.'*

2 *informal* (said of a woman) pregnant. *Mid 20th cent.*

sprat

a sprat to catch a mackerel
a small outlay made or risk taken in the hope of securing something much more valuable: a metaphor from fishing, in which sprats are used as

bait to catch larger fish. Also in early use with *herring* instead of *mackerel*. The reverse notion, *fish for a herring and catch a sprat*, is recorded in John Ray's *Collection of English Proverbs* (1670). The current phrase dates from the 19th cent.

Marryat *Newton Forster* 1831
Depend upon it, that's his plan. A sprat to catch a mackerel.

spread

spread oneself too thin
to divide one's time and effort between too many activities, making it impossible to do any of them effectively. *20th cent.*

See also spread like WILDFIRE; spread one's wings *at* WING.

spring

spring a leak
to begin to leak: originally a nautical expression, referring to the timbers of a ship springing out of position. *18th cent.*

spur

on the spur of the moment
on a sudden impulse; without any forethought: from the use of *spur* to denote speed and precipitate action. *19th cent.*

J S Mill *On Liberty* 1859
The mass do not now take their opinions from dignitaries in Church or State, from ostensible leaders, or from books. Their thinking is done for them by men much like themselves, addressing them or speaking in their name, on the spur of the moment, through the newspapers.

win one's spurs
to achieve recognition. The phrase alludes to the pair of spurs awarded to a medieval knight, and occurs in sources from Middle English, notably in John Lydgate's *Assembly of Gods* (c1425): 'These xiiii Knyghtes made Vyce that day; | To wynne theyr spores they seyde they wold asay.' Allusive uses outside the sphere of knightly gallantry date from the 19th cent.

R D Blackmore *Lorna Doone* 1869
'I pray you be not so vexatious: you always used to do it nicely, without any stool, Ruth.' 'Ah, but you

are grown since then, and become a famous man, John Ridd, and a member of the nobility. Go your way, and win your spurs. I want no lip-service.'

spy

my spies are everywhere
a humorous explanation offered by somebody who has acquired information generally thought to be secret or little known: from the literal use of the phrase in reports of political espionage. *20th cent.*

spy out the land
to check that everything is in order before beginning an undertaking. *Early 20th cent.*

square

be back to/on square one / start from square one
to be back at the starting point of a situation or undertaking. The phrase is sometimes attributed to the notional division of a football pitch into eight squares as an aid to listeners' mental reference in early radio commentaries (until the 1930s, when it was dropped): this system was explained in the issue of *Radio Times* for 28 January 1927. But 'square one' did not, in fact, correspond in any consistent way to the beginning of the game or to any notion of failure or lack of progress in it. A simpler and more likely explanation is that it refers to the squares on the board for a game such as snakes and ladders, in which landing on a penalty square could send the player back to the start, which always is 'square one'. A difficulty, however, remains with this explanation as much as with the first: that the phrase does not appear in print until the 1960s, whereas snakes and ladders is a considerably older game, and we might expect a phrase that alludes to it to be in circulation much earlier. Furthermore, the form that predominates in the first uses is, interestingly, *back in square one*, whereas an origin in board games would suggest *back on square one* or the form now current, *back to square one*. But we can all too easily be oversophisticated about these things: uses can spring up out of the blue with only a vague origin in the user's mind. I still prefer the board games theory, and all the printed evidence has this ring about it. Nonethe-

less, a question mark hovers over our conclusion. *Mid 20th cent.*

J I M Stewart *The Aylwins* 1966
I had brought him momentarily to acknowledge that he had no right to indulge his present confessional impulse at the expense of his family's happiness and security. That he had seized a chance to break off our interview at that point seemed to argue a refusal to abide by this judgement of the matter. We were back, so to speak, in Square One.

get square (with somebody)
to pay off one's debts; also in an ironic sense, to have one's revenge. *19th cent.*

Pearson's Magazine 1897
He thought he saw the means of getting square with the millionaire who had done him such an unscrupulous 'shot in the eye'.

have square eyes
to have been watching television for long periods: the image is of the eyes taking on the shape of the screen. *20th cent.*

on the square
honestly or fairly; in a straightforward manner. Several meanings of *square* are at play here. It is found from the 17th cent. in general contexts meaning 'honest, dependable'; 17th cent. uses of *on the square* (in which *square* is used elliptically without a noun) connect it with gaming boards (which are divided into squares), and it is also well attested in early use in the physical sense 'face to face'. *17th cent.*

Aphra Behn *Sir Patient Fancy* 1678
At Games of Love Husbands to cheat is fair, | 'Tis the Gallant we play with on the square.

square the circle
to achieve the impossible: based on the insoluble mathematical problem of constructing a square that is equal in area to that of a given circle. The phrase was first used in a theological context in a sermon of John Donne: 'Goe not Thou about to Square eyther circle [i.e. God or thyself].' *17th cent.*

See also settle/square accounts with somebody *at* ACCOUNT; a square PEG in a round hole.

squeeze

put the squeeze on somebody
to coerce or pressurize somebody. The sense of *squeeze* ('psychological pressure') on which the phrase is based dates from the early 18th cent. *Mid 20th cent.*

Raymond Chandler *The High Window* 1942
She hired me to … put the squeeze on Linda for a divorce.

See also squeeze somebody until the pips squeak *at* PIP[1].

squib
See a DAMP squib.

stab

stab somebody in the back
to act treacherously towards somebody; to betray them. An early use of the phrase was by G B Shaw in the context of Anglo-Irish politics in 1916: 'The cry that "England's Difficulty Is Ireland's Opportunity" is raised in the old senseless, spiteful way as a recommendation to stab England in the back when she is fighting some one else.' A *stab in the back* is a betrayal or unexpected blow. *19th cent.*

Hardy *Jude the Obscure* 1890
What dreadful things I said! And now Fate has given us this stab in the back for being such fools as to take Nature at her word!

stable

shut/lock the stable door after the horse has bolted
to take action to prevent something that has already happened. The notion goes back in many forms to Middle English and beyond, and is found in John Gower's *Confessio Amantis* (*c*1383): 'For whan the grete stiede | Is stole, thanne he taketh hiede, | And makth the stable dore fast.'

Defoe *The Farther Adventures of Robinson Crusoe* 1719
The hedge had several gaps in it, where the wild goats had gotten in, and eaten up the corn; perhaps, here and there, a dead bush was cramm'd in, to stop them out for the present, but it was only shutting the stable door after the stead was stoln.

stack

stack the cards

to arrange things dishonestly so as to be successful or achieve what one wants at the expense of others. The odds or cards are *stacked against one* when somebody else has arranged things to one's disadvantage. *19th cent.*

Twain & Harte *Ah Sin* 1877
[Broderick] *Strike another blow in that claim and you shall suffer for it.* [Plunkett] *You would not dare to –* [Broderick] *Dare! Do you think me so blind as not to see through this poor juggle? You stacked the cards there to win this from me.*

staff

the staff of life

old or humorous use bread as a staple food: from the historical meaning of *staff* 'something that provides support'. The biblical phrase *break the staff of bread* means 'to cut off a food supply', as in the curses at Leviticus 26:26 (in the Authorized Version, 1611): 'And when I have broken the staff of your bread, ten women shall bake your bread in one oven, and they shall deliver you your bread again by weight: and ye shall eat, and not be satisfied.' *17th cent.*

Edward Buckler *Midnights Meditations of Death* 1646
Our staff of life may kill: a little crumb | Of bread may choke us going down awry. | A small hair in their drink hath caused some | To breath their last. By any thing we die.

stage

hold the stage

to take the leading part in a discussion or activity. The phrase is a metaphor from the theatre: a production is said to hold the stage when it runs for a long or specified period. *16th cent.*

Sir Philip Sidney *The Countesse of Pembrokes Arcadia* a1586
And therefore since I haue named Plangus, I pray you sister (said she) helpe me with the rest, for I haue held the stage long inough; and if it please you to make his fortune knowne, as I haue done Eronas, I will after take hart againe to go on with his falshood.

set the stage for something

to make preparations for an activity, as in fitting a theatre stage with the scenery needed for a production. *19th cent.*

Henry Blake Fuller *In Such a Night* 1896
Tonight's opportunity is mine. I have allowed you to set the stage; you must allow me to direct the little drama.

stair

rain stair-rods

informal to rain heavily: *cf* rain cats and dogs *at* CAT. Stair-rods are metal rods used to keep a stair carpet in place at the bend of each step. The comparison is more straightforward than with cats and dogs, and perhaps the horizontal direction of the rods is meant to suggest wind-blown rain that seems almost parallel to the ground. *Mid 20th cent.*

The Times 1963
During the morning the rain came down like stair-rods. During the match it turned to a swirling drizzle.

stake

go to the stake for somebody/something

be prepared to defend a belief or principle against all opposition or disapproval. The allusion is to the execution of heretics in times of religious persecution, when victims were tied to a wooden stake and burned to death. *19th cent.*

Thackeray *The History of Henry Esmond* 1852
'I know I would go to the stake for you,' said Harry. 'I don't want your head,' said the Father, patting it kindly; 'all you have to do is to hold your tongue.'

pull up stakes

to move to another place to live, usually abruptly or unexpectedly: also in the shortened form *up stakes*. The notion is of pulling up the stakes in the ground that marked the area of one's property. The *OED* gives an early 18th cent. citation in a fairly literal sense; otherwise usage is predominantly from the 19th cent.

Catharine Sedgwick *A New-England Tale* 1822
And so, ma'am, as soon as the roads were a little settled, I pulled up stakes and came off. My good christian neighbours helped me up to Buffalo.

stake a claim

to assert one's ownership of something or one's right to it. The image is of marking out a site or an area of land with stakes driven into the ground. *19th cent.*

> Robert William Service *Ballads of a Cheechako* 1909
> *And while he cooked his supper on his little Yukon stove, | He wished that he had staked a claim in Love's rich treasure-trove; | When suddenly he paused and held aloft a Yukon egg, | For there in pencilled letters was the magic name of Peg.*

stall

set out one's stall

to make a show of one's abilities or qualifications: from the practice of street traders displaying their wares on a stall. *Mid 20th cent.*

> The Times 1958
> *The Australian tactics were soon apparent, with Burke setting his stall out and McDonald losing no opportunity to score.*

See also be unfit to run a WHELK stall.

stand

stand up and be counted

to make one's political views known, especially when this calls for determination because they are untypical or unpopular: first used in connection with the election campaign of Theodore Roosevelt in 1904. *Early 20th cent.*

See also hold/keep/maintain/stand one's GROUND; it stands to REASON; LEAVE somebody standing; stand somebody in good STEAD; stand on/upon CEREMONY; stand on one's own (two) FEET; stand out like a SORE thumb; stand out a MILE.

standard

raise the/one's standard

to prepare to campaign vigorously for a cause: also in variants such as *join the standard*. The phrase is originally military in sense, a *standard* being a distinctive regimental banner used on ceremonial occasions and borne into battle. *19th cent.*

> Ralph Waldo Emerson *Essays* 1841
> *The magnanimous know very well that they who give time, or money, or shelter, to the stranger – so it be done for love, and not for ostentation – do, as it were, put God under obligation to them, so perfect are the compensations of the universe. In some way the time they seem to lose is redeemed, and the pains they seem to take remunerate themselves. These men fan the flame of human love and raise the standard of civil virtue among mankind.*

standing

be in good standing (with somebody)

to be regarded favourably by somebody or on good terms with them. *Standing* here is equivalent to 'status' or 'position.' *19th cent.*

> John Esten Cooke *Ellie* 1855
> *That night the money-lender, who was in 'good standing' in his church, was reading his bible aloud magisterially to his wife.*

star

have stars in one's eyes

to be dreamily optimistic or romantic about the future. *Early 20th cent.*

> Joyce Kilmer *To My Mother* 1915
> *My love held out, against the flying death, | That clove the sea, a shield than steel more strong, | Bringing you back, where no war harrieth, | Stars in your eyes, and in your heart a song.*

reach for the stars

to be highly ambitious. The phrase is relatively modern (chiefly 20th cent.) in its current meaning, and has the ring of Hollywood and showbiz about it, but a similar image can be found in slightly different senses much earlier, for example in Thomas Dekker's drama *If It Be Not Good, The Divel Is In It* (1612): 'Thou shalt finde | A Prince there (newly crownde,) aptly inclinde | To any bendings, least his youthfull browes | Reach at Stars only, wey down his loftiest boughes | With leaden plomets.'

see stars

to feel faint from a blow: literally, to see flashes of light in one's eyes as a result of a blow to the head. *19th cent.*

Louisa M Alcott *Little Women* 1868
*Of course they bumped their heads smartly
together, saw stars, and both came up flushed and
laughing, without the ball, to resume their seats,
wishing they had not left them.*

—'s star is rising
— is becoming well known or successful. *19th
cent.*

John Kerr *Rip Van Winkle* 1826
*Columbia's star is rising, | Altho' the world des-
pising, | Say, that it soo will sink.*

thank/praise one's lucky stars
to be grateful for one's good fortune: from the
notion of the stars as influencing the course of
people's lives. The form with *praise* is recorded
from the early 19th cent., but *thank* (early 20th
cent.) is now more common. *19th cent.*

See also HITCH one's wagon to a star.

starch

take the starch out of somebody
to disconcert or humiliate somebody. *Starch* in
the sense 'stiffness or formality of manner' dates
from the early 18th cent. *19th cent.*

stare

be staring somebody in the face
1 (said of a danger or misfortune) to be immediately imminent or threatening. *18th cent.*

Royall Tyler *The Algerine Captive* 1797
*Your antagonist, with banishment from his coun-
try, and the gallows staring him in the face, will be
sure not to hit you, on his own account.*

Charles Reade *The Cloister and the Hearth* 1861
Gerard saw ruin staring him in the face.
2 (more neutrally, of facts or circumstances) to be
glaringly obvious and undeniable: typically said
of something surprising or initially unnoticed.
19th cent.

Thomas Green Fessenden *Democracy Unveiled* 1806
*Such, however, are the facts, and with these staring
us in the face, this day ought to be a Jubilee in the
United States.*

start

See start a HARE.

starter

under starter's orders
waiting to begin something. In racing, horses are
said to be *under starter's orders* when they are
waiting for the signal to start. *Mid 20th cent.*

Louis MacNeice *Canto XXIII* in *Collected Poems*
a1963
*Statues and even plays are finished before they start,
| But in a game, as in life, we are under Starter's
Orders.*

Muriel Spark *The Mandelbaum Gate* 1965
*Freddy has said to tell you we are under starter's
orders; what is starter's orders?*

state

state of play
the current situation, especially in developing or
changing circumstances: originally, the score at a
particular time during a sports match. *Mid 20th
cent.*

See also state of the ART.

stay

stay one's/somebody's hand
to restrain oneself or another person from taking
action. The phrase alludes to the words of Nebuchadnezzar of Babylon in Daniel 4:35 'He doeth
according to his will in the army of heaven, and
among the inhabitants of the earth: and none can
stay his hand, or say unto him, What doest thou?'
Although some early uses are literal in meaning,
typically referring to restraint in fighting (as in
the Shakespeare quotation below), the senses are
predominantly figurative. *16th cent.*

Shakespeare *1 Henry VI* i.iii.83 (1590)
[Dauphin to Joan la Pucelle during single
combat] *Stay, stay thy hands! Thou art an
Amazon, | And fightest with the sword of Deborah.*

See also hang/stay LOOSE; stay the COURSE; stay
PUT.

stead

stand somebody in good stead
to be useful or advantageous to somebody. *Stand
in stead*, without any qualifying word and sometimes without reference to a particular person or

group, is recorded with the same meaning from Middle English; *stand to good stead* occurs from the 16th cent. and other qualifying words such as *mighty* or (with opposite sense) *little* are also recorded. *Stead* is used in its meaning 'place or position', which has physical and abstract uses (physical in *homestead* and abstract in phrases such as *in their stead* and the phrase under consideration here).

> Thomas Churchyard *Churchyard's Challenge* 1593
> *In priests atyre, but not with shauen crowne, | I scapte their hands, that sought to haue my head, | In forckid cap, and pleycted curtal gowne: | Far from the Church, stode me in right good stead.*

> Henry Fielding *The History of Tom Jones* 1749
> *He will feel the want of these necessaries when it is too late, when he is arrived at that place where there is wailing and gnashing of teeth. It is then he will find in what mighty stead that heathen goddess, that virtue, which you and all other deists of the age adore, will stand him.*

steady

(as) steady as a rock

solid and dependable. The simile is based on the proverbial image of a rock as symbolic of firmness and dependability, and is reinforced by the New Testament account of Christ's words to the apostle Simon Peter (Matthew 16:18): 'And I say unto thee, That thou art Peter, and upon this rock I will build my church; and the gates of hell shall not prevail against it.' *Petros* in Greek means 'a rock or stone', and translates the Aramaic *cephas*, given (according to John 1:42) as a byname to Simon Peter to distinguish him from another Simon (Zelotes). *19th cent.*

> Richard Blackmore *The Kit-Kats* 1708
> *Robell, who schools and colleges did mock, | Solid, unchang'd and steady as a rock, | In these revolting times begins to shake.*

go steady (with somebody)

informal, originally NAmer to be enjoying a regular romantic or sexual relationship, in which each partner might refer to the other as *his* or *her steady*. *Early 20th cent.*

steady as she goes

gentle encouragement to somebody to carry on as they are doing: originally a nautical instruction,

in which *steady* means 'maintaining a constant course.' *20th cent.*

steady on

informal a warning to apply restraint, calm down, avoid rushing, etc: also simply *steady*. *Early 20th cent.*

---

steal

steal somebody's clothes

to claim somebody else's ideas or principles as one's own. This colourful and somewhat mischievous little phrase may have been coined by William James in 1884 along with the word *noologist* (meaning 'a rationalist'), as quoted in R B Perry, *The Thought and Character of William James As Revealed in Unpublished Correspondence* (1935): 'They always steal the clothes of the noölogists.' *19th cent.*

See also rob / steal somebody BLIND; steal a MARCH on somebody; steal the SHOW; steal somebody's THUNDER.

---

steam

gather / get up / pick up steam

to summon up one's energies to undertake a difficult or challenging activity: originally with reference to a steam engine, which needs to build up pressure to start working efficiently. Also (said of an activity) to begin in earnest and gather momentum. *19th cent.*

> Charlotte Brontë *Shirley* 1849
> *Miss Mary, getting up the steam in her turn, asked whether Caroline had attended the Bible Society Meeting which had been held at Nunnely last Thursday night.*

have steam coming out of one's ears

informal to be extremely angry or incensed. *20th cent.*

let/blow off steam

informal to release one's pent-up energies or frustrations, especially in harmless ways. The image is of releasing excess steam through a valve of a steam engine. *19th cent.*

> Edward Payson Roe *Opening a Chestnut Burr* 1874
> *One must have some way of lettin' off steam. Now my wife she purses up her mouth so tight you couldn't stick a pin in it when she's riled. I often say*

to her, 'Do explode! Open your mouth and let it all out at once.'

run out of / lose steam

informal to become tired as a result of prolonged activity or effort; to lose stamina. *Mid 20th cent.*

under one's own steam

informal by one's own efforts, without help: often used in the context of a person travelling alone or by means not needing support from others. *Early 20th cent.*

See also FULL steam ahead.

---

steer

steer clear of somebody/something

to avoid a person or thing at all costs: a nautical metaphor. *18th cent.*

> Smollett *The Life and Adventures of Sir Launcelot Greaves* 1762
> A sea-faring man may have a sweetheart in every port; but he should steer clear of a wife, as he would avoid a quick-sand.

See also steer a MIDDLE course.

---

stem

from stem to stern

from one end to the other; for the whole of something: originally with reference to a ship. The stem is the upright timber at the bow of the ship to which the planks are joined, and the stern is the rear of the ship. Figurative uses date from the 19th cent.

> Charles Reade *The Cloister and the Hearth* 1861
> Our crinoline spares the noble parts of woman, and makes but the baser parts gigantic (why this preference?): but this poor animal from stem to stern was swamped in finery.

stem the tide

to stop a forceful or seemingly endless process from continuing: a metaphor from sailing, in which the phrase means 'to acquire a velocity in sailing against the tide equal to the force of the current.' *17th cent.*

> John Banks *Vertue Betray'd* 1682
> Now I am drowning, all within's a Deluge; | Wisdom nor Strength can stem the Tide no more, | And Nature in my Sex ne'er felt the like.

Mary Hays *Memoirs of Emma Courtney* 1796
Let us summon our fortitude – let us, at length, bravely stem the tide of passion – let us beware of the criminal pusillanimity of despair!

---

step

in / out of step with somebody/something

in (or out of) harmony with a trend, fashion, attitude, requirement, etc: a metaphor based on the notion of people walking or marching together. *19th cent.*

mind/watch one's step

informal to behave or act with caution: normally used as a warning. The allusion is to walking carefully and avoiding obstacles and difficulties. *Early 20th cent.*

> Christopher Morley *The Haunted Bookshop* 1919
> 'I am a friend,' buzzed the receiver. There was a harsh, bass note in the voice that made the diaphragm at Aubrey's ear vibrate tinnily. Aubrey grew angry. 'Well, Herr Freund,' he said, 'if you're the wellwisher I met on the Bridge last night, watch your step. I've got your number.'

step by step

taking each stage in turn; methodically or gradually: literally, making progress by moving one foot at a time. *17th cent.*

> Thomas Washbourne *Divine Poems* 1654
> And as the day's each minute brighter, so | He step by step doth to perfection go.

step on it / on the gas

informal to act with speed; to hurry: literally, to press down on the accelerator of a motor vehicle to increase its speed. *Early 20th cent.*

a step too far

a decision or action that is regarded as excessive or as going beyond reasonable limits. *20th cent.*

See also be/get/step out of line *at* LINE[1]; step into the BREACH; step into —'s shoes *at* be in —'s shoes *at* SHOE; tread/step on somebody's toes *at* TOE.

---

stern

be made of sterner stuff

(said of a person) to have strength of character. The locus classicus is Antony's defence of Julius Caesar against charges of ambition in his

'Friends, Romans, countrymen' speech after Caesar's death in Shakespeare's *Julius Caesar* (1599) III.ii.93: 'Did this in Caesar seem ambitious? | When that the poor hath cried, Caesar hath wept. | Ambition should be made of sterner stuff.' *16th cent.*

---

stew

stew in one's own juice

to be left to suffer the consequences of one's own mistakes or indiscretions: *cf* French *cuire dans son jus*. The phrase occurs earlier (17th cent.) with *water* instead of *juice*, where the comparison is with oysters. *19th cent.*

> Henry James *The Ambassadors* 1903
> *Waymarsh presently said: 'Look here, Strether. Quit this ... I mean your nosing round. Quit the whole job. Let them stew in their juice. You're being used for a thing you ain't fit for. People don't take a fine-tooth comb to groom a horse.'*

---

stick^1

make something stick

to make something effective, especially to validate or substantiate an accusation: *sticking* as a metaphor for the association of (usually wrong or wicked) actions with their perpetrators dates from the early 17th cent.: *cf* Shakespeare, *Macbeth* (1606) v.ii.17, where Angus says of Macbeth 'Now does he feel | His secret murders sticking on his hands'. *Cf* stick something on somebody *below. Mid 20th cent.*

stick in somebody's throat/craw/gizzard

(said of words) to be too awkward or shameful to utter properly. The notion is of something that one can neither swallow nor spit out. The locus classicus occurs in the words of Macbeth after the murder of Duncan in Shakespeare's *Macbeth* (1606) II.ii.31: 'But wherefore could not I pronounce 'Amen'? | I had most need of blessing, and 'Amen' | Stuck in my throat.' Allusive uses are found from later in the 17th cent.

> Philip Massinger *The Bashful Lover* 1655
> *If I can feelingly express my ardor, | And make her sensible of the much I suffer | In hopes and fears, and she vouchsafe to take | Compassion on me, – Ha! compassion? | The word sticks in my throat: what's here that tells me | I do descend too low?*

> Richardson *Clarissa* 1748
> *I can think of nothing, of no-body else, but the divine Clarissa Harlowe. – Harlowe! – How that hated word sticks in my throat. – But I shall give her for it, the name of Love.*

stick something on somebody

to get somebody blamed for something: *cf* make something stick *above. 20th cent.*

stick to somebody's fingers

(said of money) to be acquired dishonestly, especially by embezzlement. *16th cent.*

See also STUCK; stand/stick out like a SORE thumb; stand/stick out a MILE; stick one's BIB in; stick one's CHIN out; stick one's NECK out; stick one's OAR in; stick to one's guns *at* GUN; stick to one's last *at* LAST^2; stop/stick at NOTHING.

---

stick^2

in the sticks

informal, originally NAmer in a remote place. The origin of the phrase is obscure, but may be connected with *sticks* as a description of flimsy things of various kinds, including furniture, with a possible extension here to buildings; alternatively, *sticks* may have an association with backwoods. *Early 20th cent.*

a stick to beat somebody with

a fact or circumstance that can be used to embarrass or threaten somebody. *17th cent.*

> Dorothy Osborne *Letter to Sir William Temple* 1653
> *What reason had I to furnish you with a stick to beat myself withal?*

up sticks

informal to move to another place, usually abruptly or unexpectedly. The phrase was originally nautical slang for setting up the mast of a ship before sailing, although some usage reflects the notion of pulling up sticks from the ground, as a variant of *up stakes* (*see* pull up stakes *at* STAKE). *19th cent.*

See also the DIRTY end of the stick; get hold of the WRONG end of the stick; the SHORT end of the stick.

sticky

batting on a sticky wicket
facing a difficult or awkward situation. In cricket, a *sticky wicket* is a pitch that has begun to dry out after heavy rain, making batting difficult; literal uses date from the late 19th cent. *Mid 20th cent.*

stiff

a stiff upper lip
stoical and determined self-control in difficult circumstances: in early use often in the form *carry* or *keep a stiff upper lip*. Based on the notion that the upper lip betrays weakness or emotion when it begins to tremble. *19th cent.*

> Harriet Beecher Stowe *Uncle Tom's Cabin* 1852
> *'Well, good-bye, Uncle Tom; keep a stiff upper lip,'* said George.

still

a still small voice
one's conscience: with allusion to 1 Kings 19:12 'And after the earthquake a fire: but the Lord was not in the fire: and after the fire a still small voice. And it was so, when Elijah heard it, that he wrapped his face in his mantle, and went out, and stood in the entering in of the cave. And behold, there came a voice unto him, and said, What doest thou here, Elijah?' *16th cent.*

still waters run deep
(proverb) a quiet or gentle outward disposition may be hiding a passionate or scheming nature. The sentiment is found in various forms from Middle English, and earlier in other languages: the Roman writer Quintus Curtius (1st or 2nd cent. AD) in his history of Alexander the Great (*Res Gestae Alexandri Magni* VII.iv.13) quotes a saying of the Bactrians that *altissima quaeque flumina minimo sono labi* 'the deepest rivers flow with the least sound'. Shakespeare uses the proverb in *2 Henry VI* (1591) III.i.53, where the Duke of Suffolk in a conversation with the King and Queen refers to the alleged machinations of the Lord Protector: '[He] did instigate the bedlam brainsick Duchess | By wicked means to frame our sovereign's fall. | Smooth runs the water where the brook is deep, | And in his simple show he harbours treason.' *Middle English*

sting

a sting in the tail
a process or activity that causes trouble or difficulty right at the end: with allusion to wasps, bees, scorpions, and other creatures that carry venom in their tails. The image is found in the New Testament (Revelations 9:10 'And they had tails like unto scorpions, and there were stings in their tails; and their power was to hurt men five months'); and in Shakespeare's *The Taming of the Shrew* (1592) II.i.210 Katherine warns Petruccio 'If I be waspish, best beware my sting.' *19th cent.*

stink

The phrases are loosely based on the slang sense of *stink*, 'a row or fuss', the image being of something unpleasant and lingering.

like stink
informal with great force or intensity. *Early 20th cent.*

raise / create / make / kick up a stink
informal to cause trouble or disagreement: *cf* KICK up a fuss. *19th cent.*

stir

stir one's stumps
to start moving or acting: *stump* here is a humorous word for 'leg.' *16th cent.*

> Peter Colse *Penelope's Complaint* 1596
> *I doubt not but poore shepheards will stirre their stumps after my minstrelsie.*

See also not lift/move/stir a FINGER.

stitch

in stitches
informal laughing uncontrollably: commonly in the form *have somebody in stitches*. The meaning involved here is 'a sharp and sudden pain in the side brought on by running or exercise' … or, in this case, by laughing. Shakespeare is an early user of the phrase in a slightly different form in *Twelfth Night* (1602), where Maria invites Sir Toby, Sir Andrew, and Fabian to spy on Malvolio (III.ii.64): 'If you desire the spleen, and will laugh yourselves into stitches, follow me.'

a stitch in time

action taken in good time: in full *a stitch in time saves nine*, i.e. prompt action saves a lot more trouble later. In 18th cent. use the form is *may save nine*. There is no particular significance in the number *nine*, other than its half rhyme with *time*; the proverb was originally a couplet. *18th cent.*

stock

on the stocks

in course of being made or prepared but not yet completed: in shipbuilding, *stocks* are the framework on which a ship is built. In its original meaning the phrase dates from the 16th cent., and figurative uses occur from the 18th cent.

Samuel Foote *The Commissary* 1765
Last week, in a ramble to Dulwich, I made these rhimes into a duet for a new comic opera I have on the stocks.

put/take stock in something

to have faith or confidence in something. *19th cent.*

take stock

to review a situation objectively, especially in order to make a decision about it: from the commercial meaning, to make an inventory of the stock of a business. *19th cent.*

R L Stevenson *New Arabian Nights* 1882
Not a man of the party escaped his sudden, searching looks; he took stock of the bearing of heavy losers, he valued the amount of the stakes, he paused behind couples who were deep in conversation; and, in a word, there was hardly a characteristic of any one present but he seemed to catch and make a note of it.

stomach

an army marches on its stomach

(proverb) working people need to be well fed to be effective. The proverb has been attributed to Frederick the Great of Prussia and to Napoleon; its use in English is relatively recent. *Early 20th cent.*

have no stomach for something

to lack the courage or inclination to undertake something difficult or unpleasant: *stomach* in its meaning 'appetite for food' dates back to Middle English, and figurative uses appear in the 16th cent.: cf Shakespeare, *The Merchant of Venice* (1598) III.v.92 '[Jessica to Lorenzo] Nay, let me praise you while I have a stomach.' *18th cent.*

on a full / an empty stomach

having had plenty (or nothing) to eat. *17th cent.*

Charles Sedley *Bellamira* 1687
The meat's hardly out of my mouth, and I am for no exercise upon a full stomach: 'tis too far to walk yet.

a strong stomach

a capacity to witness or take part in unpleasant activities without feeling squeamish: more literally, a metabolism able to cope with rich food. Reference to the stomach as the organ of digestion dates from Middle English. *17th cent.*

Margaret Cavendish *Matrimonial Trouble* 1662
He rather seem'd of a strong stomach, and a greedy appetite, by the course diet he brought men to live with.

turn somebody's stomach

to make somebody feel sick or disgusted. *17th cent.*

Jeremy Collier *A Short View of the Immorality of the English Stage* 1698
Here the poet exceeds himself. Here are such strains as would turn the stomach of an ordinary debauchee, and be almost nauseous in the stews.

stone

be carved/set/written in/on (tablets of) stone

(said of laws, decisions, etc) to be fixed and unchangeable. The phrase alludes to the account in Exodus 31:18 of the handing down of the Ten Commandments to Moses on Mount Sinai: 'And he gave unto Moses, when he had made an end of communing with him upon mount Sinai, two tables of testimony, tables of stone, written with the finger of God.' *17th cent.*

cast/throw the first stone

to make the first accusation against somebody. Used with allusion to the words of Christ in John 8:7 addressed to the scribes and Pharisees who were about to stone a woman accused of adultery (in the Authorized Version, 1611): 'He that is without sin among you, let him first cast a stone at her.' *17th cent.*

Henry King *An Elegy Upon the Most Incomparable King Charles I* 1659

How did you thank seditious men that came | To bring petitions which your selves did frame? | And lest they wanted hands to set them on, | You lead the way by throwing the first stone.

leave no stone unturned

to spare no efforts to achieve or find something. The image is found in classical Greek drama, for example in Euripides' tragedy *The Children of Herakles* (5th cent. BC), where Eurystheus says 'These children here hated me; I recalled their father's enmity. I had to leave no stone unturned [literally, 'to move every stone'] … to ensure my own safety.' The expression appears in English use from the 16th cent. in the Latin form *omnem movere lapidem*. *16th cent.*

William Patten *The Expedition into Scotland of Prince Edward* 1548

What policy hath he left unproved? What shift unsought? Or what stone unturned?

stone the crows!

informal an exclamation of amazement, disbelief, or disgust. In Britain the phrase was popularized in the 1950s and 1960s by the radio and television comedian Tony Hancock (1924–68), especially in its shortened form *stone me!* In fact the phrase originates in Australia, where it has remained in use along with other fanciful variants such as *starve the crows* (found earliest in print), *spare the crows* (a contrary notion, surely), and *stiffen the crows*. We can only guess at the origin of the phrase, the intention of which is presumably to suggest an action that is as unreal or improbable as the notion the phrase ridicules or rejects. The phrase now has a somewhat dated feel about it, in British use at least. *Early 20th cent.*

C Day Lewis *The Otterbury Incident* 1948

'Give yer sixpence if yer stays 'ere beside me for 'arf an hour, you two nippers.' 'Sixpence each,' Ted put in firmly. 'Cor stone the crows, 'ave a 'eart, young gents. I'm a poor man –'

stone deaf

completely deaf. The expression is derived from the use of *stone* in set comparisons such as *cold, dead, deaf, hard* etc *as a stone*, which date from Middle English. *18th cent.*

Sarah Scott *A Description of Millennium Hall* 1762

Thus neighbour Jane, who poor woman is almost stone deaf, they thought would have a melancholy life if she was to be always spinning and knitting, seeing other people around her talking, and not to be able to hear a word they said.

a stone's throw

a short distance away: literally, the distance that a stone can be thrown by hand. The variant form *stone throw* appears occasionally in 19th cent. use. *16th cent.*

See also have kissed the BLARNEY Stone; mark somebody/something with a WHITE stone.

stony

fall on stony ground

(said of advice or a warning) to go unheeded: with allusion to the parable of the sower in Mark 4:3–5 (in the Authorized Version, 1611) 'Behold, there went out a sower to sow: And it came to pass, as he sowed, some fell by the way side, and the fowls of the air came and devoured it up. And some fell on stony ground, where it had not much earth; and immediately it sprang up, because it had no depth of earth. But when the sun was up, it was scorched; and because it had no root, it withered away.' *17th cent.*

stool

fall between two stools

to fail because of indecision between two possibilities: based on the proverb *between two stools one falls to the ground*. The notion dates back to Roman times, and is found in Seneca (1st cent. AD). The earliest occurrences in English date from Middle English, notably in John Gower's *Confessio Amantis* (c1383). *Middle English*

stop

come to a full stop

to stop completely. *17th cent.*

Thomas Fuller *Ornithology* 1655

She therefore that hath not the modesty to die the relict of one man, will charge through the whole army of husbands, if occasion were offered, before her love will meet with a full stop thereof.

put a stop to something

to take steps to discontinue a process or activity. *17th cent.*

> Philip Ayres *The Revengeful Mistress* 1696
> *She immediately fainted, and dropt from her Chair on the Floor. This sudden Accident put a stop to the Harmony of Musick and Dancing for the present.*

stop one's ears

to refuse to listen. An early occurrence is in Wyclif's translation of Proverbs 21:13 'Who stoppeth his ere at the cri of the pore', rendered in the Authorized Version of 1611 as 'Whoso stoppeth his ears at the cry of the poor.' *Middle English*

stop short of something

to reach a certain limit or degree; (said of a person) to decline to go beyond a certain limit in one's actions or behaviour. *17th cent.*

> Jeremy Collier *A Short View of the Immorality of the English Stage* 1698
> *A second branch of the profaneness of the stage is their abuse of religion, and Holy Scripture: And here sometimes they don't stop short of blasphemy.*

> David Rittenhouse transl Lessing's *Lucy Sampson* 1789
> *That, as a man long connected with our sex, and sufficiently versed in the arts of seduction, your experience should enable you to practise too successfully to stop short of obtaining your ends, is nothing strange.*

See also catch/cop/stop a PACKET; PULL out all the stops; stop at NOTHING; stop a GAP.

stopper

put a/the stopper on something

to bring a process to an end. *Early 20th cent.*

store

in store

(usually said of something unpleasant) awaiting one in the future: from the meaning 'put aside in a store for future use.' *16th cent.*

> Thomas Beard *The Theatre of Gods Judgements* 1597
> *Notwithstanding all which hath bene spoken, and howsoeuer sinners are punished in this life, yet is certaine, that the greatest and terriblest punishments are kept in store for them in another world.*

set/lay/put store by/on something

to attach great importance or significance to something. *Middle English*

> Robert Crowley *The Psalter of David* 1549
> *And he hath made his people stronge, and hys frendes prayse worthy | The sonnes of Jacob, a people that he setteth store by.*

See also MIND the shop/store.

storm

the calm/lull before the storm

a short period of apparent quiet that ominously precedes a time of expected difficulty or trouble: from the (16th cent.) proverb *after a storm comes a calm* (and variants). *19th cent.*

> Mary Shelley *The Last Man* 1826
> *My father felt that his fall was near; but so far from profiting by this last calm before the storm to save himself, he sought to forget anticipated evil by making still greater sacrifices to the deity of pleasure, deceitful and cruel arbiter of his destiny.*

> Louisa M Alcott *Little Men* 1871
> *Mrs. Bhaer was right; peace was only a temporary lull, a storm was brewing, and two days after Bess left, a moral earthquake shook Plumfield to its center.*

go down a storm

informal (said of a performance, etc) to be very well received. *20th cent.*

> *The Face* 1991
> *The film goes down a storm with the festival audience, though the torture does send some people scurrying for the door.*

a storm in a teacup

a disproportionate fuss about something unimportant. The phrase occurs in the form *storm in a cream bowl* in the late 17th cent., and fanciful variants such as *tempest in a teapot* appear in the 19th cent. A corresponding Latin phrase *excitare fluctus in simpulo* (literally, 'to stir up a wave in a ladle') is found in Cicero (1st cent. BC). *17th cent.*

take something by storm

to impress an audience or other group of people: from the military meaning, to capture a place after a sudden assault. The phrase is used in extended metaphor from the 17th cent., and the present meaning became current in the 19th cent.

Grant Allen *The Woman Who Did* 1895
*Even northerners love Florence and Venice at first
sight; those take their hearts by storm; but Perugia,
Siena, Orvieto, are an acquired taste, like olives and
caviare.*

up a storm

informal, chiefly NAmer used to intensify a verb of
action in the sense 'with enthusiasm or energy.'
Mid 20th cent.

Billie Holiday *Lady Sings the Blues* 1953
*After Marietta taught me, I knitted up a storm and
got real fancy. I made cable-knit sweaters for Bobby
Tucker and his little boy.*

story

the story of one's life

something that one has experienced all too often:
usually said in reaction to hearing another person's experiences. *Mid 20th cent.*

to cut/make a long story short

used as a formula showing the speaker's wish to
get to the point quickly and avoid digressions.
19th cent.

Hardy *Far from the Madding Crowd* 1874
*She fleed at him, and, to cut a long story short, he
owned to having carried off five sack altogether,
upon her promising not to persecute him.*

See also END of story.

stove

slave over a hot stove

to toil long and hard in cooking: typically used
with overtones of resentment with reference to
the speaker in contrast to the person addressed.
20th cent.

straight

get something straight

informal to understand something correctly: often
used in the imperative, especially in the form
(let's) get this straight. *Keep me straight* (in the
sense 'keep me informed') is recorded from the
mid 19th cent. *Early 20th cent.*

go straight

informal (said of a criminal) to give up a life of
crime, to start behaving honestly. The phrase

occurs earlier (19th cent., also with *run* instead
of *go*) in the sense 'to act honourably.' *Mid 20th
cent.*

keep a straight face

to manage not to laugh despite being amused:
often used in negative contexts and in contexts
implying difficulty. *19th cent.*

Effie Woodward Merriman *Diamonds and Hearts*
1897
[Bernice] *Do you – do you think dhis wid prove
fadal? (Bernice makes a desperate effort to keep a
straight face as she asks this question.)*

Harper Lee *To Kill a Mockingbird* 1960
*All the time Ewell was on the stand I couldn't dare
look at John and keep a straight face. John looked at
him as if he were a three-legged chicken or a square
egg.*

the straight/strait and narrow

morally correct behaviour. The phrase ultimately
originates in the New Testament account of
Christ's words in the Sermon on the Mount
(Matthew 7:14), which need to be quoted at
length to show how the present spelling and
meaning have arisen: 'Enter ye in at the strait
gate: for wide is the gate, and broad is the way,
that leadeth to destruction, and many there be
which go in thereat. Because strait is the gate, and
narrow is the way, which leadeth unto life, and
few there be that find it.' *Strait* here means 'narrow', contrasted with the wide gate that leads to
ruin; the New English Bible translation reads 'the
gate that leads to life is small'. In current English
strait is most familiar as a noun meaning a narrow sea passage. It has the variant spelling
straight, and it has therefore been confused
with the more familiar word *straight* in the
sense 'following a direct course, without deviating'. Both spellings, *straight* and *strait*, are used in
the phrase. *Strait and narrow* is therefore a hendiadys, i.e. a pair of words reinforcing each other,
rather than a tautology (in which one word is
redundant). *Straight and narrow*, now the more
common form, uses *straight* in its meaning to do
with moral correctness. This is the form used by
J E Leeson in *Hymns and Scenes of Childhood*
(1842): 'Loving Shepherd, ever near, | Teach
Thy lamb Thy voice to hear; | Suffer not my
steps to stray | From the straight and narrow
way.' *19th cent.*

a straight fight

a contest, especially an election, in which there are only two competitors or candidates. *Early 20th cent.*

straight off

immediately; without hesitation. *19th cent.*

> George Eliot *Adam Bede* 1859
> *A man may be able to work problems straight off in's head as he sits by the fire and smokes his pipe; but if he has to make a machine or a building, he must have a will and a resolution.*

> D H Lawrence *Sons and Lovers* 1913
> *'Shall we go to the lodging straight off,' said Paul, 'or somewhere else?' 'We may as well go home,' said Dawes.*

straight up

informal truthfully and honestly: often used as an insistent reply. In the sense 'true, real', *straight up* dates from the early 20th cent. *Mid 20th cent.*

> Len Deighton *Horse under Water* 1963
> *'What's the trouble?' I asked. 'I'm being followed,' he said. 'Really,' I said. 'Straight up,' he said. 'I wasn't sure until today.'*

See also (as) straight as a die *at* DIE²; put/set the RECORD straight; a straight ARROW; straight from the SHOULDER.

strain

strain at a gnat

to make a fuss about something trivial: in full *strain at a gnat and swallow a camel,* i.e. while accepting something much worse without demur. The allusion is to Matthew 23:24, where Christ accuses the scribes and Pharisees of hypocrisy: 'Ye blind guides, which strain at a gnat, and swallow a camel.' The 16th cent. translations (Tyndale, Coverdale, Cranmer, Geneva) have '*strain out* a gnat' (Latin *excolare*), the image being of removing an insect that has fallen into wine. The Authorized Version (1611) has '*strain at* a gnat', which should probably to be understood in the same sense, as other 16th cent. uses show; this later came to be understood to mean 'to have difficulty swallowing', which gave rise to the figurative sense in which the phrase has since been used. *17th cent.*

See also strain at the LEASH; strain every NERVE.

strap

be strapped for cash

informal to be short of money. *Strapped* here is used in the sense 'bound or constricted', and was used in the 19th cent. without the additional reference to cash. Other variants are also found. *19th cent.*

> Daily News 1876
> *The tramp ... does not awaken sympathy like the 'strapped' journeyman in search of a job.*

> P G Wodehouse *Pigs Have Wings* 1952
> *A bit strapped for the ready, eh?*

straw

clutch/grasp at straws

to resort in desperation to any expedient, however inadequate: from the proverb *a drowning man will clutch at a straw.* An early reference is contained in Sir Thomas More's *Dialoge of Comfort against Tribulacion,* written during his imprisonment in the Tower of London in 1534: 'Lyke a man that in peril of drowning catcheth whatsoever cometh next to hand ... be it never so simple a sticke.' *16th cent.*

> Richardson *Clarissa* 1748
> *At his earnest request, I sat up with him last night; and, poor man! it is impossible to tell thee, how easy and safe he thought himself in my company, for the first part of the night: A drowning man will catch at a straw, the Proverb well says: And a straw was I, with respect to any real help I could give him.*

draw the short straw

to be the person chosen to do something difficult or unpleasant: from the method of drawing lots by picking from a number of straws whose length is hidden, the person drawing the short one being the unlucky victim. *19th cent.*

> Edgar Allan Poe *The Narrative of Arthur Gordon Pym of Nantucket* 1837
> *I could not bring myself to arrange the splinters upon the spot, but thought over every species of finesse by which I could trick some one of my fellow-sufferers to draw the short straw, as it had been agreed that whoever drew the shortest of four splinters from my hand was to die for the preservation of the rest. Before any one condemn me for this apparent heartlessness, let him be placed in a situation precisely similar to my own.*

have straws in one's hair

to be insane: from the notion that the insane got straw from the floor of the madhouse caught up in their hair. *19th cent.*

> Oscar Wilde *A Woman of No Importance* 1893
> [Lady Caroline] *I saw him afterwards at poor Lord Plumstead's with straws in his hair, or something very odd about him. I can't recall what.*

the last/final straw

a final unpleasant or unwelcome event or experience that makes a situation intolerable. The phrase is based on the proverb *it is the last straw that breaks the camel's back*, which originally had *feather* instead of *straw*: both words denote something very light and insignificant in itself. The phrase is 19th cent. in its current form.

> Dickens *Dombey and Son* 1848
> *'Where have you worked all your life?' 'Mostly underground Sir, 'till I got married. I come to the level then. I'm a going on one of these here railroads when they comes into full play.' As the last straw breaks the laden camel's back, this piece of underground information crushed the sinking spirits of Mr. Dombey.*

a straw in the wind

a slight indication of future developments, especially trouble or difficulty. *Early 20th cent.*

> David Graham Phillips *The Worth of a Woman* 1908
> *Was it not a straw in the wind of these times that no one of any consequence raised the cry of immorality against this play?*

See also a MAN of straw.

---

streak

be on a winning/losing streak

to enjoy a run of successes (or failures): *streak* in this sense dates from the mid 19th cent. in uses such as *a streak of bad luck. Early 20th cent.*

like a streak (of lightning)

informal with great speed or urgency. *19th cent.*

> Willa Cather *The Song of the Lark* 1915
> *Ottenburg studied the red end of his cigarette attentively. 'She might have come out to see you. I remember you covered the distance like a streak when she wanted you.'*

stream

against/with the stream

contrary to (or agreeing with) the prevailing tendency or consensus: the notion appears as an image in Middle English sources, notably Gower and Caxton. *Strive against the stream* appears in the collection of proverbs and sayings made in the 16th cent. by John Heywood.

> Henry Fielding *The History of Tom Jones* 1749
> *And now this ill-yoked pair, this lean shadow and this fat substance, have prompted me to write, whose assistance shall I invoke to direct my pen? First, Genius; thou gift of Heaven; without whose aid in vain we struggle against the stream of nature. Thou who dost sow the generous seeds which art nourishes, and brings to perfection.*

on stream

(said of a process, resources, etc) in operation; available. *Mid 20th cent.*

---

street

the man in the street / NAmer on the street

an average or typical person, as opposed to the expert or person in authority: *woman in the street* (early 20th cent.) occurs much less often, partly because of the natural conservatism of idiom but probably also because of the unfavourable connotations this might pick up from other phrases, especially *walk* (or *be on*) *the streets* (see below). *19th cent.*

> Ralph Waldo Emerson *Representative Men* 1850
> *Napoleon is thoroughly modern, and, at the highest point of his fortunes, has the very spirit of the newspapers. He is no saint ... and he is no hero, in the high sense. The man in the street finds in him the qualities and powers of other men in the street.*

not in the same street as/with somebody/something

informal not comparable with another person or thing in quality or ability. *19th cent.*

(right) up somebody's street

informal exactly what suits or appeals to somebody. *Street* has had the symbolic meaning 'a sphere of activity' from the early years of the 20th cent. Farmer and Henley's *Slang and Its Analogues* (1903) includes the entry: 'Street ... a capacity, a method; a line: e.g. "That's not in my street" = "I am not concerned" or "That's not my way of doing," etc.' The phrase appears less often in the form *down somebody's street. Early 20th cent.*

> **Evelyn Waugh** *Brideshead Revisited* 1945
> *It's hard to tell with one's own sister, but I've always thought her a jolly attractive girl, the sort of girl any chap would be glad to have – artistic, too, just down your street. But I must admit you're a good picker.*

streets ahead
informal greatly superior: a development of *not in the same street as somebody/something* (see above). To *win by a street* is to win or succeed by a comfortable margin. *19th cent.*

walk / be on the streets
1 to be homeless. *18th cent.*
2 to work as a prostitute. *18th cent.*

> **John Shebbeare** *Matrimony* 1754
> *By Heavens! I would rather hear of her being on the Streets of London, than married to so vile a Fellow.*

See also the WORD on the street.

strength

go from strength to strength
to become more and more successful or effective: originally in physical senses, e.g. with reference to growth. *17th cent.*

> **John Flavel** *The Method of Grace* 1680
> *The new creature is a thriving creature, growing from strength to strength.*

a tower/pillar of strength
a person who can be relied on for support or consolation. The phrase alludes to the Book of Common Prayer (1549) 'O Lord … be unto them a tower of strength', itself echoed in Shakespeare's *Richard III* (1593), where Richard encourages his supporters before the Battle of Bosworth (v.iii.12): 'The King's name is a tower of strength, | Which they upon the adverse faction want.' *16th cent.*

strengthen

strengthen somebody's hand(s)
to give somebody the means to act effectively: *cf* 1 Samuel 23:16 'And Jonathan Saul's son arose, and went to David into the wood, and strengthened his hand in God.' *16th cent.*

stretch

at a stretch
1 forming a continuous uninterrupted period of time. *17th cent.*

> **Smollett** *The Expedition of Roderick Random* 1748
> *Sometimes he sleeps four and twenty hours at a stretch, by which means he saves three meals besides coffee-house expence.*

2 as a maximum; with some effort or difficulty. *19th cent.*

> **George Meredith** *Diana of the Crossways* 1885
> *Others were wrangling for places, chairs, plates, glasses, game-pie, champagne: she had them; the lady under his charge to a certainty would have them; so far good; and he had seven hundred pounds per annum – seven hundred and fifty, in a favourable aspect, at a stretch.*

at full stretch
exerting oneself to the full. *17th cent.*

> **Dryden** *Aeneis* v.259 (1697)
> *They row | At the full stretch, and shake the Brazen Prow.*

by no / not by any stretch of the imagination
not conceivably. *19th cent.*

> **Theodore S Fay** *Crayon Sketches* 1833
> *Nine-tenths of the albums are nothing better than discreditable receptacles for disreputable pieces of prose and poetry that cannot, by any stretch of the imagination, ever hope to attain the dignity of print, or be incorporated in a book form in any other shape.*

See also stretch one's legs *at* LEG; spread/stretch one's wings *at* WING; stretch a POINT.

stricken

stricken in years
(said of a person) in advanced old age. The phrase is biblical and compares old age to an infirmity: for example, God addresses Joshua (Joshua 13:1, in the Authorized Version, 1611) with the words 'Thou art old and stricken in years.' *17th cent.*

stride

take something in one's stride
to manage a challenge or other undertaking comfortably: a metaphor from racing, with reference

to a horse that clears an obstacle without changing its stride. *Early 20th cent.*

strike

strike an attitude
to adopt an ostentatious or theatrical pose or manner. *Attitude* in the sense 'a posture of the body' dates from the early 18th cent. The phrase is 19th cent.

> Louisa M Alcott *Hospital Sketches* 1863
> *'Can't afford expensive luxuries, Mrs. Coobiddy.'*
> *'Turn actress, and immortalize your name,' said sister Vashti, striking an attitude.*

strike it lucky
informal to have an unexpected success. In this and the following phrase the image is based on prospecting for mineral deposits. *19th cent.*

> Mark Twain *The Adventures of Huckleberry Finn* 1884
> *All of us but Jim took the canoe and went down there to see if there was any chance in that place for our show. We struck it mighty lucky; there was going to be a circus there that afternoon, and the country people was already beginning to come in.*

strike it rich
informal to acquire great wealth. *19th cent.*

> Bret Harte *Mrs Scaggs's Husbands* 1873
> *The Old Man glibly repeated what was evidently a familiar formula, that if Johnny would wait until he struck it rich in the tunnel he'd have lots of money, etc., etc.*

strike oil
informal to become very successful or prosperous. *19th cent.*

> Sapper *The Finger of Fate* 1930
> *The general consensus of opinion was that if his cricket was up to the rest of his form, Bob had struck oil.*

three strikes and you're out
chiefly NAmer a third offence entails a severe penalty (originally as a feature of US law): occasionally used in other contexts such as election contests. The phrase is derived from baseball, in which the batsman must hit the ball by the third delivery or he is declared to be out. *Late 20th cent.*

> *The Times* 1989
> *Susan Sarandon, taking team support seriously, makes a point of bedding the most promising player of the season. Her problem is that on this occasion there are two contenders; a dim youth, played by Tim Robbins, and the ever-reliable Kevin Costner. It's a baseball film all right. After three strikes, I was out.*

See *also* strike at the ROOT of something; strike while the IRON is hot; within striking DISTANCE.

string

have a second string / two strings / more than one string (to one's bow)
to have another ability or resource that one can draw on in place of the usual one if this fails or is inadequate. The reference is to the bow used in archery, rather than to the bow used to play a stringed instrument (although this image might work as well). The phrase may well be a (16th cent.) coinage of Cardinal Wolsey, whose use is preserved in the state papers of the reign of Henry VIII (Vol.IV, 103): 'Ne totally to grounde you upon the said Quenes doinges, but to have 2 stringes to your bowe, specially whan the oone is wrought with a womans fingers.' But since the phrase appears in the near-contemporary (1546) collection of sayings made by John Heywood, it is likely to have had a wider currency than the court. *16th cent.*

how long is a piece of string?
a response to a question that cannot be answered precisely, although a precise answer seems to be expected. Various facetious pseudo-replies have been ventured, for example 'twice its length from the end to the middle.' *Early 20th cent.*

no strings attached
there are no unwelcome or adverse conditions to an offer or opportunity. The use of *string* to mean 'a limitation or restriction' dates from the late 19th cent. *Mid 20th cent.*

on a string
under one's control: in early use with *in* instead of *on*. The original reference is to leads used to guide animals, rather than to puppets (although this notion undoubtedly influences modern use of the phrase). *16th cent.*

> Brian Melbancke *Philotimus* 1583
> *Those that walke as they will, wallowing in their beastly sensualitie, perswading themselves that*

they have the worlde in a string, are like the ruffian Capaney.

Bret Harte *Tales of the Argonauts* 1875
But you know, Yorky, you got out of it well! You've sold 'em too. We've both got 'em on a string now – you and me – got to stick together now.

See also PULL strings; PULL the strings.

---

strip

See tear somebody off a strip at TEAR².

---

stroke

at a stroke
by a single action or effort: literally, by a single blow (in this meaning recorded from Middle English). The transition to figurative usage occurs during the 16th cent.

Gabriel Harvey *Pierces Supererogation* 1593
Titles, and tearmes are but woordes of course: the right fellow, that beareth a braine, can knocke twenty titles on the head, at a stroke.

Pope *Miscellanies* 1727
What a peculiarity is here of invention? The author's pencil, like the wand of Circe, turns all into monsters at a stroke.

different strokes for different folks
(proverb) different things please or satisfy different people: *stroke* here means 'a comforting or approving gesture', a use dating from the mid 20th cent. The proverb is an underlying theme in the 1960s song 'Everyday People' sung by Sly and the Family Stone: 'The butcher, the banker, the drummer and then | Makes no difference what group I'm in | I am everyday people, yeah yeah | There is a blue one who can't accept the green one | For living with a fat one trying to be a skinny one | And different strokes for different folks.' *Different Strokes* was also the title of a US television soap opera about a widowed millionaire who adopts two black boys. In recent use the connotations are often sexual. *Late 20th cent.*

Liz Lochhead *True Confessions and New Clichés* 1985
[Isabel] Its ma rule of thumb that if a wean's auld enough tae ask fur titty then he's too auld tae get, but then – [Murdo] Different strokes for different folks.

not/never do a stroke (of work)
to do no work at all. Negative uses occur earliest and now predominate; uses of *stroke* in more positive contexts (e.g. *a good stroke of business*) occur in the 19th cent. but are no longer common, except in *a stroke of genius* and *a stroke of luck* (see these below). *18th cent.*

on the stroke of —
at a specified time precisely: with reference to the striking of a clock. *Middle English*

put somebody off their stroke
to disconcert somebody or prevent them from doing something effectively: a metaphor from rowing. James Joyce appears to be the earliest user of this phrase. *Early 20th cent.*

a stroke of genius
a piece of clever or original thinking. *19th cent.*

Hardy *Jude the Obscure* 1895
'I was mistaken.' 'Oh, Arabella, Arabella; you be a deep one! Mistaken! well, that's clever – it's a real stroke of genius! It is a thing I never thought o', wi' all my experience!'

a stroke of (good) luck
an unexpected piece of good fortune. *19th cent.*

Horatio Alger *Cast Upon the Breakers* 1893
He began to consider whether he would not be compelled to pawn some article from his wardrobe, for he was well supplied with clothing, when he had a stroke of luck.

stroke somebody the wrong way
to irritate or displease somebody. The image is of stroking the hair of an animal against the direction in which it naturally lies: see also RUB somebody (up) the wrong way. *19th cent.*

with a stroke of the pen
by simply signing a document: normally used with exaggerated reference to the ease with which legal decisions and transactions can be effected. Often used rhetorically or in hyperbole. *17th cent.*

William Temple *Letter* 1668
Your Excellency with a stroak of your pen, has brought to light the most covered designs of your enemies.

strong

(as) strong as a horse / an ox

extremely strong and vigorous. The comparison is on the same lines as *eat like a horse*: see HORSE. *17th cent.*

> Thomas D'Urfey *Love for Money* 1691
> [Lady Addleplot] *Captain your arm a little, stand up strongly ye fribling fool; of my conscience the fellow begins to bend in the hams already.* [Bragg] *Who I Madam, gad y'are mistaken, I'm as strong as a horse.*

> John Cleland *Memoirs of a Woman of Pleasure* 1748
> *He was perfectly well made, stout, and clean-limb'd, tall of his age, as strong as a horse, and, with all, pretty featur'd; so that he was not absolutely such a figure to be snuffed at neither.*

> John Esten Cooke *Leather Stocking and Silk* 1854
> *Oh, you'll be as strong as an ox here in the mountains, soon, my boy.*

be (still) going strong

to remain in good health, condition, etc. *19th cent.*

be strong on something

to be good at or knowledgeable about something. *19th cent.*

> George Eliot *Middlemarch* 1872
> *The ladies also talked politics, though more fitfully. Mrs. Cadwallader was strong on the intended creation of peers: she had it for certain from her cousin that Truberry had gone over to the other side entirely at the instigation of his wife.*

be —'s strong suit/card

to be that person's particular ability or talent: a metaphor from card games. *19th cent.*

> George Ade *Fables in Slang* 1899
> *Marie was a Strong Card. The Male Patrons of the Establishment hovered around the Desk long after paying their Checks. Within a Month the Receipts of the Place had doubled.*

come it strong

informal to speak forcefully or exaggerate wildly: *cf* LAY something on thick. *19th cent.*

> Dickens *Oliver Twist* 1838
> *'If the lady will only hear the first word she has to say, she will know whether to hear her business, or to have her turned out of doors as an impostor.' 'I say,' said the man, 'you're coming it strong!' 'You give the message,' said the girl firmly.*

come on strong

informal to behave in an aggressive or forceful manner. *Late 20th cent.*

strong meat

strongly expressed ideas or language: with reference to St Paul's Epistle to the Hebrews 5:12 'For when for the time ye ought to be teachers, ye have need that one teach you again which be the first principles of the oracles of God; and are become such as have need of milk, and not of strong meat.' *19th cent.*

—'s strong point

a quality or ability in which a particular person excels. *19th cent.*

> Henry James *The Portrait of a Lady* 1881
> *She wished as much as possible to know his thoughts, to know what he would say, beforehand, so that she might prepare her answer. Preparing answers had not been her strong point of old; she had rarely in this respect got further than thinking afterwards of clever things she might have said.*

strut

strut one's stuff

informal, originally NAmer to behave flamboyantly, especially by dancing. *Early 20th cent.*

stuck

be stuck for —

informal to have no means of obtaining something, and therefore be unable to make progress. *Mid 20th cent.*

be stuck on somebody

informal to be very fond of somebody. *19th cent.*

> Clyde Fitch *The Cowboy and the Lady* 1899
> *They say every cove in Silverville is stuck on her, and each son of a gun's dead certain she's gone on him.*

> Somerset Maugham *Of Human Bondage* 1915
> *Mildred taught her to call him daddy, and when the child did this for the first time of her own accord, laughed immoderately. 'I wonder if you're that stuck on baby because she's mine,' asked Mildred, 'or if you'd be the same with anybody's baby.'*

get stuck in / into something
informal, originally Australian to involve oneself wholeheartedly in a task or undertaking. *Mid 20th cent.*

See also STICK[1].

study

in a brown study
absorbed in one's own thoughts; oblivious to what is happening around one. *Brown* is used here in an early generalized (and now otherwise disused) meaning 'dark, gloomy.' *16th cent.*

> John Lyly *Euphues* 1579
> *You are in some brown study, what colours you might best wear.*

stuff

do one's stuff
informal to do what one is expected to do; to perform a task well: a coincidental use by George Fox (1624–91), founder of the Society of Friends, in a journal entry for 1663 ('… when the priest had done his stuff …') probably has a specific meaning not connected with the general informal use, which otherwise first appears in the 1920s. *Early 20th cent.*

> T E Lawrence *Letter* 1930
> *That portable was good at Miranshah. I hope yours is doing its stuff.*

know one's stuff
informal to be knowledgeable and experienced in one's profession or field of activity. *Early 20th cent.*

> Graham Greene *Brighton Rock* 1938
> *'The medical evidence shows without any doubt that he died naturally. He had a bad heart …'*
> *'Could I see the report?' … Ida read it carefully. 'This doctor,' she said, 'he knows his stuff?' 'He's a first-class doctor.'*

See also a bit of fluff/skirt/stuff *at* BIT[1]; STRUT one's stuff; SWEAT the small stuff.

stuffing

knock/take the stuffing out of somebody
informal to cause somebody to lose vigour or vitality. The image is of stuffing being knocked out of a cushion or pillow, causing it to become limp and useless. *19th cent.*

stump

(go) on the stump
informal, chiefly NAmer to be engaged in a tour of political campaigning: from the use of a tree stump in the 18th cent. as an improvised platform for addressing a crowd. *19th cent.*

> Frederick W Thomas *Clinton Bradshaw* 1835
> *Bradshaw and Carlton had had many stern encounters on the stump. The election day approached.*

this side of / beyond the black stump
Australian, informal inside (or outside) the normal limits of civilized life. Burnt tree stumps were a common feature of the Australian landscape, and were put to all sorts of uses; these included markers in giving directions to travellers, the basis of the present phrase. *Mid 20th cent.*

up a stump
informal, chiefly NAmer unable to cope with an awkward situation. Probably a variant of *up a gum tree* (*see* GUM). *19th cent.*

See also STIR one's stumps.

suck

suck somebody dry
to exploit somebody financially or emotionally to the point of exhaustion. *16th cent.*

> John Stow *A Survey of London* 1598
> *London felt it most tragicall; for then he both seysed their liberties, and sucked themselues dry.*

suck it and see
informal find out what something is like by trying it. The image is of testing food for its taste. *Mid 20th cent.*

sudden

(all) of a sudden
suddenly or unexpectedly. The phrase dates from the 16th cent., and from the 17th cent. with *all*, and represents the only survival of *sudden* as a noun, related to its former meaning 'an unexpected need or danger'.

Thomas Beard *The Theatre of Gods Judgements* 1597
It rained so strangely and vehemently all this whole day and night, that of a sudden so huge a deluge and flood of waters overflowed the earth.

suffer

suffer fools (gladly)

to treat with patience and tolerance those one regards as foolish: normally used in negative contexts. The strand of meaning of *suffer* here is 'to tolerate, to endure the presence of', which is found from Middle English. *17th cent.*

George Wither *Carmen Expostulatorium* 1647
Suffer fools gladly, seeing ye your selves are wise.

G B Shaw *Pygmalion* 1913
He was, I believe, not in the least an ill-natured man: very much the opposite, I should say; but he would not suffer fools gladly.

sugar

See sugar the PILL.

suit

suit oneself

to follow one's own wishes, often regardless of the wishes of others. *Suit yourself* (in the imperative) is common as a response expressive of disdainful or grudging acquiescence in another person's behaviour or action. The phrase occurs more compositionally from the 17th cent. in the sense 'to accustom oneself (to surroundings, circumstances, etc).' *19th cent.*

Wilkie Collins *No Name* 1862
The parlour-maid now at St. Crux, is engaged to be married; and, as soon as her master can suit himself, she is going away.

John B Tagg *Doctor Tumble-bug* 1899
With wondrous skill | He works until, | To suit himself, he makes it | A patent Pill, | To cure or kill | The sufferer that takes it.

suit the action to the word

to act or behave in accordance with one's intentions or promises. The expression is derived from Hamlet's instruction to the players before their performance in Shakespeare's *Hamlet* (1601) III.ii.17: 'Be not too tame, neither; but let your own discretion be your tutor. Suit the action to

the word, the word to the action, with this special observance: that you o'erstep not the modesty of nature.' *17th cent.*

See also FOLLOW suit; MEN in suits; suit —'s BOOK; suit somebody down to the ground *at* down to the GROUND.

summer

See INDIAN summer.

sun

—'s sun is set

— is past their peak of achievement; — is finished or doomed. *19th cent.*

Leigh Hunt *Imagination and Fancy* 1844
Then grew the visage pale, and deadly wet; | The eyes turn'd in their sockets, drearily; | And all things show'd the villain's sun was set.

a touch of the sun

a light attack of sunstroke. *19th cent.*

under the sun

anywhere in the world: used as an intensifying phrase in negative contexts. The phrase appears in Middle English in Wyclif's translation of Ecclesiastes 1:9 ('no thing under the sunne newe'), which is translated in the Authorized Version of 1611 as 'there is no new thing under the sun'.

Anon *The London Jilt* 1683
I certifie to you according to the experience I have had thereof, and all women who have so open and frank a heart as mine, will confess as well as I do, that there is nothing under the sun that has such powerful attractions.

William Godwin *St Leon* 1799
Human affairs, like the waves of the ocean, are merely in a state of ebb and flow: 'there is nothing new under the sun'.

when the sun is over the yardarm/foreyard

the time of day when it is permitted to have alcoholic drinks. The phrase originates in naval use: the *yardarm* was the outer extremity of the horizontal spar from which a sail was hung; in northern waters the sun would reach the required position at midday. *19th cent.*

See also CATCH the sun; make hay while the sun shines *at* make HAY; a PLACE in the sun.

sunset

See RIDE off into the sunset.

sup

See sup with the DEVIL.

supper

See SING for one's supper.

sure

sure thing
informal, originally NAmer a certainty: also used
as a formula of agreement or approval. *19th cent.*

A J H Duganne *The Tenant-House* 1857
*'It is all true, then, Ferret?' 'Sure thing!' replied
Peleg.*

George Eliot *Adam Bede* 1859
*Why, it's a sure thing – and there's them 'ull bear
witness to 't.*

See also (as) sure as eggs is eggs *at* EGG.

surf

surf the Net
to browse through Internet websites, especially
in a casual or random way looking for information or entertainment: hence the words *netsurfing,
cybersurfing*, and others. The image is taken from
the sport of surfing. *Late 20th cent.*

survival

survival of the fittest
the process of natural selection, by which those
organisms that are best adapted to their surroundings are the ones most likely to survive.
The theory owes its origins to Charles Darwin
(1809–82), although the phrase as such was first
used by the philosopher Herbert Spencer in his
Principles of Biology, published in 1864. *19th cent.*

Elbert Hubbard *A Message to Garcia* 1899
*In every store and factory there is a constant
weeding-out process going on. The employer is
constantly sending away 'help' that have shown
their incapacity to further the interests of the
business, and others are being taken on … It is the*

*survival of the fittest. Self-interest prompts every
employer to keep the best.*

suspend

See suspend one's DISBELIEF.

suss

on suss
under suspicion of having committed an offence:
sus and *suss*, shortenings of *suspicion*, date from
the 1930s. *Late 20th cent.*

swallow[1] (the bird)

one swallow does not make a summer
(proverb) a single piece of evidence is not necessarily conclusive. The sentiment is found in classical antiquity: Aristotle in the *Nicomachaean
Ethics* has 'One swallow does not make a spring'
and it is spring rather than summer that appears
in Latin versions (notably Erasmus *Adages* i.7 *una
hirundo non fecit ver*). *16th cent.*

swallow[2] (verb)

swallow one's pride
to force oneself to act or speak in a humbling way
from necessity. *19th cent.*

Trollope *Dr Thorne* 1858
*Dr. Fillgrave still continued his visits to Gre-
shamsbury, for Lady Arabella had not yet mustered
the courage necessary for swallowing her pride and
sending once more for Dr. Thorne.*

swan

swan around/off
informal to wander or travel aimlessly or irresponsibly: from the literal meaning 'to swim
like a swan'. The phrase is perhaps a little unfair
to swans, with whom we hardly associate attitudes of casual irresponsibility; but the image of
gentle drifting is certainly appropriate as a metaphor. *Mid 20th cent.*

swathe

Swathe is an Old English word with many Germanic cognates: it originally denoted the space

covered by the sweep of a scythe, and then a row or line of cut grass. From the early 17th cent. the meaning broadened into 'a track or strip of land' and figurative uses developed referring to large strips or lengths of a wider range of things, even including water.

cut a swathe through something
to achieve one's ends ruthlessly or by causing much damage or harm to others. *19th cent.*

cut a wide swathe
informal, chiefly NAmer to attract a great deal of attention. Bartlett's *Dictionary of Americanisms* (second edition, 1859) has an entry that reads *'To do business with a big spoon,* is the same as to cut a big swathe.' *19th cent.*

swear

swear blind
British, informal to insist emphatically on something. *Mid 20th cent.*

See also swear like a TROOPER.

sweat

by the sweat of one's brow
by one's own physical efforts: often used humorously or ironically. The phrase is based on Genesis 3:19, which both Coverdale and the Authorized Version translate 'In the sweat of thy face shalt thou eat bread'. *Brow* first appears in this phrase in the *Art of Rhetoric* (1553) of Thomas Wilson, Tudor scholar and privy counsellor. *16th cent.*

in a cold sweat
in a state of shock or anxiety. *18th cent.*

in a sweat
extremely anxious or expectant. *19th cent.*

> Mark Twain *The Adventures of Huckleberry Finn* 1884
> *After supper she got out her book and learned me about Moses and the Bulrushers; and I was in a sweat to find out all about him.*

no sweat
informal no problem or difficulty: used dismissively. *Mid 20th cent.*

sweat blood
informal to make a strenuous effort; to work extremely hard. References to the physical sweat-

ing of blood go back to Old English; the locus classicus is the description of the sweat of Christ during his agony in the Garden of Gethsemane in Luke 22:44: 'And being in an agony he prayed more earnestly: and his sweat was as it were great drops of blood falling down to the ground.' *16th cent.*

sweat bullets
NAmer, informal to be extremely anxious or nervous. *Mid 20th cent.*

sweat it out
informal to put up with prolonged difficulty or anxiety. *19th cent.*

> Mark Twain *The Adventures of Tom Sawyer* 1876
> *'Well, it's a kind of a tight place for Becky Thatcher, because there ain't any way out of it.' Tom conned the thing a moment longer and then added: 'All right, though; she'd like to see me in just such a fix – let her sweat it out!'*

sweat the small stuff
informal to worry or fuss over trivial problems: usually in the form *don't sweat the small stuff,* said as reproof or consolation. *Late 20th cent.*

> Guardian 1989
> *My problem is that I'm the first person on either side of my family to have gone to university. I want the Ayatollah to have the blessing of opportunity. Being more secure than me, the Ayatollah doesn't seem to sweat the small stuff. His nonchalance makes me nervous; he doesn't know how hard it is out there.*

See also sweat one's GUTS out.

sweep

sweep somebody off their feet
to captivate or totally fascinate somebody. *19th cent.*

> John Keble *Lectures on Poetry* 1844
> *Most finely does the poet portray the chafing resentment of the soldiers, as he piles their indignant phrases, one upon another, while at the same time he implies that the reluctant king was borne down by stress of overwhelming pressure: as clause follows clause, the very rhythm seems to sweep him off his feet.*

> George Meredith *Beauchamp's Career* 1876
> *Renée said, 'To Venice, quickly, my brother!' and now she almost sighed with relief to think that she*

was escaping from this hurricane of a youth, who swept her off her feet and wrapt her whole being in a delirium.

See also make a CLEAN sweep; sweep the BOARD; sweep something under the CARPET.

sweet

be sweet on somebody

to be attracted to somebody or particularly fond of them, especially in a romantic or sexual way. The phrase is also recorded in the 17th cent. in a slightly different sense 'to act gallantly towards somebody.' *17th cent.*

> Head & Kirkman *The English Rogue Described* 1668
> *By this time my Mistress was so sweet upon me, that we talked very familiarly and pleasantly, and oftentimes I interlaced our Discourses with kisses and amorous sighs.*

have a sweet tooth

informal to enjoy sweet food. *16th cent.*

> Ben Jonson *The Staple of Newes* a1637
> *I have a sweet tooth yet, and I will hope the best; and sit downe as quiet, and calme as butter, looke as smooth, and soft as butter; be merry, and melt like butter; laugh and be fat like butter: So butter answer my expectation.*

keep somebody sweet

informal to ensure that somebody remains well disposed and cooperative, especially by offering them favours. *Mid 20th cent.*

she's sweet

Australian, informal everything is fine: *sweet* in the sense 'all right, well' dates in Australian use from the late 19th cent. *Mid 20th cent.*

sweet Fanny Adams

informal nothing at all: also shortened to *sweet FA* (which is also understood as *sweet fuck all*). The phrase has a grim origin: Fanny Adams was an eight-year-old girl who was raped and murdered, and her body dismembered, in 1867. To add to the macabre nature of the story, her name was adopted in naval slang to refer to the tinned meat that was first used at about the same time: hence the name became symbolic of anything unwelcome or worthless. *Early 20th cent.*

See also sweet nothings *at* NOTHING.

sweeten

See sugar/sweeten the PILL.

sweetness

be (all) sweetness and light

to put on a show of gentle affability. The phrase was first used in a physical sense by Jonathan Swift in his prose satire *The Battle of the Books* (1704): 'Instead of dirt and poison, we have rather chosen to fill our hives with honey and wax, thus furnishing mankind with the two noblest of things, which are sweetness and light.' The phrase was taken up in a more figurative sense by Matthew Arnold in *Culture and Anarchy* (1869): 'Their ideal of beauty and sweetness and light, and a human nature complete on all its sides.' *19th cent.*

swim

in the swim

informal involved in the latest business, fashions, etc: based on the meaning of *swim* 'a part of a river frequented by fish.' *19th cent.*

See also go/swim with/against the TIDE.

swing

Uses of the noun *swing* in the sense 'vigorous action' date from the late 16th cent.

get into the swing (of things)

informal to become familiarized with the task in hand. *19th cent.*

> Rider Haggard *Jess* 1887
> *Naturally of an energetic and hard-working temperament, he very soon got more or less into the swing of the thing, and at the end of six weeks began to talk quite learnedly of cattle and ostriches and sweet and sour veldt.*

go with a swing

informal (said of a social occasion) to be lively and noisy: also extended to other contexts. *Mid 20th cent.*

> G S Fraser *Letter from Asmara* 1943
> *The evocative names that make poetry go with a swing, | Gura, Nefacit, Ambulagi, Keren.*

in full swing

informal bustling with activity. *19th cent.*

Dickens *Bleak House* 1853
The fashionable world – tremendous orb, nearly five miles round – is in full swing, and the solar system works respectfully at its appointed distances.

swings and roundabouts

advantages and disadvantages that balance each other or cancel each other out: also the (early 20th cent.) proverb *what you lose on the swings you gain on the roundabouts* (and variants). The allusion is to fairground amusements, some of which are more enjoyable at different times than others. *19th cent.*

See also swing the lead *at* LEAD².

swollen

have a swollen head

1 to be suffering from a hangover: with allusion to the sensation felt in the head when suffering from the effects of excessive alcohol. *19th cent.*
2 to be extremely conceited or vain. The image here is similar to that in *bighead* and other figurative expressions denoting arrogance and conceit, presumably drawing ironically on the size of the brain as a presumed indicator of intelligence. *19th cent.*

Cullen Gouldsbury *Songs out of Exile* 1912
'Tis ever thus with the Mission bred, | Friend, thou hast gotten a swollen head!

swoop

See in/at one FELL swoop.

sword

beat/turn swords into ploughshares

to turn one's efforts to peace after prolonged warfare: with allusion to the peaceful rule of God described in Isaiah 2:4 (in the Authorized Version, 1611): 'And he shall judge among the nations, and shall rebuke many people: and they shall beat their swords into plowshares, and their spears into pruning hooks: nation shall not lift up sword against nation, neither shall they learn war any more.' A ploughshare is the pointed blade of a plough, and its symbolism of peace parallels that of the sword in fighting. The phrase is found in Middle English in Wyclif's translation of the Bible.

he who lives by the sword shall die by the sword

those who use violence can expect to suffer violence themselves. Used with allusion to Matthew 26:52, where Christ in the Garden of Gethsemane restrains a disciple who has cut off the ear of a servant of the High Priest (in the Authorized Version, 1611): 'Put up again thy sword into his place: for all they that take the sword shall perish with the sword.' *17th cent.*

put somebody to the sword

to kill somebody in war. The phrase occurs in Middle English with *do* instead of *put*. *17th cent.*

Shakespeare *As You Like It* v.iv.156 (1599)
[Jaques de Bois] *Duke Frederick ... | Addressed a mighty power, which were on foot, | In his own conduct, purposely to take | His brother here, and put him to the sword.*

sword of Damocles

a danger that threatens one: with reference to the story of Damocles, a courtier of Dionysius I of Syracuse (4th cent. BC). When Damocles declared that tyrants such as Dionysius must be the happiest of men, Dionysius demonstrated the fragility of his position by inviting Damocles to a banquet at which he placed a naked sword hanging by a thread over Damocles' head. *18th cent.*

Herman Melville *The Piazza Tales* 1856
Whoever built the house, he builded better than he knew, or else Orion in the zenith flashed down his Damocles' sword to him some starry night and said, 'Build there.' For how, otherwise, could it have entered the builder's mind, that, upon the clearing being made, such a purple prospect would be his?

See also CROSS swords; a double-edged/two-edged sword *at* EDGE.

Sydney

Sydney or the bush

Australian, informal all or nothing: said to be based on the story of a man who gambled his fortune, with the prospect of a life of luxury in the city if he won or a hard life working in the outback if he lost. *Early 20th cent.*

syllable

in words of one syllable
using simple language. *Early 20th cent.*

> **G K Chesterton** *Orthodoxy* 1908
> *It is a good exercise to try for once in a way to express any opinion one holds in words of one syllable.*

sync

in / out of sync
working well (or badly) together. These are shortenings of *synchronism, synchronization,* and related words. The phrase is first recorded in the 1920s in a technical context to do with photography in the phoneticized spelling *in sink,* although this does not recur. Early uses are largely confined to technical contexts, notably the alignment of picture and sound in early speaking films. *Early 20th cent.*

system

all systems go
everything is ready or working properly. The adjectival use of *go* to mean 'functioning correctly' dates from the early 20th cent. and became a familiar feature of US space missions in the 1970s. *Mid 20th cent.*

get something out of one's system
to rid oneself of a worry or preoccupation by indulging it to the limit. *Early 20th cent.*

T

to a T
informal completely; to perfection. The phrase is thought to allude to the precision of a designer's T-square, although this is not certain. Much less likely is an association, also postulated, with the tee of a golf course; it is difficult to see how this could be relevant. A third suggestion, that it refers to the crossing of a letter t, cannot be substantiated. A more attractive possibility is that T is the first letter of some word, and interestingly a phrase *to a tittle* (= a small stroke or point in writing) is recorded in the same meaning from the early 17th cent., about sixty years earlier than the form we are concerned with here. *17th cent.*

> **Elkanah Settle** *The Notorious Impostor* 1692
> *Ah Master, says Tom, what a parcel of brave Cattle are these. Ay Tom, replies the Master, I am sorry I saw them no sooner; these would do my Business to a T; but as the Devil and ill Luck would have it, I have laid out my whole Stock already.*

tab

The sense underlying the phrases is the North American meaning 'account or bill'.

keep tabs / a tab on somebody/something
NAmer, informal to keep a close check on a person, organization, activity, etc. *19th cent.*

> **Charles Hale Hoyt** *A Trip to Chinatown* 1891
> *By jove, I've an idea. I'll hide in here and keep tabs on that breakfast. I have some little confidence in her but none in him.*

See also PICK up the bill/tab.

table

lay something on the table

to present something for consideration or discussion, literally by putting documents on a table for members of a group to study. In North American usage, the phrase denotes postponement of discussion or action and is therefore comparable to *shelve*, which is contrary to British use. *18th cent.*

> Thomas Jefferson *Passages from his Autobiography* 1854
> *Congress proceeded the same day to consider the Declaration of Independence, which had been reported and laid on the table the Friday preceding, and on Monday referred to a committee of the whole.*

turn the tables (on somebody)

to turn a position of disadvantage to one of advantage; to put somebody in a weaker position when previously they had been in a stronger one. *Table* here means a board for chess and backgammon; *turning the table(s)* referred to the idea of reversing the position of the board and so reversing the roles of the two players (a notion not a practice). There are other explanations on offer, neither having any credibility: that wealthy collectors of furniture in ancient Rome had the tables literally turned on them by their wives when questions of extravagance arose; and a former practice in British furniture-making of finishing one side only of a table top, so that households could use the rough side for day-to-day living and turn the top to expose the good surface when company was expected. But early uses of the phrase (including the first given below) make an origin in gaming incontrovertible. *17th cent.*

> Congreve *The Double Dealer* 1694
> *I confess you may be allow'd to be secure in your own opinion; the appearance is very fair, but I have an after-game to play that shall turn the tables, and here comes the man that I must manage.*

> Vanbrugh *Aesop* 1697
> *And so Sir you turn the tables upon the plaintiff, and play the fool and knave at his door.*

under the table

completely drunk. To *drink* (or *put* or *see*) *somebody under the table* is to drink more alcohol than a companion without getting drunk oneself. *Early 20th cent.*

> Somerset Maugham *The Trembling of a Leaf* 1921
> *Walker had always been a heavy drinker, he was proud of his capacity to see men half his age under the table.*

tack

See come down to BRASS tacks.

tag

See RAG, tag, and bobtail.

tail

chase one's own tail

informal to keep doing something pointless or futile. The image is of a dog running round in circles in an apparent attempt to catch its own tail. *Mid 20th cent.*

> Steam Railway News 1992
> *One of the problems which arises from chasing one's tail in a flurry of activity is that while there is much more to write about, there is less time to write it in.*

the tail wags the dog

the least important element or factor is dominating the situation. *Early 20th cent.*

> Esquire 1992
> *At times, the relationship between my penis and the rest of my body might appear to be a classic case of the tail wagging the dog. But I've learned to stop blaming my penis for getting into a muddle when attempting to decode my hidden desires. I'm learning to live with its troublesome Jekyll and Hyde nature.*

turn tail

to turn back, especially to walk or run off: originally (16th cent.) a term in falconry, when the hawk leaves its prey without killing it. *17th cent.*

> Defoe *Robinson Crusoe* 1719
> *Upon which I ordered our last pistol to be fired off in one volley, and after that we gave a shout. Upon this the wolves turned tail, and we sallied immediately upon near twenty lame ones, whom we found struggling on the ground.*

with one's tail between one's legs

informal in a state of great shame or dejection: the image is of a sick or frightened dog slinking off with its tail tucked under its hind legs. Literal uses are found earlier (15th cent.) than the figurative uses we are concerned with here. In Shakespeare's 2 *Henry VI* (1591) v.i.152 Richard warns Clifford and York: 'Oft have I seen a hot o'erweening cur | Run back and bite, because he was withheld; | Who, being suffered with the bear's fell paw, | Hath clapped his tail between his legs and cried; | And such a piece of service will you do, | If you oppose yourselves to match Lord Warwick.' *17th cent.*

> Charles Gildon *The Post-boy Rob'd of His Mail* 1692
> *I was as obstinate altogether, in denying to correspond with his indiscretion, so that he departed with his tail between his legs, being fairly given to understand, that he must find some other nest for his master to lay his eggs in than mine.*

with one's tail up
informal feeling cheerful and confident. *19th cent.*

See also a PIECE of ass/tail.

---

take

be taken up with something
to be absorbed in a thought or idea. *17th cent.*

> Locke *An Essay Concerning Human Understanding* 1690
> *And we see, that one who fixes his thoughts very intently on one thing, so as to take but little notice of the succession of ideas that pass in his mind, whilst he is taken up with that earnest contemplation, lets slip out of his account a good part of that duration, and thinks that time shorter than it is.*

> Defoe *Robinson Crusoe* 1719
> *As I was reading in the Bible, and taken up with very serious thoughts about my present condition, I was surprised with a noise of a gun, as I thought, fired at sea.*

be taken with somebody/something
to find somebody or something appealing or likable: *cf* take a liking/fancy to somebody/something *below*. *16th cent.*

> Hobbes *Leviathan* 1651
> *So when a man compoundeth the image of his own person with the image of the actions of another man, as when a man imagines himself a Hercules or an Alexander (which happeneth often to them that are much taken with reading of romances), it is a compound imagination, and properly but a fiction of the mind.*

for the taking
(said of a person or thing) available to whoever needs them. *18th cent.*

> Smollett *The Expedition of Humphry Clinker* 1771
> *We make free with our landlord's mutton, which is excellent, his poultry-yard, his garden, his dairy, and his cellar, which are all well stored. We have delicious salmon, pike, trout, perch, par, &c. at the door, for the taking.*

have what it takes
informal to have the qualities or resources needed to achieve success: *what it takes* is recorded in North American use from the 1920s in the sense of money needed for some purpose. *If you have what it takes* is a constant cliché of job advertisements, and there are many other more or less hackneyed applications of the phrase. *Mid 20th cent.*

> Richard Dawkins *The Blind Watchmaker* 1991
> *DNA molecules … are not durable like rocks. But the patterns that they bear in their sequences are as durable as the hardest rocks. They have what it takes to exist for millions of years, and that is why they are still here today.*

on the take
informal, originally *NAmer* accepting bribes; capable of being corrupted. *Mid 20th cent.*

> *Economist* 1991
> *Mr Aichi had had to withdraw his candidature for the governorship of Miyagi prefecture when it was revealed that he had been on the take.*

take somebody apart
informal to punish or trounce somebody harshly or decisively. *Mid 20th cent.*

> *Rugby World and Post* 1991
> *But with no foundation up front, the fullback Jim Staples … , flanker Mick Fitzgibbon and fly-half Peter Russell all departing injured, the Irish were gradually taken apart.*

take it from me
an assurance that one speaks with confidence or authority on a matter: *cf* take somebody's WORD for it. *17th cent.*

> John Healey *The Discovery of a New World* c1609
> *Is it not strange that this barren country should neuer-the-lesse haue such aboundance of all necessaries, naye and superfluities also, that it may challenge all the world in a prize of wealth, and (as*

farre as their naturall fiercenesse permitteth) of delicacy too? Take it from me (quoth Hieremy Ratcliffe) they may; there is no rariety, nor excellent thing of worth in all the world, but they will haue it.

John Fletcher *The Loyal Subject* 1618
[Olimpia] *Heaven blesse the wench.* [Alinda] *With eyes that will not be denied to enter; | And such soft sweet embraces; take it from me, | I am undone else Madam: I'm lost else.*

take it from there

to continue or develop a process or undertaking from a specified point. *Mid 20th cent.*

P G Wodehouse *Jeeves in the Offing* 1960
His future hangs on this speech, and we've got it and he hasn't. We take it from there.

take it or leave it

an expression of impatience or indifference addressed to somebody who has refused or expressed reservations about an offer. *16th cent.*

Shakespeare *King Lear* I.i.203 (1606)
[Lear to Burgundy] *Will you with those infirm-ities she owes, | Unfriended, new adopted to our hate, | Dow'r'd with our curse and strangered with our oath, | Take her or leave her?*

Thomas Killigrew *Thomaso* 1664
The price is but four Royalls, that is the price, and less I know, in curtesie you cannot offer me; take it, or leave it.

take it out of somebody

to exhaust or tire somebody. *19th cent.*

Mark Twain *The Innocents Abroad* 1869
But we have taken it out of this guide. He has marched us through miles of pictures and sculpture in the vast corridors of the Vatican ... he has shown us the great picture in the Sistine Chapel, and frescoes ... pretty much all done by Michael Angelo. So with him we have played that game which has vanquished so many guides for us – imbecility and idiotic questions.

take it out on somebody

to vent one's anger or frustration on somebody. Originally the notion seems to have been of rob-bing or depriving, or exacting revenge. *17th cent.*

Sir John Suckling *The Sad One* a1642
By what thou holdst most dear, I do conjure thee | To leave this work to me; | And if ere thou canst think | That I present thee not a full revenge, | Then take it out on me.

Mrs Gaskell *Sylvia's Lovers* 1863
Yo' see, missus, there's not a many as 'ud take him in for a shillin' when it goes so little way; or if they did, they'd take it out on him some other way, an' he's not getten much else a reckon.

take it upon oneself

to agree or presume to do something. The phrase goes back in various forms to Middle English, occurring in Chaucer (see below).

Chaucer *The Pardoner's Tale* (line 612)
Ne I wol nat take on me so greet defame, | Yow for to allie unto none hasardours.

Shakespeare *As You Like It* III.ii.406 (1599)
[Rosalind to Orlando] *And thus I cured him, and this way will I take upon me to wash your liver as clean as a sound sheep's heart, that there shall not be one spot of love in 't.*

take a liking/fancy to somebody/something

to find somebody or something appealing or likable: *cf* be taken with somebody/something above. *16th cent.*

Conan Doyle *Wisteria Lodge* 1908
In some way we struck up quite a friendship, this young fellow and I. He seemed to take a fancy to me from the first, and within two days of our meeting he came to see me.

take people or things as one finds them

to form judgements about people or things impartially and without preconception. *16th cent.*

William Haughton *Englishmen for My Money* 1616
[Walgrave] *Heare you, if you'le run away with Ned, | And be content to take me as you find me, | Why ... I am yours.*

George Eliot *Middlemarch* 1872
I take the world as I find it, in trade and everything else.

take that!

said when hitting or attempting to hit somebody. Despite a few early occurrences (including one from Middle English in *Cursor Mundi*), the prin-cipal usage is from the 18th cent. onwards.

Anon *Lord George Falconbridge* 1616
He most valiantly thrust his arme (wrapped about with faire Clarabels silke scarfe) into the gaping jawes of the over-furious Lyonesse, and by the force of his manhood toare out his savage heart, (yet leaping warme in his hand) and threw it at Don

Johns face, saying; Take that thou monster of humanity, thou unprincely Potentate.

Richardson *Pamela* 1741
She hit him a good smart Slap on the Shoulder. Take that, impudent Brother, said she.

take somebody up on something

1 *informal* to accept an offer or respond positively to an opportunity that somebody provides. *I might take you up on that* is a common formula of qualified acceptance of an offer or suggestion. *Early 20th cent.*

Sinclair Lewis *Our Mr Wrenn* 1914
'We'll go Dutch to a lodging-house' … 'All right, sir; all right. I'll take you up on that.'
2 *informal* to respond to or wish to develop a particular point made by another participant in an argument or discussion. *20th cent.*

Pamela Street *Guilty Parties* 1990
'My publicity days are over, I'm afraid.' 'Afraid?' He was quick, she noticed, to take her up on any casual remark and supposed that his interest in other people's affairs and their reactions had something to do with the novelist in him.

take up one's pen

to start writing, especially to begin a literary work. *17th cent.*

Richardson *Clarissa* 1748
It was near two hours before I could so far recover myself as to take up my pen, to write to you how unhappily my hopes have ended.

George Meredith *Beauchamp's Career* 1876
Are you unaware that he met Captain Beauchamp at the château of the marquise? The whole story was acted under his eyes. He had only to take up his pen.

take up with somebody

to associate or form a friendship, especially a romance, with somebody. *17th cent.*

Alexander Oldys *The Female Gallant* 1692
Henrietta express'd a great deal of satisfaction at the sight of her brother, after so long an absence; nor was he behind hand in his expressions of joy at the sight of her; Philandra only was disconsolate, who found she shou'd dye an unmarry'd widow, unless she took up with Sir Blunder Slouch, or some such Booby of a Husband.

take something up with somebody

to raise a question or issue for discussion with somebody. *19th cent.*

George Howells Broadhurst *Man of the Hour* 1906
[Judge] *Please take the matter up with Mr. Horigan as soon as you conveniently can.*

you can't take it with you

a cliché emphasizing the impossibility of keeping material possessions after death, often invoked as an excuse for extravagance during life. *19th cent.*

See also it takes all sorts *at* SORT; take something as READ; take somebody at their WORD; take the BISCUIT; take the CAKE; take CHARGE; take somebody/something for granted *at* GRANT; take somebody for a RIDE; take it EASY; take it into one's HEAD; take it on the CHIN; take something lying down *at* LIE[1]; take the MICKEY; take somebody's name in VAIN; take no prisoners *at* PRISONER; take something on BOARD; take one OUT of oneself; take somebody's POINT; take STOCK; take somebody to the cleaners *at* CLEANER; take something to HEART; take to one's heels *at* HEEL; take somebody to TASK.

tale

dead men tell no tales

(proverb) a sinister recommendation that those who might do one harm are best disposed of. *17th cent.*

George Farquhar *The Inconstant* 1702
[2nd Bravo] *Shall we dispatch him?* [3rd Bravo] *To be sure, I think he knows me.* [1st Bravo] *Ay, ay, Dead Men, tell no Tales.*

tell its own tale

to be a clear sign of what something is like or of what has happened. *19th cent.*

Kipling *Kim* 1901
Kim looked over the retinue critically. Half of them were thin-legged, gray-bearded Ooryas from down country. The other half were duffle-clad, felt-hatted hillmen of the North: and that mixture told its own tale, even if he had not overheard the incessant sparring between the two divisions.

tell tales (out of school)

to gossip about somebody's faults or wrongdoings: originally used with reference to children. *16th cent.*

Samuel Cobb *Tripos Cantabrigiensis* 1702
Nor need you fear that I shall e'er disclose | The secrets that are whisper'd inter Nos. | For we all

know it breaks a General Rule | Of Decency, to tell Tales out of School.

thereby hangs/lies a tale

there is an interesting story to tell in connection with this: also *herein/therein lies a tale*. The form with *lie* occurs in the works of the Tudor poet John Skelton (*c*1460–1529), whereas Shakespeare, enjoying the pun on *tail*, used *hang* in place of *lie* on several occasions (e.g. in *As You Like It* (1599) II.vii.28: '[Jaques] And so from hour to hour we ripe and ripe, | And then from hour to hour we rot and rot; | And thereby hangs a tale'). Evidently Shakespeare knew it as a cliché; he also uses it in *The Taming of the Shrew* (1592), *The Merry Wives of Windsor* (1597) and *Othello* (1604). There are many ad hoc variations on the phrase (see the Fielding quotation below). *16th cent.*

> **Thomas Churchyard *A Generall Rehearsall of Warres* 1579**
> *I could tell why, but thereby hangs a tale, | Would make me blushe, and shewe of grace great lacke.*

> **Dryden et al *The Satires of Juvenal* 1693**
> *To Morrow early in Quirinus Vale | I must attend – Why? – Thereby hangs a Tale, | A Male-Friend's to be marry'd to a Male.*

> **Henry Fielding *The Adventures of Joseph Andrews* 1752**
> *I own, I could not help laughing, when I heard him offer you the living; for thereby hangs a good jest. I thought he would have offered you my house next; for one is no more his to dispose of than the other.*

See also an old wives' tale *at* WIFE.

talk

now you're talking

informal at last you are saying something interesting or exciting: used to indicate a positive reaction to a suggestion, invitation, etc. *19th cent.*

> **Mark Twain *The Adventures of Tom Sawyer* 1876**
> *'You bet I'll follow him, if it's dark, Huck. Why he might 'a' found out he couldn't get his revenge, and be going right after that money.' 'It's so, Tom, it's so. I'll foller him; I will, by jingoes!' 'Now you're talking! Don't you ever weaken, Huck, and I won't.'*

talk through one's hat / through the back of one's neck

to talk utter nonsense. *Early 20th cent.*

> **Bookseller 1993**
> *Surely Mr Taylor is talking through his hat by implying that the part that matters in Victoria Glendinning's life of Trollope is her speculation about Trollope's sex life – however interesting.*

you can talk

informal used as a spoken rejoinder to somebody who has expressed a view without being in the same vulnerable position as the speaker, or to somebody who has expressed a criticism that applies no less to themselves. Also (especially in the second sense) *you can't talk, you needn't talk*, etc. *19th cent.*

> **R L Stevenson *Treasure Island* 1883**
> *Belay that talk, John Silver ... This crew has tipped you the black spot in full council, as in dooty bound; just you turn it over, as in dooty bound, and see what's wrote there. Then you can talk.*

See also CHALK *and* talk; speak/talk of the DEVIL; talk a BLUE streak; talk DIRTY; talk somebody's HEAD off; talk the hind leg(s) off a DONKEY; talk nineteen to the DOZEN; talk SHOP; talk TURKEY.

tall

In Old and Middle English *tall* meant 'quick, prompt', from which a sense 'ready for action' and hence 'brave, valiant' developed in the 15th cent. The meaning to do with height first appears halfway through the 16th cent., and the meaning reflected in the phrases is 'grand, magnificent, high-flown', which is found from the 17th cent. in combinations such as *tall talk* and *tall writing*; this meaning became watered down in the 19th cent. to mean simply 'large'. In 1842 Dickens wrote in *American Notes*: 'We were a pretty tall time coming that last fifteen mile.'

a tall order

a demand or requirement that is difficult to accomplish. *19th cent.*

> **William Boyle *The Mineral Workers* 1910**
> *Cousin Ned Mulroy, I want my hand on your estate to carry out this project ... It's a tall order, I admit, but I have confidence in myself and in my people, and I mean to execute it.*

a tall story/tale

an account or story that is highly fanciful and hard to believe. *19th cent.*

Jerome K Jerome *Novel Notes* 1893
*Monkeys is cute. I've come across monkeys as could
give points to one or two lubbers I've sailed under;
and elephants is pretty spry, if you can believe all
that's told of 'em. I've heard some tall tales about
elephants.*

See also a tall POPPY; WALK tall.

Wilkie Collins *The Woman in White* 1860
*I shall relate both narratives, not in the words (often
interrupted, often inevitably confused) of the
speakers themselves, but in the words of the brief,
plain, studiously simple abstract which I committed
to writing for my own guidance, and for the guidance of my legal adviser. So the tangled web will be
most speedily and most intelligibly unrolled.*

tandem

in tandem (with somebody)

cooperating or working together with somebody:
from the physical meaning 'arranged or harnessed one behind the other'. The phrase was
originally used with reference to draught horses,
and gave the name *tandem* to a bicycle for two
people sitting one behind the other. *Tandem* is a
Latin word meaning 'at length', originally referring to time but used as a kind of pun in English
with reference to physical length. *Love in Tandem*
was the title of a comedy by Augustin Daly and
Henri Bocage, first produced in New York on 9
February 1892. *19th cent.*

Ian Wood *The Merovingian Kingdoms 450–751* 1994
*In 508 Theodoric continued his father's onslaught
on the Gothic south, in tandem with the Burgun-
dians.*

tangent

go off at a tangent

to diverge suddenly or unexpectedly from the
main topic of discussion or course of action: in
geometry, a *tangent* is a line touching the circum-
ference of a circle and continuing away from the
circle. *19th cent.*

H G Wells *The Invisible Man* 1897
*She turned round, as one who suddenly remembers.
'Bless my soul alive!' she said, going off at a tan-
gent; 'ain't you done them taters yet, Millie?'*

tangled

a tangled web

a confused situation, especially one arising from
human duplicity or scheming: with allusion to
Sir Walter Scott's *Marmion* (1808): 'O what a tangled web we weave, when first we practise to
deceive.' *19th cent.*

tango

it takes two to tango

informal it needs two people for certain circumstances to develop: an expression implying that
both parties involved in a particular situation are
equally responsible for it. It is based on the words
of a 1952 song written by Al Hoffman and Dick
Manning and made popular by Pearl Bailey:
'There are lots of things you can do alone! But,
takes two to tango.' This may in turn recall earlier
proverbs such as *it takes two to make a bargain*
(recorded in various forms from the 16th cent.)
and *it takes two to quarrel* (17th cent.). President
Ronald Reagan is said to have replied 'it takes
two to tango' in 1982 when commenting on the
effects on Soviet–American relations of the death
of the Soviet leader Leonid Brezhnev. *Mid 20th
cent.*

Economist 1991
*It takes two to tango, the United Nations secretary-
general observed after pre-war talks with Saddam
Hussein. The commanders of Operation Desert
Storm are beginning to feel the same way. After a
week of fighting, Mr Hussein's war machine has
done virtually nothing but hunker down and wait
to be attacked.*

tap

on tap

(said of a facility, benefit, etc) readily available on
demand: originally with reference to liquids that
could be drawn from a tap. *19th cent.*

Ambrose Bierce *Californian Summer Pictures* a1909
*Assembled in the parlor | Of the place of last resort,
| The smiler and the snarler | And the guests of
every sort – | The elocution chap | With rhetoric on
tap.*

tape

breast the tape

to achieve success. The image is of crossing the finishing line of a race, where the winner's chest is thrust forward to break the tape. The phrase is often used in extended metaphor. *Early 20th cent.*

> James Joyce *Ulysses* 1922
> *Judge of his astonishment when he finally did breast the tape and the awful truth dawned upon him anent his better half, wrecked in his affections.*

> *Financial Times* 1995
> *Manchester was wondering whether to get out of its track suit and run the race. Now it's ready to breast the tape. The dozen or so small venture groups in the city, such as Barclays Development Capital and NatWest Ventures, have outstripped the national average.*

get/have something taped

to have the measure of a problem or undertaking: probably from the physical meaning of measuring somebody or something with a tape measure, a more likely explanation than the use of tape to tie or secure things. *Early 20th cent.*

> James Joyce *Dubliners* 1914
> *I never saw such an eye in a man's head. It was as much as to say: I have you properly taped, my lad. He had an eye like a hawk.*

tapis

on the tapis

under consideration: a part translation of the French phrase *sur le tapis* meaning 'on the carpet' (*see* CARPET). *17th cent.*

> Eliza Haywood *The History of Miss Betsy Thoughtless* 1751
> *One evening, as the family were sitting together, some discourse concerning Oxford coming on the tapis, Mr. Francis spoke so largely in the praise of the wholesomeness of the air, the many fine walks and gardens with which the place abounded, and the good company that were continually resorting to it, that Miss Betsy cried out, she longed to see it.*

> Disraeli *Tancred* 1847
> *There is a grand affair on the tapis. The son of the Duke of Bellamont comes of age at Easter; it is to be a business of the thousand and one nights; the whole county to be feasted.*

tar

be tarred with the same brush

to have the same faults or weaknesses. The phrase is first recorded with *stick* in place of *brush* by Sir Walter Scott in *Rob Roy* (1817: 'they are a' tarr'd wi' the same stick – rank jacobites and papists') and *The Heart of Midlothian* (1818) and then, in the present form, in Cobbett's *Rural Rides* (1823). The form with *stick* is also used by Charles Reade in the 1860s. *19th cent.*

> Dickens *Our Mutual Friend* 1865
> *I find … that there are suspicions against both men, and I'm not going to take upon myself to decide betwixt them. They are both tarred with a dirty brush, and I can't have the Fellowships tarred with the same brush. That's all I know.*

tar and feather

to smear somebody with tar and cover them with feathers as a form of punishment or humiliation. The practice is recorded as early as the 12th cent. as a punishment in the English navy, though not in a form corresponding to the present phrase; in this form it first appears in the context of mob justice in the US in the mid 17th cent.

> Washington Irving *A History of New York* 1809
> *Sixty nine members spoke most eloquently in the affirmative, and only one arose to suggest some doubts – who as a punishment for his treasonable presumption, was immediately seized by the mob and tarred and feathered.*

See also spoil the SHIP for a ha'porth of tar.

tartan

See the tartan ARMY.

Tartar

See CATCH a Tartar.

task

take somebody to task

to rebuke or scold somebody for a mistake or wrongdoing. The phrase has earlier meanings that are no longer current; in the 16th cent. *take to task* meant 'to take something on as a task', and from this developed the neutral sense of dealing with a person or matter (17th cent.), from which the present use developed. *17th cent.*

Aphra Behn *The History of the Nun* 1689
*The Bishop, kinsman to Isabella, took him to task,
and urg'd his youth and birth, and that he ought not
to waste both without action.*

Richardson *Pamela* 1741
*Was it not sufficient, that I was insolently taken to
task by you in your letters, but my retirements must
be invaded? My house insulted?*

and other public services without (so it is alleged)
significant or noticeable benefits. Also *tax-and-spend*, used as an adjectival phrase. *Late 20th cent.*

Keesings *Contemporary Archives* 1992
*It explicitly rejected both the do-nothing govern-
ment of the last 12 years and the big government
theory that says we can hamstring business and tax
and spend our way to prosperity.*

taste

a bad/bitter/nasty taste in the mouth
a feeling of unease or disgust about something
one has experienced or encountered. *19th cent.*

Mark Twain *The Tragedy of Pudd'nhead Wilson* 1894
*He had touched both men on a raw spot and seen
them squirm; he had modified Wilson's sweetness
for the twins with one small bitter taste that he
wouldn't be able to get out of his mouth right away;
and, best of all, he had taken the hated twins down a
peg with the community.*

See also taste BLOOD; a dose/taste of one's own
MEDICINE.

tatters

in tatters
(said of hopes, ambitions, etc) completely ruined
or in disarray: from the physical meaning referring to clothes or other soft materials that are
badly torn or ruined. A E Housman in *A Shropshire Lad* (1896) includes the lines: 'And the tent of
night in tatters | Straws the sky-pavilioned land'.
Tatters is derived from an Old Norse word meaning 'rags.' *19th cent.*

Mary Jane Holmes *Hugh Worthington* 1865
*Southern people, born and brought up in the midst
of slavery can't see it as the North do, and there's
where the mischief lies. Neither understands the
other, and I greatly fear the day is not far distant
when our fair Union shall be torn in tatters by
enraged and furious brothers.*

tax

tax and spend
to keep taxes at a high level in order to sustain
public spending: normally used disapprovingly
– by their opponents – of governments that put
large amounts of money into education, health,

tea

all the tea in China
an imagined huge reward or prize: used in negative contexts in comparisons of rejection, as in *not
for all the tea in China*, meaning 'not in any circumstances'. The allusion is to China as a major
producer of tea. The phrase is said by Eric Partridge (*Dictionary of Slang*, 1937) to date from the
1890s in Australian use. But Partridge provides
no evidence and none was apparently known to
the editors of the *Australian National Dictionary*
(1988), and so this date should be regarded with
caution. The core phrase is in any case much
earlier. *19th cent.*

Scott *Rob Roy* 1817
*Martha, the old housekeeper, partook of the taste of
the family at the Hall. A toast and tankard would
have pleased her better than all the tea in China.*

tea and sympathy
consolation offered, along with supporting
refreshment, to somebody in distress. *Tea and
Sympathy* was the title of a film released in
1956. *Mid 20th cent.*

Rodney Brazier *Constitutional Texts* 1990
*After four and a half months of deliberation, the
committee presented its report. It offered neither tea
nor sympathy. To meet an estimated budget deficit
for 1932 of 120 million, a majority of the committee
recommended cuts in Government expenditure of
97 million.*

teacup
See a STORM in a teacup.

teach

that will teach — (not to —)
informal so-and-so will have been punished or
fairly dealt with for doing something wrong or

unwelcome: normally used to signal retribution or revenge. *19th cent.*

John Poole *The Hole in the Wall* 1813
[Fanny] *I hope you're satisfied, sir; and, as for you, Mr. Jeremy, take that. – (Slaps his face and exits.)* [Jeremy] *O Lord! this is the reward of honesty.* [Stubborn] *That will teach you to see clearer another other time, blockhead.*

P G Wodehouse *Laughing Gas* 1936
Maybe that will teach you not to go crawling to directors so that they will let you hog the camera!

you can't teach an old dog new tricks
somebody who is old and experienced will not want to use new methods of doing things they are familiar with. *16th cent.*

See also teach one's GRANDMOTHER to suck eggs.

---

tear¹ (noun, rhymes with *fear*)

without tears
without any trouble or difficulty. The phrase is typically used in the context of learning a language or subject; it was formerly common in the titles of course books (e.g. *Reading Without Tears*, 1857), and *French Without Tears* was the title of a highly successful comedy by Terence Rattigan, first produced in 1936. The phrase occurs frequently in 18th cent. and 19th cent. literature in the more literal meaning 'without showing any emotion' (as in the Fielding quotation below, and in Jane Austen's *Pride and Prejudice* (1813) 'By the middle of June, Kitty was so much recovered as to be able to enter Meryton without tears'). *18th cent.*

Henry Fielding *The History of Tom Jones* 1749
I am ashamed, Mr. Jones, of this womanish Weakness; but I shall never mention him without tears.

See also shed/weep CROCODILE tears.

---

tear² (verb, rhymes with *bear*)

tear one's hair (out)
informal to show extreme feelings of frustration or desperation: *tear one's hair* is also recorded in early use with reference to mourning. *19th cent.*

Tom Taylor *Going to the Bad* 1858
That's what I call action. Now, if I had been a spooney like you, where should I have been? Tearing

my hair in Chichester Barracks, while the party was tearing hers in Belgrave Square.

tear somebody off a strip
informal to scold or reprimand somebody: originally used in RAF slang. The reference may be to skinning or flaying a person. *Mid 20th cent.*

Joan Beech *One WAAF's War* 1989
More than one of them remarked on how pleasant it was to return to base in the early hours, cold, cramped and tired out, to see our welcoming smiles as they called in at the office on their way down to the Mess, even though they had probably only called in to tear us off a strip for having given them a rotten weather forecast.

---

teeth

get/sink one's teeth into something
informal to start enthusiastically on a stimulating or challenging task or undertaking: the image is of taking a huge bite out of food, or perhaps of sinking one's teeth into the flesh of an opponent: *cf* come/get to grips with something *at* GRIP. *Mid 20th cent.*

lie through one's teeth
to lie flagrantly or shamelessly: also earlier *lie in one's teeth*. *18th cent.*

Thomas Holcroft *Anna St Ives* 1792
But why the devil does she treat me thus? It is something to which I am unaccustomed, and it does not sit easily upon me. If I tamely submit to it may I — ! I lie, in my teeth! Submit I must, bounce how I will.

like pulling/drawing teeth
informal (said of a task or ordeal) long and arduous with little result. *19th cent.*

Bartley Campbell *Little Sunshine* 1873
[Gabriel Flint] *You must be a very extravagant family! That's all I have to say! Why, on eight dollars a-week a family of five ought to live in absolute luxury. Your plea for exemption is a very flimsy one, Miss Rice. My dear [to Mrs. Flint], put down one dollar opposite Miss Rice's name. [To Miss Rice] One dollar is the very least we can assess you, and you ought to consider yourself lucky to get off so – it should be two dollars. There pass on to your work, for here comes Miss Brown and you must not block the passage way. [Miss Rice] What*

will become of us? [Mrs. Flint] *That was like drawing teeth.*

Guardian 1985
The next time I saw the manager, who worked in a back office and was rarely available, I mentioned the murder. The shutters came down in his face and getting any information was like pulling teeth.

show one's teeth

to behave threateningly, especially in contrast to one's normal demeanour or reputation. The image is of an animal uncovering its teeth by pulling back its lips, as a sign of aggression, although showing the teeth is also common in 19th cent. literature in the context of grinning and laughing. *18th cent.*

O Sansom An Account of the Life of Oliver Sansom 1710
I had occasion to expostulate our case with one of those three justices that committed us; namely, Thomas Fettiplace ... He somewhat appeared at the sessions at Wantage, shewing his teeth in what he could, and thereby discovering what lodged in his heart against us, but what he said there was but little heeded by any; he being inferior to all or most of the rest.

George Eliot Romola 1863
After all the talk of scholars, there are but two sorts of government: one where men show their teeth at each other, and one where men show their tongues and lick the feet of the strongest.

See also TOOTH; ARMED to the teeth; (as) rare as hen's teeth *at* HEN; CAST something in somebody's teeth; SET one's teeth; set somebody's teeth on EDGE; sow dragon's teeth *at* DRAGON.

teething

teething troubles

problems experienced in the early stages of an enterprise, typically accepted as understandable or even inevitable. A common context is the world of computing and information technology, in which the machinery is invariably blamed for an assortment of ills that arise in the initial stages of an enterprise. *Teething* is the discomfort and slight illness usually suffered by a baby while its first teeth are beginning to grow, during which parents likewise take comfort from the transitory nature of the problem. In its literal sense the phrase dates from the 19th cent.

Trollope Barchester Towers 1857
Mr. Harding had his violoncello, and played to them while his daughters accompanied him. Johnny Bold, by the help either of Mr. Rerechild or else by that of his coral and carrot juice, got through his teething troubles. There had been gaieties too of all sorts.

telegraph

See the BUSH telegraph.

tell

tell somebody where to get off / where they get off

informal to rebuke or dismiss somebody in no uncertain terms. The image is presumably based on summary rejection of an unwelcome fellow-traveller. *Early 20th cent.*

Laura Martin Garden of Desire 1993
'Don't I get any thanks for offering to put you up for the weekend?' Robyn looked at him and flirted with the idea of telling him where to get off.

tell somebody where to put / what to do with something

informal to reject an offer or suggestion rudely or bluntly. The allusion, now remote to usage but sometimes still implied, is to putting something unwanted up one's own anus. *Mid 20th cent.*

that would be telling

that would be revealing private or secret information: used as a coy refusal to be indiscreet. *19th cent.*

Mrs Henry Wood East Lynne 1861
'What was that you were reading over with her?' pursued the indefatigable Miss Corny. 'It looked like a note.' 'Ah, that would be telling,' returned Mr. Carlyle, willing to turn it off with gaiety. 'If young ladies choose to make me privy to their love-letters, I cannot betray confidence, you know.'

there's no telling

informal one can never know for certain about a situation. *18th cent.*

Frederic Reynolds Fortune's Fool 1796
I don't know whether it was the front of her I saw – for now-a-days women are so bamboozl'd in their rigging, there's no telling the stem from the stern.

Dickens *Pickwick Papers* 1837
I'm a goin' to leave you, Samivel my boy, and there's no telling ven I shall see you again. Your mother-in-law may ha' been too much for me, or a thousand things may have happened by the time you next hears any news o' the celebrated Mr. Veller.

you're telling me

informal used to express strong agreement with something just said, or prior knowledge of it: the title of a 1932 song by Gus Kahn. A more recent form of the expression is *tell me about it. Mid 20th cent.*

See also see/tell/spot something a MILE off; tell tales (out of school) *at* TALE; tell that to the (horse) marines *at* MARINE.

temper

lose/keep one's temper

to become (or restrain oneself from becoming) extremely angry. *Temper* in the meaning 'mental or emotional composure' dates from the early 17th cent.: cf Shakespeare, *Measure for Measure* (1605) II.ii.185 '[Angelo] Never could the strumpet, | With all her double vigour – art and nature – | Once stir my temper.' *Keep one's temper* is early 18th cent., as is *lose one's temper. Keep oneself within temper* is recorded in the late 17th cent.

Jeremy Collier *A Short View of the Immorality of the English Stage* 1698
To go on to Euripides, for Sophocles has nothing more. This poet in his Phoenissae brings in Tiresias with a very unacceptable report from the Oracle. He tells Creon that either his son must die, or the city be lost: Creon keeps himself within temper, and gives no ill language.

Smollett *The Adventures of Ferdinand Count Fathom* 1753
This account, which totally overthrew the other's doctrine, was so extremely agreeable to the audience, that the testy doctor lost his temper, and gave them to understand without preamble, that he must be a person wholly ignorant of natural philosophy, who could invent such a ridiculous system.

tempt

tempt fate/providence

to act in a way that invites trouble or retribution. *17th cent.*

William Cavendish *The Humorous Lovers* 1677
'Tis not good to tempt providence; we shou'd not run into unnecessary dangers.

Defoe *Robinson Crusoe* 1719
He afterwards talk'd very gravely to me, exhorted me to go back to my Father, and not tempt Providence to my ruin.

ten

ten out of ten

recognition of complete success in an undertaking: from the awarding of a maximum of ten marks in a school exercise. *Late 20th cent.*

The Times 1987
Any organization which can draw on the words of such disparate sources as Pope John Paul II, Hugh Gaitskell and the UN Declaration on Human Rights to lend weight to its arguments certainly deserves ten out of ten for imaginative research.

See also two/ten a PENNY; COUNT (up) to ten.

tenterhooks

be on tenterhooks

to be in a state of great anxiety or suspense about what might be about to happen. A *tenterhook* was a sharp hooked nail used for fastening cloth for drying and stretching on a special frame called a *tenter. 17th cent.*

Head & Kirkman *The English Rogue Described* 1668
In this comfortless condition we remained for the space of three days, having neither money nor any thing to make money of; being thus sadly necessitated, my father and I set our witts upon the tenterhooks which way to recruit our decayed estate.

Harper Lee *To Kill a Mockingbird* 1960
I waited, on tenterhooks, for Uncle Jack to tell Atticus my side of it. But he didn't.

term

come to terms with something

to learn to accept or resign oneself to an unpleasant or unwelcome circumstance: from the literal

meaning 'to reach a legal or political agreement.'
Early 20th cent.

in no uncertain terms

in a forthright or unequivocal manner: especially with reference to giving advice, information, rebukes, etc. Similar forms, e.g. *with no uncertain voice*, are recorded from an earlier date. *19th cent.*

> Bayard Taylor transl Goethe's *Faust* 1871
> [Prologue] *The earnest reader will require no explanation of the problem propounded in the Prologue. Goethe states it without obscurity, and solves it in no uncertain terms at the close of the Second Part.*

on terms

in a state of acquaintance or friendship: a shortening of the expression *on terms of friendship* (or *amity, intimacy*, etc). *18th cent.*

> Frances Sheridan *Memoirs of Miss Sidney Bidulph* 1761
> *And to be sincere with you, my Cecilia, I did think Lady Sarah deserved this mortification, though it did not so far influence me as to make me desirous of being on terms with her: as for my brother, I was governed by no other motive than affection towards him.*

territory

come/go with the territory

informal to be an inevitable consequence of a situation or course of action. *Territory* is probably used here in the (chiefly North American) marketing sense of an area covered by a distributor or sales representative. *20th cent.*

> *Esquire* 1992
> *Size, as the actress said to the Bishop, is part of the problem. There are 2,000 acres of vines in England, compared with 2.6 million in France ... And then there's the weather. You need sunshine to ripen grapes and in England unpredictability comes with the territory.*

test

test the water

to find out people's opinions about a matter: from the literal use (late 19th cent.). *Late 20th cent.*

See also the ACID test.

tether

See at the END of one's tether.

Thames

See SET the world alight / on fire / set the Thames on fire.

thank

no thanks to —

the person named has been no particular help in resolving a difficulty, providing information, etc: in early use in the form *no thank to*. *17th cent.*

> Dryden *Cleomenes, The Spartan Hero* 1692
> [Coenus] *Y'are Cleomenes.* [Cleomenes] *No thanks to Heaven for that: I shou'd have dy'd,* | *And then I had not been this Cleomenes.*

> Dickens *Hard Times* 1854
> *'I am serious; I am indeed!' He smoked with great gravity and dignity for a little while, and then added, in a highly complacent tone, 'Oh! I have picked up a little since. I don't deny that. But I have done it myself; no thanks to the governor.'*

thanks for the buggy ride

informal thank you for your help. *Early 20th cent.*

> Ngaio Marsh *Artists in Crime* 1938
> *When the spot of trouble comes along it's 'Thanks for the buggy ride, it was OK while it lasted'.*

thanks a million

informal used to express profound gratitude, usually ironic. *Mid 20th cent.*

> Bernard Cornwell *Crackdown* 1990
> *'I suppose I like you,' she said after a moment's thought, 'because you lack guile. You remind me of a cocker spaniel I once owned.' 'Oh ...Thanks a million.'*

See also thank one's lucky stars *at* STAR.

that

and all that

and so forth; and other things of the same kind. *18th cent.*

> Jane Austen *Northanger Abbey* 1818
> *'You know he is over head and ears in love with you.' 'With me, dear Isabella!' 'Nay, my sweetest Catherine, this is being quite absurd! Modesty, and*

all that, is very well in its way, but really a little common honesty is sometimes quite as becoming.'

for all that

in spite of everything; even so. *17th cent.*

> Thomas Brown *Amusements Serious and Comical* 1700
> *All the world are agreed, that both one and the other are scoundrels, yet for all that we esteem 'em when they excel in this Art.*

that's that

informal that is the end of the matter; there is no more to be said or done. *19th cent.*

> Samuel Butler *Erewhon* 1872
> *For a moment they looked at me and at each other in great amazement; then they gave a little frightened cry, and ran off as hard as they could. 'So that's that,' said I to myself, as I watched them scampering.*

them

them and us

informal those with power or authority on the one hand, and the ordinary people on the other. *Them* is recorded in this sense from the early 20th cent., and *they* from the 1880s. *Mid 20th cent.*

> Oates & Ezra *Advice from the Top* 1989
> *The younger generation is having a favourable impact on the need to rid Britain of the 'them and us' syndrome that has plagued industry for so long and been at the root of so many of its ills.*

there

be all there

to be shrewd and alert; to have all one's faculties. Somebody who is *not all there* is slightly crazy or eccentric. *See also* not RIGHT in the head. *19th cent.*

have been there/here (before)

informal, originally NAmer to be familiar with a situation from one's own experience. *19th cent.*

> Cullen Gouldsbury *Songs out of Exile* 1912
> *It chanced one night that Dinges was down with fever pretty badly; | Temperature up to a hundred and four | (You'll know the game if you've been there before), | Head like a stove, and mouth like a drain, | And a kind of a dull, all-overish pain.*

See also been there, done that *at* BE; BE there for —.

thick

(as) thick as thieves

very friendly or intimate: also *as thick as glue, as thick as three in a bed* (though not with the modern resonance that this might have). This meaning of *thick* dates from the mid 18th cent. *19th cent.*

> Mark Twain *The Adventures of Huckleberry Finn* 1884
> *So the king sneaked into the wigwam, and took to his bottle for comfort; and before long the duke tackled his bottle; and so in about a half an hour they was as thick as thieves again, and the tighter they got, the lovinger they got; and went off a snoring in each other's arms.*

(as) thick as two short planks

informal extremely slow-witted or stupid: the meaning of *thick* referring to wits dates from the 16th cent. (cf Shakespeare, *2 Henry IV* (1597) II.iv.262 '[Sir John, with reference to Poins] He a good wit? Hang him, baboon! His wit's as thick as Tewkesbury mustard; there's no more conceit in him than is in a mallet'). *Late 20th cent.*

> Susan Gates *The Lock* 1990
> *Like I said, she's thick as two short planks but she's useful. I get a lot of information out of her. She thinks I'm in love with her, see.*

a bit thick

informal blatantly unfair or unreasonable. *Early 20th cent.*

give somebody a thick ear

informal to hit somebody hard, especially on the head. *Early 20th cent.*

> John Masefield *Poems* 1946
> *'Don't stare, but did you do it? Answer, please.' The Bosun turned: 'I'll give you a thick ear! Do it? I didn't. Get to hell from here! I touch your stinking daubs?'*

in/into the thick of something

involved in the most intense, intricate, or complicated part of something. *17th cent.*

> Mary Shelley *Falkner* 1837
> *Brought up in the thick of fashionable life, no person of her clique was a stranger; and if any odd people called on her – still they were in some way entertaining.*

thick and fast

rapidly and copiously. *17th cent.*

Margaret Cavendish *The Description of a New World*
1666
*As soon as the Duchess's Speech was ended, Folly
and Rashness started up, and both spake so thick
and fast at once, that not onely the Assembly, but
themselves were not able to understand each other.*

through thick and thin

in circumstances of all kinds, favourable and
unfavourable: used especially in the context of
loyalty or steadfastness. *Middle English*

Chaucer *The Reeve's Tale* (line 4066)
*He strepeth off the brydel right anon. | And whan
the hors was laus [= loose], he gynneth gon |
Toward the fen, ther wilde mares renne, | And forth
with 'wehee', thurgh thikke and thurgh thenne.*

Dryden *Absalom and Achitophel* 1681
*Doeg, though without knowing how or why, |
Made still a blundering kind of melody; | Spurred
boldly on, and dashed through thick and thin, |
Through sense and nonsense, never out nor in; |
Free from all meaning, whether good or bad, | And,
in one word, heroically mad.*

See also be thick/thin on the GROUND; have a thick
SKIN; LAY something on thick.

thief

See (as) THICK as thieves; HONOUR among thieves.

thin

have a thin time

informal to have an unhappy or difficult time.
Early 20th cent.

D H Lawrence *Nettles* 1930
*But wages go down, and really, Auntie, we get a
pretty thin time. | But so long as we know that
Auntie loves us we'll try to act up sublime.*

thin on top

informal, euphemistic becoming bald: in early use
in the form *thin on* (or *at*) *the top. 19th cent.*

Conan Doyle *The Lost World* 1912
*I noted the details of a face which was already
familiar to me from many photographs – the
strongly-curved nose, the hollow, worn cheeks, the
dark, ruddy hair, thin at the top, the crisp, virile
moustaches, the small aggressive tuft upon his
projecting chin.*

See also (as) thin as a rake *at* RAKE[1]; be skating on
thin ICE; be thick/thin on the GROUND; into thin
AIR; the thin end of the WEDGE.

thing

be all things to all men/people

to be able to please different people by adapting
one's behaviour and attitudes accordingly: with
allusion to St Paul's declaration about salvation
in the First Epistle to the Corinthians 9:22 (in the
Authorized Version of the Bible, 1611) 'To the
weak became I as weak, that I might gain the
weak: I am made all things to all men, that I
might by all means save some.' There is an earlier
reference to St Paul, using similar wording, in the
Posies of George Gascoigne Esquire, a collection of
secular and devotional verse made by the soldier
and poet of the title and published in 1575, some
years before the appearance of the Authorized
Version: 'And to conclude, he became all things
to all men, to the end that he might thereby win
some to salvation.' So we can date the emergence
of this phrase to the later part of the 16th cent.
Allusive uses that are free of the immediate context predominate from the 18th cent. and 19th
cent.

Maria Edgeworth *Belinda* 1801
*His chameleon character seemed to vary in different
lights, and according to the different situations, in
which he happened to be placed. He could be all
things to all men – and to all women.*

Byron *Don Juan* 1824
*Courteous and cautious therefore in his county, |
He was all things to all men, and dispensed | To
some civility, to others bounty, | And promises to
all.*

be / put somebody on to a good thing

informal to be (or put somebody) in a position to
take advantage of favourable circumstances. *19th
cent.*

do one's own thing

informal to act or behave independently or
according to one's own inclinations. *19th cent.*

have a thing about something

informal to be preoccupied or obsessed with a
particular matter. *Mid 20th cent.*

Julian Barnes *Talking It Over* 1992
For a start, have you ever looked at ... the sort of old men who seduce young women? The roguish high-bummed stride, the fuck-me tan, the effulgent cufflinks ... They demand, they expect ... It's disgusting. I'm sorry, I've got a thing about it. The thought of liver-spotted hands clamped on tense juve breasts – well, hie me to the vomitorium pronto!

have a thing with somebody
informal to have a sexual relationship with somebody. *Mid 20th cent.*

Martin Amis *Money* 1985
Seems that Prince Charles had a thing with one of Diana's sisters, way back, before he fingered Lady Di as the true goer of the family.

know / teach/tell somebody a thing or two
to have (or impart) a great deal of experience. *18th cent.*

Mary Robinson *Walsingham* 1797
'Look'ye, old star-gazer,' interrupted the prisoner, 'I know a thing or two; you can't humbug me with your canting morality'.

make a thing of something
informal to emphasize the importance or value of something. *Mid 20th cent.*

W J Burley *Wycliffe and the Cycle of Death* 1991
We go in mainly for first editions of the classics but we do have some rather nice botanical books, floras mostly, sought after for their plates ... We make a thing of local-interest books.

there's only one thing for it
we have no alternative; there is only one possible course of action. *19th cent.*

Tom Taylor *Still Waters Run Deep* 1855
Well, there's only one thing for it – we must rig the market. Go in, and buy up every share that's offered.

See also do the DECENT thing; other/all things being EQUAL; things that go BUMP in the night.

---

think

have (got) another think coming
informal to be mistaken and have to reconsider: often used as an emphatic admonition following a proposition beginning 'If you think ...' *Mid 20th cent.*

Independent 1989
If they think I'm going to do physical jerks and sing the company song before I start my shift, they've got another think coming.

put one's thinking cap on
to ponder on a problem or difficulty. *19th cent.*

C F Holder *Marvels of Animal Life* 1885
Several lessons of this kind evidently made his toadship put on his thinking cap.

think again
to reconsider; to reflect on previous thoughts. *18th cent.*

Robert Bage *Man As He Is* 1792
In one month, such is the prevalence of good company, Sir George began to think again, this world had its pleasures; in two, he partook of these pleasures liberally.

Wilkie Collins *Armadale* 1866
As a matter of course, we set to work at once, and found out who she was. Her name is Mrs. Oldershaw – and if you think of her for my stepmother, I strongly recommend you to think again before you make her Mrs. Bashwood.

think nothing of something/somebody
1 to be dismissive of something or somebody or have a low opinion of them. *18th cent.*

Eliza Haywood *Anti-Pamela* 1741
After he was gone, the Woman of the Shop began to banter me, and told me, I had made a Conquest; but I seemed to think nothing of it, and went away as soon as I had got my Silk.

George Eliot *Middlemarch* 1872
'I shall be jealous when Tertius goes to Lowick,' said Rosamond, dimpling, and speaking with aery lightness. 'He will come back and think nothing of me.'

2 to be entirely unconcerned about something: often *think nothing of it*, used in the imperative as a formula dismissing thanks or apologies or expressing reassurance. *19th cent.*

J T Trowbridge *Martin Merrivale* 1854
'I am quite a child, – I act very foolishly, I know. If you can forgive and forget, why should I remember?' The cloud cleared from his brow, and a cheerful sunshine broke through, illumining his features with a light as pure and happy as that of an infant's smile. 'O, sir, think nothing of it,' murmured the agitated woman regarding Martin with

suffused features. 'You are welcome here – heartily welcome, believe me.'

think twice

to reflect on a possibility or decision before finally committing oneself: in its negative form *not think twice* means 'not to hesitate (to do or think something).' *17th cent.*

> Fanny Burney *Evelina* 1778
> *There are a great many other ladies that have been proposed to me, – but I never thought twice of any of them, – that is, not in a serious way.*

think the unthinkable

to consider an eventuality or course of action that might seem to be desperate or to have unwelcome consequences, typically in order to rectify or improve a bad state of affairs. The phrase is often encountered in the context of difficult or unpopular political decisions. An identical expression occurs in 19th cent. philosophical writing as the theoretical notion of 'thinking what cannot be thought', which is used as a step in an argument rather than a cogent proposition in itself. But these uses are coincidental, and the modern meaning dates from the 1950s. *Mid 20th cent.*

> *Guardian* 1985
> *In the afterglow of 1983, it was possible and politically attractive for ministers to think the unthinkable about welfare state restructuring. But as the next election begins to grip political minds there is a degree of self doubt which was not there before or at least seemed less immediate.*

think the world of something/somebody

to regard something or somebody very highly. *19th cent.*

> Mark Twain *The Gilded Age* 1873
> *I have been reading up some European Scientific reports – friend of mine, Count Fugier, sent them to me – sends me all sorts of things from Paris – he thinks the world of me, Fugier does.*

See also give somebody furiously to think *at* FURIOUS; think on one's FEET.

---

third

get the third degree

to be vigorously or aggressively interrogated. *Third degree* has been used in denoting progression since the 16th cent. In Shakespeare's *Twelfth Night* (1602), Olivia tells the jester Feste (I.v.130) 'Go thou and seek the coroner, and let him sit o' my coz [her cousin, Sir Toby Belch], for he's in the third degree of drink, he's drowned.' It marks various special ranks, e.g. the highest rank in freemasonry, and the most serious degree in the classification of burns, involving the death of all layers of skin. *19th cent.*

> Harriet Ford *The Argyle Case* 1912
> [Kayton] *I'd like to speak to Miss Masuret alone if you don't mind.* [Bruce] *I'm not going to have her put through any third degree!*

third time/time's lucky

(proverb) one is often successful in one's third attempt. The notion is derived from an earlier maxim *all things thrive at thrice*, which dates from the 17th cent.; the present form is found from the 19th cent. It is recorded in Alexander Hislop's *Proverbs of Scotland* (third edition, 1862); at an earlier date (1840) Robert Browning had written in a letter that ' "the luck of the third adventure" is proverbial'.

third way

a third possible ideology or way of proceeding, especially as an alternative to extreme or discredited systems. Use of the phrase in general contexts is well established, but it has acquired recent specific social and political applications denoting more liberal and progressive alternatives to conservative ideas, and was notably used as a slogan of New Labour in Britain in the late 1990s. *Late 20th cent.*

> *Economist* 1990
> *It is not that one part of Solidarity supports the free-market experiment and another doesn't. 'There is no third way for Poland,' says Mr Jan Litynski.*

Thomas

See a doubting Thomas *at* DOUBT.

---

thorn

on thorns

constantly anxious or uneasy. *18th cent.*

> Robert Paltock *The Life and Adventures of Peter Wilkins* 1750
> *Youwarkee found Walsi sat on Thorns, wanting to be gone; but Youwarkee asking Question upon Question, Walsi got up, and begged she would*

excuse her, she would come and stay at any other time.

Harriet Beecher Stowe *My Wife and I* 1871
Mamma and Aunt Maria are on thorns, to get me off their hands and well established.

a thorn in one's side
a person or thing that causes constant trouble or difficulty. The phrase is a biblical allusion to Numbers 33:55 'But if ye will not drive out the inhabitants of the land from before you; then it shall come to pass, that those which ye let remain of them shall be pricks in your eyes, and thorns in your sides, and shall vex you in the land wherein ye dwell.' The image occurs in other forms from Middle English. *17th cent.*

Mary Pix *The Spanish Wives* 1696
I'll be a thorn in thy side, I'll warrant thee, old Father Iniquity.

See also there is no ROSE without a thorn.

thought
See SECOND thoughts.

thread

hang by a thread
to be extremely vulnerable or in a precarious situation: often used with allusion to the story of the sword of Damocles (*see* SWORD). *17th cent.*

lose the/one's thread
to become distracted and unable to remember the sequence of a story or argument. *18th cent.*

Sarah Fielding *The Adventures of David Simple* 1744
Here our gentleman's breath began to fail him, for he had utter'd all this as fast as he could speak, as if he was afraid he should lose his thread, and forget all that was to come.

pick/take up / resume the thread
to resume or assume a course of action after a pause. The phrase appears first in variant forms including *recover* and *resume the thread* (of a story, etc). *17th cent.*

Fanny Burney *Diary* 1782
We laughed so violently ... that he could not recover the thread of his harangue.

three

threescore (years) and ten
the age of seventy: based on biblical references to this as the span of a person's life (e.g. Psalms 90:10 'The days of our years are threescore years and ten; and if by reason of strength they be fourscore years, yet is their strength labour and sorrow; for it is soon cut off, and we fly away'). *17th cent.*

Shakespeare *Macbeth* II.iv.1 (1606)
[Old Man] *Threescore and ten I can remember well, | Within the volume of which I have seen | Hours dreadful and things strange.*

See also three sheets in the wind *at* SHEET; three strikes and you're out *at* STRIKE.

thrill

thrills and spills
informal the excitement of dangerous and challenging activities. *Late 20th cent.*

Daily Telegraph 1992
Joseph O'Neill's first novel lifts the lid off the arcane world of the law and paints a wry picture of the humdrum, uninspiring existence which lies beyond the thrills and spills of the courtroom.

throat

be/fly at one another's throats
to be quarrelling violently. The throat here symbolizes the most vulnerable point of attack. *18th cent.*

Jane Robe *The Fatal Legacy* 1723
[Creon] *My Royal Nephews, at each other's Throats | Demand the Theban Throne with lifted Swords.*

George Meredith *The Ordeal of Richard Feverel* 1859
But let the world fly into a passion, and is not Bedlam its safest abode? What seemed inviolable barriers are burst asunder in a trice: men, God's likeness, are at one another's throats, and the Angels may well be weeping.

cut one's (own) throat
to cause one's own downfall. *19th cent.*

John Neal *Rachel Dyer* 1828
Burroughs would have interrupted him, but he was hindered by his crafty law-adviser, who told him to

let the worthy gentleman cut his own throat in his
own way, now he was in the humor for it.

force/ram/shove something down somebody's throat

to force somebody to accept an idea or suggestion, typically by constant repetition of it. *18th cent.*

Thomas Betterton The Amorous Widow 1706
Then whoever told you, is a rascal; and were he here,
I'd ram the lie down his throat, or make him eat a
piece of my sword.

Wilkie Collins Man and Wife 1870
Do wait a little, Arnold! I can't have Milton
crammed down my throat in that way.

See also stick in somebody's throat *at* STICK[1].

throw

be thrown back on something

to have to rely on a final resource or support when there is no alternative. *19th cent.*

James Fenimore Cooper The Crater 1847
Disappointed in this respect, they found themselves
thrown back on resources that were far from being
equal to the emergency.

throw away the key

informal to lock up a place or imprison somebody indefinitely or for a very long period. *19th cent.*

George W Lovell The Wife's Secret 1850
A thousand times she has said, when you came
home, | If come you should (and then she wept
again), | She'd never see it more, but lock it up, |
With all its memories of care inside, | And throw
away the key.

Eugene O'Neill Ah, Wilderness 1933
[Miller] You'd better not repeat such sentiments
outside the bosom of the family or they'll have you
in jail. [Sid] And throw away the key.

throw one's hand in

to abandon or withdraw from a contest or undertaking: a metaphor from card games, especially poker, in which throwing in one's hand meant retiring from play. The metaphorical meaning occurs early in the history of the phrase. *19th cent.*

Conan Doyle The Noble Bachelor 1892
The richer pa grew the poorer was Frank; so at last
pa wouldn't hear of our engagement lasting any
longer, and he took me away to 'Frisco. Frank

wouldn't throw up his hand, though; so he followed
me there, and he saw me without pa knowing
anything about it.

throw in the towel / throw in/up the sponge

informal to withdraw from a contest or admit defeat: from the practice of a boxer's second in throwing a towel or sponge into the ring to signify a contestant's admission of defeat. *19th cent.*

Trollope The Prime Minister 1876
I shan't throw up the sponge as long as there's a
chance left, Sir Alured. But it will go badly with me
if I'm beat at last.

throw one's rattle/toys out of the pram

informal to behave in a petulant or childish manner. The image is of a young child throwing a tantrum. *Late 20th cent.*

The Times 1988
Bates was warned for 'verbal abuse' of a line judge
but Castle was more consistently prone to throw his
rattle out of the pram.

throw stones

to make accusations or cast aspersions: from the proverb *those who live in glass houses should not throw stones* (the implication being that the accusers are themselves vulnerable). The image occurs in Chaucer, although the proverb and the allusive phrase in its current form are later. *17th cent.*

See also fling/throw down the GAUNTLET; not TRUST somebody as far as one can throw them; pour/throw COLD water over something; throw the BABY out with the bathwater; throw DUST in somebody's eyes; throw good MONEY after bad; throw in one's LOT with somebody; throw somebody to the dogs *at* DOG; throw somebody to the lions *at* LION; throw somebody to the wolves *at* WOLF; throw one's WEIGHT about/around; throw a WOBBLY.

thumb

hold one's thumbs

South African to wrap the finger round the thumb as a gesture inviting good luck. *Cf* CROSS one's fingers. *20th cent.*

Guardian 1992
Germans and Swedes do not cross their fingers, they
hold their thumbs.

thumbs up/down

a gesture of approval or disapproval. The reference is to the signals made by Roman crowds at gladiatorial shows, although these were the reverse of the forms reflected in the English phrases. The Latin phrase denoting a favourable verdict, i.e. that the defeated gladiator's life was to be spared, was *pollicem premere* 'turn the thumb downward' and for an unfavourable verdict was *pollicem vertere* 'turn the thumb upward'. The phrase dates from the 19th cent. in its current form.

> William Ware *Probus, or Rome in the Third Century* 1838
> 'Nay, as for that,' he rejoined, 'there were some stout voices raised in his behalf to the last, and some thumbs down, but too few to be regarded.'

twiddle one's thumbs

informal to pass the time idly because one has nothing to do: literally, to put one's hands together and continuously rotate the thumbs round each other, as an expression of idleness or boredom. *19th cent.*

> Trollope *Barchester Towers* 1857
> The bishop was sitting in his easy chair twiddling his thumbs, turning his eyes now to his wife, and now to his chaplain, as each took up the cudgels.

under somebody's thumb

completely dominated or controlled by somebody. *18th cent.*

> Richardson *The History of Sir Charles Grandison* 1753
> She remembers her late act of delinquency; so is obliged to be silent. I have her under my thumb.

See also be all fingers and thumbs *at* FINGER; thumb one's NOSE.

thunder

steal somebody's thunder

to anticipate or preempt what somebody else is planning to say or do, thereby reducing or destroying its effect. The phrase is said to have originated in an exclamation by the playwright and critic John Dennis (1657–1734) in reaction to a special effect of thunder during a performance of Shakespeare's *Macbeth*: 'Damn them! They will not let my play run, but they steal my thunder.' He was supposedly referring to his own use of the same special effect in his play *Appius and Virginia*, which had been staged shortly before this but was a failure. The story is told by the contemporary actor and dramatist Colley Cibber (1671–1757) in his anecdotal work *Lives of the Poets*, and it also features in Alexander Pope's mock-heroic satire *The Dunciad*, in which Cibber was made the hero in the final edition of 1743. The long gap between this anecdotal origin and the first recorded uses of the expression in the relevant sense in the middle of the 19th cent. may be hard to explain, but in any case the notion of stealing thunder from the gods is the ultimate origin (see below). *Early 20th cent.*

> Charles Johnson *The Successful Pyrate* 1713
> 'Tis false, he is not dead, | Yonder he rides upon a Purple Cloud, | Cloath'd in soft Light – see, see, he steals the Thunder | From nodding Jove.

> Theodore Winthrop *Life in the Open Air* 1863
> I am not about to report the orator's speech. Stealing another's thunder is an offence punishable condignly ever since the days of Salmoneus.

> Max Beerbohm *Zuleika Dobson* 1911
> 'I covered my eyes and rushed upstairs, rang the bell and tore my things off. My maid was very cross.' Cross! The Duke was shot through with an envy of one who was in a position to be unkind to Zuleika. 'Happy maid!' he murmured. Zuleika replied that he was stealing her thunder: hadn't she envied the girl at his lodgings?

tick¹ (verb)

what makes — tick

informal what interests or motivates a particular individual. *Mid 20th cent.*

> W H Auden *The Age of Anxiety* 1947
> Most of them are under the illusion that their lack of confidence is a unique and shameful fear which, if confessed, would make them an object of derision to their normal contemporaries. Accordingly, they watch others with a covert but passionate curiosity. What makes them tick? What would it feel like to be a success?

tick² (the mite)

(as) full/tight as a tick

completely full, usually in the sense 'extremely drunk': with reference to the swelling of ticks when they suck blood. *17th cent.*

tick³ (trust or credit)

on tick

informal on trust; now usually in the sense 'on credit'. This word *tick* is short for *ticket* in the sense of an IOU or slip recording a debt or obligation to pay. *17th cent.*

John Oldham *Works* 1684
Reduc'd to want, he in due time fell sick, | Was fain to die, and be interr'd on tick.

ticket

be (just) the ticket

informal, dated to be exactly what is needed: also *that's the ticket*, expressing approval or agreement. There are several suggestions for the meaning of *ticket* here: the political meaning (a list of candidates), the slips of paper formerly given by charities to paupers and exchangeable for food and clothing, and the winning ticket in a lottery. It is likely, however, that the origin is more generalized and that no particular meaning can be isolated. A 19th cent. suggestion (e.g. in *Notes & Queries* June 1865, p.505) that the phrase is a corruption or adaptation of French *c'est l'etiquette* is typical of the linguistic contortions contributors went through to explain the origins of English phrases when the straightforward and obvious were not good enough. *19th cent.*

Trollope *Doctor Thorne* 1858
'He's a well-meaning fellow, is the doctor,' said Sir Louis, when his guardian was out of the room, 'very; but he's not up to trap – not at all.' 'Up to trap – well, I should say he was; that is, if I know what trap means,' said Frank. 'Ah, but that's just the ticket. Do you know? Now I say Dr. Thorne's not a man of the world.'

have tickets on oneself

Australian, informal to be extremely conceited or vain. The image is of buying tickets for a notable event, or perhaps of placing a bet, with oneself regarded as the thing 'fancied'. *Early 20th cent.*

B Reynolds *Dawn Asper* 1918
There is a current slang phrase … 'She hasn't many tickets on herself!' Now, as far as Dawn Asper was concerned, this was perfectly true – she had <u>no</u> tickets on herself.

work one's ticket

to secure one's discharge from the army or prison: from the use of *ticket* to refer to the warrant given to a soldier or sailor on discharge, stating the amount of pay owed. *19th cent.*

Margery Allingham *The Tiger in the Smoke* 1952
He … attempted to work his ticket to one of these new-style open prisons.

write one's own ticket

informal to be in a position to dictate one's own terms. *Early 20th cent.*

P G Wodehouse *Money for Nothing* 1928
'But Oil's the stuff, and if you want to part with any of that Silver River of yours, Tom,' he said, 'pass it across this desk and write your own ticket.'

tickle

be tickled pink / to death

informal to be highly amused or entertained by a remark, etc. The meaning of *tickle* 'to excite or amuse' dates from Middle English, and *pink* is the colour produced by prolonged tickling. *Be tickled to death* dates in extended metaphor from the 17th cent., and figuratively from the 19th cent.; *be tickled pink* dates from the early 20th cent.

Thomas Heywood *The Royall King, and the Loyall Subject* 1637
This Lord is of an unwonted constancy, He entertaines his disgraces as merrily as a man dyes that is tickled to death.

Charles Augustus Davis *Letters of J. Downing, Major* 1834
The Gineral was tickled to death with this story, but our folks didn't like it a bit.

See also tickle somebody's FANCY.

tide

go/swim with/against the tide

to follow (or resist) the prevailing mood or fashion. The phrase, which dates from the late 16th cent., is found in early use with *stream* as well as *tide*, as in Shakespeare's *2 Henry IV* (1597) v.ii.34: '[Clarence to Lord Chief Justice] Well, you must now speak Sir John Falstaff fair, | Which swims against your stream of quality.'

Austin Saker *Narbonus* 1580
But Fidelia, I strive against the winde, and weare my words without perfourming of workes: I swimme against the tide, and strive against the hill: seeinge therfore my departure is pronounced, and my lotte layde before me.

tide somebody over
to enable somebody to survive a difficult period until circumstances improve: typically used with reference to money or help. The relevance of the tide is not immediately clear (hence the occasional erroneous substitution of *tie* for *tide*, as a kind of etymological correction), but the image is in fact a powerful and vivid one. *Tide*, in its meaning to do with the sea, produced a verb form in the 17th cent. in the sense 'to carry or surge with the tide', and to *tide somebody over* is to carry them like the surging tide over a difficult or dangerous patch, rather like Shakespeare's image, spoken by Brutus in *Julius Caesar* (1599) IV.ii.270: 'There is a tide in the affairs of men | Which, taken at the flood, leads on to fortune.' First uses of the phrase in the 1820s are intransitive: one *tides over* a difficulty oneself, rather than have something tide one over. Another form, *tide out*, is recorded earlier (17th cent.) but did not survive for long. *19th cent.*

Trollope *Framley Parsonage* 1861
He is always looking for money; I believe that in all his hours of most friendly intercourse, – when he is sitting with you over your wine, and riding beside you in the field, – he is still thinking how he can make use of you to tide him over some difficulty.

See also STEM the tide.

tie
See bind/tie somebody HAND and foot; fit to be tied *at* FIT[1]; have one's hands tied *at* HAND; the OLD school tie; tie somebody in knots *at* KNOT; tie the KNOT.

tiger

have a tiger by the tail / ride a tiger
to become involved in an activity that proves to be dangerous but cannot easily be given up: with allusion to the 19th cent. proverb (of Chinese origin) *He who rides a tiger is afraid to dismount.* There are many variants of the phrase. *Early 20th cent.*

a tiger in one's tank
informal energy or vigour: based on *put a tiger in your tank*, an advertising slogan of the Esso Petroleum Company in the 1960s. *Mid 20th cent.*

tight

run a tight ship
to manage an organization or enterprise with strict economy and control of expenditure: widely known as a slogan of governments and senior managements whose main concern is to limit the resources of those who do the real work. A tight ship was one in which the rigging was tight and well maintained, but at least the ship sailed. *Late 20th cent.*

a tight corner/spot
a difficult or awkward predicament. *19th cent.*

Mary Jane Holmes *Hugh Worthington* 1865
'You ask a steep sum,' he said, crossing one fat limb over the other and snapping his whip at Rocket, who eyed him askance. 'Pretty steep sum, but I take it, you are in a tight spot and don't know what else to do.'

See also (as) full/tight as a tick *at* TICK[2]; keep/put a tight REIN on somebody/something.

tighten
See tighten one's BELT; put the screws on somebody / tighten the screw(s) *at* SCREW.

tile

(out) on the tiles
having an enjoyable time late into the night away from home. The phrase originates in the wanderings of cats over rooftops at night, as a colourful exchange in Thackeray's *The Newcomes* (1854) makes clear: ' "They say the old dowager doesn't believe in God nor devil: but that she's in such a funk to be left in the dark that she howls and raises the doose's own delight if her candle goes out. Toppleton slept next room to her at Groningham, and heard her; didn't you, Top?" "Heard her howling like an old cat on the tiles," says Toppleton.' *19th cent.*

Stirling & Dickens *The Old Curiosity Shop* c1840
I hope you'll excuse my appearance, but to tell the truth, I was out on the tiles last night.

till

have one's fingers/hand in the till

to steal or embezzle money from an employer (in the quotation, taking money without implications of dishonesty). *19th cent.*

Joseph Neal *Charcoal Sketches* 1838
My hours ain't my own – my money ain't my own – I belong to four people besides myself – the old woman and them three children. I'm a partnership concern, and so many has got their fingers in the till that I must bust up.

tilt

Tilt here is used in its early senses to do with jousting and combat. *To tilt* is 'to thrust with a weapon', and the noun originally means 'a joust or bout of combat', and later 'a thrust'.

(at) full tilt

at great speed. An earlier form of the phrase, *run a-tilt*, draws on the same image and occurs mockingly in Shakespeare's *1 Henry VI* (1590) III.iii.11: '[Bedford] O let no words, but deeds, revenge this treason. [Joan] What will you do, good graybeard? Break a lance | And run a-tilt at death within a chair?' *17th cent.*

Edward Ward *Hudibras Redivivus* 1705
For sure, say they, no Christian Patr'ots | Would ever make such wicked Statutes, | That Conscience should have Toleration | To run full Tilt upon Damnation.

tilt at windmills

to attack imaginary opponents: used earlier in the form *fight with windmills*. With reference to the story in Cervantes' novel of Don Quixote attacking windmills in the belief that they were giants. *17th cent.*

John Cleveland *Poems* a1658
Thus the Quixots of this Age fight with the Windmils of their own heads.

time

behind the times

old-fashioned in one's outlook. *19th cent.*

Disraeli *Coningsby* 1844
We have all of us a very great respect for Manchester, in course; look upon her as a sort of mother, and all that sort of thing. But she is behind the times, sir, and that won't do in this age. The long and the short of it is, Manchester is gone by.

be pushed/pressed for time

to be in a hurry. *Push* and *press* are used here in their parallel meanings 'to bear hard or put a strain on a person', which is recorded (typically in passive use) from the 18th cent., as is our phrase.

Thomas Holcroft *He's Much To Blame* 1798
I hope you will be kind enough to excuse me, but I am just now so pressed for time that I have not a moment to spare.

(the) big time

great or spectacular success, especially in a field of public activity or entertainment. The phrase was first used in the later part of the 19th cent. in the sense 'a time of great enjoyment' and then came to mean 'successful or important', often as a hyphenated adjectival form in combinations such as *big-time gangster, big-time friends, a big-time hit*, and so on. *19th cent.*

from time immemorial

from a time that is too long ago for people to remember: *cf* time out of mind *below. 18th cent.*

Oliver Goldsmith *Bee* 1759
This deformity ... it had been the custom, time immemorial, to look upon as the greatest ornament of the human visage.

have no time for somebody/something

to have little respect for somebody or something. *Early 20th cent.*

in good time

1 in due course; at a suitable time. *Middle English* **2** having enough time; with no risk of being late. *16th cent.*

not give somebody the time of day

to be unfriendly or uncooperative towards somebody. *Fair* (or *good*) *time of day* is a greeting that occurs often in Shakespeare; for example in *Henry V* (1599), King Harry greets a gathering of English and French nobility (v.ii.3) with the words: 'Unto our brother France and to our sister, | Health and fair time of day.' In *2 Henry VI* (1591), Queen Margaret warns King Henry of the Duke of Gloucester's worsened temper and advises him (III.i.14) 'But meet him now, and be it in the morn | When everyone will give the time of day, | He knits his brow, and shows an angry eye.' In more recent use the phrase is generally negative in context, describing curt dismissal rather than courteous greeting. *19th cent.*

not know the time of day

informal to be astonishingly or shamefully uninformed about an important topic. *20th cent.*

(only) time will tell

a judgement can only be made after time has passed. *17th cent.*

James Mabbe *The Spanish Bawd* 1631
For, it is better to lose his service, then my life in serving him. But Time will tell me what I shall do.

Thomas Holcroft *The Adventures of Hugh Trevor* 1797
You must excuse me, Mr. Trevor. I shall say no more, at present. You say I mistake your intentions. I hope I do. Time will tell. When you are my friend, I shall be very glad to see you; and so will Lady Bray. Good morning to you, Mr. Trevor.

pass the time of day

to exchange greetings or everyday remarks. *19th cent.*

Will Carleton *Poems* 1871
Awhile I leave this noise and strife, | To sing of country scenes and life | ... | Of guide-posts, showing you along; | Of folks who pass the time of day; | And when you ask of them the way, | They do their best, and tell you wrong!

time and tide wait for no man

(proverb) one should take one's opportunities when they are offered, or the chance will be lost. In modern use *tide* is understood in its sense to do with the sea (which dates from the mid 15th cent.), although in Middle English it had the same meaning as *time* and therefore formed an alliterative phrase.

Chaucer *The Clerk's Tale* (line 118)
For thogh we slepe, or wake, or rome, or ryde, | Ay fleeth the tyme; it nyl no man abyde.

time is money

a person's time is an important resource. The notion occurs in other forms (e.g. *time is precious*) from the 16th cent., and the phrase is first used in its current form by Benjamin Franklin in his *Advice to a Young Tradesman* (1748): 'Remember that time is money. He that can earn ten shillings a day ... and ... sits idle one half of that day ... has really ... thrown away five shillings.' The same expression is found in the Glossary to Maria Edgeworth's historical novel *Castle Rackrent* (1800): 'More astonishing is the number of those, who, though they are scarcely able by daily labour to procure daily food, will nevertheless, without the least reluctance, waste six or seven hours of the day lounging in the yard or hall of a justice of the peace, waiting to make some complaint about – nothing. It is impossible to convince them that time is money.' *18th cent.*

time out of mind

for longer than one can remember. This phrase and *from time immemorial* (see above) owe their origin to legal usage, in which the term *beyond legal memory* alludes to a statute of 1275 which identified a date (the accession of Richard I in 1189) as the earliest that the law could take into account. In 1452 the inhabitants of the Hampshire fishing port of Lymington petitioned 'that through time out of mind there were wont many diverse ships to come in to the said haven'. *Cf* from time immemorial *above. 15th cent.*

Thomas Nash *The Unfortunate Traveller* 1594
I ... discourst unto him what entire affection I had borne him time out of mind.

time was

there used be a time (when such-and-such happened or existed): an inversion of *(there) was a time. 16th cent.*

Shakespeare *All's Well That Ends Well* IV.iv.5 (1603)
Time was, I did him a desirèd office, | Dear almost as his life.

watch the time

to make sure one knows how late it is, especially so as to finish a task in time or so as not to miss an engagement. *18th cent.*

David Garrick adapting Shakespeare's *Romeo and Juliet* 1750
Let come what may, once more I will behold, | My Juliet's eyes, drink deeper of affliction: | I'll watch the time, and mask'd from observation | Make known my sufferings, but conceal my name.

See also in the NICK of time; ONCE upon a time; take time by the FORELOCK.

tin

have a tin ear

1 to be tone deaf or poor at discriminating sounds. *Early 20th cent.*

> The Times 1975
> *Manson had a tin ear but ... the Beach Boys recorded at least one of his songs.*

2 to be unwilling to listen to somebody or something. *20th cent.*

> Karl Miller Authors 1989
> *So what is wrong with Levi and his Levi-like writings? ... He was 'cursed with a tin ear for religion'. He could not get on with the believing Jews from Eastern Europe whose religion and traditions he neither shared nor understood.*

See also little tin GOD; put the tin LID on.

---

tinker

not give/care a tinker's curse/cuss/damn

not to care at all. The most natural explanation of the phrase is that it relates to the bad language supposedly used by tinkers. The earliest form (found in Thoreau's *Journal* for 1839) is with *damn*. An alternative origin attempts to salvage the tinkers' reputation and to find a more appealing explanation, but it won't do. According to this, it is the tinker's *dam* (not *damn*) that we are concerned with, a small plug of dough used for stopping a leak in a pot, and useless once removed when the pot had been repaired. This involves a change of word (and spelling) and takes no account of the *curse/cuss* variant, which unmistakably identifies the original form as *damn*. *19th cent.*

> Artemus Ward Artemus Ward, His Book 1862
> *Albert Edard, who wants to receive you all on a ekal footin, not keerin a tinker's cuss what meetin house you sleep in Sundays.*

> Conan Doyle The Adventure of the Illustrious Client 1924
> *It's not out of love for you I'm speaking. I don't care a tinker's curse whether you live or die. It's out of hate for him and to spite him and to get back on him for what he did to me.*

tip[1] (verb)

reach the tipping point

to reach the decisive point in a gradual or cumulative process at which action or change is brought about. The image is of a truck or other device with a tilting mechanism that is tipped to the point where the contents begin to slide out. *Mid 20th cent.*

> The New York Times 1959
> *Exactly when the 'tipping point' of white acceptance will be reached will depend upon the attitude of the individual white parent and upon the general white community attitude.*

tip one's hand/mitt

informal, chiefly NAmer to disclose one's intentions inadvertently. *Hand* is used in the sense to do with card games: *cf* keep/play one's cards close to one's chest *at* CARD. *Early 20th cent.*

> George Ade Letter 1917
> *For a time in the play it should appear that the plans of the smooth citizen are working out perfectly. He becomes confident and over reaches himself, 'tips his hands', so to speak.*

tip one's hat/cap

to touch or lift one's hat in greeting or acknowledgement. *19th cent.*

> Melville D Landon Eli Perkins 1875
> *First the polite drill-master appeared before them, smiling in his most placid manner – then politely tipping his hat he saluted the line, and proceeded to shake hands with the entire regiment.*

tip somebody off

to give somebody a hint or warning, typically in a furtive or confidential manner. *19th cent.*

> Clyde Fitch The Woman in the Case 1904
> [Walters] *I'm to come in with a note to Mr. O'Neill. He will have tipped off Klauffsky to get away, too, and they'll both make a break to go. That's the plan.*

tip the scales/balance

to be the deciding factor in a situation: from the literal meaning in weighing, which dates from the 19th cent. In early use *tip the beam* (= the arm of a balance) was also used. *See also* tip/turn the scales *at* — *at* SCALE[1]. *19th cent.*

Henry James *The Portrait of a Lady* 1881 [Preface]
Place meanwhile in the other scale the lighter
weight (which is usually the one that tips the bal-
ance of interest): press least hard, in short, on the
consciousness of your heroine's satellites, especially
the male; make it an interest contributive only to the
greater one.

tip somebody the wink
to give somebody special or private information,
originally signalled with a wink of the eye. *17th
cent.*

Vanbrugh *Aesop* 1697
Wou'd I cou'd but see the statesman sick a little, I'd
recommend a doctor to him, a cousin of mine, a man
of conscience, a wise physician; tip but the wink, he
understands you.

tip² (noun)

on/at the tip of one's tongue
1 (said of words or facts) at the ready for quoting.
16th cent.

Gabriel Harvey *A New Letter of Notable Contents*
1593
Reconciliation is a sweet word: but entire recon-
ciliation a rare thing, & a strange restorative: whose
sweetnesse lyeth not in the tip of the tongue, or in
the neb of the pen, but in the bottome of the hart, &
in the bowells of the minde.

Daniel Defoe *Moll Flanders* 1722
As we were parted by mutual consent, the nature of
the contract was destroy'd, and the obligation was
mutually discharg'd. She had arguments for this at
the tip of her tongue; and in short, reason'd me out
of my reason; not but that it was too by the help of
my own inclination.

2 about to be uttered, or almost remembered as
something to say. *19th cent.*

Jane Austen *Northanger Abbey* 1818
When the entertainment was over, Thorpe came to
assist them in getting out. Catherine was the
immediate object of his gallantry; and, while they
waited in the lobby for a chair, he prevented the
inquiry which had travelled from her heart almost to
the tip of her tongue, by asking, in a consequential
manner, whether she had seen him talking with
General Tilney.

Dickens *A Tale of Two Cities* 1859
'Now your dinner is done,' Carton presently said,
'why don't you call a health, Mr. Darnay; why
don't you give your toast?' 'What health? What
toast?' 'Why, it's on the tip of your tongue. It ought
to be, it must be, I'll swear it's there.' 'Miss Man-
ette, then!' 'Miss Manette, then!'

See also the tip of the ICEBERG.

tired

tired and emotional
drunk: commonly used from the 1960s (and in
other forms such as *tired and overwrought*) by the
satirical magazine *Private Eye*. *Mid 20th cent.*

John Parker *The Joker's Wild: Biography of Jack
Nicholson* 1991
Rip Torn, who was first choice for the part that
Nicholson eventually played had finally rejected the
pleadings of Fonda and Hopper and pulled out of the
project ... There were rows between him and
Dennis, who could become exceedingly tired and
emotional.

tiswas

all of a tiswas
informal in a state of confusion or bewilderment.
Tiswas is probably a fanciful variant of *tizzy*,
which has the same meaning. *Mid 20th cent.*

M Cecil *Something in Common* 1960
Gets you all of a tiswas, when he's up the wall.

tit

tit for tat
the return of one blow or insult for another; an
equal exchange of blows, insults, etc. Another
form *tip for tap* occurs earlier, and both are probably largely onomatopoeic. *16th cent.*

John Heywood *The Spider and the Flie* 1556
If (quoth the butterflie) the flies do here pike: | That
quarell to spiders, in customes usacion [= usage]. |
That is tit for tat, in this altricacion.

toast

have somebody on toast
informal to have somebody at one's mercy, to be
able to deal with them as one wishes: with allusion to food served up on a piece of toast. *19th
cent.*

George Robert Sims *The Referee* 1891
The landlord came and locked the door, | This piece of news imparting: | 'His lordship's had me twice on toast, | So now, as you are going, | I'd like to ask,' exclaimed mine host, | 'Who'll pay me what is owing?'

tod

on one's tod

informal on one's own, alone: rhyming slang from *Tod Sloan*, the name of an American jockey (1874–1933). *Mid 20th cent.*

Julian Critchley *The Floating Voter* 1993
But there was Hyacinth Scragg. He rang her hotel, and after a long wait she came to the phone. 'Hyacinth, it's Dave, David Swan. I'm on my tod. Carole's gone home to mother … Would you care for a bit of supper, and then we could look in at the Area Ball. I know I'm not John Major, but I'm better looking.'

toe

be/keep on one's toes

informal to be alert and ready for action. To *keep somebody on their toes* is to make sure they remain alert and ready. *Early 20th cent.*

J Dos Passos *Three Soldiers* 1921
If he just watched out and kept on his toes, he'd be sure to get it.

make somebody's toes curl

to cause somebody to react strongly from embarrassment or revulsion. *20th cent.*

toe the line

to follow the rules or conventions of a particular organization or group; to be cooperative and supportive. The original meaning is 'to place one's toes on a line', especially at the start of a race or fight, at a shooting match, or in a parade. Other terms of the same kind as *line* have since disappeared: formerly one could toe a *mark*, a *scratch* (an improvised line used in prize fighting to start a bout), a *crack*, or a *trig* (a line marked on the ground in various sports, found also in the phrase *foot the trig*). There are descriptions of this kind of procedure in sea stories from the 19th cent.: in Captain Marryat's *Peter Simple* (1833), and in R H Dana's *Two Years Before the Mast* (1840), in which 'The chief mate … marked a line on the deck, brought the two boys up to it, making them "toe the mark"'. From these literal uses a figurative sense developed, 'to make oneself ready', and the present meaning 'to be cooperative' is an extension of this. Other explanations relating the phrase to specific rules about where people should stand (e.g. members of parliament in former times, to avoid the risk of fighting in the chamber; convicted prisoners at their execution; and others) are no more than fanciful elaborations that often arise with words and phrases of obscure origin, and they have no substance. Uncertainty about these origins has resulted in a popular re-etymologizing of the phrase, adopting an alternative spelling with *tow* instead of *toe*, and implying an alternative literal meaning of 'towing' or pulling on a 'line' (in the sense 'rope'), an image that is plausible in itself but historically incorrect. *19th cent.*

J T Trowbridge *Martin Merrivale* 1854
'I thought all along you'd turn out right, and I'm glad, – I'm delighted,' he added, jerking his head back with an air of importance, and laying his hand on Martin's shoulder, – 'I may say I'm gratified to see you toe the mark in this here handsome way.'

Mark Twain *A Connecticut Yankee at the Court of King Arthur* 1889
We would make up the rest of the standing army out of commonplace materials, and officer it with nobodies, as was proper … and we would make this regiment toe the line, allow it no aristocratic freedom from restraint, and force it to do all the work.

tread/step on somebody's toes

to offend or inconvenience somebody, especially by encroaching on their sphere of activity. The image is vivid in combining interference with physical over-proximity. *19th cent.*

Charles Augustus Davis *Letters of J. Downing, Major* 1834
I know you well enough to know it will be an honest view of things, and I don't care whose toes you tread on. I have no interest in these matters further than to do my duty.

turn up one's toes

informal to die. *19th cent.*

John Godfrey Saxe *Rampsinitus and the Robbers* 1889
'Now I feel that I am going; | Swift ebbs the vital tide; | No longer in this wicked world | My spirit may abide.' | And so this worthy gentleman | Turned up his toes and died.

See also a foot/toe in the DOOR.

toffee

not be able to do something for toffee
informal to be completely inept at doing something. The notion is presumably of failing to win even the smallest prize. *See also* not be able to do something for NUTS. *Early 20th cent.*

> Dorothy L Sayers *Have His Carcase* 1932
> *The Morgan wouldn't start, not for toffee.*

token

by the same token
for the same reason; applying the same principle. The precise meaning of *token* underlying this phrase is difficult to pin down, but it belongs to the general sense 'something offered as evidence or proof of a statement or position' (as in a token of one's love). From the 17th cent. there is a second meaning in logic, denoting the application of an additional argument to substantiate a conclusion or premiss; but the current meaning is the older one. The phrase is first recorded in the Paston Letters, a collection of letters exchanged between members of a wealthy 15th cent. Norfolk family: 'To this [course] Maister Markham prayed you to agree by the same token ye mevyd [= moved] hym to sette an ende be twyx you and my masters your brethern.'

> Shakespeare *Troilus and Cressida* I.ii.277 (1602)
> [Cressida] *Adieu, uncle.* [Pandarus] *I'll be with you, niece, by and by.* [Cressida] *To bring, uncle?* [Pandarus] *Ay, a token from Troilus.* [Cressida] *By the same token, you are a bawd.*

Tom

a peeping Tom
a person who furtively spies on other people's private activities; a voyeur. The phrase is derived from the story of Lady Godiva, the 11th cent. wife of Leofric, Earl of Mercia. When Lady Godiva pleaded on behalf of his harshly treated tenants, Leofric agreed to remove a particularly onerous tax if she would ride naked through the streets of Coventry. This she did, her modesty protected by her long hair, and Leofric was true to his word. According to a later addition to the story, the inhabitants of Coventry stayed indoors when she rode by, but one citizen of the town, a tailor known as 'peeping Tom' ever since, peeped at her as she passed by and was struck blind in consequence. The allusive use in the phrase is relatively late; it first appears as an entry in Grose's *Dictionary of the Vulgar Tongue* (1796), where it is defined as 'a nick name for a curious prying fellow.' *18th cent.*

Tom, Dick, and Harry
ordinary undistinguished people. The phrase is based on three common English personal names. Variants occur from an early date: for example in Shakespeare's *1 Henry IV* (1596) II.v.8 Prince Harry declares 'I am sworn brother to a leash [= three] of drawers [= tavern-keepers], and can call them all by their christen names, as "Tom", "Dick", and "Francis".' *18th cent.*

> Samuel Pratt *Hail Fellow! Well Met!* 1805
> *The lord and fine lady must labour and dig – | To Tom, Dick, and Harry, must cap-in-hand fall, | For the world's a Free House where there's no servants' hall: | Where the maid is the mistress, the master the man, | For higgledy piggledy now is the plan.*

Tom Tiddler's ground
a source of easy money or profit: based on the children's playground game in which an area is marked out as belonging to one of the players, who has the role of Tom Tiddler. The other players try to encroach on this area and steal his money, those being caught assuming the role of Tom Tiddler in turn. *19th cent.*

> Dickens *Dombey and Son* 1848
> *Now, the spacious dining-room, with the company seated round the glittering table, busy with their glittering spoons, and knives and forks, and plates, might have been taken for a grown-up exposition of Tom Tiddler's ground, where children pick up gold and silver.*

tomorrow

as if there was no tomorrow
informal recklessly; without any regard for consequences in the future. *19th cent.*

tomorrow is another day
(proverb) other opportunities will come in time. In early use in the form *tomorrow is a new day*. The phrase in its current form is famous as the closing words of Margaret Mitchell's novel *Gone with the*

Wind (1936), spoken by Vivien Leigh as Scarlett O'Hara in the film version of 1939: 'I'll think of some way to get him back. After all, tomorrow is another day!' *16th cent.*

> Richard Johnson *A Crowne-Garland of Goulden Roses* 1612
> *Say to her thy true-loue was not here, | remember, remember: | To morrow is another day.*

ton

See come down on somebody like a ton of bricks *at* BRICK.

tongue

the gift of tongues

the ability to speak in languages one doesn't know, regarded as a divine gift. The phrase refers to the biblical account in Acts 2:2–8 of the appearance of the Holy Spirit before the apostles at Pentecost. *See also* SPEAK in tongues. *16th cent.*

with one's tongue hanging out

longing for something delicious and expected: with allusion to the panting of a thirsty dog. *19th cent.*

> Kipling *The Day's Work* 1897
> *They've been waiting for this youth with their tongues hanging out.*

(with) tongue in cheek

with irony or lack of sincerity. The phrase is derived from the image of putting one's tongue in one's cheek as a sign of contempt or sly derision, as in Smollett's *The Expedition of Roderick Random* (1748) 'I signified my contempt of him, by thrusting my tongue in my cheek, which humbled him so much, that he scarce swore another oath during the whole journey', and in Charlotte Brontë's *Jane Eyre* (1847) 'Eliza and Georgiana, evidently acting according to orders, spoke to me as little as possible: John thrust his tongue in his cheek whenever he saw me.' The phrase dates from the 19th cent. in its developed form and has also given rise to an adjectival phrase *tongue-in-cheek*.

See also have a SHARP tongue; have a SILVER tongue; HOLD one's tongue; a SLIP of the pen/ tongue; with forked tongue *at* FORK.

tooth

fight tooth and nail

to fight fiercely and with all one's strength. The image is of fierce fighting using any weapons available. Figurative uses date from the 16th cent., including an early use in William Tyndale's translation of Erasmus' manual of Christian piety entitled *Enchiridion Christiani principis* ('Education of a Christian Prince'): 'Take and holde this with toth and nayle, that to be honour onely which springeth of true vertue.'

See also TEETH.

top

at the top of one's form

in very good form; performing or working extremely well. *Mid 20th cent.*

at the top of the tree

having reached the highest rank in one's career or profession. *18th cent.*

> Fanny Burney *Cecilia* 1782
> *I dare say if any lady was to take a fancy to him, she'd find there was not a modester young man in the world. But you must needs think what a hardship it is to me to have him turn out so unlucky, after all I have done for him, when I thought to have seen him at the top of the tree, as one may say!*

at the top of one's voice

extremely loudly. *19th cent.*

> Lewis Carroll *Alice's Adventures in Wonderland* 1865
> *'Turn a somersault in the sea!' cried the Mock Turtle, capering wildly about. 'Change lobsters again!' yelled the Gryphon at the top of its voice.*

have something up top

informal to have a good brain, to be intelligent: *up top* refers to the head. The phrase is often used in negative forms, e.g. *not have much up top*. *Mid 20th cent.*

on top of the world

informal in high spirits; exhilarated. *Early 20th cent.*

over the top

informal (said of remarks, actions, etc) exaggerated or taken much too far; absurdly excessive. The phrase originates in theatrical use, and is influenced by the military sense from the First

World War, of going over the parapet of a trench to launch an attack on the enemy (used figuratively from the 1920s). John Buchan in *A Prince of the Captivity* (1933), included the advice that 'life's a perpetual affair of going over the top', pre-echoing later usage. In modern figurative use the phrase is often abbreviated to *OTT*. *Early 20th cent.*

top and tail

1 to cut the ends off fruit or vegetables. *19th cent.*
2 *informal* to wash the face and bottom of a baby or small child. *Early 20th cent.*

> H de Sélincourt *Cricket Match* 1924
> She topped and tailed each small boy with the same rubber sponge.

See also at the top of the HEAP; out of the top DRAWER; top the bill *at* BILL[1]; top/big BRASS.

torch

carry a torch for somebody

to retain affection for somebody although they do not reciprocate. The torch is symbolic of personal love, and sometimes appears as an attribute of the goddess Venus. *Early 20th cent.*

> Vanity Fair (New York) 1927
> When a fellow 'carries the torch' it doesn't simply imply that he is 'lit up' or drunk, but girl-less. His steady has quit him for another or he is lonesome for her.

hand/pass on the torch

to continue a tradition, especially an enlightened or educational one: with allusion to the passing of a torch from one runner to the next in a relay race. The word *tradition* is itself derived from a Latin word meaning 'to hand over', and in the philosophical work *De Rerum Natura* (ii.78) of the Roman poet Lucretius (1st cent. BC), *vitae lampada tradunt* 'they hand over the torch of life' is used to symbolize the succession of generations. *Torch* as a symbol of learning and guidance dates from the 17th cent. *19th cent.*

put something to the torch / put a torch to something

to set fire to a place and destroy it. *19th cent.*

> Edgar Rice Burroughs *The Return of Tarzan* 1913
> They had looked in vain for the owner of the voice which had frightened off the men who had been

detailed to put the torch to the huts, but not even the keenest eye among them had been able to locate him.

toss

not care/give a toss

informal not to care at all; to be totally indifferent: based on the meaning of *toss* 'a tossing of a coin', the idea being of the arbitrary and hence casual nature of making a decision in this way. *19th cent.*

toss one's cookies

NAmer, informal to vomit. *Mid 20th cent.*

> J D Salinger *Catcher in the Rye* 1951
> The cab I had was a real old one that smelled like someone'd just tossed his cookies in it. I always get those vomity kind of cabs if I go anywhere late at night.

See also ARGUE the toss.

touch

lose one's touch

to find that a usual ability or skill eludes one. *Early 20th cent.*

a soft/easy touch

informal a gullible or over-compliant person; a person who is easily imposed upon or taken advantage of. *Mid 20th cent.*

touch and go

an uncertain or precarious situation. The current meaning developed from an earlier sense used to describe a brief encounter (as in the first quotation below), in which one person is regarded as touching another and then passing on quickly. (*Old touch and go* was also an occasional derogatory form of address to somebody unpleasant or bad-tempered.) Other theories associate the phrase with the movement of vehicles and boats, specifically when the wheel of one road vehicle briefly touches that of another without causing damage (but it is difficult to see how such a rare occurrence can account for a popular phrase) and when a boat caught in shallow or dangerous water is swung round the moment it touches the bottom to get it back into deeper or safer water. In its early sense, the phrase is found in the 17th cent., and in the modern sense from the early 19th cent.

Richard Head *The English Rogue Described* 1665
*I love thee still for better and for worse; | He that
divorc'd us let him have my curse. | Sure 'twas a
red Nos'd fellow, for I know, | He coming near, it
was but touch and go. | But let him keep thee, for
thou'lt useless be | To him, thick cloaths suits best
with knavery.*

Marryat *Peter Simple* 1833
*'That's all he can do now, Mr. Simple,' observed
Swinburne; 'he must trust to them and to Providence. They are not more than a mile from the beach
– it will be touch and go.'*

See also hit/touch rock bottom *at* ROCK[1]; the
MIDAS touch; not touch something with a BARGE-
POLE; touch BASE; touch BOTTOM; a touch of the
SUN; touch WOOD.

---

tough

(as) tough as old boots

(said especially of a person) extremely tough or
resilient. *19th cent.*

tough it out

informal to endure a period of hardship or difficulty stoically. *19th cent.*

Mary Jane Holmes *Edna Browning* 1872
*Thank your uncle for inviting me to his house, but
tell him I prefer my own bed and board to anybody's
else. I've toughed it out these thirty years, and guess
I can stand it a spell longer.*

---

towel

See THROW in the towel.

---

tower

See a tower of STRENGTH.

---

town

go to town

informal to do something with great enthusiasm
or extravagance. *Mid 20th cent.*

on the town

informal enjoying the entertainments and attractions of city life: in 18th cent. use in the form *upon
the town*, sometimes apparently meaning little
more than 'in town' (as in 'newly come upon

the town'). In the 19th cent. the phrase often
referred to the activities of prostitutes. *18th cent.*

Susanna Rowson *The Fille de Chambre* 1792
*She informed Rebecca that after they left Lincoln-
shire Serl commenced gamester, sharper and
swindler; that his daughter went on the town, and
turned an abandoned profligate.*

town and gown

the non-academic inhabitants (*town*) of a university city and the members of the university (*gown*,
i.e. the academic dress of the university). The
phrase was first used in this form in the early
19th cent. with reference to Oxford and Cambridge, although conflicts between citizens and
students are recorded from a much earlier date:
for example, the St Scholastica's Day (10 February) riot in Oxford in 1355, which began when a
group of students complained of the quality of
the wine provided by a local vintner. It lasted for
three days and sixty-three students were killed.
19th cent.

See also PAINT the town red.

---

toy

See THROW one's rattle/toys out of the pram.

---

trace

See KICK over the traces.

---

track

the beaten track

familiar and popular places. The phrase occurs in
various guises: to *tread the beaten track* is to stick to
what is familiar and established, and to *leave* (or
forsake) *the beaten track* is to try new ideas and
situations (which are also said to be *off the beaten
track*). *17th cent.*

John Oldham *Horace His Art of Poetry* 1683
*Those, who know no better than to cloy | With the
old musty Tales of Thebes and Troy: | But boldly
the dull beaten track forsook, | And Subjects from
our Country-story took.*

in one's tracks

immediately and without warning, in the middle
of some activity: especially in the context of a
surprise or interruption, e.g. *be stopped in one's*

tracks. The image is of a vehicle coming to an abrupt halt. *19th cent.*

> Emerson Bennett *Wild Scenes on the Frontiers* 1859
> *Pete Blodget fell down dead in his tracks, killed by my first shot, jest when two seconds more o' his life would hev ended mine.*

keep/lose track of something/somebody
to keep (or fail to keep) oneself informed about developments or whereabouts: the image is of tracking a quarry. *19th cent.*

> John William De Forest *Seacliff* 1859
> *He had forgotten what he had told me five minutes before about the cessation of intercourse between himself and Westervelt, senior. He often lost track of his own stories thus, this short-sighted Hunter.*

make tracks (for a place)
to set out with determination for a place. *19th cent.*

> George Lippard *Memoirs of a Preacher* 1849
> *That's done. Now I'll make tracks for home, and have a talk with Fanny.*

on the right/wrong track
informal following a course of action that is likely (or unlikely) to be successful or produce results. The phrase occurs from an early date in extended metaphor about losing and finding one's way (as in the first quotation below). Its fixed form dates from the 19th cent.

> William Painter *The Palace of Pleasure* 1567
> *Thou wandring for thy better disport, missing the right way, so strangely didst straggle, that hard it is to reduce thee into the right track again.*

> R D Blackmore *Lorna Doone* 1869
> *I managed so to hold my peace that he put himself upon the wrong track, and continued thereon with many vaunts of his shrewdness and experience, and some chuckles at my simplicity.*

on the wrong side of the tracks
informal in the poorer or less prosperous parts of a town: with allusion to the division of a town into areas separated by railway tracks. An American source of 1929 (T Smith, *Stray Lamb*) refers to this social phenomenon: 'In most commuting towns … there are always two sides of which the tracks serve as a line of demarcation. There is the right side and the wrong side. Translated into terms of modern American idealism, this means, the rich side and the side that hopes to be rich.' Notions of

sides denoting favourable and unfavourable aspects underlie several phrases: *cf* get out of BED on the wrong side; be born on the wrong side of the BLANKET. *Mid 20th cent.*

> Sinclair Lewis *Cass Timberlane* 1945
> *I thought at first that she was from the wrong side of the railroad tracks, but she seems to have settled down to being a nice little lady and a good war worker.*

See also COVER one's tracks; JUMP the rails/track.

trail

trail one's coat
to go out of one's way to start a quarrel or fight: from the Irish custom of trailing one's coat behind one in the expectation that somebody will step on it and provide the excuse needed. *19th cent.*

> Charles Lever *Tom Burke* 1844
> *Certain it is, nations, like individuals, that have a taste for fighting, usually have the good luck to find an adversary – and as your Emperor here seems to have learned the Donnybrookfair trick of trailing his coat after him, it would be strange enough if nobody would gratify him by standing on it.*

tread

tread the boards/stage
to be a professional actor on the stage. *17th cent.*

> Anthony Pasquin *Miss Kemble* in *Poems* 1789
> *The sisters assume the great cast of the play, | And, as heroines both, they must both lead the way; | As one treads the boards, by fair Genius attended, | With t'other's presumption the House is offended.*

tread water
to make no progress despite much effort: from the literal meaning of moving one's hands and feet in water to remain afloat in an upright position without changing location. *19th cent.*

> Nathaniel Parker Willis *Dashes at Life with a Free Pencil* 1845
> *It is uncomfortable for pride to be always 'treading water', as the swimmers say. Better sink, and sink, and sink, till you come to your true level – anybody will say.*

See also tread on AIR; tread on somebody's toes *at* TOE.

treat

Used with *a* as an intensifying word in favourable contexts from the end of the 19th cent.: the phrases below are especially common.

do something a (fair) treat

to act or work with great effectiveness and panache. *19th cent.*

> Daily News 1899
> *This air makes yer liver work a fair treat.*

look a treat

informal to look particularly attractive or appealing: an extension of uses such as 'a treat to look at', as in Dickens' *David Copperfield* (1850): '"There's a friend!" said Mr. Peggotty, stretching out his pipe. "There's a friend, if you talk of friends! Why, Lord love my heart alive, if it ain't a treat to look at him!"' The phrase in its current form dates from the mid 20th cent.

> John Masefield *Poems* 1946
> *And one, the second clown, a snub-nosed youth, |*
> *Fair-haired, with broken teeth, discoloured black, |*
> *Muttered, 'He looks a treat, and that's the truth. |*
> *I've had enough: I've given him the sack.'*

tree

out of one's tree

informal, chiefly NAmer acting irrationally; eccentric or crazy. *Late 20th cent.*

> Fiona Cooper *I Believe in Angels* 1993
> *The madwoman in the attic. In a padlocked world of her own, up the pole, off her rocker, out of her tree.*

up a tree

informal, chiefly NAmer caught in a difficult situation with no apparent means of escape. The phrase was used several times by Thackeray (see below). *19th cent.*

> Thackeray *Vanity Fair* 1848
> *He was deploring the dreadful predicament in which he found himself, in a house full of old women, jabbering French and Italian, and talking poetry to him. 'Reglarly up a tree, by jingo!' exclaimed the modest boy, who could not face the gentlest of her sex – not even Briggs – when she began to talk to him.*

See also be barking up the wrong tree *at* BARK; — does not GROW on trees.

tremble

in/with fear and trembling (of somebody/ something)

extremely scared of a person or thing, especially when one has to deal with them constantly: with allusion to St Paul's Epistle to the Philippians 2:12 (in the Authorized Version, 1611) 'Wherefore, my beloved, as ye have always obeyed, ... work out your own salvation with fear and trembling.' *17th cent.*

> Aphra Behn *Love-Letters Between a Noble-man and His Sister* 1684
> *She ordered her porter to be call'd, and gave him orders, upon pain of life, not to tell of my being in the house, whatever enquiry should be made after me; and having given the same command to her page, she dismiss'd 'em, and came to me, with all the fear and trembling imaginable.*

trial

trial and error

a process of trying out different methods so as to find the one that is most effective: based on a mathematical process called (among other names) the *rule of trial and error*, in which an unknown quantity is found by assuming values for it and then testing these values against the known data. *19th cent.*

> Egbert Martin *The Magic View* 1883
> *Stripped of this what else is rife | But trial, error, and vexation.*

> G B Shaw *Man and Superman* 1903
> *They will tell you that the proof of the pudding is in the eating; and they are right. The proof of the Superman will be in the living; and we shall find out how to produce him by the old method of trial and error, and not by waiting for a completely convincing prescription of his ingredients.*

trice

in a trice

suddenly or instantly, usually with an element of surprise: recorded earlier (late Middle English) in the form *at a trice* and (16th–17th cent.) in the forms *on* or *with a trice*. The original meaning was 'with one pull or tug'. *Trice* is confined to these phrases and is based on an obsolete verb *trice* meaning 'to pull or snatch'. *16th cent.*

Shakespeare *The Tempest* v.i.241 (1613)
[Boatswain] *On a trice, so please you, | Even in a dream, were we divided from them, | And were brought moping hither.*

---

trick

do the trick
informal to achieve exactly what is wanted: also in American use in the form *turn the trick*. 19th cent.

Charles Reade *Hard Cash* 1863
He determined to win Dr. Wycherley altogether by hook or by crook, and get a certificate of sanity from him. Now a single white lie, he knew, would do the trick.

every trick in the book
every available way of getting what one wants. *Mid 20th cent.*

Today 1992
Westminster is now in for a furious bout of behind-the-scenes arm twisting as Government whips try every trick in the book to persuade the waverers back into the fold.

how's tricks?
informal, originally NAmer used as a greeting formula, an elaboration of *how are you? Early 20th cent.*

Celia Brayfield *The Prince* 1990
Out of sight behind the orange trees she loosened the string at the neck of her blouse and readjusted the straps of the overalls. A quick dab of Youth Dew and then she sauntered over to join him. 'Hiya, kid,' he greeted her sleepily. 'How's tricks?'

the oldest trick in the book
a familiar ruse or stratagem that will deceive nobody. *Mid 20th cent.*

Len Deighton *Billion Dollar Brain* 1966
He used a hair-piece to cover a bald patch on top of his head ... He blacked out a couple of his front teeth with stage cosmetics and made his breath smell with chemical – oldest trick in the business to prevent people looking you in the face close to.

a trick of the trade
a clever way of doing something, known mainly by those who do it professionally: from the 16th cent. meaning of *trick* 'a clever device or idea', found in Shakespeare, *Love's Labour's Lost* (1594) v.ii.466 '[Biron] I see the trick on't ... Some Dick |

That smiles his cheek in years, and knows the trick | To make my lady laugh.' The phrase is 17th cent., with allusive uses mainly from the 19th cent.

Maria Edgeworth *Patronage* 1814
Solicitor Babington, the solicitor employed against us in that suit ... knows, without practising them, all the tricks of the trade.

trick or treat
a request for a small gift, made by children at Hallowe'en when calling on neighbouring houses: the implication, slightly sinister because it is mentioned first, is that the householder will suffer a 'trick' or penalty if he or she refuses. The practice originated in North America and has spread to Britain in recent years. The phrase is also used to refer to the practice itself, and has produced derivatives such as *trick-or-treating*. *Mid 20th cent.*

a trick worth two of that
a much better plan or idea: with reference to Shakespeare, *1 Henry IV* (1596) II.i.36 '[Gadshill] I prithee lend me thy lantern to see my gelding in the stable. [Carrier] Nay, by God, soft. I know a trick worth two of that, i'faith.' *16th cent.*

John Day *Humour out of Breath* 1608
[Florimell] I purposed, thou in the habit of Hortensio, shouldst under pretence of removing Aspero to a new prison, have freed him out of the old one. [Page] Tut, I can tell you a trick, worth two of that.

turn a trick
1 *informal* (said of a thief) to succeed in committing a robbery: also in the form *do a trick. 19th cent.*

Julius Madison Cawein *The Republic* 1913
His chance was now | To serve the Whiteman out somehow. | He would get even for many a kick. – | Now was his time to turn a trick.

2 *informal* (said of a prostitute) to entertain a client: from *trick* in the (early 20th cent.) sense 'sexual act.' *Mid 20th cent.*

Bernard Cornwell *Crackdown* 1990
Getting laid has never been so cheap in all history. Go to a crack house, Nick, and you can buy anything you want in the way of human flesh. Do you think I want to see my kids turning tricks for a smear of white powder?

up to / at one's (old) tricks

behaving in a characteristic (and usually unwelcome) way: *trick* in the sense 'personal habit or trait' dates from the late 16th cent. *18th cent.*

William Godwin *Things As They Are* 1794
My conductor, without answering this apostrophe, bid her push an easy chair which stood in one corner, and set it directly before the fire. This she did with apparent reluctance, muttering, Ah, you are at your old tricks; I wonder what such folks as we have to do with charity! It will be the ruin of us at last.

See also a BAG of tricks; a BOX of tricks; not MISS a trick.

tried

tried and tested/true

(said of a process, method, etc) used before and known to be reliable. *Mid 20th cent.*

trim

in trim

in good condition; fit and healthy. *19th cent.*

Dickens *Bleak House* 1853
Grandfather Smallweed has been gradually sliding down in his chair since his last adjustment, and is now a bundle of clothes, with a voice in it calling for Judy. That Houri appearing, shakes him up in the usual manner, and is charged by the old gentleman to remain near him ... 'Ha!' he observes, when he is in trim again. 'If you could have traced out the Captain, Mr. George, it would have been the making of you.'

trim one's sails (to the wind)

to adapt one's behaviour or way of life to suit new or unexpected circumstances. In sailing, to trim the sails is to adjust them according to the direction of the wind. *19th cent.*

Scott *Redgauntlet* 1824
The sharks have been at and about him this many a day, but Father Crackenthorp knows how to trim his sails – never a warrant but he hears of it before the ink's dry.

trip

trip the light fantastic

to dance: with allusion to Milton, *L'Allegro* (1645) 'Trip it as you go | On the light fantastic toe'.

Milton uses *trip* in its original sense 'to move nimbly, to dance' and *fantastic* in the sense 'making fantastic (i.e. fanciful) movements (in dancing)'. The phrase first appears in its present form, as a humorous reference to dancing, in 19th cent. literature.

Mary Jane Holmes *West Lawn and the Rector of St Marks* 1874
She wouldn't let him waltz, – thought it was very improper, and I was told made several remarks not very complimentary to my style of tripping the light fantastic toe.

trivet

See (as) RIGHT as a trivet.

Trojan

like a Trojan

informal with great courage and vigour. The phrase is used (often in trivialized contexts) with allusion to the fabled bravery of the people of ancient Troy as reflected in the Homeric poems. Some early uses (perhaps including the first quotation below) are more literal in sense, making a direct rather than allusive comparison. *17th cent.*

Nahum Tate *Brutus of Alba* 1678
The blow, he drew, I drew, he thrust, I thrust, | And like a Trojan pass'd him through the heart.

Catharine Sedgwick *The Linwoods* 1885
By the living jingo, she eats like a Trojan, don't she? This way she'll soon get the blood back to her pretty cheeks.

a Trojan horse

1 a person or thing that undermines an organization from within: with reference to the story told in the second book of Virgil's *Aeneid* of the Greeks' ruse to gain entry to the besieged city of Troy by hiding in a large wooden statue of a horse left outside the city walls and taken into the city by the Trojans (*see* beware/fear the Greeks bearing gifts *at* GREEK). *17th cent.*

Edmund Elys *Divine Poems* 1659
My Mind keeps out the Host of Sin, | Sense lets 'em in: | I'th' Phant'sie, as i'th' Trojan Horse, | They Hide their Force, | Till Opportunity they find | To Sally, and Subdue the Mind.

2 in computing, a maliciously intrusive program that appears to be part of the normal operating software but causes damage to a system or allows an unauthorized user to bypass a system's security. *Late 20th cent.*

trolley

off one's trolley

informal completely irrational or deranged: from *trolley* meaning 'a low truck without sides that runs along a track in a factory or on a railway', or alternatively the sense as in *trolleybus*, i.e. a pulley running along an overhead wire for transmitting power to the vehicle. *19th cent.*

> George Ade Artie 1896
> *Any one that's got his head full o' the girl proposition's liable to go off his trolley at the first curve.*

trooper

Originally a cavalry soldier in the English army in the 17th cent. Troopers had a reputation for coarse language and behaviour, reflected in the similes associated with them.

swear like a trooper

to use bad language habitually. The phrase was already familiar by the middle of the 18th cent., as a passage in Richardson's *Clarissa* (1748) shows: 'Bless me! said I, how I heard one of them swear and curse, just now, at a modest meek man, as I judge by his low voice, and gentle answers! – Well do they make it a proverb – Like a trooper!' Other comparisons, equally unfavourable, include *drinking*, *lying*, and *snoring*.

> William Clark Russell The Wreck of the Grosvenor 1878
> *At eight o'clock I called Stevens, and saw him well upon deck before I ventured to enter the boatswain's berth. I then softly opened the door, and heard the honest fellow snoring like a trooper in his bunk.*

trot

on the trot

1 *informal* busy, especially kept on one's feet for long periods: a metaphor from riding. *17th cent.*
2 *informal* in rapid succession, as though moving past at a trotting pace. *Mid 20th cent.*

> The People 1956
> *I want to be between those posts again when Manchester City reach Wembley next year for the third time on the trot!*

troth

See PLIGHT one's troth.

trouble

See be asking for trouble *at* ASK; be looking for trouble *at* LOOK; MEET trouble halfway.

trousers

catch somebody with their trousers down

informal to find somebody unprepared or in an awkward or compromising situation: *see also* catch somebody with their PANTS down. *Mid 20th cent.*

> Malcolm Hamer Sudden Death 1991
> *It caused a lot of financial pain to a lot of people, and especially to the fast operators in the City who were over-extended with investments in secondary stocks … I would also guess that you were one of those caught with their financial trousers down.*

wear the trousers

informal to be the dominant partner in a relationship or household: based on the traditional role of the husband in a family. *Mid 20th cent.*

trout

old trout

informal an unkind epithet or form of address for a middle-aged or elderly woman. The phrase is first recorded in the modern sense from the end of the 19th cent. and overlaps slightly with *old trot* (based on a Middle English word for an old woman) which fell out of use at the beginning of the 20th cent.; so probably the word became assimilated to the familiar word for the fish. *Trout* occurs in the 16th cent. and 17th cent., though not later, as a more affectionate term for a person in phrases such as *old trout*, *true trout*, and *trusty trout*. In early use the fishing metaphor was often extended to include references to tickling (as in the 1679 quotation below).

Robert Greene *Orlando Furioso* 1594
Sounes Orgalio, why sufferest thou this old trot to come so nigh me?

John Leanerd *The Counterfeits* 1679
This is right, and the old trout rarely tickled. Nor was there any other means of getting Peralta from his house, before the design'd marriage was consummate.

Robert Dixon *Canidia* 1683
Next day th' old man is at a loss, | And swears, his stone had gathered moss. | He for his part was laid secure, | Next morn the old trout was ta'ne dead sure.

trowel

See LAY something on thick / with a trowel.

truck

want/have no truck with somebody/something

to refuse to have any dealings with a person or thing. *Truck* is an archaic (16th cent.) word meaning 'commercial dealings, bartering', derived from a Middle English verb with corresponding meaning. *19th cent.*

Conan Doyle *The Sign of Four* 1890
'How can I decide?' said I. 'You have not told me what you want of me. But I tell you now that if it is anything against the safety of the fort I will have no truck with it, so you can drive home your knife and welcome.'

true

come true

(said of a dream or prediction) to happen in real life; to come to fruition. *17th cent.*

Alexander Radcliffe *The Ramble* 1696
Then may they find him turn a dreamer too, | And live themselves to see his dream come true.

Robert Bage *Man As He Is* 1792
Things that I have foretold have come true a thousand times; and won't be less true because you won't believe them.

out of true

not of the right shape or in the right position. *19th cent.*

J Rose *Complete Practical Machinist* 1876
If the face plate of the lathe is a trifle out of true, the eccentric will only be out to an equal amount.

true to form/type

speaking or behaving in accordance with one's character or reputation: also *run true to form*, a metaphor from horseracing. *Early 20th cent.*

true to life

(said of a depiction or description) realistic; authentic. *19th cent.*

I Mitchell *The Asylum* 1811
Did we not tell you that we were detailing facts? that we held the pencil of nature? that our portraits were true to life? Shall we disguise or discolour truth to please your taste?

trump

come/turn up trumps

informal to achieve an unexpected success: from the use of *trumps* as a special suit in card games. To *turn up trumps* is to produce a trump card during play. In early use often in extended metaphor (as below). *17th cent.*

George Farquhar *Love and a Bottle* 1698
[Pindress] No consideration; the bus'ness must be done hand over head. [Leanthe] Well, I have one Card to play still; and with you, Pindress. [Pindress] You expect tho' that I shou'd turn up Trumps? [Leanthe] No, not if I shuffle right.

play one's trump card

informal to use a special advantage to produce a decisive effect or make a crucial difference at the most opportune moment. The image, though not the exact phrase, occurs in Byron's *Don Juan* (1823) viii.25: 'If he warr'd | Or loved, it was with what we call "the best | Intentions", which form all mankind's trump card, | To be produced when brought up to the test.' *19th cent.*

Louisa M Alcott *Little Women* 1868
'What shall we do when we can't eat any more?' asked Laurie, feeling that his trump card had been played when lunch was over.

trumpet

blow/sound one's own trumpet

informal to boast about one's own achievements or abilities: *cf* blow one's own HORN. The notion of sounding a trumpet or horn as a signal of achievement dates in other forms from the 16th cent. (e.g. in a source of 1576 'I will ... sound the trumpet of mine owne merites'). Normally one blows a trumpet on one's own behalf when nobody else does so. *18th cent.*

Christopher Bullock *Woman is a Riddle* 1717
As for my part, but no matter – I'll not speak – A man shou'd not sound his own trumpet you know – but I have put my hand in the lyon's mouth.

Edgar Allan Poe *The Business Man* 1840
The truth is, that few individuals, in any line, did a snugger little business than I. I will just copy a page or so out of my Day-Book; and this will save me the necessity of blowing my own trumpet – a contemptible practice of which no high-minded man will be guilty.

trust

not trust somebody as far as one can throw them / spit

to distrust somebody completely. The image behind the phrase is often stretched to breaking point, as in the quotation below. *20th cent.*

Guardian 1990
Though I wouldn't trust Hollywood as far as I could throw it on these matters, it does look as if there is plenty of talent around to foster if they look hard enough.

truth

truth is stranger than fiction

real events and situations are often more remarkable or incredible than those made up in fiction. First used by Byron in *Don Juan* (1824) xiv.101: 'Truth is always strange, | Stranger than Fiction.' *19th cent.*

William Alexander Carruthers *The Knights of the Horseshoe* 1845
We could multiply instances and illustrations, were we disposed to digress, and show at the same time that 'truth is stranger than fiction', but we leave the matter to be tested by the experience of each reader.

the truth, the whole truth, and nothing but the truth

the complete and unadulterated truth: with allusion to the formula used in the oath of truthfulness sworn by witnesses in lawcourts. *19th cent.*

Hazlitt *The Spirit of the Age* 1825
If the mind of man were competent to comprehend the whole of truth and good, and act upon it at once, and independently of all other considerations, Mr. Bentham's plan would be a feasible one, and the truth, the whole truth, and nothing but the truth would be the best possible ground to place morality upon.

truth will out

the truth will always be discovered in the end: a phrase parallel to *murder will out* (and often overlapping with it; see the Shakespeare quotation below). An early occurrence is in John Lydgate's *Life of St Alban* (1439): 'Trouthe wil out ... Ryghtwysnesse may nat ben hid [= righteousness may not be hidden].' The notion appears in other forms, e.g. in Shakespeare's *The Merchant of Venice* (1598) II.ii.73, where the clown Lancelot says to his father Gobbo 'Truth will come to light; murder cannot be hid long – a man's son may, but in the end truth will out.' *Middle English*

Roger Boyle *Mr Anthony* 1690
[Cudden] You are the better provided. [Antony] O, am I the better provided? Truth will out at last. Acknowledge but that to my brace of Mistresses, and that shall serve me as much against all thy pretensions.

Henry Fielding *The Universal Gallant* 1735
He is a very close Fellow, and proper to be trusted with a Secret, I can tell you; for he told me just the contrary; but Truth will out, Sister: besides, did you not hear my Wife confess it?

See also be ECONOMICAL with the truth; the GOSPEL truth; the NAKED truth.

try

try a fall with somebody

to compete or contend with somebody: a metaphor, established early, from wrestling (in which sense it is used for example by Shakespeare in *As You Like It* (1599) I.ii.192 in the context of the wrestling bout between Charles and Orlando). An early figurative use is by Charles Cotton in the fifth edition (1676) of Isaac Walton's *Compleat Angler*, where the reference is to catching a fish: 'Let him come, I'll try a fall with him.' *17th cent.*

try something for size

informal to consider an idea or proposition. In the form *try this for size*, a favourite line in story books and cartoon captions, often accompanied by a hefty blow. *Mid 20th cent.*

try one's hand (at something)
to attempt something new in order to determine how well one does it. *18th cent.*

> Boswell *The Life of Samuel Johnson* 1791
> *I never heard him mention the subject; but at a later period of his life, when Sir Joshua Reynolds told him that Mr. Edmund Burke had said, that if he had come early into Parliament, he certainly would have been the greatest speaker that ever was there, Johnson exclaimed, 'I should like to try my hand now.'*

See also try conclusions with somebody *at* CON-CLUSION.

tube

go down the tube(s)
informal (said of a business, activity, etc) to fail or be lost or wasted completely. The image is similar to that in *go down the drain* (see DRAIN). *Mid 20th cent.*

> Punch 1992
> *'How's things?' he asked. 'Not too good,' I said, 'I've just been told that* Punch *is closing.' A groan of real sympathy came down the line. 'Bloody hell!' he said. 'That's a bit of history gone down the tubes, eh? The lads always used to drink in there before mid-week matches' ... I explained that the Punch Tavern in Fleet Street was perfectly safe and identified the real victim. 'Oh!' he said. 'The magazine!'*

tug

tug of love
a situation involving conflict over the care or custody of a child, for example between the child's separated or divorced parents, or between natural and adoptive parents. The phrase originates as the title of a comedy by Israel Zangwill (1907), but its main uses are since the 1970s, when newspapers began to use the phrase in (often sensationalized) reports of child custody disputes. *Early 20th cent.*

tug of war
a struggle for supremacy: an older use than that referring to the athletic contest, which dates from the late 19th cent. The origin of the phrase lies in the literary proverb *when Greek meets Greek, then*

comes the tug of war (see Lee quotation below). *17th cent.*

> Nathaniel Lee *The Rival Queens* 1677
> *When Greeks joyn'd Greeks, then was the tug of war,* | *The labour'd battle sweat, and conquest bled.*

> R H Dana *Two Years Before the Mast* 1840
> *On one of these expeditions, we saw a battle between two Sandwich Islanders and a shark ... The line soon broke; but the Kanakas would not let him off so easily, and sprang directly into the water after him. Now came the tug of war. Before we could get into deep water, one of them seized him by the tail, and ran up with him upon the beach.*

tune

be tuned in
informal to be receptive to what is being said; to understand well: the image is of a radio or television tuned to a particular station. *Mid 20th cent.*

there's many a good tune played on an old fiddle
(proverb) ability and success are not confined to the young. *Early 20th cent.*

to the tune of —
amounting to (usually a large or surprising amount of money): derived from an earlier and now obsolete meaning 'in accordance with', originally as a metaphor from music. *17th cent.*

> Charles Gildon *The Post-boy Rob'd of His Mail* 1692
> *Her father left you a legacy of one hundred pounds, a better husband than father; besides your joynture, and the housewifly elucubrations of your own industry, to the tune of five times that sum.*

See also CALL the shots/tune; CHANGE one's tune.

tunnel

light at the end of the tunnel
signs of more hopeful or promising circumstances in the near future, especially during a time of difficulty. In early use with *daylight* instead of *light*. *Early 20th cent.*

> Guardian 1989
> *If Shostakovich was writing now, he wouldn't have had the same material. Many of his symphonies dealt with desolation – no light at the end of the tunnel.*

turkey

like turkeys voting for Christmas
(said of a suggestion or eventuality) highly inappropriate or absurd. *20th cent.*

talk turkey
informal to talk frankly and openly, especially on business affairs. This is the meaning now, although in earlier 19th cent. use the phrase meant rather 'to talk agreeably about pleasant things'. The current meaning, which evolved in the early 20th cent., was influenced by the phrase (American in origin) *cold turkey* meaning 'plain talk'. The origin of our phrase is unclear, but it most likely has something to do – in its original meaning – with American families getting round the table to eat a turkey dinner at Thanksgiving in November. An alternative suggestion connects it with the first contacts of the American settlers with the native population, when trading in turkeys, or 'talking turkey', was a regular topic of conversation; but this has all the ring of invention and none of historical foundation. *19th cent.*

Harriet Beecher Stowe We and Our Neighbors 1875
'Dinah can tell to a T, how long a turkey takes to roast, by looking at it. Here, Dinah, run over, and "talk turkey" to Mrs. Henderson.' Dinah went back with me, boiling over with giggle.

Aldous Huxley After Many a Summer 1939
'I'll make it worth your while,' he said. 'You can have anything you care to ask for' … 'Ah,' said Dr. Obispo, 'now you're talking turkey.'

See also go/take COLD turkey.

turn

do somebody a good turn
to help somebody; to give somebody an unexpected favour. The phrase is recorded earlier in the opposite form *do an ill turn*, and *turn* has been used since Middle English in the sense of an act or service with a qualifying word that indicates whether it is beneficial or harmful to others. Chaucer's *The Pardoner's Tale* includes lines about the sharing of gold (lines 813–15) 'But nathelees, if I kan shape it so | That it departed were [= be divided] among us two, | Hadde I nat doon a freendes torn to thee?'; and our phrase itself appears in *The Romaunt of the Rose* (lines 6945–8): 'Another is this, that if so falle | That

ther be oon among us alle | That doth a good turn, out of drede, | We seyn it is our alder dede [= a deed of us all].'

Dryden Secret Love 1668
[Asteria] *Which of the Ladies are you watching for?* [Celadon] *Any of 'em that will do me the good turn to make me soundly in love.*

one good turn deserves another
(proverb) a favour done calls for a favour in return. The proverb dates from Middle English and is earlier (14th cent.) in French (*lune bonté requiert lautre*).

serve the/somebody's turn
to be useful or suit a purpose. This meaning of *turn*, 'purpose or convenience', is largely confined to phrases. *16th cent.*

Sir Thomas North The Lives of the Noble Grecians and Romanes 1579
[Preface] *They alledge further, that in matters of war, all things alter from yeer to yeer; by means whereof the sleights and policies that are to be learned out of books, will serve the turn no more then mines that are blown up.*

Shakespeare Love's Labour's Lost i.i.284 (1594)
[King] *This 'maid' will not serve your turn, sir.* [Costard] *This maid will serve my turn, sir.*

to a turn
to exactly the right degree or level: used especially in cooking, originally with allusion to the turning of a spit. *18th cent.*

a turn-up (for the book)
informal a surprise, especially a welcome one. There are two allusions here: to the turning up of a particular card or face of the dice in gambling, and to the use in racing, in which an unexpected winner 'turns up', giving the bookmaker a welcome windfall (the *book* being the record of bets made). *19th cent.*

J Palgrave Simpson Second Love 1857
Come, that's jolly – ha, ha, ha! Here's a turn up! The colonel will have to pay the postman, I take it, and pretty handsome, too.

See also Buggins' turn *at* BUGGINS; earn/turn an HONEST penny; not turn a HAIR; tip/turn the scales *at* SCALE¹; turn one's BACK on somebody/something; turn CAT in pan; turn the CORNER; turn a DEAF ear; turn one's face to the WALL; turn one's HAND to something; turn somebody's

HEAD; turn heads *at* HEAD; turn in one's GRAVE; a turn of the SCREW; turn on one's heels *at* HEEL; turn the other CHEEK; turn over a new LEAF; turn the tables *at* TABLE; turn TAIL; turn to (dust and) ashes *at* ASH; turn a TRICK; turn TURTLE; turn up like a bad PENNY; turn up one's NOSE.

turtle

turn turtle
to turn upside down, as a turtle is turned on its back to render it helpless and easy to kill. *17th cent.*

> **Ben Jonson** *The Case is Altered* **1609**
> *Will you, because your Lord is taken prisoner, |*
> *Blubber and weepe and keepe a peevish stirre, | As*
> *though you would turne turtle with the newes.*

twain

never the twain shall meet
two people or things are totally different and incompatible: with allusion to Kipling's *Ballad of East and West* (1892): 'Oh, East is East and West is West, and never the twain shall meet, | Till Earth and Sky stand presently at God's great Judgment Seat.' *Twain* is an archaic word for 'two'. *19th cent.*

twelve

twelve good men and true
dated an emotive phrase for a jury in a lawcourt. *17th cent.*

> **Richard Brome** *Madd Couple Well Matcht* **1653**
> *Nay of five hundred | That now might overheare us*
> *(I meane not only | Gallants, but grave substantiall*
> *Gentlemen) | Could be pick'd out a twelve good*
> *men and true, | To finde you guilty, I would then*
> *condemne you, | But such a Jury must be pannell'd*
> *first.*

twice
See THINK twice.

twiddle
See twiddle one's thumbs *at* THUMB.

twinkle
See in the blink/twinkling/wink of an EYE.

twist
See get one's KNICKERS in a twist; ROUND the bend/twist; twist somebody's ARM; twist somebody round one's little FINGER.

two

put two and two together
to draw a clear conclusion from known circumstances: but if you *put two and two together and make five*, you have made a wrong conclusion, however reasonable it might have seemed at the time. The phrase in its present form is recorded from the middle of the 19th cent., but the notion of two and two making four as a paradigm of the obvious conclusion dates from several centuries earlier. *19th cent.*

> **Hardy** *A Pair of Blue Eyes* **1873**
> *'Well, I have done a great many things, if not that.*
> *And I have done one extraordinary thing.' Knight*
> *turned full upon Stephen. 'Ah-ha! Now, then, let*
> *me look into your face, put two and two together,*
> *and make a shrewd guess.'*

that makes two of us
informal used conversationally to declare, often ironically, that one shares the predicament or sentiments of the previous speaker. *Mid 20th cent.*

> **Alistair MacLean** *Santorini* **1987**
> *'You said you had powerful suspicions. What sus-*
> *picions, sir?' 'I suspect that it can't be de-activated.*
> *In fact, I'm certain the process is irreversible. The*
> *second suspicion is also a certainty. I'm damn sure*
> *that I'm not going to be the one to try.' 'That makes*
> *two of us.'*

two can play at that game
a warning that a person's bad behaviour can be imitated to their disadvantage. *19th cent.*

> **Thomas Hughes** *Tom Brown's Schooldays* **1857**
> *'Gently, young fellow,' said he; ''tain't improving*
> *for little whippersnappers like you to be indulging*
> *in blasphemy; so you stop that, or you'll get*
> *something you won't like.' 'I'll have you both licked*
> *when I get out, that I will,' rejoined the boy,*
> *beginning to snivel. 'Two can play at that game,*

mind you,' said Tom, who had finished his examination of the list.

a two-way street
a situation in which two people or groups work interactively or share a responsibility. *Mid 20th cent.*

See also another bite / two bites at the CHERRY; a double-edged / two-edged sword *at* EDGE; for two pins I would — *at* PIN; in two shakes (of a lamb's tail) *at* SHAKE; it takes two to TANGO; two heads are better than one *at* HEAD; two a PENNY.

twopenn'orth

add / put in one's twopenn'orth
informal to make a casual contribution to a discussion. *Mid 20th cent.*

> George Melly *Owning Up* 1965
> *After it* [the band] *broke up I used to go along every other Tuesday to 'The Three Brewers' … and put in what Mick would call 'my two penn'orth'.*

ugly

(as) ugly as sin
extremely ugly or unpleasant. The phrase is also recorded in variant forms from the same conceptual domain, e.g. with *the devil* or *hell* substituted for *sin*. *17th cent.*

an ugly duckling
a person or thing that appears unattractive in its early stages but develops into something outstandingly beautiful or successful: from the story by Hans Christian Andersen of the duckling that is rejected by the rest of the brood but surprises everybody by growing into a magnificent swan. *19th cent.*

> Louisa M Alcott *Little Women* 1868
> *'You know as well as I that it does make a difference with nearly every one, so don't ruffle up, like a dear, motherly hen, when your chickens get pecked by smarter birds; the ugly duckling turned out a swan, you know'; and Amy smiled without bitterness, for she possessed a happy temper and hopeful spirit.*

umbrage

take umbrage
to take offence or show resentment at somebody's words or actions: *give umbrage* is recorded from the same date but is now less common. The use is developed from earlier meanings based on the image of being 'under a shadow' (implying variously 'protection' or 'threat'); *umbrage* is derived from Latin *umbra* meaning 'shade.' *17th cent.*

> W H Prescott *History of the Conquest of Mexico* 1843
> *From this wholesome admonition the monarch himself was not exempted, and the orator boldly reminded him of his paramount duty to show respect for his own laws. The king, so far from taking umbrage, received the lesson with humility:*

and the audience, we are assured, were often melted into tears by the eloquence of the preacher.

unacceptable

See the unacceptable face *at the* acceptable FACE.

uncertain

See in no uncertain terms *at* TERM.

uncle

cry/say/yell uncle

informal, chiefly NAmer to give in or acknowledge defeat; to ask for mercy. How uncles come into the picture here is not at all clear, and most explanations offered are more confusing than helpful: attempts to rationalize rather than seek evidence. The phrase first appears in America around 1918; there is no British evidence that helps. The journal *American Speech* for 1976 (published in 1980) offered the following explanation: 'Most American schoolboys are ... familiar with the expression cry uncle or holler uncle, meaning "give up in a fight, ask for mercy". *Uncle* in this expression is surely a folk etymology, and the Irish original of the word is *anacol* (*anacal, anacul*) "act of protecting; deliverance; mercy, quarter, safety", a verbal noun from the Old Irish verb *aingid* "protects".' This far-fetched suggestion hardly clarifies anything; still less does a proposed origin in a Latin expression *patrue mi patruissime* ('uncle, my best of uncles') used by Roman boys in trouble or facing punishment. The matter remains unresolved. *Early 20th cent.*

> Eve Merriam *The Company Agent* 1956
> *Sweat it out. Sit tight. Wait and see.* | *You'll see, by tomorrow they'll come around* | *Howling the blues, ready to toss in the towel and cry Uncle –* | *Tom.*

Uncle Sam

the United States of America. The origin of the name cannot be placed precisely, but from an early date it has been explained in terms of the coincidence of initial letters, while suggestions based on various government officials having the name Sam or Samuel are probably just rationalizations or attempts to add colour to a prosaic origin. The name first appears in a New York newspaper in 1813: 'Loss upon loss, and no ill luck stirring but what lights upon Uncle Sam's shoulders'. *19th cent.*

> R H Dana *Two Years Before the Mast* 1840
> *She was called the Catalina, and, like all the other vessels in that trade, except the Ayacucho, her papers and colors were from Uncle Sam.*

Uncle Tom Cobley and all

everybody imaginable: with allusion to the names listed at the end of the ballad known as 'Widdicombe Fair' (*c1800*): 'Tom Pearce's old mare doth appear gashly white | Wi' Bill Brewer, Jan Stewer, Peter Gurney, Peter Davy, Dan Whiddon, Harry Hawk, old Uncle Tom Cobleigh and all, | Old Uncle Tom Cobleigh and all.' *Mid 20th cent.*

> Raymond Hitchcock *Fighting Cancer: A Personal Story* 1989
> *Proudly and angrily, I had maintained my independence. No one could approach me without my authority. Now here they were: in-laws, out-of-laws, Quakers, Uncle Tom Cobley and All.*

under

under age

not yet an adult in the eyes of the law: first recorded in Spenser's *Faerie Queene* (1590) II.x.64: 'Three sonnes he dying left, all under age.' *16th cent.*

> J S Mill *On Liberty* 1859
> *If protection against themselves is confessedly due to children and persons under age, is not society equally bound to afford it to persons of mature years who are equally incapable of self-government?*

See also under one's BELT; under one's BREATH; under a CLOUD; under somebody's NOSE; under one's own STEAM; under somebody's THUMB; under the WEATHER.

understand

give somebody to understand

to give somebody a good reason or indication for believing that something is the case: often used in contexts in which the belief is misguided or a misunderstanding later arises. *16th cent.*

Shakespeare *The Merchant of Venice* ii.viii.7 (1598)
The ship was under sail. | But there the Duke was
given to understand | That in a gondola were seen
together | Lorenzo and his amorous Jessica.

Bunyan *The Holy City* 1665
These words ... give us also to understand the
manner of her strength.

university

the university of life
knowledge and experience gained from practical
experience as distinct from formal learning. *19th
cent.*

Elizabeth Rundle Charles *Chronicles of the Schonberg-
Cotta Family* 1864
Many of us had completed our academical course,
and were already entering the larger world beyond –
the university of life.

unkind

the unkindest cut of all
the worst kind of personal betrayal or treachery.
The phrase comes from Shakespeare's *Julius Caesar* (1599), where Mark Antony in his 'If you have
tears, prepare to shed them now' speech after the
assassination of Caesar refers to Brutus's blow
(iii.ii.181) with the words: 'This was the most
unkindest cut of all.' (*Unkind* here means 'unnat-
ural' as much as 'cruel'.) Allusive uses are found
from the early 19th cent.

Maria Edgeworth *The Absentee* 1812
Now lady Chatterton was the greatest talker extant;
and she went about the rooms telling every body ...
how shamefully Soho had imposed upon poor lady
*Clonbrony – 'and lady Clonbrony's being a stran-
ger, and from Ireland, makes the thing worse.' From
Ireland! – That was the unkindest cut of all.*

unknown

an unknown quantity
a person or thing that is too little known to be
regarded as dependable: in algebra, the
unknown quantity is the quantity that has to be
determined by means of equations. *19th cent.*

Henry James *Washington Square* 1881
*Doctor Sloper's opposition was the unknown
quantity in the problem he had to work out. The*

natural way to work it out was by marrying
Catherine; but in mathematics there are many
shortcuts, and Morris was not without a hope that
he should yet discover one.

unpleasantness

the late unpleasantness
used euphemistically to refer to a recently-ended
war, originally with reference to the American
Civil War (1861–5). *19th cent.*

David Ross Locke *The Struggles of Petroleum v. Nasby*
1872
Are women, frail as they are, to fill positions in the
government offices? I asked her sternly, 'Are you
willing to go to war? Did you shoulder a musket in
the late unpleasantness?'

unstuck

come unstuck
informal to encounter failure or difficulty, the
implication being that it is entirely one's own
fault and fully deserved: in early use also with
undone and *unput* instead of *unstuck*. *Early 20th
cent.*

Kipling *Diversity of Creatures* 1911
'Don't apologise,' said Gilbert, when the paroxysm
ended. 'I'm used to people coming a little – unstuck
in this room.'

unvarnished

the unvarnished truth
the simple facts of a matter without any attempt
to elaborate or disguise them or to hide their
unpleasantness: *see also* the NAKED truth. *18th
cent.*

William Godwin *St. Leon* 1799
All Hungary has resounded for thirty years with the
atrocities of the sieur de Chatillon; what is here
recorded contains the whole and unvarnished truth
on the subject.

unwashed

the great unwashed
the general population, especially the working
classes regarded by the middle and upper
classes. *19th cent.*

Thackeray *Pendennis* 1849
Gentlemen, there can be but little doubt that your
ancestors were the Great Unwashed.

---

up

be/run up against something

informal to face a difficulty or setback: to *be up*
against it is to be severely tested or face a hefty
challenge. *19th cent.*

Willa Cather *The Song of the Lark* 1915
'No occasion for you to see,' he said warmly.
'There'll always be plenty of other people to take the
knocks for you.' 'That's nonsense, Ray.' Thea spoke
impatiently and leaned lower still, frowning at the
red star. 'Everybody's up against it for himself,
succeeds or fails – himself.'

be (well) up in/on something

informal to be well informed on a subject. *19th*
cent.

R H Dana *Two Years Before the Mast* 1840
He hesitated, looked a little confused, and admitted
that he was not as well up in certain classes of
knowledge as in others.

it's all up with —

informal the person named faces failure or death.
19th cent.

Dickens *Pickwick Papers* 1837
He went into the infirmary, this morning; the
doctor says his strength is to be kept up as much as
possible ... I'm afraid, however ... that it's all up
with him.

on the up and up

1 *informal* making progress; prospering. *Mid 20th*
cent.

Harpers & Queen 1991
He describes how in the midst of turning around
Ebury Press to a £5 million enterprise, she would
still wake up early enough to devote the early
morning hours and after work to their children,
Georgia, four, and Grace, one. 'Our marriage has its
ups and downs, but it is mainly on the up and up',
observes Gould.

2 *informal* honest and straightforward. *Mid 20th*
cent.

Karl Jay Shapiro *Bellow in Collected Poems* 1940–78
Mixing a powerful sense of fidelity with an equally
powerful sense of the absurd, he evolves Yiddish,

language without pedigree. Poetry with him is on
the up-and-up, only there isn't any.

something is up

something strange or untoward seems to be happening or to be about to happen. *19th cent.*

Mrs Gaskell *Letter* 1838
I did not mention a word to Lucy but she must have
guessed something was 'up'.

Theodore Dreiser *Sister Carrie* 1900
At last, the chief comedian, singing in the centre of
the stage, noticed a giggle where it was not expected.
Then another and another. When the place came for
loud applause it was only moderate. What could be
the trouble? He realised that something was up.

up and about/doing

active again after a period of sleep or illness in
bed. *19th cent.*

George Borrow *Lavengro* 1851
You must be up and doing, sir; it will not do for an
author, especially a young author, to be idle in this
town.

up and running

1 (said of equipment) installed and working: in
computing, *up* has a special significance as the
opposite of *down* = not working. *Late 20th cent.*

Crispin Aubrey *Melt Down: Collapse of a Nuclear*
Dream 1991
In the event, the coal crisis didn't materialize, but
nuclear power was by that time up and running.

2 (said of processes, undertakings, etc) active and
continuing. *Late 20th cent.*

J King et al *Community Care* 1993
Joseph expects the department to be involved in
advocates' training, to ensure they understand
procedures and what child protection means. But
once it's up and running, they may want to develop
their own skills and expertise.

up for it

informal ready and eager to take part in an activity. *19th cent.*

R D Blackmore *Lorna Doone* 1869
'Think thou could'st ride her, lad? She will have no
burden but mine. Thou could'st never ride her ...'
Mr. Faggus gave his mare a wink, and she walked
demurely after him ... 'Up for it still, boy, be ye?'
Tom Faggus stopped, and the mare stopped there;
and they looked at me provokingly.

up to it

informal capable of performing a particular role or task. *18th cent.*

Mary Robinson *Walsingham* 1797
'You must plead your own cause, if you hope to succeed.' 'Dash me, but I'm not up to it,' replied my pupil.

See also be up the CREEK; have something up TOP; not up to MUCH; raise/up the ANTE; up for grabs *at* GRAB; up HILL and down dale; up in ARMS; up the POLE; up the SPOUT; up sticks *at* STICK²; up to one's ears in something *at* EAR; up to the MARK; up to a POINT; up to SCRATCH; up to SNUFF; up to one's tricks *at* TRICK.

upgrade

on the upgrade
making progress; improving. *19th cent.*

Daily News 1892
In the iron trade ... demand seems to be on the up grade.

J Tey *Daughter of Time* 1951
'You not feeling so good today?' 'Don't you worry. I'm on the up-grade. Even my temper has improved.'

upper

have/gain the upper hand
to have or gain the advantage in a situation. The phrase occurs in Chaucer in the form *higher hand*. *Middle English*

Chaucer *Prologue* (line 399)
If that he faught, and hadde the hyer hond, | By water he sente hem hoom to every lond.

on one's uppers
informal in a state of poverty; short of money: literally, wearing shoes with the soles worn away to reveal the *uppers* to which the soles are attached. *19th cent.*

Somerset Maugham *Of Human Bondage* 1915
Betty was one of the maids in the little red brick house in Kensington. Four or five years ago I was on my uppers, and I had seven children, and I went to my wife and asked her to help me. She said she'd make me an allowance if I'd give Betty up and go abroad.

the upper crust

informal the upper classes, the aristocracy. An *upper crust* is originally the top part of a loaf or pie, and this is the image that underlies the phrase in its social use. (It is also found in the 19th cent. as a slang name for the human head.) A glossary of Northamptonshire words from the 1850s records Mrs Upper Crust as a name invented for anybody who unreasonably assumes an air of superiority. The phrase is also used with a hyphen as an adjective, as in *upper-crust circles*. *18th cent.*

Edward Ward *The Parish Gutt'lers* 1732
And thus the poor, to most mens wonder, | Betwixt the upper crust, and under, | Are choak'd with bread, as many think, | For want of pence to purchase drink.

W S Gilbert *HMS Pinafore* 1878
Two tender babes I nussed: | One was of low condition, | The other, upper crust, | A regular patrician.

upset

See upset the APPLE cart.

upstairs

See KICK somebody upstairs.

uptake

be quick/slow on the uptake
informal, originally Scottish to be quick (or slow) to understand or learn something. *19th cent.*

Scott *Old Mortality* 1816
A gude tale's no the waur o' being twice tauld, I trow; and a body has aye the better chance to understand it. Everybody's no sae gleg [= quick, keen] at the uptake as ye are yoursell, mither.

upwardly

See upwardly MOBILE.

Henry Fielding *The History of Tom Jones* 1749
It may seem remarkable, that, of four persons whom we have commemorated at Mr. Allworthy's house, three of them should fix their inclinations on a lady who was never greatly celebrated for her beauty, and who was, moreover, now a little descended into the vale of years.

vain

take somebody's name in vain

to use a name, especially a divine name, profanely or without proper respect: with allusion to the third of the commandments given to Moses (Exodus 20:7): 'Thou shalt not take the name of the Lord thy God in vain.' The phrase occurs in Middle English (in the *Cursor Mundi*), and in the form *in ydel* (= idly) in Chaucer (*The Parson's Tale*, line 595: 'And therfore every man that taketh Goddes name in ydel').

vale

the vale of tears

the sorrows and tribulations of the world. The phrase occurs earlier in different forms, especially *vale of misery*. *16th cent.*

William Dunbar *Poems* c1500
Provyd thy place, for thow away man [must] pas, | Out of this vaill of trubbill and dissait [deceit].

Mary Wollstonecraft *A Vindication of the Rights of Woman* 1792
Religion, pure source of comfort in this vale of tears! how has thy clear stream been muddied by the dabblers, who have presumptuously endeavoured to confine in one narrow channel, the living waters that ever flow towards God – the sublime ocean of existence!

the vale of years

a person's old age, regarded as a period of decline: with allusion to Othello's admission in Shakespeare, *Othello* (1604) III.iii.270 'Haply for I am black, | And have not those soft parts of conversation | That chambers have; or for I am declined | Into the vale of years – yet that's not much – | She's gone.' *17th cent.*

vanish

See do a disappearing/vanishing ACT.

variety

variety is the spice of life

(proverb) change and new opportunities are what makes life interesting. The sentiment is at least as old as Greek drama, but the first recorded use of the proverb in English in its current form is in William Cowper's *The Task* (1785): 'Variety's the very spice of life, | That gives it all its flavour.' *18th cent.*

Frederic S Cozzens *The Sayings of Dr Bushwacker and Other Learned Men* 1867
This is a very healthy condiment, sir; in the tropics it is indispensable; there is a maxim there, sir, that people who eat Cayenne pepper will live for ever. Like variety, it is the spice of life, sir, at the equator.

veil

beyond/within the veil

in a hidden or unknown state or place, especially after death: with allusion to St Paul's Epistle to the Hebrews 6:19 (in the Authorized Version, 1611) 'Which hope we have as an anchor of the soul, both sure and stedfast, and which entereth into that within the veil'.

draw/cast/throw a veil over something

to avoid mentioning or referring to a subject that is unwelcome or embarrassing. *18th cent.*

Charles Lamb *Rosamund Gray* 1798
Fain would I draw a veil over the transactions of that night – but I cannot – grief, and burning shame, forbid me to be silent – black deeds are about to be made public, which reflect a stain upon our common nature.

take the veil

to become a nun: with reference to the traditional headdress worn by nuns on taking their vows (the oldest sense of *veil*). *Middle English*

vengeance

with a vengeance

to a great degree, especially in the sense of making up for a previous deficiency or shortcoming. *Cf* with a MISCHIEF. *16th cent.*

Milton *Paradise Lost* iv.170 (1674)
So entertained those odorous sweets the Fiend | Who came their bane, though with them better pleased | Than Asmodeus with the fishy fume, | That drove him, though enamored, from the spouse | Of Tobit's son, and with a vengeance sent | From Media post to Egypt, there fast bound.

vent

The meaning involved here is 'an opening for the escape of a gas or liquid', and the corresponding verb 'to provide with a vent or opening'. Once the sense is identified the source of the metaphor is self-evident.

give vent to something

to relieve a feeling or a sense of frustration by expressing it strongly and openly. *17th cent.*

Richard Braithwait *The Two Lancashire Lovers* 1640
But little did these reasons satisfie jealous Euryclea ... To whom we must now returne, and see what extreames she is brought to; who in this her languishing plight intimates her griefes; and in a secret repose, to give more vent to passion, imparts her discontents in this private pensive relation.

vent one's spleen on somebody

to criticize somebody fiercely and vindictively or for one's own gratification: from the early identification of the spleen as the source of ill-humour and peevishness. *17th cent.*

Locke *Letter Concerning Toleration* 1692
This ... is ... like an engaged enemy, to vent one's spleen upon a party.

Henry Fielding *The History of Tom Jones* 1749
Western ... heartily hated his wife; and as he never concealed this hatred before her death, so he never forgot it afterwards; but when anything in the least soured him, as a bad scenting day, or a distemper

among his hounds ... he constantly vented his spleen by invectives against the deceased, saying, 'If my wife was alive now, she would be glad of this.'

verify

See always verify your references *at* REFERENCE.

victory

See a PYRRHIC victory.

view

take a dim/poor view of somebody/something

to regard a person or thing with suspicion or disfavour: both forms of the phrase appear to date from the 1940s, and probably originate in services' slang. *Mid 20th cent.*

Esquire 1993
Halfway through the night, he was at it again. After a few minutes, his breathing quickened and he started making noises that might have come from a monkey-house at feeding time. Suddenly he was apprehended by an irate Scout master who took a dim view of being woken at such an hour.

villain

the villain of the piece

the principal culprit in a dramatic or unpleasant series of events: from theatrical language, referring to the character in a play or novel (the 'piece') who is chiefly associated with evil intentions and actions. *19th cent.*

Louisa M Alcott *Little Women* 1868
'If I can go down easily, I'll drop; if I can't, I shall fall into a chair and be graceful; I don't care if Hugo does come at me with a pistol,' returned Amy, who was not gifted with dramatic power, but was chosen because she was small enough to be borne out shrieking by the villain of the piece.

vine

wither on the vine

to deteriorate from neglect or inactivity. The image of the withered vine occurs in Shakespeare's *1 Henry VI* (1590) II.v.11 '[Mortimer, referring to himself] Weak shoulders, overborne with burdening grief, | And pithless arms, like to a withered vine | That droops his sapless branches to the ground.' It is also found as a biblical symbol of spiritual degeneration, but allusive uses in the current form are surprisingly uncommon before the 20th cent.

> Hugh MacDiarmid *Celebratory Ode* 1976
> *The Theological Society, the Griskin and Poker Club,* | *The Soaping Club and even the Cape* | – *All withered on the vine!*

virtue

make a virtue (out) of necessity

to gain credit or an advantage from an unwelcome obligation or duty. *Middle English*

> Chaucer *Troilus and Criseyde* IV.1586
> *Thus maketh vertu of necessite* | *By pacience.*

> Scott *Rob Roy* 1817
> *While I endeavoured to make a virtue of necessity, and recall my attention to the sermon, I was again disturbed by a singular interruption.*

visit

visiting fireman

informal, chiefly NAmer a person who is especially welcome in a place because of the position they hold or the function they exercise. *Early 20th cent.*

> Susannah James *Love Over Gold* 1993
> *They had woken in the morning, stiff and damp, rushed into the house to warm themselves in the huge old-fashioned bathtub, cooked an enormous breakfast and driven back to the city so Cameron could interview some visiting fireman from Washington.*

voice

See a STILL small voice; a voice (crying) in the WILDERNESS.

vote

See vote with one's FEET; SPLIT the vote.

wag

See the TAIL wags the dog.

wagon

on the wagon

informal, originally NAmer abstaining from alcoholic drink. The wagon is an alcohol-free *water wagon*, as early uses of the phrase in this fuller form make clear. Anybody who starts drinking again is said to *come off the wagon. Early 20th cent.*

See also FIX somebody's wagon; HITCH one's wagon to a star.

wait

wait and see

to wait for developments before acting or making a decision. Evidently first used by Defoe (see below), the phrase was once commonly associated with the cautious political stance of the Liberal politician H(erbert) H Asquith (1852–1958). An article in *Blackwood's Magazine* in 1910 ridiculed him for using the phrase: 'Mr. Asquith has deemed it not incompatible with the gravity of his office to elude the curiosity of his opponents with the absurd formula, "Wait and see".' In more recent times, the phrase has become associated with similarly cautious attitudes to Britain's joining the European single currency (the euro). *18th cent.*

> Defoe *Robinson Crusoe* 1719
> *Our seizing those seven men on shore would be no advantage to us if we let the boat escape, because they would then row away to the ship, and then the rest of them would be sure to weigh and set sail, and so our recovering the ship would be lost. However, we had no remedy but to wait and see what the issue of things might present.*

D H Lawrence *Sons and Lovers* 1913
*Annie, Arthur, Paul, and Leonard were waiting in
the parlour anxiously. The doctors came down. Paul
glanced at them. He had never had any hope, except
when he had deceived himself. 'It may be a tumour;
we must wait and see,' said Dr. Jameson.*

wait for it
used, typically as an aside, to create a feeling of
suspense in one's hearers that something unexpected or exciting is coming, and commonly used
ironically to introduce an anticlimax when what
follows is familiar or predictable. *Mid 20th cent.*

wake

be a wake-up call
informal (said of an unexpected event, especially a
disaster) to jolt people out of a sense of complacency and alert them to a hidden and continuing
danger: a *wake-up call* is literally an alarm call to
wake somebody early in the morning. The phrase
achieved a special currency after the terrorist
attacks in America on 11 September 2001, events
that have since been widely regarded in this
light. *Late 20th cent.*

John E Newman *How to Stay Cool, Calm & Collected*
1992
*Wake up to what stress is doing to you. Use the
following Wake-Up Call Checklist to clarify the
impact stress is having on your life.*

be/take a wake-up to somebody/something
Australian and NZ, informal to be fully aware of
the intentions or implications of a person or
thing: a use of the expression *wake-up* meaning
'an observant and resourceful person', recorded
in Australian and New Zealand use from the
beginning of the 20th cent. *Early 20th cent.*

D Whitington *Treasure upon Earth* 1957
*I should have been a wake up to you. I should have
known you for the bastard you are.*

wake up and smell the coffee
informal to face the realities of an unpleasant
situation. *Late 20th cent.*

New Musical Express 1992
*'I do care. I went to very liberal schools, I'm at
Boston University now, and if you saw the attitudes
and prejudices there, the absolute indifference,
you'd be horrified. I was horrified at the lack of
concern ... but that's not the kind of thing this band*

*addresses.' Fair enough, I suppose ... Whether or
not the Drop Nineteens should wake up and smell
the coffee, the dogshit in the streets and the rest of
the real world, is hard to say.*

wake (up) to something
to begin to appreciate a situation, especially an
unwelcome or threatening one that has been present for some time. *19th cent.*

Harriet Beecher Stowe *Uncle Tom's Cabin* 1852
*So much has been said and sung of beautiful young
girls, why don't somebody wake up to the beauty of
old women?*

walk

be a walking encyclopedia
to have a wide range of knowledge of facts about
the world: *walking dictionary* is also recorded
from about the same date, and *walking library*
occurs in a 17th cent. source. *19th cent.*

Louisa M Alcott *Little Women* 1868
*Mr. Brooke was a grave, silent young man, with
handsome brown eyes and a pleasant voice. Meg
liked his quiet manners, and considered him a
walking encyclopaedia of useful knowledge.*

walk (all) over somebody
1 *informal* to treat somebody thoughtlessly or
without respect. *19th cent.*

Herman Melville *Moby Dick* 1851
*Oh, master! master! I am indeed down-hearted
when you walk over me.*

Mark Twain *Huckleberry Finn* 1884
*The average man's a coward. In the North he lets
anybody walk over him that wants to, and goes
home and prays for a humble spirit to bear it.*

2 *informal* to defeat somebody easily and
decisively. *Late 20th cent.*

walk away from something
1 to escape unharmed from an accident or attack.
Mid 20th cent.

Today 1992
*Amazingly, Adam walked away from the crash with
just a graze on his left shoulder.*

2 to refuse to consider or become involved in a
situation, especially a problem or difficulty. *Mid
20th cent.*

Ann Wroe *Lives, Lies and the Iran-Contra Affair* 1991
As North pointed out, these objectives were almost universally wished for. It was simply that most people, while wanting the ends, preferred to walk away from the means.

walk off with something
1 to steal something, especially something in one's care or to which one has ready access. *18th cent.*

Fanny Burney *Camilla* 1796
It's really a piece of good luck that he was not taken with a fancy to leave us upon my island; and then we might all have been soused by this here rain: and he could just as well have walked off with my bridge as with the ladder.

2 *informal* to win awards and prizes with ease or regularity: also with *away* instead of *off. Mid 20th cent.*

Today 1992
Nigel Mansell walked off with four awards at a lunch held by the British Racing Drivers' Club yesterday.

walk of/in life
a person's regular occupation or profession: in early use also with reference to social rather than professional status. *18th cent.*

Henry Fielding *The History of Tom Jones* 1749
He had served three years as clerk to an attorney in the north of Ireland, when, chusing a genteeler walk in life, he quitted his master, came over to England, and set up that business which requires no apprenticeship, namely, that of a gentleman, in which he had succeeded, as hath been already partly mentioned.

walk on eggs/eggshells
to act or speak with extreme caution, in order to avoid causing trouble or offence. *17th cent.*

Sir John Harington *Orlando Furioso* 1607
He takes a long and leisurable stride, | And longest on the hinder foote he staid, | So soft he treds, although his steps were wide, | As though to tread on eggs he were afraid.

walk the talk
informal, chiefly NAmer to make one's actions suit one's words; to behave according to one's stated principles. *Late 20th cent.*

walk tall
informal to have a self-confident and proud demeanour; to have dignity. *19th cent.*

Thomas Bangs Thorpe *The Hive of 'The Bee-Hunter'* 1854
Well, I will walk tall into varmint and Indian; it's a way I've got, and it comes as natural as grinning to a hyena. I'm a regular tornado – tough as a hickory – and long-winded as a nor'-wester ... I must fight something, or I'll catch the dry rot.

See also tread/walk on AIR; (try to) RUN before one can walk; walk the PLANK; walk the streets *at* STREET.

walkabout

go walkabout
1 *informal, originally Australian* to go off on an impromptu and casual walk, now typically associated with 'meet-the-people' forays by royalty or other celebrities during official visits: with allusion to the practice of Australian Aboriginals who leave settled society from time to time and wander into the bush in order to re-establish contact with their spiritual roots. *Mid 20th cent.*
2 *informal* to be missing and presumed stolen. *Late 20th cent.*

walkies

go walkies
informal to be missing and presumed stolen: originally a childish expression in relation to taking a dog for a walk. *Late 20th cent.*

wall

go over the wall
to escape from a prison or confinement, literally by scaling a wall to freedom. *Mid 20th cent.*

go to the wall
1 to lose a conflict or struggle: from the proverb *the weakest go to the wall*, recorded in the Coventry Plays (15th cent.) and based on the notion of people seeking refuge in churches in the Middle Ages, where seating was often placed round the walls. *16th cent.*

Stephen Gosson *The Ephemerides of Phialo* 1579
If this [religion] be corrupted, Justice perisheth; | And if Justice shrinke, this goes to the wall.

2 (said of a business or institution) to fail or become obsolete. *19th cent.*

> Mark Twain *Life on the Mississippi* 1883
> *Butter don't stand any show – there ain't any chance for competition. Butter's had its day – and from this out, butter goes to the wall. There's more money in oleomargarine than – why, you can't imagine the business we do.*

go/climb/run up / drive somebody up the wall
informal to be affected by (or to affect somebody with) extreme frustration or exasperation. *Mid 20th cent.*

> Woman 1991
> *What would you do if a crowd of crazy relatives turned up to stay? Kirstie Alley solves her problem by moving to a tent in the garden. They still drive her up the wall – and no one acts it out quite as well as Kirstie.*

off the wall
1 *informal, chiefly NAmer* odd or unusual: the image is probably of a ball bouncing off a wall in an unpredictable direction. *Mid 20th cent.*

> Belfast Telegraph 1990
> *Its appeal, he said, is the excitement it generates in the search for off the wall ideas … not to mention the opportunities it creates for involvement in radio.*

2 *informal, chiefly NAmer* ridiculous or foolish. *Mid 20th cent.*

> Mike Ripley *Angel Hunt* 1991
> *The Russians would much rather deal with a right-wing conservative any day because they know where they stand, rather than a left-wing liberal who might do something off the wall, like act on principle, for heaven's sake.*

turn one's face to the wall
to be ready for death: with allusion to biblical accounts of the deaths of kings, e.g. 2 Kings 20:2 'Then he [Hezekiah] turned his face to the wall, and prayed unto the Lord'. Allusive uses predominate in literature of the 19th cent.

> Trollope *Doctor Thorne* 1858
> *To whom else could she in such plight look for love? When, therefore, she heard that he was slain, her heart sank within her; she turned her face to the wall, and laid herself down to die: to die a double death, for herself and the fatherless babe that was now quick within her.*

walls have ears
(proverb) used as a warning to be discreet in case of being overheard. *16th cent.*

> Thomas Duffett *Psyche Debauch'd* 1678
> *Here one may kiss, and laugh, and think no harm:* |
> *For Countrey Love has neither joyes nor fears,* |
> *And Bushes break no Trust, though Walls have ears.*

wall-to-wall
informal complete and uninterrupted, occupying all the available space. Originally used with reference to a fitted carpet that covers the entire floor area, the phrase has been rapidly extended to cover all manner of things from music and dancing to crowds, traffic, and sex. *Mid 20th cent.*

> Today 1992
> *John Hunt, manager of Marks & Spencer, said: 'There are wall-to-wall customers. You wonder where all the money is coming from, they are spending like mad.' Tailbacks affected all roads into Leeds and there was a two-mile queue on the M1.*

See also the WRITING (is) on the wall.

wallaby

on the wallaby (track)
Australian, informal (said of a person) vagrant, homeless: a *wallaby track* was a path followed by a person living in the bush and going in search of seasonal work. *19th cent.*

waltz

See waltzing MATILDA.

war

have been in the wars
informal to show the results of having been hurt or injured: use of *the wars* (plural) with a meaning equivalent to the singular dates from Chaucer. *19th cent.*

> Fanny Burney *The Wanderer* 1814
> *The wind just then blowing back the prominent borders of a French nightcap, which had almost concealed all her features, displayed a large black patch, that covered half her left cheek, and a broad black ribbon, which bound a bandage of cloth over the right side of her forehead. Before Elinor could utter her rallying congratulations to Harleigh,*

upon this sight, she was stopt by a loud shout from Mr. Riley; 'Why I am afraid the demoiselle has been in the wars!' cried he.

a war of nerves

a conflict or state of opposition involving psychological pressures. The phrase was first used in the context of Nazi propaganda in the Second World War (1939–45), although its current use is as often concerned with the relations between individuals as with international politics. *Mid 20th cent.*

Rachel Elliot *Lover's Charade* 1992
She flashed him her most saccharine-sweet and blatantly insincere smile, mentally notching up a point for herself when irritation tightened his lips. In this war of nerves, it was infinitely reassuring to know she could at least get the occasional barb past that glacial exterior.

a war of words

a continued or prolonged dispute or argument: first used by Pope in his translation of Homer's *Odyssey* (1725) 11.96 'O insolence of youth! whose tongue affords | Such railing eloquence and war of words'. *18th cent.*

Hardy *Tess of the D'Urbervilles* 1891
The young man much resented this directness of attack, and in the war of words which followed when they met he did not scruple publicly to insult Mr. Clare, without respect for his grey hairs.

a war to end all wars

a war that will render future wars impossible or unnecessary: used especially in relation to the First World War (1914–18). The phrase probably alludes to the title of a book by H G Wells, *The War That Will End War* (published in 1914); the same expression was used by G B Shaw in *Back to Methusaleh* in 1921. *Early 20th cent.*

warm

(as) warm as toast

agreeably or comfortably warm: occurs earlier (16th cent.) in the form *hot as toast*, and *dry as toast* appears in the 19th cent. *19th cent.*

John William De Forest *Playing the Mischief* 1875
There she was, as dry as a bone, and as warm as toast, all curled and tucked up on her seat.

keep something warm for somebody

to hold a position or post temporarily so as to protect it until a designated person becomes able to take it over. The allusion is to keeping a seat warm by sitting on it while its usual occupant is absent. *19th cent.*

Hardy *The Trumpet-Major* 1880
I didn't think there was any danger, knowing you was taking care of her, and keeping my place warm for me.

See also warm the COCKLES of somebody's heart.

warn

warn somebody off

to advise somebody to keep away from an imminent difficult or dangerous situation. *17th cent.*

Dryden *King Arthur* 1691
[Merlin] *Be that thy care, to stand by falls of Brooks, | And trembling Bogs, that bear a Green-Sword [= greensward] show. | Warn off the bold Pursuers from the Chace.*

Francis Parkman *Vassall Morton* 1856
In a few minutes, several men were seen at a distance on the railroad, running forward with a handkerchief tied to a stick to warn off the train.

warpath

on the warpath

informal angry with somebody or something and seeking redress from them: from the literal use with reference to Native Americans setting out for battle. *19th cent.*

Upton Sinclair *The Jungle* 1906
Marija is just fighting drunk when there come to her ears the facts about the villains who have not paid that night. Marija goes on the warpath straight off, without even the preliminary of a good cursing, and when she is pulled off it is with the coat collars of two villains in her hands.

wart

warts and all

in an imperfect state, without removing every fault or blemish: from a story about Oliver Cromwell, who instructed his portrait painter Peter Lely to depict him as he really looked, including the warts on his face. The story is told by Horace

Walpole (*Anecdotes of Painting in England*, 1763): 'Mr Lely, I desire you would use all your skill to paint my picture truly like me, and not flatter me at all; but remark all these roughnesses, pimples, warts and everything as you see me, otherwise I will never pay a farthing for it.' But uses of the phrase do not occur for nearly two centuries after this, the first allusive use on record being that of Somerset Maugham in *Cakes and Ale* (1930): 'Don't you think it would be more interesting if you went the whole hog and drew him warts and all?' Current uses refer to written as well as visual descriptions. *Mid 20th cent.*

wash

come out in the wash
1 *informal* to become known in the course of time: at an earlier date Trollope uses the form *come out in the washing* (*The Prime Minister*, 1876: 'The effects which causes will produce, ... the manner in which this or that proposition will come out in the washing, do not strike even Cabinet Ministers at a glance.'). *Early 20th cent.*

> P G Wodehouse *The Man with Two Left Feet* 1917
> A sort of fate, what? Heredity, and so forth. What's bred in the bone will come out in the wash.

2 *informal* to reach a satisfactory conclusion eventually. *Mid 20th cent.*

wash one's hands of somebody/something
to disclaim further responsibility for a person or situation: with allusion to the New Testament account of Pontius Pilate's washing his hands as a token of his dissociation from the guilt of putting Christ to death (Matthew 27:24 'When Pilate saw that he could prevail nothing ... he took water, and washed his hands before the multitude, saying, I am innocent of the blood of this just person: see ye to it'). *16th cent.*

> Shakespeare *Richard III* I.iv.267 (1593)
> [Second Murderer] A bloody deed, and desperately dispatched! | How fain, like Pilate, would I wash my hands | Of this most grievous, guilty murder done!

— won't wash
a particular argument or suggestion is not valid or convincing. *19th cent.*

> Mark Twain *The Adventures of Tom Sawyer* 1876
> 'It's a dirty business,' said Joe, without moving. 'What did you do it for?' 'I! I never done it!' 'Look

here! That kind of talk won't wash.' Potter trembled and grew white.

See also wash one's dirty LINEN in public.

waste

waste not, want not
(proverb) careful use of one's resources will prevent shortages and poverty in the future: with play on the two meanings of *want*, i.e. 'lack' and 'desire'. *18th cent.*

> Maria Edgeworth *The Parent's Assistant* 1800
> The following words ... were written ... over the chimney-piece, in his uncle's spacious kitchen – 'Waste not, want not.'

a waste of space
informal a person who is regarded as useless or incompetent. *Late 20th cent.*

> New Statesman and Society 1992
> We both look forward to seeing you at the end of this term, and to those warm family evenings of good food, relaxation and talk. So fuck off and die, Rodney. You're such a waste of space you make a crab-louse look like Mother Teresa ... Your loving father.

watch

watch one's back
to be vigilant against attack from an unexpected direction. *20th cent.*

> Colin Forbes *Shockwave* 1990
> He had little doubt that if anything went wrong Buckmaster would let him drop over the cliff. Which, he reflected, is why he pays me one hundred thousand pounds a year. But, he also reflected, it means I'll have to watch my back. Treachery was the name of the game in politics.

the watches of the night
the middle of the night, especially when regarded as a time of wakefulness: from the use of *watch* to denote each of the four or five periods into which the night was divided for purposes of guard duty. In Shakespeare's *Othello* (1604) I.i.125 Roderigo warns Brabanzio against sending Desdemona 'At this odd-even and dull watch o'th' night | ... | To the gross clasps of a lascivious Moor.' *19th cent.*

Dickens *A Tale of Two Cities* 1859
Young Jerry was ordered to bed, and his mother, laid under similar injunctions, obeyed them. Mr. Cruncher beguiled the earlier watches of the night with solitary pipes, and did not start upon his excursion until nearly one o'clock.

watch it
informal to take care: often used as an ironic or token threat. *Early 20th cent.*

John Steinbeck *The Grapes of Wrath* 1939
But watch it, mister. There's a premium goes with this pile of junk and the bay horses – so beautiful – a packet of bitterness to grow in your house and to flower, some day. We could have saved you, but you cut us down, and soon you will be cut down and there'll be none of us to save you.

watch one's mouth
to take care to speak respectfully and avoid bad language. *Late 20th cent.*

Mary Jane Staples *Sergeant Joe* 1992
'Oh, you daft loony,' she said, 'call yourself a sergeant?' 'Watch your mouth, Private Nobody.'

See also count/watch the pennies at PENNY; mind/watch one's STEP; watch my SMOKE; watch this SPACE; watch the TIME.

water

like water
in large quantities: normally used with reference to supplies, resources, etc. *19th cent.*

Mark Twain *The Innocents Abroad* 1869
The Sultan has been lavishing money like water in England and Paris, but his subjects are suffering for it now.

of the first/finest/purest water
of the highest quality: based on *water* as a term denoting the lustre and transparency of diamonds, the three highest grades being classed as of the *first*, *second*, and *third water*. The term was used in transferred meanings, especially of the eyes, from the 18th cent. *19th cent.*

Washington Irving *Alhambra* 1832
With all this she was a little of a slattern, something more of a lie-abed, and, above all, a gossip of the first water; neglecting house, household, and every thing

else, to loiter slipshod in the houses of her gossip neighbors.

water under the bridge / NAmer over the dam
past events that are no longer relevant to what is happening now: also *much water has flowed under the bridge* (and variants) = much has happened in the meantime. *Early 20th cent.*

See also BLOW something out of the water; cast one's BREAD upon the waters; like water off a duck's back at DUCK.

Waterloo

meet one's Waterloo
to be finally defeated after a long period of success: with allusion to the defeat of Napoleon at the Battle of Waterloo in 1815. The phrase was first used by the US politician and abolitionist Wendell Phillips in 1859. *19th cent.*

Edward Bulwer Lytton *Glenaveril* 1885
He made but a poor fight of it, that's true! Silenced his batteries … At the first shot! Dealt him his Waterloo! The victory was incontestable!

wave

make waves
to have an effect, especially a disturbing one, on a hitherto untroubled situation. Also more generally, to make an impact on one's surroundings; to achieve success. *Mid 20th cent.*

Independent 1989
Katharine Hamnett has many friends who accept her quirks and continue to admire. Colin Barnes, the fashion illustrator, who has known her since St Martin's, says, 'Of course outspoken people tread on toes, but they are often the ones who make waves and achieve something.'

the wave of the future
the next thing to be fashionable or trendy: from the title of a book about the future of fascism by Anne Morrow Lindbergh (1906–2001, wife of the American aviator Charles Lindbergh), *The Wave of the Future: A Confession of Faith* (1940). *Mid 20th cent.*

Mario Puzo *The Godfather* 1969
The business I am in is the coming thing, the wave of the future.

wavelength

on the same wavelength
sharing the same attitudes and tastes. *20th cent.*

> Clothes Show 1991
> *I encourage hairdressers to avoid jargon ... then teach them how to check they are both on the same wavelength.*

wax

An Old English verb superseded by *grow* except with reference to the phases of the moon and in certain literary uses and fixed expressions.

wax lyrical (about somebody/something)
originally *NAmer* to speak or write with self-conscious fervour or enthusiasm about somebody or something: now normally used humorously. *Mid 20th cent.*

> E Current-Garcia O. Henry 1965
> *Once again O. Henry waxes lyrical about the gold and silver delights of New York.*

way

go out of one's way
to make a special effort, especially to do something that would not normally be expected of one. *18th cent.*

> Addison in the Spectator 1712
> *Virgil went out of his way to make this reflection upon it* [Turnus dressing up in the spoils of Pallas], *without which so small a circumstance might possibly have slipped out of his reader's memory.*

go one's own way
to act as one wishes, to follow one's own inclinations. *19th cent.*

> Kipling By Word of Mouth 1888
> *Those two little people retired from the world after their marriage, and were very happy. They were forced, of course, to give occasional dinners, but they made no friends thereby, and the Station went its own way and forgot them.*

have a way with one
to have a likable or persuasive manner. *18th cent.*

> Thomas Morton Education 1813
> [Rosine] *Ah, that roguish eye! – But how did you persuade her?* [Sir Guy] *I had a way with me – Says*

I, *'there stand your family, that want to make you miserable, here stands your lover, that will make you happy.'* [Rosine] *Bravo! Excellent! And what did she do?*

make way for somebody/something
to allow precedence to a person or thing; to concede one's place to a successor: literally, to allow somebody to pass. *18th cent.*

> Samuel Speed On Little Sins 1677
> *If sin seems greater by one breadth of hair | Than mercie doth, it makes way for despair. | No sins are little: 'tis the Devil's cheat | So to surmise; for ev'ry sin is great.*

> Wilkie Collins The Moonstone 1868
> *The three men prostrated themselves on the rock before the curtain which hid the shrine. They rose – they looked on one another – they embraced. Then they descended separately among the people. The people made way for them in dead silence. In three different directions I saw the crowd part at one and the same moment.*

mend one's ways
to improve one's behaviour. *19th cent.*

> Louisa M Alcott Little Women 1868
> *Some of the girls I know really do go on at such a rate I'm ashamed of them. They don't mean any harm, I'm sure; but if they knew how we fellows talked about them afterward, they'd mend their ways, I fancy.*

on the way out
informal becoming less popular or fashionable. *Mid 20th cent.*

put somebody in the way of something
to provide somebody with an opportunity. *18th cent.*

> John O'Keeffe The Irish Mimic 1795
> *That was Miss Melcomb's servant, run after him, he'll put you in the way of seeing his lady.*

there are no two ways about it
there can be no doubt about something; an alternative conclusion or course of action is impossible. *19th cent.*

> Henry James The Ambassadors 1903
> *Chad had been absent from the Boulevard Malesherbes – was absent from Paris altogether; he had learned that from the concierge, but had nevertheless gone up, and gone up – there were no two ways*

about it – from an uncontrollable, a really, if one would, depraved curiosity.

the way of the world
the way people normally behave and treat each other. The phrase was famously used as the title of a comedy by William Congreve, produced in 1700, although it is found earlier. Shakespeare anticipates this use of *way*, meaning 'the customary manner of behaving', in *Henry VIII* (1613) III.i.156, in a passage in which Cardinal Wolsey addresses Queen Katherine: 'Why should we, good lady, | Upon what cause, wrong you? Alas, our places, | The way of our profession, is against it.' *17th cent.*

> Robert Dixon *Canidia* 1683
> *They that won't the way of the World go, | Must resolve to be crusht and kept low, | All Affronts and Wrongs undergo.*

ways and means
resources, especially money, at one's disposal for a particular purpose. *Middle English*

> John Bunyan *The Holy War* 1682
> *The first project of the Diabolonians in Mansoul is like to be lucky, and to take; to wit, that they will by all the ways and means they can, make Mansoul yet more vile and filthy.*

See also have it BOTH ways; LOOK the other way; LOSE one's/the way; SET in one's ways.

wayside

fall by the wayside
(said of an enterprise or hope) to fail or come to nothing: with allusion to the parable of the sower in Mark 4:4 (in the Authorized Version, 1611): 'Behold, there went out a sower to sow: And it came to pass, as he sowed, some fell by the way side, and the fowls of the air came and devoured it up.' (The same account occurs in Luke 8:5.) Allusive references, i.e. uses that do not refer directly to this biblical passage, predominate from the 19th cent.

> Harold Frederic *The Damnation of Theron Ware* 1892
> *The hope that even a portion of them would stop away, and that their places would be taken in the evening by less prejudiced strangers who wished for intellectual rather than theological food, fell by the wayside.*

weak

(as) weak as water
extremely weak or feeble. A late 17th cent. source describes the phrase as 'a vulgar proverb.' *17th cent.*

> Hardy *Far from the Madding Crowd* 1874
> *'Tis a poor thing to be sixty, when there's people far past four-score – a boast weak as water.*

the weak link
the most vulnerable or least dependable part of an organization, system, team, etc: often with allusion to the (19th cent.) proverb *a chain is no stronger than its weakest link.* Early 20th cent.

See also weak at the knees *at* KNEE.

wear

See wear one's HEART on one's sleeve; wear the TROUSERS; wear two hats *at* HAT; wear one's years well *at* YEAR.

weasel

use weasel words
to use words that are deliberately and usefully ambiguous, or that compromise the meaning of other words in the sentence. The term *weasel words* was invented by the American writer Stewart Chaplin in a story published in *Century Magazine* in 1900, and popularized by Theodore Roosevelt in a speech delivered in 1916 that criticized the incumbent president, Woodrow Wilson (as reported in *The New York Times*): 'Colonel Roosevelt began the day's speechmaking by opening his guns upon President Wilson … He accused Mr Wilson of using "weasel words" in advocating universal military training, but "only the compulsion of the spirit of America". A weasel, the Colonel explained, would suck all the meat out of an egg and leave it an empty shell.' *Early 20th cent.*

weather

keep a weather eye on something
to be vigilant for changes and developments in a situation: originally a nautical term meaning to keep watch for bad weather at sea. *19th cent.*

Rider Haggard *She* 1887
The lady having retreated, Job returned in a great state of nervousness, and keeping his weather eye fixed upon every woman who came near him.

make heavy weather of something

informal to find great difficulty in doing something that should be straightforward: from the nautical meaning referring to a ship pitching and rolling in heavy seas. *Early 20th cent.*

W B Maxwell *We Forget Because We Must* 1928
I'm afraid I seem to make heavy weather of my interesting condition.

under the weather

informal not completely well; slightly ill or depressed. *19th cent.*

William Dunlap *Thirty Years Ago or Memoirs of a Water Drinker* 1836
Why the squire looks a little thinnish, I must say ... He seems a little under the weather, somehow; and yet he's not sick. He looks as if he had been jaded like.

See also fine weather for ducks *at* DUCK.

weave

See GET cracking/going/weaving.

wedge

the thin end of the wedge

informal something apparently insignificant that will lead to a more important (and usually unwelcome) development: the image is of a wedge being driven into a space and doing its work as the thicker part penetrates. *19th cent.*

George Meredith *Beauchamp's Career* 1876
Carpendike would not vote for a man that proposed to open museums on the Sabbath day. The striking simile of the thin end of the wedge was recurred to by him for a damning illustration.

weep

See enough to make the angels weep *at* ANGEL.

week

a week is a long time in politics

(proverb) a lot can happen to change political circumstances in a short time: associated with the Labour Prime Minister Harold Wilson (1916–95) during the years after his election to power in 1964, and much used since. Wilson is said to have intended the maxim as an encouragement to take long-term views, whereas the phrase is mostly used now in a more literal way about short-term political changes and unexpected developments. *Mid 20th cent.*

weigh

See weigh something in the BALANCE.

weight

throw/chuck one's weight about/around

informal to act in a bullying or domineering manner. *Early 20th cent.*

a weight off somebody's mind

relief from an anxiety or responsibility: cf take a LOAD off somebody's mind. *19th cent.*

Dickens *A Christmas Carol* 1843
Oh, a wonderful pudding! Bob Cratchit said, and calmly too, that he regarded it as the greatest success achieved by Mrs. Cratchit since their marriage. Mrs. Cratchit said that now the weight was off her mind, she would confess she had had her doubts about the quantity of flour.

worth one's/its weight in gold

extremely valuable or useful: *weight in* (or *of*) *gold* as a phrase denoting value dates from Middle English. *15th cent.*

George Turberville *Tragical Tales* 1587
Her yelding necke, that to thy yoke doth bowe, | With such good will as may not well be tolde, | So faire a frend is worth her weight in gold.

John Phillips *Maronides* 1678
And there stout Numitor behold | Who shall be worth his weight in Gold.

welcome

you are welcome to —

informal an ironic rejection of something that one would rather be without. *Mid 20th cent.*

Chris Kelly *The Forest of the Night* 1991
Mungo took a sip ... He bared his teeth in a grimace. 'Whisky?' he asked. Emily nodded. 'It's the stuff to give the troops, Jos says.' 'Well, the

troops are welcome to it,' Mungo said. 'It's disgusting.'

See also join / welcome to the CLUB.

welfare

welfare-to-work
payment of state benefits to unemployed people on condition that they actively seek work. *Late 20th cent.*

welkin

make the welkin ring
to make a loud din or racket: *welkin* is a poetic word of Old English origin meaning 'the sky, the firmament' and hence 'the celestial regions, the heavens'. The phrase occurs in many variant forms: e.g. Sir Toby Belch in Shakespeare's *Twelfth Night* (1602) II.iii.56 invites Sir Andrew to sing with the words 'Shall we make the welkin dance indeed? Shall we rouse the night-owl in a catch that will draw three souls out of one weaver?' *16th cent.*

John Taylor *All the Workes* 1630
Another takes great paines with inke and pen, | Approuing fat men are true honest men. | One makes the haughty vauty welkin ring | In praise of Custards, and a bag pudding. | Another, albe labours inke and paper, | Exalting Dauncing, makes his Muse to caper.

well

all very well
acceptable up to a point but with reservations or other factors to take into account. The phrase originated in longer declarations such as 'all very well in its place [but …]', as in the quotation below. *18th cent.*

Ann Radcliffe *The Italian* 1797
'The benevolence of your nature may be permitted to rejoice, for justice no longer has forbade the exercise of mercy.' 'This is all very well in its place,' said the Marchesa, betrayed by the vexation she suffered; 'such sentiments and such compliments are like gala suits, to be put on in fine weather. My day is cloudy; let me have a little plain strong sense: inform me of the circumstances which have occasioned this change in the course of your observations, and, good father! be brief.'

David Garrick *High Life Below Stairs* 1759
[Kitty] Well, Phil, what think you? Don't we look very smart? – Now let 'em come as soon as they will, we shall be ready for 'em. [Philip] 'Tis all very well; but – [Kitty] But what? [Philip] Why, I wish we could get that snarling Cur, Tom, to make one.

leave/let well alone
to avoid interfering in or trying to improve something that is satisfactory or working well. The sentiment goes back to the time of Chaucer, often in the sense of not trying to exceed one's capabilities; it is found notably in Shakespeare's *King Lear* (1606) I.iv.326: 'Striving to better, oft we mar what's well.' In its developed form the phrase dates from the 18th cent., with *let* somewhat earlier than *leave*.

George Cheyne *Essay on Regimen* 1740
When a person is tolerably well, and is subject to no painful or dangerous distemper, I think it his duty to let well alone.

Marryat *Jacob Faithful* 1834
You're well off at present, and 'leave well alone' is a good motto.

See also be well endowed *at* ENDOW.

welly

give it some welly/wellie
to try harder: typically used as an encouragement to somebody to put more effort into whatever it is they are doing. The notion is of giving a massive kick, as if wearing a wellington boot: first uses, in the 1970s, are in contexts in which this is more realistic, such as driving a racing car. *Late 20th cent.*

Daily Mirror 1977
The girl they call 'Daredevil Divi' gave the car a bit more wellie. In racing language, this meant she was stepping on the accelerator.

west

go west
informal to be lost or destroyed; to meet with disaster: apparently services' slang in the First World War. The origin of the phrase is probably based on the notion of the setting sun symbolizing disappearance or finality. In myth, the Fortunate Isles or Islands of the Blest, where the souls of the good are made happy, were located

in the western ocean. This association appears early in the history of the phrase (see *Notes & Queries* August 1918, p.218). An alternative suggestion, that convicts condemned to die on the gallows at Tyburn were taken west up Oxford Street (*Notes & Queries* November 1915, p.391), is hardly plausible given the first appearance of the phrase only much later. *Early 20th cent.*

Siegfried Sassoon *The War Poems* 1919
A sniper shot me through the neck; the shock | Is easy to remember. All the rest | Of what occurred that morning has gone west.

---

wet

wet the baby's head
to drink a toast on the birth of a child: the phrase is found in many variant forms. *19th cent.*

William Westall *The Old Factory* 1885
Why my wife was brought to bed last night of a little lass as we are going to call Mabel, and I'd like us to drink to her health. That's what we call wetting a child's head in these parts.

wet behind the ears
informal young and inexperienced: originally services' slang. The reference is to a young animal shortly after birth or later being washed by its mother. *Mid 20th cent.*

Pamela Bennetts *Topaz* 1988
Why should a man like Rossmayne take such trouble over a gypsy? It's bad enough that Timothy's mooning over her like a schoolboy, wet behind the ears. Surely the marquis hasn't fallen in love with her as well.

a wet blanket
a person who dampens others' enthusiasm or casts a gloom over an occasion. The phrase is derived from the notion of a wet blanket used to smother a fire and in early use appears in forms closer to the original (as in the quotation below). In 19th cent. use the phrase refers to an event or circumstance, e.g. Mrs Gaskell, *Mary Barton* (1848) 'It was a wet blanket to the evening'; from this use the meaning was rapidly personalized. *19th cent.*

Theodore Dreiser *Sister Carrie* 1900
This little pilgrimage threw quite a wet blanket upon his rising spirits. He was soon down again to

his old worry, and reached the resort anxious to find relief.

wet one's whistle
informal to have an alcoholic drink. The phrase is based on an old use of *whistle*, dating back to Chaucer, denoting the mouth or throat (especially in the context of speaking or singing). A modern invention for the origin of this phrase, that drinkers would blow on a little whistle fitted inside their beer mugs when they wanted a refill, is patent nonsense: no such mugs ever existed except as a joke based on the spurious notion itself. The phrase has occasionally been reconstructed as *whet* (i.e. sharpen) *one's whistle* and then *whet one's whittle* (a *whittle* is a kind of scythe), which adds confusion to its obscure origins. *Middle English*

Chaucer *The Reeve's Tale* (line 4155)
To bedde he goth [= goes], and with hym goth his wyf. | As any jay she light was and jolyf [= merry], | So was hir joly whistle wel ywet.

---

whack

The underlying meaning is generally 'a portion or share', which dates from the 18th cent.

full/top whack
informal the maximum amount, especially of money. *Late 20th cent.*

Practical PC 1992
Some companies offer low-cost and free upgrades only to registered users of the product in question. If you're not registered, and want the latest version, you've got to pay the full whack.

L Pemberton *Platinum Coast* 1993
Michael was cooking the books. He was selling Gary Druer from Travel Enterprise rooms at rock-bottom rates, and Gary was retailing them to the client for top whack, trading on our reputation. He and Michael were splitting the profits.

get one's whack
informal to receive one's share: originally criminals' slang. *Whack* in the sense of 'share or portion' is recorded in Francis Grose's *Dictionary of the Vulgar Tongue* (1785). The phrase dates from the 19th cent.

Thackeray *The History of Pendennis* 1849
I'll come up after dinner, fast enough ... I don't care about much wine afterwards – I take my whack at

dinner – I mean my share, you know; and when I have had as much as I want I toddle up to tea.

get/have a whack at something

informal to make an attempt at something. *19th cent.*

> **Ernest Lawrence Thayer *Casey at the Bat* 1888**
> *A straggling few got up to go in deep despair. The rest | Clung to that hope which springs eternal in the human breast; | They thought if only Casey could but get a whack at that – | We'd put up even money now with Casey at the bat.*

out of whack

informal, chiefly NAmer not working properly. *19th cent.*

> **William James *Pragmatism* 1907**
> *At any rate he and we know off-hand that such philosophies are out of plumb and out of key and out of 'whack', and have no business to speak up in the universe's name.*

whale

have a whale of a time

informal, originally NAmer to enjoy oneself enormously. *Early 20th cent.*

> **Simon Brett *Cast in Order of Disappearance* 1975**
> *On Saturday 1st December, your father Marius Steen went to the party on stage at the King's Theatre … He enjoyed the party, danced, drank and generally had a whale of a time. The following day, Sunday 2nd December, your father, because of his exertions, suffered a second heart attack, and died.*

wham

wham-bam-thank-you-ma'am

informal sexual intercourse performed hurriedly and with little feeling. *Late 20th cent.*

> **Melvyn Bragg *Rich* 1989**
> *He was, it appears, neither rapacious nor peremptory, no 'for kicks', no 'wham bam, thank you, mam!' – he tried to make sure both of them enjoyed the time; and he was fun.*

whammy

double whammy

informal, originally NAmer two simultaneous blows or setbacks, typically resulting from a single action or event. The phrase originates in the US and is particularly associated with the 1950s comic strip *Li'l Abner*: a *whammy* is an evil influence, as in *put the whammy on somebody*. It was brought into more widespread use in Britain during the general election of 1992, when the Conservative Secretary of State for Scotland, Ian Lang, who risked losing his Cabinet job along with his seat, exclaimed to his supporters: 'Scotland has rejected separatism. Britain has rejected socialism. It's a double whammy!' *Triple whammy* also occurs occasionally. *Mid 20th cent.*

> **Hansard 1992**
> *Does my right honourable friend agree that the disposable income of 10 million mortgage payers is affected by two factors – income tax and interest rates? Is he aware that the Labour party will put up both – a double whammy?*

what

and/or what not / what have you

informal, originally NAmer and other things of the same kind: used at the end of a list as equivalent to 'and so on.' *18th cent.*

> **Thomas Paine *American Crisis* 1780**
> *As individuals we profess ourselves Christians, but as nations we are heathens, Romans, and what not.*

> **Louis MacNeice *Autolycus* 1945**
> *O master pedlar with your confidence tricks, | Brooches, pomanders, broadsheets and what-have-you.*

what with

because of; taking into account (used to introduce a number of items or factors that the speaker thinks relevant): recorded earlier (Middle English) in the form *what for*. *15th cent.*

> **Shakespeare *Measure for Measure* I.ii.80 (1605)**
> [Mistress Overdone] *Thus, what with the war, what with the sweat, what with the gallows, and what with poverty, I am custom-shrunk.*

See also GIVE somebody what for; KNOW what's what.

wheat

See separate the wheat from the CHAFF.

wheel

(as) silly as a wheel

informal, chiefly Australian extremely silly. *Mid 20th cent.*

> **T A G Hungerford** *The Ridge and the River* 1952
> *Oscar was sound, but silly as a wheel.*

a big wheel

informal an important or influential person: one of a number of similar expressions (others being *big cheese*, *big gun*, *big noise*, *big shot*, etc), probably based on the notion of a wheel as controlling a mechanism and perhaps influenced by the fairground entertainment of the same name (recorded from the early 20th cent.). *Mid 20th cent.*

> **Candida Lycett Green** *The Perfect English Country House* 1991
> *Robert was sent as an apprentice to an upholsterer in Covent Garden at the age of fourteen, progressed up the ladder, bought the business, and became a big wheel.*

a fifth wheel (to the coach)

a person or thing that is not needed: the image appears in a play by Dekker (*Match Mee in London* (1631) 'Thou tyest but wings to a swift gray Hounds heele, | And add'st to a running Charriot a fift wheele') but is otherwise not attested until the late 19th cent.

> **Henry James** *The Portrait of a Lady* 1881
> *That same day Caspar Goodwood came to see him, and he informed his visitor that Miss Stackpole had taken him up and was to conduct him back to England. 'Ah then,' said Caspar, 'I'm afraid I shall be a fifth wheel to the coach. Mrs. Osmond has made me promise to go with you.'*

had one but the wheel fell off

informal a meaningless statement made by a participant in a conversation as an admission of inattention or failure to understand what has gone before. *Mid 20th cent.*

set/keep the wheels in motion

to make preparations for a process or activity to begin or continue. *18th cent.*

> **Smollett** *The Adventures of Ferdinand Count Fathom* 1753
> *None of these observations escaped the penetrating eye of Fathom, who, before he pretended to seat himself in his machine, had made proper inquiry into all the other methods practised, with a view to keep the wheels in motion.*

> **William Blackstone** *Commentaries on the Laws of England* 1765
> *Such a spirit … sets all the wheels of government in motion, which under a wise regulator, may be directed to any beneficial purpose.*

wheel and deal

informal to be a shrewd or unprincipled operator in business or politics. The expression, along with its derivative *wheeler-dealer* ('an unscrupulous politician or business person'; a contraction of *wheeler and dealer*), appears first in American dictionaries in the 1960s, and must have been current in informal speech for some years before then. *Wheel and deal* is entered in the 1961 edition of *Webster's New International Dictionary*, and, along with *wheeler-dealer*, in Wentworth and Flexner's *Dictionary of American Slang* (1961). *Wheel* in this sense is derived from its use as a noun meaning a gang leader or 'big shot' (itself a figurative use of the sense relating to parts of machinery), recorded in American use from the 1930s (and see *big wheel* above). The jazz singer Billie Holiday borrowed the term in her autobiography *Lady Sings the Blues* (1956): 'After I got to be a wheel in the kitchen, I used to take care of Marietta by saving her the best of the food.' This use of *wheel* alone is unfamiliar in British English, but *wheeler-dealing* is not. *Mid 20th cent.*

> **A R Ammons** *Tape for the Turn of the Year* 1965
> *the jay was out | before sunrise | wheeling & dealing | & around noon | a covey of quail | enjoyed (apparently) | the sunlit margin | between the back lawn | and the sumac grove*

> **J I M Stewart** *A Memorial Service* 1976
> *'What's in the wind is a little quiet wheeling and dealing about the black sheep of the family.' … 'Why should the Provost wheel and deal about you?'*

the wheel of Fortune/Providence

chance or luck in life, regarded as a wheel turned by a personified Fortune. In the 18th cent. *wheel of fortune* was also the name of a lottery wheel. *Middle English*

> **Chaucer** *Troilus and Criseyde* IV.323
> *O ye loveris, that heigh [= high] upon the whiel | Ben [= been] set of Fortune, in good aventure, |*

*God leve that ye fynde ay love of stiel, | And longe
mote [= must] youre lif in joie endure!*

wheels within wheels

the intricacies of a complex organization or operation. The image is of a complex set of cogs in a
machine: recorded earlier (17th cent.) in the form
wheel within a wheel, with possible allusion to the
vision in Ezekiel 1:16 'The appearance of the
wheels and their work was like unto the colour
of a beryl: and they four had one likeness: and
their appearance and their work was as it were a
wheel in the middle of a wheel.' *18th cent.*

> Lord Shaftesbury *Characteristics of Men, Manners,
> Opinions, and Times* 1711
> *Thus we have wheels within wheels. And in some
> National Constitutions ... we have one Empire
> within another.*

See also a FLY on the wheel; GREASE the wheels;
REINVENT the wheel; the wheel has turned/come
full CIRCLE.

whelk

be unfit to run a whelk stall

to be incapable of managing the simplest task or
enterprise: used in variant forms to denote
incompetence in those who aspire to power.
The phrase was first used by the British socialist
politician John Burns (1858–1943) in a speech in
January 1894 in which he referred to the Social-
Democratic Federation as 'men who fancy they
are Admirable Crichtons ... but who have not got
sufficient brains to run a whelk stall'. As
President of the Board of Trade in 1914, Burns
was the first working-class member of a British
Cabinet, although he resigned on the outbreak of
war in that year. The origin of the phrase was the
subject of a correspondence in *The Times* in 1976,
which resurfaced in 2002 when an article published in the same newspaper described the Blair
government as 'barely fit to run a whelk stall'.
The choice of whelk stalls was probably fanciful
and taken from their leisurely seaside associations to be symbolic of work that ought to be
straightforward, to the chagrin of many who
have tried it themselves. Nowadays the incompetent are more likely to be accused of being unfit
to *organize a piss-up in a brewery. 19th cent.*

whet

whet somebody's appetite

to make somebody want more of something.
Whet in the sense 'to sharpen or stimulate' occurs
from Middle English, and with *appetite* from the
early part of the 17th cent. Shakespeare wrote of
whetting thoughts (as in *Twelfth Night* (1602)
III.i.103, where Viola addresses Olivia:
'Madam, I come to whet your gentle thoughts
on his [Orsino's] behalf').

> Margaret Cavendish *The Presence* 1668
> [Observer] *The old Lady has whet his appetite.*
> [Spend-all] *I confess old Women make wanton
> young Men.*

> Smollett *The Adventures of Peregrine Pickle* 1751
> *In this circle of amusements our hero's time was
> parcelled out, and few young gentlemen of the age
> enjoyed life with greater relish, notwithstanding
> those intervening checks of reason, which served
> only to whet his appetite for a repetition of the
> pleasures she so prudently condemned.*

while

worth (one's) while

advantageous or beneficial to one. The phrase is
recorded in Middle English in the form *worth the
while*, and *worth while* is found from the 17th cent.
The hyphenated or one-word form *worth(-)while*
occurs from the second half of the 19th cent.
17th cent.

> Andrew Marvell *The Rehearsal Transpros'd* 1672
> *Were it not that I do really make conscience of using
> scripture with such a drolling companion as Mr
> Bayes, I could overload him thence both with
> authority and example. Nor is it worth ones while to
> teach him out of other authors, and the best prece-
> dents of the kind, how he, being a Christian and a
> Divine, ought to have carried himself.*

> Locke *An Essay Concerning Human Understanding*
> 1690
> *It is not worth while to be concerned what he says or
> thinks, who says or thinks only as he is directed by
> another.*

whip

have the whip hand

to be in control. The *whip hand* was the hand that held the whip in riding, and is hence symbolic of control and dominance. *17th cent.*

> Dryden *The Satires of Decimus Junius Juvenalis* 1693
> *Yet the Arch-Angel, in the former example, when discord was relative, and would not be drawn from her belov'd monastery with fair words, has the whip-hand of her, drags her out with many stripes, sets her, on Gods-name, about her business.*

> Jane Austen *Sense and Sensibility* 1811
> *'Aye, you may abuse me as you please,' said the good-natured old lady, 'you have taken Charlotte off my hands, and cannot give her back again. So there I have the whip hand of you.'*

whips of something

Australian and NZ, informal large amounts of something. *19th cent.*

See also a fair CRACK of the whip.

whirl

give something a whirl

informal, originally NAmer to give something a try, to have a go: from the meaning 'swift or rapid movement', e.g. of a top (i.e. giving something a whirl meant starting it going). *19th cent.*

> P G Wodehouse *Damsel in Distress* 1920
> *'Well, it's worth trying,' said Reggie. 'I'll give it a whirl.'*

whirlwind

reap the whirlwind

to suffer the consequences of one's actions: with allusion to Hosea 8:7 'For they have sown the wind, and they shall reap the whirlwind', the source of the (16th cent.) proverb *they that sow the wind shall reap the whirlwind. Middle English* (in Wyclif)

> Charles Kingsley *Westward Ho!* 1855
> *Ah, Raleigh! you can afford to confess yourself less than some, for you are greater than all. Go on and conquer, noble heart! But as for me, I sow the wind, and I suppose I shall reap the whirlwind.*

whisker

have (grown) whiskers (on it)

informal to be very old or familiar: used especially of a joke, story, etc. The allusion is to the facial hair typical of older men. *Mid 20th cent.*

> Dorothy L Sayers *Gaudy Night* 1935
> *'That old story I was ass enough to rake up –' 'The Viennese dancer?' 'Singer ... Please forget that. I mean, it's got whiskers on it – it's six years old, anyway.'*

within a whisker of something

informal having come very close to (doing or achieving) something: based on the (early 20th cent.) sense of *whisker* 'a very small amount.' *Late 20th cent.*

> *Punch* 1992
> *We know a travel agent who came within a whisker of losing his job, all for innocently caressing a colleague's bum while she was closing a sale on a two-week package to Alicante on the phone.*

See also the cat's whiskers at CAT.

whistle

blow the whistle (on somebody/something)

informal to expose somebody's illicit or clandestine activities to the responsible authorities with a view to having them ended. The phrase alludes to the act of blowing a whistle as a signal to end an activity, especially by a sports referee to bring play to a halt because of an infringement or at the end of a period of play. *Mid 20th cent.*

> *Daily Mirror* 1992
> *BNP stickers were found bearing the slogans: Love the White Race, Outlaw Homosexuality and Protect Us From AIDS. The report says the management was so weak it failed to control the savagery and racism. And staff members went to war on each other. Anyone who tried to blow the whistle on the violence was intimidated or threatened.*

whistle something down the wind

to abandon or dismiss something: in falconry, a bird was cast off downwind with a whistling sound when it was being released (but cast off against the wind to attack its prey). Cf Shakespeare, *Othello* (1604) III.iii.266 '[Othello speaking of Desdemona] If I do prove her haggard [= wild, intractable] | ... | I'd whistle her off and let her down the wind | To prey at fortune.' *Whistle Down the Wind* is the title of a novel by Mary Hayley Bell about three country children who befriend a fugitive hiding in their barn and become convinced that he is Jesus Christ, and of a 1961 film based on this story. *17th cent.*

> Dr Johnson *Taxation no Tyranny* 1775
> *The Dean of Gloucester has proposed ... that we should ... release our claims, declare them masters of themselves, and whistle them down the wind.*

> Mrs Gaskell *Mary Barton* 1849
> *The counsellor for the prosecution prepared himself by folding his arms, elevating his eyebrows, and putting his lips in the form in which they might best whistle down the wind such evidence as might be produced by a suborned witness, who dared to perjure himself.*

whistle in the dark
informal to assume a pretence of courage; to disguise one's fear with a jaunty manner. *Early 20th cent.*

> Henry James *The Ambassadors* 1903
> *Wasn't he writing against time, and mainly to show he was kind? – since it had become quite his habit not to like to read himself over. On those lines he could still be liberal, yet it was at best a sort of whistling in the dark.*

whistle in the wind
to speak or act to no effect. *20th cent.*

> Gerald Seymour *Condition Black* 1991
> *All the scientists had gathered one evening to formulate a demand for a 40 per cent pay rise. Whistling in the wind, that had been, because they had settled for half, and never recovered from the shame of behaving in the same way as the typists and fitters and laboratory assistants.*

See also (as) CLEAN as a whistle; WET one's whistle.

---

white

(as) white as a sheet
intensely white or pale. *White as a cloth* is recorded earlier (18th cent.), and *white as milk* occurs in Shakespeare's *Pericles* (1608) xv.22: 'Be't when they weaved the sleided [= sleeved] silk | With fingers long, small, white as milk' and, more strikingly, in a figurative sense in *The Merchant of Venice* (1596) III.ii.86: '[Bassanio,

aside] How many cowards whose hearts are all as false | As stairs of sand, wear yet upon their chins | The beards of Hercules and frowning Mars, | Who, inward searched, have livers white as milk?' *19th cent.*

> Mark Twain *The Adventures of Tom Sawyer* 1876
> *'Nobody will get lost in that cave any more.'*
> *'Why?' 'Because I had its big door sheathed with boiler iron two weeks ago, and triple-locked – and I've got the keys.' Tom turned as white as a sheet. 'What's the matter, boy!' ... 'O, judge, Injun Joe's in the cave!'*

mark somebody/something with a white stone
to regard somebody or something as particularly fortunate or happy: with reference to the ancient use of a white stone as a memorial of fortunate events. *17th cent.*

> Dryden transl Persius 1692
> *Let this auspicious morning be exprest | With a white stone distinguished from the rest, | White as thy fame, and as thy honour clear, | And let new joys attend on thy new added year.*

show the white feather
to act in a cowardly way: from the belief that a white feather in the tail of a game bird indicates an inferior breed. *19th cent.*

> Harold Frederic *The Damnation of Theron Ware* 1896
> *He'll be just an average kind of man – a little sore about some things, a little wiser than he was about some others. You can get along perfectly with him, if you only keep your courage up, and don't show the white feather.*

a whited sepulchre
a hypocrite. The expression alludes to the simile applied by Christ to the scribes and Pharisees in Matthew 23:27 'Woe unto you, scribes and Pharisees, hypocrites! For ye are like unto whited sepulchres, which indeed appear beautiful outward, but are within full of dead men's bones, and of all uncleanness.' *16th cent.*

a white elephant
something apparently attractive or valuable that proves to be a burden to its owner; also, an idea or scheme that has no practical use or value. A white elephant was an albino breed that was much prized in Asian countries, but was costly and difficult to maintain: this gave rise to the

story (recorded in English from the 17th cent.) of the kings of Siam making presents of these animals to courtiers and dignitaries they wanted to punish, because the cost of keeping the animal brought ruin on its owner. The phrase is 19th cent. in allusive use.

> Samuel Butler *The Way of All Flesh* 1903
> *Before many days were over he felt his unfortunate essay to be a white elephant to him, which he must feed by hurrying into all sorts of frantic attempts to cap his triumph, and, as may be imagined, these attempts were failures.*

a white knight
1 a helpful but ineffectual person: with allusion to the White Knight in Lewis Carroll's *Through the Looking-Glass* (1871), who had these characteristics. *19th cent.*
2 a hero or champion. *Mid 20th cent.*
3 a company or individual that finances a company to rescue it from a hostile takeover bid. *Late 20th cent.*

> Peter Hardy *A Right Approach to Economics?* 1991
> *Distillers, the Scotch whisky firm, when faced with an unwanted takeover bid from Argyll, the supermarket chain, in December 1985, attempted to merge with Guinness, using it as a white knight (i.e. a friendly rescuer) in an attempt to thwart this move.*

the white man's burden
the supposed responsibility of the white colonial powers to bring civilization to other peoples: originally the title of a poem by Kipling (1899) on this theme: 'Take up the White Man's burden – | Send forth the best ye breed – | Go bind your sons to exile | To serve your captives' need.' *19th cent.*

whiter than white
completely honest or morally sound. The phrase in its physical sense is popularly associated with advertising slogans for soap powder, but the notion and even the wording are very much older, occurring for example in Shakespeare's mythological poem *Venus and Adonis* (1593) line 398: 'Who sees his true-love in her naked bed, | Teaching the sheets a whiter hue than white, | But when his glutton eye so full hath fed | His other agents aim at like delight?' In its figurative use of *white*, however, the phrase is relatively recent, often alluding to the advertising associations in extended metaphor. *Early 20th cent.*

> Stewart Lamont *In Good Faith* 1989
> *The new heroes are bright young CIA-types who clean up the baddies in the Establishment, or journalists who oppose the abuse of political power, or expose nuclear power Policy. These are the new improved, biological, whiter than white heroes.*

See also big white CHIEF; BLEED somebody dry/ white.

who
See KNOW who's who; who goes there? at GO.

whole
See go the whole HOG; a new / different / whole new ball game at BALL[1].

whoop

not care/give a whoop
informal, chiefly NAmer not to care at all; to be totally indifferent: based on the meaning of *whoop* 'a loud shout or cry'. *Early 20th cent.*

> Jack London *The Call of the Wild* 1903
> *It's not that I care a whoop what becomes of you, but for the dogs' sakes I just want to tell you, you can help them a mighty lot by breaking out that sled. The runners are froze fast. Throw your weight against the gee-pole, right and left, and break it out.*

whoop it/things up
informal to have fun; to enjoy oneself extravagantly and noisily. *19th cent.*

> Charles Hale Hoyt *A Temperance Town* 1891
> *You'll just come home and whoop things up in the woodshed! You're a nice man to leave me home doing all your work besides my own, while you come here and drink up all both of us can earn. You ought to be ashamed of yourself!*

whoopee

make whoopee
informal to celebrate wildly and noisily. 'Makin' Whoopee' is the title of a song by Gus Kahn written for the Broadway musical *Whoopee*, produced in 1928. *Early 20th cent.*

> *The Times* 1986
> *I met her at the bus stop, she turned around and looked at me, you get the picture? She lived on*

Princesa, opposite the best old magic shop in town, Rey del Magia. For me, she, and Barcelona, are la Reina de Magia and a very happy hunting ground for making whoopee.

why

the whys and wherefores
the precise reasons for something: *why* and *wherefore* are balanced with each other in writing from the end of the 16th cent., but the present plural form of the phrase does not appear until the 1830s. *19th cent.*

> Mark Twain A Tramp Abroad 1889
> *Art retains her privileges, Literature has lost hers. Somebody else may cipher out the whys and the wherefores and the consistencies of it – I haven't got time.*

wick

The meaning or meanings involved in the phrases are unclear; the word as used here may be derived from *Hampton Wick*, rhyming slang for *prick* (= penis). But in the second phrase it could also be a fanciful synonym for *nerves* (as in the parallel phrase *get on somebody's nerves*: see NERVE).

dip one's wick
informal (said of a man) to have sexual intercourse. *Mid 20th cent.*

> James K Baxter A Small Ode on Mixed Flatting 1980
> *I blundered through the rain and sleet | To dip my wick in Castle Street, | Not on the footpath – no, in a flat, | With a sofa where I often sat.*

get on somebody's wick
informal to irritate or annoy somebody, especially cumulatively over a long time. *Mid 20th cent.*

> Kingsley Amis I Like It Here 1958
> *I wish he wouldn't think he'd got the right to knock the English. That's what really gets on my wick.*

wicked

no peace/rest for the wicked
used to express ironic resignation in the face of life's everyday obligations and anxieties, with allusion to Isaiah 48:22 'There is no peace, saith the Lord, unto the wicked.' *Mid 20th cent.*

Noel Barber The Other Side of Paradise 1992
I had heard a fair amount of noise from the garden, and now Miss Sowerby announced, 'There's half a dozen patients, Doctor, including one who's hurt his head badly.' 'Let's start work,' Dr Reid sighed. 'There's nae peace for the wicked.'

wicket

See batting on a STICKY wicket.

wide

See give somebody/something a wide BERTH; off / wide of the mark *at* off the MARK.

widow

a widow's mite
a modest contribution or donation, but all one can afford: with allusion to the account in Mark (12:41–4) of Christ's observation of those who came and gave money to the Temple in Jerusalem. After a succession of rich donors, a poor widow came and gave two mites, a tiny sum but all the money she had. *16th cent.*

See also a widow's CRUSE.

wife

an old wives' tale
a traditional story or account that has little basis in fact. *Wife* here is used in its old meaning 'woman'. A similar form of the phrase occurs in early English translations of the Bible at 1 Timothy 4:7, e.g. in that of Tyndale (1525): 'Cast away ungostly and olde wyves fables.' The Authorized Version (1611) has 'Refuse profane and old wives' fables, and exercise thyself rather unto godliness.' *16th cent.*

> Marlowe Dr Faustus v.137 (1590)
> *Think'st thou that Faustus is so fond | To imagine that after this life there is any paine? | Tush, these are trifles and mere old wives' tales.*

a wife in every port
female lovers all over the world: used as a token of sexual promiscuity traditionally associated with sailors. *18th cent.*

Isaac Bickerstaffe *Thomas & Sally, or the Sailor's Return* 1761

'Tis pretty sport, for one that gets a wife at ev'ry port.

wig

wigs on the green

a violent quarrel or altercation. Although the first evidence in print is from the 19th cent., the expression must have arisen in Irish use in the 18th cent. when men wore wigs; the associations are still chiefly Irish. The image is of the wigs being the first things to be pulled off in a tustle. *19th cent.*

Dion Boucicault *Belle Lamar* 1874

[Philip] *Are you as fond of a fight as ever?*
[Remmy] *I don't know. It's so long since I had a taste of one, sir! But now your honour is come, plaze God, there will be sticks out and wigs on the green.*

James Joyce *Ulysses* 1922

Edy Boardman asked Tommy Caffrey was he done and he said yes, so she buttoned up his little knickerbockers for him and told him to run off and play with Jacky and to be good now and not fight. But Tommy said he wanted the ball and Edy told him no that baby was playing with the ball and if he took it there'd be wigs on the green but Tommy said it was his ball and he wanted his ball and he pranced on the ground, if you please. The temper of him!

See also FLIP one's lid/wig.

wild

wild and woolly

1 lacking refinement; uncivilized: first used of the American West, probably with allusion to the sheepskin fleeces worn by the earlier pioneers. *19th cent.*

2 impractical; not properly thought out. *Mid 20th cent.*

R S Lambert *Ariel and All His Quality* 1940

At the Empire Marketing Board – then on the point of demise – Sir Stephen Tallents and John Grierson looked with scepticism upon a plan which they regarded as wild and woolly, and in any case trenching upon the ground of their own Film Unit and Film Library.

a wild-goose chase

a hopeless or fruitless pursuit of something unattainable. The phrase first appears in Shakespeare's *Romeo and Juliet* (1596) II.iii.66, where Mercutio says to Romeo 'Nay, if our wits run the wild-goose chase, I am done, for thou hast more of the wild goose in one of thy wits than I am sure I have in my whole five.' The reference here is to a kind of horse race in which the leader has to be followed on an erratic course by another horse; the use is figurative and refers to people rather than horses. The current meaning first appears towards the end of the 17th cent.

John Davies *Wits Bedlam* 1617

Two Gallants needs would fight; Sword, Time, & Place, | Appointed were, & all agreed vpon: | Then both rode out, and ran a Wild-goose-chase; | But both mistooke the place: so, both, alone, | Returnd againe, both swearing they were there.

See also sow one's wild oats *at* OAT.

wilderness

a voice (crying) in the wilderness

a plea for change or reform that goes unheeded: with allusion to the biblical description of John the Baptist (Isaiah 40:3 in the Authorized Version, 1611: 'The voice of him that crieth in the wilderness, Prepare ye the way of the Lord, make straight in the desert a highway for the Lord'; identified with John the Baptist in Matthew 3:3). Allusive uses are found from the 18th cent.

Richard Graves *The Spiritual Quixote* 1773

Wildgoose might as well have thought of preaching the Gospel in the deserts of Arabia, as on the Cotswold hills. He would have been like the Preacher, whose discourses generally produced such a solitude in his church, that he was facetiously called, 'the voice of one crying in the wilderness'.

wildfire

spread like wildfire

to become rapidly and widely known: also in early use with *run* instead of *spread*. *Wildfire* was a kind of projectile made of highly combustible substances, formerly used as a weapon of war. It was also a name for erysipelas and other highly contagious inflammatory diseases with eruptions of the skin. Figurative uses occur from Middle English, and there is a vivid use by Shakespeare in *The Rape of Lucrece* (1594): 'The well skilled workman this mild image drew | For perjured Sinon, whose enchanting story | The credulous old Priam after slew; | Whose words like wildfire burnt the shining glory | Of rich-built Ilion.' The phrase in its present form dates from the 18th cent. (with *run*) and from the 19th cent. (with *spread*).

> Oliver Goldsmith *The Citizen of the World* 1762
> *Though I was at that time rich in fame – for my book ran like wild-fire – yet I was very short in money.*

will

at will

according to one's wishes or inclinations. The phrase goes back to Middle English and is found in the *Cursor Mundi*, a northern English poem dating from about 1300.

> Spenser *Epithalamion* line 364 (1595)
> *Ye sonnes of Venus, play your sports at will, | For greedy pleasure, careless of your toyes, | Thinks more upon her paradise of joyes, | Then what ye do, albe it good or ill.*

where there's a will there's a way

(proverb) one needs to be determined to overcome difficulties: the sentiment occurs at an earlier date in other forms, e.g. in George Herbert's 17th cent. collection of proverbs translated from other languages (*Outlandish Proverbs*, 1640): 'To him that will, ways are not wanting.' The proverb is first found in the 19th cent. in its developed form.

> Dickens *Nicholas Nickleby* 1839
> *'Nay noo,' replied the honest countryman, reining in his impatient horse, 'stan' still, tellee. Hoo much cash hast thee gotten?' 'Not much,' said Nicholas, colouring, 'but I can make it enough. Where there's a will there's a way, you know.'*

with the best will in the world

despite one's best intentions: used to suggest the difficulty or impossibility attached to an undertaking. *19th cent.*

> Catharine Sedgwick *Hope Leslie* 1827
> *Poor Cradock now interposed with one of his awkward movements which, though made with the best will in the world, was sure to overturn the burden he essayed to bear.*

with a will

enthusiastically and energetically. *19th cent.*

> R H Dana *Two Years Before the Mast* 1840
> *'Sogering' [= hanging back] was the order of the day. Send a man below to get a block, and he would capsize everything before finding it, then not bring it up till an officer had called him twice … and after the tackles were got up, six men would pull less than three who pulled 'with a will'. When the mate was out of sight, nothing was done.*

willies

have / give somebody the willies

informal, originally NAmer to have or give somebody a feeling of nervous irritation: *willies* is just a fanciful concoction of a word without any clear-cut derivation. *19th cent.*

willow

wear the green willow

to grieve for the death of a loved one. The 'Willow Song' sung by Desdemona in Shakespeare's *Othello* (1604) IV.iii.49 includes the words 'Sing all a green willow must be my garland', and may have drawn on a poem by John Heywood (c1497–c1580) entitled 'The Green Willow': 'All a green willow, willow; | All a green willow is my garland.'

win

win friends and influence people

to succeed in one's career and social life, used as a slogan of self-improvement: the title of a book by the US writer Dale Carnegie, published in 1936. *Mid 20th cent.*

> *Economist* 1993
> *The anti-golfers may yet find their campaign bunkered. For the upwardly mobile Thai or Malaysian businessman, the golf course is the place to win friends and influence people. The smartest new housing developments in Malaysia, Thailand and Indonesia often come with golf courses attached.*

you can't win them all

informal, originally NAmer one can't always be successful: used as a formula of self-justification or consolation for failure. Also in the form *win some, lose some. Mid 20th cent.*

Raymond Chandler *The Long Goodbye* 1953
Wade took him by the shoulder and spun him round. 'Take it easy, Doc. You can't win them all.'

See also carry/win the DAY; win by a NECK; win one's spurs *at* SPUR; win the wooden SPOON.

---

wind[1] (noun)

between wind and water

at the most vulnerable point: with allusion to the part of a ship's side near the waterline, which dips below the surface with the movement of the ship and is therefore particularly vulnerable if damaged. The phrase is first recorded in its literal meaning in a document listing naval losses of 1588, the year of the defeat of the Spanish Armada: 'One of the shot was between the wind and the water, whereof they thought she would have sunk.' It was evidently popular as a risqué pun, referring to the groin, in 17th cent. drama (see below).

Beaumont & Fletcher *Philaster, or Love Lies a-Bleeding* 1620
[Dion] *He looks like an old surfeited stallion after his leaping, dull as a dormouse: see how he sinks; the wench has shot him between wind and water, and I hope sprung a leak.*

break wind

to release wind from the anus. *16th cent.*

Smollett *The Adventures of an Atom* 1769
He strutted with an air of importance. He broke wind, and broached new systems.

get wind of something

to hear a rumour of something or become aware of it. *19th cent.*

R L Stevenson *Kidnapped* 1886
'Ye must find a safe bit somewhere near by,' said James, 'and get word sent to me. Ye see, ye'll have to get this business prettily off, Alan. This is no time to be stayed for a guinea or two. They're sure to get wind of ye, sure to seek ye, and by my way of it, sure to lay on ye the wyte of [= blame for] this day's accident.'

gone with the wind

disappeared without trace: from verses by Ernest Dowson (1896) 'I have forgot much, Cynara! gone with the wind', used as the title of a 1936 novel by Margaret Mitchell about the American Civil War and of the film based on it. The phrase occurs a

few years earlier than the Dowson poem in a slightly different sense in a work by Celia Thaxter (*The Shag*, 1879): 'But the shag kept his place on the headland, | And when the brief storm had gone by, | He shook his loose plumes, and they saw him | Rise splendid and strong in the sky. | Clinging fast to the gown of his sister, | The little boy laughed as he flew: | 'He is gone with the wind and the lightning! | And – I am not frightened, – are you?' *19th cent.*

in the wind

about to happen; astir or afoot: from the physical meaning of odours being carried by the wind and being perceptible in the direction in which the wind is blowing. *16th cent.*

Chaucer *Epilogue to The Man of Law's Tale* (line 1173)
Our Hoste answered, 'O Jankyn, be ye there? I smell a Loller [= Lollard] in the wind,' quod he.

Shakespeare *The Comedy of Errors* III.i.70 (1594)
[Dromio of Ephesus] *They stand at the door, master. Bid them welcome hither.* [Antipholus of Ephesus] *There is something in the wind, that we cannot get in.*

it's an ill wind (that blows nobody any good)

some good is normally found in the worst of circumstances: a nautical metaphor. In Shakespeare's *3 Henry VI* (1591), a soldier, carrying in his arms the body of a dead man who shortly after is revealed to be the soldier's own father, says (before he knows this) to King Henry (II.v.55): 'Ill blows the wind that profits nobody.' *16th cent.*

Thomas Forde *Love's Labyrinth* 1660
[King Damocles] *It is an ill wind that blows no man good; | Though the Thessalian lad have got the prize | In his possession, it shall not be long, | But I will have them both in mine.*

Jane Austen *Sense and Sensibility* 1811
After a short silence on both sides, Mrs. Jennings, with all her natural hilarity, burst forth again. 'Well, my dear, 'tis a true saying about an ill-wind, for it will be all the better for Colonel Brandon. He will have her at last; ay, that he will. Mind me, now, if they ain't married by Midsummer.'

put the wind up somebody

informal to scare or alarm somebody: to *get the wind up* is to be affected in this way. *Early 20th cent.*

Wilfred Owen *Letter* 1918
The Munchie I ate over a period of several days &
nights; and the fact that it was once eaten under a
particularly nasty & accurate bombardment –
(shells so close that they thoroughly put the wind up
a Life Guardsman in the trench with me – so that he
shook as the Guards shake on parade) these cir-
cumstances, I say, have not taken the good savour
from Munchie-munchie.

raise the wind
informal, dated to procure funds for some enterprise: literally, to make a wind blow, an attribute
commonly associated with spirits and witches in
the Middle Ages. In the first scene of Marlowe's
Dr Faustus (1590), Faust declares as he ruminates
on the wonders of magic (i.58–63): 'All things that
move between the quiet poles | Shall be at my
command. Emperors and kings | Are but obeyed
in their several provinces, | Nor can they raise
the wind or rend the clouds; | But his dominion
that exceeds in this | Stretcheth as far as doth the
mind of man.' *16th cent.*

see how / which way the wind blows
to see how events develop before making a decision or taking action: metaphors based on the
blowing of the wind as a sign of changing events
are recorded from the 15th cent. *19th cent.*

James Fenimore Cooper *The Prairie* 1829
'Now, old trapper,' retorted Paul, 'this is what I call
knowing which way the wind blows! You ar' a man
that has seen life, and you know something of
fashions; I put it to your judgment plainly.'

spit into/against the wind
to do something that is ineffectual or pointless: in
early use in the forms *beat the wind* and *speak to the*
wind. 16th cent.

take the wind out of somebody's sails
to compromise the force or effectiveness of a
person's words or actions by anticipating them
in some way: another nautical metaphor. *19th*
cent.

Henry James *The Portrait of a Lady* 1881
'All the same what you say is very true,' Isabel
pursued … 'I look at life too much as a doctor's
prescription. Why indeed should we perpetually be
thinking whether things are good for us, as if we
were patients lying in a hospital? Why should I be
so afraid of not doing right? As if it mattered to the
world whether I do right or wrong!' 'You're a

capital person to advise,' said Ralph; 'you take the
wind out of my sails!'

to the four winds
in all directions: the *four winds* correspond to the
four compass points, i.e. north, south, east, and
west. The expression is based on uses by Milton,
one in *Areopagitica* ('A Speech … for the liberty of
unlicenc'd printing', 1644): 'Truth indeed came
once into the world with her Divine Master …
but when He ascended, and His Apostles after
Him were laid asleep, then straight arose a
wicked race of deceivers, who … took the virgin
Truth, hewed her lovely form into a thousand
pieces, and scattered them to the four winds', and
the other in *Paradise Lost* (1667) ii.516 'Toward the
four winds four speedy Cherubim | Put to thir
mouths the sounding Alchymie.' *17th cent.*

the wind of change
a new climate of opinion, leading to political and
social change. The phrase was popularized by the
British Prime Minister Harold Macmillan
(1894–1986) in a speech given to the parliament
of South Africa on 3 February 1960: 'We have
seen the awakening of national consciousness in
peoples who have for centuries lived in dependence upon some other power … The wind of
change is blowing through the continent, and,
whether we like it or not, this growth of national
consciousness is a political fact.' *Early 20th cent.*

D H Lawrence *Mornings in Mexico* 1927
The place of after-life and before-life, where house
the winds of change.

See also SAIL close to / near the wind.

wind² (verb)
See twist/wind/wrap somebody round one's little FINGER.

windmill

fling/throw one's cap over the windmill(s)
to behave recklessly or with complete abandon: a
translation of French *jeter son bonnet par-dessus les*
moulins. 19th cent.

George Meredith *One of Our Conquerors* 1891
A visit … to the Italian cantatrice separated from
her husband, would render the maiden an accom-
plished flinger of caps over the windmills.

See also TILT at windmills.

window

go window shopping
originally NAmer to enjoy oneself by browsing in shop windows without buying anything (or at least without intending to). *Early 20th cent.*

Sinclair Lewis *Babbitt* 1922
There were many women who had nothing to do ... They ate chocolates, went to the motion-pictures, went window-shopping, went in gossiping twos and threes to card-parties, read magazines, thought timorously of the lovers who never appeared.

out of the window / NAmer out the window
informal completely lost or discarded, like something thrown or blown out of a window. *Mid 20th cent.*

Dogs Today 1992
If your dog has a party piece don't be afraid to show it off. It could be a trick, an impression ... Feel free to bring any props you might require. Competitions for the most handsome dog and prettiest bitch need no explanation. Suffice to say Kennel Club standards will be out the window on Top Dog Day.

a window of opportunity
a brief period during which a particular action or activity is possible: commonly used from the 1960s in the context of launching space missiles and of the cold-war arms race (the reverse position being sometimes called a *window of vulnerability*), and more recently with reference to various peace initiatives – especially in the Middle East – which seem to receive a boost from particular events. *Late 20th cent.*

Keesings Contemporary Archives 1990
The assertion in early March by United States President Bush that the Gulf war had provided a 'window of opportunity' for Israel and the Arab states to advance toward a comprehensive peace settlement appeared unduly optimistic in late May.

---

windward

to windward of somebody/something
in a position of advantage in relation to somebody or something. The phrase is a nautical metaphor: a ship that was *to windward* had the wind behind it. Early figurative uses were in the context of seafaring and trade (see below). *19th cent.*

R H Dana *Two Years Before the Mast* 1840
The Rosa ... took off nearly a thousand hides, which had been brought down for us, and which we lost in consequence of the south-easter. This mortified us; not only that an Italian ship should have got to windward of us in the trade, but because every thousand hides went toward completing the forty thousand which we were to collect before we could say good-by to California.

---

wine

new wine in old bottles
new ideas or innovations imposed on an older system or organization, usually with the implication of incompatibility. The phrase is based on the proverb *you can't put new wine in old bottles*, which alludes to the passage in Matthew 9:17 in which Christ speaks of the new order his earthly mission will bring (in the Authorized Version, 1611): 'Neither do men put new wine in old bottles: else the bottles break, and the wine runneth out, and the bottles perish: but they put new wine into new bottles, and both are preserved'. Allusive uses date from the 17th cent.

George Wither *Predictions of the Overthrow of Popery* 1660
With new Wine our old Bottles must be fill'd, | (Endangering Wine and Bottles to be spill'd) | Till such as are in power be pleased to hear | The Counsel of a slighted Engineer.

Henry David Thoreau *Walden* 1854
Perhaps we should never procure a new suit, however ragged or dirty the old, until we have so conducted, so enterprised or sailed in some way, that we feel like new men in the old, and that to retain it would be like keeping new wine in old bottles.

wine and dine
to enjoy oneself or entertain somebody with good food and wine: recorded slightly earlier in the reverse order *dine and wine. 19th cent.*

Hugh MacDiarmid *Penny Wheep* 1926
And, dined and wined, | Solicitors find | Their platitudes assume | The guise of intuitions that illume | The hidden heart | Of Human Art.

wine, women, and song
a life of enjoyment traditionally sought after by men: references to wine and women are recorded from the 17th cent.; Byron in *Don Juan* refers to

'wine and women, mirth and laughter' (and 'sermons and soda water the day after'); and *song* was added later in the 19th cent.

Thackeray The Adventures of Philip 1862
Then sing as Doctor Luther sang, | As Doctor Luther sang, | Who loves not wine, woman, and song, | He is a fool his whole life long.

wing

in the wings
in the background; available when needed: often in the form *waiting in the wings*. The wings of a theatre are the areas to the side of the stage and out of sight of the audience, where actors wait to make their entrances. The transition to metaphor can be seen in an article by Henry James published in *Atlantic Monthly* in 1876: 'The author has given him a mother who ... has been kept waiting in the wing, as it were, for many acts.' *19th cent.*

on the wing
on the move; active: a metaphor from the flight of birds. *16th cent.*

Shakespeare Hamlet II.ii.133 (1601)
[Polonius to the King and Queen] But what might you think, | When I had seen this hot love on the wing, | As I perceived it – I must tell you that – | Before my daughter told me, ... | If I had played the desk or table book, | Or given my heart a winking, mute and dumb, | Or looked upon this love with idle sight?

on a wing and a prayer
informal relying entirely on hope in a difficult situation or predicament: originally the title of a song (in full 'Comin' in on a Wing and a Prayer'), and referring to the emergency landing of aircraft. *Mid 20th cent.*

Today 1992
Wright has lightning pace and a fabulous eye for goal. He's a wing and a prayer player, a nervous performer who hasn't really got a clue how good he is.

spread/stretch/try one's wings
to try out new ideas or activities. *19th cent.*

Trollope The Prime Minister 1876
When I found myself the son-in-law of a very rich man I thought I might spread my wings a bit. But

my rich father-in-law threw me over, and now I am helpless.

under somebody's wing
in somebody's care or patronage, especially while trying new ventures or experiences. *Middle English*

Fletcher & Massinger The Custom of the Countrey 1647
His childhood I passe, as being brought up | Under my wing; and growing ripe for study, | I overcame the tendernesse, and joye | I had to looke upon him, and provided | The choicest Masters, and of greatest name | Of Salamanca, in all liberall Arts.

winged words
words that are full of meaning and significance: an image taken from Homer and first used in translations of the *Iliad* and *Odyssey* by Chapman, Dryden, and others. In Homer *epea pteroenta* are not necessarily utterances full of meaning and significance but simply communications that reach the hearer, as distinct from those (*aptera*) that remain unspoken or go unheard. They occur, for example, in book XVII of the *Odyssey*, when Telemachus greets his mother Penelope and tells her to bathe her face and put on fresh clothes and prepare for the arrival of a guest: a typical translation is 'the words he spoke did not go unheeded'. Chapman and his fellow translators presumably intended in their translations the same as Homer, but their readers misunderstood and invested 'winged words' with an unintended grandeur. The metaphor also occurs in Spenser's *The Faerie Queene* (1596): 'So he the words into his ballaunce threw, | But streight the winged words out of his ballaunce flew.' *16th cent.*

See also CLIP somebody's wings.

wink

The oldest meaning, from Middle English and reflected in some of the phrases, is 'the closing of the eyes in sleep'.

(as) easy as winking
informal extremely easy: also slightly earlier in the form *like winking* = very easily or readily. *Early 20th cent.*

William Fox *Willoughby's Phoney War* 1991
Peregrine didn't think he was important enough to interest the Special Branch. Compared with Charity, he was a mere minnow capable of slipping through the net as easy as winking.

not sleep a wink
to stay awake all night, especially from worry or excitement. The phrase goes back in various forms to Middle English.

Head & Kirkman *The English Rogue Described* 1674
It was past midnight, they all slept better than the Countrey-man, who could hardly sleep a wink for thinking of his Misfortunes.

See also have FORTY winks; in the blink/twinkling/wink of an EYE; a nod's as good as a wink *at* NOD.

wipe

wipe the floor with somebody
informal to defeat or humiliate somebody decisively. *Mid 20th cent.*

Owen Chadwick *Michael Ramsey: a Life* 1991
Young John Lucas, who lived hard by and sat on Professor Ramsey's head to recite Greek verbs, heard stories from his father of Ramsey taking on atheists in the university in public debate and wiping the floor with them.

wipe the smile off somebody's face
to shock somebody out of a mood of self-satisfaction or glee: also in variant forms with *grin*, *scowl*, *leer*, etc. The use of *wipe* in the figurative sense of obliterating or effacing dates from the 16th cent.: in *1 Henry IV* (1596), the Earl of Northumberland tells Morton, who has brought news (1.i.210), 'I knew of this before, but, to speak truth, | This present grief had wiped it from my mind.' The present phrase dates from the early 20th cent.

William C De Mille *Strongheart* 1905
Every one of you men has got to realize what depends on this. Nelson, wipe that smile off your face.

See also wipe the SLATE clean.

wire

get one's wires crossed
to misunderstand or confuse one's information: with allusion to having a crossed line in telephoning. *Early 20th cent.*

Edward Peple *A Pair of Sixes* 1914
[Coddles] *You can't catch me – you can't catch me! … I've got me fingers crossed! I've got me fingers crossed!* [Johns] *You've got your wires crossed.*

P G Wodehouse *Hot Water* 1932
Can we by any chance have got the wires crossed? … It was the idea, wasn't it, that we should pile on to a pot of tea together?

See also be a live wire *at* LIVE².

wisdom

in his/her/their wisdom
for reasons that do not seem justified or well founded: originally in the form *God in his wisdom* with reference to divine actions that are difficult to comprehend, and then used ironically to express doubt about the wisdom of what somebody has said or done. *19th cent.*

Kipling *The Madness of Private Ortheris* 1888
I ordered him to wait where he was until it was dark enough for me to ride into the Station without my dress being noticed. Now God in His Wisdom has made the heart of the British Soldier, who is very often an unlicked ruffian, as soft as the heart of a little child.

wise

(it is easy to be) wise after the event
(proverb) we are all better aware of the right course of action in a situation when it is over and the implications are clearer. The phrase is first found in its current form in the 17th cent., although the notion is found earlier in other forms.

Ben Jonson *Epicoene, or the Silent Woman* 1620
Away, thou strange justifier of thyself, to be wiser than thou wert, by the event.

be none the wiser / not be any the wiser
1 to be unaware of something that has happened. *16th cent.*

Shakespeare *Henry V* iv.i.193 (1599)
[King Harry to Williams, an English soldier] *I myself heard the King say he would not be ransomed. [Williams] Ay, he said so, to make us fight cheerfully, but when our throats are cut he may be ransomed, and we ne'er the wiser.*

2 to know no more than one did before, typically because the information given is useless or unintelligible. *17th cent.*

James Fenimore Cooper *Pathfinder* 1840
It may be all as you say, friend Cap, but I am none the wiser for your words; and, in ticklish times, the plainer a man makes his English, the easier he is understood.

put somebody wise (to something)
informal to give somebody the necessary information to understand a situation or correct a misapprehension. *19th cent.*

See also a (wise) man of GOTHAM.

wish

if wishes were horses (beggars would ride)
(proverb) a warning not to rely too much on one's hopes and suppositions. The modern currency of the phrase owes much to the inclusion of the nursery rhyme in James Halliwell's collection of 1846: 'If wishes were horses | Beggars would ride; | If turnips were watches, | I would wear one by my side.' There have been many variants, some going back to the 17th cent., for example 'If wishes were butter-cakes beggars would bite', 'If wishes would bide, beggars would ride.' The second of these marks a transition to the form that is now familiar.

the wish is father to the thought
we often believe something because we want it to be so: with allusion to Shakespeare, 2 *Henry IV* (1597) iv.iii.221 '[Prince Harry] I never thought to hear you speak again. [King Henry] Thy wish was father, Harry, to that thought. I stay too long by thee, I weary thee.' Allusive uses are uncommon before the 19th cent. *16th cent.*

William Crafts *The Sea Serpent* 1819
[Molly] *E'en when I sleep, my thoughts to thee are carried, | And oft I dream, heigho: that we are married. [Tom] Thy wish was father, Molly, to that thought, | And if we are not married, why we ought.*

Thackeray *The Adventures of Philip* 1862
'Father and mother's orders,' shouts Philip, 'I daresay, Mrs. Pendennis; but the wish was father to the thought of parting, and it was for the black-amoor's parks and acres that the girl jilted me.'

See also wish somebody JOY of something.

wit

The noun *wit*, which underlies most of the phrases below, has several strands of meaning, the oldest of which denotes human intellect and reasoning. From Middle English the plural form *wits* referred to mental capacity and the power to think and reason. One could be *out of one's wits* just as one could be *out of one's senses* (see below). From this core meaning the notion of good intellectual capacity developed, and then cleverness and capacity for intelligent humour, which is the predominant modern sense of the word. The verb *wit* (derived from Old English *witan* 'to know') is present in *to wit*, which survives in modern use as a conscious archaism.

be at one's wits' end
to be utterly baffled about what to do: formerly written as *wit's* (singular), but now usually understood as *wits'* (plural), the meaning in both cases being 'the faculty of thinking and reasoning'. The phrase is found in Middle English in Langland's poem *Piers Plowman*, and in Chaucer (see below).

Chaucer *Troilus and Criseyde* iii.931
But whether that ye dwelle or for hym go, | I am, til God me bettre mynde sende, | At dulcarnoon [= in a perplexed state], right at my wittes ende.

Thomas Dekker *The Shoemaker's Holiday* 1600
[Hodge] *My Lord, we are at our wits end for roome, those hundred tables wil not feast the fourth part of them.*

be frightened/scared out of one's wits
to be terrified: *in* (or *out of*) *one's wits*, referring to a person's sanity, dates from the 15th cent. The expression occurs in Shakespeare's *The Merry Wives of Windsor* (1597) ii.i.131 '[Mistress Page] Here's a fellow frights English out of his wits', and *King Lear* (1606) iv.1.56 '[Edgar] Poor Tom hath been scared out of his good wits.' *16th cent.*

gather/collect one's wits
to recover one's composure or equanimity. *16th cent.*

Robert Greene *Gwydonius* 1584
Valericus … was so rapte in admiration of her eloquence, and so ravisht in the contemplation of hir beautie, that he stoode in a maze not able to utter one word, until at last gathering his wits together, he burst foorth into these speeches.

have/keep one's wits about one
to be mentally alert. *17th cent.*

Dekker & Webster *Westward Hoe* 1607
Well said; wast not a most treacherous part to arrest a man in the night, and when he is almost drunk, when he hath not his wits about him to remember which of his friends is in the Subsedy.

live by one's wits
to make a living by clever or unscrupulous methods rather than by regular work. *19th cent.*

Edgar Allan Poe *The Man of the Crowd* 1840
Very often, in company with these sharpers, I observed an order of men somewhat different in habits, but still birds of a kindred feather. They may be defined as the gentlemen who live by their wits. They seem to prey upon the public in two battalions – that of the dandies and that of the military men.

pit one's wits against somebody/something
to use one's mental resources competitively. *Early 20th cent.*

Edgar Rice Burroughs *The Monstermen* 1929
Von Horn stepped aboard. He was armed only with a brace of Colts, and he was going into the heart of the wild country of the head hunters, to pit his wits against those of the wily Muda Saffir.

to wit
namely, that is to say. *Wit* here is the Old English verb *witan*, which was eventually superseded by *know*, although it is cognate with the noun *wit* which is still in use. *To wit* is a shortening of an older (Middle English) expression *that is to wit* meaning 'that is to say'. The phrase now sounds dated or even archaic. *16th cent.*

Shakespeare *Henry V* I.ii.50 (1599)
Charles the Great having subdu'd the Saxons, | There left behind and settled certain French | Who, holding in disdain the German women | For some dishonest manners of their life, | Established there this law: to wit, no female | Should be inheritrix in Salic land.

witch

the witching hour
the middle of the night, when witches are said to be abroad: with allusion to Shakespeare, *Hamlet* (1601) III.ii.377 '[Hamlet] 'Tis now the very witching time of night, | When churchyards yawn, and hell itself breathes out | Contagion to this world.' *17th cent.*

David Garrick *Cymon* 1766
Nothing can controul | The beating tempest of my restless soul! | While I prepare, in this dark witching hour, | My potent spells, and call forth all my power.

withdrawal

get/have/experience withdrawal symptoms
to suffer from a state of depression when deprived of something enjoyable. The phrase was originally used as a medical term describing the physical and emotional effects of ceasing to take an addictive drug or indulge in an addictive habit such as smoking. It rapidly took on extended meanings referring to all sorts of pleasures, habits, and ways of life that are taken away or come to an abrupt end for any reason. Like many such phrases of medical origin, it has been much trivialized. *Early 20th cent.*

Janet Mattinson et al *Marriage Inside Out* 1989
Even a career woman will have organized her life and work to take account of the children in a way men, at present, rarely have to do. So it is the woman who will experience the first withdrawal symptoms. Some will revel in having more time for themselves; others will feel lost.

wither
See wither on the VINE.

wobbly

throw a wobbly
informal to have a tantrum or a fit of nerves. *Wobbly* is a noun use of the adjective meaning 'unsteady, tending to wobble.' *Late 20th cent.*

She 1989
If your marriage is on the rocks, the thing to do is throw a wobbly on a motorway at night so that your husband will put you out at the next lay-by.

wolf

cry wolf
to raise a false alarm, risking the possibility of not being taken seriously when help is genuinely needed. The phrase alludes to the fable of the shepherd boy who repeatedly called for help against an imaginary wolf; when a wolf did appear, nobody believed him. The phrase appears as part of this story in translations of Aesop (e.g. by L'Estrange, 1692), and allusive uses in free context date from the 19th cent.

> Browning *The Ring and the Book* 1842
> *Such an one, to disprove the frightful charge,* | *What will she but exaggerate chastity,* | *Err in excess of wifehood, as it were,* | *Renounce even levities permitted youth ...* | *Cry 'wolf' i' the sheepfold, where's the sheep dares bleat,* | *Knowing the shepherd listens for a growl?*

have/hold a wolf by the ears
to be in a dangerous situation: from Latin *lupum auribus tenere*. Cf have a TIGER by the tail. *16th cent.*

> Nahum Tate *Injur'd Love* 1707
> [Zanche] *You love the Infidel, have sworn it to her.* [Flamineo] *I own I have made Love to the Moor,* | *And I do Love her – just as a Man holds* | *A Wolf by the Ears.*

keep the wolf from the door
to have enough money or food for survival: there are earlier (including biblical) references to the wolf as a symbol of impending hunger or famine. The phrase is entered in John Heywood's collections of proverbs of 1546. *16th cent.*

> Francis Kirkman *The Unlucky Citizen* 1673
> *He always had a plentiful estate, and wherewith at the worst to keep the wolf from the door.*

throw somebody to the wolves
to save one's own position by betraying a friend or ally to one's rivals or enemies: from the former travellers' practice of casting one person off a sleigh when attacked by a pack of wolves. Cf throw somebody to the lions *at* LION. *Early 20th cent.*

Kristy McCallum *Driven by Love* 1993
'*Kate, I need your co-operation. I'm fed up with being the target for all those unattached girls who fancy that being seen with me will give them a leg-up in their dubious careers! Don't worry, I won't really throw you to the wolves. You'll just have to put up with being labelled as my latest girlfriend!' 'I can't think of anything I'd loathe more!'*

a wolf in sheep's clothing
a person who appears friendly but conceals hostile intentions. The phrase is recorded earlier (15th cent.) in the form *a wolf in a lamb's skin* and other variants (as in Shakespeare, *1 Henry VI* (1590) I.iv.54: '[Gloucester to Winchester] Thee I'll chase hence, thou wolf in sheep's array') and sometimes used with allusion to Matthew 7:15: 'Beware of false prophets, which come to you in sheep's clothing, but inwardly they are ravening wolves.' The phrase dates from the 18th cent. in its current form.

woman

See a man/woman of letters *at* LETTER; a man/woman of the WORLD.

wonder

the eighth wonder of the world
informal something wonderful or exciting, especially an innovation: also applied ironically to a self-satisfied or arrogant person. Such a person or thing joins the traditional 'seven wonders' of the ancient world, a canon of magnificent buildings and monuments drawn up in Hellenistic times (3rd–2nd cent. BC) and comprising: the Pyramids of Egypt, the Hanging Gardens of Babylon, the Mausoleum (tomb of Mausolus of Caria) at Halicarnassus, the Temple of Artemis at Ephesus, Pheidias' statue of Zeus at Olympia, the Colossus (colossal bronze statue of the sun god Helios) of Rhodes, and the Pharos (lighthouse) at Alexandria. Other versions of the list were drawn up in later times to include more recent buildings such as the Leaning Tower of Pisa and Stonehenge. The title 'Wonder of the World' (unnumbered) was applied to several medieval rulers, including the Holy Roman Emperor Otto III (980–1002) for his scholarship rather than his political wisdom. In the 17th cent. the phrase was also applied to

the Escorial, the royal palace of Philip II of Spain (1556–98). *17th cent.*

Philip Ayres The Revengeful Mistress 1696
The other palace ... is that celebrated house, the Escurial, built by King Philip the Second ... The Spaniards term this magnificent pile the Eighth Wonder of the World: And well they may; for 'tis of so prodigious a bulk, that it seems capacious enough to lodge the inhabitants of a small city.

no/small/little wonder
it is hardly surprising and only to be expected (that something has happened, is the case, etc). *Middle English*

Chaucer The Summoner's Prologue (line 1673)
This Frere [= Friar] bosteth that he knoweth helle, | And God it woot [= God knows] that it is litel wonder; | Freres and feendes [= fiends] been but lyte asonder [= are not far apart].

work/do wonders
to bring considerable benefits, especially of a dramatic or unexpected kind: originally with reference to acts of a miraculous nature attributed to supernatural powers. *Middle English*

Francis Bacon Essays 1601
And yet boldness is a child of ignorance and baseness, far inferior to other parts. But nevertheless it doth fascinate, and bind hand and foot, those that are either shallow in judgment, or weak in courage, which are the greatest part; yea and prevaileth with wise men at weak times. Therefore we see it hath done wonders, in popular states.

See also a NINE days' wonder.

wood

be out of the woods
to be no longer in danger. *18th cent.*

Edgar Allan Poe X-ing the Paragrab 1849
The great Bullet-head sat up until day-break, consuming the midnight oil, and absorbed in the composition of the really unparalleled paragraph, which follows: 'So ho, John! how now? Told you so, you know. Don't crow, another time, before you're out of the woods!'

not see the wood for the trees
to fail to understand the essential point because of paying too much attention to the details involved. *16th cent.*

Nathaniel Woodes The Conflict of Conscience 1586
Doo your lyps blinde your eyes? Why, I was in place long before you came: But you could not see the wood for the trees.

touch / knock on wood
to avert bad luck by touching a wooden object: often used as an involuntary exclamation to accompany a boast or a claim that tempts providence in some way. *Knock on wood* is the usual American form of the phrase. The magic worked by wood is a common feature of folklore, normally playing protective roles, and there are many ancient associations: the pagan belief in tree spirits, the transfer of disease to trees by walking round them or drilling holes in them, the wood of the Christian cross, the practice of touching wood to avert danger or capture. In fact the earliest occurrences of the phrase in print are surprisingly recent and are closely associated with children's tag games, in particular the taunt when being chased: 'Tiggy, tiggy, touch wood, I've got no wood.' *19th cent.*

wooden

See accept a wooden NICKEL; win the wooden SPOON.

woodshed

something nasty in the woodshed
informal something unpleasant that is kept hidden away. The phrase comes from Stella Gibbons' novel *Cold Comfort Farm* (1932), a humorous parody of contemporary novels about country life, in which a cheerful young heroine, Flora Poste, visits her cousins in a dreary Sussex farmhouse dominated by an eccentric Aunt (Ada Doom). In her childhood, as she keeps reminding everyone including herself, Aunt Ada had a traumatic experience ('When you were very small – so small that the lightest puff of breeze blew your little crinoline skirt over your head – you had seen something nasty in the woodshed. You'd never forgotten it ... You told them you were mad. You had been mad since you saw something nasty in the woodshed, years and years and years ago.'). Exactly what this experience was (or whether it occurred at all) is left to the reader's imagination, but Aunt Ada exploits it ruthlessly to feign her madness and as

a pretext for demanding constant attention from the family around her. *Mid 20th cent.*

> Beryl Bainbridge *Another Part of the Wood* 1968
> *They had all, Joseph, brother Trevor, the younger sister … come across something nasty in the woodshed, mother or father or both, having it off with someone else.*

take somebody to the woodshed

informal, chiefly NAmer to reprimand or punish somebody discreetly: also in variant forms. From the traditional practice of taking a badly-behaved child for punishment out of the sight and hearing of other people. *Early 20th cent.*

woodwork

crawl out of the woodwork

informal to appear suddenly or mysteriously: usually with reference to somebody or something unpleasant or unwelcome, the image being of insects or vermin crawling out of crevices and other hidden places in a building. To *crawl back into the woodwork* is to vanish in similar circumstances. *Mid 20th cent.*

> John Le Carré *Smiley's People* 1979
> *George Smiley, sometime Chief of the Secret Service … had one night come out of the woodwork to peer at some dead foreigner.*

wool

all wool and a yard wide

informal of the finest quality: originally applied to cloth. *19th cent.*

> Harold Frederic *The Damnation of Theron Ware* 1896
> *He's a trifle skittish sometimes when you don't give him free rein; but he's all wool an' a yard wide when it comes to right-down hard-pan religion.*

pull the wool over somebody's eyes

informal, originally NAmer to deceive somebody with evasions and untruths. The allusion is generally thought to be to the wearing of wigs, which with their tight curls have a woollen appearance. To pull the wool over somebody's eyes was to pull their wig down and make it impossible for them to see. We might expect more 18th cent. evidence if this is the true origin, unless the phrase arose in legal circles (in which wigs are still worn). Another proposed association with sheep farming, and pulling the fleece over the sheep's eyes to calm it during shearing, is less likely, and has the ring of popular etymology about it. *19th cent.*

> Horatio Alger *Cast upon the Breakers* 1893
> *Look here, Mr. Wheeler, if that is your name, you can't pull the wool over my eyes. You are a thief, neither more nor less.*

word

eat one's words

to be forced to retract something one asserted earlier, especially in a humiliating or public manner. Eating is a common metaphor for this kind of personal climbdown: *see also* eat one's HAT; eat HUMBLE pie. *16th cent.*

> Henry More *Philosophical Poems* 1647
> *What sober man will dare once to avouch | An infinite number of dispersed starres? | This one absurdity will make him crouch | And eat his words.*

have a word in somebody's ear

to speak to somebody privately or in confidence. *See also* (a word) in your shell-like ear *at* SHELL. *16th cent.*

> Shakespeare *Much Ado About Nothing* IV.ii.27 (1598)
> [Dogberry to Borachio] *Come you hither, sirrah. A word in your ear, sir.*

a man/woman of few words

a reserved or taciturn person, somebody who does not say much. There is play on words and actions in Shakespeare's *Henry V* (1599) III.ii.34 '[Boy] For Nim, he hath heard that men of few words are the best men, and therefore he scorns to say his prayers … But his few bad words are matched with as few good deeds – for a [= he] never broke any man's head but his own, and that was against a post, when he was drunk.' And in *Much Ado About Nothing* (1598), Don John, the villain of the piece, is a malign presence because he is so taciturn; at I.i.151 he replies to Leonato's welcome with the words 'I thank you. I am not of many words, but I thank you.' A *man* (or *woman*) *of many words*, by contrast, would be a talkative or verbose one; but this version is normally used in the negative, and is therefore equivalent to our original phrase (e.g. Jane Austen's description of Mrs Ferrers in *Sense and Sens-*

ibility (1811) as 'not a woman of many words'). *16th cent.*

a man/woman of his/her word

an honest and dependable person. *19th cent.*

Dickens *Pickwick Papers* 1837
'He says if he can't see you afore to-morrow night's over, he vishes he may be somethin'-unpleasanted if he don't drownd hisself.' 'Oh no, no, Mr. Weller!' said Arabella, clasping her hands. 'That's wot he says, miss,' replied Sam. 'He's a man of his word, and it's my opinion he'll do it, miss.'

not have a good word (to say) for somebody/ something

to dislike or be contemptuous of a person or thing. *19th cent.*

Henry William Herbert *The Lord of the Manor* 1844
And oh! why will he associate himself with comrades such as Lord Henry, and this Captain Spencer, of whom no man or woman had ever yet one good word to say – whose very glance is poison!

not the word (for it)

hardly the right description for a person or thing: normally used as an ironic comment on something another speaker has said. *The word* in the sense 'the right or appropriate word' dates from the 16th cent. (e.g. Shakespeare, *Cymbeline* (1610) v.v.247 '[Jailer] Come, sir, are you ready for death? [Posthumus] Over-roasted rather; ready long ago. [Jailer] Hanging is the word, sir. If you be ready for that, you are well cooked'). *19th cent.*

Wilkie Collins *The Moonstone* 1868
'I am glad to find, from what I have seen upstairs,' I said, 'that you resisted the secret Dictate.' 'Resisted isn't the word,' answered Betteredge. 'Wrostled is the word. I wrostled, sir, between the silent orders in my bosom pulling me one way, and the written orders in my pocket-book pushing me the other.'

say/give the word

to give the order to proceed: *word* in the sense 'order, command' dates from Old English, and in the form *the word* from the 16th cent. *16th cent.*

Shakespeare *Henry V* iv.vi.38 (1599)
[King Harry] *The French have reinforced their scattered men. Then every soldier kill his prisoners. Give the word through.*

take somebody at their word

to interpret what somebody says literally, and act or expect them to act accordingly. *16th cent.*

Shakespeare *The Comedy of Errors* i.ii.17 (1594)
[Antipholus of Syracuse to Dromio of Syracuse] *For with long travel I am stiff and weary.* | *Get thee away.* [Dromio] *Many a man would take you at your word,* | *And go indeed, having so good a mean.*

take somebody's word for it

to believe what somebody has said without seeking further evidence or proof: *take my word for it* is used in speech as an assurance that the speaker is telling the truth. *16th cent.*

Marmion Shackerley *A Fine Companion* 1633
[Aemillia] *By the title page of your face, I should judge you to be somewhat ancient.* [Dotario] *Take my word for it, the index is false printed, if you please to turne to the booke, you shall find no such thing written.*

too — for words

(used with an adjective) extremely —; literally, so — that words cannot be found for it. *Early 20th cent.*

Clyde Fitch *The Woman in the Case* 1904
[Julian] *Any news?* [Margaret] *Yes, dear Julian! And the same good news always! Everyone I know, believing in you absolutely, – fighting for you! Everyone too kind for words to me! I've not heard a soul who doubts that the trial will be a triumph for you.*

word for word

using exactly the same words. *Middle English*

Chaucer *The Legend of Good Women: The Legend of Dido* (line 1001)
I coude folwe, word for word, Virgile, | *But it wolde lasten al to longe while.*

—'s word is his/her bond

so-and-so keeps his or her promises. *19th cent.*

R L Stevenson *Kidnapped* 1886
'There,' said he, 'that'll show you! I'm a queer man, and strange wi' strangers; but my word is my bond, and there's the proof of it.'

—'s word is law

so-and-so must be obeyed unquestioningly. *18th cent.*

Henry Fielding *The History of Tom Jones* 1749
As he could not prevail on himself to abandon these [his dogs], he contrived very cunningly to enjoy their company, together with that of his daughter, by insisting on her riding a-hunting with him.

Sophia, to whom her father's word was a law, readily complied with his desires, though she had not the least delight in a sport, which was of too rough and masculine a nature to suit with her disposition.

the word on the street
current popular opinion or gossip. *20th cent.*

New Musical Express 1992
Cell ... from Hoboken, New Jersey, slung a 45 out on Thurston Moore's Ecstatic Peace! label a couple of months ago and the word on the street was that here comes the New Nirvs! Cell have got all that – and more – going for them, without having to resort to drooling over Kurt Cobain's toe caps.

a word to the wise (is enough)
(proverb) a hint or tip should be sufficient warning for somebody: also in early use in variant forms such as *few words may serve the wise.* The Latin version is *verbum sapienti sat est* (also abbreviated to *verb. sap.*). *16th cent.*

Ben Jonson The Case is Altered 1609
[Juniper] *Presto. Go to, a word to the wise, away, flie? vanish.*

See also by word of MOUTH; have/say the last word *at* LAST[1]; in words of one SYLLABLE; put words into somebody's MOUTH; winged words *at* WING; a word in your shell-like ear *at* SHELL.

---

work

do its work
to have the expected or desired effect. *18th cent.*

Frances Sheridan Conclusion of the Memoirs of Miss Sidney Bidulph 1767
Mrs. Askham, said she, smiling, and taking me by the hand, as I sat at her bed-side, I'll tell you a secret; then lowering her voice (for her waiting-maid was in the room) I am going very fast, said she; this last blow has struck home and effectually done its work. I was obliged to whip out my handkerchief, and could only answer, God forbid, madam!

Dickens Pickwick Papers 1837
The brandy and water had done its work; the amiable countenance of Mr. Pickwick was fast recovering its customary expression.

give somebody the works
1 *informal* to tell somebody everything, to give them the whole story. *Early 20th cent.*

Alice T Ellis Unexplained Laughter 1985
Another regrettable aspect of her personality impelled her to smile specially at this man. She had lost her love, and in her cottage was a woman preparing a possibly sapphic salad; so Lydia gave him the works. His casual, countryman's demeanour altered perceptibly and he stood still, looking at her.

2 *informal* to kill somebody. *Early 20th cent.*

C F Coe Hooch 1929
This man never was bumped here at all. They gave him the works some place a long way off.

3 *informal* to give somebody the best or most elaborate treatment (either pleasant or unpleasant). *Early 20th cent.*

Michael Dibdin Ratking 1989
I want that car brought in, turned over to the laboratory and given the works.

in the works
informal, chiefly N Amer in process of development or completion: *cf* in the PIPELINE. *Late 20th cent.*

Esquire 1991
Seth's new career earned him a fifty-thousand dollar advance for the paperback edition, and a European version was in the works.

a nasty/filthy piece/bit of work
somebody very unpleasant or threatening. In modern use *nasty* is more usual. *17th cent.*

Shakespeare Timon of Athens I.i.203 (1609)
[Timon] *Wrought he not well that painted it?* [Apemantus] *He wrought better that made the painter; and yet he's but a filthy piece of work.*

Mike Ripley Just Another Angel 1989
I sat down on the sofa next to her and patted her hand. 'He's a nasty piece of work and if he comes back you treat him just the same as this afternoon. He has a nasty track record, you know. He follows young girls home from school.'

work to rule
to follow the rules of one's work precisely and so reduce efficiency, especially as a form of industrial protest (called a *work-to-rule*). *Mid 20th cent.*

M Holborn et al Sociology: Themes and Perspectives 1991
Weber suggests that individual manual workers who are dissatisfied with their class situation may respond in a variety of ways. They may grumble, work to rule, sabotage industrial machinery, take

strike action or attempt to organize other members of their class in an effort to overthrow capitalism.

See also have one's work CUT out; work one's ass off *at* ASS[2]; work one's fingers to the BONE; work like a BEAVER; work one's TICKET.

---

workman

a bad workman blames his tools
(proverb) somebody who has done a job badly will try to blame the lack of good equipment rather than admit to poor performance. The proverb is recorded in George Herbert's *Outlandish Proverbs* (published posthumously in 1640) in the form *never had ill workeman good tooles*. Despite a gap of three centuries the English version is possibly related to the medieval French proverb *mauvés ovriers ne trovera ja bon hostill* 'a bad workman never finds a good tool'. But platitudes are always capable of random re-invention. *17th cent.*

---

world

all the world and his wife
everybody imaginable; a great crowd. The phrase was first used by Jonathan Swift in his satirical dialogues called *A Complete Collection of Polite and Ingenious Conversation* (1738): '[Miss] Pray, Madam, who were the Company? [Lady Smart] Why, there was all the World, and his Wife.' Lord Byron, writing to Sir Walter Scott in 1822, refers to the expression as a proverb: '"All the world and his wife", as the proverb goes, were trying to trample upon me.' Then, some forty years later, Dickens (in *Our Mutual Friend*, 1865) was elaborating on it: 'All the world and his wife and daughter leave cards.' *18th cent.*

(be in) a world of one's own
to be absorbed in one's own thoughts and oblivious of one's surroundings. The phrase in a recognizable form dates from the 18th cent., although earlier writers come close to the notion, notably Charles Cotton in his English versions of Lucian (*Burlesque upon Burlesque*, 1675): 'But she is gone (I speak it quaking, | The sleeping Lioness for waking) | To write in a new world of her own making.'

Richard Steele *The Tender Husband* 1705
You must understand, the young lady by being kept

from the world, has made a world of her own – She has spent all her solitude in reading romances, her head is full of shepherds, knights, flowery meads, groves and streams, so that if you talk like a man of this world to her, you do nothing.

the best of all possible worlds
life as it is, for better or worse. The phrase is derived from the words spoken by Pangloss in Voltaire's *Candide* (1759): *tout est pour le mieux dans le meilleur des mondes possibles* ('all's for the best in the best of all possible worlds'). This extended proverbial form is also found in English. *Candide*, in which Pangloss's words are ridiculed by a series of disastrous events, is a parody of the philosophy of optimism propounded by the German philosopher Leibniz (1646–1716). *Possible* is used in its philosophical sense 'logically conceivable'. The phrase occurs in 18th cent. translations of Voltaire, and allusive uses free of this context date from the 19th cent.

W Rider transl Voltaire's *Candide* 1759
Pangloss read Lectures in Metaphisico-theologo-cosmolonigology. He demonstrated that there can be no Effect without a Cause, that in this best of possible Worlds, the Baron's Castle was the finest, and my Lady the best of all possible Baronesses.

James Hall *Tales of the Border* 1835
The priest mourned over the depravity of the human race, and especially deprecated the frivolous habits of his countrymen; the valet not only believed this to be the best of all possible worlds, but prided himself particularly in being a native of a country which produces the best fiddlers, cooks, and barbers, on the habitable globe.

G B Shaw *The Shewing-up of Blanco Posnet* 1911
The administrative departments were consuming miles of red tape in the correctest forms of activity, and ... everything was for the best in the best of all possible worlds.

R Aldington *The Colonel's Daughter* 1931
The smug bastards who declare that all is for the best in this best of all possible worlds.

the best of both/all worlds
advantages derived from more than one set of circumstances at the same time. The phrase is partly derived from the proverb *all is best in the best of all (possible) worlds*, itself derived in translation from Voltaire's *Candide* (see above), but the meaning is somewhat different. *18th cent.*

carry the world before one

to be spectacularly successful. *19th cent.*

> Kipling *The Second Jungle Book* 1895
> *A berg that seemed ready to carry the world before it would ground helplessly, reel over, and wallow in a lather of foam and mud, and flying frozen spray, while a much smaller and lower one would rip and ride into the flat floe, flinging tons of rubbish on either side.*

come into the world

to be born. The phrase is used with (conscious or unconscious) allusion to the biblical passage John 1:9 (in the Authorized Version, 1611) 'That was the true Light, which lighteth every man that cometh into the world.' The phrase is found in early Bible translations, including Wyclif. Shakespeare's *The Comedy of Errors* (1594) concludes with the two Dromios leaving the stage, one saying to the other (v.i.429) 'We came into the world like brother and brother, | And now let's go hand in hand, not one before another.'

come up in the world

to improve one's social status, especially by becoming wealthy: early uses have *get up* instead of *come up*. *Come up* alone was used in the 16th cent. with the same meaning, but is now obsolete. *19th cent.*

> George Borrow *Lavengro* 1851
> *But as he got up in the world he began to look down on me. I believe he was ashamed of the obligation under which he lay to me.*

go/come down in the world

to suffer a decline in social status; to become poorer. *19th cent.*

> Dickens *Oliver Twist* 1838
> *Nor were there wanting other indications of the good gentleman's having gone down in the world of late; for a great scarcity of furniture, and total absence of comfort, together with the disappearance of all such small moveables as spare clothes and linen, bespoke a state of extreme poverty.*

look/sound for all the world like somebody/something

to resemble somebody or something so closely that nobody can tell the difference: *for all the world* is recorded in the sense 'in every respect' or 'utterly' from the time of Chaucer. *18th cent.*

> Henry Fielding *The History of Tom Jones* 1749
> *One of them is dressed as fine as any princess; and, to be sure, she looks for all the world like one.*

a man/woman of the world

a person who is widely experienced in dealing with people. A *man of the world* was originally a secular person as distinct from a cleric, then a worldly or irreligious person (used as such in the Prayer of David at Psalms 17:14 '[Keep me] from men of the world, which have their portion in this life'), and the current meaning developed from this. *18th cent.*

> Henry Fielding *The History of Tom Jones* 1749
> *This gentleman whom Mr Jones now visited, was what they call a man of the world; that is to say, a man who directs his conduct in this world as one, who being fully persuaded there is no other, is resolved to make the most of this.*

out of this world

1 *informal* excellent; superb beyond description. *Early 20th cent.*

2 *informal* bizarre or repulsive: less common than the first meaning. *Mid 20th cent.*

the world, the flesh, and the devil

the sum total of human temptations: the three are associated in this way from the time of Chaucer. *Middle English*

> Chaucer *The Tale of Melibee* (line 1610)
> *Thou hast doon synne agayn* [= sinned against] *oure Lord Crist, for certes, the three enemys of mankynde – that is to seyn, the flessh, the feend* [= the devil], *and the world – thou hast suffred hem* [= them] *entre in to thyn herte wilfully by the wyndowes of thy body.*

See also not be LONG for this world; SET the world alight/on fire; THINK the world of something/somebody; the world is one's OYSTER.

worm

even a worm will turn

(proverb) the gentlest or most humble person will retaliate if provoked enough. *16th cent.*

> Shakespeare *3 Henry VI* II.ii.17 (1591)
> *The smallest worm will turn, being trodden on, | And doves will peck in safeguard of their brood.*

a worm's-eye view

a view of something as seen from the ground or regarded from a humble position: modelled on *a bird's-eye view* (see BIRD). *Early 20th cent.*

Punch 1908
We fear the population will develop balloon-necks through trying to get a worm's-eye view of the gas-bags in the haze.

See also FOOD for worms.

wormwood

wormwood and gall

a cause of great affliction and grief: with allusion to Lamentations 3:19 'Remembering mine affliction and my misery, the wormwood and the gall.' Both words are symbolic of bitterness: *gall* is bile secreted by the liver, and *wormwood* is a bitter-tasting aromatic plant, attested in allusive use from the 16th cent. The phrase in its current form is found from the 19th cent.

Charlotte Brontë *Jane Eyre* 1847
Exhausted by emotion, my language was more subdued than it generally was when it developed that sad theme; and mindful of Helen's warnings against the indulgence of resentment, I infused into the narrative far less of gall and wormwood than ordinary. Thus restrained and simplified, it sounded more credible: I felt as I went on that Miss Temple fully believed me.

worse

none the worse for something

not harmed or badly affected by something, or not made inferior by it. *19th cent.*

Dickens *Great Expectations* 1861
It occurred to me that if I could retain my bedroom in Barnard's Inn, my life would be agreeably varied, while my manners would be none the worse for Herbert's society.

Hardy *A Pair of Blue Eyes* 1873
'Admitting that Elfride could love another man after you,' said the elder, under the same varnish of careless criticism, 'she was none the worse for that experience.' 'The worse? Of course she was none the worse.'

so much the worse for —

used as a dismissive comment about somebody who is in an unfortunate situation but deserves no sympathy. *19th cent.*

Henry James *The Portrait of a Lady* 1881
Afterwards, however, she always remembered that one should never regret a generous error and that if Madame Merle had not the merits she attributed to her, so much the worse for Madame Merle.

the worse for wear

1 *informal* (said of a person) dishevelled or untidy, or showing signs of physical stress: from the (18th cent.) literal meaning 'deteriorated from extended wear', with particular reference to clothing. *Mid 20th cent.*

Morrell & McCarthy *Some Other Rainbow* 1993
When the agony abated he was prepared to laugh with me. It wasn't just a joke, but a reflection of his need to fight back. Often, this attitude had left him physically the worse for wear, but not mentally.

2 *informal* (said of a person) suffering from the effects of too much alcohol; slightly drunk. *Mid 20th cent.*

M Brown *Richard Branson: The Inside Story* 1989
Six weeks before the baby was due, Branson attended a dinner at the Venue. It was a long evening, and he arrived home at two in the morning, much the worse for wear. Shortly after falling into bed, he was awakened by an urgent voice in his ear, 'Richard. It's happening.'

worst

do one's worst

to do what harm or damage one can: often used as an ironic challenge. *15th cent.*

Shakespeare *King Lear* IV.v.134 (1606)
No, do thy worst, blind Cupid! I'll not love.

get/have the worst of it

to suffer defeat or disadvantage. *17th cent.*

Thomas D'Urfey *The Campaigners* 1698
[Kinglove] Oh 'tis without dispute, that we had the worst of it at Steenkirk by much, though our Men fought bravely 'tis true.

if the worst comes to the worst

if the bad circumstances envisaged actually come about: normally used to introduce some feared contingency. The form as given is attested earliest; a variant form *if the worse comes to the worst* occurs in Defoe, Thackeray, Mark Twain, Edgar Rice Burroughs, and other writers from the early 18th cent. to the 19th cent. and is still occasionally found. Some have argued that this is the more logical form (e.g. a contributor to *Notes & Queries* for October 1890, p.325), but if the notion is of a progression we would expect *bad* and not *worse* – which is no improvement on *worst* – as the starting point of the phrase, and such a form is not found. Arguably, the alignment *worst … worst* is indeed logical in the sense 'if the worst in imagination becomes the worst in fact'. Whatever the case, few phrases better illustrate the futility of demanding transparent logic from the formation of idiom in English or any language. *16th cent.*

> George Farquhar *The Constant Couple* 1700
> [Errand] *Telling the Truth hangs a Man, but confessing a Lye can do no harm, besides, if the worst comes to the worst, I can but deny it agen – Well, Sir, since I must tell you, I did kill him.*

See also be one's own worst ENEMY.

worth

for all one/it is worth

using all one's energy and enthusiasm. *19th cent.*

> Mark Twain *A Connecticut Yankee at the Court of King Arthur* 1889
> *One thing at a time, is my motto – and just play that thing for all it is worth, even if it's only two pair and a jack.*

for what it is worth

used to express reserve about the value or truth of a following statement. *19th cent.*

> Conan Doyle *The Lost World* 1912
> *'My own reading of the situation for what it is worth' – he inflated his chest enormously and looked insolently around him at the words – 'is that evolution has advanced under the peculiar conditions of this country up to the vertebrate stage, the old types surviving and living on in company with the newer ones.'*

See also not worth a fig *at* FIG¹; worth one's SALT; worth one's WEIGHT in gold; worth one's WHILE.

wrap

keep something under wraps

informal to keep something secret, especially a new idea or product: from the wrapping placed over newly developed machines before their official launch. *Mid 20th cent.*

> *Economist* 1993
> *Secure Ministers spent a weekend at Chevening in Kent pondering the future of social security. They debated more precise targeting of benefits, and persuading high earners to opt out of the state pension. Their conclusions were kept under wraps.*

wrap a car round a lamppost

informal, originally NAmer to wreck a car by crashing it into a lamppost: also in other forms depending on the circumstances, the notion being of the impact bending the vehicle into a shape that encircles the post (or whatever has been hit). *Mid 20th cent.*

wring

wring one's hands

to be openly distressed: literally, to clasp the hands together and twist them in distress or grief. *Middle English*

> Spenser *The Faerie Queene* VI.xi.23 (1596)
> *What now is left her but to wayle and weepe, | Wringing her hands, and ruefully loud crying?*

wring the withers

to stir the feelings or emotions: with allusion to Shakespeare, *Hamlet* (1601) III.ii.231 '[Hamlet to King Claudius, commenting on the play and its effect on their consciences] 'Tis a knavish piece of work; but what o' that? Your majesty, and we that have free souls, it touches us not. Let the galled jade wince, our withers are unwrung.' The withers of a horse are the bony ridge between the shoulder blades which can be chafed by a badly fitting saddle. John Lyly's prose romance *Euphues* (1580) includes the advice 'Wring not a horse on the withers, with a false saddle.' *17th cent.*

wringer

put somebody through the wringer

informal to make somebody go through a difficult or stressful experience, especially an intensive interrogation: the phrase has many variants. The image is of clothes being squeezed through a mangle or wringing machine. *Mid 20th cent.*

> *Today* 1992
> *Charles and Diana were anxious to stress they will carry on providing a secure and loving environ-*

ment. But the finality of the announcement is another cruel blow to the young princes who have already been through the wringer over revelations in the Andrew Morton book.

wrinkle

See IRON out the wrinkles.

wrist

See a SLAP on the wrist.

writ

writ large

recorded or appearing in an extended or magnified form: literally, written or printed in large characters. *Writ* is an archaic participial form of *write*. 17th cent.

> Milton *On the New Forcers of Conscience under the Long Parliament* 1646
> *When they shall read this clearly in your charge | New Presbyter is but Old Priest writ Large.*

write

nothing to write home about

informal not particularly interesting or significant: the image is of including news in a letter home from abroad. *Early 20th cent.*

> Penelope Gilliat *Nobody's Business* 1990
> *'What shall we celebrate?' I said. 'I give you a toast,' he said, waving a doubled-over piece of waffle on his fork in salute. 'To your beauty,' he said, though my looks at the time were nothing to write home about, 'coupled with the birthday of the King of Bulgaria.' 'The ex-King?' I said, which was hurtful, so I toasted the man in coffee.*

write the book on —

informal, originally NAmer to be an authority on a particular subject: typically used in the form *so-and-so has written the book on it. 20th cent.*

See also write one's own TICKET.

writing

the writing (is) on the wall

there are signs of impending disaster or retribution: with allusion to the biblical account of the sumptuous feast of Belshazzar of Babylon, in which a disembodied hand appeared and wrote a message on the wall predicting the fall of Babylon to the Persians (Daniel 5:5–6: 'In the same hour came forth fingers of a man's hand, and wrote over against the candlestick upon the plaster of the wall of the king's palace: and the king saw the part of the hand that wrote. Then the king's countenance was changed, and his thoughts troubled him.'). The phrase dates from the 19th cent. in allusive use.

> Dickens *David Copperfield* 1850
> *I could not help glancing at the scar with a painful interest when we went in to tea ... There was a little altercation between her and Steerforth about a cast of the dice at backgammon, when I thought her, for one moment, in a storm of rage; and then I saw it start forth like the old writing on the wall.*

wrong

get hold of the wrong end of the stick

informal to misunderstand somebody or something: developed from an earlier and now obsolete meaning 'to lose the advantage in a contest' (and correspondingly *get the right end of the stick* meaning 'to gain the advantage'). *19th cent.*

> Robert Bell *The Ladder of Gold* 1850
> *'In this country, Mr. Trumbull,' replied Rawlings, 'every man is free to embrace the principles he thinks best calculate to promote the general good.' 'But if a man holds on to the wrong end of the stick,' cried Mr. Trumbull, 'he'll be knocked clean off, and no mistake.'*

get somebody wrong

informal to misunderstand somebody: often used in the form *don't get me wrong* as a formula correcting a possible misunderstanding. *Early 20th cent.*

> P G Wodehouse *Money in the Bank* 1942
> *I was telling Chimp yesterday about you and the Cork dame, sweetie ... We got Soapy all wrong, Chimp. He's explained everything. It seems he was just trying to sell her oil stock.*

go (down) the wrong way

(said of food being eaten) to fall into the windpipe instead of the gullet, causing choking: the form with *down* is now usual. *18th cent.*

Dickens *Oliver Twist* 1838
'That's what it is, sir,' replied the constable,
coughing with great violence; for he had finished his
ale in a hurry, and some of it had gone the wrong
way.

See also be born on the wrong side of the BLANKET;
get/start off on the right/wrong FOOT; get on the
wrong side *at* be/get/keep on the right SIDE of
somebody; get out of BED on the wrong side; if
ANYTHING can go wrong, it will; in the wrong
BOX; on the wrong side of the tracks *at* TRACK.

X

X marks the spot
informal this is the exact place: with reference to
the use of a cross to mark a point on a map or
chart where something may be found or is
thought to be located. *Early 20th cent.*

yard

by the yard

informal in large quantities; at great length: used especially of writing and talking. The image is of lengths of cloth measured in yards. *19th cent.*

> Rider Haggard *King Solomon's Mines* 1885
> *I can see the whole picture now as it appeared night after night by the light of our primitive lamp, Good tossing to and fro, his features emaciated, his eyes shining large and luminous, and jabbering nonsense by the yard.*

not in my back yard

not where I live: a slogan typically used about plans and ideas – such as dumping nuclear waste or siting a multistorey car park – that people recognize to be necessary as long as they are located where they don't have to see them or be exposed to possible dangers arising from their proximity. The phrase has been reduced to an acronym *nimby* (and a derivative *nimbyism*), which is said to have been coined in the US in the 1980s by Walter Rodger of the American Nuclear Society. *Late 20th cent.*

> *Financial Times* 1984
> *The benefits of a nuclear station or a nuclear-waste repository were broadly distributed among the nation as a whole but the social costs and risks were carried by a small, localised minority, he said. He proposed that the way to overcome what he called the Nimby syndrome – 'not in my back yard' – was to provide compensation or insurance.*

yarn

spin a yarn

informal to relate a long and intricate story: originally used in nautical slang, with allusion to making ropes from lengths of yarn. This phrase accounts for the use of *yarn* to mean 'a long story or chat', which occurs from the mid 19th cent. *19th cent.*

> Marryat *The Pacha of Many Tales* 1835
> *'You must tell lies, and you will have gold.' 'Tell lies! that is, spin a yarn; well, I can do that.'*

yea

yea and nay

to prevaricate or be indecisive. A 17th cent. reference in the *OED* refers to Jesuits being able to 'thou and thee, and yea and nay, as well as the best of them', the 'best of them' here meaning the Quakers.

> Richard Hovey *Launcelot and Guinevere* 1898
> [Merlin] *Weal and woe! A dark saying! Yeaing and naying! How shall I know?*

year

wear/bear one's years well

to continue to look young when one is older. The form with *bear* is older but no longer current. *17th cent.*

> Philip Massinger *The City-madam* 1658
> [Millescent] *You look now as young | As when you were married.* [Ladie] *I think I bear my years well.* [Millescent] *Why should you talk of years? Time hath not plough'd | One furrow in your face; and were you not known | The mother of my young Ladies, you might passe | For a Virgin of fifteen.*

> James Kirke Paulding & William Irving Paulding *Antipathies* 1847
> [John Progress] *He has experienced reverses, but never been disheartened, and wears his years well, by reason of having never disquieted himself about the welfare of poor humanity at large.*

put years on somebody

to make somebody look or seem much older than their true age: used especially of arduous experiences, or more trivially of clothes or other aspects of physical appearance. *20th cent.*

year in, year out

constantly over a long period; every year without exception. Also in the form *year in and year out*. *19th cent.*

Conan Doyle *The Adventure of the Copper Beeches* 1892
Look at these lonely houses, each in its own fields, filled for the most part with poor ignorant folk who know little of the law. Think of the deeds of hellish cruelty, the hidden wickedness which may go on, year in, year out, in such places, and none the wiser.

See also for donkey's years *at* DONKEY; the VALE of years; the year DOT.

yes

yes and no
partly so and partly not: used to express a qualified reply of affirmation or agreement when a more straightforward answer is not possible. *19th cent.*

> Bram Stoker *Dracula* 1897
> *'Must we make an autopsy?' I asked. 'Yes and no. I want to operate, but not as you think.'*

yesterday

yesterday's man/woman
a formerly famous or influential person whose career is now past its peak. *Mid 20th cent.*

yesterday's news
a person or thing that is no longer interesting or important. *20th cent.*

> Liverpool Echo 1993
> *The season is only three months old and yet Leeds, Liverpool, Sheffield Wednesday and Manchester United are yesterday's news.*

See also not BORN yesterday.

yonder
See the wide/wild BLUE yonder.

you

you and yours
you and your family and friends. The phrase is found in Middle English in the *Cursor Mundi.*

zero

go from zero to hero
informal, originally NAmer to achieve sudden and spectacular success; to come from nowhere or 'rise without trace'. A person who does this is sometimes – paradoxically – called a *zero hero*. Conversely, to *go from hero to zero* is to suffer a sudden decline or fall dramatically from favour. *Late 20th cent.*

> Sunday Times 1994
> *Control's shares, which had tumbled amid a welter of rumour and allegation, were suspended; and six months later Virani and his brothers were ousted from the Control board. His decline from hero to zero had been brutally swift.*

> The People 1994
> *Boli went from zero to hero yesterday after scoring the Rangers goal.*

zero hour
the time fixed for a momentous event or undertaking: from the count of zero as the final stage in a countdown. *Late 20th cent.*

> Robert Kee *A Crowd is not Company* 1993
> *All set? I think I should begin to get changed now if I were you. We want everybody to be ready to fall into their places five minutes before zero hour.*

zero option
an option to disarm, especially to withdraw nuclear weapons from a potential theatre of war: current towards the end of the cold-war period in the 1980s, when the US proposed to withdraw all short-range nuclear missiles from Europe if the Soviet Union did the same. Disarmament of short- and intermediate-range weapons was called the *zero-zero-option* (or *double-zero option*), which came to fruition in the INF (intermediate-range nuclear forces) Treaty agreed in 1987, as a result of the thawing of the cold war during the Gorbachev years. In this

phrase and the next, *zero* has a conceptual rather than numerical meaning, i.e. 'none at all' rather than 'nought'. The phrase is also used in other contexts. *Late 20th cent.*

Ski Survey 1991
Ino insisted on our sampling a white Pinot Noir from one of the localities I remembered crawling through in the train. This is the exception to prove the rule. Much too good for the animals. Last night was the zero option. Menu gastronomico valdostano or zero.

zero tolerance

a total refusal to tolerate a certain type of activity or behaviour, without reserve or qualification. The phrase originated in the US in the context of tough (and mostly successful) measures taken to combat crime in major cities, especially New York. It has since extended to British use in a wider range of contexts, including social behaviour and even the correct use of punctuation. *Late 20th cent.*

Economist 1993
The real conflict between Detroiters and suburbanites is in their different approaches to handling corruption. Suburban communities swiftly expel sleazy politicians and weed out corrupt practices. Zero tolerance prevails. To the amazement of suburbanites (many of whom once lived in the city), Detroiters continue to re-elect politicians who are less than squeaky clean.